A HISTORY OF THE JEWISH PEOPLE

A. Malamat
H. Tadmor
M. Stern
S. Safrai
H. H. Ben-Sasson
S. Ettinger

A HISTORY OF THE JEWISH PEOPLE

Edited by H. H. Ben-Sasson

HARVARD UNIVERSITY PRESS
CAMBRIDGE, MASSACHUSETTS

English translation © 1976 by George Weidenfeld and Nicolson Ltd

Copyright © 1969 by Dvir Publishing House, Tel Aviv

Third printing 1976

Library of Congress Catalog Card Number 75–29879

ISBN 0–674–39730–4

Printed in the United States of America

Contents

Illustrations

---

20 A relief on the arch of Titus in Rome, erected to commemorate the victory of Rome over the Jews, showing Roman soldiers carrying off the Temple's holy objects to a Roman shrine in a victory parade.

21 An inscription of the Roman governor Pontius Pilate (26–36 CE) discovered in Tiberius' temple at Caesarea.

22 A letter from Bar Kokhba to Yeshua ben Galgula threatening to place him in fetters if he does not obey an order.

23 Two coins of the Bar Kokhba period, the larger one (a silver tetradrachma) showing the façade of the Temple and a *lulav* and *etrog,* the smaller one (a silver dinar) showing a harp and the inscription 'Simeon'.

24 One of the many catacombs with decorated stone sarcophagi at Beth-shearim, in the Galilee, from the Talmudic period.

25 The remains of the synagogue in Capernaum, on the shore of the Sea of Galilee, which was used during the second to sixth centuries CE.

26 Wall frescoes uncovered during archaeological excavations of the synagogue at Dura Europos in Syria.

Between pages 564 and 565

27 Part of a business letter from the eighth century written in Persian in Hebrew characters, found during excavations in east Turkistan.

28 An eleventh-century wooden door, with sixteen carved panels, from the Ezra Synagogue in Fostat, Egypt, in which (according to tradition) the Rambam worshipped.

29 Caricature of a Norwich Jew on the ramparts of the local castle (1233), from the Public Record Office.

30 This entry of the Forest Roll of Essex, England, includes the earliest dated sketch of a mediaeval Jew (1277).

31 A Christian depiction of the Jewish slave trade. A bishop is redeeming manacled Christian slaves from Jewish merchants in a bronze relief from the door of the church in Gniezno, Poland (twelfth century).

32 A capital from the monastery of San Martin in Fuentidueña, Spain, from the second half of the twelfth century.

33 A 'Synagogue' sculpture from the Trier Church (c. 1250).

34 Hannah and her seven sons before their tormentors, among the symbols of *kiddush hashem,* from a Hebrew Prayer Book (fourteenth or fifteenth century) in the Hamburg Library.

35 The burning of Jews (1349) in an illumination from a chronicle written on the Black Death between 1349 and 1352.

36 An illuminated Bible manuscript page written in Burgos, Spain (1260).

37 The wall carvings and stained-glass windows of the fourteenth-century synagogue in Toledo, which became the Il Transito Church after the expulsion of the Jews from Spain.

38 View of the exterior of the Altneuschul in Prague, built during the last third of

the thirteenth century. Next to it is the meeting place of the Jewish community, used towards the close of the Middle Ages.

62 A tent camp, complete with gardens, set up to house temporarily new immigrants to Israel in 1948–9.
63 A camp of tin huts built outside Tiberias to house immigrants to Israel during the years of mass immigration in the early 1950s until permanent housing could be provided.
64 Jewish soldiers on their way to Jerusalem to break the siege of the city in 1948.
65 A pro-Israel rally in front of the United Nations organized by American Jewish organizations in the autumn of 1974.

Photographic Acknowledgements

The publishers wish to thank the following institutions and individuals for their permission to use the photographs reproduced in this book: Musées Royaux d'Art et d'Histoire, Brussels, 1; Hebrew Union College, Jerusalem, 2; Professor Yigael Yadin, Hazor excavations, 3; Staatliche Museen von Berlin, 4; Cairo Museum, 5, 6; Trustees of the British Museum, 7, 11, 27; University Museum, Philadelphia, 8; Israel Department of Antiquities and Museums, 9, 10, 12, 13, 17, 21; Archaeological Museum, Istanbul, 14; Israel Museum, Jerusalem, 15, 22, 23, 28, 39, 41, 44, 45, 46, 47, 48, 49, 51, 55, 56, 59; Brooklyn Museum, N.Y., 16; Kadmon Museum of Numismatics, Ha'aretz Museum, Tel Aviv, 18; Nir Bareket, 19; Scala, Florence, 20; David Harris, 24; Werner Braun Archive, 25; Yale University, 26; Public Record Office, Norwich, 29; Public Record Office, Essex, 30; Bildarchiv, Marburg, 31, 40; The Metropolitan Museum of Art, The Cloisters Collection, on loan from Spain, 32; Bischöfliches Museum, Trier, 33; Staats- und Universitäts-Bibliothek, Hamburg, 34; Bibliothèque Royale, Brussels, 35; National and University Library, Jerusalem, 36, 50; Foto-Mas, 37; Jewish Museum, Prague, 38; T. Kollek Collection, 43; National Portrait Gallery, London, 52; Bibliothèque Nationale, Paris, 54; Hulton Picture Library, Radio Times, 58; Yad Vashem, Jerusalem, 60, 61; Anna Rivkin-Brick Collection, Keren Hayesod, Jerusalem, 62, 63; Magnum, 64; UPI, 65.

List of Maps

PART I

Origins and The Formative Period

Abraham Malamat

1

Introduction

The People and Its Land

The early history of the Israelites was not confined to the borders of Palestine alone but was connected by numerous strands to the ancient Near Eastern lands lying to the north, north-east and south-west. On one flank stretched Mesopotamia, land of the Hebrews' origins, and centuries later of Israelite setbacks. For when Assyria and Babylonia eventually deprived them of national independence, the leading citizenry of the kingdoms of Israel and Judah established there a large centre of exile, from which a revitalized nation later emerged. On the other flank lay Egypt, the land of the Nile, which for generations offered a refuge for the Hebrew tribes and served, together with the bordering Sinai Peninsula, as a crucible for the maturation and consolidation of the people of Israel.

Although the history of the early Hebrews may be traced across this broad geographical expanse, it was not until the nation was ensconced within its own Promised Land – 'a pleasant land, a goodly heritage of the host of nations' (Jeremiah 3:19) – that its national image and historic activity became crystallized. The bond between the people and their spiritual mission, as well as their affinity to the Holy Land, became sanctified in the people's consciousness as a supreme religious ideal. It shaped the entire corpus of their national and religious values, set the Israelites apart from other nations and served as their expression of selfhood. Thus emerged the national synthesis to which they aspired and which, even after its disintegration, continued to be cherished in the heart of the nation as a source of inspiration and vitality throughout the long and wearisome years of exile, a strength stemming largely from the notion of their being a Chosen People belonging to a Promised Land.

The migration from their ancestral home to the Promised Land and the tribulations of their subsequent wanderings there as aliens remained ever present in the nation's memory. Indeed, according to biblical concept, a people's right to a particular land is not to be justified by its birth within the borders of that land but solely by the privilege granted by Divine Will, which determines the boundaries of nations, bequeathing lands to some and uprooting others from their abode, all as part of a master plan based on moral considerations. Here, then, was a concept that placed history in a more dynamic context.

The relationship between Israel and the Holy Land was determined by the Lord's

3

command to Abraham, the first of the Patriarchs, 'Get thee out of thy country, and from thy kindred, and from thy father's house, unto a land that I will show thee' (Genesis 12:1). Abraham's obedience to this command marked a turning-point in the history of civilization and the inauguration of an historical process whose culmination still remains to be seen. It transformed the land of Canaan into the Land of Israel, engendering that complex relationship between Israel and the indigenous peoples of Canaan. It is true that originally (in the second millennium BCE) Israel was a negligible factor within the over-all play of powers in Canaan. With the passage of time, however, Israel gained in strength until, by the final quarter of the second millennium, it played a decisive role. Within the next thousand years, Israel determined the history of the area. Eventually Israel became recognized as a people who had exerted an influence on human history out of all proportion to its numerical size or to the area or natural wealth of its land.

Palestine Among the Lands of the Ancient Near East

The land that experienced the vicissitudes of Israelite history during the biblical period was a narrow strip some 130 kilometres wide at the most, bounded by the Mediterranean Sea on the west and the Arabian Desert on the east. It is located at the south-western extremity of a series of lands stretching like a crescent from the Persian Gulf to the Sinai Peninsula. This area is known as the Fertile Crescent, a term that aptly expresses its geophysical superiority to the Arabian Desert and the encompassing barren heights. To the south-west of Palestine is the productive Nile Valley and the intervening Sinai Peninsula, while to the north the country constitutes a physical extension of Syria. Syria and Palestine comprise a geographical entity of sorts – and, to a lesser degree, an historical unit – extending from the bend of the Euphrates to the 'River of Egypt' (the present-day Wadi el-Arish), a region referred to in cuneiform sources from the seventh century on as *ēbir nāri*, 'beyond the [Euphrates] river'. Palestine thus constituted a bridge or corridor joining Asia and Africa. The Mediterranean to the west and the desert fringes to the east served as a window onto the Aegean world and onto the nomadic tribes of the Arabian Desert, respectively. Palestine, moreover, actually nestled between two seas, for the Gulf of Eilat in the south-eastern corner provided access to the Red Sea and thence to the lands washed by the Indian Ocean.

This geographical location at an intersection of the ancient world gave rise to turbulent changes in the destiny of the land's inhabitants. It left its impress on all aspects of life, spiritual and material, economic and demographic, and affected most of all the political and military spheres.

From the cultural viewpoint the country was primarily exposed to continued influences emanating from the oldest centres of civilization in the Near East – Mesopotamia and Egypt – centres that had emerged into prominence towards the end of the fourth millennium. Moreover, the cultural forces of Anatolia also penetrated into Palestine via Syria, as did those of the Aegean Basin, sweeping in from the west specifically in the Mycenaean phase. These major cultures of the day often came into conflict there, but even more frequently clashed with the various local

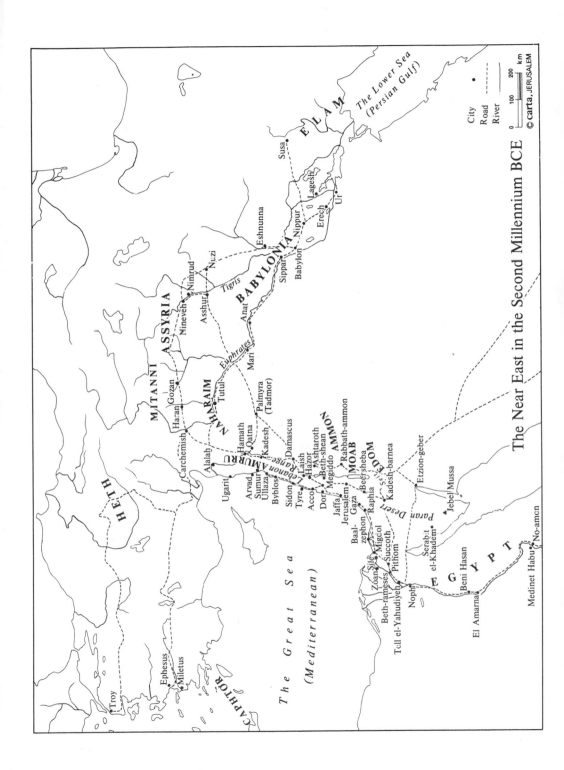

The Near East in the Second Millennium BCE

ELAM

The Lower Sea
(Persian Gulf)

Susa
Lagesh
Erech
Ur

Eshnunna
Nippur
Sippar
Babylon

BABYLONIA

Nimrud
Nineveh
Asshur
Nuzi
Anat

ASSYRIA

Tigris

MITANNI

Gozan
Haran
Carchemish

NAHARAIM

Tutul
Mari

Euphrates

Hamath
Qatna
Kadesh
Palmyra (Tadmor)

Alalah
Damascus

Ugarit
Arvad
Sumur
Ullaza
Byblos
Sidon
Tyre
Acco
Dor

AMURRU

Lebanon Range
Laish
Hazor
Ashtaroth
Beth-shean
Megiddo

AMMON

Rabbath-ammon
Beersheba

MOAB

Jaffa
Jerusalem
Gaza
Raphia

EDOM

Seir
Kadesh-barnea

HETH

Etzion-geber

Jebel Mussa

Baal-
zephon
Migdol
Succoth
Pithom

Serabit
el-Khadem

EGYPT

Zoan
Sile
Beth-rameses
Tell el-Yahudiyeh
Noph

Beni Hasan

El Amarna

Medinet Habu • No-amon

Troy
Ephesus
Miletus

CAPHTOR

The Great Sea
(Mediterranean)

Paran Desert

km
0   100   200

City
Road
River

© carta, JERUSALEM

cultures, foremost among these being that of the Canaanites. At times, however, symbiosis was attained. The net result was the engendering on the soil of Palestine of a dynamic spiritual and material creativity that expressed itself in continual change and renewal and never lapsed into tranquil passivity.

Palestine and Syria, in their dual capacity as areas of transit and junction, served as a nodal point for a complex of intersecting roads. On the one hand were the trade caravans plying the international transport routes between the Nile Valley and the Euphrates, as well as Asia Minor. There were also the caravan routes extending further afield to Arabia and even to the land of Sheba and the sea lanes leading towards busy seaports, notably those of Phoenicia. The commercial significance of Syria and Palestine, however, did not lie solely in their role as lands of transit – a circumstance exploited to the full by their inhabitants – but lay also in their various natural resources. Pre-eminent among these were the forests, the cedars of Lebanon in particular. The timber from these forests was in great demand among the rulers of Mesopotamia and Egypt, where such essential material was lacking, and its import became a matter of personal prestige. Canaan was famed as the land of the seven species – wheat, barley, grapes, figs, pomegranates, olives and honey (Deuteronomy 8:8) – and these blessings of nature find expression both in ancient Egyptian accounts (the Sinuhe tale of the twentieth century BCE) and in lists of goods destined for export to Egypt (see, e.g., page 15) and to Mesopotamia, as witnessed by the Mari documents (on these texts see pages 37ff.).

Geopolitical Factors

Throughout the ages Palestine and Syria constituted a challenge to the rulers of the ancient Near Eastern powers, as hegemony over these areas ensured both economic and political advantages of the first order. As a result, these lands were caught up for lengthy periods in repeated struggles between various nations intent on subjugating them, and they enjoyed relatively few periods of tranquillity or autonomy. Thus the region west of the Euphrates was a bone of contention between Egypt and the continually changing powers to the north and north-east. Command over the region was essential to these monarchies, primarily in order to establish their status as international powers or full-fledged empires. Without such control they were relegated to a purely local framework, whether in Africa, Mesopotamia or Asia Minor. In addition, Palestine was strategically important as a bridge-head, and its conquest was a prerequisite for any attack by one power upon another. It is not surprising, therefore, that Palestine and Syria served as international battle-grounds more often than any other area in the ancient world. In addition, there were stubborn enemies to the east and west, in the form of desert marauders and seafaring peoples. However, these could not compare in sheer power to the mighty forces that had come into being beyond the northern and southern frontiers.

In the geopolitical sense, then, Syria-Palestine found itself caught between the imperial or political forces to the north and south whose ambition it was to gain control of the region's routes. These geographically opposed powers differed appreciably in the degree of their internal uniformity and stability and in the extent of their physical and demographic intervention in the affairs of Palestine. Throughout the biblical period there lay south of Palestine a single country with a single people inhabiting it – namely, Egypt. There was, true enough, a succession of dynastic changes among the rulers there, as well as differences in their degree of aggressiveness. Palestine and extensive portions of Syria suffered from Egypt's heavy hand during the Twelfth, Eighteenth, Nineteenth and Twentieth Dynasties – that is, throughout the second millennium – as well as from attempts at renewed conquest by the Twenty-second and Twenty-sixth Dynasties during the following 500 years. Yet never once during all these conquests was any attempt made to settle an Egyptian populace within Palestine.

The relative uniformity of Egypt in ethnic and political composition was in decided contrast to the regions north of Palestine, which presented a patchwork of peoples and states, several entering upon the stage of history at one and the same time, others following upon each other in rapid succession. Unlike the south, this northerly area had, throughout the ages, sent massive population groups into Syria and Palestine, thereby altering the character of these lands. Archaeological finds in Palestine have made it possible to distinguish an influx of population from the north during the latter part of the fourth and the early third millennia and once again during the twenty-fourth century (the so-called *Beth yerah* culture). For the period of the second millennium, historical sources bear additional witness to incursions from the north. It was at the turn of the third and second millennia that the country was flooded with West Semitic tribes (known to scholars as Amorites), followed by Hurrians and even some Indo-Aryan elements. Finally, at the end of the second millennium, Syria and northern Trans-Jordan were infiltrated by Aramean tribes and Syria – and to a lesser extent Palestine – by Anatolian elements as well. Every power that rose in the northern regions made attempts to occupy parts of Syria or to deepen its penetration there. It was not until the first millennium, however, that any ventured as far south as Palestine proper, when the empires of Assyria, Babylonia and Persia extended their conquests into that country, thereby impeding any reversion to Egyptian hegemony.

The military history of Syria and Palestine represents, on the one hand, a continuous chain of conquests and oppression directed by the various powers against the local population. On the other hand, struggles were being waged simultaneously among the would-be conquerors, each aiming to enhance his own power status. It is apparent that these international squabbles and the 'cold war' being waged by the powers created an atmosphere of political and economic insecurity in Palestine. The recurring campaigns of subjugation and plunder sapped the country's vitality and natural resources. A side effect of this rivalry among the various powers of the day and of their struggle for hegemony was a series of severe disputes among the local forces within Syria and Palestine, which in any case had previously been at loggerheads with each other. It is a picture that emerges with decided clarity in the second half of the second millennium, at the time of the clash between Egypt and the Kingdom of Mitanni and, subsequently, the Hittites, when Syria-Palestine was broken up into scores of diminutive kingdoms. But severe differences also erupted during the second quarter of the first millennium, this time among the people of

Israel. The question at issue was whether to pursue a 'northern' or a 'southern' orientation in the power contest being waged between Assyria (and subsequently Babylon) and Egypt. One discerns a note of protest at this state of affairs in the words of the prophet Jeremiah directed towards Judah: 'And now what hast thou to do in the way of Egypt, to drink the waters of Sihor [the Nile]? or what hast thou to do in the way of Assyria, to drink the waters of the river [the Euphrates]?' (Jeremiah 2:18).

In short, Palestine and Syria were drawn into the power struggles with greater force than the other Near Eastern countries, and their inhabitants frequently became the victims of these international manoeuvrings.

Israelite Sovereignty over Palestine

Geopolitical conditions thus inhibited independence and national cohesion in Palestine, while dependence upon one or another of the major powers, as well as internal strife, had become almost habitual. In order to gain release from vassalage and to establish themselves in autonomous political frameworks, Palestine's inhabitants needed that rare political moment when the northern and southern powers would simultaneously be on the wane. Coupled with this external development, there would have to be an awareness of national destiny on the part of the local population.

Such an opportune moment came about in the last quarter of the second millennium, with the collapse of the Hittite Empire to the north and the decline of Egyptian power to the south, while Assyria had not yet become a decisive factor in the Levant. Hence circumstances were propitious for the liberation and upsurge of the peoples living in Syria and Palestine in order to establish themselves as new national entities. Foremost among these were the Israelite tribes in the south and the Arameans in the north. This process marked the commencement of intra-regional struggles to determine hegemony over Palestine. The Israelites now played a major role, eventually emerging victorious and bringing about a major change in the fortunes of the country, which, for the first time, experienced autonomous rule embracing all the land 'from Dan to Beersheba'.

A national achievement of this calibre was no mean matter. The country's topography weighed heavily against the creation of a unified political body intended to embrace the entire land of Palestine. The difficulty lay in the country's peculiarly varied physical structure and its highly differentiated and contrasting landscapes. These natural variations are particularly apparent in the country's west–east topography. Running lengthwise down the land are striplike zones – the coastal plain, the mountains and the Jordan depression. To the south extends the vast, semi-arid expanse of the Negev and Arabah, while in Trans-Jordan rise the heights of the plateau with the desert behind. The greater part of western Palestine is taken up by the hill country and its slopes, this region, too, being cut by numerous valleys. The ancients themselves described it as 'a land of hills and valleys' (Deuteronomy 11:11).

This geophysical partition, accompanied by appreciable variation in climate and precipitation, gave birth to specific ecological factors in the region. To a considerable extent these moulded the economic and social patterns of the settlers, their culture and political systems; and the imbalance created between these various aspects (noticeable in the development of different ways of life in the various geographical sectors) is thus, first and foremost, a product of the morphology of the land. The wooded mountain areas and the desert fringes, where livelihood was dependent primarily on grazing, were economically and culturally backward; while, in contrast, fertile valleys and lowlands – suitable for intensive agriculture and the maintenance of dense settlement – saw a flourishing economy and material advancement. However, it was the mountain area, isolated by its very nature, that was more conducive to the inner development of the Israelite genius and of its religious spirit. The Mediterranean Basin played only a marginal role in the history of the country. Unlike the Phoenician coast to the north, Palestine was virtually devoid of any natural bays or harbours that might lend themselves to the founding of port cities worthy of the name.

The outcome of this natural division into relatively small land areas is most noticeable in the obvious lack of political and territorial cohesiveness and in the chequered ethnic patterns that typified Canaan prior to the advent of the Israelites. Egyptian sources, particularly from the latter half of the second millennium, as well as numerous biblical passages, provide clear illustrations of this heterogeneity. For example, the Bible frequently mentions seven nations, and on one occasion the number rises to ten (Genesis 15:19–21). The spies' report to Moses stresses the ethno-geographic subdivision of the land: 'The Amalekites dwell in the land of the south: and the Hittites, and the Jebusites, and the Amorites, dwell in the mountains: and the Canaanites dwell by the sea, and by the coast of Jordan' (Numbers 13:29). Characteristic of this fragmentation is the listing of the thirty-one (or, according to the Septuagint, thirty) Canaanite kings smitten by Joshua (Joshua 12), while the fourteenth-century El-Amarna documents serve to augment this picture.

From the foregoing it is clear that a phenomenal change occurred in the history of the country once the Israelites overcame the natural divisions, established a uniform political and administrative structure and evolved a national culture within a sovereign framework encompassing both banks of the Jordan. Exploiting to the full the kaleidoscopic patterns on the international scene, they succeeded in the course of time in building an extensive kingdom that made of Palestine, for the first time in its history, a political factor of high order within the Near Eastern arena. The people of Israel was unique among the nations in that it bestowed upon the land of Canaan, the classic land of transit, a relatively lengthy period of political sovereignty and national autonomy.

The political vicissitudes of the nation from its settlement until the destruction of the First Temple are themselves an expression of an ardent endeavour for unity against the disjunctive tendencies embedded in the country's very landscape. On the other hand, the spiritual history of the Israelites is no less representative of the extreme efforts exerted to uphold its religious values and culture in the face of the great external influences brought to bear upon it at the time. For it was this struggle for selfhood that gave the emerging culture of Israel its unique character as a nation and forged its singular legacy to human civilization.

2

Canaan – Before and During the Israelite Conquest

The Political and Cultural Framework in the Middle of the Second Millennium

Our knowledge of the land of Canaan prior to the middle of the second millennium is fragmentary. By way of contrast, from the mid-second millennium we are in possession of a comparatively complete and continuous description of the land's history and civilization. This picture is of considerable importance in its bearing upon Israelite history, revealing as it does the back-drop to Israel's early development and at times even the actual course of its events.

In the mid-second millennium certain changes occurred in the ethnic, cultural and political patterns of the ancient Near East, including Palestine. With the founding of the New Kingdom, Egypt became the dominant power in Canaan from the sixteenth to the twelfth centuries (the Eighteenth to the Twentieth Dynasties). From an opposing quarter increasing pressure was being exerted upon Canaan by the Kingdom of Mitanni in Upper Mesopotamia, which reached its zenith in the fifteenth century. The Hittite Empire followed fast upon Mitanni, which it replaced as the dominant power in Syria from the second quarter of the fourteenth century until its disintegration towards the close of the thirteenth. With the Hittite collapse and the waning of Egypt, a new element was drawn to Canaan from overseas – the Sea Peoples, foremost among them being the Philistines. This situation eventually enabled the Assyrians, about the year 1100, to bring to fruition their age-old ambition to establish a foothold on the Mediterranean coast, and for a short spell they dominated the Phoenician coast. A detailed discussion of these developments will follow later in this chapter.

Prior to the mid-second millennium, there had already begun an increasing flow of Hurrian and even certain Indo-Aryan elements from Mitanni into Canaan with its numerous petty kingdoms, the heritage of previous political situations. Despite their numerical inferiority to the indigenous Canaanite population, the foreign intruders managed to wrest control from many of the city-states by use of their technological and military superiority, relying primarily upon chariot warfare. Eventually this non-Semitic *élite* was assimilated by the native populace to create a cultural symbiosis: in the spiritual sphere the Canaanite tongue and religious practice retained the upper hand, whereas the material, social and cultural patterns testify to a decided influence on the part of the foreign element of the population.

The historical development of Canaan during this period is attested to only by sporadic and infrequent documentation from within the country itself. It is indeed a truism that this region served as the cradle for one of mankind's major cultural achievements, the invention of the alphabet. This script, the palaeo-Hebrew or Phoenician, assumed its final form only towards the end of the second millennium. From earlier times there are only meagre remnants of linear alphabetic inscriptions (the so-called 'proto-Canaanite' script) at sites such as Shechem, Gezer and Lachish. These inscriptions, owing to their laconic character, are of little historical worth. Consequently, one must turn to cuneiform and hieroglyphic documents, which are, however, rare in Palestine. The main reason for this rarity appears to lie in the fact that Palestine came within the Egyptian sphere of influence, in which papyrus, a perishable material, was employed for written communication, except for communication in the political and diplomatic realms (see pages 16, 17ff.). Syria, on the other hand, lay within the sphere of the northern civilizations, where cuneiform and Akkadian were employed for daily purposes too. Extensive archives were discovered at Alalaḫ (from the seventeenth and fifteenth centuries) and, in particular, at Ugarit (from the fourteenth and thirteenth centuries). These archives have made it possible to probe deeply into the contemporary political and social structure and the economic and legal patterns, as well as the intellectual and religious life, of the Syrian city. The latter is most likely a counterpart to the Canaanite city-state, which, in turn, exerted an appreciable influence upon the workings of the Israelite city.

At the head of the city-state there was generally a ruler wielding a high degree of power in internal affairs. At his side were the *maryannu,* an aristocratic class of charioteer-warriors of Hurrian and Indo-Aryan descent, who provided the military and administrative backbone of the city-state. There was a class of landowners, including farmers, artisans and merchants, some of them private citizens, others in royal employ. With the passage of time, the *maryannu* aristocracy lost power in favour of the 'middle class', which rose to meet the changing needs of the rulers. The lowest rung within the free citizenry was the landless element, the serfs, from whom were drawn the labourers for the royal palace and the estates of the nobles. Detailed lists are extant indicating different professional categories, such as soldiers, builders, smiths, sculptors and tanners, potters, weavers, bakers, fullers and perfumers, hewers of wood and drawers of water. All were organized in craft corporations, technical knowledge in the various occupations being passed on from father to son. The priesthood maintained an honoured position but was also subservient to the king.

The extensive literary documents written at Ugarit, in a dialect closely akin to Canaanite and using a special alphabet in cuneiform script, have for the first time thrown light upon the religion, mythology, epic narrative and poetry that were the shared heritage of Syria-Palestine. Hitherto this sphere of literature had been no more than vaguely suggested by comparatively late documentation, such as the Bible and even Greek or Roman sources. From the Ugaritic evidence one now learns that the Canaanite pantheon was headed by El and his principal consort, Asherah. Other central deities were their offspring: Baal, the god of storm and fertility; his brother and rival, Moth, the deity of death and the nether world (Jeremiah 9:21; and Habakkuk 2:5); and the goddess Anath, their sister, excelling in beauty and prowess. Closely allied to these was the hitherto unknown Kothar, the patron deity of all crafts and the equivalent of the Greek Hephaestus. This rich store of Ugaritic literary creativity, at whose core stands the fertility myth of Baal, Moth and Anath, has been of inestimable importance in elucidating the origin and nature of biblical poetry and of early Hebrew epic style.

None the less, we have only a rudimentary knowledge of social and intellectual life in Canaan. In contrast to the paucity of epigraphic finds in Palestine, intensive archaeological activity there during the past half century has thrown much light on its material culture. We now know that a new and magnificent chapter in its history commenced close to the middle of the second millennium, the period known as the Late Bronze Age (1550–1200). The civilization of the Late Bronze Age was revealed in all its splendour at such places as Hazor, Megiddo, Taanach and Beth-shean in the north, Shechem, Tirzah and Bethel in the central mountain district, and recently at Aphek (Rosh ha-'Ayin) in the Sharon Plain. The Shephelah and southern hill region are represented by Gezer, Beth-shemesh, Lachish and Tell Beit Mirsim (assumed by some scholars to be the site of ancient Kirjath-sepher). Along the sea coast, Tell el-'Ajjul, Ashdod and Jaffa figure most prominently, while in the northern Negev mention must be made of Tell Jemmeh, Tell el-Far'ah and Tell esh-Shari'a. To the archaeological sites in western Palestine must be added the excavations conducted during recent years in Trans-Jordan, at Tell Deir Alla (perhaps ancient Succoth) and Tell es-Sa'idiyeh (either Zaphon or Zaretan), on the edge of the Jordan Valley.

From archaeological remains and from Egyptian reliefs depicting Canaanite cities, it appears that they were dominated by citadels situated on an acropolis. These enclosed the royal palace and, in most instances, a sanctuary, forming a unified complex. Surrounding the entire city were heavy walls with a fortified gate. These defensive measures reflect the precarious situation prevailing among the Canaanite city-states. The wealth of archaeological material also reveals the various arts and crafts of Canaan. To cite one example of advanced craftsmanship, there are remarkably fine ivory inlays from Megiddo. There were also ramified trade activities flourishing in this period. Commercial relations are known to have reached as far as the Aegean world, as witnessed by imported Mycenaean ware. The major occupations for which the Phoenician coastal towns were famous included textile manufacture and dyeing. It is even assumed by some scholars that the very name Canaan, as well as Phoenicia, were etymologically linked to this vocation and originally denoted the purple dye or (at a later stage) the merchants dealing in it (cf. the expression 'the Canaanite' in Proverbs 31:24 and elsewhere).

The archaeological and epigraphic material from Palestine, however, fails to provide a satisfactory picture of the historical continuum of events in Canaan. To fill the gaps we must rely to a large extent on variegated Egyptian sources, mainly records of Egyptian kings on their expeditions into Canaan. To a lesser degree information is provided by the royal Hittite archives unearthed at Boghazköy, the ancient capital of Hattusha.

The Campaigns of Thutmosis III and the
Establishment of an Egyptian Province in Canaan

Once the Hyksos domination of Egypt had been crushed, the first rulers of the Eighteenth Dynasty embarked upon extensive campaigns into Asia in order to secure Egypt from the Hyksos threat still present in Canaan. It was also intended to re-establish in Palestine and Syria the Egyptian hegemony that had been lost following the Twelfth Dynasty and that flourished during the twentieth and nineteenth centuries. Amosis I (1570–45), the founder of the Eighteenth Dynasty, after having subdued the Hyksos capital at Avaris, pressed on to Sharuhen (modern Tell el-Far'ah). This site (later included within the tribal area of Simeon [Joshua 19:6]) had served as a Hyksos base in the western Negev, controlling the route to Egypt. The Egyptians were forced to besiege it for three years before it finally fell. This, and other lengthy sieges in Canaan, illustrates the superiority of local defence techniques in the face of Egyptian assaults. With the capture of Sharuhen, Egypt established a bridge-head in Canaan that remained under its control until the termination of the Eighteenth Dynasty, facilitating frequent and far-reaching incursions into Asia.

No direct accounts are extant concerning the military expeditions of Amenophis I, the son of the aforementioned Amosis. On a shard found in Amenophis' tomb, however, there appears the name of the land of Kedem, previously known from the Sinuhe tale of the twentieth century, as well as from several biblical references. It seems to have referred to Syria's eastern frontier. An expedition into Asia was undertaken by Amosis' grandson, Thutmosis I, reaching as far as Naharin, that is, the Kingdom of Mitanni. He crossed the Euphrates and, in the fashion of the great Near Eastern conquerors, erected a stele on its bank to mark the furthermost limit of his conquests. His son and heir, Thutmosis II, also fought in northern Syria. It is during his reign that we first hear of battles against the Shasu (*cf.* the biblical term *shosim*), Bedouin tribes that led a nomadic existence along the southern and eastern frontiers of Canaan and even penetrated into its hilly regions, undermining Egyptian rule there throughout the New Kingdom. All these military expeditions were aimed primarily at the accumulation of booty. It was left to Thutmosis III (1490–36) to achieve a permanent conquest of Canaan.

Thutmosis III, the architect of the Egyptian Empire, realized that in order to transform Egypt into a power of major significance he had to annex Palestine and Syria. He attained this by undertaking a systematic campaign of conquest reaching as far as the Euphrates and by establishing an Egyptian administration in the conquered areas. Control of Palestine and Syria was no easy matter, however, as the city-states made every effort to maintain their independence. The petty sovereigns of these areas, ordinarily at odds with each other, banded together in broad alliances backed by the Kingdom of Mitanni. This coalition was led by the Kingdom of Kadesh on the Orontes River in central Syria. Thutmosis III was compelled to wage seventeen Asian campaigns, gradually extending his hold northwards. Most of his energies, however, were devoted to quelling recurrent rebellions among the subjected rulers. But along the entire southern coastal strip, contiguous Egyptian

13

control was assured, as we may infer, *inter alia,* from the fact that Gaza (which was then also called by an Egyptian name) and Jaffa were no longer regarded as newly conquered territories in subsequent lists of conquests.

Thutmosis' initial campaign (*c.* 1469), extensively described in his annals, was the basis for all his subsequent conquests. It would appear that this expedition was directed against a Canaanite move to forestall Egyptian designs. This theory would explain the broad Canaanite coalition that had aligned itself against Egypt at Megiddo less than a month after Thutmosis' army had set foot on Asian soil. According to one inscription, the confederation included 330 rulers and was the most comprehensive coalition ever to confront Egypt.

At the outset the Egyptian Army crossed Sinai to Gaza at the rate of 15 miles per day. Progress then slowed down, probably because of Canaanite resistance. Thutmosis made his way along the Sharon Plain to Yehem (Khirbet Yemma), south of the entrance to Wadi Ara, the principal pass to the north. Overriding the objections of his generals, he traversed this narrow, dangerous defile, which was heavily forested in that period. Exploiting the element of surprise, he assaulted Megiddo, the key to all northern Palestine. The city finally surrendered after a siege of seven months, and Thutmosis himself described the capture as being equivalent to 'the conquest of a thousand towns'. At this same time the Egyptians also took Yanoam, on the Jordan near its outlet from the Sea of Galilee, as well as several towns further north in the Lebanon Valley. These were subjected to an annual tribute dedicated to the temple of Amon in Egypt's capital. One of Thutmosis' commanders, Thuti, captured the port city of Jaffa, as is evidenced by an Egyptian tale that relates how warriors were smuggled into the city after the style of Ali Baba and the forty thieves.

The Canaanite cities subjugated by Thutmosis during his first campaign are apparently included in his 'shorter' geographical list of Asian cities, specifying 119 sites in Palestine and southern Syria. Most lay along the Via Maris, the highway and its various branches along the coastal plain, the valleys of Jezreel and Bethshean and the Valley of Lebanon. Others were located in Galilee and northern Trans-Jordan. Almost entirely absent from these lists are the country's interior mountain region, the Negev and central and southern Trans-Jordan – all areas of minor importance to Egypt where only nominal rule was exercised. In brief, the lowland areas were subjugated, while the hilly sectors maintained their independence.

In subsequent campaigns Thutmosis penetrated more deeply into Syria, finally subduing the main resistance at Kadesh. During his eighth expedition – the crowning achievement not only of his own but of all Egyptian Asiatic campaigns – he set out to vanquish the king of Mitanni himself. The Euphrates was crossed and the Mitanni ruler, Egypt's most powerful rival in Syria, was forced to retreat. Rule over this distant area, however, was transient. During the coming years Mitanni established an anti-Egyptian coalition in northern and central Syria. On the other hand, the Egyptians retained a firm grip on the Phoenician coast; port cities such as Byblos and Sumur became important bulwarks of Egyptian control. Apart from the importance of the coastal towns of Phoenicia as granaries for the produce of Canaan and thus for provisioning the Egyptian Army, they were also vital as administrative headquarters for all of Syria and to ensure free communication with the Egyptian homeland.

The conquests of Thutmosis III thus laid the foundations for an Egyptian province in Palestine and Syria. Despite the later loss of its northern part, the provincial administration as fashioned by Thutmosis retained its basic character until the waning of Egyptian power in Asia. He instituted a tightly knit civil and military control, headed by governors and including both fiscal officials and overseers, who supervised the exaction of tribute and governmental matters. They were supported by small military garrisons in the principal cities. Thutmosis also fortified key points such as Megiddo (and Beth-shean?), as is evidenced by the archaeological remains there, and others in the Lebanon region, as reported in his inscriptions. The main Egyptian base in Asia was at Gaza, which, it would seem, served as headquarters for the Egyptian high commissioner. As a rule the local kings who submitted peaccably were retained, though hostages from among their kin were sent to Egypt to be brought up at the court. This system served to further the Egyptianization of Canaan, for these hostages, once returned home, were relied upon to act in the interest of Egypt in all spheres.

An effective colonial rule was thus established in the Asian territories conquered by Egypt. The region's economic potential was thoroughly exploited, as is clearly revealed in the tribute and booty lists of Thutmosis and his officials, as well as in numerous bas-reliefs on Egyptian temples and tomb paintings. A considerable supply of manpower was conscripted for work in the province itself, and both male and female slaves were shipped to Egypt to work in the palace or in the various temples, as well as on the estates of high-ranking officials. Large quantities of booty were seized and annual taxes exacted, and their listings give a clear picture of Canaan's products. Most prominent were agricultural products, namely, grain and oil, together with construction timber (including the famed cedars of Lebanon). Copper also reached Egypt, as did semi-precious stones, luxury wares, art products and, understandably enough, implements of warfare. Large quantities of animal stock were transported to Egypt, especially horses for whose breeding Palestine and Syria were noted. In addition, exotic creatures of these lands, including the Syrian bear and elephant, as well as plants, were brought to grace the royal zoological and botanical gardens. These imports were no doubt intended to enhance the prestige of Egypt's rulers and to testify to the range of their domains.

The Campaigns of Amenophis II *and Thutmosis* IV

The political and administrative methods of Thutmosis III in Asia served as a model for his successors, who were also impelled to conduct repeated military campaigns into Canaan in order to quell local uprisings. Amenophis II (1439–06), the immediate successor to the throne, waged three such campaigns in Asia. The first was to put down a revolt in the land of Tahsi (the biblical Thahash, one of the 'sons' of Nahor [Genesis 22:24]), south of Kadesh, comprising a confederation of at least seven tribal chieftains. Several years later he was forced to move against northern Syria, where another revolt had broken out, probably with the support of Mitanni. On his return the Egyptian king captured the important port city of Ugarit and marched via Kadesh and the forests of Labu (the biblical Lebo Hamath) to the Sharon Plain. There his troops intercepted a messenger of the Mitannian ruler bearing a tablet (apparently in cuneiform script). This detail is illustrative of the fact that the diplomatic and subversive activities instigated by Mitanni against Egypt were not restricted to the north but extended into southern Palestine as well. Amenophis' last campaign, in his ninth year, was a punitive expedition against rebellious Canaanites, including the semi-nomadic inhabitants of the Sharon Plain. He reached as far as Anaharath (later within the tribal confines of Issachar [Joshua 19:19]) in eastern Lower Galilee, apparently Tell el-Mukharkhash at the entrance to Wadi Bireh. On his return he encamped in 'the environs of Megiddo', where he replaced a rebellious king from the Carmel region with a ruler loyal to Pharaoh, a common practice in the Egyptian occupation.

At the time Megiddo was an important Egyptian base, as is clear from archaeological findings there and from the Akkadian archives discovered at Taanach, some $4\frac{1}{2}$ miles to the south-east. The Taanach tablets – the most comprehensive cuneiform find in Palestine – bring to life the everyday problems and interrelations of the petty Canaanite rulers during the latter half of the fifteenth century. Ties among the Canaanite cities could occasionally stretch far afield, as in the case of Taanach and the Beth-shean area. One letter relates that the king of Taanach had been urgently commanded by the Egyptian authority to dispatch an armed force to Megiddo, to be accompanied by a payment and special 'gifts' for the sender of the missive. The order was issued by a high-ranking Egyptian named Amenophis. This same person, in another letter, reprimands the king of Taanach for failing to supply soldiers and for not having presented himself at Gaza. He may have been none other than Amenophis II, who during his campaign in Palestine had ordered the Canaanite rulers of cities along his route of march to furnish him with military reinforcements. Furthermore, the complex ethnic character of the area is evident from these tablets in the variety of proper names they contain. While the bulk of the inhabitants were of West Semitic, Canaanite stock, Hurrian (and Indo-Aryan) elements also made a strong appearance. The variegated population pattern of Canaan is similarly depicted by the lists of captives transported to Egypt by Amenophis II. These lists contain entire ethnic groupings, as well as social and professional classes.

The military ventures of Thutmosis IV (1406–1398), the son of Amenophis, are by no means as well documented as those of his forbears. It is possible, none the less, to learn a good deal about his conquests in Canaan from allusions in his own, as well as his officials', inscriptions. He was in fact referred to by his contemporaries as 'the conqueror of the land of Haru [Hurru]', the common Egyptian appellation for Syria-Palestine in the New Kingdom. On the chariot found in his tomb at Thebes, there are depictions of battles in Canaan showing, *inter alia,* the Shasu-Bedouin, an element increasingly troublesome to the Egyptian authorities. One of his tomb inscriptions mentions captives from Gezer, thus implying the capture of this city. This would accord with the contents of a letter unearthed at Gezer proper, in which the sender demanded a declaration of loyalty from the local king, as well as the supply of victuals to an agent who was about to arrive at Gezer, no doubt to obtain provisions for the Egyptian forces. This letter is similar in content and style to several from the El-Amarna archives dispatched from Egypt to various Canaanite kings, among whom may be noted the kings of Achshaph and Ashkelon. The above message may well have been dispatched by Thutmosis IV himself to the king of Gezer during a campaign to Canaan, and when the local ruler failed to respond the city was attacked.

Additional details about Thutmosis IV's Asiatic campaigns may be inferred indirectly from the El-Amarna correspondence, wherein the Canaanite rulers refer at times to the campaigns of former Egyptian kings. Thus the king of Byblos proclaims to Amenophis III that his town had remained loyal to the latter's father (Thutmosis IV), who had appeared in person on the Phoenician coast in order to oversee Egypt's vassal territories. This coincides with what is recorded in yet another of Thutmosis IV's inscriptions – that he went to fell cedars in the land of Retenu. Retenu, one of the most ancient designations for the land of Canaan in Egyptian sources, refers in this instance specifically to the region of the Lebanon range.

Thutmosis IV was the last of the rulers of the Eighteenth Dynasty to embark upon military expeditions into Asia. His successors, Amenophis III and IV (and Tutankhamon), were apparently content to administer Palestine from afar, until, in the second half of the fourteenth century, Egyptian rule there collapsed completely. The geographical lists of Amenophis III offer no clear evidence of campaigns in Asia. If they were not merely copies of place names listed by his predecessors (particularly where northern Canaan is concerned), at most they indicate commercial or other ties with these places. Of great interest is an additional geographical list, only recently published and referring to places hitherto unknown in Egyptian sources, such as Raphia on the southern coast and En-shasu, a settlement of nomads near a spring, also mentioned in the El-Amarna documents. A place called 'land of the Shasu Y-H-W(A)' located either in the Sinai Peninsula or in the Negev, is particularly intriguing. The name Y-H-W(A) and its location in Sinai are reminiscent of the theophany of Yahweh before Moses (see page 45). Surprisingly enough, further names refer to the Aegean realm and Greece: Knossos on Crete, the island of Cythera near the Peloponnesus, Nauplia, Messenia and Mycenae and perhaps even Ilion (*i.e.,* Troy). This suggests connexions with overseas lands, as does a cache of cylinder seals in the Syro-Akkadian style recently discovered at Thebes in Greece.

The Political Constellation During the El-Amarna Period

The fullest and most instructive portrayal of the land of Canaan in the second millennium – and one indirectly bearing upon the early history of Israel – is from the second quarter of the fourteenth century, the El-Amarna period. El-Amarna is the modern name of a site in central Egypt, ancient Akhetaten, the new Egyptian capital of Amenophis IV (1369–53), which briefly replaced Thebes. A rich state archive has gradually come to light there since 1887, containing the diplomatic correspondence of Amenophis IV, as well as that of the later years of his father Amenophis III. It includes more than 350 letters, almost all of which are in the

Akkadian language, the lingua franca of the Near East at that time. While some of the documents are letters between the Egyptian king and the heads of other ruling powers, roughly half of the archive consists of correspondence with vassals and quasi-vassals in Palestine and on the Phoenician coast. The bulk of these missives are addressed to the Egyptian king, and only a few are copies of letters from the king or his officials to petty rulers in Canaan.

It is clear from the correspondence that the Egyptian hold in Canaan had weakened appreciably and that the security situation throughout the province had severely deteriorated. One reads of repeated pillaging of caravans and of helplessness in the face of marauders (*e.g.,* the Shutu tribe) and roving bands such as the Ḫabiru (see page 41). The latter would often hire themselves out as mercenaries to local potentates. Thus, although during the reigns of Amenophis III and IV Egypt reached its zenith in various respects (particularly in the cultural sphere), its power in Asia had declined precipitously. The religious reform in Egypt, to which Amenophis IV had applied himself, has been thought to have had some bearing on the religion of Israel. The worship of the sun-god Aten was raised to the status of a state cult, and the king even named himself Akhenaten, 'glory of Aten'. This innovation, however, whose influence upon Israel's monotheistic faith has been greatly overrated in some quarters, remained no more than a transient episode and on the death of Amenophis IV was regarded as no more than a heresy. Despite his political weaknesses, Amenophis IV did not entirely neglect the Egyptian administration in Canaan. There are various indications of his interest in Asia, and he seems even to have planned a full-fledged military campaign to this area, though it seems never to have taken place. At all events, both he and his father succeeded in maintaining their authority in Canaan and on the Phoenician coast, employing the time-honoured principle of *Divide et impera* by encouraging intrigues and feuds among the native rulers.

The El-Amarna archive, our main source of information on the Egyptian colonial apparatus in Asia, reveals the role played by Palestine within the context of the imperial framework. Canaan proper was the southernmost of three Asiatic provinces, with its centre at Gaza. It included the whole of western Palestine, stretching along the coast northwards to Tyre and later extending as far as Byblos, while in Trans-Jordan it encompasses the city-states of Zaphon and Pella in the south and the Golan and Bashan areas in the north. The province was administered by an Egyptian commissioner, whose Akkadian title was *rabiṣu,* the Canaanite *sōkinu* ('agent'). In contrast to the Egyptian administration in Nubia, this officer was directly responsible to the king. Such commissioners superintended the local city-state rulers, often known by the Akkadian title *ḫazannu,* which was the equivalent of mayor or governor. The designation was intended to impress upon them subservience to the Egyptian masters who confirmed them in their office; among themselves, however, they continued to address one another as 'king'.

The backbone of Egyptian rule consisted, therefore, of client kings in Canaan working in close association with Egyptian officials. Under their command stood garrisons of Egyptians and sometimes 'Cushites', *i.e.,* Nubians. These armed units were small in size, as may be judged by the modest requests for reinforcements submitted by the city rulers; for example, one hundred men to be sent to Megiddo or a mere fifty soldiers requested by Jerusalem and Gezer. Weapons supply was also limited, as is illustrated by a contemporary letter from Tell el-Hesi stating a local ruler's need for six bows, three daggers and three swords. For larger-scale military operations, an expeditionary force would be sent from Egypt. This was the 'army of archers', a force of chariotry combining the manoeuvrability of the chariot and the striking-power of the bow.

The prime significance of the El-Amarna letters for the history of Palestine (as well as for early Israel) lies in the light they throw upon the individual Canaanite city-states – the fluid relations between them, their strife and enmities, their alliances and their occasional broadly based coalitions. The cross references provided by these letters, together with contemporary documents from the Hittite archives at Hattusha (as well as the more recently discovered archive at Ugarit), serve to underline the delicate situation of these kingdoms, particularly in Syria. The latter, held in a vicelike grip between Mitanni and the Hittites, found themselves torn, at the same time, between the two poles of Egypt and Hatti. Such a predicament could lead only to military machination and political duplicity. Hatti became a forceful adversary to Egypt, the powerful Hittite king Shuppiluliuma disposing of Mitannian hegemony in Syria and penetrating as far as Damascus and the Lebanon Valley. Indeed, many of the states in Syria preferred the Hittites to an Egyptian overlord, as the former displayed greater skill and pliability in their dealings with vassals and granted more effective military protection. The tripartite competition among the powerful rivals, Egypt, Hatti and the declining Mitanni, for the fealty of the Syro-Palestinian rulers upset the delicate power balance throughout the region.

Despite the unstable political situation, Egypt remained master in Palestine and was still held responsible for the country's inhabitants. To cite but one instance, Burnaburiash II, the king of Babylon, sued Amenophis IV as a result of the pillaging of one of his caravans and the murder of Babylonian merchants in the town of Hannathon within the vale of Netophah (later within the tribal allotment of Zebulun [Joshua 19:14]): 'Canaan is your land and its kings your servants. In your land was I robbed. Bind them [the murderers] and the money they have stolen, make good. And the people who killed my servants, kill them and let the blood be avenged.'

Egypt's dominion in the north extended to the northern edge of the Valley of Lebanon, a line of demarcation recognized by the Hittites. Consequently, the penetration by Shuppiluliuma into the land of Amqi, south of this border, was considered an infringement of Egyptian territory even in Hittite historiography, which associated this violation with the severe plague that subsequently struck their land. Nevertheless, the growth of Hittite power in Syria and the weakening of Egypt encouraged the Ḥabiru to step up their marauding. Several of the local rulers – largely in the central hill district and in Amurru in the north – joined with them to cast off the Egyptian yoke. Acts of resistance among local rulers were on the increase owing to the ineffectiveness of the Egyptian authorities. Thus in northern Palestine a clash occurred between the two most important centres, Ashtaroth in the Bashan region and Hazor, which was attempting to expand eastwards across the Jordan and westwards towards the coast. In the lowlands, however, including the Valley of Jezreel, the Sharon Plain and the coastal strip – some of which constituted Egyptian royal estates and were vital to Egypt's economy – the Egyptian hold remained fairly firm throughout this period. Indeed Biridiya, the prince of Megiddo, carried out extensive agricultural work on the Plain of Jezreel on the Egyptian king's behalf, using forced labour assembled from various places. Further south Jaffa also was an Egyptian administrative centre and contained royal granaries. According to a later Egyptian document (Papyrus Anastasi I), this city was also known as a centre for leather work and armament.

As regards the central mountain area, the El-Amarna documents supply us with the names of two city-states destined to fill important roles in the Israelite Conquest and Settlement: Shechem and Jerusalem. Labaya, the ruler of Shechem, who was a sworn enemy of Egypt, had extended his rule over the hills of (later) Ephraim and Manasseh. Aided by the Ḥabiru, he laid siege to Megiddo. On the east his control reached as far as the mountains of Gilead and westwards to the Sharon region. Together with Milkilu, the ruler of Gaza (a former opponent but now an ally), Labaya and his progeny after him maintained constant pressure upon Jerusalem and even more southerly places, such as Lachish and Ashkelon.

Jerusalem itself remained an enclave loyal to Pharaoh, and its king, Abdi-Ḥepa (this apparently is the correct reading and not Puti-Ḥepa), actually assumed an Egyptian military title. In his letters he pleads with his overlord to send military assistance to enable him to cope with the marauding Ḥabiru and other enemies. Among these he lists the rulers of Shechem, Gezer, Gath, Lachish and Ashkelon. Specifically he complains of subversive acts along his north-western border: the waylaying of one of his caravans in the Valley of Ajalon; the capture of the nearby city of Beth-horon and of Rubute (a town as yet not clearly identified); and an attempt to undercut his rule at Keilah (Khirbet Qila) on the south-western border. The predicament of Jerusalem is indicative of the dangerous isolation of several Canaanite city-states and, concomitantly, of temporary alliances between them. One illustration of such wide-ranging coalitions, intended to meet a specific situation, is the request for military aid against the Ḥabiru made by Abdi-Ḥepa and Shuwardata (the ruler of Hebron or Gath) to the kings of Acco and Achshaph in the distant northern coastal region.

The Jerusalem 'diplomatic file' found in the El-Amarna archive has not only revealed the complex problems and struggles that beset this Canaanite city-state fighting to maintain its territorial integrity and very survival; it has also shed indirect light on the biblical account of the status and fortunes of early Jerusalem. Only a few generations separated these episodes from the Israelite invasion of Canaan. This invasion apparently took place in the border region between the kingdoms of Shechem and Jerusalem, the two political entities in the mountain district, as disclosed by the El-Amarna documents. For all the differences in political and military alignment at the time of Joshua, the strategic position of the Kingdom of Jerusalem resembled that in the El-Amarna period (see Chapter 4, page 57). The composite ethnic make-up of Jerusalem's populace is reflected in the very name of Abdi-Ḥepa: the first component is Canaanite and the second is the name of a Hurrian-Hittite goddess. A similar picture is conveyed by the biblical reference to Hittites who had settled in the town side by side with the ancient Canaanite-Amorite inhabitants (*cf*. 'Uriah the Hittite' of Jerusalem; and Ezekiel 16:3). The Jebusites, settlers in pre-Israelite Jerusalem, were most probably linked to the former. Furthermore, the literary form and flowery style of the El-Amarna letters from Jerusalem, with their plethora of Canaanite idioms, indicate that the city was an important centre of scribal craft. With its conversion under David into Israel's capital, the city could well have assumed a major position in facilitating the absorption of Canaanite civilization, in addition to transmitting methods of government to the Israelites.

Canaan at the Time of the Israelite Conquest

The decline of Egypt's power in Asia, upon the disintegration of the Eighteenth Dynasty in the latter half of the fourteenth century, facilitated ever-deeper incursions by nomadic and semi-nomadic tribes from the eastern frontier into the arable area. These elements, who came with the purpose of settling, included the Israelites and kindred tribes, as well as inhabitants of southern Trans-Jordan – the Edomites, Moabites and Ammonites (see Chapter 4).

During the reign of Horemheb, who had usurped the throne of Egypt, an attempt was made to re-establish Egyptian authority in Canaan, though this was unsuccessful. Of particular interest are the reliefs in Horemheb's tomb, depicting the physiognomy typical of captives from Palestine and possibly Syria, noticeable among whom are bearded Semites, as well as Hittites. These clearly attest to the multifaceted composition of Canaan's population during this period. With the advent of the Nineteenth Dynasty, towards the close of the fourteenth century, an eastward orientation became a dominant feature of Egyptian foreign policy. Rule in Asia, albeit on a smaller scale than under Thutmosis III, was regained. Symptomatic of the strengthened ties with Canaan under this dynasty is the extraordinarily large number of contemporaneous Egyptian documents found in Palestine. Conversely, Canaanite influence within Egypt reached its peak at this time, as is evidenced by the many Canaanite deities included in the Egyptian pantheon and the extensive adoption of Canaanite words in Egyptian literature.

The successful expeditions of Seti I (1308–1290) into Canaan are recorded on several steles (at Beth-shean, Tell esh-Shihab in northern Gilead and Tyre), by the geographical lists of captured Canaanite cities and by a unique series of reliefs (with accompanying inscriptions) in the temple of Amon at Karnak. The reliefs are a highly detailed source of information on the military route taken by the Egyptians along the northern Sinai Peninsula towards Raphia. Depicted there are some twenty forts and fortified wells dispersed along the route. We are informed of the capture of 'the [city of] Canaan', apparently referring to Gaza, the conquest of Yanoam near the outlet of the Jordan from the Sea of Galilee and the conquest of Kadesh. It is doubtful, however, whether this refers to Kadesh-on-the-Orontes for, despite Seti's stele at this site, it remains unclear whether he did in fact capture so northerly a point. The fortress city of Kedesh in Upper Galilee is more likely. Alongside depictions of Canaanite strongholds and their characteristic landscapes, the reliefs include scenes of the wild Shasu-Bedouin, of Canaanite warriors, of 'the great princes of Lebanon' felling cedars for Egypt (*cf*. I Kings 5:20) and even of

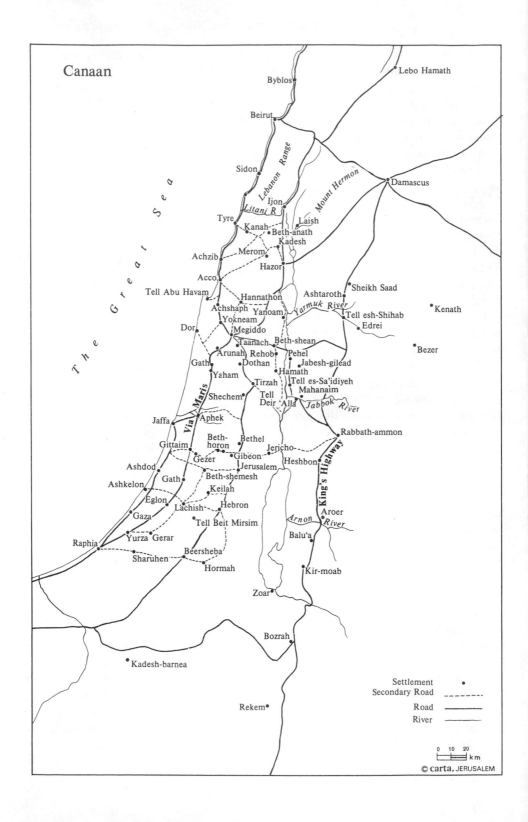

Canaan

Lebo Hamath

Byblos

Beirut

Sidon

Lebanon Range

Mount Hermon

Damascus

Ijon

Litani R.

Tyre

Laish

Kanah

Beth-anath

Kadesh

Achzib

Merom

Hazor

Acco

Sheikh Saad

Tell Abu Havam

Hannathon

Ashtaroth

Kenath

Yarmuk River

Achshaph

Yanoam

Tell esh-Shihab

Dor

Yokneam

Edrei

Megiddo

Taanach

Beth-shean

Bezer

Arunah

Rehob

Pehel

Gath

Dothan

Jabesh-gilead

Yaham

Hamath

Tirzah

Tell es-Saʿidiyeh

Shechem

Tell

Mahanaim

Deir ʿAlla

Jabbok River

Jaffa

Aphek

Rabbath-ammon

Via Maris

Beth-
horon

Bethel

Jericho

Gittaim

Gibeon

Heshbon

Gezer

Ashdod

Jerusalem

King's Highway

Gath

Beth-shemesh

Ashkelon

Keilah

Eglon

Lachish

Hebron

Aroer

Gaza

Tell Beit Mirsim

Arnon River

Yurza

Gerar

Baluʿa

Raphia

Beersheba

Sharuhen

Hormah

Kir-moab

Zoar

Bozrah

Kadesh-barnea

The Great Sea

Settlement   •
Secondary Road   -----
Road   ———
River

0   10   20
km

Rekem

© carta, JERUSALEM

turned to the movement after the pogroms. Great credit is due to Moses Leib Lilien-blum (1843–1910), who was won over from social radicalism and a desire for religious reform to Ḥibbat Zion and became one of its most active members and an ideological leader. Lilienblum emphasized that there was no remedy for anti-Semitism, nor for the alienation of the Jews in their places of residence, other than settlement in their historical homeland. Only in the land of their forefathers could the people achieve national renaissance.

Pinsker's Auto-Emancipation

Lilienblum's partner in nationalistic activity was Dr Leon Pinsker, a *maskil* who had formerly advocated the integration of the Jews into Russian life, had distinguished himself as a physician in the Crimean war and was one of the leaders of Ḥevrat Marbei Hahaskalah be-Ercẓ Russia (Association for the Dissemination of Jewish Enlightenment in Russia) with its russification tendencies.

In the summer of 1882, Dr Pinsker published an anonymous pamphlet in German entitled *Auto-Emancipation*. His basic assumption was that the hatred of the Jews was rooted in Judophobia – a fear of the Jews' disembodied, abnormal existence, resembling the fear of a ghost. Only the return of the Jews to a normal political condition, *i.e.,* a country of their own, could make them a nation and eradicate gentile hatred. But this objective called for the transformation of the consciousness of the people and the crystallization of a national self-awareness. Emancipation had been a gift bestowed by those peoples among whom the Jews lived, while national consolidation and political concentration would be acts of self-liberation, of 'auto-emancipation'. It was therefore necessary to set up a national directorate to purchase land for the settlement of millions of Jews and above all of those Jews suffering from persecution in Russia, Rumania and Morocco. In order to achieve this aim, it was essential to approach the 'existing alliances' and with their aid to convene a Jewish 'national congress'. Thus it would be possible to gain the objective: 'In place of the many refuges which we have been accustomed to request, we want one single refuge, but its existence must be safeguarded politically as well.' The 'refuge' need not necessarily be Palestine: 'We need a homeland of our own, if not the land of our own fathers.'

Pinsker wrote his pamphlet in German because he hoped to win over the Jews of the West to his ideas and to establish the centre of his movement in those countries in which political activity was unhampered. But he was to be disappointed; scarcely any of the Western Jews were willing to accept his theory in full, or to devote them-selves to nationalistic activity. A year later Pinsker responded to the request of the Hovevei Zion (Lovers of Zion) movement and joined them. Together with Lilien-blum he set up the Zerubabel Society in Odessa, which became the centre for contacts with other associations. At the urging of the Warsaw association, it was decided to convene a general assembly of all the Hovevei Zion associations on the one-hundredth birthday of Sir Moses Montefiore, the dedicated patron of Jewish settlement in Palestine.

The Organization of the Ḥovevei Zion Movement

The first convention of the Ḥovevei Zion associations opened in Katowice on 6 November 1884, with the participation of some forty delegates, most of them from Russia and Rumania and a minority from Germany and England. At that time the widespread public enthusiasm for national projects, including settlement in Palestine, had entirely died out. Volatile and radical youth shunned the movement because of its hesitant nature and because of the influence wielded within it by rabbinical and bourgeois elements. This was reflected in Pinsker's remarks at the Katowice Conference. He emphasized how grave was the predicament of the Jews, but instead of the radical plans of 'auto-emancipation' and political rule in a 'national homeland' he laid stress in his opening and concluding speeches on the old projects of the *maskilim,* agricultural settlement and work. It was decided to call the organization Mazkeret Moshe be-Ereẓ Hakodesh (The Testimonial to Moses in the Holy Land) in honour of Montefiore and to establish its central office in Berlin. But a protracted search failed to produce capable organizers in the West, and the centre remained in Odessa, headed by Pinsker and Lilienblum, with a secondary centre in Warsaw. The movement sank into a rut of 'little deeds'. Not only did it fail to provide the momentum for settlement in Palestine, but its ability to aid those settlements already established (Gederah and to some extent Petaḥ Tikvah) was extremely limited. Most of the colonies were under the patronage of Edmond de Rothschild, the famous philanthropist, and the Ḥovevei Zion were afraid of antagonizing him. Within the movement itself, there was friction between associations in the various towns and between the orthodox and the *maskilim*. The heads of the movement did not despair of obtaining official Russian authorization for the legal activities of an association for Jewish settlement in Palestine, but this authorization was in fact long delayed.

On the instigation of the Bialystok association, headed by the town rabbi, R. Samuel Mohilewer, and the Moscow and Vilna associations, the second Ḥovevei Zion conference was convened in the summer of 1887 at Druskininkai. It was attended by representatives of several dozen associations, but the weakness of the movement was apparent. Mohilewer wanted to transform it into a religious movement led by rabbis, but a considerable number of the young secular delegates were vehemently opposed to this. Eventually a compromise was proposed: Pinsker remained at the head of the movement, and six other leaders, three of them rabbis, were also elected. In actual fact neither the leadership nor the methods of operation of the movement underwent any change.

There was a slight upsurge of Ḥovevei Zion activity in 1890 when, thanks to the efforts of Alexander Zederbaum, editor of *Hameliẓ,* the authorities finally approved the statutes of The Society for Support of Jewish Farmers and Craftsmen in Syria and Palestine, and conditions conducive to legal activity of the movement were created in Russia. The society's committee was located in Odessa and was therefore known as the Odessa Committee. The foundation meeting of the committee was attended by many delegates from all over Russia and large sums were collected, which facilitated the extending of support to Palestinian settlement. But enthusiasm for the idea soon waned, and the activities of the Odessa Committee became increasingly philanthropic in nature, like those of Jewish organizations in the West.

The Nationalism of Aḥad Ha-Am

In this period of depression a young *maskil*, the son of a distinguished ḥasidic family, joined the movement in Odessa. Asher Ginzberg (1856–1927), later known as Aḥad Ha-Am ('one of the people'), did not concur with the movement's methods, as he was convinced that they were incapable of bringing economic and social redemption to Jewish individuals or to the people as a whole. The petty assistance to the settlers, in which the Ḥovevei Zion movement engaged, appeared valueless to Aḥad Ha-Am. After his visits to Palestine in 1891 and 1893, he wrote a series of articles entitled 'Truth from Ereẓ Yisrael', which contained savage criticism of the methods employed by Ḥovevei Zion in purchasing land, consolidating settlements, etc. He believed that the movement should engage in 'preparing hearts', in the spiritual and moral resurrection of the people. Palestine could not serve as a 'balm for the sorrows of the Jews'; but if a 'national spiritual centre' were established for the elect, it could provide a solution for the 'sorrows of Judaism', since it would radiate beneficial spiritual influence to the Diaspora and strengthen Jewish nationalism. Since he regarded preparation of the younger generation as the most vital task, he collaborated in 1889 in the establishment of a semi-clandestine organization – which later operated under his inspiration – known as Benei Moshe (Sons of Moses). The Benei Moshe association was a kind of order, and members were expected to dedicate themselves to the national ideal, to be of outstanding moral character and to engage in activity aimed at furthering the renaissance of Hebrew spirit and culture. Many of the most active members of Ḥovevei Zion joined Benei Moshe. The association endured for only eight years and never numbered more than 200 members, but it served as the focus of nationalist activity at a time when Ḥovevei Zion was in its decline. Ahad Ha-Am himself later described Benei Moshe as an 'unsuccessful experiment'.

Because of his attachment to the idea of a 'national spiritual centre' – which actually emanated from his contempt for popular action – Aḥad Ha-Am never became the leader of the movement. But he made a great contribution to the dissemination of Hebrew culture: the Aḥiasaf publishing house, the journal *Ha-shiloaḥ* and the first Hebrew school in Jaffa were founded on his initiative and with the aid of his associates in Benei Moshe. They also introduced into Russia the 'reformed *ḥeder*', in which the language of instruction was Hebrew rather than Yiddish. Aḥad Ha-Am left his mark on several of the more important Hebrew writers of his day, such as Bialik, Berdyczewski and Klausner, and also influenced young *maskilim* who later became the leaders of the Zionist movement in several countries.

Theodor Herzl and The Jewish State

As we have noted, the Ḥibbat Zion movement did not at first arouse widespread response among Western Jews. Graetz, who initially agreed to join the movement, requested shortly afterwards that his name be erased from the list of committee members. But not all the reactions to Pinsker's *Auto-Emancipation* were negative. In the West, the active members were mainly students of East European origin, such as those who set up the Kadimah association in Vienna in 1882. The moving spirit of these circles was Viennese-born Nathan Birenbaum, who founded the *Selbstemanzipation* journal in 1885 (the first to employ the term 'Zionism', after Mount Zion in Jerusalem, to designate the aim of Jewish revival as an independent nation in Palestine). In time Ḥovevei Zion associations were also established in Galicia and throughout Austria, in Germany, England, France, the United States and even Canada.

In 1893 Birenbaum published a pamphlet advocating national renaissance in Palestine and began to call for the convening of an international Zionist congress to establish a political movement for the implementation of this aim. At the beginning of 1894, a conference of Zionist associations of various countries was convened in Paris, but it did not succeed in establishing a long-lived organization. Demands for the convening of a Zionist congress continued, but the first steps towards implementation were taken only after Dr Theodor Herzl (1860–1904), a leader of outstanding spiritual presence and ability, joined the supporters of Zionist ideology.

Herzl, a renowned journalist and writer, came from an assimilated home, was remote from Hebrew culture and knew nothing about the national activity that had preceded him. From his youth he was aware of the anti-Semitism that prevailed in Austria, but he regarded France as the land of progress and culture. As he himself testified, he was therefore stunned by the anti-Semitic outbursts in Paris at the time of the Dreyfus trial. (Herzl was then Paris correspondent of the Viennese paper, *Neue Freie Presse*.) His Jewish and human pride, the dominant trait in his personality, was deeply affected. This led him to devote profound thought to the 'Jewish problem', to seek possible solutions and to come into contact with various Jewish personalities, such as the well-known writers Max Nordau and Israel Zangwill, and with active members of Ḥovevei Zion in the West. Previously, in May 1895, he had met with Baron de Hirsch and tried unsuccessfully to arouse his interest in a plan for the evacuation of the Jews from Europe to a country of their own. At the beginning of January 1896, Herzl published an article on this subject in the London *Jewish Chronicle,* and in February he expounded his ideas in a book entitled *The Jewish State: An Attempt at a Modern Solution of the Jewish Question*. In his opinion, anti-Semitism would never vanish; yet, he also believed that the Jews were 'one nation'. Therefore he felt that there could be no solution to the 'Jewish problem' – which to him was basically a national question – except by the establishment of a Jewish state. This could be done if 'we are granted sovereignty over some area of land on this earth, to fulfil the justified needs of our people; all the rest we ourselves will provide.' In order to facilitate the exodus of the Jews from their countries of residence and their settlement in their new land, a 'Jewish association' of scientific and political nature should be established, as well as a 'Jewish society' to administer property.

The publication of *The Jewish State* aroused a wave of enthusiasm among Zionists all over Europe. Many approached Herzl to express their loyalty and support and began to aid him in his activities. This brought him into contact with Zionist projects and Palestine. Since Baron de Hirsch had died, Herzl tried to obtain the aid of the Rothschilds in the implementation of his plans, but they refused to support him. He went to Constantinople in order to propose the settlement of the Turkish Empire's financial problems in return for the granting of Palestine as an independent state for the Jews, but the Sultan refused to grant him an audience. Herzl nevertheless remained resolute in his conviction that there was room for negotiation with the Turkish authorities on this question.

Political Zionism and the Zionist Congress

Herzl believed that the best way of implementing his plan was through political activity and was strongly opposed to any 'infiltration' into Palestine not based on explicit political guarantees. He therefore disapproved of the settlement project of Hovevei Zion in Palestine and of the plans of the Baron de Rothschild. He tried to interest the leaders of British Jewry in his programme, but encountered the opposition even of the Hovevei Zion leaders among them. His meeting with Rothschild was also fruitless: the Baron claimed that he had no confidence in the Turkish Government and that he feared the hasty immigration of tens of thousands of *shnorrers* ('beggars') who would be in need of financial support.

In order to further his plans, Herzl decided to rally all those who did share his views. He won the support of several Berlin Hovevei Zion, and, eventually, a conference of Austrian and German Zionists was held in Vienna at the beginning of March 1897. This gathering decided to convene a Zionist congress in Munich at the end of August. A special emissary was sent to arouse the Russian Zionists, and in fact most of them favoured the idea. There was, however, extensive opposition from many Jews, amongst them distinguished rabbis in Central and Western Europe. Herzl devoted himself heart and soul to the struggle for the congress: in the journal *Die Welt,* which he had founded, in articles, in speeches and in the many letters he sent to various public figures. It was in this period that his organizational abilities were revealed and his image as a leader was shaped.

The First Zionist Congress was convened in Basle on 29 August 1897, with the participation of some 200 delegates. It encompassed all Zionist forces, with the exception of a few sceptics, and aroused widespread interest in Jewish and European circles: the appearance of a Jewish organization offering an independent Jewish political plan constituted a revolutionary innovation both inside and outside the Jewish community. In a programmatic speech at the congress, Max Nordau depicted the situation of the Jews in the world in a way which aroused enthusiastic response and nationalistic activity. The congress accepted the 'Zionist' or 'Basle Programme': 'Zionism aspires to the securing of a national home for the Jewish people in Palestine, guaranteed by public [*i.e.,* international] law.' This spelled victory for Herzl's conviction that the Jewish project in Palestine needed international guarantees.

Professor Hermann Schapira proposed at the congress the establishment of a 'national fund' to purchase land in Palestine for the nation, and out of this grew the idea of the Jewish National Fund.

After the congress, Herzl continued his diplomatic efforts as well as his consolidation of the organization. The number of Zionist associations increased considerably. The Second Zionist Congress in the summer of 1898 decided to encourage settlement in Palestine (even before political guarantees were obtained) and to engage in cultural activity. In November, Herzl met the German Kaiser Wilhelm II in Palestine, but did not succeed in winning him over to his cause. At the Third Congress (1899) Herzl declared that the objective of his activities was to obtain a 'charter' from the Turkish Government for Jewish settlement in Palestine. But his further journeys to Turkey proved fruitless. In actual fact no Jewish capitalists supported his plan to solve the financial problems of the Ottoman Empire, whilst the Great Powers, and particularly France, were exerting increasing diplomatic and economic pressure on Turkey, so that her economic and political recovery seemed unlikely. Herzl's efforts to raise funds for Jewish settlement with the aid of a popular bank, to be based on two million shares of £1 each, were also unsuccessful. It was only with great difficulty, after two years of effort, that the bank succeeded in rounding up signatures for a quarter of a million pounds, enabling it to commence activity according to official regulations. It is clear that these modest efforts could not play an important part in Herzl's grandiose plans for the settlement of the Turkish national debt.

Opposition to Herzl

Opposition to Herzl had existed in Zionist circles from the beginning of his activities, but at first Aḥad Ha-Am was the only person who openly scoffed at the idea of concentrating the majority of the Jewish people in their own country and at Herzl's political programmes. But Herzl continued to devote himself to diplomatic activity, adhering to his belief that 'policy is shaped from above', and as most of his activities – namely, the negotiations with the Sublime Porte and contacts with various European politicians – proved fruitless, the number of critics and sceptics grew.

Three of Herzl's principles aroused particular criticism. The first was his emphasis upon diplomatic activity, which was in practice always a one-man show; this condemned other members of the movement to passivity, and even his close friends, such as Max Nordau, resented it. The critics argued that the liberation of the Jewish people should be carried out by the people itself and not by external forces, *i.e.*, the Great Powers. It is true that Herzl himself asked Turkey and other countries only for 'political guarantees', for which the Jews would then supply the content. But the hoped-for 'charter' was still far from attainment. He thus arrived at the second principle: in order to avoid arousing the anger of the Powers or impelling them to oppose the Zionist plans, Herzl demanded of the Zionists that they refrain from intervening in the internal political problems of these various countries. This demand condemned the Jews to inactivity on many vital political questions, particularly in Eastern Europe. His approach alienated from Zionism the more active and impulsive elements among the Jews, at a time when Jewish communities were just beginning to stir. The third principle was the neglect of cultural activity. Despite his statements on the need to return to Judaism and despite the resolutions of the Second Congress, Herzl himself was remóte from the Hebrew language and culture. When he published his utopian novel *Altneuland* in 1902, in which he prophesied the social and techno-logical achievements of future Jewish settlement in Palestine, he did not dwell on problems of culture and language. Herzl believed that the immigrants would bring to their new country the languages of the lands in which they had lived and that the strongest, probably German, would prevail. The Jewishness of the country is not evident in Herzl's descriptions – which could apply to an African state, as Aḥad Ha-Am noted in his satirical and bitter critique. But, above all, Herzl feared contro-versy in the Zionist camp between the orthodox and the free-thinkers, as they were particularly divided on the cultural question because the rabbis were afraid of the penetration of secular tendencies into traditional education and literature.

As a result of all these factors, an open opposition group was formed in 1901 composed of young *maskilim,* notably of Russian origin. This group appeared at the Fifth Zionist Congress at Basle in December 1901 under the name of 'the Democratic Faction'. It was headed by Jacob Bernstein-Kogan, Leo Motzkin, Chaim Weizmann, Martin Buber, Berthold Feiwel and others. This faction demanded a new emphasis on the national elements of Zionism, a firm stand in the face of religious prejudice, the maintenance of internal democracy in the composition of the congresses and in Zionist institutions, a clarification of ideology and an intensification of cultural activity. Despite Herzl's firm stand, a compromise was eventually reached, and the congress elected cultural committees for several countries. This led to the organiza-tion of the orthodox opponents of the 'Faction', and at a conference held in Vilna in February 1902 it was decided to establish a special group, Mizrachi (a Hebrew abbreviation for 'spiritual centre'), with the aim of defending political Zionism and opposing cultural activity by the Zionist Organization. Within a short time the Mizrachi became the central force of the religious Zionist camp.

The Uganda Crisis and Herzl's Death

The Fifth Congress constituted a turning-point in the development of the Zionist movement and a change in Herzl's political activity. He despaired of Turkey and be-gan increasingly to pin his hopes on Britain. The first opportunity was afforded him when he was invited to testify before the British Royal Commission on Immigration in 1902. Lord Rothschild, who was a member of this commission, invited him for a talk, and thus the first contact was established between the Zionist leader and the House of Rothschild. Herzl also succeeded in meeting the British Colonial Secretary, Joseph Chamberlain, and the Foreign Secretary, Lord Lansdowne, and he took the opportunity of submitting a plan for Jewish settlement in El Arish in the Sinai Peninsula. This also did not materialize.

In despair, in the summer of 1903, he agreed to discuss an existing plan for Jewish settlement in East Africa, in Uganda (now part of Kenya). Without awaiting the final results of the negotiations, Herzl left for Russia in an attempt to persuade the authorities to intervene with the Sultan on behalf of his project and to permit open

Zionist activity in the Russian state. He wanted to encourage the Jewish masses in that country, who were still shaken by the Kishinev pogroms. Many reservations were voiced about this journey, even among the Zionist leaders of Russia itself, since direct negotiations with the Russian Minister of the Interior, Plehve, who was believed to be directly responsible for the bloodshed in Kishinev, were not likely to raise the prestige of the Zionist movement in the eyes of Russian society. In fact Plehve did not intend to legalize Zionist activity, but Herzl left Russia with the hope that there was some chance of alleviating the situation of the Zionist movement there, on condition that the Jews refrained from independent Jewish activity. He was also profoundly affected by the terrible state of Russian Jewry and the hopes they pinned on his own activities: he received a tumultous welcome by masses of Jews on his way. It is possible that this was the main reason for his decision to bring the proposal for settlement in Uganda before the Sixth Zionist Congress, held shortly after his return from Russia in August 1903 at Basle.

The proposal came as a surprise to the delegates, who knew nothing about the negotiations with the British Government. Many did not know what position to adopt, but there was heavy opposition to Herzl, particularly among the Russian delegates, members of 'the Democratic Faction'. The main spokesman for the programme at the congress was Max Nordau, although he himself was unenthusiastic; he emphasized that Palestine remained the final objective of Zionism, and Uganda would serve as a *Nachtasyl* ('refuge for the night') for the hundreds of thousands of persecuted Jews. The proposal submitted to the congress was to dispatch a delegation to examine the local situation. It was approved by 295 votes to 178, with 132 abstentions. Those who voted against it, headed by Jehiel Tschlenow, one of the leaders of Russian Jewry, left the assembly hall.

The Zionist Organization was not split, but the 'Zionists of Zion' initiated a vigorous campaign against the Uganda scheme. At a gathering held in Kharkov in October 1903, and chaired by Menahem Ussishkin, it was resolved to send an ultimatum to Herzl and demand that the Zionist Organization refrain from dealing with any territorial project outside the borders of Palestine and Syria. In the meantime the British Government withdrew its offer, as a result of the controversy aroused in Britain over the plan. At a meeting of the Zionist Executive in April 1904, Herzl delivered an emotional speech, reiterating his loyalty to the idea of Palestine. The opposition leaders formally declared that they were satisfied with the efforts of the leadership with regard to Palestine. Peace was restored to the movement, but shortly afterwards, on 3 July 1904, Herzl died.

The Split Between 'Zionism of Zion' and Territorialism

The death of Herzl reopened the split that had begun to heal after the meeting of the executive, even though East Africa had now been found unsuitable for settlement. Several of the extreme 'political' Zionists, such as Israel Zangwill, Max Mandelstamm and Nachman Syrkin, proposed a search for new territories for which charters might be obtained, since this was not for the moment feasible with regard to Palestine. Zangwill's slogan was: 'Better Zionism without Zion than Zion without Zionism' –

the very fact of territorial concentration and statehood would bring about the rebirth of the people and prepare it for future achievements in Palestine. There were also those who went further and denied the indissolubility of the tie between Zionism and Palestine.

At the same time the 'practical' tendencies of the 'Zionists of Zion' were increasing. Menahem Ussishkin, who was elected head of the Odessa Committee, put forward proposals that actually implied the revival of the old activity of Hovevei Zion. In a pamphlet that he published at that time, entitled *Our Programme,* he proposed that the Zionist Organization resume its settlement activities in Palestine without delay. For this purpose he proposed the establishment of a new organization, like Bilu in its day, to be composed of Jewish youth who would volunteer for agricultural work in Palestine for three years. The Jewish National Fund (or Keren Kayemet, 'perpetual fund', in Hebrew), which had been approved by the Fifth Congress, should establish model farms in cooperation with ICA. The Hebrew character of education in Palestine should be guaranteed.

These two viewpoints clashed openly at the Seventh Congress held in Basle in July 1905. The 'Zionists of Zion' won a large majority, while the minority seceded from the Zionist Organization and founded the Jewish Territorial Organization (I.T.O.). Among those who remained, a sharp controversy developed between the 'political' and the 'practical' Zionists. Max Bodenheimer claimed that neither money nor efforts should be invested in Palestine before political guarantees were obtained, while the head of the Palestinian committee, Professor Otto Warburg, delivered a positive report on the potential of Palestine and recommended the continuation of settlement activity despite political conditions. The congress adopted this latter view. The Zionist Executive was composed of three political and three practical Zionists, and David Wolffsohn (1856–1914) was elected president of the Zionist Organization.

The influence of the territorialists was particularly strong in England and to a lesser extent in Russia and the United States. They engaged in sharp polemics with the Zionists, but in fact faced the same difficulties as had once confronted Herzl. The heads of I.T.O. emphasized the importance of diplomatic effort and established a 'geographical committee' which examined proposals for settlement in Angola, Cyrenaica, Mesopotamia, Australia and South America. The attempt to continue negotiations with the British regarding settlement in Uganda proved a failure. The Portuguese authorities agreed to grant concessions to Jewish settlers in Angola, but would not agree to Jewish self-rule in the colony.

Differences arose between the leadership of I.T.O. and its supporters in Russia, who demanded a greater stress on the national and democratic character of the organization. I.T.O. won greater success among rich Jews, who were willing to help direct the mighty wave of Jewish migration from Eastern Europe to suitable places. Attempts were made to send immigrants from Europe to the port of Galveston in Texas in order to prevent their congregating in the East Coast cities of the United States. In this sphere, cooperation developed between I.T.O. and the Alliance Israélite. The successes of the territorialists were limited. On publication of the Balfour Declaration, Zangwill rejoined the Zionist Organization.

The Zionist Movement in Russia and Austria

At the First Zionist Congress, the great majority of Russian Zionists joined Herzl's camp. But as the Second Congress approached, it became clear that certain fundamental problems needed to be discussed, particularly in the light of Aḥad Ha-Am's criticism of Herzl and his methods. The first conference of Russian Zionists was held secretly in Warsaw in August 1898 with this purpose in mind; it represented 373 Zionist organizations then active in Russia. At this gathering Aḥad Ha-Am expounded his views, although his remarks were more conciliatory than his previous comments in *Hashiloah*. During the deliberations there was considerable friction when the rabbis demanded that cultural activity be supervised by the Committee of the Great Orthodox Rabbis.

The second conference of Russian Zionists was held openly in Minsk at the beginning of September 1902, after both camps – the supporters of the 'Democratic Faction' on the one hand and the Mizrachi on the other – had defined their positions. The main subject of debate was the question of cultural activity. Aḥad Ha-Am and Sokolow were the main advocates of national-cultural activity, while the orthodox representatives were opposed to it. Eventually a compromise was reached, and it was decided to set up two committees for cultural activity for the two schools of thought – the traditional and the progressive. The conference also recommended settlement in Palestine and declared that the work of the Odessa Committee was an essential part of general Zionist activity. As a result of these decisions, a controversy arose in the orthodox Mizrachi movement, and a part of its membership seceded from the Zionist movement, fearing the domination of the secularist progressives. Some of them were among the founders of the ultra-orthodox Agudat Israel in 1912.

In the interval between the second and third conferences – the latter was held at Helsingfors (Helsinki) at the beginning of December 1906 – a basic change took place in the political activities of the Russian Jewish community in general and the approach of the Zionists in particular. This was caused by the 1905 Russian Revolution. At the beginning of that year an Alliance for the Attainment of Full Equal Rights for Russian Jews was founded, with the participation of all the non-socialist Jewish groups. It was the Zionists (and other nationalists) who insisted that the platform of the Alliance include the demand for 'national rights' and 'national-cultural self-determination with all this implies', and this proposal was accepted. At the second conference of the Alliance in November 1905, the demand was voiced that an 'all-Russian Jewish national assembly' be convened to decide on the forms of national self-determination. At the third conference (February 1906) the chief spokesman of the autonomists, the historian Dubnow, as well as the Zionists, proposed that the Jewish deputies elected to the Duma organize themselves into an independent parliamentary group. Only when those active in the Russian liberal K.D. (Constitutional Democrats) party threatened a split did the former withdraw their demand.

The Russian Zionists were faced with important political decisions. There were still echoes at the conference of the struggle with the territorialists: the 'charterism' of political Zionism was strongly attacked, and various proposals were put forward regarding the purchase of land and settlement activities in Palestine; it was argued that it was no longer possible to await developments in passive idleness. But the main discussion was devoted to national-political work in Russia – namely, 'immediate action'. The conference resolved to demand 'national rights for the Jewish population' to be defined 'on the basis of a petition [worked out by] an all-Russian Jewish national assembly'. These would include 'national self-rule' in the spheres of education, health, mutual aid, migration and religious worship. It also demanded the right to observe the Sabbath and to maintain Jewish matrimonial law among other things. But the most revolutionary resolution of the Zionists was to stand at the forthcoming elections to the Duma as an independent body or in coalition with other parties. This was a radical departure from Herzl's approach. It also led to the dissolving of the Alliance. Shortly afterwards, however, the counter-revolution occurred in Russia (July 1907), which in practice annulled all the democratic freedoms and abolished all possibility of legal political activity until the 1917 Revolution.

A similar development occurred in Austria. The tension between the national groups and the need to safeguard various Jewish interests, such as the right to open shops on Sunday, led the Zionists to engage in political activity in their places of residence. But the heads of the Zionist Organization were not ready to accept this. The fourth conference of Austrian Zionists, held in Prague in June 1905, decided that the Zionist Organization was not an Austrian political party and that members could participate in political activity of other parties only on condition that this activity did not affect Zionist programmes. These decisions aroused great opposition, particularly in Galicia, where organized Jewish activity was essential in the face of Polish pressure.

It is not surprising that there was public ferment in Zionist circles, particularly in light of the political changes occurring in Austria and the growing campaign to change the electoral system by abolishing the electoral curiae, based on social status, and introducing representation according to national groups, defined on the basis of the mother tongue. In July 1906 an extraordinary conference of Austrian Jews was convened, which decided on the establishment of a Jewish national political party to conduct the political struggles of the Jews of the empire for national rights, and to be led by the Zionists. Such a party was indeed established in western Austria, and, in addition to voicing democratic demands, it called for Jewish national autonomy, government support for Jewish schools and the establishment of a legally recognized association of Jewish national communities. In Galicia the Zionist Organization itself organized political activity. The test of the new policy was the May 1907 elections. Because of the distribution of the electoral regions and the government pressures, Jewish nationalists achieved a very limited success. Nevertheless, an independent Jewish parliamentary faction of four deputies was established in the Reichsrat after the elections.

In May 1910 an all-Austrian conference of the Jewish National Party was held in Cracow, its objective being to unite all the Jewish forces in the empire in a struggle for Jewish rights, particularly in the light of the forthcoming population census, which provided the opportunity for demanding official recognition of the Jewish nationality as equal to others – Germans, Poles, Ruthenians (Ukrainians), etc. It was decided to establish a Jewish nationalist organization for Austria, to encompass all the Jews belonging to the various national political organizations. The conference declared the Zionists alone to be the standard-bearers of Jewish nationalism.

The activity arising from the census led to severe clashes between the nationalists on the one hand and the assimilationists and authorities on the other. The registration of first language for the purpose of defining nationality was accompanied by threats, fines and arrests, particularly in Galicia, as Yiddish was not recognized as a national language. Tension was also created by the elections to the Reichsrat in 1911, during which not even one Zionist deputy was elected. Nevertheless, the Zionist influence grew steadily until the outbreak of the First World War.

The Zionist Organization in the Decade Before the War

The balance achieved within the Zionist Executive between the 'political' and the 'practical' Zionists after the Seventh Congress hampered the activities of the organization. The movement did not disintegrate after Herzl's death, as many of its opponents had prophesied, but neither did it attain any real achievements. The fact that several important Zionist associations, such as those of Russia and Austria, turned to the local political scene, also restricted the scope of world-wide Zionist activity. The consistent 'political' Zionists, headed by Nordau, never resigned themselves to political work in the Diaspora. An additional cause of ferment within the Zionist Organization was the consolidation of the religious Mizrachi and socialist Poalei Zion (Workers of Zion) ideological factions.

The Eighth Zionist Congress (Hague, August 1907) decided on the establishment of a Palestine Office, headed by Arthur Ruppin, and of Ḥevrat Haksharat Hayishuv (Society for Land Reclamation) to purchase land in Palestine and prepare it for cultivation. Chaim Weizmann appeared at the congress and advocated the creation of a synthesis between political and practical Zionism. The successful 1908 revolt of the Young Turks in the Ottoman Empire aroused new hope in the hearts of the 'political' Zionists. They hoped that the new rulers would recognize Zionist aspirations. Victor Jacobson became active in Constantinople, mainly by appealing to Ottoman public opinion through the press. When the centralizing and Ottoman-nationalistic tendencies of the Young Turks became evident – and this spelled death to the hopes of extensive autonomous rights for other nationalities in the empire – voices were raised in the Zionist camp for a re-examination of the 'Basle Programme' and the abandonment of the charter idea, as well as of the demand for the recognition of Palestine by international law as a Jewish national home. At the Tenth Zionist Congress Wolffsohn declared: 'We are not aspiring to a Jewish state, but to a national home [*Heimstätte*] in the land of our fathers.' But despite all this, there was no alleviation of the suspicion and even hostility of the Turkish authorities towards Zionist aspirations.

At the Ninth Congress (Hamburg, December 1909) the clashes between the leadership, headed by Wolffsohn, and the opposition, led by Jews from Russia (Weizmann, Tschlenow, Ussishkin) became intense. The resentment increased even after the congress, and, as a result, Wolffsohn eventually expressed readiness to concede several important organizational points, such as the transfer of the Zionist Executive from Cologne, his own home, to an important Jewish centre, to grant representation to various factions and to grant the right to elect the leader to the Executive. At the Tenth Congress (Basle, August 1911) Wolffsohn resigned as president and was replaced by Professor Otto Warburg (1859–1938), who had done much for Palestinian settlement as chairman of the Palestinian Committee of the Zionist Organization. East European Jews – Nahum Sokolow, Shmarya Levin and Victor Jacobson – were co-opted onto the Executive. At the Eleventh Congress (Vienna, September 1913) they were joined by Jehiel Tschlenow.

The new executive regarded the Zionist Organization as a body uniting various streams and trends. It encouraged organizational and journalistic activity, student and sport associations. Cultural activity, which the Tenth Congress had debated in Hebrew, was extended. The Mizrachi wanted to prevent discussion of these questions and in order to allay its apprehensions, a resolution was passed promising that cultural activity in Zionist institutions would not deal with religion. Increasing attention was devoted to problems of migration.

The Eleventh Congress, the last before the First World War, served as the arena for an attack by the 'political' opposition on the 'practical' leadership, but the influence of the former was waning. The congress decided to devote further effort to settlement and gave special attention to the founding of a Hebrew university in Jerusalem and the inclusion of Hebrew as part of Jewish education in the Diaspora. The Zionist Organization did not really widen its horizons before 1914, but it had become an important and influential factor in Jewish life.

The Socialist Movement Among Jews Before the First World War

Activities in the 1880s and 1890s

The Jewish socialist movement began to emerge in the second half of the 1870s. Within the next ten years, there commenced the organized struggle of Jewish workers in Russia, England and the United States for the amelioration of their living conditions. In Russia Jewish workers' associations proved their strength by organizing impressive strikes in several towns in the Pale of Settlement. In England and in the United States they helped new immigrants to introduce slight improvements in the terrible conditions prevailing in the sweatshops. The representatives of the socialist intelligentsia, particularly students, began to form workers' circles for the dissemination of education and socialist ideas. As in other socialist parties in their early days – and perhaps more than in most – the press served as a lever and an instrument of first-rate importance in the Jewish socialist movement. Morris Vinchevsky, who produced the Hebrew socialist journal *Asefat Ḥakhamim* ('Assembly of the Wise'), a continuation of Liebermann's *Ha'emet* in Koenigsburg in 1877–8, began to publish a Yiddish weekly *Der Poilishe Yidl* ('The Polish Jew') in London in 1884. This transition from Hebrew to Yiddish as the language of propaganda denoted the tendency to approach the broader masses of Jewish workers and not just the young Jews educated in *yeshivot*, as Liebermann had done.

An important factor in this change was the rise in the number of Jewish socialists who abandoned the theory, advanced by the Russian Narodniks, that the Jews all belonged to the parasitic class, exploiting the rest of the population. In 1880 a pamphlet was published in Geneva by 'a group of Jewish socialists' announcing the establishment of a printing press to publish socialist literature in Yiddish. The same pamphlet also explained that there were among the Jews, in addition to the intelligentsia, artisans and manual workers who could provide scope for socialist propaganda. The author was the Jewish socialist Leizer Zuckermann, who was supported in his new approach by the Ukrainian democrat M. Dragomanov.

The decision of the Jewish students and *maskilim* in Russia 'to return to their people' at the time of the 'southern tempests' affected not only the drive towards Ḥovevei Zion and migration, but also the clarification of the Jewish problem from a socialist viewpoint. One of the expressions of this was an article by Ilya Rubanovich, one of the leaders of the Narodniks, published in 1886 in his party's organ under the title 'What Should Russian Jews Do?' This was the first open discussion of the Jewish problem in the revolutionary press. Rubanovich wrote that it was not the Jewish bourgeoisie but rather the Russian revolution that would bestow liberty and equal rights on the Jewish proletariat. The revolution would also enable poor rural Jews to found their own agricultural colonies; revolutionary Jewish youth had so far paid no heed to the situation of Jewish workers and had not fulfilled their duty to conduct revolutionary propaganda among their people.

In England a monthly (later weekly) in Yiddish entitled *Der Arbeiter Freind* ('The Workers' Friend') began to appear in 1885, and after some time began to display a clear tendency towards anarchistic views. Generally speaking, anarchistic views were quite common among Jewish immigrant workers in England and in the United States. The more important anarchists in the United States, such as Emma Goldman and Alexander Berkman, were Jewish by origin. In Russia, too, anarchist groups gained strength, particularly during the first revolution (1905–7), and their courage and readiness for sacrifice made a great impression on public opinion in that country. When the anarchist character of *Der Arbeiter Freind* became evident in 1891, Vinchevsky and several of his associates left the paper and founded their own journal entitled *Die Freye Velt* ('The Free World'), which was later expanded into the weekly *Der Veker* ('The Awakener'). In his greeting to the editors, the dean of Russian revolutionaries, Peter Lavrov, wrote: 'A nation which, in the nineteenth century, produced Karl Marx and Lassalle, surely has a natural, or a historically developed tendency to absorb socialist principles.'

In 1892 there appeared in London, under a Narodnik imprint, a pamphlet signed by E. Khasin and entitled *A Jew to Jews*. The author was Dr Chaim Zhitlowsky, a Jewish Narodnik who eventually became an active leader of the Jewish workers' movement. In this essay he made an attempt to associate the Jewish people's hopes of renaissance with their direction to agricultural settlement in Russia itself, in the spirit of the agrarian socialism of the Narodniks. On the other hand, he criticized the Russian revolutionary intelligentsia for their unwillingness to comprehend the situation of the Jewish workers and condemned the Jewish intelligentsia for their detachment from the people and their lack of desire to operate among them and to guide them. But the majority of the revolutionary circles in Russia at that time leaned towards Marxism rather than Narodnik ideology.

A clear expression of the transition from propaganda in small circles to propaganda aimed at a wider public was provided by the May Day festivities of Russian Jewish workers, the first of which was held in Vilna in 1892. Two male and two female workers addressed an audience of about 100 and described the plight of Jewish workers as a result of the economic and political conditions prevailing in Russia, rejecting the Zionist solution in Palestine and pinning their hopes on the future revolution. A celebration held in Vilna in 1895 was attended by Julius Martov (Zederbaum), who was to become one of the leaders of Russian social democracy and the leader of the Menshevik group. He called for the establishment of an independent social-democratic organization of Jewish workers, since the Jewish movement was one of the strongest in the country. Though strongly opposed to nationalism, he considered that if Russian and Polish workers endured the bitter struggle and were obliged to make some concession, they would do so first and fore-most at the expense of the specific Jewish demands. Therefore 'national and class consciousness should go hand in hand', for 'a class does not deserve liberty if it does not know how to win it for itself.'

Organization of the Bund

The idea that Jews in general and Jewish workers in particular had their own special interests, and were therefore in need of a separate organization to achieve their aims, spread rapidly among the active members of the Jewish workers' movement. After various deliberations, representatives of Jewish socialist circles met in Vilna in October 1897 and founded the General Union of Jewish Workers in Lithuania, Poland and Russia, known in Yiddish as Der Bund.

The Bund did not regard itself solely as a political party and devoted a considerable part of its activity to the trade-union struggle of the workers. It also drew its main strength from the trade unions established in the various branches. It therefore did not define its organizational nature in a clear-cut fashion. Its political programme, as formulated at the first gathering, regarded war on Tsarist autocracy as the main objective.

The Bund did not consider itself a separate party, but rather a part of Russian social democracy, which was maintained in the form of scattered groups and as-sociations. Because of its relative strength, the Bund played an important part in the establishment of the All-Russian Social Democratic Party in March 1898. It is no coincidence that the first conference of this party was convened in Minsk, a Pale of Settlement town in which the Bund operated, and the latter placed an illegal printing press at the disposal of the party. It was agreed at the conference that the Bund would enter the party as an autonomous organization, independent on all questions relating to the Jewish working class.

The fact that the police succeeded in arresting the central committee of the new party and the majority of the Bund 'activists' shortly after the conference did not affect the activities of the Bund: its influence spread rapidly among Jewish workers. It increased particularly after one of its members, Hirsch Lekert, made an attempt upon the life of the Vilna provincial governor, who had ordered the whipping of Jewish workers for participation in the 1902 May Day demonstrations. Lekert was executed and became the martyr of the movement. Although the Bund was basically opposed to individual terror as a weapon in the political struggle – in accordance with Marxist theory – Bundist leaders endeavoured to justify Lekert's action because of the widespread public response.

National Development of the Bund

The first conference of the Russian Social Democrats proclaimed as part of its programme the right of every nation to self-determination, but the Bund, in its early days, did not submit any particular Jewish national demand, with the exception of civil equality. At the third conference, held in Kovno in December 1899, the view was voiced that 'national rights', *i.e.,* rights as a group, not only as individuals, should be demanded for the Jews, but this was rejected by most of the participants.

The fourth conference of the Bund (Bialystok, May 1901) was, for many reasons, a milestone in its development. It decided on the intensification of the political struggle, as separate from the economic struggle. But the main turning-point was the national question. The conference decided to demand the transformation of Russia into a 'federation of nations, each of them with complete national autonomy, independent of the territory on which it resides. The conference recognizes that the term "nation" also applies to the Jewish people.' But, taking into consideration the conditions prevailing in Russia, the conference did not demand this national auton-omy immediately, in order to avoid 'obscuring the class consciousness of the pro-letariat'. A resolution was also passed condemning Zionism.

When one of the leaders of the Bund, V. Kossovski, published a pamphlet calling for the organization of the Russian Social Democratic Party as a federation of national parties, the idea encountered the vigorous opposition of the main section in this party, which was formed around the journal *Iskra*. At the second congress of the Russian S.D., held in summer 1903, the Bund demanded that its autonomous status be recognized as the 'sole representative of the Jewish proletariat'; this met with the opposition of the majority, which rejected the federative principle in party organization. The main opponents of the Bund in this matter were Jewish Social Democrats such as Martov, Trotsky and others. (Out of forty-five delegates to the conference, twenty-five were Jewish, including five representatives of the Bund.) The Bund announced its secession from the party, and, subsequently, there was increased friction between them and the S.D. because of their parallel activities in the Pale of Settlement.

The political activities of the Bund grew in scope, and its influence over the Jewish public increased after it began organizing self-defence units in the period of the 1903–7 pogroms. It played an active part in the 1905 Revolution, and at that time the number of its members had reached 35,000. The fourth congress of the Russian S.D. agreed to approve the autonomous status of the Bund and to refrain from deciding on the question of the national programme. On the basis of this decision, the seventh conference of the Bund (Leipzig, 1906) decided to return to the ranks of the party.

With the onset of political reaction, there was a considerable decrease in the activity of the Bund, as of all other revolutionary parties. Some of its active members migrated to the United States, and others devoted themselves to cultural activity in Yiddish. The eighth conference of the Bund (Lvov, 1910) called for a struggle for the rights of Yiddish as the language of the Jews even before the attainment of national auton-omy. It also decided to participate in communal life as part of its struggle for sec-ularization. The regime was called on to grant the population the right to choose their own day of rest (Friday for Moslems, Saturday for Jews, Sunday for Christians). In 1912 the Bund was among the initiators for convening various sections of the Russian S.D., against the policy of the Bolsheviks, who had declared their faction to constitute the entire party. This gathering, which was held in Vienna in August, recognized the principle of 'cultural national autonomy' for which the Bund had been fighting for ten years and declared that it did not contradict the principles of the party. This was the first recognition by a large section of the Russian S.D. of a fundamental clause in the Bund programme.

Syrkin and the Beginnings of Socialist Zionism

Nachman Syrkin (1868–1924) is regarded as the father of socialist Zionism. In 1898 he published an article entitled 'The Jewish Question and the Socialist Jewish State' in which he demanded the establishment of a socialist Jewish state in Palestine. Only such a state, he thought, was capable of providing a solution to the Jewish question, which was insoluble under the conditions of capitalism. In 1901 he issued an 'Appeal to Jewish Youth' in which he demanded the establishment of a mass Jewish social democratic organization to achieve these aims. In this same period, numerous groups of varying leanings began to emerge in Russia, bearing the name Poalei Zion (Workers of Zion). Some of these groups, like that in Yekaterinoslav, advocated specifically socialist objectives. But the main trend among them, 'the Minsk stream', did not regard itself as socialist at all. It stressed the central role allotted to the workers in the Zionist movement, but expressed reservations regarding political activity in the Diaspora. It also held aloof from the intelligentsia for fostering ideologies that did not take into consideration the predicament of the worker and common man. The first conference of the 'Minsk' group of Poalei Zion was held in that city in December 1901 and was associated with the Fifth Zionist Congress, which was shortly to be convened, and the activities of 'the Democratic Faction', which Isaac Berger, the leader of Poalei Zion, supported.

The Poalei Zion associations continued to proliferate and to hold varying views. The Uganda crisis exacerbated the split, with the accent on territorialist and autonomist trends. An important expression of the ideology of Poalei Zion was provided by the Vozrozhdeniye (Renaissance) group, which was established after the 1903 Kiev convention, and which formulated a programme differing from that of the Minskites. It demanded national and cultural autonomy and the establishment of a central representation of the Jewish people in Russia.

Proletarian Zionism began to develop in Austria in 1903 on the initiative of the Jewish Shop-Assistants Association of Galicia and a similar group in Vienna. A German-language journal, *Der jüdische Arbeiter* ('The Jewish Worker') began to appear under the editorship of Saul Raphael Landau, who had been one of Herzl's close associates. This journal was later transferred to Cracow, where it appeared in Yiddish. In 1904 the Alliance of Workers and Shop Assistants was established in Austria, and in 1906 it took on the name of The Jewish Socialist Workers Party, Poalei Zion.

Socialist-Nationalist Parties in Russia

The Uganda crisis, the strengthening of the territorialist mood and the extensive political activity following the revolution aroused considerable ferment in Poalei Zion circles. Some of these groups completely abandoned the idea of an independent

Jewish territory, at least in the near future, and put their faith in the attainment of Jewish autonomy in Russia. There can be no doubt that they were influenced by the historian Simon Dubnow, one of the formulaters of the autonomistic theory concerning the maintenance of nationalism in the countries of residence of the Jews. Dubnow, an opponent of socialism, was active on behalf of this cause in the Alliance for the Attainment of Full Rights for Russian Jews, and after its dissolution he tried to set up a political body known as the Folkspartei (People's Party), for the attainment of these aims.

Other groups of Poalei Zion were influenced by the territorialist claim to the extent that they reached the conclusion that the 'real interests of the Jewish masses are not located in Palestine', and they therefore did not recognize 'the connection between Zionism and Palestine'. Only a small number of Poalei Zion groups maintained contact with Palestine and with the Zionist Organization. As a result of the ferment and polemics three socialist-nationalist parties were consolidated in the years 1904–6:

1 The Zionist Socialist Workers' Party (S.S.), which began to take shape in 1904 under the impact of the territorialist mood and on the inspiration of Nachman Syrkin. Its basic assumptions were that there was no possibility of normal economic development for the Jewish people in Russia and that the pétit bourgeois who was forfeiting his status was not undergoing a process of proletarization, but rather turning into a 'pauper'. Nor could emigration to developed countries change this situation, since the Jews were absorbed there in marginal economic branches, connected with consumption and commerce, rather than in basic branches. Only if the Jews built up their own economic framework from the foundations, could desirable social development be ensured. Hence the search for a suitable territory and the cooperation with I.T.O. The S.S. exerted considerable influence over workers' circles, which conducted extensive trade-union activity. For this reason their relations with the Bund were strained to the point of physical clashes. They conducted lively polemics against Zionism and autonomism, which they regarded as a 'bourgeois utopia'.

2 The Jewish Socialist Workers' Party (Sejmists). This party continued the ideas of the Vozrozhdeniye. Its members did not regard themselves as Marxists and were close to the Russian Social Revolutionary Party. Although they did not deny the need for an independent territory, they regarded this aspiration as unrealizable in the near future. Their main struggle was for extensive national autonomy within the framework of Russia, which was to become a federative state composed of various nationalities. Each nation should be headed by its own representative body, a 'sejm', with wide powers. The Sejmists were among those who initiated the convention of representatives of Russian socialist-nationalist parties, inspired by the S.R.

3 The Social Democratic Workers' Party, Poalei Zion, founded in Poltava in February 1906. Its leader and the shaper of its image was Ber Borochov (1881–1917). He commenced his political activity with a vigorous campaign against territorialist trends, endeavouring to prove that only Palestine could provide the solution to the Jewish problem. Borochov was close to Russian social democracy, but in time he formulated his own ideological framework, a kind of 'historical materialism' similar

in spirit to that of Bogdanov, a member of the Russian S.D. who evolved his own independent philosophy. In his programmatic essay 'Our Platform', Borochov claimed that Palestine was the most suitable territory for creating a 'working area' for the Jewish labourer and for the maintenance of a framework within which the class struggle could be properly conducted. Poalei Zion participated in self-defence activities, but enjoyed limited influence in labour circles. Shortly after the establishment of the party, the 1907 coup d'état occurred, which in effect put an end to the activities of the socialist-nationalist parties.

In 1907 the Social Democratic Poalei Zion established a World Alliance that brought together the parties in Russia, Austria, Palestine, the United States, England and Argentina; its office was located in Vienna. A fund was established to aid workers emigrating to Palestine and to help them settle there. In 1909, on the initiative of Zhitlowsky, all the socialist-nationalist groups in the United States united under the Poalei Zion banner, although their programme differed from that of their Russian counterparts. The socialist-nationalist parties recovered strength only after the outbreak of the 1917 Russian Revolution, or after the end of the First World War.

60

The Growth of the Jewish Centre in Palestine Before the British Occupation

The Continuity of Jewish Settlement in Palestine

After the great flowering of the Jewish centre in Palestine in the sixteenth century (see Part V), the community underwent a steep decline in the seventeenth century. The unstable security situation, natural catastrophes, the small number of immigrants and the abandonment of the towns transformed Palestine into a remote and desolate corner of the Ottoman Empire, with a weak and poverty-stricken Jewish population. In the eighteenth century there was a slight recovery. At the beginning of the century, R. Yehudah Hehasid ('the Pious') immigrated together with more than 1,000 of his followers, but the group rapidly disintegrated after the death of its leader – partly as a result of the opposition aroused by the presence of many Sabbateans among the immigrants. The Committee of Notables and Officials of the Land of Israel in Constantinople was meanwhile endeavouring to consolidate the Jewish community in Jerusalem. In 1740 R. Hayyim Abulafia, rabbi of Izmir, renewed Jewish settlement in Tiberias and its environs, under the patronage of Daher el Omar, Governor of Galilee. In 1742 R. Hayyim ben Atar of Morocco organized a group of immigrants from his country and from Italy, and the majority of them settled in the same year in Jerusalem. The great majority of the Yishuv (Jewish community) was composed of Sephardim and immigrants from the Arab countries, with only a few Ashkenazim. The authorities restricted the number of Jews permitted to reside in Jerusalem, and there was no Ashkenazi community there at all, as the Ashkenazim were held responsible for the debts left by R. Yehudah Hehasid's group. Settlement in Palestine received renewed impetus with the immigration of *Hasidim* from Lithuania, headed by R. Menahem Mendel of Vitebsk in 1777. Not only were they relatively numerous (more than 300), but they were also the first immigrants who for some time maintained living contact with their country of origin and received material and spiritual support from their brethren there. R. Menahem Mendel continued to guide the congregation in Vitebsk from Palestine, so that the relationship was reciprocal. At first the *Hasidim* contemplated settling in Safed, but, because of the opposition this aroused, the majority of them moved to Tiberias and some settled in Peki'in. The *Hasidim* augmented the Jewish community in Galilee and extended the Ashkenazi community to settlements outside Safed, where it had been concentrated till then. In the years 1808–10, some disciples of the

Gaon of Vilna, the *perushim,* immigrated and settled in Safed. In 1816 a number of them moved to Jerusalem and laid the foundations of Ashkenazi settlement there.

Despite these waves of immigration and the consolidation of the Yishuv in the 'four holy lands' (Jerusalem, Safed, Tiberias and Hebron), as well as for a time in Acre and elsewhere in Galilee, the Jewish community in Palestine at the beginning of the nineteenth century numbered only some several thousand souls, who suffered from the weakness of the Ottoman regime and from various natural catastrophes, such as plagues, earthquakes and drought. Its survival was dependent on the arbitary will of the local rulers and on the extent of the protection and patronage they chose to grant the Jews. The political and internal security situation were considerably affected by the fellaheen rebellions and attacks by marauding Bedouin. The central authority had also been weakened when European countries established a protectorate ('capitulations') over their nationals within the Ottoman Empire. After Napoleon's campaign in the East (1798–9), there was increased interest in Palestine within the European states, and they began to demand protection of the Holy Places and of the various Christian sects. In time the Jews were also included in this protective system.

In 1831 the Egyptian ruler, Mohammed Ali, sent his son Ibrahim Pasha at the head of his army to conquer Palestine and Syria. The Constantinople authorities made no resistance to this campaign, and the local rulers surrendered almost without putting up a fight. The Egyptians introduced many legal and administrative reforms in Palestine, but the local population, including the Jews, suffered greatly when rebellions that broke out against the invaders were being suppressed. In 1840 the Egyptians retreated under pressure from the Great Powers, and the Turks returned to rule the country.

Despite the numerous political changes during the first half of the nineteenth century, the Yishuv continued its slow development. Jerusalem once again became the leading community, and in 1824 Ashkenazim were again permitted to settle there – after they had succeeded in freeing themselves of responsibility for the old debts. The synagogue known as 'Ḥurbat' ('the ruin') of R. Yehudah Heḥasid was reconstructed, as were several other ancient synagogues. The number of Jews in Safed once again reached 2,000 families, and the settlement in Tiberias also grew. But the great earthquake of 1837, in which 2,000 Safed Jews and 700 in Tiberias were killed, reduced the communities. Many of the Safed Ashkenazim moved to Jerusalem.

The Old Yishuv

In the forty years that elapsed between the return of the Turks to Palestine and the commencement of Zionist immigration (1840–81), the Jewish community in Palestine became consolidated and its leadership patterns were determined. Sir Moses Montefiore played an important part in this process, and in his many visits to the country he aided the Yishuv in various spheres. The number of Jews in the country rose from 10,000 in 1840 (according to several sources, even less) to approximately 24,000. The great majority were concentrated in Jerusalem; according to one estimate there were some 14,000 Jews in Jerusalem in the seventies, and they constituted the majority of the city's population. In 1860 Jews began to settle outside the walls of the Old City and to build their own quarters – Mishkenot Sha'ananim, Maḥaneh Yisrael, Naḥalat Shiv'ah, Me'ah She'arim and Even Yisrael.

After the restoration of Turkish rule, Jerusalem became a district capital and, in accordance with the administrative regulations of the Ottoman Empire, its chief rabbi became a *Ḥakham Bashi,* with recognized authority. In practice his authority extended only to the Sephardim, who were Ottoman subjects and constituted the majority of the Jewish population. Most of the Ashkenazim were foreign nationals under the protection and jurisdiction of the foreign consuls according to the 'capitulation' agreements, which accorded the consuls judicial authority over their subjects, thus placing them outside the reach of Ottoman legislation. During and after the Crimean War (1853–4), the consuls became more powerful, and the significance of the 'capitulations' was extended to empower them to take under their protection not only their own nationals but other groups as well. This situation considerably affected the internal organization of the Jews of Palestine. The Sephardi community preserved its unity, but the Ashkenazim split into a large number of *kolelim,* or communities, in accordance with place of origin. These *kolelim* sent out emissaries to obtain financial support from their countries of origin.

The great majority of the Jewish Yishuv at this time (some authorities believe as many as 85%) lived off the *halukah,* which originated in the dispatch of rabbinical emissaries to collect funds, and the proliferation of 'Palestinian funds', or *Kuppot Rabbi Meir Ba'al Hanes.* These funds developed towards the middle of the nineteenth century into a ramified network of fund-raising for residents of the Holy Land. An important centre of this activity was the 'Committee of Officials and Administrators' in Amsterdam, founded by R. Zevi Hirsch Lehren and which received annual donations from the important communities in Western Europe and transferred them to the leaders of the Yishuv without specifying which communities were to benefit. The *perushim* had their own collection centre in Vilna, and in time most of the *kolelim* established their own fund-raising centres, which were redistributed from time to time by various agreements and compromises.

The fund distribution system of Sephardim and Ashkenazim differed. After payment of taxes and levies for all the town-dwellers and for maintenance of the Holy Places, the Sephardim distributed the major part of the funds to scholars and notables, and even the more prosperous took their share, since they regarded it as a kind of prize for their sacred work in the Holy Land. The result was that there was a disparity between the notables and the many poor members of the community, since family status was not reflected in the central distribution. On the other hand, a large number of the Sephardim engaged in trade and crafts, while most of the Ashkenazim, who were relative newcomers unacquainted with living conditions in the country or with the language of its inhabitants, lived mainly off the *halukah,* which was distributed on a per capita basis. But one-third, or even more, of all the funds were distributed as payments to scholars or notables outside of the per capita distribution. Despite the large number of persons in Europe engaged in collecting alms for the Holy Land, the sums distributed did not suffice for livelihood, particularly as the authorities appropriated a proportion of them and the years of drought and other natural catastrophes had led to a steep rise in prices. When the *kolelim* split up, a gap was created between the wealthier groups – those based on countries in which the Jewish communities were prosperous, such as Holland and Germany or Hungary – and the poorer ones based on Austria and Volhynia. A General Committee for All *Kolelim* was set up to create some form of unity, but the *kolelim* continued to operate separately.

Outside Jerusalem, the largest concentration was in Safed. In the 1840s there were some 1,500 Jews there, and by the end of the seventies more than 5,000; at first only one-third but eventually more than three-quarters of them were Ashkenazim. Next came Tiberias with between 1,000 and 2,000 Jews, and then there were several hundred in Hebron. In Jaffa there was no real community until the seventies; and there was still a small number of Jews in several other places in Galilee, such as Acre, and in Nablus and Haifa.

The way of life was rigidly conservative, with the rabbis strictly supervising the observance of all religious injunctions, however slight. But the Sephardim (even the rabbis among them) were more open to associating with their non-Jewish surroundings, studying languages and crafts and using the hospital founded in Jerusalem in 1854 by Jewish philanthropists. The Ashkenazi leaders launched an attack on the founding of schools in which secular subjects and languages were taught, such as the Lemmel School, established in Jerusalem in 1856. They also objected to the study of Hebrew grammar.

Nevertheless, a tendency to study various trades and even to engage in agricultural work began to emerge in the Yishuv, and above all among the Ashkenazim. These trends were supported by Sir Moses Montefiore, who invested considerable effort in them, and they were also advocated by the first Hebrew newspapers, *Halevanon* and *Haḥavaẓẓelet*, which began to appear in Jerusalem in the sixties, and more regularly in the seventies. These tendencies were further encouraged when the Alliance Israélite Universelle founded the Mikveh Yisrael agricultural school in 1870, not far from Jaffa. Eventually some younger members of the Yishuv made an attempt to found agricultural colonies in 1878 – Petah Tikvah ('Gateway of Hope'), north of Jaffa, and Gai Oni (Ja'ūni) in Galilee – but both were abandoned shortly afterwards because of the obstacles encountered by the settlers.

The First Aliyah. *The First Agricultural Colonies*

The first wave of Jewish immigration (*aliyah*), which commenced in 1881, completely changed the condition of the Jewish community. The number of immigrants was not great, but they came to the country with a clearly defined national aim: to found agricultural colonies as the basis for Jewish settlement in the historic homeland and as the main step towards the return of all Jews to Palestine. They regarded themselves as the vanguard of the people, aware that there was a great resurgence in their countries of origin and that they were backed by a public movement in the Hovevei Zion associations. The members of the Bilu association, who immigrated in an organized group, and the emissaries of other associations, such as Zalman David Levontin, sought ways of realizing this national aim. In the summer of 1882 the

Va'ad Ḥaluẓei Yesud Hama'alah ('Committee of Pioneers') was established in Jaffa, and it endeavoured to provide systematic aid to settlers and to set up a central body that would utilize the experience acquired. It attempted to prevent the repetition of errors, as well as exploitation by profiteers, and to formulate suitable principles on which to base the new settlement – Jewish tradition, national aspirations and Narodnik influences.

As soon as immigration began to increase, the Turkish authorities became apprehensive and tightened the regulations for entry into the country. In May 1882 they prohibited immigration completely. The immigrants were forced to enter the country secretly, often bribing officials. But despite these difficulties the first agricultural colonies were founded in 1882 (and have endured to this day). The immigrants from Russia established Rishon le-Zion, while those from Rumania set up Zikhron Ya'akov in Samaria and Rosh Pinah in Galilee. In 1883, Petaḥ Tikvah was resettled and Yesud Hama'alah was set up in the Huleh Valley. But as these initial steps were being taken, it became clear that the first settlers, for all their vision and courage, had no clear knowledge of agricultural work, particularly under Palestinian conditions, and that they lacked the financial means for consolidating the new colonies. The Ḥovevei Zion associations in Russia and Rumania could not provide the necessary support. The new colonies faced the threat of disintegration in their first summer. It was then that Jospeh Feinberg of Rishon le-Zion and R. Samuel Mohilewer, one of the leaders of Ḥovevei Zion in Russia, appealed to Baron Edmond de Rothschild for aid, since he had displayed an interest in Jewish agricultural settlement and was sympathetic towards Ḥibbat Zion.

The 'Well-known Philanthropist' and His Officials

Baron Rothschild, who was later called the 'well-known philanthropist', because his support was at first extended anonymously, and also the 'father of the Yishuv', invested more than £1.5 million in the Palestinian settlement activities over a period of fifteen years from the time he first began to aid the colonies. He supported those who had already settled in the colonies but also purchased additional land and helped several farmers from Russia to settle in Mazkeret Batyah near the ancient city Ekron (1883). Only the Bilu colony of Gederah, founded in 1884, was supported solely by Ḥovevei Zion in Russia, and its financial situation was always extremely precarious. (Throughout this period the funds raised by Ḥovevei Zion for the Palestinian colonies did not total more than £100,000.)

The 'philanthropist' sent a trained horticulturalist to train the settlers in agricultural work and, in particular, in order to introduce viniculture into the colonies, supplying them also with the necessary equipment and seeds. At the same time he demanded of the settlers that they unquestioningly obey the officials he appointed to manage the colonies. The planning of the work and the running of the farms was controlled entirely by the officials, and the settlers regarded themselves as hired workers carrying out orders. Interest in the success of agricultural efforts and harvests waned, as most of the farmers received financial aid distributed according to family size. The officials were remote from any nationalistic sentiment, did not understand the feelings of the settlers and treated them with contempt as recipients of charity. Instead of being the pioneers of a great national liberation movement, the settlers became farmers dependent on the arbitrary will of the Baron and his officials. Disputes and even rebellions against the Baron's officials broke out. However, as the incompetence of Hovevei Zion in Russia and other countries removed all hopes of wide-scale settlement, the Baron, despite all the reservations, undoubtedly saved the Jewish settlement project in its early stages.

The Odessa Committee and ICA as Settling Agencies

In 1890, as we have noted, the Russian Government approved the status of the Society for Aid to Jewish Farmers and Craftsmen in Syria and Palestine, known as the Odessa Committee. The awakening that followed both extended and reinforced the activity of the Russian Hovevei Zion. The consolidation of the first colonies over the years also served as proof that it was indeed possible to maintain agricultural settlement in Palestine. Hovevei Zion established an executive committee in Jaffa, headed by Vladimir (Ze'ev) Tiomkin, which drew up a far-reaching plan for settlement, and the flow of immigrants to Palestine increased in the years 1890–1. From this new wave there emerged two colonies set up by private enterprise: Rehovot, south of Rishon le-Zion, a well-planned colony whose founders possessed sufficient funds for consolidation, and Haderah, south of Zikhron Ya'akov, in a swampy area. Malaria took its toll of a large number of the settlers. The courage of the Haderah settlers became the ideal of the young Jewish settlement movement. On the other hand, various associations were established that sent emissaries to purchase land for settlement and, as a result, promoted land-profiteering. The Turkish authorities redoubled the strict control on entry into Palestine and prohibited land purchases by Jews. Within a short time a grave crisis broke out in the settlement project.

During the years of crisis no new colonies were established, and it was only in 1896 that the Russian Hovevei Zion established Be'er Toviyyah in the south as a labour settlement, and Baron Rothschild set up Metulah in the north. In 1899 the Baron handed over management of the settlements under his patronage to ICA, which then began to operate in Palestine. In contrast to the methods employed by the Baron's officials, the ICA planners sought to foster self-help and individual responsibility of the settlers. Financial support was abolished, the planning of agricultural work and internal administration were entrusted to the settlers. In order to decrease their dependence on market fluctuations, ICA encouraged the development of field crops rather than plantations, and a training farm was set up in 1899 in Ilaniyyah (Sejera) to train the settlers in new agricultural methods. At the turn of the century the colonies of Kefar Tavor, Yavne'el and Menahemiyya were set up in Galilee and several years later Kinneret was founded. According to the ICA settlement arrangements the settlers were at first regarded as lessees, and only after they had demonstrated their abilities as farmers did they become settlers, owners of their own plots, obliged to pay ICA interest on the capital invested.

One of the central problems confronting the settlers – veterans and newcomers alike – was the question of agricultural labourers. At first the work was carried out by the settlers themselves, their families and Jewish workers trained at the training-farm. But within a short period, Arabs from the neighbouring villages began to be absorbed as labourers in the colonies. They were cheaper, more experienced in farming and more accustomed to the climate and conditions. As in most non-European countries where Europeans settled, Palestine too was faced with the danger that the Jewish economy would be founded on native labour.

The cultural and spiritual life of the new Yishuv had also reached a crossroads. Some of the colonists had lost interest in the development of a national Jewish culture, which had been the ambition of the first settlers. And although in 1897 there were some twenty schools in the country in which the language of instruction was Hebrew, interest in the French language and culture increased under the influence of the Alliance Israélite and the Baron's officials. The sons of the colonists were uninterested in agricultural work and began to move to the towns and even to travel abroad to Paris in order to complete their education. Some even left the country for good and emigrated to the United States and Australia. During the Uganda controversy, which raged in the Zionist movement in 1903, the advocates of Uganda were influential in the colonies. On the face of it, the twenty years of Jewish agricultural settlement in Palestine had proved a limited success from the economic point of view and a total failure in its national and cultural aspects.

The Nature of the Second Aliyah

The decisive change in the national renaissance project in Palestine was wrought by the immigrants of the Second *Aliyah,* the earliest of whom, including A. D. Gordon, reached Palestine at the beginning of 1904. In 1905, one of the Hebrew teachers in the country, Joseph Vitkin, issued an appeal to young Jews in Russia, calling on them to immigrate to Palestine and save the nationalist enterprise. There began to arrive young Jews who had been shocked by the helplessness of the large Russian Jewish community in the face of the Kishinev pogroms. Their ranks were swelled by members and supporters of various parties, who had pinned their hopes on the First (1905) Russian Revolution, but had become disillusioned by its outcome. The ten years of the Second *Aliyah* (1904–14) brought some 40,000 immigrants to Palestine, the majority of whom were young. Although most of them eventually left the country again, members of this *Aliyah* not only enlarged and strengthened the Yishuv, but also completely transformed its character, institutions and aspirations. In 1914 there were some 85,000 Jews in the country: 45,000 in Jerusalem, 10,000 in Jaffa, 7,000 in Safed, 5,000 in Tiberias, 3,000 in Haifa and 12,000 in agricultural colonies. In 1909, the suburb of Ahuzat Bayit was founded near Jaffa, which soon developed into the first all-Jewish city, Tel Aviv.

The Second *Aliyah* was distinguished by the fact that it was composed of idealistic young people who were ready to devote their lives to the ideal of national renaissance. Thus they revived the pioneering traditions of the early days of the First *Aliyah,* the Biluites and others of similar views. Almost all these young people came from Russia and were influenced, to varying extents, by the socialist ideals disseminated in that country during the years of revolution. The main social frameworks they set up in the country were the labour parties and associated institutions.

The Palestinian Labour Parties

One of the outstanding personalities among the members of the Second *Aliyah* was Aaron David Gordon (1856–1922), an original thinker, who immigrated to Palestine in middle age, and whose theories served as a focus and expression of the ideological and moral aspirations of Jewish workers in Palestine. Gordon believed in the revolutionary and beneficial power of labour, of physical work, and of the return to nature and regarded them as the central motive in the regeneration of the Jewish people. The Jews, who, because of historical conditions, had been detached for centuries from creative work, could return to it only in their historic homeland. Cultivation of the soil, which would redeem the land from its barrenness, would also bestow the moral right to ownership of the land and bring about the moral and spiritual rebirth of the people. The Hapo'el Haza'ir (Young Worker) Party, established at the end of 1905 under Gordon's inspiration, saw its central task as 'the conquest of labour' – namely, basing Jewish agriculture on the work of Jewish labourers and the introduction of Jewish workers into all sectors of the economy. In addition, it advocated spiritual renaissance based on the Hebrew language as both the everyday tongue and the language of cultural creation. The best literary forces in the country rallied around the organ of this party, also named *Hapo'el Haza'ir* (its literary section was edited for a time by the writer Joseph Hayyim Brenner).

At the same time that the Hapo'el Haza'ir party was established, members of the social democratic Poalei Zion party in Russia who had arrived during the Second *Aliyah* established the Social Democratic Hebrew Workers' party (Poalei Zion), affiliated to the world federation of these parties in the Diaspora. In its programme it defined itself as aspiring to create a socialist world order (the only means being a class struggle, whose form was dependent on conditions of time and place), while its goal in Palestine was political independence for the Jewish people. Its short-term objective was to create for the Jewish worker in Palestine normal social and political conditions in order to implement these ideals. In practice, the two labour parties resembled one another in method: in the 'conquest of labour', the emphasis on national aims and the fostering of Hebrew culture.

Poalei Zion, which at first issued its programmatic statements in Yiddish, also began to publish a Hebrew journal by the name of *He'ahdut* ('Unity'). The joint efforts of these two labour parties laid the foundation for new forms of agricultural settlement. Nuclei of national autonomy were created, which developed in time into the Yishuv's independent institutions. It is not surprising that the active members of these parties and their associates in the Second *Aliyah* – Berl Katznelson, David Ben-Gurion, Izhak Ben-Zvi, Yosef Aharonovitch, Joseph Sprinzak and others – played a leading part in the leadership of the Yishuv during the mandatory period and in the independent State of Israel.

One of the first steps towards 'conquest of labour' were the attempts to break the resistance of the colony farmers to the employment of Jewish workers. The Jewish labourers began to compete with the Arabs, who were more experienced and were content with lower wages. This competition was a severe test for the young intellectual workers, and a considerable number failed. In order to foster the Jewish worker in Palestine, it was proposed that Jews from Yemen, accustomed to hard work and to a lower standard of living, be brought to the country. Some of those who had arrived during the First *Aliyah* had adapted themselves smoothly to the working conditions of the country. The immigration of the Yemenites commenced in 1909, and they were directed to agricultural work in the colonies. But despite the efforts and the successes, the number of Jewish workers remained relatively small. At the time of the First World War there were some 1,500 of them in the Jewish colonies, as against 6,000 Arab labourers who were employed there.

In addition to their struggle for the right to work, the Jewish workers also sought to improve their working conditions. They were characterized from the first by their developed sense of mutual aid. In 1911 an Association of Agricultural Workers was organized in Judea and shortly afterwards similar associations were set up in Galilee and Samaria. In 1912 a workers' sick fund (Kuppat Holim) was established, and a year later Poalei Zion founded the Palestinian Workers' Fund (Kapai), with the aim of recruiting funds among Jewish workers in the Diaspora in order to help workers in Palestine and their institutions.

Communal Settlement and Guard Duties

There was controversy between the labour parties as regards the place of the workers in the settlement project. The Odessa Committee and Menahem Ussishkin, its leader at that time, claimed that the workers should not aspire to their own settlement. In order to concentrate workers in the colonies, they tried to establish labour settlements for them, with auxiliary farms. This stand was supported by most members of Hapo'el Haza'ir. But many members of Poalei Zion and non-party members tended to support independent labour settlement, and in 1907 the Hahoresh workers' association was founded; its objective was to create in Palestine a class of 'workers and fellaheen'. The establishment of the Palestinian Office, headed by Arthur Ruppin, and the founding of the Hevrat Hakhsharat Hayishuv (Land Reclamation Society) impelled the Zionist Organization to seek new methods of agricultural settlement. At the end of 1909, Ruppin agreed to hand over to a group of workers the management of a farm on Jewish National Fund land on their own responsibility. This experiment proved successful, and in 1910 a new group of workers settled in Lower Galilee on the shores of the Sea of Galilee at Deganyah. This new type of settlement served as the nucleus for communal labour settlement and for a communal (kibbutz) movement, which later played a decisive role in the development of the Jewish community in Palestine. But, in contrast to this project, an experiment conducted between 1911 and 1914 to establish a communal farm at Merhavyah on the basis of the programme of the Zionist economist Franz Oppenheimer – an attempt to combine the advantages of a large farm's rational methods with the drive of small farming – proved a failure. Despite the progress it made in certain spheres, the experiment failed because the manager of the project disdained the ideological motivation of the Jewish workers. Nevertheless, the Merhavyah experiment served as the basis for the development of the moshav (small-holders' cooperative settlement) in a later period.

It was not only the innovations in settlement forms that characterized the Zionist settlement activities in this period, but also the examination of the economic foundations of settlement in general. The colonies of Judea and Samaria were founded on plantations and the Galilee colonies on field crops, and for this reason they were sensitive to price fluctuations or natural catastrophes such as drought. Concentration on one branch precluded rational exploitation of the soil and full utilization of the labour force. On the basis of the experiments of the agronomist Yitzhak Wilkansky at Ben Shemen, new mixed farming methods were evolved, encompassing varied branches.

An important problem that preoccupied the Jewish settlements from the outset was the question of guard duty. Both the nomadic Bedouin and the fellaheen of the neighbourhood harassed the new settlements and damaged their property. In order to prevent this, the settlements entrusted guard duties to Arab sheikhs, who often exploited them or conspired with the thieves and marauders. This impelled settlers in several locations to employ Jews as watchmen. But this arrangement also aggravated the tension between the settlers and their Arab neighbours. A group of Jewish workers associated with Poalei Zion undertook, in 1907, the task of guarding Jewish property and established the Bar Giora association for this purpose. Its members took on the task of guarding Ilaniyyah and Kefar Tavor. During Passover 1909, the Hashomer (Watchman) association was established; its aim was to take over the guarding of Jewish settlements and to ensure for the watchmen fair living conditions. This association was headed by the watchmen Israel Giladi, Mendel Portugali and Israel Shochat. The Hashomer watchmen were later given the task of safeguarding ownership of those lands purchased by Jews but not yet settled.

Relations Between the Yishuv and the Arabs

The expansion of Jewish agricultural settlement and the intensification of Zionist activity in Palestine led to the consolidation of Arab opposition. During the last years of the nineteenth century, the opinion was already being voiced among the Arabs that the sale of land to Jews should be prohibited. But there was a far-reaching change in 1908, after the Young Turks' revolution, which provided the impetus for the establishment of an organized Arab nationalist movement.

As we have noted, the Zionist leadership pinned its hopes on the Young Turks' revolt, but was disappointed. Not only did the elections to the Turkish parliament create cohesion among the Arabs of Palestine and lead them to take up a political stand hostile to Zionism, but among the new freedoms granted to the local population was the right to purchase arms. The number of attacks on Jewish settlements increased, and their security situation deteriorated. The heads of the Yishuv and the Zionist leadership gradually became conscious of the need to acquire arms and concern themselves with self-defence. In a message to the President of the Zionist Organization, David Wolffsohn, written in May 1909, Ruppin wrote:

> . . . in all the Palestinian settlements the settlers want to purchase arms. There is a widespread movement based on this. As an argument they point to the fact that since the sale of arms has been permitted in Turkey as a whole, the Arabs everywhere are equipping themselves with arms and, as a result, are permitting themselves to attack the Jewish settlements which lack arms, both in word and deed. They would cease doing this if they knew that the settlers also had arms.

As the centralizing nature and anti-Zionist tendencies of the Turkish authorities became increasingly evident, the Yishuv became more security-conscious. At the same time the Zionist leadership made some attempts at negotiation with the Arab representatives, though without success.

Cultural Life

The philanthropic organizations, the French Alliance Israélite and the German Hilfsverein der deutschen Juden, which established and managed most of the schools in the country, endeavoured to accentuate the languages of their own countries in these schools. Nevertheless the concept of Hebrew education took root in the country, and Hebrew gradually became the main language of instruction. An important role in this process was played by the Association of Hebrew Teachers in Palestine, established in 1903, and the Teachers' Centre, which headed it. It also drew up the first curriculum for elementary schools. In 1906 a Hebrew high school was founded in Jaffa, and Boris Schatz established Bezalel, a school of arts and crafts. The Hebrew Gymnasia (high school) was founded in Jerusalem in 1909.

The 'language dispute' played a decisive role in bringing about the triumph of Hebrew education in Palestine. The Hilfsverein decided upon the establishment of a Technical Institute in Haifa and an affiliated high school with the aid of funds donated by philanthropists in Russia and the United States. Since the teaching of the Hebrew language was of central importance in the educational programme of this society, the Zionists supported the plan. But at a meeting of the board of directors at the end of 1913, it transpired that the Hilfsverein intended to teach the sciences and technical subjects in German, claiming that the Hebrew language was not sufficiently developed for this purpose. This decision aroused a wave of protest in the Yishuv. Most of the pupils of the Hilfsverein schools went on strike, and the teachers resigned. The Teachers' Centre announced the opening of new schools, and a Hebrew teachers seminary was inaugurated with the aid of Hovevei Zion. Most of the pupils and teachers of the Hilfsverein network were absorbed into the new schools, while the opening of the Technion was postponed. It was finally inaugurated after the First World War, by which time Hebrew was strongly entrenched in the educational network of the country.

The Yishuv During the First World War

The war caused great hardship in the Yishuv by cutting it off from those countries that had formerly supplied immigrants and financial aid. The abolition of the capitulations by Turkey in September 1914 affected the status of many Jews who remained without protection and, in fact, without legal status. When Turkey joined the war on the side of the Central Powers in October 1914, an edict was issued exiling all 'enemy subjects' from Palestine to the interior of the Empire. On the intercession of diplomatic representatives in Constantinople, they were given the opportunity of obtaining Ottoman nationality, and many chose this way out. Nevertheless, some 10,000 exiles left the country in the first year of the war.

The Governor of Syria and Arabia, Jamal Pasha, then opened an outright campaign against Zionism. On his instructions harsh persecution began, accompanied by arrests and banishment. The economic condition of the Yishuv deteriorated. As long as the United States remained neutral, the American Provisional Executive for Zionist Affairs helped the Yishuv considerably by sending food and money. Within the Yishuv itself, an extensive network of mutual aid was organized. But at the beginning of 1917, when the British began to plan their attack on Palestine, Jamal Pasha published an edict banishing to the north of the country all Jews from Jaffa and the southern region. The inhabitants of Galilee extended aid to their brethren from the south.

The political situation became even graver in September 1917, when an espionage network of young Jews operating on behalf of the British (the Nili Association) was uncovered by the Turks. It was headed by the director of the agricultural research station at Atlit, Aaron Aaronsohn. Despite the fact that most of the Yishuv was opposed to this activity, it served Jamal Pasha as a pretext for cruel persecution of the Jewish community and particularly of the agricultural colonies. Many people were arrested and tortured, including Sarah Aaronsohn, one of the active leaders of Nili, who committed suicide. Hundreds were exiled to Damascus, where they were incarcerated under rigorous conditions, and many of them died there. Mass arrests were carried out on the pretext of searching for deserters from the Turkish Army. Several of the exiles in Damascus, together with local Jews, organized a committee for aid to the exiles, which saved many victims of persecution.

Despite all these vicissitudes the Jewish community in Palestine held firm. The number of Jews in the country was reduced from 85,000 before the war to 56,000 in 1918. But the agricultural colonies were not destroyed, and several new settlements were even established in Upper Galilee, such as Tel Ḥai and Kefar Giladi. The aid of the American Joint Distribution Committee and the German and Austrian Jewish organizations was instrumental in setting up these colonies. And despite the differences between the Old and the New Yishuv, the internal organization of the Jewish community stood up to the test. The British attack, which commenced on 31 October 1917, liberated the south, and in December 1917 (during the Feast of Chanukah), General Allenby entered Jerusalem at the head of his army. In 1918 the entire country was liberated from Turkish rule and came under British military administration.

The Growth of the New Jewish Culture: the Strengthening of Ties Between Jewish Communities and Their Increasing Role in Gentile Society

The Intensification of Conflicting Trends in Jewish Life

The development of the Jewish people at the end of the nineteenth and beginning of the twentieth centuries fluctuated between two extremes: on the one hand there was the outbreak of anti-Semitism in Central and Western Europe, which was a reflection of the unwillingness of wide circles to accept the Jews and assimilate them; and, on the other hand, there was a strengthening of radical tendencies among the Jews themselves, both in the national and in the socio-political spheres. Even those Jews who had not yet grasped the significance of the new processes and still believed in the possibility of complete integration, or, at least, of living peacefully among the nations – and these constituted the majority of the Jewish people at that time – could not escape the increasing tension between the cohesive and disruptive forces operating in Jewish history. The Jews associated their future with their countries of residence, absorbed the culture of their host countries and took an active part in the life and struggles of these nations; but, at the same time, they created special Jewish organizational frameworks for mutual aid and support of their persecuted brethren in Eastern Europe, Asia Minor and North Africa. They also, directly or indirectly, fostered the resurgence of Jewish national culture and the development of modern Hebrew and Yiddish literature.

This dichotomy was particularly evident in the period under discussion, during which Jewish integration into the national and cultural life of Western and Central Europe ceased to be the minority choice and encompassed the great majority of the Jewish communities in these countries. This integration and activity within the political, economic and cultural frameworks of the countries was not brought about by Jews as a group or community but by individuals who used their rights and fulfilled their obligations as individual citizens of the state. The hostile reaction to Jewish activity, on the other hand, did not take the form of opposition to individuals, but of a campaign against 'Jewish domination', the 'Jewish spirit' and other such anti-Semitic concepts. The Jews of these countries were therefore obliged to organize themselves in self-defence and to take part in the social and political struggle not as individuals but as a group repelling attack. They began to set up Jewish organizations for various purposes, but their central aim was to safeguard their right to integrate into the society around them and to constitute an organic part of it. The existence, however, of special Jewish organizations with their own specific social and political goals – even when they were clearly philanthropic in nature and were established in order to aid Jewish students or immigrants – served as proof both for declared anti-Semites and for many other European circles that 'Jewish unity', 'Jewish separatism' and hence the ambition for 'Jewish domination' really existed. These reactions were naturally even more likely to be aroused by Jewish bodies of specifically national and political orientation. Thus a vicious circle was created: the onslaughts, suspicions and discrimination intensified Jewish activity, while this in its turn increased suspicion and hostility. The outcome was the terrible price that the Jewish people paid during the two world wars and in the intervening period.

The Activities of Jewish Organizations on Behalf of Their Persecuted Brethren

In the 1860s and 1870s the Alliance Israélite was the main body combating anti-Semitic persecution and trying to abolish discrimination in Morocco, Switzerland and Rumania. In 1878 the Joint Foreign Committee, which had been established in Britain by the Board of Deputies together with the Anglo-Jewish Association, participated in this activity. The committee endeavoured to persuade the British Government to intervene on behalf of the persecuted Jews in Russia and in the East. After the 'southern tempests', the riots in south Russia at the beginning of the eighties, a Russo-Jewish Committee was established in Britain, which organized public protest against the persecution of Russian Jews and tried to aid them. A special publication entitled *Darkest Russia,* edited by Lucien Wolf, began to appear in 1912.

At the beginning of the twentieth century, the main initiative in this struggle was taken up by the Hilfsverein der deutschen Juden, founded in 1901. After the Kishinev pogroms in 1903, it convened representatives of the more important Jewish organizations in various countries in order to discuss the efforts that should be made on behalf of Russian Jews. In the years 1905–6, Paul Nathan, head of the Hilfsverein, approached leading figures and circles close to the Russian monarchy on this matter. In 1906 he organized a new convention of Jewish representatives in Brussels devoted to the same question. After the 1907 'agrarian riots' in Rumania, Paul Nathan approached the Premier with the demand that he compensate the Jews of his country for the damage caused them. In 1912, again mainly on Nathan's initiative, another gathering of Jewish organizations was convened in Brussels and the Union des Associations Israélites was established. Its purpose was to defend Jewish interests against the hazards of the Balkan wars. During the First World War the Hilfsverein also intervened with the German military authorities on behalf of the Jews of the occupied territories.

Similarly, extensive activity was carried out by the American Jewish Committee, founded in 1906 with the aim of rallying all sections of American Jewry to defend the rights of Jews all over the world. Like Jewish organizations in Europe, it directed its main efforts towards aiding Russian Jewry. As the Russian Government imposed restrictions on Jews with American citizenship who visited the country, the committee demanded of the U.S. authorities that they retaliate. Despite the unwillingness of the authorities to respond to the demand, the committee initiated a widespread public campaign and, with the help of public opinion, influenced Congress' position. A resolution was passed in Congress terminating the treaty between Russia and the United States, which had been violated by the Russian Government. A few days later, the Russian Minister for Foreign Affairs was notified that the United States had decided to abrogate the treaty.

During the Beilis blood libel, the committee brought before the American public systematic reports of the conduct and background of the trial. After the Balkan wars, the U.S. Government, at the demand of the committee, asked all countries that had been involved to safeguard the equal rights of the populations of annexed territories. This referred primarily to part of Bulgaria, which had been annexed to Rumania and in which there was ground for apprehension that the Jews might suffer discrimination.

Migration and Settlement – Baron de Hirsch and ICA

It was not only against the background of political and diplomatic cooperation that contacts between Jewish communities in various countries were strengthened. The communities were even more united in their joint efforts centred on the great migratory movement. This migration brought the Jews of the West closer to their brethren in the East and to their sufferings. While the refugees of the Russian pogroms were being cared for in the Austrian border town of Brody in 1881–2, conferences of Jewish representatives from various countries were held. Despite the fact that these organizations did not succeed in directing and controlling migration, they were instrumental in aiding immigrants and protecting them against exploitation by agents of shipping companies and various scoundrels. When the first wave of immigration commenced, the Hebrew Immigrant Aid Society was established in the United States.

In 1891, when the second wave of immigration reached its peak, a German Central Committee for Russian Jewry was organized in Berlin, with the aim of concentrating all aid to immigrants. Together with Jewish organizations in France, England and Austria, it established committees on the German and Austrian borders that classified the immigrants, examined their papers and supplied them with tickets to Hamburg or to the United States. The committee also concerned itself with the livelihood of the immigrants till they boarded ship (although there was no shortage of complaints on the part of the immigrants regarding the attitude towards them). The motive for this activity was twofold: a desire to aid persecuted brethren, and an attempt to find them a refuge overseas out of fear that they might remain in the West (in the propaganda of German and French anti-Semites, the 'incessant flow of Russian and Polish Jews' played an important part).

A new development in Jewish immigration plans occurred in 1891, when Baron Maurice de Hirsch (1831–96) published a programme for rescuing the millions of Russian Jews from their plight by their gradual evacuation from that country over a period of twenty-five years and their settlement on the soil in another country. In September of the same year in London he founded for this purpose the Jewish

Colonization Association with a capital investment of some £2 million, the largest sum ever allocated to a philanthropic purpose (this sum later grew to more than £7 million). The shares of the association were given to the important communities in the West (Berlin, Brussels, Frankfurt) and to the Anglo-Jewish Association.

Hirsch purchased large areas of land in Argentina on behalf of ICA and devoted considerable effort to the development of agricultural settlement there. The evacuation programme for Russian Jews as he first envisaged it – which included the attainment of autonomous status for Jews in various spheres of their new country (as he put it, 'a kind of Jewish state') – was completely abandoned. But achievements in the settlement sphere were considerable, despite all the difficulties and errors. In the six years of his activity in this field, until his death, five large colonies were established in Argentina, in which more than 6,700 people lived. After the Baron's death ICA's statutes were altered and its field of activity was extended. It began to operate in Palestine, opened hundreds of branches to aid immigrants in Russia, founded credit funds for craftsmen in Eastern Europe and fostered vocational training. But its main effort was still concentrated on Argentina: on the eve of the First World War there were more than twenty colonies there with a population of nearly 20,000.

The expansion of Jewish immigration in the twentieth century intensified the activities of the large organizations active in this field. This was partly motivated, as we have noted, by the fear that mass migration of poor Jews might arouse anti-Semitic reactions; accordingly, the poor were also assisted in their own countries, and some migrants were returned to their original homes. But extensive effort was invested in directing migration, in alleviating the suffering of the immigrants and in accelerating their absorption in their new countries of residence. In cooperation with other organizations, the Hilfsverein established a central office for migration affairs, which operated twenty-five committees that helped convey hundreds of thousands of Jewish migrants from Eastern Europe to the great European ports. Immigrant-aid associations were also set up in Holland, Belgium and Britain.

The Baron de Hirsch Fund, founded at the beginning of 1891, helped further the absorption of Jewish immigrants in the United States. It supported agricultural settlers in that country, aided the dispersion of the Jewish immigrants throughout the country, as they otherwise tended to concentrate in the East Coast ports, helped young Jews to study various occupations and encouraged 'Americanization' – namely, the study of the English language, local culture and values, and the acquisition of citizenship. When, at the turn of the century, a movement emerged in the United States directed against the new immigration in general and Jewish migration in particular, the American Jewish Committee initiated a vigorous campaign to frustrate plans for restricting immigration. On the other hand, an increasing number of societies began to engage in assisting the immigrants, in addition to the old charitable associations and the Baron de Hirsch Fund. In 1909 these associations amalgamated and set up the Hebrew Sheltering and Immigrant Aid Society (HIAS). HIAS cared for the Jewish immigrant from the moment he reached port; it extended legal assistance to those who were not permitted to disembark, helped find housing and employment, dealt with naturalization and so on. The president of HIAS tried to establish a joint body together with the large Jewish organizations in Europe in order to deal more effectively with the problems of the immigrants, but the outbreak of war frustrated the plan.

At the beginning of the war, American Jewry rallied to the aid of Jews in the battle areas of Eastern Europe. For this purpose the three main aid organizations amalgamated into the American Jewish Joint Distribution Committee (or Joint), and, with the aid of the American Embassy in Russia and through ICA, they transferred large sums of money to the Jewish Committee for Support of War Victims, which operated through numerous local committees. Money was also conveyed to the German-occupied territories through the Hilfsverein and the Israelitische Allianz. Shortly afterwards an independent Joint delegation began to operate in these areas. After the United States entered the war, the Joint continued to operate through its branch in neutral Amsterdam, established especially for this purpose.

Educational and Research Activity

The Jewish organizations attributed great importance to the educational sphere, in which, no less than in the political and social fields, conflicting trends became apparent. On the one hand they established schools for Jewish youth where the language of instruction was French or German, supported students who attended European and American universities, helped the Jewish masses to integrate into their new surroundings with regard to language and culture and did everything possible to accelerate this process. But, on the other hand, they also concerned themselves with Jewish learning – religious studies, knowledge of Hebrew and Jewish history – in the special Jewish schools established with their help, in the special classes for Jews in general institutions of education and in their subsidizing of rabbinical seminaries and research institutes.

In Western Europe and even in the United States the rapid cultural integration of the Jews into their surroundings soon made special Jewish schools a rare phenomenon. Jewish knowledge was inculcated during religious classes in general schools or through the teaching of basic Hebrew and prayers at 'Sunday school'. In Eastern Europe, in Galicia and even in parts of Hungary, the majority of Jewish youth at this time continued to study at a *heder* or *yeshiva*. It was only under the influence of the national movement that 'improved *heders*' were established, in which studies were conducted in Hebrew but secular subjects were also taught. In several *yeshivot* in Central Europe secular studies were also introduced. But the attraction of secular schools was already evident in this period even in orthodox circles in Eastern Europe. In the Near East and North Africa, where there was no state educational network, the standard of the *heder* was extremely low and the whole question of education was controlled by the great Jewish philanthropic organizations. The Alliance Israélite founded an extensive network of educational institutions in these countries. Its attempts to do the same in Russia encountered the opposition of the authorities. The Hilfsverein established a network of schools, kindergartens and vocational schools in Galicia, the Balkan countries and the Near East.

The rabbinical seminaries of the various religious trends were an important factor in furthering Jewish study and research. The first of these were established in Italy and France: the Padua seminary in 1827, with the moving spirit of Samuel David Luzzatto, and the Metz rabbinical seminary in 1829, which transferred to Paris in 1859. After the death of Luzzatto, the Italian seminary was moved to Rome and from there to Florence, where it blossomed again. In the 1850s the Jewish Theological Seminary was founded in Breslau by Zacharias Frankel, who tried to base Jewish studies there on the conservative spirit of 'positive-historical Judaism'. It was there that the *Monatsschrift für Geschichte und Wissenschaft des Judentums* was published, at first under Frankel's editorship and later with Graetz as editor. In 1872 the Higher Institution of Jewish Studies was founded in Berlin, headed by Abraham Geiger, and in 1879 an orthodox rabbinical seminary was founded by R. Azriel Hildesheimer. In 1874, a rabbinical seminary was founded in Budapest, and in 1893 a Jewish theological seminary in Vienna. In England, Jews College was founded in the sixties as a Jewish school, and only in the eighties did it become a higher institution for the training of rabbis. In the United States, Hebrew Union College was established in Cincinnati in 1875 as a reform rabbinical seminary, and the Jewish Theological Seminary of America was founded in New York in 1902, headed by one of the more important exponents of Jewish learning, Solomon Schechter, who also advocated the conservative 'historical' approach. In Russia, where rabbinical seminaries could not be established, 'Courses in Oriental Studies' were initiated in 1907 by Baron David Günzburg, and the subjects that were taught encompassed most fields of Jewish studies.

The widespread activity of these institutions in the sphere of Jewish studies and the scientific journals they published provided the impetus for Jewish studies at the turn of the century. In addition to the Breslau *Monatsschrift,* the *Revue des Etudes Juives* appeared in Paris from 1880, the *Jewish Quarterly Review* in London from 1889, *Yevreyskaya Starina* in St Petersburg from 1909, as well as several others. Information about Jews and Judaism was disseminated through publications, encyclopaedias (such as the *Jewish Encyclopaedia* in English and the *Yevreyskaya Entsiklopediya* in Russian, both of which appeared at the beginning of the century) and in literature for children and youth.

The Flowering of Hebrew Literature

Jewish education in Eastern Europe laid the foundation for the development of the Hebrew language from traditional literary forms to new patterns, and the creation of a new Hebrew literature. From the 1880s onwards the polemical or highflown didactic literature of the *Haskalah* writers began to be replaced by writing reflecting the life and aspirations of the people. The flowering of this new Hebrew literature is associated with the national renaissance movement. Dulitzki, Imber and Mani, for example, began to write poetry about Zion. In place of the scepticism of the *Haskalah* writers towards tradition, we now find sympathetic descriptions of the 'integrated Jewish life' of the past. There was increased interest in the literature of earlier periods and in folklore. Eliezer Ben-Yehuda, who believed that only in

Palestine could the people and its culture be reborn, emigrated to Jerusalem and commenced his endeavours to transform Hebrew into a living language. The publishing houses of Aḥi'asaf and Tushiyyah in Warsaw began to publish the works of the mediaeval Spanish Jewish poets, translations of works in Jewish studies, books of philosophy, textbooks and literature for the young. The Hebrew press played a particularly important role in bringing Hebrew culture closer to contemporary problems: *Hayom*, edited by Kantor, and *Haẓefirah*, edited by Sokolow, helped develop modern Hebrew journalism; Aḥad Ha-Am's articles were the classic expression of modern Jewish national thought.

The great national poet of this era was Ḥayyim Naḥman Bialik (1873–1934), comparable to Judah Halevi in the Middle Ages. His work fused delicate lyrical force with the tremendous power of poetic fury, in the tradition of the prophets. His spiritual uniqueness (and in this he reflected the main trend in the national renaissance) lay in his attempt to create a synthesis between the continuity of Hebrew cultural traditions and the creative efforts of his day. It was not by chance that the ineffectiveness of the great Russian Jewish community after the Kishinev pogroms aroused him to harsh condemnation of his people. As against this spiritual enslavement he raised the banner of renaissance, of the profound revolution in the life of the people that was eventually to lead them to full redemption in their ancient homeland.

The destruction of the patriarchal past under the cruel pressure of new developments and the conflict it aroused in the hearts of the people found its expression in the works of Feuerberg, the conflicts of Berdyczewski, the bitterness of Brenner. Hebrew literature took on new and varied forms, from the mysticism of I.L. Peretz and Berdyczewski to the pagan worship of nature and the materialistic love of life of Saul Tchernichowsky and those poets who imitated him – Zalman Shneour and Yaakov Cahan; from the naturalism of Mendele's heirs to the symbolistic psychologism of Peretz, David Frischmann and their followers.

Yiddish Literature

After the initial success of the works of Mendele and Linetsky in the sixties, the circle of Yiddish readers expanded greatly in the seventies. The popular novels in the vulgar style of Shomer began to be widespread, and the first plays by Abraham Goldfaden laid the foundations of the popular Yiddish theatre. The development of the national movement and the creation of great immigrant centres in the United States marked a new phase in Yiddish literature. Shalom Aleichem and M. Spector went out to battle against cheap popular fiction. At the beginning of the eighties, there began to appear the annuals *Der Hoisfreind,* edited by Spector, and the *Yiddishe Folksbibliotek,* edited by Shalom Aleichem, and shortly afterwards Peretz's *Yiddishe Bibliotek.* Mendele (who was still active), Shalom Aleichem and Peretz constituted the 'golden chain' of Yiddish literature. Shalom Aleichem (Shalom Rabinowitz, 1859–1916), whose work encompassed several types of literary genres, was undoubtedly one of the most important realistic humourists in modern European literature. His powerful influence is clearly evident in modern Yiddish and Hebrew literature. Younger authors also appeared as the heirs of the classic Yiddish writers – Shalom Asch, H. D. Nomberg, A. Reizen, I. M. Weissenberg, Der Nister (Pinkhes Kahanovich) and many others.

In the United States Jacob Gordin continued to write plays, which, to a large extent, were responsible for the development of the Yiddish theatre in immigrant centres. Morris Rosenfeld reflected the New York Jewish ghetto life in his poetry, as well as the hopelessness of the sweatshop workers. Yehoash translated the Bible into Yiddish.

At the turn of the century Hebrew and Yiddish writings occupied a niche of their own in modern literature. Considerable sections of the Jewish intelligentsia began to regard them as an important cultural asset, a vital part of their spiritual lives and their Jewish identity. But the unique nature of Jewish historical development left its mark in this sphere as well, for the creative forces were divided. Hebrew literature became the main foundation of the Zionist national renaissance and brought about the evolutionary transformation of the Hebrew tongue into a living language; it was not only spoken by the Yishuv in Palestine but served as the literary language of wide sections of the Jewish people, particularly in Eastern Europe. On the other hand, the non-Zionist radical intelligentsia that supported the Bund, and later the Folkists, transformed Yiddish and its literature into a primary element of their national and spiritual aspirations, showing great devotion and even fanaticism in their allegiance.

The struggle between Hebrew and Yiddish was of considerable importance in the history of Jewish spiritual creation and self-awareness during the years preceding and following the First World War. The theory that the Jewish people had always been bilingual (based on the argument that Jews had in the past written and spoken Aramaic, Greek, Arabic, Spanish, etc. in addition to Hebrew) did not succeed in lessening the differences between the two groups. Considerable effort was invested in – or squandered on – futile squabbles over the language dispute and the question of Jewish creativity. But this agitation undoubtedly engendered a lively awareness of the problem among the Jewish intelligentsia.

The Role of the Jews in the Cultural Life of Other Nations

At the end of the nineteenth century there was a great increase in the number of Jewish scientists, journalists, writers, artists, sculptors and musicians who took part in and influenced the cultural life of Europe and the United States. Their work had little connexion with specifically Jewish subjects; at the same time their attitude towards the Jewish people and their problems differed from that of the Jewish intelligentsia in the early stages of cultural integration in Europe. Originally, the Jewish intellectual had endeavoured to prove that he had totally detached himself from his Jewish heritage and was in no way to be differentiated from his new cultural surroundings. There could be no greater compliment for Jewish intellectuals of this type than to be told that they did not seem Jewish. At the turn of the twentieth century the situation changed. There were many cases where Jewish intellectuals appeared in their own fields not simply as 'men', but as Jews, and emphasized not only their desire to resemble their environment, but also their right to be different from it. For many of them the Jewish heritage had ceased to be 'the suffering of generations', a source of inferiority, but had become instead a source of pride as an ancient and honourable cultural tradition, an important contribution to human creativity. Thus their Jewishness became a more influential factor in the life and culture of their surroundings. At the end of the eighteenth and the beginning of the nineteenth centuries, the Jewish intellectual had tended to regard his Jewish brethren as occupying the lowest rung of society, and his only desire was to raise them to the cultural and moral level of the non-Jewish world, which he regarded as the supreme criterion for human achievement. At the end of the nineteenth and beginning of the twentieth centuries, on the other hand, a considerable number of educated Jews began to seek out those elements in the Jewish heritage that could help to correct the defects of human society as a whole. Thus, consciously or unconsciously, they came to support the viewpoint that the Jews had a special mission to fulfil in European culture, or joined those who identified themselves with the national movement.

In this period scientific research attained greater importance in Europe, and the Jews began to play an increased and more varied role in it. In the eighties most of the Jewish students in Germany studied medicine; it is therefore not surprising that many Jews distinguished themselves in medical subjects, some attaining outstanding achievements, such as Paul Ehrlich (1854–1915) the immunologist, one of the fathers of modern biological thought. In applied medical science important achievements were attained by the Russian-born bacteriologist Waldemar Mordecai Haffkine (1860–1930), who fought cholera and plague in India and founded the Bombay Institute, which still bears his name.

Many Jews were prominent in another field with a lengthy Jewish tradition – mathematics, and some discovered within it new fields of research, such as Georg Cantor (1845–1918), founder of the theory of set groups, and Hermann Minkowski (1864–1909), who provided the mathematical basis for the connexion between space and time. In time more and more Jews or men of Jewish extraction began to engage in physics, including a number who attained oustanding achievements, such as Albert Abraham Michelson (1852–1931), famous for his experiments in determining the speed of light; Heinrich Hertz (1857–94), who studied electromagnetic waves; and Albert Einstein (1879–1956), the father of the theory of relativity, who brought about the greatest revolution in physics since the days of Newton.

The number of Jewish scientists in the humanities was smaller than in the exact sciences, as most universities refrained from appointing Jews to teaching posts in 'sensitive' areas. Nevertheless several Jews distinguished themselves in oriental studies; the most important of them is Ignaz (Isaac Judah) Goldziher (1850–1921), who is regarded as one of the founders of Islamic studies.

A number of Jews were prominent in the field of philosophy. Hermann Cohen (1842–1918) was the founder of the 'Marburg school' (named after his native town), which aspired to revive philosophical idealism on the basis of Kantianism. Cohen criticized Spinoza's theories for identifying good deeds with the recognition of what was true and differentiated between the laws governing nature and the morality based on man's will. He regarded the word of God, as handed down by the prophets, as the bridge between these two concepts. Hence Cohen's desire to find an identity between idealistic thought and the foundations of Judaism. Another extremely influential thinker of Jewish origin was Henri Louis Bergson (1859–1941), who also attacked the mechanistic-materialistic viewpoint and advocated a spiritual approach based on intuition. Bergson differentiated between 'true internal continuity' and the physical concept of time. In his view the freedom of the creative spirit was the Divine Will.

In the study of logic Edmund Husserl's (1859–1938) phenomenological approach was of great importance. In psychology Sigmund Freud was of outstanding significance (1856–1939); he was the father of psychoanalysis, which exerted an influence far beyond the cure of psychological disturbances, at which it was aimed. In sociology both Georg Simmel (1858–1918) and Emile Durkheim (1858–1915) made important contributions.

In these years there was an increase in the number of Jews engaged in the plastic arts. Whereas in earlier periods Jewish artists and sculptors had been few and far between, now many young Jews became interested in art. Camille Pissarro (1830–1903) was one of the founders of the Impressionistic school of painting, and his son Lucien (1863–1944), who lived most of his life in England, followed in his footsteps. In Holland, Isaac Israels (1865–1934), son of the artist Jozef Israels, belonged to this school. In Germany the best-known representatives of Impressionism were Max Liebermann (1847–1935) and Lesser Ury (1861–1931). In Russia there was Leon Bakst (1868–1924), an artist who worked closely with the ballet. One of the most important artists in Russia at the end of the nineteenth century was Isaac Levitan (1861–1900) who responded with unusual sensitivity to Russian landscape, his exclusive subject. In the years before the First World War, a new revolutionary school of art, 'the Paris school', developed in the French capital, in which Jews played an outstanding part. The most important among them were Amadeo Modigliani (1884–1920), Jules Pascin, Chaim Soutine and Marc Chagall. For some of them Jewish subjects formed central themes in their work.

There were many Jews writing in German in this period. Generally, they did not concentrate on Jewish themes, but their Jewish origin or the influence of their childhood environment often found expression in their work. Peter Altenberg (1859–1919), Arthur Schnitzler (1862–1931), Jacob Wassermann (1873–1933), and Franz Kafka (1883–1924) played a prominent role in German literature. There were also several Jewish writers in other languages who preoccupied themselves with Jewish themes and who appealed principally to Jewish readers: the writings of Israel Zangwill (1864–1926) can be defined as Anglo-Jewish literature, just as Lev Levanda (1835–88) and the poet Shimon Frug (1860–1916) were the founders of Russian-Jewish literature. But in England and Russia, as had been true in Germany, Jewish literature in the vernacular existed only for a short transitional period. Subsequently the work of Jewish writers merged completely into the general literature of their countries, although attempts were also made by critics – both sympathetic and hostile – to point out their singular traits. Thus, for example, the French writer André Gide wrote in his diary at the beginning of 1914:

But why should I speak here of the shortcomings [of the Jews]? It is enough for me that the virtues of the Jewish race are not French virtues; even if the French were less intelligent, less long-suffering, less virtuous in all regards than Jews, it is still true that what they have to say can be said only by them, and that the contribution of Jewish qualities to literature (where nothing matters but the personal) is less likely to provide new elements (that is, an enrichment) than it is to interrupt the slow explanation of a race and seriously falsify, intolerably even, its meaning.

It is absurd, it is even dangerous to attempt to deny the good points of Jewish literature [namely, literature written in French by Jews]; but it is important to recognize that there is today in France a Jewish literature that is not French literature, that has its own virtues, its own meanings and its own tendencies. What a wonderful job could be done and what a service could be rendered both to the Jews and to the French by anyone who would write a history of Jewish literature – a history that would need not have to go back far in time, moreover, and with which I can see no disadvantage to fusing the history of Jewish literature in other countries, for it is always one and the same thing.

Jewish Participation in Political Life and in Social Conflicts

An even more characteristic expression than participation in cultural life was the political activity of the Jews both in political parties and social struggles. In the period under review, several Jews attained high political office in European countries, particularly those with stable liberal and democratic regimes. In England the Jews served in Liberal cabinets and also in the coalition cabinets during the First World War (*e.g.,* Herbert Samuel, Lord Reading and Edwin Montagu). In France several Jewish members of the Republican and Radical parties served as Ministers. In Italy Luigi Luzzatti was appointed Premier in 1909.

On the other hand, in the Germanic countries the importance of the Jews dwindled during this period even in the liberal camp because of the rise of anti-Semitism. In these countries as well as in Eastern Europe, the Jews attained outstanding importance only in the socialist parties. In Germany Paul Singer held one of the most important posts in the Social Democratic Party. Eduard Bernstein appeared at the beginning of the twentieth century as father of the new 'revisionist' trend, which denied some of the basic tenets of Marxism. In the 'orthodox' wing (so named by the 'loyal' Marxists), one of the important theoreticians was Rosa Luxemburg, who had formerly, together with Leon Jogiches (Tiszko) founded the Polish and Lithuanian Social-Democratic Party. In Austria Victor Adler was the accepted leader of the party.

Jews also played a prominent part in the Russian socialist movement. Among the outstanding leaders of the Social Democratic Party were Pavel Axelrod, Julius Martov (Zederbaum) and Lev Trotsky (Bronstein). In S.R. circles leading roles were played by Grigori Gershuni (head of the military organization), Ilya Rubanovich, Michael Gotz, Osip (Joseph) Minor and Chaim Zhitlowsky.

This political activity was in accordance with the declared principles of the liberal state based on law, which was the accepted form of government in Western and Central Europe. But among wide sections of the population its legality was not accepted as self-evident, particularly against the background of specifically Jewish organizations and of specifically Jewish political activity. The majority of the Jews accepted the conflicting trends in the development of Jewish society and culture as a fact, but many, and perhaps even most Europeans, regarded the abolition of the special Jewish entity as a pre-condition for Jewish emancipation and as the price of equality.

New Trends in the Development of the Jewish People After the First World War

Intensification of Jewish Political Activity After the War

The year 1917 witnessed the outbreak of the Russian Revolution, the disintegration of the multinational empires and President Wilson's declaration of his 'Fourteen Points', which in principle were aimed at safeguarding national independence, cooperation between nations and world peace through the League of Nations. These three events aroused great, almost messianic expectations among the peoples of Europe, who had suffered greatly throughout the war years. The hopes caught on even more rapidly among the millions of Jews of Eastern and Central Europe, who not only thought that the great hour had arrived when they would live as equals in their countries of residence, but also celebrated a great political achievement in the publication of the Balfour Declaration. They hoped that this document would guarantee the uninterrupted growth and development of the Jewish National Home in Palestine.

The triumph of the principle of national self-determination and the publication of the Balfour Declaration raised the prestige of the Zionists to a new height among the Jews of Eastern Europe and of the United States. The longed-for national goals appeared near realization both in Palestine and in the countries of the Diaspora. It is against this background that one should understand the new surge of idealistic vigour and political activity among large sections of the Jewish people, including the majority of the younger generation.

One spontaneous expression of independent Jewish political activity was the establishment of *nationalraten* ('national councils') in many parts of Austria-Hungary, Germany and Russia during 1918 and 1919, as soon as the fighting died down, or after the signing of cease-fire agreements. Political boundaries were non-existent, military units were being shifted from place to place, and members of various nationalities, often with opposing political trends, began to voice their demands. The Jewish national councils of Austria, Czechoslovakia, Western and Eastern Galicia, Poznan district, Congress Poland, Ukraine, Lithuania, Bukovina and Transylvania were established in order to ensure representation of Jewish interests, to arrive at an understanding with representatives of the other peoples of the region and to avoid conflict with them, to help preserve the public order and to ensure supplies and vital services. These councils were generally composed of representatives of the various Jewish parties, with the Zionists playing the most active part in their organization and direction. Groups of Jewish ex-servicemen, who were then beginning to return from the front, helped keep order and protect life and property. When clashes occurred between national armies or over the question of boundaries for the new states, the Jewish councils generally maintained a neutral stand.

The programme of these councils was generally uniform in outline. The assumption was that the principle accepted for all nations – namely, the right to national self-determination – also applied to the Jewish people. Hence they demanded that, simultaneously with the granting of equal rights to Jewish citizens as individuals, their right to national group representation and autonomy should also be recognized. In other words, the Jews as a national group should be represented in central government institutions and be permitted to organize their internal life as they saw fit, particularly in the sphere of religion, education and social aid. The national councils also supported the establishment of the Jewish National Home in Palestine. They all pinned great hopes on the Peace Conference that was due to open in Paris and hoped for official sanction for their demands. Several councils even raised the demand that the Jewish people be granted representation in the projected League of Nations as one of the liberated nations.

For a short time it appeared that the road to a combination of independent Jewish national aspirations and civil equality and activity in their countries of residence was open and promised success. But the intoxicating illusion did not endure for long. Attempts at national autonomy in several places in the Diaspora failed or dwindled away. The attitude of the British military administration in Palestine towards Zionist aspirations was guarded and even hostile. The ability of the Zionist Organization to commence a sweeping settlement project proved disappointingly limited, while the activities of the national councils were prohibited, cancelled or reduced in scope when the period of political uncertainty passed and boundaries and regimes were fixed and determined.

The Activities of Jewish Delegations at the Paris Peace Conference

At the beginning of 1919, diplomatic activity in Paris became the main focus of the various attempts to fulfil Jewish aspirations. Many Jewish delegations descended on Paris: they represented the American Jewish Congress, the Alliance Israélite Universelle, the Joint Foreign Committee of British Jewry and the national councils of various regions in Eastern and Central Europe. There were also representatives of the Jewish community assemblies in the Crimea, Georgia, Bessarabia, White Russia, Greece and Italy. There were delegations of B'nai B'rith, of the Zionist Organization and of the Jewish National Assembly in Palestine. Most of the deputations were nationalist and Zionist in nature and submitted their demands in this spirit. The Alliance Israélite delegation, which regarded itself as the host and as the most important because of its connections with the French authorities, demanded civil and political rights for the Jews of all countries; but it was opposed to any kind of nationalist demand and regarded such demands as a contradiction of the principles of emancipation. Neither did the British delegation support nationalist principles, but it was ready to recognize group demands, such as the right to autonomous Jewish educational and welfare institutions and the right to observe Saturday as a day of rest. In the American Jewish Congress delegation, a prominent role was played by representatives of the American Jewish Committee (such as Louis Marshall) who were not enthusiastic about the demand for national rights. Nevertheless the delegation as a whole agreed to submit a joint programme, to be known as the 'Jewish Bill of Rights', which included the right to national autonomy in the fields of culture and welfare, proportional representation for minorities in national parliaments, recognition of Saturday as a day of rest and so on. In Paris an attempt was made to establish a joint body representing all the Jewish delegations. This proved a failure because of the basic differences of opinion between the 'Easterners' and the French and British representatives. At the end of March 1919, the Comité des Délégations Juives Aupres de la Conference de la Paix was established, encompassing all the deputations, with the exception of the Alliance Israélite and the British Joint Foreign Committee. This Comité des Délégations Juives was headed by Julian Mack of the American delegation, who was shortly replaced by Louis Marshall. The moving spirit of the Comité, formally elected as its head in July 1919, was Nahum Sokolow. Several attempts were made to co-opt the 'Westerners', but the opposition of the Alliance Israélite delegates to any form of national rights foiled these efforts.

The Comité des Délégations Juives continued to exist even after the conclusion of the Conference and served as a forum for publicizing Jewish suffering in the new states and for arousing Western public opinion. Jewish representatives, headed by Leo Motzkin, participated in the deliberations of the minority congresses, which met annually from 1925 onwards, and discussed the status of minorities in various countries. (The driving force at these congresses and in activity on behalf of minority rights were representatives of the German minorities in the different countries.) This cooperation continued until the Nazis began to control this activity.

The Policy of Insistence on Minority Rights and Its Consequences

The Comité des Délégations Juives composed a memorandum on minority rights, demanding national autonomy for minorities in various spheres. It was discussed time after time by the representatives until it was finally submitted to the Peace Conference on 10 June 1919. But even before they were submitted, these principles served as the basis for meetings and negotiations of the Comité heads with representatives of the Great Powers. It is difficult to evaluate the extent to which this memorandum influenced the principles and clauses included in the various treaties safeguarding minority rights, since even before the Peace Conference opened it was clear to President Wilson and several of his advisers that it would be necessary to protect the minorities, and particularly the Germans and the Jews, against the Slav majority. The first idea in this direction was to include an appropriate clause in the Covenant of the League of Nations; but this idea encountered opposition. On the other hand the idea of including clauses for the protection of minorities within the treaties with the defeated nations and the new states was accepted, and for this purpose 'new states' was taken to refer to all those nations that had acquired extensive new areas. This policy introduced a radical change in Jewish awareness and altered the Jews' attitude to their surroundings, as well as the gentiles' attitude towards them.

In order to implement this policy, the Supreme Council of the Peace Conference established on 1 May 1919 a special Committee on New States and for the Protection of Minorities. This committee drew up the treaties with the new states and included within them guarantees of the rights of minorities, including the Jews. The treaty with Poland was intended to serve as an example of such guarantees. Despite the vehement opposition of the new states, the treaties included clauses regarding the protection of minorities and autonomous rights in the spheres of education and religion. But no procedure for supervising implementation or punishing violation was specified, and the problem of minorities was considered to be under the control of the Council of the League of Nations and disputes could be referred to the Permanent Court of International Justice in the Hague. Therefore, from the beginning, the treaties were of no great practical value. At the same time the opposition of these states towards their Jewish residents became more bitter, as the latter were regarded as being responsible for this restriction on their national sovereignty. In due course the League of Nations worked out a complicated procedure for the submission of petitions to the League Council regarding the violation of minority rights; but in order to reduce as far as possible the tension between the state and its minority, the minorities as organized bodies were precluded from submitting such complaints themselves, and this could only be done by one of the members of the League or a recognized organization. Thus the Jews were at a disadvantage, for other minorities had 'mother countries' that were League members and that could protect their interests. Several of the Jewish organizations, such as the Comité des Délégations Juives, the Joint Foreign Committee of British Jewry or the Alliance Israélite submitted petitions to the League, which drew attention to violation of treaties with regard to the Jews, but the nations involved, such as Poland or Hungary, replied that this constituted intervention by 'foreign factors' in their internal affairs. And when the Joint Foreign Committee and the Alliance Israélite submitted a petition concerning the *numerus clausus* in Hungarian universities, representatives of Hungarian Jewry protested against this step for fear that it would lead to a worsening of the attitude of the authorities towards them.

Furthermore, within the League itself there were those who questioned the objective of the minority treaties. The representative of Brazil declared in February 1926 that in his opinion the authors of the treaties 'did not dream of creating within certain states a group of inhabitants who would regard themselves as permanently foreign to the general organization of the country'. In his opinion, the protection of minority rights was intended solely for a transitional period, which might gradually prepare the way 'for the conditions necessary for the establishment of complete national unity'. He was supported by the British Foreign Secretary, Sir Austen Chamberlain, who declared that the purpose of the treaties was 'to secure for the minorities that measure of protection and justice which would gradually prepare them to be merged in the national community to which they belonged' (though later he regretted his use of the word 'merged', which could mean cultural assimilation as well). Such interpretations undermined even the moral validity of the treaties. The great hopes that Jews and other minorities had pinned on international recognition and support were doomed to disappointment.

Radical and Revolutionary Activity

At the time when the great majority of the Jews in Eastern and Central Europe was becoming inspired by the national ideal, the educated class, which had integrated both culturally and emotionally into the European environment, was turning to political activity in order to realize its aspirations in the ideological, social and political spheres. This path was taken at first only by small radical groups, because of the strength of conservative forces and anti-Semitic pressures in European society. The slogans of the French Revolution and the dreams of a society based on principles of universal justice were born anew. The new forces that emerged in many countries and strove to rebuild society on new foundations without regard for the traditions of the past, for origin or for religious affiliation, opened up new horizons of activity for Jewish statesmen of liberal-democratic propensities, particularly those with radical-revolutionary views. The great political and social expectations of nations and social classes that had experienced the suffering of the war, served as an appropriate background for this development. People of Jewish origin, such as Trotsky, Zinoviev, Kamenev, Sverdlov and many others were prominent among the leaders of the Russian Bolshevik revolution. Jews were also extremely active in the socialist parties that came to power or attained political importance in many European countries. They were even more prominent in the communist parties that split from the socialists and established the Third International. The ranks of the revolutionary parties were swelled by many young Jews who at first had tended towards nationalist aspirations but had been caught up in the catchwords of universal human brotherhood, or who were disillusioned by the limited success of the nationalist movement.

The active role of the Jews in the socialist revolutions of Central European countries made a considerable impression on European public opinion. In Bavaria a 'people's republic' was established at the beginning of November 1918, headed by Kurt Eisner, a Jewish socialist. After his assassination on 12 February 1919, socialist, communist and anarchist elements came to power. At the beginning of April, Bavaria was declared a Soviet republic and Jewish writers and revolutionary thinkers such as Gustav Landauer and Ernst Toller played important roles in it; Eugen Leviné was chairman of the Council of Commissars (Prime Minister) of the republic. (Landauer was murdered, and Leviné was executed after suppression of the revolt.) The communist revolt in Hungary (March–August 1919) was also headed by a Jew – Béla Kun; several other Jews fulfilled important functions in his government. In Germany the veteran revolutionary, Rosa Luxemburg, was one of the leaders of the revolutionary group Spartakusbund (Spartacus Union). She was murdered, together with her associate, Karl Liebknecht (a non-Jew), by nationalist officers at the beginning of 1919. Hugo Haase was the leader of the radical Independent

Socialist Party in Germany and its representative in the first revolutionary government. (He too was assassinated.)

Jews also attained positions of power in the democratic regimes. The leaders of the Mensheviks in 1917, at the time when they enjoyed considerable influence among the workers and soldiers, included many Jews, among them Martov, Dan and Abramowitz. The same is true of the German S.D. Party (Eduard Bernstein, Otto Landsberg and Rudolf Hilferding, who was Minister of Finance in several German socialist governments) and the Democratic Party (Hugo Preuss, author of the Weimar constitution, and Walter Rathenau, German Foreign Minister, who was also assassinated by nationalists in 1922). In short, never before in European history had so many Jews played such an active part in political life and filled such influential roles as during the first few years after the Russian Revolution and the end of the First World War (1917–22).

The Reaction of the Non-Jewish World to Jewish Political Activity

The great majority of non-Jews reacted negatively to the intensification of Jewish political activity, and it became one of the important factors in the exacerbation of differences between Jews and their surroundings that cast its shadow over the two inter-war decades. Jews and Judaism seemed to be involved in the three main conflicts that had become most acute in that period: revolution versus conservatism, cosmopolitanism versus national sovereignty and imperialism versus the colonial peoples' struggle for freedom and independence.

In the early days of the Russian Revolution it looked as if all the Jews had flocked to the revolutionary banner. They succeeded in abolishing discrimination and were granted equal rights by the democratic republic in March 1917. They supported the Soviet regime against the 'White' armies, which sought to restore the old conditions and conducted pogroms against the Jews. It was apparently the emigrants who fled the Russian Revolution who brought to the West the claim that Bolshevism was a Jewish affair (the old anti-Semitic argument regarding 'Jewish domination' in new guise). As proof of their accusation, they pointed to the role of Jews in the Soviet regime and in attempts to organize revolutions in the West and to their activities in communist parties. This argument was adopted by nationalistic right-wing forces in Germany, who began to blame the Jews for Germany's defeat in the First World War. They accused the Jews of having aroused the workers and soldiers to revolt against the Kaiser – despite the high number of Jews in the German Army during the war and their active role in the German war effort (outstanding in this sphere was Walter Rathenau, who distinguished himself in the mobilization of economic resources when the military situation deteriorated). In this propaganda campaign a considerable role was played by Catholic circles in many countries (*e.g.,* France, Austria and Britain), possibly at the instigation of the Vatican, and by the aristocracy and capitalists in the West (the most well-known being Henry Ford).

The new national states, such as Poland and the Baltic states, established in

Europe as a consequence of the war, took up arms in their early days in order to safeguard their national sovereignty against the influence of 'Jewish capital', which supposedly exerted control over ruling circles in the Western countries. The treaties for protection of minorities, which the Allies had imposed on the new states, were described as a measure employed by rich Western Jews to aid their brethren in the East at the expense of the political independence of the small states. This resentment was exploited for the fostering of nationalist tendencies in those countries and for the dismissal of the Jews from governmental posts, from many economic branches and from institutions of higher education. This brought about a basic change in the years after the First World War: equal rights were theoretically maintained in most countries, but in practice there was an entire network of regulations and procedures discriminating against the Jews in all spheres of life. Even government circles announced that many Jews (in Poland, one million) were superfluous in their countries of residence and that the way for the citizens to attain national independence in the economic, cultural and social spheres was to conduct a war on the Jews, to reject them and banish them from these fields of activity. It is not surprising that this policy on the part of many of the national states intensified radical, communist or Zionist propensities among the Jews of these countries, and this, in turn, served as a basis for the accusation regarding the disloyalty of the Jews, who were supposedly agents of the Bolsheviks or the Germans, of Rothschild or the British. Hatred of the Jews and their persecution became one of the distinguishing features of patriotism in those states.

Zionism, the national liberation movement of the Jewish people, which found itself trapped between its partnership with Britain and the desire of imperial circles to annul this partnership, was slandered by both Arab nationalists and communist activists as the emissary of imperialism, as hindering the oppressed peoples in their struggle for liberation. Several of these accusations were based on statements made by Zionist leaders who emphasized and reiterated the identity of interests between Zionism and Britain and depicted Zionism as the loyal watchman of the road to India and guardian of similar imperialistic objectives. In fact, British political and military circles, fearful of forfeiting their influence in the Moslem countries of the East, particularly among the Moslems in India, themselves demanded the cessation or limitation of the 'Zionist experiment'. The leaders of the Arab nationalist movement in Palestine, who bitterly opposed any dialogue with the Zionists, tried to recruit support for their cause among the Moslem peoples, and the radicals among them were even ready to cooperate with the Communists, depicting Zionism as a reactionary and oppressive movement. They chose to ignore the fact that the Yishuv was characterized by a democratic regime and turned a blind eye to the egalitarian and socialist trends that distinguished the labour movement in Palestine and the collective agricultural settlement, in contrast to the tribal-feudal relations prevailing in the countries of the East. The consequence was, as has been noted, that Jews came to be regarded as being involved in several central political struggles at the time and were often strongly attacked by various – and sometimes opposing – camps.

The Decline in Natural Increase, Reduction of Migration and Occupational-Social Structure

The growing opposition of the gentile world towards the Jews, as well as the increased Jewish integration into that world after the First World War, brought about drastic changes in the Jews' rate of increase, their migratory habits and their places of residence. Natural increase steeply declined. It was estimated at 1.8% annually in the years before the war, while in the twenties it reached only 1.1%, and in the thirties not more than 0.8%, lagging far behind the increase rate for non-Jews, even in Eastern Europe.

There were several reasons for this decline: disturbances and persecution in East European countries in the first few years after the war, which caused extensive loss of life; a drop in the birth-rate because of the concentration in cities and abandonment of the traditional way of life; an increase in mixed marriages, the offspring of which were usually brought up as non-Jews; the world economic depression of 1929 and the aggravation of anti-Jewish discrimination that followed.

Of these phenomena, the newest in scope and the most complex in character was that of mixed marriage, which was particularly prevalent in the smaller settlements in Western and Central Europe, where it was difficult for a Jew to find a suitable partner within his own community. On the other hand, there was an increase in the number of mixed marriages in larger centres, in which the process of cultural and social assimilation was rapid. In Germany at the beginning of the thirties about one-quarter of all Jewish marriages were mixed; in Hamburg and Prague it was almost one-third; in Trieste (1927) more than half. On the other hand, the percentage was still low in Eastern Europe (with the exception of central Russia, where the percentage reached 17% by the middle of the twenties) and the United States. Of the children born of mixed marriages in Germany only 20–25% were brought up as Jews.

The concentration of Jews in urban settlements also increased at a rapid pace in the post-war years. In the thirties, town-dwellers constituted more than 90% of the Jews in Latvia and Canada, some 85% in Germany, some 80% in Hungary, more than 75% in Poland and some 70% in Rumania. Furthermore, Jews tended to drift in ever-increasing numbers to the larger towns and capital cities. In this period all the Jews of Uruguay were concentrated in one city – the capital, Montevideo; 96.7% of Danish Jewry lived in Copenhagen; 92.9% of the Jews of Austria in Vienna; 75.9% of Greek Jews in Salonika; 64.8% of French Jews in Paris; 63.2% of the Jews of Great Britain in London; 57% of Dutch Jews in Amsterdam; 55.7% of Bulgaria's Jews in Sofia; 51.8% of the Jews of Argentina in Buenos Aires; almost half of the Jews of the United States in New York – which was the largest Jewish concentration in the world; 46% of Hungarian Jews in Budapest; and 45.2% of Tunisian Jews in Tunis. Shortly before the Second World War there were, apart from New York with a Jewish population of two million, another eighteen cities in the world with more than 100,000 Jews each. More than one-third of the Jewish people was therefore concentrated in only nineteen cities.

After the First World War the number of Jews in the world was estimated at approximately fourteen million. The dispersion map had altered considerably. In place of the multi-national empires of Russia and Austro-Hungary, where some two-thirds of the Jewish people had lived, the Jewish communities were now divided among numerous countries. The largest Jewish concentration was in the United States, with 3.5 million Jews, followed by independent Poland with close to three million, Soviet Russia with more than 2.5 million, Rumania with nearly three-quarters of a million, and Germany and Hungary with about half a million each.

There were also changes in Jewish migration in the post-war period, both in scope and direction. In the years 1901–14, some 1,615,000 Jews emigrated overseas, about 80% of them to the United States. In the years between the wars, 1,120,000 emigrated in all – only 400,000 (36%) to the United States and 330,000 (30%) to Palestine; the other third was scattered through various countries.

These figures in themselves are insufficient to highlight the extent of the change in direction. Of particular interest is the period from 1926 to 1938. At about this time grave restrictions were imposed on immigration to the United States, particularly of Jews. Various waves of persecution in Europe had transformed Jewish migration into quite literally a question of life and death. In those years the dimensions of migration were as follows: total Jewish migration – 652,824 people, of whom some quarter of a million (38%) went to Palestine; 115,000 (18%) to the United States; 60,000 (9%) to Argentina. In short, migration, which had played a vital role in Jewish life before the war, declined considerably in the inter-war period, when it offered the only chance of escape, and its dimensions shrank mainly because of the closing of the gates by the main host countries.

Furthermore, the frequent economic crises in the West in this period slowed down the rise in the standard of living that had previously accompanied immigration and caused extensive suffering to large groups of immigrants. It was not only the larger immigrant centres in the United States and Western Europe that were affected, but many Jews in Eastern Europe who were partly or mainly supported by funds sent by their emigrant relatives felt the difference.

At the same time there were no far-reaching changes in the occupational and social structure of world Jewry. In Soviet Russia and several East European countries, more Jews now engaged in manual labour, but on the other hand, there were less manual workers in the United States and other countries of immigration. The children, and even more so the grandchildren, of the immigrants gradually abandoned manual labour and turned to commerce, services and the liberal professions. The Jewish working class, which had expanded rapidly in the previous period, now grew at a much slower pace. There was also a decline in the number of Jewish capitalists and financiers, mainly as a result of the Russian Revolution and of the anti-Jewish policies in new national states. The middle class played an increasingly important role within the Jewish people, but its security and economic stability were considerably undermined.

Cultural Variegation and Religious Trends

A similar process occurred in cultural life as well. The immigrants to the West abandoned the ghetto areas in the large coastal towns and moved to more prosperous areas. This transition was accompanied by a process of adaptation to the language, culture and way of life of their environment. The Yiddish literature, theatre and press, which had flourished in the period of mass immigration, now began to decline. The numerous immigrant organizations, and even the trade unions, began to wither. Yiddish language and literature became less important to the sons and grandsons of the immigrants. On the other hand, Yiddish flourished in the twenties in Soviet Russia and several East European countries, and the importance of Hebrew language and literature increased in Palestine and in these same countries (with the exception of Russia). But here, too, as in the economic sphere, there was no basic change in the conflicting trends of adherence to or abandonment of national culture. The situation in general resembled that of earlier periods.

The same was true of religious development. In Eastern Europe there was a rapid disintegration in the traditional way of life: the hasidic dynasties lost control of large sections of youth, there was a drop in the number of those applying to *yeshivot,* and increasing abandonment of religious values. On the other hand, there was organized activity in religious circles, particularly among the Zionists, aimed at adapting the religious way of life to modern society. In the West, and particularly in the United States, there was a gradual expansion of the activities and influence of the conservative 'historic' trend and of the reform trend among those Jewish circles that had never before maintained any contact with the synagogue or with Jewish affairs. The reform trend, distinguished from the first by its extremely negative approach to Jewish nationalism and Zionism, now reached a compromise with them. In short, there was a great change in the forms of expression and the attitude of large sections of the Jewish public towards religious and cultural affairs as well; but their standing and influence over the people as a whole did not change greatly in this period.

44 A seventeenth-century etching of the Portuguese Synagogue in Amsterdam.

45 A portrayal of Rosh Hashanah in the Portuguese Synagogue in Amsterdam in a book on religious ceremonies by Bernard Picart (1673–1733).

Opposite 46 A nineteenth-century etching of the Street of the Jews in Frankfurt on Main.

Top 47 A wooden synagogue from Zabludnow, Poland, built in the seventeenth century.

Bottom 48 An early nineteenth-century lithograph of Jewish children in Poland.

49 Two medallions with anti-Jewish themes; (*top*) Suess Oppenheimer, a court Jew (1738), and (*bottom*) a Jewish grain merchant (1694).

50 A ceremonial assembly of the Great Sanhedrin, which met by order of Napoleon in Paris in 1807 and consisted of rabbis from France and Italy.

51 A sermon in a Christian church that the Jews of Rome were forced to attend depicted in an etching from 1826.

Opposite 52 A portrait in oil of Lord Rothschild, the first Jewish peer, by B.S. Marks.

Above 53 'Your purse or the whip!', a caricature on the exploitation of Russian Jewry by Tsar Nicholas I in a lithograph by Honoré Daumier (1885).

Musée des Horreurs

N: 6

le Traître!

54 A French caricature of Alfred Dreyfus.

Top 55 A settlement of Zionist pioneers, Ein Harod, in the Jezreel Valley, in the 1920s.

Bottom 56 Agricultural workers in the early 1920s in an area called Shekhunat Borochov, now part of urban Tel Aviv.

КТО АНТИСЕМИТ?

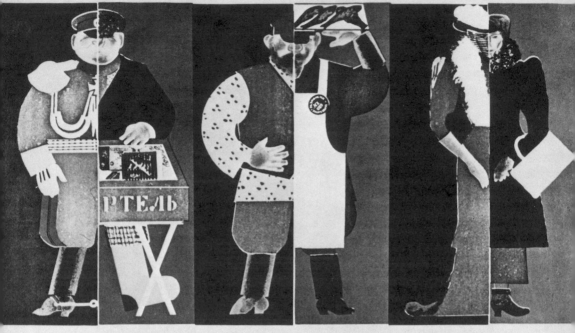

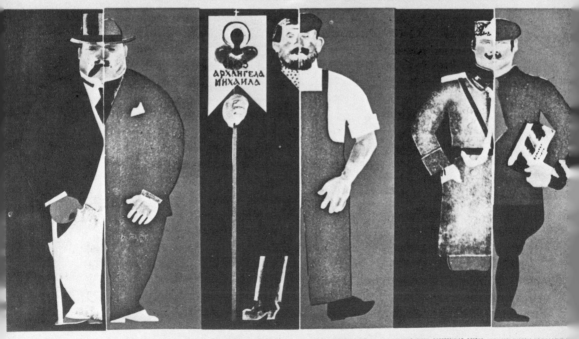

ЭТИ-ТО ЛЮДИ, ОТ ЗЛОБЫ ЗВЕРЕЯ,
ТЕМНЫХ НАУСЬКИВАЮТ НА ЕВРЕЯ.

Opposite 57 A poster published soon after the Russian Revolution condemning anti-Semitism. Its text reads: 'Who is an anti-Semite? These are people who, out of malice, spite and wickedness, incite ignorant people against the Jews.'

Above 58 Judah Magnes (the university's first rector), Lord Balfour and Dr Chaim Weizmann at the opening of the Hebrew University in Jerusalem (1925).

Top 59 An etching and aquatint entitled 'Vorletzte Station' by the contemporary artist Leo Haas, depicting the deportation of Jews to concentration and death camps by the Nazis.

Bottom 60 Jews in Vienna being forced to wash the streets after the *Anschluss* in 1938.

61 The surrender of members of the Jewish resistance after the fall of the Warsaw Ghetto.

62 A tent camp, complete with gardens, set up to house temporarily new immigrants to Israel in 1948–9.

63 A camp of tin huts built outside Tiberias to house immigrants to Israel during the years of mass immigration in the early 1950s until permanent housing could be provided.

Right 64 Jewish soldiers on their way to Jerusalem to break the siege of the city in 1948.

65 A pro-Israel rally in front of the United Nations organized by American Jewish organizations in the autumn of 1974.

63

Jews as a National Minority in East and Central European Countries Between the Wars

Recognition of the Jews as a National Minority and
Autonomistic Theories

Independent national states were established as an outcome of the Versailles Peace Conference on the principle of the right to self-determination, which was interpreted as the right of every nation to its own sovereign state. In practice, however, it was not possible, under the ethnic and geographical conditions then prevailing in Europe, to bestow on all nations (and in many cases not even on all sections of a particular nation that enjoyed sovereignty in a certain area) the right to self-determination. Thus the solution of the old national problems created new national dilemmas. Several of the new states established (*e.g.,* Czechoslovakia and Yugoslavia) were multi-national from the outset (*i.e.,* they were intended to be partnerships of several peoples), while in others, which in theory encompassed one nationality, national minorities constituted a large section of the population (as in Poland, where minorities accounted for about one-third of the population). Among the nations that gained independence and control of the new states extreme nationalist sentiment was rife, combined in some cases with violent anti-Semitism; from the early days of independence these feelings were reflected in pogroms and attacks on Jews. This situation impelled the Allied leaders to heed the advice of representatives of the new national minorities, and, above all, of the Jewish delegations to Paris, and to devise a method of safeguarding minority rights.

This development was in line with the expectations of the Jewish political parties that, even before the First World War, had included in their programmes in Russia and Austria-Hungary demands for national autonomy. To substantiate these demands Jewish socialists pointed to the example of the Austrian Social Democratic Party, which had also demanded that the Empire be transformed into a federation of autonomous nations on a personal basis, *i.e.,* affiliation to each of these nations would not depend on residence in a certain territory, but on the national definition of the individual.

The formulator of the principles of Jewish autonomy was the historian Simon Dubnow (1860–1942). In a series of articles, published in the Russian-Jewish journal *Voskhod* ('Sunrise') in the years 1897–1903, and later in a book, *Letters on Old and New Judaism* (1907), Dubnow argued that national loyalty took precedence over political allegiance. Therefore no nation had the right to deprive any national group of its national rights. He regarded the cultural-spiritual nation as a more advanced stage of national development than the territorial-national people. The Jews, in his opinion, had reached this advanced stage in group development and should base their spiritual and cultural activity on the organizational framework of the community. In the Middle Ages the Jews had preserved their national individuality within the framework of the community, while modern assimilationists had renounced it voluntarily. Now it was necessary to re-establish Jewish self-rule within the framework of the secular national community.

Despite the unanimity of opinion of Jewish political parties and organizations on this question, the principle of Jewish national autonomy was nowhere accepted before 1918. Even the Austrian Social Democrats, who supported this principle, would not agree to regard the Jews as a people with the right to autonomy, and this was explicitly stated by Otto Bauer – one of their leaders and himself a Jew – in his book *Problem of Nationalities and Social Democracy,* published in 1907. At the Versailles Conference, however, the Great Powers agreed to regard the Jews as a 'religious or ethnic' minority, entitled to a considerable degree of protection and even to autonomy. Jewish life as a whole, its various spheres of activity, and the attitude of the non-Jewish world, were perceptibly affected by this recognition of the existence of a separate national entity in the Jewish minority.

The Treaties for the Protection of Minorities and the Struggle for Their Implementation

The clauses in the treaties that safeguarded minority rights promised a considerable amelioration of the Jews' civil rights. The Great Powers recalled Rumania's evasiveness with regard to the granting of equal rights to the Jews after the 1878 Berlin Congress on the pretext that they were 'foreigners'. This time Rumania was obliged to grant civil rights 'according to a simple law, and without formal procedures, to those Jews residing in all Rumanian territories, who do not possess any other citizenship'. In addition to safeguarding civil rights, the minority treaties included clauses granting freedom of religion to the Jews and the right to observe their Sabbath. For example, the Polish minorities treaty prohibited the summoning of a Jew to a court of law or to any government agency on Saturday (with the exception of military service and national defence). The state further guaranteed not to hold elections on a Saturday, lest Jews be precluded from voting. But the endeavours of the Jewish delegations to obtain for Jews the right to open shops on Sunday instead of Saturday, lest they forfeit 'one-sixth of their economic potential', proved unsuccessful.

Autonomy was granted in the sphere of education. The minorities were ensured the right to use their national language in public and to maintain schools in their own languages. Support for a separate educational network was promised from 'public funds' to be granted to the educational committee of the minority group. But the demand that these schools be granted official status through government recognition of their certificates was rejected.

As we have noted, the new states all opposed the treaties, and after being forced to accept them either limited their validity or totally disregarded them. It is not surprising, therefore, that in a memorandum submitted on 10 April 1929 to the League of Nations by The Council for the Rights of Jewish Minorities (which had replaced the Comité des Délégations Juives) in the name of 5.75 million Jews in Poland, Rumania, Hungary, Czechoslovakia, Austria, Lithuania, Turkey, Greece, Latvia, Yugoslavia and Estonia, to whom the minority treaties applied, it was stated: 'To our regret it is a known fact that a considerable part of the rights granted to the Jews in the peace treaties have not yet been implemented. In various countries these rights are still the object of protracted efforts by the Jews wishing to obtain civil, political and ethnic rights.' Any regard for the minority treaties was achieved only through the pressure of the Western governments and public opinion, because of the political, economic and cultural influence they wielded in various Central and East European countries. To the extent that the Allies' influence waned and those demanding detachment from the Western Powers and even a pro-Nazi Germany orientation increasingly took control, so opposition to the very existence of the treaties grew. Poland, the country with the largest Jewish community in Europe, unilaterally informed the League of Nations on 13 September 1934 that it no longer recognized the validity of the minority treaty. Still the Polish government claimed that its minorities would continue to enjoy protection under the 'basic laws of Poland'.

The only state in which the government supported the definition of the Jews as a national minority was Czechoslovakia. In this country there was a large German minority and a sizable Hungarian group. Czech Jews generally adopted German language and culture, while the Slovakian Jews spoke Hungarian. The inclusion of the Jews in these minorities in accordance with their spoken language increased their proportion in the general population and expanded their areas of linguistic and cultural autonomy. (According to the Czechoslovakian constitution, only if 20% of the population of a region belonged to a certain minority could it establish schools in its own language.) As a result the authorities preferred to register the Jews in census-taking as belonging to the Jewish nation and not to the German or Hungarian, although in certain areas they also discriminated against the Jews.

Karl Renner, the socialist Premier of Austria, said in the legislative assembly in 1919: 'We cannot regard the Jews as a nation as long as they themselves do not agree on this point. Some of them aspire to create a Jewish nation and others wish to integrate into Western nations . . . I believe that it is premature for the government to intervene in this controversy . . . '

Attempts at Jewish National Autonomy in the Ukraine

The most comprehensive attempt to realize national autonomy was carried out in the Ukrainian Republic; the right of the Ukraine to self-rule (with federative ties to Russia) was recognized by the Russian Provisional Government in July 1917. Three Deputy-Secretaries (Ministers) of National Affairs – a Jew, a Russian and a Pole – were appointed in the Ukrainian Republic, and no law relating to the internal affairs of any of the national minorities could be promulgated without the signature of the Deputy-Secretary of that minority. In September 1917 a Jewish Secretariat began to administrate Jewish education and community organization. Representatives of the Jewish parties united and established a Jewish National Council. On the suggestion of the Jewish Secretariat a Law of National Autonomy was passed on 9 January 1918, which granted each nationality the right to independent organization of its internal life and to establish for this purpose a 'national association'. This association would be entitled to an allocation of funds from the government and would have the right to tax its members. Membership in the national group was determined according to a 'national list', and affiliation was voluntary. A 'national assembly' was to be elected according to this 'national list' and was to be the legislative assembly of the people, from which an executive 'national council' would be chosen. But the areas of 'national life' that these institutions would be authorized to administrate were not clearly defined.

This plan was never implemented, as the Germans commenced their invasion of the Ukraine a short time after passage of the law; at the end of April the republic was abolished, and *hetman* rule was introduced (this had been the title of seventeenth- and eighteenth-century Cossack leaders). In July 1918 the *hetman* revoked the autonomy law. A 'provisional national assembly' of representatives of Jewish parties nevertheless met at the beginning of November, after the German revolution and the abolishment of the rule of the *hetman,* which was replaced by a new government, named the 'national directorate', that renewed the autonomy law. But because of the incessant pogroms, the representatives of left-wing Jewish parties refused to cooperate with the new authorities. The Jewish Secretariat was re-established, but did not even attempt to implement the comprehensive national plan and contented itself with extensive autonomy for the local Jewish communities. From the spring of 1919, however, the Ukraine became the arena of bitter fighting between the Bolsheviks, the 'White' armies and Ukrainian nationalists. The independent Ukrainian government ceased to exist, and in 1920 its territories were divided up between Russia and Poland; no vestige of the attempts at autonomy remained, since neither the Russian nor the Polish authorities recognized them.

Jewish Autonomy in Lithuania and the Baltic Countries

Another attempt, more limited in scope but more protracted, was made in the Lithuanian state, where a special Jewish ministry was established at the end of 1918, and the Jewish parties organized a 'national council'. Lithuanian representatives at the Peace Conference, who wanted to win the support of the influential Jewish delegations and to persuade the Jews to vote in the referendum for the inclusion of Vilna within Lithuania, published, in August 1919, principles 'which constitute now and will constitute in the future part of the basic laws' of the Lithuanian state. These included the right of the Jews to enjoy representation in all legislative institutions in proportion to their percentage of the population and to be 'safeguarded by the creation of a Jewish national curia or otherwise'; the right to free use of their language not only in educational and cultural institutions, but also in 'law courts and government institutions'; the right to observe the Sabbath and the safeguarding of the legal status of rabbis 'equal to all other priests':

The Jews will enjoy autonomy in internal affairs, *i.e.,* religion, charity, social aid, teaching and all spiritual and cultural matters. The sphere of activity of national autonomy will be defined exactly in legislation and ensured in basic laws.

The institutions of Jewish autonomy are the local communities and the community federation. The establishment of communities and of the federation and their forms of representation will be defined in a special law. Study at Jewish elementary schools will be compulsory, general and free, if such arrangements are made for other elementary schools. The Jewish national autonomous institutions will be regarded as state institutions according to the example of territorial autonomy. They will be granted the right, within their sphere of activity and authority, to publish regulations, binding on all their nationals. Furthermore they are granted the right to impose special taxes on their members to cover expenditure. As regards civil rights, Jewish communities and the federation of communities will enjoy the rights of a legal body corporate. They will be permitted to accept contributions from living persons or through legacies. They will also receive government support, if such subsidy is granted to similar institutions of other nationalities.

The Lithuanian Foreign Minister approved these principles in his letter to the Jewish National Council at the end of 1920, but the declaration of minority rights delivered at the Lithuanian Tariba (parliament) on 12 May 1922 considerably restricted these rights – the Peace Conference had ended meanwhile, and Vilna had been captured by the Polish Army.

Extensive traces of autonomy nevertheless remained: wide powers for the communities, including the right to impose taxes; autonomous management of the Jewish educational network and government subsidy of it; and a central Jewish bank was established to support Jewish cooperatives of artisans and tradesmen. The Jewish Ministry and the National Council retained a certain degree of authority. But as the Lithuanian nationalist party gained force, a rapid process of cancelling Jewish autonomy commenced. The government that was established in the summer of 1924 no longer included a Ministry of Jewish Affairs, and, at the end of 1924 and the beginning of 1925, the National Council was dissolved and the autonomous federation of communities was abolished. Subsequently, until the Second World War, autonomy was retained only in the sphere of education.

In Estonia, cultural autonomy was granted to all minorities, including the Jews. In Latvia, as well, the Jews managed their own educational network. The appointment of a Jewish director of education needed the approval of the Jewish members of the Latvian parliament.

The Public Attitude Towards the Jews in the New and Defeated States

The winning of political independence brought about an upsurge of national feeling among the majority peoples of the new states. The jubilation at newly found independence, the desire to settle accounts with old 'enemies' and the lack of confidence in the stability of the new state institutions led the leaders of the nationalistic parties and the general public in those states to adopt a hostile attitude towards the minorities, to seek to reduce their influence and value as far as possible and to force them to assimilate or emigrate. They acted in this fashion even towards those minorities that were backed by a 'mother country' capable of intervening on their behalf, and all the more so towards the Jews. This nationalist awakening aroused the apprehension of the minority groups, and above all of the Jews, impelling them to seek guarantees of their security in minority treaties, at the League of Nations or through Great Power intervention. But these appeals only intensified hostility and persecution in Poland, Rumania and Hungary. In several East European countries pogroms began to break out.

These pogroms were most savage and widespread in the Ukraine. A long history of anti-Semitism combined with the hostility that the peasants, who constituted the great majority of the population, sensed towards the town-dwellers and the Bolsheviks. In wide areas of the Ukraine, Jews constituted the majority of the town-dwellers and were also politically active; as a result anti-Semites tended to identify them with the Communists. The Ukrainian socialists, thanks to whom the national autonomy law had been passed, rapidly lost their influence over the masses. The pogrom movement commenced under their rule and spread rapidly under the *hetman* and the Germans. Anarchical elements began to prevail in the Ukraine. The army steadily disintegrated, and the troops became the nuclei of gangs that began roaming the Ukraine. Even in the Ukrainian National Directorate, in which the socialists were extremely influential, nationalism and anti-Semitic feeling prevailed. The pogrom movement spread at the end of 1918 and in 1919, when Denikin's 'White' (anti-Bolshevik) armies invaded the Ukraine, spelling death for Jews everywhere. The Ukraine became the field of battle between the 'Whites' and the 'Reds' and between the Polish and Bolshevik armies. Under these conditions the mass slaughter of Jews became a common occurrence. Despite the opposition of the Soviet authorities to pogroms, and despite the heroism of Jewish self-defence, the number of Jews murdered in the Ukrainian pogroms from the end of 1917 until 1920 is estimated at 75,000. Many of them were murdered in the most brutal fashion, or horribly tortured. Thousands were injured, women were raped, and the meagre belongings of the poor were plundered and destroyed. Even for some time after the consolidation of Soviet power in the Ukraine, army forces continued to hunt down gangs that lived off the robbery and murder of Jews. This slaughter was unparalleled in previous periods, so much so that when Shalom Schwarzbard shot and killed the former head of the Ukrainian National Directorate, Simon Petlyura, in a Paris street in 1926, in revenge for the murder of his relatives in a small Ukrainian town, he was acquitted by a French court after it heard evidence of the terrible slaughter.

The birth of Polish independence was also accompanied by anti-Jewish riots. Members of the legions who fought for the liberation of Poland, including Poles from the United States, broke into Jewish homes, murdered and plundered, raped women, shaved off the beards and sidelocks of the men and carried out all sorts of persecution. It is true that *only* several thousand were killed, but the savageness of these acts stunned Polish Jewry and evoked protests throughout the world. On hearing of the murders, President Wilson sent a deputation headed by Henry Morgenthau, a Jew opposed to Jewish nationalism, to investigate the attitude of the Poles towards the Jews, and similar delegations were sent from England and France. These groups encountered violent opposition from the Polish people; the nationalist press raised an outcry against the intervention of 'international Jewry' in Polish affairs and engaged in crude incitement against the Jews.

In Hungary, 'patriotic' gangs operated till 1923, wreaking vengeance on the Jews for their alleged role in the attempted Communist revolution of the spring and summer of 1919, and aspiring to cleanse the state of 'the Jewish Bolshevik spirit'. In Rumania, anti-Semites, particularly students, acted with the approval of the government in rioting and murdering Jews. The Rumanian press was filled with anti-Semitic articles; propaganda leaflets and anti-Semitic cartoons were widely circulated. In 1924, several students were arrested for planning the murder of Jews; they confessed but were acquitted in court. Another student, Codreanu – who later became the leader of the anti-Semitic Iron Guard organization – murdered the chief of police of Jassy, who had opposed anti-Semitism. The murdered man's widow could not find, in all Rumania, a lawyer who would plead her cause, and the murderer was acquitted. When Rumanian students assembled for a conference in Transylvania in December 1927, they moved from town to town in the region, conducting pogroms against the Jews. In several parts of Rumania the Jews lived in constant fear of such pogroms.

Government Policy Towards the Jews in the Twenties and Thirties

Despite the theoretical equality granted in the constitutions of the various states and the guarantees included in the minority treaties, government policy in most Central and East European countries was aimed at discrimination against the Jews. The main areas of discrimination were:

1 *Citizenship.* Despite the obligation imposed on Rumania in the minority treaty to grant citizenship to all Jews residing within her borders, a new law was passed on 23 February 1924 that revoked the citizenship of many Jews by demanding proof of the period of their residence: those Jews who could not prove, with the aid of documents, that they had been residents of Bessarabia before 1918, were deprived of their citizenship. In Transylvania and Bukovina they were expected to prove that they had resided there since before the war. Poland thus discriminated against the 'Litvaks', *i.e.,* those Jews who had reached central Poland from the former Russian Pale of Settlement; while in Austria discrimination was exercised against Galician Jews who had fled to Vienna on the outbreak of war or even earlier.

2 *Government service.* In the new states scarcely any Jews were accepted into government service. In Poland, where they constituted more than 10% of the population, they accounted in 1923 for only 2.23% of government officials, and even these few had been appointed by the Austrian authorities in Galicia before the war. The tremendous increase in the number of government employees in the following

years further reduced the proportion of Jews, till it totalled only 1% in 1930–1. Although they composed 30% of the urban element in Poland, the Jews accounted for only 2–3% of municipal officials. In Rumania there were no Jews in government service. Even when there was a shortage of physicians in rural areas in 1936, not a single Jewish physician was admitted into government service. In Austria, where the Jews constituted 2.8% of the population in the mid-thirties, 0.4% of them were employed in government service, and in practice they were not allowed to serve as policemen, teachers, etc. In Czechoslovakia, the most liberal country in that region, the number of government employees dropped from 9,920 in 1921 to 5,601 in 1930, although the general number of government employees rose in that period by 60,000.

3 *Equality of language.* The Czechoslovakian Credit Note Law (1927) invalidated notes written in Hebrew letters (*i.e.,* in Hebrew or Yiddish). In Rumania it was compulsory to conduct bookkeeping in the language of the country, and any document written in another language was liable to double taxation. In the other countries of the region, discrimination against Jewish languages was carried out by means of administrative measures.

4 Numerus clausus *in institutions of higher learning.* In most countries of the region the authorities introduced restrictions on the number of Jewish students in institutions of higher learning. The pretext was the 'destructive influence' of Jews in higher education, and the need to adapt the number of Jews in the liberal professions to their proportion within the population. (It is, however, generally accepted that mainly town-dwellers apply for admission to such institutions, so even according to this contention, the role of the Jews in these institutions should have been adjusted to their proportion in towns and not to their proportion in the general population.) At all events, the Hungarian Government passed a law determining that the number of people of a specific national origin studying at universities should be commensurate with their proportion to the total population. When Jewish organizations from outside Hungary protested against this move – even as far as a complaint to the League of Nations – a law was passed (1928–9) making university study dependent on the occupation of the parents, with preference granted to the sons of farmers, government officials, etc. – namely, those occupations in which the Jews were poorly represented, if at all. Thus discrimination against the Jews endured.

In Poland there were no explicit restrictions, both because of the opposition of the Polish intelligentsia and because of outside pressures (French President Poincaré, in particular, intervened on behalf of the Jews); but the attacks on Jewish students and discrimination against them led to a considerable decrease in their number. While the number of non-Jewish students rose by 37% from 1923 to 1936, the number of Jews dropped by 35% in the same period. In 1935, the official Polish-government paper wrote that in no university did the percentage of Jews among the students exceed their percentage in the population. In Hungary the decline was even steeper: the percentage of Jews within the total number of students dropped from 31.7% in 1917–18 to 10.5% in 1931–2 (among students of medicine from 51.5% to 14.3%). In Latvia the percentage of Jewish students shrank between 1920 and 1931 from 15.7% to 8.5.% (and among medical students from 25.7% to 6.9%).

Economic Oppression and Impoverishment

The discriminatory policy in itself severely affected the economic status of the Jews, but, in addition, many governments in this part of Europe engaged in open economic warfare against them. Taxation policies were aimed at placing a heavy burden on Jewish enterprises and even at ruining them. In Poland and Rumania artisans who employed apprentices were obliged to pass examinations in their knowledge of the vernacular and their level of secular culture. In fact, these tests served as a means of evicting many Jews from their occupations. According to a Lithuanian law of 1934, not only artisans were obliged to take these tests but also bookkeepers, domestic servants, drivers and so on.

In the difficult years that followed the 1929 economic crisis, government credit became a further means of exerting pressure on the Jews. In Rumania several Jewish firms were obliged to take Christians as partners as a condition for obtaining credit. In Austria the closing down of Jewish banks led to the dismissal of half the Jewish bank employees; the bankruptcy of the Phoenix insurance company at the end of the thirties brought economic ruin to hundreds of Jewish agents, employees and clients.

One of the economic developments that affected the status of the Jewish trader and middleman was the great expansion of cooperatives among peasants. The governments extended vast support to these cooperatives and encouraged the tendency to regard them as competitors of Jewish trade – Jews, obviously, were not included in their operation and management. Needless to say, Jewish cooperatives won no official encouragement. In 1931 the Polish Federation of Credit Associations received eight times as much money in government loans as the Jewish associations, although there was no perceptible difference between them with regard to capital and number of members. The impoverishment of the Jewish artisan and small trader in Poland, Rumania, Lithuania, Latvia and Greece in the years between the wars was a deliberate and continuous process.

The Jews were often harassed by governmental disregard for their religion and its injunctions. In addition to voluntarily closing their shops and places of business on the Jewish Sabbath and festivals, they were forced also to close them on Sundays and Christian festivals, *i.e.,* seventy-three days annually more than non-Jews. No government permitted the Jews to trade on Christian holidays, as had been demanded by the Jewish delegations at Paris. Moreover, in several countries the demand was raised that Jewish ritual slaughter be prohibited, for allegedly humanitarian reasons. In Poland, a law was passed in 1936 permitting kosher slaughter only in quantities sufficient to supply Jewish requirements. On the assumption that half the clients of Jewish butchers were non-Jews, the amount of meat permitted for kosher slaughter was determined at half the previous quantity.

However, the main damage to the economic status of the Jews resulted from increasing official intervention in economic life. In addition to the government monopoly on tobacco, liquor, salt and matches, the Polish Government took over the mines, forests, chemical and military-supply industries. In 1925 the number of people employed in government enterprises in Poland was estimated at 14–16%

of the urban population; in the mid-thirties some 25% of the Polish trade and commerce was in government hands. And Jews were not only excluded from these firms, but the power of the state economy was exploited in order to evict Jews from other branches of the economy. It is not surprising, therefore, that the role of Polish Jews in commerce and industry, their main sources of livelihood, decreased as the state economy expanded.

In Rumania, a Law for the Defence of National Labour was passed in July 1934, under which 80% of all employees in any enterprise had to be Rumanians. While this law was being debated in the Rumanian parliament, the Premier declared that the Jews were Rumanians under this law. But in 1935 the Ministry of Trade and Industry demanded an examination of the ethnic origin of all workers in order to calculate that same 80% and even appointed a special committee to implement this order. Firms that violated the law were fined heavily (up to ten million lei), and thus Jewish companies were forced to dismiss many Jewish employees.

In Latvia it was estimated that one-third of the national property was now in government hands; in Lithuania it was some 40% and about one-third of all the commerce and industry. Almost all the forests were government-owned. Many Jews who had formerly engaged in the forestry and timber trade, or in the export of agricultural produce now forfeited their source of livelihood.

The Effect of the Rise of Nazism

In the 1920s there were blatant anti-Semitic trends in government and public circles in most of the countries of Central and Eastern Europe (with the exception of Czechoslovakia and Bulgaria). Nevertheless, the Western countries exerted a restraining influence, and consideration for both the League of Nations and the minority treaties constituted an important factor.

There was a turn for the worse at the beginning of the thirties, when anti-Semitic elements gained strength in all these countries, encouraged by the success of the Nazis in Germany. In Poland and Rumania, which belonged to the Petite Entente led by France, there was growing pressure on the part of various public circles for a *rapprochement* with Germany. The expulsion of the Jews from economic life, the 'purging of the cities' (*i.e.,* of Jews) and even pressure to force them to emigrate became, sooner or later, the policy of these governments. The Polish Premier declared: 'We must not strike the Jews – but as to boycotting them, with pleasure!'

Attacks on Jewish students increased, and in 1937 the Polish Minister of Education officially approved the introduction of 'ghetto benches' for Jewish students. Various university departments refused to accept even one Jewish student. But the gravest phenomenon was the spread of pogroms: the National Democrats (a right-wing nationalistic party) and the National Radicals established spearhead units that organized a boycott, attacked Jews in the streets and concealed explosives in Jewish places of assembly. At their meetings and in their pamphlets they demanded that Jews be deprived of civil rights and expelled from fortified areas. The United Peasant Party also declared in its 1935 programme that emigration of the Jews was the sole solution to the Jewish problem. Even in the Socialist Party (P.P.S.), which opposed anti-Semitism, there were some who claimed that only those Jews who were willing to assimilate into the preponderant national and cultural *milieu* should be allowed to remain in Poland, while all the others should be forced to emigrate. From the middle of 1935 onwards, pogroms against Polish Jewry became a common occurrence. In March 1936, a savage pogrom took place in the townlet of Pszytyk; the local peasants not only robbed Jewish shops but also murdered Jews in their homes. In 1937–8, the wave of pogroms and attacks swelled, and as Polish fear of their mighty German neighbour increased, government and public anti-Semitism was intensified.

The situation in Rumania appeared even worse. The veteran anti-Semitic leader Cuza established, together with Goga, an anti-Semitic National Christian Party, which achieved widespread influence; the fascist Iron Guard was officially dissolved at the end of 1933, but continued to incite people against the Jews and to engage in physical violence and murder. The government not only supplied funds but also supported the boycott organized by the National Christians, placed trains at their disposal in order to transport their supporters to meetings and gave instructions to officials to be helpful to them. The pogroms did not cease.

There was a further deterioration in the situation in 1937, when the King entrusted the formation of a new government to Goga. This granting of power to an explicitly anti-Semitic party soon produced racist laws resembling Nazi legislation; associations of physicians and lawyers expelled their Jewish members; the 'Rumanization' of economic enterprises owned by Jews was intensified; and Jews were prohibited from employing non-Jewish domestic servants. But the Goga government did not last long: it fell under Western pressure, though this did not alter the official anti-Jewish policy.

The coups d'état that brought semi-fascist dictatorships to power in the Baltic countries also brought in their wake increased anti-Semitic activity. An anti-Semitic association operated in Lithuania in order to 'Lithuanize' the cities; in Latvia the main slogan of the anti-Semites was 'Latvia for the Latvians'. In both Hungary and Austria those circles that demanded the introduction of racist laws gained strength.

For all these reasons, the Jews of Central and Eastern Europe lived in a state of constant terror during the last few years before the Second World War, fearing for their lives and security and afraid to voice their apprehensions in public. Their contacts with non-Jews were in many cases broken off. The economic situation of the Jews – not only the small traders and artisans (and needless to say, the large stratum of recipients of charity), but also the intelligentsia – became desperate. Many were reduced to poverty. And it was in this precarious situation that the Jews of these countries fell into the hands of the Nazis.

The Political Activity of the Jews in Eastern and Central Europe

As soon as the First World War ended, the Jews of most Central and East European countries began to engage in extensive political activity. Jewish parties were established or revived: the Agudah (Agudat Israel – ultra-orthodox, non-Zionist),

Mizrachi (orthodox Zionist), the General Zionists, Poalei Zion, the Bund, the Folkists ('People's Party', Yiddishist), as well as the assimilatory and Communist organizations, became active in Jewish circles.

The country in which Jewish activity took on the widest dimensions was Poland. At the end of December 1918, the Zionists and Mizrachi set up a 'provisional national council', which submitted a list of its own to the elections to the Polish constituent assembly. At these elections, eleven Jewish deputies were elected (six from the National Council, two from the Folkists, two from Agudat Israel and one from Poalei Zion), who together set up a national Jewish faction. The main spokesman of this faction was Yizhak Gruenbaum. In order to hinder the government's attempts to deprive minority representatives of their rights in the Sejm through faulty electoral procedure, the Jewish faction initiated cooperation with other national minorities in elections and Sejm work and conducted a bitter parliamentary struggle. For several years this minority bloc was an important factor in Polish internal politics.

During the 1922 elections, the Jewish faction won thirty-four seats in the Sejm (out of 444, the minority bloc numbered eighty-seven) and twelve in the Senate. The government tried to break up the minority bloc, at first through concessions to the Ukrainians and later (July 1925) through an attempt at compromise (*ugoda*) with Jewish deputies, mainly those from Galicia. According to the compromise proposal, the Polish Government would recognize the autonomous organization of Jewish communities, cancel all restrictions against the use of Hebrew and Yiddish, recognize and support Jewish schools, facilitate the observance of the Sabbath and so on. The Polish Government hastened to publicize this agreement abroad, but made no effort to implement it in practice. On the contrary, the economic pressure and harsh methods of tax-collection led to an increased exodus of Jews from Poland, some of them making their way to Palestine (the 'Grabski *aliyah*', so called after the Polish Premier of the day).

Many Jews, Sejm deputies among them, were critical of the *ugoda*. And, in fact, after Pilsudski's political coup d'état of May 1926, an attempt was made to revive the 'minority bloc'. In the 1928 elections, however, Agudat Israel and the Folkists appeared as a separate list, which won government support. The number of Jewish deputies elected was therefore much less than at the preceding elections (thirteen in the Sejm, five in the Senate). This time Jews even appeared on the government list – a new phenomenon under Polish conditions, which led to a split of Jewish votes among government and opposition groups. As a result, the independence and political influence of Polish Jewry were severely affected.

In Lithuania, after the revoking of autonomy, the Jewish parliamentary representatives fought the anti-Semitic tendencies of the public and the discriminatory policies of the government. In Rumania, a Jewish party was organized; it did not generally win parliamentary representation because of the distorted electoral system, but served as the focus of Jewish political activity. The Zionists constituted the central force in this party. In Czechoslovakia there was also a Jewish party led by the Zionists, which participated in parliamentary activity and in the organization of Jewish life.

In most of these countries there was an Agudat Israel party or some other extreme orthodox body that represented part of the Jewish public. These parties generally tended to cooperate with the authorities – even the most reactionary and anti-Semitic – for they regarded this as the best way of defending Jewish interests under given conditions. In this way they generally split the political force of the Jewish community in their particular country.

On the home front the Jewish parties were split into several trends. The extreme orthodox elements, represented by Agudat Israel, generally won the support of the ḥasidic courts, most of the *yeshiva* heads and a considerable section of the rabbis and other religious dignitaries. The majority of the Jewish public in these countries was influenced by various shades of Zionist opinion emanating from Mizrachi, the General Zionists, labour Zionist parties and their respective youth movements. Immediately after the First World War, the latter began to lean further left. Poalei Zion was split, and the leftist Poalei Zion came close to the Communists; they even tried to gain entry to the Third International. But their influence rapidly dwindled, as those who believed in this ideology took up directly with the Communists. In contrast, the influence of the right wing of Poalei Zion increased. It amalgamated with the socialist Ze'irei Zion and established the United Jewish Workers' Party, Poalei Zion (1923) and later the Socialist Jewish Labour Party, Poalei Zion (Z.S., 1925). Among the left-wing youth movements, Gordonia emerged, and Hashomer Haẓa'ir, which also moved left, became stronger. At the end of the twenties and the beginning of the thirties Heḥaluẓ, with its expressed aim to prepare young people for *aliyah* by learning agricultural work, vocational training and study of Hebrew, became the central mass movement among socialist youth in Poland and several other countries.

Outside the Zionist camp, the Bund played an important part in Polish Jewish life. In the struggle with the anti-Semitic Polish right, the Bund wielded considerable influence in safeguarding democratic rights and in trade-union activity. In its early days in independent Poland it was also open to Communist influences, but it soon adopted a firm anti-Communist line. The main activities of the Communists were outside Jewish frameworks, but since many of their active members were Jews, they were obliged to take a stand on Jewish questions. Jews played a large part in Communist parties in all these countries. In most they operated under difficult underground conditions and their dedication and self-sacrifice made a great impression on Jewish youth and increased their prestige.

The Jewish Community

The community played a central role in Jewish life in this part of Europe – in addition to its religious functions, it was of considerable social significance – as did the institutions of mutual aid and cooperation. In most countries the authorities granted legal recognition to the communities. In Poland during the First World War, the German-occupation authorities recognized the communities as free religious associations, headed by elected committees. This situation was also reflected in the first independent Polish law regarding communities, which was passed on 7 February 1919. Towards the end of 1927 the government granted the communities the right to impose taxes and to deal with matters of education and charity. In theory a supreme Jewish council was established to serve as a national body supervising the communities, but the council was never convened.

Most sections of the Jewish population, and almost all parties, participated in communal activity in Poland. But the most active were Agudat Israel and Mizrachi (there was a clause in the community constitution depriving membership in the community to anyone who spoke out openly against religion), and because of its government support, Agudat Israel gradually predominated. But as anti-Semitism increased and general Jewish political activity was restricted, other groups began to take an interest in the communities, and the Bund achieved considerable success there at the end of the thirties. This was caused, on the one hand, by the general resentment in Jewish circles against those elements that collaborated with the government, and, on the other hand, by the vehement response of the Bund to several manifestations of anti-Semitism, which thereby raised its prestige in Jewish circles.

In Lithuania the communities were legally recognized on 4 March 1920 as basic units of national organization connected with the National Council and administered by the Ministry of Jewish Affairs. But after the abolition of these institutions in 1925 the communities were deprived of the right to impose taxes and in 1926 were stripped of official recognition. From 1927 onwards only synagogue committees remained, as in Tsarist Russia.

In Rumania the government initially recognized only the individual communities, and it was not until 22 April 1928 that official sanction was given to the 'association' of communities. (The Sephardi communities and the ḥasidic communities of Transylvania remained outside this body.) This recognition was also reflected in the fact that the rabbi of Bucharest represented the Jews in the Rumanian Senate. The communities wielded only a very limited influence in matters outside synagogue and legislative affairs. In Czechoslovakia the communities were free associations, organized according to the various religious trends, while in Yugoslavia according to a law from 1929 there was a central organization that was recognized and subsidized by the authorities.

In light of the worsening economic plight of the Jews, the mutual-aid institutions were of particular importance, and they proliferated. With the assistance of the American Joint and other Jewish organizations in the West, cooperative credit institutions were developed, and loans were granted to small traders and artisans in order to rescue them from bankruptcy and confiscation of their property. Special emphasis was placed on vocational training for Jewish youth in ORT schools and other institutions.

Religious and Cultural Life

A large part of East European Jewry still lived, even in the inter-war period, in accordance with their age-old traditions. The courts of the ḥasidic ẓaddikim flourished in various parts of Poland, in Carpathian Russia and Transylvania. The great yeshivot of Lithuania and Poland served as a source of religious authority for large sections of the people. Particularly renowned was the Ḥafeẓ Ḥayyim yeshiva in Radin. There also were still many ḥeders and talmudei Torah.

During this period, increasing numbers of young people began to study at secular schools. In widespread areas of Hungary, Czechoslovakia and even Poland this was the rule. In Lithuania and eastern Poland a network of Jewish schools, both private and those supported by various organizations, was developed in this period, constituting a departure from the traditional pattern. In Lithuania the great majority of Jewish youth obtained a secular education in both Hebrew and Yiddish. In several countries the network of Tarbut Hebrew schools, founded by the Zionist Organization, expanded rapidly, as did Hebrew teachers' seminaries founded by the same body. The number of students at these institutions reached tens of thousands in Poland alone. The Mizrachi also established its own Hebrew religious schools – the Tahkemoni network.

Yiddish education also developed considerably. The left-wing parties of Bund and Poalei Zion in Poland established a school network that was run by Zisha (Zentraleh Yiddishe Shul-Organisatzie, or Central Organization of Jewish schools), which in time came wholly under Bund control and influence. In Lithuania the Yiddishists were active in education, but had less pupils than the Hebrew schools.

The Hebrew, Yiddish and vernacular press played an important part in Jewish cultural and social life. Dozens of daily papers, hundreds of weeklies and monthlies of various political trends and areas of interest reached all sections of the population, reflecting their aspirations and fighting their battles. Jewish publishing was also highly developed, and thousands of books on Jewish and general subjects appeared in this period. Nor did Yiddish and Hebrew literature decline. Side by side with veteran writers like Shalom Asch, a new group of writers grew up: Aaron Zeitlin, Melech Ravitch, Joel Mastbaum, I. J. Singer and many others. The outstanding Hebrew writers were Yaakov Cahan and Itzhak Katzenelson. In the post-war years a group of radical writers, called Khaliastre, was consolidated; at the time it was composed of Uri Zevi Greenberg, Perez Markish and others. Another group, created in Vilna, the centre of the new Yiddish culture, was the Yung Vilne (Young Vilna) group, whose members included the poet Chaim Grade. Theatre did not rise to such heights of achievement but the 'Vilna Troupe' and Esther Rachel Kaminski's theatre in Warsaw – both in Yiddish – won renown and honour in the Polish Jewish community.

A Jewish educational institute (Yidisher Visenshaftlikher Institut, or YIVO) for the study of Jewish history, language and culture was founded in Vilna in 1925. It later opened branches in the United States and Argentina and was a trail-blazer in several spheres of Jewish studies. Jewish historiography also attained considerable achievements in these years. The most prominent Jewish historian of the time, S. Dubnow, lived in Riga in Latvia; in Poland there were several scholars active in the study of Jewish history – Meir Balaban, Ignacy Schiper and Emanuel Ringelblum.

In short, despite the harassment on the part of anti-Semitic elements and the pressures of nationalistic governments, despite the impoverishment and decline, the Jewish communities of Eastern and Central Europe were united and militant and nurtured a rich national culture. It was in these countries that Jewish cohesion, pride and self-awareness found impressive expression in social and cultural creativity.

64

Soviet Jewry Between the Wars

The Flowering of the Soviet Jewish Community

The revolution that broke out early in 1917 in Russia put an end to the Tsarist regime and resulted in a republic headed by a provisional government. The new government abolished discrimination and granted the Jews equal rights. But not only did this legal equality characterize the new situation of the Jews in post-revolutionary Russia, the atmosphere of freedom that now prevailed greatly affected the large Jewish community, which had suffered so much. For the first time in the annals of Russian Jewry they were able to organize their life as they saw fit and to further their own chosen objectives. As a result, all the social and cultural forces latent in this community now erupted.

The Jewish parties, which had restricted or even totally suspended their activities during the reactionary period from 1907 onwards, now awoke to great activity and became extremely influential in the Jewish world. There was a particularly strong revival of the Ze'irei Zion, the United Party (an amalgamation of the S.S. and the Sejmists), Poalei Zion and the Bund. After the prohibition imposed during the war years on all publications in Hebrew lettering, the Hebrew and Yiddish publishing houses now resumed their activities, and dozens of periodicals and even several newspapers began to appear. An extensive network of Jewish education was developed. In the space of a few months, some 250 Hebrew educational institutions were established, ranging from kindergartens to teachers' seminaries.

The conventions of Jewish parties and their publications unanimously demanded the right to Jewish national autonomy, but while the Bund was content with autonomy in the field of education and culture alone, the other parties expanded their demands for autonomy in more comprehensive areas, such as welfare and mutual economic aid, legal recognition of Jewish matrimonial laws, the right to observe the Jewish Sabbath, etc. The Zionist parties demanded both national autonomy in Russia and Jewish political independence in Palestine. This situation differed from that at the turn of the century, for now the non-Jewish parties began to support the idea of Jewish national and cultural autonomy. In 1917 this was the decision of the S.R., the Mensheviks and the Constitutional Democrats (Kadets). The only leftist or centrist party that was against this was the Bolshevik Party, which, despite the considerable number of Jewish activists in its ranks and even among its leaders, lacked any real influence in the Jewish *milieu*.

The initial objectives of the Jewish parties in Russia included the restoration of community life (the basic nucleus of national autonomy) and the establishment of an all-Russian Jewish representation. In fact, during the second half of 1917, democratic elections were held for community councils and for an all-Russian Jewish conference. This conference was supposed to bring the demands of Russian Jewry before the all-Russian Constituent Assembly – elections to which were held at the same time. During the first elections the Zionists won approximately two-thirds of the votes; these results encouraged the British and French Zionist leaders, who were then petitioning their governments to support their demands concerning Palestine. At the elections to the Constituent Assembly the nationalist parties stood as a united Jewish-national list, and the elected deputies agreed to unite into an independent faction to act in accordance with the resolutions of the all-Russian Jewish conference.

The October 1917 Bolshevik Revolution frustrated all these plans. The Jewish Conference was not convened, and the Russian Constituent Assembly, in elections to which the S.R. won a decisive majority, was dispersed by force by the Bolsheviks immediately after its convocation on 5 January 1918. The Jewish public did not submit: in July 1918, community representatives met in Moscow and elected a central bureau whose task was to co-ordinate the activities of Jewish institutions. But both the community federation and the parties were subjected to increasing pressure and persecution on the part of the Soviet regime.

The Jewish Commissariats and the Communist 'Sections'

The relations between the Soviet authorities, or Bolshevik Party, and the Russian Jewish community after the consolidation of Bolshevik rule are unique, even in eventful Jewish history. On the one hand, these relations were based upon the supposedly emancipatory and egalitarian intentions of the Bolsheviks towards the Jews; for the most part, the Jews and their institutions carried out the policy of the regime, and the Jews under Soviet rule were initially offered a secular Yiddish culture to replace their old traditions. On the other hand, there were the immanent assimilatory tendencies of the Bolsheviks, who reintroduced Russification methods in the Soviet Union, that eventually created the basis for a straight-forward anti-Semitism. The prejudices and hostility of the past were fused with what appeared to be revolutionary innovation; hence, the intensity and the dialectical tension of this historical development, despite its brief span.

After the seizure of power, it became clear to the Bolshevik Party that it had no instrument of influence among the Jews. Not only were there no Communist publications in Yiddish, but the party had no people capable of conducting propaganda in this language. A special Jewish commissariat was therefore established in January 1918 within the framework of the Soviet Ministry for Nationalities; its function was to organize Communist activity among the Jews in their own language. The active members of this commissariat were emigrants to the United States who had returned to Russia after the revolution. It opened local branches, and its initial move was to take control of Jewish schools and to combat the influence of the Jewish parties. At first representatives of the left-wing S.R. and Poalei Zion participated in the Jewish commissariat. Its first publications spoke of the establishment of local Jewish soviets or of the creation of Jewish sections in the general soviets, and even of convening an all-Russian convention of these soviets to decide on the organization of Jewish life in Russia and the election of the Commissar of Jewish Affairs. The declared aim was, therefore, to develop life within Jewish frameworks and fill it with Communist content.

But all these plans and aims were soon cancelled. At the beginning of July 1918, the representatives of the non-Communist parties were expelled from the Jewish commissariat, and Communist sections, which served as emissaries of the party among the Jews, were set up within it. The activists of the Jewish sections regarded themselves as members of the general party, each belonging to a local cell besides working within the 'Jewish *milieu*'. The heads of the sections were not elected by the public, nor by the sections themselves, but were functionaries appointed by the party.

At the first convention of commissariats and sections in October 1918, it was explicitly stated that the establishment of these institutions had not been decided upon 'because we demand national autonomy' for the Jews, but in order 'to disseminate the ideals of the October Revolution among the Jewish working masses, and for this reason alone. You may be sure that the commissariat will not become a Jewish parliament.' The new institutions were, therefore, nothing but a party instrument for action among Yiddish-speakers, but their activists were not ardent supporters even of the Yiddish language. 'It has not become "holy Yiddish" for us as for the Jewish nationalists. The language in itself is unimportant to us,' declared one of the commissariat leaders, S. Dimanstein.

The Cessation of Independent Jewish Activity

In the first stage the main function of these Jewish sections was to fight against the Jewish parties and against independent Jewish organizational patterns. For the left-wing parties, the section advocated propaganda based on the importance of 'unity'. As the Red Army conquered more and more areas of the Ukraine, there was increasing pressure on these parties from outside, augmented by the pro-Communist tendencies of its members from within. Not only did the Communists appear to many members of these parties as their sole defenders against the extermination of the Jewish people by the White Army and by various nationalistic Ukrainian gangs, but they also believed that they could rely on the Communists to safeguard the future of the Jewish people.

The outside pressure together with this inner belief served to dissolve the Jewish leftist parties. In February 1919 there was a split in the Ukrainian Bund, and the left-wing majority took the name of Combund, *i.e.*, Communist Bund. A similar process occurred in the United Party: the left wing established the United Jewish Community Party. The majority of Poalei Zion also tended to a pro-Communist orientation. In May 1919 these groups united in the Ukrainian Communist Union

(Comfarband). This Union wanted to amalgamate at once with the Communist Party, but the latter refused, demanding the dismantling of the Jewish organization and insisting that its former members join the Communists as individuals; it was only after the military situation of the Bolsheviks in the Ukraine worsened that the Communist Party agreed to allow the Union to join it as an organized unit (August 1919). The degree of confidence that the Union placed in the national policy of the Communist Party is attested to by the following decision: 'Special political guarantees for national minorities, such as autonomy . . . or the right to national self-determination, should be demanded only of the bourgeois state . . . the interests of the proletariat now necessitate full concentration of power . . .' In other words, at that fateful hour of struggle to maintain the Soviet regime, no political demands should be put forward that might lead to a division of power. This implied their confidence that, when the war ended, the Communist regime would concern itself with safeguarding the national rights of Russian Jews.

In White Russia, the weak Soviet regime agreed to permit the Communist Bund, which wished to maintain its autonomous status in the party, to organize itself into a Jewish Communist Party (January 1919). A considerable number of its members demanded national autonomy and Jewish activity within special frameworks. As a compromise it was agreed, in this region as well, to establish a Communist Union of White Russia and Lithuania (February 1919), but soon it too joined the Communist Party. The demands of this group that the Jewish sections of the Communist Party should constitute an autonomous Jewish body within it were rejected at the third all-Russian conference of Jewish sections (July 1920). This conference reiterated that the sections were a mere technical instrument for the implementation of party policy among the Jews. The remaining section of the Bund also declared at the time that it accepted the Communist programme, but demanded the right to continue as a separate organization within the framework of the party. The Communist leaders refused, and in 1921 the Bund was obliged to announce its dissolution.

The Zionist parties were disbanded in a different fashion. In the summer of 1919, the Ukrainian Communist Union demanded that Zionist activity be prohibited, and, in fact, all Zionist organizations and parties were ordered to hand over their property and documents to a 'liquidation committee'. At that time the Soviet regime had not yet established a uniform or comprehensive stand as regards the official suppression of the movement, but contented itself with imposing restrictions on its activity. Only when an all-Russian Zionist conference was convened in Moscow in April 1920 were all its members and guests arrested; in the summer of the same year, a clandestine circular was distributed by the Soviet political police, ordering the prevention of assemblies, the interception of mail and confiscation of the apartments of members of Zionist organizations. This was the beginning of a long history of cruel persecution. Thousands of Zionists of various outlooks were thrown into prison, incarcerated in concentration camps or exiled to Siberia or central Asia.

But despite all these measures, Zionist activity did not cease in Soviet Russia in the twenties. Some Zionists carried out their activities in underground or semi-underground conditions. The most extensive activity was conducted by Heḥaluẓ, the association for agricultural and labour training that was established mainly on the initiative of Ze'irei Zion, but soon became an independent non-party organization. The founder and father of the Russian Heḥaluẓ was Joseph Trumpeldor, one of the leaders of the Palestinian labour movement, who had distinguished himself as an officer in the Russian Army and had lost an arm fighting in the Russo-Japanese War. Heḥaluẓ established agricultural training farms and maintained contact with Palestinian labour parties and with large Jewish organizations, encouraging Jews to engage in agricultural work. It also promoted cultural activity in Hebrew. From 1924 onwards the authorities clamped down on the Heḥaluẓ movement as well, but it stood firm for another two years, when it was finally eliminated. After the Hebrew publishing houses were closed down, a group of Hebrew writers and poets founded in 1925 a literary journal entitled *Bereshit,* but it ceased publication after the first issue. A Hebrew theatre, Habimah, was founded in Moscow and operated there until 1925. The Jewish Communist party, Poalei Zion, was finally suppressed in 1928.

In addition to the parties and organizations, communities that immediately after the Revolution had organized themselves into democratic bodies representing the Jewish public began to be rapidly suppressed. The very first conference of the Jewish commissariats and sections in October 1918 had demanded the liquidation of these 'bourgeois institutions'. The commissariat decided on the abolition of the communities in April 1919, but published the edict only in June of that year, as it was incapable of taking over at one move the numerous and varied community institutions, including hospitals, orphanages and old-age homes. The liquidation order claimed that the communities had rallied around them the 'enemies of the working class', were 'obscuring the class consciousness of the Jewish working masses' and were appropriating state functions, such as education and culture, and implementing them in an 'anti-proletarian spirit'. The communities should therefore be permanently dissolved and their property and assets handed over to the Jewish commissariats. In practice, the communities were again reduced to the status of synagogue committees, as in Tsarist times. But they were subjected to increasingly strict control, particularly with regard to the prohibition of religious instruction, including the teaching of Hebrew, to those under the age of eighteen. The maintenance of Jewish organization and Jewish awareness was made immeasurably difficult. The government's attitude put an end to attempts to introduce Jewish autonomy and independent Jewish activity into existing frameworks. But it also spelled the end of the Jewish commissariats. They were replaced by a Jewish Department in the People's Commissariat (Ministry) for Nationalities in 1920, but this too disappeared after the liquidation of this Ministry. Only the Jewish section of the Communist Party (the *Yevsektsiya*) continued to be active among the Jews.

Suffering During the Civil War and the 'War Communism' Era

Lenin and the Bolshevik leaders regarded the special status of the Jews under Tsarism as the consequence of a deliberately discriminatory government policy and of official anti-Semitic incitement. It was for this reason that they demanded equal rights for the Jews, which would inevitably lead to rapid assimilation, as they believed had occurred in the West. But the realities of Russia in the first post-revolutionary years refuted these assumptions and hopes. The White armies and nationalistic groups advocated a violently anti-Semitic policy, conducted pogroms against the Jews and incited the population against them, claiming that Bolshevism was 'a Jewish regime'. The Soviet government attempted to resist anti-Semitism by educating the public and even employed punitive measures against the organizers of the pogroms. According to a government order signed by Lenin and published in July 1918:

> The council of people's commissars declares that the anti-Semitic movement and the pogroms against the Jews are damaging to the interests of the revolution of the workers and peasants, and calls on the labouring people of socialist Russia to fight this evil by all possible means. National hatred weakens the revolutionary ranks and the united labour front, irrespective of nationality, and can only help our enemies. The council of the people's commissariat orders all the *Sovdeps* [local councils] to take all appropriate measure in order to uproot the anti-Semitic movement; the organizers of pogroms and those inciting to pogroms should be outlawed.

This policy enlisted the sympathy of many Jews on behalf of the new regime, but did not reduce anti-Semitism. Opposition to the Bolsheviks was exacerbated when increasing numbers of Jews began to occupy important posts in the new regime and its administration; many Russian officials and members of the intelligentsia left government and public service because of their resistance to the Soviet regime and were replaced by educated and semi-educated Jews, who in Tsarist times could not have hoped to obtain such positions.

The wave of savage pogroms in the Ukraine, the activities of gangs in White Russia, the transformation of the Pale of Settlement into the main arena of battle between the 'Whites' and the 'Reds' and between Poles and Russians brought terrible suffering for Russian Jews and totally undermined their economic security. The world war and the civil war (1918–20), which ruined Russian industry and communications and severely affected the large farms and estates, destroyed the foundations of Jewish livelihood in the 'Pale' and wiped out their main economic and social function – mediation between the town and the village. The town now had nothing to offer the village in return for agricultural produce. This situation was aggravated by several years of severe drought in various parts of Russia.

In 1920–1, the hungry towns were joined in their distress by widespread famine-stricken rural areas. Almost the sole source of livelihood that remained to the Jews in villages and small towns was conveying foodstuffs and other goods from place to place, or smuggling contraband – though this involved danger of robbery and expropriation. But under the conditions of 'war Communism' (the name given to the first period of Bolshevik rule, during which foodstuffs were obtained for the towns by forced seizure from the peasants by military units), this activity was regarded as 'speculation', and offenders were shot. The numerous Jewish artisans could only obtain raw materials by what were regarded as illegal methods, and they were also punished with excessive severity. The impoverished and hungry Jewish masses, who had hoped that the Soviet regime would at least bring them security, suddenly found themselves regarded as 'class enemies'. There were instances in which Jewish hostages were arrested in border areas and sometimes executed. There were even armed clashes between Jews in small towns and the Soviet authorities. Under the new rule, the peculiar conditions of Jewish life were even more strongly emphasized.

The Change in the Years of the New Economic Policy (NEP)

One of the gravest consequences of the 'war Communism' era was the deterioration of the Jewish *shtetl*. Anyone who was able to escape from the *shtetl* did so. The young people who had been unemployed for months or years, through no fault of their own, moved to the larger towns or to central Russia, eagerly looking for any opportunity of obtaining employment or of studying there. Even when the New Economic Policy replaced 'war Communism' and opened up opportunities for economic activity through private enterprise, there were still immeasurably greater possibilities in the towns, and this, too, stimulated departure from the *shtetl*. Only those who were supported by relatives abroad, maintained contact with local peasants or had themselves become semi-peasants cultivating plots of land, remained in their homes. But even under the conditions of the NEP, the situation in the *shtetl* areas was more difficult than in the towns; the local authorities imposed stricter control, and most of the new workshops, businesses or shops were soon ruined by the heavy burden of taxation. Needless to say, when all these businessmen (NEP-men) were declared to be 'deprived of rights' (*lishentsy*), including the right to medical care, when their children were expelled from school and were sometimes even driven out of their homes, their situation was much worse in small townlets; in towns and cities undesirable 'social origin' could be obscured through joining a cooperative or taking up some employment in a large plant. The Jewish townlet was doomed to extinction.

However, the move to larger towns and the mass migration to central Russia created new problems. The concentration of unemployed Jews in towns where there was already a high rate of unemployment and where living conditions were very poor created severe competition, and the plaint was heard that 'the Jews are conquering Moscow'. The increase in the number of Jewish businesses, particularly in the central cities, gave rise to the claim that most of the NEP-men were Jews. This again aroused acute anti-Semitism, which in the second half of the twentieth century became a common and severe phenomenon. There were increasing attacks on Jews, and even instances of murder. But above all, wide circles were influenced by anti-Semitic propaganda: 'We spilled our blood for the sake of the Revolution and only the Jews are benefiting from it.'

The NEP itself was only a brief episode. Even the partial rehabilitation of the nationalized industry was sufficient to ruin private enterprises, which lacked sources for the supply of raw materials and struggled for survival under the ruinous tax burden. When the NEP was abolished, the *lishentsy* remained without means of livelihood or any hope of integrating into the labour force. The second generation could not gain admittance to secondary or higher institutions of learning, which now began to pay stricter attention to 'social origin'. The sufferings of the *lishentsy* increased particularly during the years of collectivization, when there again was a severe shortage of food and in many areas actual famine prevailed. Rationed food distribution was introduced; each social group received a different quantity, and the *lishentsy* were deprived of ration-cards altogether.

Agricultural Settlement Programmes and Territorial Concentration

The Soviet regime could not disregard these developments and was obliged to re-examine its attitude towards the Jewish problem. When industry was ruined, and even veteran workers found themselves out of work, the sole method of preventing the transformation of the 'little profiteers' into a dangerous 'anti-social element' and of saving them from actual hunger lay in directing them to agriculture. This had been discussed by the Jewish sections back in 1919. It was not a specifically socialist solution, but a continuation of the drive for 'productive occupations' – a legacy from previous generations. In desolate Russia it was clear to both the authorities and the Jews that only the farmer could be sure of his daily bread. Furthermore, Jewish organizations abroad also proposed similar plans and promised to extend aid to the settlers.

The Soviet regime adopted such plans, but only arrived at their systematic implementation a few years later. On 29 August 1924 the Soviet Presidium decided to establish 'a committee for the settlement of Jewish workers on the soil' (*Komzet*), and a year later, in June 1925, it approved plans to transfer 100,000 Jewish families to agricultural settlement within the space of a few years. These aims were never achieved, but Jewish agricultural settlement developed rapidly. According to the December 1926 population census, there were 155,400 Jews in the agricultural population, some 6% of all Jews; and in 1928 they totalled 220,000, or 8.5%. In October 1930, the total number of Jews who found their livelihood in agriculture totalled 10.1% – an all-time record for Russian Jews.

The success of agricultural settlement reinforced nationalistic trends among the Jews, particularly in light of the strengthening of Ukrainian and White Russian nationalism in the twenties. In White Russia, Yiddish was recognized as one of the four official languages of the republic and was widely employed, but there were no autonomous Jewish regions, and the number of soviets (local councils) where business was conducted in Yiddish was small: twenty-two in 1927 and twenty-seven in 1935. On the other hand, there were three autonomous regions in Ukraine – which never developed into important Jewish centres despite the fact that new agricultural settlers were sent there – and a considerable number of rural and urban Jewish soviets: in 1929 there were soviets of this type in seventy-seven villages and sixty-nine townlets, and in 1932, in 113 villages and fifty-five townlets. In the Ukraine in 1931 there were forty-six courts where business was conducted in Yiddish (as against ten in White Russia and eleven in central Russia).

As a result of these developments, even several members of the *Yevsektsiya* began to speak of the possibility of creating an autonomous Jewish territory within the framework of the Soviet Union. Since the great majority of the heads of the *Yevsektsiya* had once been Bundists or territorialists, the differences between them sometimes took on the form of disputes between the positions of their 'parent parties' regarding the nature of Jewish autonomy. In any case there were those who claimed that the 'proletarian dictatorship' created the possibility of Jewish national-territorial consolidation, or even stressed that only such concentration could prevent anti-Semitism. Despite the attacks of Chemeriski, secretary of the *Yevsektsiya,* against this 'nationalistic deviation', it was Kalinin, head of the Presidium of the Soviet State (in a speech at the Conference of Ozet, the public association for the support of Jewish settlement), who supported the 'Jewish desire to preserve their nationality' by explaining that this accounted for the Jewish leaning towards agricultural settlement. In addition to the influence of economic factors, he also recalled that 'among the Jewish masses there has developed a sense of self-preservation, the struggle for nationality' and that agricultural settlement was 'one of the most efficient means of preserving the independent existence of the Jews as a nation'.

Although this view was not universally accepted in government circles, it undoubtedly provided additional momentum for the search for a territory in which continuous Jewish settlement could be developed. Such a territory was required also because Jewish settlement on a small scale in the Ukraine and White Russia had already succeeded in arousing the opposition of local farmers. Jewish settlement in the Crimea had even stimulated a wave of anti-Semitism; despite the lack of water and the soil salinity in Crimea, which had particularly hampered Jewish settlement there, an outcry was raised in Russia alleging that the best lands in the country, in the supposedly fertile south, were being handed over to the Jews. For these reasons, and out of strategic and political considerations, the authorities concentrated their search on the Far East. The need to populate the area close to the Chinese border and to fortify it against the traditional enemy, Japan, was one of the major concerns of the regime, and the establishment of a Jewish territorial unit there could, in theory, further this goal. In addition, as Kalinin had stated at the above-mentioned Ozet conference:

> The Jews as a nation are one of the most lively and influential peoples, politically speaking, although as a people they do not entirely constitute one complete entity. The Jews are an energetic people, and in certain cases have demonstrated this. We should therefore consider the question if, under the existing situation, in conditions of capitalistic encirclement it is important or not that the mass of the Jews will display the warmest attitude towards the Soviet Union. If the pétit bourgeois Jewish masses, small traders, artisans, etc., outside the borders of the Soviet Union, display warm feelings towards the Soviet Union will this be of any value to the revolution? Of course it will. And if so, it is clear that from this point of view as well, the establishment of a Jewish republic will be of tremendous value . . .

The territory chosen was Birobidzhan. In the summer of 1927 an investigatory commission was sent there, and although it could not carry out a thorough study, the first Jewish settlers left for the region in April 1928. Despite the extensive support provided by various Jewish organizations abroad, which also extended aid to Jewish settlement in the Crimea, the Ukraine and White Russia, the Birobidzhan project did not meet with great success. In the first five years, some 20,000 settlers arrived there, of whom about 60% later left. The climatic and soil conditions were poor, and the aid extended proved insufficient. All the same, in May 1934, Birobidzhan was declared to be 'an autonomous Jewish district', despite the fact that the Jews constituted not more than 20% of the population.

It is clear that one of the main reasons for the lack of success in Birobidzhan lay in the widespread opportunities that opened up to Jewish youth elsewhere with the commencement of the Five-Year Plans (1928–9). But there were also other more basic reasons, as we may see from a report by A. Merezhin, one of the *Yevsektsiya* leaders, to an Ozet council in 1929, on a group of graduates of a Minsk agricultural school, from which the

> entire graduate class went to Birobidzhan and founded a commune there. And in this commune – in contrast to other settlements in the same region which lost their herds – not one horse, not one cow was lost. This is because they are the children of peasants, because they graduated from agricultural schools and know how to look after cattle in an expert fashion. They renounced personal comfort, started by building cowsheds, saved the herds, and even said to the others: don't be discouraged, don't think that Siberian fever cannot be overcome. Raise the standard of proficiency as we have and you will not lose even one head of cattle. But would we have obtained this commune without the slogan 'to the land of the Jews'. Would the entire graduating class of an agricultural school have gone there? I doubt it very much. I also doubt whether the large number of workers we needed would have gone there without the slogan 'to the land of the Jews'. Would the present number of settlers have held firm there without this slogan?

The main attraction of Birobidzhan lay in the catchphrase 'to the land of the Jews'. But it soon became clear to the settlers that their dream of Birobidzhan as the 'land of the Jews' would not be realized under the conditions of Soviet Russia.

The Suppression of Hebrew and the Flowering of Yiddish Culture

The main struggle within the Jewish population occurred in the early twenties between the *Yevsektsiya* and the pre-Soviet parties and organizations. From the mid-twenties it raged between orthodox Jewry and the advocates of secular Jewish culture.

Despite the prohibition against religious instruction for the young, there were still *ḥeders* and even *yeshivot* in the first few years. The number of pupils at state schools was limited. But the Soviet authorities initiated an anti-religious propaganda campaign with public debates, trials and arrests. Rabbis, ritual slaughterers and teachers were warned, expelled or arrested, and synagogues were closed. The study of Hebrew subjects continued clandestinely. The printing of religious books, even prayerbooks, was discontinued at the end of the twenties. In the thirties there were only a few groups (outstanding among them in their cohesion were the *Ḥabad Ḥasidim*) who maintained their traditional way of life under constant threat.

The objection of the leaders of the *Yevsektsiya* to 'cultural autonomy' made itself felt only after they took over the educational network and the Jewish cultural and social welfare institutions. They abolished the study of Hebrew and based education on Yiddish, probably realizing that otherwise there would be no chance of influencing the public. According to the 1926 census, more than 90% of White Russian Jews, more than 75% of Ukrainian Jews and more than 50% in central Russia declared Yiddish to be their mother tongue. As a substitute for the prohibited Hebrew language and religion, the Jews were offered a secular Communist culture in Yiddish. In the small towns the number of pupils at schools where teaching was carried out in Yiddish increased rapidly: at the beginning of the thirties there were 30,000 pupils at such schools in White Russia and close to 90,000 in Ukraine. However, the Yiddish schools in Soviet Russia not only failed to inculcate any Jewish cultural or historical values, but also attempted to eradicate and uproot them. It soon transpired that these schools were not to the liking of the Jews; observant parents and assimilated families alike preferred to send their children to general schools, mainly Russian. In the smaller towns the *Yevsektsiya* officials forced Jewish parents to send their children to the Yiddish schools and prohibited them from entering general schools. In the larger towns of the Ukraine the Yiddish schools never encompassed more than a small percentage of Jewish pupils.

Despite the tension, the struggles and the conflicts – or perhaps as a result of them – there was a great cultural flowering in Yiddish in the 1920s. The number of newspapers had been reduced as a result of the suppression of the Jewish parties, but a large number of books and pamphlets appeared in Yiddish, published by state publishing houses. Soviet Jewish literature flourished. Not only did several young Communist writers, such as Izi Kharik and Itzik Fefer, emerge, but several non-Communist writers, who had left Russia after the revolution, began to return out of the belief that only in this country did suitable conditions exist for the growth of Jewish culture. Thus, in the late 1920s an important school of writers emerged in Soviet Russia, who described in their works the life of the Jewish townlet and the vicissitudes of its disintegration; the problems of adaption to the new realities also found expression in this literature. Several of these writers described the past and its values with love and nostalgia. They included David Bergelson, Perez Markish, Der Nister (Pinkhes Kahanovich), David Hofstein, Moshe Kulbak, Leib Kvitko and others. Jewish theatres also attained considerable achievements, and several of them, such as the Moscow Jewish Theatre directed by Solomon Mikhoels, reached a remarkably high standard. In Moscow, Kiev and Minsk there were also Yiddish drama schools.

The study of Jewish history and literature continued in the twenties. There were still several scholarly societies whose publications appeared in Russian, but they were finally liquidated at the beginning of the thirties. In the twenties, two Communist scholarly institutes were established, which conducted their work in Yiddish: the Institute of Jewish Proletarian Culture, affiliated to the Ukrainian

Academy of Sciences, and the Jewish Section of the White Russian Academy. They published several linguistic and literary studies, essays on social ferment, on the class struggle among Russian Jews in the eighteenth and nineteenth centuries and on the history of the Jewish labour movement. But their main efforts were devoted to 'exposing the image of bourgeois scholarship' in the past and the struggle against the 'anti-revolutionary and fascist' trends of Jewish scholarship outside Russia.

After the suppression of the Jewish parties – and throughout the twenties – the *Yevsektsiya* was regarded as the representative of Soviet Jewry. This, however, never was the view of the Jews themselves. Those who lived in the townlets or remained within Jewish frameworks feared this body and were hostile towards it, while those who had moved to large towns or to central Russia were absorbed into broader frameworks and did not want recourse to its aid. There were those who claimed that the *Yevsektsiya* was responsible for the negative attitude of the Soviet authorities towards independent Jewish activity, though this was not so – the *Yevsektsiya* was only one of the agencies of the government. But it did at least symbolize the fact that the Soviet regime recognized the existence of a 'Jewish problem', which called for treatment and consideration, and the need for a special Jewish framework. The dissolution of the *Yevsektsiya* marked the beginning of a process of disregard for Jewish existence and its eventual suppression. When several of its officials displayed over-enthusiasm for the fostering of Yiddish cultural activity or wanted 'to maintain the specific weight of the Jews' – namely, to preserve their special role in the population (as the White Russian *Yevsektsiya* claimed with regard to agricultural settlement projects in that republic), they were accused of 'nationalistic deviationism', and in January 1930 all the *Yevsektsiyas* were disbanded.

The Changes in Russian Jewish Life in the 1930s

The shift in the attitude of the Soviet regime towards the Jewish community resulted in part from changes in the way of life of the Jews in the twenties and early thirties and partly from the changes in methods of government – particularly its growing opposition towards nationalistic sentiment and the intensification of its suppressive measures.

The 1920s were a period of far-reaching change in Jewish life as a result of the transition to agriculture and manual labour and the increased involvement in institutions of learning; it was expressed in a rapid process of 'proletarization' and cultural assimilation. Between 1926 and 1935 the number of those engaged in manual labour tripled, until they constituted almost half of all Jewish wage-earners. There was also a rapid increase in the percentage of Jewish youth studying at higher institutions. The Jews were less than 2% of the total Soviet population, but constituted 14.4% of all students in 1927–8; and despite the tremendous expansion of the number of students in the following years, they still accounted for 13.3% of the total in 1935. These revolutionary processes, which occurred over a very brief span of time, naturally produced far-reaching effects on Jewish society and a transformation of the cultural and spiritual image of the Jews.

During the thirties there was a decisive change in the occupational structure of the

Soviet Jewish community, and the following trends emerged among Jewish bread-winners: the abandonment of agriculture, a change-over to skilled industrial work, a more important role for the technological intelligentsia and professionals, such as teachers, physicians, scientists and artists, and the proliferation of officials (commercial employees, bookkeepers, etc.).

Agriculture was abandoned because of the new opportunities that opened up in the towns as a result of the Five-Year Plans. The Jews, who had always been town-dwellers, turned to agriculture only when this offered the sole solution to their hope-less economic situation and seemed to promise a minimal livelihood. But as soon as it became possible – even if through arduous labour – to make a living in town, they preferred this alternative. Hence there was a drop in the number of those who turned to agricultural settlement in the early thirties. An additional factor was collectivization, which eradicated all private initiative in the agricultural economy and converted the collective farms into estates managed by officials. The Jewish settlers, who had been the first to set up communal farms of their own free will, now began to leave them. This process was particularly influenced by the fact that the Jewish communes were generally created by people who were in any case close to one another; they maintained their own way of life within the village, observed religious traditions, maintained synagogues and sometimes even employed a rabbi, and so they were imbued with a sense of social and national cohesion. When the slogan of 'internationalization of the kolkhoz' was first bandied about in the early thirties, implying the amalgamation of Jewish and non-Jewish farms into a single unit, in practice, all the advantages of belonging to a commune evaporated and only the disadvantages remained.

The nationalist aspect of agricultural settlement in a 'Jewish territory' was also affected. Those who had feared for Jewish national existence now tired of the inces-sant attacks on 'nationalistic deviation' and the pronouncements that the raising of pigs was the symbol of Jewish liberation. The consequence was that the number of Jews engaged in agriculture in 1939 was low, not only in comparison with the peak figures of the early thirties, but also in comparison with those of 1926. The process of proletarization was also checked. The industrial development of the Five-Year Plans absorbed the unemployed Jewish labour force, and these Jews rapidly adjusted to the new working and living conditions, as well as to the language and concepts of their environment. Within a few years most of them had become skilled workers: the data of the 1939 population census reveals that 50% of the Jewish workers were skilled labourers, 40% semi-skilled and only 10% unskilled. Some of them graduated, within the industrial enterprises themselves, from manual labour to organizational and managerial positions; in 1939 there were less manual labourers among the total number of Jewish wage-earners than at the beginning of the thirties (43% as compared to 50%). But the most important change was that many of those who underwent the process of proletarization – or in some cases their children – succeeded in com-pleting their studies at higher institutions and moved up to become part of the intel-ligentsia.

At the end of the thirties, those engaged in clerical work and liberal professions constituted the largest group among Jewish. bread-winners. The liquidation of privately owned shops and the development of state commerce and the complicated methods of administration and economic control opened up – for those Jews who were acquainted with the vernacular – the gateway to state employment, even for those who had not completed secondary or higher education. The ranks of the intelligentsia were augmented by students at higher institutions during the late twenties and early thirties. Tens of thousands of Jewish engineers, physicians and teachers were absorbed into the state machinery. Several of them attained high standing in their respective fields. Some of the most important scientists in the Soviet Union were Jews, *e.g.,* the physicists Abraham Joffe, Leonid Mandelstam, Lev Landau and Grigori Landsberg. Prominent in artistic life were poets such as Osip Mandelshtam, Boris Pasternak and Samuel Marshak, writers such as Isaac Babel and Ilya Ehrenburg, and musicians such as David Oistrach, Emil Gilels and Mark Reizin.

This change in occupational predominance came simultaneously with increased Jewish dispersion throughout the Soviet Union, since graduates of higher institutions were obliged to serve, after completion of studies, wherever they were sent. Yet they increasingly concentrated in the larger towns, as these were the administrative, economic and cultural centres. In 1939 some 40% of all Soviet Jews lived in only six cities: Moscow, Leningrad, Odessa, Kiev, Kharkov and Dnepropetrovsk.

At the same time Yiddish began to forfeit its importance in Jewish life. Even in the townlets of the Ukraine and White Russia, parents endeavoured not to send their children to Yiddish schools, as there were no higher institutions that taught in these languages and without education in Russian or one of the major languages it was impossible to find a post in the bureaucracy or in academic professions. The authorities also increased their onslaught on 'nationalistic deviation' and tried to raise the prestige of the Russian language as that 'uniting all the peoples of the Soviet Union'. Jews who acquired Russian education not only made considerable progress towards adopting Russian culture, but also served as a 'russificatory' factor in the national republics of the Soviet Union.

Thus we find that all the achievements of the cultural and social flowering of the twenties – Yiddish schools and courts, soviets and autonomous regions – were rapidly dwindling in the mid-thirties. Literary creativity was also affected, and at the beginning of 1939 there were those who proposed that Yiddish literature be published from the outset in Russian translation or in Ukrainian. The persecution of 'nationalistic deviationism', which was intensified in the period of the 1936–8 trials and terror, gravely affected many of those active in Jewish culture in the Ukraine and White Russia and totally destroyed the burgeoning of this culture in Birobidzhan. The war against anti-Semitism, which increased between 1927 and 1931, was also completely suspended during these years.

Parallel to the rapid linguistic assimilation, religious persecution was renewed, and the activities of foreign Jewish organizations within the Soviet Union (the Joint, ICA and ORT) were suspended. Jewish identity became obscured, mixed marriages increased, and the young Jewish generation was almost totally detached not only from Jewish tradition and culture, but also from the Jewish way of life.

The rapid assimilation of Soviet Jews, and the important position that many of them began to attain in economic and cultural life might, under different circumstances, have led to a negative reaction on the part of the non-Jews around them and an intensification of anti-Semitism. But hostility towards the Jews was not sharply felt in the Soviet Union at the end of the thirties, as, on the one hand, this was a period of Jewish expulsion from political life – not only were many Jews, who were veteran Bolsheviks and had held important positions, murdered or exiled in the years of terror, but, in addition, because of the desire to placate Nazi Germany, Jews were rapidly ejected from the party machinery, diplomatic service and such; and, on the other hand, even if there existed jealousy and hostility towards the Jews, the regime, which cruelly suppressed any public expression of opinion, prevented them from emerging.

The Effect of the Annexation of Areas in the West

In 1939 and in 1940 Russia annexed extensive areas in the west (eastern Poland, the Baltic states, Bessarabia and Bukovina), which were densely populated by Jews. Some two million Jews were added to those three million already living in the Soviet Union. Despite the administrative barriers that the regime strictly observed between the 'old' Soviet Union and the annexed territories, contact was rapidly established between the Jews of the two areas. Many of the Jews of the older Soviet territories were vastly impressed by the lively and independent Jewish life in the annexed territories: the existence of organizations and parties, the religious and communal life, Jewish schools and cultural institutions. This contact with the 'western' Jews (as the residents of the annexed territories were called) revived among Jews from various sections of Jewish society memories of the past and helped reshape the national awareness that had gradually become obscured.

For some time the Soviet regime was obliged to maintain some of the independent institutions of the Jews in the annexed territories – for example, schools – but, generally speaking, the rapid liquidation of Jewish life commenced at once. Parties and organizations were disbanded and their members arrested, the cultural and social institutions were dissolved or integrated into the state systems, under Communist control. Furthermore, the Soviet regime began mass expulsion of 'untrustworthy elements' from the new areas to Siberia and Kazakhstan. Thousands of Jews were arrested and exiled. The brief period (less than two years) between the annexation of the western areas and the Nazi attack on the Soviet Union was sufficient to destroy independent Jewish life in those regions. But the dispersal of the 'westerners' throughout the Soviet Union strengthened the Jewish consciousness of those Jews who had been living for more than twenty years under Soviet rule.

The *rapprochement* between the Soviet Union and Nazi Germany led, as we have noted, to an acceleration in the pace of Jewish expulsion from influential positions. It was forbidden to refer openly to Nazi anti-Semitism and the persecution of the Jews in Germany and Central Europe. On the day when Germany invaded the Soviet Union, the vast Jewish community of the U.S.S.R., numbering almost five million, stood helpless and defenceless, abandoned to the Nazi mass-extermination plan.

65

American and West European Jewry Between the Wars

The Struggle for Free Immigration and Its Effect in the West

The struggle to attain recognition of the Jews as a national group and the demand for national autonomy almost entirely bypassed the Jewish communities of Western Europe, the United States and several Central European countries, such as Germany and Italy. In those countries, which at the time enjoyed stable constitutional government, the Jews believed that the laws of equality safeguarded their status in society and their right to be considered a part of the dominant nations. Jewish independent activity endured only in the sphere of religion and philanthropy (including political activity on behalf of persecuted brethren). Even circles with nationalistic tendencies and supporters of the Zionist movement, who were relatively numerous in Britain and the United States, assumed that Zionism would solve the problems of the Jews of Eastern Europe, the Middle East and North Africa rather than their own.

However, the vast migration movement westwards reversed this trend. The hundreds of thousands of Jews who came to the new centres before the First World War carried with them the ideological, social and nationalist trends that had prevailed in the Jewish communities in the East; furthermore, their presence highlighted the problem of Jewish solidarity. The arrival of masses of Jews aroused extensive debate over the 'Jewish question' in the countries of the West. As President Benjamin Harrison of the United States rightly noted in a message to Congress in 1891: 'It is estimated that over one million will be forced out of Russia within a few years.' The policy of the Russian authorities was therefore a weighty factor in the life of other countries since 'a decree to leave one is in the nature of things an order to enter another country.' It is not surprising that in the last years of the nineteenth century and at the beginning of the twentieth century there was considerable opposition in the United States to the new immigration from the countries of Eastern and Southern Europe, which was mainly composed of Catholics and Jews. There were those who claimed to be protecting the 'Old Americans' against the flood of undesirable races and religions and even an Immigration Restriction League was organized. The press, which was harnessed to this campaign, emphasized the physical weakness of the Jews, their poverty, their 'arrogance' and their tendency to concentrate in ghettos in large cities.

Under pressure from these circles, the U.S. immigration authorities began to register not only the country of origin of the immigrant but also his race, and, thus, from 1898 onwards, the term 'Hebrew race' appears in the lists. In 1907 Congress appointed a special committee to investigate the causes of immigration from the various countries and to seek methods of control. This controversy over freedom of immigration was aggravated by specifically anti-Semitic leanings of the non-Jewish immigrants, who brought their anti-Semitic traditions with them to the New World. In reaction, various Jewish circles began to conduct propaganda for free immigration and to attempt to explain its beneficial influence. In 1913 the Chicago B'nai B'rith established the Anti-Defamation League in order to combat manifestations of anti-Semitism in the United States.

Even in England, the proclaimed haven of the persecuted, there was a public outcry against the flood of 'destitute aliens'. On several occasions royal commissions were appointed to clarify the problem. One of these, appointed in 1902 to examine *inter alia* the causes of Jewish migration from Russia, heard the evidence of various experts, including Dr Theodor Herzl. The Liberals remained loyal to the principle of freedom of migration, but among both the Conservative and Labour parties the views of those favouring restrictions, including some with clearly anti-Semitic prejudices, prevailed. After a vociferous public campaign, the Aliens Act was passed in 1905, which considerably restricted immigration into Britain.

Migration therefore became one of the focal points of public life in the Anglo-Saxon countries, which had formerly only been marginally affected by anti-Semitic propaganda. Anti-Jewish trends in these countries were strengthened as a result of this controversy. But, on the other hand, it helped to consolidate the living contact and solidarity of interest between Jewish communities in the West and the East.

The Intensification of Anti-Semitism in the West.
The Protocols of the Elders of Zion

The First World War, with all the suffering and destruction it wrought, aroused a new wave of anti-Semitism. Despite the patriotism of German Jewry and their sacrifices during the war, anti-Jewish feeling grew even before the war had ended. After the armistice it became greatly aggravated, and in right-wing circles the idea was fostered that the defeat had resulted from a 'stab in the back' by the Jews and the socialists. This was augmented by the post-war economic crisis and inflation and the fierce political tension between left and right, which at times resulted in civil strife. For this, too, conservatives, and particularly Junker circles, blamed the Jews: it was allegedly they who had benefited from inflation, organized the revolutions, signed the 'humiliating treaty' of Versailles, and dragged German policy from bad to worse (the appointment of a Jew, Walter Rathenau, as German Foreign Minister aroused particular fury).

Anti-Semitic incitement was particularly stimulated by a number of nobles from the Baltic countries, who had formerly been estate-owners, officers or government officials in Tsarist Russia. They were imbued with the Russian brand of anti-Semitism and had escaped to Germany after the 1917 Revolution. It was they who were the main distributors of 'anti-Bolshevik' literature in Germany and the West, and particularly of anti-Semitic works, above all *The Protocols of the Elders of Zion*.

The *Protocols* were almost certainly composed by members of the Russian secret police in Paris during the last few years of the nineteenth century. The authors took a pamphlet by a French lawyer, Maurice Joly, which had appeared in the 1860s and was directed against Napoleon III, leaving it almost untouched but substituting the leaders of world Jewry as the object of attack. The term 'Elders of Zion' apparently points to the proximity of time between the forging of the *Protocols* and the holding of the First Zionist Congress. According to the *Protocols* there existed a world-wide Jewish leadership operating constantly and secretly against all other nations to further the rule of evil and of Judaism. The leaders of these Jews were striving to set the Christian nations at each other's throats, to undermine them economically, socially, morally and politically. Thus they hoped to achieve Jewish domination of the world.

At the beginning of the twentieth century, the *Protocols* fell into the hands of a Russian mystic, who for a time was one of the Tsar's henchmen; he printed them, but at the time the work made little impression in Russia. Even when it was reprinted during the 1905 Revolution it aroused little response. On the other hand, it made a great impression when it was published in many European languages after the First World War.

In Germany, the *Protocols* won attention because of the claims of 'experts on the Russian question' (*i.e.,* the Baltic Germans mentioned above) that the Russian Revolution had been organized by Jews and that the Soviet Government and the Communist International were headed by Jews – Lenin (whose mother was allegedly Jewish), Trotsky, Zinoviev, Kamenev, Sverdlov, Joffe, Radek, Sokolnikov and others – who had all operated on the instructions of the 'Elders of Zion'. One member of this group of 'experts', the future Nazi theoretician, Alfred Rosenberg, who subsequently published an anti-Semitic book *The Myth of the Twentieth Century,* wrote extensively on the *Protocols*.

In France, the *Protocols* and other anti-Semitic literature served as a propaganda weapon for ecclesiastical circles that, since the eighties, had been fighting 'Judaism and freemasonry'. After the war all of France's problems were blamed on 'Jewish masonry' by the extreme right-wing elements, such as the Action Française and the Croix du Feu. It is not surprising that they displayed great interest in the *Protocols*.

The most serious response occurred in Britain. The Russian Revolution so shook English public opinion that widespread circles began to pay attention to the claim that a connexion existed between this event and 'international Jewry'. The conservative *Morning Post* devoted a series of articles to the *Protocols* in July 1920. On 8 May of the same year, the *Times,* the most respected British paper, published an article calling for public investigation of the truth of the accusations contained in the *Protocols*. Only a year later, in August 1921, did this paper publish the comments of its Constantinople correspondent, who had come upon a copy of Joly's pamphlet against Napoleon III and thus uncovered the literary forgery. But this discovery did not eradicate the influence of the *Protocols* nor did it end anti-Semitic propaganda, particularly in Catholic circles in Britain. In his book *The Jews,* the Catholic writer

Hilaire Belloc wrote: 'It is the unique mark of the Russian Revolution and its attempted extension elsewhere that it repudiates patriotism and the division of property [*i.e.*, private property]. In that it differs from all others and it is markedly, obviously Jewish.' Hence his conclusion: 'The Bolshevik movement was a Jewish movement.'

In the United States, the *Protocols* won widespread circulation under the title *The Jewish Peril*. It was fostered particularly by the weekly owned by the tycoon Henry Ford, which published a series of articles on the 'international Jew' and printed them as a separate pamphlet. Only in 1927 was Ford obliged to admit that the accusations were groundless. White Russian immigrants were active in the United States too in incitement and the dissemination of anti-Semitic propaganda, which won widespread response particularly among those who had fought for closing the United States to immigration. The Ku Klux Klan, which renewed its activity during the war years, added the Jews to the list of 'enemies of America', which already included the Negroes and the Catholics. This propaganda was effective even in educated circles. Nevertheless, even during that period, anti-Semitism never took on the dimensions of a public movement.

Restrictions on Immigration and Economic and Social Discrimination. Increasing Nazi Influence in the West

Among the gravest consequences of the upsurge of anti-Semitic propaganda in the West were the severe restrictions imposed on Jewish migration. After the First World War there was a general trend towards restricting immigration to the United States and Western Europe. But it was the specific anti-Semitic tendencies that led to special discrimination against Jewish immigration.

The laws restricting entry into the United States were based on 'national quotas', but the preference of members of the 'Nordic race' particularly affected the Jews. The 1921 law restricted the number of immigrants per year to 3% of the total of that nationality already residing in the United States in 1910, while the 1924 Quota Act restricted it to 2% of the 1890 figures. The number of Jews entering the United States, which in certain earlier years had fluctuated between 100,000 and 150,000, was now reduced – at first to 49,000 annually and eventually to 11,000. At the end of the 1920s the United States was no longer the main country that absorbed Jewish immigrants.

France, which had accepted a considerable number of Jewish immigrants immediately after the First World War, now also began to close its gates. The main opposition to the Jews came from the socialist trade unions, which claimed that immigration encroached on the achievements of the worker. The 'cheap labour' of the immigrants supposedly undermined organized labour.

The grave economic crisis of 1929 and the slump that followed, and lasted for several years, also served as a convenient background for the intensification of anti-Semitic propaganda in the United States. It took on wider dimensions after the rise to power of the Nazis in Germany, particularly when they began to invest considerable funds and organizational effort to foster anti-Jewish feeling abroad. They initiated the establishment of 'Aryan' and 'Christian' organizations, mainly to disseminate anti-Jewish propaganda, and they placed large sums of money at the disposal of these groups. The most active were the German-American Bund and the 'silver shirts'. Anti-Semites even attacked the New Deal policy of President Roosevelt as a 'Jew Deal' and accused 'Jewish capitalists' of causing the economic slump. After Roosevelt's victory in the 1936 elections, this propaganda died down to a certain extent and the number of anti-Semitic organizations dropped. But in 1938 a new wave commenced, particularly after a Catholic priest, Father Coughlin of Detroit, initiated a widespread anti-Semitic campaign in sermons, on the radio and in the press.

For all these reasons economic and social discrimination increased in the United States. The employment columns of the press printed an increasing number of advertisements specifying that 'Christians only' would be considered. Several universities introduced an unofficial *numerus clausus*, and a few were completely closed to Jews. Banks, large firms and the majority of great industrial trusts did not, in practice, employ Jews, a fact that influenced young educated Jews in choosing a profession. Many clubs, hotels and recreation centres also discriminated against Jews.

The barriers and tension between the Jew and his surroundings grew and were further aggravated as the Second World War approached. The right-wing and anti-Semitic groups were mainly isolationist, that is, opposed to U.S. intervention in European affairs, and hoped for conciliation with Hitler; while the Jews naturally identified with those who were convinced that war against Nazism was unavoidable. Thus, on the one hand, the Nazis helped intensify anti-Semitism in the United States with considerable success but, on the other hand, their efforts made the 'Jewish question' part of the general struggle over the image of American society and over government policy.

In England the influence of Nazism was less evident; nevertheless, it aroused grave apprehension in the hearts of the Jewish community, particularly after the leader of the small British Union of Fascists, Oswald Mosley, visited Germany and began preaching emulation of Nazi methods. The Fascists organized marches through Jewish areas of East London and provoked clashes. The tension reached such heights that young Jews, supported by socialist groups, organized for self-defence. Also influential in the public, though not specifically anti-Semitic, were the 'appeasers'. They advocated an agreement with Hitler and regarded the Jews as an obstacle to this end. Some of them claimed that the Jews were exploiting British policy for their own interests and accused them of bringing about a deterioration of relations between Germany and England.

This clash grew more acute after the outbreak of the Spanish Civil War in 1936. Liberal, Socialist and Communist circles demanded that full aid be extended to the legitimate republican government of Spain, while the right wing and the 'appeasers' called for a policy of 'non-intervention'. This afforded considerable advantage to the Fascist rebels, who were strongly supported by Hitler and Mussolini. In France these circles succeeded in weakening and bringing down the 'Popular Front' government, headed by Léon Blum. On the other hand, there were many Jews in the International Brigade that fought in Spain on the Loyalist side, and thousands of Jews volunteered for service in the brigades of various nationalities (according to some calculations they constituted between one-quarter and one-third of their members). Quite a number of the important generals of these units were also of Jewish origin. It is clear that this situation facilitated the anti-Semitic incitement of the Fascist camp.

Anti-Semitic propaganda, on the one hand, and the reservations of widespread circles in Britain and France with regard to the Jews and 'war-mongers', on the other, increased at the end of 1938, after the Munich agreement between these two powers and Hitler. The appeasers in these two countries, who believed that they had reached a compromise with the German dictator and had 'preserved peace', disregarded the sufferings of the Jews and regarded them as a nuisance. The number of Jewish refugees in Europe increased greatly, but the gates of all countries were barred to them. The British authorities checked immigration to Palestine in the hope of appeasing the Arab leaders, the majority of whom were then in close contact with the Fascist states. The French right wing openly called for a pro-Nazi orientation and for the imitation of German methods – including anti-Semitism.

Consolidation of the Jewish Centre in the United States

It was during these difficult times for the Jewish people that the Jewish community in the United States became the greatest Jewish centre in the world. The Jewish population of this country, which, at the end of the nineteenth century, had totalled some one million souls, grew to three and a half million in the early twenties, and four and a half million at the beginning of the thirties. The restriction of immigration to a minimum, the sufferings of the Depression years and the discriminatory policies brought about changes in the occupational structure and social life of the Jewish community. Although New York, with more than one and a half million Jews, remained the largest Jewish concentration in the world, there was a trend towards emergence from the 'ghettos' in the large cities of the East Coast and dispersal in suburbs, or even migration to smaller towns and to the west.

The number of Jews engaged in manual labour began to decrease. In 1933, 35% of New York Jews were engaged in commerce, 30.6% in industry, 21.6% in clerical work and 7.4% in liberal professions. In the smaller towns this was more striking: in Detroit in 1935, 54.1% of the Jews were engaged in commerce, 23.3% in industry and 9.5% in liberal professions. There was an increase in the number of self-employed: in 1937 the self-employed constituted 28.8% of all Jewish bread-winners, and wage-earners accounted for the remainder; while in the general population only 11.7% were self-employed.

Nevertheless, the Jews still played a large and influential role in the trade-union movement. In New York and several other cities in which there were still many Jewish workers and artisans, the Arbeiter Ring and other workers' circles still exerted great influence. Some large trade unions – mainly in the garment industry – such as the International Ladies Garment Workers or the Amalgamated Clothing Workers of America (founding-unions of the American Federation of Labor) were then primarily Jewish unions. They underwent a serious crisis from 1921 to 1923 and in 1925, when the Communists tried to take over control of trade-union activity by exploiting the warm relations that existed then between Jewish workers in the United States and Soviet Russia and by taking over leadership of several of the more important branches of these unions. The extreme methods employed by the Communists in strikes and trade-union struggles proved their undoing, and their influence rapidly dwindled.

There were many Jews in Communist ranks, and the Jewish section of this party was, almost certainly, the largest. The Depression years strengthened the status of the trade unions. In the thirties, when Communist influence over Jewish students and the intelligentsia grew, leaders of the trade-union movement, such as David Dubinsky and Sidney Hillman, succeeded in eradicating it in the unions.

The emergence from the 'ghettos' and integration into the surrounding society led to a decline of the Yiddish press and theatre and to the weakening of ties with the country of origin, which was previously based on affiliation with *Landsmanshaften*. There commenced a rapid process of 'Americanization'. Jews became more predominant in general cultural life – in literature, in the theatre and in the film industry. Despite some discrimination in higher institutions of learning the percentage of intellectuals and members of the liberal professions in the Jewish community grew. In this period there was the crystallization of organized communal and religious life according to religious trend: Orthodox, Conservative and Reform. Each had its own community structure, rabbinical association and rabbinical seminaries, which also served as institutes of Jewish study. The annual conventions of the various associations determined the religious and social principles that guided each trend. The communities and organizations also furthered the dissemination of Jewish education among youth – whether in Sunday schools or full-day educational institutions.

An important part was played in Jewish communal life by social and philanthropic organizations. The American Jewish Committee was maintained by a small, *élite* group, while the American Jewish Congress was a more encompassing organization, in which all the trends and opinions of American Jewish life were represented. It was founded during the early war years with the aim of protecting the rights of Jews in Eastern Europe and the Orient, but at the request of the American Government it was convened only after the war, in December 1918. Its most active members were the Zionist and radical national groups. The American Zionist Federation flowered during and immediately after the war under the leadership of Supreme Court Justice Louis D. Brandeis.

The philanthropic organizations, and particularly the Joint, did much to help the Jewish communities in Europe that had suffered during the war. They supported schools and educational institutions, vocational training, medical institutions, etc. The Joint extended aid to the Jews of Palestine and the Middle East, to the Jewish communities in Eastern Europe that had undergone pogroms and government discrimination and particularly to the Jewish farmers in the Soviet Union. The Agro-Joint was established especially to aid settlement in Crimea and Birobidzhan, and it lavished funds on this project, supplying agricultural machinery and tools, training, etc., until the Soviet Government prohibited its activity.

Jewish Political Activity in the West

During the Versailles Conference, Western Jewry was active in the struggle for the rights of their brethren in the East, but this activity was only temporary. Jewish political parties, along the lines of those in Eastern Europe and Palestine, did not exist in the West, apart from Zionist or Zionist-Socialist organizations, which did not appear as independent political bodies but as ideological trends or as associations with educational and cultural aims. On the other hand, the Jews of the West were active in the political life of their countries of residence. In Britain Jews participated in Liberal governments and in Lloyd George's coalition war cabinet. The decline of the Liberal Party after the war reduced their numbers, but Jews then became prominent in the Labour Party. In France Jews played an active role in the Republican, Radical and Socialist parties and filled government posts. In the mid-thirties Léon Blum served as premier. Jews also played an important part in the leadership of the Socialist and Communist parties in Germany, France and Italy, and in several countries were even among the founding fathers and the important theoreticians.

The rise of Nazism stimulated the political activity of Jewish, and particularly Zionist, organizations. Jewish organizations in the West initiated a widespread boycott of German goods. In order to co-ordinate defence and aid activity, a World Jewish Congress was convened in Geneva in August 1936; it passed resolutions regarding propaganda, boycott activities, the struggle against discrimination, constructive activity for rehabilitation of Jewish refugees and the changing of Jewish occupations, particularly among the younger generation. Absent from the conference were German Jewry, confined under Nazi rule, and the Jews of the Soviet Union, who were cut off from their brethren. In his speech at the Congress, the American Zionist leader Stephen Wise said:

> Such national bodies as there are among Jews – B'nai B'rith, the Hilfsverein, the Board of Deputies, the American Jewish Committee – each works separately and alone in the land of which it is a part and amid the citizenship in which its members are included. But it is not the Englishmen who are attacked, nor Frenchmen, nor Americans, nor Belgians, nor Dutch, but Jews, Jews, Jews. Not French Jews, nor British Jews, nor American Jews, not even German Jews, but Jews as Jews. Even the war of Hitlerism is not directed against German Jews. That phase of the struggle was little more than an election expedient to bring the Nazis to power. Hitlerism's real war is against World Jewry. Hitler said, *'Wir werden die Juden ausrotten'* ('we will root out the Jews'). Through the voice of the World Jewish Congress we answer: 'You shall not destroy the Jews, though you may uproot them from your own land.' For the Jew has within him the very essence of imperishableness. What Haman and Titus and Pobiedonosteff failed to achieve, Hitler will not do.

Nazism impelled the Jews of the West to organize as Jews in order to conduct their political struggle.

Cultural and Spiritual Life

Western Jewry contributed its share to Jewish spiritual creativity. Research institutes and Jewish archives were established, historical material was collected, an extensive literature grew up, and there were numerous journals dealing with Jewish life, culture and studies. In the United States, which, even after the First World War, was still a great centre of Yiddish culture, there were many writers active in this language, including H. Leivick and J. Opatoshu. There were also innovators in the field of Yiddish literature – writers with their own individualistic stamp who published a journal entitled *In-Zikh* ('Within Ourselves'). A large group of Yiddish writers, who later moved to the Soviet Union, then assembled in Berlin. There were also several Hebrew writers productive in the West, particularly in Germany.

Nevertheless, even in those intellectual circles in which there was no need for Jewish languages, there was increased interest in Jewish culture. One of the most typical expressions of this was the neo-Romantic interest in Ḥasidism, reflected in the East in the works of I. L. Peretz and Shalom Asch. In the German sphere of culture the Zionist philosopher and writer Martin Buber elucidated the basic elements of Ḥasidism to Jewish and non-Jewish readers who were remote from Jewish affairs (people such as Walter Rathenau began to display an interest in it). There was increased interest in other spheres of Jewish creativity – the Bible, Jewish philosophy and Kabbalah. Franz Rosenzweig, who, together with Buber, composed a new German translation of the Bible, also tried, in his book *The Star of Redemption,* to evolve a new Jewish philosophical system.

The awakening resulted, on the one hand, from the renewed contact of many Western Jews with their brethren in the East, both during military service in the German Army in the occupied territories of Eastern Europe during the First World War and as a result of the migration of Jews from the East to the West. The world of orthodox Jews, with all its mystery, attracted young educated Jews who had been brought up on European culture. On the other hand, the rising wave of anti-Semitism intensified the search for spiritual and historical roots and strengthened the attachment to Jewish heritage even among those Jews who were totally assimilated in language and culture.

At the same time, however, Jews became increasingly active in the field of general culture – in science, literature and art – in Germany, Western Europe and the United States. In the democratic era of the Weimar Republic, many Jews attained considerable scientific achievement and prominent academic positions in universities and research institutions. In this period German Jewry exerted great influence over the cultural life of this country, a fact that further aroused the anger of the anti-Semites.

In literature, Alfred Döblin, Stefan and Arnold Zweig and Franz Werfel became established writers, and in France, André Maurois and the playwright Georges de Porto-Riche were respected names. A considerable number of Jews from various countries were active in the great Parisian cultural centre – including the most important artists and sculptors of the day – such as Jules Pascin (Pinkas), Chaim Soutine, Marc Chagall, Jacques Lipchitz and Chana Orloff. Soviet Jewish artists –

who greatly influenced the artistic search of the twenties – such as Nathan Altman, El (Lazar) Lissitzky and Issachar Ryback, were also connected with artistic trends in the West. Jankel Adler, whose work was suffused with Jewish atmosphere, was active in Germany. In England, the sculptor Sir Jacob Epstein, who had begun his work in the New York ghetto, also achieved artistic prominence. The many Jewish artists active in the United States in this period included the painter Ben Shahn and the sculptor William Zorach.

In Germany, Max Reinhardt was a trail-blazer in the theatre. Prominent Jewish composers of this period included: Gustav Mahler, Arnold Schoenberg and Kurt Weill in Germany; Paul Dukas and Darius Milhaud in France; Ernest Bloch in Switzerland; and George Gershwin in the United States.

In brief, Jews were extremely active in the culture of their surroundings, although the situation was not uniform in all countries. Their activity was most variegated and rich in Germany. France attracted Jewish artists who were united by the universal element in their art. In the United States Jews were in the process of changing from an immigrant community to an important segment of national cultural life.

66

The Zionist Movement and the 'National Home' Between the World Wars

Zionist Policy in the War Years and the Balfour Declaration

The First World War stunned the World Zionist Organization and confronted it with numerous problems. When it became clear that Russia was allied with the Entente Powers of Britain and France, many Jews anticipated a change in Russia's anti-Jewish policy. They were harshly disappointed, however, in the first months of the war, when Jews were expelled from the front-line areas, seized as hostages and even attacked in pogroms. This disappointment only reinforced the belief of many other Jews, particularly in the United States, who from the first had supported the Central Powers of Germany and Austro-Hungary (which were later joined by Turkey). But even these Jews could not disregard the basic fact that one-half of the Jewish people resided in Russia, the most important centre of Jewish life, and that the fate of this country could decide the destiny of its Jews.

The Zionist Organization, which was centered in Berlin, endeavoured to continue Herzl's tradition and to avoid arousing the hostility of any political factor. It therefore anticipated events and opened a 'Chief Bureau' in neutral Copenhagen in order to be able to continue Zionist activity in all countries. But even among the Zionist leaders there were those with conflicting political orientation. Some, such as Vladimir Jabotinsky, claimed vehemently that only the defeat of Turkey could save the Jewish community in Palestine from destruction and open up new horizons for the Zionist movement. He therefore called for active participation in the war on the Entente side. Those with a pro-German orientation, on the other hand, argued that only Germany, which wielded considerable influence over the Turkish Government, could ensure the safety of the Yishuv.

As early as 1915, British Zionists, led by Weizmann, had begun to attempt to persuade the British Government to safeguard Jewish interests in Palestine, out of the hope that after the war the country would be under British trusteeship. Several prominent British Jews, including Herbert Samuel, presented memoranda to Cabinet ministers in this spirit. The spokesman of the Joint Foreign Committee of British Jewry, Lucien Wolf, who cooperated with the British Foreign Office in an effort to draw the sympathies of American Jewry to the Allies, also claimed that a guarantee to the Jews regarding Palestine would aid this issue. The Zionist Chief Bureau in

Copenhagen sent two representatives to Britain, J. Tschlenow and N. Sokolow, to negotiate with the British Government. A memorandum that the Zionists submitted to the British Government in October 1916 contained the demand that, after the liberation of Palestine from Turkish rule, the rights of the Jewish people in the country be recognized, free immigration be permitted and the status of Zionist institutions be legalized.

Despite the opposition of Zionist leaders, Vladimir Jabotinsky, Joseph Trumpeldor and Pinḥas Rutenberg began to agitate for the establishment of a Jewish Legion to fight on the side of the Allies. At first the British authorities expressed reservations with regard to the entire project, but at the beginning of 1915 they agreed to set up the Zion Mule Corps, drawn particularly from the Palestinian refugees in Egyptian camps. This unit was deployed in service tasks (supplying food and ammunition) under the arduous conditions of the Gallipoli Campaign. In the summer of 1917, the 38th Battalion of the Royal Fusiliers was established, mainly composed of Jews from London's East End and, after undergoing training, was sent to Palestine and participated in battles there in the following summer. Rutenberg went to the United States where, with the aid of David Ben-Gurion and Izhak Ben-Zvi, he conducted propaganda to promote volunteering to Jewish units. The volunteer movement encompassed thousands of young men and by the summer of 1918 some 4,000 had arrived in England. They composed the 39th Battalion of the Royal Fusiliers, only part of which arrived in time to take part in the fighting in Palestine.

The change of government in Britain and the worsening of the military situation induced the British authorities to respond more strongly to Zionist demands. The Allies hoped that, through a declaration recognizing the justice of Zionist aspirations, they would influence Jewish public opinion in the United States to aid them in their efforts to persuade the United States to join in the war effort. Furthermore, it became known that the German authorities were also contemplating the possiblity of publishing a declaration expressing sympathy for Zionist aspirations. For all these reasons, contact was established at the end of January 1917 between the Zionists and the British Foreign Office in order to define political objectives after the war. At the same time, Sokolow was conducting negotiations with the French Government – and even winning considerable concessions. At the beginning of June 1917, he received a note from the French Foreign Ministry, which stated:

> You consider that if circumstances permit it and the independence of the Holy Places is assured of being safeguarded, it would be a deed of justice and of reparation to assist, by the protection of the Allied Powers, in the renaissance of the Jewish nationality in that Land from which the people of Israel were exiled so many centuries ago. The French Government, which entered this present war to defend a people wrongly attacked, and which continues to struggle to assure the victory of right over might, cannot but feel sympathy for your cause, the triumph of which is bound up with that of the Allies. I am happy to give you herewith such assurances.

This document was handed over by Sokolow to the British Foreign Office, but was not published. It seems that the Zionists wanted to reassure Britain that there was no

French objection to a pro-Zionist declaration. On the other hand, in the British Foreign Office and among the military there were those who hoped, with the aid of the Zionists, to include the whole of Palestine within the British sphere of control, in contrast to the secret British-French Sykes-Picot Treaty of 1916, which divided the spheres of influence of the Allies in this area.

In July the Zionists submitted to the British Government the draft text of a proposed political declaration, in which Britain would agree with 'the principle that Palestine should be reconstituted as the National Home of the Jewish people' and the British Government 'will use its best endeavours to secure the achievement of this object and will discuss the necessary methods and means with the Zionist Organization.' The opponents of Zionism, both Jewish and non-Jewish, violently objected to this declaration, and eventually the British Government approved a much more guarded wording. In a letter that British Foreign Secretary Arthur James Balfour sent to Lord Rothschild on 2 November 1917, which was to be conveyed to the British Zionist Federation, he stated that the British Government 'views with favour the establishment in Palestine of a national home for the Jewish people and would use their best endeavours to facilitate the achievement of this object.' Despite the moderate and careful wording, the Balfour Declaration recognized both the national aspirations of the Jews in Palestine and the fact that the Zionist movement represented these aspirations. The Balfour Declaration was the first political triumph of the Zionists and the culmination of Jewish independent political activity until that time.

The Jewish Community in Palestine Under British Military Administration

At the time of the British occupation, the condition of the Yishuv was serious. Most of its leaders had been arrested or exiled; the economy was collapsing. The British officers appointed to run local affairs chose to ignore the Balfour Declaration, and many of them were imbued with a hatred of the 'Jewish Bolsheviks'. The military administration regarded its main task as the maintenance of a status quo. Not only did it fail to facilitate the activity of Jewish organizations, but it prohibited immigration and land purchase. Moreover, the official languages remained English and Arabic, as the military administration believed that recognition of Hebrew as one of the official languages would prove cumbersome from a budgetary and administrative point of view.

In the summer of 1918 an official delegation – the Zionist Commission – representing the Zionist Organization arrived in Palestine on behalf of the British Government. In addition to British Zionists, headed by Weizmann, it was composed of non-Zionist representatives of French and Italian Jewry. The commission began to organize the Yishuv and to mediate between it and the military administration. Its primary activity lay in extending economic aid (subsidies and loans), medical aid, organization of education (in July 1918 the corner-stone of the Hebrew University was laid in Jerusalem despite the objections of the military administration) and assistance to the colonies and to agricultural settlements. In the autumn of 1918, there were twenty-nine communal settlements in the country under the patronage of the Zionist Organization, as compared with only eleven before the war. The commission clashed violently with the administration. Its achievements were not great and, in most cases, necessitated the intervention of the Foreign Office in London in order to force the occupation authorities to make concessions. In 1919 Menahem Ussishkin was appointed head of the Zionist Commission; he extended its sphere of influence by the sheer force of his personality. Arthur Ruppin worked side by side with him, managing settlement affairs.

Together with the Commission there was also a representative body of the Yishuv known as the Provisional Committee for the Jews of Palestine in the Occupied Territory. The Provisional Committee was elected at the beginning of 1918 at a gathering of representatives of Jewish settlements and organizations in Palestine. At another meeting of the Provisional Committee, held in Jaffa immediately after the war on 18 December 1918, the demand was voiced for the establishment of a society for Jewish settlement in Palestine, empowered to organize the immigration of Jews from all countries and to prepare the country for their absorption. This society was to take over all the government lands and desolate areas, to be granted the authority to exploit natural resources, to develop railways and ports, to arrange credit and institute any other measures that might help Jewish settlement in Palestine. Each national or religious group in the country would be granted the right to national autonomy in matters of personal status, education, culture and social welfare. The official languages of the Palestinian Government would be Hebrew and Arabic. The country should bear the name of Ereẓ Yisrael (the Land of Israel), and its flag should be blue and white. The official rest-days should be Saturday and Jewish festivals, without encroaching in any way on the religious rights of non-Jews.

Many in the Yishuv, particularly youth and labour circles, now voiced the hope that the time was ripe for the establishment of a Jewish military force to help complete the liberation of the country and to achieve the Zionist political goals. This hope was strengthened when General Hill, one of the British commanders of the occupation army, called on the Yishuv, immediately after the conquest of Jerusalem, to volunteer for military service. This appeal found a response in the labour camp and among secondary-school students, and also among the farmers. In February 1918 the first convention of volunteers was held. Many opposed the idea, and a lively propaganda campaign was conducted for some six months. In the summer of 1918, the 40th Battalion of the Royal Fusiliers, composed of some 1,100 men from all walks of life – mostly workers but including *yeshiva* students – left for training in Egypt, but they were too late to participate in military action.

In 1919 the first post-war immigrants began to arrive – members of the Third *Aliyah*. Many of them had belonged to the Heḥaluẓ movement, which demanded of its members that they personally fulfil the Zionist ideal of agricultural or manual labour, and the fostering of Hebrew language and culture. Among the founders of this movement were the leaders of the Palestinian Poalei Zion, David Ben-Gurion and Izhak Ben-Zvi, who spent the war years in the United States. The founder and leader of Heḥaluẓ in Russia was, as previously noted, Joseph Trumpeldor. Within a relatively short period, Heḥaluẓ associations had sprung up in all the countries of Eastern Europe. At a conference in Karlsbad in 1921, the world federation of Heḥaluẓ was established.

The pioneering immigration brought about a resurgence in the labour camp in Palestine. In 1918, David Ben-Gurion of Poalei Zion, who had been a member of the Jewish Legion recruited in the United States, met Berl Katznelson of the Palestinian Battalion, who belonged to no party and was a member of the Agricultural Federation, and the two held discussions on labour unity in Palestine. In time the agricultural federations of Judah, Samaria and Galilee approached the two labour parties – Poalei Zion and Hapo'el Haẓa'ir – with a proposal for amalgamation, which Hapo'el Haẓa'ir rejected. At a labour conference held in Petaḥ Tikvah at the beginning of 1919, the Aḥdut Ha'avodah (Unity of Labour) Party was established; it was composed of members of the agricultural federations, Poalei Zion and non-party elements, together encompassing 80% of all the Jewish workers in Palestine. It set for itself the aim of uniting all Jewish workers of Ereẓ Yisrael into one national federation, which would be an alliance of trade unions and which would also undertake the constructive task of building a national economy, as well as performing cultural and political functions. In order to preserve the unity of the Zionist-Socialist movement throughout the world, Aḥdut Ha'avodah joined the world Poalei Zion movement.

The difficult economic situation, the unemployment and the incompetence that, according to the workers, the Zionist Commission had displayed in its dealings with the British military authorities created tension between the commission and the labour camp. After the French Army evacuated Upper Galilee in 1919 and before the British Army had occupied it, the three labour settlements in the region – Kefar Giladi, Tel Ḥai and Ḥamra – faced a severe potential threat. Aḥdut Ha'avodah decided that it was essential to safeguard Jewish settlement in this area, to ensure that it be included within the framework of the National Home. Ussishkin supported this view, despite the hesitant stand of the commission. Joseph Trumpeldor went to Kefar Giladi to organize the defence of the settlement, and from there he and his comrades went to the aid of the neighbouring settlement of Tel Ḥai. In an Arab attack on Tel Ḥai on 1 March 1920, Trumpeldor was killed. The defence of Tel Ḥai became the symbol of the Yishuv's struggle for its life and honour, despite the fact that the defenders were forced to evacuate both locations. Trumpeldor's dying words, 'It is good to die for our country,' became the motto of all fighters for the Yishuv.

The Struggle over the Nature of the National Home

The Balfour Declaration did not define precisely what a National Home implied. Jewish bodies, such as the American Jewish Congress, convened in December 1918 to demand the creation of conditions ensuring the 'development of Palestine into a Jewish commonwealth' under the protection of Great Britain, the latter to operate on behalf of the League of Nations (which was about to be established). Weizmann, on the other hand, warned against the enthusiastic demand that the 'Jewish State' be established at once and believed that Palestine should first be populated with a Jewish majority so as to be as 'Jewish as England is English'.

Statesmen such as Churchill, Smuts and Chamberlain also understood the declaration in this fashion – as the initial step towards a Jewish commonwealth.

Jewish representatives were invited on 27 February 1919 to appear before the Allied Supreme Council. Weizmann, Sokolow and Ussishkin (who spoke in Hebrew) presented the Jewish demands: encouragement of immigration and settlement; recognition of a Jewish council or agency to represent the Jews of Palestine and of the world; recognition of the prior rights of Jews in granting development concessions. They were followed by Sylvain Lévi, representative of the Alliance Israélite Universelle. He claimed that Palestine was too small to absorb millions of Jews and that the establishment of a Jewish political centre would create the problem of dual loyalty. Zionist representatives, to whom Lévi's remarks came as a surprise, regarded his behaviour as tantamount to treason. The American representative then asked whether the Jews desired an autonomous government in Palestine. This gave Weizmann the opportunity of reclarifying his arguments. He replied that they were not demanding an autonomous Jewish government, but that the mandatory authorities facilitate the entry of 70–80,000 Jews annually and make it possible to consolidate Hebrew education in the country; 'when the Jews formed the large majority they would be ripe to establish such a government as would answer to the state of development of the country and to their ideals.'

In those days representatives of the Yishuv and several Zionist leaders in the Diaspora were already criticizing the moderacy of the Zionist leadership. The writer Israel Zangwill, former leader of the territorialists, who returned to Zionist activity during the war, claimed that, according to these proposals, 'the Jewish National Home is to be a British Crown Colony with a predominantly Arab population. . . . It is neither Jewish, nor National nor a Home.'

On the other hand, no protest was voiced by the Arabs at the time of the publication of the Balfour Declaration. Only when differing interpretations of the significance of the Declaration were put forward, various factors began to emphasize the importance of the Arab stand towards the plan. The Zionist leaders met, therefore, in London at the end of 1918 with Feisal, son of Sherif Hussein of Mecca, and endeavoured to arrive at an understanding with him. The extent of their success can be ascertained by Feisal's remarks, as published in the *Times* of 12 December 1918. There it was stated that the two main branches of the Semitic family understand one another. The Arabs do not envy the Zionist Jews and intend to act in a spirit of 'fair play', and the Jews have promised the 'nationalistic Arabs' a similar attitude. In his memorandum to the Peace Conference in the name of the Arabs, submitted on 1 January 1919, Feisal stated: 'The Jews are very close to the Arabs in blood, and there is no conflict of character between the two races. In principle we are absolutely at one.'

After the deliberations Feisal signed an agreement with Weizmann on 3 January 1919 accepting the Balfour Declaration and agreeing to large-scale immigration and settlement:

> In the establishment of the Constitution and Administration of Palestine, all such measures shall be adopted as will afford the fullest guarantees for carrying

into effect the British Government's Declaration of the end November 1917. All necessary measures shall be taken to encourage and stimulate immigration of Jews into Palestine on a large scale, and as quickly as possible to settle Jewish immigrants upon the land . . .

The agreement noted that if any conflict should arise between the parties it should be 'referred to the British Government for arbitration'. Feisal added under his signature the qualification that he would maintain the agreement only if the Arab demands that he was submitting to the British Foreign Office were fulfilled; if not, he was not responsible for its implementation. As he had, in the meantime, in an interview with the press, expressed reservations regarding the idea of a Jewish state, additional discussions were held. Their conclusions took the form of a letter from Feisal to Professor Felix Frankfurter, one of the leading U.S. Zionists. In this letter, sent on 1 March 1919, it was stated that the Zionist proposals, as submitted to the Peace Conference, appeared to the Arab delegations both 'moderate and proper'. 'We will wish the Jews a hearty welcome home. . . . The Jewish Movement is national and not imperialistic. Our Movement is national and not imperialistic, and there is room in Syria for us both. Indeed, I think that neither can be a real success without the other.' At the same time, on 2 July 1919, a Syrian Congress, representing Arab nationalists, passed a resolution against 'the pretensions of the Zionists to create a Jewish Commonwealth in the southern part of Syria, known as Palestine', and Palestinian Arabs expressed their protests to an American commission sent by President Wilson.

Meanwhile, deliberations had commenced on the formulation of the Mandate, and the disputes between England and France regarding control of the legacy of the Ottoman Empire grew sharper. It was only in April 1920, in San Remo, that agreement was reached, and the Mandate over Palestine was entrusted to Great Britain. The San Remo resolutions were greeted with enthusiasm by the Jews and with anger by the Palestinian Arabs, particularly in light of the fact that Lloyd George asked Herbert Samuel to become the first British High Commissioner in Palestine, and Samuel accepted. Conditions appeared favourable for the implementation of the Balfour Declaration both in theory and in practice, and it seemed that the Zionist goals would be attained before long.

The Zionist Movement Between the Balfour Declaration and the Twelfth Zionist Congress

During the war years, the national Zionist associations were kept apart, and the prestige of the Zionist Executive waned. After the war, the movement began to rehabilitate its world organization. Subsequent to the Balfour Declaration and the establishment of the Zionist Commission, it was generally apparent that hegemony in the Zionist movement was now concentrated in the hands of a group of Zionists active in Britain and that Weizmann was the leader of the entire movement. Also of outstanding importance were the American Zionists and their leader, Brandeis, whose standing as a Supreme Court Justice and whose close contacts with influential circles in the United States gave him considerable influence.

During Brandeis' visit to Europe in 1919, he and Weizmann disagreed on several of the basic issues of Zionist policy. But the matter reached open conflict only at the first representative convention after the war, held in London in July 1920, with the participation of Zionists from various countries. In accordance with the new spirit then prevailing, Brandeis held that the political functions of the Zionist Organization were ended as far as Palestine was concerned and should be transferred to the mandatory authorities. The central function of the Zionist movement from then on would be the economic development of the country, which should be based mainly on private enterprise; for this reason non-Zionist financiers should be attracted to Zionist activity. Any Jew sympathetic towards the building of Palestine could find a place within the framework of the movement, but the main part of the practical work, he thought, should be conducted by experts. Brandeis strove to change the character of the Zionist movement by weakening the dependence of national associations on the centre. He did not have a high regard for nationalistic education in the Diaspora and was even actively opposed to it.

The London Conference decided to establish a special fund for the development of Palestine – Keren Hayesod (The Foundation Fund), with a capital of £25 million. Despite the differences of opinion, the conference elected Brandeis as Honorary President of the Zionist Organization, Weizmann as President and Sokolow as Chairman of the Executive. Among American Zionists there were those who advised Brandeis to resign from the Supreme Court and dedicate himself to Zionist activity, but he refused. The two camps emerged dissatisfied from the conference. When Weizmann approached the American Zionists with the demand that they raise a large sum for the Keren Hayesod, he encountered refusal. Weizmann then decided to travel the United States, together with Menahem Ussishkin and Albert Einstein, to promote the Fund. In his American activities he was supported by American Zionists of East European origin, who were resentful of the leadership of Brandeis and his associates. At the American Zionist conference in Cleveland (June 1921) there was a clash between the supporters and opponents of Brandeis, and the latter, supported by Weizmann, prevailed. Brandeis resigned from his posts in the Zionist movement, and a new leadership was elected.

At the Twelfth Zionist Congress, which was convened at Karlsbád (September 1921), the movement and its leadership were consolidated in accordance with Weizmann's objectives. All the Zionist parties were represented at the Congress. Its resolutions emphasized the national-political and democratic nature of the movement and the task of settlement in Palestine; and the hope was expressed that good relations would prevail between Jews and Arabs in Palestine and that the Mandate would rapidly be approved by the League of Nations, providing new impetus for the implementation of Zionist plans. The new Zionist leadership constructed its policy on the theory that there existed common interests between the Jewish people and Great Britain and that there could be political cooperation between them. Both the achievements and the failures of this leadership derived from this assumption.

The Mandate and Its Implementation

The discussions held between representatives of Britain and the Zionist Organization on the contents of the Mandate began as early as the spring of 1919. In July 1920 Herbert Samuel took up his post as High Commissioner for Palestine, but only in December 1920 did the British Government submit the draft formula of the Mandate to the League of Nations; it was approved by the League on 24 July 1922. The preamble to the Mandate noted that

> the Principal Allied Powers have agreed . . . that the Mandatory should be responsible for putting into effect the declaration originally made on November 2nd, 1917 by the Government of His Britannic Majesty, and adopted by the said Powers, in favour of the establishment in Palestine of a national home for the Jewish people . . . and recognition has thereby been given to the historical connection of the Jewish people with Palestine. . . . The Mandatory Power has undertaken to create conditions as will secure the establishment of the Jewish national home (article 2); to recognize an appropriate Jewish Agency, which would cooperate with the Administration of Palestine in all matters as may affect the establishment of the Jewish national home and the interests of the Jewish population in Palestine (article 4). The Administration of Palestine, while ensuring that the rights and position of other sections of the population are not prejudiced, shall facilitate Jewish immigration under suitable conditions; and shall encourage, in cooperation with the Jewish Agency, close settlement by Jews on the land, including State lands and waste lands . . . (article 6).

The Mandate was intended to serve as an implementation of the Balfour Declaration concerning the establishment of the Jewish national home.

At the beginning of Sir Herbert Samuel's activity as High Commissioner it transpired that he was not taking a clear-cut path for the resolute implementation of these guarantees. He retained many of those members of the military administration who had proved their unwillingness to implement the Balfour Declaration and endeavoured to win the trust of the Arabs through concessions to their demands. Apart from opening the gates of Palestine to immigration, the Mandatory Government did nothing to further the National Home. Samuel expected the Zionist Organization to recruit funds for the implementation of nation-wide development projects without resorting to British aid.

The 1920–1 Riots and the Policy of Appeasing the Arabs

The political tension in the country increased perceptibly even before Samuel's arrival. Various Arab circles began to organize political groups and nationalist clubs in order to arouse violent opposition to British policy and to Jewish immigration. This incitement was supported by a number of the officers serving in the military administration. Before long, attacks on Jews commenced. Outbursts on a wider scale began in April 1920, during the San Remo deliberations. An Arab mob attacked Jews in Jerusalem, mainly in the Old City, looting shops, injuring and killing, and the British Army did nothing to prevent the riots. Jabotinsky, who recruited young Jews for armed defence activity in order to induce the authorities to set up a legal Jewish military force, was arrested and sentenced to fifteen years' imprisonment – although he was speedily pardoned along with the Arab rioters.

The Jerusalem riots demonstrated that, despite the previous negotiations between Zionist and Arab leaders, there existed strong Arab opposition to the National Home plan and that the military administration had not taken sufficient steps to suppress these outbursts or to implement the Balfour Declaration in its true spirit. The Yishuv and the Zionist leadership were now confronted with the problem of safeguarding the future of the National Home.

Several Zionists already tended to view the Jewish Battalions as the nucleus of independent Jewish military force; and, in fact, at the beginning of the British occupation they were entrusted with guard-duty in various parts of the country. But, wherever they were deployed, these units encountered manifestations of Arab hostility, and the British military authorities decided to dispense with them. An attempt was made even to evacute part of the Palestinian Battalion to Cyprus, and it was only the firm stand of most of the troops which prevented this. The Jerusalem riots demonstrated that the British authorities were unwilling to hand over defence of the Yishuv to the Jewish Battalions. The attempts of a Battalion to come to the aid of attacked settlements on their own initiative were regarded as a grave breach of disipline, and the unit was disbanded. The leaders of the Yishuv reached two conclusions: there was a need for an independent Jewish defence force, and such a force would be obliged for some time to come to operate clandestinely.

The replacement of military rule by a civilian administration and the appointment of a Jewish – and Zionist – High Commissioner did not basically alter the situation. At the beginning of May 1921, Arab gangs attacked the immigrant centre in Jaffa and murdered thirteen Jews. On the following day the well-known writer, Joseph Ḥayyim Brenner, was murdered with several companions in Jaffa. The total number of Jewish dead reached forty-three. Thousands of Bedouins and Arab villagers attacked Petaḥ Tikvah, but were repelled by the population and dispersed by an Indian cavalry unit. The settlers and members of the Jewish Battalions prevented attacks on other settlements. The Arab policemen, with very few exceptions, made no attempt to defend the Jews and often participated in the attacks.

When the riots broke out, High Commissioner Sir Herbert Samuel suspended Jewish immigration and established a commission of inquiry, headed by the Chief Justice of Palestine, in order to clarify the causes of the riots. In reaction to the suspension of immigration, the Jewish institutions announced their resignation and did not retreat from this stand until the Colonial Secretary, Winston Churchill, announced the resumption of immigration. The commission found that the Arabs had been the aggressors, that the police had not acted efficiently and that several policemen had even participated in the riots. But the commission also noted that the activity of Zionist institutions, and particularly the propaganda for 'Hebrew labour' (*i.e.,* to employ only Jewish workers in Jewish enterprises), had served as convenient background for the outburst. It placed special emphasis on the declaration of Dr

Eder, deputy head of the Zionist Commission, who had voiced Zionist opinions totally opposed to those of the Colonial Secretary and the High Commissioner. According to Eder's statement, only one national home is possible in Palestine and that is a Jewish home, and Jewish predominance as soon as the number of Jews increases sufficiently. As summarized by the commission, 'He was quite clear that the Jews should and the Arabs should not have the right to bear arms, and he stated his belief that this discrimination would tend to improve Arab-Jewish relations.' He was convinced that as regards a High Commissioner for Palestine, the Zionist Organization should be afforded the possibility of explaining its objection to the choice of the British Government, or to submit its own list of candidates.

In the summer of 1921, Samuel published an interim report on his activities as High Commissioner. In this report he re-emphasized that it was possible to combine Jewish national aspirations with Arab interests, but noted: 'The degree to which Jewish national aspirations can be fulfilled in Palestine is conditioned by the rights of the present inhabitants.' 'Rights of inhabitants' meant, in actual fact, the total opposition of the Arabs to the Jewish National Home. Thus we see that the Jewish High Commissioner and the British Government regarded the fulfilment of their mandatory obligations in accordance with the degree of Arab pressure. The outcome of this policy was that the Arab opposition to the National Home grew even stronger. One of the most damaging acts from this point of view was Samuel's decision to entrust the post of Mufti of Jerusalem to a fanatic Arab nationalist, Amin el-Husseini.

When Churchill visited Palestine in March 1921, he reached an agreement with the son of Sherif Hussein, the Emir Abdullah, to place Transjordan under his rule. As a result of the Jaffa riots, not only was Transjordan (which in all previous deliberations had been considered part of Palestine) broken away, but various concessions were also offered to the Arabs of western Palestine. All these concessions were summarized and emphasized in Churchill's White Paper, published in the summer of 1922. This White Paper also stressed the adherence of the Mandatory Government to the Balfour Declaration, but at the same time promised to establish self-rule institutions in Palestine, in which most of the representatives would be elected, *i.e.,* Arabs. It also stressed that the Zionist institutions would have no part in the government and determined that the scope of immigration would be in accordance with 'the economic capacity of the country at the time to absorb new arrivals'. It was specifically noted that the government did not intend to make Palestine 'as Jewish as England is English'.

This White Paper was the first in a series of British acts of appeasement towards the Arabs, yet the Arabs remained obdurate. The Zionist Organization felt itself constrained to approve this policy, as reflected in the new White Paper, but the Arabs rejected it. Samuel's other efforts to appease the Arabs also proved fruitless: the Arabs boycotted the elections to the Legislative Council, which he announced in September 1922; those Arabs appointed to the Advisory Council – a new body established after the Arab boycott of the Legislative Council – refused to accept the nomination; they also rejected a proposal submitted at the end of 1923 to establish an Arab Agency parallel to the Jewish Agency.

Samuel himself summed up his policy in 1925 as follows: the government, he said, had bestowed on the National Home moral support, recognition of the Hebrew language and maintenance of order; 'for all the rest, it [the Jewish national movement] has had to rely on its own internal resources, on its own enthusiasm, its own sacrifices, its own men'. In other words, Britain did not revoke the Balfour Declaration and the Mandate, but she did not take any active steps to implement them.

Sir Herbert Samuel tried to bring about a compromise between the Jews and the Arabs, but without success. In fact, he was mainly interested in appeasing the Arabs. The High Commissioner who followed him, Lord Herbert Plumer (1925–8), chose the path of consistent implementation of British policy as formulated in the 1922 White Paper and acted directly and aggressively without any consideration for Arab pressure. His first achievement was to maintain quiet and security, and, in fact, during his term of office, Arab activity did not exceed the boundaries of political protest, and there were no outbursts or riots.

The Growth of the Yishuv in the Twenties

Despite all the obstacles and difficulties, the foundations of the National Home were laid in the twenties. The Yishuv grew in this decade approximately threefold and totalled 160,000. The number of agricultural settlements totalled 110 (as compared to fifty in 1920), with a population of 37,000 and a cultivated area of 700,000 dunams (175,000 acres). According to the 1929 census, there were 2,500 Jewish industrial enterprises with 11,000 workers, and the value of their products totalled £2.5 million annually. The Electricity and Potash corporations exploited their concessions and became the largest economic enterprises in the country.

But this considerable progress did not achieve the objective that the leaders of the Zionist movement had set themselves at the time of the Balfour Declaration and the Peace Conference and did not fulfil the hopes that the Yishuv and the Jewish people throughout the world had pinned on the Declaration. Jewish immigration between 1920 and 1929 encompassed approximately 100,000 persons, about one-quarter of whom subsequently emigrated; thus, the average annual increment from immigration was some 8,000. There were fluctuations in this wave of immigration: in 1925 more than 30,000 immigrants arrived, in the crisis year of 1927, only 2,713 came and 5,071 emigrated. In 1928, 2,178 entered the country, and 2,168 left. Immigration was resumed in 1929, but the sum total at the end of the twenties was small.

Conditions in the agricultural settlements did not differ greatly from the country as a whole. The authorities did not place land at the disposal of Zionist settlement, while some 100,000 acres were handed over to the Arabs in the Beth-shean Valley in 1921. Thus, the achievements of the settlements were obtained through the independent efforts of the Zionist movement and the Yishuv. The greatest purchasing project carried out by the Jewish National Fund in the early twenties, through Yehoshua Hankin, was the redemption of the Jezreel Valley lands (which was carried out without the knowledge of the Zionist Executive). There were also considerable achievements in the sphere of irrigation, producing some 15,000 acres of orange groves. With regard to settlement patterns, the majority of the farmers lived in colonies, but the number of *kevuẓot* (communal settlements) and cooperative small-holders' settlements increased rapidly (twenty-eight and twenty-four, respectively, in 1929, as compared to eleven and seven, respectively, in 1920). These settlement units cultivated some 50,000 acres of land and had a population of 7,000 by the end of the 1920s. In short, despite the important advancement of settlement, its achievements were limited when measured against national aspirations.

Jewish Self-rule

No less important than all these achievements, however, and perhaps of greater significance, was the establishment of the Yishuv's self-rule institutions. This was a fulfilment of the autonomistic principles accepted by Jewish communities after the First World War and, in practice, laid the foundations of future self-rule. Some of the institutions established were integrated into the legal and administrative frameworks of the Mandatory Government, and others were clandestine or semi-underground bodies. It is possible that this endeavour, more than any other, brought to light some basic differences of opinion. Several Western Zionists believed that, after approval of the Mandate, the main task of implementation of Zionist aims would be taken over by the mandatory authorities, while the leaders of the Yishuv, most of them of East European origin, were filled from the beginning with distrust for the alien authority.

The Provisional Committee was established immediately after the British occupation guaranteed to hold elections to a 'constituent assembly' of the Yishuv within three months, but, in fact, the representative body met only in October 1920. The structure of the Yishuv's representative bodies, under the leadership of Zionist organizations, was as follows: the local unit, the Kehillah Ivrit (Hebrew community), a modification of the historic Jewish community but secular in nature; a central representative body, the Asefat Hanivḥarim (Assembly of Delegates), which was elected by the Yishuv; and its executive body, the Va'ad Le'ummi (National Committee). Jurisdiction over matrimonial law and religion was entrusted by the mandatory authorities to the Chief Rabbinate and rabbinical courts. In February 1921 the first two chief rabbis were elected: for the Ashkenazim, Rabbi Abraham Isaac Kook, and for the Sephardim, Rabbi Jacob Meir.

Efforts to include members of the Old Yishuv in the new institutions did not meet with success, and Agudat Israel remained outside Knesset Yisrael (the designation of the Yishuv as a corporate body). Even after the authorities recognized the obligation of affiliation to Knesset Yisrael, the leaders of Agudat Israel were permitted to announce their secession and maintain their own recognized courts.

The defence of Tel Ḥai and the 1920 Jerusalem riots highlighted in all its severity the problem of protecting the life and property of the Jewish Yishuv. In the institutions of the Zionist movement there was no unanimity on this question. Some Zionist leaders hoped to achieve security through exerting pressure on the British Government to permit the establishment of a Jewish military force. Others were content with government recognition of legal Jewish defence units. The main initiative for the establishment of the Haganah (Defence Organization) emerged from labour circles.

It was decided to establish this body at a conference of Aḥdut Ha'avodah at Kinneret in 1920, and its nature as a non-party organization was stressed from the beginning. In actual fact, during most of the twenties, defence was organized by a small number of activists. The initiators were Eliyahu Golomb and Dov Hos. The Haganah was headed by Yosef Hecht, together with Shaul (Meirov) Avigur, and they were aided by local commanders, mainly in the larger towns. They recognized the authority of the Secretary of the Histadrut (in those days, David Ben-Gurion) and reported to him on their activities. Yishuv and Histadrut institutions were not very concerned about defence activities in the relatively quiet 1920s.

Education and Culture

An extensive educational network grew up in the twenties: in 1929–30 there were some 21,000 pupils in 230 schools, while 200 students attended the Hebrew University in Jerusalem. Some 30,000 persons were insured in the Histadrut Sick Fund (Kuppat Ḥolim), and the Hadassah Organization supplied a range of medical services, mainly for children and pupils. The death-rate in the Yishuv was among the lowest in the world (from 1926 to 1930, 11.66 per 1,000).

One of the most important achievements of the Yishuv in that period was the continued renaissance of the Hebrew language and extensive creativity in that language. The whole educational network, from kindergarten to university, was conducted solely in Hebrew. The Habimah theatre, which had been established in Moscow, settled in Tel Aviv and became the national theatre. The greatest Hebrew writers of the period also settled in Tel Aviv: Bialik, Aḥad Ha-Am and Saul Tchernichowsky. Not only did the language and literature serve as the basis for the Yishuv's spiritual life, but the Zionist movements – particularly youth movements – in the Diaspora were nurtured on this cultural renaissance.

The Labour Movement and Communal Settlement

The most active element in the new Jewish Yishuv was the labour movement. As we have noted, unifying tendencies began to emerge at the end of the war, and, as a result, the Aḥdut Ha'avodah Party was established. This party's aim was to establish one organizational framework for the entire labour movement to encompass labour, economy, culture and politics, but this aim was not realized. The Hapo'el Haẓa'ir Party, and several other smaller bodies, did not fit into this framework and were reluctant to abandon their own political or social frameworks. It was therefore decided to convene a general conference of the Jewish workers in December 1920, in order to set up a general labour organization to deal with labour, economic and cultural questions, within which all the political parties could operate. Thus the Histadrut, the General Federation of Hebrew Workers, came into being. Some 4,500 workers participated in the elections to the first congress. All the economic, cultural and educational institutions of the various parties now came under the jurisdiction of the Histadrut, and it controlled all settlement problems and mutual-aid projects.

Various trends emerged within the Histadrut, each of which tried, in its own way, to consolidate new patterns of communal and labour life. Each trend sought ways of educating and training youth in the Diaspora for life in Erez Yisrael. At the end of the twenties, the tendency towards political unification once again prevailed in the labour camp, and a programme was drawn up for the amalgamation of Aḥdut Ha'avodah and Hapo'el Haza'ir. Thus Mapai, the Erez Yisrael Workers' Party, was established at the beginning of 1930 and constituted a decisive majority within the Histadrut.

As a result of the grave economic situation in the post-war years, the Jewish economy, both rural and urban, was unable to provide employment for Jewish workers, and was certainly incapable of absorbing immigration. The workers organized themselves into independent groups, mainly for work on road-building, a project that the British authorities had recently undertaken. The new immigrants of the Third *Aliyah* were absorbed mostly in these jobs. The groups that undertook to carry out these projects on a contractual basis were generally organized along cooperative lines. Several had a distinct social programme, such as the Shomriah group, or the large unit that bore the name of 'The Joseph Trumpeldor Labour Battalion'.

The Labour Battalion (Gedud Ha'avodah) was established at a memorial meeting to Trumpeldor six months after his death. It was composed of autonomous groups with a common budget, and they were mainly employed on road-building. The Battalion set up two camps at Ein Ḥarod and at Tel Yosef, which served as the headquarters of units scattered all over the country. When the roadwork was completed, some of the Battalion members moved to towns and took up construction work, while others settled on the land. This eventually led to a split (mid-1923): the Ein Ḥarod settlers seceded from the Battalion and, together with other settlement groups, established the kibbutz of Ein Ḥarod. In 1927 they, together with other communal settlements, established the Hakibbutz Hame'uḥad (United Kibbutz) movement. It was associated with the Aḥdut Ha'avodah Party, and its reserve in the Diaspora was the Heḥaluz movement.

The members of the Gedud Ha'avodah at Tel Yosef were divided on an ideological question, which led to bitter conflict between the right- and left-wing components. Members of the right-wing section founded the settlements of Tel Yosef, Kefar Giladi and Ramat Raḥel near Jerusalem. The leftists on the whole left the Battalion, and one section became strongly attracted towards Communism; some forty members, headed by M. Elkinc, one of the outstanding figures in the Battalion, returned to Soviet Russia. There they established an agricultural settlement in the Crimea, called Woja Nova (New Way).

The Shomriah Labour Battalion also split into several groups, but the character of its members, all formerly affiliated to the pioneering youth movement Hashomer Haza'ir, ensured social and ideological cohesion. The Hashomer Haza'ir movement in Palestine, based on the movement of the same name in Galicia, Poland and several other East European countries, became a consolidated and clearly defined ideological trend in the labour movement. In 1927, the Hakibbutz Ha'arẓi (Erez Yisrael Kibbutz) movement was founded, which united all the Hashomer Haza'ir kibbutzim. The Gordonia movement, founded in Galicia in 1925, provided the reserve for Hapo'el Ḥaẓi'ir and the Ḥever Hakevuẓot (Association of Kevuẓot) movement associated with it.

At the beginning of the twenties, religious workers began to arrive in Palestine and subsequently formed the Hapo'el Hamizrachi organization. In 1925, 100 ḥasidic families immigrated from Poland and settled at Kefar Ḥasidim. The majority did not stay for long, and the village was later consolidated by Hapo'el Hamizrachi.

Attempts to create new social patterns, and the desire to shape a new human image, to 'conquer Hebrew labour' and to build up the country were characteristic of all the communal-settlement trends. They differed only with regard to the form that the commune should take. Those who believed that communal settlement should be a social cell, whose main function was to fulfil national aims and to absorb new immigrants, were in favour of establishing large settlements – heavily populated kibbutzim maintaining industrial enterprises in addition to engaging in agricultural work, and also performing outside jobs. This was the approach of Hakibbutz Hameu'ḥad. Ḥever Hakevuẓot, on the other hand, held that the communal cell, the *kevuẓah,* should be an intimate and organic society, engaging solely in agricultural work. Hashomer Haẓa'ir also leaned towards the latter view.

At the same time, a new form of agricultural settlement known as the moshav ovdim (small-holders' cooperative settlement) began to develop; it was characterized by the preservation of family economic units, each working independently, but cooperating in various forms of supply and marketing and in extensive mutual aid. The first such moshavim were Nahalal, Kefar Yeḥezkel and Kefar Malal.

The Histadrut regarded the fostering of all forms of communal settlement as one of its main functions. It also engaged in the establishment of workers' urban housing estates, organizing industrial and service cooperatives, contractual enterprises in agriculture and construction (Solel Boneh) and even cultural activity and the dissemination of the Hebrew language. In time a common framework was established for all the Histadrut's economic enterprises – Ḥevrat Ha'ovdim (The Labour Society). At the same time the Histadrut preserved its trade-union character, protecting the interests of the wage-earner and organizing welfare activity. It also established various funds for this purpose.

The labour camp also bore the main burden of security. There were local defence committees in the moshavot and towns, but there was no co-ordination among them. The party most closely involved in security affairs was Aḥdut Ha'avodah, in whose ranks were members of Hashomer and most of the veterans of the First World War Jewish units. Most of those active in security affairs, such as Eliyahu Golomb, were members of this party. For a time it appeared that the Gedud Ha'avodah would bear the main defence burden, but the internal friction in this unit, as well as the tension between the veteran members of Hashomer in the Battalion – who thought that security should be entrusted to 'professionals', in accordance with Hashomer practice – and the views of the new Haganah activists, who based defence on maximal recruitment of all those willing to lend a hand on a volunteer basis, greatly reduced the value of the Battalion for this purpose. For a time the ex-members of Hashomer who were living in Kefar Giladi tried to maintain their own separate military organization, Hakibbutz, which even established contact with Soviet Russia in order to acquire arms; but after part of the Battalion turned to Communism, this organization was disbanded.

The Zionist Movement in the Twenties

The tension engendered between the Zionist movement and the British Government, together with the slow pace of development of the National Home, aroused fierce controversy within the Zionist movement. Jabotinsky resigned from the Zionist Executive in protest against the White Paper of 1922 – which he had previously accepted. The Mizrachi, the 'Radical Zionists' from Poland, led by Yitzhak Gruenbaum, and Ussishkin from Palestine joined together at the Thirteenth Zionist Congress (Karlsbad, August 1923) in criticism of the leadership. They protested against the weak stand of the Zionist Executive towards Britain and against the 'surrender to non-Zionists' implicit in the proposal to introduce representatives of institutions and bodies from outside the Zionist Organization into the Jewish Agency so as to rally general Jewish support for the building of Palestine. The Congress decided to demand the convening of a world Jewish congress, which should elect the representative Jewish Agency. S. Kaplansky of Poalei Zion demanded that a programme for Jewish-Arab cooperation be drafted.

At the Fourteenth Zionist Congress (Vienna, August 1925), convened in a year of mass immigration, criticism of the leadership was more moderate. Weizmann proposed that the Jewish Agency be composed of equal numbers of Zionists and non-Zionists. Nevertheless, opposition to the leadership was strong, and more than half of the delegates abstained during the vote of confidence for the Zionist Executive.

Vladimir Jabotinsky was consistent in his criticism at this Congress and submitted a plan of his own in opposition to that of the Executive. He claimed that in order to implement the Zionist plan it was essential to demand that the Zionist Executive, and not the government, supervise immigration. Some 40,000 immigrants should be allowed into Palestine each year for twenty-five years, and thus a Jewish majority would be created. The appointment of officials in Palestine should be in the hands of the Zionist Executive. Jewish military units should be established, and desolate lands should be nationalized and transferred to the Jews. In 1925 Jabotinsky set up the Federation of Revisionist Zionists, which proclaimed its aspiration to return to the 'original Herzlian policy', demanded a re-examination of the old Basle programme and its replacement by a clear declaration of the final objective of Zionism – the establishment of a Jewish state in Palestine within its historic borders on both sides of the Jordan. But the majority of the Zionist movement did not agree with this policy – most because of tactical reasons.

The Fifteenth Congress (Basle, August-September 1927) was convened under the shadow of the severe economic crisis that had broken out in Palestine. This situation was, to a large extent, the outcome of the failure to absorb the Fourth *Aliyah*. It had been mostly composed of middle-class Polish Jews who, in the main, settled in towns and began to engage in industry, commerce and services. The great building boom, which commenced in 1924 and expanded greatly in 1925, was checked at the end of that year: businesses collapsed, workers were dismissed and unemployment rose rapidly. In 1926 more than 7,000 people left the country, and in 1927 emigration was twice as high as immigration. At this Congress the Revisionists led by Jabotinsky, and the Radicals headed by Gruenbaum, attacked the Executive. The budget of the Executive, some £250,000, seemed to them nothing but a mockery. The labour parties were more strongly represented at this Congress, but for fear of the growing force of the right-wing opposition, they bestowed their support on the Executive.

The consequences of an improved economic situation and the renewal of immigration were recognizable at the Sixteenth Congress (Zurich, July-August 1929). The labour representation, which had again greatly increased, gave its full support to Weizmann (particularly Chaim Arlosoroff, who was beginning to make a name for himself as one of the leaders of the labour movement). But the opposition – the Revisionists, the Radicals and the Mizrachi – had also gained strength. Jabotinsky again demanded a struggle for the repeal of the 1922 White Paper and called for a public proclamation of the aim of establishing a state with a Jewish majority. Ussishkin, as well as Rabbi Meir Berlin on behalf of the Mizrachi, attacked the way in which the leadership was appeasing the government and denounced the activities of the Brit Shalom (Peace Alliance) group led by the President of the Hebrew University, Judah Magnes, which had published a plan for the creation of a bi-national Jewish-Arab state in Palestine. Dr Stephen Wise, on behalf of the American Zionists, also criticized the mild attitude towards the Mandatory Government. Despite all the criticism, Weizmann was re-elected President of the Zionist Organization, and representatives of the labour parties and of the Mizrachi joined the Zionist Executive. Immediately after the Congress ended, the wider Jewish Agency – half of its members were now non-Zionists – was convened for its first session. The opportunities for Zionist activity appeared greatly improved, but the 1929 riots broke out at this point and completely altered the situation.

The 1929 Riots, the Passfield White Paper and the MacDonald Letter

During the 1920s, the Arab nationalist movement in Palestine became stronger, and its opposition to the Jews grew more intense. The Mufti of Jerusalem, Amin el-Husseini, dominated the movement and it became more extremist under his influence. Anti-Jewish leaflets were openly distributed. One of them, issued by the 'Jerusalem Arab Students', which appeared just before the outbreak of the riots, declared:

> Remember that the Jew is your strong enemy, and the enemy of your ancestors since olden times. Do not be misled by his tricks, for it is he who tortured Christ, peace be upon him, and poisoned Mohammed, peace and worship be with him. It is he who now endeavours to slaughter you, as he did yesterday. Be aware that the best way to save yourself and your Fatherland from the grasp of the foreign intruder and greedy Jew is to boycott him. Therefore boycott him and support the industry of your Fatherland and God.

Under the leadership of the Mufti, the idea of compromise with the Jews was rejected, and there was an increasing tendency to employ violence as the main method in the Arab struggle. A pretext for the renewal of tension was the dispute on the right of the Jews to pray at the Western Wall, the last remnant of the wall surrounding the ancient Temple in Jerusalem. As a result riots broke out in Jerusalem on 23 August 1929, and an Arab mob attacked the Jewish quarters. From there the attacks spread to the agricultural settlements of Moẓa, Ḥuldah and Be'er Toviyyah. There were also riots in the Tel Aviv area and in Haifa. In all these places the attackers were repelled by Jewish defence units, and only in Hebron, where the Jewish community mainly consisted of members of the Old Yishuv and *yeshiva* students, was there brutal slaughter; more than sixty Jews – including old people, women and children – were killed. Several days later there was an attack on the Jewish quarter of Safed, during which eighteen people were murdered and many homes plundered and burned down. There was also loss of life elsewhere, and the total number of Jewish victims was over 130.

The Colonial Secretary of the new Labour Government, Lord Passfield, appointed a commission, headed by Sir Walter Shaw, to investigate the causes of the riots. The commission pinned full responsibility on the Arabs, but explained that the background was the Arab hostility towards the Jews because 'the claims and demands which from the Zionist side have been advanced in regard to the future of Jewish immigration . . . have been such as to arouse among Arabs the apprehension that they will in time be deprived of their livelihood and put under the political domination of the Jews.' In conclusion the commission declared that the main task of the Palestinian Government, according to the 1922 White Paper, was to maintain the balance between the two communities in the country. 'There was no clear direction to assist either party in the fulfilment of their aspirations.' The report recommended that there be given 'directions more explicit . . . as to the conduct of policy in such vital issues as land and immigration' but its intention was clear – to place restrictions on both.

The report of the Shaw commission aroused Arab enthusiasm and was severely criticized by Yishuv institutions and the Zionist leadership, as well as certain sections of British public opinion. The League of Nations Permanent Mandates Commission also rejected the report. Nevertheless, on the basis of this report the British Government halted immigration to Palestine in May 1930.

In order to justify its policy, the government decided to appoint an investigator to examine conditions and economic opportunities in Palestine. The investigator, Sir John Hope-Simpson, gave a minimal evaluation of the amount of land available in the country and claimed that it was already insufficient to ensure a reasonable livelihood for Arab farmers. He criticized the land policies of the Jewish National Fund and the Histadrut's slogan of 'Hebrew labour'. Hope-Simpson pinned his main hope on raising the cultural standards of the Arabs and transferring both Jewish and Arab farms to intensive cultivation methods. He also proposed the introduction of strict supervision of immigration to prevent unemployment.

The Hope-Simpson report was published in October 1930, together with the Passfield White Paper on the British Government's Palestinian policy. In theory this document was intended to be a continuation of British policy as laid down in the

Churchill White Paper, emphasizing the equal British obligation towards both Arabs and Jews. In practice, it was redolent of hostility towards the Jews. The main attack on Zionist aspirations was in the reinterpretation of the term 'economic absorptive capacity' of the country. According to the Passfield White Paper this did not refer to the absorption capacity of the Jewish Yishuv, but to that of the entire country; *i.e.*, as long as there was unemployment among the Arabs, Jewish immigration should not be permitted, because the Arab population feared that the entry of additional Jews would worsen the situation.

One day after the publication of the White Paper, Weizmann resigned all his posts in the Jewish Agency and the Zionist movement, as did several other members of the Agency. Several well-known British statesmen also protested against the new policy. They were joined by Sir Herbert Samuel, who was known for his conciliatory attitude to Arab demands. Under pressure of these protests, the British Government retreated from its stand, and on 13 February 1931, Prime Minister Ramsay MacDonald published a letter to Weizmann in which he 'clarified' the White Paper in a manner more congenial to the Jews: it recognizes that the undertaking of the Mandate is an undertaking to the Jewish people and not only to the Jewish population of Palestine. Immigration would not be curbed and 'economic absorptive capacity' would be interpreted as before. 'The obligation to facilitate Jewish immigration and to encourage close settlement by Jews on the land remains a positive obligation of the Mandate.' Although quite a number of Jews distrusted the MacDonald Letter and demanded the revocation of the Passfield White Paper, the Zionist Organization accepted it and announced that the basis for cooperation with the mandatory power had been restored.

Conflicts in the Zionist Movement in the 1930s

Despite the MacDonald Letter, criticism of the Zionist leadership did not die out. The hopes that many people had pinned on the co-opting of non-Zionists on to the Jewish Agency, in order to create a new momentum for Zionist activity, had not been realized. This served as the basis for the strong criticism voiced at the Seventeenth Congress (Basle, June-July 1931) against Weizmann and his political methods. The Revisionists succeeded in winning 20% of the representation at this Congress, and many of the General Zionist and Mizrachi delegates tended to support them. Stephen Wise demanded Weizmann's resignation and attacked the MacDonald Letter and the Zionist Organization for placing trust in British promises. Jabotinsky again demanded of the Congress that it define the final objective (*Endziel*) of Zionism as the establishment of a state in Palestine, on both banks of the Jordan, with a Jewish majority and self-rule. This demand was echoed by the Mizrachi and many of the General Zionists, but Menahem Ussishkin, although he was a Zionist maximalist all his life, opposed proclamations of objectives, as he felt that any formal definition restricted the ideal of the full renaissance of the people.

Because of Ussishkin's stand and the cables that arrived from Palestine warning that any definition of the 'final objective' would lead to renewed Arab outbursts,

Jabotinsky's proposal was rejected. He demonstratively tore up his delegate's card and left the Congress. However, Weizmann was not re-elected President of the Zionist Organization and was succeeded by Nahum Sokolow. The Revisionists did not join the Zionist Executive; it was composed of members of Mapai, the Mizrachi and the General Zionists, and Chaim Arlosoroff headed the Political Department. Thus Mapai attained a central position on the Executive.

Arlosoroff was not far removed from radical political thought, as demonstrated by his letter to Weizmann, dated 30 June 1932. In this letter he raised the possibility of 'a transitional period in which the Jewish minority will rule in organized revolutionary fashion . . . and a nationalistic minority government will take over the state machinery, administration and military force, so as to forestall the threat of domination by the non-Jewish majority and of revolt'. But the attitude of Arlosoroff and of the entire labour camp towards the Revisionists became more hostile. The Revisionists, and particularly the more extreme among them, sharply attacked the Zionist Executive. Clashes occurred between members of Betar (the Revisionist youth movement) and the youth movements of the Histadrut parties. The internal struggle in the Yishuv was intensified.

During this tense period, on 16 June 1933, Arlosoroff was murdered on a Tel Aviv beach. The rumour was immediately spread that he had been murdered by the Revisionists; but this was opposed by various prominent personalities in the Yishuv, led by Chief Rabbi Kook. Against this background clashes between the two camps became more acute and were sometimes accompanied by violence.

This friction was reflected at the Eighteenth Congress (Prague, August 1933), but few political innovations resulted. The resolutions reiterated that there was no contradiction between the aspirations of Jews and Arabs and demanded that immigration be stepped up in light of the predicament of German Jewry. The labour parties, with almost half of the delegates, became the dominant factor. David Ben-Gurion, Berl Locker, Eliezer Kaplan and Moshe Shertok entered the Zionist Executive; Shertok became head of the Political Department. Towards the end of 1934, Ben-Gurion attempted to reach an agreement with Jabotinsky in order to overcome the differences, but the majority within the Histadrut, which regarded the Revisionists as a fascist movement, did not approve.

Before the Nineteenth Congress, a referendum was held among the branches of the Revisionist movement, and the majority supported secession from the official Zionist movement. The Revisionists did not participate in the Nineteenth Congress, and, shortly afterwards, they convened a conference in Vienna, at which they announced the establishment of the New Zionist Organization (1935). One of the reasons behind this move was the question of the *ha'avarah* ('transfer') – an agreement arrived at between the leaders of the Zionist movement and the Nazi authorities for the removal, in the form of goods, of part of the property of those German Jews who were immigrating to Palestine. In this period Jewish and even non-Jewish firms were subscribing to a widespread boycott of German goods, and many people believed that the transfer agreement could only weaken the boycott front. Its supporters regarded it as a method of rescuing Jewish property and an important means of developing Palestine. But the direct reason for the secession was the 'discipline clause' passed at the Zionist Executive, which prohibited all 'independent political activities' by Zionist parties.

The Nineteenth Zionist Congress (Lucerne, August-September 1935) emphasized the advancement of the Zionist movement. Despite the departure of the Revisionists, its members numbered close to 1.25 million. The Congress devoted its deliberations mainly to the increase in anti-Semitism as a result of the rise of Nazism, the situation of Jewry in Germany, Poland and several other countries, and the chances of fulfilment of the Zionist plans as a result of expanded immigration. The Congress approved the 'transfer' project; Chaim Weizmann was re-elected President of the Zionist Organization (Sokolow became Honorary President), and the Zionist Executive was made up of a coalition, with the labour camp as the central force.

The Strengthening of the Yishuv in the Thirties

The thirties were a period of rapid expansion for the Yishuv. During this decade some quarter of a million Jews immigrated (some of them illegally), while emigration was negligible. Palestine became the main refuge for the persecuted Jews of Europe. The Jewish community numbered about 250,000 in 1933 and 500,000 in 1939; about 120,000 resided in agricultural settlements. There were 233 such settlements in 1938, sixty-eight kibbutzim and kevuẓot, and seventy-one moshavim. In 1939 alone, eighteen new settlements were founded.

There were more than 150,000 dunam (37,500 acres) of citrus groves cultivated by Jews in this period, and they supplied 60% of the citrus exports in 1939. Credit institutions were established to aid the farmers – Tnuva for marketing of produce and Mekorot for water supply. The number of agricultural schools increased, and agricultural research and applied science flourished. In these same years 'mixed farming' was consolidated. This method was developed in order to free agriculture of exclusive dependence on one branch – citrus – which was affected by price fluctuations on world markets, but the main objective was to free the Yishuv of dependence on the Arab village for its food supply. The leaders of the Yishuv had already learned from experience that any manifestation of political tension checked or reduced this supply. The Yishuv was obliged to achieve self-sufficiency. At the end of the thirties, the efficacy of this type of economy was demonstrated.

Industry also expanded at a rapid rate. In 1937 there were some 5,600 industrial enterprises in the Jewish community, with some 30,000 workers, and their annual output was over £9 million. The Potash Company, which produced 9,000 tons in 1932, manufactured 63,500 tons in 1939, to the value of £428,000. Industrial expansion is attested to by the electricity output, which rose from three million kilowatt hours in 1931 to twenty-five million in 1939. Jewish capital introduced into Palestine in the years 1933–9 was estimated at £63 million, part of it in goods that German Jews brought with them as part of the transfer agreement. The immigration and import of capital lent renewed impetus to the building industry. The towns grew; the population of Tel Aviv reached 132,000 in 1939. Health and education services also developed: vocational schools were opened; the number of teachers' seminaries increased; some 1,000 students attended the Hebrew University and 500 the Technion in Haifa. A special organization known as Youth Aliyah was established for the absorption of immigrant youth from Germany; it combined general education with training for agricultural settlement. The German immigrants made a considerable contribution to the development of the Yishuv during this period.

Just as the twenties were a period of experimentation in settlement and social patterns and in the consolidation of institutions and parties, the thirties were years of development according to established lines. The settlement movements grew, and a religious settlement movement was established. The Histadrut and its branches occupied a central place in the life of the Yishuv, and its representatives filled the key leadership positions. The largest party in the Yishuv and the Histadrut was Mapai. At the elections to the third Asefat Hanivharim (Assembly of Delegates) in 1931, Mapai won thirty-one seats (out of seventy-one); the Revisionists, sixteen, and the Mizrachi, five.

Political struggles also left their mark on defence matters. In the spring of 1931, a section of the Jerusalem Haganah connected with the Revisionists seceded from the general organization and established an independent association. It was joined by right-wing groups in other towns, and the new organization became nation wide. It called itself the National Military Organization in Palestine, and was generally known by the name Irgun Bet (B). During the period of internal tension that followed the murder of Arlosoroff, its representatives appeared at the Prague Congress. They also succeeded in establishing a Committee of Public Control, headed by the leaders of the Revisionists, the Mizrachi and the General Zionists. This support greatly strengthened their organization, but the 1936 riots induced the right-wing parties to agree among themselves on the merger of the two defence organizations, and this was completed at the beginning of 1937 on a parity basis. The new defence organization undertook to accept the authority of the Jewish Agency and the Va'ad Le'ummi, and only the Revisionists, who were now outside the Zionist Organization, remained outside the agreement.

The Arab Strike and Revolt of 1936 and the Partition Proposal

The upsurge of immigration and the strengthening of the Yishuv aroused a new surge of Arab political activity. In October 1933, a wave of demonstrations, which developed into riots against the British authorities and Zionism, swept the towns of Palestine. The Arabs wanted to exert pressure on the new High Commissioner, Sir Arthur Wauchope. In 1935 the activity of the Arab nationalist movement was intensified, after representatives of the intelligentsia joined its ranks. The High Commissioner endeavoured to appease them with a proposal to establish a legislative assembly in Palestine – eleven Moslems, seven Jews, three Christians and five government officials. The Jewish representatives rejected the proposal, while most of the Arab parties expressed their readiness to discuss it. Those British parliamentary circles sympathetic to Zionism sharply criticized the plan.

Meanwhile, significant international developments, which had occurred at the beginning of 1936, greatly encouraged the extremist elements in the Arab camp: Hitler strengthened his position in Europe; and in Egypt and Syria, nationalist forces won considerable gains. Some Arabs established contact with German and Italian agents in the Near East. Nationalist gangs were formed in Palestine that began murdering Jews and plundering property. In April of the same year, the Arab Higher Committee was established, which submitted three demands to the authorities: the total cessation of immigration, prohibition of the sale of land to Jews and the establishment of an Arab 'democratic government', *i.e.,* the imposition of the Arab majority's will on the Jewish minority. A general strike was declared for the duration of six months, and it was fairly effective. At this time additional military groups had begun to operate under Fauzi al Kawakji; they blew up the oil pipeline running from Iraq to Haifa, damaged railways, mined roads and tried to cut off Jewish settlements and destroy their crops. This time the acts of hostility did not take the form of riots, but were semi-military operations carried out by units led by experienced officers. The British Government decided to send a Royal Commission, headed by Lord Peel, to examine the situation. At first the Arabs boycotted the Commission, but they later changed their decision and gave evidence.

The commission published its findings on 7 July 1937. It noted that the 'national home' had ceased to be an experiment and had become a 'going concern'. It emphasized the progress achieved by Jewish immigration, as a result of which the health situation and methods of agriculture had improved among the Arabs as well. It was thus that the commission interpreted the tremendous rate of natural increase among the Arab population. At the same time it noted the underlying causes of the disturbances: (1) the desire of the Arabs for national independence and (2) their hatred and fear of the establishment of a Jewish National Home. On the other hand, the commission stressed Britain's obligations towards the Jews in accordance with the Mandate and noted that the Jews had reason to assume that if their numbers increased greatly, a Jewish state would be established in the country. Nor did it ignore the predicament of German and East European Jewry, or the fact that Palestine had become their main refuge after the United States had drastically reduced immigration. Nevertheless, the commission arrived at the conclusion that the Arab fear of Jewish domination should be allayed through the restriction of immigration to an annual maximum of 12,000 Jews. This limitation should not be based on 'economic absorptive capacity', which had been increasing with immigration, but rather the guiding principle should be high-level political restraint. The sale of land to Jews should also be restricted, as, in the view of the commission, there was no surplus land in the country.

The revolutionary conclusion arrived at by the commission was that the national aspirations of Jews and Arabs could not be reconciled even under prevailing conditions, and it concluded that the guarantees given to both sides, and included in the Mandate, were contradictory. The commission therefore proposed as the most reasonable compromise that Palestine be partitioned into a Jewish state, an Arab state and a British enclave. The Jewish state would encompass the coastal strip, Galilee and the Jezreel Valley, the enclave would have Jerusalem, Bethlehem, Lydda, Ramleh and Jaffa, and the Arab state would consist of the Ephraim and Judean hills and the Negev. As minorities would be present in each state, it would be necessary to arrange an exchange of land and population.

The British Government published the Peel Commission report together with a White Paper that approved its recommendations. On this basis the sale of land to Jews in areas earmarked for the Arab state was prohibited, and an immigration quota of 8,000 annually was fixed for the period ending in mid-March 1938. Various reservations with regard to the partition plan were expressed in the British Parliament and at the League of Nations Permanent Mandates Commission.

The Zionist leadership welcomed the plan, but it aroused fierce controversy within the movement and in the Yishuv. The main struggle raged at the Twentieth Congress (Zurich, August 1937). The majority of Mapai supported partition, as did most of the General Zionists. In their opinion, the Yishuv was faced with the choice, as Gruenbaum put it, 'between a Jewish majority in a Jewish state and a Jewish minority in an Arab Palestine'. They thought that even a state with a small area could be an important factor in rescuing the victims of Nazism. Partition was opposed by the Mizrachi, Hashomer Haza'ir, which favoured a bi-national state, and a small group of the Hebrew State Party (Revisionists who had remained within the Zionist Organization under the leadership of Meir Grossman). Most of the membership of Hakibbutz Hame'uhad, headed by Yitzhak Tabenkin, belonged to that section of Mapai that opposed partition, but the most prominent spokesman of the opponents within Mapai was Berl Katznelson. On the right wing, the opponents of partition included Menahem Ussishkin and the entire separatist Revisionist organization – which was the fiercest of all in its antagonism. This latter group regarded the partition plan as a trap – a British plot to hand over most of the country to the Arabs and to continue to control the Jewish section.

The Twentieth Congress proclaimed in its resolutions that the Mandate was capable of implementation, and thus, in effect, rejected the partition plan as it stood. But it authorized the Zionist Executive to conduct negotiations to amend it and to increase the area of the proposed Jewish state. On the other hand, the Arab Higher Committee vehemently opposed partition and requested the support of the Arab states in its struggle. Emir Abdullah and the Nashashibi Party in Palestine, which tended to support the plan, dared not express their views openly. At the beginning of September 1937, a pan-Arab congress was convened at Bludan in Syria and drew up plans for an armed struggle. The congress resolved that 'we must make Great Britain understand that to choose between our friendship and the Jews, Britain must change her policy in Palestine or we shall be at liberty to side with other European powers whose policies are inimical to Great Britain.' At the end of the month, an armed revolt broke out among the Palestinian Arabs.

The Impact of the Arab Revolt

The Arabs of Palestine were encouraged by the support of the Arab states and also hoped for the aid of the Axis Fascist powers. Their militant elements began to engage in guerilla warfare, attacking not only Jews and Englishmen, but also moderate Arabs; several thousand Arabs were murdered by these gangs. The government dissolved the Arab Higher Committee and banished its members to the Seychelles Islands. Only the Mufti of Jerusalem succeeded in escaping to Syria, from where he left on a visit to Germany. It was only at the end of 1938, after the British had succeeded in mobilizing a considerable military force, that they began to liquidate the gangs, but the pressure of the Arab states did not lessen. In October 1938, a World Interparliamentary Congress of Arab and Moslem Countries for the Defence of Palestine was convened in Cairo. In England, a conciliatory mood was then growing stronger. The British public abhorred the thought of war of any kind, while the 'appeasers' favoured compromise with the Axis. They believed that the Middle East constituted one of the weakest points of the British Empire as far as sabotage was concerned. Therefore, those who claimed that Zionism could only bring harm to Britain became steadily more influential. The opinion was voiced that in order to check Axis influence in the East, it was essential to arrive at understanding with the Arabs, who controlled the route to India and the oil resources.

It was just at this time that a commission, sent to Palestine in April 1938 to examine in detail the partition frontiers, published its conclusions. It declared that the partition programme could not be implemented for economic reasons and because of Arab opposition. The British Government accepted this viewpoint and published a White Paper, which was submitted to Parliament in October 1938. Although it was obvious that the British Government had chosen the path of conciliating the Arabs, this document relied on the recommendations of the Partition Commission, which claimed to be the basis for 'a settlement by negotiation'. Accordingly, the government proposed the convening of both parties to the dispute in London at the beginning of 1939.

The Arab revolt did not check the Jewish settlement project: fifty-five new settlements were established in the years 1936–9. Ḥanitah which was founded in March 1938 in harsh mountain terrain on the northern border near the crossing point of the marauding gangs, became the symbol of kibbutz heroism and self-defence in that period. The *Ḥomah u-Migdal* ('Stockade and Tower') settlements, named after their defensive fortifications, were of both economic and political-strategic significance. The political importance of the new settlements increased even further after the submission of the partition plan.

Defence Measures and the Policy of 'Aggressive Defence'

The Arab revolt also demonstrated to the Zionist leadership and to the Yishuv that military force had become a decisive political factor. The new tactics employed by the Arab units rendered several of the local defensive methods ineffective: military positions capable of holding off a rioting mob could not repel trained units that laid ambushes in fields or on paths or attacked under fire. The number of victims steadily increased, and the Jewish community began to suffer from a feeling of impotence.

Several of the active leaders of the Haganah demanded retaliation – attack for attack – and this demand led to tension within the organization. There were certain groups that began to plan separate military action on their own initiative. Those

Revisionists who refused to join Irgun Bet or the Haganah set up a special military body, Irgun Zeva'i Le'ummi (Ezel), which advocated attack and retaliation; their methods included throwing grenades in Arab population concentrations, which claimed many Arab victims but did not affect the military capacity of the gangs. Their tactics led to extreme tension between the Haganah and the Irgun, and the British authorities began to hunt down the Irgun, sometimes even executing its members.

Most of those engaged in defence activity accepted the authority of the Zionist institutions and chose the path of *havlagah* ('self-restraint'), which implied refraining from reacting to Arab attacks with similar methods. On the other hand, new methods began to emerge from the field and night units, who operated in the territory around the Jewish settlements and broke the power of the gangs there.

The authority of Haganah headquarters over its branches was consolidated, the purchase and manufacture of arms were extended, and training methods were streamlined. The Haganah began to arrange for the systematic transportation of illegal immigrants to Palestine, a project that the Irgun had initiated. New methods of mobilizing and transporting manpower from the urban centres to remote settlements were developed. In cooperation with the British authorities, special police units were established: the 'gaffirs', night squads, railway squads – consisting of some 20,000 men in all. Some of them were trained by Orde Wingate, a British officer sympathetic to the Zionist cause. All these units created a legal framework for training, for the acquisition of battle experience and for the protection of illegal-arms caches. Special contributions – which became a regular tax known as *kofer hayishuv* – were levied to finance these activities.

The St James Conference and the 1939 White Paper

Representatives of the Jewish Agency, of Palestinian Arabs and of the Arab states were invited to the St James Round Table Conference convened by the British Government. Thus the Arab states were recognized, for the first time, as a party to the Arab-Jewish dispute. The Arabs refused to sit with the Jews, and therefore the British conducted separate and parallel sessions with both sides, which lasted from 8 February to 17 March. They proposed that gradual independence be granted to a Palestinian state, which would maintain an alliance with Britain, and that the transitional stage would last ten years. In the first five years, 75,000 Jews should be permitted to immigrate, and subsequent immigration would be conditional on Arab agreement. Both parties rejected the British proposals.

Meanwhile the Arab revolt had been suppressed. The British Government nevertheless published a White Paper on 17 May 1939 in which it announced that it would implement its plan without reference to the two parties. The White Paper was attacked in Parliament by Churchill, Amery and Herbert Morrison, and in the House of Lords by Samuel and Snell. The League of Nations Permanent Mandates Commission also decided unanimously in June of that year that 'the policy set out in the White Paper is not in accordance with the interpretation which . . . the Commission had placed on the Palestine Mandate.' The Arab Higher Committee demanded the immediate cessation of immigration and a shortening of the transitional period.

A wave of protest swept the Yishuv. In order to demonstrate that the Zionist project would continue, no less than twelve new agricultural settlements were established in May, seven of them in one day – 25 May 1939.

At the Twenty-first Zionist Congress (Geneva, August 1939), convened in the shadow of the approaching world war, David Ben-Gurion proposed a programme of non-cooperation with the British Government. In his opinion only an activist policy, causing considerable embarrassment to the government, could dissuade it from the policy it had adopted. Abba Hillel Silver, the American Zionist leader, was in favour of continued cooperation with Britain, since he contended that it was not possible to support Britain in her struggle against Germany while at the same time creating internal difficulties. In his view 'the White Paper is a fleeting document; it must be opposed vigorously, and there are good chances of annulling it . . . ' A few days after the Congress ended, war broke out, and the Yishuv proclaimed its willingness to join in the war effort against Hitler. Yet it seemed that the fate of this small Jewish community, half a million strong, abandoned by a British Government that was denying its obligations and surrounded by millions of Arab enemies all hoping for a Nazi victory, had been sealed – as had that of Zionism.

67

The Second World War and the Holocaust

The Rise of Anti-Semitism in Germany in the Twenties

Under the democratic conditions of the Weimar Republic, in an atmosphere of social tension and violent political clashes, anti-Semitic propaganda became one of the outstanding phenomena in political life. Various groups, often with diverse political views, advocated anti-Semitism and put forth political programmes that included anti-Semitic clauses. As early as 1920 the Deutsche-nationale Party, which leaned towards anti-Semitism, won sixty-six seats in the Reichstag, and in 1924 the number of its deputies rose to ninety-six. An extremely radical anti-Semitic group broke away from this party and joined the German National-Socialist Workers Party; together they obtained thirty-two seats in the 1924 elections. Their leader was Adolf Hitler, who from the beginning of his political career advocated an extreme anti-Semitic programme, which was to become one of the central underpinnings of all Nazi ideology. Hitler was supported by General Ludendorff, Chief of the Imperial General Staff during the First World War. The *'voelkische'* (traditional nationalists) then won some two million votes. The Deutsche-nationale Party was the second largest, after the Social Democrats.

The anti-Semitic parties drew inspiration from the numerous anti-Semitic publications that flooded Germany in the twenties, and particularly from the so-called 'scientific' anti-Semitic theories put forward in essays by various scientists and philosophers. The majority of these theories were a reflection of the anti-rational and anti-democratic mood that had taken root in Germany after the vicissitudes of the war years and the period of crisis and shock that followed. They were aimed at accentuating the importance of 'race', 'blood' and 'soil' in the life of the German people. Of considerable influence was Oswald Spengler's book, *The Decline of the West,* which was suffused with a spirit of pessimism and nihilism. Anti-Semitism was prevalent among scholars in the fields of oriental studies, biblical research and ancient history. The Assyriologist Friedrich Delitsch won particular renown at the time with an essay entitled 'The Great Delusion'. At the beginning of the century he had delivered a series of lectures, 'Babel und Bibel', in which he claimed that the Bible was nothing but an imitation of Babylonian culture; in the book, published in 1920, he attacked the Jews on the grounds that they were an immoral and criminal people, whose God was nothing but a 'caricature of the concept of divinity', who 'lacked a homeland because of their own volition' and similar spurious charges. Those with anti-Semitic proclivities were particularly attracted to racist theories, such as those expounded in a book by Hans Guenther – the future Nazi theoretician on race – published in 1922 under the title *The Racial Origins of the German People*. Guenther regarded the Nordic race as the ideal and demanded that it be nurtured through 'racial hygiene'. The Jews, in his view, were an inferior and extremely dangerous mongrel race. Many novels were written in the same spirit; for example, Artur Dinter's *The Sin Against the Blood,* of which hundreds of thousands of copies were sold.

Anti-Semitic Agitation During the 'Great Crisis' and the Nazi Rise to Power

The grave economic crisis that broke out in 1929 intensified the political conflicts in Germany. The influence of the left- and right-wing radical parties increased, and the Nazis became a powerful political factor. In the 1930 elections they won 6.4 million votes and 107 deputies in the Reichstag. But their influence was even more evident in the streets, particularly in urban centres, and was expressed in attacks by 'storm troopers', in demonstrations and in the assassination of political enemies. Intoxicated by their success, the Nazis declared a boycott of Jewish businesses, placed guards outside Jewish shops and, in September 1931, instigated pogroms against Berlin Jews. Thus, the status of the Jews had been undermined even before the Nazis came to power.

In the July 1932 elections the Nazis won some fourteen million votes (37%) and sent 230 deputies to the Reichstag, thus becoming the strongest faction. With the aid of the right-wing parties, they succeeded in taking over the reins of government. The leader of the Nazi Party, Adolf Hitler, was appointed Chancellor of Germany on 30 January 1933, and the reign of street-corner murderers was augmented by the government persecution of political opponents, particularly of Jews.

With the exception of several underground groups, there was no active opposition to the Nazi regime in Germany. In the elections to the Reichstag early in March 1933, conducted under conditions of severe terror, the Nazi Party gained seventeen million votes (44%) and 228 seats. Shortly afterwards, all other parties were dissolved, and at the elections held towards the end of the same year, the Nazis obtained 92% of all the votes cast and consolidated their one-party rule.

The Nazi plan for the Jews was open and well known. Hitler's *Mein Kampf* and Alfred Rosenberg's *Myth of the Twentieth Century* demanded that the Jews be rooted out of German life. Anti-Semitic slogans were printed in the press (in the *Voelkischer Beobachter,* for example), in propaganda leaflets and in party publications. Nazi meetings ended with the cry 'Death to the Jews!' Having taken over power, they could now give free rein to their hatred – through attacks on Jews, and particularly on Jewish government officials, judges and lawyers, through arbitrary arrests, by burning works of Jewish authors, looting Jewish shops and similar provocative acts. On 1 April 1933 a one-day boycott of Jewish businesses and members of the liberal professions was held. Shortly afterwards there followed a series of laws directed against 'non-Aryans', which led to the dismissal of government officials, to the imposition of restrictions against Jewish physicians and lawyers carrying out professional duties in public institutions, and to the dismissal of journalists and artists among others. The press was filled with verbal attacks on Jews; the most extreme paper was Julius Streicher's *Der Stuermer,* which engaged in systematic, crude and violently aggressive anti-Semitic incitement.

Old, established German institutions adopted Nazi concepts and methods towards the Jews at a more rapid pace than could have been anticipated. The medical journal of the German physicians' association, for example, stated in June 1935:

> The comparison between Jews and the tuberculosis bacilli is a telling one. Almost all people harbour TB bacilli, almost all nations on earth harbour the Jews – a chronic infection, which it is difficult to cure. Just as the human body does not absorb the TB germs into its general organism, so a natural, homogeneous society cannot absorb the Jews into its organic association; at the most they suffer them as parasites.

The Nuremberg Laws and the Reaction of German Jewry

In their first two years of rule, the Nazis published many laws and regulations affecting the Jews and discriminating against them. During this period various Jews were arrested or banished, as they were accused of being hostile towards the Nazis or of fighting them; but at the beginning of 1935 the preparation of comprehensive anti-Jewish legislation commenced, and on 15 September the decrees known as the Nuremberg Laws were published. The Nationality Law, as it was officially called, made the Jews 'subjects', without any political rights. Under this law these rights were the privilege of 'citizens of the Reich' alone – namely, of people of Aryan origin. Another law passed unanimously by the Reichstag on the same day was the Law for the Protection of German Blood and Honour. In order to 'preserve the German people perpetually', the law prohibited Jews from marrying non-Jews, employing non-Jewish housekeepers under the age of forty-five and flying the national flag. The law then defined a 'Jew' as a person with three Jewish grandparents. Those with less Jewish blood in their veins were regarded as first or second-class 'mongrels', according to the number of Jewish grandparents. In time the 'first-class mongrels' suffered the same fate as full-blooded Jews. The Nuremberg Laws were basic laws, which were supplemented over the years by various edicts and regulations that restricted and gradually cancelled the status of the Jews in all spheres of life, until they completely lacked legal standing and were under the power of the 'security police'.

In the period between the publication of the Nuremberg Laws and 1938, the expulsion of Jews from economic and social life continued. In 1937, 'Aryanization' commenced on a large scale; that is, Jewish businesses were stolen and transferred to the hands of 'Aryans', mostly those associated with the regime. This transfer was allegedly carried out through sale, but was actually implemented by force.

By the beginning of 1938, only about one-third of Germany's Jews had left the country. The majority still hoped that the wave of terror would pass. But the persecution helped strengthen the ties of individuals to the Jewish community: at the very beginning of the Nazi regime, when Jewish businesses began to be marked with the 'Yellow Badge', a Zionist paper, *Jüdische Rundschau,* wrote: 'Wear it with pride, this yellow badge. Jews, accept the Shield of David, and bear it proudly.' Most of the Jewish organizations joined a National Representation of German Jews (Reichsvertretung der deutschen Juden), which evolved into the leadership of the Jewish community, representing it under the most bitter and difficult conditions. It was headed by the Chief Rabbi of Berlin, Leo Baeck. The main functions of the Reichsvertretung were organization of emigration; teaching new trades and vocations, mainly crafts and agriculture, in place of the old sources of livelihood; running Jewish schools (even before Jewish children were officially prohibited from attending general schools, they were unable to endure the persecution of their teachers and fellow-pupils); and aiding those deprived of their livelihood. This aid was mainly supplied through funds sent by U.S. Jewry. The Jews reacted to their expulsion from cultural life by establishing a Cultural Alliance of German Jews, which arranged concerts, theatre performances and literary evenings. According to an official edict, these gatherings were open only to Jews. Thus Nazi discrimination brought about a renaissance of independent Jewish activity.

World Jewry did not stand idle in the face of German Jewry's plight. In reaction to the persecution and the boycott operated by the Nazis, Jewish and anti-Fascist groups in the democratic countries began to organize a counter-boycott of German goods. The World Jewish Congress was convened in August 1936 in order to co-ordinate this campaign, and it became a permanent body. It decided to initiate propaganda and information activity aimed at exposing the true nature of the Nazi regime and to plan defence and aid operations.

The Crisis in 1938

In 1938 there was a worsening in the attitude of the Nazi regime towards the Jews. The annexation of Austria by Hitler encountered no real opposition. The Conference on Refugee Affairs convened by the Great Powers at Evian demonstrated that they were unwilling to involve themselves in any far-reaching activity on behalf of the persecuted Jews. Hitler's self-confidence increased, and his apprehension of adverse public opinion outside Germany waned. He began to implement his anti-Jewish policies both openly and arrogantly.

The invasion of Austria in March 1938 brought to the Reich 190,000 Jews, in addition to the 350,000 still living in Germany. The restrictions and discriminations against German Jews were immediately extended to the Jews of Austria. At the end of that month, official recognition of Jewish communities was revoked throughout the Reich. At the end of April, the Jews were ordered to inform the authorities of any property in their possession worth more than 5,000 marks; in July the licences of Jewish physicians were withdrawn; in September, lawyers were also affected. In August, all Jews were obliged to take the additional name of 'Israel', and all Jewish women, the name of 'Sarah'. Simultaneously mass arrests were carried out and hundreds of Jews were incarcerated in concentration camps. At the end of October 1938, some 15,000 Jews, who were formally Polish citizens, though they had been living in Germany for years, were rounded up, loaded onto lorries and conveyed to the Polish border. The Polish authorities refused to take them in, and they were shuttled about in no-man's-land, frozen and hungry, for some time, until the Poles were forced, under political pressure, to open the border and accept some of them. Others were returned to Germany, and some were sent to concentration camps. The German pressure on Poland to accept these Jews did not ease until German troops invaded Polish soil.

On 7 November 1938 a young Jew named Herschel Grynszpan assassinated the Counsellor at the German Embassy in Paris, declaring that he was taking revenge for the injustice done to his parents, who were expelled by the Nazis to Poland. Under the pretext of retaliation, the Nazis decided to carry out a general pogrom against all the Jews under their rule: on the night of 9 November (*Kristallnacht*, as it was later called), members of the S.S. together with a Nazi mob attacked Jewish homes, beating, injuring and murdering Jewish victims. Hundreds of synagogues were burned down; some 7,500 Jewish shops and businesses were destroyed, and the number of dead totalled ninety. Immediately afterwards there commenced a series of mass arrests: 26,000 Jews, mainly well-to-do, were placed in concentration camps, and hundreds of them died as a result of brutal treatment by the S.S. A 'contribution' of one billion marks was exacted from the German Jewish community. The Jews were ordered to repair the damage caused to their own businesses and shops by rioters. Subsequently Jews were expelled from all economic enterprises and from managerial positions; Jewish children were expelled from schools; Jews were forbidden to attend cultural events, their organizations were disbanded and their publications suppressed; in practice Jewish cultural and economic life was brought to a standstill.

In June 1939 the Reichsvertretung was dissolved and was replaced by the National Association of Jews (Reichsvereinigung der Juden), which was placed under direct Gestapo supervision. All Jews and their spouses were obliged to belong to this association, and it was through this body that the Gestapo exercised its control over the Jewish community. At the same time, the Gestapo was exerting increased pressure to force Jews to emigrate. This task was carried out by a special section headed by Adolf Eichmann. The pressure was applied for more than two years, even after the outbreak of war, until Jewish emigration was totally prohibited on 31 October 1941. After war broke out in 1939, more than 150,000 Jews left Germany; more than 100,000 succeeded in leaving Austria before the war, and an additional 30,000 left before the final prohibition of emigration. (Numerical estimates concerning the Jews of Central and Western Europe in this period are not uniform because, *inter alia,* of the differences in defining a Jew, whether by religious or 'racial' affiliation.)

After the Munich Agreement the Sudeten region was annexed to the Reich. In March 1939, Czechoslovakia was divided up; Bohemia and Moravia were declared to be German 'protectorates', and anti-Jewish laws became applicable there. At the time of the outbreak of the Second World War there were some 400,000 Jews within the borders of the Reich.

Jewish Refugees and the Indifference of the World

The Nazi rise to power encouraged anti-Semitic trends in most Central and East European countries. There was greater discrimination against Jews, and pogroms increased. In 1938 the Hungarian Government published laws undermining the basis of Jewish economic survival. These particularly affected the Jews of Carpathian Russia, the section of Czechoslovakia annexed to Hungary, where ousting of Jews from their sources of livelihood took on widescale proportions.

In many countries there was increased agitation for forced Jewish emigration. In 1937, the Polish Government sent a deputation to examine the possibility of settling Jews in Madagascar. It protested against the 1939 White Paper, regarding it as an obstacle to Jewish emigration. Propaganda against the 'superflous Jews' reached its height at this time. In many countries the Jews chose in fact to emigrate, but found that those countries that had once absorbed immigrants now, without exception, closed their gates.

The problem of the Jewish refugees, who totalled hundreds of thousands, was most serious immediately after the Nazis came to power. At the end of 1933, the League of Nations had decided to appoint a High Commissioner for Refugee Affairs. James MacDonald (later the first American Ambassador to Israel) became commissioner, but two years later resigned because of the inactivity of the League of Nations. In 1936, The British Council for German Jewry was established with the participation of prominent Jewish personalities. It was instrumental, together with the Joint, in alleviating the distress of the refugees.

After the invasion of Austria it became clear to Western public opinion that the refugee problem was becoming more acute, particularly where Jews were concerned. Britain at long last began to display signs of flexibility. A plan was drawn up for the absorption of 7,500 Jewish children in England and some 3,500 in West European countries. But this was only a drop in the ocean. Under the pressure of public opinion in the democratic countries, President Roosevelt of the United States called the above-mentioned special conference devoted to the problems and fate of those refugees under threat of persecution. But the British Government, which feared demands on the Palestinian question, agreed to participate only on condition that this subject would not be included in the deliberations. It also insisted that the conference discuss only actual and not potential refugees. The conference was held at Evian in France from 6 to 15 July 1938. With the exception of the representative of the Dominican Republic, who declared his government's readiness to take in 100,000 refugees, no government expressed its willingness to help. The Dominican plan was also mainly for propaganda purposes, as the racist dictator Trujillo wanted only to improve his image in American eyes. An Inter-governmental Committee on Refugees was established, but, on the demand of the British, it was headed by Earl Winterton, who was known for his hostile attitude towards the Jews and the Palestinian Mandate. A special representative of the committee began to negotiate with the Nazis to arrange systematic emigration from Germany, but the political events of 1939 and the outbreak of war put an end to all these plans.

The Partition of Poland and the Oppression of the Jews in Nazi-occupied Territory

The Nazi invasion of Poland and its partition between Germany and the Soviet Union placed nearly two million more Jews within Hitler's power. Immediately after the occupation, pogroms were perpetrated against the Jews. The Germans endeavoured to recruit rioters from among the Poles, but their own troops also took part in the murders. Then there commenced a systematic policy of oppression.

At the end of September, a decree was published ordering all Jews – even those residing in villages and townlets – to concentrate themselves in the towns. At the beginning of October, western Poland (the areas that had belonged to the German Empire before the First World War, with the addition of Lodz district, subsequently known as Litzmannstadt) were proclaimed part of the Reich. Immediately afterwards, there commenced expulsions from these areas eastwards, to the region between the Vistula and the Bug. The Jews were expelled from all of western Poland with the exception of Lodz and its vicinity, and Bohemian and Austrian Jews were also sent to the same area. For a time, the Nazis even contemplated the establishment of a 'Jewish reserve' in Lublin, but no real measures were undertaken to implement this plan. Terrible stories of Jews forced to wander for days in frost and snow, of hundreds of people freezing to death and other atrocities reached the foreign press.

At the end of October 1939, all the Jews of the German-occupied area of Poland were obliged to wear a white or yellow badge with a Shield of David on it. On 12 December 1939 all men between the ages of fourteen and sixty were recruited for forced labour 'for two years, a period which may be extended if the educational objectives have not been achieved'. This same obligation was also imposed on Jews within the Reich, although they were forced to wear the yellow badge only in September 1941. On the other hand, their radios were confiscated and, immediately after the outbreak of war, a curfew was imposed on them. Within a few weeks the restrictive laws directed against German Jewry were also imposed on the Jews of Poland. They were prohibited from visiting public places and from attending cultural performances, and they were expelled from schools and universities; their social rights as workers were revoked; they were driven out of the liberal professions, and their shops, business and industrial concerns were confiscated. They were left no other practical choice but to engage in the simplest manual labour.

In November and December 1939, it was announced that all Jews would be obliged to move to ghettos, special quarters within the cities. The first ghetto was set up in Lodz in February 1940; the Warsaw ghetto followed in November 1940. By 1941 there were ghettos all over Poland, in most cases surrounded by a wall. At first the Germans, out of economic considerations, issued numerous permits for movement to and from the ghettos, but in time these considerations were abandoned, and, in instructions dispatched to the local authorities, it was emphasized that in dealing with the 'Jewish question' there was no room for calculations of this kind. From October 1941 the death penalty was imposed on any Jew found outside the walls of the ghetto without a permit. At the end of the same year the authority of regular courts over the Jews was annulled, and they were placed under the jurisdiction of the police and the S.D. (special security police). In actual fact, they were now left with no protection of the law. Persecution of the Jews – in the form of cutting their beards and sidelocks, harnessing them to carts, beatings and even murder – was encouraged by the Nazi authorities.

The Persecution of Jews in Occupied European Countries

Jewish suffering became more acute with each additional German invasion. In the few weeks between April and June 1940, the Germans captured Denmark, Norway, Belgium, Holland and France. Close to half a million Jews fell into their hands, and some 130,000 remained in the non-occupied area of France, which was ruled by the Vichy government. The Nazis began to expel Jews from the German-French border region (Alsace, Lorraine, Baden, Palatinate) and from occupied France to Vichy. On 3 October 1940 the first anti-Jewish law of the Vichy government was published, banishing Jews from all public activity and depriving those Jews who were not French subjects of their civil rights. At the end of March 1941, a Commissaire aux Questions Juives (Jewish Commissioner) was appointed by the Vichy government.

In the occupied area, police registration of Jews and special stamping of their papers commenced in September 1940. At the end of the year, 40,000 'alien' Jews were imprisoned in detention camps; the great majority of them were German citizens who had fled from the Nazis. In May 1941, 3,600 Polish Jews who had become nationalized Frenchmen were arrested on the basis of the Vichy anti-Jewish laws. Even the Jewish Commissioner tried to intervene on their behalf.

In Holland the confiscation of Jewish property commenced in October 1940. In November, Jews were dismissed from government service, and at the beginning of 1941 their identity papers were marked with a special stamp. The activities of the Germans and their Dutch collaborators aroused the anger of many Dutchmen. When the Nazis attacked the Jewish quarter of Amsterdam at the beginning of February, many Dutch workers came to the aid of the Jews. The Germans took Jewish hostages, tortured and murdered them. In Amsterdam a workers' strike broke out in solidarity with the Jews; it developed gradually into a general strike, but was suppressed by military force. At the time, this was a unique example in occupied Europe of public readiness to take risks on behalf of the Jews.

The German Invasion of the Soviet Union and the Beginning of Mass Extermination

The German attack on Soviet Russia on 22 June 1941 changed the whole course of the war and also brought about a worsening in the situation of the Jews. While planning the campaign against Russia, the German General Staff had discussed the murder of those political commissars who would be taken prisoner and, apparently, also of Jews. As early as the end of May the S.S. set up a special training camp for the members of the Einsatzgruppen (Action Groups), whose task was to murder commissars, Jews and gypsies. On the war front, which stretched from the Baltic to the Black Sea, there were four such groups operating, and the slaughter commenced during the first days of battle. The relations between the armed S.S. units and the army were complicated. Nevertheless, they usually worked in cooperation, and sometimes the Einsatzgruppen carried out murders on the explicit instructions of military commanders. In any case, Field-marshal von Reichenau issued a notorious Order of the Day on 10 October 1941 to the Sixth German Division: 'In the eastern territories the soldier is not merely a warrior fighting according to the rules of the art of war, but also the merciless bearer of a national ideology. . . . Therefore the soldier must comprehend the necessity of cruel but just revenge against subhuman Jewry.'

At that same time, the Rumanians also began murdering Jews. When Russian aircraft bombed the town of Jassy, members of the fascist Iron Guard spread the rumour that the Jews had signalled to the planes. On 28 June 1941 bloody pogroms were conducted there, during which 7,000 Jews were murdered. In the interval between the retreat of the Soviet Army and the entry of the Rumanians, Jews were murdered in several small towns in Bessarabia and Bukovina by Ukrainian gangs. On 30 August, the Germans and Rumanians agreed that the area between the Dniester and the Bug – Transnistria – should be administered by the Rumanians, and the latter established concentration camps there for the Jews.

At the beginning of their Russian campaign, the Germans initiated pogroms, conducted by the local population. In the north, the Nazi forces captured Kovno in the first days of the war, and Lithuanian gangs were immediately organized; within two days (25 and 26 June) they had murdered 3,800 Jews. In those same early days the Germans were still endeavouring to depict the murders as the action of the local population and ordered the halting of the slaughter, but in fact the murderers formed part of the Einsatzgruppen. In the south the Germans captured Lvov on 30 June. Immediately after their entrance into the town, a Ukrainian militia was formed, which began murdering Jews on 2 and 3 July. This was known as the 'Petlyura action' (in revenge for the murder of the notorious anti-Semitic nationalist leader in Paris in 1926), and some 7,000 Jews lost their lives. Here too the murders were halted by order of the Germans. But at the end of July and beginning of August, 3,000 Jews were murdered in Zhitomir and 2,000 at Uman and Berdichev. The Hungarians also began to expel Jews from their occupied territories, and 11,000 Jews were murdered in Carpathian Russia before September.

In smaller places the operations of the Einsatzgruppen followed a fixed pattern: immediately after entering the town, they would find out the name of the rabbi and local intelligentsia from the local population, send for them and demand that they assemble all the local Jews for registration and dispatch to a 'Jewish region'. The Jewish population, which then knew nothing about the Nazi schemes, generally obeyed (since the Molotov-Ribbentrop Agreement in 1939 there had been no information activities in Russia regarding the nature of Nazi anti-Semitism, and it was even forbidden to mention their crimes in works of fiction). The Einsatzgruppen, together with the local Ukrainian, White Russian, Lithuanian or Latvian militia, would transport the Jews outside the town and murder them all – men, women and children – by machine-gun fire within abandoned dugouts or ravines. In time there were also cases where victims were drowned in the sea or asphyxiated in special vans, which emitted poison gas while in motion. One of the greatest mass murders took place at the end of September (the Day of Atonement) 1941 at Babi Yar near Kiev. No less than 34,000 Jews were exterminated there by the Germans and Ukrainians (according to several sources, the figure was several times larger). In Odessa the Rumanians murdered 26,000 Jews at the end of October. By the end of that year mass murders had been carried out in Dnepropetrovsk, Rovno, Riga, Vilna, Kovno and Dvinsk; on 6 November, 15,000 Jews were murdered at Rovno; on 8 December, 27,000 in Riga; on 22 December, 32,000 at Vilna; on 30 December, 10,000 at Simferopol. In several places ghettos were established after the first wave of murders, but they were mainly utilized as collection points for the second wave. To replace those Russian Jews who had been murdered, Jews were brought to these ghettos from the Reich and the protectorate. There are no exact figures on the number of Jews murdered by the Einsatzgruppen and other elements, but there can be no doubt that they totalled many hundreds of thousands.

The Ghetto Regime and the Judenrats

The ghetto served two purposes for the Nazis: the main one was the concentration of the Jews for supervision and future extermination, but in the meanwhile it facilitated economic exploitation. In the large ghettos the Jews worked in various enterprises vital to the German war effort; in the smaller ghettos they were made to build roads. Workers received regular rations of food, and therefore even the hardest tasks were coveted, as those who did not work had no source of livelihood. In the early stages of the ghettos, the aid of Jewish organizations, which reached them through the neutral countries, was of considerable importance. The Jews also tried to make a living by smuggling from the 'Aryan' to the Jewish side, under constant threat of death.

The way of life in the ghetto was shaped, on the one hand, by giving in to Nazi pressure, and, on the other, by attempts to maintain the supply of vital goods and reasonable human and social relations. At first the majority of the Jewish public regarded the new vicissitudes as a temporary misfortune and hoped that it, too, would pass. To many it seemed that submission to Nazi pressure was the only way of enduring until the storm blew over. In a number of places in Eastern Europe, the Judenrats (Jewish Councils), which were insisted upon by the Nazis in all the ghettos, were regarded by the Jews as the continuation of various patterns of Jewish self-rule from previous periods, and the members of the Judenrat were elected by the community itself. Elsewhere the Judenrats were appointed from among prominent members of the Jewish community, in order to induce others to obey them and to create the illusion that Jewish existence would continue, and thus to conceal the true intentions of the Nazis. But, as was only to be expected, there was no shortage among the members of the Judenrat of certain dubious elements who served the Germans as agents and informers against their fellow-Jews, for it was compulsory for all Jewish contact with the authorities to be maintained through the Judenrat.

Affiliated to it was a Jewish police force, which helped to impose its authority on the Jewish public. The Judenrat had the right to levy taxes; in several places the Judenrats even printed money and stamps. But at the same time the Germans also favoured Jews outside the Judenrat, to whom they handed over economic concessions (such as transport within the ghetto), or who were exploited as agents and spies among the Jews. There were also those who won a certain measure of independence and special protection because of the payments they made to the Germans.

Even after the establishment of the ghettos in Poland in 1940, the life of the Jews was not entirely disrupted. Despite the large degree of suffering, Jewish society and its leadership continued to struggle for survival in all spheres of life – in economic, social and political activity, and even in cultural life and education; various schools were still maintained, theatre performances and cultural evenings were held, and writers and artists continued to be creative. Even outwardly the impression was that life was continuing. Despite the terrible overcrowding, there were shops, cafés, and even nightclubs, and mutual-aid associations distributed aid to the needy.

All this changed in the second half of 1941. The receipt of parcels from neutral countries was forbidden. Smuggling from the 'Aryan' side became even more dangerous. Hunger was intensified in the ghettos, disease increased, epidemics broke out and the death-rate rose alarmingly. In March 1942 the death-camps began to operate on a large scale, and the Nazis began to demand of the Judenrats that people be selected for transport. The Jewish representatives were faced with a tragic situation from which there was no escape. There were those who made superhuman efforts to postpone the demands for a time, to warn their brethren of the danger and to hide the candidates for transport. There were others who, after realizing the true situation, committed suicide, or who themselves accompanied the Jews on their way to extermination. But there were also those who gave in and helped assemble people for such 'actions'. There is no possibility of evaluating the activities of the Judenrats at that time of terrible trial, but it is clear that the new situation caused a grave shock in the ghettos. Jewish society in the ghetto began to die when its members were sent to the crematoria. This process brought about its disintegration, yet at the same time roused it to new and daring action. It was against this background that the resistance movement arose in the ghettos.

The Wannsee Conference and Systematic Extermination

The idea of exterminating the Jews had existed as part of the Nazi plan for some time, since the cancellation of such projects as Jewish settlement in Madagascar; but the practical decision to commence systematic extermination was apparently taken at the end of 1941. On 20 January 1942 a Nazi conference was held in Berlin, which was referred to in the material submitted to the Nuremberg international court as the Wannsee Conference – after the street in which it was held. Five of the participants were representatives of the S.S. and the Gestapo – including Heydrich, Müller and Eichmann. The remainder were representatives of various ministries at the executive level. They discussed details of the plans for exterminating the Jewish people in

Europe; according to their calculations, eleven million in all. Among the decisions for implementation taken there, the most important was that Jewish subjects of Germany, Croatia, Slovakia and Rumania would be sent 'east'. It was decided to inform the governments of those countries that the Germans were ready to organize the transport of their Jews 'eastwards'. At the time, a camp that carried out extermination by gas was already operating at Chelmno in Poland. As transpired from later activity, there was a basic guideline in the 'Final Solution' plan – to break the spirit of the Jews before killing them by worsening conditions in the ghettos, by increasing terror and by creating the illusion that those who submitted had a chance of saving themselves.

From the end of 1941, the expulsion of Jews from the borders of the Reich to Poland was revived and became a systematic operation. The Nazis had apparently decided by then to make Poland the centre for the extermination of all European Jews. The Jews of Western Europe and the Reich were sent to the ghettos of Lodz, Riga, Minsk and Kovno. In the months of March-July 1942, 80,000 Jews were expelled from Austria, Germany, Bohemia and Slovakia to the Lublin area. As early as March 1942, thousands of Jews in this region were dispatched to the extermination camp at Belzec, with the exception of those Jews in possession of work permits. Rumours regarding extermination began to spread to all the Polish ghettos and even abroad.

The Nazi leaders urged the S.S. and the Gestapo to speed up the extermination process. In a speech delivered in March 1942, Himmler declared that half of Polish Jewry should be 'resettled' (the Nazi term for extermination) by the end of the year. In a cable sent in July, he demanded that the operation be extended within the same period to *all* Polish Jews. In order to prevent resistance within the largest Jewish concentration, the Warsaw ghetto, the Nazis began to introduce more severe methods of terror. In July 1942 the elderly German troops who had been guarding the ghetto were replaced by members of the Ukrainian and Lithuanian militia, and immediately afterwards the Judenrat was ordered to hand over 6,000 Jews daily for 'resettlement in the East'. The Jewish police (*Ordnungsdienst*) began to assemble the people. Some Jews despaired and made their way to the assembly centres of their own volition. After two days of such concentrations, the head of the Warsaw Judenrat, Adam Cherniakov, committed suicide. Reliable information began to reach the ghetto about what was going on in the Treblinka extermination camp, to which the Jews of Warsaw had been dispatched.

The mood in the ghetto changed. The Germans began to cancel work permits *en masse*. Even the German factory-owners, who had made many millions out of exploiting the Jewish slave-labour in the ghetto, could no longer save their workers. Several members of the Judenrat enlisted the aid of the Lithuanian militia and carried out the Nazi orders. Resistance worthy of the name did not crystallize in the ghetto until the end of October. During the ten weeks between the end of July and mid-October, close to 310,000 Jews were sent to their deaths from the Warsaw ghetto.

Mass 'actions' for expulsion to Majdanek were carried out in the Lodz ghetto.

In a report submitted to Himmler at the end of 1942 it was stated that within occupied Polish territory some 1,274,166 Jews had been 'resettled'.

In the winter and spring months of 1943, the pace of extermination was slowed down in Poland. After the outbreak and suppression of the Warsaw ghetto revolt, about 300,000 Jews remained in occupied Poland and Russia. Some 85,000 were in the Lodz ghetto, 30,000 in Bialystok, and about 20,000 each in Sosnowiece, Lvov, Vilna and Kovno. In March 1943, the Cracow ghetto was liquidated, and some fifty ghettos were wiped out at Himmler's order in April 1943. In July-September 1943, the ghettos of Bialystok, Minsk, Riga and Vilna were obliterated. After Smolensk was captured by the Soviet Army, the last of the White Russian ghettos were wiped out. Only in Lodz and Kovno were there still Jews left in 1944. When the Soviet Army began to advance at the beginning of that year, the Germans began to expel the camp inmates to the west, forcing them to march on foot under bitter wintry conditions; very few survived these death marches.

The Ghetto Uprisings

The forces of resistance in the ghettos were organized at a late stage, and no outside force came to their aid. In Warsaw it was necessary to purchase arms, and the price of an old Italian revolver was as high as $50. The resistance movements were in contact with several left-wing groups on the 'Aryan' side, but did not enlist their aid to a large extent. The Polish government-in-exile in London, which knew all the details of the extermination, remained inactive.

The united underground forces, mainly members of the pioneering youth movements, eventually decided to act. The Warsaw ghetto uprising was headed by Mordechai Anilewicz. The first clash between the Nazis and the resistance force occurred on 18 January 1943, when Jewish members of a group earmarked for transport fired on their guards and succeeded in escaping. In carrying out their searches, the Germans encountered armed resistance. The expulsions were halted and members of the Judenrat and the Jewish Police, many of whose colleagues had already been sent to Treblinka, ceased cooperating with the Germans. The Nazis decided to wipe out the ghetto.

On 19 April 1943 a German force entered the ghetto with several cannons and armoured cars in order to exterminate the population and destroy the site. Despite systematic bombardment and burning on the part of the Germans, who progressed from block to block, the ghetto defenders held strong for five weeks. Resistance continued as long as there were defenders left alive. During the uprising some 7,000 Jews were killed, and many were burned to death within the bunkers.

From the outset, the ghetto, which was surrounded on all sides and isolated, had no hope of victory, but this uprising was a reflection of the fact that even years of Nazi terror and of indifference on the part of the Polish environment could not break the spirit of Jewish youth. It was an expression both of despair and of faith in man and in the future of the Jewish people. The heroism of the ghetto fighters proved to be as profoundly symbolic for the remnant of Polish Jewry and for the

Jewish people as a whole as the courage of the defenders of Masada had been in an earlier generation.

Resistance groups were also formed in the Bialystok, Minsk and Kovno ghettos. In Vilna, a United Partisan Organization (Fareinigte Partisanen Organisatzie) was established. When the population of the Vilna ghetto began to be exterminated in April 1943, members of this organization decided to fight inside the ghetto (which would have led to their rapid annihilation, as had occurred in the Warsaw ghetto), but the leader of the organization, Itzik Vittenberg, gave himself up to the Germans of his own free will in order to prevent the precipitation of a holocaust. In the large extermination camps as well, several revolts of Jewish prisoners broke out in the hope that they would help transmit to the outside world information about events inside the camps.

The Extermination of the Jews of Western and Central Europe

Many of the Jews of Western and Central Europe who were not dispatched to the ghettos of Poland and Russia were sent directly to the death-camps. The dimensions of the Holocaust were not uniform in all countries, but there was no Jewish community in a Nazi-occupied country or within the Axis camp (with the exception of Bulgaria and the small communities of Denmark and Finland) that was not seriously undermined.

At the beginning of 1943, the dispatch of the remnants of Berlin Jewry to Auschwitz commenced, and S.S. troops went from house to house seeking out the Jews. The Reichsvereinigung der Juden was disbanded. There were some 170,000 Jews within the borders of the 'Old Reich' on 1 May 1941, and on 1 September 1944 only 15,000 were left.

In France, expulsion to Auschwitz commenced in June 1942. On 16 July 1943 a large-scale manhunt was held in Paris and some 13,000 Jews, including 4,000 children, were arrested and incarcerated at Drancy. They were all sent to Auschwitz. The July and August transports encompassed some 25,000 French Jews, and expulsion then continued at a slower pace. All in all, about one-quarter of French Jewry was exterminated.

The great majority of Dutch Jewry was exterminated – more than 100,000 persons. The transports to Auschwitz commenced there in June 1942, but in April 1943 more than half of Holland's Jews were still living openly in their homes. The arrests were subsequently speeded up, and Jews were sent to Sobibor; in April 1944 the extermination programme was completed. The transport of Belgian Jews to Auschwitz commenced in August 1942, and by September 1943 about one-third of that community had been destroyed.

The large Jewish community of Salonika, where most of Greece's Jews were concentrated, was exterminated at Auschwitz during 1943 and 1944. Of the few Jews in Athens, most succeeded in escaping death, but some 60,000 Greek Jews were murdered.

In Slovakia and Croatia, the satellite states established by Hitler, the Jews suffered a

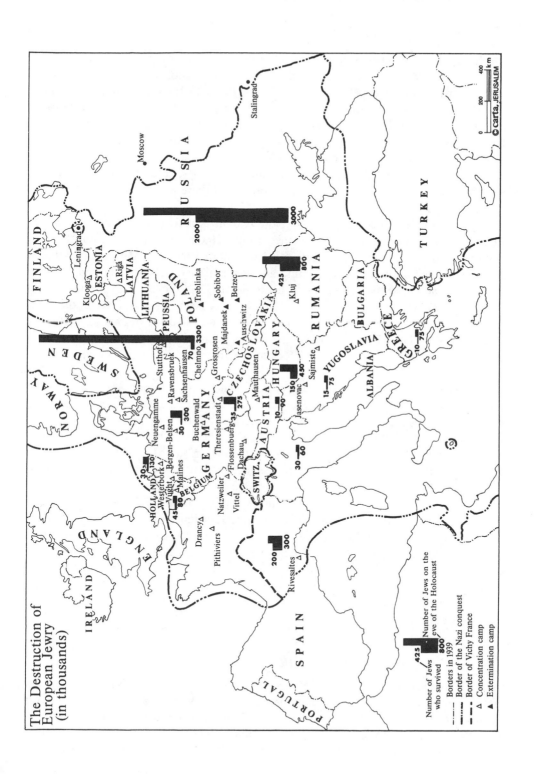

The Destruction of European Jewry (in thousands)

Number of Jews on the eve of the Holocaust
Number of Jews who survived

- Borders in 1939
- Border of the Nazi conquest
- Border of Vichy France
△ Concentration camp
▲ Extermination camp

© carta, JERUSALEM

km
0   200   400

similar fate. In March 1942, the President of Slovakia, Father Tisso, agreed to the expulsion of the Jews, and the fascist Hlinka Guard conducted a massive manhunt for the Jews of Bratislava. Some 35,000 Jews were sent 'eastwards' and were murdered at Auschwitz, Majdanek and Treblinka. Some 15,000 additional Jews, relatives of those murdered, were expelled between 15 May and 30 June. The number of those sent to extermination camps during 1942 reached 58,000. The expulsions were renewed in September 1944, after suppression of the Slovakian uprising; another 13,000 Jews were expelled, of whom about two-thirds perished. In Croatia, the Jews were concentrated in labour camps during October 1941, and some of them escaped to Italy. In 1942, some 5,000 Croation Jews were sent 'eastwards', and several thousand in the following year. But in October 1944 there were still Jews in Croatian concentration camps.

The Jews of Rumania and Hungary, the two allies of Hitler, suffered a different fate. In 1941–2 the Rumanians banished some 150,000 Jews from Bessarabia and Bukovina to Transnistria, only one-third of whom survived. More than 150,000 Jews were exterminated by the German and Rumanian armies during their advance into Bessarabia and Bukovina after hostilities began. Nevertheless some 15,000 Jews of Chernovitz survived, although the Germany Army passed through the town on several occasions. The great majority of the Jews of old Rumania (the 'Regat') remained alive. On 23 August 1944, the day of Rumania's capitulation to Russia, Eichmann was still making every effort to organize the expulsion of the Jews to death camps.

The destruction of Hungarian Jewry commenced at a later stage. Despite the country's collaboration with Nazi Germany, the Jews of Hungary were not harmed till, in March 1944, the German Army entered the country and a Fascist government was set up. Members of the Fascist organization Spearhead were immediately appointed directors of the section dealing with Jews in the Ministry of the Interior. Eichmann arrived in order to conduct the extermination operation, and between 24 April and 5 May of that year some 200,000 Hungarian Jews were arrested. On 15 May, expulsions to Auschwitz commenced, and by 30 June, 380,000 Jews had been sent there, of whom no less than 300,000 were murdered immediately. Eichmann demanded that the expulsion continue, but the Western Powers exerted pressure on the Hungarian ruler, Horthy; the government was replaced and negotiations commenced with the Soviet Union regarding surrender. This changed the situation. Nevertheless, even with the Soviet Army standing at the gates of Budapest, the Germans arrested some 40,000 Jews and sent them on a death-march to Austria. Very few survived.

The Countries that Resisted Hitler

A small number of Jews were saved because the governments of their countries did not surrender to Nazi pressure. In Finland, not only were the Jews not handed over for extermination, but they even continued to serve in the army. The Jewish community of Finland consisted of a little more than 1,000 people. In Denmark, because of the resolute stand of the government and the people against Nazi anti-Semitism, the underground succeeded in September and October 1943 in smuggling the great majority of the Jews (more than 6,000 people) to neutral Sweden. Only a few hundred were caught and sent to Theresienstadt. In Italy, anti-Jewish laws were promulgated, but the Italian Government, and above all the army, opposed dispatching the Jews to extermination, despite German pressure. Furthermore, some Jews from Yugoslavia and the south of France fled to Italy and were held there in concentration camps, but under humane conditions. After the Allies invaded Italy in 1943 and the country was occupied by the Germans, expulsions commenced from here as well, especially from Rome.

The outstanding example of active opposition to the German extermination policy, which demonstrates that by taking up a resolute stand a government could in fact resist German pressure, was supplied by Bulgaria. Despite the fact that Jews were sent to death-camps from the Bulgarian-occupied areas of Yugoslavia and Greece, close to 50,000 Jews of Bulgaria itself were saved thanks to the firm stand of the majority of the Bulgarian people and their government.

The Holocaust in Jewish History

The Holocaust was a dreadful blow for the Jewish people, more savage and inhuman than anything it had ever suffered – both in numbers and in agony. It was also a stunning spiritual and psychological shock. All the achievements and innovations of modern science and technology had been enlisted for the extermination of an entire nation; Nazi propaganda had endeavoured to reduce the Jews to the status of vermin, to exterminate them by gas and fire in order to 'purify the world'.

The Holocaust destroyed European Jewry, which, until the outbreak of the Second World War, had been the largest concentration of Jews in the world. Of the vast number of Jews in Poland, Germany, Austria, Holland, Czechoslovakia, Yugoslavia and Greece, only small remnants survived. Of the Jewish communities of the Soviet Union, Rumania and Hungary, only about half remained. There are no exact figures on the number of Jews murdered. Estimates range from 4.5 million to more than six million, but one thing is certain – the Nazi 'Final Solution' was a phenomenon unparalleled in the annals of human brutality. Even the suffering caused during the war to many peoples in Europe was incomparable to the Holocaust of the Jewish people. No nation experienced such torture, humiliation and vicious forms of murder; no nation witnessed such mass murder of women, elderly people and children; no nation lost one-third of its people; nor was any nation subjected to a deliberate plan that would not permit even one member to escape with his life.

The trials of the Nazi war-criminals at Nuremberg demonstrated that the claim subsequently bandied about in Germany that only the Nazi leaders and a select group of people around them knew about the mass extermination was unfounded. Not only did thousands of people play an active part in the murders – in government offices, in the administration of the occupied territories, in the S.S., the S.D. (security police) and the Gestapo, in the concentration and death-camps, in the Einsatzgruppen, where all were well aware of the scope of the terrible crimes they were committing – but tens of thousands of German soldiers, from field-marshals down to privates, who aided in the murders and expulsions, or witnessed them with their own eyes, were unquestionably accomplices. There were those among them who were shocked, but even they did not protest. The thousands of officials in the various ministries who drew up the record of plunder – from libraries and works of art to gold teeth, children's shoes and blood-stained coats – knew what they were doing. As the number of criminals and of those who enjoyed the fruits of crime reached hundreds of thousands, it is impossible to pretend that the German people knew nothing of what was going on. The Germans remained indifferent, and with the exception of a very few, were loyal to their *Fuehrer* almost to the end. Even resistance to him was no sign of a different attitude towards the Jews; among those who plotted against Hitler there were some who had murdered thousands of Jews. Only a very small number dared to express opposition – mainly people with Jewish spouses or those with deep religious faith. Worthy of special mention are those few righteous people who endangered their lives in the name of human dignity: the old Catholic priest Bernard Lichtenberg of Berlin, who openly prayed for the Jews and, when arrested, demanded that he be sent with the Jews (he died on his way to Dachau); or the simple housepainter Louis Birk from Wiesbaden who prophesied that the Nazi leaders would one day be obliged to build up, with their own hands, the Jewish synagogues they had destroyed – he was executed in 1943. There were very few others.

The most active accomplices of the Germans in these acts of extermination were the Ukrainians and Lithuanians, but they had many helpers among the Croatians, Rumanians, Hungarians and Slovaks. Among the Ukrainians and Lithuanians, traditional hatred of Jews was combined with the political hopes they pinned on the victory of the Germans and the fulfilment of their nationalist plans. This accounted for their extensive participation in acts of extermination carried out by the Einsatzgruppen and in wiping out the ghettos. Their police personnel were willing to search tirelessly for days and even weeks in order to hunt down one concealed Jewish child. Though Poland was notorious for her anti-Semitism, it is a fact that the number of Jews hidden and saved there by the local population was many times higher than in Soviet Ukraine and Soviet White Russia.

It is not by chance that Poland was chosen as the country of extermination. The Polish people did not cooperate with the Nazis, but neither did they lift a finger to help the Jews, even in the worst days of mass murder, or during the Warsaw ghetto uprising. There were many Poles who handed escaping Jews over to the Nazis. Nevertheless there were some Poles, mainly in the monasteries, who were shocked at the brutal murders, and particularly the slaughter of young children, and attempted to save them. Through them, several thousand Jewish children were saved in Poland.

On the other hand, in many countries, such as Slovakia, Hungary and Rumania, there was, even among the anti-Semitic leaders, an ambivalent attitude. On the one hand there was the desire to be rid of the 'alien' Jews – namely, refugees or Jews residing in annexed territories; on the other hand even they were not eager to hand over to the Germans the well-established Jews. The Germans were sometimes obliged to exert heavy pressure on their satellites in order to achieve their aim.

There were also a few countries in which the population was sympathetic towards the persecuted Jews, or where hatred of the Germans helped overcome anti-Semitic propensities. In France, Holland, Belgium, Denmark, Norway, Finland, Bulgaria, Greece and Italy, widespread circles expressed their sympathy for the Jews, and there were some who risked their lives in acts of protest or in rescuing Jews. It should be noted that even the Nazis did not dare act in Western Europe as they did in the East, and they took public opinion into consideration. In most of these countries, it was because of the public expression of sympathy that the percentage of Jews rescued was considerable. Only in Holland did the attitude of the public fail to rescue many Jews from their fate.

The attitude of the Christian churches towards the murder of Jews is a different matter altogether. The main body of the official Lutheran Church in Germany adopted a clearly anti-Semitic attitude from the earliest days of Nazi rule and did not abandon it till the end. Even when converted Jews, or Christians of partly Jewish origin, or even churchmen were affected, its stand remained unchanged. On the other hand the members of the Confessing Church were sworn anti-Nazis; they were disturbed by the wave of anti-Semitism, but, with the exception of a few individuals, there was no open protest even within this circle. Among the Catholic clergy, including parts of its leadership and in monasteries in various countries, a considerable number of people aided the Jews. Generally speaking, resistance to Nazi policy in this field was concentrated in the lowest ranks of the churches, and the rescue efforts were directed at Jews as individuals. In contrast, the higher echelons remained silent, and there were few attempts at this level to intervene on behalf of the Jews as a whole. The attitude of the Vatican is well known; throughout the years it never reacted to the extermination of the Jews. In December 1942 it rejected a suggestion to join the 'solemn resolution' of the Allies condemning Nazi crimes, and Pope Pius XII never condemned the Nazis or their deeds. The German Ambassador to the Vatican wrote to the German Foreign Office at the end of October in 1943:

> Although the Pope is under heavy pressure from all sides, he has not permitted himself to be drawn into any condemnation of the expulsion of the Jews from Rome. Although he could have expected his attitude to be criticized by our enemies and exploited by Protestants in the Anglo-Saxon countries in their propaganda against Catholics, he has done everything in his power not to strain relations with the German Government or with German circles in Rome . . .

The cardinals acted in similar fashion, as did the heads of the church in Poland and Hungary, and the Uniate Archibshop of the Greek Orthodox Church in Galicia, which recognized the authority of the Pope. They remained silent and did not protest against the terrible acts of murder occurring before their eyes; there were even some members of the Catholic clergy who spread savage anti-Semitic propaganda.

The Attitude of the Allies Towards the Holocaust

The attitude of the Allies towards the Nazi extermination policy was in principle clearly one of total opposition, but in practice it was passive. No special measures were taken to save the Jews of Europe, nor were the Nazi crimes sufficiently publicized. The Allies did issue a warning on 17 December 1942 that 'those responsible for these crimes shall not escape retribution,' but it was not followed by any action. The leaders of the democratic camp apparently feared Nazi propaganda, which persisted in claiming that the war was the result of world Jewry's scheming to control the Anglo-Saxon countries. They were even apprehensive about the transfer of several thousand Jews to neutral countries and claimed that this would arouse transportation and supply problems.

When the first information about the mass extermination reached the United States, the heads of the State Department tried to persuade the leaders of the Jewish community not to publicize the matter, lest they harm the war effort. Even when the pace of extermination was speeded up in 1943, the situation did not change. The State Department even forbade the acceptance of reports 'to be transmitted to private persons', *i.e.*, reports of extermination of Jews via governmental channels. An international conference on refugee affairs was convened at Bermuda in April 1943 under the pressure of public opinion, and although the Jewish organizations made several suggestions, such as the granting of United Nations passports to refugees, it brought no results.

The attitude of the British Government at that time is attested by several acts of hindrance, omission and evasiveness, such as the case of the *Struma,* the refugee ship from Rumania. This ship anchored in mid-December 1941 opposite the Turkish shore; the Turkish authorities refused to permit its passengers to disembark and the British refused to permit them to continue on their way to Palestine. On 24 February 1942 the *Struma* was driven away from the Turkish coast and sank shortly after. Of the 770 passengers (including seventy children), only one was rescued. When an Allied declaration condemning 'the German policy of extermination of the Jewish race' was read out in the British Parliament in December 1942, some of the members demanded that the Allies promise an immediate refuge to all those in danger. To this the British Foreign Secretary replied that 'first we must discuss security measures' and that there were 'many geographical difficulties'. At the beginning of 1943, it was revealed that 70,000 Jews could be rescued from Rumania if a certain sum of money were deposited in Switzerland, but Britain blocked this plan.

During 1943 the United States was swept by a wave of Jewish protest against its inactivity in the face of the extermination. In January of the same year, an Emergency Committee of American Jewry was established. Only after the intervention of Henry Morgenthau, Jr., Secretary of the Treasury, did President Roosevelt announce the establishment of a War Refugee Board (22 January 1944), composed of representatives of the departments of State, Treasury and War, authorized 'to take all measures within its power to rescue the victims of enemy oppression' and to combat 'Nazi plans to exterminate all the Jews.' It helped to save thousands of lives, but when a representative of the Rescue Committee of Hungarian Jews reached Istanbul with a proposal from the Nazis for a deal whereby Jews would be freed in exchange for trucks, the British arrested him and held him under detention until the end of the war. It is possible that Raoul Wallenberg, Secretary of the Swedish Legation in Budapest, was more instrumental than all the Allied committees in saving Hungarian Jews. He extended his country's protection to thousands of Jews and thus prevented their dispatch to Auschwitz. (He was arrested after the Soviet occupation and died in a Russian prison.)

The acts of the Soviet authorities against the Jews were even more cruel. After the agreement with Germany in August 1939, all anti-Nazi propaganda was abandoned, and German citizens who sought refuge in the Soviet Union (generally Communists), including a number of Jews, were handed over to the Nazis. After the outbreak of war, neither the military units nor the partisans operating behind the front-lines were ordered to display a special attitude towards the Jews in light of the dangers facing them. The acts of valour of Jewish fighters were not publicized, except in several Yiddish publications. In many partisan leaflets attacking the Nazis, published at the instigation of the Soviet authorities, the extermination of the Jews was never mentioned. There were Soviet partisan units that refused to accept Jews into their ranks. The Jewish 'family camps' of those who had fled to the forests were not supported by the Soviet partisans, and at times the latter even robbed them of arms and food. There were very few instances of the protection of such camps or of the rescue of Jews from ghettos. When a large partisan unit conducted a campaign behind the German lines in Galicia in 1943, capturing several towns, very little was done to rescue the Jews imprisoned in the ghettos. When committees 'for the investigation of Nazi crimes' began to operate during the war, not only did they fail to emphasize the systematic extermination of the Jews, but they even endeavoured to disguise it by describing the victims simply as 'Soviet citizens.'

The end of the war brought no basic change in the Allied attitude towards Jewish refugees. Immediately after the cessation of hostilities some 200,000 Jewish refugees assembled in the British and American occupation zones in Germany and, despite the change of government in Britain, it became apparent that the attitude towards Jewish refugees remained unchanged. A British general who headed the United Nations Relief and Rehabilitation Administration declared in the early days of 1946 that a secret Jewish organization was smuggling Jews from the East into Germany. He claimed that these Jews were 'well-dressed, well-fed and rosy-cheeked' and had large quantities of money in their possession. 'They certainly did not look like persecuted people.' He warned against the danger that European Jews were 'growing into a world force'. In mid-1946 the British prohibited the entry of Jewish refugees into their zone in Germany.

Soviet Jewry During the War and the Holocaust

Of all the Jewish communities in Allied countries, the Jews of the Soviet Union were marked particularly heavily by the war and the Holocaust. The horrors of war, the waves of refugees and the nightmarish fear of a German victory were a very real factor in the lives of Soviet Jewry throughout the war. The changes that these years of dread wrought in Soviet Jewish life were unique. They differed in character both from the destruction within the areas of Nazi occupation and from the reverberations and activity in the Western countries. There commenced a widespread dispersion of the Jews over the whole area of Russia. Many of those fleeing the Nazi armies, or those evacuated together with various Soviet industries, found themselves in the remotest corners of Siberia, Kazakhstan and Central Asia. The very foundations of Jewish life and what still remained of Jewish cultural institutions were totally destroyed.

An innovation brought about by the war was the establishment of a new body in the Soviet Union, which acted on behalf of the Jews. The Soviet regime was not interested in accentuating the sufferings of the Jewish people nor in depicting them as partners in the war effort, but it did want to exploit the Jews for the purpose of mobilizing public opinion in the United States. It therefore convened The First Public Convention of Representatives of the Jewish People in Moscow on 24 August 1941, which condemned the Nazi policy towards the Jews and called on World Jewry to rally for the war against Hitler.

The idea of creating a permanent Jewish representation was apparently proposed to the Soviet authorities by two leaders of the Polish Bund, Erlich and Alter, who had fled from Poland and who were in prison in the Soviet Union when war broke out. They approached the Soviet authorities in October 1941 with the proposal of establishing a Jewish committee to represent all the Jews of the occupied countries and to consist of representatives of the Soviet Union, the United States and Britain. On the basis of this proposal, negotiations were conducted with members of the Soviet leadership, but they were abruptly broken off, and the two initiators of the proposal were arrested and executed.

On 7 April 1942 the Soviet press reported that a Jewish Anti-Fascist Committee had been established, composed of representatives of the Soviet Jewish intelligentsia alone. It appealed to the Jews of the world to aid the Soviet Union in its struggle. The committee was headed by the director of the Jewish theatre in Moscow, the renowned actor Solomon Mikhoels. The regime was interested in the Jewish Anti-Fascist Committee above all as an instrument for enlisting sympathy and support for the Soviet Union. But its very existence made it the focus of Jewish life and activity in Russia. Although the committee published only one newspaper in Yiddish, *Einikeit,* which appeared three times a week, all the Yiddish writers in the Soviet Union rallied around it. This was the only paper in the Soviet Union in which the Jewish war effort and valour were reported. This material did not appear in the general Soviet press and was mainly directed at the Jewish press outside the Soviet Union. All those with any Jewish interest whatsoever approached the Committee.

In establishing the Jewish Anti-Fascist Committee, the Soviet regime recognized a phenomenon that it had denied throughout the years – the common interests and special ties existing not only between the Jews of Russia itself, but also between all Jewish communities throughout the world. The influence of the committee was mainly symbolic; for all practical affairs the committee was only one of the departments of the Soviet Ministry of Propaganda (Sovinformbureau). Under Soviet conditions just its name was significant, as it recalled the existence of the Jews and their struggle, particularly in the light of the fact that, during the war, when the Jews of the Soviet Union became aware of the Nazi acts of mass murder, there was an upsurge of national consciousness among them.

The Holocaust and Jewish suffering left a deep impression on members of the assimilated intelligentsia, on writers, economic leaders and army officers. The opinion was voiced that Jewish life should be rehabilitated, whether through fostering the Jewish centre in Birobidzhan or by establishing a Jewish centre in the Crimea. (Some of the Tartar inhabitants there had collaborated with the Nazis during the war, and therefore the entire community was banished eastwards by Stalin after the liberation of the Crimea.) Voices – though muted – were also raised in suggesting the rehabilitation of the Jews in 'the land of the Jews', *i.e.,* Palestine. For many Jews who had drifted far from Jewish affairs and interests during the thirties, the Holocaust came as a reminder of their origins. The struggle against Nazism and the Holocaust reminded the Jews of the Soviet Union – even the most detached among them – of a common Jewish destiny and served as a cohesive and unifying force in consolidating renewed Jewish consciousness.

68

The Struggle for Independence and the Establishment of the State of Israel

The War Effort of the Yishuv

When war broke out, the great majority of the Jewish community in Palestine supported Ben-Gurion's proposal at the Twenty-first Zionist Congress that 'we must fight Hitler as if there were no White Paper, and the White Paper as if there were no Hitler.' But, in practice, any idea of causing difficulties to the British Government was abandoned. The leaders of Zionism and the Yishuv began to submit proposals for the establishment of a Jewish military force to engage in the war against Hitler. They hoped that participation in the war effort would reinforce the political demands of the Jews (as in the First World War) and that, as a result, the White Paper would be revoked.

But both the British Government and the military were uninterested in setting up a Jewish fighting force at that time. The war was still progressing at a slow pace and there were no serious shortages in manpower. On the contrary, the British leaders claimed that the establishment of a Jewish fighting force would arouse resentment in the Arab states, in which the Axis powers were active, while the military force needed to suppress the Arab revolt would be immeasurably larger than any increment of manpower provided by the Yishuv. The government agreed to recruit Palestinian Jews only for the mixed (Jewish-Arab) sappers and technical units. The aim was clear – not to give open expression to Jewish participation in the war.

The German conquests during the spring and summer of 1940, the rise of a militant government in Britain under Churchill's leadership, the fall of France, Italy's entry into the war on the German side all led to a far-reaching change in the course of the war. A plan was suggested to create a Jewish army on the same basis as the Czech and Polish armies, but it was opposed by the architects of British Near Eastern policy and eventually abandoned. In September 1940 it was decided to recruit an infantry battalion in Palestine, 'the Buffs', but in order to preserve political equilibrium, it was proposed to establish an equal number of Jewish and Arab units – despite the well-known fact that the Arabs were not anxious to join the British Army or to support the war effort against Hitler and Mussolini. In fact, the battalion was predominantly Jewish.

Within the Yishuv there was no unanimity of opinion with regard to the recruitment policy. Among members of the Haganah there were those who feared that the firm stand of the Yishuv might be weakened if many men were mobilized and transported outside the country. But on this question the British Army undertook that the Jewish units would remain in Palestine. Negotiations regarding the establishment of a fighting Jewish regiment reached a certain stage, but eventually came to nought. When war broke out the British authorities even began displaying a stern attitude towards Haganah activity, to which they had turned a blind eye during the Arab revolt. At the end of 1939 and the beginning of 1940, several measures were introduced to curtail the activities of the Haganah and confiscate arms. This policy was clearly reflected in the trial of forty-three members of this organization, arrested for participation in training, and in the trial that followed the confiscation of arms at Ben Shemen.

The worsening of the general political and military situation in the summer of 1940 eased the situation of the Haganah. After the establishment of the Palestinian infantry battalion, there was increased cooperation with the British Army, particularly in light of the direct threat posed by the Vichy government's control of Syria. The successes of the Axis also intensified Arab sympathy towards that side, and the common interests of Britain with the Yishuv in Palestine became more apparent. Nevertheless, there were still obstacles to this cooperation. 'Illegal' immigrants were still reaching the country in a trickle, and the authorities treated them extremely harshly, even banishing them to remote islands. At the end of 1940, the immigrant passengers on the *Atlantic* were banished to Mauritius, while those aboard the *Patria* (which was mined by the Haganah, while under expulsion order, to disable its engines, though the explosion actually took 200 lives) were permitted to remain in Palestine as an 'act of grace'. Their number was deducted from the quota of certificates allocated according to the 1939 White Paper. This aroused considerable resentment in the Yishuv, but did not affect military cooperation.

Military Cooperation with Britain

In addition to the direct war effort, cooperation was reflected in sending skilled Jewish manpower to work in British military bases (setting up camps, maintenance, operating workshops), in intelligence activities, in strengthening guard operations. When the German forces led by Rommel reached the Egyptian border at the beginning of April 1941, the British headquarters agreed to renounce the 'parity principle' in mobilizing Jews and Arabs and, within a few months, more than 3,000 Jewish men and women had enlisted in the British Army.

The Irgun also cooperated with the British. During the pro-Nazi revolt of Rashid Ali, which broke out in Iraq during May 1941, Irgun members went there on an intelligence mission, and the leader of the organization, David Raziel, lost his life in this action. At that same time the leaders of the Haganah decided to establish a military unit – the Palmah ('striking force') – to stand at its disposal for the execution of special tasks. The first operations carried out by this volunteer force were the dispatch by boat of twenty-three fighters in an attempt to blow up the refineries in Tripoli (the boat was lost and the fate of the Palmah members remains unknown) and the participation of a platoon formed from the nuclei of the two first units of the Palmah in the Allied invasion of Syria (June 1941).

In the second half of 1941, after the British Army had succeeded in pushing the Axis forces westwards and in capturing the whole of Cyrenaica, there was a lull in the military situation in Palestine. But at the beginning of 1942, when Rommel renewed his attacks and again advanced to the Egyptian border, there was a real danger that Palestine would be invaded. The Yishuv summoned up its strength, and during the summer of 1942, more than 5,000 additional Jews joined the British Army. The Palmaḥ intensified its training, Haganah units were strengthened, and training camps for local defence were set up for thousands of citizens. Within the Yishuv stormy debates were held as to what to do in the event of a German invasion. But the danger was averted when the British Eighth Army defeated the Germans at El Alamein during the autumn of 1942.

The Political Struggle of the Zionist Leadership.
The Biltmore Programme

The Zionist leadership, which, at the beginning of the war, had not yet grasped the scope and nature of the Holocaust, envisaged millions of Jewish refugees in Europe and made every effort to facilitate their immigration to and absorption in an independent Palestine at the end of the war. In January 1942 Weizmann submitted the political demand for a Jewish commonwealth in Palestine. In order to recruit maximum support for this idea, Weizmann travelled to the United States in April 1942 and participated in a conference with representatives of numerous Jewish organizations.

At this conference, held at the Biltmore Hotel in New York at the beginning of May 1942, various resolutions were passed, which later constituted the basis for the political activity of the Zionist movement (the Biltmore Programme). These included a demand for the opening of the gates of Palestine to mass Jewish immigration; the demand that all matters connected with immigration and development of the country for absorption purposes be entrusted to the Jewish Agency; and, in particular, a call for the establishment of an independent Jewish commonwealth in Palestine. This programme was put forward with Weizmann's approval and participation, but it was David Ben-Gurion who gave it its great public impetus through the demand for 'immediate implementation', *i.e.,* as soon as the war ended, and through accentuating American aid for its implementation. This highlighted the conflict between Ben-Gurion and the members of the Zionist Executive in London, who were still basing their plans on common interests with Britain. The Biltmore Programme was brought before the Zionist Executive in November 1942 and approved by a decisive majority. Even those who did not believe in its full implementation regarded it as the basis for political negotiations on the annulment of the White Paper or on the revival of the participation plan as envisaged by the Peel Commission.

The Worsening British Attitude Towards the Yishuv

As the front-line retreated from Palestine, the apprehension of the British over the political aspirations of Palestinian Jews increased, and they displayed growing fear of a Jewish revolt. The authorities in Palestine reverted to their previous attempts to break the Haganah by confiscating arms. Furthermore, they endeavoured to restrict the authority of the Yishuv institutions, which appeared to them to constitute 'a state within a state' and hence to undermine British authority.

A search carried out in the Jewish Agency Recruitment Bureau in April 1943, accompanied by physical violence, led the Agency to announce the closing of the Bureau for three months. But even more serious was the affair of the arms trials and searches for arms in settlements. The Yishuv institutions did everything in their power to consolidate their independent force, including purchasing arms stolen by deserters from British Army stores in Palestine and the vicinity and the 'filching' of arms by soldiers. In the summer of 1943 a trial was held at which two Jews were accused of purchasing arms from British deserters. Apparently the main purpose of the trial was to discredit the Yishuv institutions in the eyes of the American public. Searches for arms at the settlements of Huldah and Ramat Hakovesh (where one member was killed by a British police officer), carried out at the end of that year, strengthened the Yishuv's awareness that an independent Jewish military force was a vital necessity and aroused strong anti-British feeling.

A no less important factor in the disrupting relations between the Yishuv and the British was the harsh stand of Britain on the question of the European Holocaust. As early as 1942 information began to reach Palestine, and even to appear in the press, regarding the murder of Jews by the Nazis, though the majority of the public treated the news with scepticism. The significance of the terrible tragedy had not yet penetrated the consciousness of the Yishuv. The proximity of the front-line in the period just before the El Alamein battle also helped to divert attention from European events. During 1943 the dimensions and significance of the Holocaust became more apparent. Nevertheless the Yishuv institutions and the Zionist movement made no attempt to establish direct, independent contact with those incarcerated in ghettos and camps, nor to organize revolts and acts of sabotage. The Jewish leadership took the well-trodden path of exerting pressure on the Allies, and particularly Britain, to force them to help in the rescue work, but without any tangible results.

Jewish institutions put forward several proposals for action to aid the remnants of European Jewry. The only one that materialized was the dispatch of parachutists to the war zone. At the end of 1943 and in 1944, thirty-two volunteers were parachuted into seven Nazi-occupied countries. Some of them did not succeed in reaching their objective, but others carried out important military intelligence operations and played an outstanding part in organizing and encouraging the Jews of those countries. Twelve of them fell captive, and seven were murdered. They became a symbol of the valour and sacrifice of the Yishuv and of the Jewish people as a whole. The names of Enzo Sereni, Hannah Szenes, Havivah Reik and their comrades symbolized the ties between the Yishuv and the Jews of Europe. In the summer of 1944 the Yishuv institutions proposed to the British Government the establishment of a camp for the training of another 100 parachutists to operate among Tito's partisans in all the Balkan countries, but the English sabotaged this plan.

The harassment of the Yishuv and its institutions and the attitude of indifference to the fate of European Jewry discredited the British in the eyes of many Jews.

The Irgun and Leḥi Against the British

It was against this background that anti-British activities were intensified by the Irgun and Leḥi (Loḥamei Ḥerut Yisrael, Israel Freedom Fighters, a group that had split from the Irgun in 1940). Until that time the founder of Leḥi, Abraham Stern, and several of his associates had been the only element in the Yishuv that took a consistently anti-British stand and tried to contact the Axis powers, particularly Italy, so as to achieve the political objectives of Zionism with their help, in a common struggle against Britain. Such an attitude could not be accepted by the Yishuv at a time when the war against the Nazis and their satellites was at its height, and this group therefore became isolated. Finally, it was almost entirely annihilated when Abraham Stern was captured by the British police in February 1942 and murdered on the spot.

The Irgun continued with its policy of cooperation with Britain during these years – the heritage of Jabotinsky – and its central aim was to force Britain to agree to a military partnership with the Jews and to recognize their role in the war. But the deterioration of relations between Britain and the Yishuv and the change of leadership within the Irgun, which occurred in 1943, led to a drastic switch in this policy. In January 1944 the Irgun announced the beginning of a 'revolt against the British conqueror'.

During 1944 the Irgun sabotaged government offices, attacked police camps, the broadcasting station and various other British installations. The anti-British sentiments prevailing in the Yishuv created sympathy for these operations. Leḥi chose the path of individual terror: they shot policemen and tried to assassinate the High Commissioner, MacMichael (August 1944). Their most extreme act was carried out on 5 November 1944 when two of their members murdered in Egypt the British Minister of State in the Middle East, Lord Moyne. This murder aroused deep resentment in Britain and a sharp reaction from Churchill. The Yishuv (including the Irgun) dissociated itself from the act. At the same time the courageous stand of the two assassins during the trial (they were both executed) made a strong impression, even on foreign journalists.

Prior to this, the British authorities had exerted pressure on the Yishuv institutions to put an end to the activities of the 'dissidents' – as the Irgun and Leḥi were called by the Yishuv institutions – either on their own or with the aid of the British police. After hesitation, the institutions of the Zionist movement decided on independent activity – by the Haganah intelligence service (Sherut Yed'iot) and by the Palmaḥ – against the Irgun. Several hundred Irgun members were arrested and imprisoned. After the murder of Lord Moyne, the movement decided also to cooperate with the British police, and some 100 of the Irgun prisoners were handed over to the C.I.D. (Criminal Investigation Department, the political department of the Palestine police force), which was also informed of the whereabouts of several other members of the organizations, who were promptly arrested by the British. Many of them were exiled to Eritrea; the total number of Irgun and Leḥi prisoners exiled during this period reached approximately 250. This action aroused great resentment in both the Palmaḥ and the Yishuv institutions (Yizhak Gruenbaum resigned from the Agency Executive as a result), as well as among the public. In March 1945, the leaders of the Haganah announced the suspension of this policy.

The Deterioration of Relations Between Zionist Institutions and the British Government

The qualified attitude óf the Yishuv institutions towards terrorism, the cooperation which endured in several military spheres, and the realization that the Jews would have to be offered some compensation at the end of the war, brought the British Government to the decision to establish a Jewish Brigade. This was announced in September 1944. At that time the political and military situation in Europe had changed to such an extent that Britain no longer feared the Arab reaction. The brigade had its own military standard and a national character. It was ready for battle by the end of the year and participated in some fighting in Italy. Later it formed part of the occupation army in Europe. In addition to its political value, the brigade, as a military force, gave its troops basic military training and was a superior fighting unit with some 25,000 troops, recruited in Palestine. It was undoubtedly of great importance to the consolidation of the military strength of the Yishuv. But of particular importance was its function in establishing contact with the remnants of European Jewry, engaging in physical rescue, encouraging the survivors and organizing 'illegal' immigration to Palestine.

Despite this particular development, the relations between the Yishuv institutions and the mandatory authorities generally deteriorated, as did those between the British Government and the leadership of the Zionist movement. The aid provided by the Yishuv to Britain during its time of severe trial in the Middle East seemed to have been forgotten. For all Churchill's sympathy for the Zionist cause over the previous decades, and despite his promise to change British policy after the war, it became clear that the cooperation between the Zionist movement and Britain was drawing to an end. The Yishuv's appeal to the American Jewish community and to American public opinion as a whole to exert pressure on the British also helped to disrupt relations. And this naturally helped strengthen the position of those Zionist leaders with a pro-American orientation, who hoped to win the support of the U.S. Government for the Jewish demands.

In fact, on 1 February 1944, Congress passed a resolution demanding the opening of the gates of Palestine to Jewish immigration 'so that the Jewish people may ultimately reconstitute Palestine as a free and democratic Jewish commonwealth.' The American Government rejected this demand out of supposedly military considerations, but President Roosevelt sent a message to an American Zionist Convention in October 1944 supporting 'the establishment of Palestine as a free and democratic Jewish commonwealth'. This attitude did not endure for long. After the Yalta Conference (February 1945) Roosevelt met with King Ibn Saud of Saudia Arabia and gave in to his pressure. A week before his death (April 1945) Roosevelt promised Ibn Saud that, with regard to the future of Palestine, nothing would be done 'which might prove hostile to the Arab people'. Thus it seemed that despite the changes in political orientation the chances of success for the Zionist movement, even after the war, were not great.

The End of the War. Meeting the Survivors of European Jewry

When the war ended, contact was established between the Yishuv in Palestine and the remnants of European Jewry, which immediately created a fateful mutual relationship. The institutions of the Zionist movement and the Yishuv made every effort to bring the survivors of the death-camps back to life and hope, while the latter became an active and decisive factor in the determination of independent Jewish policy, with the clear and unequivocal objective for the entire Jewish people of establishing a Jewish state in Palestine.

The first contact between the survivors and the Yishuv was established, as has been noted, through the Jewish Brigade. In north Italy at this time were assembled many Jews who had hidden in the mountains and in monasteries. The brigade became the address to which representatives of the survivors from all over Europe turned. It extended help, dealt with problems of health and education, organized Jewish life and assisted 'illegal' immigration. The extensive activities of the Brigade soldiers in these spheres were one of the main reasons for the rapidity with which this unit was disbanded by the British.

Immediately after the capitulation of the Nazis, tens of thousands of Jews assembled in the Displaced Persons camps of Germany. But the borders were not yet closed, and a movement westwards began from Eastern Europe. From the depths of Russia they reached Soviet Ukraine, Poland and Czechoslovakia by the hundreds of thousands. They, as well as the survivors of the concentration and death-camps, returned to their old homes in the hope of finding those members of their families from whom they had been separated during the Holocaust. The non-Jewish population generally did not welcome the Jews. There arose the problem of restoring houses, apartments or property that had been confiscated, abandoned or plundered. The dimensions of this return movement were large; some 150,000 Jews returned to Poland in 1946 from Russia alone, under the repatriation agreement between the two countries. The consequences swiftly followed: in June 1946 a terrible pogrom broke out in Kielce in which dozens of Jews were murdered. In Poland Jews were murdered by the roadside and were pushed to their deaths out of moving railway carriages. It became apparent that the Holocaust had not only failed to soften the traditional anti-Semitism of the Polish people but had even intensified it. In Soviet Russia as well there was great tension. In Kiev, for example, riots broke out over the question of restoring apartments to their rightful owners. In Bratislava in Slovakia there were actual pogroms.

The Polish Government tried to settle the returning Jews in the areas annexed after the expulsion of the Germans, but very few Jews settled there. The majority began to flee westwards: in July 1946, 17,000 Jews left Poland, in August the number rose to 35,000. According to a Czech government report, more than 200,000 people crossed its border in 1946. The refugees concentrated in the D.P. camps in Germany. Some 200,000 Jewish refugees were assembled there at the end of 1946, most of them looking forward to only one thing – peace and security among their brethren through emigration to Palestine. But the gates of Palestine were closed, and the possibilities of migrating to other countries were very limited.

Post-War British Policy on the Palestinian Question

After the publication of the 1939 White Paper, the British Labour Party continually expressed its severe criticism of the government's Palestine policy. Even while participating in Churchill's coalition cabinet, party spokesmen reiterated their support for the Jewish National Home and even demanded the creation of a Jewish majority in Palestine. In a document dealing with post-war settlements, submitted to the Labour Party Executive in April 1944, it was stated:

> There is surely neither hope nor meaning in a 'Jewish National Home' unless we are prepared to let Jews, if they wish, enter this tiny land in such numbers as to become a majority. There was a strong case for this before the war. There is an inevitable case now after the unspeakable atrocities of the cold and calculated German plan to kill all the Jews in Europe. . . . Let the Arabs be encouraged to move out and the Jews to move in. Let them be compensated handsomely for their land and let their settlement elsewhere be carefully organized and generously financed. The Arabs have many wide territories of their own; they must not claim to exclude the Jews from this small area of Palestine.

Even Jewish leaders dissociated themselves from this idea of a population transfer. In May 1945 Hugh Dalton, one of the leaders of the Labour Party, announced at the party conference that

> it was morally wrong and politically indefensible to restrict the entry into Palestine of Jews desiring to go there. . . . Close agreement and co-operation should be secured between Britain, America and Russia, particularly if they were to assure not only the settlement of the Palestine question but of those connected with the surrounding countries . . . it was indispensable that steps be taken to get common support for the policy of giving facilities for the creation of a free, happy and prosperous Jewish State of Palestine.

In July 1945 the British Labour Party came to power, but the gates of Palestine were not opened. Various factors swayed the government on this question. At the end of May the Jewish Agency demanded that the White Paper be cancelled and that Palestine be established as a Jewish state. President Truman of the United States declared in mid-August his support for the right to free Jewish immigration, and on 2 September he sent a missive to the British Prime Minister, Clement Attlee, in which he demanded that 100,000 Jewish refugees be granted immediate entry into Palestine. The Labour government ignored all these demands, as well as its own former resolutions.

Only after four months of incessant pressure did Foreign Secretary Ernest Bevin proclaim the government's Palestinian policy. In his declaration on 13 November he reiterated Britain's 'dual obligation' towards the Jews and the Arabs, the constant disputes between the two sides and the apprehension of the entire Arab world – including ninety million Moslems in India – regarding the fate of the Palestinian Arabs. The main point of Bevin's statement was that Palestine could not – and should not – solve the problems of Jewish refugees and that the Jews were called on to contribute 'their ability and talent toward rebuilding the prosperity of Europe'. But as Bevin declared to the press: 'I am very anxious that Jews shall not in Europe over-emphasize their racial position' and that they should not 'get too much at the head of the queue'.

The statement by Bevin contained only one practical proposal – the establishment of an Anglo-American Committee of Inquiry to examine the Palestine question and the situation of the Jews in Europe. Bevin announced that Palestine would be handed over to the trusteeship of the United Nations and, in time, would become a Palestinian, not a Jewish, state. The immigration quota of 1,500 certificates per month would continue even after the end of the immigration allocation under the 1939 White Paper. In short Bevin defined Labour's policy on the basis of the assumption that after the Holocaust there was no longer any need for mass immigration and that British rule could be maintained in Palestine to defend a Jewish minority within a dominant Arab majority.

The Committee of Inquiry was established with an equal number of American and English members. It commenced its investigation in Washington on 7 January 1946 and heard a considerable amount of evidence in Europe, in D.P. camps and in Palestine. On 30 April 1946 it published its recommendations. The most urgent was the proposal to grant immediately 100,000 immigration certificates to refugees in the camps. The Committee also proposed revoking the prohibition against sale of land to Jews. Regarding the political future of the country, it proposed a British Mandate to be administered by the United Nations. Immediately after publication of these recommendations, President Truman issued a manifesto in which he expressed his gratification at the fact that 'my request that 100,000 Jews be granted immediate entry into Palestine was unanimously approved by the Committee.' He emphasized that, in practice, the Committee had recommended the annulment of the 1939 White Paper, so that the Jewish National Home could continue to grow and develop. But the British Government did not intend to carry out the recommendations. Attlee announced that they would be implemented only after disbandment of 'the illegal armies' now existing in Palestine and the surrender of their arms. This was a clear evasion of obligations that the British Government had undertaken, and it constituted open provocation against the Jews.

Illegal Immigration

The Yishuv braced itself for the struggle against the British authorities, and the Zionist movement opened a political campaign against British policies. The most daring means employed by the Jews in order to force open the gates of the country was born out of the plight of the survivors of the Holocaust who were yearning for

Palestine in the D.P. camps and had found their way to the Mediterranean ports; this was the *ha'apalah* ('illegal immigration'). As early as August and September of 1945, small, battered boats, which had left from Italian ports, began to arrive in Palestine with survivors. Immigrants also began to arrive by land through Syria. Many of them were caught by the police. At the beginning of October the members of kibbutz Kefar Giladi succeeded in rescuing seventy immigrants from the police and hiding them in their settlement, despite the British siege. On 10 October 1945 Palmaḥ units broke into the detention camp at Atlit and succeeded in liberating some 200 illegal immigrants then being held there.

Anti-British sentiments brought about a *rapprochement* between the various military organizations in the Yishuv, and an attempt was made to establish an umbrella organization for the Haganah, Irgun and Leḥi; this was known as Tenu'at Hameri Ha'ivri (Hebrew Resistance Movement). On the night of 2 November 1945 an attack was launched on railway lines, bridges and railway stations. Installations were blown up and coastal patrol boats were sunk in port. The aim of these attacks was to demonstrate to the British that they could not rule the country against the wishes of the Jewish Yishuv. Subsequently coastal police stations were destroyed at Givat Olga and Sidne Ali. In reaction British military units surrounded the settlements of Givat Ḥaim and Shfayim and began to destroy the buildings and the plantations. Thousands of people gathered from the vicinity to aid the settlements. The British resorted to armed force, and several people were killed.

In the meantime, 'illegal' immigration was increasing. The British began to apprehend immigrant ships at sea. The Haganah reacted by blowing up radar installations, police cars and other equipment. In an attack on the Sarona Police station (near Tel Aviv) four Haganah members were killed, and their funeral, which was attended by tens of thousands of Tel Avivians, was transformed into a huge anti-British demonstration. There were further clashes with the police when an attempt was made to disembark immigrants in the port of Tel Aviv (26 March 1946) and when the British Army captured Biria in Galilee, a new settlement settled by the Hapo'el Hamizrachi movement, and arrested all its members.

The Militant Partnership of the Holocaust Survivors and the Yishuv

The Holocaust survivors from the death-camps were a mighty force in pressing for the opening of Palestine to immigration. Residence in camps had ceased to be a temporary phenomenon and had become a way of life for tens of thousands of Jews; it also became a way of being trained for emigration. Hebrew and Yiddish schools were opened, pioneering youth movements were established, political parties were founded; the former partisans set up their own organization, Paḥaḥ (Partisans, Pioneers and Fighters). All these activities were carried out under the guidance and inspiration of emissaries from Palestine and with the support of Jewish organizations in the Diaspora.

Some of the inmates left the camps and settled in Europe – in Germany itself or in Western Europe. There were also individuals who engaged in profiteering and trade in the German black market, and there were young people who began to study at universities. But the great majority of the camp inmates wanted to emigrate to Palestine and prepared themselves for this move. At several conventions and conferences held in the camps in the second half of 1945, firm resolutions were passed protesting against the detention of the survivors in camps and demanding immediate emigration. Many undertook the difficulties and dangers of illegal immigration.

As the struggle over illegal immigration became intensified, the Jewish refugees opened up a new front on European soil. When two illegal immigrant ships were detained under British pressure before leaving the Italian port of La Spezia, in April 1946, their passengers declared a hunger strike and threatened to sink the ships. Italian public opinion rallied to the support of the refugees, and the leaders of the Yishuv declared a hunger strike until the boats were eventually released.

When it transpired that the British Government did not intend to implement the recommendations of the Anglo-American Committee, it was decided to organize concentrated reaction; on one night Palmaḥ units blew up all the bridges on the borders connecting Palestine with its neighbouring countries. The operation was a success, with the exception of a catastrophe in which fourteen fighters were killed while placing explosives under Haziv bridge. The British Army determined to take forceful action to break the Palmaḥ and arrested as many Haganah members and leaders of the Yishuv as possible. This action, in which thousands of police and army personnel participated, was completed in one day – Saturday, 29 June 1946 (known subsequently in the Yishuv as 'the Black Saturday'). Several leaders of Jewish institutions and of the Haganah hid, but many were arrested; thousands of settlement members were forcibly detained and obliged to provide identification, which they refused to do. The attempt to discover Palmaḥ members among the detainees failed. Eventually most of them were released, with the exception of 2,000 who were sent to concentration camps at Rafiah and Latrun. The settlement of Yagur, in which a large Haganah arms cache was discovered, suffered considerable damage at the hands of the British Army.

A state of warfare now existed between the government and the Yishuv. In reaction to 'Black Saturday' the Irgun blew up the offices of the government secretariat and the military headquarters, which were located in the King David Hotel in Jerusalem, even though the building was heavily guarded. Many employees – British, Jews and Arabs – were killed in the explosion. The Irgun claimed that a warning had been given to clear the building, but the Chief Secretary denied it. This action greatly shocked public opinion in England and throughout the world. Although the Haganah had not opposed this operation at the outset, Yishuv institutions and the Zionist movement dissociated themselves from it, and this put an end to cooperation within the Hebrew Resistance Movement.

In order to uncover the saboteurs, the British set up detention camps in Tel Aviv and carried out mass arrests. Moreover, the British authorities decided to deliver a blow at the most sensitive spot in the Yishuv – immigration. Since the attempt to detain the boats at their point of embarkation had failed, the authorities published an announcement on 12 August 1946 that henceforth illegal immigrants would be sent to camps in Cyprus. Two days later 100 immigrants were transferred from two boats to a ship that conveyed them to Cyprus. On the day of expulsion the authorities declared a curfew in Haifa, so as to prevent the public from extending aid to the immigrants who resisted their transfer; the curfew was violated, the army opened fire, and there were several victims. In reaction the Palmah began to sabotage the expulsion ships.

The most daring battle in the illegal immigration fight, which moved public opinion throughout the world, was the affair of the *Exodus,* which sailed from France in July 1947 with 4,500 illegal immigrants abroad. It was attacked near the coast of Palestine by British destroyers, which opened fire on its decks and killed several of the passengers. The ship was brought to Haifa port, and instead of being banished to Cyprus, the immigrants were returned to Europe. The French Government agreed to accept them, but the passengers refused to leave the ship and were forcibly taken off at Hamburg. Not only was it a terrible shock to the Holocaust survivors to be brought back, after two years of struggle and hope, to the land of their suffering, but they actually were returned to D.P. camps. It was only natural that many boarded other illegal ships shortly afterwards. The incident aroused considerable resentment against the British in the Yishuv and throughout the world.

Despite the obstacles and the sacrifices, illegal immigration attained considerable achievements. Not only did it demonstrate how groundless were the basic assumptions of Bevin's policy, but at least 70,000 Jews sailed to Palestine in the period between 1945 and the establishment of Israel in May 1948. Fifty thousand were caught and sent to Cyprus. With the aid of emissaries from the Yishuv and Haganah members, educational, social and cultural activity, as well as semi-military training, was conducted in the Cyprus camps until the detainees were permitted to enter Palestine in 1948.

International Debate on the Palestine Problem

After the British Government had refused to implement the recommendations of the Anglo-American Committee, it attempted to submit a new programme for the solution of the Palestine problem. The Morrison-Grady Plan proposed the partition of Palestine into four areas: Jewish (17% of the area of western Palestine), Arab (40%) and two British districts (43%). The country as a whole would be headed by a British High Commissioner, and the Jewish and Arab provinces would enjoy a certain measure of self-rule; the government of the Jewish province would be granted the right to propose to the central government that it permit immigration within the limits of the 'absorption capacity' of the province. But the Morrison-Grady plan also provided for the 'immediate admission of 100,000 Jews to Palestine.'

This plan was rejected by both Jews and Arabs. The Twenty-second Zionist Congress, which was convened at Basle in December 1946 (the first post-war congress), rejected the British Government's invitation to participate in a new conference to be convened in London to discuss the future of Palestine. The Arabs of Palestine also turned down the invitation. The conference was attended only by representatives of the Arab states who demanded independence for the country and agreed to ensure 'minority rights' to the Jews residing there.

On 14 February 1947, the British Foreign Secretary, Ernest Bevin, announced that Britain could not reconcile the interests of the two peoples residing in Palestine and had therefore 'decided to refer the whole problem to the United Nations'. For this purpose a special session of the United Nations General Assembly was convened at the beginning of May, which was addressed by both Jews and Arabs. The United States and several West European and Latin American countries displayed a sympathetic attitude towards the Jewish cause. But of outstanding importance was the appearance of the Soviet representative, Andrei Gromyko, who unexpectedly supported 'the aspirations of the Jews to establish their own State. It would be unjust,' he declared 'not to take this into consideration and to deny the right of the Jewish people to realize this aspiration. It would be unjustifiable to deny this right to the Jewish people, particularly in view of all it has undergone during the Second World War.' The Polish representative also supported the idea.

The General Assembly elected a committee of investigation composed of representatives of eleven countries – UNSCOP (United Nations Special Committee on Palestine). The committee heard the evidence of various parties and at the end of August submitted its conclusions. The majority recommendation (seven members) was the partition of the country into a Jewish state, an Arab state and an international area under U.N. supervision, to include Jerusalem and its environs. In the transitional period, to commence on 1 September 1947 and to last for two years, the immigration of 150,000 Jews would be permitted. The Jewish and Arab states would be connected by an economic union. The Jewish state was to cover 62% of the area of Palestine, but did not include Jerusalem, western and central Galilee, the hills of Samaria and Judah and part of the Judean Desert. The minority (three members) recommended that Palestine be transformed into a Jewish-Arab federative state. One member abstained on both proposals.

During the debate at the U.N. General Assembly, the United States supported the partition plan, although the U.S. State Department attempted to introduce additional territorial changes and to detach the Negev from the Jewish state. Only the personal intervention of President Truman foiled this plan. The Soviet Union and the Communist-bloc countries consistently supported the establishment of a Jewish state. Several representatives of Latin America fought resolutely for the Jewish cause. Britain expressed reservations regarding the plan and announced that she would evacuate her troops from the country. A sub-committee, which studied the details of the partition plan, reduced the borders of the Jewish state until it encompassed only 55% of the area of Palestine, thus leaving Jaffa and Beersheba and its environs outside the state.

On 29 November 1947 the U.N. Assembly approved the decision to partition Palestine into two states by a majority of thirty-three to thirteen. Britain was to evacuate her troops by 1 August 1948 and to evacuate a port for the absorption of immigrants within the area of the Jewish state before 1 February of that year. The General Assembly elected a committee of five that was entrusted with implementing the Assembly's resolution.

The Yishuv During the Years of Struggle and Decision

During the years of conflict, the Yishuv continued to grow and by the time that statehood was declared, it had a population of 650,000. Settlement activity also continued; despite the White Paper policy, forty-seven agricultural settlements were established during the war years, and from 1945 to 1947 there were an additional forty-seven, of which eleven were founded on the same day – 6 October 1946 – in the Negev, in the hope that this area would be included within the borders of the Jewish state.

Yet the internal conflict did not cease. After relations between the Haganah, the Irgun and Lehi were broken off, the two latter groups intensified their attacks on government and military installations (including police stations and army camps), the oil pipeline and railways. They shot at soldiers and policemen on patrol and kidnapped hostages in order to prevent the execution of their incarcerated comrades. At first, as a result, many of the death sentences passed by the British were mitigated, but as the terrorist activity increased, sentences were carried out. At the beginning of May 1947, Dov Gruner, one of those who had attacked the Ramat Gan police station and who had refused to request clemency, was executed at Acre jail. The proud stand of the Irgun prisoners during their trials aroused considerable emotion in the Yishuv, and the execution aroused stormy reaction. Several days later, the Irgun broke into Acre jail and several dozen of their imprisoned members fled. When three of the participants in this prison-break were arrested and hanged, the Irgun, in retaliation, hanged two British sergeants whom they had taken as hostages. This act aroused fury in Britain, and there were anti-Semitic outbreaks there.

The authorities reacted to the acts of terror by imposing military law on urban Jewish settlements. In Jerusalem fortified areas were set up (referred to, mockingly, by the Jews as 'Bevingrad') as headquarters for army personnel and government officials. The Jewish quarters placed under military control were cut off from their surroundings and supplies. The number of death sentences increased greatly. The British wanted to break the spirit of the Yishuv and to create discord, but they did not succeed. This was the struggle of the entire Yishuv, and it aroused tremendous response both in Jewish communities throughout the world and among many other nations.

The 'organized Yishuv', however, increasingly dissociated itself from the 'dissenters', mainly because of differences of opinion on the measures to be employed to achieve the same objective. The heads of the Jewish Agency and the Haganah claimed that this method of individual terror, with attacks on individual Englishmen, and in particular on civilians, was morally reprehensible and that the hanging of hostages was indefensible. They severely criticized blackmail and bank-robbery as carried out by the Irgun and Lehi. But, above all, this was a dispute on the question of authority. The Jewish Agency claimed that disregarding its authority was damaging to the people's struggle; the 'dissenters', on the other hand, declared that in their consistent and daring struggle they were forcing the leadership to liberate itself from the traditional policy of cooperation with Britain.

There was also an internal struggle within the 'organized Yishuv'. In fact it was a

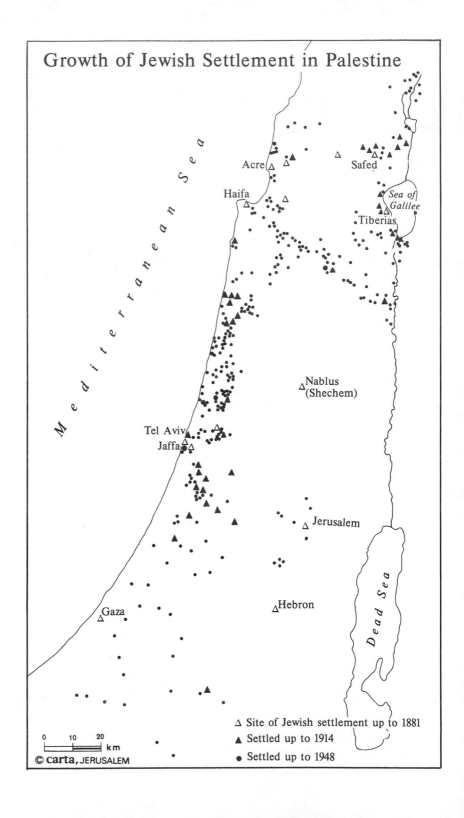

Growth of Jewish Settlement in Palestine

Mediterranean Sea

Acre

Haifa

Safed

Sea of
Galilee

Tiberias

Nablus
(Shechem)

Tel Aviv
Jaffa

Jerusalem

Hebron

Dead Sea

Gaza

0   10   20
‾‾‾‾‾‾‾‾ km
© carta, JERUSALEM

△ Site of Jewish settlement up to 1881
▲ Settled up to 1914
• Settled up to 1948

continuation of the controversy between the supporters and opponents of partition, which had commenced in 1937. Most of the opponents now advocated stepping-up the struggle against Britain. Within Mapai, the Hakibbutz Hame'uḥad element were in the 1930s political activists and evolved their own separate faction (Si'ah Bet – Faction B). Because of this development, the organizational problem became almost more important than the political questions: the majority in Mapai demanded that factions be prohibited. At the Mapai conference in Kefar Vitkin (October 1942) Si'ah Bet, to which one-third of the members belonged, boycotted the deliberations. At the elections to the Sixth Congress of the Histadrut in 1944, Si'ah Bet appeared as an independent party under the name Hatenu'ah le-Aḥdut Ha'avodah (The Movement for Labour Unity); it won some 18% of the general vote, as against Mapai's 56%. Later there was a *rapprochement* between the left-wing groups: Aḥdut Ha'avodah amalgamated with Left Poalei Zion and, in 1947, also with Hashomer Haẓa'ir. The joint left-wing body was known as Mapam (Mifleget Hapoalim Hame'uḥedet, United Workers Party)), and its joint programme included the intensification of resistance to partition, the expansion of Zionist settlement and a pro-Soviet orientation in foreign policy. However, the dividing factors within the party were stronger than the unifying elements.

During the days of struggle it transpired that, despite the break-away of Si'ah Bet, there were still profound differences of opinion within Mapai. Ben-Gurion called for 'militant Zionism' and in this he came close to the view of Aḥdut Ha'avodah; but the latter were distinguished by their negative attitude towards any partition plan. On the other hand, the Ḥever Hakevuẓot element within Mapai feared that the struggle would bring 'disaster on the entire Zionist enterprise.' The spokesman of the moderate element within Mapai, Eliezer Kaplan, led the opponents of Ben-Gurion's policies. Hashomer Haẓa'ir also dissociated itself from any extreme stand in the conflict and advocated moderation ('a constructive attitude') even in resisting the British authorities. This was particularly evident at the Twenty-second Zionist Congress, at which Hashomer Haẓa'ir strongly supported Weizmann, who symbolized the opposition to intensifying the struggle (although Weizmann supported partition, and Hashomer Haẓa'ir was consistently faithful to the idea of a bi-national state).

At this congress the Revisionists rejoined the World Zionist Organization. Weizmann was not re-elected President of the Zionist Organization, but his personality nonetheless dominated the deliberations and resolutions of the congress – to the discomfort of the majority of the 'activists'. In its appearance before UNSCOP, however, and in its political activity at the U.N. General Assembly, the Zionist leadership seemed united in its demand for the establishment of a Jewish state, even if only in part of Palestine.

The War for Independence

While the deliberations were being held at the U.N. General Assembly, the Arabs announced that they would forcibly resist the implementation of partition; Britain declared that she would not support it, nor cooperate in carrying it out. The United

Nations did not possess a military force to impose its authority and implement its resolution. The actual establishment of the Jewish state was therefore the task of the Yishuv in Palestine, with the aid of the Jewish people all over the world.

The day after the U.N. General Assembly resolution of 29 November 1947, the Arabs opened their attack on Jewish transport. They carried out raids and arson in outlying Jewish quarters in the mixed-population towns, and after various onslaughts, such as the murder of thirty-nine Jewish workers at the Haifa refineries, a dividing line was drawn between the Jewish and Arab districts. A 'Liberation Army' was mobilized in the Arab states, and the British did not oppose its entry into Palestine. With the aid of British deserters (or members of a fascist organization), Yugoslav, Polish, and even German, mercenaries, the Arabs began to initiate terror activities against Jewish civilians, and, above all, to plant explosives in the Jewish towns. Dozens of Jews were killed in explosions in Haifa and Jerusalem.

The Jewish force repelled the attacks on the outlying suburbs and isolated settlements, and contact with them was maintained with the aid of armoured cars. Checkposts were set up at the entrance to Jewish suburbs. But in March 1948 the Arabs increased their pressure (until then 1,200 Jews had been killed, half of them civilians), and Jerusalem, the Negev and western Galilee were cut off from the main territory held by the Jews along the coastline. On the political front there was further deterioration: the U.S. delegation to the United Nations announced that it was withdrawing its support for partition and proposed handing the country over to U.N. trusteeship.

In this difficult situation the leaders of the Yishuv and the Haganah decided to take the initiative. They were aided by shipments of arms that began to arrive from Czechoslovakia; these were put to use at the beginning of April in Operation Nahshon to open the road to Jerusalem, which made it possible to bring supplies into the city. At the same time the Arab 'Liberation Army', commanded by Kawakji, concentrated its efforts on capturing Kibbutz Mishmar Ha'emek with the aid of artillery, but in vain. The success of Operation Nahshon and the failure of the Arab onslaught changed the situation.

The Arab population began to flee, fearing the advance of the Jewish units. The flight became a mass exodus after the Irgun attacked the village of Deir Yassin near Jerusalem, where many women and children were killed. The Arab leaders wished to exploit the incident for propaganda purposes and in order to incite the Arab states against the Jews; but the result was a mass flight of the Palestinian Arabs.

In the month between mid-April and mid-May 1948, the Jewish forces made a supreme effort to hold continguous territory, which would be under their control when the British evacuated the country on 15 May, in order to prepare for a possible invasion by the Arab states. In fact, during this month considerable gains were made: Haganah forces took over Haifa after a short but fierce battle, and most of the Arab population left; Tiberias was liberated and thus the road to the settlements in eastern Galilee was opened; Safed, a city with an Arab majority, was captured after breaking the siege that the Arabs had imposed on the Jewish quarters. Its Arab inhabitants together with the volunteers from the neighbouring Arab countries fled. Jewish forces also broke through to western Galilee, and Acre surrendered to the Jewish army on 17 May. On the outskirts of Tel Aviv, Jaffa, which according to the partition plan was to be included in the Arab state, was surrounded and on 13 May surrendered after a joint Haganah and Irgun operation. Of its 70,000 Arabs only 3,000 remained.

The Jewish forces also initiated Operation Har'el in order to capture the strongholds on the road to Jerusalem. This objective was not achieved in full because of the behaviour of the British forces in the city: on 13 April a convoy of doctors and nurses from Hadassah hospital and some faculty from the Hebrew University made its way up to Mount Scopus, in accordance with an agreement with the British military authorities. This convoy was attacked by the Arabs, and its passengers were slaughtered before the eyes of the British forces who stood only a few paces away. They not only did nothing to halt the massacre but prevented Haganah units from extending help to the convoy. This was presumably Arab revenge for the atrocity of Deir Yassin, and the inactivity of the British was hence intended as a manifestation of their sense of justice. This incident aroused fear that the British would hand over the strongholds in Jerusalem to the Arabs. Therefore Operation Har'el was suspended and Palmaḥ units were transferred to Jerusalem to ensure Jewish control there.

In bitter fighting the quarters of Katamon and the German Colony were captured, but in the struggle for Sheikh Jarraḥ the Jewish forces were cut off and suffered heavy losses. The road to Mount Scopus remained closed, nor did the defenders of Jerusalem succeed in maintaining contact with the Eẓyon group of four settlements, which fell into the hands of the Arab Legion. The Kefar Eẓyon settlers were all slaughtered, and members of the other settlements who survived were taken prisoner. In the centre of the city the Jewish forces succeeded, after the completion of the British evacuation, in taking over the fortified 'Bevingrad area' and capturing the suburb of Abu Tor. By mid-May contact had been established between all parts of the country under Jewish rule. Only to the Negev did transports still move along dirt-roads. The convoys to Jerusalem travelled under enemy fire, as the main obstacle, the police fortress near the Latrun monastery, could not be captured because of British assistance to Kawakji's forces.

The Jewish achievements were considerable, but the numerous operations and bitter fighting weakened the forces. Some of the best commanding officers and veteran fighters fell in these battles. Equipment was still scarce. The Jewish army lacked any sort of air and armoured forces, and in mid-May, after the British evacuation, it was confronted not with the Palestinian Arab militia (although Syrian and Iraqi troops were already taking part in the fighting) but with the regular armies of the Arab states, well equipped with artillery, armour and planes.

U.N. attempts to prevent war in Palestine proved fruitless. On 16 April 1948 a special session of the U.N. General Assembly was convened and devoted itself once again to the situation in Palestine. The U.N. committee appointed to implement the partition plan reported to the session on the failure of its efforts; the British had not permitted them to enter Palestine and take control. Britain deliberately plunged the country into a state of chaos, apparently on the assumption that the Jews would not succeed in resisting the Arabs and would request the U.N. to restore British rule. But the Jews did not beg for mercy and the General Assembly was dissolved without passing any new resolutions. It only appointed an official mediator on behalf of the United Nations.

On 12 May 1948, in summing up the debate at the Minhelet Ha'am (People's Administration, then the supreme institution in the Yishuv) David Ben-Gurion reviewed the situation:

> Do we see any real possibility of withstanding the invasion [of the Arab states]? My reply is: If we can enlarge the mobilized manpower by additional recruitment in Palestine and immigration from abroad, if we increase training and acquire equipment partly through our own manufacture and even more by bringing to the country what has been purchased abroad – then we can withstand, and win victory.

The Declaration of Independence and the Arab Invasion

On Friday, 14 May 1948, the leaders of the Yishuv assembled in the Tel Aviv Museum, and David Ben-Gurion read out the Scroll of Independence: '. . . by virtue of our national and intrinsic right and on the strength of the resolution of the United Nations General Assembly we hereby declare the establishment of a Jewish state in Palestine, which shall be known as the State of Israel.' Government of the state of Israel was entrusted to the Provisional State Council (Mo'ezet Hamedinah), which elected the Provisional Government. Immediately after this declaration, the State of Israel was recognized *de facto* by the U.S. Government and both *de facto* and *de jure* by the Soviet Government.

On the following night five Arab armies simultaneously invaded Israel. On 15 May, a cable from the Egyptian Foreign Minister was submitted to the U.N. Security Council announcing that Egyptian forces had begun entering Palestine in order 'to re-establish respect for universal morality and the principles recognized by the U.N.' The Lebanese did not cross the border at Rosh Hanikrah, but entered Malkiyyah and Kadesh Naphtali. The Syrians captured Zemah and attacked the two settlements of Deganyah Alef and Bet. There was bitter fighting here as the kibbutz defenders stood firm against enemy tanks. Despite its superior equipment, the enemy was forced to retreat, leaving armour and ammunition behind. Zemah was restored to the Jewish force, which also took over two settlements previously abandoned – Massadah and Sha'ar Hagolan. The defenders of Kibbutz Ein Gev provided an outstanding example of resolute resistance. But the Syrians succeeded in capturing and destroying the colony of Mishmar Hayarden and took the last of its defenders prisoner. The Iraqis, who operated in the Arab triangle of Nablus-Tulkarem-Jenin, did not meet with success; they tried to advance as far as the Jewish town of Netanyah and to cut the coastal plan in two, but were halted. On the other hand, the Israeli forces captured Jenin (3 June 1948) but were forced to evacuate it.

The Arab Legion proved more successful. After destroying the Ezyon settlements, it entered the Old City of Jerusalem and Latrun. Despite offensives from the New City and the establishment of provisional contact between the two Jewish sections of the city, the defenders of the Jewish quarter of the Old City, who had been totally isolated long before the fighting commenced, were unable to hold out, and they surrendered on 28 May 1948. All were taken prisoner. The Jewish settlements north of Jerusalem were evacuated. The Arab Legion's control of Latrun cut off

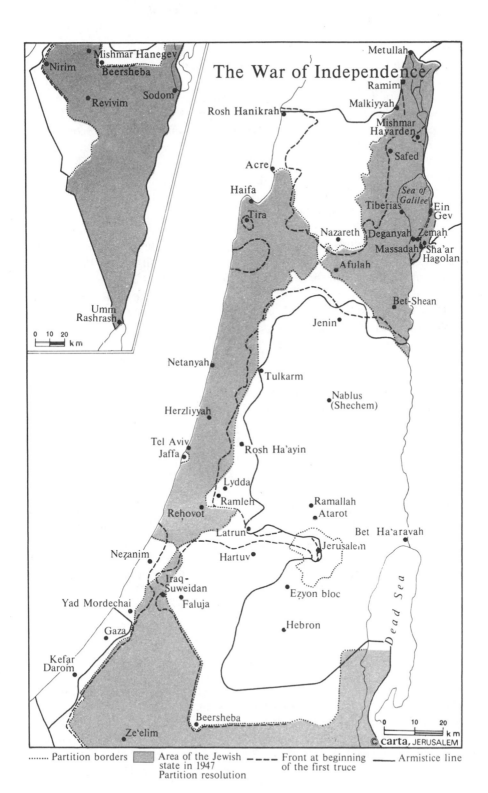

The War of Independence

Mishmar Hanegev
Nirim
Beersheba
Revivim
Sodom

Rosh Hanikrah

Metullah
Ramim
Malkiyyah
Mishmar Hayarden
Safed

Acre
Haifa
Tira

Sea of Galilee
Tiberias
Ein Gev

Nazareth
Deganyah
Zemah
Massadah
Sha'ar Hagolan
Afulah

Bet-Shean

Umm Rashrash

Jenin

Netanyah
Tulkarm

Nablus (Shechem)

Herzliyyah

Tel Aviv
Jaffa
Rosh Ha'ayin

Lydda
Ramleh
Ramallah
Atarot
Rehovot
Bet Ha'aravah
Latrun
Jerusalem
Nezanim
Hartuv
Iraq-Suweidan
Ezyon bloc
Yad Mordechai
Faluja
Gaza
Hebron
Kefar Darom

Dead Sea

Beersheba
Ze'elim

0 10 20
km

© carta, JERUSALEM

.... Partition borders [ ] Area of the Jewish state in 1947 Partition resolution ---- Front at beginning of the first truce ——— Armistice line the road joining Jerusalem. Food supplies did not get through, and the water pipeline from Rosh Ha'ayin was cut off. The city was in a state of siege, and water and food were rationed out by the Civil Defense.

The Jewish part of Jerusalem was heavily bombarded by the Arab Legion, and there was considerable loss of life among the civilian population. The Legion launched heavy attacks on the nearby settlement of Ramat Raḥel and on Mount Scopus, but these were repelled. On the other hand, three Israeli attempts to capture Latrun failed and incurred heavy loss of life. The Legion tried to attack the settlement of Ma'aleh Haḥamishah and to safeguard its strongholds near Jerusalem, but they failed. At that time contact with the city was re-established through the 'Burma Road', a dirt-track that bypassed Latrun.

On the Egyptian front heavy battles raged in the Negev and on the outskirts of Tel Aviv. The Egyptians underestimated the importance of the Jewish settlements, and the heroic stand of Negbah, Kefar Darom and Nirim disrupted their plans. There were heavy losses in the battle for the Negev, and two Jewish settlements, Yad Mordechai and Neẓanim, fell to the enemy, but the Egyptian armoured column was halted at Ashdod and was unable to break through to Tel Aviv. The most important achievement of the Egyptians was to cut off the Jewish settlements in the Negev; this was made possible after they had taken over the police station of Iraq-Suweidan, which the British had handed over to the Arabs at the time of the evacuation. The many Jewish attempts to capture it before the first truce failed.

Such was the situation on the various fronts when the truce arranged by the U.N. mediator came into force – after several delays – on 11 June. The battles had lasted less than four weeks from the day of invasion to the first cease-fire, but they had been of tremendous value for the consolidation of the state. Mobilization was completed, and on 31 May an Order of the Day was published by Defence Minister Ben-Gurion to create the Israel Defence Forces (I.D.F.). On 1 June the Irgun announced its disbandment throughout the country (with the exception of Jerusalem) and the enlistment of its members in the I.D.F., but in separate units. During these weeks arms purchased abroad began to flow into the country. The foundation of the Israel Air Force and Navy was laid. Immigrants arrived, and, after a short training period, they were sent to the front-line; volunteers also came from abroad. Amidst the bitter fighting the State of Israel demonstrated its vitality and resolve. Its army did not retreat on any of the long and winding fronts.

From the First Truce to the Signing of the Armistice Agreements

The cease-fire created an opportunity for rest and reorganization for the weary I.D.F. units. But in these very days of lull, the country was involved in stormy conflict. With the arrival on 20 June of an Irgun ship, the *Altalena,* which brought hundreds of volunteers and a large quantity of arms to the Israeli coast, the Irgun laid down various conditions regarding the ownership of these arms. The government decided to employ military force. It seems that the government decided to demonstrate that in military matters there was only one single authority. There were bloody clashes, which lasted several days and claimed a number of victims. The *Altalena,* which had arrived at Netanyah, sailed from there south to Tel Aviv, and the Irgun attempted to mobilize its supporters in order to unload the arms. Several shots fired at the ship from a cannon set it on fire. Those aboard jumped into the water, and some of them drowned. The hatred that had begun to die down after the disbandment of the Irgun now flared anew. But government control in both the military and the political sphere was safeguarded. The separate battalions of Irgun members, which still existed within the framework of the I.D.F., were now disbanded.

The U.N. mediator, Count Folke Bernadotte from Sweden, tried to exploit the lull in the fighting in order to find a new basis for a political settlement. Adopting a line similar to that of the British, he tried to replace the U.N. resolution of 29 November with one that would limit the sovereignty and borders of the Jewish state. He proposed that the Negev be handed over to the Arabs in return for the annexation of Galilee by the Jewish state; that the Negev and all the territory earmarked for an Arab state be annexed to Transjordan; and that Haifa port be placed under international control. He also suggested the political amalgamation of the Jewish state with greater Transjordan and entrusting supervision of Jewish immigration to the U.N. Both sides rejected this plan. His proposal that the truce be extended for another thirty days was also rejected by the Arabs, and they renewed the fighting. In actual fact, the mediator only succeeded in creating a control network of U.N. observers, which determined the arrangements for demilitarizing Mount Scopus.

The truce expired on 9 July. The fighting raged for only ten days, until the second truce was declared. At this point the battle was clearly going in Israel's favour. During the ten days Nazareth was captured, and the I.D.F. positions in Galilee were reinforced. On the central front the towns of Lydda and Ramleh were captured in a daring operation, and the Jerusalem corridor was widened, but attempts to capture the Latrun police fortress and to break into the Old City of Jerusalem met with failure. In the south, despite heavy fighting, Israeli forces did not manage to open a secure route to the Negev, and the Egyptians continued to hold their main positions.

The second truce came into effect when the Security Council passed a resolution threatening sanctions against the side that did not obey. Bernadotte again proposed territorial change to Israel's disadvantage and safeguarding the rights of Arab refugees to return to their homes, if they so desired, with no conditions attached. The day after submitting his report to the U.N., Bernadotte was murdered in Jewish Jerusalem by members of the 'Homeland Front', a group founded by Leḥi. The assassination antagonized world public opinion; the government ordered the Irgun in Jerusalem to disband and arrested some 200 members of Leḥi.

One of the main clauses in Bernadotte's recommendations was the annexation of the Negev to Transjordan. The Israel government therefore regarded it as a matter of vital urgency to fortify its positions in the south and, above all, to open up the road to the isolated Negev. Since the Egyptians, in violation of the truce conditions, refused to permit the passage of Israeli convoys to the Negev, the I.D.F. planned to break through. This action was known as Operation Yoav. On 15 October 1948 a convoy set out for the Negev, after the U.N. headquarters had been notified of its departure. The Egyptians opened fire on the convoy and this provocation served as the pretext for an Israeli attack. At first it was repelled, but when Israeli forces succeeded in cutting off the coastal road behind the Egyptian front-lines, the latter began to retreat. The Egyptian force at Faluja was cut off. Eventually, on 20 October, the road to the Negev was cleared, and on the same day an attack was instigated on Beersheba, which was captured on the following day. On 22 October, by order of the Security Council, the fighting ceased.

Kawakji exploited the Negev battles to open a sudden onslaught on Kibbutz Ramim (Manarah) in the north. The Israeli reaction came in the form of Operation Hiram on 28 and 19 October. In this operation, Kawakji's 'Liberation Army' was wiped out and the Galilee was almost entirely freed of Arab forces. The Negev fighting also continued, and on 9 November 1948 the police station of Iraq-Suweidan was finally captured. At the end of December, operations commenced for the final expulsion of the Egyptian forces from Palestine. The I.D.F. attacked Abu Ageila and El Arish and entered the Sinai Peninsula, which was under Egyptian rule. But as a result of a British ultimatum and a warning from the U.S. President, a retreat was ordered. On 7 January 1949 a cease-fire was declared in this region. At the beginning of March, the I.D.F. reached the Red Sea and captured the entire shore of the Dead Sea from Sodom to Ein Gedi.

On 12 January 1949 armistice talks between Israel and the Arab states opened at Rhodes; they were conducted by the acting mediator, Ralph Bunche. Discussions continued at intervals for a long time. The first agreement was signed with Egypt on 14 February, and, according to this document, the encircled Egyptian troops at Faluja – which included a young batallion commander named Abdul Nasser – were permitted to leave; the Egyptian force was obliged to retreat behind the El Arish-Abu Ageila line. The Gaza Strip remained in Egyptian hands. A mixed commission was established to supervise the armistice. On 23 March an agreement was signed with Lebanon. On 3 April 1949 an armistice agreement was signed with Transjordan, under which the entire railway line to Jerusalem was to be in Israeli hands. Accordingly, the I.D.F. entered several Arab villages south of Jerusalem and several villages in Wadi Ara and in the vicinity of Tulkarem. On the other hand Israeli territories in the Mount Hebron area were evacuated and handed over to Transjordan. Other obligations included in the agreement with the Jordanians were the possibility of free access for Jews to the Western Wall and Mount Scopus and the opening of a section of the Jerusalem-Tel Aviv road in the Latrun area, which was under the control of the Arab Legion, to Israel vehicular traffic. The armistice agreement with Syria was signed only on 20 July, after negotiations that lasted three and a half months. Iraq signed no agreement with Israel.

The area of the State of Israel within the borders of the armistice agreements included some 80% of the area of mandatory western Palestine. According to the declared aim, 'the establishment of an armistice between the armed forces of both sides is accepted as an essential step towards liquidation of the armed dispute and restoration of peace to Palestine'. In theory Israel now had sovereignty over agreed and secure borders, determined by negotiations between the sides, and with the support and approval of the Security Council. Yet, despite her impressive achievements, Israel had not achieved security and tranquillity.

69

The Diaspora After the Second World War

Changes in Jewish Geographical Dispersion

Two decisive events in Jewish history – the Holocaust and the establishment of the State of Israel – completely changed the image of the Jewish people. Of the eleven or twelve million Jews left in the world after the Holocaust, half lived on the American continent. Only one-third remained in Europe and the Soviet Union, and, of these, some 250,000 were located in the Displaced Persons camps in Germany and Austria. The great majority of the surviving Jews of Eastern Europe did not return to their pre-war homes: the rural settlements had been completely wiped out, the *shtetl* and smaller towns abandoned; the Jewish population concentrated mainly in a few urban centres; many remained in central Russia and in the places to which they had been evacuated during the war, in the eastern parts of the U.S.S.R.

The political tension in the Middle East, which resulted from the Second World War, also left its mark. Some of the Arab nationalist movements, and particularly the supporters of the Jerusalem Mufti, collaborated openly with the Fascist countries and even participated in plans for the extermination of the Jews. Popular sympathy in the Arab countries was directed towards the Axis countries. In addition, the political struggle with Britain, which the Yishuv had initiated in 1945, exacerbated the relations between Jews and Arabs in the Middle East. The establishment of the State of Israel and the Arab onslaught transformed the tension between the two peoples into open warfare, and the situation of Jews in the Arab countries became intolerable. Most of them were forced to leave their age-old homes.

As a result, some million and a half Jews were confronted with the problem of finding a new haven. In the first ten years of its existence, the State of Israel absorbed some 850,000 of these Jews, while some 150,000 went to the United States; the remainder settled in Central and West European countries, some remaining on the fringes of society.

Changes in Jewish Social Structure

The decisive factor in the effect of the socio-economic situation was the concentration of the Jews in countries with a high standard of economic and cultural development. Before the Second World War, some 8.5 out of the 10 million Jews of Europe had been residing in the backward countries of Eastern Europe and in the developing Soviet Union. Together with the 300,000 Jews of Asia (not including Palestine), the 500,000 Jews of Africa and 400,000 in Latin America, some two-thirds of the Jewish people lived in relatively backward countries. After the war, the Jews of the United States and Canada, the Soviet Union and Western Europe constituted approximately three-quarters of the Jews of the Diaspora; in other words, the great majority of the Jewish people lived in advanced countries, which increased the attraction towards assimilation into the non-Jewish society and culture.

The great majority of the Jews ceased to speak Yiddish and adopted the languages of their countries of residence. On the other hand, under the impact of the establishment of the State of Israel, there was an increase in the number of Hebrew-speakers even among Jews in the Diaspora. In Jewish institutions of education, and even within the non-Jewish universities and secondary schools in the West, the teaching of Hebrew and interest in Jewish culture began to play a more important part. Thus, in this period, there have been conflicting processes: on the one hand, cultural assimilation and integration into the gentile world, and, on the other hand, a renewed sense of unity and an increasing interest in the cultural traditions of the Jewish people.

The direct consequence of cultural assimilation was a rise in the number of young Jews who acquired a university education. But only in the 1950s and 1960s did this become the dominant trend in Jewish life. Against the background of mass entry to institutions of higher learning in America and Europe (between one-quarter and one-third of the youth), it is significant to note the fact that in the United States and the Soviet Union 75–80% of young Jews study at such institutions. This phenomenon has affected both the occupational structure of the Jews, their Jewish self-consciousness and their role in the life of the countries of their residence.

Although there are no precise statistics for this period as regards the occupational structure of the Jews in various countries, certain significant facts are known, *e.g.,* the almost total disappearance of Jewish farmers in the Diaspora. The Jewish colonies in southern Russia and the Crimea were wiped out by the Nazis; in Birobidzhan and Argentina most of the younger generation abandoned the colonies, so that, with the exception of Israel, there are almost no Jewish farmers in the world. The Jewish working class, which at the beginning of the twentieth century constituted an active section of the people, dwindled considerably. The sons of these workers found their way to secondary schools and higher institutions of learning and became physicians, engineers, teachers, economists, etc. Even those who remained in their old occupations for the most part became skilled workers or managers. The number of shop assistants and junior clerks has gradually dropped, and there is an increasingly large number of accountants, economic and commercial directors; there is now a particularly large number of Jewish scientists in various spheres.

The Role of Jews in the Surrounding Society

This process has been reflected in the activity of Jews in the life of the society around them. The number of Jews in research, technological development, mass media, literature, music and the plastic arts far exceeds their proportion in the population or even their percentage of the urban community – to which, as in the preceding era, most Jews belong. There can be no doubt that the movement of Jews towards higher education, science and cultural activity emerges to no small extent from their urban nature and their concentration in the larger towns and cities. But it derives no less from the tradition of study and intellectual activity, which always characterized the Jews, and the readiness of Jewish parents, however poor, to make great sacrifices in order to provide their children with a good education. All the obstacles placed in the path of young Jews – such as discrimination in admissions to certain universities in the United States in the 1920s and 1930s and the persecutions in the Soviet Union during the last years of Stalin's life and for some time afterwards – could not check their determination to acquire a higher education.

In the advanced industrial countries, scientific research and technological development became an economic and political factor of the highest importance; hence the growing value of Jews to these societies. All countries now appreciate the contribution of their Jewish scientists, and the steep decline of German science as a result of the dismissal of Jews from scientific institutions in Hitler's day served as a lesson.

In the Middle Ages and the era of developing capitalism, Jews gained some degree of tolerance because of their activity in the spheres of finance and administration; but after the Second World War they were appreciated for their outstanding scientific and cultural achievements. In the eighteenth and the first half of the nineteenth centuries, when very few Jews integrated in their surroundings and they were regarded for the most part as contemptible, uncultured and lacking in finesse – as the culture and manners of the Jews were alien to their surroundings and condemned by Jewish intellectuals – the Jews themselves regarded their origin and spiritual heritage as a disability and endeavoured to escape, to conceal, or to condemn them. However, once the Jews had attained distinction in areas vital to society, all this changed. They began to accept the fact of their Jewishness, even experiencing a certain pride in the historical and cultural heritage of their people. As a result, they began to stress their Jewish identity and solidarity as something self-evident and natural. Hence the further paradox that, despite the increasing integration of the Jews in the lives of other nations, their Jewish consciousness remained generally unaffected, unweakened and sometimes even reinforced.

The Old and New Centres

The post-Second World War Diaspora can be divided into two clear sections: (1) the new Jewish communities, created at the end of the nineteenth and beginning of the twentieth centuries by the great migration movement to North and South America, South Africa and Australia, and, to a less extent, to Western Europe, particularly Britain, France and Switzerland; and (2) the old communities – some of the established Jews of England, Germany and the Netherlands, the Jews of Italy and, for the most part, those of Eastern Europe, the Middle East and North Africa.

The great majority of the Jews of the Arab countries and Eastern Europe (apart from the Soviet Union) emigrated to Israel. Most of the Jews of the North African

Arab countries left – some for Israel and some for France; the French Jewish community thus grew considerably. Many Jews also left Turkey and Iran for Israel. Of the 13.5 million Jews in the world at the end of the 1960s, some six million were living in North America, some three-quarters of a million in South and Central America, and about 200,000 in South Africa and Australia. All in all there were some seven million Jews in the new communities, and with the addition of two and a half million in Israel, this made more than two-thirds of the people.

There were approximately three million Jews in Eastern Europe – only a quarter of a million of them outside the Soviet Union. This population centre had been more drastically reduced than any other area in the Diaspora during modern times. The number of Jews in the Arab states of the Near East and North Africa also dropped radically, and only about 250,000 Jews remained. In Western Europe there are more than one million Jews, more than half a million in France and some 400,000 in Britain.

The Jewish Centre in the United States

The Jewish community in the United States, which is the largest of all, fulfils a vital function in Jewish life. The aid of U.S. Jewry to the young State of Israel in its struggle for survival, in consolidating its security, developing its economy and absorbing immigrants, was tremendous. Jewish aid organizations, led by the Joint, which in the twenties and thirties had extended support to Jewish settlement projects in various countries (including the Soviet Union), for vocational training of Jewish youth and the support of persecuted Jewish communities, directed their main efforts after the war at rehabilitating the survivors of the Holocaust. The United Jewish Appeal, which was established in 1939, allocated money both to Israel for the rehabilitation of Jewish communities in Eastern Europe and for the Jews persecuted or expelled by the Arab countries.

The fate of European Jewry under Hitler aroused the consciousness of U.S. Jewry, and this found striking expression in May and June of 1967, when the Arab rulers declared that the time had come 'to wipe Israel off the map and throw the Jews into the sea'. A tremendous wave of solidarity with Israel, which was now threatened with extinction, engulfed all the Jewish communities and democratic parties and organizations all over the world. But it found its strongest echo among the Jews of the United States.

The emergence of the Jewish nationalist movement in the U.S.S.R and the obstacles that the Soviet authorities have put before Jewish emigration have brought a new outburst of activity among American Jews. As a result, public opinion in the United States strongly supported the struggle of Soviet Jews for their right to emigrate and for their national existence within the U.S.S.R.

When the Arabs attacked Israel in October 1973, the solidarity of American Jewry with Israel and its political, moral and material support became a most important factor in Israel's struggle for survival. All these developments refuted the claims that American Jewry was disintegrating.

The resurgence was also felt in the communal sphere. Numerous Jewish organizational bodies developed cultural and social activity. The number of pupils attending special Jewish schools has increased from 230,000 in 1946 to 553,000 and is still rising. At these schools emphasis is placed on the study of the Hebrew language and Jewish subjects. In more than 100 universities in the United States, there are special courses and departments of Jewish Studies. Of particular importance in disseminating Jewish education are the many summer camps for Jewish youth and the arrangements between many American and Israeli universities, under which American students may spend one year in Israel studying Hebrew and Jewish subjects. The strengthening of Jewish consciousness has left its mark on general American culture – problems of Jewish history, the Jewish cultural tradition, the psychological conflicts of Jews in non-Jewish society have found expression in American culture through literature, art, the theatre and television. American Jews whose work gives expression to Jewish problems include Saul Bellow, Bernard Malamud and Philip Roth in fiction, Arthur Miller in the theatre, Ben Shahn in art and Leonard Bernstein in music.

Under such conditions it is obvious that most young Jews do not find it a discomfort to be Jewish, and young people are replacing the older generation in the leadership of American Jewry. Yet this very sense of ease has, for many, obscured the unique traits of Judaism. Cultural assimilation has led to a superficial attitude towards the Jewish cultural and religious heritage. There has been an increase in the number of mixed marriages and there is a growing detachment from Jewish life and problems. Political and moral radicalism have also had their impact and led many young Jews to try to 'change the world' within the framework of American society as a whole rather than within the supposedly separatist framework of Jewish society. Sometimes this takes the form of a militant opposition to the Jewish establishment, or anti-Israel propaganda. Thus both centrifugal and centripetal trends continue to operate simultaneously within the American Jewish community.

Other New Centres

In the countries of South America, particularly Argentina, Brazil and Uruguay, the immigrant Yiddish culture remains alive, but here too it is on the decline. There are schools in Yiddish and Hebrew, but most of the young generation has grown up immersed in Spanish culture. The activities of Jewish bodies and of Jewish youth associations are extensive, and the Jewish communities are well organized and strong. The intensification of anti-Semitism, which was brought to these countries by those Nazis or Fascists who fled from Europe after the war, as well as by the emissaries of Arab organizations (in South America there are many Arab communities), has strengthened Jewish solidarity and cooperation between diverse Jewish bodies. Some of the young Jews in South America have emigrated to Israel, not so much because of anti-Semitic pressures, as in search of Jewish identity. The framework of communal life in kibbutzim has proved very attractive to many groups of young people. The high rate of departure from the Jewish agricultural colonies in Argentina, which were once flourishing and densely populated (they now have a population of only 8,000), has also had its effect: a number of the settlers' sons have chosen to live in Israeli kibbutzim. During the Six Day War, a wave of national resurgence overwhelmed the Jews of South America and many students abandoned their studies and volunteered to aid Israel. But there too the non-Jewish surroundings exert their attraction; particularly influential is the militant social radicalism, such as that of Castro, which takes young Jews away from Jewish matters and activities.

In Western Europe, as we have noted, there are two comparatively large Jewish centres in Britain and France. British Jews, mostly the sons and grandsons of immigrants from Eastern Europe, have completely assimilated into the cultural life of their country, and they play a prominent role, particularly in the spheres of economics and science. The fact that many important Jewish scientists, refugees from Hitler, settled in Britain, has been of great significance. Here too there is increasing interest in Jewish culture, and the number of pupils in Jewish schools has risen. Several writers and playwrights of Jewish origin (their number and impact is considerable) give expression either explicitly or indirectly to the problems and conditions of Jewish life. Anglo-Jewry is closely bound up with Israel, and the communities are well organized. It played an extraordinary role in the support of Soviet Jews, and its help to Israel after the Yom Kippur War was relatively strong. This community differs from that of the United States in that there is still a high percentage of self-employed Jews engaging in commerce and the liberal professions (some two-thirds of the total). Most of the wage-earners are white-collar workers, and only some 10% engage in manual labour.

The same does not hold true for France, which has always been a country of extensive assimilation. The established Jewish community includes many who play important roles in French life, but most are now remote from all Jewish affairs. Their ranks were swelled between the wars by young Jews from Eastern Europe who came to France to study at universities there. After the Second World War, refugees from the Nazi camps of various European countries settled there. In the fifties and sixties, after the upsurge of Arab nationalism, some 200,000 Jews arrived in France from North Africa. The two latter groups reconsolidated the Jewish communities and strengthened Jewish consciousness. In certain circles, particularly among students, there has been increasing interest in Jewish values and culture. But French Jewry only emerged as a vital factor in the Jewish world during the Six Day War, in the summer of 1967.

When the De Gaulle government, which till then had supplied Israel with most of its military equipment and declared Israel to be its 'friend and ally', betrayed her on the eve of the war by imposing an embargo on arms shipments and courting the Arabs, French Jewry organized public demonstrations on behalf of Israel's peace and security. The cream of France's intellectual, liberal and socialist forces supported this movement. French Jewry raised financial aid for Israel and sent over volunteers. Interest in Israeli problems and Jewish history increased. In November 1967, De Gaulle attempted to weaken French public sympathy for Israel by employing the classic weapon of anti-Semites; he hinted that support for Israel implied disloyalty towards France and stated that the Jews had always been an 'overbearing and domineering' people. But this appeal to the reactionary Right and to anti-Semitic instincts latent in certain circles of the French population did not change the feelings of French Jews nor those of most of the enlightened general public.

French Jews also took part in the campaign in defence of Soviet Jews and the support of Israel after the Yom Kippur War in 1973. The Jewish community in France remains in the 1970s a lively part of the Jewish people.

The Decline of Old Centres

In contrast to this situation in the new centres, organized Jewish life is steadily dwindling in the Arab countries and in Eastern Europe. Most of the Jews have left, the great majority for Israel. Jewish activity in the early seventies continues only in Rumania and Hungary. About 100,000 Jews remained in Rumania. There are still religious communities with a chief rabbi, religious institutions, Jewish cultural institutions, publications and a Yiddish theatre. In Hungary, too, which has a Jewish population of nearly 70,000, there is organized Jewish life, a rabbinical seminary and various communal and cultural institutions. An active Union of Jewish Communities continues to exist in Yugoslavia, though the number of Jews there is no more than a few thousand.

The Jewish Communities of the Soviet Union and Its Satellites

The Jews of the Soviet Union have been singled out for a special destiny. After the Holocaust, in which at least two million Jews were slaughtered, changes began to appear in the government's policy towards the Jews. As we have noted, during the war itself, large sections of the population of the Ukraine, Lithuania, Moldavia and White Russia collaborated in the mass extermination. After the war anti-Semitic feeling endured in these areas. On the other hand, the Jews of Russia underwent a process of national awakening during the war. Even those among them who had totally assimilated into Russian culture and had moved away from Jewish life began to sense the depths of the tragedy of their people and gave it expression in their work (see, for example, a poem by Pavel Antokolski, published in the journal *Znamia* in 1946). This aroused the anger of Stalin and his associates, and in early 1949, a campaign was launched against the 'cosmopolitans', 'people without origin or affiliation', 'those who advocate bowing down to the West' and similar accusations of anti-Semitic intent. The names of writers, critics and journalists of Jewish origin who had russified their names were printed with the original names in brackets. At a meeting of the plenum of the Executive of the Writers Association, the writer Constantine Simonov viciously attacked the 'cosmopolitans' (the claim that 'cosmopolitanism' expressed the Jewish spirit was first put forward in 1879 by the historian Heinrich von Treitschke, one of the fathers of modern anti-Semitism). The 'black' years' of Russian Jewry had commenced; they were to end only with the death of Stalin.

There can be no doubt that this new trend was lent momentum by the establishment of the State of Israel. The heroic stand of the Yishuv in the years 1945–7 aroused great enthusiasm among the Jews of the Soviet Union. A lecture on the Middle Eastern situation, delivered at the Moscow Popular University in the sum-

among certain intellectual circles. But the attitude of the authorities was reflected in Khrushchev's speech of March 1963, in which he attacked Ehrenburg and Yevtushenko and related an anecdote (which later turned out to be a fabrication) about a Jewish translator who had served with the Nazi General Paulus as proof of the fact that the Jews, like other nations, were divided into opponents and supporters of Hitler and that some of them even collaborated with the Nazis. It is clear that this despicable libel was aimed at encouraging (and indeed did encourage) those who had in fact collaborated with the Nazis to increased anti-Semitic activity in the Soviet Union. Hence it is clear why Trofim Kitchko, a Ukrainian who himself apparently collaborated with the Nazis during the war, was declared to be an 'expert' on Jewish affairs on behalf of the Ukrainian Academy of Sciences. His book *Judaism Unembellished* is a compilation of anti-Semitic slanders and lies drawn even from eighteenth- and nineteenth-century German and French anti-Semitic literature and from Nazi literature, under the guise of an attack on religion. Such anti-religious literature, which was distributed in hundreds of thousands of copies, certainly was not intended nor was capable of persuading believing Jews that their faith was groundless, but it was aimed at providing an allegedly scientific justification for those anti-Semites who claimed that Judaism had always been 'the most reactionary of religions' and that the Jews were 'the enemies of the human race'.

The incitement against Zionism and the State of Israel and the *Der Stuermer*-like cartoons reached their height during the Six Day War. The threats publicly voiced by the Syrian and Egyptian leaders regarding 'the hour of revenge' and 'the extermination of Israel' were declared to be 'the exaggerations of private individuals'; the concentration of tens of thousands of Egyptian soldiers in Sinai with hundreds of tanks and guns, the arbitrary and one-sided expulsion of the U.N. force from the Egyptian-Israeli border, and the closing of the Tiran Straits, an international waterway, were explained as 'defensive measures'. But Israel's self-defence against these extermination schemes was depicted as 'Israeli aggression'. The hundreds of aircraft, tanks, guns and rockets that the Soviet Union sent the Arab states (and their value is estimated by military experts at $1 billion) were not mentioned. A story was spread of a plot between the United States, West Germany and Israel for an attack on the Arab states. This distorted propaganda, which was probably greeted with total disbelief by the enlightened section of Russian public opinion, undoubtedly served as an efficient instrument for anti-Semitic incitement in the Soviet Union.

All these developments, however, had an opposite effect on Soviet Jewry, which had already learned its bitter lesson. As in previous periods of national suppression, there was an intensification of national sentiment and Jewish identity. The tens of thousands of young Jews who flock to the synagogues in the large towns on Jewish festivals in order to proclaim their affiliation to the Jewish people provide overwhelming proof of the fact that the suppression of Jewish national feeling has been unsuccessful. Among Soviet Jewish youth there has been an upsurge of interest in Jewish history and creativity. This has led to a resurgence of the Jewish nationalist movement in the U.S.S.R. and the struggle for the right to emigrate to Israel, which began after the Six Day War. This movement came as a surprise not only to the Soviet authorities but also to the majority of outside observers – Jewish and non-

Jewish alike, who considered Soviet Jewry to be a completely assimilated group. Soviet officials started a campaign of suppression and intimidation, but the dramatic appeal of eighteen Georgian Jewish families to the United Nations to help them in their struggle for emigration made a great impression on world public opinion.

A turning-point in the development of the Zionist movement in the U.S.S.R. was the trial of a group of Leningrad Jews, arrested in June 1970 for an attempt to hijack a plane and to leave for Israel. This trial was followed by other trials of Jewish activists in Leningrad, Riga and Kishinev. The severe punishments, including two death sentences, agitated wide circles outside the Soviet Union and created a world-wide protest movement against the treatment of Jews in the U.S.S.R. Under the pressure of public opinion, the Soviet authorities opened the gates of their country for Jewish emigration, but harassment and intimidation of potential emigrants did not cease. In the summer of 1972 the Soviet authorities imposed a special tax on emigrants – heavy payments as recompense for higher education and academic degrees; but after severe criticism and protests abroad this demand was tacitly abandoned.

In 1972 and 1973 more than 30,000 Jews left the U.S.S.R. each year, and the sum total for the years 1968–74 was about 100,000 emigrants. During the Yom Kippur War of 1973 and in the following months, emigration even increased. During these years Jewish activists had found new ways to express their protest against the inimical and oppressive policy of the authorities – letters and petitions sent abroad, delegations, sit-in strikes, hunger strikes – and threats, trials and imprisonment of Zionists did not diminish their demand for free emigration.

A sharp decline in the number of emigrants began at the end of 1974. It came as a result of the change in the attitude of the Soviet authorities after the passing of the Jackson amendment in the U.S. Senate, which made commercial preference of the U.S.S.R conditional upon free emigration from the country. This brought a new wave of suppression against Jews desiring to emigrate. In addition to the renewed Arab threats of war against Israel and the difficulties in absorbing new immigrants there, it brought emigration to a low ebb. After their arrival at the transfer centre in Vienna, many did not continue on to Israel, but chose to settle elsewhere.

The emigration crisis does not seem to have brought about a decline in the nationalist movement within the U.S.S.R. The social and national conflicts in the Soviet Union, which increased social anti-Semitism and governmental discrimination of Jews, are inherent to the Soviet regime. The interest among Soviet Jews in Jewish affairs continues, and the activity of Jewish nationalists remains on the increase. Though it is impossible to estimate the number of Soviet Jews who want to emigrate or those who identify as Zionists or nationalists, the growing suspicion of wide circles of the population, incited by the mass media, that all the Jews are disloyal to the Soviet Union is making the great majority of Jews, and even part-Jews, aware of their identity. In effect, Soviet conditions are fostering Jewish nationalism.

The Similarity in Development Trends

The trends in social and cultural development in the various Jewish communities are actually very similar, despite the differences in the form of government and in social relations. Some of the communities have grown stronger and expanded, while others are on the decline, but characteristic of them all are linguistic and cultural assimilation coupled with Jewish loyalty and interest in their spiritual heritage; a growing importance in the life of the various nations, yet a separate group affiliation; social and political activity in their places of residence, but a strong attachment to Israel. These traits characterize all Jewish communities, including the Soviet Union.

70

The Consolidation of the State of Israel

Two basic facts have determined the development of the young State of Israel: mass immigration, which flooded into the country immediately after its establishment and brought hundreds of thousands of Jews from different countries, united in religion, historical origin and emotional identity, but separated by language and habits, standard of living and way of life, as well as social and cultural values; and the unceasing hostility of the Arabs, their unwillingness to accept the existence of the state, their attempt to harm it in every possible way, which has created within the population of Israel a sensation of being under constant siege. Immigration served as a diversifying factor, creating tensions and undermining the stability of Israeli society, while Arab hostility was a cohesive, stimulating factor, strengthening solidarity. Immigration produced a tension between the veterans and newcomers, between 'Europeans' and 'Orientals', between the formulators of policy and the white-collar workers, between the labourers and the welfare recipients. The Arab siege and the security threat created a sense of shared destiny, a bond between the individual and the community, and the need for speedy development of the state. Nevertheless, there can be no doubt that immigration was regarded by all as a vital need for the state – its strength and the basis of its existence and future development. There was popular support for encouraging immigration and its absorption as a matter of life and death for the young state, and the acceptance of the 'integration of the communities' was proclaimed as one of the main social and cultural objectives.

The 'Ingathering of the Exiles' and the Liquidation of Diaspora Communities

The mass immigration in the first years of statehood was the result of pressure exerted by Jews waiting in D.P. camps in Germany and Cyprus and of refugees from Eastern Europe and from the Arab countries. It was aimed at fulfilling the Basle Programme, the central aim of Zionism, *i.e.,* 'the creation of a safe refuge for the Jewish people in Palestine'. Furthermore, the very establishment of the State of Israel and international support for this act came from the recognition that there was no other place for Jewish refugees, and the disturbing realization that had such a refuge existed in the 1930s at least part of European Jewry might have been saved.

But above and beyond these considerations, it was clear that in order to maintain a self-supporting entity, a state capable of defending itself and developing its land and society, there was need for a considerable increase in population, and, in fact, there were new immigrants in 1948 who were sent straight from the ship to the front-line.

The first immigrants were the inmates of the Cyprus and German camps. Immediately afterwards came the immigration of the Jews from Arab lands. By the end of 1950, some 45,000 Yemenite Jews had arrived – gathered from their places of residence to Aden whence they were flown to Israel in what was called 'Operation Magic Carpet'. In 1950–1 some 122,000 (out of a total of 130,000) Iraqi Jews immigrated. Several of the more ancient communities were almost emptied – 30,000 (out of 35,000) immigrated from Libya, 37,000 (out of 45,000) from Bulgaria. By the end of 1951, 104,000 had arrived from Poland and 119,000 from Rumania. All in all, immigrants in the first three and a half years of statehood totalled 685,000 persons, of whom 304,000 came from Eastern Europe. The Yishuv doubled its population in this period.

The absorption of immigration at this rate was a tremendous task. The new arrivals were greeted with enthusiasm and as part of the 'Ingathering of the Exiles'. The Knesset passed the Law of Return, which proclaimed that 'every Jew has the right to immigrate' (1950). But grave problems – economic, social, medical and psychological – soon emerged. The total liquidation of certain communities brought to Israel among others the sick, the disabled, criminals and welfare cases. There were young people who had spent most of their lives in camps. There were immigrants who had been torn away from mediaeval frameworks and flung headlong into advanced, modern conditions. Social relations, family hierarchies, ancient and hallowed patterns of behaviour were undermined before there was time to adopt new ones to replace them. The veteran Yishuv was confronted with the 'Second Israel', and there was an estrangement between the two. Many of the immigrants from Eastern and Central Europe, and particularly the younger generation, were totally divorced from Jewish culture and tradition, and from Zionist concepts.

The immigrants were settled in the abandoned Arab villages and towns, and when these had reached the saturation point, *ma'abarot,* or provisional urban settlements near urban centres, were established. Only a small percentage of immigrants were directed to agricultural settlement, but even these were different in quality from those who had been absorbed by the kibbutz movement after undergoing pioneering training. The kibbutz had no attraction for immigrants of this type. New settlements, into which immigrants from various countries were assembled in order to accelerate the process of integrating the different communities, experienced conflict and mass departures. Many immigrants left the agricultural settlements and drifted into urban slums.

The financial burden that rested on the young state as a result of the mass immigration was immense, and the security expenditure was simultaneously increasing because of Arab hostility. Israel's dependence on the financial aid of world Jewry, which had been considerable during the War of Independence, became even greater. Jewish farmers could only provide a small percentage of the state's food requirements. The balance-of-payments deficit increased rapidly, and there was a shortage

of basic goods. The government therefore imposed a policy of austerity and introduced rationing of foodstuffs and clothing. A black market began to flourish.

The deterioration of the situation in Israel in comparison with the improvement
in Europe created an immigration slump. In 1953–4, only some 50,000 immigrants
arrived. There was a rise in emigration, but by the end of 1952 not more than 38,000
people had left, some 5% of all immigrants. Despite the difficult situation, the government succeeded in maintaining vital services. In 1949 compulsory education was
introduced for all children between the ages of five and fourteen, which also applied
to the Arab minority. In 1953 a National Education Law was passed, which determined a uniform framework for schools, though these were divided into 'state' and
'state-religious' schools. One of the central objectives of this law was to accelerate
the integration of different communities, but despite the progress, achievements
were modest. Israel succeeded also in granting health services to all and even in
considerably raising the health standards of the immigrants. Although a large percentage of the immigrants arrived in a poor state of health, bringing with them contagious and hereditary diseases, and although many of them came from extremely
primitive conditions, were ignorant of hygiene and of modern methods of baby-care
and proper nutrition, within a few years the health services had attained a commend-
able standard, comparable to that of advanced European countries. The contagious
diseases were overcome, malaria and tuberculosis were almost completely obliterated,
and the infant death-rate declined steeply.

A new wave of immigration arrived in the years 1955–7, consisting of more than
160,000 people. Because of the intensification of Arab nationalism in North Africa,
some 70,000 Jews immigrated from Morocco and 15,000 from Tunisia. During the
political thaw in Russia and after the ferment in Poland and Hungary tens of thousands arrived from there, including some of those repatriated from the U.S.S.R. In
the same years tens of thousands of Jews arrived in Israel after being expelled from
Egypt after the 1956 Sinai Campaign. In order to absorb these immigrants temporary
asbestos huts were erected, which were cramped and inconvenient. Special arrangements were made for the absorption of university-trained personnel and special
ulpanim (intensive Hebrew courses) were established. A larger percentage began to be
absorbed into the kibbutz movement – some 10,000 immigrants during the years
1957–60.

After a short lull, there was a third wave of immigration in the years 1961–4. In
these four years some 215,000 immigrants came, including a considerable number
from Eastern Europe. In contrast, more than 100,000 Algerian Jews, who fled that
country after it attained independence in 1962, did not choose Israel as their destination. Most of them opted for the rehabilitation projects offered by the French
Government to the Algerian refugees. In 1965 immigration began to wane and with
the onset of an economic recession, it was reduced even further (some 25,000 in the
years 1966–7). After the Six Day War immigration from the affluent countries rose
significantly; several thousand Jews arrived from Poland after increased anti-Semitic
incitement there in 1968, and from Czechoslovakia after the Soviet invasion. In the
years 1968–74 about 100,000 arrived from the Soviet Union.

Those Diaspora communities in which Jews suffered persecution and discrimination have been almost totally liquidated. The fate of immigration in the seventies now depends on the extent to which Soviet Jewry and enlightened public opinion succeed in keeping the gates of Russia open for those Jews who desire to immigrate to Israel and on the continued desire of Western Jews to settle in Israel in order that they may live a full Jewish life. They expect to find in Israel high moral and cultural standards and social harmony.

Israel's Security Problems

Despite the armistice agreements the Arab states have never ceased their war against Israel. At first they initiated a diplomatic onslaught by demanding the implementation of the U.N. resolution regarding the internationalization of Jerusalem and a return to the partition borders as determined on 29 November 1947 – although it was clear that by refusing to accept this resolution, in attacking the State of Israel and capturing the area of the proposed Arab state (Judah and Samaria by Jordan, Gaza by Egypt), they themselves had defied and destroyed the basis of that same resolution. In addition there was the demand, which the U.N. supported on the recommendation of Bernadotte, to return those Arab refugees who had fled from their homes during the war, even though, at least at the beginning of the fighting, the Arab inhabitants left their places of residence on the instructions of their own leaders. It was clear to all that the return of hundreds of thousands of refugees, hostile towards Israel, to its territory, would destroy the country from within.

In the first year after the signing of the armistice agreement, King Abdullah tended to favour a separate agreement with Israel, but hesitated in the face of the pressure of other Arab states. After his assassination on 20 July 1951, all chances of peace vanished. On the contrary, in the spring of 1951 there was increased tension on the Syrian border; irregular units, and later even regular units, attacked Israeli territory in order to prevent the implementation of the drainage of the Huleh swamps, but were repelled. Egypt blocked the Suez Canal against Israeli shipping and prohibited the passage of goods earmarked for Israel. The Security Council declared, in September 1951, that the blockade imposed by Egypt on the canal flouted the armistice agreements and the principle of free maritime navigation. But the Egyptian authorities ignored the resolution, and the new regime, established after the 1952 coup d'état, intensified the blockade.

From 1952 onwards there were increased instances of infiltration from Jordan for the purpose of plunder and sabotage and, in 1953, acts of murder as well. In early 1954 a bus on its way from Eilat was attacked at Ma'aleh Akrabim and eleven passengers were murdered. At the same time, Egypt was stepping up the dispatch of infiltrators from the Gaza Strip for sabotage purposes, and in 1955 two marauder units, known as the Fedayun, were established. They carried out acts of murder, particularly among the civilian population, and penetrated as far as the centre of the country. In the period between the War of Independence and the Sinai Campaign in 1956, some 1,300 Israelis fell victim to the infiltrators.

The Israeli reaction to the acts of sabotage and murder consisted of retaliatory operations across the border, in which those Arab villages from which the saboteurs had departed or their military headquarters were attacked. In order to carry out this objective, a special fighting unit was established and in time this task was entrusted to paratroop units, which became Israel's crack fighting force. The acts of retaliation, which increased in scope, did not succeed in checking hostile infiltration nor in bringing peace to the borders. Furthermore, the destruction of the village of Kibia in 1953, in which some fifty inhabitants were killed, aroused sharp condemnation of Israel by world public opinion. The attack on Gaza in the same year led the new ruler of Egypt, Gamal Abdul Nasser, to declare that there was no possibility of arriving at an agreement with the aggressor, Israel. Within Israel herself, there were those who began to doubt the efficacy of retaliation, which produced no clear results and caused a considerable number of Israeli losses. There was a grave sense of public concern over the security situation of the state.

Israel's Foreign Relations

After the main armistice agreements had been signed and fifty-five states had recognized Israel within her first year of existence, the new state was accepted as a member of the United Nations on 11 May 1949. But in the autumn of that year she was already forced to engage in a fierce political struggle on the question of the status of Jerusalem. A coalition of several Catholic, Arab and Moslem states together with the Soviet bloc led to the passing, on 9 December 1949, of a new resolution calling for the internationalization of Jerusalem. In reaction the Israeli Government proclaimed Jerusalem to be the capital, and the Knesset was transferred there. But most countries refused to establish their diplomatic missions in that city.

From the first Israel endeavoured to preserve her neutral status in the struggle between the blocs, although, in her political structure and ties with the great Jewish community of the United States, she was closer to the West than to the East. This created a predicament with regard to an arms supplier. Neither of the blocs were interested in supplying Israel with arms, while Britain continued to equip the Arab states; their strongest army, the Jordanian Arab Legion, was under direct British command. As a result of Israel's pressure for the acquisition of arms, the three Western Powers – the United States, Britain and France – published, in May 1950, a declaration expressing their opposition to the utilization of force or threats of force between the countries of the region and guaranteeing the existing borders. This was known as the Tripartite Declaration.

As the Cold War intensified, Israel adhered with increased strictness to her non-aligned stand. She recognized the People's Republic of China, but joined the United States on U.N. resolutions regarding the Korean War. In any case the attitude of the Soviet bloc towards Israel took a turn for the worse from 1949 onwards. Soviet publications began to conceal the role of the Soviet Union in aiding the establishment of the State of Israel and disregarded Arab aggression, which had once been sharply condemned by representatives of the Soviet Union. Attacks on Zionism increased and reached their height in the 1952 Prague trial and in the 'doctors' plot' at the beginning of 1953. And when a bomb exploded in the courtyard of the Soviet Embassy in

Tel Aviv in February 1953, the Soviet Union broke off diplomatic relations with Israel. These were renewed only after the death of Stalin, when diplomatic representation was raised to the ambassadorial level.

A grave test of Israel's status came after Egypt signed a wide-scale arms agreement with Czechoslovakia in September 1955. It was clear that Nasser was doing everything in his power to prepare an attack on Israel and that Russia was endeavouring to infiltrate into the Middle East by means of equipping the Arabs. Egyptian aggression increased: Fedayun attacks became more numerous, and in 1956 Egypt blocked the entrance to the Gulf of Aqaba and placed a military unit as Ras Nasrani. After a wide-scale Israeli retaliatory action at Kalkilya on 10 October 1956, a joint Arab command was established, headed by the Egyptian Chief of Staff.

After the Egypt-Czechoslovakia arms deal, Israel tried at first to appeal to all the Great Powers to balance the situation. In the spring and summer of 1956 there was an apparent improvement in the Soviet attitude towards Israel. She proposed a 'general embargo on arms sales to the Middle East' and slightly eased the restrictions on immigration from the Eastern bloc. But she did not check the flow of arms to Egypt, while the United States refused to supply arms to Israel directly, and Britain was still trying to salvage her position in the Arab countries by continuing to court them. The only country that responded to Israel's appeal at the time was France, which was then deeply involved in the struggle with the Algerian rebels and by strengthening Israel expected to weaken Arab support for the F.L.N. in Algeria.

Within the Israeli Government, differences of opinion emerged between the firm stand of Ben-Gurion and the compromisory attitude of Moshe Sharett, both with regard to retaliation and to the attitude towards the Soviet Union and Egypt. In June 1956 Sharett was obliged to resign from his post as Foreign Minister, and Ben-Gurion became, in effect, the sole architect of Israeli foreign policy.

The Sinai Campaign and Its Aftermath

The political situation in the Middle East changed in 1956. The United States began to dissociate itself from Nasser's policy and refused to finance the building of the Aswan Dam. In reaction Nasser nationalized the Suez Canal. France and Britain began to plan military action; they found the right time when the agitation in Poland and revolution in Hungary were keeping the Soviet Union occupied. After co-ordination between Ben-Gurion and French Premier Guy Mollet, the Israeli onslaught commenced in Sinai; its objective was to disrupt Nasser's military schemes, to destroy the Fedayun bases and to open the Straits of Tiran to Israeli shipping.

On 29 October 1956 an Israeli force was parachuted to the Mitla Pass and at the same time a paratroop brigade crossed the Israel-Egypt border. After a fierce and bloody battle at the Mitla Pass, the Israeli force advanced towards the Suez Canal on 2 November. The Anglo-French ultimatum to both sides not to approach the Canal prevented further Israeli progress. The force advanced from there to Sharm el-Sheikh, while another force advanced in the same direction along the Gulf of Aqaba. On 5 November the occupation of the southern tip of the Sinai Peninsula was completed, and the Egyptian blockade was broken. Simultaneously infantry and armoured Israeli forces broke through the Rafiaḥ defences, and on 2 November the town of Gaza was captured. The Israeli forces advanced to El Arish and further along the coast. The entire campaign lasted six days, but was settled in really only three. Of no small importance was the Anglo-French invasion, which immobilized Egyptian forces behind the lines, and some value should be attributed to the aid of the French Navy. The I.D.F. captured a large quantity of arms and equipment, inflicted heavy losses on the Egyptians and took some 6,000 prisoners.

While the military operations were continuing, the U.N. Assembly was convened for a special session and passed, by an overwhelming majority, a resolution calling for an immediate cease-fire, while the United States and the Soviet Union exerted heavy pressure on Israel to withdraw. It was also decided to set up an international emergency force 'to maintain peace', but Israel announced that she would not agree to its being stationed on her borders. The Soviet Union threatened Israel with the dispatch of 'volunteers' to Egypt and revoked the previously signed oil-supply agreement. Under such threats and pressures Ben-Gurion announced on 7 November that Israel would retreat from Sinai. After an unsuccessful Israeli attempt to demand that Gaza be handed over to U.N. supervision, the evacuation was carried out unconditionally, but with an American promise that freedom of navigation in the Gulf of Aqaba would be safeguarded.

The Sinai Campaign succeeded in liquidating Fedayun activity and in opening the Gulf of Aqaba to shipping, but did not alter the borders (even in Gaza). Nor did it harm Nasser, who succeeded, through a political manoeuvre, in transforming the defeat into a victory, so that his status in the Arab world was strengthened. Israel's image suffered a blow in the eyes of world opinion and among the Afro-Asian states, as she was now regarded as a partner in an 'imperialistic plot'. On the other hand, the security of Israel's population was reinforced because of the damage to Egyptian military manpower and equipment, although these were rapidly rehabilitated with Russian aid.

After the retreat, Israeli-Soviet diplomatic relations were restored to their previous state, and relations with the United States and Britain improved. Israel's main source of arms supply was still France. In order to extricate herself from her political isolation, Israel initiated economic- and technical-aid operations to several African and Asian countries, which led to an improvement in her foreign contacts. Cooperation of sorts was created with the non-Arab states in the region – Turkey, Iran and Ethiopia.

There was also a lull on the borders with the Arab states. Although their hostility towards Israel had not decreased, internal ferment caused them to direct more attention to domestic problems. Syria, which was characterized throughout this period by extreme political instability, for three years (1958–61) maintained political union with Egypt under the name of the United Arab Republic.

Israel's foreign policy began, at the end of the fifties, to strive for *rapprochement* with Germany, and Ben-Gurion's meeting with Adenauer in New York in 1960 gave public expression to this decision. The Deputy Minister of Defence, Shimon Peres, also emphasized the importance of reliance on Germany and France, mainly because of the need for arms supplies, but also out of a desire to utilize their aid for the development of atomic energy and in order to gain entry to the Common Market. After Ben-Gurion's resignation in 1963, the new prime minister, Levi Eshkol, began once again to work for *rapprochement* with the United States and to attempt to improve relations with the Soviet Union.

The Six Day War and Its Aftermath

After the dissolution of the United Arab Republic in 1961, Syria continued to generate border tension. In 1963 she headed those demanding forcible action to prevent the completion of Israel's water-pipeline project, but Egypt did not agree. The conference of Arab leaders held in 1964 accepted the Egyptian proposal to divert the Jordan River sources in Syria and Lebanon. There were those in Israel who were in favour of a preventive war against the Arab states, but the policy eventually adopted was one of armed disruption of the diversionary work. Eventually, when the pipeline became operational, the Arab states failed to react. But the Syrians intensified border activity by repeated bombardment of the eastern Galilee settlements, harassment of fishing on the Sea of Galilee, and attacks on agricultural workers in the demilitarized zones. In addition Syrian intelligence began to train saboteurs to be sent into Israel. Once again there were marauding attacks and, in reaction, Israeli retaliatory raids. The raid on the village of Samoa in the Hebron hills, which was regarded as the departure base of the gangs, at the end of 1966, severely undermined the stability of the monarchy in Jordan and led to vigorous world condemnation of Israel. As the Arab attacks increased, the Israel Air Force took to the skies, and on 7 April 1967 Israeli planes shot down seven Syrian MIGs and hovered over Damascus.

As a result of all these developments, the Soviet press began to claim that Israel was planning to attack Syria, that there were Israeli military concentrations on the Syrian border and so forth. There are grounds for believing that Soviet officials impelled the Egyptians to act against Israel, both by informing them of Israel's alleged intention to attack Syria in May 1967 and by their false evaluation of the situation in Israel, which was supposedly close to disintegration as a result of the economic recession, emigration, unemployment and tension between the various communal groups.

It is impossible to determine whether Nasser genuinely believed that the triumphant hour had at last arrived when he could 'push the Jews into the sea', or whether he merely wished to exploit Israel's alleged weakness in order to extract political concessions and slowly strangle her. Whatever the case may have been, Nasser – having accumulated large supplies of modern military equipment from the Soviet Union over the years and after having his troops acquire battle experience in Yemen and being evacuated from there – on 15 May opened a military campagin directed at Sinai. The Egyptian Army, consisting of some 100,000 men and hundreds of tanks, took up positions in Sinai. Immediately afterwards, Nasser ordered the United Nations Emergency Force to evacuate its positions and on 22 May proclaimed the closing of the Straits of Tiran to Israeli shipping. He knew that in the eyes of Israel this would serve as a *casus belli* and openly stated that he was awaiting an Israeli attack, which would be answered by a crushing Egyptian move.

This great political success once again raised Nasser's prestige in Arab eyes. On 30 May, King Hussein of Jordan arrived in Cairo and signed a treaty for military cooperation. Iraqi units entered Jordan, and Saudi Arabia and Kuwait announced their support. Thus it appeared that a united Arab front had been created to surround and throttle Israel. Arab media threatened the Jews of Palestine with total extermination after what they regarded as their certain victory.

Israel stood totally alone in the face of the Arab threat. De Gaulle warned her of the consequences of military action and imposed an embargo on arms shipments to the Middle East; as the Arab states were continuing to receive arms from the Eastern bloc, the embargo could only affect Israel. The maritime nations, headed by the United States and Britain, denounced Nasser's actions and pronouncements, but did nothing to ensure freedom of navigation in the Straits, despite the earlier American promise delivered after the Sinai Campaign. The United States asked for respite to seek a settlement by political means, and Israel agreed. This period of waiting, which lasted some two weeks, gave the Egyptians time to consolidate their forces in Sinai, but also enabled Israel's reserve units to train under field conditions. It was for this reason that there was no apparent difference in operational level during the war between reserve and regular units. As the Chief of Staff, Yitzhak Rabin, noted in summing up the war, there was not a single unit in the I.D.F. 'which did not fulfil the task imposed on it.' On the other hand, the period of waiting created great tension among the Israeli public, and the government was severely criticized by both military and civilian elements for delaying a decision.

The military operations commenced in the early hours of 5 June, when several waves of Israeli aircraft simultaneously attacked runways in the main Egyptian airfields, putting them out of operation and subsequently scoring direct hits on grounded planes and installations in Egypt, Syria, Jordan and even one Iraqi airfield. Hundreds of enemy planes were destroyed in these attacks, and they ensured Israeli domination of the skies. The ground battles to a large extent resembled those of the Sinai Campaign, although the I.D.F. had learned several lessons from the earlier campaign, and, most important of all, had streamlined the massive deployment of armoured forces.

The battle that raged in Sinai was one of the great armoured battles in history. Although the I.D.F. had no tank that could compare in quality with the modern Soviet tanks in the possession of Egypt and Syria, it was the mobility and ability of the Israeli tank crews which won the day. Israeli units broke through the Egyptian fortifications south of Rafiah and advanced to the Canal along the coast. Other units turned north and captured the Gaza Strip. Simultaneously, other units broke through the Egyptian line at Abu Ageila and Koseima and advanced towards Ismailiya, the Mitla Pass and the town of Suez. The campaign against Egypt was settled within three days. Israeli units broke through the mighty Egyptian fortifications in Sinai, attacking from the front and from the rear. The Egyptian retreat turned into a mass flight. Hundreds of tanks and vehicles were abandoned or destroyed, and the remaining Egyptian units surrendered. Several thousand Egyptian officers and men were taken prisoner, thousands more wandered about the desert without water or food, making towards the Canal. Sinai, where Nasser had concentrated his forces, became a death-trap for the Egyptian Army.

When fighting broke out in the south, Prime Minister Levi Eshkol transmitted a warning to Hussein through the U.N. supervision force against opening hostilities, as Israel intended to maintain peace along the eastern border. But Hussein refused to heed the warning and opened fire on the U.N. Headquarters situated in no-man's-land in Jerusalem and began bombarding Jewish Jerusalem. Israeli forces responded with a counter-attack, broke through the Jordanian line, surrounded the Old City and advanced towards Ramallah and the Dead Sea. From the north, Israeli forces attacked Jenin. The Jordanian Army retreated rapidly, and East Jerusalem and the Old City were captured on 7 June; on the following day the entire area up to the Jordan River was in Israeli hands. Most of the towns of Judah and Samaria capitulated without a fight.

The Syrians contented themselves all this while with bombarding Jewish settlements in eastern Galilee, without any military consequences. The Iraqis made several abortive attempts to attack towns from the air. On 9 June the I.D.F. began to break through the mighty Syrian fortifications in the Golan Heights. Although the Syrians enjoyed all the strategic advantages – both topographical and quantitative – many of the strongholds were captured on the same day, and Israeli forces began to advance towards Kuneitra. After that town fell, the I.D.F. halted only several dozen miles from Damascus.

The Six Day War demonstrated the ability of the I.D.F. – an army built mainly on reserve forces, a people's army in the truest sense of the word, but at the same time an army that operates the most modern military equipment accurately and with great professional skill. The cooperation between the various branches (including the Medical Corps, whose efficiency saved the lives of many of the wounded), the cohesion between front line and civilians, and the readiness to make sacrifices all found sublime expression in this campaign. The soldiers and commanding officers in 1967 lived up to the standards of those who had fought in 1948 and exceeded them in military ability.

On the other hand, the weaknesses of the Arabs were made apparent in this war: the great social gap between soldier and officer, the lack of initiative of both, untrustworthy reports, poor technical skill. For all these reasons even the personal heroism of some of the Arab fighters could not change the situation. In order to conceal the fact that Israel had triumphed alone over all the Arab armies, Nasser published a fabricated story of American and English air intervention on behalf of Israel. On the night of 9 June, Nasser delivered a dramatic speech to the Egyptian nation, admitted defeat and announced his resignation. As a result of mass demonstrations in his favour (and possibly organized by Nasser himself or by highly influential Soviet elements in Egypt who feared the replacement of Nasser by a pro-Western politican), he withdrew his resignation. Egypt's *débâcle* was not only a failure of the military machine, but of the entire political – allegedly socialist – structure that Nasser had erected and of his political orientation.

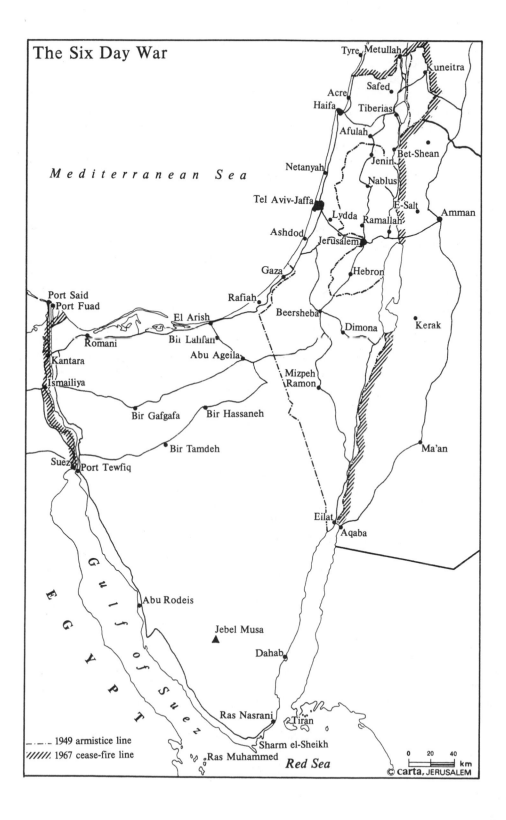

The Six Day War

Tyre Metullah
Kuneitra
Acre Safed
Haifa Tiberias
Afulah
Bet-Shean
Netanyah Jenin
Nablus
Tel Aviv-Jaffa E-Salt
Lydda Ramallah Amman
Ashdod
Jerusalem
Gaza Hebron
Rafiah
Port Said Beersheba
Port Fuad El Arish Dimona Kerak
Romani Bir Lahfan
Kantara Abu Ageila
Ismailiya Mizpeh
Ramon
Bir Gafgafa Bir Hassaneh
Bir Tamdeh
Ma'an
Suez Port Tewfiq
Eilat
Aqaba

Mediterranean Sea

*G
u
l
f

o
f

S
u
e
z*

*E
G
Y
P
T*

Abu Rodeis

Jebel Musa ▲

Dahab

Ras Nasrani
Tiran

—·—·— 1949 armistice line
/////. 1967 cease-fire line

Sharm el-Sheikh
Ras Muhammed *Red Sea*

0 20 40
km
© carta, JERUSALEM

Immediately after the outbreak of fighting, the Soviet Government approached the President of the United States with a proposal for mutual nonintervention, which was accepted. At first Russian sources published announcements of Egyptian military victories, but shortly afterwards they began to denounce 'Israeli aggression' and to demand an immediate cease-fire and the return of Israeli forces to their previous positions. Only when it became clear to them how great the Arab defeat was, did they agree to an unconditional cease-fire.

Within a few days the Soviets demanded the convening of a special session of the U.N. General Assembly, in order to discuss the Middle East situation. They apparently hoped to repeat the tactic employed after the Sinai Campaign. But this time the United States did not take the same attitude. President Johnson put forward his own programme for a Middle Eastern settlement, which expressed opposition to territorial annexations, but demanded a peace settlement and the guaranteeing of freedom of navigation in maritime straits. The Arabs and the Soviet bloc did not succeed in achieving their political aim at the Assembly. On 22 November 1967 the Security Council adopted a British resolution, which in more vague fashion put forward those same principles proposed by the United States.

After the political stalemate became clear, the Egyptians embarked in 1969 on a War of Attrition against Israel, with the help of Soviet military instructors and equipment. Both governments hoped to extract concessions from Israel by inflicting heavy human losses on her. But the I.D.F. succeeded in finding the right military answers, and the pressure on Egypt became so great that Nasser turned to the U.S.S.R. for immediate aid. Thus the dependence of Egypt on Soviet military aid had grown considerably, and with it Russian involvement in the Middle East. Nonetheless, the losses of the Egyptian Army were so heavy that Nasser was compelled to agree (in August 1970) to a cease-fire proposed by the United States.

The new Egyptian President, Anwar Sadat, was from the start under heavy pressure from forces within the country and from various groups in the Arab world to end 'Israeli occupation of Arab territories'. It seems that the U.S.S.R. refused to promise a direct military intervention in case of war, and this was the reason for the spectacular expulsion of Soviet military advisers in July 1972. In Israel it was considered as a sign of Egyptian despair and of the weakness inherent in the Arab world. The prevailing attitude of contempt for the military potential of the Arabs grew stronger, and the I.D.F. leadership proclaimed that there was no military option for Egypt. On the other hand, the terrorist Palestinian groups, which after a few spectacular hijackings of planes and other acts of terror had been suppressed by the Jordanian Army, renewed their murderous activities, mainly in various European countries. The growing dependence of Western Europe and Japan on Arab oil, and the pressure of the Arabs on the African states, increased the political influence of the Arabs. The rulers of Egypt and Syria felt that a continuation of the political stalemate could endanger the stability of their regimes, and even an unsuccessful military action could be politically expedient for them.

The mighty anti-aircraft rocket defence system supplied to Egypt and Syria by the U.S.S.R. increased their military self-confidence. Therefore they decided on a simultaneous attack on Israel from the north and the south, which opened on the

Day of Atonement (6 October) 1973. The Arab armies succeeded in deceiving Israeli intelligence, and the attack came as a complete surprise to Israel.

The Syrians placed five divisions (about 45,000 men and 1,200 tanks) on the Golan Heights against two Israeli tank brigades (about 4,500 men and 180 tanks). They were supported by 300 planes. In the southern part of the Golan, they succeeded in breaking through the Israeli defences, reaching almost as far as the Jordan River, but on the following day Israeli reserves started to arrive, and the air force became more effective once the advancing Syrians had gone beyond their missile cover. After twenty-four hours of fighting, the Syrian Army had lost half of its force, and on the next day the I.D.F. started a counter-attack. On 10 October it crossed the former demarcation line and inflicted heavy losses on the enemy on Syrian territory. The auxiliary Iraqi, Jordanian and Moroccan units also suffered losses and began to retreat. On 13 October the I.D.F. penetrated the Syrian defences in the region of Sasa, some 25 miles from Damascus, but the advance was halted to prevent possible complications with the Russians.

In the south three motorized divisions started an attack against the single brigade that was to hold the Bar-Lev line and a tank brigade which supported it. In a few hours they succeeded in crossing the Suez Canal and captured footholds on the eastern bank. Several of the Israeli strongholds fell during the first days of war; others held out nearly a week (and one did not surrender at all). The Israeli air force suffered heavy losses from the surface-to-air missiles and could not extend sufficient help to the attacking ground units. On 8 October the Israeli tanks counter-attacked; the units were almost completely destroyed, but they prevented the Egyptians from further advancement into the Sinai Peninsula.

After two tank divisions had crossed the Canal, on 14 October, the Egyptians started to advance beyond their missile umbrella. A great armour battle developed, in which the I.D.F. proved its superiority: more than 200 Egyptian tanks were destroyed and the remainder withdrew from battle. The Israeli air force, now partly transferred from the northern front, was also very effective. But the general losses of tanks and ammunition during the first week of war were very high, and on 13 October an American emergency airlift began (the Soviet air and sea deliveries to the Arab armies had begun even earlier).

On 15 October the I.D.F. initiated its audacious plan to attack the Egyptian mainland, on the west bank of the canal. It began north of the Great Bitter Lake, on the border line between the Second and Third Egyptian Armies. The crossing was executed under heavy fire, but on 17 October a tank brigade was already operating on the west bank of the canal, destroying many missile installations. This enabled the air force to develop its activity and to suppress the Egyptian fire on the bridge over the canal. One Israeli division went to the northern sector, approaching the Ismailiya-Cairo road, another moved south, cutting off the supply lines of the Third Egyptian Army and the city of Suez.

This operation changed completely the military situation and engendered Soviet diplomatic activity. Fearing a new *débâcle* of the Arab armies, the U.S.S.R. began to demand a cease-fire and invited the U.S. Secretary of State, Henry Kissinger, to Moscow. The United States, fearing possible direct military intervention by the

Russians and striving to save the policy of détente, agreed. Resolution 338 of the U.N. Security Council called for a cease-fire on the evening of 22 October. Israel and Egypt accepted the resolution, but Syria rejected it. Nevertheless, the Egyptian Third Army made several attempts to restore their lines of supply after the agreed hour for the cease-fire, but the I.D.F. repelled them and then continued to advance. In the morning of 24 October, when a new call for a cease-fire was published, the I.D.F. stood at Ras Adabie, on the shore of the Gulf of Suez and 20 miles to the east of the Canal, cutting off the Suez-Cairo road. The Third Army was now completely encircled on the east bank, and the Israeli forces were about 50 miles from Cairo.

The Egyptians claimed that Israel had violated the cease-fire and demanded the retreat of Israeli forces to the lines of 22 October. The Soviet Union put on alert several airborne divisions, threatening to send them into Egypt, but the United States declared a state of alert as well, and the cease-fire line remained as it was. The Arab states laid an embargo on oil shipments to the United States and Holland. Western Europe complied with it and published a pro-Arab declaration of the foreign ministers of the EEC. Almost all the African states severed their diplomatic ties with Israel. The dependence of Israel on the United States had grown.

On the other hand, in purely military terms, the Yom Kippur War was a decisive victory for the I.D.F.: it ended with Israel in control of 325 square miles of Syrian and about 1,600 square miles of Egyptian territory. The Third Egyptian Army (about 20,000 men and 300 tanks) was encircled. Egypt lost nearly 15,000 soldiers and officers, 8,000 prisoners of war and 1,000 tanks; Syria lost 3,500 men, 370 prisoners of war and about 1,200 tanks. Both countries lost the greater part of their air forces and fleets. The Israeli losses were more than 2,500 killed, nearly 350 prisoners of war, 100 planes downed and several hundred tanks destroyed.

Although the Arabs inflicted serious losses on Israel, and possibly broke what they called 'the barrier of fear', and despite the continuous extensive support from the Soviet Union, they were on the verge of catastrophe. The Arab leaders recognized that they were far away from any possibility of bringing Israel down by military means. Therefore, Egypt and Jordan (but not Syria) decided to participate in the Geneva Conference (opened on 21 December 1973) for the settlement of the Middle East conflict, under the chairmanship of the United States and the Soviet Union. In January 1974 an agreement on the separation of forces between Israel and Egypt was signed at Kilometre 101 of the Cairo-Suez road. The Israelis lifted the siege of the Third Army (which had already been ensured supplies and the evacuation of the wounded under the terms of the cease-fire agreement signed by the two countries in the previous November) and withdrew to a line that runs to the west of the Mitla and Gidi passes in Sinai. A U.N. military force was stationed in the demilitarized zone between the lines. Syria, opposing a settlement and being continuously supplied by the U.S.S.R., opened a new war of attrition, but after long negotiations conducted through Secretary of State Kissinger likewise signed a disengagement agreement in May 1974. Israel withdrew from the enclave in Syria and from the destroyed town of Kuneitra, and a U.N. force of 1,250 military observers was stationed between the lines.

The I.D.F. started immediately to learn the lessons of the war. There was a great shift in its high echelons; the United States continued sending military supplies. About a year after the war, according to foreign military observers, Israel was considerably stronger than it had been before 6 October 1973. On the other hand, Israel's diplomatic situation worsened, not only because the U.N. General Assembly gave a hearty welcome to Yasser Arafat, the head of the terrorist Palestine Liberation Organization, at the end of 1974, but also because the hostility of the Soviet and Afro-Asian blocs in the United Nations increased, and there was a weakening of Israel's position even in the traditionally friendly West European and Latin American countries. But the main problem Israel faced in its diplomatic struggle grew out of the fact that the United States, which gained a growing influence in the Arab states, began to increase pressure on Israel to meet Arab demands by extending its concessions more than half way.

Israel's Political Consolidation

The foundations of Israeli democracy had been laid in the midst of battle during the War of Independence. On 8 November 1948 a census of the population was held, and on 25 January 1949 elections were held to the Constituent Assembly, with the participation of 87% of the electorate. The Constituent Assembly consisted of 120 members, of whom forty-six belonged to Mapai, nineteen to Mapam, sixteen to religious parties and fourteen to Herut (there were also four Communist members). On 14 February 1949 the Constituent Assembly met for its first session and elected Joseph Sprinzak as chairman. It resolved to bestow on the Israeli legislative assembly the title of Knesset and thus the Constituent Assembly was subsequently known as the First Knesset. On 16 February Chaim Weizmann was elected as the first President of Israel. Immediately afterwards the Provisional Government, which had served since the establishment of the state, resigned, and David Ben-Gurion founded a new government based on a coalition between Mapai, the religious parties, the Progressive Party and the Sephardim. (The relations between Mapai and Mapam had deteriorated mainly because of the disbanding of the Palmah as a separate military unit in November 1948; Mapam supporters had attributed great moral and social importance to the separate existence of this unit.) In the new government Ben-Gurion served as Prime Minister and Minister of Defence, Moshe Sharett as Foreign Minister, Eliezer Kaplan as Minister of Finance, Zalman Shazar as Minister of Education and Golda Meir as Minister of Labour.

The Knesset decided not to draw up a constitution, although this was specifically mentioned in the Declaration of Independence. Only in June 1950 was it decided that there indeed should be a constitution, to be composed chapter by chapter, consisting of 'basic' laws. Over more than two decades only a few such basic laws have been passed.

Because of differences of opinion within the coalition on the question of the education of immigrant children (the religious parties claimed that the children of religious families were being sent to secular educational institutions), a government crisis erupted in the beginning of 1951. The government resigned, and since Ben-Gurion could not form a new government, the First Knesset was dissolved and new elections were held on 30 July 1951. At these elections the General Zionists made great gains (from seven to twenty-three members), a result that reflected the dissatisfaction of the public with the government's policy of austerity, and both the right-wing Herut and the left-wing Mapam showed a decline. The new government was based on a coalition between Mapai and the religious parties, but Agudat Israel seceded because of differences of opinion on the questions of education and military service for women. Ben-Gurion reached an agreement with the General Zionists for their joining the government. Levi Eshkol took over the Ministry of Finance and Ben-Zion Dinur became Minister of Education. After the death of Chaim Weizmann on 9 November 1952, Izhak Ben-Zvi was elected second President of Israel.

At the end of 1953, Ben-Gurion resigned and settled at Kibbutz Sedeh Boker in the Negev. A new government was set up in which Moshe Sharett served as Prime Minister and Foreign Minister, and Pinhas Lavon became Minister of Defence. A year later the Prime Minister announced the resignation of Lavon and Ben-Gurion's return to replace him as Minister of Defence. The public did not then comprehend the significance of this change-over, and this emerged only five years later.

In 1951–2 grave differences of opinion emerged within Mapam. Some of the members moved drastically to the left and demanded a pro-Soviet orientation. They included such personalities as Yitzhak Sadeh, one of the former leaders of the Haganah and founding-fathers of the I.D.F. On the other hand, there were many within this party who took a grave view of the anti-Semitic policy of the Soviet regime, particularly during the period of the Prague trials and the 'doctors' plot' in Russia. As a result of this controversy, part of Mapam's left-wing, headed by Dr Moshe Sneh (former Haganah chief of staff and a General Zionist leader), seceded from the party and eventually joined the Communist Party. There was also a split between the two parties that had originally established Mapam-Hashomer Haza'ir; one group maintained the name of Mapam, while the other reverted to its original name of Ahdut Ha'avodah.

One of the gravest crises in Israeli political life erupted in the second half of 1952, after the signing of a reparations agreement between West Germany and Israel on 10 September 1952. These reparations were to serve as compensation to the Jewish people for the damage caused to the Jews by the Nazis and for the property stolen from them. Under the agreement Germany guaranteed to transfer over a period of twelve to fourteen years three billion marks ($720 million) in the form of goods to Israel and to pay 450 million marks to world Jewish organizations. The money was earmarked for the rehabilitation of victims of Nazism. Wide circles, and particularly Herut supporters, vehemently opposed the agreement and claimed that it constituted monetary payment for the blood of millions and a way of whitewashing the crimes of Nazi Germany. During the Knesset discussion of the agreement, a demonstration was held in the street outside and the demonstrators clashed violently with the police. There can be no doubt that the agreement was a milestone in the reconciliation between the Jewish people and the German nation; but it is also clear that the reparations constituted, to a certain extent, restoration of stolen property, as it was Israel who had absorbed most of the survivors of the death-camps. In Israel's economic situation, after a wave of mass immigration, the reparation agreement was of great constructive value.

Elections to the Third Knesset were held after four years in the summer of 1955. At these elections the General Zionists registered losses, Herut gained, Mapam and Ahdut Ha'avodah were strengthened, while Mapai declined slightly. At the end of the same year Ben-Gurion formed a coalition government comprising Mapai, Hapo'el Hamizrachi, Ahdut Ha'avodah, Mapam and the Progressives. The religious parties left the government in 1958 after the Minister of the Interior, Israel Bar Yehudah, had instructed officials to register as a Jew any person proclaiming himself in good faith to be such, although this was not in accordance with religious law. Moshe Sharett, in disagreement with Ben-Gurion's foreign policy, resigned from his post as Foreign Minister in June 1956 and was replaced by Golda Meir.

In the early days of the Fourth Knesset (elected in November 1959), government stability continued. New Mapai ministers were appointed – Moshe Dayan as Minister of Agriculture and Abba Eban as Minister of Education – but there was no fundamental political change. Shortly afterwards the great political storm known as 'the Affair' came to light and deeply shook Israeli society and politics. It transpired that the resignation of Pinhas Lavon from his post as Minister of Defence at the beginning of 1955 had resulted from the failure of a dubious Intelligence operation carried out in Egypt in 1954, which had caused the death of several of those involved as well as political complications. A committee of two appointed by Prime Minister Moshe Sharett could not arrive at an unequivocal conclusion on the question of who had given the order to carry out the operation and, although Lavon claimed that the operation had been carried out without his knowledge, he accepted parliamentary responsibility and resigned. In 1960 new material came to light that led to the suspicion that two senior officers had given false testimony in order to cast the blame on Lavon. The Legal Adviser to the Government recommended continuing the investigation against the two officers. Ben-Gurion demanded that the matter be clarified at a committee 'with legal authority' and nowhere else.

On the proposal of Levi Eshkol, the government set up a committee of seven ministers to clarify the question, and this body cleared Lavon and cast suspicion on one of the senior officers. But the Prime Minister, who had not appointed an Inquiry Committee with legal powers and had not opposed the appointment of the committee of ministers, now voiced various accusations against the methods of this committee's investigation and its conclusions and did not place the 'senior officer' on trial. Representatives of the coalition parties demanded of Ben-Gurion that he cease his attacks on the ministers. As a result, Ben-Gurion submitted his resignation to the President on 31 January 1961. In order to dissuade him, the Mapai Central Committee decided, by 60% to 40%, to depose Lavon from his position as Secretary-General of the Histadrut.

Ben-Gurion returned and attempted to reconstruct his government, but without success. The Fourth Knesset was dissolved, and new elections were fixed for the summer of 1961. Most of the parties, in their election propaganda, attacked Mapai for its behaviour, but the election results did not produce any real change: Mapai was reduced to forty-two seats (instead of forty-seven), and the Liberals (an amalgamation of the General Zionists and the Progressives) and Communists showed slight gains. Negotiations on the formation of the government lasted several months and they were conducted not by Ben-Gurion himself but by Levi Eshkol on his behalf; eventually a coalition was established consisting of Mapai, Ahdut Ha'avodah and the religious parties and headed by Ben-Gurion.

The undermining of his public image as a result of 'the Affair', as well as foreign policy problems, were apparently among the reasons that induced Ben-Gurion finally to resign from the premiership in June 1963 and retire to Sedeh Boker. But he continued to struggle for his viewpoint and did not refrain from severely attacking his successor, Levi Eshkol, whom he himself had recommended for the post of Prime Minister. Eshkol also occupied the post of Minister of Defence, but Shimon Peres, who continued to serve as Deputy Minister, wielded extensive power. Pinhas Sapir was appointed Minister of Finance. On 23 April 1963, President Ben-Zvi died and was succeeded by Zalman Shazar.

Within Mapai there emerged a group of Ben-Gurion supporters (Dayan, Peres, Yosef Almogi, Giora Josephtal) who attacked Eshkol and the 'Old Guard' of Mapai. In 1964 Dayan resigned from the government and in mid-1965 Almogi and Peres also resigned. Mapai was split, and the dissidents established Rafi (Reshimat Poalei Yisrael, Israel Workers' List). In reaction, the Mapai leadership, together with Ahdut Ha'avodah, established the Labour Alignment, Ma'arach. This body established, from among Ben-Gurion's opponents, a public body in support of Eshkol. At the elections to the Histadrut in the autumn of 1965 Mapai forfeited her dominant position. But in the elections to the Sixth Knesset on 2 November 1965 the ruling circle maintained its position. The Alignment obtained forty-five seats; Gahal (a bloc including Herut and the Liberals) twenty-six; the National Religious Party, eleven; Rafi, ten; and Mapam, eight. A government was established, headed by Eshkol, on the basis of a coalition of the Alignment, the religious parties and Mapam. Its ministers included: Abba Eban (Foreign Minister), Yigal Allon (Minister of Labour) and Zalman Aranne (Minister of Education). Gahal and Rafi remained in the opposition. Both had failed in their efforts to establish an alternative to the existing coalition, but Rafi's failure was the greater.

When the security situation became grave, Rafi began to attack the government's 'security omissions'. In the period of waiting on the eve of the Six Day War, Rafi aroused public opinion against the government, and Eshkol personally, for its weakness and failures. It was proposed that Ben-Gurion be made Premier again and that Dayan take over as Minister of Defence. Under pressure from the religious parties, Eshkol was forced to surrender the defence portfolio, and it was handed over to Dayan several days before the fighting broke out. Rafi and Gahal agreed to join a National Unity Government.

The I.D.F.'s successful military operations confounded the critics. It transpired that Eshkol as Minister of Defence and Rabin as Chief of Staff had made important contributions to the development of the I.D.F.'s military ability and equipment. The period of waiting at the end of May and beginning of June, which had aroused such anger and tension in the public, also proved to have had its positive aspects, even in the military sphere, and increased the political possibility of withstanding pressures after the war. The National Unity Government reflected the prevalent yearning for internal peace, although after the Security Council resolution of 22 November 1967 this partnership made it difficult for the government to take up new initiatives in the political sphere, because of rigid adherence to the principles that had served as the basis of this unity. The death of Levi Eshkol in February 1969 and the appointment of Golda Meir as Premier did not change the situation. Only after the acceptance by Israel of the cease-fire suggested by the U.S. Government in 1970 did Gahal resign from the coalition and enable greater manoevrability in foreign affairs.

After the Six Day War commenced, a *rapprochement* of the workers' parties, Mapai, Ahdut Ha'avodah and Rafi, established a united Labour Party (Ha'avodah), which formed an alignment with Mapam. In the elections to the Seventh Knesset in 1969, the Alignment gained fifty-six seats, Gahal twenty-nine, the religious parties eighteen. The National Unity Government continued until 1970. Golda Meir remained Prime Minister and Allon Deputy Prime Minister and Minister of Education, with few other changes in the cabinet.

The Yom Kippur War broke out during the election campaign for the Eighth Knesset. Immediately after the cease-fire, a political ferment developed in Israeli public opinion, but it found only a partial expression in the results of the elections, which were held on 31 December 1973. A new parliamentary bloc of right-wing parties established in the summer under the name Likud now became a dangerous opponent to the ruling Alignment, which suffered a great loss in its prestige as a result of the war. Many protest groups raised their voices, calling for profound changes in government. On the other hand, a group of intellectuals, fearing a victory of the right-wing Likud, called 'in spite of it all' for support of the Alignment.

The Alignment suffered a loss in the elections, but remained the leading faction (with fifty seats); the religious parties also lost a few seats; the Likud came out with thirty-eight seats; and a new group, the Citizen's Rights List, won three seats. But the ferment did not quiet down after the elections, particularly among the demobilized. The main criticism for the lack of military preparedness and improper conduct of the war in its first days was directed against the Defence Minister, Moshe Dayan. Although a special enquiry commission under the President of the Supreme Court, Shimon Agranat, placed the main responsibility for these failures on the Chief of Staff of the I.D.F., General David Elazar, public opinion did not comply. Golda Meir resigned, and the new government of Yitzhak Rabin (which took over in June 1974), based on a coalition of the Alignment with the Independent Liberals and the Citizen's Rights List (which later left the coalition after the National Religious Party joined it) did not include Dayan and Eban. Deputy Prime Minister Yigal Allon also became Foreign Minister, and Shimon Peres was chosen as Minister of Defence.

Development of the Economy and Society

When mass immigration commenced immediately after the establishment of the State, the government introduced an austerity program and took control over the distribution of commodities and over prices, out of a desire to ensure housing, clothing and food for the immigrants, to find employment for them and for the demobilized soldiers and to safeguard vital services. In the years 1952–3 this strict control was eased, and an attempt was made to base the Israeli pound on a realistic rate. The development budget was extended and greater efforts were made to develop the economy. The years 1954–9 were marked by rapid economic development and a considerable rise in the standard of living, although the inhabitants of the development towns established in the Negev and the north in order to disperse the population were still suffering from unemployment and poor services. Until 1964 the Gross National Product increased by about 10% annually. The rate of unemployment was 10% of the labour force in the first few years but dropped thereafter.

There was a period of economic boom between 1960 and 1964, and unemployment vanished almost totally. But the gap in the balance of payments increased rapidly and reached some $570 million in 1964. In order to correct this situation the government introduced a policy of restraint, and in order to slow the rate of economic activity, it considerably reduced the development budget. This policy, against the background of the slump in immigration, gravely affected the building industry. Credit shrank, investments decreased, and output dropped. The gap in the balance of payments was lessened ($425 million in 1967), but the losses to the economy as a result of the reduction of economic activity cast doubt on the efficacy of this policy. Its main achievement was a certain stabilization of prices and wages and an improvement in the attitude of the workers towards their tasks. After the Six Day War rapid economic activity developed once more, particularly in branches of industry connected with security. Renewed immigration expanded building activity, and the increase in the national product exceeded the previous boom period.

The heavy burden of the Yom Kippur War and of the war of attrition that followed, which required the extended mobilization of the reserves, worsened considerably the economic situation. The political tension and the Arab boycott reduced new investments in Israel's industry, and the economic recession in the West, the result of inflation and high oil prices, diminished the financial support from Jewish communities abroad. Israel became more dependent on the United States not only in military and political matters but also economically.

But all in all, Israel's economic achievements have been impressive. There have been numerous achievements in all spheres of agriculture; output has increased sixfold and the number of agricultural settlements threefold in the twenty years since the establishment of the state; the number of those employed in agriculture has more than doubled. In 1967 agricultural output reached IL1.6 billion (an annual increase of 10% since the establishment of the state). But social changes have occurred in the rural population: the percentage of kibbutz members in the total population dropped during the years 1948–66 from 7.5% to 3.5%, while the proportion of moshav members rose from 3.4% to 5.4%.

There was considerable advancement in industry as well. Output increased from IL 1.5 billion in 1950 to approximately IL7 billion in 1966 (an average annual increase of 10.3%); industrial exports in these same years increased from $18 million to $375 million (an annual average increase of 20.8%); the number of workers rose from 90,000 to 222,000 (5.8% average annual increase); and output per worker rose from IL 6.5 thousand per year to IL 20.2 thousand (4.2% annual increase). Some industries remained dependent on government protection, though there was a perceptible improvement in this sphere after the Six Day War, particularly in the electronics and chemical industry. The agreement of affiliation with the European Common Market, signed in 1975, opened new possibilities before Israel's industry.

The role of minerals in industrial export increased in that same period from 8% to 14%, while tourism accounted for 3% of exports in 1952 and 7% in 1966. Electricity consumption rose from 261 million kilowatts per hour in 1948 to 3.8 billion in 1966 (an average annual rise of 16%).

Cultural Development

As we have noted, the Israeli Government, during the first few years of statehood, regarded its main task as ensuring elementary education to every child below the age of fourteen and closing the gap between the veteran Yishuv and the new immigrants, particularly from Eastern countries. Expansion of the educational network accompanied the increase in population. In 1948, 141,000 pupils attended some 1,342 Jewish and Arab institutions of education under the supervision of some 6,500 teachers. In 1968, 776,000 pupils were studying at 5,382 institutions with 42,300 teachers. In the second decade of statehood particular attention was paid to expanding secondary and higher education: in 1954, 32,000 pupils attended secondary schools, and 7,000 were studying at higher institutions; in 1965–6 the figures were 116,000 and 22,000 respectively.

In 1969 the Sixth Knesset passed a law extending compulsory education by two years – to include the fifteen- and sixteen-year-olds – and decided to implement a reform programme in education based on the establishment of junior high schools. During the sixties the veteran institutions of higher education (the Hebrew University, the Haifa Technion, the Weizmann Institute) expanded, and new institutions developed (Tel Aviv University, Bar-Ilan University, and the universities of Haifa and Beersheba).

In cultural activities there was also considerable progress. In 1965 the Israel Museum was established, which contains the Bezalel collections, the Archaeological Museum and the Shrine of the Book (containing the Dead Sea Scrolls); the Tel Aviv Museum and the Modern Art Museum of Haifa were also developed in this period. The Haifa Municipal Theatre and many other theatre troupes were set up. Television was introduced in 1968. Musical education was improved, and, in addition to the renowned Israel Philharmonic Orchestra, other orchestras were established. Each year in the summer months an Israel Festival is held, combining musical events with theatrical and folkloristic performances.

The older generation of writers and poets – Uri Zevi Greenberg, the Nobel Prize winner S. Y. Agnon, Abraham Shlonsky, Nathan Alterman – have been followed by new generations: the older ones are named the writers of the period of the War of Independence, the younger ones were shaped in the reality of the State of Israel.

Changes in the Relations Between Israel and the Diaspora

The four wars that Israel has fought in her years of existence have strengthened her ties with the Diaspora. Over the years there has also been a change in the nature of these relations. At first many young Israelis regarded the Diaspora Jew with a large measure of contempt and regarded themselves as of superior status. The character of the immigrants, most of them from backward countries or refugees from the Holocaust, strengthened this feeling among the native Israelis. Even the Holocaust itself, despite the shock it aroused among the young, did not greatly change this critical attitude.

Despite the extensive publicity given to the Holocaust and the existence of a special institute – Yad Vashem – for perpetuating the memory of the Holocaust and of Jewish heroism in resisting it, the fateful significance of the Holocaust was not clear to young Israelis. There was, to a large extent, a change in this attitude during the Eichmann trial of 1961. The prosecution case and the testimony voiced in this trial cast a new light on the Holocaust and on the stand of the Jews. This silenced the question that had often been voiced – why the Jews seemed to have gone to their deaths like sheep, without resisting. For the first time the Jewish public and the world at large was told, clearly and in detail, the story of the devilishly concealed and cunning methods by which the murderous Nazi machine and its satellites led the scattered, exhausted and defenceless victims to the death-chamber. Many young Israelis began to understand and re-evaluate the situation of the destroyed communities. Contempt was gradually replaced by a sharp sense of shared destiny, facilitating a greater understanding of Jewish history and its problems and a sense of brotherhood with the Jews of the Diaspora.

The most profound change occurred as a result of the Six Day War, when it transpired that Israel was standing alone and that her sole ally was the Jewish people throughout the world. The demonstrations organized by Diaspora Jews, their mass volunteering to fight, their generous response in mobilizing funds, their grave concern for Israel's fate reawakened the sense of a common destiny. In the Diaspora, there was a resurgence of interest in Judaism and in Jews, their culture and history. The stream of tourists, students and volunteers created an opportunity for direct contact.

The Yom Kippur War, despite its different outcome, did not change this basic tendency. Most Israelis, as well as most Jews in the Diaspora, began to realize that the factors uniting Jews all over the world were more numerous and more binding than they had assumed – and perhaps even more binding than the founders of the Jewish national movement themselves had ever imagined.

Selected Bibliography

The Biblical Period: Introductory Works

The Ancient Near East and Its People

The Cambridge Ancient History, vols. I–II (3rd ed.), Cambridge, 1970–5; vol. III, Cambridge, 1929.

Fischer Weltgeschichte: Die altorientalischen Reiche II–III, Band 3, Frankfurt a.M., 1966; Band 4, Frankfurt a.M., 1967.

Gardiner, A., *Egypt of the Pharaohs,* Oxford, 1961.

Gordon, C.H., *The World of the Old Testament* (rev. ed. of *Introduction to Old Testament Times*), Garden City, N.Y., 1958.

Hallo, W.W. and W.K. Simpson, *The Ancient Near East—A History,* New York, 1971.

Kitchen, K.A., *Ancient Orient and Old Testament,* London, 1966.

Moscati, S., *The World of the Phoenicians,* London, 1968.

Olmstead, A.T., *History of the Persian Empire,* Chicago, 1948.

Saggs, H.W.F., *The Greatness That Was Babylon,* London, 1962.

Wiseman, D.J., ed., *Peoples of Old Testament Times,* Oxford, 1973.

General Works on the History of Israel

Albright, W.F., *From the Stone Age to Christianity* (2nd ed.), Garden City, N.Y., 1957.

——, *Archaeology and the Religion of Israel* (3rd ed.). Baltimore, 1953.

Bright, J., *A History of Israel* (2nd ed.), London, 1972.

Herrmann, S., *A History of Israel in Old Testament Times,* Philadelphia, 1975.

Kaufmann, Y., *The Religion of Israel,* trans. and abridged by M. Greenberg, Chicago, 1960.

Noth, M., *The History of Israel* (2nd ed.), London, 1960.

Olmstead, A.T., *History of Palestine and Syria,* New York, 1931.

de Vaux, R., *Ancient Israel,* New York, 1961.

Archaeology and Historical Geography

Abel, A.M., *Géographie de la Palestine,* vols. I–II, Paris, 1933–8.

Aharoni, Y., *The Land of the Bible,* Philadelphia, 1967.

——, and M. Avi-Yonah, *The Macmillan Bible Atlas,* New York, 1968.

Albright, W.F., *The Archaeology of Palestine,* Harmondsworth, Middlesex, 1949.

Amiran, R., *Ancient Pottery of the Holy Land*, New Brunswick, N.J., 1969.
Avi-Yonah, M., ed., *Encyclopaedia of Archaeological Excavations in the Holy Land*, vols. I–II, Englewood Cliffs, N.J., 1975–6; vols. III–IV, Englewood Cliffs, N.J. (in press).
Kallai, Z., *The Tribes of Israel*, Jerusalem, 1967 (in Hebrew).
Kenyon, K.M., *Archaeology in the Holy Land*, London, 1960.
Winton Thomas, D., ed., *Archaeology and Old Testament Study*, Oxford, 1967.
Wright, G.E., *Biblical Archaeology* (rev. ed.), Philadelphia, 1962.
——, and F.V. Filson, *The Westminster Historical Atlas to the Bible* (2nd ed.), Philadelphia, 1956.
Yadin, Y., *The Art of Warfare in Biblical Lands*, vols. I–II, Jerusalem-Ramat Gan, 1963.

Biblical Encyclopaedias and Introductions to the Bible

Dictionnaire de la Bible, Suppléments I–X, Paris, 1928–74 (in progress).
Eissfeldt, O., *The Old Testament: An Introduction*, Oxford, 1965.
Encyclopaedia Biblica, vols. I–VII, Jerusalem, 1950–71 (in progress).
Interpreter's Dictionary of the Bible, vols. I–IV, New York-Nashville, 1962.
Sellin, E., and G. Fohrer, *Introduction to the Old Testament* (rev. ed.), Nashville, 1968.

Collections of Sources Relating to Biblical History

Breasted, J.H., *Ancient Records of Egypt*, vols. I–V, Chicago, 1906–7.
Donner, H., and W. Röllig, *Kanaanäische und Aramäische Inschriften*, vols. I–III (2nd ed.), Wiesbaden, 1966–8.
Galling, K., ed., *Textbuch zur Geschichte Israels* (2nd ed.), Tübingen, 1968.
Gibson, C.L., *Textbook of Syrian Semitic Inscriptions*, vols. I–II, Oxford, 1971–5.
Luckenbill, D.D., *Ancient Records of Assyria and Babylonia*, vols. I–II, Chicago, 1926–7.
Pritchard, J.B., ed., *Ancient Near Eastern Texts Relating to the Old Testament* (3rd ed. with a supplement), Princeton, 1969.
Winton Thomas, D., ed., *Documents from Old Testament Times*, London-New York, 1958.

Collected Essays and Studies

Alt, A., *Kleine Schriften zur Geschichte des Volkes Israel*, vols. I–III, Munich, 1953–9.
——, *Essays on Old Testament History and Religion*, Garden City, N.Y., 1968.
Cross, F.M., *Canaanite Myth and Hebrew Epic*, Cambridge, Mass., 1973.
Freedman, D.N., and J.C. Greenfield, eds., *New Directions in Biblical Archaeology*, Garden City, N.Y., 1969.
——, G.E. Wright, and E.F. Campbell, Jr., eds., *The Biblical Archaeologist Reader*, vols. I–III, Garden City, N.Y., 1961–70.
Mazar, B., *Canaan and Israel: Historical Essays*, Jerusalem, 1974 (in Hebrew).
——, *Cities and Districts in Eretz-Israel*, Jerusalem, 1975 (in Hebrew).
Noth, M., *Aufsätze zur biblischen Landes und Altertumskunde*, vols. I–II, Neukirchen-Vluyn, 1971.
——, *The Laws in the Pentateuch and Other Essays*, Edinburgh and London, 1966.
Orlinsky, H.M., *Essays in Biblical Culture and Bible Translation*, New York, 1974.
Speiser, E.A., *Oriental and Biblical Studies*, J.J. Finkelstein and M. Greenberg, eds., Philadelphia, 1967.

de Vaux, R. *Bible et Orient,* Paris, 1967.

——, *The Bible and the Ancient Near East,* London, 1972.

Wright, G.E., ed., *The Bible and the Ancient Near East: Essays in Honor of William Foxwell Albright,* Garden City, N.Y., 1961.

Origins and the Formative Period

General Works

Albright, W.F., *Yahwe and the Gods of Canaan,* London, 1968.

Bright, J., *Early Israel in Recent History Writing,* London, 1956.

Rowley, H.H., *From Joseph to Joshua,* London, 1950.

de Vaux, R., *Histoire anciennes d'Israel,* vols. I–II, Paris, 1971–3.

——, G.E. Mendenhall and M. Greenberg, 'Method in the Study of Early Hebrew History' in J. Ph. Hyatt, ed., *The Bible in Modern Scholarship,* Nashville-New York, 1964, pp. 15–43.

The World History of the Jewish People, vol. I, *At the Dawn of Civilization,* E.A. Speiser, ed., New Brunswick, N.J., 1964; vol. II, *Patriarchs,* B. Mazar, ed., New Brunswick, N.J., 1970: J. Liver, 'The Bible and Its Historical Sources,' pp. 35–62; H. Tadmor, 'The Chronology of the Ancient Near East in the Second Millennium BCE,' pp. 63–101; Y. Yadin, 'Warfare in the Second Millennium,' pp. 129–57 (for other chapters see below); vol. III, *Judges,* B. Mazar, ed., New Brunswick, N.J., 1971 (relevant chapters cited below).

Canaan: History, Society and Culture

Albright, W.F., 'The Amarna Letters from Palestine' in *The Cambridge Ancient History,* vol. II, part 2 (3rd ed.), Cambridge, 1975, pp. 98–116.

Campbell, E.F., *The Chronology of the Amarna Letters,* Baltimore, 1964.

Gray, J., *The Legacy of Canaan* (2nd ed.), Leiden, 1965.

Helck, H.W., *Die Beziehungen Ägyptens zu Vorderasien im 3. und 2. Jahrtausend v. Chr.* (2nd ed.), Wiesbaden, 1971.

Klengel, H., *Geschichte Syriens im 2. Jahrtausend v. u. Z.,* vols. I–III, Berlin, 1965–70.

Malamat, A., 'Campaigns of Amenhotep II and Thutmose IV to Canaan,' *Scripta Hierosolymitana,* 8 (1961), 218–31.

——, 'The Egyptian Decline in Canaan and the Sea-Peoples' in *The World History of the Jewish People,* vol. III, pp. 23–38, 294–300.

Mazar, B., 'Canaan in the Patriarchal Age' in *The World History of the Jewish People,* vol. III, pp. 169–87.

——, 'The Historical Development' in *The World History of the Jewish People,* vol. II, pp. 3–22.

Mercer, S.A.B., *The Tell el-Amarna Tablets,* Toronto, 1939.

Moran, W.L., 'The Syrian Scribe of the Jerusalem Amarna Letters' in H. Goedicke and J.J.M. Roberts, eds., *Unity and Diversity,* Baltimore, 1975, pp. 146–66.

Rainey, A.F., *El Amarna Tablets (359–379),* Neukirchen-Vluyn, 1970.

Reviv, H., 'Some Comments on the Maryannu,' *Israel Exploration Journal,* 22 (1972), 218–28.

Simons, J., *Handbook of the Study of the Egyptian Topographical Lists Relating to Western Asia,* Leiden, 1937.

Hebrew Origins, the Patriarchs and the Exodus

Albright, W.F., 'Abram the Hebrew,' *Bulletin of the American Schools of Oriental Research*, 163 (1961), 36–54.

——, 'From the Patriarchs to Moses,' *The Biblical Archaeologist*, 36 (1973), 5–33, 48–76.

Cazelles, H., 'Patriarches' in *Supplément, Dictionnaire de la Bible*, 7 (1961), cols. 81–156.

——, 'Les localisations de l'Exode et la critique littéraire,' *Revue Biblique*, 62 (1955), 321–64.

Cross, F.M., 'Yahwe and the God of the Patriarchs,' *Harvard Theological Review*, 55 (1962), 225–59.

Eissfeldt, O., 'The Exodus and the Wanderings' in *The Cambridge Ancient History*, vol. II, part 2 (3rd ed.), Cambridge, 1975, pp. 307–30.

Giveon, R., *Les bédouins Shosu des documents égyptiens*, Leiden, 1971.

Glueck, N., 'The Age of Abraham in the Negeb,' *The Biblical Archaeologist*, 18 (1955), 2–9.

Gordon, C.H., 'Abraham of Ur' in D. Winton Thomas, ed., *Hebrew and Semitic Studies Presented to G.R. Driver*, Oxford, 1962, pp. 77–84.

——, 'Biblical Customs and the Nuzu Tablets,' *The Biblical Archaeologist*, 3 (1940), 1–12.

Greenberg, M., *The Hab/piru*, New Haven, 1955.

Haran, M., 'The Religion of the Patriarchs' in *The World History of the Jewish People*, vol. II, pp. 219–45.

Herrmann, S., 'Das Werden Israels,' *Theologische Literaturzeitung*, 87 (1962), 561–74.

Malamat, A., 'King Lists of the Old Babylonian Period and Biblical Genealogies,' *Journal of the American Oriental Society*, 88 (1968), 163–73.

——, 'Northern Canaan and the Mari Texts' in J.A. Sanders, ed., *Near Eastern Archaeology in the 20th Century: Essays in Honor of N. Glueck*, Garden City, N.Y., 1970, pp. 167–77.

——, 'Mari,' *The Biblical Archaeologist*, 34 (1971), 2–22.

Mazar, B., 'The Historical Background of the Book of Genesis,' *Journal of Near Eastern Studies*, 28 (1969), 73–83.

Parrot, A., *Mari – capitale fabuleuse*, Paris, 1974.

Posener, G., *Princes et pays d'Asie et de Nubie*, Brussels, 1940.

Redford, D.B., *A Study of the Biblical Story of Joseph*, Leiden, 1970.

Speiser, E.A., *Genesis (Anchor Bible)*, vol. I, Garden City, N.Y., 1964.

Thompson, Th. L., *The Historicity of the Patriarchal Narratives*, Berlin, 1974.

Van Seters, J., *Abraham in History and Tradition*, New Haven, 1975.

Yeivin, S., 'The Age of the Patriarchs,' *Rivista Studi Orientali*, 38 (1963), 277–302.

Conquest and Settlement

Aharoni, Y., 'The Settlement of Canaan' in *The World History of the Jewish People*, vol. III, pp. 94–128.

Alt, A., *Kleine Schriften zur Geschichte des Volkes Israel*, vol. I, Munich, 1953, pp. 126–92.

——, *Essays on Old Testament History and Religion*, Garden City, N.Y., 1968, pp. 173–221.

Callaway, J., 'New Evidence on the Conquest of 'Ai,' *Journal of Biblical Literature*, 87 (1968), 312–20.

Glueck, N., *The Other Side of the Jordan* (2nd ed.), Cambridge, Mass., 1970.

Kaufmann, Y., *The Biblical Account of the Conquest of Palestine*, Jerusalem, 1953.

——, 'Traditions Concerning Early Israelite History in Canaan,' *Scripta Hierosolymitana*, 8 (1961), 303–34.

Kenyon, K.M., *Digging Up Jericho*, London, 1957.

Malamat, A., 'Aspects of Tribal Societies in Mari and Israel' in *XVe Rencontre Assyriologique Internationale*, Leiden, 1967, pp. 129–38.

——, 'The Danite Migration and the Pan-Israelite Exodus-Conquest,' *Biblica*, 51 (1970), 1–16.

——, 'Conquest of Canaan: Israelite Conduct of War According to the Biblical Tradition' in *Encyclopaedia Judaica Yearbook 1975/76*, Jerusalem, 1976 (in press); see also *Proceedings of the Symposium on 'The Archaeology and Chronology of the First Period of the Iron Age' in Honor of the 75th Anniversary of the American Schools of Oriental Research*, New Haven (in press).

Mazar, B., 'The Exodus and Conquest' in *The World History of the Jewish People*, vol. III, pp. 69–93.

Noth, M., *Das System der zwölf Stämme Israels*, Stuttgart, 1930.

——, 'Der Beitrag der Archäologie zur Geschichte Israels,' *Supplement to Vetus Testamentum*, 7 (1960), 262–82.

Pritchard, J.B., *Gibeon – Where the Sun Stood Still*, Princeton, 1962.

Weippert, M., *The Settlement of the Israelite Tribes in Palestine*, London, 1971.

Wright, G.E., 'The Literary and Historical Problem of Joshua 10 and Judges 1,' *Journal of Near Eastern Studies*, 5 (1946), 105–14.

Yadin, Y., *Hazor*, London, 1972.

Yeivin, S., *The Israelite Conquest of Canaan*, Istanbul, 1971.

The Period of the Judges

Anderson, G.W., 'Israel: Amphictyony: *'AM; KAHAL; 'EDAH*' in H.T. Frank and W.L. Reed, eds., *Translating and Understanding the Old Testament: Essays in Honor of H.G. May*, Nashville-New York, 1970, pp. 135–51.

Buber, M., *Kingship of God* (3rd ed.), London-New York, 1967.

Fohrer, G., '"Amphiktyonie" und "Bund",' *Studien zur alttest. Theologie und Geschichte* (Beihefte zur Zeitschrift für die alttest. Wissenschaft 115), Berlin, 1969, pp. 84–119.

Freedman, D.N., 'Early Israelite History in the Light of Early Poetry' in H. Goedicke and J.J.M. Roberts, eds., *Unity and Diversity*, Baltimore, 1975, pp. 3–35.

Malamat, A., 'The Period of the Judges' in *The World History of the Jewish People*, vol. III, pp. 129–63, 314–23.

——, 'Charismatic Leadership in the Book of Judges' in F.M. Cross and P. Hanson, eds., *Magnalia Dei: The Mighty Acts of God* (Essays on the Bible and Archaeology in Memory of E. G. Wright), Garden City, N.Y. (in press).

Meyer, E., *Die Israeliten und ihre Nachbarstämme*, Halle a.S., 1906.

Noth, M., 'Das Amt des "Richters Israels"' in *A. Bertholet Festschrift*, Tübingen, 1950, pp. 404–17.

Orlinsky, H.M., 'The Tribal System of Israel and Related Groups in the Period of the Judges,' *Oriens Antiquus*, 1 (1962), 11–20.

von Rad, G., *Der heilige Krieg im alten Israel*, Zurich, 1952.

Richter, W., *Traditionsgeschichtliche Untersuchungen zum Richterbuch*, Bonn, 1963.

Reviv, H., 'The Government of Shechem in the El-Amarna Period and in the Days of Abimelech,' *Israel Exploration Journal*, 16 (1966), 252–7.

Smend, R., *Yahwe War and Tribal Confederation*, Nashville, 1970.

Täubler, E., *Die Epoche der Richter*, Tübingen, 1950.

Wright, G.E., *Shechem—The Biography of a Biblical City*, New York-Toronto, 1965.
Zobel, H.J., *Stammesspruch und Geschichte* (Beihefte zur Zeitschrift für die alttest. Wissenschaft 95), Berlin, 1965.

The Struggle with the Philistines

Albright, W.F., 'Syria, the Philistines and Phoenicia' in *The Cambridge Ancient History*, vol. II, part 2 (3rd ed.), Cambridge, 1975, pp. 507–36.
Alt, A., *Kleine Schriften zur Geschichte des Volkes Israel*, vol. I, Munich, 1953, pp. 216–30.
Barnett, R.D., 'The Sea Peoples' in *The Cambridge Ancient History*, vol. II, part 2 (3rd ed.), Cambridge, 1975, pp. 359–78.
Dothan, T., *The Material Culture of the Philistines*, Cambridge, Mass. (in press).
Macalister, R.A.S., *The Philistines*, London, 1914.
Mazar, B., 'The Philistines and the Rise of Israel and Tyre,' *Proceedings of the Israel Academy of Sciences*, I/7 (1964).
Rahtjen, B.D., 'Philistine and Hebrew Amphictyonies,' *Journal of Near Eastern Studies*, 24 (1965), 100–4.
Wainright, G.A., 'Some Early Philistine History,' *Vetus Testamentum*, 9 (1959), 73–84.
——, 'Some Sea-Peoples,' *Journal of Egyptian Archaeology*, 47 (1961), 71–90.

The Period of the First Temple, the Babylonian Exile and the Restoration

Biblical Historiography and Chronology

Cross, F.M., *Canaanite Myth and Hebrew Epic*, Cambridge, Mass., 1973, pp. 274–89.
Freedman, D.N., 'The Chronicler's Purpose,' *Catholic Biblical Quarterly*, 23 (1961), 436–42.
Jepsen, A., *Die Quellen des Königbuches* (2nd ed.), Halle a.S., 1956.
Liver, J., 'The Book of the Acts of Solomon,' *Biblica*, 48 (1967), 75–101.
Mazar, B., 'Ancient Israelite Historiography,' *Israel Exploration Journal*, 2 (1952), 82–8.
Mowinckel, S., 'Israelite Historiography,' *Annual of the Swedish Theological Institute*, 2 (1963), 4–26.
Noth, M., *Überlieferungsgeschichtliche Studien*, vol. I, Halle a.S., 1943.
von Rad, G., *The Problem of the Hexateuch and Other Essays*, Edinburgh and London, 1966, pp. 166–221.
——, *Das Geschichtsbild des chronistischen Werks*, Stuttgart, 1930.
Tadmor, H., 'Chronology' in *Encyclopaedia Biblica*, vol. IV, Jerusalem 1962, cols. 245–310 (in Hebrew).
Thiele, E.R., *The Mysterious Numbers of the Hebrew Kings* (2nd ed.), Grand Rapids, Mich., 1965.
Weinfield, M., *Deuteronomy and the Deuteronomic School*, Oxford, 1972.
Welch, A.C., *The Work of the Chronicler*, London, 1939.

Political and Religious Institutions

Alt, A., *Essays on Old Testament History and Religion*, Garden City, N.Y., 1968, pp. 313–35.
Buber, M., *The Prophetic Faith*, New York, 1949.

Buccellati, G., *Cities and Nations of Ancient Syria* (Studi Semitici 26), Rome, 1967.

Haran, M., *Ages and Institutions in the Bible*, Tel Aviv, 1972 (in Hebrew).

Kaufmann, Y., *The History of the Religion of Israel*, II, Books 1–2, III, Books 1–2, Tel Aviv, 1946–8 (in Hebrew).

Kraus, H.J., *Worship in Israel*, Richmond, Va., 1966.

Lindblom, J., *Prophecy in Ancient Israel*, Oxford, 1962.

Malamat, A., 'Organs of Statecraft in the Israelite Monarchy,' *The Biblical Archaeologist*, 28 (1965), 34–50.

Soggin, J.A., *Das Königtum in Israel* (Beihefte zur Zeitschrift für die alttest. Wissenschaft 104), Leiden, 1967.

Tadmor, H., 'The People and the Kingship in Ancient Israel: The Role of Political Institutions in the Biblical Period,' *Journal of World History*, 11 (1968), 46–68.

Talmon, S., 'The Biblical Concept of Jerusalem,' *Journal of Ecumenical Studies*, 8 (1971), 300–16.

——, 'The Judaean "Am-Ha'areṣ" in Historical Perspective' in *Fourth World Congress of Jewish Studies*, vol. I, Jerusalem, 1967, pp. 71–6.

Thornton, T., 'Charismatic Kingship in Israel and Judah,' *Journal of Theological Studies*, n.s. 14 (1963), 1–11.

de Vaux, R., *Jerusalem and the Prophets, Goldenson Lecture for 1965*, Cincinnati, 1967.

Weber, M., *Ancient Judaism*, H.H. Gerth and D. Martindale, eds., Glencoe, Ill., 1952.

Uffenheimer, B., *Ancient Prophecy in Israel*, Jerusalem 1973 (in Hebrew).

From Samuel to the Division of the Kingdom

Albright, W.F., *Samuel and the Beginnings of the Prophetical Movement, Goldenson Lecture for 1961*, Cincinnati, 1961.

Alt, A., *Essays on Old Testament History and Religion*, Garden City, N.Y., 1968, pp. 225–309.

Evans, G., 'Rehoboam's Advisers at Shechem and Political Institutions in Israel and Sumer,' *Journal of Near Eastern Studies*, 25 (1966), 273–9.

Katzenstein, H.J., *The History of Tyre*, Jerusalem, 1973.

Malamat, A., 'Aspects of the Foreign Policies of David and Solomon,' *Journal of Near Eastern Studies*, 22 (1963), 1–17.

Mazar, B., 'The Military Elite of King David,' *Vetus Testamentum*, 13 (1963), 310–20.

——, *Canaan and Israel*, Jerusalem, 1974, pp. 208–21 (in Hebrew).

Mendelsohn, I., 'Samuel's Denunciation of Kingship in the Light of the Akkadian Documents from Ugarit,' *Bulletin of the American Schools of Oriental Research*, 143 (1956), 17–22.

Mettinger, T.N., *Solomonic State Officials – A Study of Civil Government Officials of the Israelite Monarchy*, Lund, 1971.

Rainey, A.F., 'Compulsory Labour Gangs in Ancient Israel,' *Israel Exploration Journal*, 20 (1970), 191–202.

Rost, L., *Die Überlieferung der Thronnachfolge Davids*, Stuttgart, 1926.

Soggin, J.A., *Old Testament and Oriental Studies* (Biblica et Orientalia 29), Rome, 1975, pp. 31–49.

Weiser, A., *Samuel und die Vorgeschichte des israelitischen Königtums*, Göttingen, 1962.

Yadin, Y., 'Solomon's City Wall and Gate at Gezer,' *Israel Exploration Journal*, 8 (1958), 80–6.

——, 'New Light on Solomon's Megiddo,' *The Biblical Archaeologist*, 23 (1960), 62–8.

From the Division of the Kingdom to the Time of Josiah

Childs, B.S., *Isaiah and the Assyrian Crisis* (Studies in Biblical Theology, Second Series 3), Naperville, Ill., 1967.

Cogan, M., *Imperialism and Religion: Assyria, Judah and Israel in the Eighth and Seventh Centuries B.C.* (Society of Biblical Literature, Monograph Series, vol. 19), Missoula, Mont., 1974.

Elat, M., 'The Campaigns of Shalmaneser III against Aram and Israel,' *Israel Exploration Journal*, 25 (1975), 25–35.

Eph'al, I., 'The Penetration of Arab Tribes to the Periphery of Palestine and Southern Syria in the 8th Century B.C.E.' *Fifth World Congress of Jewish Studies*, vol. I, Jerusalem, 1969, pp. 145–51 (in Hebrew).

Hallo, W.W., 'From Qarqar to Carchemish,' *The Biblical Archaeologist*, 23 (1960), 34–61.

Jepsen, A., 'Israel und Damaskus,' *Archiv für Orientforschung*, 14 (1941–1944), 153–72.

Malamat, A., 'Kingship and Council in Israel and Sumer; A Parallel,' *Journal of Near Eastern Studies*, 22 (1963), 247–52.

Mazar, B., 'The Historical Background of the Samaria Ostraca,' *Journal of the Palestine Oriental Society*, 21 (1948), 117–33.

——, 'The Campaign of Pharaoh Shishak to Palestine,' *Supplement to Vetus Testamentum*, 4 (1957), 57–66.

——, 'The Aramean Empire and Its Relations with Israel,' *The Biblical Archaeologist*, 25 (1962), 97–120.

Millard, A.R. and H. Tadmor, 'Adad-Nirari III in Syria,' *Iraq*, 35 (1973), 57–64.

Na'aman, N., 'Sennacherib's "Letter to God" on His Campaign to Judah,' *Bulletin of the American Schools of Oriental Research*, 214 (1974), 25–39.

Oded, B., 'The Phoenician Cities and the Assyrian Empire in the Time of Tiglath-pileser III,' *Zeitschrift des Deutschen Palästina-Vereins*, 90 (1974), 38–49.

Tadmor, H., 'The Campaigns of Sargon II of Assur,' *Journal of Cuneiform Studies*, 12 (1958), 22–40, 77–100.

——, 'Azriyau of Yaudi,' *Scripta Hierosolymitana*, 8 (1961), 232–71.

——, 'The Southern Border of Aram,' *Israel Exploration Journal*, 12 (1962), 114–22.

——, 'Philistia under Assyrian Rule,' *The Biblical Archaeologist*, 29 (1966), 86–102.

——, 'Assyria and the West: The Ninth Century and Its Aftermath' in H. Goedicke and J.J.M. Roberts, eds., *Unity and Diversity*, Baltimore, 1975, 36–48.

Unger, M.F., *Israel and the Aramaeans of Damascus*, London, 1957.

Weippert, M., 'Menahem von Israel und seine Zeitgenossen in einer Steleninschrift des assyrischen Königs Tiglathpileser III aus dem Iran,' *Zeitschrift des Deutschen Palästina-Vereins*, 89 (1973), 26–53.

The Last Days of Judah and the Babylonian Exile

Aharoni, Y., *Arad Inscriptions, Judean Desert Studies*, Jerusalem, 1975 (in Hebrew).

Albright, W.F., 'King Joiachin in Exile,' *The Biblical Archaeologist*, 5 (1942), 49–55.

Freedy, K.S., and D.B. Redford, 'The Dates in Ezekiel in Relation to Biblical, Babylonian and Egyptian Sources,' *Journal of the American Oriental Society*, 90 (1970), 462–85.

Greenberg, M., 'Ezekiel 17 and the Policy of Psammetichus II,' *Journal of Biblical Literature*, 76 (1957), 304–9.

Lance, H.D., 'The Royal Stamps and the Kingdom of Josiah,' *Harvard Theological Review*, 64 (1971), 315–32.

Malamat, A., 'Jeremiah and the Last Two Kings of Judah,' *Palestine Exploration Quarterly*, 83 (1951), 81–7.

——, 'The Last Kings of Judah and the Fall of Jerusalem,' *Israel Exploration Journal*, 18 (1968), 137–56.

——, 'Josiah's Bid for Armageddon,' *Journal of the Near Eastern Society of Columbia University*, 5 (1973), 267–79.

——, 'The Twilight of Judah: In the Egyptian-Babylonian Maelstrom,' *Supplement to Vetus Testamentum*, 28 (1974), 123–45.

Naveh, J., 'A Hebrew Letter from the 7th Century B.C.,' *Israel Exploration Journal*, 10 (1960), 129–39.

Tadmor, H., 'Chronology of the Last Kings of Judah,' *Journal of Near Eastern Studies*, 15 (1956), 226–30.

Wiseman, D.J., *Chronicles of Chaldean Kings (626–556 B.C.) in the British Museum*, London, 1956.

Yeivin, S., 'Families and Parties in the Kingdom of Judah,' *Tarbiz* 12 (1940), 241–67 (in Hebrew).

The Return and the Persian Period

Ackroyd, P.R., *Exile and Restoration*, London, 1968.

Alt, A., *Kleine Schirften zur Geschichte des Volkes Israel*, vol. II, Munich, 1959, pp. 316–37.

Avigad, N., *A New Discovery of an Archive of Bullae from the Period of Ezra and Nehemia*, Jerusalem (in press).

Bickerman, E., 'The Edict of Cyrus in Ezra 1,' *Journal of Biblical Literature*, 65 (1946), 249–75.

——, *From Ezra to the Last of the Maccabees*, New York, 1962, pp. 3–90.

Cross, F.M., 'Aspects of Samaritan and Jewish History in Late Persian and Hellenistic Times,' *Harvard Theological Review*, 59 (1966), 201–11.

——, 'A Reconstruction of the Judean Restoration,' *Journal of Biblical Literature*, 94 (1975), 4–18.

Galling, K., *Studien zur Geschichte Israels im persischen Zeitalter*, Tübingen, 1964.

Japhet, S., 'The Supposed Common Authorship of Chronicles and Ezra-Nehemia Investigated Anew,' *Vetus Testamentum*, 18 (1968), 330–71.

Kaufmann, Y., *The Babylonian Captivity and Deutero-Isaiah*, New York, 1970.

Liver, J., *The House of David*, Jerusalem, 1959 (in Hebrew).

Mazar, B., 'The Tobiads,' *Israel Exploration Journal*, 7 (1957), 137–45, 229–38.

Porten, B., *Archives from Elephantine*, Berkeley and Los Angeles, 1968.

Rainey, A.F., 'The Satrapy "Beyond the River",' *Australian Journal of Biblical Archaeology*, 1 (1969), 51–78.

Schaeder, H.H., *Esra der Schreiber* (Beiträge zur historischen Theologie 5), Tübingen, 1930.

Smith, M., *Palestinian Parties and Politics That Shaped the Old Testament*, New York and London, 1971.

Stern, E., *The Material Culture of the Land of the Bible in the Persian Period (538–332 B.C.E.)*, Jerusalem, 1973 (in Hebrew).

Tadmor, H., 'The Historical Background of the Edict of Cyrus' in *Oz le-David: David Ben Gurion Anniversary Volume*, Jerusalem, 1964, pp. 450–73 (in Hebrew).

The Period of the Second Temple, the Mishnah and the Talmud: Introductory Works

The Hellenistic and Roman World

Bevan, E.R., *The House of Seleucus,* vols. I–II, London, 1902.
Bikerman, E., *Institutions des Séleucides,* Paris, 1938.
The Cambridge Ancient History, vols. VII–XII, Cambridge, 1928–39.
Debevoise, N.C., *A Political History of Parthia,* Chicago, 1938.
Dessau, H., *Geschichte der römischen Kaiserzeit,* vol. II, part 2, Berlin, 1930.
Fraser, P.M., *Ptolemaic Alexandria,* vols. I–III, Oxford, 1972.
Jones, A.H.M., *The Later Roman Empire,* vols. I–III, Oxford, 1964.
Nilsson, M.P., *Geschichte der griechischen Religion,* vol. II (2nd ed.), Munich, 1961.
Préaux, C., *L'économie royale des Lagides,* Brussels, 1939.
Rostovtzeff, M., *The Social and Economic History of the Hellenistic World,* vols. I–III, Oxford, 1953.
———, *The Social and Economic History of the Roman Empire,* vols. I–II (2nd ed.), Oxford, 1957.
Tarn, W.W., *Hellenistic Civilisation* (3rd ed.), London, 1952.
Will, E., *Histoire politique du monde hellénistique,* vols. I–II, Nancy, 1966–7.

The Period of the Second Temple

General Works

Abel, F.M., *Histoire de la Palestine,* vols. I–II, Paris, 1952.
Baron, S.W., *A Social and Religious History of the Jews,* vols. I–II, New York, 1952.
Bickerman, E.J., *From Ezra to the Last of the Maccabees,* New York, 1962.
Derenbourg, J., *Essai sur l'histoire et la géographie de la Palestine,* Paris, 1867.
Juster, J., *Les Juifs dans l'empire romain,* vols. I–II, Paris, 1914.
Klausner, J., *A History of the Second Temple,* vols. I–V (2nd ed.), Jerusalem, 1951 (in Hebrew).
Meyer, Ed., *Ursprung und Anfänge des Christentums,* vols. I–III, Stuttgart-Berlin, 1921–3.
Radin, M., *The Jews Among the Greeks and Romans,* Philadelphia, 1915.
Robinson, T.H., and W.O.E. Oesterley, *A History of Israel,* vol. II, Oxford, 1932.
Safrai, S., and M. Stern, eds., *The Jewish People in the First Century,* vol. I, *Compendia ad Novum Testamentum,* Leiden, 1974.
Schlatter, A., *Geschichte Israels von Alexander des Grossen bis Hadrian* (3rd ed.), Stuttgart, 1925.
Schürer, E., *Geschichte des jüdischen Volkes in Zeitalter Jesu Christi,* vols. I–III, Leipzig, 1901–9.
———, *The History of the Jewish People in the Age of Jesus Christ* (a new English version revised and edited by G. Vermes and F. Millar), vol. I, Edinburgh, 1973.
Zeitlin, S., *The Rise and Fall of the Judean State,* vols. I–II, Philadelphia, 1962–7.

Collections of Documents, Sources and Commentaries

Abel, F.M., *Les livres des Maccabées,* Paris, 1949.
Charles, R.H., *Apocrypha and Pseudoepigrapha,* vols. I–II, Oxford, 1913.

Dancy, J.C., *A Commentary on 1 Maccabees,* Oxford, 1954.

Frey, J.B., *Corpus Inscriptionum Iudaicarum,* vols. I–II, Rome, 1936–52.

Gabba, E., *Iscrizioni greche e latine per lo studio della Bibbia,* Turin, 1958.

Grintz, V., *The Book of Judith: A Reconstruction of the Original Hebrew Text with Introduction and Commentary,* Jerusalem, 1957 (in Hebrew).

Lifshitz, B., *Donateurs et fondateurs dans les synagogues juives,* Paris, 1967.

Nikiprowetzky, V., *La troisième Sibylle,* Paris, 1970.

Rabin, C., *The Zadokite Documents* (2nd ed.), Oxford, 1958.

Reinach, T., *Textes d'auteurs grecs et romaines relatifs au judaïsme,* Paris, 1895.

Smallwood, E.M., *Philonis Alexandrini Legatio ad Gaium,* Leiden, 1961.

Stern, M., *Greek and Latin Authors on Jews and Judaism,* vol. I, Jerusalem, 1974.

——, *Documents on the History of the Hasmonean Revolt* (2nd ed.), Tel Aviv, 1972 (in Hebrew).

Tcherikover, V.A., A. Fuks and M. Stern, *Corpus Papyrorum Judaicarum,* vols. I–III, Cambridge, Mass., 1957–64.

Vermes, G., *The Dead Sea Scrolls in English,* Harmondsworth, Middlesex, 1962.

Historical Geography

Abel, F.M., *Géographie de la Palestine,* vols. I–II, Paris, 1933–8.

Avi-Yonah, M., *The Holy Land from the Persian to the Arab Conquest: Historical Geography,* Grand Rapids, Mich., 1966.

Historiography

Bunge, J.G., *Untersuchungen zum zweiten Makkabäerbuch,* Bonn, 1971.

Feldman, L.H., 'The Sources of Josephus' Antiquities, Book 19,' *Latomus,* 21 (1962), 320–33.

Momigliano, A., *Prime linee di storia della tradizione maccabaica,* Rome, 1930.

Niese, B., *Kritik der beiden Makkabäerbücher,* Berlin, 1900.

Schunck, K.D., *Die Quellen des I. und II. Makkabäerbuches,* Halle, 1954.

Stern, M., 'Nicolaus of Damascus as a Source of Jewish History in the Herodian and Hasmonean Age' in B. Uffenheimer, ed., *Studies in Bible and Jewish History Dedicated to the Memory of Jacob Liver,* Tel Aviv, 1971, pp. 375–94.

——, 'Strabo on Jews' in M. Dorman *et al.,* eds., *Essays in Jewish History and Philology in Memory of Gedaliahu Allon,* Tel Aviv, 1970, pp. 169–91.

Thackeray, H. St. J., *Josephus, the Man and the Historian,* New York, 1929.

Wacholder, B., *Nicolaus of Damascus,* Berkeley-Los Angeles, 1962.

Judea Under Hellenistic Rule

Bickermann, E., 'La charte séleucide de Jérusalem,' *Revue des Etudes Juives,* 100 (1935), 4–35.

——, 'Une proclamation séleucide relative au Temple de Jérusalem,' *Syria,* 25 (1946–8), 67–85.

Cross, F.M., 'Aspects of Samaritan and Jewish History in Late Persian and Hellenistic Times,' *Harvard Theological Review,* 59 (1966), 201–11.

Gutman, Y., 'Alexander the Macedonian in Palestine,' *Tarbiz,* 11 (1940), 271–94 (in Hebrew).

Hengel, M., *Judentum und Hellenismus* (2nd ed.), Tübingen, 1973.

Stern, M., 'Notes on the Story of Joseph the Tobiad,' *Tarbiz,* 32 (1963), 35–47 (in Hebrew).

Tcherikover, V., *Hellenistic Civilization and the Jews,* Philadelphia, 1959.

The Hasmonean Revolt and the Hasmonean State

Avi-Yonah, M., 'The Battles in the Books of the Maccabees' in J. Gutman and M. Schwabe. eds., *Johanan Lewy Memorial Volume*, Jerusalem, 1949, pp. 13–24 (in Hebrew).

Bickermann, E., *Der Gott der Makkabäer*, Berlin, 1937.

——, 'Un document relatif à la persécution d'Antiochus IV Epiphane,' *Revue de l'histoire des religions*, 115 (1937), 188–223.

Heinemann, I., 'Wer veranlasste den Glaubenzwang der Makkabäerzeit?' *Monatsschrift für Geschichte und Wissenschaft des Judentums*, 82 (1938), 145–72.

Kanael, B., 'The Beginning of Maccabean Coinage,' *Israel Exploration Journal*, 1 (1950–1), 170–5.

Mørkholm, M., *Antiochus IV of Syria*, Copenhagen, 1966, pp. 135–59.

Plöger, O , 'Die Feldzüge der Seleukiden gegen den Makkabäer Judas,' *Zeitschrift des Deutschen Palästina-Vereins*, 74 (1958), 155–88.

Rabin, C., 'Alexander Jannaeus and the Pharisees,' *Journal of Jewish Studies*, 7 (1956), 3–11.

Rappaport, M., 'La Judée et Rome pendant la règne d'Alexandre Jannée,' *Revue des Etudes Juives*, 127 (1968), 329–45.

——, 'The Hellenistic Cities and the Judaisation of Palestine in the Hasmonean Age' in S. Perlman and B. Shimron, eds., *Commentationes Benzioni Katz dedicatae*, Tel Aviv, 1967, pp. 219–30 (in Hebrew).

Shotwell, W.A., 'The Problem of the Syrian Akra,' *Bulletin of the American Schools of Oriental Research*, 176 (1964), 10–19.

Stern, M., 'The Death of Onias the Fourth,' *Zion*, 25 (1960), 1–16 (in Hebrew).

——, 'The Relations Between Judaea and Rome During the Rule of John Hyrcanus,' *Zion*, 26 (1961), 1–22 (in Hebrew).

——, 'The Political Background of the Wars of Alexander Jannai,' *Tarbiz*, 33 (1964), 325–36 (in Hebrew).

——, 'The Hasmonean Revolt and Its Place in the History of Jewish Society and Religion,' *Journal of World History*, 11 (1968), 92–106.

The Herodian Monarchy and the Roman Administration at the End of the Second Temple Period

Bammel, E., 'Die Bruderfolge im Hochpriestertum der Herodianisch-römischen Zeit,' *Zeitschrift des Deutschen Palästina-Vereins*, 70 (1954), 147–53.

Hoehner, H.W., *Herod Antipas*, Cambridge, 1972.

Momigliano, A., 'Ricerche sull' organizzazione della Giudea sotto il dominio romano,' *Annali della R. Scuola Normale Superiore di Pisa*, ser. II., vol. 3 (1934), 183–221; 347–96.

Otto, W., *Herodes*, Stuttgart, 1913.

Schalit, A., *Roman Administration in Palestine*, Jerusalem, 1937 (in Hebrew).

——, *König Herodes*, Berlin, 1969.

Sherwin-White, A.N., *Roman Society and Roman Law in the New Testament*, Oxford, 1963.

Smallwood, E.M., 'High Priests and Politics in Roman Palestine,' *Journal of Theological Studies*, 13 (1962), 14–34.

Stern, M., 'Herod's Policy and Jewish Society at the End of the Second Temple,' *Tarbiz*, 35 (1966), 235–53 (in Hebrew).

Religion, Sects and Society at the End of the Second Temple Period

Allon, G., 'The Attitude of the Pharisees to the Roman Government and the House of Herod,' *Scripta Hierosolymitana,* 7 (1961), 53–78.

Bousset, W. and H. Gressmann, *Die Religion des Judentums im späthellenistischen Zeitalter,* Tübingen, 1926.

Cross, F.M., *The Ancient Library of Qumran,* Garden City, N.Y., 1961.

Ephron, Y., 'The Sanhedrin of the Second Temple' in S. Perlman and B. Shimron, eds., *Commentationes Benzioni Katz dedicatae,* Tel Aviv, 1967, pp. 167–204 (in Hebrew).

Hengel, M., *Die Zeloten,* Cologne-Leiden, 1961.

Herford, R.T., *The Pharisees,* London, 1924.

Hoenig, S.B., *The Great Sanhedrin,* Philadelphia, 1953.

Finkelstein, L., *The Pharisees,* vols. I–II (3rd ed.), Philadelphia, 1962.

Jeremias, J., *Jerusalem in the Time of Jesus,* London, 1969.

Krauss, S., *Synagogale Altertümer,* Berlin, 1922.

Lauterbach, J.Z., 'The Pharisees and Their Teaching,' *Hebrew Union College Annual,* 6 (1929), 96–139.

Le Moyne, J., *Les Sadducéens,* Paris, 1972.

Lightley, J.W., *Jewish Sects and Parties in the Time of Jesus,* London, 1925.

Liver, J., 'The Doctrine of the Two Messiahs in Sectarian Literature in the Time of the Second Temple,' *Harvard Theological Review,* 52 (1959), 149–85.

Maier, J., and J. Schreiner, eds., *Literatur und Religion des Frühjudentums,* Würzburg, 1973.

Marcus, R., 'The Pharisees in the Light of Modern Scholarship,' *Journal of Religion,* 32 (1952), 153–64.

Moore, G.F., *Judaism in the First Centuries of the Christian Era,* vols. I–III, Cambridge, Mass. 1971.

Neusner, J., *The Rabbinic Traditions About the Pharisees Before 70,* vols. I–III, Leiden, 1971.

Safrai, S., *Pilgrimage at the Time of the Second Temple,* Tel Aviv, 1965 (in Hebrew).

Smith, M., *Palestinian Parties and Politics That Shaped the Old Testament,* New York, 1971.

Stern, M., 'Zealots' in *Encyclopaedia Judaica Yearbook 1973,* Jerusalem, 1973, pp. 135–52.

Strugnell, J., 'Flavius Josephus and the Essenes,' *Journal of Biblical Literature,* 77 (1958), 106–15.

Wagner, S., *Die Essener in der wissenschaftlichen Diskussion vom Ausgang des 18. bis zum Beginn des 20. Jahrhunderts,* Berlin, 1960.

The Diaspora

Applebaum, S., *Greeks and Jews in Ancient Cyrene,* Jerusalem, 1969 (in Hebrew).

Brücklmeier, M., *Beiträge zur rechtlichen Stellung der Juden im römischen Reich,* Speyer, 1939.

Goodenough, E.R., *An Introduction to Philo Iudaeus* (2nd ed.), Oxford, 1962.

Heinemann, I., *Philons griechische und jüdische Bildung,* Breslau, 1932.

Leon, H.J., *The Jews of Ancient Rome,* Philadelphia, 1960.

Neusner, J., *A History of the Jews in Babylonia,* vol. I, Leiden, 1965.

Tcherikover, V., *The Jews in Egypt in the Hellenistic-Roman Age in the Light of the Papyri* (2nd ed.), Jerusalem, 1963 (in Hebrew).

Wolfson, H.A., *Philo,* vols. I–II, Cambridge, Mass., 1947.

The Era of the Mishnah and the Talmud

Jabneh and the World of the Sages

Allon, G., *Studies in Jewish History in the Times of the Second Temple, the Mishna and the Talmud*, Tel Aviv, 1957, pp. 219–73 (in Hebrew); English translation, Jerusalem, 1976 (in press).
Büchler, A., *The Economic Conditions of Judea After the Destruction of the Second Temple*, London, 1912.
Finkelstein, H., *Akiba, Scholar, Saint and Martyr*, Philadelphia, 1936.
Neusner, J., *A Life of Rabban Yochanan Ben Zakkai*, Leiden, 1962.
Safrai, S., *Rabbi Akiva ben Joseph, His Life and Teaching*, Jerusalem, 1970 (in Hebrew).

Between the Destruction of the Temple and the Bar Kokhba Revolt

Allon, G., *The History of the Jews of Palestine in the Period of the Mishna and the Talmud*, vol. I, Tel Aviv, 1953, pp. 114–92, 290–354 (in Hebrew); English translation, Jerusalem, 1976 (in press).
Büchler, A., 'Die Schauplätze des Barkochba-Krieges,' *Jewish Quarterly Review*, 16 (1904), 143–205.
Yadin, Y., *Judean Desert Caves*, A, Jerusalem, 1960; B, Jerusalem, 1961.
Yeivin, S., *The Bar Kokhba Revolt*, Jerusalem, 1946 (in Hebrew).

From the Revolt to the End of the Fourth Century

Allon, G., *The History of the Jews of Palestine in the Period of the Mishna and the Talmud*, vol. II, Tel Aviv, 1957, pp. 129–48 (in Hebrew); English translation, Jerusalem, 1976 (in press).
Baer, Y., 'The Jews, the Church and the Roman Empire from the Time of Septimius Severus to the Beginning of Constantine's Rule,' *Zion*, 21 (1956), 1–9 (in Hebrew).
——, 'Johanan Levi, Julius Caesar and the Building of the Temple,' *Zion*, 7 (1941), 1–32 (in Hebrew).
Büchler, A., *Studies in Jewish History*, Oxford, 1956, pp. 179–244.
Fraenkel, Z., *The Ways of the Mishnah*, Jerusalem, 1958 (reprint), pp. 201–8 (in Hebrew).
Juster, J., *Les Juife dans L'Empire Romaine*, vols. I–II, Paris, 1914.
Klein, S., *The Galilee*, Jerusalem, 1946, pp. 71ff. (in Hebrew).
Krauss, S., 'The Martyrs,' *Hashiloah*, 46 (1925), serialized (in Hebrew).
Lieberman, S., 'Palestine in the Third and Fourth Centuries,' *Jewish Quarterly Review*, 36 (1945–6), 329–79; 37 (1946–7), 31–54.
Parkes, J., *The Conflict of the Church and Synagogue*, London, 1934.
Safrai, S., 'Sikarikon,' *Zion*, 17 (1952), 56–64 (in Hebrew).
Sperber, D., *Roman Palestine (200–400)*, Ramat-Gan, 1974.
Urbach, E., 'Status and Leadership in the World of the Sages of Palestine,' *Proceedings of the Israel Academy of Sciences and Humanities*, 2/4 Jerusalem, 1965 (in Hebrew).

From the Fourth Century to the Arab Conquest

Hilkowitz, K., 'The Participation of the Jews in the Conquest of Jerusalem by the Persians in AD 614,' *Zion*, 4 (1939), 307–16 (in Hebrew).

Hirschberg, H., *Israel in Arabia*, Jerusalem, 1946, pp. 50–110 (in Hebrew).

Juster, J., *Les Juife dans L'Empire Romaine*, vol. II, Paris, 1914.

Schwabe, M., 'The Letters of Libanius to the Patriarch in Palestine,' *Tarbiz*, 1/2 (1930), 85–110 (in Hebrew).

——, 'A New Document Relating the History of the Jews in the Fourth Century,' *Tarbiz*, 1/3 (1930), 107–21 (in Hebrew).

Voigt, J., *Kaiser Julian und das Judentums*, Leipzig, 1939.

The Diaspora

Allon, G., *The History of the Jews of Palestine in the Period of the Mishna and the Talmud*, vol. I, Tel Aviv, 1953, pp. 251–5 (in Hebrew).

Appelbaum, A., 'The Rebellion of the Jews of Cyrenaica in the Time of Trajanus,' *Zion*, 19 (1954), 23–56 (in Hebrew).

——, 'The Legal Status of the Jewish Communities in the Diaspora' in *Compendia Rerum Judaicarum*, S. Safrai and M. Stern, eds., vol. I, Assen, 1974, pp. 420–63.

——, 'The Organization of the Jewish Communities in the Diaspora' in *Compendia Rerum Judaicarum*, S. Safrai and M. Stern, eds., vol. I, Assen, 1974, pp. 464–503.

Beer, M., *Babylonian Amoraim*, Ramat Gan, 1974 (in Hebrew).

Fuks, A., 'The Jewish Revolt in Egypt (AD 115–17),' *Zion*, 22 (1957), 1–9 (in Hebrew).

Lazarus, J., 'Die Häupter der Vertriebenen,' *Jährbuche für Geschichte und Literatur*, 10 (1890), 1–170.

Leon, H., *The Jews in Ancient Rome*, Philadelphia, 1960.

Neusner, J., *A History of the Jews in Babylonia*, vols. I–IV, Leiden, 1965–70.

Obermeyer, Y., *Die Landschaft Babylonien*, Frankfurt a.M., 1929.

Tcherikover, V., *The Jews in Egypt in the Hellenistic-Roman Age in the Light of the Papyri* (2nd ed.), Jerusalem, 1963 (in Hebrew).

——, A. Fuks and M. Stern, eds., *Corpus Papyrorum Judaicarum*, vol. I, Cambridge, Mass., 1957, pp. 1–111.

Widengren, G., 'The Status of the Jews in the Sassanian Empire,' *Iranica Antiqua*, 1 (1961), 117–62.

Zuri, Y., *Rav*, Jerusalem, 1925 (in Hebrew).

——, *The Rule of the Exilarch and the Yeshivot*, Tel Aviv, 1939 (in Hebrew).

The Middle Ages

General Histories and Source Collections

Baron, S.W., *A Social and Religious History of the Jews*, vols. 3–15 (2nd ed.), New York, 1957–73.

Ben-Sasson, H.H., *Trial and Achievement: Currents in Jewish History*, Jerusalem, 1974.

Dinur, B., *Israel in the Diaspora*, I, Books 1–6; II, Books 1–6, Tel Aviv, 1961–72 (in Hebrew).

Dubnow, S., *History of the Jews*, vols. II–IV, South Brunswick, N.J., 1968–71.

Finkelstein, L., ed., *The Jews*, New York, 1960, pp. 216–49, 287–320, 854–92, 932–53, 1116–48.

Graetz, H., *History of the Jews*, vols. III–V, Philadelphia, 1967.

Journal of World History, 11 (1968).

Katz, J., *Tradition and Crisis*, New York, 1974.

Markus, J.R., *The Jews in the Medieval World*, Cincinnati, 1938.

Parkes, J., *The Jew in the Mediaeval Community*, London, 1938.

Roth, C., ed., *The World History of the Jewish People*, 2nd series, Medieval Period, vol. II, *The Dark Ages*, Tel Aviv, 1966.

Erez Yisrael, Messianism and the Aliyot

Aescoli, A., *Jewish Messianic Movements*, Jerusalem, 1956 (in Hebrew).

Assaf, S., and L. Meir, eds., *The Record of Settlement*, vol. II, Jerusalem, 1944 (in Hebrew).

Baer, J., *Galut*, New York, 1947.

Baer, Y., 'Erez Yisrael and the Diaspora in the View of the Middle Ages,' *Zion Yearbook*, 6 (1946), 149–71 (in Hebrew).

Ben-Sasson, H.H., 'Exile and Redemption Through the Eyes of the Spanish Exiles' in S.W. Baron, ed., *I. Baer Jubilee Volume*, Jerusalem, 1960, pp. 216–27 (in Hebrew).

Ben-Zvi, Y., *Erez Yisrael Under Ottoman Rule*, Jerusalem, 1967, pp. 3–261 (in Hebrew).

Dinur, B., 'The *Aliyah* from Spain to Erez Yisrael After 1492,' *Zion*, 32 (1967), 161–74 (in Hebrew).

Goitein, S.D., 'Letters from Erez Yisrael Dating to the Crusader Period,' *Yerushalaim*, 2 (1955), 54–70 (in Hebrew).

Heyd, A., 'Turkish Documents on the Rebuilding of Tiberias in the Sixteenth Century,' *Sefunot*, 10 (1966), 193–210 (in Hebrew).

Prawer, J., *The Latin Kingdom of Jerusalem: European Colonialism in the Middle Ages*, New York/London, 1972, pp. 233–51.

Scholem, G., *Sabbetai Sevi, The Mystical Messiah*, Princeton, 1973.

Yaari, A., ed., *Travellers' Tales from Erez Yisrael*, Tel Aviv, 1946, pp. 31–323 (in Hebrew).

The History of the Jews in Various Countries

Anchel, R., *Les Juifs de France*, Paris, 1946, pp. 7–152.

Ashtor (Strauss), A., *The History of the Jews in Moslem Spain*, vols. I–II, Jerusalem, 1966 (in Hebrew).

Bachrach, B., 'A Reassessment of Visigothic Jewish Policy,' *American Historical Review*, 78 (1974), 11–33.

Baer, I.F., *Die Juden im christlichen Spanien*, vols. I–II, Berlin, 1929–36.

Baer, Y., *A History of the Jews in Christian Spain*, vols. I–II, Philadelphia, 1961–6.

Ben-Sasson, H.H., *Ashkenaz Jewry*, Tel Aviv, n.d. (in Hebrew).

——, 'The Generation of the Expulsion from Spain Speaks About Itself,' *Zion*, 26 (1961), 23–64 (in Hebrew).

Bondy, G., and F. Dvorsky, *Zur Geschichte der Juden in Böhmen, Mähren und Schlesien, 906–1620*, vols. I–II, Prague, 1906.

Cassuto, U., *Gli Ebrei a Firenze nell'età del Rinascimento*, Florence, 1918.

Chasan, R., *Medieval Jewry in Northern France*, Baltimore, 1973.

Dunlop, D.M., *The History of the Jewish Khazars*, New York, 1967.

Emery, R.W., *The Jews of Perpignan in the Thirteenth Century*, New York, 1959.

Ettinger, S., 'The Legal and Social Status of the Ukrainian Jews in the Fifteenth to Seventeenth Centuries,' *Zion*, 20 (1955), 128–52 (in Hebrew).

Germania Judaica, vol. I, M. Brann and A. Freiman, eds., 1917; vol. I, part 2, J. Elbogen, A. Freimann and H. Tykocinsky, eds., Breslau, 1934; vol. II, Z. Awneri, ed., Tübingen, 1968.

Gross, H., *Gallia Judaica*, Paris, 1897.

Halperin, I., ed., *Polish Jewry*, vols. I–II, Jerusalem, 1948 (in Hebrew).

——, *East European Jewry*, Jerusalem, 1968 (in Hebrew).

Hirschberg, H., *Israel in Arabia*, Jerusalem, 1946 (in Hebrew).

——, *A History of the Jews in North Africa*, vols. I–II, Jerusalem, 1965, I, pp. 152–359; II, pp. 207–73 (in Hebrew).

Katz, S., *The Jews in the Visigothic and Frankish Kingdoms of Spain and Gaul*, Cambridge, Mass., 1937.

Kisch, G., *The Jews in Medieval Germany*, Chicago, 1949.

——, *Forschungen zur Rechts- und Sozialgeschichte der Juden in Deutschland während des Mittelalters*, Zurich, 1955.

Mahler, R., *History of the Jews in Poland*, Merḥaviah, 1946, pp. 9–230 (in Hebrew).

Mann, J., *The Jews in Egypt and in Palestine Under the Fatimid Caliphs*, vols. I–II, London, 1920–2.

Richardson, H.G., *English Jewry Under Angevin Kings*, London, 1960.

Roth, C., *The History of the Jews of Italy*, Philadelphia, 1946.

——, *A History of the Jews of England*, Oxford, 1949.

Saige, G., *Les Juifs du Languedoc autérieuxrement au XIVᵉ siécle*, Paris, 1884.

Scherer, J.E., *Die Rechtsverhältnisse der Juden in den deutschösterreichischen Ländern*, Leipzig, 1901.

Schilling, K., *Monumenta Judaica, 2000 Jahre Geschichte und Kultur der Juden am Rhein*, Cologne, 1963, pp. 9–15, 33–275, 668–98, 737–85.

Simonsohn, S., *The History of the Jews in the Duchy of Mantua*, vols. I–II, Jerusalem, 1962–4 (in Hebrew).

Sraus, R., *Die Juden im Königreich Sizilien*, Heidelberg, 1910.

Starr, J., *The Jews in the Byzantine Empire, 641–1204*, New York, 1939.

Stengers, J., *Les Juifs dans les Pays-Bas au Moyen Age*, Brussels, 1950.

Strauss (Ashtor), E., *The History of the Jews in Egypt and Syria Under Mameluke Rule*, vols. I–II, Jerusalem, 1944–70 (in Hebrew).

Economy and Settlement

Canaani, Y., 'Economic Life in Safed and Its Surroundings in the Sixteenth to Seventeenth Centuries, *Zion Yearbook*, 6 (1946), 172–217 (in Hebrew).

Caro, G., *Sozial- und Wirtschaftsgeschichte der Juden im Mittelalter*, vol. I, Frankfurt a.M., 1924.

Ettinger, S., 'The Participation of the Jews in the Colonization of the Ukraine,' *Zion*, 21 (1953), 107–42 (in Hebrew).

Fischel, W., *Jews in the Economic and Political Life of Medieval Islam*, New York, 1937.
Goitein, S.D., *A Mediterranean Society*, vol. I, *Economic Foundations*, Berkeley and Los Angeles, 1967.
Gross, N., ed., *Jewish Economic History*, Jerusalem, 1975.
Jacoby, D., 'Les Quartiers Juifs de Constantinople à l'Epoque Byzantine,' *Byzantion*, 37 (1967), 167–227.
Kellenbenz, H., *Sephardim an der unteren Elbe*, Wiesbaden, 1958.
Philipp, A., *Die Juden und des Wirtschaftsleben*, Strasbourg, 1929.
Pinthus, A., 'Studien über die bauliche Entwicklung der Judengassen in den deutschen Städten,' *Zeitschrift für die Geschichte der Juden in Deutschland*, 2 (1930), 101–30, 197–217, 284–300.
Täubler, E., 'Zur Handelsbedeutung der Juden in Deutschland vor Beginn des Städtewesens' in *Festschrift Martin Philippson*, Leipzig, 1916, pp. 370–92.
Straus, R., *Die Juden in Wirtschaft und Gesellschaft*, Frankfurt a.M., 1964.
Wätjen, H., *Das Judentum und die Anfäge der modernen Kolonisation*, Berlin, 1914.

Attitude of the Host Society to the Jews

Baron, S.W., 'John Calvin and the Jews' in *H.A. Wolfson Jubilee Volume*, New York, 1965, pp. 141–63.
——, 'Medieval Heritage and the Modern Realities in Protestant-Jewish Relations,' *Diogenes*, 61 (1968), 32–51.
Blumenkranz, B., *Juifs et Chrétiens dans le monde occidental, 430–1096*, Paris, 1960.
——, *Juden und Judentum in der Mittelalterlichen Kunst*, Stuttgart, 1965.
Browe, P., *Die Judenmission im Mittelalter und die Päpste*, Rome, 1942.
——, 'Die Judenbekämpfung im Mittelalter,' *Zeitschrift für katholische Theologie*, 62 (1938), 971–231, 248–349.
——, 'Die religiöse Duldung der Juden im Mittelalter,' *Archiv für katholisches Kirchenrecht*, 118 (1938), 3–76.
——, 'Die Hostienschändungen der Juden im Mittelalter,' *Römische Quartalschrift für christliche Altertumskunde und für Kirchengeschichte*, 34 (1926), 167–97.
Grayzel, S., *The Church and the Jews in the Thirteenth Century*, Philadelphia, 1933.
Haliczer, S., 'The Castilian Urban Patriciate and the Jewish Expulsions of 1480–92,' *American Historical Review*, 78 (1974), 35–62.
Hailperin, H., *Rashi and the Christian Scholars*, Pittsburgh, 1963.
Kamen, H., *The Spanish Inquisition*, New York, 1968.
Langmuir, G.J., 'The Jews and the Archives of Angevin England: Reflections on Medieval Anti-Semitism,' *Traditio*, 19 (1963), 183–244.
Lewin, R., *Luthers Stellung zu den Juden*, Berlin, 1911.
Liebeschütz, H., 'The Significance of Judaism in Peter Abelard's Dialogues,' *Journal of Jewish Studies*, 12 (1961), 1–8.
——, 'Judaism and Jewry in the Social Doctrine of Thomas Aquinas,' *Journal of Jewish Studies*, 13 (1962), 57–81.
Lukyn Williams, A., *Adversus Judaeos*, Cambridge, 1935.
MacKay, A., 'Popular Movements and Pogroms in Fifteenth-Century Castile,' *Past and Present*, 55 (1972), 33–67.

Pfaff, V., 'Die Soziale Stellung des Judentums in der Auseinandersetzung zwischen Kaiser und Kirch vom 3. bis 4. Laterankonzil (1179–1215),' *Vierteljahresschrift für Sozial- und Wirtschaftgeschichte,* 52 (1965), 168–206.

Seiferth, W., *Synagogue und Kirche im Mittelalter,* Munich, 1964.

Smalley, B., *The Study of the Bible in the Middle Ages,* Oxford, 1952.

Synan, E.A., *The Popes and the Jews in the Middle Ages,* Oxford, 1967.

Trachtenberg, J., *The Devil and the Jews,* New Haven, 1943.

Wolff, P., 'The 1391 Pogrom in Spain, Social Crisis or Not?' *Past and Present,* 50 (1971), 4–18.

The Jews' Response and the Resulting Confrontation

Baer, I., 'The 1096 Massacres' in M.D. Cassuto *et al.,* eds., *Assaf Jubilee Volume,* Jerusalem, 1953, pp. 126–40 (in Hebrew).

Beinart, H., *Records of the Trials of the Spanish Inquisition in Ciudad Real,* vol. I, Jerusalem, 1974.

Ben-Sasson, H.H., 'Jewish Reflection on Nationhood in the Twelfth Century' in E. Rosenthal, cd., *P'raqim, Yearbook of the Schoken Institute for Jewish Research of the Jewish Theological Seminary of America,* vol. II, Jerusalem, 1969–74, pp. 145–218 (in Hebrew).

——, 'Jewish-Christian Disputation in the Setting of Humanism and Reformation in the German Empire,' *Harvard Theological Review,* 59 (1966), 369–90.

——, 'The Reformation in Contemporary Jewish Eyes' in *Proceedings of the Israel Academy of Sciences and Humanities,* 4 (1971), pp. 239–326.

——, 'Jews and Christian Sectarians: Existential Similarity and Dialectical Tensions in Sixteenth-Century Moravia and Poland-Lithuania,' *Viator: Medieval and Renaissance Studies,* 4 (1973), 369–85.

Chazan, R., 'A Jewish Plaint to Saint Louis,' *Hebrew Union College Annual,* 45 (1974), 287–305.

Cohen, M.A., 'Reflections on the Text and Context of the Disputation of Barcelona,' *Hebrew Union College Annual,* 35 (1964), 157–92.

Ettinger, S., 'The Jewish Influence on the Religious Ferment in Eastern Europe at the End of the Fifteenth Century' in S.W. Baron, ed., *I. Baer Jubilee Volume,* Jerusalem, 1960, pp. 288–347 (in Hebrew).

Haberman, A.M., ed., *The Book of the Massacres in Germany and France,* Jerusalem, 1946 (in Hebrew).

Katz, J., 'Religious Tolerance in the *Halakha* and Philosophy According to R. Menahem Hameiri,' *Zion,* 18 (1953), 15–30 (in Hebrew).

——, *Exclusiveness and Tolerance,* London, 1961.

Kimhi, Joseph, *The Book of the Covenant,* F.E. Talmage, ed., Toronto, 1972.

Pacios Lopez, A., *La Disputa de Tortosa,* vols. I–II, Madrid-Barcelona, 1957.

Roth, C., *A History of the Marranos,* New York, 1974.

Spiegel, S., *The Last Trial,* Philadelphia, 1967.

Steinschneider, M., *Polemische und Apologetische Literatur in arabischer Sprache,* Leipzig, 1877.

Wilpert, P., ed., *Judentum im Mittelalter, Beitrage zum Christlich-Jüdischen Gespräch,* Berlin, 1966.

Self-government

Abramson, S., *Centres and Peripheries in the Time of the Geonim*, Jerusalem, 1965 (in Hebrew).

Agus, I.A., *Urban Civilization in Pre-Crusade Europe*, vols. I–II, New York, 1965.

Assaf, S., *In the Tents of Jacob*, Jerusalem, 1943 (in Hebrew).

——, *Texts and Studies in Jewish History*, Jerusalem, 1946 (in Hebrew).

Baer, I., 'The Foundations and Beginnings of a Jewish Community Structure in the Middle Ages,' *Zion*, 15 (1950), 1–41 (in Hebrew).

Baron, S., *The Jewish Community*, vols. I–III, Philadelphia, 1942.

Benaiahu, M., 'The Renewal of *Semikhah* in Safed,' in S.W. Baron, ed., *I. Baer Jubilee Volume*, Jerusalem, 1960, pp. 248–69 (in Hebrew).

Ben-Sasson, H.H., 'Sabbath Observance Laws in Poland and Their Economic and Social Context,' *Zion*, 21 (1956), 183–206 (in Hebrew).

——, *Hagut Vehanhagah, The Social Theories of the Jews of Poland in the Late Middle Ages*, Jerusalem, 1960 (in Hebrew).

——, 'The Social Teaching of R. Johanan Luria,' *Zion*, 27 (1962), 166–98 (in Hebrew).

——, *The Urban Community in Jewish and General History and in Relation to Kiddush Hashem*, Jerusalem, 1968, pp. 161–78 (in Hebrew).

Finkelstein, L., *Jewish Self-Government in the Middle Ages*, New York, 1924.

Frank, M., *Ashkenaz Communities and Their Courts from the Twelfth to Fifteenth Centuries*, Tel Aviv, 1938 (in Hebrew).

Goitein, S.D., *A Mediterranean Society*, vol. II, *The Community*, Los Angeles, 1971.

Katz, J., 'The *Semikhah* Controversy Between R. Jacob Berab and Ralbach,' *Zion*, 16 (1951), 28–45.

——, 'Towards a Rabbinate at the Close of the Middle Ages' in A. Melamed, ed., *Benjamin de Vries Memorial Volume*, Jerusalem, 1968, pp. 281–94 (in Hebrew).

Mann, J., *Texts and Studies*, vol. I, Cincinnati, 1931.

Neustadt, D., 'The Neguduth in Egypt in the Middle Ages,' *Zion*, 4 (1939), 126–49 (in Hebrew).

Stern, S., *Josel of Rosheim*, Philadelphia, 1965.

Spiritual Creativity and Religious Ideals

Assaf, S., *Sources for the History of Jewish Education*, vols. I–IV, Tel Aviv, 1925–48 (in Hebrew).

——, *The Period of the Geonim and Their Literature*, Jerusalem, 1955 (in Hebrew).

Baer, Y., 'The Socio-Religious Trends of *Sefer Hahasidim*,' *Zion*, 3 (1938), 1–50 (in Hebrew).

——, 'Rashi and the Historical Setting of His Times,' *Tarbiz*, 20 (1959), 320–32 (in Hebrew).

——, 'The Belief in Natural Equality Among the Hasidei Ashkenaz,' *Zion*, 32 (1967), 129–36 (in Hebrew).

——, 'On the Doctrine of Providence in *Sefer Hahasidim*' in *Studies in Mysticism and Religion Presented to G. Scholem* (Hebrew section), Jerusalem, 1967, pp. 47–62.

Cornbach, A., 'Social Thinking in the Sepher Hasidim,' *Hebrew Union College Annual*, 22 (1949), 1–47.

Goitein, S.D., *Methods of Education: From the Period of the Geonim to Maimonides*, Jerusalem, 1962 (in Hebrew).

Güdemann, M., *Geschichte des Erziehungswesens und der Cultur der abendländischen Juden*, vols. I–III, Vienna, 1880–8.

Güdemann, J., *Philosophies of Judaism,* New York, 1964.

Guttmann, J., ed., *Moses ben Maimon,* vols. I–II, Leipzig, 1908–14.

Kleinberger, A., *The Educational Theory of the Maharal of Prague,* Jerusalem, 1962 (in Hebrew).

Landsberger, F., 'The Jewish Artist Before the Time of the Emancipation,' *Hebrew Union College Annual,* 16 (1941), 321–414.

Mahler, R., *The Karaites,* Merḥaviah, 1949 (in Hebrew).

Malter, H., *The Works of Saadia Gaon,* Philadelphia, 1921.

Nemoy, L., ed., *Karaite Anthology,* New Haven, 1952.

Schechter, S., *Studies in Judaism,* 2nd series, Philadelphia, 1908, pp. 1–30, 126–47, 202–301.

Scholem, G., *Major Trends in Jewish Mysticism,* New York, 1965.

——, 'The Kabbala in Spain on the Eve of the Expulsion,' *Tarbiz,* 24 (1960), 167–206 (in Hebrew).

——, *Ursprung und Angänge der Kabbala,* Berlin, 1962.

Talmage, F.E., *David Kimhi: The Man and the Commentaries,* Cambridge, Mass., 1975.

Tishbi, I., and F. Lachsurer, eds., *The Wisdom of the Zohar,* vol. I (3rd ed.), Jerusalem, 1971; vol. II, I. Tishbi, ed., Jerusalem, 1971.

Urbach, E., *The Tosafists,* Jerusalem, 1955 (in Hebrew).

Werblowsky, R.J.Z., *Joseph Karo,* London, 1962.

The Modern Period

Descriptive Works, Collections of Studies and General Surveys

Altmann, A., ed., *Studies in Nineteenth Century Jewish Intellectual History,* Waltham, Mass., 1964.

Baron, S.W., 'The Modern Age' in L. Schwarz, ed., *Great Ages and Ideas of the Jewish People,* New York, 1956, pp. 315–484.

——, *A Social and Religious History of the Jews,* vol. II, New York, 1937.

Dinur, B.Z., *Israel and the Diaspora,* Philadelphia, 1969.

Elbogen, I., *A Century of Jewish Life,* Philadelphia, 1944.

Finkelstein, L., ed., *The Jews: Their History, Culture and Religion,* Philadelphia, 1960.

Grayzel, S., *A History of Contemporary Jews: From 1900 to the Present,* Philadelphia, 1960.

Katz, J., *Out of the Ghetto: The Social Background of Jewish Emancipation,* Cambridge, Mass., 1973.

Marx, A., and M. Margolis, *A History of the Jewish People,* Philadelphia, 1927, chapter 77ff.

Sachar, H.M., *The Course of Modern Jewish History,* New York, 1958.

Demography, Emigration and Economics

Aris, S., *The Jews in Business,* London, 1970.

Bloom, H.I., *Economic Activities of the Jews of Amsterdam in the 17th and 18th Centuries,* Port Washington, N.Y., 1937.

Corti, Count Egon, *The Reign of the House of Rothschild,* New York, 1927.

Emden, P., *Money Powers of Europe in the 19th and 20th Centuries,* London, 1938.

Engelman, U.Z., *The Rise of the Jew in the Western World,* New York, 1944.

Gartner, L.P., 'Immigration and the Formation of American Jewry, 1840–1925,' *Journal of World History*, 11 (1968), 297–312.

Hersch, L., 'Jewish Population Trend in Europe' in *The Jewish People: Past and Present*, vol. II, New York, 1948, pp. 1–24.

——, 'Jewish Migrations During the Last Hundred Years' in *The Jewish People: Past and Present*, vol. I, New York, 1946, pp. 407–30.

Joseph, S., *Jewish Immigration to the United States from 1881 to 1910*, New York, 1914.

Kissman, J., 'The Immigration of Rumanian Jews up to 1914,' *YIVO Annual of Jewish Social Science*, 2–3 (1947/1948), 160–79.

Lestschinsky, J., 'The Economic and Social Development of the Jewish People' in *The Jewish People: Past and Present*, vol. I, New York, 1946, pp. 361–90.

Marcus, A., 'Jews as Entrepreneurs in Weimar Germany,' *YIVO Annual of Jewish Social Science*, 7 (1952), 175–203.

Marcus, J.R., *Mass Migrations of Jews and Their Effects on Jewish Life*, Cincinnati, 1940.

Reich, N., 'The Role of the Jews in the American Economy,' *YIVO Annual of Jewish Social Science*, 5 (1950), 197–204.

Ruppin, A., *The Jews in the Modern World*, London, 1934.

Stern, S., *The Court Jew*, Philadelphia, 1950.

Strauss, R., 'The Jews in the Economic Evolution of Central Europe,' *Jewish Social Studies*, 3 (1941), 15–40.

Szajkowski, Z., *The Economic Status of the Jews in Alsace, Metz and Lorraine, 1648–1789*, New York, 1959.

Tcherikower, E., 'Jewish Immigrants to the United States, 1881–1900,' *YIVO Annual of Jewish Social Science*, 6 (1951), 157–76.

Wischnitzer, M., *To Dwell in Safety: The Story of Jewish Migration since 1800*, Philadelphia, 1948.

Jewish Centres

Adler, H.G., *The Jews of Germany*, Notre Dame, Indiana, 1969.

Baron, S.W., *The Jews in Roumania*, New York, 1930.

——, *The Russian Jew under Tsars and Soviets*, New York, 1964.

Blau, J.L., and S.W. Baron, *The Jews of the United States: A Documentary History*, New York, 1963.

Cohen, J.X., *Jewish Life in South America*, New York, 1941.

Dubnow, S., *History of the Jews in Russia and Poland*, vols. I–III, Philadelphia, 1920.

Fraenkel, J., ed., *The Jews of Austria*, London, 1967.

Gitelman, Z.Y., *Jewish Nationality and Soviet Politics*, Princeton, 1972.

Glazer, N., *American Judaism*, Chicago, 1957.

Greenberg, L., *The Jews in Russia*, vols. I–II, New Haven, 1944.

Halpern, B., *The American Jew: A Zionist Analysis*, New York, 1956.

Handlin, O., *Adventure in Freedom*, New York, 1954.

Janowsky, O.I., ed., *The American Jew: A Reappraisal*, Philadelphia, 1964.

Karp, A., ed., *The Jewish Experience in America*, vols. I–IV, New York, 1969.

Kochan, L., ed., *The Jews in Soviet Russia since 1917*, New York, 1970.

Lipman, V.C., *Social History of the Jews in England, 1850–1950*, London, 1954.

Lowenthal, M., *The Jews of Germany*, Philadelphia, 1936.

Marcus, J.R., *Rise and Destiny of the German Jew*, Cincinnati, 1934.

Meyer, M.A., *The Origins of the Modern Jew*, Detroit, 1967.

Rischin, M., *An Inventory of American Jewish History*, Cambridge, Mass., 1954.

Roth, C., *History of the Jews of Italy*, Philadelphia, 1946.

——, *History of the Jews in England*, Oxford, 1949.

Saron, G., and L. Hotz, eds., *The Jews in South Africa*, Cape Town, 1955.

Schappes, M.U., *A Documentary History of the Jews in the United States, 1654–1875*, New York, 1950.

Schwarz, S.M., *The Jews in the Soviet Union*, Syracuse, 1951.

Sherman, C.B., *The Jew Within American Society*, Detroit, 1965.

Sklare, M., ed., *The Jews: Social Patterns of an American Group*, 1958.

Szajkowski, Z., *Jews and the French Revolution of 1789, 1830 and 1848*, New York, 1970.

The Legal Status of the Jews and Jewish Autonomy

Adler, C., and A. M. Margalith, *With Firmness in the Right: American Diplomatic Action Affecting Jews, 1840–1945*, New York, 1946.

Baron, S.W., 'The Impact of the Revolutions of 1848 on Jewish Emancipation,' *Jewish Social Studies*, 9 (1949), 195–248.

——, 'Newer Approaches to Jewish Emancipation,' *Diogenes*, 29 (1960), 56–81.

Janowsky, O.I., *The Jews and Minority Rights (1898–1919)*, New York, 1933.

——, *People at Bay: The Jewish Problem in East Central Europe*, New York, 1938.

Kann, Robert, 'German-Speaking Jewry During Austria-Hungary's Constitutional Era (1867–1918),' *Jewish Social Studies*, 10 (1948), 239–56.

Lazerson, M.M., 'The Jewish Minorities in the Baltic Countries,' *Jewish Social Studies*, 3 (1941), 273–84.

Rossi, M., 'Emancipation of the Jews in Italy,' *Jewish Social Studies*, 15 (1953), 113–34.

Starr, J., 'Jewish Citizenship in Roumania (1870–1940),' *Jewish Social Studies*, 3 (1941), 57–80.

Stillschweig, K., 'Nationalism and Autonomy Among Eastern European Jewry,' *Historia Judaica*, 6 (1944), 27–68.

Wolf, L., *Notes on the Diplomatic History of the Jewish Question*, London, 1919.

'The Jewish Question': Jews in the Surrounding Society

Altschuler, M., 'The Attitude of the Communist Party of Russia to Jewish National Survival, 1918–1930,' *YIVO Annual of Jewish Social Science*, 14 (1969), 68–86.

Bauer, B., *The Jewish Question*, Cincinnati, 1958.

Bieber, H. and M. Hadas, eds., *Heinrich Heine: A Biographical Anthology*, Philadelphia, 1956.

Deutscher, I., *The Non-Jewish Jew and Other Essays*, London, 1968.

Dohm, C.W., *Concerning the Amelioration of the Jews*, Cincinnati, 1957.

Ettinger, S., 'The Beginnings of the Change in Attitude of European Society towards the Jews,' *Scripta Hierosolymitana*, 7 (1961), 193–219.

Goldberg, B.Z., *The Jewish Problem in the Soviet Union*, New York, 1961.

Hertzberg, A., *The French Enlightenment and the Jews*, New York and Philadelphia, 1968.

Katz, J., *Freemasons and Jews in Europe, 1723–1939*, Cambridge, Mass., 1970.

Lewin, K., *Resolving Social Conflicts*, G. Weiss-Lewin, ed., New York, 1948, pp. 186–200.

Liptzin, S., *Germany's Stepchildren*, Philadelphia, 1944.

Marx, K., *On the Jewish Question*, Cincinnati, 1958.

Pinsker, P., 'English Opinion and Jewish Emancipation,' *Jewish Social Studies*, 14 (1952), 51–94.

Vago, B., and G.L. Mosse, eds., *Jews and Non-Jews in Eastern Europe, 1918–1945*, Jerusalem, 1974.

Communal Life

Baron, S.W., 'Church and State Debates in the Jewish Community in 1848' in *Mordecai Kaplan Jubilee Volume*, New York, 1953, pp. 49–72.

——, 'Aspects of the Jewish Communal Crisis in 1848,' *Jewish Social Studies*, 14 (1952), 99–144.

Goren, A.A., *New York Jews and the Quest for Community: The Kehilla Experiment, 1908–1922*, New York, 1970.

Levitats, I., *The Jewish Community in Russia, 1772–1844*, New York, 1943.

Marrus, M.R., *The Politics of Assimilation: A Study of the French Jewish Community at the Time of the Dreyfus Affair*, Oxford, 1971.

Hasidism, Frankism and the Musar Movement

Buber, M., *Tales of the Hasidim*, vols. I–II, New York, 1947–8.

——, *Hasidism and Modern Man*, New York, 1958.

——, *The Origin and Meaning of Hasidism*, New York, 1960.

Dresner, S.H., *The Zaddik*, London, 1960.

Duker, A.G., 'Polish Frankism's Duration,' *Jewish Social Studies*, 25 (1963), 287–333.

Ettinger, S., 'The Hassidic Movement – Reality and Ideals,' *Journal of World History*, 11 (1968), 251–66.

Glenn, M.G., *Israel Salanter, Religious-Ethical Thinker: The Story of a Religious-Ethical Current in Nineteenth Century Judaism*, New York, 1953.

Newman, L.L., *Hasidic Anthology*, New York, 1934.

Schechter, S., *Studies in Judaism*, New York and Philadelphia, 1958, pp. 150–89.

Scholem, G., *Major Trends in Jewish Mysticism*, New York, 1965, pp. 328–50.

Ury, Z.F., *The Musar Movement: A Quest for Excellence in Character Education*, New York, 1970.

The Haskalah, the Study of Judaism, the Reform Movement and Neo-Orthodoxy

Bamberger, B., 'Beginnings of Modern Jewish Scholarship,' *Yearbook of the Central Conference of American Rabbis*, 42 (1932), 209–35.

Baron, S.W., *History and Jewish Historians*, Philadelphia, 1964, pp. 240–321.

——, 'The Revolution of 1848 and Jewish Scholarship,' *Publications of the American Academy for Jewish Research*, 18 (1948–9), 1–66; 20 (1951), 1–100.

Barzilay, I., 'The Background of the Berlin Haskalah' in *Essays in Jewish Life and Thought Presented in Honor of Salo W. Baron*, New York, 1959.

——, 'The Jew in the Literature of the Enlightenment,' *Jewish Social Studies*, 18 (1956), 243–61.

——, 'National and Anti-National Trends in the Berlin Haskalah,' *Jewish Social Studies*, 21 (1959), 165–92.

——, *Shlomo Yehudah Rapoport (Shir, 1790–1867) and His Contemporaries*, Tel Aviv, 1969.

Davis, M., *The Emergence of Conservative Judaism: The Historical School in Nineteenth Century America*, Philadelphia, 1963.

Glatzer, N.N., ed., *Leopold and Adelheide Zunz: An Account in Letters (1815-1885)*, London, 1958.

Halkin, S., *Modern Hebrew Literature: Trends and Values*, New York, 1950.

Levy, B.H., *Reform Judaism in America*, New York, 1933.

Littman, E., 'Saul Ascher,' *Leo Baeck Institute Yearbook*, 5 (1960), 184–96.

Mahler, R., 'The Social Aspects of the Haskalah in Galicia,' *YIVO Annual of Jewish Social Science*, 1 (1946), 64–85.

Maimon, Solomon, *An Autobiography*, M. Hadas, ed., New York, 1947.

Philipson, D., *The Reform Movement in Judaism*, New York, 1967.

Plaut, G.W., *The Rise of Reform Judaism*, New York, 1963.

Raisin, J.P., *The Haskalah Movement in Russia*, Philadelphia, 1915.

Rudavsky, D., 'The Historical School of Zacharia Frankel,' *Jewish Social Studies*, 5 (1963), 224–45.

Wallach, L., 'The Beginning of the Science of Judaism in the Nineteenth Century,' *Historia Judaica*, 9 (1946), 33–60.

——, *Liberty and Letters: The Thoughts of Leopold Zunz*, London, 1959.

Wiener, M., 'The Concept of Mission in Traditional and Modern Judaism,' *YIVO Annual of Jewish Social Science*, 2–3 (1947/1948), 9–24.

——, 'The Ideology of the Founders of Jewish Scientific Research,' *YIVO Annual of Jewish Social Science*, 5 (1950), 184–96.

——, *Abraham Geiger and Liberal Judaism*, Philadelphia, 1962.

The Jewish Workers' and Socialist Movements

Berlin, I., *The Life and Opinions of Moses Hess*, Cambridge, 1959.

Epstein, M., *Jewish Labor in the U.S.A.: An Industrial, Political and Cultural History of the Jewish Labor Movement*, New York, 1969.

Hetz, J.S., 'The Bund's Nationality Program and Its Critics in the Russian, Polish and Austrian Socialist Movements,' *YIVO Annual of Jewish Social Science*, 14 (1969), 53–67.

Mendelsohn, E., *Class Struggle in the Pale: The Formative Years of the Jewish Workers Movement in Tsarist Russia*, Cambridge, 1970.

——, 'The Jewish Socialist Movement and the Second International, 1889–1914,' *Jewish Social Studies*, 26 (1964), 131–45.

Mishninski, M., 'International Socialism and the Jewish Labour Movement,' *Journal of World History*, 11 (1968), 225–37.

Patkin, A.L., *The Origins of the Russian-Jewish Labor Movement*, Melbourne, 1947.

Pinson, K.S., 'Arkady Kremer, Vladimir Medem and the Ideology of the Jewish Bund,' *Jewish Social Studies*, 7 (1945), 233–64.

Tcherikower, E., *The Early Jewish Labor Movement in the United States*, A. Antonovsky, ed., New York, 1961.

Anti-Semitism, the Nazi Persecution and the Holocaust

Bernstein, P.F., *Jew-Hate as a Sociological Problem*, New York, 1951.

Bieber, H., 'Anti-Semitism in the First Years of the German Republic,' *YIVO Annual of Jewish Social Science*, 4 (1949), 123–45.

Braham, R.L., *The Destruction of Hungarian Jewry*, vols. I–II, New York, 1963.

Byrnes, R.F., *Antisemitism in Modern France*, New Brunswick, N.J., 1950.

——, 'Edouard Drumont and "La France Juive",' *Jewish Social Studies*, 10 (1948), 165–84.

Cohn, N., *Warrant for Genocide: The Myth of the World-Jewish Conspiracy and the Protocols of the Elders of Zion*, London, 1967.

Dawidowicz, L.S., *The War Against the Jews, 1933–1945*, New York/London, 1975.

Ettinger, S., 'The Origins of Modern Anti-Semitism,' *Dispersion and Unity*, 9 (1969), 17–37.

Feingold, H.L., *The Politics of Rescue: The Roosevelt Administration and the Holocaust, 1938–1945*, New Brunswick, N.J., 1970.

Fischer, J.S., *Transnistria: The Forgotten Cemetery*, New York, 1969.

Gergel, N., 'The Pogroms in the Ukraine in 1918–1921,' *YIVO Annual of Jewish Social Science*, 6 (1951), 237–52.

Handlin, O., 'American Views of the Jew at the Opening of the Twentieth Century,' *Publications of the American Jewish Historical Society*, 40 (1950), 323–44.

Heifetz, E., *The Slaughter of the Jews in the Ukraine, 1919*, New York, 1921.

Herzog, W., *From Dreyfus to Petain*, New York, 1947.

Higham, J., 'Anti-Semitism in the Gilded Age: A Reinterpretation,' *Mississippi Valley Historical Review*, 43 (1957), 559–78.

Hilberg, R., *The Destruction of the European Jews*, Chicago, 1967.

Korey, W., *The Soviet Cage – Antisemitism in Russia*, New York, 1973.

Levinger, L.J., *Anti-Semitism in the United States*, New York, 1925.

Massing, P., *Rehearsal for Destruction*, New York, 1949.

Parkes, J., *Antisemitism*, London, 1963.

Pison, K., ed., *Essays on Antisemitism* (2nd ed.), New York, 1946.

Poliakov, L., *Harvest of Hate*, London, 1965.

Reitlinger, G., *The Final Solution: The Attempt to Exterminate the Jews of Europe, 1939–45*, London, 1969.

Robinson, J., and P. Friedman, *Guide to Jewish History under Nazi Impact*, New York, 1960.

Rotenstreich, N., *The Recurring Pattern: Studies in Anti-Judaism in Modern Thought*, New York, 1964.

Samuel, M., *Blood Accusation: The Strange Story of the Beiliss Case*, New York and Philadelphia, 1966.

Silberner, E., 'Anti-Jewish Trends in French Revolutionary Syndicalism,' *Jewish Social Studies*, 15 (1953), 195–202.

Sterling, E., 'Jewish Reaction to Jew-Hatred in the First Half of the 19th Century,' *Leo Baeck Yearbook*, 3 (1958), 103–21.

Trunk, I., 'Religious Education and Cultural Problems in the East European Ghettos under German Occupation,' *YIVO Annual of Jewish Social Science*, 14 (1969), 159–95.

——, *Judenrat: The Jewish Councils in Eastern Europe Under Nazi Occupation*, New York, 1972.

Tushnet, L., *To Die with Honor: The Uprising of the Jews in the Warsaw Ghetto*, New York, 1965.

Vishniak, M., 'New Studies on the "Elders of Zion",' *YIVO Annual of Jewish Social Science*, 2–3 (1947/1948), 140–5.

Yahil, L., *The Rescue of Danish Jewry*, Philadelphia, 1969.

The Nationalist Movement: Zionism, Autonomism, Territorialism

Ahad Ha'am, *Nationalism and the Jewish Ethic,* H. Kohn, ed., New York, 1962.

Bein, A., *Theodor Herzl,* Philadelphia, 1940.

Borochov, B., *Nationalism and the Class Struggle: A Marxian Approach to the Jewish Problem,* M. Kohn, ed., New York, 1937.

Cohen, I., *The Progress of Zionism,* London, 1943.

Dubnow, S., *Nationalism and History, Essays on Old and New Nationalism,* K.S. Pinson, ed., Philadelphia, 1958.

Goldman, S., ed., *Brandeis on Zionism,* Washington, D.C., 1942.

Goodman, P., and L. Simon, *Zionist Thinkers and Leaders,* London, 1929.

Gordon, A.D., *Selected Essays,* F. Burnce, ed., Boston, 1938.

Hertzberg, A., *The Zionist Idea: A Historical Analysis and Reader,* New York, 1960.

Herzl, T., *The Diaries of Theodor Herzl,* M. Lowenthal, ed., New York, 1956.

Learsi, R., *Fulfillment: The Epic Story of Zionism,* Cleveland, 1951.

Meyer, I.S., ed., *Early History of Zionism in America,* New York, 1958.

Rose, H.H., *The Life and Thought of A.D. Gordon,* New York, 1964.

Simon, L., *Ahad Ha-Am,* Philadelphia, 1960.

Simon, L., *Studies in Jewish Nationalism,* London, 1920.

Stein, L., *The Balfour Declaration,* New York, 1961.

Syrkin, Marie, *Nachman Syrkin, Socialist Zionist: Biographical Memoir, Selected Essays,* New York, 1961.

Zangwill, I., *The Voice of Jerusalem,* New York, 1921.

The Jews in Palestine and the State of Israel

Bauer, Y., *From Diplomacy to Resistance: A History of Jewish Palestine, 1939–1945,* Philadelphia, 1970.

Begin, M., *The Revolt,* New York, 1951.

Bein, A., *The Return to the Soil: A History of Jewish Settlement in Israel,* Jerusalem, 1952.

Crossman, R., *Palestine Mission: A Personal Record,* New York, 1947.

Crum, B.C., *Behind the Silken Curtain,* New York, 1947.

Eisenstadt, S.N., *Israeli Society,* New York/London, 1967.

Halpern, B., *The Idea of the Jewish State,* Cambridge, Mass., 1961.

Herzog, Chaim, *The War of Atonement,* Boston/London, 1975.

Hurewitz, J.C., *The Struggle for Palestine,* New York, 1950.

Katznelson, B., *Revolutionary Constructivism: Essays on the Jewish Labor Movement in Palestine,* New York, 1937.

Kimche, J., and D. Kimche, *The Secret Roads,* New York, 1955.

Palestine: A Study of Jewish, Arab and British Policies, vols. I–II, Esco Foundation for Palestine, New Haven, 1947.

The Seventh Day, London, 1970.

Sharett, M., *Israel in a World of Transition,* Jerusalem, 1958.

Sykes, C., *Crossroads to Israel: Palestine from Balfour to Bevin,* London, 1965.

Index

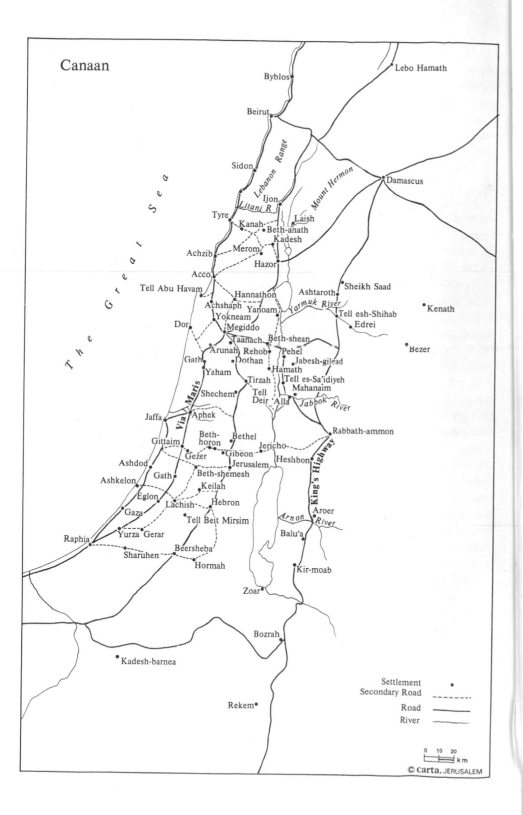

Canaan

The Great Sea

Settlement •
Secondary Road -----
Road —
River ~~~

0 10 20
km

© carta, JERUSALEM

or a mere fifty soldiers requested by Jerusalem and Gezer. Weapons supply was also limited, as is illustrated by a contemporary letter from Tell el-Hesi stating a local ruler's need for six bows, three daggers and three swords. For larger-scale military operations, an expeditionary force would be sent from Egypt. This was the 'army of archers', a force of chariotry combining the manoeuvrability of the chariot and the striking-power of the bow.

The prime significance of the El-Amarna letters for the history of Palestine (as well as for early Israel) lies in the light they throw upon the individual Canaanite city-states – the fluid relations between them, their strife and enmities, their alliances and their occasional broadly based coalitions. The cross references provided by these letters, together with contemporary documents from the Hittite archives at Hattusha (as well as the more recently discovered archive at Ugarit), serve to underline the delicate situation of these kingdoms, particularly in Syria. The latter, held in a vicelike grip between Mitanni and the Hittites, found themselves torn, at the same time, between the two poles of Egypt and Hatti. Such a predicament could lead only to military machination and political duplicity. Hatti became a forceful adversary to Egypt, the powerful Hittite king Shuppiluliuma disposing of Mitannian hegemony in Syria and penetrating as far as Damascus and the Lebanon Valley. Indeed, many of the states in Syria preferred the Hittites to an Egyptian overlord, as the former displayed greater skill and pliability in their dealings with vassals and granted more effective military protection. The tripartite competition among the powerful rivals, Egypt, Hatti and the declining Mitanni, for the fealty of the Syro-Palestinian rulers upset the delicate power balance throughout the region.

Despite the unstable political situation, Egypt remained master in Palestine and was still held responsible for the country's inhabitants. To cite but one instance, Burnaburiash II, the king of Babylon, sued Amenophis IV as a result of the pillaging of one of his caravans and the murder of Babylonian merchants in the town of Hannathon within the vale of Netophah (later within the tribal allotment of Zebulun [Joshua 19:14]): 'Canaan is your land and its kings your servants. In your land was I robbed. Bind them [the murderers] and the money they have stolen, make good. And the people who killed my servants, kill them and let the blood be avenged.'

Egypt's dominion in the north extended to the northern edge of the Valley of Lebanon, a line of demarcation recognized by the Hittites. Consequently, the penetration by Shuppiluliuma into the land of Amqi, south of this border, was considered an infringement of Egyptian territory even in Hittite historiography, which associated this violation with the severe plague that subsequently struck their land. Nevertheless, the growth of Hittite power in Syria and the weakening of Egypt encouraged the Ḥabiru to step up their marauding. Several of the local rulers – largely in the central hill district and in Amurru in the north – joined with them to cast off the Egyptian yoke. Acts of resistance among local rulers were on the increase owing to the ineffectiveness of the Egyptian authorities. Thus in northern Palestine a clash occurred between the two most important centres, Ashtaroth in the Bashan region and Hazor, which was attempting to expand eastwards across the Jordan and westwards towards the coast. In the lowlands, however, including the Valley of Jezreel, the Sharon Plain and the coastal strip – some of which constituted Egyptian royal estates and were vital to Egypt's economy – the Egyptian hold remained fairly firm throughout this period. Indeed Biridiya, the prince of Megiddo, carried out extensive agricultural work on the Plain of Jezreel on the Egyptian king's behalf, using forced labour assembled from various places. Further south Jaffa also was an Egyptian administrative centre and contained royal granaries. According to a later Egyptian document (Papyrus Anastasi I), this city was also known as a centre for leather work and armament.

As regards the central mountain area, the El-Amarna documents supply us with the names of two city-states destined to fill important roles in the Israelite Conquest and Settlement: Shechem and Jerusalem. Labaya, the ruler of Shechem, who was a sworn enemy of Egypt, had extended his rule over the hills of (later) Ephraim and Manasseh. Aided by the Ḥabiru, he laid siege to Megiddo. On the east his control reached as far as the mountains of Gilead and westwards to the Sharon region. Together with Milkilu, the ruler of Gaza (a former opponent but now an ally), Labaya and his progeny after him maintained constant pressure upon Jerusalem and even more southerly places, such as Lachish and Ashkelon.

Jerusalem itself remained an enclave loyal to Pharaoh, and its king, Abdi-Ḥepa (this apparently is the correct reading and not Puti-Ḥepa), actually assumed an Egyptian military title. In his letters he pleads with his overlord to send military assistance to enable him to cope with the marauding Ḥabiru and other enemies. Among these he lists the rulers of Shechem, Gezer, Gath, Lachish and Ashkelon. Specifically he complains of subversive acts along his north-western border: the waylaying of one of his caravans in the Valley of Ajalon; the capture of the nearby city of Beth-horon and of Rubute (a town as yet not clearly identified); and an attempt to undercut his rule at Keilah (Khirbet Qila) on the south-western border. The predicament of Jerusalem is indicative of the dangerous isolation of several Canaanite city-states and, concomitantly, of temporary alliances between them. One illustration of such wide-ranging coalitions, intended to meet a specific situation, is the request for military aid against the Ḥabiru made by Abdi-Ḥepa and Shuwardata (the ruler of Hebron or Gath) to the kings of Acco and Achshaph in the distant northern coastal region.

The Jerusalem 'diplomatic file' found in the El-Amarna archive has not only revealed the complex problems and struggles that beset this Canaanite city-state fighting to maintain its territorial integrity and very survival; it has also shed indirect light on the biblical account of the status and fortunes of early Jerusalem. Only a few generations separated these episodes from the Israelite invasion of Canaan. This invasion apparently took place in the border region between the kingdoms of Shechem and Jerusalem, the two political entities in the mountain district, as disclosed by the El-Amarna documents. For all the differences in political and military alignment at the time of Joshua, the strategic position of the Kingdom of Jerusalem resembled that in the El-Amarna period (see Chapter 4, page 57). The composite ethnic make-up of Jerusalem's populace is reflected in the very name of Abdi-Ḥepa: the first component is Canaanite and the second is the name of a Hurrian-Hittite goddess. A similar picture is conveyed by the biblical reference to Hittites who had settled in the town side by side with the ancient Canaanite-Amorite inhabitants

(*cf*. 'Uriah the Hittite' of Jerusalem; and Ezekiel 16:3). The Jebusites, settlers in pre-Israelite Jerusalem, were most probably linked to the former. Furthermore, the literary form and flowery style of the El-Amarna letters from Jerusalem, with their plethora of Canaanite idioms, indicate that the city was an important centre of scribal craft. With its conversion under David into Israel's capital, the city could well have assumed a major position in facilitating the absorption of Canaanite civilization, in addition to transmitting methods of government to the Israelites.

Canaan at the Time of the Israelite Conquest

The decline of Egypt's power in Asia, upon the disintegration of the Eighteenth Dynasty in the latter half of the fourteenth century, facilitated ever-deeper incursions by nomadic and semi-nomadic tribes from the eastern frontier into the arable area. These elements, who came with the purpose of settling, included the Israelites and kindred tribes, as well as inhabitants of southern Trans-Jordan – the Edomites, Moabites and Ammonites (see Chapter 4).

During the reign of Horemheb, who had usurped the throne of Egypt, an attempt was made to re-establish Egyptian authority in Canaan, though this was unsuccessful. Of particular interest are the reliefs in Horemheb's tomb, depicting the physiognomy typical of captives from Palestine and possibly Syria, noticeable among whom are bearded Semites, as well as Hittites. These clearly attest to the multifaceted composition of Canaan's population during this period. With the advent of the Nineteenth Dynasty, towards the close of the fourteenth century, an eastward orientation became a dominant feature of Egyptian foreign policy. Rule in Asia, albeit on a smaller scale than under Thutmosis III, was regained. Symptomatic of the strengthened ties with Canaan under this dynasty is the extraordinarily large number of contemporaneous Egyptian documents found in Palestine. Conversely, Canaanite influence within Egypt reached its peak at this time, as is evidenced by the many Canaanite deities included in the Egyptian pantheon and the extensive adoption of Canaanite words in Egyptian literature.

The successful expeditions of Seti I (1308–1290) into Canaan are recorded on several steles (at Beth-shean, Tell esh-Shihab in northern Gilead and Tyre), by the geographical lists of captured Canaanite cities and by a unique series of reliefs (with accompanying inscriptions) in the temple of Amon at Karnak. The reliefs are a highly detailed source of information on the military route taken by the Egyptians along the northern Sinai Peninsula towards Raphia. Depicted there are some twenty forts and fortified wells dispersed along the route. We are informed of the capture of 'the [city of] Canaan', apparently referring to Gaza, the conquest of Yanoam near the outlet of the Jordan from the Sea of Galilee and the conquest of Kadesh. It is doubtful, however, whether this refers to Kadesh-on-the-Orontes for, despite Seti's stele at this site, it remains unclear whether he did in fact capture so northerly a point. The fortress city of Kedesh in Upper Galilee is more likely. Alongside depictions of Canaanite strongholds and their characteristic landscapes, the reliefs include scenes of the wild Shasu-Bedouin, of Canaanite warriors, of 'the great princes of Lebanon' felling cedars for Egypt (*cf*. I Kings 5:20) and even of

Hittites, with whom the Egyptians may well have clashed in southern Syria. Seti's geographical lists suggest that his principal goal was the restoration of Egyptian sovereignty over the Beth-shean Valley, Galilee and the Phoenician coast, along which we find a series of cities from Acco to Ullaza in the north.

The two victory steles from Beth-shean, both apparently dating to Seti's first regnal year, furnish enlightening details on the region in general and on the politico-military alignment that confronted the king. One stele reports the suppression of an uprising by the ruler of Hamath, who had attacked Beth-shean further to his north and, together with the inhabitants of Pella in Trans-Jordan, had besieged the town of Rehob (Tell eṣ-Ṣarem, 3 miles to the south of Beth-shean). The other stele was erected to commemorate the Egyptian victory over the 'Apiru (the Egyptian equivalent of the Akkadian Ḥabiru or Ḥapiru [see page 41]), who had fanned out across the hills of Lower Galilee and were endangering the local populace. These are allusions to the infiltration of Galilee by nomadic groups who may have been precursors of Israelite tribes in the north of the country. This is particularly likely as Seti's geographical lists contain the first mention of Aśer, a name which appears later as that of an Israelite tribe, Asher.

During the reign of Seti's successor, Rameses II (1290–24), the struggle between the Egyptians and the Hittites for supremacy in Asia reached its climax in the battle of Kadesh on the Orontes River. The battle of Kadesh, which took place in the fifth year of Rameses' reign (1285 BCE), was the most intense clash ever between the two contenders, both sides being assisted by numerous allies. The Egyptians employed, *inter alia,* a contingent of the 'Naruna of Amurru' (an *élite* infantry corps designated by the Canaanite-Hebrew term *ne'arim*), while the Hittites included in their camp northern Syrian as well as western and northern Anatolian troops. The Ramesside temples throughout Egypt contain numerous depictions of the battle of Kadesh, extolling it as the most momentous of Rameses' victories. This self-aggrandizing account notwithstanding, the outcome was in point of fact a near debacle, for Rameses failed to attain his objective, the capture of Kadesh. The Hittites regained the land of Amurru, which had briefly defected to Egypt, and even penetrated as far south as the region of Damascus (Api), which fell for a time under Hittite suzerainty, as is known from a Hittite document.

The Egyptian fiasco at Kadesh led to a loosening of control in Canaan. Some three years later Rameses was compelled to lead an expedition into Upper Galilee to put down rebellious city-states such as Acco and Merom, near where occurred the military clash between the Israelites and the Canaanites several decades later (see page 57). Further conquests in the north are attested to by Rameses' steles at Beth-shean, Tyre, Byblos and Sheikh Saad, in the Bashan region. The monument found at the latter site, known as the 'Job Stone', mentions the Semitic deity El-kon(eh)-zaphon, which is a variant of Baal-zephon, known at Ugarit and in the Bible, and which is reminiscent of the biblical *El 'elyon koneh shamayim va'arez* (Genesis 14:19). Rameses' ties with northern Trans-Jordan are indicated also by the fact that a highly placed Canaanite official in Egypt, one Ben-azan, came from Ziri (Zer)-Bashan, a town mentioned in the El-Amarna and Ugarit archives. Rameses II did not restrict his military activities to the northern part of the country. Recently discovered evidence points to the great interest he displayed in the south as well. Excavations at Jaffa have shown that the town was destroyed and rebuilt during this king's reign, and an inscription mentioning him actually appears on the city's gate. A detailed relief from his reign, depicting the capture of Ashkelon, has long been known. Newly found geographical lists indeed support the view that Rameses subdued the entire coast, from Dor in the north to Raphia in the south, while in the south-east he overwhelmed the Shashu-Bedouin tribes in the Negev and Seir.

Particularly enlightening are the reliefs and accompanying inscriptions on a temple wall uncovered not long ago at Luxor, depicting Rameses' campaign in Moab. This record of a military expedition into southern Trans-Jordan is the first proof of Egyptian interest in this remote area. It may now provide a clue to a strange stele from the village of Balu'a in northern Moab, apparently to be attributed to the time of Rameses. The stele contains a relief in Egyptian style, depicting a Moabite ruler (could it portray 'the first king of Moab' mentioned in Numbers 21:26?), flanked by deities, and bearing an enigmatic inscription in apparently pseudo-hieroglyphic script. The recent discovery at Timnah in the southern Arabah of an Egyptian copper-mining centre (apparently employing Midianites), with an adjacent sanctuary, is of particular interest in connexion with Rameses' campaign to Moab, for the finds there include several of his inscriptions. The newly attested presence of Egyptians and Midianites in this area is equally significant for a new appraisal of the biblical Exodus and Conquest tradition, as the Arabah and southern Trans-Jordan played a prominent role for the Israelites in this period (see Chapter 4, pages 55 ff.).

The cold war between Egypt and the Hittites that followed the battle of Kadesh led eventually to the conclusion of a peace treaty (in 1269) between Rameses II and Hattusilis III. The detailed treaty contains no precise reference to an agreed border. Nevertheless, it would appear that the line of demarcation conformed to the northern frontier of the land of Canaan as described in the Bible (Numbers 34). This was the geopolitical reality that confronted the Israelites as they made their way into the land. In fact, it is reflected in the outline of the Promised Land in Joshua 1:4: 'From the wilderness and this Lebanon [i.e., the limit of Egyptian dominion] even unto the great river, the river Euphrates, all the land of the Hittites . . . [i.e., the Hittite dominion in Syria]'. Hence Egypt remained in possession of the Damascus region and as far afield as Lebo Hamath in the northern stretches of the Valley of Lebanon. With the land of Amurru under Hittite domination, Egypt's hold extended along the Mediterranean littoral up to Sumur, to the north of Byblos. Damascus and Sumur are indeed noted in Papyrus Anastasi I as, respectively, the easternmost and northernmost of the Egyptian bases in Asia; this document reflects the physical limits of Egyptian rule in Asia in the latter half of Rameses' reign.

Papyrus Anastasi I, a remarkable document composed by an Egyptian scribe in the form of a satirical letter, is a unique source of information on Canaan, a sort of 'guide-book' serving the needs of the Egyptian Army and especially the *mehir* (a Canaanite term signifying an *élite* corps). It contains a vivid depiction of the physical landscape, the country's major towns and variegated population groups and, above all, its network of highways. The provisioning of an Egyptian expeditionary force by the local populace is also mentioned in the papyrus, providing evidence of the prosperity of the cities of the plain, especially those on the coast, such as Jaffa. On the other hand, security was poor in the hill country, owing to the presence of the predatory Shasu-Bedouin and other marauders who by now may well have included the newly ensconced Israelites. The account of a heroic deed by the chief of a tribe known as Aser recalls the exploits of Samson or of David's warriors.

Relations between Egypt and Hatti during the reigns of Merneptah (1224–14) and of the Hittite king Tudhaliyas IV (*c.* 1250–20) were tranquil up to the fall of the Hittite Empire. One unifying factor was the common danger presented by the Sea Peoples (see Chapter 6, pages 80 ff.), who on the one hand, stirred up the inhabitants of western Anatolia and, on the other, launched an assault upon Egypt (in the fifth year of Merneptah's reign) in confederation with the Libyans. In his initial years the Egyptian king was compelled to quell a general uprising that had flared up in Canaan, from Ashkelon and Gezer in the south to Yanoam in the north, as we learn from a stele dating from the fifth year of his reign. This victory hymn, in which Merneptah indulges in self-praise, is of the highest import as the first extra-biblical mention of 'Israel'. In listing the vanquished nations, he proclaims: 'Israel is desolated, her seed is not.' The full significance of this reference for Israelite history and for the chronology of the Israelite Conquest will be discussed later (see pages 42, 52).

Fragmentary journals of Egyptian officials stationed on Egypt's eastern frontier and in the Sinai Peninsula supply useful information on Merneptah's renewed control in Canaan, especially over such centres as Gaza and Tyre on the sea coast and even over certain places in the hill region (Papyrus Anastasi III). Among those passing through the border posts whose movements are recorded in detail by the Egyptian authorities are army officers returning from the 'wells of Merneptah in the mountain region'. Some scholars consider this to allude to 'the fountain of the water of Nephtoah [*ma'ayan mei Nephtoah*]', a border point between Benjamin and Judah near Jerusalem (Joshua 15:9 and 18:15). The basis for such an assumption lies in the possibility that the consonant 'r' in Merneptah's name was not pronounced at that time, so that it sounded like 'Meneptah'; a Hebrew scribe could have misread the name as 'the waters of [*mei*] Neptah', leading to the awkward Hebrew form 'fountain of the waters of Nephtoah'. Indeed, various inscriptions indicate that Merneptah, like his forbears Rameses and Seti, named several sites after himself, including fortresses in Canaan and in the Sinai Peninsula.

The Twilight of Egyptian Rule in Canaan

The death of Merneptah and the consequent weakening of Egyptian rule in Canaan did not lead to an abrupt termination of contact between the two countries; archaeological evidence from Palestine indicates continued relations. A jar found at Tell el-Far'ah (ancient Sharuhen) in the western Negev bears the name of Seti II, and another from Tell Deir Alla (probably ancient Succoth) on the Jabbok River in Trans-Jordan bears the name of Seti's royal consort, Ta-usert. Further discoveries at Tell Deir Alla from this period testify to the influence of the Sea Peoples even in this remote area (see page 86). An entry in the journal of an Egyptian frontier official of this period mentions the passage of a Bedouin tribe, together with its cattle, from the land of Edom to the region of the eastern delta, the biblical land of Goshen (Papyrus Anastasi VI; see page 41). The tribesmen were in quest of a more reliable source of sustenance, and the account is reminiscent of the migrations of Israel's Patriarchs.

The end of the Nineteenth Dynasty, around 1200, was marked by widespread anarchy, during which an obscure usurper seized power. The identity of this new-comer, who bore the name Irsu, is controversial, but his designation as a 'Haru' discloses his Hurrian-Asian ancestry. This episode of a probably northern-based invasion of Egypt, known only from a later Egyptian source, may perhaps be linked to events in Palestine, echoed in the biblical narrative concerning Chushan-risha-thaim, the king of Aram-naharaim and the first oppressor of Israel in the period of the Judges (Judges 3:3–10). This enigmatic narrative presupposes an invasion of southern Palestine by a ruler from northern Syria at an early stage of the Israelite Settlement, which would accord chronologically with the end of the Nineteenth Dynasty in Egypt. Yet it is difficult to conceive that a ruler from Aram-naharaim (*i.e.,* from the Euphrates region) would undertake such a large-scale campaign for the mere purpose of subjugating the region of Judah. If one is to avoid the questionable emendation of the biblical text to read 'king of Edom' in lieu of 'king of Aram [-naharaim]', then the more likely assumption is that this king actually aimed at the conquest of Egypt. The battle with Israel would then be only incidental in character, and the biblical account would conform with the Bible's general tendency to view broader historical events within the limited framework of Israelite history. Against the larger back-drop of events in the Near East, Israel's deliverance by Othniel ben Kenaz would be related to the general defeat of the foreign invader of Egypt at the hands of Set-nakht, the founder of the Twentieth Dynasty.

Rameses III (1198–66 or, according to the 'low' chronological reckoning, 1182–50), the son and successor of Set-nakht and last of the eminent Pharaohs of the New Kingdom, succeeded in establishing Egyptian authority in Canaan for the last time. His wars were aimed primarily against the Sea Peoples who were then storming the eastern seaboard of the Mediterranean. This was a life-and-death struggle not only for Canaan but also for Egypt itself. These events will be discussed more fully in the chapter on the Philistines (see Chapter 6, pages 80 ff.); this people is first brought to our notice in the inscriptions of Rameses III. For the moment we will concentrate upon the other activities of Rameses III that affected Canaan.

Apart from his campaigns against the Sea Peoples in Canaan, Rameses successfully engaged the Shasu-Bedouin of Seir, who had been exerting increasing pressure upon the Egyptian frontier. He also fortified several Canaanite cities, notably along the Via Maris, in order to ensure his control; one of these bore his name, Migdol Rameses ('Rameses' fortress'). There is archaeological evidence of this last brief period of Egyptian rule at several sites, including numerous objects bearing Rameses III's name, such as a vase from Gezer, ivories from Megiddo and the recent finds from Timnah in the Arabah. The finds at Beth-shean are particularly indicative of this renewed Egyptian control; Rameses rebuilt the city and, indeed, a statue of him has been unearthed, as well as inscriptions of the commanders of the Egyptian garrison there. The Canaan of Rameses III saw the erection of numerous sanctuaries and steles dedicated to various deities, more, in fact, than were erected during any other period. The local Canaanite pantheon was represented in these sacred abodes alongside that of the Egyptians, evidently with the aim of legitimatizing Egyptian hegemony over the land. The temples were also of great economic significance, for they served as the depositories of the gifts and tribute of the population of Canaan. Among the extensive properties of the chief god Amon, as listed in the Great Harris Papyrus, are nine cities in the land of Haru (Canaan), probably some sort of temple estates, centres of priestly residence. These may well have served as a model for the later Israelite priestly Levitical towns known to us from the Bible.

After the death of Rameses III, Egyptian rule in Canaan rapidly approached total collapse. The latest evidence of Egyptian influence there is a statue of Rameses VI at Megiddo, dating from the mid-twelfth century. Egypt's loss of prestige even along the Phoenician littoral, which had been subject to her for centuries, is clearly attested by the tale of an Egyptian envoy, Wen-Amon, who had undertaken a voyage to Byblos at the outset of the Twenty-first Dynasty (*c.* 1080). Among the factors militating against Egyptian influence in this area were the rise of Assyria and the invasion by its aggressive ruler, Tiglath-pileser I (1114–1076), of Lebanon and the Phoenician seaboard. Three maritime cities, Arvad, Byblos and Sidon, became tributary to him. This situation enables us to understand the contemptuous treatment accorded to Wen-Amon and other Egyptian envoys paying court visits to Zakar-baal, the king of Byblos, around this time. Egypt, it seems, was attempting to establish relations with Assyria, the rising political power in the Phoenician coastal region. This is evident from the shipping of exotic Nile animals by Pharaoh – probably through Phoenician intermediaries – to the Assyrian king as a gesture of good will.

The Assyrian incursion into the west, however, was for the time being no more than a transient episode, and more than two centuries were to pass before Assyria truly entrenched itself on the Mediterranean littoral. Blocking Tiglath-pileser and his successors in their attempt to achieve a real conquest of Syria were the Aramean tribes mentioned explicitly for the first time in his inscriptions. Since the end of the twelfth century, masses of Arameans had invaded the Syrian and Euphrates regions. Their obduracy and Tiglath-pileser's inability to bring them to heel are illustrated by the fact that the Assyrian king had to wage twenty-eight campaigns across the Euphrates, pursuing them as far as the oasis of Tadmor (Palmyra) and even to the Lebanon range. Some three generations later the Arameans, having in the interim organized themselves into several states, are encountered doing battle with Saul and David for supremacy in Lebanon and northern Trans-Jordan. Within Palestine itself, where Egyptian power had collapsed and Assyria had not yet become a factor, the twelfth and eleventh centuries witnessed growing internal feuds, in which Israel assumed a dominant role. The Israelites had to deal in turn with the indigenous Canaanite element, with the Trans-Jordanian kingdoms and desert marauders on the east and finally with the Philistines in the west, the latter constituting a particularly fierce and obstinate enemy.

3

The Dawn of Israel

The Problematics of Bible Tradition

The genesis of every nation and tongue is enshrouded in obscurity, and generally there survive only a few vague recollections of limited historical value. Israel alone among the nations of the ancient Near East has preserved any organic, ramified tradition – as exemplified by the Pentateuch and the Book of Joshua – recounting its origins and vicissitudes prior to its crystallization as a true historical entity. It is possible that similar traditions had circulated among Israel's neighbours, as may be deduced from Amos' remark (9:7): 'Have not I brought up Israel out of the land of Egypt? and the Philistines from Caphtor, and Aram from Kir?' In other words, 400 years subsequent to the settlement of the Philistines and Arameans in their historic domains, echoes still reverberated concerning their origins and exodus from previous homelands. But the fact remains that of no people in the biblical period other than Israel has there been preserved such a detailed account of its protohistory or, certainly, such a complete and continuous description as is to be found in the patriarchal narrative and in the Exodus-Conquest cycle.

A cardinal question immediately poses itself and is the basis for any proper assessment of the historical beginnings of Israel: how is the biblical tradition (or, more precisely, the biblical traditions) to be evaluated from the standpoint of historical authenticity? The problem applies to the historical sketch in its broad outline as it emerges from the biblical account: the origin of the patriarchal family in Mesopotamia and its migration to Canaan; the social and religious modes of life followed by Abraham, Isaac and Jacob; the bondage in Egypt and the subsequent Exodus; the desert wanderings and the ultimate conquest of the Promised Land. Can this entire account or even a portion of it be viewed as faithfully mirroring historical reality?

The nature of the sources at the disposal of the historian poses a serious difficulty in method. He must base his reconstructed picture of Israel's beginnings on the evidence supplied by the Israelites themselves, with all the limitations presented by internal testimony of this sort. The rich store of extra-biblical material at hand today, for all its importance, must still be viewed as no more than 'circumstantial evidence' (see below). Moreover, the historian must bear in mind that the biblical evidence in its present form was formulated generations after the occurrence of the events described and on the basis of oral traditions and early written sources of diverse nature and value. The biblical tradition as it stands represents an organic, chronological whole that took its final form only after lengthy, multifarious literary activity in which sources were sifted, reworked and interwoven. This complex process may have ensued in the manner laid down by the orthodox school of Bible criticism, the so-called 'documentary hypothesis' or, rather, along the lines of the 'form criticism' and *Ueberlieferungsgeschichte* (*i.e.,* tradition-history) method, which has gained increasing ground in recent years, that postulates an amalgamation of small literary units into large complexes and 'themes'. Moreover, the simplistic, linear portrayal of Israel's protohistory is the product of a later schematic approach and of a specifically historiosophic tendency that would place the events of the Hebrews' genesis on a broadly national, pan-Israelite base (for the Conquest tradition see page 47; and on the nature of the Book of Judges, page 67). Once again, then, how is one to distinguish the early and authentic from the later, tendentious material that attached itself to the former and gave it final shape?

From the very beginnings of modern Bible criticism, scholars have striven to solve this perplexing dilemma. Some of the proposed solutions are far fetched, and only a few can be presented here in condensed form. With all the risks of generalization, it may be stated that German Protestant circles displayed, with varying degrees of severity, a predominantly negative attitude towards the historicity of the biblical account, while other scholars (of course with exceptions, notably in the United States and Israel) have evinced a greater faith in this tradition. The Wellhausen school entirely rejected its reliability, seeing in the biblical tradition mere reflections of late periods, from the days of the monarchy and even later. To cite one illustration of this approach, the contentiousness of Jacob and Esau and the preference of the former in their father's blessing are seen as mirroring the enmity between Israel and Edom under the monarchy and the subjugation of Edom by David. With the passing years the Wellhausen school has produced a number of variegated and odd theories, such as the 'mythological' approach at the turn of the present century. The proponents of this view maintained that Israel's Patriarchs were fundamentally god-figures transformed into ordinary mortals; such scholars 'deciphered' the biblical narratives describing Israel up to the advent of the monarchy according to this mythological 'key'.

The current scholarly view, an outgrowth of the Wellhausen school and accepted with varying modifications also by many historians and Bible scholars outside Germany, has best been expressed in the works of A. Alt and M. Noth (see Bibliography). According to this viewpoint, Israel was constituted as a people only on the soil of Canaan and at a relatively late date, that is to say, not before the twelfth century BCE. The process consisted of the gradual coalescence of twelve tribes, originally of unrelated groupings, that had come to share a belief in a common God, Yahweh. Noth in particular took the Greek (most specifically the Delphic) amphictyony as his model for this tribal confederation. The Israelites too, in his opinion, formed such a union around a common cultic centre, allegedly first located at Shechem, thence at Bethel and finally at Shiloh. Thus the tradition that speaks of a common origin for the Israelite tribes and a shared fate prior to their settlement in Canaan is automatically rejected. The account of a military conquest of the country also goes by the board; for these scholars conceive of the Israelite invasion rather as a quiet infiltration resulting from normal transhumance, the seasonal search for pastures that brought the semi-nomads from the fringe of the desert into the cultivated areas. An even more extreme hypothesis has recently been proposed by G. Mendenhall (see Bibliography), who denies the very idea of any sizable Israelite incursion into Canaan from the outside. He argues that the Hebrews crystallized into a religious community through withdrawal from the debauched urban Canaanite society.

In seeking a rationale for the biblical tradition as it stands, the critical school epitomized by Alt and Noth has had recourse to a technique of literary analysis based on certain premises and principles. With regard to the aetiological explanation, presumed to be a central factor in the creation of narratives in the Pentateuch and the Book of Joshua, illustrations from the Conquest cycle will be presented further on. At this point another of their theses should be noted, namely that which claims the tendentious 'nationalization' of the biblical traditions, which, according to their view, were originally of a restricted tribal and local character. These ancient traditions, maintained by the individual tribes throughout their wanderings on the desert fringe, were transplanted in Canaan upon settlement and came to be associated with the newly allocated locales (hence the name of this general approach: 'Ortsgebundenheit', i.e., attachment to a specific locality). Moreover, the cultic sites, such as Shechem and Bethel in the patriarchal tradition and Shechem and Gilgal in the Conquest account, gave rise to the final formation of the narratives. Once the tribes had coalesced as the people of Israel, the tribal epics were nationalized, that is, they donned a national garb. In this view Abraham, Isaac and Jacob were at first no more than individual tribal chieftains whose original abode was the desert fringe of Palestine. Only in later biblical tradition were they accorded pan-Israelite status in a genealogical pattern uniting Israel's ancestors. In short, this school (and similar ones) regards biblical 'history' prior to the period of the Judges as primarily fictitious.

The view adhered to here, in the present assessment of biblical tradition, is quite different. It is, of course, a moot point whether research into Israelite protohistory will ever go beyond the hypothetical stage. Perhaps biblical tradition itself intended to pass on only the early Israelites' own conjectural conception of their national antecedents. Thus it is preferable to regard this tradition, a product of the innate historical consciousness with which the people of Israel was blessed, as a working hypothesis for any attempted reconstruction of the events. This view should certainly lead to a more positive evaluation, as does the approach of the Albright school – which has gained considerable momentum in the last generation – that much of biblical tradition may serve as an authentic historical basis for reconstructing Israelite protohistory. In this respect great importance must be attached to the deeply rooted Israelite belief that all the tribes of Israel derived from the same ancestry, for this postulate provides the rationale for a national organism that was eventually to encompass both banks of the Jordan, despite severe physical obstacles (see Chapter 1, pages 8 ff.).

We must now accept the biblical premise that Israel's final settlement in Canaan was preceded by a lengthy period of nomadism, during which Israel underwent a process of national consolidation. The Bible vaguely alludes to several centres as having performed a major role in the moulding of the people: Penuel (near the Jabbok confluence in Trans-Jordan) or Bethel, where Jacob, the *heros eponymos* of the tribal alliance, was given the name Israel (Genesis 32:29ff. and 35:10ff.; *cf.* Hosea 12:5); Shechem, where Jacob acquired a plot of land and erected an altar 'and called it El-Elohei-Israel' (Genesis 33:18–20); and Kadesh-barnea, also referred to as En-mishpat (in north-eastern Sinai) – names of a cultic-juridical nature – the rallying-point of the Israelite tribes for the assault upon Canaan (see pages 44, 55). Biblical tradition points to a decline in Israel's national cohesiveness, from a state of tribal unity at the outset of its history and during the Conquest to one of fragmentation during the period of the Judges. But this does not necessarily imply the tendentiousness of a later historiography. On the contrary, it may accurately reflect the transition from a nomadic state, when the individual or small group is assured of its existence only by cleaving to a larger framework, to the phase of settlement, when tribal or familial links tend to loosen.

Much of the re-evaluation of biblical tradition has evolved from the perspective afforded by a wealth of recently discovered extra-biblical material. The Albright school of thought and, even more markedly, Yehezkel Kaufmann contested the negative approach to tradition upheld notably by the Alt-Noth trend. Kaufmann, who sets out quite persuasively, eventually goes to the opposite extreme, maintaining an almost blind respect even for the details of biblical tradition. To claim, as he does, that the arrangement of the major literary complexes of the Bible accurately reflect the objective historical-chronological scheme of events is indeed far-fetched (see Bibliography and Chapter 4). Even with a positive orientation towards biblical tradition, we must avoid the pitfalls of a fundamentalist acceptance. Quite apart from late theological reflection and dogmatic tendentious redaction, it is clear that some embellishment of legendary character, as well as later anachronistic accretions, have entered into the biblical text and can be revealed by critical scrutiny. In the subsequent sections we shall employ a dialectical approach to the biblical material – in contrast to the one-sided radical methods noted above.

The Patriarchs in the Bible and in Modern Scholarship

Scholars positively oriented towards biblical tradition agree that the thirteenth century BCE marks the date of the Exodus from Egypt and the Conquest of Canaan, at least in so far as their main phases are concerned. The dating of the 'patriarchal period', however, is more controversial. Supporters of an early dating, headed by such scholars as Albright, Glueck, Speiser, De Vaux and, in Israeli research, Yeivin (see Bibliography), have assigned the date to the first half of the second millennium, that is, the Middle Bronze Age. Among other evidence adduced as support for this hypothesis are the archaeological findings from Trans-Jordan and the Negev, as well as the Mari documents from Mesopotamia and the Execration Texts from Egypt. The Bible has been quoted to show that Israelite bondage in the land of Egypt lasted for a period of 400 or 430 years (see, respectively, Genesis

15:13 and Exodus 12:40–1). In contrast, the bulk of scholarly opinion (including Kaufmann, Gordon and Eissfeldt [see Bibliography]) proposes a fourteenth-century date, close on the Conquest and Settlement period and contemporaneous with the El-Amarna era. In this instance, too, arguments are based on biblical sources: the number of generations was carefully enumerated (Genesis 15:16: 'But in the fourth generation they shall come hither again'); Moses, who must be assumed to have lived in the thirteenth century, belonged to the fourth generation after Jacob (Jacob – Levi – Kohath – Amram – Moses). In both cases, however, biblical chronology must be regarded with scepticism. On the one hand, the significance of the absolute figures (400 or 430) is still insufficiently clear. On the other hand, the selective character of the genealogical tables precludes any great chronological value; thus the very sketchy pedigree assigned to Moses is in decided contrast to that of his contemporary, Joshua, who is ten generations removed from Jacob (I Chronicles 7:22–7).

Attempts to determine a comparatively accurate date for the Patriarchs are themselves doomed to failure, for in fact it is difficult to speak of the so-called 'patriarchal period' as a well-defined chronological entity, even where one accepts the biblical tradition as such. It would seem, rather, that imbedded in this narrative cycle are reminiscences of centuries-long historical processes that may hark back to the West Semitic migrations within the Fertile Crescent that made their way ever westwards and reached their apex during the first quarter of the second millennium. These extended time spans were telescoped in the biblical narrative into a mere trigenerational scheme – Abraham, Isaac and Jacob.

Yet, whatever interest the Bible may show in the three Patriarchs as individuals and as representatives of historical periods, it has been more concerned with their role as recipients of a twofold pledge: the proliferation of their seed to form the nation of Israel and the perpetual inheritance of the land. These are two recurrent motifs, as in God's promise to Abraham: 'And I will make of thee a great nation . . . Unto thy seed will I give this land' (Genesis 12:2, 7 and elsewhere). The Patriarchs were, consequently, the bearers of divine revelation and of a covenant with the Lord – a pact whose essential theme was the destiny of a Chosen People. The 'God of the Fathers' is an exclusive patron deity maintaining an intimate relationship with the patriarchal family and granting it protection in its wanderings. Simultaneously He is a nameless God, with generalized appellatives: 'God of Abraham, Isaac and Jacob', 'The Fear of Isaac' and 'The Mighty One of Jacob'. The deity was revealed to the Patriarchs in their encampments in Canaan, again by general appellatives: 'Everlasting God', 'The Most High God' and, in particular, 'El Shaddai' (usually translated 'Almighty God'). At times He was associated with specific locations, such as 'El Roï' or 'El Bethel'. True, these designations may allude to Canaanite deities of an originally local character, as may be gathered from the Ugaritic documents, where El stands at the head of the Canaanite pantheon (see page 11). Yet the Patriarchs invested these appellatives with their own divine conceptions. Be this as it may, the revelation of Yahweh and of a true monotheistic belief seems more appropriate for the time of Moses, their appearance in the Genesis account consequently being an anachronism (see pages 34, 45f.).

Admittedly, the wanderings throughout the land are depicted in Genesis as having a religious motivation – the sanctification of various places by means of altars and *mazzevot*. Nevertheless, the biblical source presents a clearly limned image of the Patriarchs as semi-nomads accustomed to moving from place to place within the confines of the central mountain region and the Negev, pitching their tents on the outskirts of Canaanite cities. Hence they are seen to encamp in the environs of Shechem (Genesis 12:6 and 33:18), between Bethel and Ai (Genesis 12:8), near Hebron (Genesis 13:18 and 35:27), near Beersheba (Genesis 26:25) and 'beyond the tower of Eder' (Genesis 35:21). They enjoyed the protection of the Canaanite rulers and, as a rule, entered into treaties with them, as may be learned from Abraham's relations with Melchizedek, the king of Salem (Genesis 14:18–20), and Abimelech, the ruler of Gerar (Genesis 20 and *cf.* 26). A further indication is contained in the episode of the purchase of the cave of Machpelah from Ephron the Hittite (Genesis 23). At times they would range far from their main encampment in search of pasture land, as evinced by the sons of Jacob leaving the vale of Hebron for the environs of Shechem and Dothan 'to feed their father's flock' (Genesis 37:12ff.).

There is no reason to deny this semi-nomadic aspect of the patriarchal way of life and accept the version that has recently gained ground, that the Patriarchs lived solely off the proceeds of the international caravan trade. Some scholars have gone even further afield and regarded them as 'merchant princes'. In this matter the explicit biblical testimony must be accepted in good faith when it describes the Patriarchs' existence as that of typical herdsmen whose sustenance came from their livestock and, sporadically, from seasonal farming, as in the story of Isaac at Gerar (Genesis 26:12). This social and economic colouring applies equally to their markedly patriarchal-tribal mode of existence.

In examining the historical authenticity of the patriarchal traditions, one is instantly struck by their twofold nature, alluded to in our opening remarks on Israel's protohistory. On the one hand, they contain early, authentic material and, on the other, late, anachronistic conceptions. At times the patriarchal *milieu* appears to be in surprising accord with the over-all pre-Conquest reality – in its social and legal patterns, its variegated beliefs and customs, its demographic character and its nomadic paths – as is borne out by recent discoveries (see pages 35–40). On many counts the patriarchal tradition conflicts with what is known of the later periods, the Settlement and Monarchy, or at least is devoid of any meaning in a later context. It is therefore not feasible to argue that the general background of the biblical account merely reflects later conditions. To offer one specific example: the personal names of the Patriarchs and of members of their families do not, for the most part, recur in later Israelite history; but, on the other hand, frequent onomastic parallels crop up throughout Akkadian and Egyptian sources no later than the final quarter of the second millennium. In other words, the names in the patriarchal narrative represent an early onomastic stratum. Indeed, at times it is surprising to what degree the tradition has maintained early details, so much so that their original significance eluded even later editors.

On the other hand, a painstaking analysis of this tradition will reveal that side by side with genuinely early elements there are numerous anachronisms, indicating a late date of composition for the Book of Genesis. Some of the more obvious anachronisms were pointed out by commentators as early as the Middle Ages (e.g., Ibn Ezra's commentary on the beginning of Deuteronomy), while others are less readily apparent and yield themselves only to the closest scrutiny and research. These late elements were absorbed into the various spheres of the patriarchal account, such as the monotheistic concept referred to above and the prevalent usage of the Tetragrammaton (i.e., Yahweh).

A typical anachronism encountered in the depiction of the patriarchal mode of life is its association with the camel (Genesis 12:16, 24:10, 30:43, 31:17 and elsewhere). In fact the domestication of this animal and its employment in caravans commenced only in the twelfth century (see page 72). Nor is this a matter of little consequence, for it is indicative of the decided difference between the mode of life of the fully nomadic desert dweller, possessing the camel, and that of the semi-nomad as personified by the Patriarchs. The latter resided among the sedentary population, or at least along the fringes of the cultivated area, and in their wanderings resorted to the donkey for transportation. These anachronisms are particularly numerous in the geographical and ethnographical spheres. An indication of the first is the use of the later Israelite name Dan (Genesis 14:14; cf. Rashi's commentary on this passage) for the pre-Conquest city of Laish, which is attested in both the Egyptian Execration Texts and the Mari documents (see page 38). In the ethnographical sphere we note the Philistines, referred to in the episode of Isaac and Abimelech, the king of Gerar, who is made to bear the title 'king of the Philistines' (Genesis 26:1, 14; 18) – this despite his obviously Canaanite name. In fact, the Philistines did not make their first appearance in Canaan until the beginning of the twelfth century (see Chapter 6); and only at a later stage did they appoint kings in place of the seranim or 'tyrants', who had ruled until then.

Such historical inconsistency would seem to hold true for the Arameans, too, with whom the forefathers of Israel were closely linked in the Bible. Not only was Abraham a kinsman of the Arameans, but his son Isaac and grandson Jacob established familial ties with Laban the Aramean (Genesis 25:20) and may, for that reason, have adopted the designation 'Aramean' for themselves (Deuteronomy 26:5). Furthermore, their ancestral home was called Padan-aram or Aram-naharaim (Genesis 24:10, 25:20 and 28:2). Nevertheless, the existence of the Aramean tribes is not attested by extra-biblical sources prior to the end of the twelfth century (see page 27), when they made mass incursions into the region known in the Bible as Aram-naharaim (i.e., the Jezireh, encompassing the Habor-Euphrates region). In fact this region was referred to in the earlier external documents simply as Naharaim. The Aramean element in the patriarchal stories is seemingly a later anachronism. There is thus no basis for a current scholarly contention that the Israelites were of Aramean or 'proto-Aramean' extraction. The Hebrews are, rather, to be linked with an earlier West Semitic stratum known in scholarly terminology as the Amorites (derived from the Akkadian designation 'Amurru', to be distinguished from the biblical usage of the Amorites), who first appeared in the Fertile Crescent towards the end of the third millennium. For the origin of the term 'ibri

('Hebrew') used to denote both the Israelites and the land of Canaan or a portion of it ('the land of the Hebrews' [Genesis 40:15]) and explicitly applied to Abraham, the nation's founding father (Genesis 14:13), see page 41.

The Patriarchs in the Light of Recent Discoveries

Numerous discoveries made especially in the last half century have revealed the back-drop against which Hebrew history unfolded. Many data have accumulated on the early West Semitic tribes in Mesopotamia, with whom the Patriarchs were affiliated, as has already been indicated. In addition, we now possess a more thorough knowledge of Canaan and its population in the centuries antedating the Conquest and the consolidation of Israel within its borders. True, no direct evidence or 'scientific' proof of the actual existence of the Patriarchs has yet come to light; but it is unwarranted to demand proof of this sort. It will be sufficient for our purposes if the essential *milieu* and many of the details found in the patriarchal cycle conform to the historical reality revealed by the discoveries. Illuminating in this respect is the fact that the names of several of Abraham's forbears (Genesis 11) – among them Serug, Terah and particularly Nahor – appear in earlier or later extra-biblical sources as place names in the Haran region, the ancestral home of the Hebrews (Nahor appears as a place name even in the Bible [Genesis 24:10]). While the extra-biblical material is solely circumstantial, its typological weight is considerable. Epigraphic data are of paramount importance, with strictly archaeological findings placed second in order. We shall first present some of the recent archaeological material that is significant for any evaluation of the patriarchal tradition – specifically the material from Palestine in the Middle Bronze Age, that is, from the first half of the second millennium.

As the Patriarchs were not permanently settled, nor were they creators of an urban civilization but, rather, tent-dwelling migrants, archaeology can reveal little of their way of life; but it can be more informative on their methods of burial. We may note, for example, that the Bible records a family tomb in the cave of Machpelah on the outskirts of Hebron (Genesis 23), while in another passage Rachel is noted as having died on the road during the family's travels, 'and [Rachel] was buried in the way to Ephrath, which is Bethlehem. And Jacob set a pillar upon her grave: that is the pillar of Rachel's grave unto this day' (Genesis 35:19–20). These modes of burial are at variance, yet both are typical of semi-nomadic tribes, who were constrained to bury their dead on the road or who encamped adjacent to the cities of Canaan and sought to bury their dead in cemeteries there. Both modes are illuminated by the archaeological finds in Palestine from the Middle Bronze Age. On the one hand, there are sporadic and isolated roadside burials (including the so-called tumuli), and, on the other hand, there are the familial tombs (of a later phase) surrounding such urban centres as Jericho. At this latter site there was an average of twenty skeletons per tomb, the remains of men, women and children. Dame Kenyon (see Bibliography), who uncovered these tombs, justly assumed that they were used over the course of several generations, precisely as is related of the cave of Machpelah. Thus this biblical episode can hardly be regarded as peculiar; nor can it be considered an aetiological tale, as it is by the Alt-Noth school. The details of Abraham's transaction with Ephron the Hittite for the purchase of the tomb may also have parallels in ancient business procedure, notably in the Hittite legal code. This biblical episode, illustrating as it does the distinction between an urban populace and nomadic groups seeking burial sites, may also clarify another archaeological phenomenon; for in some cases the pottery of the Middle Bronze Age found within the urban settlements (*i.e.*, the mound proper) differs surprisingly from that uncovered at the adjacent cemeteries.

Yet another conclusion, possibly of historical import, has resulted from the archaeological survey in the Negev conducted by Nelson Glueck and others during the 1950s. We now know that there were dozens of flourishing settlements there in the Middle Bronze Age I. Around 1900 BCE or somewhat later, permanent settlement there was destroyed, leaving the Negev uninhabited till the twelfth – eleventh centuries BCE. How does this picture compare with that depicted in the patriarchal narrative? The biblical text reads: 'And Abraham journeyed from thence toward the south country, and dwelt between Kadesh and Shur, and sojourned in Gerar' (Genesis 20:1); 'And Isaac came from the way of the well Lahai-roi; for he dwelt in the south country' (Genesis 24:62) – possibly implying a settled region experiencing tranquillity and security. Indeed Glueck, and Albright following him, have regarded this as conclusive evidence for fixing the patriarchal period at the beginning of the second millennium. They go even further, suggesting that the general devastation that overtook the Negev and Trans-Jordan south of the Yarmuk River (*cf.* page 52) is alluded to in Genesis 14, which preserves a vague tradition seemingly not entirely devoid of historicity. During a military campaign by four northern and eastern kings, headed by the monarch of Elam, which led down the King's Highway in Trans-Jordan towards the Negev and Sinai, five petty kings of the southern Dead Sea area were defeated and the entire region ravaged. But the semi-nomadic Patriarchs are specifically noted as clustering around urban centres – a feature entirely lacking in Canaan in the centuries prior to the Middle Bronze Age II. Indeed, the archaeological evidence from this latter period (especially the nineteenth–seventeenth centuries BCE) in Canaan far better suits the patriarchal narratives, for it reflects the dimorphic character of the population – a side-by-side existence of important, fortified cities and adjacent, open settlements.

As mentioned above, even more important than the archaeological data for revealing the historical background of the patriarchal era are the epigraphic treasures of the Near East – the tens of thousands of cuneiform documents that have come to light in Syria and Iraq and, to a lesser degree, the sources from Egypt. Palestine proper has produced few inscriptions from the second millennium, all of minor historical value. Only a few of the major discoveries of the past fifty years can be dealt with here, and we shall have to omit discussion of the Ugaritic texts from the excavations since 1929 at Ras Shamra on the north Syrian coast. The latter, for all their importance to the history and civilization of Syria, are significant in Bible studies mainly in the linguistic and literary spheres (see pages 11 f.; for possible points of contact with patriarchal history, see C.H. Gordon in Bibliography).

As for the Egyptian sources, the so-called Execration Texts take pride of place, as they shed considerable light upon Canaan. They have reached us in several groups, separated by approximately fifty years and dating from the nineteenth century and the first half of the eighteenth century. The earlier group, published by K. Sethe, consists of inscriptions on pottery bowls, while the later group, published by G. Posener, consists of inscriptions on small clay figurines symbolizing vassal kings of Egypt. A group of the latter type has been unearthed recently at Mirgissa in Nubia; this, however, is contemporaneous with the pottery bowls (see Posener in Bibliography). The inscriptions, which are magical texts meant to forestall any threat to Egyptian rule, contain lengthy lists of potential enemies, subjecting them to curses and execrations. Enumerated in the chronologically later group are some sixty Canaanite rulers and localities whose names are of great importance in revealing the ethno-demographic composition of contemporary Canaan, as well as the Egyptian spheres of influence in Asia during the Middle Kingdom.

What emerges from these texts is that the ruling dynasties in Canaan were clearly West Semitic, as is evident from the rulers' names, frequently containing such distinctive elements as: *ab* ('father'), *'am* ('kindred'), *shem* ('name', 'reputation') and the names of such deities as El and Hadad; they also include the personal name Aburahan, which evokes particular interest. No less illuminating are the many place names in Canaan, this being their first appearance in any source. The lists indicate an accelerating process of urbanization in Canaan and the subdivision of the land into scores of city-states. Preserved here are the ancient names of the country's towns, among them Laish (the later Dan), and eastern tribal frontier areas, such as Shutu (Seth) and Cushu, still occurring in biblical rhetoric as archaic equivalents for Moab ('The children of Seth' [Numbers 24:17]) and Midian ('the tents of Cushan' [Habakkuk 3:7]).

It is most instructive that the city-states are found mainly on the plains, whereas only Shechem and Jerusalem are mentioned in the central hill region. They also figure as the two most prominent centres in this area in the later El-Amarna documents (see page 20). Conversely, the patriarchal migratory movements took place in the central mountain area and in the Negev. It is significant that the Execration Texts and the patriarchal narratives represent fundamentally different geographical spheres. The absence of the Patriarchs from the country's fertile plains did not derive from a primitive mode of existence but from their inability to find a place in the already densely settled valleys and plains. Hence they turned to the sparsely populated and wooded mountain region and the Negev.

Turning now to the discoveries in Mesopotamia, the ancestral habitat of the Hebrews, we may first examine the outstanding finds from the city of Mari (modern Tell Hariri), situated on the bank of the Euphrates some 17 miles north of the Syrian-Iraqi border. Excavations at this site, begun in 1933, have revealed a palace of unique physical scope and grandeur, dating from the Old Babylonian period, when the city was ruled by West Semitic dynasties. Some 20,000 documents were found in the royal archives there, of which only a small portion has been published to date. The great potential of these discoveries for research into Hebrew origins (and for Bible scholarship as a whole) is readily apparent from the obvious bearing the Mari documents have upon early Israelite history in general and upon the patriarchal narratives in particular.

From the chronological point of view, the Mari documents date from the end of the nineteenth century and the first half of the eighteenth (according to the so-called 'middle' chronology, or about sixty-four years later as reckoned by the 'low' chronology), a period that may be reflected to a greater or lesser degree in the patriarchal narratives (cf. page 32). On the geographical plane the region of Aram-naharaim lay within Mari's horizon, and indeed Haran and Nahor – which figure in the Bible as ancestral habitats of the patriarchal family – are well documented at Mari as cities of prime importance and centres of nomadic and semi-nomadic tribesmen. Moreover, the biblical tradition that speaks of patriarchal migrations between Aram-naharaim and Canaan can now be viewed against a realistic background, as a result of the multifaceted references in the Mari documents to tribal wanderings and caravans plying between the Euphrates region, southern Syria (the land of Amurru) and northern Palestine up to Hazor. Similarly, the schematic conception of the biblical genealogy of Abraham's brother Nahor is now given more concrete form. Nahor's offspring are divided into two geographical groups (Genesis 22:20–4): he himself, together with his eight 'sons' by his wife, represents the area of Aram-naharaim, whereas his progeny by a concubine represent localities in the Valley of Lebanon and in the Upper Jordan region. Lineage through a concubine was intended here to indicate the migration of clan elements from their ancestral abode to far-off regions (as will be explained on page 63), in this instance from the vicinity of Nahor westwards to northern Canaan. If this supposition is correct, the genealogical scheme of the Nahorites could serve as an instructive parallel within the Bible for the wanderings of the Patriarchs themselves.

The 'Canaanites' as such (kinaḥnu) appear in a recently published document from Mari, pushing back their earliest attestation by several hundred years. Of actual cities in Palestine the Mari archives so far mention only Hazor (its ruler being called Ibni-adad), noted several times as maintaining diplomatic and commercial relations with Mari, and Laish, mentioned as the destination of a consignment of tin. The importance of these two towns in this period is also attested by their mention in the later group of Execration Texts, of roughly the same date, and even more so by the recent excavations at both these sites.

Great importance attaches to the ethnic and linguistic affinities between Mari and early Israel, as most of the individuals and tribes mentioned in the Mari documents, like the forefathers of the Israelites, were of West Semitic stock, speaking dialects closely akin to the earliest forms of Hebrew. This relationship is borne out by the many proper names that parallel those prevalent in Israel, especially in the patriarchal and Exodus narratives; to mention but a few: Abram, Jacob, Leah, Laban and Ishmael. On the other hand, there is a wealth of typically West Semitic expressions and loan-words in use at Mari that have their cognates in biblical Hebrew but are foreign to the Akkadian tongue in which the Mari records were composed (see A. Malamat in Bibliography). Finally, the major significance of Mari lies in the sociological realm, for the descriptions of tribalism in Mari contain most valuable insights into the nomadic and settled phases of the Israelite tribes, including the distinctive character and structure of patriarchal-tribal society and the transition from a nomadic to a sedentary existence, as well as the interrelationship with the indigenous urban population. From among the multifarious examples of tribal institutions and traditions that have close biblical counterparts (*cf.* pages 60, 68 f. and A. Malamat in Bibliography), we may note here the ritual at Mari of establishing a covenant by means of the slaughter of an animal. A parallel rite may be seen at the conclusion of the covenant between God and Abraham (Genesis 15:9–10; *cf.* Jeremiah 34:18–19).

Yet another source provides a new perspective for appreciating the patriarchal accounts of familial relations and legal practices, as well as a more general picture of their everyday life. These are the thousands of documents found at Nuzi, a city situated beyond the Tigris, near the present-day Kirkuk. These documents reveal, above all, the civilization of the Hurrians, for Nuzi during the late sixteenth and fifteenth centuries functioned as an important government centre for the Kingdom of Mitanni, whose inhabitants were mainly of Hurrian extraction (see page 10). But the Hurrians (the Horites of the Bible) had already fanned out across the Haran region and towards Syria and Palestine in earlier times. Thus they may well have left their impress upon the early ethnic and cultural character of the Hebrews, just as they did later on the Israelite tribes. Hence the importance of the Nuzi documents for a study of early Israel. The detailed material coming to light from the private archives of the city's notables and senior officials has, on more than one occasion, caused scholars to reassess the biblical narratives. Rather than purely literary creations, they have been re-evaluated as based upon solid legal and social foundations that prevailed during the middle of the second millennium but later receded into oblivion.

From the many instances that could be adduced to bear out these contentions, a few may be mentioned here (for further illustrations see C.H. Gordon and E.A. Speiser in Bibliography). There is, first of all, the account of the childless Abraham about to bequeath all his possessions to Eliezer, a servant and member of his household. However, the Lord assures him: 'This shall not be thine heir; but he that shall come forth out of thine own bowels shall be thine heir' (Genesis 15:4). The entire situation becomes readily comprehensible in the light of the accepted practice at Nuzi, whereby a childless master would eventually adopt a retainer as his heir but have the latter revert to his original status upon the birth of a natural son. Nuzian family laws conform with the practice exemplified by Sarah and Rachel, who, fearing barrenness, had given their husbands their maidservants from whom to bear children (Genesis 16:2–3 and 30:1–4). Just such a stipulation occasionally appears in Nuzi marriage contracts, making it mandatory for a barren woman to present her handmaid to her husband for the purpose of child bearing. The strange incident of Esau transferring his birthright to Jacob for a pot of lentils takes on a factual hue from certain business documents at Nuzi. One such record speaks of a birthright sale to a younger brother, with the elder recompensed by the price of three sheep. Some scholars also argue that the appropriation of Laban's *teraphim* or household gods by Rachel is based on a Nuzi custom whereby family property could at times pass on to the possessor of the household gods, which were of symbolic legal value.

Biblical instances such as the above have previously been considered unseemly deviations and were even used as grounds for denouncing the supposedly debased morality of the Patriarchs and their kin. The new information at our disposal, however, places these practices squarely within the accepted patterns of life in the ancient Near East in the mid-second millennium.

Israel in Egypt

The complete silence of extra-biblical sources on the descent of the Children of Israel into Egypt, their residence in the land of Goshen and the subsequent Exodus to Canaan does not constitute a conclusive argument against biblical tradition. From a typological point of view we are on quite solid ground, as the biblical account, in its boldest strokes as in many of its details, conjures up historical phenomena of the second millennium whose basic elements are to be found in Egyptian sources.

The Israelite settlement in the land of Goshen and Joseph's whirlwind ascent to the position of vizir of Pharaoh's court are examples ('And he hath made me a father to Pharaoh and lord of all his house and a ruler throughout all the land of Egypt', Genesis 45:8; see also Genesis 41:40–5). Joseph's appointment has been closely linked by many scholars with Hyksos rule in Egypt (during the years 1720–1570). Many rulers of Semitic descent held the reins of power under the Hyksos (Fifteenth and Sixteenth Dynasties), with their capital at Avaris (at Qantir rather than Tanis, the biblical Zoan) in the eastern delta, that is, in the vicinity of Goshen. We encouter among them such characteristic names as Yaqob-har, Anath-har, Hiyan and Ḥamudi. The Egyptian victory over the Hyksos and the ultimate expulsion of the latter from Egypt (see page 13) were indeed long ago associated with the Israelites and their Exodus under Moses (albeit in a vague manner) by Manetho, the Egyptian-hellenistic writer of the third century BCE quoted by Josephus (*Against Apion*, I, 14ff.).

There is, however, no valid support for this connexion within the Bible, as it contradicts the actual chronology of the Exodus. Also, the general Egyptian atmosphere pervading the Joseph narratives, while authentic in itself, points to a far later date. The descent of the Israelites into Egypt may, in a very general manner, be related to the continuous flow of West Semitic elements from Canaan to the land of the Nile that had commenced as far back as the end of the third millennium. Some of these newcomers occasionally rose to high state positions. This Semitic penetration, in small or large groups, was fundamentally peaceful and primarily motivated by commerce, as is attested, for example, by the well-known merchant-caravan scene depicted in the Beni-hasan tomb in Middle Egypt. Further motivation for such migration might also include a famine in Canaan or sale into Egyptian slavery. All these elements are well reflected in the patriarchal narrative.

The Egyptian documents are enlightening on this score. Thus perusal of a list of slaves on the estate of an eighteenth-century noble antedating the Hyksos (Papyrus Brooklyn, No. 35.1446) reveals numerous decidedly West Semitic names, and the position of Joseph in Potiphar's household comes immediately to mind. Another list, of the mid-fifteenth century (Papyrus Leningrad, No. 1116A), mentions *maryannu* nobility hailing from places such as Megiddo, Taanach, Hazor and Ashkelon and appearing before Pharaoh for rations of wheat and beer, just like Jacob's sons, who had gone down to Egypt to replenish their food supply. One is particularly struck by another parallel to the descent into Egypt by Jacob's sons, as well as by the families of Abraham and Isaac, due to a famine in the land of Canaan. An Egyptian frontier official notifies his superior of the passage of a nomadic tribe from the south of Palestine to the eastern delta. He writes: 'We have completed the transfer of the Bedouin [Shasu] tribes from Edom by way of the Fortress of Merneptah, which is in Tjeku [apparently the district of the town Succoth in Goshen], to the pools of Pe(r)-Atum [biblical Pithom] of Merneptah which are in Tjeku, to provide sustenance for them and their cattle' (Papyrus Anastasi VI; see page 26).

Indirect support for the Israelite sojourn in Egypt may be gleaned from the presence of groups there termed 'Apiru, referred to in documents dating from the mid-fifteenth to mid-twelfth centuries. There can be no doubt that the term 'Apiru in Egyptian usage is the equivalent of Hapiru or Habiru, prevalent in Akkadian records for about 1,000 years from the end of the third millennium on. It is employed there in the Mari and Nuzi documents and in the El-Amarna letters. There is most likely a relationship between these terms and the appellation 'Hebrew' (*'ibri*) of the Bible; some scholars assume a complete linguistic and contextual identity between the two, while others maintain only the latter relationship. Still others deny the possibility of any connexion whatsoever. The Habiru are an element of broad range in time and place, from Babylonia in the south to Anatolia and Palestine in the north and west, respectively; furthermore, their personal names derive from totally divergent languages. The inevitable conclusion is that this appellative does not denote any specific people or ethnic group but rather a social concept, though its precise nature is still the subject of scholarly dispute. At all events the term connotes an inferior social class that, owing to either the foreign elements it contained or other causes, was outside the normal social pale and legal framework, much like the *gerim* ('strangers') of the Bible.

If there is any connexion between *'ibri* ('Hebrew') and 'Apiru or Habiru, it is evident that the former term also originally denoted a social stratum. Viewed from this perspective, the concept of the *'ebed 'ibri* ('Hebrew slave') takes on a new meaning (Exodus 21:2 and elsewhere), as do other instances of the use of *'ibri*, such as 'Abram the Hebrew' (Genesis 14:13), who was a stranger in Canaan lacking full civic rights. This view would also accord with the inferior status of the Israelites in Egypt, where they lived as semi-slaves and clients of Pharaoh: 'For ye were strangers [*gerim*] in the land of Egypt'. Conceivably because of historical circumstances of this nature, the appellative 'Hebrew' stuck to the Israelites as a group; but in the Bible itself the term had taken on a decided ethnic hue. The biblical usage of 'Hebrews' as indicative of national affiliation is restricted to the Joseph and Moses narratives and to the episode of the Israelite-Philistine conflict in I Samuel. Fundamentally it is limited to denoting the Israelites as such in their confrontation with the foreigner – the Egyptians, Canaanites or Philistines. It is doubtful whether, on the basis of the eponym Eber, appearing six generations prior to Abraham (Genesis 11:14ff.), one may read into the biblical 'Hebrew' a broader meaning than that pertaining to Israel alone. Eber was patently a personification derived from *'ibri*, not *vice versa*, and in the course of time it became associated with the geographical connotation *'eber hannahar* ('beyond the River'). The Egytian term 'Apiru, in contrast, was broad in connotation, encompassing the various forced labourers of foreign origin in Egypt, who were indeed, for the most part, Semites from Canaan and thus most likely also included the Israelites.

Despite doubts as to whether it contains any specific reference to the Israelites, great interest attaches to a letter by an Egyptian official under Rameses II concerning construction work by the 'Apiru: 'Distribute grain rations to the soldiers and to the 'Apiru who transport stones to the great pylon of Rameses' (Papyrus Leiden 348). This immediately calls to mind the forced labour of the Israelites in Egypt: 'Therefore they did set over them taskmasters to afflict them with their burdens. And they built for Pharaoh store-cities, Pithom and Rameses' (Exodus 1:11). This enlightening piece of information appears authentic and tallies astonishingly with the activities of the early kings of the Nineteenth Dynasty, who, as a consequence of their strongly Asia-oriented foreign policy, had transferred their seats of government to the eastern delta. This was adjacent to the biblical land of Goshen, which was also anachronistically labelled 'the land of Rameses' in the Joseph stories (Genesis 47:11) or 'the field of Zoan' (Psalms 78:12), *i.e.,* Tanis. Rameses II, in particular, was noted for the large-scale building projects carried out during his lengthy reign (1290–24). He founded a new capital, apparently at the site of the ancient Hyksos city of Avaris, naming it in his honour Pe(r)-Rameses, 'the House of Rameses'. In addition to other sites guarding the approaches to the Sinai Peninsula, he rebuilt a city called Pe(r)-Atum, 'the House of [the god] Atum' (quite likely Tell el-Maskhutah in Wadi Tumilat, the actual location of Goshen). These two cities are indeed none other than the biblical Pithom and Rameses noted above (the 'r' in Per-Atum was not pronounced in those days, and the name would therefore have sounded like Pithom).

In all likelihood, then, Rameses II should be regarded as the Pharaoh who oppressed the Israelites and during whose long reign they may have left Egypt, perhaps in connexion with his clashes with the Shasu-Bedouin in Seir (see page 24). If, however, any historical importance is to be attached to the mention in Exodus 2:23 of the death of the Pharaoh who enslaved the Israelites, the Exodus would then have taken place under his successor, Merneptah. The victory stele of Merneptah, dating from his fifth regnal year (*c.* 1220), lends added credence to the above supposition. In this monument he boasts of having defeated 'Israel', the encounter no doubt having taken place within Canaan and not in the Sinai Peninsula (as is maintained by some), since it is mentioned in a context with Ashkelon, Gezer and Yanoam. Yet the precise meaning of the term 'Israel' here – its first appearance in any extra-biblical source – is elusive. Was it meant to encompass Israel in its entirety or merely several of the (northern) tribes? Might the hieroglyphic determinative for a people, rather than for a place, be regarded as evidence that the Israelites had not yet become ensconced in any permanent settlement or distinct territory of their own? At all events, it can be concluded from the foregoing that the episodes of the Exodus and Conquest, or at least their main phases, occurred during the thirteenth century BCE and had already reached their culmination by the final quarter of that century.

This chronological conclusion finds other support, particularly from archaeology (see page 53), but perhaps also from biblical sources. According to the chronological notation in I Kings 6:1, the Exodus took place 480 years before the construction of King Solomon's Temple (*c.* 970 BCE). The figure seems to be typological, based on a calculation of twelve generations, for a generation in the Bible was reckoned as a forty-year span (see Psalms 95:10 and the typological figures in the Book of Judges). If the more realistic computation of twenty-five years for one generation is adopted, the biblical comment can then be reckoned for an interval of 300 years, and the Exodus would then have taken place in the mid-thirteenth century. A similar dating is supported by the comment of the judge Jephthah to the king of the Ammonites (Judges 11:26), to the effect that Israelite settlement in Trans-Jordan reached back 300 years before his own time (in the early eleventh century). Using the same computation as above, this figure will be reduced to approximately 180 years, and thus the beginnings of Israelite settlement in Trans-Jordan will once again be seen to fall in the mid-thirteenth century.

The Exodus and the Revelation at Sinai

The absence of any extra-biblical sources for the Exodus and Conquest of Canaan can be accounted for, in all likelihood, by the fact that these events carried insufficient international weight to be recorded in contemporary accounts. For the Israelites, however, the tradition of redemption from the 'house of bondage' and the journey through Sinai to the Promised Land became a corner-stone of their faith, not only in the Pentateuch and the historiographical books of the Bible but also in the writings of the Prophets (*e.g.,* Hosea 11:1; Amos 9:7; and Jeremiah 2:6), as well as in the Book of Psalms (*e.g.,* Psalms 78:12–13 and 81:6). The biblical account of the Exodus and the desert trek does, it is true, bear the stamp of folklore and is interlaced with legendary material. Yet it contains authentic historical traits that are especially discernible when compared with the enlightening typological parallels in Egyptian sources.

Particularly instructive in this respect are the reports of Egyptian officials stationed on the Sinai frontier in the final quarter of the thirteenth century, to which reference has already been made (Papyri Anastasi III, V, VI). They reveal the strict surveillance of the border and the system of special permits from the Egyptian authorities for passage in either direction. These facts shed light on the persistent pleas by Moses and Aaron that Pharaoh grant the Israelites permission to leave the country. The very flight of the Children of Israel in the dead of night, once their request had been turned down, finds a partial parallel in an early Egyptian document, the tale of Sinuhe. This refugee from Twelfth Dynasty Egypt crossed the frontier under cover of darkness on his way through Sinai to Canaan. Similarly, a letter by the commander of the town of Tjeku (apparently Succoth, noted at the beginning of the biblical account of the Israelite flight from Egypt) tells of a military detachment sent in pursuit of two runaway slaves who had managed to slip through the border defences into Sinai, north of Migdol, which also is mentioned in the Exodus account (Papyrus Anastasi V, dating from the end of the thirteenth century). One of the purposes of the Egyptian boundary fortifications was thus to prevent the departure of conscript labourers. This barrier, however, was not always effective, as may be gathered from the sources, which, on the one hand, recount the successful flight of individuals and, on the other, of the 600,000 Israelite warriors and their families in the Exodus narrative (on the interpretation of this exaggerated figure, see page 62).

On the Israelites' journey through the desert, we are informed that they avoided the more direct route to Canaan 'through the way of the Philistines although that was near; for God said, Lest peradventure the people repent when they see war, and return to Egypt' (Exodus 13:17). This tradition, too, takes on a new meaning within the context of the contemporary scene, since (as noted on page 21) the 'way of the Philistines', which formed part of an international route along the coast of Sinai, was fortified with a tight network of strongholds by Seti I around 1300 BCE. Understandably enough, a guarded route of this sort might easily have become a military trap for the Israelites, and it was for this reason that they embarked upon the tortuous march they did. Despite the detailed itineraries in the books of Exodus and Numbers, it is impossible to reconstruct their route through the Sinai Peninsula and southern Palestine with any degree of certainty, for the overwhelming majority of way-stations were merely temporary encampments that cannot be precisely identified. The same applies to the whereabouts of Yam Suph, ('the Reed Sea'), and Mount Sinai. Many mediaeval commentators located both sites in the south, one in the Gulf of Suez or the Bitter Lakes, or alternatively in the Gulf of Eilat, and the other at Jebel Mussa ('the Mount of Moses') in the southern part of the peninsula, an identification going back to Byzantine times. Many modern scholars, however, insist upon moving them to sites in northern Sinai: the 'Reed Sea' to Lake Menzalah (called *'Tjouf'* in Egyptian sources, *i.e., 'Suph'* in Hebrew) or further east to Lake Sirbonis (Sabkhat el-Bardawil), a lagoon. The shallow waters of the latter permit foot passage at several points, and anyone making his way over the narrow strip of land separating the lagoon from the Mediterranean Sea finds himself surrounded by water, 'the waters being a wall to them on [the] right hand, and on [the] left' (Exodus 14:29). Mount Sinai would then be identified as one of the summits east of Kadesh-barnea, especially Jebel Ḥalal (see the atlases listed in Bibliography).

In point of fact, both hypotheses – the northern one and that pertaining to a broadly circuitous route to the south – can be supported by geographical identifications, sparse and uncertain though they be. The northern journey might be indicated by sites mentioned at the outset of the Israelite trek: Migdol and Pi-hahiroth, presumably on the ancient Pelusian arm of the Nile, as well as Baal-zephon (Exodus 14:2). The latter apparently was the Mount Casius of the classical period, a site sacred to seafarers from earliest times, located at Ras Kasrun on the narrow tongue of land enclosing Lake Sirbonis and recently examined by archaeologists. But elsewhere in the biblical text there is a definite suggestion that Yam Suph is the Gulf of Eilat. Perhaps it is not conflicting literary traditions that are reflected here, as is usually held, but rather waves of migration at different time intervals, as also occurred in the course of the campaigns of the Conquest (see pages 54ff.). In any event, the main base for the wanderings of the Children of Israel was the important oasis of Kadesh-barnea, identifiable as the present Tell Qudeirat in north-eastern Sinai, adjacent to a copious spring capable of sustaining a large encampment for 'many days' (Deuteronomy 1:46; on the significance of this site, see pages 31, 55).

Despite the historical mist enveloping both the Exodus and the Conquest, the events themselves fit well into the general pattern of the times, which saw the coalescence of certain ethnic groups into national entities striving for territorial integrity and political sovereignty. At approximately the same time, Edom, Moab and Ammon consolidated into nations (see page 52), which, unlike Israel, became independent kingdoms early in their development. Israel's transformation from a mere tribal grouping to full nationhood may well find expression in the religious metamorphosis symbolized by the revelation at Mount Sinai. This episode, however, has been regarded by several scholars as a tradition originally quite separate from the Exodus narrative, engrafted into it at a later period. Whichever view is correct, at least the biblical tradition itself attributes the transmission of this revolutionary ideology to the remarkable personality of Moses, a Levite. In the people's consciousness he remains foremost among prophets, a lawgiver and judge, a commander in battle, a statesman and the charismatic leader of Israel's departure from bondage to freedom, who saw his Maker more closely than any other mortal and who received the Law for his people and for all mankind. This spiritual metamorphosis was kindled by the revelation of the Divine Presence and of His ineffable name before Moses. In biblical tradition the God of Moses came to be identified with that of the Patriarchs. 'I am the God of thy father, the God of Abraham, the God of Isaac, and the God of Jacob' (Exodus 3:6); 'And I appeared unto Abraham, unto Isaac, and unto Jacob as God Almighty but by my name Jehovah [Yahweh] I made me not known to them' (Exodus 6:3).

Scholars have offered various explanations of the name Yahweh and of its origin. Some maintain that its roots lie in ancient religious concepts connected with the very origins of the Hebrews, a view which may now be supported by various proper names appearing in the Mari documents. Surprisingly enough, among the Hebrews themselves no proper names containing the theophoric element *yahu* or *yo* (an abbreviated form of Yahweh) appear until Jochebed, the mother of Moses. On the other hand, the so-called 'Midianite-Kenite' hypothesis on the origin of the name Yahweh is based on the fact that the divine manifestation in the burning bush and at Mount Sinai occurred in Midianite territory. Additional support for this view is found in the unique role of Jethro, the Midianite priest and father-in-law of Moses, to whom biblical tradition ascribes the introduction of legal institutions among the Israelites (Exodus 18). Now still another support for this hypothesis is the discovery of the 'land of the Shasu Y-H-W(A)' in the geographical lists of Amenhotep III and Rameses II, the former antedating Moses and the latter contemporaneous with him (see page 17). In both instances this place name is associated with Sinai or the land of Seir, an area mentioned in the Bible, even outside the Exodus context, as the site of the Lord's theophany (see Deuteronomy 33:2; Judges 5:4; Habakkuk 3:3; and Psalms 68:9).

Whatever the origin of Yahweh, the clear fact remains that this basic religious innovation – monotheistic faith – represents a specifically Israelite phenomenon, showing no indebtedness to the surrounding pagan world. It differed from the familial worship of the Patriarchs, which was at most monolatric – addressing itself to a single God but not ruling out the existence of other deities. The new monotheistic belief relied upon a polarized conception of Yahweh as both a universal-cosmic deity and a specific national god. No longer is the Covenant a mere bond with a Chosen People; it now embraces a fully developed social and moral message epitomized in the Ten Commandments. Despite the evolutionary viewpoint prevailing in Bible criticism, monotheism does not seem to have been the product of later theological speculation and, in accordance with Y. Kaufmann's view, is to be seen as an overriding historical and sociological force operating from the time of Israel's very inception as a people and pulsating in the consciousness of the tribes as they entered the Promised Land. Herein lies the real significance of the Exodus and of the revelation at Sinai.

4

Conquest and Settlement

The Conquest in Biblical Tradition

With the episodes of the Conquest and Settlement of Canaan by the Israelite tribes, we pass from the stage of protohistory to the threshold of history itself. The 'official' or 'canonical' tradition of the Bible here is clear cut. Palestine on both sides of the Jordan was, according to that account, seized by a military operation of comparatively brief duration in which all the twelve tribes participated as a unit, first under the leadership of Moses and then of Joshua. The mode of settlement was also simple in nature, according to a pre-arranged allotment of the conquered territory among the tribes. Those tribes settling in Trans-Jordan received their shares of land from Moses himself (Numbers 32; and Joshua 13:8ff.), while the others received their territories from Joshua, seven of them after casting lots (Joshua 18).

This simplified biblical account of a single pan-Israelite conquest, of continuous and organic development, accords with the tendentious and schematic approach of a late date concerning the nation's early vicissitudes (see page 29). In fact, the historical reality was immeasurably more complex. It was the later redactors who combined and interwove the various phases of long drawn-out military ventures and intricate historical processes, telescoping them into a unified, organic epic. As was often the case with other national chronicles, here, too, outstanding hero-figures – Moses and Joshua – were thrust into the foreground. Nevertheless, whatever may be the true date of the Book of Joshua (in which the bulk of the source material lies encased) or of the Book of Numbers and the first chapter of the Book of Judges (into which a lesser amount has found its way), the broad range of sources provides an historical base sufficient to allow for varying reconstructions of events, often by diametrically opposed schools of thought and even by differing scholars within one and the same school.

In brief, despite the reworking of the biblical tradition in subsequent generations, according to various historiosophical concepts that prevent us from taking the account at face value, we should not dismiss the tradition entirely nor deny the forcible occupation of Canaan by the Israelites, as do the more radical theories (see the opening remarks in Chapter 3, pages 29 f.). The most widespread of these theories, that of the Alt-Noth school, would turn the entire biblical tradition topsyturvy by predicating an originally peaceful penetration of the country. They admit the overthrow of certain Canaanite cities by the Israelites, but only as the final stage in a gradual process of infiltration on the part of Israelite tribesmen. In the biblical tradition, however, they hold that the violent terms of the final stage eclipsed the initial, peaceful stage.

We have already mentioned the assumption that the biblical account represents, in effect, a nationalization of traditions of a definitely tribal, local scale. According to this view, the Conquest narratives were considered specifically Benjaminite in origin. We should consider here a further tenet of the Alt-Noth school in their elucidation of the literary evolution of the Conquest cycle in the early part of Joshua (1–11). Occupying a prominent place in their reasoning is the aetiological factor, *i.e.,* the creation of a causal explanation for a phenomenon, especially where it is of a limited physical nature. In other words, a legend is manufactured to provide the historical-causative rationale for a supposedly bewildering occurrence.

A classic instance is the description of the fording of the Jordan and the erection at Gilgal of the twelve-stone monument at Joshua's behest:

> That this may be a sign among you, that when your children ask in time to come saying: what mean ye by these stones? Then ye shall answer them: that the waters of Jordan were cut off . . . and these stones shall be for a memorial unto the children of Israel forever. And the children of Israel did so as Joshua commanded and took up twelve stones . . . according to the number of tribes of the children of Israel . . . and they are there unto this day (Joshua 4:6–9).

The impulse to supply an explanation of this sort has been regarded as the underlying rationale for other stories as well, even when not openly stated by the source. The key expressions 'unto this day' or 'unto this very day' concluding such stories are, in these scholars' eyes, obvious clues to their aetiological make-up. This approach has been applied to the traditions affecting the captures of Jericho and Ai, Achan's transgression and the hanging of the five Amorite kings on five trees, as well as their subsequent burial in the cave at Makkedah. The treaty between the Gibeonites and Israel involving the former's inferior status and the acceptance of the Canaanite family of Rahab within the Israelite fold are further illustrations. Yet, even where such aetiological motifs in the Conquest and Settlement narratives cannot be denied, they should be regarded as no more than secondary elements in the literary evolvement of the stories. Consequently, it is invalid to negate the factual substructure of the narratives and their patent mirroring of an invasion by force.

On the other hand, one is constrained to admit that the simple and tendentious account that emerges in the 'official' version of the episodes cannot stand up to close critical scrutiny. In fact, numerous cleavages and even discrepancies are apparent in the biblical sources, only a few of which can be mentioned here. For example, there is a pronounced tendency in the Bible, as was remarked above, to assign to Moses and Joshua exploits and conquests of various periods that were, in fact, implemented by tribal groups or individuals. Thus Numbers 21 speaks of the capture of Trans-Jordan by Moses and all Israel, whereas elsewhere in this same book (Numbers 32:39–42) there appear separate accounts of conquest by the tribesmen of Machir ('son of Manasseh'), of Jair (also a 'son of Manasseh') and of one Nobah (representative of an undetermined tribal unit). By the same token, the capture of Hebron and Debir, officially ascribed to Joshua (Joshua 10:36–9), is attributed elsewhere (Joshua 15:13–19; Judges 1:10–16; and see page 66) to the clans of Caleb and Kenaz, which later became attached to the tribe of Judah. An outstanding example of the biblical tendency to assign to Joshua the victory over most of Canaan is to be found in the listing of the thirty-one (in the Septuagint version thirty) vanquished kings in Joshua 12. In contrast to the many towns whose fall is explicitly related in the record to Joshua's campaigns, not the slightest mention is made of the capture of other towns contained in this list, among them Adullam in the Shephelah, Tappuah, Hepher and Tirzah in the central hill district and Taanach and Megiddo in the Plain of Jezreel. The town of Bethel, which appears in the list, was conquered, according to a different version, 'after the death of Joshua', by the house of Joseph alone (Judges 1:22–6).

Discrepancies in biblical testimony may be clearly revealed by the fate of individual cities such as Jerusalem, Hormah and Hazor (on whose capture see page 69). All three are included in the list of Canaanite kings defeated by Joshua. There are conflicting accounts in the biblical sources of the war against Hormah (probably Tell Masos [Meshash], east of Beersheba). One version tells of an Israelite attempt during the days of Moses to enter the country from the south, culminating in ignominious defeat (Numbers 14:40–5; and Deuteronomy 1:44); another account tells of a successful venture in this direction (Numbers 21:1–3); and a third report transfers the fall of Hormah to a period later than both Moses and Joshua, considering it the exclusive achievement of the tribes of Judah and Simeon (Judges 1:17). There is also a plethora of partially conflicting versions depicting the fate of Jerusalem in pre-Davidic times. One story depicts its king, Adoni-zedek, at the head of an Amorite confederation defeated by Joshua at Gibeon, although his own city remained unconquered (Joshua 10:1ff. and 12:10). Judges 1:8 relates that after the death of Joshua the tribe of Judah campaigned southwards from Mount Ephraim, seized Jerusalem and put it to the torch. According to another account, Judah was unable to expel the city's inhabitants, 'and the Jebusites dwell with the children of Judah at Jerusalem unto this day' (Joshua 15:63); elsewhere (Judges 1:21) however, the same tradition is assigned to the Benjaminites. On the other hand, in the narrative of the outrage at Gibeah, Jerusalem is still specified in the period of the Judges as a foreign, Jebusite town 'that is not of the children of Israel' (Judges 19:11–12). In fact, Jerusalem came under complete Israelite control only under David.

These discrepancies apply only to the conquest of individual sites. Far more significant are the deviant traditions fissuring the account of the overall conquest, both of Trans-Jordan and of Palestine. The 'official' account stresses time and again that the Israelite circumvention of the south of Palestine and Trans-Jordan was made to avoid the established kingdoms of Edom, Moab and Ammon. The only alternative facing the Israelites was to force a passage (which would have proved impractical). Biblical tradition ascribes the decision for this circuitous route to divine command, in order to prevent war with nations kindred to them (Numbers 20:14–21 and 21:4, 11–20; Deuteronomy 2:1–3, 9, 13, 19; and *cf.* Judges 11:17–18). As against this prevalent version, a close analysis of the stations listed in Numbers

33:37–49 indicates something quite different. In the recounting of the itinerary of the Exodus from Egypt, mention is made of a route leading from 'Mount Hor in the edge of the land of Edom' until Abel-shittim on the Moabite Plains, in the very midst of the territories of Edom and Moab. This source, admittedly of a comparatively late date, contains not the slightest allusion to resistance to Israelite passage on the part of these peoples, nor to any armed encounter with Sihon, the Amorite ruler.

On the matter of the Israelite occupation of western Palestine, the first chapter of the Book of Judges presents a variant tradition, whether it be regarded as an additional version of the actual conquest or a description of events 'after the death of Joshua', as is stated in the opening remarks of the chapter. Several problems related to this chapter, such as the mention of the conquest of Jerusalem, Hebron, Debir, Bethel and Hormah, have already been considered. The biblical narrator, it appears, has recalled diverse conquests already made by Joshua and even Moses (e.g., Hormah), but at the same time concludes with a detailed list of Canaanite enclaves in the various tribal domains which had not yet been conquered. But the most remarkable aspect of Judges 1, in comparison with the description in the Book of Joshua, is the portrayal of particularistic, tribal conquests accomplished without a national leader. At their core stands the tribe of Judah, which campaigned from the Canaanite town of Bezek (Khirbet Ibzik, north-east of Shechem) through the central hill country in a southerly direction, first towards Jerusalem and then on to the Judean hills and the Shephelah till Hormah on the border of the Negev. Judah is even credited with the capture of Gaza, Ashkelon and Ekron, which in the Book of Joshua are regarded as 'land that yet remaineth' (Joshua 13:1–6) outside the limits of Israelite penetration (indeed the Septuagint version of Judges 1:18 negates the seizure of the Philistine towns). In short, this chapter from the Book of Judges, in its account of the Israelite subjugation of western Palestine, sketches a picture entirely different, both in detail and in general outline, from that found in the Book of Joshua.

The tangled tissue of biblical testimony thus prevents us from accepting the literary continuity of the books of Numbers, Joshua and Judges as a reliable historical account or as a chronologically consistent record of the Conquest and Settlement. The discrepancies, real or imaginary, between the different traditions leave two possibilities: either to regard them as the products of different tendentious hands describing the same events, or to seek in them the residue of complex and variegated historical processes. The latter possibility ought, in general, to be given preference, as the ensuing discussion will show. A similar discrepancy in literary evidence is to be found in the broad national conquests of other nations, for example, in the Homeric epic of the Trojan War or the Arab conquest of Palestine in the seventh century CE – which have, in recent years, been justly regarded as instructive parallels to the Israelite Conquest, as far as methodology is concerned.

The Archaeological Evidence

The problematic nature of the biblical tradition increases the importance of external sources, whether epigraphic or archaeological. An extra-biblical source of paramount significance in any attempt to reconstruct events leading up to the conquest of Canaan

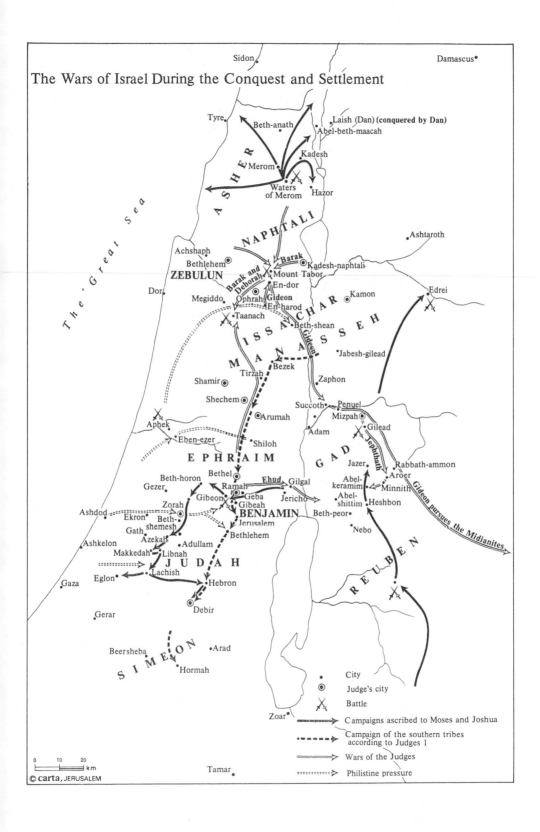

The Wars of Israel During the Conquest and Settlement

Sidon

Damascus

Tyre
Beth-anath
Laish (Dan) (conquered by Dan)
Abel-beth-maacah
Kadesh
Merom
Waters of Merom
Hazor

ASHER

Ashtaroth

NAPHTALI

Achshaph
Bethlehem
ZEBULUN
Barak
Kadesh-naphtali
Barak and Deborah
Mount Tabor
En-dor
Dor
Megiddo
Ophrah
Gideon
En-harod
Kamon
Edrei

Taanach
Beth-shean

ISSACHAR

MANASSEH

Gideon
Jabesh-gilead

Bezek
Tirzah
Shamir
Zaphon
Shechem
Succoth
Penuel
Arumah
Mizpah
Gilead
Adam

Aphek
Jephthah
Eben-ezer
Shiloh
GAD

EPHRAIM
Jazer
Rabbath-ammon
Beth-horon
Bethel
Ehud
Gilgal
Abel-keramim
Aroer
Gezer
Ramah
Minnith
Gibeon
Geba
Jericho
Abel-shittim
Zorah
Gibeah
Heshbon
Ashdod
Ekron
Beth-shemesh
BENJAMIN
Beth-peor
Gath
Jerusalem
Nebo
Ashkelon
Azekah
Bethlehem
Makkedah
Adullam
Libnah

Gideon pursues the Midianites

JUDAH
Eglon
Lachish
Hebron
Gaza
REUBEN
Debir
Gerar

SIMEON
Beersheba
Arad
Hormah

The Great Sea

Zoar

● City
◎ Judge's city
✗ Battle
▬▬▬▶ Campaigns ascribed to Moses and Joshua
▪▪▪▪▶ Campaign of the southern tribes according to Judges 1
═══▶ Wars of the Judges
▪▪▪▪▶ Philistine pressure

Tamar

0   10   20
═══════ km

© carta, JERUSALEM

is the mention of Israel in the Merneptah stele, which records Egyptian military successes in Canaan in approximately 1230 or 1220 BCE (according to the 'high' or 'low' datings, respectively [see page 42]). Other epigraphic evidence from documents of Seti I, Rameses II and Merneptah has already been presented (see pages 21 ff.), and more will be noted below. At this point we shall consider the contribution made by archaeological findings as the result of systematic excavation or provisional soundings or from archaeological surveys in Palestine.

The Israelite trek across the Negev, the Arabah and Trans-Jordan is clarified significantly by the results of the surveys conducted in these areas since the 1930s. It appears that with the destruction of permanent settlement in Trans-Jordan south of the Yarmuk River during the nineteenth century BCE, the region (save for a few key sites) remained desolate for centuries until settlement was renewed there at the start of the thirteenth century. This means, in effect, that the rise of the kingdoms of Edom, Moab and Ammon must be relegated to the earlier part of the thirteenth century, though recent excavations at Tawilan and Buseirah (biblical Bozrah) in northern Edom indicate that settlement began there much later. Using this as a chronological base, one may now conjecture the dates of the Israelite incursions as reflected in the contradictory traditions previously discussed. The account that speaks of a campaign within the borders of these countries refers, assuredly, to a penetration prior to the consolidation of the kingdoms of Edom and Moab. The other tradition, which tells of a vastly circuitous route, in reality postulates the pre-existence of these two kingdoms, which resisted the invasion of their territory. Highly indicative in this respect is the discovery of a dense system of frontier fortresses encircling Ammon on the west and south, built on a square or rectangular plan (the *kaṣr* type) or on a round plan (as Rujum el-Malfuf). This fortification system, probably instituted in the Early Iron Age, seems to be what the Bible refers to in noting the inability of the Israelites to occupy this region, 'for the border of the Children of Ammon was strong' (Numbers 21:24).

In the southern, central and northern regions of western Palestine, numerous sites that, according to biblical testimony, were conquered by the Israelite forces have been excavated. Many instances have been amply corroborated by archaeologists, for they have uncovered evidence of violent destruction towards the end of the Late Bronze Age – certainly the work of the Israelites themselves (in contrast to the opinion held by many scholars). In a few cases, however, the archaeological findings have raised difficulties, the most serious of which concerns the conquest of Ai, described in detail in Joshua 7–8. This town is undoubtedly the modern Et-Tell, about $1\frac{1}{4}$ miles 'east of Bethel' (Joshua 7:2). The modern name, like 'Ai', implies 'a ruin', and in fact the Hebrew name always appears with the definite article to imply its appellative nature. Excavations there have shown, however, that the site had lain barren for more than a millennium prior to the Israelite invasion. Far-fetched attempts have been made to resolve this difficulty, but no satisfactory solution has yet been forthcoming. Indeed, as one scholar has been moved to remark, the conquest of Ai in antiquity may prove to have been easier than the solving of its historical problems today.

The findings at Jericho also conflict with the biblical version of its fall. More recent archaeological investigations have proved that its famed walls, the focus of the biblical story, belonged to the Middle Bronze Age, that is, to the first half of the second millennium, and not to the days of the Israelite conquest. Yet, for all this, the narrative fundamentally is no mere fiction. In the fourteenth and perhaps even in the early thirteenth centuries, a relatively meagre and open settlement existed at Jericho, and in all likelihood it was this settlement that suffered destruction at the hands of the Israelites (see page 59). The biblical folk-tradition of the collapse of its walls may have derived from the visible remnants of the once-mighty defences. The story of Gibeon also has been questioned, as excavations on the site (modern El-Jib) have brought to light no Late Bronze Age stratum. Several tombs here, however, were found to contain Late Bronze Age pottery, pointing to at least a temporary settlement in that period. The inhabitants may have been recently arrived migrants, just as the Gibeonites claimed to have been before Joshua ('From a very far country thy servants are come' [Joshua 9:9]), though the Bible presents this claim as a cunning device intended to deceive the Israelites. The Gibeonites were of Hivite stock and, indeed, may have arrived not long before from parts far to the north (from southern Anatolia?). Whatever the case, the comment 'because Gibeon was a great city, as one of the royal cities' (Joshua 10:2) was most likely inserted by a later redactor at a time when Gibeon had assumed a position of central importance under the Judean monarchy.

In contrast to these three divergences between the biblical account and the archaeological findings (all of which incidentally relate to Joshua's initial campaign into the country's central region), the continuation of the biblical narrative is generally corroborated by discoveries from the excavations. Thus the cities of Lachish and most likely Kirjath-sepher/Debir and Eglon (apparently Tell el-Hesi, west of Lachish), whose capture is attributed to Joshua (Joshua 10:31ff.), were in fact utterly destroyed in the second half of the thirteenth century. It is highly significant that Hazor in the north, whose destruction the Bible vividly relates, also met a violent fate during this period. Here, in addition, excavations have illuminated the biblical comment 'for Hazor beforetime was the head of all those kingdoms' (Joshua 11:10). At the foot of the mound (upper city) stood a huge lower city spreading over an area of 175 acres, the largest site hitherto excavated in Palestine. It appears now that Bethel, in the central region, also was destroyed in the second half of the thirteenth century.

On the other hand, the recent excavations at Shechem have revealed no destruction layer from the end of the Late Bronze Age; on the contrary, there is evidence of an uninterrupted settlement until the close of the twelfth century (see page 74). These findings also accord with the biblical evidence. Apart from faint echoes of an early conquest of Shechem as recounted in the patriarchal stories – in the affair of Dinah (Genesis 34) and in Jacob's blessing bestowed upon Joseph (Genesis 48:22) – there is nothing to indicate the violent overthrow of the city prior to the later period of the Judges. Moreover, Joshua appears unhindered at Shechem and convenes there an assembly of the Israelite tribes in order to conclude a covenant with the Lord (Joshua 24). Most interesting in this connexion is the sacral precinct that has been unearthed at Shechem, which contains a temple, an altar and several steles going back to the Middle Bronze Age. This indicates that Shechem was an ancient cultic centre, and, as such, its aura of sanctity permeated the Israelite traditions of the Patriarchs and Joshua.

Shechem provides a conspicuous exception in an archaeological picture otherwise typified by general destruction. The sites of ravaged Canaanite towns served as bases for new settlements, at times almost immediately after their destruction, as at Tell Beit Mirsim and Bethel. These repopulated towns remained unfortified and were meagre in comparison with their predecessors. A striking example is Hazor, whose remains prove that after its destruction the huge lower city was never rebuilt; even the mound has nothing more to show in the following period than a provisional settlement of semi-nomads. The renewed settlements, greatly differing from the Canaanite cities in their material culture, were indisputably Israelite. Evidence of this is to be found also in the cultural continuity between this phase and the period of the Israelite monarchy. Archaeological evidence shows also that at the turn of the thirteenth and twelfth centuries intensive Israelite colonization began in areas never before settled. Many towns now sprang up on virgin soil, especially in the area of Mount Ephraim and in Benjamin (see page 61), as well as in eastern Judah. Archaeological surveys of Upper Galilee and Gilead have also revealed a series of new, small dwelling-sites. With the destruction of the Canaanite cities and the founding of Israelite settlements, the Late Bronze Age came to a close and a new era – the Iron Age – was inaugurated.

The Conquest Reconstructed

Analysis of the variegated sources relating to the Conquest shows it to have been a complex process consisting of various phases, both in Trans-Jordan and in western Palestine. Nor does the archaeological evidence indicate a single campaign of conquest. Admittedly, a good many Canaanite cities were destroyed during the latter half of the thirteenth century, but it would be an oversimplification to infer that all these sites were reduced to ruins at one and the same time. Jericho, as has already been indicated, had been destroyed several decades earlier. Thus some scholars have argued that there were several waves of Israelite penetration; their views differ, however, on the number of such invasions, on their exact chronology, on the specific invasion routes and on the identity of the tribes participating in each wave. An extremely important adjunct to the last of these questions lies in the twelve-tribe division of the Israelites, based on maternal genealogy – that is, on the basis of whether a given tribe stemmed from Rachel or from Leah (or from their respective handmaids, Bilhah and Zilpah). Since this alignment makes no sense in the light of the later tribal allotments, or in any other historical framework, it probably reflects a situation prevailing just prior to the final entrenchment of the Israelite tribes (see pages 63 ff.).

Such a premise presupposes at least two principal stages of Israelite penetration, probably separated by a short period: one accomplished by the so-called 'Leah' tribes, with Judah at their head; the other by the 'Rachel' tribes, under the leadership of the 'house of Joseph'. The tribes assigned to the handmaids – Gad and Asher to the one and Dan and Naphtali to the other – have been considered tribal appendages, possessing an inferior status in the Israelite confederacy and sometimes regarded as having made their way separately into Canaan (for another opinion see page 63).

The opinion prevailing today, as in previous generations, contends that the 'Leah' tribes preceded the 'Rachel' group in entering Palestine. Among the recent exponents of this school is De Vaux, as is Yeivin (see Bibliography), who postulates three successive waves of conquest: Asher and Naphtali forcing their way into Galilee towards the end of the fourteenth century; the 'Leah' tribes arriving about 1300; and the 'Rachel' group entering approximately one generation thereafter. More recently, however, an opposite view has gained ground, propagated mainly by Albright and later by Mazar, according to which the 'Rachel' tribes anticipated the other groups. Incidentally, rabbinical sources contain a similar allusion asserting a premature Ephraimite exodus from Egypt thirty years prior to the remainder of the tribes (see *Mechilta of Rabbi Ishmael*, Beshalah I; the Talmudic and mediaeval Jewish commentaries on Exodus 13:17 and I Chronicles 7:22; and *cf.* the Aramaic Targum on the latter verse and on Psalms 78:9). We shall present here, in broad outline, a reconstruction of the Conquest cycle based on Mazar, as it utilizes considerable source material without recourse to an excessively complicated hypothesis (see Bibliography).

According to this approach, the desert oasis of Kadesh-barnea served as the base for both waves of penetration into Canaan, that of the 'Rachel' and of the 'Leah' tribes. The first wave, led by Joshua, an Ephraimite, made its incursion about 1300 BCE through Edom and Moab (*cf.* the itinerary given in Numbers 33) – as these nations had not yet consolidated into kingdoms. Reaching as far as Abel-shittim in the Plains of Moab, the invaders forded the Jordan and, after capturing Jericho, ascended into the central mountain region. Near Gibeon they successfully engaged an Amorite confederacy and thus acquired the lands adjoining the town to the west and to the north. Thence the 'Rachel' tribes fanned out across all of Mount Ephraim, several contingents even infiltrating northwards into Galilee and, still later, as far as northern Gilead and the Bashan in Trans-Jordan.

The second wave, consisting of the 'Leah' tribes, was already compelled to circumvent the kingdoms of Edom and Moab, encountering *en route* the Amorite kingdom of Sihon, with its capital at Heshbon. This buffer state between Moab and Ammon had come into being only a short time before the Israelite invasion, for its founding, according to this theory, was linked to the aftermath of the battle of Kadesh, between Rameses II and the Hittites (see page 23). The Hittites, presumably together with their Amorite allies, had at the time penetrated into the Damascus region, while the Amorites themselves apparently continued to press farther southwards. After inflicting a defeat upon Sihon at Jahaz, the Israelites advanced steadily northwards into Amorite territory – the land of Jaazer and the domains of Og, the king of Bashan (Numbers 21:21ff.) – the tribes of Reuben and Gad taking possession of southern and central Trans-Jordan from the Arnon to the Jabbok rivers.

The resumption of this campaign of conquest into the western confines of Palestine by the second wave possibly underlies the tradition transmitted in the first chapter of the Book of Judges, whereby the Israelites, led by Judah, crossed the Jordan apparently far north of Jericho. First encountering Bezek in the hills of Manasseh, they moved southwards towards the Judean hills and the Shephelah, conquering Jerusalem on their way. At approximately the same time, in the late thirteenth century, the towns of the southern Judean hills and the northern Negev – Hebron, Debir and Hormah – were overrun by clans kindred to Judah, namely, the Calebites, Kenizzites and Kenites, which had infiltrated from the south. This account of the seizure of the southern part of the country is complemented by Joshua 10:28–39, which relates the capture of the western hill towns and those in the Shephelah – Makkedah, Libnah, Lachish and Eglon. According to this view, the war against the Canaanites in the north (Joshua 11:1–15) was initiated jointly by the 'Leah' tribes Issachar and Zebulun, which succeeded in expanding northwards from the central hill region, and the 'Rachel' tribes, which in the interim had grown in numbers and in strength.

The above hypothesis, like other reconstructions of the process of Conquest and Settlement, understandably enough remains conjectural. Thus the deliberations and conclusions hinge largely upon the degree of credence and weight placed upon the particular biblical and extra-biblical data. It would seem preferable, therefore, to treat the Conquest from a typological point of view – to consider the general phenomena, as we did in connexion with the Exodus (see pages 40 ff.) – and to determine the prevalent, underlying circumstances, thus avoiding a hair-splitting reconstruction of the actual course of events. In the following section we shall treat the Conquest from a military standpoint, but first some of the basic underlying facets of the Conquest episode will be examined.

The Israelites, upon leaving Egypt, were clearly incapable of forcing an entry into Canaan directly from the south because of Egyptian control of the Via Maris (see page 22) and the strong defences along the country's southern approaches. Any attempt from this direction was bound to end in failure, as the incident at Hormah would indicate (Numbers 14:40ff.). Hence they were compelled to make a broad flanking movement by way of Trans-Jordan and to invade Canaan across the Jordan fords. Of great chronological significance, besides its politico-military importance, is the biblical passage relating the Israelite encounter with Sihon, the king of the Amorites, 'who had fought against the first king of Moab and taken all his land out of his hand even unto Arnon' (Numbers 21:26). The advent of the Israelites, or rather a portion of them, is placed not long after the founding of the kingdom of Moab, which, as stated, is to be dated to the first half of the thirteenth century. If we accept the view that Sihon's own kingdom arose in the wake of the battle of Kadesh, that is, shortly after 1285 BCE (see pages 23, 55), an even finer degree of accuracy is possible in dating the foregoing events. In any case, the fertile region between the Arnon and the Jabbok rivers changed hands several times during the first half of the thirteenth century. At first the Moabites gained control of the southern portion of the area, with the north apparently occupied by the Ammonites. Soon thereafter the entire area fell under Sihon's dominion, only to pass eventually into Israelite hands. The Egyptian factor should now be added to the regional power struggle during this period, as is evidenced by Rameses II's expedition to Moab, in which he managed to capture towns even to the north of the Arnon (see page 24).

Two decisive military confrontations with the Canaanites stand out in the conquest of western Palestine – one in the south, at Gibeon, and the other in Upper Galilee – upon the outcome of which hung the fate of Israelite settlement in the country. The treaty that the Gibeonites (who, with the towns of Chephirah, Beeroth and Kirjath-jearim, formed the Hivite confederacy) concluded with the invading Israelites exposed the north-western flank of the Kingdom of Jerusalem and endangered the entire military disposition of the Canaanite cities to the west of the hill country. This situation evoked a sharp reaction from Adoni-zedek, the king of Jerusalem, who headed an alliance of four Canaanite city-states – Hebron, Jarmuth, Lachish and Eglon – and attacked the renegade Gibeon, whom the Israelites now hastened to defend. The Israelites' victory paved the way for their hegemony over the western slopes (Joshua 10). In the other successful encounter, the Israelites decisively routed a northern coalition of four Canaanite city-states under the leadership of Jabin, the king of Hazor, at the battle of the Waters of Merom in north-eastern Galilee (the town of Merom itself may have lain in ruins since its sacking by Rameses II [see page 23]). The next step was the destruction of Hazor itself, the focus of Canaanite power in the north (Joshua 11:1–15).

Military Aspects of the Conquest

Even after accepting the central assertion of the biblical tradition, namely, the forcible seizure of Canaan by the Israelites (which is supported by the archaeological evidence), we must still determine the basis for Israel's military success. How could semi-nomadic Israelite tribesmen, lacking in military lore and only meagrely equipped, prevail over a much superior Canaanite foe, long versed in the ways of warfare and possessing a highly developed technology? How could they succeed against powerful Canaanite fortress towns, which they saw as 'great and walled up to heaven' (Deuteronomy 1:28)? Queries of this sort had already been voiced by the ancients. Thus the third-century Jewish-hellenistic author Demetrius inquired, as did Josephus (*Antiquities* II, 16.6), as to the source of the arms in Israelite possession when they entered the country. Both these authors replied naively that the military equipment had been taken from the Egyptians drowned in the Red Sea.

The Israelites' success in the face of Canaanite military superiority becomes understandable when we consider certain factors that facilitated a relatively rapid occupation of the country, at least in the mountain areas. Among these were the impoverishment of Canaan as a result of Egyptian exploitation, the unstable security situation (clearly reflected in the El-Amarna tablets and in Papyrus Anastasi I) and, above all, the incessant internal strife among the Canaanite city-states. These bickerings had been intensified by the Egyptian policy of 'divide and rule', which, prior to the advent of the Israelites, had left the country politically fragmented, with its towns divided. The Israelites, kindled by religious and national zeal, confronted a Canaanite population devoid of any over-all national consciousness, a land unable to present a unified front against an invader. The two Canaanite coalitions mentioned previously (see above) were, after all, of limited size; the southern one, moreover, had initially aligned itself against only the Gibeonites. No one had rushed to the defence of Jericho or Ai in their hour of peril. Even the help proffered to the beleaguered Lachish by the king of Gezer (Joshua 10:33) seems to have been motivated by Egyptian policy, which made mutual defence between the cities in question mandatory. Both were important administrative centres under Egyptian rule in the final third of the thirteenth century, as may be gathered from Egyptian documents.

An additional factor expediting the Israelite seizure of control was the ethnic heterogeneity of Canaan, well reflected in the biblical sources (see page 9). The Israelites skilfully exploited the animosities existing among the various ethnic and national groupings in Canaan, as is illustrated by the separate peace concluded with the Gibeonites, who were of Hivite stock (Joshua 9:7). We may recall in this connexion that the inhabitants of Shechem, or rather a portion of them, also traced their origin to the Hivites (Genesis 34:2); their leadership at the time of the Israelite settlement was in the hands of the collective 'lords of Shechem', similar to the existence at Gibeon of the leadership of elders rather than of a single king. Shechem, too, passed peacefully into Israelite control (see page 53). We also know of the existence of Israelite elements in Jerusalem existing side by side with the Jebusites (Joshua 15:63; and Judges 1:21), which would testify to peaceful relations between these two groups. It now appears that the Jebusites traced their ancestry to northern (Anatolian?) ethnic elements similar to the Hivites and may have infiltrated into Jerusalem at about the time of the Israelite conquest or slightly earlier.

Canaanite resistance was overcome to no small extent by the specific methods of warfare employed by the Israelites and clearly implied in the biblical account. Evidently they possessed a highly developed intelligence service as may be inferred from the detailed instructions given by Moses to the twelve spies sent to reconnoitre Canaan; here one may detect the gathering not only of strictly military data but also of economic and demographic information (Numbers 13:19–20). We are informed that Jaazer and Bethel were reconnoitred (Numbers 21:32; and Judges 1:23) and that, prior to assaults, spies were dispatched to Jericho and Ai to collect information on enemy disposition. The initial Israelite defeat at Ai is undoubtedly the result of a faulty appraisal of the city's defending forces ('Let not all the people go up, but let about two or three thousand men go up and smite Ai, and make not all the people to labour thither, for they are but a few' [Joshua 7:3]).

Attention was paid also to matters of a logistic nature, such as food and general supply requirements, as can be discerned from Joshua's preparing supplies for the entire people prior to the fording of the Jordan (Joshua 1:10–11), as well as from the very timing of the invasion for the spring (on the tenth of Nisan [Joshua 4:19]), when the grain had already ripened on the Jericho Plain, so as to provide them with 'the fruit of Canaan that year' (Joshua 5:10–12). Like other invaders (cf. the Midianite raids in the days of Gideon, page 72), the Israelites followed the policy of plundering cattle and produce, which simultaneously deprived the enemy of food and provisioned their own troops (Joshua 8:27 and 11:14). Another strategic and logistic element may be discerned in the 'official' version of the Conquest, wherein Gilgal occupied a prime position as the base camp after the Jordan crossing, the site to which the Israelites repaired after each further phase of their southern campaign (Joshua 9:6 and 10:6–9, 15, 43). This astonishing fact has led many scholars to assume here a late Benjaminite tradition of a local and liturgical nature, woven about the allegedly cultic site at Gilgal. From a military standpoint, however, this was a vital bridge-head for any penetration into western Palestine from the Plains of Moab. The task-forces may have retired to this base, upon completion of long-range incursions, in order to safeguard their link with the Israelite rear across the river in Trans-Jordan.

The military problem facing the Israelites was twofold. First, there were the strong Canaanite fortress cities, formidable barriers even for the mighty Egyptian war machine (*cf., e.g.,* page 13). In addition, the Canaanites could place in the field a professional, well-trained army, with a body of overawing chariotry, as opposed to the Israelites' infantry. A close analysis of the battle accounts of the Conquest, and, in fact, of the period up to the beginning of the monarchy, reveals that this imbalance was surmounted by the so-called indirect military approach. In other words, the Israelites strove to avoid frontal assaults upon Canaanite fortifications and, wherever possible, relied on deception, military cunning and diversionary manoeuvres rather than open confrontation.

The sole example of a siege on the part of the Israelites is that at Jericho; here too, however, there is no talk of a direct assault but, rather, of the wondrous fall of the city (however, *cf.* Joshua 24:11, which implies an actual battle with its inhabitants). Of Bethel (Judges 1:22–5) and later of Jerusalem, it is explicitly stated that they fell by stealthy means and not as a result of open battle. The stories concerning the capture of Ai and Gibeah of Benjamin – the latter laid waste in intertribal warfare (see page 79) – contain detailed accounts of Israelite stratagem. Both cities were seized after a staged retreat by part of the besieging soldiers that was intended to draw away the defenders and thus enable another force, lying in ambush, to enter the town without struggle (Joshua 8; and Judges 20:39ff.). It is of particular interest that in both these instances the final conquest was preceded by truly unsuccessful attacks resulting in genuine flight on the part of the Israelites; thus the feigned retreat was designed to lull the enemy into a false sense of security. In other instances Canaanite strongholds fell after their forces had been beaten on the open battle-field. Examples of this are the fall of several of the southern fortresses after the battle of Gibeon and of the city of Hazor after the battle of the Waters of Merom (see page 57).

In these battles, as in others, Israelite arms overcame superior Canaanite forces through excellent planning and execution, at the core of which lay the element of surprise. In the battle at Gibeon, the Israelites are said to have ascended from Gilgal, some 20 miles away, climbing more than half a mile in a gruelling night march in order to exploit to the full the elements of darkness and surprise: 'Joshua therefore came unto them *suddenly* and went up from Gilgal all night' (Joshua 10:9 [author's italics]). The battle was joined apparently at the crack of dawn, as may be concluded also from the quotation from the Book of Jashar: 'Sun stand thou still upon Gibeon and thou, Moon, in the valley of Ajalon' (Joshua 10:12). This rhetorical flourish reflects the natural state found only in the early morning hours, when the moon can be seen setting in the west over the Valley of Ajalon while the sun rises in the east over Gibeon. With the enemy already dislocated at dawn, the Israelites pursued the fleeing remnants of the Canaanite forces by way of Beth-horon. Similar operations, comprising a night march followed by a dawn engagement, are found in subsequent actions, such as Gideon's encounter with the Midianites (see pages 72 f.), Abimelech's attack on Shechem (Judges 9:34) and Saul's engagements with the Ammonites and Philistines (I Samuel 11:11 and 14:36; cf. Abraham's night raid on the enemy who had taken his nephew Lot captive, in Genesis 14:15).

The surprise factor was decisive in another major campaign ascribed to Joshua – the battle of the Waters of Merom, in which the Canaanites employed their chariotry (Joshua 11:7; note the specification 'suddenly' here too). This same striking-force posed a serious problem in the battle of Deborah and Barak against Sisera, who is said to have possessed 900 iron chariots. Although the Bible recounts the episode in detail (see pages 69 ff.), the actual battle is recorded only sketchily, and its course is difficult to reconstruct. Reading between the lines, however, one may discern how carefully the Israelites exploited topographical (see pages 70 f.) and climatic factors in order to disable the Canaanite chariotry. The Israelite command, it appears, held off the assault until the rainy season, when the Jezreel Valley became one large, impassable quagmire, thereby depriving the Canaanite vehicles of their mobility; hence the allusions to heavy rain in describing the theophany in the opening verses of the Song of Deborah (Judges 5:4–5), as well as the emphasis upon 'bounteous rain' in a passage of the Book of Psalms referring to the war of Deborah (Psalms 68:10), the poetic description of the swollen Kishon River (Judges 5:21) and the fact that Sisera himself was forced to abandon his chariot, which had bogged down, and to flee for his life on foot (Judges 4:17).

Tribal Settlement and Its Aftermath

For all their military efficiency, the Israelites gained the upper hand only in the mountainous regions of the country; in the lowlands they were held in check by the enemy's main weapon, the chariot, which prevented them from dislodging the foe. The Bible itself underscores this point, once in reference to the 'house of Joseph' (Joshua 17:16–18) and once in reference to Judah: 'And he drave out the inhabitants of the mountain, but could not drive out the inhabitants of the valley because they had chariots of iron' (Judges 1:19). Israelite supremacy in the hill country and inferiority in the lowlands are reflected, generations later, in the words of Ben-hadad, the king of Aram-damascus: 'Their gods are gods of the hills; therefore they were stronger than we. But let us fight against them in the plain, and surely we shall be stronger than they' (I Kings 20:23). Accordingly, many Canaanite enclaves remained within the various tribal areas, especially in the Valley of Jezreel, and several became tributary to Israel in the course of time (see the list of unconquered cities within the tribal domains, in Judges 1:21–35; and Joshua 16:10). Those Israelites who succeeded in settling in the lowlands suffered at first from Canaanite subjugation. This is stated outright in Jacob's blessing of Issachar, whose tribal allotment was in the eastern Jezreel-Beth-shean valleys: 'And [Issachar] bowed his shoulder to bear and became a servant unto tribute' (Genesis 49:15). The Hebrew terms used in this verse (the verb *sabal* and the noun *mas*) indicate forced labour;

their Akkadian cognates (*siblu* and *massu*) appear in the Mari and El-Amarna letters, respectively, which describe in detail how such corvée was exercised.

To sum up, Israelite settlement at the outset was concentrated primarily in the country's hill regions, which were only sparsely populated by the Canaanites, and only there did Israel achieve sovereign status. In these 'empty' mountainous sectors, lands were made arable for extensive settlement mainly by clearing the forests, as may be gathered from Joshua's directives to the children of Joseph, who were eager for areas of settlement: 'But the mountain shall be thine for it is a wood, and thou shalt cut it down and the outgoings of it shall be thine' (Joshua 17:14–18). The intensive felling of trees and settling of hitherto unpopulated areas brought about a radical change in the country's landscape, which, prior to the coming of the Israelites, had been described (especially in Egyptian sources) as a land of vast forests. In clearing these areas for cultivation, the settlers were greatly aided by newly acquired technology, such as the use of the plaster-lined cistern, which enabled them to store rain-water (*cf.* Mishnah *Aboth* 2:8: 'A plastered cistern which loses not a drop') and, as a result, created conditions for populating additional areas. A significant technological innovation that was common in the lands to the north, especially among the Hittites, and was apparent in Palestine only from the eleventh century on was the manufacture of iron utensils. Such implements proved far more efficient in mountain farming and in the clearing of forests – not to mention in weaponry – than the copper and bronze tools previously in use.

Large-scale settlement was thus made possible both in Trans-Jordan, especially in the Ajlun region north of the Jabbok River, and in the Galilee and central mountain regions of western Palestine. It is clear from biblical and especially archaeological evidence that intensive settlement began especially in the land of Benjamin and in the adjoining hills to the north and south. Some of the Canaanite towns that had lain in ruins for varying periods – among these Bethel, Ai and Mizpah (Tell en-Nasbeh) – were now resettled, but the main task was the founding of new sites, such as Gibeah of Benjamin, Geba, Michmash, Ramah, Anathoth and Azmaveth. In all likelihood the initial area of settlement for many of the Israelite tribes was concentrated in the midst of the central hill district. Only in later stages, with the rapid growth in population, did tribal units move to the areas forming their 'historical' allotments. In this sense the process of Israelite settlement is, in many instances, conceivable as a centrifugal movement from the central mountains to the intervening valleys and the peripheral areas on either side of the Jordan River. This was an expansion motivated by demographic pressure and the inability of the Israelites to retain a foothold in their original locations.

The fate of Dan, which provides the sole explicit biblical illustration of the migration of a single Israelite tribe (Judges 17–18), is symptomatic of the general settlement process. This tribe failed to strike roots among the western hills of the Benjaminite-Judean territory, finding itself between the Amorites to the west (Judges 1:34) and the Israelite tribes to the east. Part of the tribe was forced to secure a new inheritance, while the remainder stayed in the south, at Mahaneh-dan ('the encampment of Dan'), bereft of any inheritance, as is indicated by the Samson cycle. The movements of the other tribes may be inferred from the Danite episode, which may be regarded as a sort of diminutive model of the entire Exodus and pan-Israelite Conquest cycle. With the Danites, too, intelligence and reconnaissance preceded the actual military campaign. Five tribal notables (as against twelve in the Exodus narrative) were dispatched from Zorah and Eshtaol in search of land suitable for settlement. The new inheritance was found at Laish on the north-eastern border of Palestine (for all the intervening territory was already occupied by the Israelites). Furthermore, Laish and its environs were especially suitable for conquest and settlement, as the spies themselves acknowledged: 'A large land . . . a place where there is no want of anything', and 'the people that were therein . . . dwelt careless after the manner of the Sidonians, quiet and secure . . . and they were far from the Sidonians and had no business with any man' (Judges 18:7–10). In other words, Laish, though within the Phoenician coastal sphere of influence, was completely isolated as a result of its distance from its 'protectors', and it could quite easily be overcome. Recent excavations at Tel Dan (Tell el-Qadi) have, indeed, confirmed the town's destruction and resettlement in the Early Iron Age.

Yet another item typical of the military campaigns is the number of warriors who rallied to Dan's cause: 'Six hundred men appointed with weapons of war' (Judges 18:11), which seemingly represents a complete regiment in biblical convention. The parallel that comes to mind is that of the 600,000 foot-soldiers of the Exodus from Egypt, surely a typological figure patently indicative of a thousand such 'regiments' and signifying a vast army. Another characteristic feature prominent in the Danite narrative is the engagement of a priest for oracular purposes, to determine 'whether our way which we go shall be prosperous' (Judges 18:5). Similarly, we are informed in the Exodus epic of the priest Eleazar, who consulted 'the judgement of Urim before the Lord: at his word shall they go out, and at his word shall they come in, both he and all the children of Israel with him, even all the congregation' (Numbers 27:21ff.). And just as the Tabernacle, which had accompanied the Israelites on their desert trek, is said to have been placed in Shiloh after the completion of the Conquest (Joshua 18:1), so did the Danites deposit Micah's image at Laish, their final destination, after having transported it all along the way. The change of the name Laish to Dan after the town's destruction and resettlement also represents a phenomenon common in the Conquest tradition. Kirjath-arba became Hebron and Kirjath-sepher became Debir; Zephath was renamed Hormah and Luz changed to Bethel (Judges 1:10–11, 17, 23). Like Laish, several sites in northern Trans-Jordan were renamed to conform with the tribal units that captured and resettled them, such as Jair and Nobah (Numbers 32:41–2; see pages 48 f.).

The experience of Dan – the split into subdivisions, some of which eventually were forced to migrate – was shared by other tribes. This process can only be inferred indirectly, however, as the Bible has presented us solely with the final picture of the Settlement, the ultimate boundary system of the various tribal areas (Joshua 13–19). Yet there is no doubt that this end-product was preceded by a dynamic and well-ramified process of tribal movement, allusions to which occur throughout the biblical sources. While some traces are discernible in the descriptions of the tribal domains, of special interest in this respect are the genealogical lists of the individual tribes, as well as three documents outlining their status and characteristics: the blessing of Jacob (Genesis 49), the blessing of Moses (Deuteronomy 33) and the Song of Deborah (Judges 5). To offer one illustration, the statement on Zebulun in Jacob's blessing, 'Zebulun shall dwell at the haven of the sea, and he shall be for an haven of ships, and his border shall be unto Sidon' (Genesis 49:13), contradicts the delineations of this tribe's boundaries as they appear in Joshua 19:10–16, where Zebulun is confined to inland Lower Galilee, its territory not yet touching the sea coast. Jacob's blessing indicates, therefore, the tribe's possession of a larger territory at a certain period (perhaps after Deborah's victory), with Zebulun's area shrinking at a later date when the tribe of Asher expanded.

The Settlement as Reflected in Tribal Genealogy

A prime source for reconstructing the settlement process is found in the genealogical lists of the individual tribes (specifically those contained in I Chronicles 2–9), which are unique in ancient Near Eastern sources. Only the Arab genealogists of the Islamic period offer similar examples. These tables provide a schematic view of the internal tribal structure and, at the same time, indicate continual inter-tribal regroupings, the rise and decline of the various sub-units within the tribal frame and their dissolution and eventual merger, as well as the migratory movements of branches to new tribal territories and their frequently distant wanderings from region to region. The significance and historical implications of the intricacies of the family trees have not yet been fully elucidated. However, some key to their interpretation is supplied by the very system adopted by the lists' compilers. The use of ordinary familial concepts and relations is indubitably intended to convey a definite symbolism. Hence wherever marriage ties are indicated, they must, in point of fact, be taken to imply the merger of two tribal units. When a clan is identified as the first-born within its familial frame, it must be assumed that it was the oldest or strongest unit within the tribe. 'Daughters', on the other hand, represent either clans or settlements that were dependent on and subject to the protection of a principal urban centre, as is conveyed by the expression 'the city, and all the daughters thereof'. Union with a concubine may portray a fusion with foreign or inferior ethnic elements (*cf.* I Chronicles 7:14). A lineage traced back to a concubine or maidservant probably indicates clan migration from the ancestral home to peripheral regions, based upon the custom actually followed in the ancient world whereby families often expelled the offspring of these secondary wives (see the stories of Hagar and Ishmael and the lot that befell the progeny of Abraham's concubines, in Genesis 25:6; and that of Jephthah, in Judges 11:1–2). One may perhaps find an explanation here for the situation of the Israelite tribes descended from the maidservants of the Matriarchs – Gad, Naphtali, Dan and Asher – all four of which eventually dwelt on the eastern and northern periphery of the Israelite settlement framework. For Dan, and most likely also for Asher (see page 64), we have evidence of their departure from the central portion of the country to northern Palestine.

The genealogical tables will be adduced here mainly to throw light on the migratory movement of tribal units from the central mountain district towards the settlement perimeter, a phenomenon reflected in part by the recurrence of identical clan names in different tribal genealogies. A striking example is the genealogy of Asher (I Chronicles 7:30ff.), many of whose familial branches are linked to the central mountain region. Among them were Beriah, Japhlet, Shual and Shelesh or Shilshah, whose names are identical with those of clans and frontier sectors between Ephraim and Benjamin (Joshua 16:3; and I Samuel 9:4 and 13:17). From the identity of names it may be deduced that groups of these families, like the Danites, failed to gain a foothold within their original localities and, being caught between the various tribes, made their way far afield in the direction of western Galilee, where they consolidated themselves within the Asherite framework. In this context it is instructive that the majority of the Asherite families claimed descent from Heber (literally 'association'), apparently no more than a symbolic name personifying a confraternity of clans linked by their joint wanderings, as may be gleaned from the usage of the cognate term *ḥibrum* in the Mari documents (*cf.* Heber the Kenite, who 'had severed himself from the Kenites' and wandered towards the Valley of Jezreel; Judges 4:17). In the Asherite pedigree 'Heber son of Beriah' consequently included those clans of the Beriah stock who may have migrated northwards together, in contrast to other offshots of Beriah who had remained in their southern home and become part of the tribes of Ephraim and Benjamin (I Chronicles 7:23 and 8:13).

Evidence exists that clans of Issachar and Manasseh as well resided at first in the central mountain sector and only later moved northwards into the valleys of Jezreel and Beth-shean and into Lower Galilee. There is an interesting statement about the first of the minor Judges: 'Tola the son of Puah, the son of Dodo, a man of Issachar, and he dwelt in Shamir in Mount Ephraim' (Judges 10:1; see page 68). Tola and Puah represent chief families in the tribe of Issachar (I Chronicles 7:1; *cf.* there an additional 'son' of Issachar – Shimron – apparently connected with the above place name, Shamir, or else with Shemer, the original owner of the hill of Samaria); yet its leader, Tola, is found in the early days of the Judges dwelling in the hill country of Ephraim. That Manasseh, too, infiltrated northwards is to be concluded from the peculiar description of its northern border, which did not lend itself to accurate delineation but only to a vague outline: 'and they met together in Asher on the north and in Issachar on the east. And Manasseh had in Issachar and in Asher Beth-shean and her towns . . . ' (Joshua 17:10–11). Enumerated in the continuation of the verse is a series of Manassehite enclaves within the domains of its northern neighbours. It is fair to assume that one such enclave inside the area of Issachar was the town of Ophrah, the birthplace of Gideon, who traced his ancestry to the clan of Abi-ezer of the Manasseh tribe (Judges 6:15; see page 72 and the map on page 51).

The primary outlet for the population surplus in the central mountain range was the broad expanse of terrain in Trans-Jordan, the fertile land of Gilead and, in particular, the sparsely populated areas north of the Jabbok River. Indeed, from the genealogical lists and other biblical allusions it may be concluded that a large-scale migratory movement had taken place by all the mountain tribes eastwards of the Jordan. Chief among these was Manasseh, and in fact the Bible speaks explicitly of 'half the tribe of Manasseh' that took up an abode extending from northern Gilead as far as Bashan. Most of this eastern half tribe was assuredly of Machirite stock, which the Song of Deborah still recognizes as a tribal entity in the central hill country of Cis-Jordan (Judges 5:14). Yet all the genealogical lists already refer to Machir as 'the father of Gilead' and 'the son of Manasseh' (Joshuah 17:1; I Chronicles 7:14; and elsewhere). The inference is clear: Machir, or more precisely 'half of the sons of Machir' (Joshua 13:31), had migrated eastwards and overrun areas in Gilead and Bashan (Numbers 32:39; and Joshua 17:2); with the passage of time, it was integrated into the overall Manassehite tribal framework. This latter fact is reflected also in the tradition relating the birth of 'the children of Machir son of Manasseh . . . upon Joseph's knees' (Genesis 50:23). Such migration holds true for many Ephraimite elements as well. They had infiltrated into Gilead, as may be deduced from the existence of a 'forest of Ephraim' there (II Samuel 18:6), where Absalom was later ensnared, as well as from the fratricidal strife in Trans-Jordan in Jephthah's day (see page 78).

The tribe of Benjamin was particularly hard pressed, being wedged into a tiny hilly portion between the tribes of Ephraim and Judah, while to the west a foreign population held it in check. It is no wonder, therefore, that Trans-Jordan proved a convenient outlet for Benjamin's surplus population. Indeed, several clues are provided in the Bible on the close-knit relations existing between Benjamin and the inhabitants of northern Gilead, for example, the conspicuous absence of Jabesh-gilead in the pan-tribal punitive action against Benjamin and, conversely, the military aid that the Benjaminite Saul rushed to that city (see page 79). Such ties are also indicated in the genealogical lists, where identical family names appear under the headings of both Benjamin and the several Trans-Jordanian tribes: Manasseh, or more precisely Machir, father of Gilead (the clans Shuppim and Huppim; I Chronicles 7:12 as against verse 15); Reuben (the clan Bela; I Chronicles 8:1 as against 5:8); and Gad (the clan Ezbon; I Chronicles 7:7 as against Genesis 46:16). In accordance with the biblical terminology dealing with Manasseh and Machir, it is thus possible to speak of 'half the tribe of Benjamin' whose abode was east of the Jordan. Repercussions of this expansion have indeed reached us in Obadiah's prophecy that 'Benjamin shall possess Gilead' (Obadiah 1:19). The same holds true for the tribe of Judah, when the Bible relates of one of its major subunits: 'And afterward Hezron went in to the daughter of Machir, the father of Gilead, whom he married . . . and she begat Segub, and Segub begat Jair' (I Chronicles 2:21–2). Hence families of the ramified Hezron clan, which claimed descent from both Judah and Reuben (I Chronicles 4:1, 5:3), had migrated to the land of Gilead, intermingled there with the settling Machirites and absorbed additional semi-nomadic tribes of foreign extraction roaming in the region.

This latter illustration reveals a widespread phenomenon also evident from the genealogical lists, namely, the assimilation or absorption of foreign elements by the settling tribes of Israel. This was achieved either by means of actual ethnic merging or by incorporating earlier Canaanite sites within the Israelite system, particularly in the tribal portions of Judah, Ephraim and Manasseh (*e.g.,* the city of Shechem, mentioned as a 'son' in the Manassehite genealogy). The tribe of Judah especially lends itself to close scrutiny of its settlement process because of the highly detailed description of its physical inheritance (Joshua 15), as well as the ramified family lists, recorded as a result of the special interest attached to this tribe by the Bible narrators

(I Chronicles 2 and 4:1–23). These lists elucidate the complex anatomy of Judah that resulted from its expansion in the south of the country – in the hill regions, the Shephelah and the Negev perimeter – where, on the one hand, a sizable earlier Canaanite and Horite element existed and, on the other hand, there were tribes still undergoing a settlement process resembling that of the Israelites. The strong foreign admixture is indicated at the very opening of Judah's genealogy, where three of his five immediate progeny are attributed to a Canaanite wife (I Chronicles 2:2–3; *cf.* the affair of Judah and Tamar in Genesis 38). The extent of this merger with the local population can be deduced from the numerous Canaanite and Hurrian names contained in the lists. Judah, above all, shows the absorption of kindred groups who, at the time of the Israelite Conquest, were wandering along the southern perimeter of the country, including the Kenites, the Kenizzites, the Jerahmeelites and the Caleb-ites. Some of the Calebite elements reached as far north as Hebron and Bethlehem and became a prominent ethnic ingredient in the ultimate coalescence of Judah.

While the absorption of foreigners into Judah was relatively easy, other tribes exercised stricter control in preserving the purity of their stock. Initially Israel's tribal society seems to have encouraged marriage within the group, as is reflected in the patriarchal custom of marrying near blood-relations. This endogamic principle gave way during the process of settlement to an increasingly exogamic tendency, es-pecially among the tribes encountering large foreign populations in the locale of their permanent habitat. Aside from Judah, this tendency is most prominent in the tribe of Simeon, which remained semi-nomadic even after settlement and whose wanderings along the country's fringes led to close contact with both the Canaanites and the southern desert nomads. One of Simeon's main offspring traced his lineage to a Canaanite woman (Genesis 46:10), while two others, Mibsam and Mishma, bear names identical with those of Ishmael's sons (I Chronicles 4:25 as against Genesis 25:13–14). The tribe's exogamic leanings are also hinted at in the Baal-peor episode describing the Simeonites' turning aside to the daughters of Midian (Numbers 25:6, 14–15).

These remarks on tribal settlement seen in the light of the genealogical lists may be concluded with an instructive biblical quotation attesting to the transfer of birthright among the various Israelite tribes, thereby implying a change in the tribal power structure within the pan-national framework: 'Now the sons of Reuben the first-born of Israel – for he was the first-born; but, forasmuch as he defiled his father's bed, his birthright was given unto the sons of Joseph the son of Israel: and the geneal-ogy is not to be reckoned after the birthright. For Judah prevailed above his brethren, and of him came the chief ruler; but the birthright was Joseph's' (I Chronicles 5:1-2). Thus the tribe of Reuben, which, like Simeon, continued to be semi-nomadic, had fallen from its former prominence and position of primogeniture (see Genesis 49:3–4; and Deuteronomy 33:6). The Joseph tribes were now in the ascendant; but ultimately the pre-eminence would move to Judah. On the other hand, the growing im-portance of Ephraim within the 'house of Joseph' during the period of Settlement is indicated by the transfer of Manasseh's birthright to his younger brother, Ephraim, in the blessing of Jacob to his grandchildren (Genesis 48:13–20; *cf.* page 79).

5

The Period of the Judges

The Rule of the Judges

Any historical survey of the era of the Judges must inevitably base itself on the collection of narratives in the Book of Judges itself, aside from a very few intimations in other biblical sources. The historiosophical framework into which the individual stories were integrated is the product of a twofold doctrine: the concept of historical periodicity and the tendency towards a pan-Israelite outlook. The former views the events of the period as recurrent cycles based on successive stages: the nation's reverting to idolatry, its subsequent subjugation by foreigners, its appeal for divine aid and its ultimate redemption by a deliverer who ushers in an extended period of tranquillity. This cyclic view of history imposed on the Book of Judges a seemingly chronological sequence, which cannot be accepted at face value. The same holds true for the pan-Israelite outlook (see page 29), which elevates tribal events and the activities of the individual Judges to a broad, national level. Exaggerated as this may be, the historical reality of the period none the less indicates that, as a rule, several tribes were victimized simultaneously by a foreign oppressor and that release from such pressure entailed joint action by a group of tribes.

Following the sociologist Max Weber, some historians have aptly described this régime of the Judges as constituting a leadership based on personal charisma. As such it is to be distinguished from the traditional patriarchal leadership of elders and clan chiefs, as well as from the institutionalized authority of the later monarchy (see Part II). Charismatic rule thrives on a people's belief in the appearance in a time of crisis of a divinely favoured personage enjoying a close relationship with God, experiencing divine revelations and possessed of outstanding courage. This type of leadership is characteristically spontaneous and specifically personal, with no leanings towards social class or status and devoid of any bureaucratic apparatus. Nor is the authority hereditary. The clamour for a champion in a time of distress would produce a voluntary gathering of the people around this person, a feeling of total dependence upon him and a national religious awakening. As a result, the political régime of the Judges was loose knit and of a sporadic nature, with the routine of daily affairs managed by the heads of families and the institution of elders. Yet patriarchal authority itself within the tribal units began to weaken during this period because of the increasingly sedentary nature of Israelite life, the firmer hold upon the soil and a partial adaptation to the Canaanite urban environment. These, in turn, led to a preference for territorial bonds rather than those of clan and kinship (see page 31 and A. Malamat in Bibliography).

The charismatic Judges who delivered the people in times of distress were (in the order of the Book of Judges) Othniel, Ehud, Gideon, Deborah (and Barak), Jephthah, Samson (though he lacked a popular following) and probably Shamgar ben Anath, whose exploits are recorded in a single verse (Judges 3:31). This book also focuses attention upon a different type, the 'minor' Judges, to whom no acts of deliverance are attributed but who, to all appearances, were men of standing in their respective tribes: Tola ben Puah (of Issachar), Jair the Gileadite, Ibzan of Bethlehem (perhaps in Zebulun), Elon the Zebulonite and Abdon from Pirathon in Mount Ephraim (Judges 10:1–5 and 12:8–15).

A prevailing scholarly view maintains that the minor Judges held a pan-Israelite office, a post passed on successively. Unlike the saviour-Judges, they allegedly served in the capacity of jurists and arbiters, even promulgating legislation in pre-monarchal days. At the same time it is often assumed that a late redactor of the Book of Judges (the so-called 'Deuteronomist') reworked the original accounts of the deliverer-Judges, adapting them to the pattern of the minor Judges; that is to say, he converted the charismatic figures into judges in the ordinary sense of the term. These premises are, however, untenable – particularly the assumption that the concept *shofet* ('judge') as applied to a charismatic leader is the result of later editing and supplanted the supposedly more archaic term *moshia'* ('saviour'). In fact, extra-biblical sources reveal that the term *shofet* and its derivatives are an ancient West Semitic usage implying primarily governorship and rule rather than juridical power. The Mari texts prove that the term was already in use in the first quarter of the second millennium, denoting a prominent tribal figure whose authority extended far beyond mere legal judgement. The title means 'magistrate' or 'ruler' in Phoenician (particularly in Punic; *suffetes* in Latin transcription) and perhaps in Ugaritic documents as well.

The root *shafat,* therefore, whether applied to major or minor Judges, denotes leadership over the people – including the juridical functions, it is true, but referring principally to their deliverance of the people from an enemy. The sharp distinction in the Bible between the deliverer-Judges and the minor Judges in all likelihood stems from the different literary sources relied upon by the compilers of the Book of Judges. While the exploits of the major Judges have been recorded as folk-tales, data on the minor Judges are derived from family chronicles and are limited only to such particulars as tribal origin, place and duration of office, burial site and number of descendants.

That the minor Judges, too, may have excelled in military leadership (see Judges 10:1) need not be ruled out, though no record of their activity has been preserved for posterity within the Book of Judges itself. Jair the Gileadite may be a case in point, for several sources in the Bible outside this book refer to his military exploits in northern Trans-Jordan (see Numbers 32:41; and *cf.* I Chronicles 2:22). Conversely, the deliverer-Judges are often portrayed in the style of the minor Judges, as in the cases of Gideon and Jephthah, where details typical of the latter group are inserted at the end of their accounts (Judges 8:29–32 and 12:7), or in the example of Deborah, whose renown even prior to her part in war lay in her meting out justice to the Israelites in the area of Ramah and Bethel (Judges 4:4–5). The interrelationship between the two types of Judges is evidenced also by Joshua, who, in addition to his military function, also fulfilled the function of inter-tribal arbitrator – as when he was called upon by the 'children of Joseph' to deal with their demand for further territory (Joshua 17:14ff.).

With all its short-comings, the Book of Judges remains of great value as an historical source depicting the mode of life and the setting typical of the period in question. The story of Ruth is another portrayal of the general scene 'in the days when the Judges ruled' (Ruth 1:1). In selecting the stories in the Book of Judges, the compiler seems to have had a paradigmatic intent: seeking singularity in his models, he avoided duplication in the Judges' tribes, in the types of foes encountered and in the regions involved, while highlighting the problems specific to the particular confrontation. Thus, the Deborah episode describes a clash with indigenous Canaanite inhabitants in the north; the Gideonite narrative epitomizes the encounter with nomadic desert marauders from the east; underlying the stories of Ehud and Jephthah is the strife with the nations on the Trans-Jordanian perimeter – the Moabites and Ammonites; finally, the Samson cycle records the Israelite response to the Philistine challenge in the west.

Deborah's Battle for Freedom

The growing strength and numerical increase of the Israelites transformed the demographic character of the country and affected the indigenous settlers, who were dispossessed of appreciable portions of their land. This led to the most fateful confrontation experienced by Israel during the days of the Judges – the battle of Deborah and Barak with the Canaanites. Like the other Israelite wars under the Judges, this was fundamentally a war of self-defence thrust upon the people. The Canaanites were apparently attempting, in a last comprehensive effort in the north of the country, to turn back the clock of history.

Serious problems of chronology arise in connexion with this battle because of its dual tradition, in poetry and in prose (Judges 4 and 5), and because of the apparent contradiction between it and the battle of the Waters of Merom and the fall of Hazor, as outlined in Joshua 11:1–15 (see page 57). The difficulty as regards Joshua is not necessarily in the name of the Canaanite king Jabin, who figures in both clashes with the Israelites; this may merely have been a dynastic name at Hazor. What is truly perplexing is the actual mention of Hazor as the focus of broad Canaanite leagues in both encounters. It is inconceivable that Hazor, which the Bible claims to have been razed to the ground by Joshua, should have played a major role in a Canaanite confederacy several generations later. Moreover, the excavations at Hazor prove that the city was completely destroyed in the latter part of the thirteenth century (see page 53) and that until the Solomonic era it existed only as a meagre, unfortified settlement.

A likely solution for the dilemma is to regard the name Hazor in the Deborah episode, and presumably the name Jabin as well, as later interpolations inspired by the rather similar events recorded in the Book of Joshua. Indeed, both Hazor and Jabin find only incidental mention in the Book of Judges, and neither of them suits the topographical or military framework of the Deborah account. It was, of course, Sisera, the commander of Harosheth-hagoyim, who led the Canaanites on the field of battle – an entirely different picture from that painted in the Book of Joshua. Alternatively, the encounters both of Deborah and at the Waters of Merom have been regarded as two closely linked phases of a single military conflict; the Deborah campaign would thus anticipate Joshua's battle and refer to a period when the Kingdom of Hazor was still potent. But this assumption would contradict biblical chronology and, on the basis of the Hazor excavations, would entail placing Deborah's campaign at least as early as the third quarter of the thirteenth century – a most improbable dating indeed.

It appears that Deborah's war took place only in the late twelfth century, as may be assumed from certain details mentioned in the Song of Deborah. The song, for example, makes reference to Shamgar, the selfsame deliverer who smote 600 Philistines (a complete 'regiment') and thereby saved Israel (Judges 5:6; whether he was of Israelite or Canaanite stock is uncertain). Yet a clash of this kind, presumably in the north of the country, could not have taken place before the early twelfth century, when the Philistines made their initial appearance in Canaan (see pages 80ff.). Deborah's war occurred only after this event. Another piece of evidence favouring a comparatively late date for the Deborah episode is the mention, in the song, of Dan as being located between Gilead and Asher, indicating that the migration of this tribe to its northern habitation had already taken place (see page 64). In this connexion it is interesting to note that the Song of Deborah locates the battle arena at 'Taanach by the waters of Megiddo' (Judges 5:19), not at Megiddo itself. This may imply that this important city lay in ruins at that time, and thus it has been proposed that Deborah's campaign took place in the interval between the destruction of stratum VII at Megiddo and the founding of stratum VI (c. 1125 BCE). The latter date would accord with the results of the recent excavations at Taanach, which prove that this Canaanite town still existed in the late twelfth century, after which there followed a long gap in its occupation. This fact, on the other hand, would rule out any proposed dating of the battle in the eleventh century.

In reconstructing the Deborah episode, one must rely upon both the later prose account and the song itself, which is indubitably early and perhaps even contemporaneous with the events it describes. Though the two sources seem contradictory, they may actually complement one another. The major discrepancies between them – the number of tribes participating in the battle and the topography of the battle-field – apparently reflect different stages of the same war. Naphtali and Zebulun bore the brunt of the battle, as only they are mentioned in both the poem and the narrative. The myriad warriors placed in the field by the two tribes were led to Mount Tabor by Barak ben Abinoam of Kedesh-naphtali. As a military base of operations, this mountain had obvious advantages: it offered an extensive field of vision for keeping a check on enemy movements and gave the Israelites the possibility of assembling forces beyond the reach of Canaanite chariotry, thus enabling initiative in attack. The enemy, on his part, was compelled to concentrate his troops at the foot of

Mount Tabor, in the narrow, rugged valley terrain hardly suitable for the deployment of chariotry. We have already mentioned the Israelite operational plan to exploit weather conditions as a means of depriving the enemy's chariotry of its manoeuvrability (see page 60).

The subsequent sequence of events seems to have been preserved accurately in the song. The beaten enemy, retreating to the western edge of the Jezreel Plain, encountered a further obstacle – the rain-swollen Kishon brook. Here the final and decisive engagement took place. Perhaps it was only in this last phase that the central hill tribes of Ephraim, Benjamin and Machir joined in, as happened in the battle under Gideon, in which the Ephraimites appeared only when the enemy was already in headlong flight. Sisera, who had fled the battle-field, met his death at the hands of Jael in the encampment of Heber the Kenite. The Kenite clan had cultivated friendly relations with both the Canaanites and the Israelites (with whom it had familial ties; Judges 4:11, 17), but upon the Israelite victory abandoned its neutrality.

Deborah's campaign marks the high point of national solidarity against foreign oppression during the entire period of the Judges – from Benjamin in the south to Naphtali in the north. It is no coincidence that, of all the tribes, it was those dwelling in the mountain areas that took the military initiative. Having suffered less from Canaanite pressure, they were more disposed to rise against the enemy. In contrast, the lowland tribes, which would benefit most from the defeat of the Canaanite oppressor, were in a more precarious position and less able to initiate resistance (*cf.* page 60). A consequence of Israel's victory was the strengthening of its position in the Plain of Jezreel and the securing for the first time of territorial contiguity between the tribes in Galilee and those in the central region of the country.

Gideon's Campaign Against the Desert Marauders

Deborah's victory over the Canaanites appears to have opened the way to a new danger to Israelite settlement in the north. This military success largely undermined the Canaanite power structure in the north and thus the security situation in general, exposing the country to raids, particularly by marauders from the desert. Incursions of desert nomads into the cultivated and settled areas was a recurrent historical phenomenon in Palestine in times of political and military laxity, such as in the period of the Israelite Settlement. This situation was only rectified finally by the stable régime under King David. The proximity of the Deborah and Gideon accounts in the Book of Judges seems, therefore, to be valid historically and may not be due to late arbitrary editing.

The nomads, for their part, continued to penetrate from the desert fringe in rather loose-knit confederations. A single group would stamp its imprint upon the entire tribal alliance – at one time the Midianites and at another the Amalekites, Hagarites or Ishmaelites. Spearheading the wave of marauders at the time of Gideon were the Midianites, who reached their peak in the thirteenth and twelfth centuries; they were joined by the Amalekites and the 'Children of the East' (Judges 6:3 and 7:12). The area of Midianite concentration was the perimeter of southern Trans-Jordan, which explains their special ties with Moab and the Amorite Kingdom of Sihon

(Numbers 22:4ff.; and Joshua 13:21), as well as their clash with the Israelites in the days of Moses (Numbers 25 and 31). Their full nomadic domain, however, sprawled across an enormous tract, from Egypt on the west to the Euphrates region in the north; offshoots reached even to Sheba in South Arabia. Such distant wanderings, as well as a general flourishing of the desert tribes, resulted from the large-scale breeding and domestication of the camel, which had already begun in the early twelfth century. By now the camel had become the main economic factor in the Arabian wastes and even served military purposes.

The Midianite incursion in Gideon's day – apparently towards the end of the twelfth century – was aimed at the Beth-shean and Jezreel valleys and beyond to the fertile coastal plains. Deep inroads as far as Gaza (Judges 6:4) were facilitated by the decline of the Canaanite city-states, coupled with the slackening of Egyptian rule along the Via Maris during the latter half of the twelfth century (see page 27). In the style of desert predators, hordes of Midianites, men, women and children, descended upon the cultivated areas at harvest time, plundering and destroying the crops. The rural Israelite population was especially vulnerable to these depredations; living as they did in open settlements, they were forced to prepare 'hiding-places in the mountains and caves and strongholds' (Judges 6:2) in order to preserve their lives and their crops. They laboured in an atmosphere of threat, as exemplified by Gideon's threshing of wheat in the winepress so as to 'hide it from the Midianites' (Judges 6:1). This insecurity appears to be confirmed by archaeological findings, such as the discovery of numerous grain-pits within a village for concealing stored crops from marauding bands.

The initiative in this war of liberation was taken by Gideon ben Joash, the Abi-ezrite from the tribe of Manasseh. As instanced by other battles in the period of the Judges, the actual military encounter followed a national religious awakening. But only in Gideon's case are details of the religious reform given, namely, the liquidation of the Baal-Asherah cult at his birth-place, Ophrah. This act parallels Saul's elimination of the foreign cults prior to his decisive battle against the Philistines (I Samuel 28:3; see Part II). In addition to his own tribesmen, Gideon summoned to the battle against the Midianites tribesmen from Asher, Zebulun and Naphtali and, at a later stage, from Ephraim too.

Gideon's campaign is described with sufficient topographical and military detail to enable a close reconstruction of the actual course of battle. The Midianites encamped 'to the north of Gibeath Hamoreh which is in the valley' (Judges 7:1). According to an allusion in Psalms 83:11, where events of the era of the Judges are reviewed, this took place at En-dor in the plain extending from the hill of Moreh to Mount Tabor. Gideon and his men were perched on the slopes of the Gilboa range above En-harod – as with Barak, beyond the enemy's reach. The military problem facing the Israelites at this time was their opponent's numerical superiority and his skilful use of the camel, both of which demanded novel strategy. Gideon found the tactical solution in a night assault, which nullified the enemy's advantages. The meticulous planning and successful execution of this operation made it a classic example of the way in which a small, ill-equipped force could overcome a much larger and more powerful opponent.

Under cover of darkness Gideon exploited to the full the factors of surprise and psychological warfare, thereby creating total confusion in the enemy's midst. This led to a panicky flight at dawn towards the Jordan Valley. Thus Gideon's tactics were a complete success, and his brilliant victory was preserved as a model for future generations and remembered as 'the day of Midian' (Isaiah 9:3). As was customary among nomadic bands, the beaten enemy now attempted a hasty withdrawal into the desert wastes. In order to forestall their escape, Gideon, aided by the Ephraimites, blocked the enemy's line of retreat. He seized the Jordan fords and, at the same time, embarked upon a daring, long-range pursuit of the remnants of the fleeing Midianites. At Karkor in Wadi Sirhan, he again surprised the encamped enemy and even succeeded in capturing the two Midianite rulers, Zebah and Zalmunna. On his return he meted out punishment to the uncooperative authorities of Succoth and dealt most severely with the recalcitrant town of Penuel, killing its inhabitants and razing its citadel – all this because the populace of both towns had earlier refused to supply his troops for fear of Midianite reprisal.

Moves Towards Monarchy

The desire to stabilize and perpetuate this sporadic leadership of charismatic figures – a tendency familiar elsewhere under this type of rule – led to efforts to replace the Judges by a dynastic monarchy. The initial attempts met with internal opposition. Just as the crown was offered to Saul (at least according to one biblical version) after his triumph over the Ammonites (I Samuel 11), so had 'the men of Israel' approached Gideon, some generations earlier, to enthrone him over Israel after his magnificent defeat of the Midianites. Gideon's classic rejoinder was: 'I will not rule over you, neither shall my son rule over you; the Lord shall rule over you' (Judges 8:23), whereby he stressed that the appointment of mortal kings contravened the concept of the kingship of God. Whether Gideon actually made this statement or some editor put it into his mouth, the remark is not necessarily the product of a late theocratic ideology but seems to be a faithful reflection of the mood prevailing during the period of the Judges, with its firm belief in the freedom of the individual and egalitarianism.

An even more pungent expression of antimonarchism in this period is to be found in the parable of Jotham, which depicts kingship as a futile, absolutist institution. Yet, while strong opposition continued to be evinced to any such innovation, the very proposal made to Gideon (as well as Jotham's adage) suggests that at least certain circles had begun to think seriously of institutionalizing the charismatic leadership. The same attitude also underlies Jephthah's insistence that he be recognized as 'the head of all the inhabitants of Gilead'; this meant that he wished to act as supreme sovereign – in peace as in war (see page 77).

Despite Gideon's refusal of the kingship, his military triumph gave him great prestige, and he wielded broad powers both in the governmental and in the religious spheres (*e.g.,* the setting up of the *ephod* at Ophrah, converting the site into a cultic centre). Yet he made no arrangements for succession, and in fact a bloody internecine dispute resulted among his large progeny after he had passed on, 'hoary with age'. Abimelech, the offspring of Gideon's political marriage into an aristocratic family of Shechem, exploited his family connexions to rid himself of his brothers and seize power in the foreign city. The 'lords of Shechem', the city's oligarchic ruling clique, backed Abimelech's claim to kingship for political and economic reasons, but also because they were long accustomed to the Canaanite monarchal tradition. The plan, however, went wrong. Having gained control over the northern part of the central hill area with the help of a hireling band of 'vain and light persons', Abimelech abandoned Shechem as his royal residence and became a political and economic competitor to the city's nobility. This then provided the background for the ensuing friction between the two factions. Gaal ben Ebed in the meantime incited the inhabitants of Shechem to rebellion, exploiting the social (and possibly racial) tension among the various demographic elements in the city. What occurred, apparently, was that Gaal had conspired with the long-established local aristocracy – which traced itself back to 'Hamor the father of Shechem' (Judges 9:28) – against the rest of the Canaanite populace, specifically those loyal to Abimelech, at the head of which group stood Zebul, 'the ruler of the city'. The uprising was cruelly suppressed by Abimelech, who razed the city to the ground and symbolically strewed salt over the ruins.

Indeed, excavations at Shechem have unearthed clear evidence of the utter destruction of the town at the end of the twelfth century. Furthermore, it is now clear that Shechem of this period was divided into a lower city and an acropolis upon a foundation of beaten earth – apparently the '*beth millo*' (Judges 9:6). In the latter two towers flanked the entrance to a large building complex that served as both fortress and temple (see page 53). This must have been the biblical 'tower of Shechem' to which was attached the 'hold of the house of El Berith' (Judges 9:46), where the men of Shechem fled for safety after the fall of the lower city. A similar course of events overtook the town of Thebez, which had also raised the banner of revolt against Abimelech. There, too, it would seem, after the capture of the lower city the inhabitants withdrew to the security of 'the tower of strength' or the fortress-temple, where they again sought the highest part of the building, the 'roof of the tower' (Judges 9:51). At this juncture, however, Abimelech met his death, the victim of a millstone flung at him as he approached the wall. The manner of his death was to serve as a classic warning against the dangers of siege warfare some generations later (*cf.* II Samuel 11:21).

Abimelech's system of government was of a dual nature, representing a combination of rule over a Canaanite urban centre, on the one hand, and an Israelite tribal entity, on the other. Furthermore, his rule drew its inspiration from the Canaanite monarchal model and found support among the foreign populace after a blood bath among his own people. Little wonder that this experiment was doomed to failure after a short time and that biblical tradition could see in Abimelech neither king nor judge, but simply a despot: 'And Abimelech held sway [*vayyasar*] over Israel for three years' (Judges 9:22). His leadership, devoid of all charisma, such as Saul or David possessed, and lacking any legitimacy as far as Israelite tradition was concerned, was merely an abortive attempt at kingship. The time was not yet ripe for the establishment of a monarchy in Israel.

Encounters with the Peoples of Trans-Jordan

The growth in numbers and power of the Israelite settlement brought in its wake an ever-increasing tension not only with the populace in Cis-Jordan but also with neighbours in Trans-Jordan. In contrast to the indigenous Canaanites, in Trans-Jordan the Israelites were confronted by peoples ethnically akin to themselves, who were recent arrivals experiencing a process of settlement similar to their own (see page 52). The open clash here was with the Moabites and Ammonites. Edom was beyond the Israelite sphere of interest, and even in the extensive and sparsely settled areas of Trans-Jordan north of the Jabbok, Israelite and Aramean expansion did not come to any real clash. It has been suggested that Chushan-rishathaim – the first oppressor of Israel, according to the Book of Judges, who was finally overpowered by Othniel ben Kenaz – was a king of Edom and not of Aram-naharaim (in the Euphrates region) as the Bible has it (Judges 3:8); but this argument is not convincing (see page 26).

The situation in the flourishing sector between the Jabbok and Arnon rivers was different, for here nature had been most generous with her gifts, and the rapid demographic increase soon reached the saturation-point. The limited living-space of this area, which was bounded by the desert to the east and the Jordan River to the west, led to a deterioration in the relations between the local Israelite tribes and Moab and Ammon, as well as between the latter two kingdoms themselves. Geopolitical conditions in the region were thus instrumental in initiating a fierce struggle, as there was insufficient space for two neighbouring forces to prosper simultaneously.

By combining the information and allusions scattered throughout the biblical sources, one may perceive a cyclic process in the regional power structure. The rise of Moab under King Eglon meant the weakening of both the neighbouring Israelite tribes and the Kingdom of Ammon. The latter's inferior status to Moab may possibly be deduced from the fact that Ammon had to provide auxiliary troops in the Moabite war with Israel (Judges 3:13). Moab's control over the desert fringes may also be indicated by Amalekite participation in the same campaign. On the other hand, with the defeat of Moab by the judge Ehud, a strengthening of her three neighbours – Israel, Ammon and Edom – must have ensued. The way was now open for a strong flow of Israelite elements from the west into Moab, including some degree of inter-marriage with the Moabites, as emerges from the Book of Ruth and the genealogical lists of Judah and Benjamin (see I Chronicles 4:22 and 8:8). On the other hand, Ammonite ascendancy over Moab may be echoed in the exchange between Jephthah and the king of Ammon (Judges 11:12ff.). The latter appears in this dispute also in the role of suzerain of the land of Moab, or at least of its northern areas, which enabled him to press territorial claims against Israel.

As for Edom, an instructive comment has been preserved in the list of Edomite kings informing us that Edom's king, Hadad ben Bedad, smote the Midianites in the 'field of Moab' (Genesis 36:35). The inference may be that Moab alone was incapable of repelling the desert marauders, or it may even indicate actual Edomite control over Moab. The above-mentioned Edomite ruler reigned some five generations prior to Saul or David, that is, around 1100, a short time before the advent of

Jephthah. In the interim, we gather, Moabite sovereignty was reduced; only when Ammon was defeated at the hands of Jephthah and, even more so, by Saul in the late eleventh century could Moab regain its former position. However, we possess no chronological evidence for dating Moab's earlier prosperity under King Eglon and the blow it received from Ehud, but these must have been during the twelfth century.

The rise of Moab as a significant political factor is linked to her northern expansion beyond the Arnon River, including the fertile tableland and the 'plain of Moab' (which was of strategic importance in addition to its fertility, as it controlled the Jordan fords). With this as the starting-point, Moab under Eglon extended its control over the Jordan River's western bank, subduing the territory of Benjamin. Israel's battle of liberation was initiated by Ehud ben Gera, the scion of a noble Benjaminite family that was still well known in David's day (Genesis 46:21; and II Samuel 16:5). Ehud must previously have assumed a dominant role in his tribe, having headed the delegation that brought tribute to the Moabite ruler, in the manner in which heads of vassal states would appear before their overlord.

The folkloristic aura of the Ehud tale is readily apparent in the elaboration on Ehud's personal prowess and the assassination of Eglon, as opposed to the actual facts of the war, which are only briefly sketched (Judges 3:12ff.). The vague topographical details do not allow for a reconstruction of the course of events, though the realistic description of Ehud's deed does enable us to perceive the clever stratagem devised by the Israelite hero. Ehud's scheme was to rely on his distinctive physical characteristic, the fact that he was 'a man left-handed' or, more precisely, trained in the left-handed use of his weaponry, as were the rest of his tribal kinsmen (Judges 20:16). His short sword ('of a cubit length') was thus surely strapped, in contrast to normal practice, on his right thigh, which enabled him to draw it in an unanticipated left-hand motion in order to kill the king. After the king's death, which left the enemy without a leader, the revolt spread against the Moabite forces occupying western Palestine, whence they were driven out. The enemy incurred heavy losses at the Jordan fords, which had been seized by the Israelites in the time-honoured method used by them on several occasions during the period of the Judges. Ehud scored a decisive victory over the Moabites that, according to the Bible, resulted in eighty years of tranquillity – denoting actually a time span of two generations. No other act of deliverance during the period of the Judges produced so long a period of security.

In the wake of Moab's decline, the Kingdom of Ammon consolidated its power in the early eleventh century and renewed the threat to Israelite settlement in Trans-Jordan. An additional factor in the Ammonite rise was Gideon's blow to the Midianites, as well as that of the Edomite ruler Hadad around 1100 BCE. Ammon was situated on the desert fringes, which had suffered more than other areas from the rapacious assaults of marauding nomads. Once this danger was removed, Ammon could set itself to the task of efficient control of the caravan trade, from which it derived great economic prosperity. Its physical location enabled Ammon to dominate the road junctions and especially a section of the 'King's Highway', the international artery that linked Syria with the Gulf of Eilat and the Arabian Peninsula.

When it had consolidated its power, Ammon spread out westwards, far beyond its tiny confines around the capital, Rabbath-ammon, to the fertile el-Buqeia' region, encompassed by the curving Jabbok River, and towards the territory of Gilead. However, merely controlling the land up to the Jordan River was not sufficient; Ammon's ambitions extended into the territories of Ephraim, Benjamin and Judah. The Bible chronicler makes the large Ammonite offensive against the Israelites from the east coincide with the growing pressure exerted by the Philistines from the west (Judges 10:7–9) – which does, in fact, tally with the historical situation in the first half of the eleventh century. The Israelite response was not long in coming once the danger threatened Gilead, which was thickly populated by the tribe of Gad and the half tribe of Manasseh. In their distress the Gileadite elders called upon the same Jephthah, the son of a harlot, who had previously been expelled from his father's patrimony. Jephthah had at his call a band of brigands, and it was this private army that helped him assume the leadership of the cause of liberation. In this respect his rise to power resembled that of Gideon, Abimelech and David, or Rezon ben Eliadah in Damascus, all of whom had armed bands at their personal disposal. After wearisome negotiations with the elders, Jephthah acquired the dual status of 'captain' and 'head', by which was meant that he would be ruler of Gilead in times of both war and peace (Judges 11:5ff.).

The Israelites deployed their force at Mizpah, the religious and political focus of the Gileadites, hallowed already in patriarchal tradition (Genesis 31:48). Encamped directly opposite, in the 'city of Gilead', were the Ammonites. Jephthah at first refrained from forcing the issue, preferring negotiations with the enemy ruler. Although the actual wording of these diplomatic negotiations bears telltale signs of late (Deuteronomistic) editing, it nevertheless remains an important historical source, indicative of the claims of both parties to the disputed territory between the Jabbok and Arnon rivers. Jephthah presented a twofold argument: he pointed out that the Israelites had formerly wrested control over the area from Sihon, the king of the Amorites, not from Ammon or Moab; and that they held ownership rights by virtue of an uninterrupted 300-year residence there (for the true chronological implications, see page 43). The Ammonite counter-claim seems to have rested on supposedly original ownership of the region by the Ammonites, prior to the take-over by the Amorites.

Upon the breakdown of negotiations, Jephthah launched an assault upon the defensive line of Ammon's western border, 'from Aroer even until thou come to Minnith even twenty cities and unto Abel of the vineyards' (Judges 11:33). The Aroer mentioned here is not the well-known city on the bank of the Arnon River but a more northerly point, 'Aroer that is before Rabbah [Rabbath-ammon]' (Joshua 13:25); the twenty towns were no doubt minor border forts encircling Rabbath-ammon to the west and south (see page 52). The Ammonite capital nevertheless remained impervious to Jephthah's attempts at penetration; nor was his victory lasting, for only some two generations later, on the eve of Saul's assumption of the crown, the Ammonites again embarked on a campaign far to the north, laying siege to the city of Jabesh-gilead.

Fratricidal Strife

In the aftermath of Jephthah's war with the Ammonites, a tragic event occurred in the history of the Israelite tribes – the outbreak of a cruel and bloody feud between the Gileadites and the Ephraimites. The underlying issue appears to have been Ephraim's aspiration to dominate the Israelite settlement in Gilead, being aided in all likelihood by the many Ephraimites who had migrated there, for 'ye Gileadites are fugitives of Ephraim' (Judges 12:4; cf. page 65). The Ephraimites went up to the town of Zaphon (listed in Gad's tribal allotment and apparently identifiable with Tell es-Sa'idiyeh in the eastern Jordan depression), probably intending to continue on to Mizpah, the residence of Jephthah. On being routed they attempted to escape to their ancestral territory on the west bank of the Jordan River, but were massacred as they tried to steal across the river. It is in this connexion that the Bible introduces an illuminating detail, recording how the Ephraimites were identified by the peculiar pronunciation of the password *shibboleth* as *sibboleth* (Judges 12:6). This is a rare testimony to the linguistic individuality of Ephraim and may be indicative of more general differences of dialect among the Israelite tribes. Faint echoes of these internecine events may still be heard in the remark by Hosea that 'Gilead is a city of them that work iniquity and is polluted with blood' (Hosea 6:8).

The inter-tribal strife in Jephthah's day flared up over the complaint of the Ephraimites that they had not been summoned to war (Judges 12:1). A similar charge was directed by the people of Ephraim against Gideon after his initial defeat of the Midianites, but Gideon appeased them by inviting them to join in the pursuit of the retreating enemy and thus enabled them to effect a sizable military achievement (Judges 7:24 and 8:3; cf. Isaiah 10:26). There were, however, also occurrences of a reverse type, in which internecine resentments were instigated by the outright refusal by a town or tribe to help their brethren in times of danger. We have had occasion to point out (see page 73) how Gideon avenged himself upon the inhabitants of Succoth and Penuel for failing to provision his troops as they pursued the Midianites. Still another outstanding example of failure to provide aid is mentioned in connexion with Deborah's campaign against the Canaanites, when, in her song, the tribes of Reuben, the Gileadites, Dan and Asher and the town of Meroz, in particular, were castigated 'because they came not to the help of the Lord, to the help of the Lord against the mighty' (Judges 5:23).

Inter-tribal disputes were largely a consequence of strained relations or even open rift between the settlers on either side of the Jordan. There was not a single battle for freedom in which both banks joined forces, whatever the cause may have been. Perhaps it was this lack of solidarity that occasioned the repeated biblical stress upon the commitment by the two-and-a-half Trans-Jordanian tribes to take the lead in the conquest of western Palestine. The antagonism between the two parts of the nation is also reflected in the tradition contained in Joshua 22, on the setting-up of an altar by the Trans-Jordanian tribes 'over against the land of Canaan, in the borders of Jordan', which these tribes explained on the following grounds: 'And if we have not rather done it for fear of this thing saying, in time to come your children might speak unto our children saying: What have ye to do with the Lord God of

Israel?' (Joshua 22:24). The western tribes remained unconvinced, seeing the act as an attempt to compete with the Shiloh sanctuary, and they were in fact about 'to go up against them to war'. Their anger subsided only after the altar's purpose was defined as a national, unifying factor rather than a divisive, cultic instrument.

The principal instigator of the various inter-tribal clashes was the tribe of Ephraim, which feared for its primacy of status. It became involved in disputes with all the neighbouring tribes once these had gained in prestige after the victories of Gideon the Manassehite, Jephthah of Gilead and Ehud the Benjaminite. Indeed, Ephraim was the driving force behind the pan-tribal assault on Benjamin over the issue of the concubine of Gibeah; this adventure culminated in the broadest and most bitter inter-tribal conflict during the period of the Judges. Although, according to the biblical account, the reason for this fratricidal war was the dastardly crime committed on Benjaminite soil, the true cause lay in the contest for tribal hegemony.

The episode of the outrage at Gibeah, in Judges 20:19–21, reflects an ancient historical tradition (*cf.* the references to 'the days of Gibeah' in Hosea 5:8 and 9:9), though many have doubted the authenticity of the story as such, owing to its tendentiousness and literary embellishments. Chronologically, the account can be sandwiched between Jephthah's day (indicative as it is of the continuing enmity between Ephraim and the Gileadites, the former being the true instigator of the punitive action against Jabesh-gilead) and Saul's accession to the throne some decades later. The story of the concubine highlights the special ties of friendship between Benjamin and the people of Jabesh-gilead, the only group in all of Israel refusing to participate against Benjamin and, as a consequence, suffering severely (Judges 21:5ff.). These facts, as such, link up well with the happenings on the eve of Saul's reign: the previously weakened town of Jabesh-gilead was pounced upon by the Ammonites, and its inhabitants appealed to Benjamin rather than to the closer Ephraim. In fact, it was Saul, of the tribe of Benjamin, who hastened to their assistance.

The Gibeah episode is replete with illustrative details on social, institutional, military and religious facets. One such instance is the information that Bethel served as a religious centre, 'for the Ark of the Covenant of the Lord was there in those days' (Judges 21:27). Especially instructive is the depiction of the primitive democracy of the Israelites, whose central organs were the 'congregation' (*'edah*) and 'general assembly', which enjoyed supreme legislative and military authority (Judges 20:1ff.). In this episode the army was summoned by the gruesome means of dispatching a portion of the concubine's corpse to each of the tribes – similar to the method employed by Saul in his war against Ammon and to other instances in primitive tribal warfare in the ancient Near East. The intrinsic importance of the Gibeah episode lies in its being the sole illustration from the era of the Judges of concerted action by a pan-tribal alliance (excluding the punished tribe), led not by a judge nor yet by a king, but by its representative institutions.

6

The Struggle Against the Philistines

The Invasion of the Sea Peoples and the
Destruction of the Coastal Cities

The Philistine incursion along the Palestinian seaboard formed part of a larger assault by the Sea Peoples throughout the eastern basin of the Mediterranean, repercussions of which reverberated throughout all the adjacent lands. Around 1200 BCE the Hittite Empire collapsed after flourishing for hundreds of years; Egypt was approaching its eclipse, and along the Syrian-Palestinian coast many port towns succumbed. On the Greek mainland and the Aegean isles, the magnificence of the Mycenaean world lay forlorn, soon to be finally extinguished. Far-reaching changes were affecting the ethnic and political map of the Near East. A new ethnic regrouping in Asia Minor was followed by a shift in population from the area's southern part to Syria (and perhaps even further southwards), and a foothold was gained in Cyprus and Palestine by new elements (of which the Philistines were only one) hailing from the Aegean sphere. To the west Doric tribesmen invaded Greece, and there was a migration of Indo-European elements into Italy and the neighbouring islands. This swirling movement may not, indeed, be traceable to one sole historical factor, but the Sea Peoples, beyond any doubt, played a dominant role and were the instigators of a chain reaction felt throughout three continents.

The first wave broke across the western delta of Egypt during Merneptah's fifth regnal year (*c.* 1220; see page 25). He managed to repulse the invaders, but more powerful waves came crashing against the eastern shores of the Mediterranean during the days of Rameses III, sweeping across the isle of Cyprus and such lands as Amurru and Djahi, in Syria and Palestine. The war between the Egyptians and the invaders, both on land and sea, reached its pinnacle in the eighth year of Rameses' reign, immortalized in his numerous reliefs (see pages 83 f.). Of special significance in this connexion is the explicit mention of the Philistines – their first appearance in extra-biblical sources (*c.* 1198, 1187 or 1162 BCE, according to the 'high', 'middle' – to be preferred – or 'low' chronology). It may well mark the date of the Philistines' initial arrival in the country to which they were eventually to bequeath their name – Palestine. As a rule they head the list of the Sea Peoples in Rameses' inscriptions, a fact that may testify to their importance. Closely related to the Philistines were the Tjeker, who settled farther to the north along the Palestinian coast. A century after the Sea Peoples' incursion, the Egyptian envoy Wen-amon informs us of a Tjeker kingdom at the port city of Dor, on the Carmel coast, and of their buccaneering vessels off Phoenicia. In all likelihood they established settlements in Cyprus as well.

Traces of the catastrophe that overtook the eastern seaboard of the Mediterranean have been discovered at many coastal and also some inland sites. Archaeological excavations have revealed that several of the ravaged port towns never rose again, or at least never regained their former status (among them Alalaḫ and Ugarit to the north), while others were to rise from the ashes after a brief lapse. Jaffa, Ashdod and Ashkelon on the Philistine coast illustrate several such towns newly resettled by the Sea Peoples. The devastation of the Phoenician harbour towns for which archaeological evidence is lacking is intimated in a late tradition preserved by the Latin historian Justinus. He speaks of a victory by the king of Ashkelon (probably already under the dominion of the Sea Peoples) over the inhabitants of Sidon, who, upon the destruction of their city, 'founded the city of Tyre one year before the fall of Troy'. Tyre was then in ruins, according to this information, and was reconstituted by the Sidonians, a tradition that also found its way into the writings of Josephus.

The cataclysm caused by the Sea Peoples has been dramatically brought to life by the correspondence discovered in recent years in the royal archive at Ugarit, dating from the eve of the city's fall. In one letter a Cypriot ruler warns the last king of Ugarit of an approaching enemy (whose identity is not disclosed) and advises him to make urgent preparations against the forthcoming invasion. The king of Ugarit, on his part (in what may be a reply to this letter), reports an initial landing by commando forces of the Sea Peoples: 'Now seven enemy ships have arrived here and have caused us great harm. If further enemy vessels appear, please inform me, so that I may know [of them].' From another letter we may gather that an enemy fleet made a surprise attack on a fleet from Ugarit; in another case, no less than the Hittite king himself reports that the enemy – probably the Sea Peoples and their allies – has penetrated into his land, and he implores the king of Ugarit to speed food supplies to him because of the heavy famine that has descended upon his country. It is difficult to determine accurately the date of the fall of Ugarit and the other port towns. They may perhaps have succumbed as early as the final quarter of the thirteenth century, with the initial onslaught of the Sea Peoples in the reign of Merneptah. On the other hand, they may have been conquered a generation later, at the time of the final destruction of the Hittite Empire. In any case, it has become clear that the massive invasions by the Sea Peoples in the days of Rameses III were preceded by successive raids against the coasts of Palestine and Syria.

Rameses III managed to block the way of the Sea Peoples into Egypt proper, but he could not prevent their extensive penetration into Palestine. In order to ward off the danger threatening his own land, Rameses evidently sought a modus vivendi with the Sea Peoples, particularly the Philistines, allowing them to settle in Canaan and subsequently exploiting them as an instrument of Egyptian policy. Biblical sources do indeed indicate that the Philistines flourished in precisely those areas that had formerly been under Egyptian control, that is, the southern coastal plain of Palestine, as well as the valleys of Jezreel and Beth-shean. Together with other groups of Sea Peoples, they were probably employed as garrison troops in such administrative centres as Gaza in the south and Beth-shean in the north and proved useful in quelling local uprisings. With the decline of Egypt's rule in Palestine, the Philistines became the natural heirs, particularly in the bitter struggle with the people of Israel.

The Philistines – Their Origins and Civilization

According to biblical testimony, which undoubtedly is based on Philistine tradition, the original home of the Philistines was Caphtor, the ancient name of Crete or of the entire Aegean region (*e.g.,* in Amos 9:7; see page 28). Like the late hellenistic writers, whose works contain references to the migrations of the Philistines and other nations related to the Sea Peoples, so the prophet Amos preserves allusions to the origin of the Philistines, approximately four centuries after their arrival in Palestine. The prophet may have been acquainted with a Philistine epic glorifying their advent in their new homeland, just as the Israelites cultivated their Exodus tradition. Jeremiah still saw the Philistines as a 'remnant of the isle of Caphtor' (Jeremiah 47:4), and their kinship with the Caphtorites is alluded to elsewhere in the Bible (Genesis 10:14; and Deuteronomy 2:23). Further biblical references juxtapose the Philistines and the Cretans (Ezekiel 25:16; and Zephaniah 2:5); their relationship with the Cretans is confirmed also by the description of the western Negev as the 'Negev of the Cherethites [Cretans]', which formed part of the Philistine pale, as well as by David's mercenary corps, 'the Cherethites and Pelethites', the latter obscure term apparently a variant of 'Philistines'. Indirect evidence of the Cretan origin of the Philistines may perhaps be found in the so-called Phaestos disc, discovered in Crete and dating from the middle of the second millennium. Its script is as yet undeciphered, but one of the pictographs recurring on the disc portrays the head of a man wearing the typical feathered headgear of the Philistines.

Biblical tradition in this respect tallies with the 'Aegean' hypothesis, which argues that the Philistines and the Sea Peoples in general hailed from the Aegean isles and the Greek mainland. Counter to this view is the 'Anatolian' hypothesis, which favours a homeland along the western and southern seaboard of Asia Minor. Support for this latter theory has been sought within Greek epic tradition, where Perseus and Mopsus, linked to the Daneans (one of the Sea Peoples) and to Asia Minor, do battle in the coastal towns of Palestine – the first fighting a sea monster off Jaffa and the second actually conquering Ashkelon. But the main support for this view is drawn from late classical historians who, for instance, would trace the Philistine homeland to Lydia or describe the head-dress of the people of Caria as identical to the type of feathered helmet worn by the Philistines. The conflicting views on the origins of the Sea Peoples may in fact be resolved by relying on those classical traditions of which Herodotus is an example, which argue in favour of a Cretan origin even for the peoples of western Asia Minor (such as the Lydians and Carians). Unfortunately, the historical value of these traditions is doubtful. The geographical dividing line that has been seized upon by both the 'Aegean' and 'Anatolian' schools, however, seems unwarrantedly rigid and artificial. Indeed, for seafaring nations of the calibre of of the Sea Peoples, the coasts of Asia Minor and Greece, together with the Aegean isles, formed one organic world where inextricable links connected shore with shore.

Hence the thrust of the Sea Peoples, the Philistines among them, swept across from both the Aegean Sea and the coasts of Asia Minor.

In addition to these geographical aspects, the ethnic and linguistic identity of the Philistines has proved a vexing problem for historians and philologists. The very few Philistine words and proper names that have survived offer only limited clues. The most distinctive term, *seren* (the Bible, incidentally, knows only the plural, *seranim*), the appellative of the rulers of the Philistine cities parallels the Greek τύραννος in form and meaning, though the term seems in fact to have entered Greek from some early Indo-European language. Other apparently Philistine words are *qova* or *kova*, 'helmet', and *argaz*, 'box', for which Indo-European etymologies have been suggested. Two distinctly Philistine personal names in the Bible are Goliath and Achish ('Αγχοуς in the Septuagint), the ruler of Gath. The first has been compared to the name of the Lydian monarch Alyattes (Walwatta in its earlier form) and the second to the Homeric hero Anchises, of Illyrian descent and mentioned in the Illiad. Recently several names of apparently Philistine rulers appearing in the Wen-amon tale have been identified as characteristic of the south-west Anatolian or Luwian dialect group (an Indo-European language with very early Anatolian admixtures). From all this it has become clear that the Philistines, like the other Sea Peoples, were of Indo-European stock – but of which specific branch remains unclear. They have variously been defined as Luwians or Illyrians (*i.e.,* tribes originating in the Balkans, evidence for which supposedly lies in the names of the Palaeste and the river Palaistinos in Illyria), or even as the mysterious Pelasgians (referred to in the sources as the pre-Greek population of Greece, the Aegean islands and the western seaboard of Asia Minor). The two latter opinions are not necessarily contradictory, as some affinity does exist between the Pelasgians and the Illyrians.

Above all, the Philistine material civilization, unearthed in Palestine and alien to the local culture, reveals strong links with the lands of the eastern Mediterranean Basin. This affinity is most marked in the Philistine pottery, which is derived from the late Mycenaean ceramic ware (known as Mycenaean III C 1) found at Cyprus, Rhodes, the southern Anatolian littoral and even the Greek mainland. The Philistine pottery of the twelfth and the first half of the eleventh century is characteristically bichromatic (red and black), bearing geometric and animal designs, with fish and bird motifs taking pride of place. In addition to wares intended for daily use, vessels and clay figurines of a ritual character have been discovered at sites such as Ashdod and Gezer, these too being reminiscent of the late Mycenaean style. Several seals bearing marks of Aegean influence also have been found in Philistine levels at Megiddo, Tell Qasile, Tell el-Far‘ah (Sharuhen) and Ashdod (those at the last site even bearing signs resembling Cypro-Minoan script). Another find often indicative of the Philistines and other Sea Peoples (though adapted from the Egyptians) are the anthropoid clay coffins discovered at Tell el-Far‘ah, Lachish and Beth-shean. The head-ornamentation as seen on the coffin lids, especially at Beth-shean, strongly resembles the Philistine soldiers with their characteristic helmets, as depicted on Egyptian reliefs from the period of Rameses III.

These reliefs in Rameses' temple at Medinet Habu, near Thebes, offer a clear notion of the physical appearance of the Philistines and other Sea Peoples and of their armament. They also depict their warships and chariots, as well as their wagons for transportation. Certain of the details of weaponry differ somewhat from the biblical description of Goliath (I Samuel 17:4–7); a combination of the two sources, however, produces the impression of a tall people, clean shaven (in this respect unlike the Semites) and armed in the finest tradition of the Aegean and Homeric warrior. Goliath is described wearing a bronze helmet, a coat of mail and bronze greaves. According to the biblical narrative, the heavily armed soldiers often had recourse to a shield bearer, while offensive weaponry consisted of the spear and a long, straight-blade sword. The bow was not at first used by them, but it may have been introduced later (see I Samuel 31:3). An instructive remark in the Goliath story refers to the head of his spear as being made of iron, an innovation in Palestinian weaponry (although for 'spear' perhaps one should read here 'sword', which appears further along in the story but is absent from the details of his armament). Iron manufacture must indeed be listed among the technological attainments of the Philistines, one that accounted for their military success (see page 86). Actual iron objects from the twelfth and eleventh centuries have been discovered at sites with which the Philistines had direct and indirect contact, for example Tell Qasile, Tell Jemmeh, Tell el-Far'ah, Tell Aiytun, Tell el-Ful and Megiddo.

Philistine material culture may be defined as eclectic from its very inception. As the Philistines absorbed various influences in the course of migration and later as colonists in Canaan, their culture tended to adapt rapidly to the immediate environment, to the point that its own distinctive character was completely submerged. Thus the distinctive Philistine pottery steadily deteriorated until it disappeared completely in the latter half of the eleventh century. The assimilative process was most marked in the non-material sphere, such as in the change-over to the Canaanite tongue and essentially also in their adoption of the Canaanite religion. The Philistine pantheon, as revealed in the Bible, is clearly Canaanite, with gods such as Dagon, in whose honour they erected sanctuaries at Gaza, Ashdod and Beth-shean (Judges 16:23; I Samuel 5:1–7; and I Chronicles 10:10); or Baal-zebub (more correctly to be read as Baal-zebul), whose cult was practised in Ekron (II Kings 1:2ff.). Both these deities, it should be noted, had been venerated earlier, especially at the port city of Ugarit, where, interestingly, many Ashdodite merchants seem to have settled. Recently, however, remains pointing to a specific cult among the Philistines were discovered at Ashdod (a figurine of a female deity) and at Tell Qasile (a complete sanctuary).

Philistine Hegemony in Palestine and the Wars with the Israelites

Although culturally the Philistines assimilated quite readily into the indigenous population of the country, on the political and military level they attained country-wide supremacy as heirs to the weakened Egyptian rule in Palestine during the second half of the twelfth century – a position that they lost only in the days of David. Philistine settlement, initially under the aegis of Egypt, was concentrated along the country's fertile southern coastal plain. The sector, known in the Bible as 'all the borders of the Philistines', extended 'from Sihor which is before Egypt even unto the borders of Ekron northward' (Joshua 13:2–3). Five major Philistine towns were established here, three on or near the coast – Gaza, Ashkelon and Ashdod – and two, Gath and Ekron, in the Shephelah further east. The first three were Egyptian centres until relatively late, as is indicated by a reference to them in an Egyptian document (known as the 'Onomasticon of Amenope') dating from the late twelfth century. At Ashdod, furthermore, an Egyptian inscription of the Nineteenth or Twentieth Dynasty was found on a lintel of the city gate. On the other hand, it seems that Gath (perhaps Tell eṣ-Ṣafi) and Ekron (probably Khirbet el-Muqanna were built by the Philistines at a later stage, on the ruins of Canaanite settlements that had been semi-independent.

According to the Bible, the Philistines were not united in a national state with a single ruler at its head (*cf.* page 34); they had established a confederacy of city-states with a central sanctuary. At its peak this league included all five cities – the Philistine pentapolis (Joshua 13:2; Judges 3:3; and I Samuel 6:4, 16–18) – headed by the five local *seranim*, in whose hands lay supreme political, military and religious control. In fateful hours they would convene and act upon a majority decision (see I Samuel 5:8–11 and 29:1–7). The confederacy of five cities, as has been noted, seems to have crystallized only at a late stage, perhaps on the eve of the battle of Aphek, in the mid-eleventh century. It may be no mere coincidence that the Samson cycle, reflecting an earlier historical phase, makes reference only to Gaza and Ashkelon, even though the other three cities were closer to the scene of Samson's exploits. Most surprising is the complete absence of Ekron, in the vicinity of Timnah (the latter figuring in the Samson cycle as the major town in the Sorek Valley); the reason for this must surely be sought in the fact that Ekron achieved status as a member of the confederacy only at a later date. Conversely, we note that the stories dealing with the battle at Aphek and the subsequent moving of the Ark of the Covenant do mention Ashdod, Gath and Ekron; Timnah, on the other hand, is absent here despite its location on the route from Ekron to Beth-shemesh, along which the Ark travelled when being returned to the Israelites.

Moreover, it is apparent that the Philistine league was not a static organization. With the passage of time, its centre of gravity shifted from one city to another, at least as far as its confrontation with Israel was concerned. Initially it appears that Gaza functioned as the focal point, inheriting its central position from the Egyptian administration of Canaan (see page 15). This may be inferred from the Samson narrative, which relates that the judge was brought there and that the Philistine leaders convened in its temple (Judges 16:23). From there the focus transferred to Ashdod, the primary force in the war of Aphek; at this point it was the temple of Dagon at Ashdod to which the sacred Ark of the Israelites was transported as a trophy. Only later did the centre of power pass to Gath and Ekron (I Samuel 5:1ff.). Towards the end of the eleventh century, Gath apparently assumed the primacy, as may be gathered from its status as the main Philistine city at the time of Saul and David.

From the coastal region the Philistines and the other Sea Peoples who had settled in the country fanned out eastwards, a process that was accelerated by population growth and the influx of new migrants. The various directions that this movement took may be gleaned from archaeological findings, in particular the typical Philistine pottery found in fair abundance and dating from the late twelfth and early eleventh centuries. At two important junctions *en route* from the Shephelah to the hill district – Gezer and Beth-shemesh – a wealth of Philistine pottery has been uncovered. Varying quantities were also discovered along the northern perimeter of the Negev, at such sites as Tell esh-Shari'a and Tel Masos, west and east of Beersheba, respectively, and along the Via Maris, at Aphek (Rosh ha-'Ayin), Megiddo and Afula. Interestingly enough, Philistine pottery has recently been unearthed even at Dan in the north, but such widespread distribution may be attributed to trade rather than actual settlement. Another surprising recent discovery is that of Philistine-type pottery at Tell Deir Alla (probably ancient Succoth) in Trans-Jordan, which points to the influence of the Sea Peoples even in this distant spot. In a slightly earlier level at this site, clay tablets have been found inscribed in a script that has so far defied decipherment; it bears some similarity to Minoan Linear script, yet another allusion to an Aegean source. Here too the appearance of Sea Peoples must surely have followed in the wake of Egyptian rule (see pages 25 f.).

The increasing Philistine penetration into the interior of the mountain areas and the growing Philistine dominion over much of the Israelite populace are borne out mainly by biblical, but also by archaeological, testimony. Philistine pottery has turned up at such places as Tell Beit Mirsim and to the north-east in the tombs at Tell Aiytun, at Beth-zur in the Judean hills and at Bethel and Mizpah in the central mountain range. It is even possible that the fortress at Tell el-Ful (Gibeah of Benjamin), dating from the latter half of the eleventh century, is also Philistine. The Bible speaks of Philistine governors at Gibeath-elohim, which was probably identical with this Gibeah (I Samuel 10:5), and at Geba (I Samuel 13:3), as well as at Bethlehem in the Judean hills (the text in II Samuel 23:14 reads: 'the *garrison* of the Philistines', while the parallel in I Chronicles 11:16 reads: '*commissioner* of the Philistines' [author's italics]).

The Philistines obtained dominion over the Canaanites and the Israelites by virtue of their technological and military superiority, which in turn was the outcome of perfected weaponry and a professional, well-trained army led by a military *élite*. The organization of the armed forces in Philistine warfare at the time of Saul is indicated by two terms: *mashhith* and *mazzab* (I Samuel 13:17, 23). The first designated mobile expeditionary forces that made forays from bases in Philistia, while the second referred to small garrison units stationed in strategically placed towns in the interior of the country. In this dual division, as well as in other military matters, the Philistines patterned themselves on the system of the Egyptian occupation forces in Canaan, as may be deduced, for instance, from the El-Amarna documents. Like the Egyptians, the Philistine striking-force was supported by chariotry (I Samuel 13:5), which acted in concert with archers. This may be inferred also from a synoptic reading of I Samuel 31:3 and II Samuel 1:6, both noting that Saul was hard-pressed at Mount Gilboa – in the one instance by archers and in the other by chariotry. The Philistine *mashhith* was sometimes deployed in three detachments (I Samuel 13:17), in the style of Seti I's punitive expedition in the Beth-shean Valley (see page

23). With the aid of such units, the Philistines were able to suppress any Israelite attempt at rebellion, exact taxes from them and make matters even more difficult by maintaining a monopoly over metal manufacture. In this way they achieved the two-pronged goal of preventing both Israelite rearmament and the development of its industry (I Samuel 13:19–22).

Hints of the tangled relationship between the Philistines and the Israelites during the period of the Judges can be perceived in the Samson cycle. For all its legendary and anecdotal aura, the tale accurately depicts the fluctuations in these relations, from the evolvement of good-neighbourly ties and even occasional nuptial bonds to strife that erupted into bloody encounters. Although Samson represents the tribe of Dan, the cycle is basically an expression of Philistine pressure upon Judah, several of whose districts had already fallen to the Philistines (Judges 15:11). The decisive moment in the struggle between Israel and the Philistines occurred in the middle of the eleventh century, in the battle of Eben-ezer and Aphek. At this time the tribes of the 'house of Joseph', which had hitherto preserved their independence in the central hill country, went down in defeat (I Samuel 4). The real goal sought by the Philistines in this campaign is revealed by their selection of Aphek (Tel Rosh ha-'Ayin), at the western approaches to Mount Ephraim, as their rallying-point. The Israelites, opposite them at Eben-ezer (in the vicinity of Migdal-zedek), attempted to intercept the enemy advance into the heart of the hill region but were routed and their centre at Shiloh destroyed. Its destruction is not explicitly mentioned in the biblical account but would appear to be confirmed by archaeological excavations at the site, as well as at other key places that were razed at the time. The sacking of Shiloh and the total defeat of the Israelites remained a grim recollection in later Scripture (Jeremiah 7:12–14 and 26:9; Psalms 78:60; and *cf.* the poetic passage in Deuteronomy 32:21ff., which may also allude to these events).

The severity of the disaster looms even larger when one recalls the status previously enjoyed by Shiloh. It had served as the primary (though not the sole) national and religious centre, where the holy Sanctuary and the Ark of the Covenant reposed. Here was the seat of the priestly house of Eli, and it was to Shiloh that the Israelites repaired for festivals and convocations (Judges 21:19; and I Samuel 1:3ff.). Eli's two sons, Hofni and Pinhas, were killed in the battle, followed soon thereafter by their father's death. (Eli's priestly lineage is not fully known, but his descendants continued in their sacral tasks until the days of Solomon.) Israel's grief was compounded by the Philistine capture of the Ark of the Covenant, which had hastily been brought to the field of battle. Its seizure symbolized the subjugation of the entire tribal confederacy of Israel. From now on the Philistines ruled without restraint, at least over the Israelites in the central part of the country.

However, at this difficult period for Israel, redemption was approaching in the guise of Samuel, the prophet and judge, who was to lead the nation to liberation and revive its flagging spirits. The defeat that threatened Israel's very existence led to a fundamental transformation in the life of the nation, giving new meaning to the phrase 'The Glory of Israel will not fail' (I Samuel 15:29). Awakening to its own latent potential in the struggle for life and death against the Philistine oppressor, the nation of Israel constituted itself as a monarchy in the final quarter of the eleventh century.

PART II

The Period of the First Temple, the Babylonian Exile and the Restoration

Hayim Tadmor

7

The United Monarchy

Samuel the Seer

The bleak period from the destruction of Shiloh to the beginning of Saul's war against the Philistines is spanned by the leadership of Samuel, the 'seer' (c. 1050 BCE). The biblical books that bear his name offer only a fragmentary account of his activities, and from the sources it is difficult to obtain a coherent picture of this religious and political leader. On the one hand, he was a judge (his sons also served as judges in Beersheba [see I Samuel 8:2]) who played an important role as a charismatic leader of the people until the advent of the monarchy. The sphere of his activities was the territory of Benjamin and Ephraim which, at the time, was under severe pressure from the Philistines. On the other hand, he was apprenticed to a priest in the Sanctuary of the Lord at Shiloh, and he offered up sacrifices at central shrines. Both a Mishnaic reference and a Dead Sea Scroll fragment refer to him as a 'Nazirite' and as a 'seer', foretelling the future through oracles. However, his relation to institutional prophecy is not very clear, although in I Samuel 19:20 he is described as heading a guild of ecstatic prophets known as 'the sons of the prophets', an active religious and social force. This guild helped to instigate the national awakening that was eventually to lead to the foundation of the monarchy and to liberation from the Philistine yoke. Another factor of significance is that Samuel's leadership passed on to his sons. He appointed them as 'judges over Israel . . . in Beersheba' (I Samuel 8:1–2). Their only right to rule derived from the fact that they were the sons of the recognized leader of the people. This fact, in itself, is of importance when one comes to consider the demand of the people for a permanent, hereditary leadership, that is a king.

The last stage of Samuel's career is recorded in the sources in greater detail. I Samuel 9–10 attributes to him the selection and coronation of Saul, the first king, despite his personal opposition to the institution of monarchy. With great reluctance he acceded to the popular demand: 'Make us a king to rule [lit., to 'judge'] us like all the nations' (I Samuel 8:5). The biblical account stresses that Samuel supported Saul during his initial period as monarch but finally quarrelled with him and withdrew from political activity, shifting his support to David, the newly emerging leader. The historicity of this account has often been questioned, especially as the Books of Samuel, which were edited in a spirit hostile to Saul and favourable to

David, attempted in their portrayal of Samuel to link together the last leader of the period of the Judges and the founder of the permanent royal dynasty, while excluding Saul's family.

King Saul

It is difficult to assess the historical validity of the conflicting traditions concerning Saul's accession to the throne. It appears, however, that Saul emerged as a military leader, on the pattern of the leaders in the period of the Judges, when he came to the rescue of Jabesh-gilead, the Trans-Jordanian city whose inhabitants were related to his tribe, the Benjaminites (see Judges 21:8ff.). There he defeated the Ammonites, whereupon he was crowned king at Gilgal near the Jordan (I Samuel 11:15).

After this victory he naturally turned his efforts towards Israel's main enemy, the Philistines, and his struggle with them dominated the remainder of his reign. The long conflict opened with Saul's victory over a Philistine garrison situated between Geba and Michmash (I Samuel 14:5), where he employed tactics familiar from the period of the Judges – a misleading feint followed by a sudden attack. This victory marked the onset of full hostilities throughout the mountain area of Benjamin and Ephraim. It is described in epic style as a 'one-day' war, a literary device employed by the biblical narrator when dealing with campaigns that are decisive for their eras, such as Joshua's war at Gibeon. The close of this first campaign, as of those that followed, is recorded with the utmost brevity: 'Then Saul went up from following the Philistines: and the Philistines went to their own place. So Saul took the kingdom over Israel, and fought against all his enemies on every side, against Moab, and against the children of Ammon, and against Edom, and against the kings of Zobah, and against the Philistines: and whithersoever he turned himself, he vexed them' (I Samuel 14:46–7). We are given no information about his other wars, except the one against Amalek (I Samuel 15:1–9), which is included only to point out that Saul lost his crown through failing to obey Samuel's orders. Yet, in the final analysis, with his base of power at his birth-place, Gibeah (which has been identified as Tell el-Ful, some 5 kilometres north of Jerusalem), Saul succeeded in uniting most of the tribes of Israel. Socially and politically, Saul's reign was a period of transition. The tribal and patriarchal systems gave way to fresh developments that were fully implemented only in the days of David and Solomon. In his personal character Saul was a brave soldier, free from regal pomp (unlike the Canaanite kings) and, above all, a charismatic leader (I Samuel 10:10, 11:6, 22:6). These qualities indicate that the first king was rooted in the Israelite society of the period of the Judges, sharing its conceptions and way of life. Indeed, these are valid reasons to regard Saul as the last of the 'Judges' as well as the first of the kings.

Saul introduced major innovations in the military sphere. His objectives did not allow him to remain satisfied with warrior bands that responded to the summons of their leader in emergencies and returned to their tribes and estates when the war was over. A standing army was needed; thus 'when Saul saw any strong man, or any valient man, he took him unto him' (I Samuel 14:52). Though divided into units of hundreds and thousands (I Samuel 22:7), this new army continued to be organized on the basis of the traditional tribal and territorial structure. Thus, for example, all the sons of Jesse (David's father) served in the same army unit (I Samuel 17:18).

The major change that came about in Saul's time concerned the social structure. A new class arose with a special relationship to the king, and it was drawn, naturally, from members of his family and tribe. Saul granted them estates (see I Samuel 22:7), apparently from lands conquered from the Philistines or taken from the Gibeonite cities. Until his time the latter had maintained an autonomous framework (see Part I), but Saul ruthlessly crushed them (see II Samuel 21:1–5). The granting of land to those close to the leader was novel in Israel but customary in ancient Near Eastern states. A close parallel is offered by the Akkadian documents from the royal archives of Ugaritic kings that date from the fourteenth and thirteenth centuries BCE. These documents illustrate 'the manner of the king' as described in I Samuel 8:11ff., such as the right of the monarch to recruit men for his army and impose a tithe on agricultural produce. He was also entitled to exempt court officials ('royal servants') from all such obligations. (The technical term for this right in Ugaritic documents is *zukku,* literally, to make one 'clean', that is, exempt or free [see I Samuel 17:25].)

In Israel there was considerable opposition to these changes. The narrator expressed this by the sharp criticism of autocracy, ascribing this criticism to Samuel himself (I Samuel 8:1). The warning 'this will be the manner of the king that shall reign over you' continues with a detailed survey of royal actions that formed the essence of this practice. The condemnation repeatedly stresses that violent and arbitrary confiscation, exploitation of the individual and seizure of his property by the ruler constitute the outstanding characteristics of monarchy. The survey ends ominously: 'And ye shall cry out in that day because of your king which ye shall have chosen you; and the Lord will not hear you in that day' (I Samuel 8:18). In other words, once the monarchy has been established there will be no respite from its tyranny. As against this royal exploitation, the narrator portrays, in the words of Samuel, the modesty and benevolence of the traditional 'Judge': 'I am old and grayheaded . . . and I have walked before you from my childhood unto this day. Behold, here I am: witness against me . . . whose ox have I taken? or whose ass have I taken? or whom have I defrauded? whom have I oppressed? or of whose hand have I received any bribe to blind mine eyes therewith?' (I Samuel 12:2–3).

Indeed, the final period of Saul's reign is marked by the struggle between an increasingly tyrannical king and the traditional leadership that had formerly ruled. In the biblical narrative this opposition appears in the form of antagonism between Saul and Samuel. It may be that the slaying of the priests of Nob on Saul's orders (I Samuel 22:16–18) was part of the struggle between these two social elements. David, the young rival of Saul, shrewdly exploited these differences and derived the maximum benefit from them.

Many of the stories in the first Book of Samuel describe David's rise at Saul's court. Although they have been edited in a manner hostile to Saul, intended to glorify David in retrospect, the figure of Saul towards the end of his life emerges as that of a torn and tragic individual. It is possible that this internal struggle for power in the youthful Kingdom of Israel led the Philistines to believe that the time had come to strike a final blow at Saul and his kingdom. Saul's last battle at Gilboa is described indirectly in the sources. It seems that the Philistines employed a completely new stratagem. They sent their forces to the weakest point in Saul's kingdom, the remnants of the Canaanite cities in the Jezreel and Beth-shean valleys, which apparently were still semi-autonomous. Perhaps their intention was to split his kingdom in two, or to force him to descend from the mountains into the valley, where they could exploit the military superiority of their chariots. Saul had no alternative but to join battle in the foot-hills of the Gilboa range (I Samuel 28:4 and 29: 1ff.). His army was defeated, and he, along with his sons, met a heroic death. The Philistines occupied Beth-shean, and, although nothing is recorded of their penetration into the mountain areas, it may be assumed that they imposed their authority over the entire area of Saul's former kingdom. The outcome of the defeat was that Saul's kingdom was split in two. While the area across the Jordan and in the mountains remained faithful to Saul's son Eshbaal (or Ish-bosheth) and Saul's general and strongman, Abner, in the south David was appointed king of Judah.

The Reign of David (1004–965)

The Davidic era offers the most comprehensive and detailed account of any period in biblical history. In common with the great kingdoms of the ancient Near East, the Davidic court employed scribes trained to record the manifold needs of the growing and prosperous state. Both the census (see II Samuel 24) and the division of lands for taxation purposes required written records and led to the compilation of geographical lists delineating tribal and familial boundaries, as well as detailed genealogies. This valuable historical material is preserved in the first nine chapters of I Chronicles and in Joshua 15–16. Yet the main source for the Davidic period is the narrative centred around David himself, recounting David's origins, his struggle against Saul for the throne (I Samuel 18–26), his reign and finally the tragic struggle for succession among his sons (II Samuel 10–20). This narrative is unique in the historical literature of the ancient Near East. Written realistically and with a rare literary talent, it gives the reader an insight into the social life of the royal household. Its singularity lies in the author's application of moral standards in the account of his hero. For example, the exalted king is depicted as having had committed a grave sin by sending Uriah the Hittite to his death so that he could marry Uriah's wife. As a result, the personal calamities within his family – the murder of Amnon and the revolt of Absalom – are regarded as a divine punishment for this deed: 'The sword shall never depart from thine house' (II Samuel 12:10). The use of such standards in respect to the 'Lord's anointed', the founder of the dynasty, shows a degree of literary freedom not witnessed anywhere else in the ancient Near East. Thus the very compilation of the history of King David's era was influenced by a novelty that matched the revolutionary and innovatory character of his reign.

The Rise of David

The historical material indicates four stages in the rise of David. The first is from the emergence of David, the son of Jesse of Bethlehem, at the court of King Saul until his marriage to the king's daughter Michal. There are two versions or traditions concerning this stage. One (I Samuel 16:16ff.) tells of the 'man that can play well' who is brought from the flocks to the royal court in order to play on the harp for Saul when the king is distressed by 'the evil spirit'. Saul loved him 'and he became his armourbearer' (I Samuel 16:21). According to the other version (I Samuel 17), Saul came to know David only after the youth had slain a Philistine champion in the Valley of Sochoh. What the two traditions relate in common is that in due course David became a successful and highly popular military leader.

In the second stage David escapes from Saul's jealousy, when the latter attempts to kill him, and flees from place to place, hiding in the borderlands of the tribe of Judah. He becomes the head of a roving band that includes both the persecuted and those outcasts who cannot find their place in the established social order, 'every one that was in distress, and every one that was in debt, and every one that was discontented . . . and he became a captain over them' (I Samuel 22:2). His followers initially numbered 400 men and grew to 600. Their nucleus was 'the thirty', the unit of warriors whose names and origins have been preserved in II Samuel 23 and I Chronicles 11. Most of the warriors came from Judah and Benjamin and a few from the neighbouring peoples. Basically, this troop resembled the companies of 'vain and light persons' (Judges 9:4 and 11:3), landless and marginal groups in society, who have already been mentioned in connexion with Abimelech and Jephthah. These groups, of course, constituted a threat to the established tribal society. Mainly for this reason, neither David nor his men found support even within his own clan. The southern clans, comprised mainly of shepherds, remained faithful to Saul, who had defended them in the past from the Amalekites. David was therefore compelled to move out into the desert, where he again found no refuge. In due course he even collaborated with the Philistines, the traditional enemy of Israel, and became a protégé of Achish, the king of Gath, from whom he received the city of Ziklag near Lachish, at the south-western approaches to Judah. At this, the third stage, David found himself between the hammer and the anvil: on the one hand he had to prove his loyalty to the Philistines as an enemy of Israel, while at the same time he sought to establish ties with the elders of the clans of southern Judah, the Calebites, the Jerahmeelites and the Kenites of Hebron. In order to win their favour, he followed Saul's practice of raiding their traditional enemy, the Amalekites.

During the severe political crisis that followed Saul's defeat and death at Gilboa, the ties between Judah and the northern tribes were weakened, giving David the opportunity to establish himself within the territory of Judah. David, his household and his whole company therefore proceeded to Hebron, 'and they dwelt in the cities of Hebron' (II Samuel 2:2–3). The elders of Judah, now faced with this *fait accompli,* came to terms with David by making him the king of Judah. The reason for this was not so much fear as the desire that his efficient army protect them from their enemies.

This action to some extent restored the situation to what it had been in the days of the Judges, when Judah had been separate from the other tribes.

The coronation of David in Hebron marked the fourth stage in his rise to power. According to II Samuel 2:11 and 5:5, David ruled over Judah in Hebron for seven years and six months, although the exact length of his stay and the order of events are not completely clear. The period of his rule in Hebron was marked by bitter fighting between the forces of Abner, who represented the Saulite dynasty, which was regarded as legitimate by the northern tribes, and of Joab, who headed David's army. Saul's son Eshbaal was killed, as far as can be judged, only two years after he had been made king (see II Samuel 2:10); yet some time passed before the northern tribes recognized David as the king of Israel. At this transitional stage, while Ishbosheth was still alive, Abner, the regent of the Saulite dynasty, entered into collusion with David, concluded a pact and promised him the support of all Israel. His price was that he would become David's general in place of Joab. The role of the general as the strongman at court is illustrated by the story of Abner's murder (II Samuel 3:27–39). Joab, who assassinated Abner in a blood feud, was only reprimanded. All David could do was to lament Abner's death and state that Joab and his brother were 'too hard' for him and that the matter of punishment must be left to divine justice (*ibid.*, 39).

The death of Ishbosheth and Abner marked the end of the Saulite dynasty. At this point the elders of Israel came to Hebron and offered David the monarchy (II Samuel 5:1–3), apparently because it became evident that now David was the only leader capable of heading the people in the war against the Philistines. The form of his election assumed the character of a covenant between David and the elders of Israel that was confirmed 'before the Lord', that is, in the local temple of Hebron. This covenant was later to determine the course of events at critical moments of David's reign. Until the end of his rule, David remained the king of Judah and Israel, that is, of two bodies separate from each other both institutionally and in the eyes of their own inhabitants.

David, King of Israel

When David became the king of all Israel in the year 1004, he faced the same objectives as had Saul – liberation of the country from the Philistine yoke and its unification under his rule. The sources do not indicate clearly the order of David's wars against the Philistines, nor the stages in which the country was unified. The historical chronicles (the most significant of which are II Samuel 8 and 10) have preserved only a summary account of his campaigns against the neighbouring peoples of Moab, Ammon, Edom and Aram, as well as of his forays against the Philistines. The latter campaigns must have commenced while he was still in Hebron and increased in intensity after the conquest of Jebus (Jerusalem). The major clashes apparently took place in the vicinity of Bethlehem and Jerusalem (II Samuel 5:17–24). In a series of battles in which he more than once risked his own life (see II Samuel 21:15–17), David succeeded in forcing the Philistines out of the mountains and driving them to the edge of the foot-hills. It may be assumed that at the end of these campaigns the five cities of Philistia concluded a treaty with David and probably even acknowledged his sovereignty over them. In point of fact, from the time of David until after the death of Uzziah the Philistines never attacked Judah or infringed upon its territory. The age-old animosity with Philistia had come to an end. We even find Cretan and Philistine units (referred to as Cherethites and Pelethites) serving David, as well as a military commander named Ittai of Gath, with his force of Gittites who originated from the time of David's stay at Gath (II Samuel 15:18) and who remained loyal to David during the revolt of Absalom.

After defeating the Philistines, David appears to have annexed the remaining large Canaanite enclaves, such as Megiddo, Taanach and Beth-shean. The biblical account makes no express mention of such annexations, with the single exception of Jerusalem, whose conquest prepared the way for closer ties between Judah, Benjamin and the northern tribes. As a 'neutral' area not belonging to any of the tribes, an area that had become the personal property of the king by right of conquest, Jerusalem was particularly well suited to serve as his capital. By this move David demonstrated his pan-tribal status as the king of both Judah and Israel. The topographical situation of the city made it a natural fortress, increasing the king's security and stabilizing his position. David not only concentrated his ministers and warriors in Jerusalem, but he also brought there the symbol of tribal unity, the Ark of the Covenant (I Samuel 14:3, 22:9, 20), together with the priestly family of the sons of Abiathar, descendants of Eli, the priest of Shiloh. In this way he also transformed his new capital into a religious centre.

With the geographical unity of Israel thus accomplished, David turned his attention to imperial expansion, an ambition that was considerably aided by the international situation. The large empires that had determined the fate of western Asia on the eve of the Conquest were now in a period of decline. Egypt's greatness was past, the Hittite Kingdom had been destroyed two centuries before and Assyria had not yet emerged as a major power. After the defeat of the Philistines, the principal rivals of Israel were the Aramean states in Syria, headed by Aram-zobah. The struggle with them was to determine the position of David's kingdom in the contemporary international balance of power, although David did not initiate the inevitable war. It arose from a dispute between Israel and her eastern neighbours beyond the Jordan River, the Ammonites (see Part I on the early relations between the tribes of Israel and Ammon), who called on Aram-beth-rehob, Aram-zobah and the king of Maachah for aid (II Samuel 10:6). In the bitter campaign that followed, there were three decisive engagements. The first battle, near Rabbath-ammon, was fought on two fronts: the royal guard faced the Ammonites, while 'the choice men of Israel' fought against the Arameans (II Samuel 10:9). The second battle, against the Aramean confederacy of states drawn from both sides of the Euphrates, was fought at Helam in Bashan. In the third engagement David attacked Hadadezer, the king of Zobah, when the latter, it would appear, was engaged in a war with the Assyrians (II Samuel 8:3–6). He defeated Hadadezer, conquering Damascus and extending his dominion as far as the Euphrates.

With the conquest of Moab and Edom, the Kingdom of Israel expanded beyond the geopolitical framework of Canaan and its immediate neighbours to exert an active influence on international trade policy, for now the king had gained control over the entire length of the important trade route known as the 'King's Highway', running from Edom to Damascus. In the north the boundaries of David's realm reached the neo-Hittite state of Hamath, which had been under pressure from Aram-zobah. Toi, the king of Hamath, recognized the hegemony of David and sent him gifts (II Samuel 8:9–10). In the north-west David's influence reached the Phoenician ports of Tyre and Sidon, with which he established a close alliance that was to grow even firmer during the days of Solomon. This alliance, which served the interests of both states, opened new economic horizons for David's kingdom. Now Israel could supply oil and grain to Tyre, receiving in return cedar wood, copper and various luxuries for the royal court.

In this newly flourishing kingdom, far-reaching social and administrative changes occurred. The court had become the administrative centre and had thus given rise to a new class, the court officials, who were given the new title of 'royal servants'. In setting up this new administration, David followed the established patterns of the ancient cities of Canaan and of certain neighbouring countries. Indeed, it has been generally assumed that several of David's leading officials, such as Shavsha, (or Sheva) the scribe, and Adoram, in charge of the corvée, were non-Israelites in origin, as their names and the very nature of their offices imply.

A list of David's leading court officials is to be found in II Samuel 8:16–18 (see also I Chronicles 18:15–18) and II Samuel 20:23–6. Both lists are headed by the commander-in-chief of the army, Joab, who is described as commanding 'over the host' in one list and as commanding 'over all the host of Israel' in the other. Another military office was that of the commander of the Cherethites and the Pelethites, the king's body-guard. The lists include several offices belonging to what would today be called the diplomatic and civil administration and which, as far as can be seen, were new to Israel. As was mentioned, the names of the individuals and the definition of their duties show that they were modelled after the pattern found in the state administrations and royal courts of the region. There appear a *mazkir* ('recorder'), most probably the royal herald who announced royal edicts, and a *sopher* ('scribe'), whose principal responsibility was the exchange of correspondence with neighbouring rulers and who, therefore, required a familiarity with foreign languages and with contemporary diplomatic protocol. These offices became an inseparable part of the royal court. Even after the division of the kingdom, Judah retained David's system of administration, and the offices of the herald and the scribe continued until the destruction of the Temple. When Sennacherib invaded Judah in the reign of Hezekiah, both officers appear in the three-man delegation headed by the official 'over the household' (II Kings 18:18), an office that was apparently introduced after David's time (see I Kings 4:6) and that corresponded to the man 'in charge of the house' or 'in charge of the palace' at the courts of Assyrian kings. Another important office-bearer, who is referred to only after the revolt of Absalom, was Adoram (or Adoniram), who was 'in charge of the corvée [*ha-mas* in Hebrew]'and whose importance increased particularly during the reign of Solomon. Two other ministers not included in the lists of II Samuel are mentioned in the narrative, namely, 'David's counsellor', Ahithophel (II Samuel 15:12), and

'David's friend', Hushai the Archite (II Samuel 15:37). Some description of their offices is to be found in the story of Absalom's revolt, when the rebel prince required their advice concerning general policy and military tactics (II Samuel 16:15ff.). Most instructive in respect to the economic history and the contemporary status of the kingdom is the list of ministers of 'the king's treasures' found in I Chronicles 27:25–31. This list, though appearing in a late historiographic composition, is apparently authentic. It records those in charge of the various economic branches: the king's storehouses in the field, the cities, the villages and the citadels; those engaged in field work and the tilling of the soil; the vineyards; the produce of the vineyards intended for the wine cellars; the olive trees and the sycamore trees in the plain and the stores of oil; the cattle grazing in the Sharon and the cattle in the valleys; the camels (which are in the charge of 'Obil the Ishmaelite'); and the breed-asses and the flocks. This list, the only one of its kind for the entire biblical period, reflects the various branches of the extensive agricultural economy. It also provides evidence of the notable increase in royal property, which gave the king a considerable measure of economic independence.

Another phenomenon of major importance for the new dynasty was the emergence of the ideology of a covenant between the God of Israel and the Davidic dynasty, patterned after the Covenant of Sinai between Israel and its God. The new ideology is expressed in the court Psalms: 'I have made a covenant with my chosen/I have sworn unto David my servant/Thy seed will I establish for ever/and build up thy throne to all generations' (Psalms 89:3–4; and see Psalms 132:10–14). The corollary of this court ideology was that the king had a sacral status and the right to engage in cultic functions. A clear expression of this view is found in Psalm 110, apparently addressed to the king by a court poet: 'The Lord hath sworn, and will not repent, Thou art a priest for ever after the order of Melchizedek.' This establishes a nexus between the king of Israel, whose capital is Jerusalem, and Melchizedek, who in this psalm symbolizes the priest-king of Jerusalem in the pre-Israelite tradition (see Genesis 14:18). It is not surprising, therefore, that David's sons officiated as priests (II Samuel 8:18). The chronicler, who viewed this as an aberration, emended 'priests' to read 'chief about the king' (I Chronicles 18:17). This reference and the fact that the lists of royal ministers include also the priests Abiathar (of the family of Eli) and Zadok, who, according to I Chronicles 16:39, had formerly served at the great high place in Gibeon, indicate that the priesthood was entirely subordinated to the crown.

The Revolt of Absalom

Despite David's political and military achievements and the efficient tools of administration that he introduced, the new régime was unable to become quickly and deeply rooted in the national life. The new administrative system and the rapid political and social changes that had occurred within a brief period primarily affected the traditional institutions of the people. The rise of a new class of 'royal ministers and servants' considerably diminished, although it did not annul, the power and status of the elders and the patriarchal-tribal institutions from the pre-monarchal period. Among certain sections of the people, particularly among the northern tribes, there was a growing dissatisfaction with the regime that found remarkably spontaneous expression in the revolt of Absalom.

The story of the revolt, written almost contemporaneously with the events it describes, is a notable document. It gives us one of our deepest insights into the social structure of ancient Israel by bringing into relief the rift between the old institutions surviving from the period of the Judges and those established by the king. Absalom was supported by two groups, 'the elders of Israel' and 'the men of Israel'. It is clear that these two terms are not used synonymously, for the sources are careful to differentiate between the two, as well as between them and 'the servants of David'. The phrase 'the men of Israel' is not a figure of speech; it is a technical term for the people's militia, called to arms in times of national emergency. It seems to have been the method of expressing national will, as is evidenced by the remarkable fact that as soon as the news of the revolt spread David was left practically without support. Only a few close colleagues, a handful of his ministers and his mercenaries – the Cherethites and Pelethites, who were by definition an alien force – stood by him. It is not even certain whether David's renowned 'thirty mighty men' remained loyal to the king.

There were apparently two main reasons for the early success of the revolt and for Absalom's ability to win over the elders and the national militia. First, there were his promises to revive the ancient forms of government. The new administration with which David had replaced them was regarded by the people as a barrier between them and the king, to whom they looked for justice. Absalom's promises were therefore the ideal tactic for gaining popular support; it is not known whether they were regarded as more than this by the prince, a scion of a royal family on his mother's as well as his father's side (II Samuel 3:4) who could hardly have had a strong attachment to popular institutions. When Absalom entered Jerusalem and assumed the throne, he took care to give the elders of Israel the status of a consultative body to the king even in matters of warfare (see II Samuel 17:4), an arrangement that in any case could not have survived long and that disappeared with the end of the revolt.

The second factor in Absalom's success was the continued existence of the *eleph* ('a thousand' or 'extended family'), the basic military unit of the pre-monarchal army. When the people were recruited to the army on the basis of family and tribe, they were assembled 'by their thousands'. In spite of all his military innovations, David had continued this system of recruitment, thereby retaining the influence of the elders over the army and the people. Thus, when the family heads, the elders, decided to support Absalom, they were easily able to persuade 'the men of Israel' to do the same. Consequently, when David heard that 'the hearts of the men of Israel are after Absalom' (II Samuel 15:13), he realized that virtually the entire country was against him, and he took the only course open to him – flight. Even when David succeeded in gathering forces (mostly from Trans-Jordan) for a confrontation with the rebels, the source states explicitly that it was 'the servants of David' who defeated 'the people of Israel' (II Samuel 18:7).

Changes at the End of David's Reign

The revolt led David to the conclusion that henceforth he had to gain a foothold in the traditional tribal power structure, a decision that had a profound influence on the fate of the united monarchy. He decided to abandon the aims of intertribal equality, according to which he had been operating until then, and to secure himself loyal support within the military and tribal structure of 'the men of Judah', the social and military force of his own tribe. This decision finds expression in the fact that 'the men of Judah', not 'the men of Israel', conducted David and his household across the Jordan (II Samuel 19:41–2) and in the replacement of Joab by Amasa, Absalom's former commander who represented the militia of Judah. This preferential treatment now granted to Judah and not previously attested formed the background of a fresh revolt that broke out among 'the men of Israel' – the term this time designating the militia of the northern tribes only – who declared their disaffection from David even though they had decided, once the death of Absalom was known, 'to bring the king back to his house' (II Samuel 19:11). The leader of this revolt was Sheba ben Bichri of the tribe of Benjamin.

The rebels now called for a separate union of the northern tribes (perhaps under the leadership of a Saulite king [see II Samuel 16:1–8]), as is evident from the cry attributed to their leader: 'We have no part in David, neither have we inheritance in the son of Jesse: every man to his tents, O Israel' (II Samuel 20:1). The aftermath of Absalom's revolt perhaps gave the first indication of the rift between the two entities that were to separate at the fall of the united monarchy. David may have realized that this division could be the consequence of the northerners' slogan, hence his apprehension at Sheba's revolt, as expressed in his words to Abishai: 'Now shall Sheba the son of Bichri do us more harm than did Absalom' (II Samuel 20:6).

Sheba's revolt was suppressed in its early stages, but not by 'the men of Judah', whom Amasa attempted to call together. David sent the 'guard', his professional army, to deal with Sheba, and Amasa, having failed in the task that David had set him, was slain by Joab. Sheba, who had fled to Abel-beth-maachah in Upper Galilee, was executed by the townspeople, and internal peace was restored. David returned to Jerusalem and re-established the royal institutions but did not long survive this rising.

The embers of resistance were still liable to flare up, as we learn from an incident at the end of David's life, when his son Adonijah attempted to win popular support and establish a party of his own. In order to ensure the continuity of the dynasty and prevent its disruption after his death, David elevated Solomon, the son of his favorite wife, Bath-sheba, to the throne while he was still alive. In so doing, he passed over several older sons. Adonijah, David's eldest son after the death of Absalom, was supported by the veteran ministers, including Joab and Abiathar; but Solomon succeeded in establishing himself firmly, and with the aid of Benaiah ben Jehoiada, the head of the retainers, he killed all his opponents and became the undisputed king of Israel and Judah.

The Reign of Solomon (965–928)

Solomon has, like David, been given full and detailed treatment by the biblical historiographer, although in a very different manner, in accordance with the changed circumstances. The focal point had shifted, and the biographical account of an outstanding personality is now replaced by a chronicle – 'the book of the acts of Solomon' – with a totally different grasp of the moving forces of history (I Kings 11.41). The narrator, in recounting the Solomonic period, attributes the political tranquillity and economic well-being of the reign to the king's divine wisdom. He apparently belonged to the circle of wisdom writers, whose ideology finds its most striking expression in the Book of Proverbs, traditionally attributed to the monarch who 'was wiser than all men'. His wealth, his outstanding political acumen and his juridical genius are all regarded as emanating from 'the wisdom of God in his heart', which he received as a heavenly gift when he mounted the throne. Furthermore, Solomon is portrayed not only as a wise king but as the father of wisdom in Israel. 'And Solomon's wisdom excelled the wisdom of all the children of the east country, and all the wisdom of Egypt. For he was wiser than all men; than Ethan the Ezrahite, and Heman, and Chalcol, and Darda, the sons of Mahol: and his fame was in all nations round about. And he spake three thousand proverbs: and his songs were a thousand and five. . . . And there came of all people to hear the wisdom of Solomon. . . .' (I Kings 4:30–4). Indeed, it is not surprising that Solomon is depicted in these exaggerated terms. During his long and almost entirely peaceful reign, united Israel became a great and wealthy kingdom with widespread influence, highly honoured as the leading state between Egypt and Asia Minor. Evidence of the high standing of Solomon's kingdom can be seen in his marriage to 'the daughter of Pharaoh'. Certainly Pharaoh would not have given his daughter in marriage outside her own country had there not been good diplomatic and political reasons.

The Kingdom of Solomon Within the Ancient Near East

The kingdom of Solomon included all David's conquests: Edom, Moab, Ammon and Aram-damascus. Moreover, it had a common frontier with Hamath, the important neo-Hittite kingdom in northern Syria that may quite possibly have been included, politically speaking, within the area under Solomon's hegemony. Since he was the sole ruler over the chief trade routes connecting Mesopotamia and Syria to Egypt, including both the King's Highway east of the Jordan and the 'Sea Road' or Via Maris passing through Philistia, he enjoyed many political and commercial advantages. Thus he was in control of the Arabian trade, which was chiefly in spices, myrrh and frankincense. This trade began to develop on a large scale in the tenth century and reached considerable proportions. The spices and other luxuries originated in Sheba (in South Arabia) and were in great demand in the courts of Syrian and Mediterranean rulers. Since this trade was largely in the hands of the people of Sheba, whose trading-posts were in North Arabia, there is good reason to accept the historicity of the story concerning the visit paid to Jerusalem by the Queen of Sheba to establish commercial ties.

The United Kingdom (David and Solomon)

Legend:
- Judah and Israel
- Conquered kingdom
- Spheres of influence

The Great Sea

PHOENICIANS

ARAM-DAMASCUS

HAMATH

MAACAH

GESHUR

I S R A E L

AMMON

JUDAH

PHILISTINES

MOAB

EDOM

Desert

Dead Sea

Arvad
Hamath
Tadmor
Byblos
Lebo
Sidon
Damascus
Tyre · Abel-beth-maacah
Dan
Kadesh
Hazor
Acco
Ashtaroth
Dor
Megiddo
Beth-shean
Ramoth-gilead
Hepher
Jabesh-gilead
Succoth
Shechem
Mahanaim
Jaffa
Rabbath-ammon
Beth-horon
Jazer
Gezer
Gibeon
Ekron
Jerusalem
Ashdod
Beth-shemesh
Bethlehem
Medeba
Ashkelon
Gaza
Hebron
Aroer
Arad
Beersheba
Kadesh-barnea
Sela
Teman
Ezion-geber

0   30   60
km

© carta, JERUSALEM

The increasing importance of Solomon's kingdom in international trade and the economic progress that resulted created close bonds between Israel and the neighbouring states, particularly with Tyre, which at this period was of rising importance as the largest trade centre on the Phoenician coast. The two states complemented each other economically: Solomon supplied Hiram, the king of Tyre, with agricultural surpluses and in return received the raw materials he needed for his buildings, particularly cedar wood. The close economic ties led to a joint maritime enterprise: the establishment of a shipping route from Ezion-geber on the Red Sea coast to Ophir, which seems to have been situated on the east coast of Africa. The purpose of Solomon and Hiram was to deal without intermediaries with the sources for the leading luxury goods of their period, especially ivory, gold, rare woods (*almug,* formerly translated 'coral' but probably identical with the Akkadian *elammakku* or sandalwood), rare beasts and birds. The collection of rare animals for a royal zoo was an established monarchal custom and is known from the courts of Assyrian kings in the eleventh to ninth centuries.

Through the Tyrians and the neo-Hittite kingdoms of northern Syria, Solomon reached the sources of metals: copper from Cyprus and iron from Asia Minor. The copper was chiefly used for vessels of the Temple and the iron for tools and weapons. From the land of Que (Cilicia) in Asia Minor came horses that were sold to Egypt in return for ornamented chariots (apparently used for processions and ceremonies). The latter were sold to the neo-Hittite kingdoms in the north. Trade was conducted by 'the king's merchants', who functioned either as officials or as agents with a semi-independent status. Agents of this kind were among the economic innovations of Solomon's reign (I Kings 10:28–9).

The flowering of trade was only one aspect of the country's economic expansion. The long period of peace also gave impetus to improved means of production. Ploughs with iron blades appeared, which enlarged the areas under cultivation and led to agricultural surpluses that could be exported to neighbouring countries.

A clear sign of the economic progress of the period was the widespread building throughout the land. This construction work, which the archaeologist's spade is bringing to light, was marked by a new style: dressed stones and proto-Aeolian capitals now became accepted elements of royal architecture. The cities were fortified according to a uniform architectonic style: a massive wall and an intricate gate, examples of which have been found in Megiddo, Gezer and Hazor. The greatest attention was paid to the building of Jerusalem, 'the royal city'. It was expanded towards the north, where the royal palace and Temple were built, and was improved and fortified far beyond the boundaries of 'the City of David'. In the construction of the Temple, Solomon was aided by Tyrian experts, and it seems to have been planned in the style of the temples of northern Syria. The scale of the new and magnificent Temple was a complete novelty for Israel, as indeed were the form and symbolism of the cultic vessels made especially for it. Adjacent to the Temple and possibly attached to it was the royal palace, the construction of which took thirteen years. Thus Solomon physically transformed Jerusalem into a royal city and a temple city in accordance with David's design of making his new capital the cultic centre of his kingdom. However, the establishment of a temple to the God of Israel in a formerly alien city that had no place in tribal traditions undoubtedly led to opposition on the part of the old religious centres, which still played a decisive role in the life of the people. The fact that the Ark of the Covenant had been transferred to the Jerusalem Temple was apparently insufficient to gain it acceptance. The religious dissatisfaction with Jerusalem may have been one of the main factors behind the revolt that broke out after the death of Solomon.

An important element in the consolidation of the monarchy and in raising the status of Jerusalem and the Temple was Solomon's organization of the cultic personnel both in the Temple and in the governmental administration. Although the descriptions of these matters date from the Second Temple (I Chronicles 23–6), they still may provide a genuine reflection of Solomonic, or possibly even Davidic, measures. From this point of view, it has been suggested that the intention was to transform the landless Levites into a special class of royal officials distributed throughout the administrative cities and centres of the land (see the list of cities of refuge in Joshua 21 and I Chronicles 6) and that the rebel Jeroboam dismissed these cultic officials because of their loyalty to the house of David, appointing others in their place (I Kings 12:31).

The Levies Imposed on the People

Solomon's large-scale building works, particularly the construction of the Temple, were implemented through the corvée (*ha-mas*) and the levy (*sebel,* from a term that originally meant carrying baskets for earthworks). This seasonal recruitment for royal service was imposed on all Israel (excluding Judah) and was strictly implemented. The Solomonic chronicler tells of 70,000 'that bare burdens', 80,000 quarriers in the mountains supervised by 3,300 'officers which were over the work' and 30,000 who were sent in rotation, 10,000 each month, to Lebanon to provide lumber (I Kings 5:13–16). The Solomonic chronicler states that this seasonal compulsory labour was imposed not only on part of the Israelites, but primarily on the remaining Canaanites (I Kings 9:20–3), who had become permanent forced labourers engaged in royal projects. The corvée, a new phenomenon for Israel, produced a bitterness that in due course found expression in rebellion.

Another levy was the provision of supplies for the royal court and the army, which was chiefly encamped in Jerusalem, as well as being stationed in the special garrison and fortress cities. It appears that this army consisted largely of a chariot force, which might have been founded by David and became the backbone of the army under Solomon. Chariotry by its character required a permanent class of highly trained soldiers accompanied by retainers. Therefore a number of fortresses and garrison cities were built for this *élite* (I Kings 9:15–19). In these cities archaeological excavations have revealed the remains of buildings and impressive fortifications that indicate that they were military and administrative centres. The uniformity of the city gateways at Gezer, Megiddo and Hazor confirms that there was centralized planning for the fortifications of this period.

In order to provide for these large forces and for the numerous officials, a tax was imposed and collected throughout the kingdom. The country was divided into twelve districts, a detailed list of which is given in I Kings 4:7–19. The meticulous care taken to ensure that each district should fulfil its duties to the king and his court is certainly another of Solomon's innovations. A striking feature of this list is the omission of Judah from the twelve regions that were obligated to support the king. Judah enjoyed special rights as a royal district; this privileged position, which began after the revolt of Absalom, established even closer ties between Judah and the royal house, a fact that proved decisive when the kingdom split. The increasing wealth of the royal court and the rise in the status of the ministers, as well as the taxes and corvée, increased the gap between the populace in general and the new nobility. This polarization was intensified at the end of Solomon's reign when, it appears, the kingdom underwent a political and economic crisis. Evidence of the distress in which the state found itself can perhaps be deduced from the passage in I Kings 9:11–13, which relates that Solomon handed over to Hiram twenty cities, the land of Cabul (apparently the entire stretch of coast from Tyre to south of Acco), an important and fruitful region that remained thereafter in the hands of the Sidonians. Solomon was not, it would seem, in a position to pay Tyre for the raw material received, so he settled his debt by handing over inhabited cities.

The Crisis

The international situation also changed decisively in the second half of Solomon's reign. About the year 945 there was a change of dynasty in Egypt. The founder of the new dynasty (the Twenty-second), Shishak, was hostile towards Solomon, who was connected by marriage to the preceding dynasty. Some time later rebellions began in Aram and Edom, the north-eastern and south-eastern extremities of Solomon's kingdom. Solomon suppressed the revolt in Edom, but the rebel leader found refuge with Shishak. He did not succeed in overcoming the revolt in Aram, where Rezon ben Eliadah, the Aramean, established an independent royal dynasty in Damascus, severing Aram from Solomon's empire (I Kings 11:23–4). This reduced the king's income from trade and also increased the expenditure on the upkeep of the army in the north of the country, as well as forcing him to accelerate the fortification of the cities along the Egyptian frontier. At the same time Jerusalem was also fortified and the *millo* ('massive earthwork') was constructed. It was apparently against this background that the revolt against Solomon broke out. Jeroboam ben Nebat, who was in charge of the corvée workers recruited from Ephraim to fortify Jerusalem, 'lifted up his hand against the king' (I Kings 11:27). The account in I Kings 11 does not preserve details of the revolt, but an additional passage in the Lucian version of the Septuagint relates that Jeroboam actually captured Tirzah in Ephraim and took refuge there. It may even be that his symbolic name Jeroboam, which in Hebrew means 'he who quarrels for the people', was a nickname given to him by his followers. Jeroboam was eventually forced to flee to Egypt, where Shishak gave him asylum. There he waited for a suitable opportunity, which came when Solomon died and his son Rehoboam ascended the throne.

According to I Kings 11, the prophet Ahijah of Shiloh played a decisive part in Jeroboam's rebellion, prophesying the division of the kingdom and initially supporting Jeroboam. It is very possible that he belonged to the house of Eli, the important priestly family that had served in Shiloh but had been passed over in favour of Zadok for service in the Temple of Jerusalem. It is likely that he was not alone but represented a circle of prophets who actively propagated the traditionalist viewpoint.

Solomon's historiographer in I Kings does not stress the crisis of his later years. In the historical traditions Solomon remained the monarch who symbolized the flourishing days of tranquillity. He was portrayed as the builder of the Temple, the ruler in whose days Judah and Israel were as numerous 'as the sand which is by the sea in multitude, eating and drinking, and making merry' (I Kings 4:20). The difficulties of his last years were explained as punishment for allowing idolatrous cults to penetrate the court when his alien wives diverted the heart of the aged king (I Kings 11:14).

The Division of the Kingdom

When Rehoboam ascended the throne in 928, resistance was on a far larger scale than before. The first and most striking sign was given at the coronation ceremony. True, there was as yet in Israel neither a fixed place nor traditionally accepted forms for crowning a king, but efforts were made by David and Solomon during their reigns to ensure that Jerusalem should be the centre of the united nation. Solomon, in fact, went to great lengths to achieve this. It should have been natural for the people to come to Jerusalem, the capital, in order to crown his son and heir. Yet the heads of Israel gathered in Shechem and demanded that the coronation take place there. This demand clearly shows that the northern tribes of Israel were rallying as a unit separate from Judah. The situation seemed so serious that Rehoboam was forced to submit and went to meet them at Shechem. This in itself was an expression of the readiness of the new king to come to terms. According to one version in I Kings 12, the spokesman on behalf of the people was the rebel Jeroboam, who had returned from Egypt upon the death of Solomon; but in another version, in I Kings 12:20, he was invited back only after the breach.

The confrontation between Rehoboam and the heads of the people is portrayed in a critical and even slightly humorous fashion. Undoubtedly, the account was written by the same historiographer from the wisdom circles responsible for 'the book of the acts of Solomon' (see page 102). The very same standards by which Solomon was judged and found to be wise are now applied negatively to Rehoboam. He is censured for being foolish, because he did not learn from the older royal advisers but permitted himself to be misled by the inexperienced young men. The story outlines the request of the people (here called also 'the assembly') for relief from the corvée, the main levy imposed upon them by Solomon. The request is formulated briefly: 'Make thou the grievous service of thy father, and his heavy yoke which he put upon us, lighter, and we will serve thee' (I Kings 12:4). Rehoboam is called upon to proclaim a reform, like the Akkadian *andurarum* or *misharum,* a proclamation made by Babylonian kings in the second millennium upon ascending the throne (although the content of the Babylonian *andurarum* was concerned with release from debts, not from corvée). According to this account, Rehoboam did not listen to his elderly advisers who had 'stood before Solomon'. Their advice was that the new king should compromise with the people for a while and appease them, on the assumption that once in power he could regain his full authority. Rehoboam did not favour this advice but accepted that of 'the young men that were grown up with him, and which stood before him', namely, the young ministers of the new generation, his contemporaries, who were accustomed to the authoritarian method of rule that took no account of popular opinion. The king's response was formulated in a coarse and arrogant phrase: 'My father hath chastised you with whips, but I will chastise you with scorpions' (I Kings 12:11). In responding the assembly used the familiar formula that had already been uttered in the revolt of Sheba ben Bichri: 'What portion have we in David? neither have we inheritance in the son of Jesse: to your tents, O Israel: now see to thine own house, David' (I Kings 12:16). The demands were fundamentally social and economic, but the revolt and the split came about along lines of demarcation that had clearly emerged long before (see page 101). From here it was but a step to the actual division of the kingdom, the separation of Judah and Israel, of north and south. The historical circumstance that led to the division was primarily the weakness of the ties between the two, which had temporarily been strengthened by the outstanding efforts of David and had been maintained by the force of his personality. Yet, in spite of the superhuman efforts that David had made to unite the two sectors, neither he nor his son had succeeded in erasing the deep historical differences between them. The special status of Judah within the kingdom, as laid down after the revolt of Absalom, helped to bring about the split. Rehoboam reaped what his forefathers had sown.

It is surprising that Rehoboam quietly acquiesced in this situation and did not even attempt, as did David, to lead his forces out to suppress the revolt. The conditions must have been different. He may have been apprehensive of Shishak of Egypt, the patron of Jeroboam, who was waiting for an opportunity to strike at the kingdom. In any case, he preferred conciliation and sent Adoram, who was in charge of the corvée and now an old man, apparently to negotiate concessions. However, it was too late. The revolt was already well established, and Adoram, who represented the hated institution of the corvée, was stoned, while Rehoboam barely succeeded in escaping to Jerusalem.

Thus the united monarchy of Israel broke apart after a century of existence. During this time the royal institutions had become so firmly established that even during the split the rebels – apparently the vestiges of the earlier tribal and patriarchal leadership – made no attempt to dissolve the kingship. The two separate states, the Kingdom of Judah and the Kingdom of Israel (which on the eve of its destruction in the seventh century was also known as Ephraim), did not encompass the entire area that had been ruled by David and Solomon. Ammon, Moab and Edom broke away and became independent. The cities of Philistia grew stronger and conducted raids in the direction of the Valley of Ajalon. The political influence of each of the two kingdoms was obviously far less than that of the united monarchy had been. Their economic structure was damaged, for they were both affected by their separation from the trade routes beyond the Jordan. The crisis had less of an effect on

Judah, as the royal treasury in Jerusalem was not yet empty and the court still possessed economic reserves. The larger Kingdom of Israel, which included the entire country north of Benjamin, was the chief heir to the united monarchy. Its population and natural resources far exceeded those of Judah, whose land was less fertile and whose economic structure was based largely on cattle-raising. As the revolt was shaped by the ideology of pre-monarchic tribal institutions, on the one hand, and as the 'royal servants' – Solomon's former officials – were naturally unfit for service in the new administration, on the other, it took quite a while for the kings of Israel to re-establish the instruments of power and administration. Symptomatic of this process were the numerous violent dynastic upheavals in the northern kingdom, which will be discussed below.

8

The Period of the Two Kingdoms

Relations Between the Two Kingdoms

The two separate kingdoms of Israel and Judah existed side by side from the split in 928 BCE until the fall of Samaria in 720. These two centuries may be divided into five periods: (1) consolidation of the two independent units; (2) close alliance; (3) decline in both kingdoms; (4) renewed expansion; (5) the Assyrian conquest and the destruction of the Northern Kingdom.

Although Israel and Judah were constantly competing politically and even fought one another from time to time, the bonds uniting them were far stronger than the divisive factors. The national consciousness as expressed in the literature of the entire period of the two kingdoms was that of a single people separated into two states. The political boundaries were incapable of breaking the natural economic unity of such a small country, and an economic crisis in one state inevitably led to a decline or crisis in the other, while periods of growth and expansion usually occurred simultaneously in both kingdoms. In spite of the different centres and forms of worship, the common elements of national, religious and historical consciousness continued to play their part. At the same time the differences between the two kingdoms are self-evident. The outstanding feature of Judah's political history was the continuous rule of a single, Davidic dynasty. The dynastic stability ensured continuity of government and spared Judah the internecine warfare that was waged by the claimants to the crown of Israel. There were several reasons for this phenomenon: the sanctity that had surrounded King David and was extended to his descendants; the close ties between the royal household and the Temple; and the fact that this kingdom was based mainly on the tribe of Judah and its offshoots, a long-standing, homogeneous entity. The unconditional acceptance of the sole legitimacy of the Davidic dynasty by the populace of Judah guaranteed this remarkable dynastic stability in the Southern Kingdom for over 350 years.

Of special significance was the concept of a covenant between the God of Israel and the Davidic dynasty, best expressed in Nathan's oracle: 'Now therefore so shalt thou say unto my servant David, Thus saith the Lord of hosts, I took thee from the sheepcote, from following the sheep, to be ruler over my people, over Israel. . . . And when thy days be fulfilled, and thou shalt sleep with thy fathers, I will set up thy seed after thee, which shall proceed out of thy bowels, and I will establish his kingdom. . . . And thine house and thy kingdom shall be established for ever before thee: thy throne shall be established for ever' (II Samuel 7:8–16). This concept of a divine covenant, which originated in the Davidic court and was further emphasized during the Solomonic period, assumed that the God of Israel had chosen David to rule over all Israel, 'to shepherd them' ('shepherd' is the common appellative for a Mesopotamian king in his capacity as 'the fountainhead of justice'). Moreover, this divine authority was attributed not only to David himself but to his whole line in perpetuity. Certain psalms composed by court poets, such as 89 and 132, reflect this view: 'I have found David my servant; with my holy oil have I anointed him: With whom my hand shall be established: mine arm also shall strengthen him. The enemy shall not exact upon him; nor the son of wickedness afflict him. And I shall beat down his foes before his face, and plague them that hate him. But my faithfulness and my mercy shall be with him: and in my name shall his horn be exalted. I will set his hand also in the sea, and his right hand in the rivers. He shall cry unto me, Thou art my father, my God, and the rock of my salvation. Also I will make him my firstborn, higher than the kings of the earth. My mercy will I keep for him for evermore, and my covenant shall stand fast with him. His seed also will I make to endure for ever, and his throne as the days of heaven' (Psalms 89:20–9).

The Psalms introduce yet another element: the divine selection of Jerusalem as God's sole legitimate seat (the original name, 'the City of David' [*'Ir David*], was supplanted in the Psalms by the name 'Zion', a poetic, pre-Davidic term). Thus, in this concept, three elements are inseparably intertwined: the divine selection of David, the perpetuity of his dynasty by virtue of that selection and the designation of Jerusalem as the divine seat.

In contrast to Judah, the history of the Northern Kingdom is one of repeated dynastic changes accompanied by the extermination of the dethroned royal family. Every change of dynasty not only rooted out those associated with the preceding rulers but also produced radical changes in the administration and methods of government. The longest surviving dynasty in Israel, the house of Jehu, lasted only four generations. The frequent change of rulers in Israel should not, however, be attributed to any difference in ideology between Israel and Judah, such as the Northern Kingdom's rejection of an hereditary monarchy. The view that Israel accepted charisma as the sole criterion for kingship, while Judah accepted the dynasty in principle – a view that in recent years has gained support among many eminent scholars – is hard to reconcile with the facts. The concept of non-hereditary kingship was totally alien to the ancient Near East, of which Israel was always an integral part. Dynasties fell not through lack of charisma but because of political weakness. The most likely cause of instability in the north was its social and demographic composition. Not only was the Northern Kingdom far larger in area than Judah, but it also contained a more heterogeneous population. The interests of the various parts of the country often ran counter to one another; the social structure was more varied than Judah's, and social conflicts within it were more acute. It was this combination of factors, rather than ideological principles, that set its stamp on the political history of the country. The seesaw of opposing forces prevented any single dynasty from exercising sovereignty long enough to establish its authority as inviolate, in contrast to the Davidic dynasty in Judah where, when kings were assassinated, their sons were enthroned in their place. In addition, the influence of the army increased steadily within Israel. Successful army leaders claimed the crown more than once; indeed, dynastic revolts frequently germinated in army camps or during wartime. In the Northern Kingdom the early prophets, such as Ahijah the Shilonite (I Kings 11:29), Jehu ben Hanani (I Kings 16:1) and Elisha (II Kings 9:1), were an influential political force, as their support gave these revolts the seal of both divine and popular approval.

The Historical Sources

The history of the two kingdoms from the division until the destruction of Judah is found in the Books of Kings and the Books of Chronicles. Although they were finally edited only after the destruction of the Temple (the Books of Kings at the end of the Babylonian exile and the Books of Chronicles in the fourth century BCE), they rely on earlier sources that are in part preserved within them. In writing the synchronic history of the two kingdoms, the original author and the later editor of the Books of Kings made few changes in the sources that preceded them. The author of the Books of Chronicles, on the other hand, reworked his source material considerably, describing events at length and in the language of his time. The authors of both these historiographical accounts made use of a wide variety of sources. The author of the Books of Kings had at his disposal documents from the archives of the kings of Israel and Judah that recorded the history of each reign and each monarch's most important acts. Frequently he refers to 'the book of the chronicles [in Hebrew, *sefer dibrei hayamim*] of the kings of Israel' and 'the book of the chronicles of the kings of Judah' (*e.g.,* in I Kings 14:29, 15:23, 31 and 16:27). It appears that these books were a sort of semi-official historical composition in the manner of the Assyrian Chronicles of the thirteenth to eleventh centuries BCE and the Babylonian Chronicles of the eighth to sixth centuries BCE. They probably contained factual biographical material, an account of the enterprises of the king, his wars, the buildings he constructed and much valuable chronological data that the later editors reworked. The author of the Books of Kings used also the records of the Temple in Jerusalem, which listed important events in the Temple's history. From this source apparently came the description of the cultic reforms, as well as information about the fate of the Temple treasury. One excerpt from the Temple records is the passage in I Kings 14:25–8 that recounts the consequences of the campaigns of Pharaoh Shishak in the fifth year of Rehoboam's reign, when the Temple and palace treasuries were paid to him as tribute. Another example is the passage in II Kings 18:14–16 that records the tribute of Hezekiah to Sennacherib, the king of Assyria, in 701 (see page 143).

A source on which the editors relied extensively was the collection of stories about the prophets, particularly the early prophets of the ninth century. To this source belong the Elijah and Elisha cycles (I Kings 17 to II Kings 10), which preserve important historical details of the period: the history of Ahab in the Elijah cycle;

and the description of Jehu's revolt and the period of subjugation to Aram (in the time of Jehoahaz) in the Elisha cycle. Another cycle of prophetic stories incorporated into the Books of Kings centres on the prophet Isaiah and his relations with Hezekiah, the king of Judah. Originally a separate unit, this cycle was also attached to the collection of prophecies of Isaiah preserved and transmitted by his disciples.

These rich and varied historical sources were edited during the sixth century BCE, at the end of the Babylonian exile. The author's and the editor's outlook directed both the selection and the presentation of events. Their narration focuses on the kings, and they state clearly their approval or disapproval of each historical personality. Their main criterion is correct cultic practice, rather than the moral and social standards typical of the prophetic literature. Consequently, those kings who introduced cultic reforms and abolished the *bamot* (the local centres of worship usually referred to as the 'high places') in favour of a centralized cult at the Jerusalem Temple are considered just and righteous. This Deuteronomic ideology of the seventh and sixth centuries (see page 150) centred on Jerusalem and the Temple and denigrated the kings of Israel, all of whom 'did evil in the eyes of the Lord' by the very fact of their withdrawal from the cultic centre. Still, this consistent view did not prevent the author and the editor of the Books of Kings from providing sporadic information, occasionally accompanied by positive assessments, on various achievements on the part of even those kings of Israel whom they regarded as sinners. An illuminating example of this can be found in the description of Jeroboam II, who 'did that which was evil in the sight of the Lord: he departed not from all the sins of Jeroboam the son of Nebat, who made Israel to sin.' Yet, at the same time, 'he restored the coast of Israel from the entering of Hamath [Lebo Hamath] unto the sea of the plain [Arabah], according to the word of the Lord God of Israel, which he spake by the hand of his servant Jonah, the son of Amittai, the prophet, which was of Gath-hepher. For the Lord saw the affliction of Israel . . . . But he saved them by the hand of Jeroboam the son of Joash' (II Kings 14:24–7).

Historical material reflecting the spiritual and social conditions in Israel and Judah is included in the books of the literary prophets Amos, Hosea, Isaiah and Jeremiah. Here the later editors did not impose their views on the material, as was the case in the Books of Kings; in addition, these books contain first-hand historical information not to be found elsewhere in the Bible, the remarkable precision of which has often been validated.

For example, the passage in Isaiah 20:1, 'In the year that Tartan came unto Ashdod, when Sargon the king of Assyria sent him, and fought against Ashdod, and took it', is supported by the Assyrian 'Eponym Chronicle' (whose chronological accuracy is unimpeachable), which states that during the year in question, 712, Sargon stayed in Assyria proper. This version, though contradicted by the Annals, in which the king boasts that he himself conquered Ashdod, seems to be historically correct. In spite of Sargon's claim in the Annals, Ashdod was conquered not by Sargon in person but by his deputy (*turtanu,* in Akkadian, hence biblical Tartan) who commanded the Assyrian Army, precisely as described at the beginning of Isaiah 20.

Another important source of information is the epigraphic material – Hebrew,

Aramaic, etc. – unearthed since the last century. The best known of this material is the Mesha Stone (or the 'Moabite Stone'), still the major surviving royal inscription from the biblical period, which supplements the account in II Kings 3. The only surviving official or semi-official Hebrew epigraphic record on stone is the 'Siloam Inscription' of the Siloam Tunnel, dating from the time of Hezekiah.

Valuable material shedding light on the administrative and social conditions in Israel and Judah has been found in ostraca. Of these the best known are the Samarian ostraca from the eighth century BCE; the Lachish letters dating from the last days of Judah; the letters and administrative documents recently discovered in Arad; and a letter from Metzad Hashavyahu from the time of Josiah. Of special importance are inscribed seals and seal impressions stamped on pottery vessels. It has been suggested that the latter may reflect the administrative division of Judah at the end of the First Temple period, but their exact meaning is still uncertain.

Egyptian sources for this period are relatively few, the most informative being the list of cities conquered by Pharaoh Shishak, inscribed on the walls of his temple at Karnak in Egypt. The cuneiform material, on the other hand, is particularly abundant and varied, beginning with Assyrian and followed later by Babylonian documents. The kings of Assyria who conducted military campaigns into ancient Syria and Palestine sometimes gave details of the course of their campaign or at least mentioned, in their historical inscriptions, the name of the king of Israel who fought against them or sent them tribute. Of these sources the best known are the Annals of Shalmaneser III which mention Israel's kings Ahab and Jehu; the historical inscriptions of Tiglath-pileser III and Sargon, who campaigned in the country until they finally destroyed the Northern Kingdom; and the Annals of Sennacherib, which describe in great detail his punitive expedition against Judah. Since they were usually composed a short time after the events described had taken place, the records of the Assyrian kings are likely to be more precise than the historical books of the Bible. However, they are also liable to be more biased than the biblical account since, by their very nature, they were written in praise and thanksgiving to the gods of Assyria, mainly to Ashur, the supreme god, for the military victories they had granted the king. The Assyrian royal historiographer would not record a defeat; therefore these documents are obviously one sided, even to the point of listing imaginary victories. A good example is the assertion of Sargon in his Annals that he captured Samaria in his first regnal year, 721 – a statement that cannot be true as other sources confirm that he remained in Assyria during that year. Only in 720, his second regnal year, did he quell the rebellion in the west by reconquering Samaria, which had been taken in 722 by his predecessor, Shalmaneser V. The biblical account in II Kings 17:3–6, which states that Shalmaneser conquered Samaria, is therefore more trustworthy.

Somewhat more objective are the neo-Babylonian Chronicles covering the years 745–538. These works, the peak of Babylonian historical writing, were not official documents designed to glorify god and king; consequently, they have preserved information also about the defeats of the kings of Assyria and Babylonia. Particularly important is the chronicle dealing with Nebuchadnezzar II, which supplement the information in II Kings and Jeremiah about the last days of Judah.

Independent Consolidation

Very little is preserved in I Kings on the administrative and military measures of Jeroboam, who founded the Northern Kingdom of Israel. There is, however, reason to assume that, in his efforts to set up separate institutions for the state he had created, Jeroboam retained the Solomonic administrative-district division, though not the controversial corvée. Unlike Solomon, Jeroboam did not establish one permanent capital; he changed his place of residence several times, his capitals being variously Shechem, Penuel and Tirzah (see I Kings 12:25 and 14:17). On the other hand, ample details of his cultic reforms are provided by the author of the Books of Kings who, as we have stated, was highly critical of Jeroboam's innovations and motives: 'Whereupon the king took counsel, and made two calves of gold, and said unto them, It is too much for you to go up to Jerusalem: behold thy gods, O Israel, which brought thee up out of the land of Egypt. And he set the one in Bethel, and the other put he in Dan. And this thing became a sin: for the people went to worship before the one, even unto Dan. And he made an house of high places [*bet-bamot*], and made priests of the lowest of the people, which were not of the sons of Levi. And Jeroboam ordained a feast in the eighth month, on the fifteenth day of the month, like unto the feast that is in Judah, and he offered upon the altar. So did he in Bethel, sacrificing unto the calves that he had made: and he placed in Beth-el the priests of the high places which he had made' (I Kings 12:28–32).

To this day modern research remains puzzled by the nature and significance of Jeroboam's calves. They are viewed by the author of the Books of Kings as a complete novelty and a fundamental deviation from established cultic practices. However, since Jeroboam came to the throne with the support of the conservative tribal forces, he must have taken into consideration the strength of conservative sentiment in his kingdom. Any attempt to describe the calves as a foreign cult, such as the cult of Apis, the Egyptian bull-god, cannot therefore be accepted, particularly since, in a revolutionary step of this kind – the introduction of an alien god – Jeroboam would have been acting against those very religious beliefs of the tribal society of Israel that had set him on the throne. Even if there were some innovative aspect to these calves, they could not have been a complete novelty. According to one view, the calf, a derogatory term for a young bull, was actually an ancient representation of the God of Israel that went back to an old Aaronite tradition derived from Canaanite iconography (see Exodus 32:1ff.), even as the form of the proclamation 'behold thy gods, O Israel' (I Kings 12:28) goes back to Aaron (Exodus 32:4). Another view, however, which has gained wide acceptance, treats Jeroboam's calves not as divine images but as a pedestal upon which the God of Israel was believed to be enthroned. Representations of divinities standing erect upon animal-shaped pedestals were common in the ancient Near East. This motif is a familiar one in Syro-Phoenician and Mesopotamian art and always takes the form of a male or female figure standing on the back of a winged ox, bull, sphinx (the biblical cherub), lioness or the like. Yet, in the biblical description, no mention is made of any such human figure. It is therefore taken to imply that in his new temple Jeroboam deviated from the Jerusalem tradition by setting up a different divine pedestal – not in the form of cherubs as in Solomon's Temple, but in the form of a bull, apparently an old, even pre-Israelite, symbol upon which the God of Israel was believed to be enthroned.

The very location of his new shrines was not a complete novelty either: Bethel was associated with patriarchal traditions as the place of theophany in the story of Jacob's dream (Genesis 28). It remained an uncontested (and later the major) religious centre of the Northern Kingdom (see Amos 7:13). Although the religious origin of Dan is not completely clear, its priests seem to have claimed Mosaic descent, in contrast to the Aaronite descent claimed by the priesthood in the Solomonic Temple (see Judges 18:30, where 'the son of Manasseh' is an ancient emendation for 'the son of Moses').

Another innovation on Jeroboam's part was the celebration of the Feast of Tabernacles on the fifteenth day of the eighth month, one month later than in Jerusalem. Here too it is likely that he revived an ancient Northern practice. It also seems that Jeroboam could not rely on the loyalty of the Levites, who had remained faithful to the Jerusalem Temple and had close ties with the royal household of Judah, having served in administrative posts under the Davidic dynasty. In his sanctuaries Jeroboam therefore ordained a new class of priests who, according to I Kings 12:31, did not belong to the Levites but were selected 'from among all the people [literally 'fringes']' (interpreted by some scholars not as the lowest class but as the sons of notables).

The kingdom of Jeroboam underwent a severe political and military test at its start. Five years after the division of the country, Shishak of Egypt 'went up against Jerusalem' (I Kings 14:25). The list of cities he conquered contains about 150 names, of which the great majority were in the Kingdom of Israel. He conquered Gezer, pillaged the Valley of Succoth and the valleys of Beth-shean and Jezreel and then returned to Egypt, leaving in ruins most of the fortified cities of Jeroboam, his former protégé. In Megiddo, which is mentioned in the list, part of a stele erected by Shishak has been discovered. Judah was less affected. Jerusalem was spared after Rehoboam paid a heavy tribute, handing over to the invader the treasures of the Temple and of the royal palace.

In spite of the havoc wrought to the country, Shishak's campaign proved to be no more than a passing episode. He died soon afterwards, and his heirs discontinued his aggressive policy. Rehoboam spent the years following the campaign fortifying and strengthening Judah. He appears to have learned a lesson from the invasion, for his main achievement was the erection of a chain of fortresses along the western and southern frontiers of his kingdom. II Chronicles preserves a detailed list of these fortresses: 'And Rehoboam . . . built cities for defence in Judah. He built even Bethlehem, and Etam, and Tekoa, and Beth-zur, and Shocoh, and Adullam, and Gath, and Mareshah, and Ziph, and Adoraim, and Lachish, and Azekah, and Zorah, and Ajalon, and Hebron, which are in Judah and in Benjamin fenced cities' (II Chronicles 11:5–10). Building operations on such a scale undoubtedly involved a major effort on the part of the small, independent kingdom and laid a considerable burden upon its inhabitants. But apparently Judah was able to bear it and both at the end of Rehoboam's reign and, even more so, during that of his son, Abijam, succeeded in pushing its frontier northwards. It was the weakness of Jeroboam after the invasion by Shishak that encouraged Judah to engage in warfare against the Northern Kingdom (II Chronicles 13:2–19). Abijam won an important victory and conquered the southern approaches to the hill country of Ephraim, including the important religious centre Bethel and the frontier city Jeshanah. This major defeat of Jeroboam and the failure in the war he waged against the Philistines, who advanced as far as Gibbethon (I Kings 15:27), were instrumental in the collapse of the dynasty in the time of his son Nadab. The revolt, which broke out not long after Jeroboam's death, began in the ranks of the army that was then besieging Gibbethon. The commander, Baasha ben Ahijah of the tribe of Issachar, murdered the entire family of Jeroboam and ascended the throne himself (906–883).

Baasha was more successful than his predecessors both in the internal organization and administration of the state and in the military field. Not only did he recover from Judah the southern part of the hills of Ephraim, but he also seized Ramah, a Judean fortress (I Kings 15:17). However, the estrangement between the two kingdoms inevitably had its effect. Asa, the king of Judah, turned to Ben-hadad I of Damascus, sent him gifts and requested aid (I Kings 15:18–19). Ben-hadad came, capturing the fortresses of the land of Naphtali in western Galilee: 'And [he] smote Ijon, and Dan, and Abel-beth-maachah, and all Cinneroth, with all the land of Naphtali' (I Kings 15:20). This crushing defeat of the Northern Kingdom, which is assumed to have occurred in the last year of Baasha's reign ('the six and thirtieth year' in II Chronicles 16:1 should probably be emended to read 'the six and twentieth year'), seems to have been disastrous for his dynasty. Soon the fate of Jeroboam's dynasty was to be repeated; there was a revolt against the king caused by a military defeat suffered by the young state.

The rebel was Zimri, the captain of 'half of the chariots'. According to I Kings 16:9–10, 15, Zimri assassinated Elah ben Baasha while the army of Israel was waging war against the Philistines and had renewed the siege of Gibbethon. The strength of the army and its growing influence within the state gave new power to the generals, and various forces briefly raised their generals to the throne. Zimri himself was supported by only part of the army, namely, the charioteers, who constituted a group of young nobles and of whom Zimri in fact commanded only 'half'. When the revolt became known to the army beleaguering Gibbethon, they hastened to crown Omri, their commander, in place of the dead king Elah. Omri and his troops marched upon Tirzah, and Zimri perished in a fire within that besieged city.

Part of the army, apparently the section that was stationed in the north against Aram, did not recognize Omri and chose as king Tibni ben Ginath, probably also a general, like Omri. These two rivals contested the throne for four years, and only after the death of Tibni did Omri become king 'over Israel' (I Kings 16:22–3). During his brief reign the new king succeeded in normalizing the situation in the country, and thus he founded the first stable dynasty of the Northern Kingdom.

The Period of Close Alliance

We do not possess much information about the long reign of Asa, the king of Judah (908–867). The cultic reform that he carried out, in particular the removal of his mother, Maachah, from the position of *gebirah, i.e.,* 'queen mother', invested with executive power, won the approval of the biblical historian. The reason was purely religious: she was punished for having made a *mifletzeth* of Asherah, a derogatory name used here to mean an image of the well-known Tyrian goddess. Indeed, it is likely that the queen had belonged to some family of foreign princes. A late tradition preserved in II Chronicles 15:10–15 mentions another, more comprehensive reform that Asa carried out in the fifteenth year of his reign, but the trustworthiness of this tradition is uncertain, as is that of the account of the invasion by Zerah the 'Ethiopian' from the south (II Chronicles 14:9–15). Neither the story of his miraculous defeat near Mareshah nor the identity of Zerah have so far been confirmed, though some scholars have identified Zerah with Osorkon I, king of Egypt.

During the reigns of Jehoshaphat, the king of Judah, and of Omri and Ahab, the kings of Israel, a number of decisive changes occurred in the mutual relations between the two kingdoms and in their relations with the neighbouring states, as well as in the internal administrative and cultic structure. These kings had come to realize that the military struggle between the two sister states must be brought to an end and that a close alliance would benefit them both, even if it involved a renunciation of Judah's long-desired goal to restore its hegemony over the united monarchy. The alliance was strengthened by a marriage between Jehoram, the son of Jehoshaphat, and Athaliah, the daughter of Omri and sister of Ahab (or, according to another tradition, the daughter of Ahab). Indeed, the course of events endorsed this approach. The alliance between Judah and Israel led to a period of peace and prosperity for both states.

A detailed though late tradition in II Chronicles 17 ascribes to Jehoshaphat far-reaching reforms. He removed the high places and took steps to disseminate the Law (II Chronicles 17:6–9); he strengthened the army and built fortresses and storage cities (II Chronicles 17:1–2, 12–19); he set up judges in the fortified cities of Judah and established a supreme judicial institution in Jerusalem with the participation of the Levites, the priests and the heads of families (II Chronicles 19:5–11). However, it is very difficult to isolate the authentic historical elements in this tradition, which clearly bears the stamp of the late period when the Books of Chronicles were composed. Nor is it clear according to what set of rules Jehoshaphat's judges, *i.e.,* the elders and priests, functioned. It is difficult to believe that they followed a rigid written code. Almost certainly, local custom and traditional practices played a decisive part in shaping the judicial decisions of his time, as they did when David pronounced: 'As his part is that goeth down to the battle, so shall his part be that tarrieth by the stuff: they shall part alike. And it was so from that day forward, that he made it a statute and an ordinance for Israel unto this day' (I Samuel 30:24–5). As a matter of comparison, it may be pointed out that the judicial 'codes' of Mesopotamia, such as the 'Law Code' of Hammurabi, served not as the actual basis for day-to-day decisions but rather as a summary of judicial practice, together with some legal theory. In Mesopotamia as well, cases were decided according to traditional local customs. References to 'written law' in the Bible and in Mesopotamian sources should not, therefore, be confused with modern legal codes; the ancient law codes were literary compositions rather than legislative instruments.

The reign of Omri (882–871) and more particularly that of his son Ahab (871–852) opened a new epoch in the history of the Northern Kingdom. Like Solomon, Omri struck up a close alliance with Ethbaal, the 'king of the Sidonians' and founder of a new dynasty in Tyre. In accordance with the accepted practice in ancient Near Eastern states, the treaty was confirmed by a royal marriage between Omri's son Ahab, and Ethbaal's daughter Jezebel.

Omri proved very successful in southern Trans-Jordan, where he fought and defeated the Moabites under *Kmšyt,* the father of Mesha. The Mesha Stone ('Moabite Stone') has this to say about him: 'And he afflicted Moab for many days, Kemosh being wroth with his land, and his son replaced him, and likewise said, I shall afflict Moab.' Moab must have suffered a severe defeat, and, though Israel's dominion over Moab lasted only a few years, it was still remembered by the Moabites at the end of Mesha's reign as a period of prolonged servitude.

It is not clear whether Omri succeeded also against the Arameans in northern Trans-Jordan. Relations between Aram and Israel are reflected in the text of I Kings 20:34 in connexion with the negotiations between Ahab and Ben-hadad II after the latter had been defeated by Israel. There the text gives the following quotation: 'The cities, which my father took from thy father, I will restore; and thou shalt make streets for thee in Damascus, as my father made in Samaria.' The passage seems to be a dialogue. If the opening words were actually said to Ahab by Ben-hadad (and not to Ben-hadad by Ahab, as some scholars suppose), they mean that the Arameans had once enjoyed a victory over Omri and had been granted the privilege of a free market for their merchants in Samaria. But if the opening sentence belongs to Ahab, then the precise opposite might have been implied, indicating that Omri defeated Ben-hadad and conquered cities from him. The question must be left undecided, though the first possibility seems preferable.

The most significant manifestation of Omri's security and independence is the fact that, like David, he established a new capital. Built in the territory of Issachar in the hills of Ephraim, possibly the region where his family had originated, it was on the main trade route leading to the north. According to I Kings 16:24, he named it Samaria (in Hebrew, Shomron) because he bought it from Shemer, the original owner of the land. This, however, is a late aetiological explanation. No founder ever named his royal city after the previous owner, especially in a case such as this, where the land had been acquired legally, as Omri had paid a full price for it. So strong was the traditional system of landholding that even a king could not acquire land except by purchase. (When, for example, Sargon II of Assyria decided to build a new capital, Dur Sharrukin [Khorsabad], he bought the land from its owners at the full price, and we even possess the royal charters detailing the conditions of the sale.)

The name Samaria clearly points to the fact that the capital was built on the site of an existing village, whose name it took and perpetuated. A reasonable name for Omri's capital would have been 'House [or City] of Omri'. But this was already the name of the dynasty; Beth Omri (Bit Humri in the Assyrian inscriptions, literally 'the House of Omri') remained the official name for the Kingdom of Israel even after the fall of Omri's dynasty, according to Assyrian documents. Similarly, in the Assyrian records the states of Gozan, Arpad and Damascus bear the names of their ruling dynasties – Bit Bahian, Bit Agusi and Bit Hazael.

Ahab, who was apparently a co-regent with his father during the last years of the latter's reign, continued Omri's policy and developed it further. During his reign the Kingdom of Israel became one of the most important states in the entire region, enjoying economic prosperity through the development of commerce and industry, along with territorial expansion and increased urbanization. During the period of peaceful coexistence with Judah, Israel became an economic and political centre linking Judah with Tyre through common trade routes. Indeed, it is probably this alliance and its economic needs that induced Jehoshaphat to reconquer Edom in order to take possession of the Arabian trade routes as well, with all the accruing benefits. The King's Highway, running the length of eastern Trans-Jordan to North Arabia, was now under Judean and Israelite control.

It may have been the struggle for control of the Trans-Jordanian trade routes that led to the wars between Aram and Israel. On this assumption, it would be reasonable to date them to the beginning of Ahab's reign and not to the end, as the text in I Kings 22:1 seems to imply. In the early stages Ben-hadad II had the upper hand, but later Ahab succeeded in defeating him several times and even took him prisoner (I Kings 20). After this victory Ahab made a diplomatic initiative of the utmost importance: he, Ben-hadad and the neo-Hittite Kingdom of Hamath entered into an alliance that became the most significant military factor in his reign. The reason for the extraordinary *rapprochement* between these traditional enemies was the rise of Assyria during the ninth century as an aggressive, militant power that threatened the peace and security of Damascus, Hamath and Samaria alike.

The Assyrian Challenge

Assyria under Ashur-nasirpal II (884–859) and his son, Shalmaneser III (859–824), became, through its annual military campaigns, the leading threat to the kingdoms west of the Euphrates. This situation is particularly conspicuous in the time of Ashur-nasirpal, whose inscriptions describe in detail the cruel measures taken in regard to the neo-Hittite and Aramean states of northern Mesopotamia and northern Syria.

Assyria's might was based on its highly efficient military force, which featured a powerful core of war chariots and advanced siege techniques. The pillaging expeditions were intended mainly to bring home spoils from the wealthy states of northern Syria – gold, silver, luxury items and especially raw materials to be used in the construction of Ashur-nasirpal's new capital, Calah (Tell Nimrud). The numerous captives taken in these expeditions were brought to Assyria and employed in the building of Calah, and later some of them were settled in the new capital.

Shalmaneser III continued the Assyrian expansion westwards; but the situation had now changed, and his powerful military machine was faced by two alliances:

one of the north Syrian and south Anatolian states, the other of 'the Twelve Kings of Hatti [Syria] and the Sea Coast'. The 'Kurkh Monolith', a stele from the sixth year of Shalmaneser's reign, lists the participants in the latter alliance: it was headed by Damascus and Hamath, followed immediately by 'Ahab the Israelite'. Other minor members were the cities of Phoenicia, the Arabs (who find their first historical mention here) and a token auxiliary force from Egypt. The stele goes on to describe the decisive battle fought between Assyria and the alliance of the twelve kings at Qarqar in northern Syria. The complete list of the participants and their forces reads as follows:

1 1,200 chariots, 1,200 cavalry horses, 20,000 infantry of Adad-idri (*i.e.,* Hadadezer) the Damascene.
2 700 chariots, 700 cavalry horses, 10,000 men of Irhuleni the Hamathite.
3 2,000 chariots, 10,000 men of Ahab the Israelite.
4 500 men of Byblos (Gebal; a preferred reading to the previously accepted Que-Cilicia).
5 1,000 men, the Egyptians.
6 10 chariots, 10,000 men, the Arkites.
7 200 men of Matan-baal the Arvadite.
8 200 men, the Usnuites.
9 10,000 men of Adoni-baal the Sianite.
10 1,000 camels of Gindibu the Arabian.
11 30 chariots, (. . .) men of Baasha 'son of Rehob' (*i.e.,* the King of Beth-rehob) from Mount Amana (Anti Libanus).

It is interesting to note that the chariot force of Israel exceeded that of all the other allies. Here is evidence of the military and economic power of Israel on the eve of the battle of Qarqar.

Shalmaneser was not victorious in the battle of Qarqar, and the fight was repeatedly resumed in 849, 848 and 845. However, in contrast to the battle of Qarqar, we have no detailed knowledge of these campaigns, which the Assyrian sources mention with the utmost brevity, and it is not known whether Israel participated in them. In any case, a prophetic tale in I Kings 22 (whose historicity has been questioned) relates that Ahab met his death in a battle that he and Jehoshaphat fought at Ramoth-gilead against Ben-hadad (probably an appellation of Hadadezer). This battle should be dated to 852, only about a year after the battle of Qarqar in which Israel and Aram were still allies. It is doubtful whether the alliance – which, according to the biblical version was broken by Ahab – was renewed by his son Jehoram and whether, after the battle of Qarqar, Israel continued to participate in the league of 'the Twelve Kings of Syria and the Sea Coast'.

The Religious and Social Ferment and the Revolt of Jehu

The close economic and military ties between Israel and the Syro-Phoenician states, in particular Tyre, led to increased cultural and religious influences from these areas upon Israel. These influences, augmented by the marriage of Ahab to Jezebel, the daughter of the king of Tyre, found expression both in the adoption of Phoenician art motifs (as manifested by the Samarian ivories) and in the introduction of the cult of Melqart, the Tyrian Baal, into the royal court.

A temple to Baal, in which Tyrian priests officiated, was erected in Samaria. Presumably, extensive sections of the higher classes, such as state officials and courtiers, followed the royal lead. The sudden-prosperity of merchants and court circles in the newly erected capital must have brought into sharp focus the growing polarization between them and the conservative rural population. Although biblical sources provide no details, the story of Naboth of Jezreel is an illustration of the internal struggle that placed the prophet in the role of opponent to the court. Two points stand out prominently in the story in I Kings 21. One is the vitality of the principles of patriarchal society, still powerful in the Kingdom of Israel, whereby even the king was not permitted to appropriate a man's inheritance against his will. Ahab himself did not dare challenge this hallowed tradition of the individual's right to his land. The second point is the decline of public institutions. The elders of the community are presented as being not only powerless but actually corrupt, having no qualms about engaging in judicial murder at the queen's behest. The character of this queen from Tyre and her contempt for justice and civil rights are drawn in brief and dramatic strokes. She mocks the weak king, who finds that the rights of the individual infringe upon his desires: 'Dost thou now govern the kingdom of Israel?... I will give thee the vineyard of Naboth the Jezreelite' (I Kings 21:7). With arrogant cynicism she exploits an ancient and widely respected legal principle whereby the death sentence is imposed on anyone who curses 'God and the king': Queen Jezebel orders the elders to sentence Naboth to death and to confiscate his property on the basis of false evidence, with the acquiescence of the king and the judges.

In this decisive clash the prophetic movement is revealed as the spokesman for justice and human rights. The king's act is condemned in Elijah's immortal outburst against the tyrannous ruler: 'Hast thou killed, and also taken possession?' (I Kings 21:19). This collision between the prophetic movement and the royal family reached its zenith in another prophetic tale, the dispute on Mount Carmel (I Kings 18–19). In this story Elijah fights a lone battle against the queen and her prophets of the Tyrian Baal and brings the people face to face with an unequivocal choice: 'How long halt ye between two opinions? if the Lord be God, follow him: but if Baal, then follow him' (I Kings 18:21). For the first time ironical polemics are used against idolatry: 'Elijah mocked them, and said, Cry aloud: for he is a god; either he is talking, or he is pursuing, or he is in a journey, or peradventure he sleepeth, and must be awaked' (I Kings 18:27) – a motif that was to appear again in classical prophecy (Isaiah 44:12–15). Yet at this stage Elijah and *bnei hanebi'im* ('the sons of the prophets') were not strong enough. Their movement failed temporarily. Despite Elijah's failure, the beliefs for which the prophets stood were not extinguished and found supporters even in the royal court – Obadiah, for example, concealed some of the prophets from Jezebel's persecution.

It was not long before the prophetic movement gained strength and the prophets could openly oppose the policy of the royal family, at that time headed by Jehoram, Ahab's son (851–842). By that time they were no longer headed by Elijah, their recognized leader being his disciple and spiritual heir, Elisha ben Shaphat, a farmer from Trans-Jordan.

One of the main causes of the decline of the Omride dynasty was the disastrous military record of Jehoram. About 850, shortly after Ahab's death, he went to war against Moab in an attempt to suppress the revolt of Mesha. Though aided by Judah, he proved ignominiously unsuccessful. The allies besieged Kir-moab, Mesha's capital, but could not take the city. The narrative in II Kings 3 (again a prophetic tale that underwent later redaction) concludes with a striking detail: Mesha sacrificed his first-born son to Kemosh, his god, apparently in a ceremony on the walls of the beleaguered city. The Moabites finally prevailed and regained their independence. A further set-back occurred in the war between Israel and Aram. About 843 Ben-hadad died or was killed, and Hazael, the head of his army, ascended the throne. These dynastic changes in Damascus induced Jehoram to engage in a war to regain the entire Golan and Bashan, held by Aram since the time of Ben-hadad I. In a battle at Ramoth-gilead, which marked the southern limit of Aramean expansion east of Jordan, Jehoram's army was defeated and he himself was wounded. In addition to these military mishaps, there was a severe drought during his reign (II Kings 4.38–41) which must have caused an economic crisis. The result was that the army mutinied. The revolt was headed by Jehu ben Nimshi, one of the generals; but according to II Kings 9, the initiative came from Elisha. The prophet's messenger, one of 'the sons of the prophets', arrived at the army camp in Ramoth-gilead and secretly anointed Jehu king, thus investing him with the authority to destroy the house of Ahab. As soon as this became known to the other army officers, 'they hasted, and took every man his garment, and put it under him on the top of the stairs, and blew with trumpets, saying, Jehu is king' (II Kings 9:13). Standing at the head of the army, Jehu marched upon Jezreel, the winter capital of the kingdom. He killed Jehoram and proceeded to Samaria, where he executed Jezebel as well as Ahaziah, the youthful king of Judah, who was either Jehoram's cousin or nephew. The revolt climaxed with the extermination of all Ahab's offspring and all those who served the Tyrian Baal, along with the destruction of the temple of Baal. In this last act Jehu was assisted by the Rechabites, a sect of desert hermits who zealously observed the pure worship. Some scholars believe that Elijah originally came from this group. The objective of the revolt was now fully achieved. The house of Omri was destroyed and the worship of the Baal of Tyre was eradicated, never to reappear in Israel. Politically and religiously, the year 842 was a turning-point in the history of Israel.

9

The Decline, Rise and Destruction of the Kingdom of Israel

The Decline

Jehu's revolt succeeded in eliminating foreign influences, mainly in cultic areas, but the consequences were disastrous for both Israel and Judah. From the time of Jehu, Israel experienced a period of decline lasting about forty years, one of the gravest periods in the history of the two kingdoms.

The dramatic events of the year 842 had far-reaching political consequences. The alliance of Israel, Judah and Tyre, which had existed from the time of Ahab and Jehoshaphat, broke apart. The Northern Kingdom stood alone against its historic enemy, Aram-damascus, which under the ambitious and energetic rule of Hazael had been transformed into a major power.

The alliance of 'the Twelve Kings of Syria and the Sea Coast', which had ensured stability in the region during the final years of Ahab and the greater part of Jehoram's reign, was based on the containment of the traditional animosity between Israel and Aram and between Aram and Hamath. However, as this was essentially a treaty between the ruling dynasties, it was only natural that when those changed in both Aram and Israel the alliance ceased to exist, and Shalmaneser III of Assyria finally had the opportunity to force his way into the region. In 841 Assyria advanced against Damascus. Hazael was defeated; the Assyrian Army reached Hauran and then advanced to 'Mount Baali-rasi', which may have been Mount Carmel or Rosh Hannikra. On the way Shalmaneser received tribute from the king of Tyre and from Jehu, the king of Israel, whom the Assyrian inscriptions name 'Jehu son of Omri', meaning the one ruling over the Kingdom of Bit Humri, *i.e.,* 'the House of Omri' (see page 120). The scene depicted on the 'Black Obelisk' from Calah is probably that of the tribute received in 841.

A few years later Shalmaneser abandoned Syria-Palestine and turned to southern Anatolia. Relieved of the Assyrian pressure, especially after the death of Shalmaneser, Aram grew steadily until it regained hegemony over southern and central Syria. This process was continued and consolidated by Hazael's son Ben-hadad III.

Already in Jehu's lifetime Hazael had conquered Gilead (from Bashan to the Arnon River), thus making Ammon, Moab and Edom his tributaries. In 814 he conducted a military expedition through the territory of Israel, received considerable tribute from Judah, reached as far as Gath of the Philistines and very probably imposed his rule over the whole of Philistia. These events occurred during the last year of Jehu's reign.

The reign of Jehu's son Jehoahaz (814–800) marked the nadir in the history of the Northern Kingdom, as the king became little more than a vassal of Hazael and Ben-hadad III. The weakness of Israel is reflected by the statement in II Kings 13:7: 'Neither did he leave of the people to Jehoahaz but fifty horsemen, and ten chariots... for the king of Syria had destroyed them, and had made them like the dust by threshing.' This period of decline is also reflected in the cycle of Elisha stories in II Kings 5–7. Although Jehoahaz is not mentioned there by name, he is probably the one referred to as 'the king of Israel' who was ordered to cure Naaman, the general of Aram, of his skin disease (leprosy) and who found himself helpless to withstand the numerous raids of the Arameans (II Kings 5:6 and 6:8–23). The prophetic tales give an authentic echo of the degree to which the king of Israel was subject to Aram during that period. There is much to be said for the view that this period is also reflected in the 'prophesies against the nations' in Amos 1–3. They condemn events that preceded Amos by several generations – the cruelty of the Arameans ('because they have threshed Gilead with threshing instruments of iron' [Amos 1:3]) and of the Ammonites ('because they have ripped up the women with child of Gilead, that they might enlarge their border' [Amos 1:13]).

Paradoxically, Israel was delivered by the Assyrians. Adad-nirari III (810–782) revived Assyrian ambitions in the west. He defeated Arpad and his allies in northern Syria and then resolved to break the Aramean hegemony over central and southern Syria. In 796 he struck a decisive blow at Damascus; claiming that he had entered the city itself, he exacted heavy tribute from its king. A stele of Adad-nirari found recently in Tell el-Rima in Iraq commemorates his Syrian campaigns: it mentions, alongside the defeat of the king of Aram, the tribute received from Joash of Samaria. It appears that, like Jehu in 841, Joash sought Assyrian protection against Damascus and, by paying tribute, acknowledged Adad-nirari's supremacy. as an arbiter, if not actually a protector, of the Syro-Palestinian states.

Another source, the 'Nimrud Slab', supplements our knowledge of these events. It appears that not only Israel but also Ammon, Moab and Edom acknowledged the supremacy of Assyria. Yet Assyria had not yet assumed its later powerful role, and for half a century, under Jeroboam, the son of Joash, Israel succeeded Aram as the leader in Syria-Palestine.

The defeat of Damascus receives only the faintest echo in the biblical record: 'And the Lord gave Israel a saviour, so that they went out from under the hand of the Syrians' (II Kings 13:5). From this time on the position of Israel began to improve, and Joash (800–784) succeeded in regaining an appreciable part of its former territory: 'And Jehoash the son of Jehoahaz took again out of the hand of Ben-hadad the son of Hazael the cities, which he had taken out of the hand of Jehoahaz his father by war. Three times did Joash beat him, and recovered the cities of Israel' (II Kings 13:25). The prophetic circles, headed by the venerable Elisha, encouraged the king of Israel to engage in a campaign of national liberation and to fight Aram to the end (II Kings 13:19). Hatred of Aram was characteristic of the prophetic movement during this period, just as it had been earlier (see I Kings 20:35–43).

Judah also underwent significant changes during the period of Aramean hegemony. At the death of Ahaziah in 842, his mother, Athaliah, seized power. The biblical narrator in II Kings 11 accuses her of a dreadful, if unlikely, crime: the slaughter of the entire royal family, including, presumably, her own grandchildren, in order to secure the throne. Since the pattern of ancient Near Eastern kingship was that women ruled as regents rather than as queens in their own right, this crime would seem to be self-defeating, unless it was an act of irrational frenzy. It seems likely that the narrator accused Athaliah of crimes she hardly could have committed, especially since a massacre of royal princes in Judah already had taken place in the days of Jehoram, Athaliah's husband (II Chronicles 21). The key to the narrator's antagonism towards Athaliah seems to lie in the fact that, like Jezebel in Samaria, Athaliah introduced the worship of the Tyrian Baal into Judah, building a temple of Baal near Jerusalem under the priesthood of Mattan, whose name suggests he was Tyrian. The course of events that brought Athaliah's rule to an end is detailed in the same narrative (II Kings 11) and in a parallel source (II Chronicles 23) that is dependent upon it. The already dubious narrative in II Kings employs well-known literary stereotypes: the sister of the slain king concealed the smallest of the king's sons, kept him hidden for six years and in the seventh year prepared a plot against Athaliah. The queen was killed and the infant prince, Jehoash, was crowned in the Temple in an impressive public ceremony. 'And [Jehoiada, the High Priest] put the crown upon him, and gave him the testimony; and they made him king, and anointed him; and they clapped their hands, and said, God save the king. . . . The king stood by a pillar, as the manner was, and the princes and the trumpeters by the king, and all the people of the land rejoiced, and blew with trumpets' (II Kings 11:12–14). The leader of this revolution was Jehoiada the High Priest, Jehoash's uncle, and the chief partners in the plot were the Temple guard, as well as the 'runners', a force that apparently served as one of the units in the palace guard. The role of the priesthood was indeed decisive: the coronation was confirmed in a covenant established between the God of Israel, the king and the people – on the one hand, between the people and their God, 'that they should be the Lord's people', and, on the other hand, 'between the king also and the people' (II Kings 11:17).

At the coronation of Jehoash, 'am ha-arez ('the people of the land') appears as an active participant both in the revolt and in the destruction of the temple of Baal. If this mention of 'am ha-arez is not anachronistic, i.e., an editorial slip in place of the original term, it would be the first appearance of that important institution in Judah. Subsequently, during the last decades of Judah, 'the people of the land' were to appear time and again with the specific authority to choose a king whenever the normal order of succession was disturbed.

The singular conditions under which Jehoash ascended the throne were decisive in respect to the status of the Temple and the priests of Judah. Until this time there had been no reference to priestly intervention in political affairs. On this occasion, as a result of the leading part played by Jehoiada in restoring the crown to its legitimate holder, the priest appears as the defender of the Davidic dynasty. During the minority of the king, while Jehoiada served as regent, the exalted political status of the High Priest was further consolidated. This may account for the conflict later in Jehoash's reign between the king and his counsellors on the one hand, and between the king and the Temple priesthood on the other (see II Chronicles 24:17). One of the reasons for the conflict must have been the clash for authority over control of the Temple's income. According to the account in II Kings 12, taken from Temple records, the priests neglected the upkeep of the building, which was part of their responsibility. Jehoash altered this state of affairs and required the priests 'to receive no more money of the people' (II Kings 12:8). At the same time he conducted an extensive popular collection of funds, all of which were dedicated to the restoration of the building. An additional source of conflict seems to have been the tribute paid by Jehoash to Hazael of Aram in 841, which was taken from the Temple treasury (II Kings 12:18). The repeated conflicts between the king and the priesthood, as well as the economic difficulties that arose from the country's territorial isolation and separation from the trade routes with Syria and Phoenicia, were now supplemented by Judah's political subjugation to Hazael and Ben-hadad III. It was against this background of internal strife and political decline that Jehoash was assassinated by two of his attendants.

In the reign of Jehoash's successor, Amaziah (798–769 BCE), a short-lived change occurred in Judah's political fortune. By some process unknown to us, the new king managed to reconstruct Judah's army and conduct a successful campaign against Edom, which had won independence from his grandfather Jehoram some forty years previously (II Kings 8:22). He defeated Edom (II Kings 14:7) and captured the city of Selah ('Rock', probably the Edomite capital), though he did not succeed in reaching the shores of the Red Sea. This rise in the military power of Judah may account for the obscure incident described in II Kings 14:8, according to which Amaziah challenged Joash, the king of Israel, to a military confrontation. There might have been an unsuccessful attempt on Amaziah's part to force Joash to sign a treaty between the two kingdoms – an attempt that preceded the challenge and occasioned the strange reply of Joash (II Kings 14:9–10). It has also been suggested that Amaziah's act was motivated by a desire to avenge the murder of his grandfather at the hand of the founder of the Jehu dynasty. In any case, the outcome was a defeat for Judah in a battle fought at Beth-shemesh. Amaziah himself was taken captive, Joash proceeded to Jerusalem, and for the first time in the history of Judah the city walls were breached and the city captured. The king of Israel plundered the Temple treasures and took captives and hostages back to Samaria. Amaziah was subsequently set free; however, for the next fifteen years he probably was compelled to share power with his son, Uzziah, the co-regent (II Kings 14:17, note the word 'lived', not 'reigned'). After he was killed by conspirators, 'all the people of Judah' intervened and crowned Uzziah (Azariah) king (II Kings 14:21; and II Chronicles 26:1).

'All the people of Judah' cannot be taken literally, as it is improbable that a larger number of persons participated on this occasion than at other coronations. This term should be associated with the later 'people of the land', a popular assembly, the largest body through which the community participated in any political or state activity. Its designation was civic, in the same way that 'the men of Israel' of David's time (see page 100) was military.

It is difficult to reconstruct the chronology of the kings of Judah at this particular period. Apparently, Amaziah's defeat took place in his fourteenth year, which must be equated with the penultimate year of Joash of Israel (785/4). There is reason to believe that Uzziah came to the throne not after his father had been assassinated at Lachish, following a reign of twenty-nine years, but earlier, shortly after the battle of Beth-shemesh, when Amaziah was taken captive to Samaria. According to this hypothesis, Uzziah reigned as prince-regent for fifteen years during his father's lifetime and these years were included in his total reign. His reign therefore should be reckoned as 785/4–734/3.

Israel Under Jeroboam II

The long reigns of Uzziah of Judah and Jeroboam ben Joash of Israel (784–748) were almost contemporaneous and mark a period of prosperity and success following the long decline. This improvement was due not only to the weakening of Aram-damascus and the end of its hegemony over Syria-Palestine but also to the close commercial and economic ties between the two kingdoms during this half century.

Only fragmentary information is available about Jeroboam's wars and the size of his kingdom. This was certainly the greatest period in the history of the Northern Kingdom, but ironically the only statements about Jeroboam's conquests are that 'he restored the coast of Israel from the entering of Hamath [Lebo Hamath] unto the sea of the plains [Arabah]' (II Kings 14:25) and that 'he recovered Damascus, and Hamath, which belonged to Judah in Israel' (II Kings 14:28). The expression 'Judah in Israel' is not found elsewhere, and its significance remains obscure. (Indeed, the traditional English translation of the phrase was 'Judah for Israel', which is no less obscure.) In other words, he gained control of both Syria and Trans-Jordan as far south as the Dead Sea. The successive stages of this territorial expansion and their respective dates are not known, but it was presumably at the very beginning of his reign that he fought against the Arameans for control of Trans-Jordan. It has been suggested that Amos' statement 'You who rejoice in lo-debar, who say "have we not by our strength taken karnaim for ourselves"' (Amos 6:13) refers apparently to two early victories over the Arameans: one at Lo-debar in Gilead and the other at Karnaim in Bashan. In any case, it was only after Aram was defeated by Adad-nirari III in 796 (see page 125) and subsequently by one of his successors in 773 that Damascus itself came under Israel's rule; exactly how long after, however, is not known. The history of both Israel and Assyria of this period suffers from a lack of sources, and the years 796–745 are poorly documented. The best we have are the laconic statements in the Assyrian 'Eponym Chronicle' that recount the most significant event of the year. These statements indicate that, in the years 772–765 and again in 755 and 754, Assyria conducted military campaigns in the Arpad and Hadrach areas of northern Syria. It is from another source, the Urartaean royal inscriptions, that we gain some insight into the history of western Asia in those years. Indeed, this was the period when Urartu (the biblical Ararat, modern Armenia) was becoming dominant. In the second quarter of the eighth century it became a leading kingdom in eastern Anatolia, and both northern Syria and Assyria faced the constantly increasing pressure of Urartaean invasions on their north-western frontiers. The kings of Assyria could no longer fight on two fronts simul-taneously and restricted their efforts to preserving their hold in the area of Arpad in northern Syria. Hence it can be assumed that Jeroboam's conquest of Damascus was not carried out against the will of Assyria and may even have suited its policy of destroying Aram's power. Thus Jeroboam was given an opportunity to engage in conquest and to become overlord of the lands south of Hamath. It is quite possible that Hamath itself recognized Israel's hegemony, as in the time of David and Solomon.

Jeroboam's reign was also a period of economic growth and consolidation. Israel ruled once again over the main trade routes joining Mesopotamia and Anatolia with Egypt. The conquest of Bashan and Hauran, once the wheat granary of Israel, restored the firm economic and agricultural basis that had been lacking for so long. In order to strengthen the renewed Israelite rule over northern Gilead, Bashan and Hauran, the regions were opened to widespread Israelite settlement. The genealogical list in I Chronicles 5, which seems to reflect a census following popula-tion diffusion, indicates that the Gadites reached the Hermon, while the Reubenites grazed their flocks as far as the Euphrates. Henceforward the population of Gilead was of increasing importance in the Northern Kingdom. Of the four last kings of Israel who forced their way to power, three were from Gilead.

The economic prosperity of Jeroboam's reign left its mark also on the speed and scale of building operations. Finds excavated at Samaria – especially the ivory furniture inlays – indicate the splendour of the royal palace in that period. The increasing wealth of the ruling classes of Israel unquestionably enhanced the already acute social contrasts. Our chief source on social conditions in the days of Jeroboam is Amos, a prophet from the village of Tekoa in Judah, who denounced the oppres-sion of the poor and the perversion of justice. Amos condemned the ruling classes, who alone benefited from the prosperity during this period of peace and tranquillity. But, at the same time, a different tone can be heard in sections of his prophecy, leading to the reasonable assumption that by the end of Jeroboam's reign this stability was giving way and the prosperity was reaching its end. Natural disasters, such as drought and a locust plague, precipitated the crisis. Especially severe was the plight of the landless and the very poor, exploited by rich landowners who stored their surplus crops from plentiful years in order to sell them at inflated prices during years of drought. As a result, 'they sold the righteous for silver, and the poor for a pair of shoes' (Amos 2:6). These sharp social contrasts endangered the very foundations of the society. The fact that such bitter prophetic denunciations could be uttered in public without awakening a mass reaction against the prophet would seem to indicate that the people at large approved of and identified with his words. Even though Amaziah, the High Priest of the temple at Bethel, warned the king, saying, 'Amos hath conspired against thee in the midst of the house of Israel: the land is not able to bear all his words' (Amos 7:10), the 'plotter' was not brought to judgement. Clearly the prophets were a viable force even during Jeroboam's life-time; all the more so when, following his death, the ferment exploded into the open.

The Literary Prophets

The prophetic movement, which had fought for the 'true worship' of the God of Israel and against the intrusion of foreign deities in the days of Ahab and which had been a prime factor in encouraging resistance during the period of subjugation to Aram, underwent another drastic change with the victories of Jeroboam II. It stands to reason that prophets like Jonah ben Amittai, who predicted the rise of Israel and the defeat of Aram (II Kings 14:25), now became close to the court, if not actually 'official' court prophets. Thus the traditional critical stance of the prophetic movement vis-à-vis the king and his court, their religious practices and ideology, took an about-face. Instead of dealing with questions of social justice and the like, the prophets apparently were more concerned with fostering national-istic expectations, promising the imminence of the 'day of the Lord', when the God of Israel would punish all and defeat Israel's historical enemies (*cf.* Amos 5:18; and Joel 3:16).

Amos was a new phenomenon. His declaration 'I was no prophet, neither was I a prophet's son; but I was an herdman, and a gatherer of sycamore fruit' (Amos 7:14) was an avowal that he was not one of the professional soothsayers who lived by their prophecy (see I Kings 14:3; and II Kings 4:42), but was economically independent, supporting himself as a cattle-breeder (probably the correct meaning of *boker,* 'herdsman') and a cultivator of sycamore figs (for cattle-fodder). His prophecy has no connexion with omens, wonders or ecstasies, and he did not belong to any of the politically active prophetic guilds. His main concern was social justice as the supreme criterion in the existence of the people and the state. Hence his rejection of the official cult, especially those sacrifices offered by the rich and the rulers who perverted justice to oppress the poor: 'I hate, I despise your feast days, and I will not smell in your solemn assemblies. Though ye offer me burnt offerings and your meat offerings, I will not accept them: neither will I regard the peace offerings of your fat beasts. . . . But let judgement run down as waters, and righteous-ness as a mighty stream . . . said the Lord whose name is the God of hosts' (Amos 5:21–7). This theme, which was to be developed and receive greater emphasis in the prophecies of Isaiah, became the theme of the later prophetic message.

Amos can be regarded as the first of the 'literary prophets', whose insistence on social justice is unique among the ancient Near Eastern civilizations. It is not by chance that this movement originated in the Northern Kingdom, for in the days of Jeroboam II the social contrasts there were more acute than in Judah, which remained a basically agricultural society and retained its traditional stability.

Judah's Zenith, the Reign of Uzziah/Azariah

Uzziah is referred to in II Kings 15 as Azariah. It is possible that these two forms are variations of the same name. His long reign, described very briefly in II Kings but in greater detail in II Chronicles 26, a trustworthy historical source, marked a period of greatness not achieved since the division of the kingdom. Once he had firmly established his power, Uzziah continued to war against Edom. He soon conquered Eloth (*i.e.,* Eilat, on the Red Sea), thus completing the conquest of Edom and achieving control of the important trade routes passing through its territory. To strengthen his hold over the Arab caravan routes in northern Sinai, he also conquered and fortified the central oasis of Kadesh-barnea, whose remains have been uncovered in archaeological excavations. During this campaign he defeated the Meunites, a nomadic Arab tribe that, according to an Assyrian source, was based in northern Sinai and whose wanderings extended as far as the Egyptian border. His goal of control over the trade routes led Uzziah into a war with Philistia, the first in the history of Judah since the period of David. He took Jabneh and built cities about Ashdod, and among the Philistines' (II Chronicles 26:6), that is, settlements and fortresses along the northern section of the coastal trade route. Once again, as in the days of the united monarchy, Judah controlled the two great trade routes that passed through her territory, thereby deriving a large income from international commerce. The economic recovery of Judah showed itself not only in trade and commerce but also in extensive agricultural enterprises, particularly in the Negev. Uzziah was the only king of Judah of whom it is said 'for he loved husbandry' (II Chronicles 26:10), a phrase that indicates his deep personal interest in agriculture.

In fact, archaeological surveys and excavations conducted in the Negev during the last decade have revealed impressive remains from that period: fortresses built far away from settlements, surrounded with walls and towers. Several of the latter, it appears, were watch towers over trade routes and pastures.

Uzziah also reorganized the army and equipped it with new weapons: 'Shields, and spears, and helmets, and habergeons, and bows, and slings to cast stones' (II Chronicles 26:14). Special measures were employed to improve the defence system of the capital: 'And he made in Jerusalem engines, invented by cunning men, to be on the towers and upon the bulwarks, to shoot arrows and great stones' (II Chronicles 26:15).

Having safeguarded the state both politically and economically, Uzziah then demanded the right of participation in the Temple cult. This royal prerogative had deep historical roots, as both Solomon and his brothers before him participated in religious ceremonies (see II Samuel 8:18). For many generations, however, particularly since the time of Uzziah's grandfather Joash, there had been a well-defined separation between the royal and the priestly domains. Consequently, according to a late priestly tradition in II Chronicles 26, when Uzziah attempted to offer incense on the altar, he met with the fierce opposition of the priests. This source also interprets Uzziah's skin disease (leprosy) as a punishment for profanation: 'Then Uzziah was wroth, and had a censer in his hand to burn incense: and while he was wroth with the priests, the leprosy even rose up in his forehead' (II Chronicles 26:19). A later priestly tradition preserved in Josephus developed this legendary story further, adding the motif of an earthquake (known to be historical from Amos 1:1 and Zechariah 14:5) that occurred while the king was interfering in the Temple service: 'His heart became corrupt with excessive pride ... and on the occasion of an important festival ... the king arrayed himself in priestly garb and entered the Temple precinct. The priest who tried to prevent him he threatened with capital punishment . . . yet while he was still speaking a great earthquake shook the ground and the Temple was cleft and a dazzling radiance of the sun flashed and fell on the face of the king who was immediately smitten with leprosy' (Josephus, *Antiquities* IX, 10.4). Striking proof of Uzziah's illness is a tombstone dating to the Second Temple period inscribed in Aramaic. The inscription reads: 'To here were brought the bones of Uzziah, king of Judah. Do not open!' Evidently the body of the 'leper' king was buried not in the royal cemetery but separately and was found later and reburied with a new tombstone.

Jotham, the son of Uzziah, assumed power during the final years of his father's life, when the king's ailment officially prevented him from taking an active part in public affairs. Chronologically, the reign of Jotham should be included within the fifty-two-year reign of Uzziah, as his regency is to be dated to 758–743. Jotham, who continued his father's policy of growth and expansion, is reported to have defeated the Ammonites and exacted heavy tribute from them (II Chronicles 27:5). We do not know whether this advance into Trans-Jordan was conducted by agreement with Jeroboam II, the king of Israel, but there is reason to believe that such was indeed the case. A partial proof can be adduced from the fact that the names of both Jotham and Jeroboam are mentioned in a reference to a census that took place in Trans-Jordan: 'All these were reckoned by genealogies in the days of Jotham king of Judah, and in the days of Jeroboam king of Israel' (I Chronicles 5:17). Censuses and genealogical investigations of this kind were usually undertaken during times of territorial expansion and new settlement.

Though the political rise of Israel preceded that of Judah, the Southern Kingdom now began to show increased political strength. The process became evident in the final years of Jeroboam's life, and it is possible that after his death Judah gained hegemony over the entire territory of Israel and perhaps Aram as well. This supposition would be bolstered if, indeed, Uzziah/Azariah is identified with Azriyau of Tiglath-pileser's Annals (see page 133).

The death of Jeroboam in 748 marked the beginning of a decline in the Kingdom of Israel. His son Zachariah, together with the remainder of Jeroboam's family, was murdered six months after he had ascended the throne. The new king, Shallum ben Jabesh (who came from Jabesh in Gilead), held the throne for only one month and was then murdered by Menahem ben Gadi (possibly from the tribe of Gad). He succeeded in partially restoring the internal stability of Israel but not its former political influence. Menahem's seizure of power seems to have been accompanied by atrocities, in particular the massacre of an entire city: 'Then Menahem smote Tiphsah [the correct reading is probably Tappuah, according to a Septuagint version] . . . and all the women therein that were with child he ripped up' (II Kings 15:16; see similar earlier atrocities in II Kings 8:12 and Amos 1:13).

The critical period following the death of Jeroboam is reflected in the prophecies of Hosea ben Beeri. Internal criteria make it clear that Hosea should be placed in this period rather than later, as is usually supposed. Strangely enough, in his prophecy Aram is not mentioned as a independent political and military factor and Assyria does not yet constitute a danger to Israel. On the contrary, strange as it may seem, Assyria is regarded as a potential ally: '. . . and they do make a covenant with the

Assyrians . . .' (Hosea 12:7; *cf.* 14:3). There is no express mention of the loss of Galilee and Trans-Jordan to Assyria and the exile of their inhabitants, on which he could hardly have failed to comment had they already occurred.

The Destruction of Israel by Assyria

At the period when the Northern Kingdom was beginning to disintegrate internally, the political balance of power throughout the ancient Near East underwent a radical change. Tiglath-pileser III, who ascended to the throne in 745, transformed Assyria into a world empire that cruelly and effectively ruled the ancient Near East for the next century. Like his great predecessors of the ninth century, he directed his main drives against Urartu to the west and the north. By a series of consecutive conquests, he defeated this rival as well as its ally, Arpad, the leading Aramean kingdom in northern Syria. Within three years Arpad was conquered and annexed. The Assyrian frontier now reached Hamath in central Syria, and Tiglath-pileser clearly aimed at penetrating as far as the Egyptian frontier in the south.

Judah played a decisive role at this point, but the events of these years are not at all clear. The biblical narrative makes no reference to them, while the inscriptions of Tiglath-pileser have been preserved only in fragmentary form. A surviving section of his Annals refers to a certain Azriyau, who apparently headed an alliance of north-Syrian states resisting Assyria in about 738. However, the identity of this Azriyau has haunted scholars for over a century. It was generally assumed in the past that he was a king of Sam'al (Zenjirli) in southern Anatolia, whose rulers called themselves 'the kings of Ya'adi'. While the kings of Sam'al are well known from Aramaic and cuneiform sources, not one of them is named Azriyau. Moreover, Sam'al was a minor state of no geopolitical significance and therefore an unlikely candidate to head an alliance.

The most startling clue to Azriyau's identity, however, is the fact that the name is a Hebrew form, not an Aramaic one (the Aramaic would be Idri-yau, [*cf.* Adad-idri, king of Damascus]). The bearer could therefore have been an Israelite or a Judean. The most probable candidate is Uzziah/Azariah, king of Judah, as no other Azariah/Azriyau has come to light in all of the Syro-Palestinian states of that period. If this is indeed so, then we may conclude that at this perilous and decisive stage in the history of Syria-Palestine, Judah, with its strong army, became the leader of a league against Assyria. Yet the Annals of Tiglath-pileser describing the events of those years (743–738) are very poorly preserved, and therefore no conclusive picture of Uzziah/Azariah's role can be determined from them. Unless further discoveries provide new and more definitive evidence, the riddle of Azriyau's identity cannot be satisfactorily solved.

Even in their fragmented state, Tiglath-pileser's Annals make one thing very clear: by 738 the kings of southern Anatolia, Syria and Palestine – among them Menahem, the king of Samaria (see also II Kings 15:19–20) and Rezin of Damascus – were paying tribute. The tribute list illustrates the wealth and diversity of the region's economic bases: 'Gold, silver, tin, iron, elephant hides, ivory, multi-coloured garments, linen garments, wool [dyed] bluish-purple and reddish-purple, maplewood and boxwood . . . horses, mules, cattle and sheep, camels, she-camels with their young'.

The events of 743–738 marked the turning-point in the political fortunes of Israel and Judah. About that time Rezin, the king of Damascus who established a new dynasty, succeeded in restoring to Aram the disputed lands in Trans-Jordan – Bashan, Golan and northern Gilead. The area of Aram-damascus now spread (admittedly, for a brief period only) from Lebanon to Bashan and Ramoth-gilead, the historic frontier-point with Israel. As in the past the rise of Aram in the north involved the re-emergence of an independent state in Edom. Soon after 738 Edom successfully revolted against Judah, which lost all its possessions beyond the Jordan. At the same time it also lost control of Philistia and the Ashdod district. The Philistines actually burst into Judah, devastating the area up to the Ajalon Valley: 'The Philistines also had invaded the cities of the low country [Shephelah], and of the south [Negev] of Judah, and had taken Beth-shemesh, and Ajalon, and Gederoth, and Sochoh with the villages thereof, and Timnah with the villages thereof, Gimzo also and the villages thereof: and they dwelt there' (II Chronicles 28:18). Uzziah's grandson, Ahaz, who succeeded his father, Jotham, as Uzziah's co-regent, struggled hopelessly to preserve Judah's predominance. A heavy blow was inflicted on him in 734 when Tiglath-pileser advanced with his army from northern Syria and passed along the Mediterranean coast from Phoenicia to Philistia. After the northern Philistine cities submitted, the Assyrians took Gaza and advanced as far as the 'Brook of Egypt', where Tiglath-pileser set up a stele to commemorate his victory and to mark this remote point of his empire. The list of tribute in the Annals of Tiglath-pileser noted that among those paying was Ahaz, the king of Judah (referred to by his full name, Yauhazi, *i.e.,* Jehoahaz), together with seven other monarchs of Philistia and Trans-Jordan who had previously been subject to Judah. Although at that stage Tiglath-pileser took no further steps towards annexation proper, the mere passage of the vast Assyrian Army through Syria-Palestine must have had immediate political repercussions.

Rezin the Aramean and Pekah ben Remaliah, the new king of Israel who had overthrown Menahem's dynasty with the support of Rezin (*c.* 735/4), plotted an attack on Judah. The plan was to dethrone Ahaz and replace the Davidic dynasty with a certain Ben-Tabeal (Isaiah 7:6), perhaps a Trans-Jordanian prince. According to II Kings 16:5 and Isaiah 7:1, the allies advanced on Jerusalem and besieged the city. At this desperate point Ahaz appealed to Tiglath-pileser for aid. The appeal is couched in the words of a vassal to his lord: 'I am thy servant and thy son: come up, and save me out of the hand of the king of Syria, and out of the hand of the king of Israel, which rise up against me' (II Kings 16:7). Fittingly, Ahaz dispatched rich gifts from the royal and Temple treasures (II Kings 16:8). Following this plea Tiglath-pileser invaded the country; during the next two years (733–732) he entered Aram, taking its fortified cities one after the other and besieging Damascus, which he finally captured in 732. Rezin was killed, and Aram-damascus ceased to be an independent state, becoming an Assyrian province with Damascus as its administrative centre. A similar fate befell Israel. The Assyrian Army invaded Galilee and took Ijon, Dan, Abel-beth-maachah, Hazor and many other cities in the hills of

Naphtali and in the Valley of Beth-netophah (II Kings 15:29). A fragmentary Assyrian source mentions that 13,150 exiles from these areas were led away to Assyria.

Tiglath-pileser III, whose genius was not merely military, introduced several major innovations which were perfected by his heirs and which reshaped the entire history of the region. The first and most obvious was the transformation of conquered states into Assyrian provinces administered by Assyrian governors, mostly high courtiers. However, in respect to its radical character and subsequent influence on the history of Israel, his most important innovation was the development and perfection of the process of mass deportation and resettlement that henceforth became the outstanding feature of Assyrian imperialism. Deportation took the form of enforced exchanges of population: selected residents, outstanding craftsmen and soldiers were taken from the newly conquered provinces in the west and were resettled either in regions of Assyria that had been depopulated by the ravages of the ninth century, particularly the district of Gozan, or on the northern and northeastern borders of the empire (in Media). In place of these deportees, Aramean and Chaldean tribes from Babylonia were brought as colonists to the western provinces. In this way the power of the conquered peoples was broken, because they were deprived of their *élite* and because the new colonists intermingled with them to form a hybrid culture that was predominantly Aramean and loyal to Assyria.

As for Israel, Tiglath-pileser apparently annexed Galilee, which he conquered in 733–732; subsequently it became known as the province of Magiddu, with the city of Megiddo as its centre. As only a section of the population was deported and a considerable Israelite element remained, it is not at all clear whether Galilee was resettled with foreign colonists. In any case, we have no evidence of a new ethnic entity consisting of a mixture of Israelites and colonists coming into being in Galilee, as was the case in Samaria (see page 137). The inhabitants of Trans-Jordan, whether ruled by Israel or Rezin, also were exiled to Assyria during the years 733–732. The frontier of the Assyrian Empire now ran from Trans-Jordan through the Jezreel Valley, extending as far as the Valley of Acco, which at that time belonged to Tyre.

The defeat of Israel and the loss of two-thirds of its territory led to political turmoil that culminated in yet another coup d'état. Pekah ben Remaliah, who had relied on Damascus, was killed and replaced by Hoshea ben Elah, who ascended to the throne in 732 and was confirmed by Tiglath-pileser in the following year. After the loss of Galilee and Trans-Jordan, nothing more was left to the Kingdom of Israel than Samaria, in fact little more than the hills of Ephraim. Yet even at this stage Israel would not accept defeat, and Hoshea turned to Egypt, Assyria's traditional foe. According to II Kings 17:4, he sent a delegation to 'So king of Egypt'. The customary suggestion of scholars that this is Shabako, a Nubian king (see page 141), has been proved unlikely. *So* might be a corrupt form of Osorkon IV, the last pharaoh of the Twenty-second Dynasty. Yet it is possible that *So* is not the name of a ruler but the Hebrew form of Sais, a major city in the Nile Delta and the seat of the powerful rulers Tephnakhte and his son Bocchoris. Apparently, Egyptian aid was promised to Hoshea, for he ceased to send tribute to Assyria. It is quite possible that the decision to revolt was quickened by the death of Tiglath-pileser III in the winter of 727/6 and by the ascent of his son Shalmaneser V to the throne (727–722). The death of the great conqueror raised hopes among the vassals and increased their expectations that Assyria would now be unable to maintain her vast empire. It was against this background, it seems, that Isaiah gave his prophetic warning to one of the vassals: 'rejoice not thou, whole Palestina [Philistia] because the rod of him that smote thee is broken: for out of the serpent's root shall come forth a cockatrice, and his fruit shall be a fiery flying serpent' (Isaiah 14:29).

Since no Assyrian documents have survived from the reign of Shalmaneser V, no details of the war against Hoshea are known. It may be assumed that when the Assyrian forces appeared in the country Hoshea realized that resistance was pointless and surrendered. He was taken captive by Shalmaneser and exiled to Assyria. Shalmaneser invested Samaria, yet the city managed to withstand the Assyrians for about two years despite the absence of a king; it fell in the winter of 722/1. A Babylonian Chronicle relates laconically that Shalmaneser had 'vanquished Shamara'in', which is the Aramaic rendering of Samaria. Shalmaneser V may have died soon after, or he may have been killed in a revolt. In any case, it seems probable that internal upheavals in Assyria led the army to withdraw in the winter of 722/1 or the spring of 721 and to return home. A new ruler, who was not directly in line for the throne, seized power, pretentiously adopting the name Sargon, after the founder of the Kingdom of Akkad 1,700 years earlier. A revolt that spread throughout the Assyrian Empire west of the Euphrates raised hopes of liberation in Israel and in other provinces; not only the territories that had preserved a certain measure of independence, such as Gaza, revolted, but also the newly established provinces, such as Hadrach and Damascus. A new Syro-Palestinian alliance was now formed, headed by Hamath and the cities of Philistia, principally Gaza. Egypt promised active military aid to this unfortunate alliance.

In his second year of reign, in 720, Sargon gathered his forces to quell the revolts west of the Euphrates. In a series of swift actions, he defeated the king of Hamath and invaded Philistia. At Raphia, at the gates of Egypt, he joined battle with the Egyptian Army. The Annals of Sargon relate that the Egyptians were defeated and their commander fled 'like a shepherd whose flock has been stolen from him'. On their way back the Assyrians took Gaza and proceeded against Samaria, which was still in a state of upheaval following Shalmaneser's death. Sargon set up a governor and made it the centre of the new Assyrian province of Samerina. He relates his conquest of Samaria in the Annals: 'I captured Samaria, 27,290 people dwelling in it I took as spoil, 50 [or 200] chariots I requisitioned from within it, and the rest of them I settled in Assyria. I rebuilt the city of Samaria and made it bigger than it was [before]. People from the lands which I had conquered I settled in it and directed them in their own particular [probably technical] skill. I placed over it my palace-official as governor and imposed upon them a tax payment as on the citizens of Assyria' (Sargon's Annals, reconstructed text).

Samaria was resettled with colonists deported from other parts of the Assyrian Empire. In 716 Sargon settled there the nomad tribes conquered that same year. The Assyrian inscriptions do not give any additional information on these deportations to Samaria, but II Kings 17 lists the origins and forms of worship of the new settlers. According to this late source, they were sent to Samaria 'from Babylon, and from Cuthah, and from Ava, and from Hamath, and from Sepharvaim' (II Kings 17:24), but the locations of Ava and Sepharvaim are unknown, nor is it clear whether this Hamath is the one in Syria or a city of Media with the same name. As Sargon was an enthusiastic adherent of Babylonian culture and a supporter of the Babylonian temple cities, there is some difficulty in assuming that he actually exiled the people of Cuthah, a sacred Babylonian city. It seems more probable that his anti-Babylonian son and successor, Sennacherib, who conducted several campaigns against Babylonia and carried off many thousands of its population, was responsible for the exile of the inhabitants of Babylon and Cuthah to Samaria. The narrator in Ezra 4:2, 10 states that both Esarhaddon and Asnapper (apparently Esarhaddon's son, Ashurbanipal) had exiled people to Samaria. It would appear that these exiles were brought from Media and Elam.

At first the new peoples still worshipped their own gods, but in the course of time they intermingled with one another and with the remaining Israelite inhabitants of Samaria (II Kings 17). The biblical narrative adds an instructive detail here regarding the stages by which the foreign exiles took root. Some were attacked by lions and appealed to the king of Assyria saying: 'The nations which thou hast removed, and placed in the cities of Samaria, know not the manner [in Hebrew, *mishpat*, 'law'] of the God of the land: Therefore he hath sent lions among them and they slay them.' In reply the king of Assyria sent a priest of the exiled Israelites, and he taught them 'the manner of the God of the land' (II Kings 17:26–7). An instructive comparison, showing the education of exiles by the authorities, is found both in the previously quoted account of the fall of Samaria and in the description of the building of Sargon's new capital, Dur Sharrukin (Khorsabad). It is related that Sargon brought to his new capital 'people from the four corners of the earth, who speak a strange tongue and confused language, dwellers of the mountains and the plain. . . . These exiles', related Sargon in his 'Cylinder Inscription', 'I unified and settled them therein. Assyrians, fully competent in every skill, I dispatched to them as superintendents and supervisors to teach them how to fear god and king.'

In other words, the Assyrians regarded it as a primary state function to unify the heterogeneous ethnic elements in the main cities of the kingdom and the provinces and to turn them into cohesive local units within an Assyrianized society. Thus, towards the Persian period in Samaria, there came into being a new ethnic and religious entity, the kernel of what later became known as the Samaritans.

Little information is preserved about the ten tribes that were exiled to Assyria, whose fate was to serve later generations as a subject of legendary speculation and messianic hopes. What transpired was that most of those exiled were settled in the vicinity of Gozan on the Habor River. This region, one of the most important of the western Assyrian provinces, had been laid waste both at the end of the tenth century and during the ninth century, in the course of the military campaigns of Ashur-nasirpal II, and had gradually been restored from the time of Tiglath-pileser III onwards. Others were settled in Media, where they apparently served as garrison troops in units organized within the Assyrian Army. This method of annexing into the Assyrian Army complete units from the armies of conquered peoples was widespread. Sargon, for instance, took fifty chariots from Samaria (or 200, according to another version) and added them to his royal guard; while Sennacherib absorbed Hezekiah's *élite* corps. This practice may help to explain the presence in the Assyrian Army of an officer named Hilkiyau, *i.e.,* Hilkiah, who is mentioned in a document from the time of Sargon recently discovered in Calah. Assyrian documents from Gozan itself also contain a few names that testify to the fact that an Israelite community still existed there in the seventh century. One document mentions two Gozan officials named Paltiyau and Niriyau. These, however, are scraps of information. It may be assumed that a part of the exiled tribes that still existed as a separate and conscious group in the days of Jeremiah and Ezekiel (see Jeremiah 31:8; and Ezekiel 37:19–22) subsequently joined the exiles from Judah upon their return. The majority, however, were assimilated into the surrounding Aramean population, thus sharing the fate of every ethnic community displaced by the Assyrians and subjected to their policy of enforced Assyrianization. The spread of Aramaic as the lingua franca of the Assyrian Empire, especially in the west, hastened that process.

Nor should it be supposed that Judah entirely escaped the consequences of Assyrian cultural policies; II Kings 16:10ff. relates that Ahaz went to the camp of Tiglath-pileser soon after the fall of Damascus in 732 and had a copy of an Aramaic altar made for use in the Jerusalem Temple. It appears that Ahaz had decided to become an Assyrian vassal, not only politically but also culturally and religiously, which in the west involved the adoption of Aramaic manners, religious symbols and even language. This trend is especially evident in the reign of Manasseh, who transplanted patterns of Aramaic cult to Jerusalem in blatant contravention of the religious practice of his forefathers.

10

Judah from the Fall of Samaria to the Fall of Jerusalem

The Reign of Hezekiah

After the fall of Samaria, the kings of Judah regarded themselves as the natural successors to the kings of Israel and tried to extend their protection and influence over the inhabitants who had not been exiled. At the same time they also endeavoured to spread northwards into the areas that had formerly been held by Israel.

These objectives guided the policy of Hezekiah (727–698). Like his father, he was careful not to take part in the various attempts at revolt against Assyria. He did not participate in the revolt of Israel under Hoshea ben Elah that brought about the destruction of the Kingdom of Samaria. For this reason the end of the reign of Ahaz and the greater part of his own rule were peaceful periods that enabled Judah to consolidate both politically and economically. The fruits of this stability were a growth in population and the extension of building. Hezekiah succeeded also in expanding the southern frontiers of Judah, particularly in the Negev. Although he paid tribute to Assyria, during his reign Judah emerged as the most important state between Assyria and Egypt.

It was in the latter part of his reign that Hezekiah became involved in the struggle between Egypt and Assyria over the Plain of Philistia and the roads leading to Egypt. In 716, the Assyrians reappeared in Philistia, uncomfortably close to the Egyptian border. Sargon's forces reached 'the City of the Brook of Egypt', where he appears to have established an Assyrian military garrison. The Assyrians had a strong economic motive in opening up Egypt to trade. A fragmentary passage in Sargon's Annals – unique in its mention of aspects other than military – states: 'I opened the sealed [harbour, or border] of Egypt, the Assyrians and Egyptians I mingled to[gether] and I made them trade [with each other].' Egyptian reaction was divided: the weak Pharaoh Osorkon IV (Shilkanni in Assyrian sources), accepted the Assyrian presence and sent Sargon gifts, which the latter regarded as tribute. However, other elements in Egypt continued a policy of inciting rebellion among the vassal states bordering on Assyria. At the same time, emerging from the south of Egypt was a warlike Nubian dynasty that was destined to extend its hegemony over the whole of Egypt and revive Egyptian strength to the point that it could challenge Assyrian domination of Palestine.

A prelude to coming events occurred in 712, when Ashdod revolted. Anti-As-

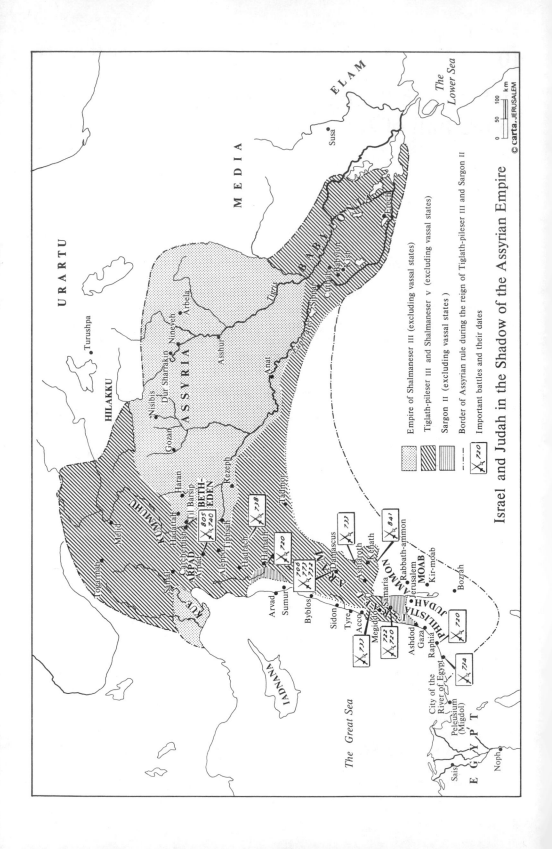

Israel and Judah in the Shadow of the Assyrian Empire

syrian extremists overthrew the city's vassal king and replaced him with a leader named Yamani. This ambitious Philistine leader, realizing Ashdod's inability to face Assyrian displeasure alone, tried to establish a broad alliance of vassal states that was to have involved all the other cities of Philistia, as well as Edom, Moab and Judah. He had contacts with the 'Pharaoh King of Egypt' (as designated in Sargon's inscription), who promised him military assistance.

When Sargon learned of the revolt, he swiftly sent his army, headed by his deputy, the *turtanu* (see page 113) to quell the rebellion in a distant and sensitive zone (Isaiah 20:1). On its way the Assyrian Army took several fortified cities on the borders of Philistia and Judah. It proceeded to Ashdod, conquered it after a short siege and made it an Assyrian province (Asdudi). Remains of the stele that Sargon set up to commemorate this victory were recently unearthed in the excavations at Ashdod. The Egyptian Pharaoh could not come to Yamani's assistance since, in the meanwhile, Egypt was completely overrun by the Nubian princes of Egypt, who established Egypt's Twenty-fifth Dynasty. The new king, Shabako, apparently was better disposed towards Assyria, so that when Yamani sought asylum at the Nubian court, he was extradited and delivered to Sargon in chains. Hezekiah had barely managed to avoid involvement in this upheaval. At the decisive moment he withdrew support from Yamani and escaped with almost no loss.

Hezekiah remained a faithful Assyrian vassal. But his ultimate aim was clear, and when the Nubian dynasty began to adopt a more anti-Assyrian policy, he was quick to cooperate with them. The opportunity for action came in 705, with Sargon's death in battle in a distant province. The unprecedented circumstances (his body was not recovered) were taken as an omen by his discontented vassals, who seized the opportunity to instigate a widespread rebellion. In Babylon, Assyria's old enemy, the Chaldean Merodach-baladan, seized power and re-established the rule that he had exercised during the first part of Sargon's reign. In the west another change had taken place. The energetic Nubian Pharaoh likewise viewed Sargon's death as an opportunity to reassert Egyptian hegemony in Philistia. This coincided with Hezekiah's view that Assyrian domination could not survive the death of Sargon. He therefore headed an alliance in which Ashkelon and Ekron took an active part. Hezekiah and his Philistine allies would hardly have made such an open challenge to Assyrian power had they not been able to rely on the active support of the Nubian king of Egypt.

It also appears that Hezekiah and Merodach-baladan, the Chaldean king of Babylon, were in close alliance. Isaiah 39 describes a diplomatic mission from Merodach-baladan to Jerusalem. Whether it took place during the Ashdod incident in 712 or after Sargon's death in 705 is still debatable, but it illustrates Judah's importance among the forces that could still resist Assyria's might.

Hezekiah realized that the Assyrian Army would almost certainly besiege Jerusalem, so he prepared the city and fortified its walls. Food was stored, and a water supply was readied by driving the Siloam Tunnel from the spring of En-gihon to a point inside the walls. It was a remarkable engineering operation, for the 400-metre tunnel was hewn through solid rock from both ends simultaneously. An inscription describing the work was discovered in 1880 on the wall of the tunnel itself; it is one of the best-known Hebrew epigraphic remains of the biblical period.

Sargon's heir, Sennacherib (705–681), could not deal with Hezekiah's revolt until he had gained control of Babylon in 702. About a year later, in the spring of 701, he set out at the head of a great army, advancing along the Phoenician coast. His Annals, almost contemporaneous, describe the subsequent events in great detail. Near Tyre he received the tribute of those vassals who had not revolted or who had decided to submit, among them the kings of Ammon, Moab and Edom (strangely enough, a king of Ashdod is also mentioned among them). From here he advanced along the coast to Philistia. After he had taken Jaffa and the vicinity, which belonged to Ashkelon, the latter city submitted and a new king was appointed. Sennacherib then besieged Ekron, at which point the promised Egyptian relief force arrived. The two great armies met in the Plain of Eltekeh. Sennacherib's description of this battle as a great victory appears to be exaggerated; more likely, the result was inconclusive, as he failed to pursue the Nubian troops after the battle. Instead of the expected list of booty, which usually follows a victorious battle, the Assyrian court historiographer treats us to an account of the punishment of Ekron and the capture of Eltekeh and Timnah, two insignificant cities nearby.

From there Sennacherib turned to deal with Hezekiah. The well-known description of this war against Hezekiah is one of the most detailed extra-biblical sources, and the comparison between it and the biblical account remains an often-disputed problem in biblical historical research. According to the Annals, composed several months after the campaign, the Assyrian Army besieged and captured forty-six of Hezekiah's 'strong walled cities as well as the small cities in their neighborhood'. The Annals do not list them by name, but the Judean stronghold Lachish, in which Sennacherib set up his camp, was singled out. The royal artists, in decorating the palace of Sennacherib at Nineveh, depicted in relief upon slabs of stone the assault on Lachish and its fall and pillage. Among the surviving reliefs from Sennacherib's palace, this is the most elaborate and detailed plastic description of the conquest of an enemy fortress. The next step in the campaign, according to the version in the Annals, was the siege of Jerusalem. Sennacherib claimed that he had invested Jerusalem and completely sealed it off: Hezekiah was shut up 'like a caged bird', and 'the going out of his city gate I made utterly impossible [literally, 'taboo'],' so that even Judah's *élite* force (*urbi,* an Aramaic and Hebrew term for shock troops) could not be employed. At this point the Assyrian account becomes abrupt: Hezekiah, overcome by the 'awe-inspiring radiance' emanating from Sennacherib, decided to submit and reaffirm his vassalage. After Sennacherib's departure Hezekiah delivered a heavy tribute to Nineveh, enumerated in most unusual detail (this is the longest list of tribute in Sennacherib's Annals): 'Thirty talents of gold, 800 talents of silver, choice antimony, large blocks of carnelian, beds [inlaid] with ivory, chairs [inlaid] with ivory, elephant hides, ivory, ebony-wood, garments with multi-coloured trim, garments of linen, wool [dyed] red-purple and blue-purple, vessels of copper, iron, bronze, and tin, chariots, slings, lances, armour, daggers for the belt, various kinds of arrows, countless trappings and implements of war, together with his daughter, his palace-women, his male and female musicians he had sent after me to Nineveh, my royal city, and he dispatched his personal messenger to deliver the tribute and to do obeisance' (the 'Rassam Cylinder' of Sennacherib).

The biblical account is more perplexing. It has been analysed as consisting of two sources:

1   II Kings 18:14–16 is an excerpt from a Temple chronicle recording the exact amount of the monies rendered as tribute, as well as the silver that was given to Sennacherib both from the Temple treasury and by stripping the silver veneer from its doors and pillars.

2   II Kings 18:13; 18:17–19:37; and Isaiah 36–7 form a prophetic story originating in a larger cycle of prophetic narratives about Isaiah and Hezekiah. That cycle comprises three stories, which probably should be arranged in the following order: (a) Hezekiah's illness in the fourteenth year of his reign (713) and his miraculous cure marked by the omen of the shadow on Ahaz's sundial moving back 10 degrees (II Kings 20:1–11; and Isaiah 38); (b) Merodach-baladan's delegation to Hezekiah (see page 141) and Isaiah's opposition to Hezekiah's political flirtation with Babylon, which was indeed Judah's main enemy but not until over 100 years later (II Kings 20:12–19; and Isaiah 39); (c) Sennacherib's invasion of Judah and Jerusalem's miraculous salvation, as foretold by Isaiah (II Kings 18:13; 18:17–19:37; and Isaiah 36–7).

Source 2, however, is a composite and consists of two closely interwoven strands, each of which contains an address (delivered, most unexpectedly in Hebrew) by *rab-shakeh,* Sennacherib's chief butler and envoy to the besieged city demanding immediate surrender, as well as Isaiah's reply and the story of Jerusalem's salvation. Only the second and perhaps later strand has the motif of the miraculous salvation of the city when 'the angel of the Lord went out, and smote in the camp of the Assyrians an hundred fourscore and five thousand: and when they arose early in in the morning, behold, they were all dead corpses' (II Kings 19:35). According to the earlier strand, Sennacherib would return to Assyria upon hearing a rumour and would be assassinated: 'Behold, I will send a blast upon him, and he shall hear a rumour, and shall return to his own land; and I will cause him to fall by the sword in his own land' (II Kings 19:7). Isaiah's prediction therefore is vindicated by the end of this story: 'So Sennacherib king of Assyria departed, and went and returned, and dwelt at Nineveh. And it came to pass, as he was worshipping in the house of Nisroch his god, that Adrammelech and Sharezer his sons smote him with the sword: and they escaped into the land of Armenia [in Hebrew, Ararat; in Assyrian, Urartu] and Esarhaddon his son reigned in his stead' (II Kings 19:36–7).

The inconsistency between the prophetic narrative as a whole, describing Sennacherib's miraculous defeat, and Sennacherib's own account, claiming victory, has been a matter of scholarly debate from the very time that his Annals were deciphered in the early days of Assyriology. This inconsistency, as well as the fact that the prophetic narrative (II Kings 19:9; Isaiah 37:9) mentions 'Tirhakah [Egyptian Taharqa] King of Ethiopia [*i.e.,* Nubia]' as the king of Egypt (who ascended the throne only in 690), while the Nubian king who fought Sennacherib at Eltekeh must have been his predecessor, led several scholars to suggest that Sennacherib had in fact led two expeditions to Palestine. The first, in 701, described in the Annals and in the account in biblical source 1, ended in Judah's submission to Assyria.

The second campaign is supposed to have taken place during the years 688–681, a period for which official historical records are lacking. This campaign was supposed to have ended in Sennacherib's defeat and to have been the basis for the account in biblical source 2. However, the supposition of two campaigns cannot be upheld. There is no independent evidence from Assyrian sources that could lead us to postulate an additional campaign against Judah on the part of Sennacherib. On the contrary, there is reason to suppose that Sennacherib had no further interest in the west after his campaign of 701. He had abandoned his father's expansionist policies, concentrating on his enormous building projects, especially the transformation of Nineveh into his new capital. Sennacherib consciously acquiesced in the *de facto* independence of Judah and the Philistine cities, being content with their remaining vassal states as a buffer between Assyria and the growing power of the Nubian dynasty. It was only under his son Esarhaddon (681–669) that Assyria reverted to the Sargonic imperial policy in the west. Indeed, Esarhaddon's first campaign, in 679, was to the 'Brook of Egypt' to re-establish the Assyrian domination in Philistia that had declined during his father's reign. Esarhaddon's main enemy was Tirhakah, with whom he and his son Ashurbanipal fought one battle after another until Assyria finally conquered Egypt. The supposition of an extra campaign seems to be untenable also on methodological grounds.

The existence of two conflicting accounts emanating from the two parties to the conflict should not surprise us, as it is a common feature in history. In this case the two contemporary sources (Sennacherib's Annals and the account in biblical source 1) are in striking agreement. It is only the late prophetic story of source 2 that presents a problem. This story, probably written in the second half of the seventh century, dates from fifty years after the event; it stresses the veracity of Isaiah's prophecy that Jerusalem would survive Sennacherib. Indeed, the prophetic account telescopes events: Sennacherib's assassination at the hands of his sons is presented as following immediately upon his return from Judah to Nineveh, while in fact it took place twenty-one years later. (The same practice of telescoping events is used in a Babylonian chronicle that relates the death of a thirteenth-century Assyrian king, Tukulti-Ninurta I, implying that it resulted from his desecration of Babylon, although his death occurred almost thirty years later.) The mention of Tirhakah may be a result of the same process, according to which the name of a well-known king who had repeatedly fought against Assyria supplanted that of the less-known Nubian who was the adversary of Sennacherib. Still, it is, of course, not impossible that Tirhakah, the crown prince (who is now believed to have been a young man at the time of the campaign), was indeed nominal head of the Egyptian army at Eltekeh.

Sennacherib's account of the events of 701 leaves open the main question as to what motivated his sudden return to Nineveh, forsaking even Hezekiah's tribute. Various reasons for this hasty departure have been suggested: he might have been weakened by the battle with the Nubians at Eltekeh; or perhaps, as the prophetic account hints, some crisis at home (the 'rumour') demanded his presence or, indeed, as some biblical scholars believe, an epidemic spread through his camp. An echo of Sennacherib's sudden departure is found also in a late Egyptian tale recorded by Herodotus (XII, 14). It relates the defeat of Sennacherib, whom it calls 'king of the

Assyrians and the Arabs', at Pelusium in the Egyptian approaches. The tale relates (XII, 141) that field-mice overran the camp of Sennacherib and ate the bows and shield handles of the soldiers; the next day, when this was discovered, all the army fled. This story has been seen by some as an indication that Sennacherib's army was afflicted with bubonic plague, which is carried by mice. At all events, the fact that Sennacherib and his huge army could devastate most of Judah but not take its capital was considered by the following generations as indeed a miracle. Until then the Assyrian military machine had seemed invincible, crushing every western rebel, annexing its territory and exiling its people. The very fact that the Assyrian Empire did not conquer and annex Jerusalem, though it lay only about 10 miles south of the imperial border, was seen as a clear sign of the divine plan as revealed by Isaiah: to punish Judah through Sennacherib but not to destroy her utterly.

Jerusalem had escaped the fate of Samaria, yet the country was gravely affected by the war. Many of her cities were in ruins; thousands of her inhabitants had been deported to Assyria (Sennacherib claims 200,150 deportees); Judah was reduced in size, with sections being handed over to the Philistines. Yet, at the same time, the status of Jerusalem as a Temple city under divine protection was enhanced, and the prophetic circles, who preserved and handed down the oracles of Isaiah, naturally stressed the role of Isaiah, the prophet of deliverance, at the crucial moment of Judah's history. (The prestige of this prophecy and the concept of the inviolability of Jerusalem, which stemmed from the outcome of the siege of 701, contributed to the later Josianic reforms.)

Isaiah, the foremost of the classical prophets, took an active part in the political life of Judah. Though socially a member of the nobility, he followed the tradition of Amos as a prophet of protest on behalf of the poor and oppressed, whom he regularly referred to as 'my [God's] people'. Social justice rather than cult or military strength should be, in his opinion, Judah's real concern. Therefore, Judah should not rely on 'horse and chariot' or on aid promised by Egypt. In fact, she should not rebel against Assyria. The existence of this arrogant heathen conqueror did not conflict with the idea of divine control over history and Judah's special role in it. The Assyrian emperor was a mere tool in the hands of the God of Israel and he would be destroyed in his turn after having unconsciously fulfilled his functions. Hezekiah, therefore, should refrain from rebellion and devote his energies to internal reform (Isaiah 30:1–18). However, with all his opposition to the king's political ambitions, he remained an ardent Davidite, extolling the role of the righteous 'rod out of the stem of Jesse' (Isaiah 11:1) and of the Jerusalem Temple at 'the end of days', that is, after Assyria's inevitable downfall in the not-too-distant future. Then 'out of Zion shall go forth the law, and the word of the Lord from Jerusalem,' and universal peace will prevail (Isaiah 2:3).

It was only natural that Isaiah's attitude to Sennacherib's campaign was ambivalent: on the one hand, he welcomed Assyria as the bearer of punishment for Judah's iniquities; yet, on the other hand, when Jerusalem and the house of David were in danger of extinction (the inevitable consequence of the city's surrender), he reacted vehemently to the *rab-shakeh*'s abusive speech, promising the forthcoming downfall of Sennacherib.

It is very likely that, in spite of the later transformation into literary form, the biblical text preserves a kernel of the original orations of Isaiah delivered during that period of crisis. 'Therefore thus saith the Lord concerning the king of Assyria, He shall not come into this city, nor shoot an arrow there, nor come before it with shields, nor cast a bank against it. By the way that he came, by the same shall he return, . . . saith the Lord. For I will defend this city to save it for mine own sake, and for my servant David's sake' (Isaiah 37:33–5).

This prophecy of hope should be contrasted with those of Micah, his contemporary, who did not share Isaiah's belief in Jerusalem's inviolability. Because of blatant social injustice on the part of Judah's leaders, Jerusalem and the Temple would not escape the fate of Shiloh (Micah 3:12). Yet he too believed in the universal role of the Temple and the Davidite reigning in Zion at 'the end of days' (Micah 4).

Finally, a moot point in the history of Hezekiah's reign is the date of his cultic reforms. 'He removed the high places, and brake the images, and cut down the groves, and brake in pieces the brasen serpent that Moses had made: for unto those days the children of Israel did burn incense to it: and he called it Nehushtan. He trusted in the Lord God of Israel; so that after him was none like him among all the kings of Judah, nor any that were before him' (II Kings 18:4–5).

These reforms, intended to abolish centres of worship outside Jerusalem, thus increasing the importance of the Temple and purifying its cult, are described at great length in a late and dubious tradition in II Chronicles 29–31. There they are dated to the first year of Hezekiah's reign (726), although there is reason to assume that the reforms were in fact carried out somewhat later in his reign. One possibility is to place them shortly after the fall of Samaria, still during Sargon's reign; another view is that they date from the years 705–701, from the occasion of his rebellion against Assyria. Whatever their exact date, the abolition of syncretistic practices and the elevation of the Temple as the sole legitimate place of worship were not only a demonstration of piety on the part of the king but also a calculated move to consolidate his control over the cult and the priesthood.

The Reign of Manasseh

Hezekiah died a few years after Sennacherib's campaign, and his son Manasseh ascended the throne while he was still a boy. He reigned for fifty years, and during most of that time he was a faithful vassal of Assyria. In II Kings and in later biblical tradition, he is described as an apostate and archsinner. Not only did he abandon the cultic reforms of his father, but he went so far as to introduce the worship of foreign gods into the Temple:

And he did that which was evil in the sight of the Lord, after the abominations of the heathen, whom the Lord cast out before the children of Israel. For he built up again the high places which Hezekiah his father had destroyed; and he reared up altars for Baal, and made a grove, as did Ahab king of Israel; and worshipped all the host of heaven, and served them. And he built altars in the house of the Lord, of which the Lord said, In Jerusalem will I put my name. And he built altars for all the host of heaven in the two courts of the house of the Lord. And he made his son pass through the fire, and practised soothsaying, and used enchantments, and dealt with familiar spirits and wizards: he wrought much wickedness in the sight of the Lord, to provoke him to anger. And he set a graven image of the grove that he had made in the house, of which the Lord said to David, and to Solomon his son, In this house and in Jerusalem, which I have chosen out of all tribes of Israel, will I put my name for ever (II Kings 21:2–7).

Manasseh's idolatry is regarded as the immediate cause of Judah's downfall. Even Josiah's reforms could not overcome the iniquities of the earlier king. The prophetess Huldah, in response to Josiah's query, responded that the land was doomed despite the king's righteousness (II Kings 22); while Jeremiah explicitly stated that prayer had lost all efficacy 'because of Manasseh the son of Hezekiah king of Judah, for that which he did in Jerusalem' (Jeremiah 15:4).

What was the character of Manasseh's cultic innovations? The first step was a retreat from Hezekiah's cultic centralization and the re-establishment of the local shrines. This in itself was not a heathen act but merely a cultic practice that had recently been outlawed by the Deuteronomic movement. But he also introduced into the Temple altars to foreign gods and sponsored the Assyrian astral cult throughout Judah. Lastly, he passed his son through a fire – i e, dedicating him to Molech (or Moloch; II Kings 21:6).

Extra-biblical research has recently elucidated in detail the exact nature of these elements. The worship of celestial bodies, the sun and moon discs, is well attested in ancient Palestine, Syria and Anatolia in the second millennium BCE. It is only under the Assyrian Empire, however, that they enjoyed universal popularity. Thus, where we are told that Josiah abolished the horses and chariots sacred to the sun (II Kings 23:11), he must have been dealing with one of Manasseh's cultic innovations. (White horses sacred to the sun-god and moon-god are attested to in Assyrian documents from that period.) The passage in II Kings 21 also accuses Manasseh of introducing practices of divination. In Assyria this was the golden age of divination; astrologers and haruspices were prominent at the royal court, especially under Esarhaddon. The cult of Molech may be derived from the Aramean practice of dedicating children to Adad – the major Aramean-Assyrian deity – by 'passing them through fire', both as an act of divination and as a sacrifice. The Aramean component of Assyrian civilization was already predominant in Judah from the middle of the eighth century, as is evidenced by the innovations introduced in the Temple cult by Manasseh's grandfather Ahaz (II Kings 16:10–18).

Was the introduction of these new cultic practices into the Judean court and the Temple cult a deliberate act on the part of Manasseh, in order to demonstrate his loyalty as an Assyrian vassal? Or was it merely the immediate influence of a particularly intensive Assyrian military presence in the area during his reign that motivated his apostasy? There is no clear answer at present. In any case, one matter that recently became clear is that the Assyrian emperors did not require their vassals to adopt their religious practices. Whatever the reason for it, Manasseh's idolatry was regarded by many of his contemporaries as an aberration and by the criteria of later generations as Judah's worst sin.

Manasseh's reign was the time of the heaviest Assyrian impact on Judah. It was the period of repeated Assyrian campaigns in the west aimed at the defeat of Egypt. Esarhaddon (681–669) reasserted the Assyrian domination of Philistia, forcing out the Nubian army of Tirhakah, but he was badly defeated at the gates of Egypt. In 671, however, he returned and this time succeeded in invading Egypt and conquering the Delta. He died while conducting another campaign to Egypt in 669, but his son, Ashurbanipal, continued his military enterprises, finally conquering and pillaging the southern capital of Thebes. The Nubian presence in Egypt was ended. In these campaigns the measure of Judah's involvement in Assyrian imperial policies is illustrated by the fact that Manasseh participated with his army in one of Ashurbanipal's campaigns to Egypt. It was only after the Assyrian withdrawal from Egypt (after 656) that the burden upon Judah may have been eased, although uninterrupted Assyrian control of the country continued until at least 649, as is testified by the Assyrian administrative tablets from Gezer. Meanwhile, internal difficulties were increasing in Assyria. The power of the empire was exhausted by the prolonged wars in Babylonia and Elam. Finally, the threat from the north became real: the Cimmerians were encroaching upon the north-western borders of the empire. This combination of circumstances was bound to give rise to hopes for the liberation of Judah from Assyria, which were actually fulfilled in the days of Josiah, the grandson of Manasseh.

A story in II Chronicles 33 of certain purported events in Manasseh's reign still remains a historical crux. Manasseh is said to have been arrested by the king of Assyria, apparently on a charge of conspiracy and rebellion, and imprisoned in Babylon, where he prayed to the Lord and was forgiven. After his return to Jerusalem, he took steps to fortify the city. Whether this late tale has a historical basis is still an open question; but it is possible that the easing of Assyrian pressure towards the end of Manasseh's reign resulted in his fortifying the outer defences of Jerusalem (II Chronicles 33:14).

Another obscure historical problem is the murder of Manasseh's son Amon, after only two years on the throne. His death may have been connected with religious movements in Judah that came into the open during Josiah's reign. At any rate, the conspirators were unable to exploit their initial success. 'Am ha-arez, 'the people of the land', intervened and placed Amon's eight-year-old son, Josiah, on the throne (the same body was later responsible for elevating to the throne a successor to Josiah). It is important to note that 'the people of the land' did not include the nobles, priests and (official court) prophets – in other words, classes connected with the court or Temple (see Jeremiah 1:18; and Ezekiel 22:26–9).

The Reign of Josiah

Although events during the latter years of Ashurbanipal are obscure, it may be assumed that by that time the ties between the more distant provinces, including Judah, and the centre of the Assyrian Empire had grown weak. In Philistia, Egypt's power was again on the increase: according to the tradition preserved by Herodotus (II, 157), Psammetichus I (656–610), the founder of the Twenty-sixth Dynasty, conquered Ashdod from the Assyrians. The death of Ashurbanipal in 627 precipitated a major crisis in the empire. Babylon revolted in that same year and gained independence under the Chaldean prince Nabopolassar, who was to found the neo-Babylonian (Chaldean) Empire. Assyria itself may have suffered internal strife: a war broke out between Ashur-etil-ilani (627–623), the son of Ashurbanipal, and his brother, Sin-shar-ishkun (623–612), and the empire was probably split for some years between two rival administrative centres, each with its own eponyms. Against this background a movement towards liberation from Assyria developed in Judah after decades of continuous vassalage. Judah's growing independence, which seems to have been achieved gradually and without bloodshed, is expressed in two actions of the utmost significance undertaken by its young king: Judah encroached upon the southern part of the province of Samaria, now apparently abandoned by Assyria; and, internally, Josiah conducted a fundamental reform in cult practices. These were but two facets of the same national and religious revival in Judah – the last before its fall.

Josiah's reform, which chiefly involved the elimination of the foreign cultic practices characteristic of Manasseh's age, is described in great detail in II Kings 22–3. According to the account presented there, the reforms resulted from a covenant formed upon the finding of a 'book of the law' in Josiah's eighteenth year. Moreover, the reforms were compressed into what was evidently a brief period between the formation of the covenant (II Kings 23:3) and the celebration of Passover (II Kings 23:21). Neither of these assessments can be considered accurate, as the reforms must have involved a longer process and do not necessarily have to stem from the finding of the 'book of the law'. Therefore a variant account found in II Chronicles 34:3, which dates the reforms of Josiah to his twelfth year (628), is apparently to be preferred. Though the author of the Books of Chronicles ('the chronicler') is suspected of rewriting history according to his preferences and of distorting chronological sequence to suit his theological views, in this case it stands to reason that Josiah's reforms in fact began at the earlier date, that is, at the very close of Ashurbanipal's reign with the weakening of Assyria's empire in the west.

Probably in the early stage of the reform, Josiah removed the chariots of the sun, the vessels for Baal and Asherah and the houses for Asherah, ancient cultic symbols originating from Phoenicia (II Kings 23:4, 11). The next step was the elimination of the high places (the *bamot*) from all over the country (II Kings 23:8; and II Chronicles 34:6). These actions culminated in the destruction of the old and venerated cultic centre of Bethel, which remained Israel's main place of worship even after the fall of Samaria. Other steps that he took included the concentration of the priests of the *bamot* in Jerusalem, although they were prohibited from offering sacrifices in the Temple (II Kings 23:9). Naturally, these measures strengthened the position of Jerusalem and the Temple as the sole and undisputed sanctuary and reinforced the Davidic king's claim to be the legitimate ruler of all Israel.

The high point of the reform was in the eighteenth year of Josiah's reign (622/1), when a 'book of the law' was discovered in the course of repairs carried out on the Temple in Jerusalem and was read before the king: 'And Hilkiah the high priest said unto Shaphan the scribe, I have found the book of the law in the house of the

Lord. And Hilkiah gave the book to Shaphan, and he read it. . . . And Shaphan the scribe shewed the king, saying, Hilkiah the priest hath delivered me a book. And Shaphan read it before the king' (II Kings 22:8, 10).

The problem of the identity of this book is central to biblical research. It is generally accepted that the 'book of the law' was Deuteronomy or at least a considerable part of it, in particular the covenantal curse (Deuteronomy 28ff.). It is the only book that stresses the absolute prohibition of worship anywhere except in the chosen city (Deuteronomy 12:5). Recent research has shown that Deuteronomy was drawn up as a covenant between Israel and its God; it is actually a treaty in which Israel takes upon herself vassalage to its God, the overlord. A breach of the covenant would bring about, as accepted in similar treaties of vassalage of that period, exceedingly harsh punishments – in particular, extermination of the population and destruction of the kingdom. The covenant is sealed by a list of curses (Deuteronomy 28) that are similar to the curses in recently discovered vassal treaties from the time of Esarhaddon, the king of Assyria.

The profound influence of the discovery of the book and the subsequent effects are described in detail in II Kings 22–3.

> And it came to pass, when the king had heard the words of the book of the law, that he rent his clothes. And the king commanded Hilkiah the priest, and Ahikam the son of Shaphan, and Achbor the son of Michaiah, and Shaphan the scribe, and Asahiah a servant of the king's, saying, Go ye, enquire of the Lord for me, and for the people, and for all Judah, concerning the words of this book that is found: for great is the wrath of the Lord that is kindled against us, because our fathers have not hearkened unto the words of this book, to do according unto all that which is written concerning us (II Kings 22:11–13).

Disturbed by the words in the newly discovered book of the covenant, Josiah summoned the representatives of the people to Jerusalem: 'And the king went up into the house of the Lord, and all the men of Judah and all the inhabitants of Jerusalem with him, and the priests, and the prophets, and all the people, both small and great: and he read in their ears all the words of the book of the covenant which was found in the house of the Lord' (II Kings 23:2). The words of the newly discovered book were read in public, and a covenant was entered upon in an impressive ceremony. The essence of this new covenant was the insistence upon eliminating all foreign cults, total abolition of the high places and the centralization of worship in 'the place which the Lord your God shall choose . . . to put his name there' (Deuteronomy 12:5), which was understood to mean Jerusalem's Temple. The great national and religious awakening culminated in the celebration of the Passover festival in Jerusalem, for 'there was not holden such a passover from the days of the judges that judged Israel, nor in all the days of the kings of Israel, nor of the kings of Judah' (II Kings 23:22). Apparently both the people and the king believed that henceforth a new era was opening in the history of Israel, as Manasseh's alien gods had been removed, the *bamot* had been abolished, Bethel utterly destroyed and Jerusalem, 'the place that the Lord had chosen', had emerged as the sole legitimate centre of worship. Indeed, this reform, together with the Deuteronomic movement that accompanied it, played a decisive part in the history of Israel. It brought about a revival of those national values rooted in Israel's historic tradition as expressed in terms of the Covenant at Mount Sinai.

The new movement gave birth to a novel historiographic composition that forms the basis of the present Books of Kings. A contemporary historian in Jerusalem set out to describe the history of Israel up to his own time from a critical viewpoint based on two main assumptions: (1) the Northern Kingdom had been destroyed because of its rejection of Jerusalem's Temple; thus Jeroboam I was the first 'sinner', and his 'sin' was repeated by every one of his successors; (2) the Davidic dynasty was the only legitimate dynasty, reigning by virtue of the divine covenant with David; thus the cultic transgressions of the Judean kings, their leniency towards the high places and idolatry, did not result in Judah's destruction but only in the temporary chastisement of the particular king. In this framework a link was established between Jeroboam's initial 'sin', worshipping the God of Israel at the altar of Bethel, and the destruction of the same altar by Josiah some 300 years later. The historian even took the liberty of putting a most unusual prophecy, clearly a *vaticinium ex eventu,* into the mouth of a prophet of Judah, who addresses the altar at Bethel while Jeroboam is sacrificing there: 'O altar, altar, thus saith the Lord; Behold, a child shall be born unto the house of David, Josiah by name; and upon thee shall he offer the priests of the high places that burn incense upon thee, and men's bones shall be burnt upon thee' (I Kings 13:2). This same historian describes in II Kings 23:15-18 the fulfilment of his prophecy during Josiah's purification of Bethel. Josiah's reign marked the end of one era, that of cultic sin and its punishment, and the beginning of a new one inaugurated by the new covenant. This outlook is congruent with the fact that Josiah's reign, his reforms and Judah's long-awaited independence coincided with the decline and fall of the seemingly invincible Assyrian Empire.

The reign of Josiah was also a period of territorial expansion and economic prosperity. As we have noted, he hoped to unite under his rule the remnant of the Northern Kingdom. In the initial stage of this expansion, Judah spread from Geba in the hills of Ephraim to Beersheba in the south and later may have reached even as far as Galilee. Archaeological excavations have shown that there was considerable activity in the Negev as well. In the west Josiah advanced into northern Philistia and regained control of the coastal trade route. Evidence of his control of this route comes from a recently excavated fortress, Metzad Ḥashavyahu, on the sea-shore north of Ashdod. The king settled the area with either colonists or serfs, one of whom complained in a letter that an officer had taken away his garment because he had not done the necessary amount of work. This fortress may have been built to meet pressing military needs in connexion with the expansion of Egyptian rule over Philistia and the conquest of Ashdod by the Egyptian king, Psammetichus I. These events were bound to clash eventually with Josiah's expansion from the north.

The final years of Josiah's reign were a time of upheaval and change. In the bitter struggle between Assyria and Chaldean Babylonia, the latter gradually gained the upper hand, mainly with the help of the now unified and independent kingdom of the Medes, who had spread their rule over most of Iran, waiting for the right moment to attack the weakening Assyria. (The tradition in Herodotus that Scythians took part in these wars and even invaded as far south as Ashkelon is not borne out by contemporary sources.) A third power also emerged on the scene, the Twenty-sixth Dynasty in Egypt, and when Assyria grew weak, Psammetichus I came to her aid. We do not know the circumstances of this alliance nor its exact date (it might have originated in the latter half of Ashurbanipal's reign, that is, after Assyria's withdrawal from Egypt), but in 616 we find Egyptian forces fighting in Mesopotamia alongside the Assyrians. This assistance was of no avail, however, and in 614 the city of Ashur fell to the Medes. Two years later, while the Assyrian Army was engaged in Babylonia, the Medes descended upon Nineveh and looted and destroyed it. The impact of the fall of Nineveh on Assyria's former subject peoples was enormous, and its echoes can be heard clearly in the prophet Nahum's 'Vision of Nineveh', which expressed in no uncertain terms Judah's delight in the fall of its tyrannical master. On the ruins of the once-mighty city, the victorious king of the Medes made an alliance with Nabopolassar, the king of Babylon. The Assyrian Army nevertheless withdrew to the west and continued to fight. It took up positions in Haran, where Ashur-uballit II (Ashurbanipal's young son) became Assyria's last king. However, Haran could not hold out against the overwhelming strength of the Medes and Babylonians. It fell in 610, but the last king of Assyria may have managed to extricate himself and withdraw to Carchemish, where he awaited Egyptian help. No clear information is available about the political orientation of Judah during these years of confusion, nor is it clear why Josiah, in 609, attempted to block the passage of Necho, the son of Psammetichus, who, on ascending the throne, immediately hastened towards Carchemish in order to help the remains of the Assyrian forces. Josiah was probably apprehensive of Egypt's growing strength, or he may have feared the revival of Assyria and been unwilling to forfeit the independence that Judah had gained through Assyria's decline. He tried to halt the Egyptian Army near Megiddo, a key spot on the route between Egypt and the north, but he was severely wounded at the beginning of the battle and soon died (II Kings 23:29).

The Last Days of Judah and the Destruction of the Temple

No two other decades in the history of Judah are better documented than the years 609–586, for the most part spent under Babylonian suzerainty. The detailed description in II Kings 24–5 and in Jeremiah is supplemented by the Babylonian Chronicles and Hebrew epigraphic material, notably ostraca, seals and seal-impressions.

It was a period of intense conflicts: political confusion in Jerusalem; a struggle between militant extremists favouring insurrection against Babylonia and moderates acquiescing to foreign rule; the prophetic condemnation of the court and king; and a growing oppression of the poor. The pace of events quickened. Omens of catastrophe were already apparent, but very few perceived them. Those who did became the supporters of Jeremiah, the prophet of doom. Although Jeremiah's prophetic career began in 627, the thirteenth year of Josiah's reign (Jeremiah 1:2), it was only from 609 that his admonitions elicited any response.

Within this twenty-year period, the throne changed hands four times. Upon Josiah's death 'the people of the land' placed his son Jehoahaz on the throne. (It is possible that Jehoahaz was not the first-born but was preferred to his elder brother, Eliakim.) When Pharaoh Necho returned three months later from his unsuccessful siege of Haran, he dethroned the newly elected king, demonstrating his prerogative as the suzerain of Judah. Jehoahaz was carried off to an Egyptian exile, while Necho crowned Eliakim king and changed his name to Jehoiakim. The reason for name changes among the later Judean kings is obscure. However, in this case it is obviously a sign of Jehoiakim's new status as vassal to Egypt.

Jehoiakim's brief reign (609–598) witnessed many changes. First came three years of Egyptian sovereignty. Then, in 605, the decisive battle of the Egyptian-Babylonian war was fought. The two armies clashed at Carchemish on the Upper Euphrates. Nebuchadnezzar, Nabopolassar's heir and the commander of the army, defeated the Egyptian Necho.

The Babylonian Chronicle, describing Nabopolassar's and Nebuchadnezzar's reigns, reads: 'In the twenty-first year, the king of Akkad [Babylon] stayed in his own land, Nebuchadnezzar, his eldest son the crown prince, mustered [the Babylonian Army] and took command of his troops; he marched to Carchemish which is on the bank of the Euphrates, and crossed the river [to march] against the Egyptian Army which lay in Carchemish. . . . They fought with each other and the Egyptian Army withdrew before him. He accomplished their defeat [so quickly that] no weapon reached them. In the district of Hamath, the Babylonian troops overtook and defeated them so that not a single man [escaped] to his own country.' (The exact date of this battle is crucial for biblical chronology in this period; Jeremiah 46:2 explicitly dates it to Jehoiakim's fourth year of reign.)

Nebuchadnezzar did not penetrate Palestine that year. Shortly after the battle at Carchemish, he succeeded his father as king of Babylon. Not until 604/3 did he consummate his victory. For six months, the Babylonian Chronicle states, he 'marched about unopposed' in Syria and Phoenicia. He then turned south and marched against Philistia.

Philistia still enjoyed a special status deriving from the days of Assyrian rule. The kings of Assyria officially governed the large Philistine cities, from Ekron in the north to Gaza in the south, but at the same time these cities had close ties with Egypt. This connexion was mainly historical, as Philistia was under nominal Egyptian rule at the beginning of Saul's reign and, as far as we can tell, again during part of Solomon's rule. For this reason the kings of Assyria more than once revealed a certain flexibility in their treatment of rebellious Philistine cities and leniency in their punishments. At the end of Ashurbanipal's reign (towards the close of the seventh century), Egypt renewed its direct involvement in Philistine affairs, becoming the dominant power and supplanting Assyria. Philistine kings swore allegiance to Pharaoh and became Egyptian vassals.

The close ties between the Philistine cities and Egypt are succinctly illustrated by a fragment of an Aramaic letter discovered in Sakkarah in Egypt. A Philistine king (the name of his city has not survived, but it was apparently Ashdod or Gaza) begged Pharaoh to come to his aid on the grounds that the troops 'of the king of

Babylon have advanced as far as Aphek and have be[gun to . . .] For Lord of Kings, Pharaoh knows that [thy] servant [cannot stand alone against the king of Babylon. May it therefore please him] to send a force to succor me. Let him not forsake m[e. For thy servant is loyal to my lord] and thy servant remembers his kindness, and this region [is my lord's possession. But if the king of Babylon takes it he will set up] a governor in the land . . . ' (H.L. Ginsberg's translation and restoration). The exact date of this letter is still debated, but it plainly reflects the suzerain-vassal relationship and the expectation of Egyptian assistance.

The most prominent of the northern Philistine cities was Ashkelon, which, as a large port, had an especially close relationship with Egypt. Now it became Nebuchadnezzar's target. The Ashkelonites decided not to submit, having apparently been guaranteed Egyptian military support. The city was beseiged and taken and paid heavily for resisting Babylonian rule. The king was captured, the people led off into Babylonian exile, the city plundered and destroyed – in the words of the Babylonian Chronicle, 'turned into a mound and heap of ruins'.

Ashkelon was a warning to Egypt and to the other Palestinian city-states still wavering between Babylon and Egypt. Jehoiakim panicked; his ardent belief in Egyptian power was shaken and a fast was proclaimed 'before the Lord to all the people in Jerusalem, and to all the people that came from the cities of Judah unto Jerusalem' (Jeremiah 36:9). The fast is dated to the ninth month of Jehoiakim's fifth year. The relevance of this date became clear after the publication of the Babylonian Chronicle, relating Nebuchadnezzar's reign. It revealed that Nebuchadnezzar's campaign against Ashkelon occurred in the very same month.

At this critical moment, before the impending approach of the Babylonians, Baruch ben Neriah, Jeremiah's scribe, read before the people assembled in the Temple a scroll of Jeremiah's prophecies compiled the previous year, that is, under the impact of the Babylonian victory at Carchemish. Jeremiah's message was that Nebuchadnezzar was an instrument of Divine anger. The king of the Chaldeans was fulfilling a divine plan to chasten all the lands, especially sinful Judah. But the period of chastisement would be limited to seventy years. (The literary notion of seventy years of affliction is linked in the prophetic literature of Assyria and Judah to the span of a man's life [see Isaiah 23:15].) It will be at the end of that period, 'when seventy years are accomplished, that I will punish the king of Babylon, and that nation, saith the Lord, for their iniquity, and the land of the Chaldeans, and will make it perpetual desolations' (Jeremiah 25:12).

Jeremiah's vision of imminent destruction enraged Jehoiakim, who snatched the scroll, 'cut it with the penknife, and cast it into the fire' (Jeremiah 36:23). Jeremiah went into hiding to avoid punishment for treason. It is still unclear whether Jehoiakim submitted to Babylon in that year or during Nebuchadnezzar's campaign to the region in the following year. The Babylonian Chronicle at this point is damaged, and the name of the city conquered in the campaign is missing, but it might have been Gaza. Thus all Philistia and Judah came under Babylonian sway.

Jehoiakim, like the majority of his advisers, did not believe the Chaldean rulers of Babylon would be able to hold Palestine against the armed might of Egypt. Chaldean Babylonia was a new phenomenon in the Near East, and therefore its longevity was in doubt. Egypt was much closer geographically, and the pharaohs had never employed the harsh methods of the Assyrians and Babylonians. Jehoiakim's attachment to Egypt was therefore very deep, and his fidelity to the erstwhile Babylonian conqueror consisted only of lip-service. Seeming proof of Nebuchadnezzar's weakness came in the winter of 601/600. The Babylonian king attacked Egypt but was repulsed. The site of the battle is unknown, but it was probably somewhere in southern Philistia. The Babylonian set-back inspired Jehoiakim to withhold his customary vassal tribute and declare a rebellion. For a short time it appeared that he would be successful. The defeated king of Babylon reorganized his army and did not return to Philistia and Judah for almost three years. In the winter of 598, he invaded Judah. At this fateful moment Jehoiakim died – while the Babylonian Army was approaching Jerusalem. His eighteen-year-old son, Coniahu (or Jehoiachin), was raised to the throne in time to surrender Jerusalem to the besieging Babylonian forces. 'And Jehoiachin the king of Judah went out to the king of Babylon, he, and his mother, and his servants, and his princes, and his officers' (II Kings 24:12).

The fall of Jerusalem is described briefly in the Babylonian Chronicle of Nebuchadnezzar: 'In the seventh year, the month of Kislev, the king of Akkad (Babylon) mustered his troops, marched to the Hatti-land, and encamped against [besieged] the "city of Judah" and on the second day of the month of Adar he seized the city and captured the king. He appointed there a king of his own choice [literally, heart], received its heavy tribute and sent [them] to Babylon.'

Jehoiachin's submission saved Jerusalem for a time, but the price was high. The king and his court were led to Babylonia. The Temple and king's treasuries were plundered, and 10,000 people, mainly choice troops and artisans, were taken captive and brought to Babylonia. Jehoiachin's uncle, Mattaniah, was enthroned, and his name was changed to Zedekiah.

The capture of Jerusalem is dated to the second of Adar in the Babylonian Chronicle. However, as the practice of Babylonian kings was to be present at the beginning of Nisan for the New Year's ceremonies, it would seem that Nebuchadnezzar departed after the city's fall, leaving a subordinate king and probably Babylonian commanders to carry out the orders for the exile. Several months must have elapsed in organizing the exile. The 10,000 people (a round number) were accompanied by their families, and it is likely that they were transferred to Babylonia in groups (see Jeremiah 52:28). It was in the next year, 596, that Zedekiah truly became king.

Zedekiah's first year witnessed extremely difficult conditions in Judah. The new, inexperienced leadership that had replaced the exiled court tended to be more militant and, surprisingly, even adamantly anti-Babylonian. The prophets too were sharply divided: while Jeremiah and his few followers aligned themselves with the moderate factions (which were actually entire families, as each family maintained a consistent political stance), the nationalistic prophets (such as Hananiah ben Azur [see Jeremiah 28]) predicted the destruction of Babylon within a short period. Some of the latter group agitated among the exiles and, as a result, were severely punished by Nebuchadnezzar (Jeremiah 29:21-2). This group, although designated as false prophets by Jeremiah, exerted significant influence upon the remaining populace in Jerusalem, as well as on the king.

Zedekiah's position was made tenuous by the fact that he was actually a regent, not the king. Although in exile, Jehoiachin was given deferential treatment by Nebuchadnezzar, to the extent that he was allowed to retain his manors in Judah, overseen by his own stewards. According to Babylonian administrative texts from the thirteenth year of Nebuchadnezzar, Jehoiachin and his five sons received food rations from the royal store, and Jehoiachin bore the title 'king of Judah'. (Jehoiachin's treatment was not unique: the exiled kings of Ashkelon, Ashdod and Gaza, as well as artisans of Egyptian, Tyrian, Lydian and even Greek origin, received food allocations from the royal court.) For the exiled Judeans and probably for many of those remaining, Jehoiachin was the only legitimate ruler. The exiles and those remaining in Judah had frequent contacts with each other; thus rumours of Babylonian events soon spread to Judah. At the end of 595, word of an insurrection in Babylonia reached Jerusalem, raising hopes for the deliverance of the captives.

Shortly afterwards, in 594, Pharaoh Necho of Egypt died and was replaced by his son Psammetichus II, a warrior known for his military prowess. This change forced a re-evaluation of the political situation by the Palestinian states, and a meeting of ambassadors from Edom, Moab, Ammon, Tyre and Sidon was held, probably in secret, in Jerusalem. The main topic, obviously, was their relations with Babylonia, as is evident from Jeremiah's warning:

> And now have I given all these lands into the hand of Nebuchadnezzar the king of Babylon, my servant; and the beasts of the field have I given him also to serve him. And all nations shall serve him, and his son, and his son's son, until the very time of his land come: and then many nations and great kings shall serve themselves of him . . . [and] the nation and kingdom which will not serve the same Nebuchadnezzar the king of Babylon . . . but that nation will I punish, saith the Lord (Jeremiah 27:6–8).

In that same year Nebuchadnezzar conducted two campaigns to Palestine in order to reinforce the Babylonian presence. Unfortunately, our main source for these events, the Babylonian Chronicle covering Nebuchadnezzar's reign breaks off in 594, and we do not have details concerning the last days of Judah from any other external source. In all probability, word of the above-mentioned meeting reached Nebuchadnezzar. In any case, Zedekiah soon paid a visit to Babylon to offer tribute and reaffirm his loyalty (see Jeremiah 51:59).

At this stage Judah's political double-game reached an ominous phase. On the one hand, Zedekiah swore a vassal oath to Nebuchadnezzar. Yet, on the other hand, he was firmly drawn into Egypt's sphere of influence. There is some evidence that Judean soldiers had been sent to Egypt to help Psammetichus in his campaign against the king of the Ethiopians. Apparently this took place in Psammetichus' fourth year, 592. It is not known whether the Judean soldiers were hired by Egypt as mercenaries or whether, as is most likely, this help was part of a secret treaty concluded between the two kings. Thus Zedekiah, the vassal of Babylon, at the same time became an Egyptian ally – if, indeed, not a subordinate. In the next year Egyptian messengers toured Judah on a special mission. Judah became central to the Egyptian goal of regaining control of Palestine. The decision to revolt was apparently reached in that or the following year, with Psammetichus giving full assurance that he would assist Zedekiah when needed. It is not clear exactly when the rebellion broke out, but moves probably began shortly after Psammetichus gave his guarantees. However, the pharaoh died in 589 and was succeeded by Apries (the biblical Hophra), and Nebuchadnezzar felt that the dynastic change in Egypt presented the proper moment to invade Judah.

The exact date of the last siege of Jerusalem and its fall is still debated. Opinions are divided between two or three sets of dates for these events. The confusion is due to uncertainty as to the proper mode of counting regnal years in Judah. The regnal year began either in the spring with Nisan, the first month, or in the fall with Tishri, the seventh month. (Months were counted from the spring.) If the regnal year did indeed begin in the spring, then the siege of Jerusalem began in the middle of the winter of 587, which was in Zedekiah's ninth year and Nebuchadnezzar's seventeenth.

The Egyptians were faithful to their word. The Egyptian Army advanced to Judah's aid and effected a temporary break in the siege of Jerusalem (Jeremiah 37:5). No information has survived about the probable Egyptian-Babylonian confrontation. But it is clear that the Egyptians retreated, and Jerusalem was left to her own defence. The desperate situation in the city is illustrated in the prophecies of Jeremiah and is reflected in the general release of slaves by their masters during the siege. (Ironically, when the Babylonian Army met Hophra's forces, these liberated slaves were recaptured.) It is quite possible that the cities north of Jerusalem (the area of Benjamin) capitulated to the Babylonians and were most probably spared from deportation. But other fortified cities of Judah fell under siege and were captured one by one. It is believed that the Lachish letters illustrate this last stage of the war, when Lachish and Azekah (mentioned in one of the letters) struggled in their final resistance (see Jeremiah 34:7).

Despite the onslaught of the Babylonian military machine, Jerusalem withstood its attackers until the summer of 586. Resistance was broken by a growing famine and lack of water. Finally, the city wall was breached and the city captured. Zedekiah fled but was quickly overtaken (II Kings 25:5). He was brought before Nebuchadnezzar at the victor's camp at Riblah in the Valley of Lebanon and was cruelly punished. His children were slain before his eyes, and he himself was then blinded, the legal punishment for violating a vassal oath. The humiliated king was then taken to Babylon in chains.

The true end of Judah came with the absolute destruction of Jerusalem and the Temple, as described in detail in II Kings 25:8ff.:

And in the fifth month, on the seventh day of the month, which is the nineteenth year of king Nebuchadnezzar king of Babylon, came Nebuzaradan, captain of the guard, a servant of the king of Babylon, unto Jerusalem: And he burnt the house of the Lord, and the king's house, and all the houses of Jerusalem, and every great man's house burnt he with fire. And all the army of the Chaldees, that were with the captain of the guard, brake down the walls of Jerusalem round about. Now the rest of the people that were left in the city, and the fugitives that fell away to the king of Babylon, with the remnant of the multitude, did Nebuzaradan the captain of the guard carry away.

Along with the remnants of the people, excluding the poor, who were left to farm Judah, Nebuzaradan carried away the spoils of the city, including the king's treasury and the vessels from the Temple.

The narrator related these events in a style more terse than that common to the rest of II Kings. It is not accidental that the historiographer who wrote Chapter 25 and appended it to the earlier Book of Kings chose a dry chronicler's style, without the inclusion of value judgements that is so typical of the book itself. His proximity to these tragic events and their magnitude imposed on him an uncommon reserve. His narration is unadorned; he is yet unable to comment and can only record.

A poetic response to the destruction of Jerusalem followed shortly after: 'The Lord was as an enemy: he hath swallowed up Israel, he hath swallowed up all her palaces: he hath destroyed his strong holds, and hath increased in the daughter of Judah mourning and lamentation' (Lamentations 2:5).

11

The Babylonian Exile and the Restoration

The Biblical Sources

In contrast to the First Temple period, narrated in the books of Samuel and Kings, the period of the Restoration lacks a unified historical account. Our information is derived from heterogeneous sources whose validity has often been debated, and the result has been varied historical reconstructions of the period. Only two chapters within this period are adequately documented: the first is the era from the Edict of Cyrus (538) to the completion of the Second Temple (515); the other is from the appearance of Ezra (458) to the end of Nehemiah's office as the governor of Judah (*c.* 430). The main biblical sources for these periods are the prophetic works of Deutero-Isaiah, Haggai and Zechariah 1–8, the Aramaic documents quoted in the Book of Ezra and especially the memoirs of Nehemiah and narrative of Ezra, which were edited into a single book perhaps even as early as the close of the Persian period.

The Books of Chronicles, probably composed in Jerusalem in the early fourth century, are another source for this period. Although the books as a whole are concerned with the history of the First Temple, certain aspects reflect the time in which they were written. The emphasis that author – 'the chronicler' – placed on genealogical lists (I Chronicles 1–9) is indicative of the importance of such lists during a period when people renewed their claims upon ancestral homes and needed evidence to substantiate their status in the community of the returnees. An even more intense concern with genealogical evidence is shown by the authors and redactors of the books of Ezra and Nehemiah. The concern of the chronicler with the Temple and the cultic personnel, especially the Levites, shows the central role of the Temple in the life of the community in Judah. His own attempt to glorify the personalities of David, Solomon and other Judean kings, in contrast to the critical attitude prevailing towards them in the books of Samuel and Kings (utilized by him), shows that the period of the Davidic monarchy was looked upon as the Golden Age. Finally, the emphasis placed on the role of the remnants of the Northern Kingdom of Israel in the cultic reforms in Jerusalem under Hezekiah and Josiah might indicate that the chronicler did not share the isolationist ideologies of Ezra and Nehemiah. However, a proper reassessment of the work of the chronicler as a source for the Persian period is as yet impossible for several reasons. First, we do not know what group he represented at the time of his writing. Second, we are still unable to differentiate reliably between authentic sources from the First Temple period and the chronicler's later adaptation of them. Furthermore, whether the work is the product of a single author, the chronicler, or of several hands working in successive periods is still a much-debated question. What does emerge clearly, however, is that the commonly held opinion that the chronicler was also the author of the Book of Ezra and/or the redactor of the combined Book of Ezra and Nehemiah does not stand up to critical philological scrutiny.

The apocryphal books of Judith and Tobit, composed towards the end of the Persian period, also reveal certain attitudes towards isolationism, though their historical kernel is hard to assess. No documents have been discovered that validate the story preserved in the Book of Esther, though it describes vividly and accurately the manners in the court of the Persian emperor. The importance of these books for the history of the Jews is that they are the first narratives describing communal life in the Diaspora and the first evidence of those virulent anti-Jewish attitudes that were to become so frequently directed at major Jewish communities there.

Of special significance is the contemporaneous epigraphic and archaeological material: the Elephantine papyri and the recently discovered Samaritan papyri from Wadi Daliyeh; ostraca, coins, seals and other remains of material culture. These sources are especially valuable in filling the gap between the end of Nehemiah's office and the Macedonian conquest. For that later stage in the history of Judah under the Persians, important information is preserved in Josephus' *Antiquities,* as well as in fragments from the extant writings of hellenistic, Roman and Byzantine historians.

The Aftermath of the Destruction

After the destruction of Jerusalem and the exile to Babylon, the territorial framework of Jewish history expanded from Judah proper into wider areas. It now included not only those who remained in Judah but also the diasporas of Babylonia and Egypt and, in due course, of Asia Minor as well. At first the Jewish communities that arose far from the boundaries of Palestine preserved their religious, national and cultural character. Later their fate varied from place to place, in accordance with their legal situation and the historical circumstances that brought them into existence.

For the history of Judah during the period of the Babylonian exile there are very few sources, and scarcely any information has survived. From the description in Jeremiah 32ff. and in II Kings 24–5, it is clear that the devastation was widespread and that only the poor remained in the country, 'to be vine-growers and husband-men'. Assumptions vary as to the total number of exiles: 10,000 persons were exiled with Jehoiachin, (see page 155) but it is uncertain whether this figure refers to heads of families or the total number of exiles. As against this high number, even if it stands for individuals, the sources mention surprisingly few exiles from Jerusalem: 832 at the time of the destruction of the Temple and 745 after the murder of Gedaliah (Jeremiah 52:29–30). There can certainly be no doubt that a great many left Judah during the war or immediately after the destruction and fled in all directions – to

Samaria, Edom, Moab, Ammon or Egypt. The archaeological excavations that have been carried out in Tell Beit Mirsim, Beth-shemesh, Lachish and Ramat Rachel, bear witness to the dimensions of the destruction. The remains show clear marks of devastation, the results of cruel fights and battles in the last years of Judah's independence. At the same time, several cities lying north of Jerusalem, *e.g.*, Bethel, Mizpah and Gibeon, were not destroyed at all, and it is now assumed that this region – the land of Benjamin – submitted to the Babylonians in 588, with the commencement of the war, and thus escaped destruction. Mizpah could therefore serve as the seat of Gedaliah ben Ahikam. The grandson of Shaphan, Josiah's scribe, and apparently a leader of the moderate faction that opposed the rebellion in Judah, Gedaliah was appointed governor of whatever remained in Judah after the destruction of 586. When the Babylonian armies left Judah, the dispersed soldiers and officers gradually assembled in Mizpah.

Gedaliah's first and foremost reform was to legalize the status of the usurped lands by recognizing as owners those occupying or tilling them. Thus the 'poorest of the land', those not exiled, took possession of the lands through this exceptional measure. Gedaliah's primary purpose was to normalize life in Judah. His policy is formulated in the statement reported in Jeremiah 40:9–10: 'Fear not to serve the Chaldeans: dwell in the land, and serve the king of Babylon, and it shall be well with you. As for me, behold, I will dwell at Mizpah, to serve the Chaldeans, which will come unto us: but ye, gather ye wine, and summer fruits, and oil, and put them in your vessels, and dwell in your cities that ye have taken.' This move coincides with the view that the land belonged by right to those who took physical claim to it, as evidenced by slogans quoted in Ezekiel: ' . . . They that inhabit those wastes of the land of Israel speak, saying, Abraham was one, and he inherited the land; but we are many; the land is given us for inheritance' (33:24) and ' . . . unto us this land is given in possession' (11:15). The fate of the Israelites and other peoples exiled into Assyria had taught that generation that exiled people never return to their native lands. Hence those who remained in Judah viewed themselves as the only survivors of the people – a view strongly opposed by the prophet Ezekiel.

However, Gedaliah's brief rule was ended by his assassination at the hands of a member of the royal family. The assassin, Ishmael ben Nethaniah, must have considered Gedaliah a traitor. It is also very likely that he was hired by the king of Ammon, who apparently desired to occupy parts of Judah. In any case, this signalled the end of the last manifestation of Judah's autonomy.

Fearing Babylonian vengeance, the 'captains of the guards' and the people of Mizpah decided to flee to Egypt, taking with them the prophet Jeremiah. It is through the eyes of the elderly prophet that these tragic events are reported in great detail (see Jeremiah 40–4). Indeed, the day of Gedaliah's murder (the third day of the seventh month) became a fast day and was observed even at the time of the Babylonian exile, as was the ninth day of Ab (Zechariah 8:19).

Although the neo-Babylonian Empire continued the Assyrian pattern of administration, it deviated in its policy towards exiles. There is no evidence that the policy of a two-way, enforced exchange of population existed, but only that of a unidirectional deportation of conquered people to Babylonia, which at the time required an augmented population to resettle the areas destroyed in the wars with Assyria. Skilled craftsmen and workers for the building operations throughout the country, especially in the city of Babylon were also needed; consequently, Nebuchadnezzar did not transfer any new inhabitants to the devasted Judah, nor to Ashkelon, which had been destroyed even earlier, but let the territories lie in ruins. Indeed, they may purposely have been allowed to remain waste in order to serve as a buffer area with Egypt. As a result of this policy, the returning exiles met no outside opposition upon their return to their own homes, although the Edomites seem to have encroached upon the territory of Judah from the east and south and to have expanded almost as far north as Hebron. Nothing is known about the organization or history of the land of Judah from 586 until the Return in 538. On the other hand, there is considerable information about the Judean exiles in Babylon during the reign of Nebuchadnezzar, mainly from the Book of Ezekiel, a prophet deported with King Jehoiachin to Babylonia while still young.

The Exiles in Babylonia

The Judean exiles were settled on the Chebar River, an important irrigation canal near the city of Nippur (Ezekiel 1:1). The choice of this territory seems not to have been accidental. Nippur had served as the stronghold of the Assyrians in Babylonia in the days of Ashurbanipal, particularly during the wars between his heirs and Nabopolassar, and had in large degree been laid waste. It is quite possible that the inhabitants who had remained faithful to Assyria were killed or deported. The names of other sites settled by the Judean exiles point to a similar situation. They all indicate destruction and ruin: Tell-abib, 'the place destroyed as though by the flood' (abūbu in Akkadian); Tell-melah, 'Mound of Salt', i.e., a ruin on which salt was strewn to symbolize that nothing should ever grow upon it; and Tell-harsa, 'a ruin covered with potsherds'. The new settlers were mainly engaged in agriculture. Others, chiefly craftsmen and skilled workmen, were transferred to Babylon itself and were employed in the building projects of Nebuchadnezzar. The economic documents from Babylon that record the food allocation in 592 for Jehoiachin, the deported king of Judah, and his five sons (see page 156) also list a number of other Judeans: Gadiel, Semaḥyahu and Shelemyahu the gardener. (The same documents also mention exiles from other countries: sailors and singers from Ashkelon; 126 Tyrians, of whom more than 100 were sailors; carpenters from Byblos and Arvad; Elamites; Medes; Persians; and Egyptians. There were also Greek and Lydian craftsmen.)

The Judean exiles preserved the social structure of family units, as evidenced by the genealogical lists in Ezra 2 and Nehemiah 7. Jehoiachin, the exiled king, the nobility and the priests are never mentioned directly by Ezekiel. The only leaders that the prophet encounters are the 'elders', the traditional leadership (Jeremiah 29:1; and Ezekiel 8:1 and 20:3).

The Book of Ezekiel bears witness not only to the social organization of the exiles; its main significance lies in the fact that it reflects in many ways the longings, conflicts and hopes of the exiles, their psychological condition and their spiritual attitude.

The first wave of exiles, those carried off with Jehoiachin, regarded their captivity as temporary. They expected the imminent defeat of the young neo-Babylonian Empire and their consequent return to Judah along with the captured Temple vessels. It is against this vain hope that Jeremiah and Ezekiel directed their utterances, prophesying time and again the approaching destruction of Jerusalem and the Temple. Yet the optimism of the exiles, enhanced by the activity of the so-called 'prophets of redemption' – condemned by Jeremiah as false prophets – precluded their acceptance of the prophets of doom. Their false optimism was shattered and led to intense despair upon the actual destruction of the Temple in 586. It is this depression that Ezekiel depicts so vividly. The people now felt the full burden of their sins and especially those of their fathers. Against this Ezekiel emphasized personal responsibility: 'The son shall not bear the iniquity of the father, neither shall the father bear the iniquity of the son' (Ezekiel 18:20). The generation of Jehoiachin and Zedekiah was not punished for the sins of Manasseh, he argued, but for its own iniquities. Only repentance could obviate the punishment. After the destruction the people perceived the strength of their captors and realized that the exile meant a total break with their now-desolate homeland. In response to the lament then current, 'Our bones are dried, and our hope is lost' (Ezekiel 37:11), Ezekiel countered with his 'Vision of the Dry Bones' in which the bones are reclothed in flesh (Ezekiel 37:1–10).

No doubt the activity of Ezekiel bore fruit, although little is known of the spiritual life of the exiles. We are aware, however, that a decisive change took place in the religious and cultural perceptions of the exiled community. The syncretistic idolatry and fetishism that was still evident at the end of the First Temple period seems to have disappeared. A decisive factor was the feeling of repentance for the cultic transgressions of Manasseh and his age. As in Babylonian and Assyrian religious concepts, destruction and exile were regarded as manifestations of divine wrath. Only the elimination of sin and its atonement could restore divine grace. This attitude was clearly paralleled by the Babylonian historians of the period. The destruction of Babylon in 689 by Sennacherib, the king of Assyria, was explained as the punishment of the Babylonian chief god Marduk as a result of his fury at the sins of the inhabitants. (According to an Assyrian version from the days of Esarhaddon, Babylon was destroyed not because of cultic sins but because of social and moral transgressions – homicide, civil war and the decline of morality.) Similarly, in a later inscription of Nabonidus, the destruction (in 610) of Haran (the last capital of Assyria and the centre for the worship of Sin, the moon-god) was interpreted as divine punishment: 'Sin king of the gods was angered with his city and his temple [of E-hul-hul] and went up to heaven. The city [of Haran] and the people that were in it became desolate.' It was only when the 'appointed period of affliction' was completed that 'his wrath was calmed . . . he was reconciled' and agreed to return to his city and his temple, restored by his ardent follower Nabonidus.

The religious and spiritual change that the exiles underwent at that period was a sign of isolationist tendencies, a desire for complete separation from the imposing foreign surroundings. Yet it was also a period in which some secular Babylonian influences penetrated deeply. This is noticeable in the Babylonian names adopted by some exiles, even members of the royal family of Judah, such as Zerubbabel (Zēr-bābili, literally, 'seed of Babylon'), the name of Jehoiachin's grandson. Another significant change was the adoption of the Babylonian names of the months – Nisan, Iyyar, Sivan, etc. – instead of the original Israelite system of numbering them serially as the first, second, third month, etc. There was also a change influenced by Aramaic, the lingua franca in Babylonia and the western part of the Persian Empire, whereby Aramaic cursive replaced the ancient Hebrew script.

Babylonian influence is recognizable in the literary sphere too. Thus the Books of Kings (see page 112) were re-edited as a synchronic chronicle on the pattern of the Babylonian Chronicles. Especially reworked was the chronological framework: the dates of the kings of Judah were harmonized with those of the kings of Israel. The whole composition was brought up to date up to the year of 561, the liberation of Jehoiachin from his imprisonment by Evil-merodach, Nebuchadnezzar's successor (II Kings 25:27–30). (The circumstances of Jehoiachin's imprisonment are obscure. His legal status at the beginning of Nebuchadnezzar's reign was that of an exiled king; see page 156.)

The Fall of Babylon and the Rise of Persia

The last years of the Babylonian Empire witnessed far-reaching changes. In 556 the throne was seized by the elderly Nabonidus, a high official (probably of Aramean stock, from a family originating in Haran) who was strongly connected with the worship of the moon-god. Unlike other kings of Babylon, he was literate and profoundly interested in the Babylonian past and in divination. However, from the beginning of his reign his main concern was to elevate the cult of Sin, the moon-god, above that of other Babylonian deities. As a result of his cultic reforms, he came into conflict with the priests of the chief Babylonian temple cities, left Babylon and sojourned ten years at Teima in northern Arabia. His son, Bel-shar-uṣur (Belshazzar of the Book of Daniel), was regent during his absence.

During the years Nabonidus spent at Teima (552–543), the political balance of power in the area shifted drastically. At that time the mountain range of what is now Iran, Kurdistan and Turkey was ruled by the Medes, whose king was a Babylonian ally. In 550, however, Cyrus of Anshan (Persia), a vassal of the Median emperor Astyages, rebelled against and defeated his overlord, captured the capital of Ecbatana and founded the Persian Empire, thus succeeding Media. He then engaged in a series of wars to consolidate and expand his kingdom, turning towards the west. In 546 Cyrus conquered Sardis (Sepharad in Obadiah 20), the capital of Lydia, then the leading state in Asia Minor. He then awaited a suitable opportunity to attack Babylon, still the undisputed leader of western Asia.

Upon his return from Teima in 543, Nabonidus was confronted by increasing dissatisfaction among the priesthood in the major Babylonian cities. Especially dissatisfied were the temple administrators, who now found themselves economically restricted by the crown, which had seized the temple treasuries. The dissatisfaction became even more pronounced after Nabonidus had completed the restoration of E-hul-hul, the temple of Sin in Haran. Favourable conditions had now been created for Cyrus to advance against Babylon, and there is even good reason to assume that the leaders of the opposition to Nabonidus, mainly the priests of Marduk in Babylon and those of Nabū in Sippar, conspired against him and secretly invited Cyrus to 'liberate' Babylonia. Whether he was actually crowned king of Babylon prior to its conquest or there was only a favourable attitude towards him on the part of a considerable section of the Babylonian population, Cyrus claimed to be the legal king of Babylon, appointed to his post by her gods. Unlike the Medes, he was not considered a barbarian by the Babylonians, but a legitimate king from the outset – a phenomenon unparalled in the history of Mesopotamia.

In 539 Nabonidus transferred the statues of the gods from the temples of several Babylonian cities to the capital itself, in anticipation of a Persian attack. This act, too, was regarded as sacrilegious, thus strengthening the position of his opponents. At this point Cyrus moved against Babylonia proper; Sippar, a major Babylonian temple city, submitted to his forces, and Babylon itself fell without a battle. While Nabonidus fled, Cyrus was joyously welcomed and entered Babylon, was recognized immediately as the Babylonian monarch and bore the title 'King of Babylon, King of the Lands', a title employed thereafter by the Persian emperors in Babylonian legal documents.

Cyrus' first steps were to abolish the reforms of Nabonidus and return the statues of the gods to their sanctuaries. Thus he appeared as a restorer of religion and order in Babylon and as the benefactor of all the peoples over whom he had established himself. He even claimed to have restored ancient sacred sites (such as Ashur, Akkad and Eshnunna) that had been destroyed many centuries before. However, this claim should not be taken at face value.

At the beginning of Cyrus' reign, the Babylonian royal scribe composed the following text inscription glorifying the new monarch:

When I [Cyrus] entered [the city of] Babylon peaceably and established to jubilation [my] royal seat in the Palace of the Ruler, the great Lord Marduk, [turned] the hearts of the many inhabitants of Babylon [to love me] and I daily sought to worship him. My vast armies paraded peacefully about Babylon, I did not let one frighten the people of [Shumer] and Akkad. I shepherded in peace within Babylon and all the sacred cities. The people of Babylon, upon whom he [Nabonidus] against the will of gods imposed the yoke which did not befit them, I relieved of their sorrows and removed their burden. Upon which Marduk the great Lord rejoiced at my virtuous deeds and graciously blessed me – Cyrus the King who worships him, Cambyses my son the offspring of my loins, and all my army; and in harmony before him, we praise his supreme divinity. All the Kings of the world from the Upper Sea to the Lower Sea, those who inhabit [. . .] and [all the] nomad kings of the West, the tent dwellers, brought their sumptuous gifts into Babylon, and kissed my feet. From [Nineveh] to the cities of Ashur, Shushan, and Akkad, the Land of Eshnunna and the cities of Zamban, Meturnu, Der and as far as the boundary of the Land of the Gutians [*i.e.,* highlanders of Kurdistan], across the Tigris, whose temples were destroyed in the distant past, [to all of these] I have restored and returned their own gods and I have set them up on their eternal seats. I have assembled all their [dispersed] people and restored them to their habitations ('Cyrus Cylinder', lines 22–32, new translation by author).

The Edict of Cyrus

The Edict of Cyrus to the exiles of Judah in Babylon, permitting them to rebuild the Temple in Jerusalem, is another expression of this policy of restoration. The original version, probably in Aramaic, has not survived. However, a brief Hebrew version is preserved in Ezra 1:2–3: 'Thus saith Cyrus king of Persia, The Lord God of Heaven hath given me all the kingdoms of the earth and he hath charged me to build him an house at Jerusalem which is in Judah. Who is there among you of all his people? his God be with him, and let him go up to Jerusalem, which is in Judah and build the house of the Lord God of Israel, he is the God, which is in Jerusalem.' In structure, style and terminology, this Edict in Ezra resembles other documents of the period. According to the heading, it was issued in the first year of Cyrus' reign, that is, it would seem, in the first year of his reign as the king of Babylonia (538 BCE), perhaps in the course of the New Year festivities. At the same time an Aramaic version, found in Ezra 6, was prepared for the use of the royal chancellery. It gives the measurements of the Temple and states expressly that the funds of rebuilding should be taken from the royal treasury (Ezra 6:3–5). The restoration of temples throughout the empire, including those of the conquered nations, served as an important factor in the policy of religious toleration displayed by the subsequent emperors of Persia, although it is possible that, to begin with, it was intended only to serve the political interests of Cyrus in his conquest of Babylon.

The conquest of Babylon by Cyrus was met with enthusiasm and awakened a national renaissance expressed in the words of the anonymous prophet usually referred to as Deutero-Isaiah. In line with the prophetic ideology that regarded the great empires of the ancient Near East merely as divine instruments for punishing sinful Israel or Judah (Isaiah 10:5ff.; and Jeremiah 25:9ff.), Deutero-Isaiah proclaims that the sole purpose of the rise of Cyrus and his conquest of the world – especially of Babylon – was to benefit Israel. But Deutero-Isaiah employs extraordinary terminology, referring to Cyrus as 'the Lord's anointed' (in Hebrew, *mashiaḥ*). This term was originally used solely in reference to Saul and David (I Samuel 26:23; II Samuel 19:22), and in this context it has been suggested that it means 'messenger', rather than 'anointed'. 'Thus saith the Lord to his anointed, to Cyrus, whose right hand I have holden, to subdue nations before him; and I will loose the loins of kings, to open before him the two leaved gates; and the gates shall not be shut; I will go before thee, and make the crooked places straight: I will break in pieces the gates of brass and cut in sunder the bars of iron: And I will give thee the treasures of darkness, and hidden riches of secret places, that thou mayest know that I, the Lord, which call thee by thy name, am the God of Israel. For Jacob my servant's sake, and Israel mine elect. . . . ' (Isaiah 45:1–4; see also 44:25–8). This exaltation of Cyrus might seem astonishing, but it is fully explicable in the light of the general attitude displayed towards Cyrus in Babylon immediately after its conquest in 539.

While Cyrus, as 'the Lord's anointed', plays an important role in Deutero-Isaiah's world view, no role is reserved for the Davidic dynasty in the forthcoming restoration. In contradistinction to the prophets of the First Temple period, for whom the Temple and the Davidites were an inseparable entity, this later prophet almost ignores the royal house of David. The Temple will be restored and Jerusalem rebuilt, but 'the sure mercies of David' (Isaiah 55:3), that is, the everlasting Covenant with the Davidic dynasty (see Psalm 89), will now be extended to the nation. A new everlasting Covenant with Israel is indeed a central motif in Deutero-Isaiah's prophecy: 'For the mountains shall depart, and the hills be removed; but my [covenantal] kindness shall not depart from thee, neither shall the covenant of my peace be removed, saith the Lord that hath mercy on thee' (Isaiah 54:10). Deutero-Isaiah does not explicitly reject the restoration of the Davidites, but in his vision the elevated role of the Davidic ruler as the just and righteous prince (Isaiah 11:1–10) is replaced by the glory of the rebuilt Jerusalem:

> Lift up thine eyes round about, and see: all they gather themselves together, they come to thee: thy sons shall come from far, and thy daughters shall be nursed at thy side. Then thou shalt see, and flow together, and thine heart shall fear, and be enlarged; because the abundance of the sea shall be converted unto thee, the forces of the Gentiles shall come unto thee. The multitude of camels shall cover thee, the dromedaries of Midian and Ephah; all they from Sheba shall come: they shall bring gold and incense; and they shall shew forth the praises of the Lord. All the flocks of Kedar shall be gathered together unto thee, the rams of Nebaioth shall minister unto thee; they shall come up with acceptance on mine altar, and I will glorify the house of my glory.... And the sons of strangers shall build up thy walls, and their kings shall minister unto thee: for in my wrath I smote thee, but in my favour have I had mercy on thee. Therefore thy gates shall be open continually; they shall not be shut day nor night; that men may bring unto thee the forces of the Gentiles, and that their kings may be brought. For the nation and kingdom that will not serve thee shall perish; yea, those nations shall be utterly wasted. The glory of Lebanon shall come unto thee, the fir tree, the pine tree, and the box together, to beautify the place of my sanctuary; and I will make the place of my feet glorious. The sons also of them that afflicted thee shall come bending unto thee; and all they that despised thee shall bow themselves down at the soles of thy feet; and they shall call thee, The city of the Lord, The Zion of the Holy One of Israel (Isaiah 60:4–14).

Clearly, this poetic imagery bears little resemblance either to the traditional prophetic descriptions of Jerusalem or to the reality of that age. Indeed, behind it lies rather the city of Babylon in all its splendour. Babylon, the centre of a world empire, richly rebuilt and adorned by Nebuchadnezzar II, was referred to in similar terms in the inscriptions of the neo-Babylonian kings. Thus Deutero-Isaiah introduces a completely new element into the biblical rhetoric – the exaltation of Jerusalem, a theme reiterated in later Jewish literature.

The Return and Restoration

The Edict awakened enthusiastic hopes. The very granting of permission to rebuild the Temple in Jerusalem from the funds of the royal treasury was an incentive to return. As early as 538, the year of the proclamation, the first group of returnees was organized. The number recorded is 42,360 (Ezra 2:64), together with 7,337 men and women servants and more than 200 male and female musicians. These figures presumably constitute the total of the several waves of returnees during the reign of Cyrus and his successors, and some assume that they actually include the returnees in the days of Ezra and Nehemiah as well. It is plausible that the return ceased for some time during the wars waged by Cambyses in Egypt. Obviously, a considerable number of exiles decided to remain in Babylonia, despite the enthusiastic urging of Deutero-Isaiah that they depart immediately from the 'land of the Chaldeans'. Apparently, these exiles had struck roots in Babylon and their economic situation was sound. It should be remembered that the overwhelming majority were natives of Babylonia and therefore remained unswayed by promises of a distant homeland that they had never seen.

The first wave of the returnees was headed by Sheshbazzar, 'the prince of Judah' (Ezra 1:8); possibly he should be identified with Shenazar, the son of Jehoiachin (I Chronicles 3:18). It was Sheshbazzar who received the vessels of the Temple from the Persian treasurer. The honorific title 'the prince of Judah' is identical to that used by Ezekiel in his vision of a restored monarchy in Judah. However, this does not indicate that Cyrus necessarily intended a restoration of the monarchy; indeed, his main purpose was to rebuild the Temple in Jerusalem. The structure of the Persian Empire left no place for vassal kings, only for 'governors', some of whom may have been descendants of local dynasties. It is possible that Sheshbazzar was actually appointed governor (*peha*) of Judah, as Ezra 5:14 might indicate. At a later stage Sheshbazzar is no longer mentioned in the sources. His place as the *peha* of Judah is taken by Zerubbabel son of Shealtiel, the grandson of Jehoiachin, whose political activities belong chiefly to the days of Darius I.

The Edict of Cyrus referred only to the Temple in Jerusalem, while the rest of Judah was not mentioned at all. It may even be assumed that the Jerusalem Temple was exempted, at least in the initial stage, from all the forms of taxation usually imposed in the Persian Empire. On the other hand, it appears that the people of Judah were subject to taxes and to corvée duties as was customary among the subjects of the Persian Empire (Ezra 4:12–16). Cyrus and his successors adopted the same policy in several other provinces of the empire, exempting some temples from corvée and taxes. In this way the priestly class was bound to the Persian rule, its faithfulness secured by economic privileges.

The order of events in the construction of the Second Temple, as well as the identity of the leadership of that time, is still open to debate. According to Ezra 3, Jeshua son of Jozadak, the Priest, and Zerubbabel, the son of Shealtiel, headed the returnees, their first step being to erect the altar in its place and reinstitute the sacrifice. The next step, 'in the second year of their coming unto the house of God at Jerusalem' (Ezra 3:8), was to lay the foundation of the Temple amid celebration and rejoicing

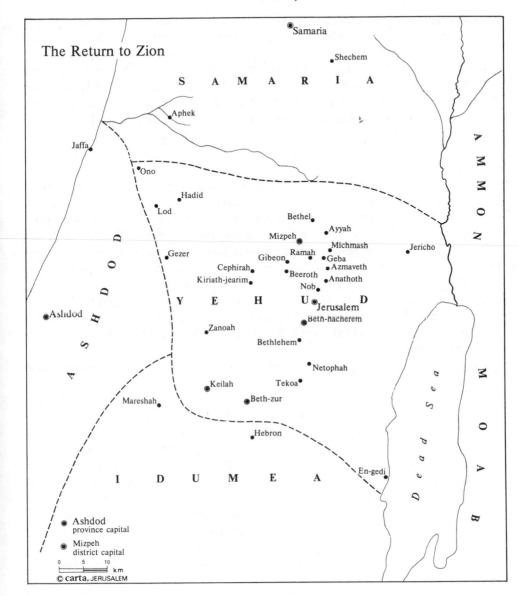

The Return to Zion

Samaria
Shechem

S A M A R I A

Aphek

Jaffa

Ono

Hadid

Lod

Bethel
Ayyah
Mizpeh
Michmash
Ramah
Gibeon Geba
Cephirah Azmaveth
Kiriath-jearim Beeroth
Nob Anathoth

A S H D O D

Gezer

Ashdod

Y E H U D
Jerusalem
Beth-hacherem

Zanoah

Bethlehem

Netophah

Keilah Tekoa

Mareshah Beth-zur

Hebron

I D U M E A

En-gedi

Jericho

A M M O N

M O A B

Dead Sea

Ashdod
province capital

Mizpeh
district capital

0   5   10
km
© carta, JERUSALEM

('a great shout' [Ezra 3:11]). According to Ezra 4, the rebuilding was stopped and was resumed only in the second year of Darius I (Ezra 4:24), that is, in 520. At that stage, too, Zerubbabel and Jeshua led the people. The prophets Haggai and Zechariah issued prophecies of encouragement to both, urging them, and especially Zerubbabel, now called *peḥa* ('governor' [Haggai 1:1]), to hasten the work. The impression received, especially from Haggai 2:15 ('before a stone was laid upon a stone in the temple') and 2:18 ('from the day that the foundation of the Lord's temple was laid'), is that the Temple was completed only in the days of Darius. In addition, an Aramaic document referring to the rebuilding under Cyrus states: 'Then came the same Sheshbazzar, and laid the foundation of the house of God which is in Jerusalem: and since that time even until now hath it been in building, and yet it is not finished' (Ezra 5:16). To explain this dilemma it has been suggested that Zerubbabel and Jeshua belong only to the second period, that of Darius, and that their earlier appearance is the result of a later editorial addition. On the other hand, Zerubbabel and Jeshua may well have belonged to both phases. In 538, when Sheshbazzar was governor and officially responsible for the rebuilding, Zerubbabel and Jeshua were the popular leaders, while by the later stage (520) Zerubbabel had become the Persian governor of Judah.

It is unlikely that Darius would have appointed a governor in a minor western province in 522/1, when he was attempting to quell a rebellion spreading throughout his kingdom. It therefore stands to reason that Zerubbabel was appointed prior to that, either in the later years of Cyrus or during the reign of Cambyses. It has also been suggested that another group returned to Judah during Cambyses' reign. In any case, it is clear that no restoration work was carried out for a considerable time. Haggai, a witness to the events (1:2), clearly indicted the people, who maintained that 'the time is not come, the time that the Lord's house should be built,' while the historian in Ezra 4:1–5 blames the delay on 'the adversaries of Judah and Benjamin', who 'troubled them in building, And hired counsellors against them, to frustrate their purposes'.

Even in the earliest stages, grave conflicts developed between the returnees and 'the people of the land' (Ezra 4:4), who regarded themselves as co-religionists: 'For we seek your God, as ye do; and we do sacrifice unto him since the days of Esarhaddon king of Assyria, which brought us up hither' (Ezra 4:2).

This group requested that they be allowed to participate in the restoration of the Temple. The answer of Zerubbabel and the other leaders was unequivocal: 'Ye have nothing to do with us to build an house unto our God; but we ourselves together will build unto the Lord God of Israel, as king Cyrus the king of Persia hath commanded us' (Ezra 4:3). The question of the identity of these 'adversaries of Judah and Benjamin' is another debated point. The accepted opinion, following the above statement in Ezra 4:2, is that they were the descendants of the foreign settlers deported to Samaria by the Assyrian kings, a group later known as the Samaritans. It has, however, been suggested that the rejected group were the descendants of the original Israelites or of the unexiled Judeans.

It may be assumed that the local Persian governors, particularly the governor of Samaria, who was himself subject to the governor of Trans-Euphrates (*Abarnahara*), took advantage of the dispute between the 'adversaries of Judah and Benjamin' and the returnees in order to impede the restoration. The local governors obviously would not be interested in the rise of Jerusalem as an administrative and religious centre that could compete with Samaria and could have placed numerous obstacles in the way of implementing the Edict.

Cyrus himself was apparently no longer interested in maintaining his policy of granting special privileges for the restoration of desolate religious centres. His efforts were now directed towards consolidation of the empire and expansion into the east. He died in 530, while fighting the Scythians on the eastern outskirts of Iran. His son Cambyses renewed the Persian interest in western expansion and led a successful campaign to Egypt. He invaded Egypt, defeated the last ruler of the Twenty-sixth Dynasty and became, as Cyrus had in Babylon, the king of Egypt. By marrying the daughter of the deposed Pharaoh, he claimed a retroactive legitimacy for his rule in Egypt. His feats were commemorated in hieroglyphic inscriptions that paid homage to the gods of Egypt. Cambyses' brief reign finds no mention in the Book of Ezra, which resumes the narrative in the second year of Darius' reign.

Upon the death of Cambyses and the ascent to the throne of Darius I (a member of a rival royal branch) in 522, revolts erupted throughout the Persian Empire, from Media itself, where the nobility revolted against Darius, to Elam, Babylonia and Asia Minor. It was only in 519, the end of his second and the beginning of his third year, that Darius assumed control of the entire empire. There is no evidence that the countries to the west, particularly Egypt, also revolted. In any case, in his second year the restoration of the Temple was resumed. Echoes of disturbances in the Persian Empire are reflected in the prophecies of Haggai and Zechariah, the last of the literary prophets. In the sixth month of the second year of Darius (520), Haggai aroused the people and the leaders to recommence the building of the Temple (Haggai 1:14). In conjunction with the rebuilding, there arose the hope of renewing the kingship under the Davidic dynasty, and this hope was naturally connected with the personality of Zerubbabel:

> And again the word of the Lord came unto Haggai in the four and twentieth day of the month, saying, Speak to Zerubbabel, governor of Judah, saying, I will shake the heavens and the earth; And I will overthrow the throne of kingdoms, and I will destroy the strength of the kingdoms of the heathen; and I will overthrow the chariots, and those that ride in them; and the horses and their riders shall come down, every one by the sword of his brother. In that day, saith the Lord of hosts, will I take thee, O Zerubbabel, my servant, the son of Shealtiel, saith the Lord, and will make thee as a signet: for I have chosen thee, saith the Lord of hosts (Haggai 2:20–3).

The vision of Zechariah, dated to the same period, reflects some sort of conflict between Zerubbabel and Jeshua, the High Priest, although no details are available as to its exact nature. Zechariah shared the same hope of resuming the Davidic dynasty under Zerubbabel, whom he called 'my servant the Branch' (Zechariah 3:8; the Hebrew word *tzemah*, 'a branch', designated an offspring of the Davidites [see Jeremiah 23:5]). Yet he believed that in the leadership of Judah there was a place for both a prince and a priest: 'Thus speaketh the Lord of hosts, saying, Behold the man whose name is The Branch; and he shall grow up out of this place, and he shall build the temple of the Lord: Even he shall build the temple of the Lord; and he shall bear the glory, and shall sit and rule upon his throne; and he shall be a priest upon his throne: and the counsel of peace shall be between them both' (Zechariah 6:12–13).

The restoration of the Temple proceeded slowly. When news of the rebuilding reached Tatnai, the newly appointed governor of Trans-Euphrates, he challenged the legal right of the returnees to build their Temple and reported the affair to Darius (Ezra 5:3–17). As the Edict had been proclaimed verbally and the written text, retained for the official records, was not in Jerusalem, they could not prove that they were indeed acting with the authorization of the king. Darius ordered that a search be conducted in the royal archives at Ecbatana (Achmetha), where the original document was discovered, and instructions were issued to complete the Temple and supply the expenses from the treasury of the satrapy (Ezra 6:1–12). Darius' order contained the additional requirement that in the completed Temple a sacrifice be made for the welfare of the king and his sons. From then on this became regular practice in the Second Temple period, and it continued until the Great Revolt against the Romans in 68 CE. The building of the Temple was completed in the sixth year of Darius' reign (516/15) and was marked by the joyous celebration of Passover (Ezra 6:15–20).

From Zerubbabel to Ezra

It is of special significance that the completion of the Temple occurred exactly seventy-one years after its destruction. There is evidence that Jeremiah's original prophecy of seventy years of affliction (Jeremiah 25:11) was reinterpreted during and after the exile. It is clearly alluded to in Zechariah 7:5: 'Speak unto all the people of the land, and to the priests, saying, When ye fasted and mourned in the fifth and seventh month, even those seventy years, did ye at all fast unto me, even to me?' It is, therefore, possible that the returnees, aware of the validity of Jeremiah's prophecies of doom, endeavoured to finish the rebuilding at the end of the seventy-year period, thus implying that the period of divine wrath was indeed over and that the new epoch, that of divine grace, was to begin.

At this point, however, the records break off. The period between the completion of the Temple and the arrival of Ezra the Scribe in 458 – more than half a century – is hardly documented. Zerubbabel is no longer mentioned, and it is assumed that he was summoned back to Persia, since one of his descendants (Hattush) returned with Ezra (Ezra 8:2; and I Chronicles 3:22). It seems reasonable to suppose that the disappearance of Zerubbabel resulted in the rise of the High Priest. The primacy of the High Priest, who was also the administrator of the Temple and of the adjoining area, would be in accordance with the Persian practice in the cultic centres throughout the empire. Another characteristic of this period was the close ties that developed between the families of the High Priest, leading nobles and officials in Jerusalem and the leading families in Samaria. The latter regarded themselves as belonging to Israel, and, though excluded from participation in the rebuilding of the altar in the days of Cyrus, they now became an influential and, indeed, decisive force in Jerusalem. The religious and cultural differences no longer seemed significant. The nobility in Samaria accepted Jerusalem and the Temple as their religious centre and, it would seem, recognized the authority of the High Priest in Jerusalem in all matters affecting worship and religious leadership. It is most probable that the religious leadership in Jerusalem perpetuated the universalist and anti-exclusivist outlook expressed in the books of Zechariah and Deutero-Isaiah (Zechariah 2:11

and 8:23; Isaiah 56:3–7). However, the religious reawakening in the Babylonian diaspora about the middle of the fifth century, which brought Ezra and Nehemiah to Judah, was destined to interrupt this state of affairs.

The eventful reign of Xerxes (Ahasuerus, 483–465) and his Greek campaigns have left little impression in the biblical sources. Although an accusatory letter about the inhabitants of Judah and Jerusalem (Ezra 4:6) was sent to the king at the beginning of his reign (the letter has not survived), there was apparently no change in the status of these areas. Only in the reign of Artaxerxes I (464–424) did external affairs affect the fate of Judah. The Athenians, with the aid of the Delian League, intensified their war against the Persians, and in 460 their fleet assisted an Egyptian prince in his revolt against Persia.

The revolt lasted several years. In 456 the satrap of Abar-nahara (Trans-Euphrates) invaded Egypt, and in 454 he captured the Egyptian rebel. It was against this background that in 458, the seventh year of Artaxerxes' reign, the king granted permission to Ezra the Scribe to lead another wave of returnees to Judah. Most likely, the Persian attitude was that ties with distant Judah would be solidified by the presence there of new settlers loyal to the empire.

We lack documentary evidence on the development and history of the Jewish diaspora in Babylonia. Our only evidence is the cuneiform archive of the large Babylonian family of Murashu found in Nippur, which mentions a considerable number of Jews – alongside some other ethnic communities – participating in various economic activities. Their names are recognizable by the element 'yau' (written 'yama' and pronounced 'yaw'): Hananiyama, Gadaliyama, Tubiyama, Zabadaiyama (*i.e.,* Hananiah, Gedaliah, Tobiah, Zebadiah). Yet some had Babylonian or Persian names. They were engaged in agriculture, fishing and minor government service. Trade was still unattested among them. Although fully at home in Achamenid Babylonia, the Jewish community remained linked to their original home. They stressed religious exclusiveness, but unlike the Jewish community in Elephantine (see page 180), they did not build a temple to their God. Worship was now decentralized. Apparently each community met in an assembly (*kinishtu,* an Aramaic loan word in Babylonian, hence *knesset* in Mishnaic Hebrew), and it might be supposed that their house of assembly became a place of worship. If so, this was the origin of the synagogue, the focal point of the Jewish community in later times. A natural interest would develop in the forms of worship and religious expression and especially in the religious laws. It may further be assumed that the leaders of the community, like Ezra, were personally involved in the codification and preservation of major segments of Mosaic law. Thus their feeling of exclusiveness vis-à-vis Babylonian society was strengthened by their assertion of special rules of 'purity' typical of the priests, to which class Ezra belonged (their own appellative, [see Ezra 9:2 – lit. 'seed of holiness'] expressed their separatist world view). This exclusiveness was destined to clash with the view predominating among the Jerusalem priesthood and apparently shared by many others in Judah.

Opinions differ with regard to the chronological sequence of Ezra's and Nehemiah's activity. Some scholars are of the opinion that the biblical order should be reversed and that Ezra should not be placed in the days of Artaxerxes I, that is, before Nehemiah, but in the reign of Artaxerxes II, about fifty years after Nehemiah. Some have suggested a compromise between the two views by dating the year of Ezra's arrival as the thirty-seventh year of Artaxerxes I, *i.e.,* 428, or at all events after the time of Nehemiah.

Actually, more methodological problems are posed by assuming that Ezra came after Nehemiah than by accepting the view that he preceded Nehemiah. The difficult conditions in Judah prior to Ezra's arrival, as described in the Book of Ezra, hardly fit the period following Nehemiah's successful mission. As there is no definitive evidence to justify a change in the order transmitted by the editor, the sequence Ezra–Nehemiah should be preferred.

Ezra 'the Scribe'

Ezra arrived in Jerusalem in the fifth month of the year 458, carrying with him an official authorization (*nishtevan* in Persian) empowering him to appoint judges and to judge in accordance with the 'law of the God of heaven'. Whoever would not observe the 'law of the God of heaven' and the law of the king would be subject to heavy punishment (Ezra 7:26). It is still disputed whether or not Ezra's authority extended over those who observed the 'law of the God of heaven' in Judah and in the province of Trans-Euphrates (the fifth satrapy of the Persian Empire) or was restricted solely to the community of the returnees from Babylon (*bnei hagolah,* see below).

The king also authorized Ezra to receive a special allocation from the royal treasury and to reinstitute in the Temple of the 'God of heaven' in Jerusalem sacrifices for the well-being of the king and his family. He also furnished the Temple with vessels of silver and gold, on the pattern of Babylonian kings who endowed temples in sacred cities. Moreover, it is specifically stated that those accompanying Ezra (1,500 people in all, including priests, Levites, singers, gate-keepers, etc.) would be free from the payment of royal tolls, taxes, levies and imposts. If this authorization and the account in Ezra 8 are indeed authentic, this would mean that Ezra, as the leader of the returnees, was given outstanding privileges – a sign of high position. Perhaps as 'the scribe of the law' he was actually the highest official of the Jewish community in Babylonia. The Book of Ezra even credits him with a priestly genealogy dating back to the Aaronites (Ezra 7:1–5).

Ezra's main concern, as it appears from fragments of his own memoirs, as well as from the editorial narrative in the Book of Ezra, was to separate the community of the returnees in Judah from those who had not undergone the experience of exile. Indeed, the community to whom Ezra addresses himself is continually called *bnei hagolah* or *kahal hagolah* ('the people of the exile', or 'the congregation of the exile'). His adversaries are referred to as 'the peoples of the land' (a plural form of *'am ha-arez*), by which he implied gentiles. Thus the term *'am ha-arez,* which denoted the concept of populace and their sovereignty at the end of the First Temple period (see page 148), was transformed by Ezra into a derogatory expression. However, these 'peoples of the lands' included those who had not gone into exile and especially the new adherents to the religious practices of the Jews and above all to worship in the Jerusalem Temple. This apparently underlies Ezra's efforts against intermarriage with gentile women, a practice that was widespread among the nobles and leading priests.

After several months of persuasion and activity, Ezra assembled the people together in Jerusalem on the twentieth day of the ninth month (winter of 458) and by virtue of the authority vested in him, imposed a revolutionary demand on them, particularly on the heads of the leading families – that they separate from their alien wives. Ezra 10:18–44 preserved a list of the priests and Levites who 'had taken strange wives'. At this point (Ezra 10:44) the source breaks off. It is possible that at this stage Ezra was compelled to retract his order owing to changes in the international situation or complaints lodged on behalf of the noble families in Jerusalem who were affected by his far-reaching measures.

There is no information about Ezra's whereabouts until he reappears fourteen years later, when he is mentioned together with Nehemiah (Nehemiah 12:26). Perhaps Ezra journeyed to his community in Babylonia and returned years later, or he may have stayed in Judah as a teacher and scribe of the Law.

In the period between the mission of Ezra and the coming of Nehemiah, the situation in Syria, Palestine and Egypt underwent a number of changes. The sedition in Egypt was suppressed in 454, but later Megabyzus, the satrap of Trans-Euphrates, rebelled against the Persian overlord. After some time the two reached a settlement, and the king reappointed Megabyzus to his former post.

Perhaps as a result of this turmoil, the Jerusalem community decided that the time had come to restore the city walls (although temple cities without walls did exist). This episode is not narrated by the editor of the Book of Ezra, nor has the date survived. However, among his Aramaic documents, the editor did include one pertaining to this event, although it seems to have been placed out of chronological sequence. It is a hostile petition composed by Rehum and written by Shimshai the scribe and their collegium in Samaria. The latter included Babylonians and Elamites exiled to Samaria by Asnapper (Ezra 4:10), *i.e.,* Ashurbanipal, the king of Assyria. It is remarkable that this group of inhabitants of Samaria, exiled 200 years before, should stress in a letter to the Persian court their noble origin and kinship with the Persian overlords, thus separating themselves from the rest of the people of Samaria. Their argument was that if the city of Jerusalem were fully restored and its walls completed, the revenues to the crown might diminish, as Jerusalem had been a rebellious city since time immemorial. It is reasonable to assume that the version given in Ezra 4:8–16 is authentic. Apparently the denunciation was succesful. The nobles and officials of Samaria were given the necessary authority to come to Jerusalem and, in a show of force, put an end to the rebuilding (Ezra 4:23). Ezra's mission appears to have ended in failure.

The Reforms of Nehemiah

Nehemiah, the son of Hachaliah, appeared in Jerusalem as the governor of Judah in 445, thirteen years after the arrival of Ezra. Our only source for the history of these times is the book of memoirs bearing his name, which gives no indication of his background. This unique document is the first in the genre of authentic first-person memoirs in the Bible. It begins abruptly in the twentieth year of the reign of Artaxerxes I, when Nehemiah, a cup-bearer to the king and thus a courtier of the highest rank, received word from what appears to have been a delegation from Jerusalem about the unsuccessful attempt to rebuild the wall: 'And they said unto me, The remnant that are left of the captivity there in the province are in great affliction and reproach: the wall of Jerusalem also is broken down, and the gates thereof are burned with fire' (Nehemiah 1:3). Nehemiah describes his sorrow and anguish and notes his long prayer delivered on that occasion (1:4–11).

Nehemiah felt that, as the highest Jewish official in the Persian court, it was his duty to intervene with the king. Four months elapsed before he confronted the king with the unusual request to be relieved of his post and to be sent 'unto Judah, unto the city of my fathers' sepulchres, that I may build it' (Nehemiah 2:5). The suspicious ruler granted his permission and gave Nehemiah letters to the governors of the provinces of Trans-Euphrates and to the keeper of the king's forests (probably in Lebanon), who was to supply timber for rebuilding the gates of the fortress of the Temple, the wall of the city and the new governor's house in Jerusalem.

Although the tersely written memoir relates Nehemiah's piety, the wickedness of his opponents and his achievements, it is possible to perceive behind these events the calculated acts of a skilled statesman. His first concern was to rebuild the city wall. This work, described in Nehemiah 3–4, aroused enthusiasm among the populace, which formed volunteer teams, each of which rebuilt one section. The entire construction took only fifty-two days.

During the two generations preceding Nehemiah's arrival in Jerusalem, the social polarization in Judah had become very acute. While the nobles, the higher officials and the priestly families were relatively prosperous, drought, famine and taxation hit the peasants and small landowners, so that bondage and enslavement became a common phenomenon. Their condition found expression in the outcry directed to Nehemiah: 'We have mortgaged our lands, vineyards, and houses, that we might buy corn, because of the famine. . . . And we bring into bondage our sons and our daughters to be servants, and some of our daughters are brought unto bondage already: neither is it in our power to redeem them; for other men have our lands and vineyards' (Nehemiah 5:3–5). Nehemiah resorted to a radical solution: the cancellation of debts and the restoration of the fields to their impoverished owners. These acts were carried out by virtue of his authority as the Persian governor of Judah, which apparently permitted him to take extreme measures at critical moments. However, in this case Nehemiah shunned the easy method of simply imposing the reforms, preferring to use another means of persuasion. He convened the people in an extraordinary 'great assembly' (Nehemiah 5:7) in Jerusalem, where the richer segments of the population were apparently in the minority. By verbal persuasion and by relying on the will of people and his own authority, he was able to proclaim the above-mentioned reforms. The nobles had to swear publicly before the assembly that the reforms would be implemented immediately.

Such far-reaching social reforms were unusual but not unique in the history of Israel and the ancient Near East. These acts are reminiscent of the *andurarum* legislation of Babylonian kings when ascending the throne. Similar extraordinary enactments were demanded of Rehoboam (see page 107); and Zedekiah resorted to the same type of measures when Jerusalem was beseiged. In the classical world such measures, coupled with agrarian reform, were not infrequent. While the most prominent example is that of Solon in sixth-century Athens, Nehemiah's acts bear a closer resemblance to those of contemporary tyrants in fifth-century Ionia and Sicily.

Another major reform, introduced later in Nehemiah's career, was the enlargement of Jerusalem's population by an order requiring ten per cent of the populace to settle there. This also was in line with similar enactments of late Greek and hellenistic practice – *synoikismos,* a compulsory transfer of the population from rural settlements to an urban centre.

A further set of Nehemiah's reforms was connected with the Temple, even though Nehemiah himself was a layman. Nehemiah must have felt that in bolstering the status of the Temple and the priestly classes he would likewise be strengthening the position of Jerusalem by securing a solid economic basis for the Temple and the city. He provided for regular payment of the tithe, the most common impost of temple cities in Mesopotamia in the sixth and fifth centuries. His major change in this area regarded the priestly classes. The poorer priests and the Levites had lost their incomes (the hereditary portions or prebends, *isku* of the Babylonian temples), while a few priestly families had gained control of the treasury and were in charge of the gifts of agricultural produce brought to Jerusalem. It appears that Nehemiah took particular pains to ensure an economic basis for the Levites, the poorest priestly section. He renewed their portions and assigned new positions for them as gate-keepers and guards in the Temple area.

Of special significance is Nehemiah's insistence on strict observance of the Sabbath. This is not surprising as Sabbath observance had become one of the outstanding characteristics of Jewish communities in the Diaspora. The strict enforcement of the Sabbath law was entrusted to the Levites. 'And it came to pass, that when the gates of Jerusalem began to be dark before the sabbath, I commanded that the gates should be shut, and charged that they should not be opened till after the sabbath: and some of my servants set I at the gates, that there should no burden be brought in on the sabbath day' (Nehemiah 13:19).

It is only natural that such controversial measures met with strong opposition. The foremost opponent was Sanballat, the governor of Samaria. Though bearer of a Babylonian name (Sin-uballit) and called a Horonite by Nehemiah (perhaps a reference to the city of Haran, the centre of the Sin cult), Sanballat was a devotee of the Jerusalem Temple and the God of Israel (which is manifested in the names of his sons, Delaiah and Shelemiah, later governors of Samaria, see page 179). Indeed, Nehemiah never accused him of being a heathen. The second adversary, usually mentioned in conjunction with Sanballat, was Tobiah the Ammonite. Though referred to as a 'slave' by Nehemiah (apparently a pun on his official title 'king-slave'), he was a representative of the most influential landowning family in Ammon. The family of the Tobiads, of Judean origin, was to become the most prominent in Jerusalem about two centuries after Nehemiah. A third adversary, noted by Nehemiah, was Geshem the Arab, apparently the king of the Kedarites, a powerful

North Arabian tribal confederation in possession of monopolies over the profitable incense trade.

Yet another adversary was Eliashib, the High Priest in Jerusalem. His opposition, was not as obvious as that of Sanballat or Tobiah, and he is not depicted negatively in Nehemiah's memoirs. However, his close ties with the two other adversaries are evident: Eliashib's grandson was married to Sanballat's daughter, and Tobiah, undoubtedly a layman, had a private chancellery at the Temple. Here too Nehemiah resorted to extreme measures. He evicted Tobiah, cancelling his special rights, and during his second term of office (after 432) banished Eliashib's grandson from Jerusalem.

The latter move was connected with the 'purification' of the Judean community. Nehemiah adhered to the isolationist ideology of Ezra, typical of the Babylonian diaspora. Intermarriage again became the major issue. As stated above, Ezra did not mention Nehemiah in his memoirs, yet both were associated with the expulsion of gentile women, an act that culminated in a national convocation in which the 'book of Moses' was read.

The only mention of this event in Nehemiah's memoirs occurs in Nehemiah 13:1, whereas the historiographer who edited and combined the books of Ezra and Nehemiah (apparently at the close of the third century) eloquently detailed, in the third person, the events of 'the seventh month' in Jerusalem in Nehemiah 8–10. His description, whose veracity has been questioned, is placed in the midst of Nehemiah's own memoir. The convocation culminated with the signing of a covenant by Nehemiah, the governor, followed by the priests, the Levites and the heads of families (Nehemiah 10:1ff.). The central point of the covenant was their separation from 'the peoples of the land' (Nehemiah 10:29–31). Other items dealt with the obligations of the people to the Temple and a per capita tax of a third of a shekel for the Temple (Nehemiah 10:30–40).

Nehemiah's personal position ensured some success for his reforms. It can be assumed that a majority of the people in Judah followed him, although the family of the High Priest continued its opposition. Nehemiah's final departure to Persia, after his second term of office, terminated not only his book of memoirs but also our main source for the history of the period. From this point until the fall of the Persian Empire, we have no first-hand written documents recording the history of Judah. It is here that the archaeological and epigraphic evidence must be used to shed light on the period. Apparently, Nehemiah left his brother, Hanani, in charge of Jerusalem and perhaps of Judah (his title is 'Governor of the Fortress'). In 419 the Jewish military community of Elephantine addressed a query about Passover to a certain Hananiah in Jerusalem who might be Hanani, Nehemiah's brother. The Elephantine papyri mention a certain Bagohi as governor of Judah. To judge by his name, he was apparently a Persian, although in Ezra 2:2 we find a Jew with another version of the same name (Bigvai). Josephus (*Antiquities* XI, 7) relates that Bagohi (Bagoaz in Greek) supported Joshua, the grandson of Eliashib the High Priest, in his quarrel with his brother Johanan over accession to the position of High Priest. When Joshua was murdered in the Temple, Bagohi imposed a heavy fine on Johanan and the Jerusalemites.

Yehud, Samaria and Elephantine

The status of Judah as a separate administrative unit with an autonomous internal administration is attested to by coins bearing the word 'Yehud' – Judah in Aramaic, the official language of administration in the western portion of the Persian Empire. Provinces were heavily taxed by the central government, which received payment in silver and gold. Each province was also obliged to support the local governor and his court ('the bread of the governor' [Nehemiah 5:14]; Nehemiah emphasized that he did not collect the tax but supported himself). The province also taxed its own inhabitants in order to support the administration and the army. Coins, seals and seal impressions from this period (mainly the fourth century) reflect a certain fiscal autonomy in the province. While only the central government could issue silver coins of high denominations, the local authorities in Judah struck very tiny coins of small denominations.

Judah was subdivided into districts, each with its own officials. In the south the frontiers reached the vicinity of Hebron; in the north they extended beyond Bethel; and in the west as far as Lydda and Ono. The foot-hills and the coastal territory were held by the Ashdodites. At the close of the Persian period, the Phoenicians who had colonized the coastal plain of Palestine penetrated inland. They established Sidonian colonies in Judah, one of which was Mareshah in the southern part of the hill country. The south was in the hands of the Edomites, soon to be called Idumeans, who reached as far as Hebron and had settled in the entire Judean Negev. These boundaries of Judah were extended only under the Hasmoneans (see Part III).

Aramaic papyri found in the caves of Wadi Daliyeh in the Jordan Valley have illuminated the history of Samaria and its community. It appears that Hananiah, the son of Sanballat, was the governor of Samaria in 354. His father must have been Sanballat II, the grandson of Nehemiah's contemporary and the governor of Samaria in the first half of the fourth century. A third Sanballat, apparently the son of Hananiah, was the governor of Samaria at the time when Alexander the Great conquered the east. It is the latter Sanballat, described in a story of Josephus (*Antiquities* XI, 306–12), whose daughter Nicaso married Manasseh, a member of a family of High Priests in Jerusalem. According to Josephus, the elders of Jerusalem expelled Manasseh, whereupon he went to Samaria and, with Sanballat's aid, built a temple on Mount Gerizim near Shechem. He was then installed as the High Priest of this new centre of worship. However, in the midst of these events Alexander the Great destroyed the city of Samaria in revenge for the murder of his governor and resettled it with Macedonian colonists. This crisis coincided with the building of the place of worship on Mount Gerizim, which marked a step towards the final separation between the so-called Samaritans (or Shechemites) and Jerusalem, which occurred in the late hellenistic period.

A fair amount is known about the Jewish soldiers living on the Island of Yeb, or Elephantine, near Syene in southern Egypt, the modern Aswan. Aramaic papyri and parchment scrolls discovered in Elephantine have indicated that a Jewish settlement known as 'the Jewish Force', largely a military group, existed there. Its families were organized into military units, and their religious centre was a temple to Yahu, that is, the God of Israel, where sacrifices were offered. Apparently, the building resembled the Temple in Jerusalem (as did the temple of Onias, subsequently built at Leontopolis in Egypt). It is not known definitely when this military colony began, but presumably it commenced under the Egyptian kings of the Twenty-sixth Dynasty, *i.e.,* in the sixth century. According to the Jews of Elephantine, their temple had already been standing when Cambyses conquered Egypt (525). In addition to the Jews, there were other soldiers, chiefly Arameans, and their common language was Aramaic. The fate of this Jewish colony was sealed at the end of the Persian period in Egypt, with the restoration of the Twenty-ninth Dynasty, commencing in 399. In addition to Elephantine, there were other centres of Jewish soldiers in the service of the Persian kings in Egypt, such as those in Migdol, though it is not known whether the latter had a separate religious centre. The Jews of Elephantine regarded themselves as bound by close ties to the Temple in Jerusalem, and evidence of this can be seen in the letters they wrote to Jerusalem requesting assistance and intervention on their behalf, as well as asking for instruction on major holidays, such as Passover. The letters date chiefly from the fifth and early fourth centuries. Their dependence on Jerusalem and the Temple, not only in matters of faith, worship and observance of the festivals, but also with regard to their very existence and the defence of their sanctuary, indicates that in spite of the physical distance close ties existed between the Diaspora and Jerusalem throughout the Persian period. These persisted and were intensified later in hellenistic and Roman times.

The last years of Persian rule in Palestine were marked by Persian campaigns to suppress the many insurrections that had broken out, especially in the coastal area. Here again archaeological excavations supplement the scant historical information. It appears that Nepheritis, who founded the Twenty-ninth Egyptian Dynasty and re-established a short-lived Egyptian autonomy (the last during the Persian period), occupied the southern coastal plain as far as Gezer. His successor extended this rule to Tyre and Sidon and the northern coast. At some point, approximately in 380, the Persians reconquered the area. Again, in about 360, the western satrapies revolted with the help of Egypt. The last revolt was that of Sidon in 345 – joined by the king of Cyprus – which was harshly suppressed by the Persians, who burned and razed Sidon and various neighbouring cities along the northern coast. A late Byzantine tradition speaks of the banishment of Jewish captives to Hyrcania, near the Caspian Sea; another late tradition relates that Artaxerxes destroyed Jericho. Scholars therefore suggested that Judea apparently participated in that revolt and that it was punished by the destruction of Jericho and with the banishment of its population. Yet the entire question remains obscure, and its relationship to this revolt is still problematic. At last the revolt in the west was suppressed. Cyprus was punished; Egypt was reconquered by the Persians in 343/2, but this was the last military victory of that empire. In 334/3 Alexander the Great defeated the Persians at Granicus, in Issus, and proceeded to capture Phoenicia, Philistia and, in 332, Egypt. Only Tyre and Gaza attempted to withstand the Macedonians, but they fell after several months of siege. Elsewhere the new victors were accepted. Josephus (*Antiquities* XI, 338) records that representatives of the Jews went to greet Alexander and that he allowed them to live according to their own laws. Thus Alexander continued the Persian system of non-intervention in the religious affairs of the conquered peoples. The High Priest in Jerusalem was considered the direct representative of the people of Judah to the Macedonian rulers, and the political status of Jerusalem as a temple city remained, for a time, an unaltered factor in the rapidly changing course of Jewish history during the hellenistic age.

Epilogue

We have attempted in this survey to delineate the political and social history of Israel during a period of 700 years, from its beginnings as a national monarchy to its transformation into an autonomous, ethno-religious community in the Persian period. Neither the history of the religion of Israel nor the history of biblical literature have been included, as they are subjects adequately treated by biblical scholarship.

The importance of this period for our time is that it witnessed the development of certain institutions and ideas that have not only been crucial to the course of Jewish history up to the present day but have also had a profound effect upon the nature of Western civilization.

The first of these institutions was the monarchy and in particular the Davidic monarchy. The image of David was elevated from that of a founder of a dynasty to the symbol of an ideal monarch. His was the 'kingdom of truth and of righteousness', which, after the Babylonian exile, when the monarchy ceased to exist as a political force, continued its existence as part of an eschatological scheme in which 'the son of David' became a national as well as a universal redeemer – the Messiah who would ultimately bring peace and justice.

Closely associated with the monarchy were its two major manifestations, Jerusalem the capital and the Temple. The importance of the latter is expressed by our very terminology: the period of the First Temple. The destruction of these symbols signified the close of an era, and the period of the 'return to Zion' is integrally linked to the restoration of the Temple and the city. In fact, the entire image of Jewish history in the Persian period is dominated by Jerusalem and its Temple.

The prophetic movement – the outstanding critic of the monarchy and the Temple cult – is another of the most significant developments of this period. The prophets were instrumental in elevating kings to the throne as well as in exposing and criticising their failings and transgressions and guarding the traditional rights of the people against the excesses of the monarchial establishment. As the prophets strove to establish a system of ethical and social values as the criterion for national existence, their underlying principle was the Covenant between Israel and its God, an idea that originated at the dawn of Israel's history and found its clearest expression in the code of Deuteronomy. According to prophetic ideology, the breaking of this Covenant leads to exile. Indeed, the stress on the Covenant was not specific to the prophets alone. It epitomizes the very essence of the religious ideology of Israel from its inception; and of all the peoples of the ancient world, Israel – so far as we know – was the only society that based its relationship to its God on a formal treaty.

Furthermore, the covenant (phrased as a vassal treaty) became the *leitmotif* throughout the period: the covenant of Abraham, the covenant at Sinai and their assertions by Josiah and Nehemiah.

During this period, for the first time in Jewish history, the people were subjected to two cataclysmic phenomena: destruction and exile – the destruction and exile of the 'ten tribes' of Israel by Assyria; the destruction and exile of Judah by Babylonia. By their very impact, these events serve as milestones. When the Northern Kingdom was destroyed, Judah perpetuated the traditions of 'all Israel'. When Judah was destroyed and exiled to Babylonia, Jewish history adopted a new pattern: a vital Diaspora coexisting in a symbiotic relationship with the community in the homeland. Beginning with the Babylonian exile and throughout the Persian period, the Jewish community witnessed the crystallization of patterns of communal organization, religious outlook and social concepts that were to become paradigmatic of the encounters between the Jewish Diaspora and its environment from the hellenistic period onwards. Moreover, this first Jewish diaspora attempted to impose its own self-image on the community of Judah – as evidenced by the activities of Ezra and Nehemiah – and this self-assertion, to one degree or another, became a central facet of the relationship between the homeland and the Diaspora that has characterized Jewish existence up to the present day.

PART III

The Period of the Second Temple

Menahem Stern

12

Palestine Under the Rule of the Hellenistic Kingdoms

The Political Background

Until the latter part of the fourth century BCE, Palestine fell within the sphere of influence of the great eastern empires (Egypt, Babylonia and Persia [see Parts I and II]). Its political history was shaped by the balance of forces that determined the rise or fall of those powers. From the end of the fourth century until the victory of Islam in the seventh century CE, Palestine, like its neighbouring countries, was included among those states whose civilization was inspired by the Greek and later the Roman world. The first traces of Greek influence in the East, including Palestine, had been noticeable even before the fourth century, but governments containing a markedly Greek element developed in the East only after Alexander the Great had defeated Persia and his heirs had consolidated their positions in the conquered lands = that is to say, at the end of the fourth century. The Macedonian conquest therefore marked the beginning of a new era in the history of the Near East. Since the nineteenth century historians have referred to it as the 'hellenistic' period and to its civilization as 'Hellenism'.

Alexander's conquest of Palestine, in 332 BCE, was rapid. The cities did not resist his armies, with the sole exception of Gaza, where the Persian garrison made a desperate stand. Alexander did not remain long in Palestine, however, and the conquest was completed by his generals, who also laid the foundations of hellenistic rule in the country.

After Alexander's death in 323, the entire East was swept by a wave of wars, the wars of the *diadochs* or 'successors', who fought over the inheritance. Palestine changed hands several times, with disastrous results for its towns and population. In 301 it finally fell to Ptolemy I of Egypt, and it remained under Ptolemaic rule until the year 200, at which time its history remained linked for many years to that of Ptolemaic Egypt.

Ptolemaic rule in Palestine in the third century was not uncontested. The other great Macedonian dynasty, the Seleucids, who had established themselves in Syria, Mesopotamia and other areas, also laid claim to Palestine. Ptolemaic rule in a country so close to the Seleucid heartland was scarcely a matter of indifference to the Seleucids; while for the Ptolemies, as for all Egyptian rulers since time immemorial (see Part I), Palestine was of major strategic importance as an advance base for the defence of Egypt – and its economic worth was no less than its military value. Thus the country became a bone of contention between the two great hellenistic dynasties. During most of the third century, the Ptolemies had the upper hand, and only with the accession of Antiochus III (223–187) to the Seleucid throne were the Syrian rulers able to gain the initiative. During the early part of his reign, he succeeded in conquering most of the country, but in 217 he was defeated by Ptolemy IV Philopator at Raphia and lost all that he had won. After a while he resumed his attempts to conquer Palestine, and in the year 200 his troops won a decisive victory near the sources of the Jordan (the battle of the Panium). As a result, control of Palestine passed from the Ptolemies to the Seleucids, though the Ptolemies tried to recoup their losses, sometimes by open war and sometimes by interfering in Syrian struggles for succession, or even by dynastic marriage. In fact, the duration and continuity of Ptolemaic rule in Palestine exceeded those of any other foreign power from the fall of Persia to the beginnings of the Roman domination; and the patterns and institutions of government, no less than the cultural and economic influences that developed in the Ptolemaic period, remained in force until Roman times.

In Egypt itself the Ptolemies adopted a highly centralized system of administration and did not favour the development of urban life of a *polis* type. But in the remaining parts of their kingdom they usually followed the practice of other hellenistic rulers and encouraged the founding of Greek cities.

Palestine's Borders and Its Place in the Hellenistic Administration

Under Ptolemaic rule Palestine was not a separately defined administrative district of the kingdom. The name Palaistine, already familiar to such classical Greek writers as Herodotus and Aristotle, had no political or administrative significance whatever in the hellenistic period. To the Ptolemies its territory formed part of the region that Ptolemaic documents refer to as 'Syria and Phoenicia'. The borders of Syria and Phoenicia were not fixed, for they fluctuated according to the military balance of power between the Ptolemaic and Seleucid kingdoms. At all events, it is certain that throughout most of the third century the Ptolemaic Syria and Phoenicia included both western Palestine and Trans-Jordan, as well as Tyre and Sidon.

Syria and Phoenicia were ruled, it appears, by a governor with the title *strategos* who exercised supreme military and civil power. As a result of the frequent wars with the neighbouring power, the *strategos* was usually an experienced soldier. He was assisted by a chief finance officer, who was in charge of state revenue.

Syria and Phoenicia were divided into smaller administrative units called *hyparchies*. We may assume that their boundaries corresponded in general to the historical division of the land as it had developed in earlier times. The *hyparchies* were in turn subdivided into yet smaller administrative units (*nomes* or toparchies). In the main, this division remained in force until the end of the Second Temple period. The areas included within the boundaries of the *hyparchies* were not of a uniform legal-economic nature. Some were regarded as royal domain and were cultivated by the local farmers, who inevitably became tenants and had to pay high rents. But it seems that only a small proportion of the country's land became the property of the crown, the rest remaining in private hands.

A considerable part of the country was defined by its ethnic character; that is to say, the status of a region was determined according to the nation or *ethnos* to which its population belonged (*e.g.,* Judea, Samaria, Edom). These territories were included within the framework of the established administrative division, and part of their land also belonged to the crown. In areas with a clear ethnic character, the Ptolemaic authorities were forced to consider local traditions and leadership.

Changes in the Population and the Hellenistic Cities

Among the most important results of hellenistic rule in Palestine were the changes that occurred in the ethnic composition and patterns of organization within the population. Until the Greek conquest the majority of the population of Palestine – whether Jewish, Phoenician, Samaritan, Edomite or Nabatean – had lived there since ancient times. The interior districts were inhabited by the Jews and Samaritans and most of the coastal plain by the Phoenicians; in the south the Nabateans, who had dispossessed the Edomites from their ancestral lands, formed the strongest element, while the Edomites had turned to the north and settled in the Hebron hills and in Marissa, up to Beth-zur. In the wake of the conquest, a new ethnic element, the Macedonians and Greeks, entered the field. In fact, even in Persian times Greek traders and mercenaries had played a role in the life of the country, but the number of actual Greek settlers must have been very small and the extent of their influence limited. Only after the conquest did Greek settlement begin to assume considerable dimensions. Greek military colonies were then founded; even the country's ancient towns underwent change, and the influence of the hellenistic cities set its imprint on the country's life. The large majority of hellenistic cities in Palestine were ancient towns that had assumed a Greek image, adopting the governmental and social patterns of the Greek *polis*. The upper classes of the local population soon joined the settlers who had come from Greece. The Phoenicians went furthest in this respect and did not take long to become the standard-bearers of hellenization in Palestine. Among the most important centres of the new way of life were Gaza and Ashkelon on the southern coast, Acco (Ptolemais) north of the Carmel and Jaffa and Dor between them. In addition to the Greek cities of the coastal plain, urban centres of a hellenistic nature emerged also in Trans-Jordan and in the vicinity of the Sea of Galilee. Many of the Greek settlements in Trans-Jordan date from the very beginnings of hellenization in Palestine. Philadelphia, the successor to the ancient Rabbath-ammon, had become an important centre by the time of Ptolemy Philadelphos (285–246). In Trans-Jordan the urban tradition was not as strongly rooted as in the coastal area, but in the course of time its people developed a Greek civilization that was in no way inferior to that of western Palestine. The most famous of the Trans-Jordanian cities of the hellenistic period was no doubt Gadara, which produced several authors famous in the Greek literature of their time. The hellenistic cities in Trans-Jordan maintained close connexions with Beth-shean, which became known by its Greek name, Scythopolis.

About the system of government of these cities, no hard and fast rules can be laid down. In the earlier stages of hellenistic rule, they were closely linked to the state, had garrisons and paid taxes to the royal exchequer. Apparently, some of the towns won the status of *polis* at an early date. In other towns the *polis* system developed more gradually, and their independence increased as the power of the hellenistic kingdoms declined.

In the interior of the country, the hellenization process was slow and the towns and villages preserved their original Semitic character. The only exception was the city of Samaria (Shomron), where Macedonians began to settle from the start of the hellenistic period and determined the pattern of life. Hellenistic penetration was also marked in Idumean Marissa (Tell Sandahanna), which controlled the road from the south-west to Jerusalem and became the centre of the Ptolemaic administration in southern Palestine. The standard-bearers of the hellenistic trend in Idumea were hellenized Sidonians; but, generally speaking, hellenization struck far shallower roots in Idumea than in the coastal plain.

The Attitude of the Ptolemaic Government to Different Sections of the Population

The authorities drew a clear distinction between the Greek settlers and hellenized upper-class elements, on the one hand, and the ordinary local population, on the other. From an ordinance of King Ptolemy Philadelphos, we learn of tension between the former and the latter and of the local population's struggle not to become enslaved to the Greek settlers. The government sided with the local population and did not allow the upper classes to exploit it at will. The ordinance that has come down to us forbids, in no uncertain terms, the enslavement of the local population. It also shows that the authorities had no objection to the establishment of permanent relations between soldiers and local women, a trend that was to play an important role in the integration of the different ethnic elements and in the ways in which Hellenism and the East affected each other.

The main interests of the Ptolemaic authorities in Palestine were the regular levying of taxes and concern for security conditions. In order to make tax-collection in the different districts more effective, the Ptolemies operated wide-branching tax-gathering organizations, based on the custom prevailing in Egypt. They even made the local upper classes share in the responsibility for the total amount of taxes collected in their district and consequently farmed out the taxes of towns and villages to men of substance, who in turn would travel to Alexandria in order to receive these privileges. The taxes of a town or district went to the leading citizens who bid the highest, with the latter sometimes contracting for other towns as well.

These tax-gatherers, whose property served as a guarantee for the total amount of the revenue, had an interest in raising the amount of taxes collected to the maximum, for the balance remaining after the agreed payment to the royal treasury went into their own pockets. We witness, therefore, the development of a class of capitalists who cooperated with the royal government and were usually hated by the population. Tax-collection often led to friction and helped to increase the tension between the rulers and the ruled. The government attempted to alleviate the burden of the people by limiting the profits of the tax-gatherers; but, on the other hand, it encouraged denunciations in order to prevent the increasing evasion of taxes and ordinances.

Defence and Administration

Another problem that occupied the Ptolemies was the military situation in Palestine. Palestine was, to all effects, a borderland, and the Ptolemies regularly kept considerable forces there. The defence forces of the Ptolemaic Kingdom consisted of several elements: contingents of mercenaries raised from all parts of the Greek world and stationed as garrisons in the major towns and fortresses; and the military colonists, who ordinarily farmed the land but in times of war were liable for military service and reinforced the ranks of the royal armies. Apparently, the Ptolemies attempted to bolster the military strength of their kingdom by granting land to settlers of varied origin in return for military service in times of emergency. The armed forces also included the citizens of the Greek cities, who in times of danger were required to defend their city but were not liable to service in foreign lands.

In general outline the hellenistic administration underwent little change with the conquest of Palestine by the Seleucids. All the districts that had belonged to the Ptolemies were now given the collective name of Coele-Syria and Phoenicia. Their administration was entrusted to a royal governor with the rank of *stategos* who also served as the high priest of the royal cult in the district subject to his authority. His residence was apparently in Acco (Ptolemais). On the whole, the Seleucids did not change the administrative division of the country that had existed under the Ptolemies. This division was abolished only after the victory of the Hasmoneans, which resulted in the disbandment of the former administrative organization and the creation of new patterns appropriate to the new conditions.

Economic Life

Palestine shared in the economic prosperity of the Ptolemaic Kingdom during the time of its greatness. Economic progress was due as much to the development of trade with Egypt and other parts of the kingdom as to the introduction of more rational methods, particularly in agriculture. Farming in Egypt benefited greatly from the immigration and settlement of Greeks. Under Ptolemy Philadelphos, large tracts of land that had been neglected were converted into flourishing agricultural holdings; often they were given to high officials and courtiers as land grants, on the condition that the recipient would improve the soil and use the land efficiently. It is not easy to follow this process in all its details, but the method adopted by the Ptolemies in Egypt seems also to have worked under Palestinian conditions. In attempting to obtain the largest possible crop yields from their holdings, the Greek landlords introduced considerable improvements in Palestinian farming methods, and the local landowners shared in the benefits derived from the Greek methods.

On trade relations more information has been preserved than on agriculture.

Palestine, it appears, was an important link in the economic system of the Ptolemaic Kingdom. It was a major exporter of commodities that were common within its own borders or those of southern Syria, but were scarce in the Nile Valley. Even more important was its role as a transit station for goods from remote countries, a factor that did much to maintain the Ptolemaic trade balance. Though Egypt had a reputation as one of the greatest granaries of the world in those days, we hear of Syrian grain being exported to Egypt from Palestinian ports. Another export commodity was high-quality oil; for the kinds of oil found in Egypt were inferior and not to the taste of the Greek colonists. Consequently, Palestine became one of Egypt's main suppliers of good oil. Specifically Palestinian exports included also asphalt from the Dead Sea, which the Egyptians of those days used for embalming their dead. Another product of considerable economic importance was the balsam, which grew in groves near Jericho and at En-gedi. Slaves also were exported from Palestine. The papyri mainly speak of young boys and slave-girls. Local notables as well as Greeks engaged in the slave-trade. The slaves brought from Palestine were used mainly in domestic service rather than in the fields, which were cultivated by the Egyptian tenant peasantry itself.

To cater to the needs of the Greek population and of the garrisons stationed in the Palestinian towns and fortresses, there were also imports, such as wine, from the Aegean islands. Handles of Rhodian amphorae, found in great quantity in the citadels of Beth-zur, Gezer, Samaria and elsewhere, testify to the volume of exports from Rhodes to Palestine. Next to Rhodian wine, the wines of Cnidos and Thasos were also popular. Of great importance, as we have noted, was the role of Palestine in the Ptolemaic economy as a transit country. The Ptolemaic rulers of Egypt set a high value on goods imported from the east. Some of these imports – perfumes, spices, silks and ivory – were intended for the use of the royal court and the temples; the remainder was re-exported to the countries of the Aegean Sea and formed an important source of revenue for the Ptolemaic treasury. The main trade route for these goods ran from South Arabia to the Nabatean capital Petra and from there to Gaza and on to Egypt, by land or by sea (see Parts I and II). Palestine's role as a transit station for goods bound for Egypt was enhanced by the fast land and sea routes between the two countries.

13

The Social and Governmental Structure of Judea Under the Ptolemies and Seleucids

Judea and the Jews Within the Hellenistic Kingdoms

Until the Hasmonean Revolt, Judea was a self-contained unit, one of the many that formed the Ptolemaic administrative division of Syria and Phoenicia and in later years one of the units of the Seleucid province of Coele-Syria and Phoenicia. Thus the identity of the province Yahud (Judea) was established from the days of Persian rule (see Part II), and even its Greek name, *Ioudaia*, was similar. To the Ptolemies and Seleucids, Judea, with its population of *Ioudaioi*, was a nation (*ethnos*), with its centre in Jerusalem.

The Autonomy of Judea and Jerusalem: The High Priest and the Gerousia

Jerusalem was not only the capital but the major city of Judea. Until the changes introduced under Antiochus Epiphanes, Jerusalem had neither the status nor the institutions of the *polis*, though its relation to the entire territory of Judea was in a way comparable to that between the Greek cities and their territories. Governing the autonomous territory of Judea was left to the High Priest and the Council of Elders or the Gerousia. Thus the pattern of government in Judea remained, to all intents, the same as that which had developed under Persian rule (see Part II). The Gerousia, despite its Greek name, which appeared throughout the Greek world, had few of the characteristics of Greek systems and was a direct continuation of the council of 'the elders of Judah' from Persian times.

The High Priests were Zadokites of the priestly course of *Yedaya* (one of the twenty-four divisions of the priesthood) and were all descendants of Joshua ben Jozadak, the High Priest during the period of the restoration of the Temple (see Part II). The office was passed on from father to son; if the lawful heir was too young to hold the position, it was customary to appoint a brother or uncle of the deceased High Priest. The High Priest held office for life (only Antiochus Epiphanes broke this custom), and Jews and strangers alike regarded him as the leader of the nation. 'The Jews have no king at all. The leadership of the nation is regularly entrusted to a priest regarded as superior to his colleagues in wisdom and virtue, whom they call the High Priest.' Thus reads a description of the High Priest by

Hecataeus, a gentile historian of the beginning of the hellenistic period (quoted by Diodorus Siculus, *Bibliotheca Historica* XL, 3.5). The High Priest was therefore not only the religious head but also the political leader of the nation. He exercised supreme authority over the Temple, which included responsibility for the capital's security and its regular water supply. He also presided over the Gerousia and was responsible for the gathering of royal taxes.

In fact, the influence of the High Priest depended largely on his personality. A High Priest such as Simon, the son of Onias II, set his imprint on the development of the entire nation. It is interesting to see with what enthusiasm Ben Sira describes him:

> Great among his brethren, and the glory of his people,
>> Simon, son of Yohanan the Priest,
> In whose time the House was renovated
>> And in whose days the Temple was fortified.
> In whose time a reservoir was dug
>> A water-cistern like the sea in its abundance.
>> I shall tell thereof among the multitude.
> In whose days the wall was built
>> With turrets for protection like a royal palace
> He cared for his people, to preserve them from robbery
>> And fortified his city against the enemy.
> How glorious when he gazed out from the Tent
>> When he came forth from the Sanctuary!
> Like a morning-star from between the clouds
>> Like the full moon on festivals.

(Ben Sira 50:1–6)

On the other hand, Simon's father, Onias II, had to cede part of his powers and influence to Joseph ben Tobias of Trans-Jordan. Even within the Temple itself, the High Priest had his rivals. Under Seleucid rule, during the time of Onias III, the son of Simon, one hears of another priest named Simon who served as governor of the Temple and, in doing so, clashed with the High Priest.

The High Priest was assisted by the Gerousia. Presumably, it ranked above him officially; such, at least, was the case at the end of the third century. In addition to the leaders of the priesthood, the Gerousia also included heads of families who represented the interests of the provincial towns of Judea. The custom of the hellenistic kings was apparently to give precedence to the Gerousia over the High Priest in their documents, but when the Hasmonean dynasty consolidated its position and the office of High Priest passed to its members, the documents began to name the High Priest before the council. This change reflected the shift in the balance of power in Judea following the Hasmonean Revolt.

The sources also tell of assemblies of the people of Jerusalem that took place in the Temple courtyard. They did not meet regularly, and one doubts whether they had a clearly defined function, as did the *ecclesiai* of the Greek cities. Apparently, they met only on extraordinary occasions when particularly important decisions were called for. It was such an assembly that approved the embassy of Joseph ben Tobias to Alexandria. For decisions of a constitutional nature, the entire people of Judea were convened. Such assemblies were known as *haknesset ha-Gedolah* ('the Great Assembly').

The foreign monarchy confirmed the 'ancestral laws' of the Jews as the binding code for the entire territory of autonomous Judea. These ancestral laws in effect consisted of the Law of Moses as interpreted by the recognized leadership of Judea. By virtue of this royal confirmation, the autonomous authorities of Jerusalem were even empowered to compel the entire population of Judea to comply with the precepts of the Torah and to ban idolatry throughout the land. Besides the rights that the government granted the Jews, it also imposed duties on them. Judea, as part of the Ptolemaic or Seleucid Kingdom, had to pay heavy taxes to the royal exchequer, which were a burden on its farmers as long as foreign rule lasted. From an order issued by Antiochus III after the conquest of Jerusalem, we learn that the population of Judea paid not only land-taxes but also other taxes, including a sort of poll-tax. We also know of the existence of a salt-tax and a crown-tax. The latter was at first a gift expressing the people's participation in joyous events in the royal house, but eventually it became an oppressive and compulsory contribution. In addition to direct taxes, the Judeans paid heavy duties on imported goods, even if they were merely carried from one district to another.

On the whole, the Seleucids left the tax system in Judea as it had been under the Ptolemies. Antiochus III granted the Jews a certain measure of relief from the payments required under the previous administration because of the military assistance that the Jews of Jerusalem had extended to him in fighting the Ptolemaic garrison and in order to win the sympathies of his new subjects for the future. The relief also constituted a royal contribution to the repair of Jerusalem after the heavy damage it had suffered in the course of the war.

From a valuable document preserved in I Maccabees 10 (a letter of Demetrius I of Syria in which he offers the Jews relief from various taxes), we learn that in the author's time the royal exchequer received one-third of the field crops and half of the fruit from trees, apart from the salt-tax, the crown-tax and other payments. It seems, however, that this document reflects the changes in tax rates and in methods of collection resulting from the punitive laws of Antiochus Epiphanes, rather than conditions throughout the hellenistic period. On the other hand, it is possible that even before Antiochus Epiphanes the situation was more or less the same, though the rates of taxation were somewhat lower.

The Temple and Priests

The focus of religious, political and social life in Judea was the Temple. The Greek historian Polybius, who lived in the second century BCE, defined the Jews as a nation dwelling around the famous Temple of Jerusalem (quoted in Josephus, *Jewish Antiquities* 12.136). Unlike other Eastern temples, the Temple of Jerusalem was not rich in landed estate. The livelihood of the priests and Levites was, according to the precepts of the Torah, the concern of the entire nation, which was required to render to them gift offerings and tithes. At the same time, the Torah had imposed no regular tax for the maintenance of the Temple, the daily sacrifices and so forth. Nehemiah (see Part II) was the first to levy from all of Judea a tax of one-third of a shekel (Nehemiah 10:33) to cover the expenditure of the Temple. To what extent this custom persisted between the days of Nehemiah and those of the Hasmoneans is not clear, but we know that the Temple revenue included sums of money from the gentile monarchy, which contributed to the financing of the daily sacrifice. Because of its particularly sacred character, the Temple also served as a depository for capital sums, such as money belonging to widows and orphans or to the rich, who feared for their capital under the often insecure conditions that prevailed in the land.

The *élite* of hellenistic Judea were the priests, one of whom was the High Priest, the acknowledged head of the nation. They furnished part of the membership of the Gerousia, as well as most of the important functionaries. To foreigners Judea was a land ruled by priests who enjoyed many privileges, not least of which were those in the economic field. Ben Sira warned his compatriots to hold the priesthood in due respect:

Fear God with all thy heart
　And revere his priests.
With all thy strength love Him that made thee,
　And forsake not his ministers.
Glorify God and honour the priests
　And provide their portion as has been commanded.
(*Ben Sira* 7:29–31)

Many priests lived in country towns and villages but customarily went to Jerusalem to serve in the Temple when the turn of their watch came, as well as for the three festivals of Passover, Pentecost and Tabernacles. The entire priesthood was divided into twenty-four watches, which served in the Temple in rotation.

The members of the priesthood did not all enjoy equal standing, for the interests of the leading priests and the lay priests or of the priesthood, on the one hand, and the Levites, on the other, were not always identical. The Torah had laid down the original distribution between priests and Levites of revenue from gift offerings, tithes and other dues, but during the time of the Second Temple, when the number and influence of the Levites had shrunk, the priests appropriated the bulk of the tithes, which, according to the Torah, were the Levites' share. As we can see from the books of *Judith* and *Tobit,* which may go back to Persian times, as well as from I Maccabees, the tithes were brought to Jerusalem and were not distributed on the spot by the farmers. This concentration of the tithes in Jerusalem brought them directly within the sphere of influence of the High Priest and the central authorities in the capital, thus making the masses of the priests and Levites even more dependent upon the upper stratum of the priesthood.

There were several prominent priestly families, besides that of the High Priest, that played important roles in the social and political life of the Jews. One of them was the house of Hakotz. Johanan ben Hakotz was the man who negotiated with

Antiochus III to secure the rights of Jerusalem after the conquest. His son Eupolemos led the delegation sent to Rome by Judah the Maccabee. Another important priestly family was that of Bilga; its members included Simon, Menelaus and Lysimachus, who undermined the position of the lawful High Priests and became pillars of the hellenization movement. Simon held the office of Temple governor, and Menelaus actually replaced the High Priest. Also from one of the priestly families came Jose ben Joezer, one of the greatest Jewish sages of his time. A relative of his, Jakim-Alcimus, was appointed High Priest by the Syrian king Demetrius I during the Hasmonean Revolt. In the Second Temple period, the leading priestly families made a practice of endogamous marriage; but under suitable circumstances they were not unwilling to establish matrimonial ties with influential families not included among the priesthood.

The House of Tobias

Undisputedly first among the non-priestly families that achieved an important status in Judea in the third century was the house of Tobias, an ancient clan whose rise dates back to the days of the First Temple. Its power was based in southern Gilead, where it had its family estates, known by the name of 'the land of Tobias'. The Tobiads gained in influence under the Persians. In the days of Nehemiah, Tobias allied himself by marriage with influential residents of Jerusalem and became one of the chief opponents of the religious-national policy of Ezra and Nehemiah. One of his descendants, the Tobias who was the contemporary of Ptolemy Philadelphos, stood at the head of a military colony in 'the Citadel of Ammon' that was composed of Jews and gentiles. The Ptolemies needed the Tobiads in order to stabilize their rule in Trans-Jordan. We have papyri testifying to the fact that Tobias was a well-known personality at the Ptolemaic court and corresponded with Apollonius, the royal finance minister. He also sent rare animals to King Ptolemy. Tobias married the sister of the High Priest Onias II and thus increased his prestige in Jerusalem. The influence of the house of Tobias reached its peak with Joseph, Tobias' son.

Joseph ben Tobias was a faithful pupil of his father. He established even closer relations with the court in Alexandria and shifted the centre of his activities from Trans-Jordan to western Palestine. When relations between the High Priest Onias II and the Ptolemaic authorities grew tense, Joseph's ambitions found new channels. He succeeded in narrowing the High Priest's field of activity considerably and even won the support of the people's assembly in the Temple courtyard, which authorized him to represent Judea at the royal court.

However, Joseph's main strength was derived from his positions outside Judea. He acted as a royal tax-farmer on a scale that hellenistic Judea had never known before. The scope of his activities even included the Greek cities. In this respect he enjoyed the support of the royal government and displayed a surprising determination in pursuing his tax-gathering activities. It seems that many Jews from the higher ranks of Jerusalem's society also were involved in his affairs and thus came into closer contact with the gentile capitalists of Ptolemaic Syria. While the earlier Jewish leaders, from Nehemiah onwards, had retained their specifically Jewish viewpoint, Joseph ben Tobias and his circle adopted a more Palestinian outlook; Joseph was no less at home in Samaria than in Judea. His business methods attracted much capital to Judea and strengthened Jewish influence in various parts of Palestine. With the introduction of new capital into the Jewish sector, there was also an influx of customs and modes of existence that were common in third-century hellenistic Palestine and which threatened the traditional Jewish way of life. However, the increasing identification of Joseph and his circle with the upper classes of Palestinian society in general was counterbalanced by his thoroughgoing methods of collecting taxes, which left a heavy substratum of enmity in the hearts of the gentile population and even created tension between Jews and gentiles in various parts of Palestine.

The rise of the Tobiads, who supplanted the High Priest in certain fields of public life, and the cultural and economic results of their policy aroused strong opposition among wide circles in Jerusalem that did not benefit from the new economic prosperity, and the anti-traditional atmosphere that began to prevail in Jerusalem was widely resented. Class tension, caused by the gap between the rich and the poor, grew throughout the land:

What peace can the hyena have with the dog,
　Or what peace the rich with the poor?
The wild asses of the desert are food for the lion
　Even so the poor are the pasture of the rich.
Humility is an abomination to pride
　Even so are the poor an abomination to the rich.
　　　　　　(*Ben Sira* 13:18–20)

Within the house of Tobias, a deadly quarrel broke out between Hyrcanus, Joseph's youngest son, and his brothers. Under the Seleucids, Hyrcanus took the side of High Priest Onias III against his brothers, who attempted to depose Onias and replace him by a High Priest from a priestly family sharing their views and aspirations. After one of the members of this family, Simon, had become governor of the Temple, his brother Menelaus was appointed High Priest by Antiochus Epiphanes. Both brothers worked together with the Tobiads in attempting to uproot the principles of Jewish life that had been established by Ezra, Nehemiah and their successors.

The Influence of Hellenism

The protracted influence of Hellenism in the cultural and social field, the Ptolemaic and Seleucid administrative system and the material achievements of hellenistic civilization in agriculture, town planning and finance all combined to create far-reaching changes even in Judea. We must not forget that the settlements of the Jewish population in Palestine – whether in Judea or elsewhere – were surrounded by a hostile gentile population; and while this population was of widely differing ethnic origins, hellenistic rule provided it, stratified as it was, with something like a united hellenized leadership. Formerly, only the Jewish side was distinguished by its unity, but now a Syrian-Greek bloc took shape, and the crucial question arose as to whether the Jewish nation could hold its own as a force to be reckoned with in Palestine, or whether it would lose its specific national, religious and cultural character and become one of the many units that were the bearers of hellenistic civilization in Palestine, just as it had lost its political independence and become one of the many units of the polity of Syria and Phoenicia. Around the year 200 it seemed that the victory of Hellenism was assured; the outer glamour and material superiority of the dominant civilization seemed liable to endanger the continuity of Judaism or at least to deprive the leadership class of its Jewish character. The upper classes – the priests and others – increasingly adapted their way of thinking and style of life to those of the corresponding classes of the non-Jewish sections of the population. Trends that had never completely disappeared emerged in full strength again: opposition to the accentuation of Jewish particularism and the desire to merge into the upper strata of the gentile society. The other classes also came increasingly under the influence of the general hellenistic atmosphere. Many Jews lived in towns where the majority of the population was hellenized, and Jewish merchants who traded with far-off foreign cities acquired Greek civilization together with their merchandise and passed it on to their fellow Jews.

The hellenistic influence in Judea reveals itself primarily in the field of material civilization. The coins of Yehud of the Persian period imitated the Athenian coinage, and it seems that hellenistic finance gradually conquered Jerusalem. Hellenistic influence was evident also in architecture and art. The spread of Greek names among the Jews was an external sign of the hellenization of Judea; Greek names were no longer used only by those Jews who had detached themselves from Jewish tradition. In the third century Greek names were still rare among the Jews: even the son of Tobias had a Hebrew name; but by the year 200 or thereabouts, Greek names began to be common at different social levels, including even the family of the High Priests. Also known by his Greek name is one of the greatest Jewish sages of those days, Antigonus of Socho, and we find Greek names among the officers of Judah the Maccabee. They were particularly common among Jerusalem's upper class and in districts bordering on hellenized gentile populations. Only in part of the country towns and in the villages of Judea and southern Samaria did this custom fail to strike root: none of the sons of Mattathias the Hasmonean, for example, was called by a Greek name.

Nevertheless, it must be stated that by the year 200 Greek civilization had not yet struck deep roots in Judea. While contacts with neighbours and with the royal administration had made the Jews conversant in the Greek language and Greek words began to find their way into Hebrew, one doubts whether there were many in Judea who were literate enough in Greek to read the classics of Greek literature and philosophy, and, although certain Greek ideas gained acceptance in the Jewish literature of Palestine of those days, they merely reflect the influence of the general cultural background and cannot be regarded as serious evidence of any direct influence of Greek literature on Judaism. Even in such books as Ecclesiastes and *Ben Sira,* it is difficult to detect any strong influence of the Greek spirit.

Jewish Expansion Beyond Judea

Only a portion of the Jews in Palestine lived within the administrative boundaries of autonomous Judea. Since the end of Persian rule, the number of Jews in the country had increased steadily, and Judea – from Beth-zur in the south to Bethel in the north – could no longer contain them. Jews therefore lived beyond Judea itself. The Jewish population was particularly dense in the three districts of southern Samaria – Lydda, Ephraim and Ramathaim. Politically and administratively these districts were part of Samaria, but their inhabitants remained, in all matters concerning religion and nationality, Jews in the fullest sense of the word and therefore connected with the Temple in Jerusalem. Naturally, some of them also sought political union with Judea, and during the Hasmonean Revolt the Jews from the hills to the north and north-west of Jerusalem and from the Plain of Lydda were among the most valiant of the fighters. Even the actual cradle of the revolt, Modi'in, seems to have lain outside Judea, in the district of Lydda.

Another considerable Jewish concentration existed in north-western Samaria. Its population may be presumed to have been composed of ancient Israelite elements mixed with Judean settlers; but whatever the origin of these Jews, from the national-religious viewpoint they formed part of the Jewish nation, whose centre was the Temple in Jerusalem. The Jewish population of western Galilee, which had to fight for its life against the expansion of the hellenistic cities of Acco (Ptolemais) and Tyre, should be regarded as an offshoot of the Jewish concentration in north-western Samaria. There was also a considerable Jewish population in eastern and central Galilee. Many Jews, for instance, lived in Arbel, and during the revolt its inhabitants proved their loyalty to the Jewish nation by their valiant resistance to the Seleucid general Bacchides when his large army advanced against Jerusalem in 160 BCE. In fact, the continuity of the old Israelite settlement in the north of the country had never been interrupted, and even the founding of the hellenistic cities on the edge of Galilee and the development of large estates in the hellenistic fashion made but few inroads upon it.

Jewish concentrations existed also east of the Jordan, part of them in the region of the Tobiad estates, others further to the north. There were Jews in Scythopolis (Beth-shean), where relations with the gentile neighbours were better than those between Jews and gentiles elsewhere. There were Jews also in the cities on the coast, such as Jaffa. All these Jews, though they lived outside the boundaries of Judea, took an active part in Judean public and spiritual life. Neither the Tobiad leaders of the hellenistic movement nor the Hasmoneans, who headed the revolt against hellenistic domination, came from Jerusalem; their homes were in places that were officially outside the borders of Judea. Jose ben Joezer, one of the greatest sages of his time, came from Zereda in southern Samaria, and another famous scholar, Nitai the Arbelite, likewise one of the men who left his imprint on the spiritual development of his time, came from Arbel in eastern Galilee.

Outside the consolidated national-religious body of the Jews stood the Samaritans in central Samaria who lived around their separate temple on Mount Gerizim. The founding of the temple, towards the end of the Persian era, enhanced the standing of Shechem in the life of Samaria; but the main impulse for the resumption of urban life in Shechem came down from the changes that took place in the city of Samaria, which became a Macedonian colony and therefore could no longer serve as the centre of the Samaritans. In the hellenistic era the Samaritans became the people that 'dwelt in Shechem'. This situation is clearly borne out by the archaeological findings, which show that Shechem, after an interruption of centuries, again became an important settlement. It seems that the beginning of Seleucid rule led to economic prosperity for Shechem which, however, ended when the political situation deteriorated after the decrees of Antiochus Epiphanes. About the political status of hellenistic Shechem we know virtually nothing. That it did not become a *polis* is certain, but apparently it had a council (Boule), which also represented the Samaritan community in its dealings with the royal authorities.

The Number of Jews

The sources available to us show clearly that in the Persian and hellenistic era the number of Jews in Judea and the whole of Palestine increased considerably; so much so that foreign observers, as early as the beginning of the hellenistic era, felt compelled to find explanations for the rapid increase of the Jewish population. We have only limited data on the numbers of Jews in Palestine, and they are not always of unimpeachable reliability. Thus Hecataeus (quoted in Josephus, *Against Apion* 1.197) stated that the city of Jerusalem had a population of 120,000, and in the Aristeas letter (see page 294) we read of 100,000 Jewish captives being exiled to Egypt by Ptolemy I. More realistic are the numbers of Jewish soldiers reported in connexion with the military campaigns of the Hasmonean Revolt. We are told that Judah the Maccabee had 8,000 men under his command on his march to Gilead in the year 164 (I Maccabees 5:20), and at the same time 3,000 Jews fought in western Galilee under his brother Simon. The highest number of Jewish soldiers quoted by any source is 40,000 – the figure given for the force with which Jonathan the Hasmonean set out against Tryphon (I Maccabees 12:41).

Relations Between the Jews of Palestine and the Diaspora

There were also large Jewish populations outside Palestine. The people of Judea had, of course, a special bond with the Jews who remained in the Babylonian exile from which they themselves had returned. Under the Ptolemies, however, the Jews of Palestine were cut off from the Jewish masses living in Babylonia and other parts of the Seleucid Empire, while closer relations developed with Egyptian Jewry.

Early in the hellenistic period, there was an increase in the migration of Jews from Palestine to Egypt. In part it was voluntary and was a result of the attraction of the easy economic conditions of Ptolemaic Egypt; but it was also partly a matter of compulsion, for many Jews were captured and enslaved by the Ptolemaic armies that passed through Palestine in the frequent wars of the early hellenistic times. The fact that Egypt and Palestine were under the same Ptolemaic rule helped to establish closer ties with these Jews: high-placed Judeans often visited Alexandria on private business or public missions and established connexions with the Jews in Egypt. That Egyptian and Palestinian Jewry remained in contact is evident also from the fact that literary works written in Palestine in Hebrew, such as the book of *Ben Sira,* were translated into Greek for the use of the Jewish community in Egypt.

Relations between the Jews living in Judea and those in the Diaspora were largely determined by the political status and aspirations of the Palestinians as shaped by the competition between the Ptolemaic and Seleucid dynasties. When Palestine became detached from the Ptolemaic realm, the bond with the Jews of Alexandria would weaken, while a Seleucid victory was likely to result in the resumption of contacts with Babylonian Jewry.

14

The Decrees Against the Jewish Religion and the Establishment of the Hasmonean State

The Beginnings of Seleucid Rule

Antiochus III (223–187 BCE), the Seleucid conqueror of Palestine, changed little in the pattern of government and customs that had prevailed in Ptolemaic and, to all intents, Persian Judea. He allowed Judea to maintain its traditional system of government and even granted the Jews additional privileges: the remission of all royal taxes for three years, a one-third reduction in the rate of taxation and an exemption from all taxes for the Temple singers and members of the Gerousia. This situation continued under Seleucus IV, Antiochus' son. But the political and financial crisis that befell the Seleucid Kingdom produced changes in its domestic policy. Antiochus III's defeat in the war against Rome and the peace of Apamea (188) had saddled the Seleucid administration with a heavy financial burden of indemnities to be paid to the Roman republic. As a power, the Seleucids had lost much of their international prestige and were to remain in continual financial straits, which were reflected in the central authorities' attitude towards the different nations of the realm. The Seleucid kings deemed themselves forced to raise money wherever they could and saw no reason for overlooking the enormous treasures kept in the ancient, wealthy temples of their kingdom. Antiochus III, in fact, met his death while attempting to plunder a famous Elamite temple. This situation also explains the attempt of his son, Seleucus IV, to appropriate money from the treasury of the Temple in Jerusalem. In so doing, Seleucus had no intention of offending the Jewish religion but acted out of simple financial considerations; however, it must be regarded as the first stage in the clash between the Jews and the Seleucid Kingdom.

Jewish Political Trends and Activities Until the Reign of Antiochus Epiphanes

In assessing Jewish political activity in the years preceding the Hasmonean Revolt, we must bear in mind that the achievement of full independence and the re-establishment of the ancient Jewish kingdom in all its glory was not, in practice, the main policy of the Jewish leadership. Its actual aim, which moulded its relations with the central authorities, was to maintain and foster Jewish autonomy. In their military activities the Judeans were connected with both of the hellenistic powers, always in the hope of obtaining more privileges from the royal government or some measure of territorial improvement in the borders of autonomous Judea. Nevertheless, in the country towns and villages of Judea there would be occasional clashes between the local population and representatives of the central government, due largely to the natural tension between the heavily taxed Judean peasantry and the foreign administration. From time to time relations between the Jews and their immediate neighbours also reached the point of conflagration. The expansion of the Jewish population into the areas of Palestine adjoining Judea and the natural desire of these areas then to become part of Judea resulted in frequent friction between the Jews and their neighbours, mainly the Idumeans and Samaritans, which only the ever-watchful eye of the foreign rulers seems to have prevented from escalating into a major war. The hostile attitude of the Jews to their neighbours in those days is reflected in the writings of Ben Sira:

For two nations doth my soul feel abhorrence
  Yea, and for a third which is not a people;
The inhabitants of Seir and Philistia
  And that foolish nation that dwelleth in Sichem.
                    (*Ben Sira* 50:25–6)

However, quite apart from actual policies, the hope that their subjugation was only temporary and that the greatness of Israel would be restored had remained alive in the hearts of the Jews even during the years prior to the revolt. They were conscious throughout that the 'heritage of their fathers' (see the words of Simon the Hasmonean in I Maccabees 15:33) was the entire Land of Israel, which by right belonged to the Jews. These hopes for the rebirth of the Hebrew nation inspired not only messianic visionaries and fiery zealots but even a moderate like Ben Sira himself:

Renew the signs and repeat the wonders,
  Glorify the Hand, and praise the Right Arm,
Waken indignation and pour out wrath
  Subdue the foe and expel the enemy
Gather all the tribes of Jacob
  That they may receive their inheritance as in days of old
Have mercy on the people that is called by Thy name,
  Israel whom Thou hast called Thy first-born
Give testimony to the first of Thy works,
  And fulfil the vision proclaimed in Thy name.
                    (*Ben Sira* 36)

Antiochus Epiphanes (175–164) and the Changes in Judea

The reign of Antiochus Epiphanes marked a turning-point in the history of the Jewish nation. It was a period of intensive activity in both the political and military spheres. As his father's defeat in the war against Rome had deprived the Seleucid

Kingdom of much of its manpower, Antiochus sought to fill the gap from the resources that existed within the kingdom by accelerating the hellenization of the lands under his rule. At no time in the history of the Seleucid dynasty, apart from the first days of its establishment, were so many cities founded as were under Antiochus Epiphanes, though they were not actually new cities but existing towns to which Antiochus gave a new status in order to encourage speedier hellenization. In general, modern scholars have over-estimated the number of cities founded by Antiochus Epiphanes.

In the first seven years of his reign, his political and military activity was focused on the southern border of his kingdom – the border with Ptolemaic Egypt. Hence much importance was attached to Judea as a buffer state between his realm and that of the Ptolemies. From the very first Antiochus displayed a great interest in all that happened in Palestine and a tendency to intervene in Jerusalem's internal affairs. The High Priest, Onias III, was deposed by his order and replaced by his brother Jason, a man of hellenistic inclinations who, moreover, had promised the king to raise more taxes than his predecessor. With Antiochus' consent, Jason also introduced far-reaching changes in Jerusalem's political and social structure. The aim of these changes was to convert Jerusalem into a *polis,* which was to be named Antiochia. Establishing the new *polis* required the introduction of Greek political and cultural institutions into the life of the Jewish capital.

The most outstanding of these institutions was the gymnasium, one of the hallmarks of all Greek cities and the centre of their social life. The atmosphere surrounding the gymnasium gave serious offence to Jews who had kept to their faith, for the traditions of the gymnasium were rooted in Greek paganism and connected with the cult of Heracles and Hermes. While it is unlikely that Jason actually introduced the cult of foreign gods in Jerusalem, the atmosphere that the gymnasium imposed on Jerusalem must have been imbued with paganism. It did not take long for the gymnasium to replace the Temple as the focus of Jerusalem's social life. II Maccabees 4:14 relates with implacable bitterness how the priests abandoned their duties in the Temple to attend the competitions in the gymnasium.

Faithful to the system of the Tobiads and their faction, Jason made every effort to integrate the new *polis* into the cultural life of hellenistic Syria. The new Antiochia (Jerusalem) was represented by a delegation at the games in honour of the Tyrian Heracles (Melqart) – a major step towards the abolition of Jerusalem's specific character. But Jason did not last long as High Priest and head of the *polis* Jerusalem. Antiochus, on the brink of war against Ptolemaic Egypt, apparently did not think him trustworthy enough at such a crucial moment. He was replaced (in 171) by Menelaus, who did not belong to the family of the High Priests. Menelaus, in his loyalty and submissiveness to the king, was, in effect, like any ordinary official of the royal administration. The large amounts of money that he offered the king – which he could raise only by cruelly extorting the people of Judea and robbing the Temple treasury – must also have been welcome to the chronically impecunious king. The relations between the Seleucid Kingdom and the institutions of autonomous Judea were now placed on an entirely different footing. The High Priest, who had been the representative of the Jewish nation and its interests, now became the representative of the crown in Judea – Antiochus' governor in Jerusalem, as it were, and his main partner in carrying out his Judean policy.

Meanwhile, important events had taken place in the political and military sphere. The Ptolemaic Kingdom had declared war on Antiochus in order to recover southern Syria and Palestine, and Antiochus had taken up the challenge. It did not take him long to turn the tables on Alexandria; Egypt was invaded and the Nile Valley transformed into a battle-field. In 168 Antiochus was about to conquer Alexandria, the capital of Ptolemaic Egypt, and depose the dynasty. Only the intervention of the Roman Republic saved Egypt from annexation by the Seleucids. Antiochus was forced to abandon his conquests and returned home in a fit of depression (Daniel 11:29–30: 'At the time appointed he shall return, and come toward the south; but it shall not be as the former, or as the latter. For the ships of Chittim shall come against him: therefore he shall be grieved, and return, and have indignation against the holy covenant . . .').

Antiochus' wars against Egypt were closely connected with significant developments in Judea. On the way back from his first invasion of Egypt, the king, assisted by Menelaus, had plundered the vast treasures of the Temple and, in doing so, had aroused the anger of the Jews, who regarded this act as a serious blow to Judean autonomy and a deliberate insult to all they held holy. In 168, during Antiochus' last campaign against Egypt, rumours of his death circulated in Judea and set off revolts in several cities in the south of the kingdom, including Jerusalem. Jason, the deposed High Priest, returned to Jerusalem – perhaps at the instigation of the Ptolemaic court – and took control there; but as soon as Antiochus had returned from Egypt, after Rome's intervention against him, he retook Jerusalem. As a punitive measure and in order to secure his control of the city for the future, he settled a foreign colony on the Acra, the citadel of the town. The foreigners were joined by the extreme hellenists of Menelaus' faction. No decrees had as yet been promulgated against the Jewish religion, but the very fact that non-Jewish elements and extreme hellenists – the latter differing but little from the former – now controlled the capital of Judea deprived it of its character as the holy city of the Jews and turned it into a pagan town teeming with idolatrous cults. The gentile settlers had brought their gods with them, and Menelaus' hellenists did nothing to stop them. To many of the Jews, this situation was unbearable. Disgusted by the prevalence of foreign cults in Jerusalem, they left the city and sought an escape in the deserts to the east and south-east or in the villages and country towns to the north and north-west.

Religious Persecution

In 167 Antiochus took a decisive step: he forbade observance of the Jewish religion in Judea – and later also in other districts – and imposed the death sentence on any Jew who circumcised his children or observed the Sabbath. The authorities even forced the Jewish population to participate in pagan rites and eat forbidden foods, particularly pork, and the Temple was desecrated and rededicated to Olympic Zeus.

Polytheism is in general regarded as naturally tolerant, and it is a fact that Antiochus did not resort to religious compulsion in respect to other nations in his kingdom. The priests of the Babylonians and other nations continued to live their traditional religious lives and to serve their gods. Antiochus himself was particularly inclined towards the cult of Olympic Zeus, as is evidenced by the coins he struck; but there are no grounds for assuming that this attachment induced him to humiliate other cults, with the exception of the Jewish religion, which he persecuted mercilessly. Apparently, the long-lasting tension in Judea made the king realize that the Jewish religion with its militant monotheism lay behind the stubborn resistance of the Jews to the innovations that he wished to introduce in their country and that this resistance endangered the security of his southern border. It also seems likely that his personality was strongly repelled by the Jewish religion, which contradicted his entire outlook on life. This combination of power politics and personal revulsion from Jewish monotheism offers an explanation of Antiochus' new policy. Moreover, he was aggressive and daring by nature and not averse to using unconventional means or unusual methods.

The policy that he chose seemed eminently practicable, for he could rely on the full cooperation of the extreme hellenists among the Jews and, first and foremost, on their leader, Menelaus. Apparently, he failed to realize how thin this upper crust was, for their willing cooperation led him to assume that the entire upper class of the Jews would support him against the elements hostile to his rule and that the latter drew their main support from the lower classes. Actually, Menelaus and his followers had no real foothold among the Jewish people. The hellenists had nothing to lose by Antiochus' new policy, for they no longer had any spiritual bond with the Jewish faith, and by detaching themselves even from the bulk of the priesthood they had cut themselves off from the fabric of the Jewish social structure. This group followed Antiochus until it was swept away entirely by the powerful current of events; after the Hasmonean Revolt there remained no trace of them among the Jewish nation. Antiochus' decrees and the indignation they aroused among those faithful to Judaism changed the entire course of Jewish history. Contrary to the king's expectations, the large majority of the Jewish nation remained loyal to its religion, and at all social levels there were people ready to give their lives for the sake of their ancestral faith. The whole-hearted and uncompromising dedication of the Jewish masses to their beliefs was deeply rooted. Even in earlier times the Jews had proved that they would not hesitate to sacrifice their lives when religion commanded it, but now, for the first time in human history, the world witnessed a spectacle of mass martyrdom. The deeds of the martyrs and the devout in these times of religious persecution were to become an example for Jews and non-Jews in all ages to come.

As was to happen so often in the future, martyrdom was accompanied by heightened eschatological yearnings. There was a growing belief that a time of divine retribution, which would bring with it the downfall of the kingdom of evil, was approaching and so would fulfill the prophecy of the 'end of days'. In the face of attempts to hellenize them forcibly, there arose among the faithful a renewed and strengthened loyalty to the religion of Israel.

The Significance of the Hasmonean Revolt

Throughout Judea and southern Samaria, among the group that had been active in the desert since the time of the first governmental changes in Jerusalem and among the rural Jewish population of northern Judea and the Plain of Lydda, a powerful movement of resistance against the Syrian authorities emerged. It did not take long for this movement to be converted into a mighty fighting force, led by the Hasmoneans, a priestly family living in Modi'in in the Lydda district and headed by a priest named Mattathias. The Hasmonean family, which belonged to the Watch of Jehoiarib, was held in high regard in Jewish circles and was an example and source of inspiration to the masses. For the next 130 years, the Hasmonean family was to occupy the central place in Jewish history.

Jews loyal to their faith occasionally faced severe trials, as they had during the persecution of the prophets of the Lord under Ahab and Jezebel and during the reign of King Manasseh, when foreign cults were imposed by force (see Part II). Yet it seems that Judaism had never been in such danger of complete extinction as it was during the systematic, relentless persecutions sanctioned by the decrees of Antiochus Epiphanes. In those years the large majority of the nation lived under Seleucid rule, whether in Palestine or elsewhere. And though there were Jews also outside the borders of the Seleucid Kingdom – in Egypt, in Cyrene, in Asia Minor and in parts of the Middle East that were not under Antiochus' rule at the time – it is doubtful whether those communities were materially and spiritually strong enough to keep the nation alive or to renew it should the Palestinian centre be destroyed or lose its identity. The continuation of the Jewish nation's existence, with all the impact it was to have on world history, was secured by the struggle of the Hasmoneans and the valiant stand of the population of Judea in the fourth decade of the second century BCE.

The Reasons for the Revolt's Success

The outcome of the conflict, in military and political terms, was determined by a series of internal and external factors. Perhaps the most important of these was the boundless loyalty of the Jewish masses to their religion. The ideals that had evolved in Jerusalem and Judea during the centuries preceding the persecution had penetrated to the masses of the nation. The Torah had become part of the everyday life of tens of thousands of farmers in Judea and was regarded as an essential element in their existence. This spirit inspired the ranks of the insurgents with an enthusiasm and confidence that stood them in good stead in times of trial. As we have seen, there was a minority among the upper class – Menelaus' followers and the Tobiads – that followed Antiochus to the bitter end. Not so the moderate hellenists, who at the decisive moment placed their power and talents at the disposal of the leaders of the revolt, helped wage the war and exerted their influence in establishing foreign contacts.

The manpower available to the Hasmoneans in their war against the Seleucids was relatively large. Judea and the other centres of Jewish population were densely inhabited and, when necessary, their peasantry made excellent soldiers. To the extent that the clash would be confined to the population of Palestine, there was no doubt that the Jews would have the upper hand. The danger to Judea lay in the Seleucid Kingdom's well-trained regular armies. If the Seleucids could engage their entire military strength on the Judean front, they might well be able to suppress the revolt. For even after the withdrawal from Egypt in 168, under Roman pressure, Antiochus' army remained the mightiest military force in the East and could have stood up to any other power in the Mediterranean, except the Roman Republic. It could field a force of more than 70,000 men, consisting of infantry drilled in the use of the Macedonian phalanx, cavalry, elephants, war chariots and auxiliary contingents of various origins. But the political and military conditions of the time did not allow the deployment of this large military force on the Judean front; for while part of the royal army fought in Judea under a succession of generals, other forces under the king's own command were engaged in campaigns and defensive duties in the eastern satrapies of the kingdom. Nevertheless, the military position of Judea was precarious, for even Antiochus' forces on the near side of the Euphrates were far more numerous and better trained than the fighters who gathered under the banner of the Hasmoneans.

It was the Jews' good fortune that the house of Seleucus was divided against itself. After the death of Antiochus Epiphanes, struggles for the succession broke out again and again. These struggles, which assumed the form of open warfare among the various pretenders, divided the army and provided the enemies of the Seleucid realm with an opportunity to exploit the situation and play off the different sides against each other.

Finally, the victory of the Jews was in no small measure due to the fact that in opposing the Seleucids they had the support of foreign powers. In the first place, Rome was interested in weakening the chief hellenistic power. Before the death of Judah the Maccabee, the Roman Senate made a formal treaty with the Jews, which later would be renewed several times. The practical importance of this alliance is difficult to assess, but undoubtedly it was helpful in consolidating Judea's international standing. The Ptolemies in Egypt, the age-old enemies of Seleucid Syria, also welcomed the progress made by Judea. Even the Nabateans were allies of the Jews in the first years of the revolt and assisted in their military operations across the Jordan.

In Judah, Jonathan and Simon, the sons of Mattathias the Hasmonean, the revolt had leaders of outstanding mettle, military talent and executive ability who, at the same time were statesmen of vision capable of using the constellation of forces to the best advantage, as well as inspiring loyalty and admiration among the masses. In the course of time, they also learned to use the military tactics and strategy of their day. Under Jonathan and Simon the Jewish armies proved that they were not confined to the hilly terrain of Judea and could successfully engage the royal armies even in the plains, far from their bases. Their campaigns took them well beyond the borders of Palestine, to Damascus and even to Antioch, the capital of the kingdom.

The Revolt up to the Conquest of Jerusalem and the Purification of the Temple

The first clash between the Hasmoneans and the king's forces occurred when the latter came to Modi'in in order to force the local population to take part in a pagan sacrifice. Mattathias, the head of the Hasmonean family reacted with the utmost determination:

> And Mattathias answered and spake in a loud voice: If all the nations that are in the King's dominions obey him and by forsaking every one of them the worship of their fathers have chosen for themselves to follow his commands, yet will I and my sons and my· brethren walk in the covenant of our fathers. Heaven forbid that we should forsake the Law and the ordinances! (I Maccabees 2: 19–21).

One of the Jews, who obeyed the royal command and approached the pagan altar that had been set up in Modi'in for the sacrifice, was slain by Mattathias.

After this incident Mattathias and his sons could no longer stay in Modi'in. They and their supporters took to the hills, where they were joined by many who shared their views. Soon Mattathias became the recognized leader of the entire community of the *Ḥasidim* and was instrumental in adopting several important decisions that were accepted by all the insurgents. Perhaps the most important of these was the ruling that permitted the Jews to take up arms even on the Sabbath in order to repulse attacks. In Mattathias' days the insurgents were still reluctant to wage open warfare against the king's armies and confined themselves to guerilla operations. Mattathias' activities addressed themselves to consolidating the organization of the insurgent bands, undermining the foreign ruler's authority in the villages and country towns and liquidating those Jews who collaborated with the Syrians in implementing their religious policy. As a result of these operations, the area of Judea under Seleucid control was gradually reduced, and Jerusalem, with its citadel and garrison, was to all intents cut off from the army bases and the other administrative centres in Palestine.

After Mattathias' death the leadership of the revolt passed to his sons, among whom Judah, known by the nickname 'Maccabee', stood out by reason of his military talents. Under Judah's command the activities of the insurgents endangered the Seleucid hold on Jerusalem itself to the extent that it was considered necessary to take determined steps in order to maintain control of the capital of Judea. The assignment of breaking the Jews' military strength and re-establishing contact with the garrison in Jerusalem was given to Apollonius, the governor of Samaria. His attempt to break through to Jerusalem from the north failed dismally; he himself fell in an engagement that ended in Judah's first victory over Antiochus' regular forces. What Apollonius had failed to do another Seleucid general, Seron, attempted to set right; but Judah inflicted a decisive defeat on Seron as well, on the slopes of Beth-horon. After these two victories it was evident that Judah commanded a force to be reckoned with, too strong to be defeated by local commanders. Ptolemy, the son of Dorymenes, the governor of Coele-Syria and Phoenicia and one of the most consistent supporters of Antiochus' anti-Jewish policy, assigned a strong army to

Judea under the command of two of his principal officers, Gorgias and Nicanor. The plan was to approach Jerusalem from the west, through Emmaus. A Seleucid victory seemed absolutely certain, so much so that slave merchants followed in the wake of the invading forces in the hope of being able to buy Jewish captives for next to nothing. Judah's army stood at Mizpeh, north of Jerusalem. The atmosphere of fighting for a sacred cause that prevailed in the camp, inspired by memories of ancient traditions and institutions as much as by the dangers of the present, was poignantly described by the author of I Maccabees:

> And they gathered themselves together and came to Mizpeh over against Jerusalem, for in Mizpeh there had been aforetime a place of prayer for Israel. And they fasted that day and put on sack-cloth and covered their heads with ashes and rent their clothes . . . and they brought the priestly vestments and the first-fruits and tithes and they shaved the Nazirites whose vows were fulfilled. And they cried out loudly unto Heaven, saying: What shall we do with these men and where shall we bring them? For Thy Holy Place is trodden down and defiled, and Thy priests are in mourning and brought low. And behold the gentiles are gathered together against us to destroy us. Thou knowest what things they plan against us. Shall we be able to stand against them unless Thou help us? And they blew their trumpets and cried out in a loud voice (I Maccabees 3:46ff.).

In a daring march to the south-west against the camp at Emmaus, Judah took his enemies by surprise and won one of his most brilliant victories.

After this victory, Lysias, Antiochus' lieutenant in the Cis-Euphratian part of the kingdom, realized that conditions in Palestine were deteriorating to the point that they might seriously endanger the peace of the entire realm. Determined to lead the campaign against Judea in person, Lysias assembled a huge force and decided to approach Judea from the south, through the lands of the Idumeans, who were hostile to the Jews. In a battle near Beth-zur, on the border between Judea and Idumea, the fortunes of war once again favoured the Jews, and the fourth and most threatening attempt to suppress the revolt was, like the others, defeated.

Judah the Maccabee, now at the head of an army flushed with victory, prepared to take Jerusalem itself. The military potential of the kingdom made it improbable that the revolt could be suppressed by force of arms. Judah's victories had also attracted the attention of the Roman legates who were visiting Syria at the time, and they volunteered their good offices as mediators in negotiations between the Jews and the royal court. Even those Jews who had remained loyal to the Seleucid dynasty throughout the war, including Menelaus himself, were now ready for a compromise. Lysias had no choice but to appease the Jews. At his insistence a decree was issued to the Jewish Gerousia granting a free pardon to any Jew who would return to his place of residence by a stated date and proclaiming freedom of religion to all Jews. However, the implementation of the decree was entrusted to the High Priest Menelaus, in disregard of Judah the Maccabee and his men. As a further conciliatory gesture, Ptolemy the son of Dorymenes was deposed as governor and replaced by Ptolemy Macron, whose attitude to the Jews was one of compromise.

Judah was unimpressed by these concessions and determined to use his temporary military advantage in order to gain control of Jerusalem. He did so in the month of Kislev (December) in the year 164, shortly after Antiochus had died in the east. The conquest of Jerusalem represented the complete success of the revolt. Only in the Acra did an encircled enemy garrison continue to hold out. The Temple was purified, the pagan cult abolished and the Temple service entrusted to priests of the Hasmonean camp, though Judah did not assume the dignity of the High Priest for himself. In memory of the purification of the Temple, the yearly festival of Hanukkah was instituted.

By establishing control of Jerusalem and the Temple, the insurgents had in effect temporarily detached Judea from the kingdom, though no such act was formally proclaimed. Nearly all the Jewish manpower in Palestine was now at the disposal of the leaders of the revolt, and in the months following the conquest of the capital the number of soldiers who gathered to Judah the Maccabee's banner increased markedly.

The Fight Against the Non-Jewish Population of Palestine

In the wake of the war between the king and the Jews, relations between the gentile population and the Jews living among them became tense throughout Palestine. Judah's victories served only to increase the tension and revive old quarrels. During the earlier days after the purification of the Temple and Antiochus' death, Judah's soldiers were often required to come to the aid of their brethren in remote parts of Palestine. The Seleucid authorities, as a matter of course, took the part of the gentiles, their faithful allies throughout the years of the disturbances; but Ptolemy Macron himself did not intervene in this conflict and left the initiative to the local commanders. In the fighting between the Jews and the gentiles, the military superiority of the Jews and their almost absolute control in all parts of the country became even more evident. Judah and his brothers invaded Bashan and fought in Idumea and western Galilee. They were able to capture the enemy's fortresses, and the local commanders were, in most cases, roundly defeated. These victories heralded the advent of a new era of Jewish expansion all over Palestine, but at this stage no distant areas were annexed to Judea. The immediate aim was to rescue Jews who were in danger of extermination and to evacuate them from such places. Simon the Hasmonean evacuated Jewish communities from western Galilee and transferred them from the surroundings of Acco and Tyre to Judea, while the Jews of Bashan and Gilead were rescued as a result of Judah's own campaign in those parts.

Judah's Final Campaigns

The royal authorities could not remain indifferent for long to the activities of the Jews, nor could they allow Judea to be completely cut off from the body of the kingdom. There was an increasing fear that Judah would take the Acra, whose settlers sent repeated appeals for aid to Antiochus. Lysias, who acted as the *de facto* regent for young King Antiochus v, decided to try his luck at invading Judea once more. Ptolemy Macron was accused of treason and committed suicide; he was replaced by another governor. Lysias, accompanied by the young king, set out to conquer Palestine at the head of a mighty army, larger than any that had ever fought in Judea in the past. The fortress of Beth-zur was besieged, and heavy fighting broke out near Beth-zakhariah in the Hebron hills; Eleazar, Judah's brother, fell in battle. Beth-zur surrendered to the Seleucid Army, which continued its advance and besieged Judah on the Temple Mount. But disputes in the kingdom forced Lysias to lift the siege, the more so as Judah, at the head of his *élite* troops, offered stubborn resistance. The two sides agreed to come to terms. The royal government abandoned Antiochus' religious policy unreservedly and, as a gesture of appeasement to the Jews, made Menelaus the scapegoat of that policy's failure and executed him. The office of High Priest was given to one of the moderate hellenists, Alcimus. In other words, the court did not acknowledge Judah the Maccabee as the leader of the Jewish nation, but he remained at the head of his loyal Jewish regiments. The Jews' main achievement in the peace treaty was that the royal government accorded them full freedom of religion. After that there were no further attempts by the foreign authorities to convert the Jews. But, from the military and political viewpoint, the agreement amounted to no more than an armistice, for it soon became apparent that the Seleucids were unable to impose Alcimus as High Priest on the people of Judea, and the supporters of the Hasmoneans effectively deprived him of all influence in Temple affairs.

With the appearance of a new king in Syria, the situation in Judea again became tense. Demetrius I (162) embarked on a determined campaign to set the entire kingdom in order and his rule was generally much more forceful than those of his immediate predecessors. With the intention of coming to Alcimus' aid and breaking the military superiority of the Hasmoneans in Judea, he dispatched a strong force with Bacchides, his best general, in over-all charge and Nicanor directly responsible in the field. While the king himself was engaged on the eastern front, his generals implemented his policy in Judea. At first the plan seemed certain to succeed. At the sight of the mighty Seleucid Army, many abandoned the ranks of the opposition, particularly since the religious persecution had not been resumed. Alcimus was reinstated, and many of the *Hasidim*, who had supported Judah all along, showed themselves reluctantly prepared to regard Alcimus as the High Priest. Afterwards, however, many were repelled by the vengeful cruelty of Bacchides and Alcimus, and almost the entire Jewish nation rose in revolt against them. Judah resumed his operations against his opponents and was in *de facto* control of all the rural areas of Judea, while Alcimus' influence was confined to Jerusalem itself. There were attempts to reach a compromise, but it soon became evident that the Hasmoneans and their supporters would never be prepared to recognize a High Priest appointed by the Seleucids and were ready to fight to the bitter end. Again the campaign was fought in the hilly terrain north-west of Jerusalem, the main battle taking place at Adasa, near Beth-horon. Here Judah won his last great victory, on the 13th of Adar in the year 161 (Nicanor's Day). Nicanor fell in battle, and Jerusalem was captured by Judah for the second time.

With the victory over Nicanor, the Hasmoneans regained the control of Judea that they had held three years earlier, after the purification of the Temple. Judah was now determined to win political independence at any price, and establishing good relations with Rome seemed to be one way of doing so. The treaty concluded between the Jews and Rome (in 161) marked the official recognition of Judea by the Roman Republic and was a first and highly valuable step on the road to political freedom from Rome. As we have already seen, Rome was interested in these relations because they were liable to affect the power and unity of the Seleucid Kingdom. The two main provisions of the treaty between Rome and Judea, which was drawn up in the form of a Senate resolution (*senatus consultum*), were friendly neutrality and mutual defence. It should be noted that the treaty was formally written as an agreement between equals and involved no interference on the part of the stronger power in the sovereignty of the weaker one.

Whether the treaty had any immediate consequences is not clear; it certainly did not deter Demetrius from sending his armies against Judea again. At any rate, the Hasmoneans valued the alliance for several reasons. First, it gave Judea its entrée as a state into the international arena. Second, notwithstanding many disappointments, it operated, in the course of time, as a partial deterrent against Seleucid Syria and also against Ptolemaic Egypt, for the Roman Senate closely followed developments in both kingdoms, and an awareness that they could not hold their own against the Roman legions was a determining factor in the considerations of the various hellenistic rulers.

Judah did not long enjoy the fruits of his victory over Nicanor. Demetrius overcame his enemies in the east and was thus able to divert large forces to Judea under Bacchides' command. In 160 Judah fell in battle. With his death the nation was deprived of its ablest leader and the Hasmonean family lost the most outstanding personality that it had produced.

Jonathan

Judah's brothers, Simon and Jonathan, gathered the remaining fighters under their banner but were unable to return to Jerusalem. Bacchides was in control of the city and returned Alcimus to power. The Hasmoneans were forced to resort to their old methods of guerilla warfare again. The focus of their activities was shifted to the Judean desert. In order to prevent a recurrence of the situation that had existed at the beginning of the revolt – when the royal armies were confined to garrisoning a few strongholds and were forced to leave the insurgents with freedom of movement everywhere else – Bacchides now fortified and garrisoned a number of forts, with the purpose of completely subduing the northern part of Judea with its dense Jewish settlement. He also fortified Beth-zur, Gezer and the Acra of Jerusalem. But for all these and other strong measures, his plan failed dismally and the Hasmoneans were able to keep the spark of resistance alive. The death of Alcimus (159/158) left the Jewish opponents of the Hasmoneans leaderless and Judea without a High Priest. Bacchides besieged the insurgent forces at their desert fortress but failed to subdue them. Jonathan and Simon were by now strong enough to force the Seleucid general to deal with them.

Under Jonathan the Jews gained control of most of the rural areas of Judea,

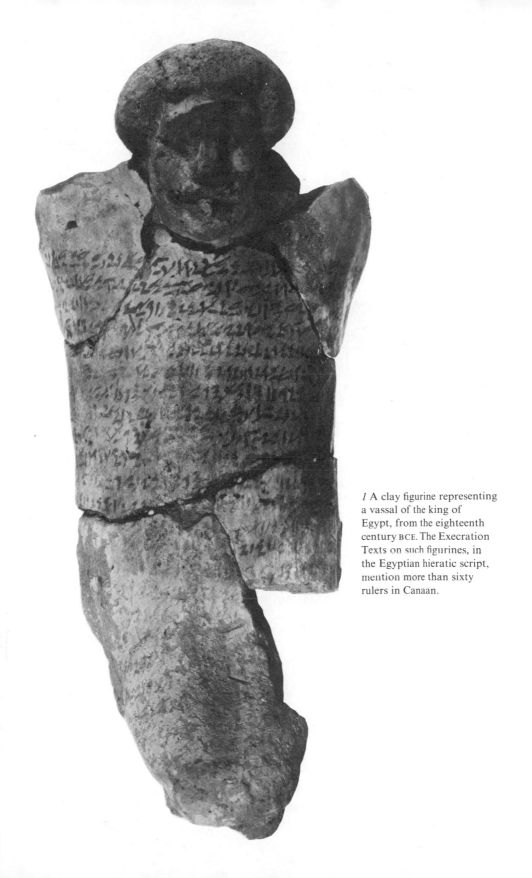

1 A clay figurine representing a vassal of the king of Egypt, from the eighteenth century BCE. The Execration Texts on such figurines, in the Egyptian hieratic script, mention more than sixty rulers in Canaan.

Top 2 A stone stele and altar at the high place of Gezer from the middle Canaanite period (1600 BCE).

Bottom 3 A pottery mask from Hazor dating from the late Canaanite period (fourteenth to thirteenth century BCE).

Opposite 4 A fortified Canaanite city in an Egyptian relief from the reign of Seti I (*c.* 1300 BCE). Alongside the fortress, designated 'City of The Canaan', are Bedouin warriors.

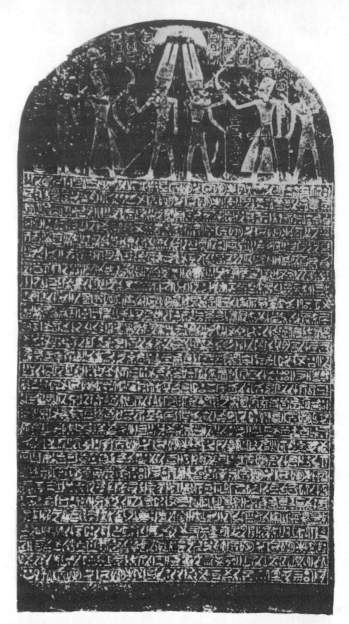

5, 6 The victory stele of Pharaoh
Merneptah (from Thebes, c. 1220
BCE), which mentions the name of
Israel for the first time in an extra-
biblical source (see detail).

Top 7 Jehu, king of Israel, submitting to Shalmaneser III, king of Assyria, in a relief on the 'Black Obclisk' of Shalmaneser from Calah (Nimrud). The inscription in cuneiform script above the relief (not shown) reads: 'A tribute of Jehu, son of Omri [the king of the "house of Omri", *i.e.*, Israel]'.

Bottom 8 The archaeological excavations at Gibeon uncovered a water pool (probably from the period of the united monarchy) with a staircase leading down into it. At the bottom of the pool is the opening to a tunnel hewn out of rock that leads to the water source. The depth of the pool is 12 metres and its diameter is 11 metres.

Top 9 An ivory plaque decorated with the figure of a sphinx (cherub) from the royal palace at Samaria (ninth century BCE). Plaques of this type served as decorative inlays on palace furniture.

Bottom 10 A woman looking out of a window – a common motif in Phoenician art – depicted on an ivory plaque from the royal palace at Samaria (ninth century BCE).

Top 11 Sennacherib, king of Assyria, seated on a throne while the captives of Judah are brought before him (701 BCE) on a relief from Sennacherib's palace at Nineveh.

Bottom 12 Fragments of Sargon's victory stele set up in Ashdod after the abortive rebellion of 712. These and further fragments were found during the excavations of that city.

Top 13 The Siloam Tunnel (about 500 metres in length) leading the waters of the Gihon Spring to the Siloam Pool. It is generally accepted that the tunnel was cut in the reign of Hezekiah, king of Judah, during his rebellion against Assyria (705–701 BCE).

Bottom 14 The 'Siloam Inscription', which relates the story of the cutting of the tunnel (see above). The rock-cut inscription was discovered fixed to the passageway in 1880 and is now in the Archaeological Museum, Istanbul.

15 A coin bearing the name of the province 'Yahud' (Judea) from the fourth century BCE.

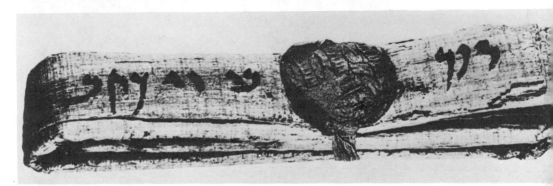

16 A deed from Elephantine, written on papyrus, folded, tied and sealed.

17 A silver ladle and bowl from the period of Persian rule in Palestine found at Tell Far'ah in the western Negev.

18 Coins of the Hasmonean dynasty: Alexander Jannai and Mattathias Antigonus.

19 An aerial view of the fortress of Masada, including Herod's palace in the left foreground.

20 A relief on the arch of Titus in Rome, erected to commemorate the victory of Rome over the Jews, showing Roman soldiers carrying off the Temple's holy objects in a victory parade.

21 An inscription of the Roman governor Pontius Pilate (26–36 CE) discovered in Tiberius' temple at Caesarea.

22 A letter from Bar Kokhba to Yeshua ben Galgula threatening to place him in fetters if he does not obey an order.

23 Two coins of the Bar Kokhba period, the larger one (a silver tetradrachma) showing the façade of the Temple and a *lulav* and *etrog*, the smaller one (a silver dinar) showing a harp and the inscription 'Simeon'.

24 One of the many catacombs with decorated stone sarcophagi at Beth-shearim, in the Galilee, from the Talmudic period.

25 The remains of the synagogue in Capernaum, on the shore of the Sea of Galilee, which was used during the second to sixth centuries CE.

26 Wall frescoes uncovered during archaeological excavations of the synagogue at Dura Europos in Syria.

including the country towns. The Hasmoneans' main base was again transferred to the north, to Michmash, north of Jerusalem, a locality saturated with ancient memories from the days of Jonathan, the son of Saul (see Part II). 'And Jonathan dwelt at Michmash, and Jonathan began to judge the people and he destroyed the evildoers in Israel' (I Maccabees 9:73).

When Alexander Balas set himself up as a rival to Demetrius I, new prospects opened for Judea's advance towards independence. Alexander Balas conquered Acco (Ptolemais) and made it his temporary capital. The strength of the two Seleucid camps was balanced, and each was interested in winning over every possible ally. Thus the importance of Jonathan, the leader of the Jews, increased considerably, for he commanded the strongest military force in Palestine. This force, moreover, was located close to Alexander's temporary capital and could interfere with its overland routes to Egypt – and connexions with Ptolemaic Egypt were important to Alexander. Demetrius was the first to attempt to win over Jonathan; he permitted him to recruit soldiers and gave orders for the release of Jewish hostages kept in the Acra. The Seleucid garrisons abandoned Judea, and Jonathan, returning to Jerusalem as victor, began to fortify the city. But he thought Alexander the more reliable ally, and Alexander paid a higher price – he made Jonathan the High Priest. Through this appointment the family that had led the revolt became the acknowledged holders of the High Priesthood; thus the Jewish nation received from the Greeks a leadership with wide popular support. This change in the system of government and the society of Judea was to have far-reaching consequences. The leader of the insurgents was acknowledged by one of the representatives of the Seleucid dynasty as the legitimate head of the nation. On the Sukkot festival of the year 152, Jonathan exercised the functions of the High Priest for the first time, and for the next 115 years the office was held by a Hasmonean.

By this decisive measure Alexander Balas made Jonathan his loyal ally in all the wars he waged in the following years. Jonathan was also invited to Acco when Alexander met his father-in-law and ally, Ptolemy Philometor, and he was received with great honour. It was Jonathan's first official appearance outside the boundaries of Judea. Alexander confirmed him as the military and civil governor of Judea, and the complaints against him by the hellenists were rejected. Soon Jonathan was given an opportunity to prove to Alexander the advantage of his alliance with the Jews. In 147 Demetrius II, the son of Demetrius I, invaded Syria in order to recover his ancestral kingdom. Once more all of Syria, including Palestine, became the scene of a fratricidal war. Jonathan took Alexander's side and mounted a campaign in the coastal plain. The Jews took Jaffa and held it for a while and also overran the Ashdod area. Jonathan's services were fully acknowledged by the court; he was rewarded with the gift of Ekron and its surroundings as his personal estate.

In 145, after Alexander had been defeated and killed by his rival Demetrius, Jonathan was forced to come to terms with the victor. Demetrius also valued the support of the High Priest of the Jews. Considerations of political and military advantage made him prefer Jonathan as an ally rather than the hellenists, who came to present their complaints. He confirmed Jonathan as the High Priest and gave his royal stamp of approval to the full annexation by Judea of the three districts in southern Samaria that had been settled by Jews (Aphaerema, Ramathaim and Lydda). This annexation was the realization of a long-standing ambition of the Jews and was one of the main achievements of the Hasmoneans.

The continuation of Demetrius II's struggle against his opponents within the Syrian empire provided the context for a new stage in Jonathan's military and political activities. At first he stayed on Demetrius' side and even sent a Jewish army to help suppress a revolt by the citizens of Antioch. Shortly afterwards, however, Jonathan deserted Demetrius for his enemy Tryphon, who was acting on behalf of Antiochus VI, Alexander Balas' son. In the wake of this alliance, Jonathan's brother Simon was appointed royal governor of the coastal plain, from the Ladder of Tyre to the border of Egypt. Jonathan's campaigns were not confined to Palestine; he invaded Syria and advanced as far as Damascus. Meanwhile, his brother Simon reduced the fortress of Beth-zur and even gained control of Jaffa, where he stationed a Jewish garrison on the pretext that the populace planned to surrender the city to Demetrius.

Jonathan did not content himself with winning battles and taking towns but began a project of fortifying Jerusalem and other key positions in Judea as an obstacle to future enemy invasions. He also indulged in widespread diplomatic activity, sending envoys to Rome to renew the treaty with the Roman Republic and fostering friendly relations with Sparta. The increasing strength of Judea under Jonathan was a source of envy to his ally, Tryphon, the more so as Jonathan was able to field an army strong enough to defeat any force Tryphon might dispatch against him. Realizing that he could not overcome Jonathan by open warfare, Tryphon resorted to treachery and imprisoned Jonathan during a visit to Acco. From the viewpoint of the political consequences, the plot miscarried: under the command of Simon, Mattathias' last son, Judea offered strong resistance to Tryphon's army, and he was forced to withdraw again. The victim of his rage was Jonathan, whom he executed.

Jonathan's rule was a decisive period for Hasmonean Judea. He proceeded from victory to victory and showed great skill in exploiting the internal difficulties of the Seleucid realm in order to benefit Judean interests. As a result of Jonathan's appointment as the High Priest, in his time the Hasmoneans became the official ruling family of Judea. Politically, he converted Judea into the dominant element in all of southern Syria, capable of affecting the fate of the entire Seleucid dynasty. Among the territorial gains during Jonathan's reign, the most prominent were the annexations of southern Samaria and the Ekron area, but in fact the Jews also controlled the port of Jaffa; and even the Greek cities on the southern coast of Palestine came within their sphere of influence. Simon, his successor, continued his policy and won official recognition for the freedom of Judea from the Seleucids.

Simon the Ethnarch

The enmity between Hasmonean Judea and Tryphon automatically made Simon a natural ally of Tryphon's opponent, Demetrius II. One consequence of this alliance was that Demetrius exempted Judea from paying tribute to the royal exchequer (in 142). Thus the independence of Judea was acknowledged by the official representative of the Seleucid dynasty. The Jews themselves reckoned Jewish sovereignty from this year: 'And the people of Israel began to write in their instruments and contracts: In the first year of Simon, High Priest, commander and leader of the Jews' (I Maccabees 13:42). After twenty-five long years of struggle, Judea had become a sovereign state in every respect. The war, which had begun as a desperate revolt against the religious policy of Antiochus Epiphanes, had gone far beyond its original aims and resulted in the re-establishment of the Jewish state after an interruption of more than 440 years.

In several directions Simon carried on where Jonathan had left off. In foreign affairs he was forced to maintain a state of belligerency against those elements within the Seleucid realm that were hostile to Judean independence and objected to the extension of Judean rule to territories outside Judea proper. In order to secure Judea strategically, Simon found it essential to liquidate the last enemy strongholds remaining on Judean soil and to provide an outlet to the sea by the final annexation of the port of Jaffa. Like his brothers before him, he attached great importance to relations with foreign powers, especially with Rome and its allies. Internally, Simon sought to achieve a constitutional settlement that would provide his rule and that of his descendants with a legal basis and to widen the support of Hasmonean rule by winning over as many elements of the population as he could.

Soon after his accession Simon sent an army against Jaffa, under the command of Jonathan ben Absalom, with orders to expel the foreigners and secure the port as part of Judea. The fraternal wars in the Seleucid Kingdom provided him with an opportunity to remove the last serious threat to Judea by conquering Gezer, which controlled the road to the coast, and the Acra, which since the time of Antiochus Epiphanes had endangered the security of Jewish Jerusalem. The conquest of these places was made possible by the rapid progress of the Jewish Army in siege techniques. Gezer was invested according to all the rules of that art and attacked with the sophisticated siege engines that were in use in the hellenistic armies. The population was expelled, pagan cults abolished and the city resettled with Jews faithful to their religion. Simon also built himself a palace in Gezer, which became one of the administrative centres of Judea. John Hyrcanus, Simon's son, was appointed governor of the city. An even greater impression on contemporaries was made by the conquest of the Acra, for as long as the citadel was inhabited by hellenists and garrisoned by gentiles Judea's independence could not be assured. On the 23rd of Iyyar in the year 141, Simon's forces entered the Acra: 'And they entered into it on the three and twentieth day of the second month in the one hundred and seventy first year [of the Seleucid era] with psalms and palm branches and with harps and cymbals and with viols and hymns and songs for a great enemy had been destroyed out of Israel' (I Maccabees 13:51). The day of the citadel's conquest was made a permanent feast day.

Simon also renewed the alliance with Rome and Sparta. In a letter to various states and cities, particularly in the eastern Mediterranean, one of the Roman consuls announced the renewal of the treaty with Judea (in 142) and requested the extradition to Simon of criminals who had fled from his country (presumably members of the extreme hellenist group).

215

After Demetrius was captured by the Parthians, the conduct of the war against Tryphon was taken over by his brother, Antiochus VII Sidetes (138), the last great personality of the Seleucid dynasty. At first, as long as he was not yet firmly in the saddle, Antiochus attempted to maintain close and friendly relations with Simon and to avail himself of his assistance in the war against Tryphon. He confirmed Simon in his office and even authorized him to strike coins. Once he had grown stronger than his enemies, however, he no longer sought the assistance of the Jews and determined to reduce the influence of the Jewish High Priest, to subject him once more to Syrian suzerainty and to re-establish the supremacy of the Seleucids in Judea. Antiochus' most insistent demand was that Jaffa, Gezer and the Acra of Jerusalem be returned. Simon replied to the king's envoy: 'We have neither taken other men's lands nor have we taken possession of that which belongeth to another but only of the inheritance of our fathers; howbeit it was held in the possession of our enemies wrongfully for a certain time' (I Maccabees 15:33). No agreement was reached. Antiochus ordered his governor on the coastal plain to commence hostilities against the Jews from his base in Jabneh. Under the command of Simon's sons, the Jewish army, 20,000 strong and now also including cavalry, took the field against the invaders and beat them back beyond Ashdod. It was the last time during Simon's life that Antiochus Sidetes resorted to open military intervention in Judea.

From the beginning Simon sought from the Jews legal authority for his rule, in the form of an acknowledgement of his family's status as the hereditary dynasty of Judea. Soon after Jonathan was captured by Tryphon, a popular assembly approved the appointment of Simon as his deputy. In 140 a Great Assembly was convened in Jerusalem and confirmed Simon as ethnarch, High Priest and supreme commander of the Judean nation and declared these offices hereditary 'until a true prophet shall arise' (I Maccabees 14:27ff.). The hereditary High Priesthood of the Hasmoneans was therefore confirmed in disregard of any claims by the family that had held the office before the revolt. On the other hand, though there is no explicit reference to messianic hopes and to the future rights of the house of David, the limiting clause must be taken as a formal expression of hallowed national hopes. This resolution of the Great Assembly became the corner-stone of Hasmonean rule and reflected the merging of the highest sacral, civil and military offices, which were exercised by representatives of one and the same family – a condition that was characteristic of the entire development of the Jewish state under Hasmonean rule.

Simon, as we have noted, made efforts to win over circles basically opposed to Hasmonean policy. Prominent among these were men of local influence in different parts of the country, including Simon's own son-in-law Ptolemy, whom he appointed governor of Jericho. Apparently Ptolemy attempted to supplant Simon in Judea with the aid of Antiochus Sidetes. Simon and two of his sons, Mattathias and Judah, were assassinated by Ptolemy when they visited Jericho in 134. But the murder, like that of Jonathan before it, completely failed to achieve its purpose; loyalty to the Hasmonean dynasty was firmly rooted among the majority of the people, and Simon's remaining son, John Hyrcanus, until then the governor of Gezer, assumed the rule of Judea with the enthusiastic support of the population.

15

The Hasmonean State

The General Political Background

Just as the beginnings of the Hasmonean state of Judea had largely been determined by political developments in Syria as a whole, so were its growth and expansion affected by the processes that led to the gradual disintegration of the Seleucid Empire. The focus of the military conflicts shifted to the successor states of the empire – the independent cities and principalities that took over the areas adjoining Judea – although occasionally a Seleucid king appeared as Judea's main enemy. The protracted dynastic struggles completely exhausted the military and financial power of the remnants of the Seleucid Empire and left Syria powerless against the dangers that threatened it from outside and the ferment that weakened it internally. Characteristic of the entire period was the secession of the large Greek cities from the empire. Nearly all the important cities demanded and were granted political independence by the kings as they increasingly lost power. Occasionally, the cities also warred against each other and thus invited the intervention of foreign forces.

Hasmonean Judea was not the only state to benefit from the disintegration of the Seleucid Empire. Parallel to the rise of Judea, the Nabatean Kingdom, whose development also directly affected that of Judea, gained in power. One of the main aims of the Nabatean kings was to control the roads through their capital, Petra, linking South Arabia to Gaza and Egypt on the one side and to Damascus and the Phoenician cities on the other. In Judah's and Jonathan's time, the Nabateans had been allies of the Jews in the war against their common enemy, the Seleucids; but when the Hasmonean state flourished, Petra was usually among its sworn enemies. To a large extent this was due to the manner in which the lines of expansion of the two states intersected. Eastern powers far from the region also began to cast their shadow over its development. The most powerful of these was the Parthian Kingdom, which had won its independence in an armed revolt against the Seleucids. Some kingdoms in Asia Minor also gained in international importance, particularly Pontus and Armenia. At one point (early in the fourth decade of the first century BCE), Armenian armies stood at the gates of Acco and it seemed that it would take all of Syria and Palestine under its wing; but the Armenian advance was brought to a complete halt by the Romans. Throughout these years the Ptolemaic state also continued to be a political factor of the first order in Palestine. Though much beset by internal dissension, it was able to preserve its unity, unlike Syria, and only out-lying parts, such as Cyprus, were at times detached from the centre at Alexandria.

John Hyrcanus

Soon after he had come to power and overcome his enemies at home, John Hyrcanus had to face an invasion by Antiochus Sidetes, who had raised a large army in order to recover Palestine. The war was hard and long (134–132). Some of the king's counsellors attempted to give the war a religious character and to renew the edicts of Antiochus Epiphanes, but Sidetes did not follow their advice. This time the Jews were not able to resist the royal army outside Jerusalem, as they had done under Jonathan and Simon, and when the siege of the capital dragged on, an agreement was reached. Antiochus acknowledged John Hyrcanus as the ruler of Judea proper, while John agreed to pay tribute for the cities that the Hasmoneans had conquered outside the Judean borders. He also undertook to provide military aid to Antiochus in a campaign against the Parthians. Thus the political ties between Judea and the Seleucid dynasty were briefly resumed; but after Antiochus lost the war that he had decided to wage against the Parthians (129), the entire structure of the kingdom virtually collapsed. John was then able to recover in full Judea's political indepen-dence and to begin expanding in various directions.

John Hyrcanus' wars were essentially a continuation of those begun by his father and uncles, but were pursued on a larger scale and, to some extent, by different means. In principle, John's position was the same as that previously formulated by Simon in his reply to the envoys of Antiochus Sidetes – that the whole of Palestine was the ancestral heritage of the Jewish nation. In that heritage there was no room for foreign cults, as evidenced by the conversion of Idumea and the destruction of the Samaritan temple on Mount Gerizim. Under John Hyrcanus territorial ex-pansion proceeded in various directions – south, north and east – with decisive consequences for the history of the people and the land.

It is doubtful whether John Hyrcanus would have been able to begin extensive conquests immediately upon learning of Antiochus Sidetes' death were it not for the fact that Demetrius II, having returned from his Parthian captivity and set on recovering at least part of his ancestral kingdom, began to interfere in Egyptian affairs. The reaction of the Ptolemies gave John his opportunity. The Alexandrian court set up Alexander (known by the nickname Zabina) as a rival to Demetrius II, and John found himself in the same camp with Alexander and his Ptolemaic backers. During the years in which the two rivals fought each other, John was able to re-establish full Jewish rule in the areas where it had been limited by the agreement with Antiochus Sidetes. In those years – the second decade of the second century BCE – he also succeeded in annexing most of Palestine, except for the areas under the control of the large Greek cities. From the viewpoint of its stability and its consequences in times to come, the most important expansion was probably that which took place in the direction of Idumea in the south. Idumea, with its two main centres of Adora and Marissa, was annexed to Judea, and its population was con-verted to Judaism. In John Hyrcanus' view this operation was designed to strengthen the Jewish nation. The fact that the Idumeans of the Second Temple period lived in the ancient patrimony of biblical Judah must have confirmed him in the conviction that his policy befitted the circumstances and that the Jewish population of the country was strong enough to succeed in the wholesale absorption of the Idumeans. The conversion of the Idumeans was the first of its kind, as it was of an entire race rather than of a few individuals. The Jewish religion fell on fertile soil in Idumea; the Idumeans soon became an integral part of the Jewish nation, and before long their upper classes occupied key social and governmental positions in the Hasmonean Kingdom. From then on the Judaization of the whole of Palestine became a permanent element of Hasmonean policy.

John Hyrcanus also turned to Trans-Jordan, where the Jewish population of the Tobiad estates served as a convenient base for expansion. He conquered Medaba and Samoga (Khirbet Samikh). He also mounted a campaign against the Samaritans, conquered their centre in Shechem and destroyed the temple on Mount Gerizim.

In his last years John Hyrcanus resumed his campaigns in Palestine, which culminated in the capture of the two largest hellenistic cities, Samaria and Beth-shean (Scythopolis). A pretext for the war against Samaria was furnished by its inhabitants' hostilities against the nearby Jewish settlement at Merus (Khirbet el-Mahruna, east of the Valley of Dothan in Samaria). The siege of Samaria was protracted and called for a great effort on the part of the Jewish forces, for an attempt to relieve the town was made by Antiochus IX Cyzicenus, one of the kings who contested the Seleucid throne, and by Ptolemy Lathyrus, the son of Queen Cleopatra III of Egypt, who henceforward became one of the most stubborn enemies of the Hasmonean Kingdom. Nevertheless, the town was taken and destroyed (c. 107). The road to Galilee was now open, and it seems that considerable parts of this district were annexed even during John Hyrcanus' lifetime.

At the time of John Hyrcanus' death, in 104, the Jews were expanding their borders everywhere in Palestine. His son and heir, Judah Aristobulus I, and the latter's younger brother, Antigonus, had been among the chief implementers of their father's policy during his lifetime. Now they completed the conquest of Galilee and defeated the Ituraeans, who seem to have ruled over part of Upper Galilee. Like the Idumeans before them and in line with the policy developed by John Hyrcanus, they were converted; but their conversion played no decisive role in the Judaization of Galilee, where a Jewish population had apparently existed without interruption since ancient Israelite times.

The conquests by John Hyrcanus and Aristobulus increased Judea to several times its former size. Not only had virtually the entire population outside the territory of the hellenistic cities come under Jewish rule and become part of the Jewish nation, but even some of the hellenistic settlements, such as Beth-shean, Samaria and Marissa, were taken. However, the main Greek cities on the sea coast, such as Gaza, and those in Trans-Jordan remained outside the borders of the Jewish state; only part of them were later annexed by Alexander Jannai.

When his rule was expanded to include most of the area of Palestine, John Hyrcanus benefited greatly from the relations he had established with some of the leading powers of his day – particularly the Roman Republic and Ptolemaic Egypt –

and with some of the pretenders to the Seleucid throne who were allied with one or the other of these powers. After the murder of his father and two brothers in 134, Antiochus Sidetes presented a threat to Judea, and John immediately attempted to renew the treaty with Rome in order to preserve the status quo. The Roman Senate responded favourably to his request. Shortly after Sidetes' death the Senate again decided in favour of the Jews, and in 112 it took John Hyrcanus' side against Antiochus Cyzicenus.

Another important element of John Hyrcanus' policy was his friendship with the Ptolemaic court, a friendship that he maintained no less steadily than that with Rome. He was an ally of Alexander Zabina, who also had Alexandria's support; later he fought on the Egyptian side – with Roman support against Antiochus Cyzicenus. The development of relations between Ptolemaic Egypt and Judea was furthered by the considerable influence and close ties with the royal court of the Egyptian Jewish community of those days.

The alliance with Rome paved the way to further international ties. As Jonathan and Simon had maintained relations with Sparta, so did John develop connexions with Pergamum and Athens and presumably with other cities as well.

Alexander Jannai

Alexander Jannai (103–76) succeeded to the throne after the death of Judah Aristobulus I, his elder brother. The history of the kingdom's foreign affairs during his reign is a succession of conquests and wars. Under his rule Hasmonean Judea reached its largest territorial size. Syria remained throughout in the throes of fraternal wars between the different pretenders who were linked with a dynastic dispute within the house of Ptolemy. Queen Cleopatra III was engaged in incessant strife with her son and sometime co-regent Ptolemy Lathyrus. In 107 she finally managed to oust him and drive him out of the country. Ptolemy then entrenched himself in Cyprus, from where he continued the war against his mother, occasionally threatening Egypt and often interfering in Syria and Palestine. In her struggle against Ptolemy Lathyrus, Cleopatra availed herself of the assistance of Jewish officers and soldiers. After her death relations between her heir in Alexandria, Ptolemy Alexander, and Ptolemy Lathyrus continued to be tense. In Syria, Ptolemy Lathyrus usually backed a pretender of his choice, while Alexander Jannai was often to be found in the role of a member of the counter-alliance. The great cities on the sea coast, such as Gaza and Ashkelon, also sided with one party or the other, depending on the circumstances. They enjoyed an independent status and prospered greatly; thus they were able to affect the balance of power. Gaza, as the sea outlet for goods from South Arabia and India, was closely linked with the Nabatean Kingdom, which apparently was on less than good terms with Alexandria, due to Egyptian attempts to control the Red Sea trade. In the confrontation with the Nabateans, Jannai found himself in line with the Ptolemies, while Gaza, which in the past had been outstanding in its loyalty to Egypt, now drew away from Alexandria under the influence of its Nabatean allies.

In the history of Alexander Jannai's reign we may distinguish three main stages.

The first stage extends from his accession till about the year 95, when Jannai gained full control of the Palestinian sea coast from the Carmel to the Egyptian border (with the exception of Ashkelon). Although at the beginning of this period Jannai suffered defeat at the hands of Ptolemy Lathyrus, the set-back was soon offset by the aid he received from Cleopatra III. The period culminated with the conquest of Gaza and of Gadara in Trans-Jordan.

At Alexander Jannai's accession Judea was in a stage of accelerated expansion; after the conquest of Idumea, Samaria and Galilee, it was the turn of the coastal plain. Acco in the north and Gaza in the south were strong cities, and a clash with the tyrant of Dor and Straton's Tower was also in the offing. They all combined to resist the Jewish onslaught, with assistance from the Phoenician cities north of Acco, particularly Sidon. Jannai's first target was Acco, while Ptolemy Lathyrus' plans called for an advance through Galilee to Trans-Jordan, where he proposed to join forces with Jannai's Trans-Jordanian enemies, notably Theodorus, the tyrant of Amathus. In a surprise attack, on the Sabbath, Ptolemy took Sihin in the western part of the Bet Natopha Valley, but an attempt on Sepphoris miscarried. He therefore abandoned his designs on Sepphoris and continued his march to Trans-Jordan. Near Zaphon, not far from Amathus, Alexander Jannai's army was defeated and his enemies invaded Judea, terrorizing the population with their barbaric conduct. Jannai was saved by Cleopatra's intervention. Ptolemy Lathyrus was driven off, and at Scythopolis (Beth-shean) Jannai concluded a military alliance with Cleopatra, which left him free to settle accounts with Ptolemy's Palestinian allies. After a ten-month siege, he took Gadara, the most famous of the Greek cities of Trans-Jordan of the time, and Amathus, 'the largest of the fortresses found in Transjordan' (Josephus, *Jewish Antiquities* 13.356). Theodorus put up a valiant fight to prevent Jannai from bringing the district under his control but was unable to hold out long.

After his great victories in Trans-Jordan, Jannai turned to the southern part of the coastal plain. He took Rafia and Anthedon without much effort; the only place where he had to face serious resistance was in Gaza. But Aretas II, the king of the Nabateans on whose aid the Gazans relied, disappointed them, and internal quarrels among the city's defenders also made Jannai's work easier. Nevertheless, the siege of Gaza took a full year.

The second period of Jannai's military and political activities covers the late nineties and most of the eighties of the first century BCE. From the viewpoint of internal history, it was a time of overt conflict between the Hasmonean dynasty and large sections of the nation. The background is marked by the rising power of Ptolemy Lathyrus, who in the mid-nineties had succeeded in establishing one of his candidates in Damascus and other parts of Syria and in the year 88 gained control of Alexandria. Cities that had supported Cleopatra, such as Ashkelon, came to his side after he had become king of Egypt. Now Alexander Jannai was in serious difficulty. Ptolemy's Syrian ally, Demetrius III, pushed him to the brink of disaster in the early eighties, and Jannai's political opponents were given asylum in Alexandria. On the other hand, once Ptolemy Lathyrus had consolidated his hold on the Egyptian crown, he seems to have been anxious not to annoy his influential Jewish subjects beyond reason. What his relations with the Nabateans were, we do not know; he may well have inherited the tension between his Egyptian predecessors and the Nabatean kings, a tension that arose from the commercial rivalry between the two kingdoms.

The third stage – Alexander Jannai's last five years – brought renewed prosperity to the Hasmonean Kingdom and, from the viewpoint of territorial expansion, was the culmination of the Hasmonean era. Jannai had overcome the internal crisis in his kingdom, which had tied his hands in the preceding years, and he no longer feared intervention on the part of Ptolemy Lathyrus, who had died in the year 80. He overcame the Nabateans, invaded the territory of the rich city-league of the Decapolis and marched into Gaulanitis. He died of an illness while besieging the fortress of Regev in Trans-Jordan; it fell soon after his death.

What enabled Alexander Jannai to gain these victories during his last five years was not only the weakness of the hellenistic kings in the region but also the military superiority that he succeeded in establishing over Aretas III, the king of the Nabateans. Only a few years earlier, Jannai had still been on the defensive against the Nabatean forces, but now the Nabateans proved unable to resist him and were forced to cede territories that they regarded as essential. This state of military preponderance over the Nabateans continued after Jannai's death, throughout the reign of his wife, Shelomziyyon (Salome) Alexandra. The strife between her sons after her death was the only opportunity the Nabateans had to make major gains at Judea's expense.

Queen Alexandra and Her Sons

Under Shelomziyyon Alexandra (76–67), foreign policy continued along the lines established in Jannai's time. The increasing influence of the Pharisees and their virtual control of domestic policy did not substantially change the country's foreign policy, though the pace of conquest was slowed down. Alexandra continued the siege of Regev until the fortress fell to the Jews and made it her concern to maintain a large army. She is said to have doubled the strength of the Jewish armed forces and to have raised so large an army of mercenaries 'that she struck terror into the local rulers round her and received hostages from them' (Josephus, *Jewish Antiquities* 13.409). She also maintained the principal fortresses of the land, which she entrusted to experienced commanders. But the most daring of her plans miscarried. She sent out an army under her younger son, Aristobulus, to take Damascus, but he returned without achieving anything. Only once during Alexandra's reign was Judea seriously threatened, when Tigranes, the king of Armenia, was on the point of invading Judea at the head of a large army. While he was besieging Acco, the queen sent envoys to appease him and establish relations with him. The Armenian danger was lifted entirely when the Roman legions invaded Armenia.

The appearance of the Romans in Syria and its annexation to the Roman Republic were a direct consequence of the victories won by the Roman generals Lucullus and Pompey over the kings of Pontus and Armenia. Once Rome had decided to annex Syria, its intervention in Judea became inevitable. The fraternal war that broke out in Judea between Alexandra's two sons, Hyrcanus and Aristobulus, only accelerated the intervention; and the war waged by Aristobulus' party against the Romans merely determined the form, not the fact, of annexation.

The death of Alexandra (67) plunged Judea into a war between brothers. Aristobulus ousted his elder brother, Hyrcanus, from the kingdom and the High Priesthood, but Hyrcanus was not prepared to stay out of power for long. Through one of his friends – Antipater the Idumean, a man with considerable influence in the south and close ties with the Nabateans – he reached an agreement with Aretas III: in return for territorial concessions, the Nabatean ruler was to help Hyrcanus regain his ancestral throne. The concessions included part of Jannai's conquests. The joint armies of Hyrcanus and Aretas overpowered Aristobulus and laid siege to him in Jerusalem. Meanwhile, however, the legates of the Roman general Pompey appeared in Syria. After taking Damascus they intervened on Aristobulus' behalf and forced Aretas to withdraw from Judea. On the way home he was soundly defeated by the pursuing forces of Aristobulus.

Roman Domination

It was left to Pompey himself to decide the matter of the Hasmonean succession. He withheld his decision for a while but was inclined to award the kingdom to Hyrcanus. After long hesitation Aristobulus surrendered to Pompey, and the road to Jerusalem was open to the Romans. Hyrcanus' men opened the city gates for them; only at the Temple Mount did they meet with fierce resistance, the defence being led by Aristobulus' uncle Absalom. After a siege of three months, the Temple Mount was also reduced (63) and thousands of its defenders were killed. Thus the independence of Hasmonean Judea came to an end; it had lasted for some eighty years and resulted in the political consolidation of Palestine under Jewish rule.

The conquest of Judea by the Romans resulted in decisive political changes. Syria became a Roman province, but Judea was granted autonomy, though its territory was reduced and its ruler's authority was dependent on the provincial administration of Syria. The autonomous state of Judea was shorn of all Jannai's conquests and part of those of Simon and John Hyrcanus. It was forced to surrender the entire coastal plain from the Carmel to Raphia including Jaffa; this deprived it of any outlet to the sea, and in that respect the situation reverted to what it had been before the Hasmonean Revolt. In addition, part of Idumea (Marissa) and the bulk of Samaria were detached. As a result, the Jewish population of Palestine was no longer territorially continuous, and contact between Jerusalem and the Jewish centre in Galilee could be maintained only through the Jordan Valley. The fact that Pompey freed the large hellenistic cities in Trans-Jordan and Scythopolis from Judean rule was only to be expected; they formed themselves into the Decapolis or Union of Ten Cities and resumed their life as independent cities. The Greek cities on the coast were also freed. What remained to Hyrcanus II was Judea (including southern Samaria, which had been annexed under Jonathan), most of Idumea, the parts of Trans-Jordan closely settled by Jews (the Peraea), and Galilee.

The tendency of Pompey and his successors, the first proconsuls of Syria, was to

223

rehabilitate the Greek urban settlements at the expense of the Jewish population, which had so remarkably gained in strength during the period of the Hasmonean Kingdom. But the hands of the clock could not be set back entirely, and for many years to come the Jewish population of Palestine was to exceed the gentiles in strength and numbers. The absorption of the gentile population, excluding the hellenized cities and the Samaritan concentration around Mount Gerizim, as a result of the proselytizing policy of John Hyrcanus and his successors, was irreversible.

Territory was not all that Judea lost in the Pompeian settlement, for the renewed subjection to foreign rule was no less detrimental than the territorial diminution. Hyrcanus II was deprived of the title of king and recognized only as the ethnarch and High Priest, and the country was again obliged to pay tribute – the hallmark of servitude. The Jews of Palestine did not quietly accept the new dispositions, and we hear of frequent rebellions, usually led by the branch of the Hasmonean family represented by Aristobulus. Antipater, on the other hand, remained consistently loyal to the Romans. Insurrections were particularly frequent during the proconsulate of Gabinius in Syria (57–55). He, more than any other Roman governor, was concerned with renewing Greek city life and reducing the unity and strength of the Jews. Soon after his arrival a rebellion broke out under Aristobulus' son Alexander, who succeeded in raising a force of several thousand and taking the fortresses of Alexandrion and Machaerus. With the help of Jewish supporters of Hyrcanus and Antipater, the rebellion was suppressed, and Gabinius seized the opportunity to impose even further reconstruction of the government of Jewish Palestine. He divided the country into five administrative-fiscal districts, each headed by its own local synhedrion. The seats of these synhedria were Jerusalem, Jericho, Amathus, Sepphoris and another town whose identity is a matter of controversy. As a result of this settlement, Hyrcanus in effect no longer directly ruled the entire Jewish population of Palestine, and all that was left to him was the dignity of the office of High Priest. The new settlement, however, was no stronger a bar to rebellion than the old one had been, and twice more Gabinius was forced to suppress serious Jewish insurrections: one under Aristobulus, who had escaped from Rome, where he had been kept by the Romans from the time of Pompey, and the other under Alexander's son. The rebellions proved to the Roman authorities that Judea was unlike other Eastern lands and that its people would not readily accept the loss of their freedom.

The Rise of the House of Antipater and the End of the Hasmonean Dynasty

Under Julius Caesar relations between Rome and the Jews of Palestine improved markedly. He showed himself sympathetic to the Jews throughout the Roman Empire, regarding them as valuable allies. Hyrcanus and Antipater were among those who joined Caesar after his victory over Pompey (48), and they rendered sorely needed assistance when he was in danger in Alexandria by providing him with a Jewish expeditionary force. The fact that Hyrcanus joined Caesar's camp also influenced the Jews of Egypt, who held key points on the approaches to the country. After Caesar had extricated himself, he concentrated, among other things, on settling the affairs of Palestine, and he decided a number of issues in favour of Hyrcanus II and the Jews. Hyrcanus was confirmed as the hereditary ethnarch of Judea and as High Priest. The unity of the Jewish population, which Gabinius had abolished, was re-established. Caesar's settlement also increased Antipater's influence, and his sons were given some of the highest administrative posts in the country. The elder son, Phasael, became the governor of Jerusalem, while the younger one, Herod, was entrusted with the administration of Galilee – an office in which he gave the first indications of his high regard for Roman interests and his harsh treatment of his Jewish subjects. He maintained close relations with the proconsul of Syria and executed many Jews without trial, among them one named Hezekiah, whose descendants were to play a significant role among the anti-Roman freedom-fighters.

Caesar's assassination (44) dragged Judea into the turmoil of the civil war that encompassed the entire Mediterranean world. After the murder, Cassius, one of the main conspirators, came east and took control of Syria and Palestine. Antipater and his sons gave him support, although Cassius' main concern was to extort as much money as possible from Judea. (The population of four Jewish towns [Gophna, Emmaus, Lydda and Timnah] was sold into slavery.) Antipater himself fell victim to the internal strife in Judea, but his sons continued to cooperate with Cassius and even succeeded in increasing their influence. The defeat of Caesar's murderers and Antony's assumption of power in the east (42) brought no change in the position and influence of Antipater's sons.

Major changes occurred only when the Parthians invaded the eastern provinces of the Roman Empire in the year 40. Mattathias Antigonus, Aristobulus' youngest son, whose claims to the throne of Judea had been rejected by Caesar and Antony, joined Rome's enemies as a means of regaining his patrimony. The Parthian Army advanced along the coast. The Jews in the areas surrounding the Carmel and Apollonia (Arsuf) rushed to Antigonus' banner, and it soon became obvious that a substantial majority of the nation had remained loyal to the Hasmoneans and favoured Antigonus. Phasael and Hyrcanus, who had gone to negotiate with the Parthians, were imprisoned by them; Phasael committed suicide, and Hyrcanus' ears were cropped to make him ritually unfit for the High Priesthood. Herod escaped from Jerusalem and left for Rome to seek military aid. Meanwhile, Antigonus became the king of Judea. Thus the Hasmonean Kingdom was restored, after having been abolished by Pompey twenty-three years earlier.

Herod was received in Rome with great honour, for Antony and Octavian realized that he was Rome's only remaining ally in Judea. It was decided to entrust the rule of Palestine to him, and in order to enhance his status he was given the title of king. Meanwhile, the Roman generals had pushed the Parthians back and Antigonus' position had become precarious. Returning to Palestine, Herod, with Roman assistance, succeeded in gaining control of Idumea and Samaria and, after overcoming the resistance of the Jews near Arbel, also of Galilee. Nevertheless, neither his forces nor the Roman contingents that came to his aid were strong enough to take Jerusalem, nor to prevent the general renewal of hostilities. It was only after the final defeat of the Parthians in 38 that larger Roman forces were available to complete the war in Samaria and Antigonus' army was defeated at Isana in Samaria, on the way from Shechem to Jerusalem. Antigonus' fate was sealed. After heroically withstanding a five-month siege, Jerusalem finally fell to the Roman legions (37). The defenders of the city were put to the sword, and Antigonus, the last of the Hasmonean kings, was executed. His death marked the end of the Hasmonean dynasty, which, more than any other family during the days of the Second Temple, had left its mark on the political history of Judea.

The Expansion of Hasmonean Judea

One of the outstanding characteristics of Hasmonean Judea was its territorial expansion and the changes that came in its wake. The Hasmonean conquests in effect reversed the inroads that Hellenism had made and halted the domination of the Greek cities and the mixed Greco-oriental elements in western Palestine. As a result of the Hasmonean conquests, the bulk of the non-Jewish population of the country became an integral part of the Jewish nation and what had been mere islands of Jewish settlement became normal districts of the Jewish kingdom. The name Judea no longer referred only to the area bounded by Jericho and Modi'in, Bethel and Beth-zur; it became the common appellation of the whole of Palestine: 'The interior above Phoenicia as far as the Arabs, between Gaza and Antilebanon, is called Judea,' wrote the Greek historian and geographer Strabo in the first century BCE (*Geography* XVI, 2.21). Judea remained the official name of the country until the time of Hadrian (the second century CE), which is but another clear reflection of the ethnic changes and the balance of forces that resulted from the conquests of the Hasmonean rulers.

The expansion of Hasmonean Judea took place gradually. Under Jonathan, Judea annexed southern Samaria and began to expand in the direction of the coastal plain. The great achievement of Simon's days was gaining control of Jaffa and thereby acquiring an outlet to the sea. The main ethnic changes were the work of John Hyrcanus, who acted on the premise that the entire country was the heritage of the Jewish nation. It was in his days and those of his son Aristobulus that the annexation of Idumea, Samaria and Galilee and the consolidation of Jewish settlement in Trans-Jordan was completed. Alexander Jannai, continuing the work of his predecessors, expanded Judean rule to the entire coastal plain, from the Carmel to the Egyptian border – with the exception of Ashkelon – and to additional areas in Trans-Jordan, including some of the Greek cities there. He also attempted to impose a Jewish character on the new conquests. The city of Pella (Fahal) in Trans-Jordan was razed because its inhabitants refused to convert to Judaism; so also were Gaza and Philoteria at the southern end of the Sea of Galilee. Generally, the organizational and social institutions of the conquered hellenistic cities (Gadara, Gerasa, Scythopolis, Dor and Gaza) were disbanded, though their citizens did not become Jews. Nevertheless, it is almost certain that, even after those cities had been deprived of their political structure, their inhabitants continued to live in or near

The Hasmonean Kingdom

Tyre

Mediterranean Sea

GOLAN

Gush Halav

Acco
(Ptolemais)

Taricnaea
(Migdal Nunya)

Gamala

Shikmona

Sihin

Arbel

Hippus

Dium

GALILEE

Sepphoris

Philoteria

Abila

Yarmuk River

Geba

Mount Tabor

Gadara

Beth-shean
(Scythopolis)

Narbata

Pella

SAMARIA

Gerasa

Apollonia

Samaria

Shechem

Amathus

Alexandrion
(Sartaba)

Gador

Jaffa

Philadelphia

Lydda

Gophna

Ofrayim

Modi'in

Lower Beth-horon

Upper Beth-horon

Jabneh

Gezer

Jericho

Emmaus

Jerusalem

JUDEA

Azotus

Bethlehem

Dead Sea

TRANS-JORDAN

Medeba

Ashkelon

Beth-zur

Marissa

Anthedon

Hebron

Machaerus

Gaza

Adora

En-gedi

Arnon River

Raphia

Masada

Rabbath-moab

Rhinocorura

Kerak-moab

Elusa

Jewish area in the period
of Judah the Maccabee

Kingdom of Alexander Jannai

Independent city

■ Fortresss

0   15   30
km

© carta, JERUSALEM

them. This may be concluded from the relative ease with which the Roman rulers re-established most of the old hellenistic cities.

Among the non-urban and non-hellenized population, however, Judaism obviously took root. They were apparently more ready to adopt the Jewish religion, as may be seen from an incidental remark in a hellenistic source (Strabo, *Geography* XVI, 2.34), that 'the Idumeans joined the Jews and shared their customs,' without any indication that this was the result of imposed conversion. The Idumeans indeed became faithful Jews, and the Judaization of the non-hellenized population of Palestine became an established fact that even the Roman conquest did not reverse. Only in one place did the religious-ethnic policy of the Hasmoneans fail: in central Samaria; and the destruction by John Hyrcanus of the cultic centre on Mount Gerizim did not heal the rift between the Jews and Samaritans. With the decline of the Hasmonean dynasty, the Samaritans again became an independent and often hostile element. All in all, in most of the areas conquered by John Hyrcanus and Aristobulus I, the ethnic and religious structure of the population was profoundly and lastingly affected. On the other hand, the impact of Alexander Jannai's conquests, which were mostly in Greek-colonized territory, was short-lived.

The main achievement of the Hasmonean's ethnic-territorial policy may be defined as a Jewish victory over the religious and cultural determination of the non-Jewish population of inland Palestine. As a result, for centuries after the Hasmonean dynasty was ousted, Palestine remained a country with a Jewish majority, with all that this implied in the political, cultural and religious respects. The Hasmonean conquests were presumably accompanied by a mass migration of Jews from Judea and the surrounding districts to the fertile farmlands of the coastal plain and Trans-Jordan. The conquest of towns on the coast also attracted Jews to commerce and seafaring. Jaffa, in particular, played a prominent role in this respect. The Shephelah and Sharon up to the Carmel were densely settled by Jews; the strength of the Jewish population in the Carmel area is indicated by the part it played in the fight on behalf of Antigonus. The expansion of the Jewish population throughout the country stimulated the growth and development of such local centres as Sepphoris in Galilee. The increasing strength of Hasmonean domination was accompanied by the destruction of hellenistic civilization in Palestine, which had been reflected in the highly developed life of the *polis* and the integration of the Jewish *élite* into the social and cultural patterns of Hellenism. Famous hellenistic cities such as Gadara, Scythopolis and Gaza were conquered by the Jews, and though some of the members of the Hasmonean dynasty adopted the trappings of hellenistic life, Greek public opinion saw them mainly as the destroyers of Hellenism.

The tension existing between Greeks and Jews in Egyptian Alexandria and, to a lesser extent, in other parts of the Diaspora also contributed to the deterioration in the popular Greek view of the Jews. If the early hellenistic literature reflects an attitude of respect and appreciation of Judaism, the tone from the second century BCE onwards becomes aggressive and at times scurrilous. Even moderate authors, who generally did not allow themselves to be carried away by anti-Jewish prejudice, represented Judaism as being in a state of decline and degeneracy. Typical in this respect is what Strabo had to say in the sixteenth book of his *Geography*. According to him, Moses was one of the Egyptian priests who was disgusted by the Egyptian animal cult and had as little use for the anthropomorphous Greek religion. Strabo claims that Moses taught that 'God encompasses us all and encompasses land and sea, He is what we call heaven, or universe, or the nature of all that exists' – a view that led him to reject idols and graven images. His ideas were accepted by a few enlightened contemporaries, who accompanied him to Jerusalem, where he founded a system of government that conformed with his doctrine. For some time his successors followed in his footsteps, but then the priesthood fell into the hands of superstitious and, later, tyrannical elements. They were the ones who introduced such practices as circumcision. As a result of their rule, robbery became widespread, strangers were deprived of their property and large parts of Phoenicia and Syria were enslaved. These charges of robbery and dispossession of others appealed all the more to the hellenized population because of the assumption that the inhabitants of the hellenistic cities of Palestine were the true heirs of the original Canaanite population and that the Jews had unjustly supplanted them.

The Jews felt impelled to answer this hostile propaganda. They did not content themselves with the religious argument that it was God's will that the Jews should inherit the land, but developed the argumentation that the land had always been destined for the sons of Shem and that Canaan had wrongly conquered it: 'And his father Ham and his brethren Kush and Mizraim said unto him: Thou hast settled in a land which is not thine and which has not fallen unto us by lot. Do not do so' (*Jubilees* 10.30).

Constitutional Developments in the Hasmonean Kingdom

The constitutional development of Hasmonean Judea was based on the decree of the Great Assembly of 140 BCE, which also provided the legal authority for the status of the Hasmoneans as the rulers of the Jewish state. This decree confirmed the *de facto* situation that had developed as a result of the political reality established in the course of the revolt, whereby the Hasmoneans, by reason of their outstanding achievement, had risen to a position of military leadership within the nation. The bond between the Hasmonean family and the office of High Priest was a natural consequence of the situation that had come into existence under Persian rule, when the High Priesthood became the first office of the nation and was regarded as the expression of its autonomy. If the Hasmoneans had relinquished the High Priesthood and allowed it to fall into other hands, their political power would have been undermined and their other offices deprived of all real substance, for the people had grown accustomed to regarding the High Priest as their supreme leader. Domestically also the office of High Priest ranked above the other functions of the Hasmonean rulers; it is this title that was usually stressed in the Hebrew inscriptions on the coins struck by them, including the last of the dynasty, Mattathias Antigonus. The Hasmonean High Priests also continued to officiate personally in the Temple, mainly on the Day of Atonement and on the three Pilgrimage Festivals.

In foreign relations the position of the Hasmonean rulers was at first reflected in the title of ethnarch. Simon had already held this title, and John Hyrcanus used it to the end of his days. A major change occurred only under Judah Aristobulus I (104–103), who was not content with the title of ethnarch and assumed the trappings of royalty. His main reason was to put himself on an equal footing with other rulers in his part of the world. With regard to their Jewish subjects, however, the Hasmoneans were, in fact, careful not to draw too much attention to their new title; to them they remained first and foremost High Priests. Only Alexander Jannai, during part of his reign, disregarded the feelings of those Jewish circles that considered the kingship of the Hasmoneans as contrary to the traditional Jewish way. Some of Jannai's coins are inscribed 'Yehonathan the King'. Generally, though, the coinage of Antigonus was more characteristic of the practice in Judea: his custom was to use the title king in the Greek text, while the Hebrew lettering referred to him as the High Priest.

The conversion of Judea into a monarchy gradually increased the influence of the ruler in comparison with the traditional institutions that had previously led the nation. Before the Hasmonean Revolt the Gerousia had outranked even the High Priest, at least officially; but after the revolt official documents named Jonathan and Simon before the Gerousia. The composition of the Gerousia also changed, as some of the hellenistic elements were ousted and pro-Hasmonean elements from among the people were co-opted into it. After the monarchy had become established in Judea and had taken its place within the political environment, the institution began to lose some of its traditional Jewish aspects and to resemble the royal councils common to hellenistic kingdoms. The change seems to be reflected in the new name given to it: Synhedrion or Sanhedrin, the name by which the hellenistic crown councils were customarily known. Nevertheless, the traditional characteristics of the Gerousia continued to be reflected in the image of the Sanhedrin as the central institution of the kingdom; it always remained a composite body within which different elements competed for the dominant role.

Strong though their position had become, the Hasmonean rulers, with the possible exception of Alexander Jannai, never regarded themselves as absolute monarchs nor excluded the people from all governmental affairs. In domestic matters, at least, they always took pains to stress that the entire people shared the sovereignty with the regent. Clear examples may be found in the coinage struck by the different rulers ('Judah the High Priest and the Commonwealth of Jews', 'Jonathan the High Priest and the Commonwealth of Jews'). Even in the final days of the Hasmonean monarchy, under Hyrcanus II, documents addressing themselves to the outside world still acknowledged the official status of the Jewish nation together with that of its High Priest and ethnarch.

The Army and the Court

In order to protect the kingdom and to realize their plans for conquest, the Hasmoneans needed to maintain an army capable of standing up to those of their neighbours. Most of the Hasmonean soldiers were Jews, but there were also units of foreign mercenaries. The first to hire non-Jewish soldiers was John Hyrcanus. His successors, including Queen Alexandra, the mainstay and prime supporter of the Pharisees, followed his example. The mercenaries came from various places, though as a matter of principle the Hasmoneans avoided recruiting soldiers from Syria, because of the Syrians' hatred for the Jews. In their mercenary contingents the Hasmoneans had at their disposal professional soldiers trained in hellenistic methods of combat. Alexander Jannai also had recourse to Pisidia and Cilicia in Asia Minor for supplementary forces. For such a ruler a mercenary force was important also out of considerations of domestic policy, as he could rely on its loyalty in case of a conflict with his adversaries within Judea itself.

In addition to maintaining the army's strength, the Hasmoneans were also intent on fortifying the towns of their kingdom and building strong fortresses. Jerusalem was known as an unusually strong city and several times had to withstand heavy sieges. Inside Jerusalem the Temple compound was a fortress in its own right; its defenders made a desperate stand against Pompey and kept up their resistance for three months. Other great cities also proved their ability to resist the enemy valiantly; thus Sepphoris in Galilee put up a strong defence against Ptolemy Lathyrus, who was unable to reduce it. In particular, the Hasmoneans made their mark by building strong fortresses, which played an important role in the military history of the Second Temple period. They were required to fulfil a double task: as strongholds in a war against a foreign enemy, who had gained control of the countryside in the course of hostilities, and as points of support against domestic adversaries. Among the most famous fortresses of the kingdom of Judea were Hyrcania and Alexandrion in western Palestine and Machaerus in Trans-Jordan.

Gradually, the Hasmonean court began to assume the manners, appurtenances and atmosphere of the royal households of the hellenistic orient. Along with the outward pomp, the usual trademarks of Eastern royalty began to infiltrate into the court of the Hasmonean kings. The king was surrounded by a bodyguard who protected his life but also to some extent prevented direct contact with his subjects. The usual court intrigues were not lacking. The succession to the throne sometimes became an occasion of tension and conflict between pretenders. Indicative of this was the situation that evolved after the death of John Hyrcanus. The king had left his wife with extensive executive powers but his intentions were defeated by his eldest son, Judah Aristobulus. The latter imprisoned his mother and brothers and allowed only one of them, Antigonus, to become his partner in power. After the death of Judah Aristobulus, another problem arose in the succession. The dead king's widow released his two brothers from prison and helped one of them, Alexander Jannai, to seize the throne.

This development was accompanied by a process of external hellenization, which was reflected, among other things, in the assumption of Greek names by the Hasmonean rulers. Judah the Maccabee and his brothers had been known only by Hebrew names, but the son of Simon, for example, added the Iranian name Hyrcanus to his Hebrew name Johanan. From the time of Judah Aristobulus onwards, the Hasmoneans always retained Greek as well as Hebrew names, as did most of the more important officials in the Hasmonean administration, the army and the diplomatic service. Aristobulus I, the first to assume the royal crown, made a point of demonstrating his positive attitude towards Hellenism by assuming the cognomen

'Philhellene'. But, for all that, the gulf between the Greek world and the Hasmonean dynasty was never bridged. Despite all the changes in the government of the kingdom and the atmosphere prevailing at the court, the Hasmonean kings never dreamt of disowning the essentially Jewish and theocratic nature of their rule, which had had its origin in a religious war and whose whole existence was pervaded by the traditions of the Jewish faith.

Economic Life

Agriculture continued to be the mainstay of the Jewish economy. The measuring rod of a country's prosperity or poverty, as it was understood during this era, was the state of its agriculture. One of the results of the Hasmonean policy was, as we have seen, the annexation of good farmland in the Shephelah, Sharon, Samaria and Galilee, which in turn attracted Jewish farmers *en masse*. An enthusiastic description of the fertility of the Land of Israel may be found in the letter of Aristeas (paragraph 112), written in the second century BCE:

> For great is the energy they expend on the tillage of the soil. The land is thickly planted with multitudes of olive trees, with crops of corn and pulse, with vines too, and there is abundance of honey. Other kinds of fruit trees and date palms cannot be compared with these. There are cattle of all kinds in great quantity and a rich pasturage for them.

Apart from the usual farm products, particular importance was attached to the balsam groves in the Jordan Valley, which were a valuable source of revenue for the Hasmonean kings. Fishing also played an important part in the Jewish economy. The town of Tarichaeae (Migdal Nunya) on the western shore of the Sea of Galilee was famous for its fish preserves.

With particular fondness the national records record the peaceful years of Queen Alexandra as a time of agricultural prosperity (*Safra Behukotai*: 'In the days of Simeon Ben Shetah and in the days of Queen Shelomziyyon, the rains used to fall from one Friday night to the other, until the wheat grains grew as big as kidneys'). But we also have reports of poor farming years and drought. Long wars and heavy fighting on Palestinian soil always brought severe economic damage, particularly in the days of Alexander Jannai and in the early years of Roman rule. Many were killed, many left the country and not a few settlements were razed. The number of those captured in war and sold as slaves also was considerable.

Not only agriculture and associated trades flourished; crafts also developed and commerce prospered. Even before the Hasmonean Revolt, Jerusalem had an abundance of artisans of all kinds; and the letter of Aristeas refers to it as a city of many trades. The country played a role of importance as a transit station in international commerce. With the conquest of the coastal plain, Judea's share in this commerce increased, and certain classes of Jewish society made their fortune in it.

It should be noted that even though the region that included Palestine was divided into numerous and variable political units and was plagued by continuous warfare, its trade never ceased to prosper. While the Seleucids lost all their wealth, the states and cities that arose in their place developed lively economic activities. Advances in the manufacture of glass insured the fortunes of the Phoenician coastal cities; the better organization of trade with China via the Parthian Empire resulted in increased imports of Far Eastern commodities, which were in great demand in the markets of Rome and Italy. Changes also occurred in the ports through which the wares from the interior of Asia were exported. In the third and in much of the second century, this trade was mainly channelled through the ports of Asia Minor; but when the Attalid kings of Pergamum lost their power, towards the end of the second century, trade began to shift to the south. At the same time contact between the Phoenician and Palestinian coastal cities and Ptolemaic Egypt improved once again, and this trend increased with the rise of the markets of the West (Italy) and the relative decline of those of Asia Minor and the Greek mainland.

The author of the letter of Aristeas describes this trade in glowing terms (paragraph 114ff.):

> And moreover, a great quantity of spices and precious stones and gold is brought into the country by the Arabs. For the country is well adapted not only to agriculture but also to commerce, and the city is rich in the arts and lacks none of the merchandise which is brought across the sea. It possesses too suitable and commodious harbours at Ascalon, Joppa, and Gaza, as well as at Ptolemais [Acco].

Social Change and the Rise of the Sages

The development of the Hasmonean family into a ruling dynasty and of the system of government into a monarchy was accompanied by substantial changes in the structure of Jewish society. Essentially, the Hasmoneans were a respected priestly family, and in their own rise they likewise carried along allied families to the upper social levels. At the same time other persons and families, mainly those who had been close to Menelaus and the Tobiads, disappeared from the national political scene. Although, one of the characteristics of the social developments during the revolt was the cooperation between the Hasmoneans and a considerable part of the Jewish upper class that had objected to the extreme conclusions that Menelaus and his party had drawn concerning the hellenistic way of life. At the decisive moment these circles came to the support of the Hasmoneans. A clear case is that of the priestly house of Bnei Hakotz.

We know little about social developments during the rise of the Hasmoneans, but the little known to us indicates certain important trends. (1) During the period preceding the revolt, when even the stronger families, such as that of the High Priests or the Tobiads, were no more than *primi inter pares,* there had been a good deal of variety within the leadership; while under the rule of the Hasmoneans, the royal family overshadowed all the other families. As in the time of David and his descendants, here too we have a clear instance of a royal dynasty. While the ruling family, as we have seen, brought other families within its compass, the Hasmoneans and members of related houses occupied all the highest military and administrative offices. (2) Since the Hasmoneans were priests, it is self-evident that the hegemony of the priestly families remained a permanent feature of the Jewish social structure. (3) The policy initiated by Simon of establishing close ties with influential elements outside Judea proper was faithfully followed by his successors. Particularly important, in view of the later consequences, were the relations that the Hasmoneans established with one of the leading families of Idumea, the house of Antipas. Antipas himself was appointed governor of Idumea after its conquest by the Hasmoneans; his son Antipater gained an even more central position in Jewish society; whereas, the grandson of Antipas was Herod, the man who eliminated the Hasmonean family and founded a new dynasty in its place. Malik, Antipater's rival for influence in Judea during the rule of Hyrcanus II, also seems to have been of southern origin. (4) The most interesting aspect of the social development of the Jewish nation during these times was undoubtedly the rise of the *hakhamim* or sages as an influential and prestigious group. They were scholars of the Torah and religious tradition who became a factor of the first importance in the Second Temple period and set their stamp on religious and secular life.

The study of Torah and the development of the *halakhah* (see page 283), which determined the patterns of everyday life – religious, ceremonial, justice and government – in Hasmonean Judea, attracted the cream of the nation's intellectual and spiritual elements, who devoted their lives to it. Even in the generations preceding the revolt, the study of Torah and the shaping of the nation's spiritual life had, in practice, ceased to be the exclusive affair of the priests and had become the concern of men who did not belong to the priestly caste. Whoever was willing and able could achieve the status of a Torah scholar. While the number of priests among the sages remained considerable even in generations to come, there were many prominent men in the field who originated from different sections of the Jewish population in Palestine and elsewhere. Even descendants of converts were to be found among the most respected *hakhamim*. 'Disciple of Aaron' became a more honourable title than 'son of Aaron'. This circumstance gave the image of the *hakham* a popular aspect that, on the whole, was preserved in later generations.

The great sages of the Hasmonean era were teachers who gathered circles of students and disciples around themselves. Some of them taught in the Temple, but already in these days there were presumably *batei midrash* ('houses of study') headed by famous sages who, in addition to playing an important role in the development of the *halakhah* and law, appeared to the nation as exalted figures surrounded by an aura of holiness and moral purity. Their ethical teachings were no less generally accepted than were their *halakhic* rulings. Some of them earned a bare living by physical labour; others were members of the Sanhedrin and influenced political life. They were generally involved in everyday activities and initiated rules that governed a wide range of subjects, in accordance with the needs of the time. Whether or not these rules were officially sanctioned by the Sanhedrin and the organs of the state – at times when the *hakhamim* had a decisive voice in these institutions – they were accepted as binding and gained currency among the entire nation by virtue of the repute of the sages who had instituted them. The *hakhamim* were the mainstay of the *Perushim* (Pharisees), the largest and most well-rooted sect in the days of the Hasmoneans, as well as in later periods.

We know of great sages who lived and worked during the second and first centuries, until the time of Hillel the Elder. In chronological order, tradition mentions Antigonus of Sochoh, Jose ben Johanan of Jerusalem, Jose ben Joezer from Zereda in southern Samaria (who lived at the time of the Hasmonean Revolt), Joshua ben Perahiah and Nittai of Arbel in Galilee, Simeon ben Shetah, Judah ben Tabbai, Shemiah and Abtalion. The most famous of these figures was undoubtedly Simeon ben Shetah, whose activity, with that of his colleague Judah ben Tabbai, extended through the stormy rule of Alexander Jannai and the days of Queen Alexandra. The name of Simeon ben Shetah is connected with several rulings that were seminal for the development of Jewish society and its spiritual life. He was the author of the directives that obligated a husband to be liable to the value of his entire property for fulfilment of the marriage contract with his wife and prescribed that children should attend school. He also played a crucial role in the conflict with Jannai and the *Zedukim* (Sadducees, see page 237). As the Talmud was to put it: 'The world was desolate until Simeon ben Shetah came and restored the Torah' (Babylonian Talmud, *Kiddushin* 66a).

The span of time between Simeon ben Shetah and Hillel the Elder was bridged by the figures of Shemaiah and Abtalion, both presumably of proselyte origin. Their families may have belonged to the non-Jewish population of Palestine that was converted by the Hasmoneans. The fact that two such men could rise to become the heads of the *hakhamim* is a clear sign of the thorough spiritual integration of the Palestinian population into Hasmonean Jewry.

Religious Currents

The *hakhamim* were the moving spirit of the most important religious current among the Jews of the Second Temple era – the Pharisees, who set their imprint on the entire internal development of Judea and in effect even laid the foundations of Judaism as it was to be after the destruction of the Temple. In the main, the Pharisees carried on a trend that had its origins in the Persian era and had encompassed the activities of the *soferim* and interpreters of the Torah in the days of Ezra and thereafter. Their immediate predecessors were the *Hasidim*, who chose martyrdom in the persecutions under Antiochus Epiphanes.

The basic tenet of the Pharisees was unswerving faithfulness to the Torah and its infusion into all aspects of life. The Torah to which they referred differed considerably from the text of the Scriptures, for it also encompassed the entire living tradition of the *halakhah* as it had evolved in the course of generations (see page 283), based on the assumption that the Torah must be able to provide an answer to any question that arises in actual life. This 'oral Torah', which was the Pharisaic tradition arrived at by interpretation of the written Torah – with results that, on the face of it, often seem to be contrary to the plain reading of the written text – encompassed all aspects of religion, ritual, law and social order. In the legal field the Pharisaic tendency was to humanize penal law; in theology the Pharisees occupied what may be regarded as the middle ground between the determinist beliefs held, for instance, by the Essenes, and the doctrine of free will. They believed in the immortality of the soul and in individual reward and punishment after death and shared the eschatological beliefs of the people. Their spiritual and social activity was what preserved Jewish religion in those days as a vital, active faith, and some of them also served as the main spokesmen in the proselytizing movement throughout the Diaspora.

One of the most characteristic trademarks of the Pharisees was their strictness in all that concerned ritual purity and impurity and their punctiliousness in fulfilling the duties of tithing, which in a sense created a division between those who were meticulous about these matters and the common people, who treated them with greater latitude. Some even believe that the name *Perushim* is derived from the sect's ritual avoidance of impurity and a separatist way of life.

The Pharisaic influence extended far beyond the direct adherents of the sect. Their followers included the bulk of the nation, who regarded the Pharisees as their natural leaders and Pharisaic *halakhah* as the self-evident expression of Jewish religion. Their main opponents during the existence of the Hasmonean state were the Sadducees. In terms of religion the Sadducees were essentially the conservative element. They held only the written Torah holy and did not concede to the Pharisaic *hakhamim* authority to proclaim their self-inspired interpretations as oral Torah and as the source of laws equivalent to the written word. In many matters that were connected with the Temple service, with legal affairs and with daily life, they differed from the Pharisees. In matters of faith and philosophy, they believed in free will and rejected many of the popular beliefs of their time, including the resurrection of the dead and the important functions of the angels. Socially, they formed the upper stratum of the Jewish community, the aristocracy and plutocracy and above all the senior priestly families; in short, the elements that had been the social and political leadership of the nation at the outbreak of the Hasmonean Revolt. Even their name, *Zedukim,* was apparently derived from their nexus with the priesthood and the Zadokites. 'The Sadducees have their support only among the rich, and the people do not follow them, while the Pharisees have the people for their ally' (Josephus, *Jewish Antiquities* 13.298).

Religious life in the days of the Hasmonean Kingdom was rich in its variety. It would be wrong to assume that the Pharisee-Sadducee controversy alone reflects the entire complex of trends and subtrends that gave expression to the fervent spiritual life of the times. Among the other sects one should mention the Essenes (see page 272), whose tightly knit organization, holiness in daily life, belief in the prophetic inspiration of their ways and other such qualities characterized their position in Jewish society. However, the battle for the soul of the nation and the character of the kingdom was primarily fought between the Pharisees and the Sadducees.

Opposition to the Hasmoneans

At first the Hasmoneans were upheld by a combination of religious and national enthusiasm. In the eyes of many, theirs was the only family to which the salvation of Israel could be entrusted. But, from the very first, domestic developments contained the seeds of division, for the supporters of the Hasmoneans were far from homogeneous. The *hasidic* extremists and the representatives of the priestly aristocracy who had joined the Hasmonean ranks could not always find a common language. At first the Hasmoneans were the natural leaders of those circles influenced by the Pharisees, and, until the last years of John Hyrcanus, Pharisaic *halakhah* officially determined the rules of procedure and law that were binding throughout the kingdom. Under John Hyrcanus the rift between the Hasmonean rulers and the Pharisees became apparent for the first time. It widened under John's sons, until the Hasmonean dynasty once again came to terms with the Pharisees. The latter's standing improved vastly under Queen Alexandra.

It is not difficult to understand some of the reasons for the disturbed relations between the Hasmoneans and the Pharisees and the circles close to them. The outward hellenization of the royal household and the royal administration and certain tyrannical attitudes could not coexist with such Pharisaic ideas as the rule of the Torah and holiness in everyday life. The fact that the Hasmoneans gradually came to rely on the support of a range of social elements throughout Palestine, some of which were foreign to the hallowed ideals that had marked the rise of the dynasty, contributed to the increase in tension. Some opposed the very conversion of Judea into a monarchy and regarded it as an open break with the traditional lawful order of the Jewish nation. The monarchic system of the Hasmonean state resulted, as we have seen, in the decline of the highest representative institution of the nation, which became a mere privy council with most of its members appointed by the king. Another clear characteristic of one-man rule was the growth of the mercenary army, which began under John Hyrcanus and continued under the rulers who followed him. The enlistment of gentile mercenaries was a thorn in the side of most Jews. Their displeasure was due as much to religious motives as to the realization that the mercenary army strengthened the hold of the monarchy and enabled the king to disregard the will and institutions of the nation.

Even at the summit of the Hasmonean dynasty's power some opponents agreed that it retain secular authority, if only it would surrender the High Priesthood. But the circumstances of the times made such a solution impracticable, and the Hasmoneans, of course, rejected it. On the other hand, there were circles whose main objection was to the Hasmoneans' assumption of the royal crown. This objection was inspired by the belief that, by ascending the throne 'on which no stranger shall sit', the Hasmoneans had in effect become usurpers and had assumed a glory that was exclusively reserved for the house of David.

Nevertheless, the prestige of the Hasmoneans among the nation was high, and even the Pharisaic leaders were ready to compromise, as long as their particular objections were reckoned with. First among the Pharisees to show this inclination was Simeon ben Shetaḥ. Under Queen Alexandra, the successor of Jannai, he seems to have achieved his purpose. Pharisaic *halakhah* was reinstated, and the Pharisaic laws again became the law of the land, as they had been before the dispute between John Hyrcanus and the Pharisees broke out. The most severe crisis in relations between the rank and file of the nation and the Hasmoneans occurred during the reign of Alexander Jannai. On one occasion riots broke out in Jerusalem on the Festival of Sukkot and resulted in numerous casualties. After the defeat that Jannai suffered in Gaulanitis at the hands of the Nabateans, a dangerous insurrection broke out in Judea, and the king was able to suppress it only after a war that lasted six years and in which the Seleucid king Demetrius III intervened. After winning the war that had threatened to put an end to his rule, Jannai treated the insurgents, with excessive severity. Many were executed, and many others fled abroad to save their lives. Hints of these events may be found in the interpretation offered by *Pesher Nahum,* which was discovered among fragments of the Qumran scrolls: 'Its interpretation concerns the Lion of Wrath . . . when he hangs men up alive.' But even Alexander Jannai realized that he could not rule long against the will of the nation, and in the latter days of his reign he apparently made many concessions in order to come to terms with at least a portion of his Jewish opponents. His latest victories also won him wide sympathy in Judea.

The reign of his wife, Alexandra (76–67), was a time of cooperation between the Hasmonean royal house and the Pharisees. While she occupied the throne, the chief Pharisees to all intents took over the administration of the kingdom, and their traditions and rulings, which had been invalidated under John Hyrcanus, became law once again.

16

The Political and Social History of Judea Under Roman Rule

The defeat of Antigonus the Hasmonean by the Romans gave Herod full control of Palestine. Herod's reign was above all a product of Rome's oriental policy. The borders of the kingdom of Herod were determined by the needs of Roman rulers – first of Antony, later of Augustus. They approved of Herod as the ruler of Palestine because they found him strong, capable of preserving the existing order and at the same time unflinchingly loyal to and dependent upon Rome. It was to the Roman legions that Herod owed his victory over the Hasmoneans and his confidence that he would be able to deal with any Jewish insurrection. Since the Jews formed the majority of the population in Palestine, it made sense even from the Roman viewpoint that the king of the land should be a Jew. On the other hand, if Herod's kingdom were to include a large non-Jewish population, particularly the inhabitants of the large hellenistic cities, it was preferable that the kingdom should not be a theocracy, as that of the Hasmoneans had been, and that the functions of the king and the High Priest should not be combined in the person of a single ruler. In this respect Herod certainly met the requirements of Roman policy; moreover, his character assured his lifelong military and political cooperation with Rome's representatives in the East. Roman support for a Jewish king in Palestine served also as a gesture of goodwill towards the Jewish masses in the Diaspora, who were particularly numerous in the eastern provinces of the empire and whose sympathy was of great importance for the Romans in consolidating their hold on that part of the world. Admittedly, Herod was unpopular with many Jews because he had ousted the Hasmoneans, but at a distance his cruelty was less noticeable, while his close connexions with influential circles in Rome were highly useful to the vital interests of the Jews in the Diaspora.

Herod's kingdom was no exception in the Mediterranean world. There were other regions within the borders of the Roman Empire that the central government thought unsuitable for integration into provincial administration and that were maintained as separate kingdoms. The rulers of such territories were chosen from the dynasties that had ruled them prior to the Roman conquest or were persons who owed their high rank to the assistance they had given to the leaders of Rome. Herod was merely one of the most prominent among these rulers. The settlement between him and the Roman state was in keeping with the usual pattern of relations between

Herod's Kingdom

Mediterranean Sea

PHOENICIA

Caesarea Philippi

GAULANITIS

GALILEE

Gush Halav

Ptolemais (Acco)

Tarichaeae

Tiberias

Geba   Sepphoris

BATANAEA

TRACHONITIS

Dora

Caesarea

Scythopolis

D   Pella

Narbata

E

Sebaste

Gerasa

Shechem

DECAPOLIS

Antipatris

Jaffa

Sartaba   Gador

Lydda   Timnah

JUDEA

Beth-horon

Jabneh

Emmaus   J   Jerusalem   Jericho

Azotus

Betar   Hyrcania   Khirbat Qumran

Esbus

Ashkelon

Herodion

Machaerus

Dead Sea

Gaza

Masada

Fortress   ■

Territories gained up to 30 BCE

Territories gained after 23 BCE

0   10   20
km

© **carta**, JERUSALEM

the empire and its vassal kingdoms. Herod enjoyed all the trappings of royalty that had developed in the hellenistic East and bore the title of an ally of the Roman people. Practically, though, his hands were tied in all matters of political importance and particularly in the sphere in which political independence is characteristically reflected – foreign policy.

Herod's foreign policy was confined to the vicissitudes of Roman politics. When Antony was predominant, Herod was the faithful instrument of his policy. In those days a Roman legion was stationed in Jerusalem to safeguard Herod's position as long as some remnants of the Hasmonean supporters still held out. Herod's main problem at the time was how to react to the plans of Queen Cleopatra of Egypt, to whom Antony had made a present of parts of Palestine and who had designs on the Kingdom of Judea as well. The policy of Antony and Cleopatra also involved Herod in a clash with the king of the Nabateans (in 31). From the Jewish viewpoint it was one more stage in the Jewish-Nabatean conflict that dated back to the times of Alexander Jannai. The fortunes of war sometimes favoured Herod, at other times the Arabs. Finally, Herod's military talents prevailed and gave him a decisive victory over the Nabateans, which incidentally showed the Romans how valuable he was as the man responsible for order and security in his part of the world.

After Augustus' victory over Antony, the victor confirmed Herod in his kingship of Judea (30) and even enlarged his domain. Herod's position in the Roman Empire was consolidated even further when the general political situation was stabilized through the establishment of the Augustan principate in the second decade of the first century BCE. Under the Augustan principate Herod's kingdom extended to include nearly the whole of Palestine, with the exception of the enclave of Ashkelon and the coastal belt north of the Carmel, which did not form part of the Jewish state during the Second Temple era. Generally speaking, the Kingdom of Judea once more became what it had been under Alexander Jannai. An important gain for Herod was the incorporation under his rule of Trachonitis, Batanaea and Auranitis in the year 23; other areas, near the mouth of the Jordan, were annexed a few years later (20 BCE).

Herod's position in the empire was founded not so much on official arrangements as on his skill in developing personal relations with the heads of the Roman state and on an intricate network of contacts with the leaders of Roman society, from Augustus himself downwards. These relations and his admiration of the emperor were reflected in the cities that he built and named after him all over his kingdom and in the special temples that he established in his honour. Of no less concern to Herod was the establishment of excellent relations with Agrippa, the greatest Roman general of his generation and Augustus' right hand. Agrippa was regarded as Herod's personal friend; he visited Jerusalem and even brought large sacrifices to the Temple in the year 15. Herod maintained continuous contact with some of his friends in Rome and was thus kept constantly informed of the situation in the imperial capital. He also took their advice in matters of domestic policy.

Herod's considerable influence in high places in the empire stood him in good stead in assisting Jewish communities in the Diaspora. When a serious dispute developed over the rights of the Jews in the cities of Asia Minor and the issue was left for Agrippa to decide, Agrippa ruled in favour of the Jews. Diaspora Jewry therefore had the feeling that in the king of Judea they had a powerful advocate in their relations with the Roman Empire.

In ruling his own subjects, Herod rarely exercised any self-restraint. They were deprived of practically all rights, and the king dealt with them according to his own whim. The only limitation on him was his fear that the people might lose patience and revolt against him, which would diminish his prestige in the eyes of the Romans. Generally, he succeeded in preserving the peace throughout his kingdom; as long as he lived, the dissatisfaction of the people did not rupture into an open revolt. By means of an iron hand and timely concessions, as well as of police supervision and preferential treatment of the social elements dependent upon him for their social and economic position, Herod succeeded in holding on to the throne to the end of his life.

The capture of Jerusalem by Herod in the year 37 BCE marked the end of any residue of the old Jewish system of government. The traditional Jewish synhedrion was deprived of all political power. Herod set up a synhedrion of his own, a privy council that, in composition and nature, was not connected with the Hasmonean past and in which all important affairs of state were discussed. Another central institution that lost much of its prestige in Herod's time was the High Priesthood. Since Herod himself did not belong to the priestly caste and was not qualified to hold the office of High Priest, he was forced to surrender this function to others. He chose men who had no strong bonds with the Hasmonean past and who would owe him a debt of gratitude for the high distinction that he had conferred on them.

The external splendour of the Herodian state was visibly reflected in the royal court, which resembled in every way those of the hellenistic kings of the East. In Herod's entourage, there were 'royal friends' and 'royal kinsmen', official titles conferred on the holders of the state's main offices that expressed their direct dependence on the king. Many of his principal ministers were of Greek descent. His entourage also included some of the luminaries of the Greek literature of the day; best known among them was Nicolaus of Damascus, one of the great Greek historians whose universal history includes a detailed account of Herod's reign. Nicolaus had first been in the service of Antony and Cleopatra, but after their defeat he took up residence in Jerusalem and became the king's confidant and agent on special diplomatic missions. The tutor of the king's sons, his bodyguard and his secretary were also foreigners. Herod's fame and his international contacts attracted visitors from different parts of the Greek world (*e.g.,* Cos and Sparta) to his court; at times they played roles of some importance in the events that took place in the royal household. Herod's court was also a centre for actors, musicians and athletes.

Herod took many women in marriage and had sons and daughters by them: among them were Antipater by his first wife and Alexander and Aristobulus by Mariamne the Hasmonean, his second wife. After Mariamne's execution more marriages followed. His wives included a Jewess from an Alexandrian family, a Samaritan and a native Jerusalemite. The presence at court of sons by different wives, all wanting to succeed their father, resulted in a troubled atmosphere. Particularly bitter was the rivalry between Herod's two sons by Mariamne and his first wife's son, Antipater. All three were executed by their father on charges of conspiring against him – Antipater only a few days before Herod's own death. This atmosphere of suspicion, intrigue and executions often cast a cloud over the external splendour and material success that Herod enjoyed throughout most of his life. It also tinged his reign with a chill of terror that detracted from the king's reputation abroad no less than at home and even affected his relations with the emperor.

Herod excelled every Jewish ruler of the Second Temple era as a builder of magnificent cities and structures in Roman style. In this activity he found an outlet for his natural energy, which by virtue of international conditions was frustrated in the political sphere, and regarded these projects as a means of enhancing his fame. His main achievements in this field were the founding of Caesarea (on the site of Straton's Tower) and of Sebaste (in place of Shomron). In Caesarea he constructed the largest seaport on the Palestinian coast, which soon played a central role in the country's economy. In Sebaste he settled many of his army veterans, to whom he distributed fertile lands, and he fortified and adorned the city. Both cities were patterned on the hellenistic cities of the orient, and their establishment did much to upset the existing balance of forces in the country, for their prosperity resulted inevitably in the weakening of the Jewish element. Caesarea also attracted a large Jewish population, whereas Sebaste seems never to have had a Jewish community worthy of mention. Among the smaller towns built by Herod were the fortress Herodion south-east of Jerusalem, Phasaelis in the Jericho Valley and Antipatris near Rosh ha-'Ayin. He also restored the fortress of Machaerus and improved and beautified Masada. Jerusalem itself became, thanks to Herod's building enterprises, one of the most magnificent capitals in the entire East. Among the building works of the city mention should be made of the royal palace, the reconstructed Temple (the 'Herodian' Temple), the mighty towers of the Upper City (Hippicus, Phasael and Mariamne), the fortifications of the Antonia Fortress, the theatre and the amphitheatre. Other luxurious Herodian palaces were built in Jericho, in Ashkelon (which lay outside the boundaries of his kingdom), at Beth-haramata in Trans-Jordan and elsewhere.

Herod's Relations with the People

From the viewpoint of developments in the Jewish life of Palestine, Herod's reign must be considered a revolution second only to the one that followed in the wake of the Antiochan persecution and the Hasmonean Revolt. Once more the old order collapsed; part of the upper classes of the Hasmonean era was killed, others lost their economic power, and most were deprived of their influence. In their place new elements rose to the upper echelons of Jewish society. Some came from outlying areas of the country, from Idumea and perhaps also from Galilee. But more important was another trend, which the king explicitly encouraged: the integration of leading families from the hellenistic or Babylonian diaspora into the Jewish society of Palestine. Among the great houses of the hellenistic diaspora, particularly in such major centres as Alexandria, the prevailing ideas, manners and mentality were often closely related to those of Herod. Cooperation with Roman rule was their guiding principle and the basis on which they maintained their high economic and social positions in their respective places of residence. It was to families from the hellenistic diaspora (the families of Boethos and Phiabi) that Herod later entrusted the High Priesthood. Likewise, he did much to attract Jewish immigrants from Babylonia, as the first High Priest whom he appointed was Hanamel the Babylonian. Another Babylonian family (Bnei Bathyra) became one of the pillars of Herodian rule in northern Trans-Jordan. This process of the rise of Babylonian families to the upper stratum of Jerusalem society is reflected also in the history of the house of Hillel, whose rise was no doubt assisted considerably by the general trend to give prominence to families and individuals who had not been involved in the Hasmonean past. Those who came from the hellenistic diaspora were close to Herod in inclination and views; those from the Parthian Kingdom demonstrated his ties with the Jews of Babylonia.

To a remarkable degree Herod's policy reflected the same attitude, though in different political circumstances, as had that of the Tobiads. Just as the rule of the Tobiads had expressed a mentality whose orientation was primarily Palestinian and hellenistic, so Herod's outlook was marked by a Palestinian and hellenistic trend, which was embedded in the specific environment of the Roman Empire and its tendencies. Under Herod's rule hellenistic elements penetrated into the structure of the Jewish state. As we have seen, the administration, the army, the education of his sons and diplomacy were entrusted to Greeks or people who had adopted the Greek way of life. They held the key positions in the Herodian hierarchy; and next to the royalty these 'Hellenes' formed the backbone of Palestine's system of government. But the element of stability was lacking: the penetration of Greek elements did not lead to their fusion with the existing Jewish structure. The Jewish religion was too solid an obstacle to allow for such assimilation. Also, there are no indications that the king advocated any intermingling of Greek and Jewish elements in the society of Jerusalem or in the new cities that he founded in various parts of his kingdom.

Herod had ascended the throne against the express wishes of the overwhelming majority of the Jewish people in Palestine, who had fought desperately for Antigonus and the Hasmoneans. The hostility between Herod and the people at large continued to the end of his life, and his rule was generally regarded as a time of tyranny, despite his efforts to win the sympathy of the nation. He did much for the Jews of the Diaspora, built a splendid temple that aroused the enthusiasm of all who saw it, occasionally reduced taxes, and in times of starvation he even sold the crown jewels in order to buy grain. Sometimes he would convene the people in order to explain his policy and describe the achievements and benefits that had accrued to the Jewish nation by reason of his connexions with powerful figures in Rome. He showed a great deal of consideration for the Pharisee leaders and paid respect to Menahem the Essene, an important personality among the members of the sect. Certain circles that he helped settle in the country, such as the Babylonian Jews across the Jordan, followed him whole-heartedly. But all this could not obscure the contrast between his reign and the aspirations of the nation. The liquidation of the remnant of the Hasmoneans and the execution of the sons of Mariamne the Hasmonean highlighted the contrast between his rule and the tradition of the former dynasty. Admittedly, Herod remained faithful to the Jewish religion and, on the whole, took care not to transgress its commandments, at least in areas possessing a Jewish majority; when asked to give his sister in marriage to a Nabatean nobleman, he insisted that the bridegroom convert to Judaism. Nevertheless, his general conduct often offended the religious sensibilities of the Jews. For instance, his order that thieves should be sold abroad as slaves was an open violation of the Torah and of Jewish custom and even rendered the future Jewishness of the victims questionable. But that was not all. The non-Jewish atmosphere prevailing at his court, the pursuit of conspicuous splendour, his complete alignment with the ideology of the Roman principate, to the extent of introducing the cult of the emperor and building temples in his honour (outside the areas of Jewish settlement), his unlimited admiration of physical strength and his lack of consideration for human life in the pursuit of selfish political aims all served to widen even further the gap between the king and the people. The handing over of the administration to hellenistic officials of foreign origin, the founding of new cities with a hellenistic character to serve as fortresses against the Jewish nation and the feeling that Herod impoverished his Jewish subjects in order to ingratiate himself to foreigners made the people realize the substantial harm caused by the king's policy.

Herod's rule in Judea could be upheld only by a system of harsh oppression based on military power and a chain of fortifications and by stringent prohibitions against associations and assemblies which were enforced by an elaborate network of spies. Only by virtue of an efficient civil service and by timely concessions and acts of appeasement when necessary did Herod succeed in preventing the outbreak of serious disorders in Judea during his lifetime. There were indeed plots against his life, but they failed. Thousands of Pharisees persisted in their refusal to swear loyalty to him and incurred heavy fines. The overt discontent reached a peak towards the end of Herod's life. Extreme zealots, inspired by the sages Judah ben Zerifa and Mattathias ben Margalit, removed the eagle that the king had suspended above the Temple gate and were executed at his orders. When the king died, the entire people breathed a sigh of relief.

Jewish dislike of Herod is reflected throughout Jewish literature. In the Talmud he is remembered as a cruel tyrant, 'a slave of the Hasmonean House' (Babylonian Talmud, *Bava Batra* 3b) who treacherously rose against his masters. In the New Testament he is characterized as a murderer of infants. An uncompromisingly negative attitude is presented in the pseudepigraphic *Assumption of Moses* (6.2ff.), composed not long after Herod's death:

> And an insolent king shall succeed them [*i.e.,* the Hasmoneans] who will not be of the race of the priests; a man bold and shameless, and he shall judge them as they shall deserve. And he shall cut off their chief men with the sword, and shall destroy them in secret places, so that no-one may know where their bodies are. He shall slay the old and the young, and shall not spare. Then the fear of him shall be bitter unto them in their land. And he shall execute judgements on them as the Egyptians executed upon them, during thirty and four years, and he shall punish them (tr. R. H. Charles).

Herod's Heirs

After Herod's death, in the year 4 BCE, his kingdom disintegrated. In his will he bequeathed the chief part of the kingdom – Judea, Idumea and Samaria, with the large urban centres of Jerusalem, Caesarea, Sebaste and Jericho – to his son Archelaus. Another son, Herod Antipas, inherited Galilee and the Peraea; while Philip's share was the north-eastern parts of the kingdom. Herod's death was a signal for the people to demand relief from taxation and changes in the methods of government.

When these demands were not fulfilled, serious riots broke out. They were put down only after determined military intervention by Varus, the governor of Syria. Augustus confirmed the general outline of Herod's testament but denied Archelaus the title of king, and he had to content himself with the title of ethnarch. Archelaus, as cruel as his father but immeasurably less capable, failed to win the hearts of his Jewish and Samaritan subjects. The latter complained against him to the emperor, who deposed him and reorganized his domain as a Roman province (in 6 CE).

Direct Roman Administration

During the last sixty years before the destruction of the Temple, the large majority of the Palestinian Jews was subject to the rule of Roman governors, with only one brief interruption, when the government of the entire country was entrusted to the Jewish king Agrippa I (41–4 CE). When Archelaus was deposed from the ethnarchy in 6 CE, Judea proper, Samaria and Idumea were converted into a Roman province under the name Iudaea. Galilee and the Trans-Jordanian parts of Herod's kingdom remained within the vassal states of Herod's other sons, Herod Antipas and Philip.

Augustus' disposition of Palestine was the result of a considered decision on his part, for after Archelaus was exiled he could, in theory, have chosen another ruler from among Herod's relatives and place him in charge of Judea. However, in practice, this option was not open to him, because of the lack of a suitable candidate and because so large a part of the Jewish population was strongly opposed to the Herodian dynasty. Alternatively, Augustus could have annexed the country to Syria, but there were weighty considerations against such action – primarily, the particular nature of the Jewish population with its history and religion, which were completely different from those of Syria. The situation in Palestine had to be dealt with on a separate basis. As long as the empire lasted, the Roman emperors never forgot this fact and did not entirely integrate Palestine into Syria. Augustus chose to turn it into a provincial unit in its own right. According to his well-known system of provincial organization, provinces not requiring large military forces were generally entrusted to the direct administration of the Senate. Those in which large numbers of legionaries were stationed (*e.g.*, Syria) were administered by governors appointed by the emperor, who were also of senatorial rank. Yet there were also provinces to which Augustus and the emperors succeeding him used to appoint men of equestrian rank. As Augustus did not at first see any need to send Roman legions to Judea, since he thought that a garrison of auxiliaries would suffice to assure internal security and to suppress possible disorders, there was no point in sending an important personality of senatorial rank; a Roman knight would be sufficient. At first the governor of Judea held the title of prefect; only after Agrippa's death (in 44) did procurator become the official designation.

We even have some information on the antecedents of several of the governors of Judea. Tiberius Alexander was a Jew by origin but had abandoned his ancestral religion; Felix was a Greek freedman; Florus was a Greek from one of the cities of Asia Minor. Thus at least three of the last seven procurators were neither of Roman nor of Italian origin but came from the hellenistic East. And it was only natural that governors of Greek origin would be sympathetic to the hellenized urban population.

When Judea was converted into a Roman province, Jerusalem ceased to be the administrative capital of the country. The Romans moved the governmental residence and military headquarters to Caesarea. The centre of government was thus removed from Jerusalem, and the administration became increasingly based on inhabitants of the hellenistic cities (Sebaste, Caesarea and others). But Jerusalem, the most populated city of the province and the focus of riots, clashes and turbulent life in general, was nevertheless frequently visited by the governor. At the same time Roman rule continued to follow the tradition of identifying Judea with the entire area of Palestine, and, by continuing to call the province by the old name, Iudaea, it gave expression to the fact that the Jews formed the majority of the population.

The late republican era is usually regarded as a time when the Romans oppressed their provinces, and much is made of the improvement of conditions under the principate. In fact, this improvement was limited. The measure of power and authority concentrated in the person of the governor was such that control from afar was not easy. Moreover, it was not possible to bring a man to trial in Rome as long as he held a governmental office. We know that the residents of Judea required special permission from the governor himself to send a delegation to the emperor. Even if it had been possible to complain to Rome against the governor, it was very doubtful whether such a step would have been effective, since the governor usually had connexions and influence in Rome; thus it would have been necessary to enlist a considerable amount of interest against him at the court in order to succeed. The one consideration likely to restrain a governor was the fear that his actions would drive his subjects to revolt, with all that this implied. Even an aggressive governor such as Pilate sometimes retreated before the uncompromising stand of the Jews. In addition, the governor always had to reckon with the possibility that he might have to stand trial after completing his term of office; and the influence of the Jews in Rome itself was not a matter to be taken lightly during the Julio-Claudian era. It was, for instance, the influence of Agrippa II that enabled the Jews to win their case when they complained against the governor Cumanus, who was sentenced to exile. Even harsh governors sometimes sought to appease the people before leaving Judea. Albinus, for instance (in 64 CE), freed all the prisoners held in Judean jails, except those who had been condemned on capital charges.

Intervention in Judean affairs by the governor of Syria also was frequent. In some cases this may be explained by the special powers that the emperor had vested in the governor of Syria, but this explanation did not always apply. In any case, the auxiliary troops stationed in Judea were obviously insufficient to put down serious insurrections, and the governor of Judea was, in practice, dependent upon the assistance given him by the governor of Syria. The latter was not an ordinary provincial governor but the most respected of all the imperial representatives, the commander-in-chief of the entire Roman East and the person responsible for the Parthian border. The office of governor of Syria was reserved for the cream of the Roman aristocracy; his prestige was immeasurably greater than that of the governor of equestrian rank who held office in Judea. Consequently, the province of Judea may be regarded as a satellite of Syria, though, in view of the measure of independence left to its governor in domestic affairs, it would be wrong to say that in the Julio-Claudian era Judea was legally part of the province of Syria.

The Roman governor of Judea was, in the first place, the commander of the forces stationed in the province. The armed forces of the Roman Empire were based on two main components: the legions and the auxiliary contingents. The legions consisted of Roman citizens; the auxiliaries (with the exception of the officers) were usually recruits who were not Roman citizens when they enlisted but were granted Roman citizenship on their discharge. The garrison of Judea consisted of auxiliary contingents that had largely been recruited from among the people of Sebaste and Caesarea and had their main base at the provincial capital, Caesarea; but a regiment of infantry was usually stationed in Jerusalem as well. The latter's main task was to preserve order during the High Holidays, which was an inexhaustible source of friction between the Jews and the Roman authorities. The Great Revolt and, after it, the revolt of Bar Kokhbah made the Roman government aware of the dangers presented by the unrest in Judea and led to the conclusion that legions must be stationed in Judea as well.

Like all the other provinces, Judea was required to pay tribute to Rome. This was not the first time, for previously Pompey had imposed a tribute after taking Jerusalem; however, after the settlement in the days of Hyrcanus II and Herod, there no longer was direct contact between the Roman authorities and the Jewish taxpayers. When the province of Judea was established, it became necessary to organize the collection of taxes in accordance with the new situation. The Roman tax system was based on a general census of the entire population involving detailed declarations of the personal status and property of every individual. These declarations were checked from time to time in surveys conducted on behalf of the administration.

Under the Roman governors the basic element of the tax system continued to be taxes levied on the land. In addition, there was a kind of poll-tax; although these by no means completed the list. We hear, for instance, of a house-tax that the inhabitants of Jerusalem were required to pay and from which Agrippa I exempted them. For the collection of direct taxes, the Roman authorities did not use tax-farmers but availed themselves of the local governmental institutions. As in other Roman provinces, so in Judea the tax burden lay heavily on the people. The Roman historian Tacitus, when writing of the events of the year 17, noted that 'Syria and Judea were tired of the burden of taxes and requested their reduction' (*Annals* 2.42). In addition to the various taxes, the people were irked also by the many customs duties that were levied at the borders and ports of the province and even within the country. Particularly heavy duties were charged on perfumes imported from Arabia, for which the main caravan transit point was Petra. Other important customs stations were established in Gaza and the other seaports (Caesarea and Jaffa). We also know of customs collectors in different parts of the country itself. We hear of a chief customs collector named Zakkai, who was stationed in Jericho, no doubt on the border between the Peraea – which was ruled by Herod Antipas – and the province of Judea. This Zakkai stood at the head of a group of publicans and was notorious for his wealth. From the Gospels we know also of many customs agents at Capernaum. Apparently, the activities of these customs officers were not confined specifically to customs duties but also included other government revenues. Since they could avail themselves of the aid of the military, they were able to act high-handedly. Many of them grew wealthy, and some, like the publican John of Caesarea, even rose to a high position in society. But the general attitude of the Jewish population towards them was hostile and contemptuous, and they were regarded as virtual criminals.

Since the needs of provincial rule were many, the governors' interest was to extract as much money as possible from the people. Notorious in this respect was Pilate's use of the Temple treasury to finance the water supply of Jerusalem. One of the fears besetting the heads of the community was that the governor might rob the Temple treasury; and indeed Florus, the last governor before the revolt, removed 17 talents from the Temple treasury on the pretext that the money was required to meet the emperor's needs. The Roman government also enjoyed considerable revenues from the private estates of the imperial house in Palestine, which had been inherited from the Herodian rulers. They included, among others, Jabneh and the balsam groves near Jericho. In addition to taxes and levies, there were contributions in the form of forced labour, for the authorities used to seize men and animals to supply the needs of the government. It was a system that prevailed throughout the entire hellenistic world, and Jewish Palestine was no exception.

One of the hallmarks of provincial rule was that criminal jurisdiction was vested in the governor. The general view held in Roman ruling circles was that the local courts were, in principle, unsuitable for trying criminal cases and certainly could not be entrusted with the power of life and death. The official justification for leaving criminal jurisdiction in the hands of the governor was concern for public security, a term that could be interpreted as widely and flexibly as the situation demanded. Indeed, the procurators of Judea made frequent use of their criminal jurisdiction. Sometimes they did not pass sentence themselves but sent people to Rome for trial before the emperor. This was usually done when there was something unusual about the case and when the sentence might have serious consequences. Those residents of Judea who were Roman citizens formed a separate category and enjoyed special privileges. They probably had the choice in capital cases of standing trial in the province before the governor or of being sent to Rome to be tried by the emperor. However, the evidence is scanty and we do not know enough about the exact workings of the system. Many of the Roman citizens were freedmen, who, in accordance with Roman law, became citizens by virtue of their emancipation. Some Jews were even of Roman equestrian rank.

Jewish Self-government

In general, Roman rule left the local Jewish institutions a great deal of autonomy. They were held responsible for maintaining law and order, for collecting direct taxes and for supervising the Jewish population in general. The most respected of the Jewish institutions was the Sanhedrin in Jerusalem, the Great Court, which had its seat on the Temple Mount and was the highest legal and religious authority of the Jewish nation. In the administrative sphere the powers of the Sanhedrin were confined to Judea proper, but in matters of religion and religious regulations its authority extended far beyond the boundaries of the country.

The tasks of the Sanhedrin were therefore greatly varied. It served as the highest authority in matters of religion and ceremony, passed religious and legal rules and controlled religious life inside and outside Palestine. It was in charge of supervising the Temple service and handling the specific affairs of the priestly and Levitic castes and had the authority to proclaim the New Moon and the leap-year.

Apparently, the Roman authorities were incapable of dealing with the great volume of trials and cases that required speedy decisions and, as a matter of course, left them to the local Jewish authorities, who continued to exercise civil jurisdiction. One thing is certain: jurisdiction over capital cases was taken over from the Jewish institutions by the Roman authorities. Explicit evidence is found in the Talmudic literature: 'More than forty years before the Temple was destroyed, capital cases were removed [from the authority of the Beth Din]' (Jerusalem Talmud, *Sanhedrin* I 18a); and the Talmudic comment is borne out by the Gospel of John (18:31): 'It is not lawful for us to put any man to death.' Nevertheless, we sometimes get the impression that the Jews were accustomed to trying capital cases. A comparative study of the sources leads to the following conclusions: (1) in principle, criminal jurisdiction was indeed transferred from the Jewish institutions to the Roman administration; (2) in the case of offences directly involving desecration of the Temple, the Sanhedrin was entitled to pass death sentences, though even here there was a measure of supervision by representatives of the Roman administration; (3) the degree of supervision was liable to change according to the circumstances: under a governor such as Pilate it was stricter than under less aggressive governors, and when the circumstances were favourable the Jews could give a broader interpretation to their residual powers of capital jurisdiction and include religious offences connected only indirectly with the Temple; (4) even in matters that were not in any way related to the Temple or its cult, the Roman authorities sometimes voluntarily authorized the Sanhedrin and the High Priest to try capital cases.

The Sanhedrin consisted of seventy (or seventy-one) members. We know this fact not only from the *halakhah* but also from actual information available about the composition of the highest institutions during the Great Revolt. The Sanhedrin included priests, Levites and commoners. The priests, particularly the circle of the High Priesthood, formed a coherent group within the larger body. Besides them, there is mention of elders or of elders and scribes (*soferim*), the term scribes here meaning *hakhamim* or representatives of the Pharisees. These also formed a consolidated group, which became increasingly important and influential through the whole-hearted support that it received from the people. Their opinion usually carried the day. The chiefs of the priesthood, who were of Sadducean persuasion, rarely dared take decisions against the express wishes of the Pharisaic *hakhamim* in the Sanhedrin.

In keeping with its national function, the Sanhedrin included not only residents of Jerusalem but also townspeople from the countryside of Judea. We even hear of elders who used to come to the sessions from their homes in Trans-Jordan. When the High Priest was present, he presided over the session. In addition to the High Priest, who was the official head of the Sanhedrin, the Pharisaic group maintained its separate leadership. This was entrusted to the great men of the house of Hillel, Rabban Gamaliel the Elder and his son Rabban Simon. One of the functions exercised by the Sanhedrin was that of municipal council of Jerusalem. Whether Jerusalem as it existed at the end of the Second Temple era can be regarded as a city with the constitution of a hellenistic *polis* is more than doubtful. It had no cultural-social institutions in the Greek manner, such as gymnasia; nor were regular popular assemblies, held at a set time and place, among its constitutional characteristics. The members of the Sanhedrin, which served as the municipal council, were not chosen by democratic election; but we must bear in mind that considerable changes had occurred during the development of the hellenistic cities of the East and that they had moved away from the traditional democratic system of the *polis*. On the other hand, the governing institutions of Jerusalem adopted, at least outwardly, some of the accepted terminology of the hellenistic-Roman East. Thus the Sanhedrin began to be referred to as Boule and its members as Bouleutai. Some of the characteristics of Greek city organization also found their way into Jerusalem; as in other cities of the empire, we have records of the existence of *decaprotoi:* a committee of notables concerned in particular with the management of municipal finances.

In contrast to Jerusalem, which in its organization and institutions bore little resemblance to a *polis* and continued to develop, for the most part, in accordance with Jewish tradition, Tiberias was an example of a city with an absolute Jewish majority that, from the very beginning, was built and organized on the Greek *polis* pattern. Tiberias had its Boule and its popular assemblies, although in regard of its Jewish character, the city sometimes held its assemblies in the synagogue. At the head of the city's executive stood an archon, and control of economic life was entrusted to an *agoranomos*. The city also contained a large stadium.

Relations Between the People and the Roman Authorities

Under the first Roman governors, with the exception of Pilate, relations between the Jewish nation and the Roman Empire were not markedly hostile. A large part of the nation had hated the rule of Herod and Archelaus so implacably that at first direct Roman government was a welcome change. Others, mainly from the upper classes, who at the time had cooperated with Herod, later switched their allegiance to the Roman governors. But even in those years groups with a revolutionary ideology began to take shape, regarding any non-Jewish government as objectionable on the grounds that Jews should not be slaves to a king of flesh and blood, since God alone was their master. This ideology resulted in disorders from the very beginning of the establishment of direct Roman government. But after the first agitation (which occurred in the wake of the first Roman census) had faded out, we no longer hear of bloodshed in Judea until the days of Pilate. From the time of Pilate onwards, reports of unrest and riots become more frequent, and a gradual disillusionment from the hopes that had been attached to Roman rule is evident.

The Roman authorities attempted at first to find ways of keeping the peace in Judea, by showing consideration for Jewish religious feelings. This consideration was reflected, for instance, in the prohibition against bringing pictures and statues into Jerusalem. But the two sides were not always able to achieve real understanding. The presence of a garrison consisting of a regiment of auxiliaries, who generally disliked the Jewish population, was in itself enough to lead to clashes. Another source of irritation to the Jewish masses was the power granted to the governor to appoint High Priests, to have custody of the High Priest's vestments and to supervise the Temple cult. The heavy taxes, the harsh conduct of governors such as Pilate and the lack of communication between ruler and subject also contributed to the growth of the Jews' hatred of Roman rule. On the other hand, there were Jewish circles that sincerely believed in Rome's omnipotence and attempted to settle the differences, fearing that a direct conflict with Rome would bring disaster upon the entire nation, upon Jerusalem and upon the Temple. These circles included not only men with a direct interest, such as the representatives of the Herodian family, but also others who acted out of a sincere concern for Judea's future. When the Roman administration threatened the very existence of the Jewish religion in the days of Caligula's persecution, nearly all parts of the nation were ready to adopt the attitude of the rebels of the Hasmonean Revolt.

The first serious deterioration in the relations between the Jews and the Roman administration did not occur until the days of Pontius Pilate (26–36), who is remembered as a harsh, stubborn governor, not easily appeased. One of the most dangerous incidents during his term of office was his decision to bring the banners of a Roman army unit, bearing the image of the emperor, into Jerusalem. This was contrary to the custom of the earlier governors and a demonstration of contempt for Jewish religious feelings. The governor's measure aroused the entire nation. Masses of Jews gathered at Caesarea to plead with the governor. An attempt to intimidate them by surrounding them with troops had no effect. When the governor realized how devoted the Jews were to their faith and that they were prepared to die for it, he relented and ordered the banners removed from Jerusalem. On another occasion, thinking he would be upheld by the central government, Pilate insisted on having his way – he took money from the Temple treasury, in disregard of the objections of the Jews, in order to bring water to Jerusalem. This time he used troops against the Jewish crowd. Yet another dispute broke out when Pilate wanted to bring shields dedicated to the emperor Tiberius into Jerusalem. The Jews put up an organized, determined resistance, led by four of Herod's sons. Following intervention by the emperor himself, the shields were removed from Jerusalem to Caesarea.

Nor were these the only clashes during Pilate's term of office. On one occasion there was a blood bath among the pilgrims from Galilee, 'whose blood . . . mingled with their sacrifices' (Luke 13:1). His harsh attitude towards the Jewish nation was reflected also in the bronze coins that were struck in Judea during his governorship. His predecessors had generally shown consideration for the Jews' religious feelings and had not used human or animal figures or cultic implements and symbols of an explicitly pagan nature on their coins. In this respect, too, Pilate was an exception. The coins struck by him between the years 28 and 32 bear pagan symbols in the form of cultic objects of the kind found in other parts of the empire. It seems that Pilate's conduct in Judea was inspired by Tiberius' minister Sejanus, the real power behind the throne in those days. After Sejanus' fall in 31, Pilate's influence gradually dwindled, and when he treated the Samaritans too severely, he was recalled (in 36).

The Herodians Under Roman Rule

Even when Rome ruled Judea directly, the princes of the Herodian dynasty remained important figures. Herod Antipas remained the ruler of Galilee and the Peraea (until 39), and his brother Philip was in charge of the north-eastern part of the country. Both were succeeded by Agrippa I, who was the first Herodian after Herod himself to bear the title of king in Palestine and who, in his last three years, was the king of all Palestine.

Rome regarded the Herodians as a friendly dynasty whose princes could be used for the purposes of Roman policy even outside Palestine. Some of them became kings of Chalcis and of Armenia. The Herodian rulers, inside and outside Palestine, ranked highly among the kings of their kind; their relations with the rulers and high society of Rome were generally very close. Herod's sons customarily had their own agents and representatives in Rome who kept them in touch with events in the capital and maintained contact with the central administration. Some of Herod's sons succeeded in becoming fully integrated into the Roman upper class. At the same time they became the natural advocates of the Jewish nation at the court, even when they did not actually rule in Judea. They also maintained close ties with the great families of the hellenistic diaspora. Agrippa's daughter Berenice was married to the son of the Alexandrian Jewish leader Alexander, the brother of Philo, and her sister, Mariamne, was married to another leader of the Alexandrian Jews, Demetrius.

Among the Herodians active at the time of the first governors, the one who ranked highest was undoubtedly Herod Antipas, one of Herod's sons from his marriage with the Samaritan woman. For more than forty years, he ruled Galilee and Jewish Trans-Jordan (the Peraea), with the title of tetrarch, and set his imprint on those districts, which contained the largest Jewish population after that of Judea. Herod Antipas attempted to follow in his father's footsteps with respect to widening his reputation in foreign lands and building new towns within his own realm. More than any other Herodian of his time, Antipas distinguished himself by building new cities or rebuilding old ones that had fallen into ruin or insignificance. Soon after coming to power, he considered it necessary to rehabilitate two major cities that had suffered much in the disorders following his father's death. One of them was Sepphoris, which had been laid waste; Antipas restored it and rebuilt its wall. The other was Beth-haramata in Trans-Jordan, which he renamed Livias, after Livia, the wife of Emperor Augustus. The crowning glory of Herod Antipas' activity was the founding of Tiberias (between the years 17 and 22). Eastern Galilee needed an administrative centre, as there was not a single city worth mentioning in the entire district after Philoteria had been razed during the time of Alexander Jannai. The establishment of Tiberias was designed to fill this void; in fact, the city not only became the administrative capital of its district but also competed with Sepphoris for the status of capital of all Galilee. Of all Herod Antipas' works, Tiberias was to prove the most lasting, as it continues to exist to this very day.

In order to build Tiberias and convert it into a large urban centre within a short time, Antipas had to resort to unusual measures. Settlers for the new city were assembled from many places. In the manner of the hellenistic rulers, he forced many of them to leave their homes and settle in Tiberias. In order to keep the people from leaving, Antipas built houses for them at his own expense and gave them land. The new settlers included people from different classes; many were poor and not a few had been slaves whom Antipas had set free. Faithful to the Herodian tradition, he named the new city after Tiberius, who was emperor at the time. What made the town unique was that it was the only *polis* in Palestine with a clear majority of Jewish residents (see page 251). Herod Antipas also made it his concern to beautify the city with public buildings, the most conspicuous of which was the royal palace. The latter was a thorn in the side of many Jews because of the animal figures with which it was decorated.

Since the population of Galilee and the Peraea was overwhelmingly Jewish, Herod Antipas was forced to consider its feelings, as we learn from his coins. In Jerusalem he had no official standing, but his influence made itself felt all the same. He certainly could not have imagined that the religious ferment among his subjects in Galilee would produce one of the greatest revolutions of world history – Christianity. It was within his tetrarchy that most of the activity of John the Baptist took place. John preached against the marriage of Herod Antipas to his brother's wife, was thrown into prison and later was executed. Jesus of Nazareth also lived and worked in Herod Antipas' land.

With the death of Tiberius (37), Herod Antipas' prosperity also came to an end. His attempts to win over the new emperor, Gaius Caligula, failed, and he had to witness his brother-in-law, Agrippa, being made a king, while he himself remained a mere tetrarch. At the urging of his wife, he left for Rome in order to solicit a royal crown. His efforts bore no fruit; he was even accused of hoarding arms for use against the Roman Empire and of having entered into a secret alliance with the Parthians. He was sentenced to exile in Gaul (39), and his lands were annexed to Agrippa's kingdom.

The Crisis Under Gaius Caligula

The reign of Gaius Caligula (37–41) witnessed the first open break between the Jews and the Julio-Claudian empire. Until then – if one excepts Sejanus' heyday and the trouble caused by the census after Archelaus' banishment – there was usually an atmosphere of understanding between the Jews and the empire, and in the countries of the hellenistic diaspora there was even an informal alliance between the Jewish communities and the Roman authorities. These relations deteriorated seriously during Caligula's reign, and, though after his death the peace was outwardly re-established, considerable bitterness remained on both sides. The Jews had learned what danger foreign rule posed for the very existence of the Jewish faith and what was to be expected from an absolute, all-powerful monarchy where everything hinged on the whim of a single individual. The times of Antiochus Epiphanes seemed to have returned and the onset of a similar persecution became an ever-present danger. The Roman historian Tacitus showed a sound grasp of the situation when he wrote that 'the fear remained that some emperor might issue an identical order' (*Annals* 12.54).

The trouble started in Alexandria, where the Greeks quarrelled with their Jewish neighbours. The tension rapidly spread to Palestine as well, where the non-Jewish inhabitants exploited Caligula's dangerous illusions. He was completely convinced of his own divinity and demanded that his subjects worship him as a god. The first clash over this issue broke out in Jabneh, a town with a mixed population, the majority of which was Jewish. The non-Jewish minority realized that this was an opportunity to cause trouble between the Jews and Rome, and in the town they set up an altar for the cult of the emperor. The Jews of Jabneh, who would tolerate no pagan practices on Judean soil, destroyed the altar. The emperor, whose entourage included some of the Jews' most rabid enemies, from Egypt or from among the non-Jewish population of Palestine, learned of the incident. As punishment for the destruction of the altar, Caligula ordered that a golden statue of himself be set up in the Temple in Jerusalem. Petronius, the governor of Syria, was commanded to implement the order; since it was obvious that he would have to act against the opposition of the entire Jewish nation, he was instructed to proceed with the support of the legions. Two legions – half the legionary force stationed in Syria – and large auxiliary contingents were given marching orders. Petronius chose Acco as his starting-point and planned to proceed from there to Galilee and Judea.

Philo says of Petronius that 'apparently he himself had some glimmerings of Jewish philosophy and religion' (*Legatio ad Gaium* 245). Whether this was a result of sympathy for the Jewish religion or objective political calculation that the good of the empire required some appeasement of the Jews, the fact is that Petronius doubted the wisdom of the emperor's policy. When the report of the decree spread, the Jews gathered in their masses at Acco to seek its repeal. When Petronius moved his headquarters to Tiberias to study the situation at close range, they followed him, abandoning their homes and farms and demonstrating their readiness to die rather than permit the abomination from being brought into the Temple. The mass demonstrations were supported by the heads of the Jewish community, who begged Petronius not to drive the entire nation to acts of desperation and to write to the emperor and inform him of the true situation. Agrippa also acted with determination and courage: he went to Rome to persuade his friend the emperor to abandon his plan. He found Caligula in a responsive mood; the order to set up the emperor's statue in the Temple was rescinded, though Petronius was ordered to punish all who had interfered with the raising of altars to or statues of the emperor and his family. This imperial instruction, touching on a point that was vital to the entire Jewish nation, carried with it the danger of further rioting. Only Caligula's death, at the hands of Roman conspirators (41), prevented the outbreak of a Jewish-Roman war that might well have spread to the entire East.

Agrippa I

The reign of Agrippa I, the son of Aristobulus and a grandson of Herod and Mariamne the Hasmonean, separated the two periods of direct Roman rule in Judea. Even during Caligula's short reign, Agrippa had made his mark as the leading personality among the Jews of the Roman Empire. As a boy, he had been educated in Rome and had had an opportunity to move in the highest circles of Roman society. After years of changing fortune and adventures for Agrippa, the rise of his friend Caligula resulted in his being given royal rank and made ruler of the northern and north-eastern parts of Palestine, which had previously belonged to his uncle Philip. From then on he became one of the most important figures in Roman society, where he won greater influence than had any Jew before him. His grandfather Herod had been an outsider in the eyes of the Romans; they valued his services and his great talents, but deprecated his barbarian manners. But Agrippa moved among the great of Rome as their equal in every respect. Perhaps it was his inside knowledge of Roman society and policy, with all their strengths and weaknesses and the whims of the emperors and their relatives, that explained why, towards the end of his life, he was reluctant to identify himself fully with Rome. Among all the great Herodians, he was the only one to make the Jewish nation and its welfare his main concern and to become the greatest Jewish statesman of his time. In his last seven years, Agrippa identified himself entirely with the Jewish people and its needs as he understood them, and he had the consent and support of the large majority of the Palestinian Jews and their acknowledged leaders.

After Herod Antipas was exiled, Galilee and the Peraea were added to Agrippa's kingdom. At the time of Caligula's death, Agrippa happened to be in Rome; by virtue of these circumstances, he was able to intervene in the course of affairs, thus affecting the entire empire. The military had proclaimed Claudius emperor, but a considerable part of the Senate indulged in thoughts of re-establishing the republic. It was Agrippa who negotiated between the parties. Once Claudius was firmly in the saddle, he showed his gratitude to Agrippa, and in the course of a general settlement of the empire's affairs he enlarged Agrippa's kingdom by adding Judea and Samaria to it. Thus Agrippa became king of all Palestine (41), and in the territorial sense at least, Herod's former kingdom was re-established. The relations between Claudius and Agrippa were formally confirmed by an imperial decree, deposited at the Capitol in Rome, ordering the enlargement of Agrippa's kingdom.

When Agrippa became king of all Palestine, Judea's existence as a province was temporarily suspended. Gradually the king began to buttress his political standing in the east and to strengthen the defences of his kingdom. Departing from the traditional policy of the Herodian kings, who had always been the faithful instruments of Roman policy, he relied on the fact that his personal relations with the emperor and with many high-placed Romans would enable him to act with impunity where other rulers could not have hoped to escape imperial wrath. His position as the senior member of the Herodian family and a friend of the emperor gave him a standing in the Eastern world far exceeding that which Herod Antipas had enjoyed at the summit of his career. But not all Agrippa's plans were crowned with success. A clear instance of the limitations to which he was subjected was the failure of his attempt to strengthen the fortifications of Jerusalem and to build a wall around the New City – a project that at least in Josephus' opinion (*Jewish Antiquities* 19.326), would have made Jerusalem impregnable. In order to finance this plan, Agrippa even had recourse to the Temple treasury. But he was not allowed to complete the project. The Syrian governor, Marsus, informed Claudius, who ordered Agrippa to desist. Another incident gives further indication of Agrippa's inclinations and circumstances. His high and respected position among the vassal kings of Rome, together with his personal charm, won him the sympathy of other kings, with whom he developed close relations. At his insistence, the kings of Commagene, Emesa, Lesser Armenia, Pontus and, of course, Herod's brother, the king of Chalcis, met for a conference in Tiberias. Thus, most of the vassal kings of the Roman East would have been brought together and the meeting would have been Agrippa's crowning glory; however, Marsus was highly suspicious of the conference and of Agrippa's plans, fearing that they would result in a political and military constellation that might prove embarrassing to Rome and ultimately drive the kings into the arms of Parthia, Rome's enemy. He unexpectedly appeared in Tiberias and ordered the kings to disperse, and they complied.

The relatively long period of Roman government, the frequent and serious clashes with Pilate and, above all, the terrors of Caligula's reign had opened the eyes of many to the advantages of Jewish rule, even if it were only a semi-independent one. On his part, Agrippa made every effort to secure the Jews' sympathies. On becoming king, he dedicated to the Temple a golden chain that the emperor had given him and brought large numbers of thanksgiving-offerings. There were those who were dissatisfied even with Agrippa and his conduct, but the king merely attempted to appease them and reach an understanding and took no action against them. Nor did he neglect his connexions with the Jews of the Diaspora; in this respect he followed the example of his grandfather Herod. His task was made easier by the fact that these relations were an established tradition that had merely to be maintained and fostered. Agrippa was in every respect a Jewish king who sought the good of the Jewish cause throughout Palestine. During those years many Jews regarded him as the lawful and deserving successor of the Hasmoneans, rather than an heir of the house of Herod. Since the land he ruled also included large numbers of non-Jews among its inhabitants, he was forced to seek a modus vivendi with them as well, and he followed the example of the Herodians by attempting to enhance his reputation in the non-Jewish cities. Nevertheless, the gentile population regarded him as its enemy. When he died the people of Sebaste and Caesarea did not conceal their contempt for his memory. The Jews, on the other hand, openly showed their love for him during his lifetime and their feelings of bereavement after his death.

The Last Procurators

Agrippa's death (44) restored direct Roman rule to Judea. The twenty-two years from then until the outbreak of the Great Revolt may be summed up as a period that marked the decline of that rule and the progressive deterioration of the relations between the Roman authorities and the general Jewish population. Agrippa II did not succeed his father as king of Judea. After a while the Romans allowed him to rule in the north and north-east. Because of the high regard in which the Herodian dynasty was held in Rome and the special status allowed Agrippa II in the appointment of the High Priests, he and his family continued to enjoy considerable influence in Jerusalem. They continued to cooperate with the Roman Empire and occasionally even tried to appease the local Roman representatives and improve the lot of the Jews. But it was obvious that none of them acted out of the same complete identification with the Jewish cause as had motivated Agrippa I in his last years.

The re-establishment of Roman administration in Judea also brought with it the recurrent quarrels between the Jewish community and the procurators. First a dispute broke out over the custody of the High Priest's vestments. In a special missive to the official institutions of Jerusalem, Emperor Claudius ordered that the sacred vestments should be in the exclusive custody of the Jews. More serious were the results of a clash between the hellenistic city of Philadelphia and the Jews of Trans-Jordan. The Jews took the law into their own hands and defeated the Philadelphians, but the procurator Fadus (44–6) intervened on the latter's side and executed one of the Jewish leaders. The beginnings of a new outburst were inherent also in a new messianic movement that arose in those days. A man named Theudas assembled a great multitude and led them to the Jordan, which he proposed to convert miraculously into dry land. Fadus sent a detachment of horses after them, and Theudas was decapitated. The situation did not become any less tense in the days of the next procurator, Tiberius Alexander (46–8), of Jewish descent and a nephew of the Alexandrian philosopher Philo. The procurator showed a strong hand and ordered Jacob and Simon, the sons of Judah of Gamala (see page 274), to be crucified. The severe droughts that prevailed during Tiberius Alexander's administration did nothing to improve the situation.

Under the next procurator, Cumanus (48–52), the people grew even more restless. Pilgrims from Galilee were attacked by the Samaritans in northern Samaria (near the present Jenin). Immediately, large numbers of Galileans gathered to fight the Samaritans. Jerusalem was in an uproar. The riots resulted in Roman intervention, and the leaders of both factions were brought to trial before the emperor. Cumanus was deposed and replaced by Felix.

Felix (52–60) began his administration with an attempt to appease the Jews, whose leaders – notably, the former High Priest Jonathan ben Ḥanan – had even made efforts to assure his appointment. But his term ended with an open break between the Roman government and the Jews. During his administration the extremist freedom-fighters increased their activity and became a major, permanent element in the life of Judea. At first Felix attempted to halt the movement's spread, as his general policy was to discourage messianic hopes among the Jews. Many of the group were executed, and Eleazar ben Dinai, who had led the Jewish campaign against the Samaritans during Cumanus' rule, was imprisoned. Another movement, which had arisen in the wake of the prophecies of an Egyptian Jew who promised to bring down the walls of Jerusalem by a verbal command, was totally suppressed by Felix. Troops were sent against the soothsayer and staged a blood bath among his followers. That was the end of the Egyptian prophet's power; he was never heard of again.

The strong hand displayed by Felix did not produce the intended results. On the contrary, by the end of Felix' rule, Roman control in the villages and country towns and on the mountain paths of Judea had collapsed entirely. The extremist groups increased their activity and grew in strength throughout the country, encouraging the people to revolt against the Roman rulers and to win back the freedom of which they had been robbed. The extremists also passed death sentences on those who refused to obey their orders, raided the houses of the rich and the villages of their opponents and slaughtered their enemies. Terrorist violence had become the obverse of Roman tyranny.

The riots and clashes during Felix' administration were not confined to Judea proper. The main focus of the disorders was the provincial capital, Caesarea. The conflict here arose from a dispute over civic rights between the Greco-Syrian majority of the population and the large Jewish minority. The Jews claimed ownership of the city, as it had been founded by the Jewish king Herod; the Greco-Syrians based their claim on the city's former name, Straton's Tower, and its essentially non-Jewish character. Moreover, they argued, if Herod had wanted to found a basically Jewish city, he would not have set up temples and statues in it. Gradually, the dispute resulted in armed clashes. The Jewish minority had the advantage in wealth and physical strength, but their opponents relied on the city's garrison, which consisted of men of Sebaste and of Caesarea itself, who were naturally sympathetic towards their fellow Greco-Syrians. The Roman authorities attempted to put down the disturbances at their very beginning but had little success. When one of the clashes ended in a Jewish victory, Felix sent in troops, who killed many Jews and looted their property.

Under the last three procurators before the Great Revolt – Festus, Albinus and Florus – the conditions that had developed under Felix continued to run their course. The extremist freedom-fighters operated unhindered in the villages and country towns of Judea, and even Jerusalem itself was no longer secure. The heads of the priestly oligarchy and other men of influence in the city recruited their own bands of strongmen, who competed for control of the streets of Jerusalem. At the same time a fight for political and economic power developed between the party of the High Priests and the rank and file of the priestly caste. The matter at issue was the tithes. The great priestly families were accustomed to send their retainers to the granaries to collect the tithe, so that the common priests were deprived of their revenues and became impoverished. Concurrently, there was a standing dispute between the priests and the Levites, who made a bid for a status equal to that of the priests. Albinus (62–4) maintained the cooperation with the Jewish upper class and particularly with the former High Priest Hananiah ben Nedebai; but under

Florus, the last procurator before the Great Revolt, the break between Rome and the Jewish nation came out into the open. Neither the Roman administration nor the official institution of autonomous Jewish rule was strong enough to preserve its former prestige and influence. Anarchy grew apace in the streets of Jerusalem as much as in the rural districts of Judea.

The Jewish Population on the Eve of the Revolt

At the end of the Second Temple era, the majority of Palestine's population, as we have seen, was Jewish. Most of the Jews were concentrated in Judea, Galilee and the Peraea, but many lived in the other parts of the country. There were considerable Jewish communities in the hellenized coastal cities, such as Caesarea, Ashkelon and Acco, and further inland, in such places as Scythopolis and Gerasa in Trans-Jordan. Idumea was Jewish by now, and though the Idumeans made some attempt to preserve their separate identity, that did not exclude them from the Jewish nation. The Jews had also spread to the north-eastern part of Trans-Jordan, and to Gaulanitis and Batanaea east of the Sea of Galilee. They made up the bulk of the population of the Narbata district in north-western Samaria. Only one part of Palestine had kept itself apart and made no room for Jews faithful to the Temple in Jerusalem – central Samaria, which consisted of Shechem and Mount Gerizim, where the Samaritans continued to maintain their religious and ethnic centre. (The *ḥakhamim* used to refer to it as 'a patch of Kutaeans [Samaritans]'.) Neither do we hear of Jews in the rural parts of the Samaritan district or in the hellenized city of Sebaste. The Samaritan population was like a wedge driven between two of the centres of Jewish settlement, Judea and Galilee, and its very existence was a thorn in the side of the Jews, although the Jews and Samaritans occasionally found themselves in the same camp in the struggle against Roman rule.

At the end of the Second Temple era, the village system was still the pattern of settlement and social cohesion for many Jews, though a considerable minority already lived in settlements that were urban in size and in form of organization. Some of these had a clear Jewish majority and were places that, by the standards of the times, deserved the designation city in every respect – these included Jerusalem, Jericho (the second largest town in Judea proper), Sepphoris and Tiberias. An intermediate place was held by the chief towns of the districts (toparchies), which for the most part did not achieve the status of city as far as their form of local government was concerned. One such settlement, for instance, was Lydda. A considerable proportion of the Jews lived in the hellenized cities; in some of them, such as Caesarea and Scythopolis, they accounted for a large percentage of the population. Between the urban and rural population there often prevailed a state of tension, which occasionally led to open hostilities, not only between Jewish country dwellers and nearby hellenistic cities (as in the case of the Jewish settlers of the Peraea and the citizens of Philadelphia) but also between the Jews themselves. The friction between the villages of Galilee and Tiberias is one example.

We have no reliable statistics on the Jewish population of Palestine at the end of the Second Temple era – neither for the total population of the country nor for any particular district or town. The ancient sources usually gave exaggerated figures. Josephus (*Bellum Judaicum* 6.420) gave the number of dead in the siege of Jerusalem as 1,100,000 and the number of prisoners as more than 97,000. On the basis of a count of the Passover sacrifices offered shortly before the Great Revolt, the same historian arrived at the incredible number of three million participants in the Passover celebrations in Jerusalem (*Bellum Judaicum* 2.280; *cf.* Babylonian Talmud, *Pesaḥim* 64b). The Roman historian Tacitus (*Historiae* 5.13) says that 600,000 were besieged in Jerusalem. Of Galilee, Josephus wrote that it contained 204 towns and villages (*Vita* 235), none of which had a population of less than 15,000 (*Bellum Judaicum* 3.43). It is hard to take these figures at face value. More reasonable seems to be the figure given by Josephus for the total number of defenders of Jerusalem during Titus' siege, which he puts at 23,400 (*Bellum Judaicum* 5.248–50). In any case, it is obvious that the entire country was quite densely settled. In this respect Palestine did not differ from its neighbours Syria and Egypt, which also had remarkably large populations for the days of the Roman Empire.

The three centres of Jewish settlement in Palestine – Judea, Galilee and the Peraea – were in many respects treated by the Mishnah as separate countries for the purposes of *halakhah,* and each developed a life style and populace of its own. Particularly marked were the differences between Judea and Galilee. Judea still ranked first among these centres, mainly because of Jerusalem and the Temple. If one takes the enormous population of Jerusalem into account, it seems likely that Judea also led in numbers. Judea proper stretched from the Jordan (Jericho) to Jaffa. The capital, Jerusalem, overshadowed all the other settlements within its boundaries. The Temple and, no less so, the great schools of the Pharisee sages made Jerusalem the capital of the entire Jewish nation and the symbol of its uniqueness. As Philo of Alexandria put it, 'Jerusalem is not only the metropolis of the single country of Judea, but of most other countries also' (*Legatio ad Gaium* 281). The time had passed when the world heard of Jerusalem only vaguely and when Greek and Roman writers, such as Polybius and Livy, referred to it mainly as a temple. In the last years of Jerusalem's existence, it was spoken of in a very different vein. To the Roman author Pliny (*Naturalis Historia* V, 14.70), Jerusalem was the most famous city not only of Judea but of the entire East. Jerusalem was the linchpin that held the Jewish population of Palestine together and a focus of attraction for Jewish pilgrims from the Diaspora, for converts and for pious gentiles. Its fortifications were a source of pride and security to the Jews of the entire country. And from Jerusalem the Torah and *halakhah* went forth to inspire Jews in all the countries of the Diaspora.

The *élite* of Jewish society was concentrated in Jerusalem. As the site of the Temple, it was also the residence of most of the priestly families and their relatives. The city also attracted men of rank who did not belong to the priesthood but wanted to live permanently, or for long periods, at the nation's centre in order to keep a finger on the pulse of political life. Members of the Herodian family, even if their dominions lay in remote parts, often maintained a residence in Jerusalem.

Jerusalem was also the hub of intellectual life. The representatives of the house of Hillel, Rabban Gamaliel the Elder and his son Simon, lived there permanently;

their Babylonian origins were a matter of the past, and they were regarded as full-fledged Jerusalemites. *Ḥakhamim* from other parts of the country also took up residence in Jerusalem. Its centres of Torah study were always alive with Jews from other areas of Palestine and even from the Diaspora who had come in search of wisdom. Jerusalem's religious and administrative position and the fact that it contained the largest population in Palestine helped turn it into the main focus of economic life. Here the cream of the artisans and craftsmen of Jewish Palestine gathered – weavers, potters and perfumers. The Temple alone required many hands skilled in the building trades and crafts, and the Temple service encouraged the development of skills needed for cultic purposes. The city attracted merchants and businessmen from far and near.

The other large Jewish centres were mainly in the northern parts of Judea, the second largest city of Judea being Jericho. The fertile land surrounding the city, its situation on the road from Trans-Jordan to Jerusalem, the administrative function that it fulfilled in the Jordan Valley and the interest in the region taken by Herod and his successors all contributed to the prosperity of Jericho at the end of the Second Temple era. Other important centres in northern and north-western Judea were Gophna, Lydda and Emmaus, all three of which were capitals of toparchies. The southern part of Judea seems to have been less densely populated. Its main landmarks were Herodion, a fortress built by Herod that also served as the capital of its district, and En-gedi, which, after a period of decline, regained its prosperity. Also connected with Judea proper were the cities of Jabneh and Jaffa. In Jabneh the Jews were in the majority, but the non-Jewish minority that had established itself in the town created trouble for the Jewish majority in the days of Caligula.

Jewish Trans-Jordan reached from the hellenized city Pella (Fahal) in the north to Machaerus, east of the Dead Sea, in the south. Its western border was the Jordan River, and in the east it extended until the territory of the Greek cities Gerasa and Philadelphia. The settled area of the Peraea was divided into two parts. The smaller and doubtlessly less populated area lay north of the Jabbok. Its most important settlement was Amathus, a strong fortress from the hellenistic period that had been conquered by Alexander Jannai and had become a Jewish town of some importance, the seat of a local Sanhedrin in the days of Gabinius and the capital of a toparchy. However, the majority of the Jews in Trans-Jordan lived south of the Jabbok, across the river from north-eastern Judea. The capital of this region was Gador (Es-Salt), which was considered the capital of the entire Peraea. South of Gador lay Abila (Abel-shittim) and Beth-haramata, and still farther to the south was the fortress Machaerus. Thus, geographically, the situation of Jewish Trans-Jordan was marked by two characteristics: its nearness to and common border with Judea and its location within the generally hostile neighbourhood of the Greek cities to the east and north.

The Jews of the Peraea followed the fortunes of Judea. They played an important role in the insurrection after Herod's death, burning the royal palace at Beth-haramata; and in the Great Revolt the people of the Peraea fought side by side with those of Judea. One of the insurgent commanders was Niger of Trans-Jordan. A particularly valiant fight was put up by the men of Machaerus, who held out even after Jerusalem had fallen.

The political and administrative boundaries of Galilee were less stable than those of either Judea or the Peraea. Several important Galilean cities, such as Tiberias and Tarichaeae (Migdal Nunya), were annexed to the kingdom of Agrippa II only a few years before the revolt but did not cease sharing in the life of Galilee; on the contrary, as far as the feelings of the population were concerned, they continued to belong to it. Usually Galilee was considered to be bordered by the territory of Acco and the Carmel in the west, Samaria and the lands of Scythopolis in the south, Tyre and its territory (which reached far inland) in the north and Gaulanitis and the Greek cities Hippos and Gadara in the east.

At the end of the Second Temple era, Galilee prospered and contained a multitude of towns and villages. The large majority of its inhabitants were Jews. The most important cities in Galilee were Sepphoris, Tiberias, Tarichaeae and Gabara ('Arab). At first Sepphoris was the provincial capital of Galilee, but it suffered heavily in the days of Varus, after Herod's death. After it was rebuilt and again dominated many of the surrounding villages, Sepphoris remained consistently loyal to Roman rule and opposed the Great Revolt. Of all the Jews of Palestine, those of Sepphoris were most inclined to compromise with the Romans, and it seems that after its restoration the city received special treatment from the Roman authorities. We have no means of knowing how many non-Jews lived in Sepphoris, but it is obvious that there was a clear Jewish majority.

Sepphoris' rival for first place in Galilee was Tiberias, a city that was mainly Jewish but had the constitution of a Greek *polis*. The atmosphere of Jewish Tiberias in those days seems to have differed considerably from that of Jerusalem or of the villages of Galilee. It was not by mere chance that Tiberias produced in that period an author such as the Jewish historian Justus, whose Greek was better than that of Josephus. The Jews of Tiberias were not as keen on rising against Rome as were those of the Galilean villages, but they were by no means as strongly opposed as were the people of Sepphoris. Most of the Jews of Tiberias joined the insurgents, and those who escaped even took part in the defence of Jerusalem. Relations between Tiberias and the nearby Greek cities were tense, and at the beginning of the revolt villages within the territories of Hippos and Gadara were set on fire. But the relations between Tiberias and Jewish cities in Galilee, such as Tarichaeae and Sepphoris, were also less than peaceful.

Tarichaeae was situated on the Sea of Galilee, north of Tiberias. Its population was entirely Jewish and was notorious for its determined opposition to the Romans. Nevertheless, its people also imitated the Greek way of life to some extent, for the city had a large hippodrome for chariot races that occasionally served also as the meeting-place for popular assemblies.

An important centre of Jewish settlement in Lower Galilee was Gabara, where Rabban Johanan ben Zakkai lived and taught in the last years before the revolt. Other major settlements in Lower Galilee were Jotapata, the fortress that became the focus of resistance against Vespasian in that part of the country, and Japhia, 'the largest of the villages of Galilee' (*Vita* 230). We also know of the existence in the eastern part of Upper Galilee of several prosperous towns, such as Giscala and Capernaum; Cabul, another large, rich village, lay on the western border of Galilee, near Acco. Many Jews lived in Gaulanitis, and the mighty fortress of Gamala, situated in that area, was one of the hardest places to conquer. The Jews of Gaulanitis were considered to be part of the Galilee and were sometimes reckoned among the Galileans.

Some of the most important trends in Jewish religious and political life came into existence in Galilee. It was here that Christianity was born; here began the extremist freedom movement, headed by Judah ben Hezekiah; out of Galilee came John of Giscala, one of the two chief leaders of Jerusalem during the siege, and Eleazar, who converted the royal house of Adiabene to Judaism. Many of the Galileans maintained close relations with the heads of the Jerusalem community; a characteristic instance is the ties between John of Giscala and Rabban Simon ben Gamaliel.

The toparchy of Narbata in the north-west was inhabited mainly by Jews. Jews lived also in the hellenized coastal cities, such as Acco, Dor and particularly Caesarea. In all these cities friction between the Jews and the gentile population among which they lived was a standing feature. Better relations between the Jews and their non-Jewish neighbours prevailed in Scythopolis and in Trans-Jordanian Gerasa: when the Great Revolt broke out, the people of Gerasa let the local Jews choose whether to stay or leave. In Hippos and Gadara relations between the non-Jewish majority and the Jewish minority were less cordial.

The Temple and the Jewish Oligarchy

After its renovation by Herod (see pages 243, 244), the Temple in Jerusalem successfully competed in splendour with other famous cultic centres. It was the centre for Jews of the entire country; priests from all parts of the country, even if they were not permanent residents of Jerusalem, came in their multitudes to serve in the priestly division ('watch') to which they belonged. The Jewish masses made pilgrimages, mainly on the High Holidays, and were joined by many others who came from the Diaspora. The men did not go up to Jerusalem alone but took their wives and children along. Philo of Alexandria (*The Special Laws* 1.69) described this mass movement of Jews to the Temple in terms that reflect his pride and joy:

> Countless multitudes from countless cities come, some over land, others over sea, from east and west and north and south at every feast. They take the Temple for their port as a general haven and safe refuge from the bustle and great turmoil of life, and there they seek to find calm weather and, released from the cares whose yoke has been heavy upon them from their earliest years, to enjoy a brief breathing-space in scenes of genial cheerfulness (tr. F.H. Colson, Loeb. ed., vol. VII).

This gathering of the masses provided a suitable context for interaction between different circles from various parts of the country as well as from the Diaspora, who thus had an opportunity to learn of and exchange new ideas. Hence the pilgrimages on the High Holidays were notorious as occasions of unrest, revolt and mass riots.

The Temple Mount was also the seat of the Sanhedrin and a centre for the propagation of Jewish learning. Some of the greatest *hakhamim,* such as Rabban Simon ben Gamaliel and Rabban Johanan ben Zakkai, taught in the Temple. It is also reported that Jesus preached his gospel in the Temple, as did the first members of the Christian community in Jerusalem.

The expenses occasioned by the public sacrifices, the costs of maintaining the Temple and all other financial outlays were borne by the Temple treasury, which was replenished by funds sent from all over Palestine and the Diaspora. The revenue received from the payment of the half shekel and from other contributions made it possible to use the treasury's funds also for the municipal needs of Jerusalem; the Temple treasury was in fact a source of financial strength for the entire nation. The management of Temple affairs was entrusted to the High Priest and the chiefs of the priesthood, who nevertheless were supervised by the Roman governors. Throughout this period (from Herod till the Great Revolt), we witness the increasing consolidation of a priestly oligarchy consisting of a number of priestly families that claimed the office of High Priest as their exclusive privilege. Herod's policy with respect to the High Priesthood was similar only to that of Antiochus Epiphanes before him. Before and after Antiochus Epiphanes, until the reign of Herod, the office of High Priest had been handed down within the same family, from father to son. Under Herod this practice changed. From then onwards the appointment was limited to a specific term. Sometimes a High Priest stayed in office for years, as in the cases of Joseph Caiaphas (eighteen years, from 18 to 36) and Hananiah ben Nedebai (twelve years, from 47 to 59); in other instances the term was reduced to a year or even just a few months. Herod and the Roman governors in fact acknowledged that the office of High Priest was the preserve of a few families. Only the Zealots of the Great Revolt departed from these customs and changed the system entirely.

The Babylonian Talmud preserves a doggerel that provides us with a fairly complete picture of the composition of the priestly oligarchy, its influence over the people and the discontent of the *hakhamim:* Abba Saul ben Bothnith said, in the name of Abba Joseph ben Hanin:

Woe is me because of the house of Boethos,
Woe is me because of their staves.
Woe is me because of the house of Hanin,
Woe is me because of their whippings.
Woe is me because of the house of Kathros,
Woe is me because of their pens.
Woe is me because the house of Ishmael the son of Phiabi,
Woe is me because of their fists!
For they are High Priests
And their sons are treasurers
And their sons-in-law are overseers
And their servants come
And beat us with staves.

(Babylonian Talmud, *Pesahim* 57a, Tosefta Menahot 13.21)

The great priestly families jealously preserved their collective supremacy. Their members not only served as High Priests but also took over all the other important offices connected with the Temple and greatly affected the composition of the class structure of Jewish society.

One of the most prominent houses within the priestly oligarchy was the family of Boethos, which had risen to greatness under Herod and set its imprint on domestic affairs for several generations. Its history reflects all the characteristics of the social development of Palestine in those days. The Boethos family formed part of the stratum that had achieved prominence together with Herod, and its interests were intertwined with those of the Herodians. Like many of the great families of those days, the house of Boethos was not of Palestinian origin but came from the Diaspora – from Alexandria in Egypt – and several of its members later became High Priests. Its chief rival was the house of Hanan, which produced some of the most important statesmen and personalities of Judea in the last decades before the Great Revolt. Outstanding among them were Jonathan ben Hanan and Hanan ben Hanan. The latter was a militant Sadducee and the acknowledged leader of the Jewish upper classes during the revolt. The greatness of the third priestly family, the house of Phiabi, which also seems to have come from Egypt, is reflected in the fact that it supplied three High Priests: the first, Joshua ben Phiabi, held office under Herod himself; the second, Ishmael ben Phiabi I functioned as High Priest under the early Roman governors; the third, Ishmael ben Phiabi II, was appointed by Agrippa II. The High Priest was assisted by a staff of high Temple officers. The most important of them is known in the Greek sources as the '*strategos* of the Temple'. Other important functionaries were the *amarcalim* ('overseers') and treasurers.

Relations with the Diaspora

The close relations with the Jewish masses in the Diaspora (concentrated primarily in the eastern provinces of the Roman Empire [Egypt, Cyrenaica, Syria, Asia Minor and the Greek islands] and under Parthian rule) played an important role in the social development of Palestine at the end of the Second Temple era. Gradually relations with the Jews in the western part of the empire also became more important, primarily those with the Jews of Rome, who were close to the imperial court. The Roman authorities were forced to consider the reactions of the Jewish masses in different parts of the empire – and outside it – towards their policies in Judea. No less important were the social, economic and cultural consequences of these relations. Contact with the Diaspora was maintained in several ways: through the pilgrimages of Diaspora Jews to Jerusalem; through the settlement of many of them in Palestine and the establishment in Jerusalem of Diaspora Jews grouped by country of origin; and through the contributions by Diaspora Jewry to the Temple in Jerusalem of the half shekel and votive donations.

Many Diaspora Jews observed the commandment of pilgrimage, and on the High Holidays in Jerusalem one might have met Jews from such different lands as Parthia, Media, Elam, Mesopotamia, Cappadocia, Pontus, Asia Minor, Phrygia, Pamphylia, Cyrene, Crete, Rome and Arabia. Jews who lived in nearby countries such as Syria would make frequent pilgrimages; first fruits offered by the Jews of Syria were accepted in Jerusalem, because 'buying in Syria is like buying in the suburbs of Jerusalem' (Mishnah Ḥalla 4.11). Some Diaspora Jews remained to study Torah in the famous academies of Jerusalem. One such instance was that of Saul of Tarsus, later known as the apostle Paul, who came from a city in Cilicia to study under Rabban Gamaliel the Elder.

In many cases these Jews preserved the way of life they had brought with them from the Diaspora, and we can witness the formation of groups based on country of origin. One point of distinction was the language of daily use: there were 'Hebrew' Jews, who spoke Hebrew or Aramaic, and 'hellenistic' Jews, who spoke Greek and came from Egypt, Cyrene, Asia Minor and Cyprus. Some of the Jews of Diaspora origin who had settled permanently in Jerusalem played a formative role in Jewish society at the end of the Second Temple era. Among them were the Boethos and Phiabi families, who, as noted previously, came from Egypt, and the families of Hillel and Bnei Bathyra, who had their origin in the Babylonian diaspora. Hanamel, the first High Priest under Herod, also was a Babylonian, and some of the leading *ḥakhamim* (Nahum the Median, for instance) were of Diaspora origin. Jews from the Diaspora sometimes played a leading role in religious disturbances, as did the Egyptian prophet of Felix's days (see page 259). The establishment and rise of hellenistic Jews in Palestine resulted in the spread of Greek knowledge in Judea and the development of a Jewish-hellenistic way of life. One circumstance that accompanied their rise was the increase in the number of Jews possessing Roman citizenship. Occasionally, sons of respected Jewish families in the Diaspora married into the Judean upper class. One of the leading Jews of Cyprus married a woman of the Herodian family, and two of Agrippa I's daughters were married to notables in Alexandria.

Diaspora Jewry's main material support for Jewish Palestine was the half-shekel payment. From the time of the Hasmoneans on, we have evidence of the participation of Diaspora Jewry in the maintenance of the Temple. Augustus explicitly confirmed the right of Jews in different parts of the empire to send the Temple tribute to Jerusalem without hindrance. His intervention took place after the Greek citizens of several cities had tried to prevent the Jews from transferring these moneys to Judea. The arrangement became permanent, and there were hardly any attempts to interfere with it. Contributions came not only from Jews but also from proselytes and sympathizers. The oriental Jews under Parthian rule did not lag behind their brethren in the Roman Empire in this respect. The Jews of Babylonia, we are told, used to send all the half-shekel contributions to Nisibis, and the caravan that took them to Jerusalem was escorted by masses of Jews, for fear of robbers.

The contributions of Diaspora Jewry were by no means confined to the half shekel; many gave large additional donations. Particularly outstanding were the gifts of the rich Jews of Alexandria, who greatly enhanced the external splendour of the Temple. During the restoration of the Temple under Herod and later under the Roman governors, individual Jews from the Diaspora were given an opportunity to build certain parts of the Temple, such as gates and doors: Nicanor's gate is frequently mentioned in Talmudic literature. Another instance of the generosity of the Alexandrian Jews was the plating of the Temple doors in gold by Alexander, the brother of Philo. Sometimes the Temple invoked the aid of Alexandrian Jews also for other purposes. On one occasion an attempt was made to import tradesmen from Egypt in order to break the monopoly held by certain families (Garmo and Abtinas) that had specialized in preparing the shewbread and the incense. In effect, the religious and social ties between the Jews of Palestine and those of the Diaspora served to establish closer economic relations.

Economic and Socio-economic Stratification

The economic development of Palestine at the end of the Second Temple era was first and foremost a result of the protracted peace that reigned in the Roman Empire during the Julio-Claudian age. Peace encouraged economic progress in the Mediterranean world and provided opportunities for closer contact between its different parts. Nevertheless, Palestine was in some respects an exception to the rule, for during a considerable part of this period it was involved in disturbances and clashes between the Roman authorities and the Jews and between its Jewish and non-Jewish populations. The unrest disturbed economic life and interfered considerably with the course of commerce. Palestine shared in the benefits that peace brought to international trade, though the main beneficiaries were the coastal towns and some of the towns in Trans-Jordan. The fact that many Diaspora Jews made their fortunes during this period of peace also had an indirect effect on the situation of the Palestinian Jews.

The economy of Palestine continued to be based on agriculture, as it had been throughout antiquity. In a famous passage (*Contra Apionem* 1.60), Josephus wrote: 'Ours is not a maritime country; neither commerce nor the intercourse which it promotes with the outside world has any attraction for us. Our cities are built inland, remote from the sea, and we devote ourselves to the cultivation of the productive country with which we are blessed' (tr. H. St. John Thackeray, Loeb ed.). Though this is a one-sided and exaggerated statement, it is basically true, for the large majority of the Jews in Palestine was engaged in various forms of agriculture. This respect for work on the land is expressed also in the literature of the Second Temple era: 'Bow down your back unto husbandry, and toil in labours in all manner of husbandry, offering gifts to the Lord with thanksgiving'; 'And leaving husbandry they will follow after their own wicked devices, and they shall be dispersed among the Gentiles and shall serve their enemies' (*Testaments of the Twelve Tribes, Testament of Issachar* 5.3 and 6.2, tr. R. H. Charles).

The general picture of the country at the end of the Second Temple era as portrayed by Josephus (*Bellum Judaicum* 3.42ff.) is that of a prosperous agricultural country that provided an honest living for its inhabitants. Galilee, according to his description, was a fertile land with pastures, various types of trees and crops so rich that even the most indolent people were tempted to devote themselves to agriculture. The entire land was under cultivation, hence the large population of Galilee. Though the area of Galilee was smaller than that of Jewish Trans-Jordan (the Peraea), it was richer and more populous, for the soil was fertile, while the Peraea consisted mainly of uncultivated hilly ridges and was not suitable for fruit trees. Yet the Peraea also possessed fertile parts. In the valleys there was a large variety of fruit trees, with olives, date-palms and vines in particular being cultivated. The streams descending from the mountains saturated the soil, and the springs gave water throughout the year, even in the heat of summer, when most springs are dry. Josephus expanded particularly on the fertility of the Valley of Gennesar,

> a region whose natural properties and beauty are very remarkable. There is not a plant which its fertile soil refuses to produce, and its cultivators in fact grow every species; the air is so well tempered that it suits the most opposite varieties. The walnut, a tree that delights in the most wintry climate, here grows luxuriantly, beside palm-trees which thrive on heat, and figs and olives which require a milder atmosphere. One might say that nature had taken pride in thus assembling, by a tour de force, the most discordant species in a single spot, and that by a happy rivalry, each of the seasons wished to claim this region for her own (*Bellum Judaicum* 3.516f., tr. H. St. John Thackeray).

Speaking of Samaria, Josephus said that it did not differ in nature from Judea, for

> both regions consist of hills and plains, yield a light and fertile soil for agriculture, are well wooded, and abound in fruits, both wild and cultivated; both owe their productiveness to the entire absence of dry deserts and to a rainfall for the most part abundant. All the running water has a singularly sweet taste, and owing to the abundance of excellent grass, the cattle yield more milk than in other districts. But the surest testimony to the virtues and thriving condition of the two countries is that both have a dense population (*Bellum Judaicum* 3.49f., tr. H. St. John Thackeray).

A special place in his description of the country is given to the Valley of Jericho (*Bellum Judaicum* 4.467ff.), with its pleasant, densely planted orchards and its dates known by different names and possessing different tastes. Most precious of all was its balsam, 'and it would be no misnomer to describe as "divine" the spot in which the rarest and choicest plants are produced in abundance.'

The three main crops, as in earlier times, were grain, wine and olives. In normal years the country supplied sufficient grain to meet its own needs and even to export some from Galilee to Tyre and Sidon; but when there was a drought grain had to be imported from abroad. Thus we are told that when Queen Helena of Adiabene came to Jerusalem it was a year of hunger and she sent messengers to Alexandria to buy grain and to Cyprus to get a shipload of dry figs.

From Josephus' general description we gain the impression that he valued orchards above plough-land, a preference that we later find among the Tannaites. Among the tree crops, olives ranked first. They grew in most of the areas inhabited by Jews. Judea was rich in olive groves, which supplied the oil required for the Temple; but the richest olive country was Galilee. The Peraea also produced many olives, and the oil of Regev was particularly famous. Olive oil was an export commodity, as it had been even in hellenistic times. After the olive next in importance were figs, dates and vines. Figs, fresh or dry, played a large part in the Palestinian diet. The dates of Judea and particularly of Jericho were famous throughout the world and became, to some extent, a symbol of Judea. Balsam occupied a prominent place because of the reputed medical properties of its juice.

A large part of the land of Palestine was owned by the farmers themselves, who, together with their entire household, cultivated it by the sweat of their brow. On the other hand, we have records of large landholdings owned by the government or by landlords. We read of large quantities of grain being delivered to Beth-shearim from the surrounding villages, which belonged to Queen Berenice. Beth-shearim was the centre of a private estate that Berenice had inherited from her Hasmonean and Herodian ancestors; the old royal estates in the western Jezreel Valley for the most part remained the property of the last members of the house of Herod, while their other lands were taken over directly by the Roman authorities. There were also wealthy Jewish landlords who did not belong to the royal family and who usually leased their lands to tenant farmers.

Next to agriculture in economic importance among the Jews of Palestine were animal husbandry and fishing: 'In the summer I caught fish, and in the winter I grazed the flocks with my brethren' (*Testaments of the Twelve Patriarchs, Testament of Zebulun* 6.8). The Jewish fishermen of the Sea of Galilee sometimes worked on a cooperative basis. After farming and fishing, trades and crafts became important in this era. Ben Sira still regarded the artisan with a certain contempt, but by the end of the Second Temple era we hear of leading *hakhamim* in Jerusalem who engaged in one or another of the crafts. The tradesmen included master goldsmiths, perfumers, weavers, blacksmiths and potters. Many Jerusalemites were hired labourers engaged in a wide range of building crafts that were in great demand under Herod and after him. Some of them were employed on the restoration of the Temple, which was begun under Herod and completed only a few years before its destruction. Tradesmen directly connected with the Temple cult sometimes established a monopoly in their trade and demanded high wages for their labours. The crafts clearly played an important role in the life of Jerusalem. Craftsmen were organized in guilds, and their workshops were concentrated by trade in special parts of the city.

The Jews of Palestine had also begun to engage increasingly in commerce. Jerusalem's special position as the centre of Jewish life encouraged its development also as a commercial centre. Many Jewish merchants were to be found also in the coastal cities. We hear of many rich Jews who lived in Palestine at the end of the Second Temple era. Among them were members of the Herodian family and of the priestly oligarchy. The High Priest Hananiah ben Nedebai was exceptionally wealthy, and the Talmud (Babylonian Talmud, *Gittin* 56a) has preserved a tradition of three rich men of Jerusalem, Nicodemus ben Gorion, Ben-Kalba Savua and Ben-Ẓiẓit Hakkesset who among them were able to supply Jerusalem with all that was needed to withstand a siege for years. We also know of many Jewish communities famous for their prosperity; for example, the Jews of Caesarea were richer than the non-Jewish population of the city. Living close to the best of the country's harbours, they engaged in overseas trade as well as in customs farming; one of their leaders was known as Johanan the publican. Sometimes the sources mention in passing that certain villages, especially in the north of the country, were particularly prosperous: the houses of the village of Cabul were a source of admiration; they were as good as the houses of Tyre, Sidon or Beirut (*Bellum Judaicum* 2.504).

On the other hand, we hear of a great deal of abject poverty among the masses, large numbers of insolvent debtors and many workmen who remained unemployed when the restoration of the Temple was completed and who sometimes were employed on other public works, such as paving the streets of Jerusalem. The roads between Jerusalem and other parts of the country were no longer safe – not only the road from Galilee to Samaria and Judea but even the road from Jerusalem to Jericho. The causes of the insecurity were the general dissatisfaction of the people and the harsh economic conditions; and the lack of security resulted, in turn, in further economic deterioration. The farmers suffered under the heavy taxes, and the arbitrary conduct of harsh governors such as Florus added to the general depression. Tenant farmers had to surrender a considerable portion of their crops to the landlord; many farm hands were mere seasonal labourers; and even rank-and-file priests, who often depended on the tithe for their livelihood, sometimes fell into desperate straits, for the tithes were often seized by the oligarchs of the great priestly houses. Landless farmers, refugees from various places and unemployed temporary labourers constituted the reserves from which the increasingly frequent riots and rebellions drew their manpower.

The Sects

The main religious trends of Hasmonean times had continued in their viability and their influence on the Jewish community. The Sadducees remained faithful to their ideas and religious concepts; in social terms they represented a restricted circle among the upper class. The new priestly oligarchy that had developed under Herod and the Roman governors was essentially Sadducean; the appellatives 'Boethusian' and 'Sadducee' were almost synonymous. Some allusions to the Sadducees' social thinking have been preserved: they took pride in their way of life and beliefs and mocked the abstinence of their adversaries. They are said to have 'used silver and gold plate all their lives; not because they were ostentatious, but on the basis of the Sadducee saying: "The Pharisees have the tradition of afflicting themselves in this world; yet in the world to come they will have nothing" ' (*Aboth Derabbi Nathan* 5, versio I, S. Schechter, ed., p. 26). Next to the house of Boethos, the High Priests of the house of Hanan were the most faithful spokesmen of the Sadducean persuasion. Because of the decisive influence of their Pharisaic opponents ('Their power among the masses was so great that their word was law even if they spoke against the king or against the High Priest' [Josephus, *Jewish Antiquities* 13.288]), the Sadducees had no choice, even while they held the highest offices, but to make many concessions to Pharisaic opinion. Only on rare occasions did they attempt to enforce their own views in various areas of public life and religious ceremonial. Particularly daring in this respect was the High Priest Hanan ben Hanan, who in the year 62 established a Sanhedrin that judged capital cases with all the stringency of Sadducean doctrine. Here and there, as in the following passage, Talmudic literature has preserved something of the conflict between the Sadducees and the

Pharisees over points of Temple ceremonial:

> And why do they require an oath of him? Because of the Boethusians, who said: let him cense from outside and let him enter from inside. We are told of one who did so, and when he came out, someone said to his father: 'Though ye have taught this all your lives, ye have never done so until this man came and did it.' The other replied: 'Though we have taught so all our lives, we have done as the ḥakhamim willed and I wonder whether this man will live long.' It is said that there were no easy days until he died; and some said that worms came out of his nose (Jerusalem Talmud, *Yoma* I 39a).

The whole Second Temple period was dominated by the leadership of the Pharisees. We have no way of knowing how many Pharisees there were at the end of the era; all that can be said is that the number of Pharisees in Herod's time who refused to swear an oath of loyalty to the crown was more than 6,000. But these were only the solid core of the faction; its sympathizers were far more numerous. As a matter of course, the Pharisees were led by the most famous *ḥakhamim* of the time. In the Sanhedrin itself the Pharisees were represented by a united faction of Torah authorities whose influence on Sanhedrin decisions was enormous. The Pharisaic camp also included many priests, some of whom were from respected families, such as the historian Josephus.

The very fact that Pharisaism had become the leading doctrine in the Jewish community at large created rifts in matters of national importance. Where religion was concerned all the Pharisaic groups stood on common ground, the differences arose over political issues and, above all, over relations with the Roman authorities. In fact, it was the Pharisees who produced the extremist freedom movement (see page 274), although the majority remained faithful to the house of Hillel, whose representatives were acknowledged by the entire nation as the leaders of the Pharisees and whose attitude towards Rome was much more moderate than that of the Zealots.

The Essenes, whose beginnings also go back to Hasmonean times, likewise still existed at this time and were active at the end of the Second Temple era. The description of them by Philo of Alexandria (located in a fragment preserved by Eusebius, *Evangelical Preparation* 8.11) tells us that they lived in the towns and villages of Judea and owned no private property. Some of them engaged in agriculture and were remarkably skilful at sowing and planting, while some were herdsmen or bee-keepers. Others preferred the crafts, but they would hand over their wages to the treasurer whom they had chosen among themselves, and he would buy what was required for their common needs. According to Philo, the Essenes were celibate.

Elsewhere (in *Every Good Man Is Free* 75ff.), Philo had much the same to say; he added that the Essenes numbered more than 4,000 and that they sacrificed no living creatures. Philo also reported that some of the Essenes engaged in agriculture and others in the crafts, but that they hoarded neither silver nor gold; of all men they alone were by their own choice without riches, nor did they engage in the manufacture of weapons, and they rejected commerce in all its forms. There were no slaves among them, and none of them possessed a house of his own. Not only did they live together and organize themselves in communities, but their homes were open to men of similar views. Their treasury, expenses, clothing and meals were all communal. They cared for the sick and aged and supplied all their needs.

A detailed description of the Essenes is provided also by Josephus (*Bellum Judaicum* 2.119ff.). He too stresses their completely communal life. The priests, he says, had a special place in their prayers and in the blessings offered at their communal meals. The rejection of marriage, according to his report, was due not to objections in principle to married life but to their views about the basic corruption of woman. He adds, however, that in addition to the common Essenes there was another type who married in order to propagate the human race. In matters of theology, Josephus stresses that the Essenes believed in predestination (*Jewish Antiquities* 18.18).

Neither Philo nor Josephus related the Essenes in any way to the Dead Sea. This connexion occurs only in non-Jewish writings and is, in fact, the main addition to our knowledge of the Essenes contributed by Pliny (*Naturalis Historia* V, 17.73; a Greek author, Dio Chrysostomus, also mentions the connexion between the Essenes and the Dead Sea). In view of what Josephus and Philo relate, it would be wrong to conclude from Pliny that the only permanent settlements of the Essenes were near the Dead Sea. One of their largest and most important settlements was located there, but they lived elsewhere as well. In Jerusalem, for example, we know of an 'Essenes' Gate'. The specific character of the Essenes and the atmosphere of holiness that surrounded them gave them an important place in the Jewish community. Josephus placed them on an equal footing with the Pharisees and Sadducees. Their numbers were also not inconsiderable. Philo, we have seen, praised their pacifism highly. Nevertheless, we find that some of them fought in the Great Revolt, and one of them, John the Essene, was made commandant of the toparchy of Timnah. Apparently, they too were swept along by the wave of national enthusiasm, which is why the Romans treated them harshly during the war.

The great discoveries made at Khirbet Qumran from 1947 onwards have revealed the regulations, way of life and literature of a sect that dwelt in the Judean Desert. For weighty reasons most of the scholars engaged in the study of the Qumran scrolls tend to identify this sect with the Essenes; and they seem to be right. The religious views and social structure of the sect are remarkably similar to those of the Essenes as we know of them from other literary sources, and the archaeological evidence also supports the identification. In addition to the Qumran scrolls, we have the 'Covenant of Damascus', which was discovered much earlier and reflects one of the trends and stages in the development of the sect.

At the very beginning of one of the Qumran scrolls, a document known as the Rule Scroll, which records the main rules, tenets, organizational structure and aspirations of the sect, we are told that the members of the sect propose

> to do what is good and just in His eyes, as He has commanded us through Moses and through all his servants the Prophets, to love all that He has chosen and to hate all that He has despised, and to keep far from all evil and cleave to all that is right . . . and to love all the sons of light, each according to his destiny, as God

has counselled, and to hate all the sons of darkness, each according to his sin as God in his vengeance wills. And all the truly munificent shall contribute all they know and can and have to [the community of goods of all the members of the sect] . . . and neither advance nor postpone their set times [a reference to the special calendar of the sect, which did not accept the lunar year commonly observed by the Jews] nor depart from the laws of His truth to the right or left (Licht, ed., part I, chapter 1, pp. 59ff.).

The sect's belief in predestination is apparent further on in the scroll:

From the God of knowledge all have come into existence, and before they existed, He prepared all their thoughts, and when they were brought into existence as designed by the thought of His honour they shall fulfil their function, which is unchangeable. In His hand is the judgement of all, and He supplies all their wants (*ibid.*, pp. 90ff.).

The Zealots

One of the most important developments in the life of Jewish Palestine at the end of the Second Temple era was the emergence of sects that agreed with the religious viewpoint of Pharisaic Judaism but were more extreme than most of the Pharisees in fighting for political freedom and liberation from Roman rule. It is usual to designate all these sects by the common name Zealots, although the term referred at one point only to one trend in the activist liberation movement.

Josephus connects the beginnings of the extremist movement with the census held under the supervision of Quirinius, the legate of Syria, soon after Judea had been converted into a Roman province (6 CE). As founders of the movement, he mentions Judah of Gamala in Gaulanitis and Zadok the Pharisee (*Jewish Antiquities* 18.4). He also names the movement as a fourth Jewish sect, after the Pharisees, Sadducees and Essenes. Following his usual habit of explaining matters in terms comprehensible to the non-Jew, he refers to the movement as a 'philosophy'. According to him, Judah of Gamala was a Pharisee with his own system of thought: his 'philosophy' was in every respect the same as that of the Pharisees, but his followers had a boundless love of liberty; God alone was their lord and master, and they were ready to suffer any kind of unnatural death, along with their entire family, rather than acknowledge a mortal as their master. Thus the characteristic feature of the movement was that it raised freedom to the rank of a religious tenet of the first order and regarded submission to the rule of the Roman emperor as one of the most serious sins, similar to sacrilege. As there could be no compromise in matters of idolatry, so there could be none regarding submission to Roman rule. The kingdom of God, in its literal sense, was to be brought nearer by purposive action against foreign rule, and God would help those who performed His will. The practical implications of this philosophy were that it served as a permanent incitement to revolt; it instilled in its believers a readiness to lay down one's life for the hallowed ideal and it led to a series of attempts to impose these views by whatever means, irrespective of realities, on those who were not prepared to go to war against Rome.

This movement, whose basic principle was freedom, was the product of a combination of various social elements. One of them drew its strength from certain circles in the north, in Gaulanitis and Galilee. Its first leader was Judah, the son of Hezekiah (the Gaulanite or the Galilean, who had fought Herod and had been executed at his orders). This element was joined by an explicitly Pharisaic group under a man named Zadok. We have no certain knowledge of the origins of Zadok the Pharisee or of his followers, but they seem to have belonged to the Jerusalem priesthood. As the freedom movement developed, it continued to consist of several trends that maintained their separate identities in matters of ideology and social ties. The Galileans remained loyal to the leadership of the family of Judah the Galilean. Thus we see that forty years after Judah's time his two sons, Jacob and Simon, were the central figures in an insurrection and subsequently were executed by Tiberius Alexander (46–8). The leading personality of the Galilean circles at the beginning of the Great Revolt was Menahem, who tried to assume the royal crown and was the object of messianic expectations. His rise was also connected with the outbreak of the social revolution in Jerusalem. Menahem was killed in a clash with Eleazar ben Hananiah, the leader of the Jerusalem rebels. The remnants of Menahem's band, among them Menahem's relative Eleazar ben Jair, escaped to Masada. We hear of no more action by Menahem's supporters in Jerusalem itself, but the men who fled to Masada were to have the honour of being the last defenders of Judean freedom. The ideas that had from the first inspired Judah's movement were restated in Eleazar ben Jair's famous Masada address: they included the principle of freedom and the acknowledgement of God's exclusive sovereignty.

As far as basic principles are concerned, there was not much to distinguish the men associated with Menahem and Eleazar ben Jair, whom Josephus refers to as 'Sicarii', from the Jerusalem activists, for whom he reserves the name of Zealots and who seem to have continued the tradition of Zadok the Pharisee; some of the latter, as we have seen, were priests, and their leaders also belonged to the priesthood. The main differences indicated by a comparison between the Sicarii and the Zealots were (1) the Jerusalem Zealots never attached themselves to one particular family and never proclaimed any of their leaders king; (2) the Sicarii had their original base in Galilee, while the Zealots were concentrated in Jerusalem; (3) the Galilean Sicarii were fighting for a social revolution, while the Jerusalem Zealots placed less stress on the social aspect, though they too attempted to eliminate the oligarchy that had come to dominate the High Priesthood and the Temple, and, when they were in control during the revolt, they abolished the exclusive claim of the great priestly families to the office of High Priest.

By far the most important leader of the Jerusalem Zealots was Eleazar ben Simon, who belonged to a priestly family. However, even during the height of his power he was not the sole leader of his party, and we learn of a Zachariah ben Abculus, also a priest, who was associated with him. It seems that some of their other leaders also were prominent members of Jerusalem society. Ideologically related to the leaders of the Jerusalem Zealots was John ben Levi of Giscala in Galilee. John never claimed the royal crown and was not regarded as the Messiah by his followers. At the beginning of the revolt, he even belonged to the moderate party, but the events of the war changed his outlook. After the conquest of Galilee by the Romans, he escaped to Jerusalem, where he played an important role. Gradually, he came to think in more extremist terms, and after he had gained control of the Temple Mount even the Zealots to some extent regarded him as their leader, though they always insisted on maintaining their separate identity.

Completely different from John of Giscala in character and social connexions was his main rival in the final stages of the Great Revolt, Simon bar Giora, a Trans-Jordanian who had no contacts with upper-class circles in Jewish Palestine. Simon remained primarily the leader of the lower classes throughout the country. Unlike John of Giscala and the leaders of the Jerusalem priests, who never assumed a royal title, Simon seems to have been paid royal honours by his followers, at least at a certain stage in his career. What distinguished him in particular was his attitude towards the various classes of Jewish society: he freed the slaves and caused great harm to the wealthy, both in life and in property.

In many respects Simon bar Giora brings to mind the Jewish leaders who emerged in Palestine after the death of Herod (4 BCE). One of them, also named Simon and a former slave of the late king, operated in Jewish Trans-Jordan and proclaimed himself king. We have similar reports of another rebel leader of the same period, a shepherd named Athronges, who was assisted by his four brothers. He also assumed the royal crown. Athronges' career was remarkable in that he did not refrain from harming Jews if it were to his advantage. The common denominator of both these earlier movements was that their originators came from the lower classes, apparently primarily motivated by social discontent. The atmosphere in Judea was saturated with messianic expectations and this no doubt made it possible for certain social groups, mainly of the lower class, to create messianic kings, the last of whom was Simon bar Giora. The royal style of Menahem of Galilee formed part of the same phenomenon, but, unlike Simon, Menahem came from a family that had produced heroes for several generations. Simon never belonged to Menahem's Sicarii, though some of them probably joined him in the course of time. This would explain the total absence of the Sicarii as an organized group during the siege of Jerusalem and the large number of Simon bar Giora's men in comparison with the other groups that operated in the city.

17

The Jewish Diaspora in the Second Temple Era

One of the most prominent aspects of the history of the Jewish nation in the hellenistic-Roman era was the existence of a large Diaspora, which was partly a residue from the Persian era and partly an outgrowth of the period of Greek rule, when new Jewish communities developed as offshoots of those already existing. A number of factors contributed to the geographical and numerical expansion of the Jewish Diaspora: expulsion, political and religious oppression in Judea, attractive economic prospects in prosperous countries, such as Egypt in the third century BCE, and a proselytizing movement whose roots reached back to the beginnings of the Second Temple era and which reached its peak in the first century CE. In the times of Augustus, the Greek historian and geographer Strabo (quoted in Josephus, *Jewish Antiquities* 14.115) could write that in the entire inhabited world there was hardly a place where the power of the Jews had not made itself felt.

The greater part of the Jewish Diaspora lived under the sway of hellenistic-Roman civilization, and its development was determined by those political, social and economic events that moulded the Mediterranean world as a whole during the period of the hellenistic 'balance of power' and later under the centralistic government of imperial Rome. Only one large Jewish centre – Babylonia and the other parts of the Parthian Kingdom – lived during practically the entire period outside the hellenistic and Roman sphere of influence and developed its own patterns of life, which in due course were to influence the entire nation. Particularly numerous were the Jews in the two countries adjoining Palestine, Egypt and Syria (including Phoenicia). The Jewish community in Egypt had already played an important role under Persian rule, and the fact that at the beginning of the hellenistic era Egypt and Palestine were parts of the same kingdom stimulated Jewish migration to the Nile Valley. Jews were to be found in every town and village in Egypt, from Alexandria, the capital, in the north to Syene in the south. Philo, the Alexandrian Jewish philosopher, claimed (*Contra Flaccum* 43) that the Jewish community in Egypt numbered one million. Alexandria was one of the greatest Jewish centres in the world. It had a Jewish quarter from the very beginning of Jewish settlement there, and in the course of time the Jews predominated in two out of the city's five quarters.

The Jewish community in Cyrenaica is to be regarded as a direct offshoot of the

Egyptian community since, most of the time, the two lived under the same government. The Jews were numerous in the large cities of Cyrenaica, such as Cyrene and Berenice, as well as in the rural areas. Syria is mentioned by Josephus (*Bellum Judaicum* 7.43) as a land with a particularly large Jewish population, which is understandable if one considers the geographical propinquity of Syria and Palestine. Large Jewish concentrations existed in the capital Antioch, in Damascus and in Apamea. In Asia Minor, Jewish settlement was greatly encouraged by the policy of the Seleucid kings. We know of the existence of Jewish communities from the beginning of Roman rule, under the Julio-Claudian principate, in most of the important cities of Asia Minor – Ephesus, Pergamum, Miletus, Sardis and Phrygian Apamea. Asia Minor was also the home of, or at least a transit point for, Jews who settled on the northern shore of the Black Sea. No less numerous were the Jews on the islands of the eastern Mediterranean. Here the oldest Jewish colony was no doubt the one on Cyprus, as it is so close to Palestine. But there were also many Jews on Crete, Delos, Melos and other islands.

Greece itself, which during the late hellenistic and Roman era was losing its economic strength and diminishing in population, attracted fewer Jewish settlers than did Egypt or Asia Minor. Nevertheless, there were Jews in most of the larger cities of Greece and Macedonia (Athens, Delphi, Corinth and Thessalonica). The first record testifying to a Jewish presence in Greece is an inscription from the third century BCE at Oropus on the border of Boeotia, that refers to a Jewish slave. By Philo's time Jews had already settled in most of the main districts of Greece (*Legatio ad Gaium* 281).

The Jews of Italy and particularly of Rome, which gradually became the political capital of the entire Mediterranean world, fell into a different category. Jews began arriving in Rome in the second century BCE, and by the time of Pompey's conquest of Jerusalem their numbers had increased considerably. Jewish captives taken by Pompey and his successors accelerated the growth of Rome's Jewish community. Julius Caesar did much to consolidate its position, and under Augustus and his successors the Jews numbered in tens of thousands and had synagogues in several quarters of the city. Their activities are reflected in the writings of the major Augustan poets, such as Horace and Ovid. Police action under Tiberius and Claudius did little to restrain the growth of the Jewish community in the capital, where it had become a permanent feature of Roman life. Certain quarters were particularly noted for their Jewish concentrations. Gradually, Jewish communities developed in other Italian towns also, mainly in the south, and they even spread to the western provinces of Gaul and Spain. Of great importance was the Jewish community in the Roman province of Africa.

A further category was the Jewish diaspora in the Parthian Kingdom, namely, Babylonian Jewry and its offshoots in Persia, Media, Elam and the adjoining countries. It was not only an ancient but also a very large part of Jewry. The Jewish population in Babylonia itself was particularly large. A considerable Jewish community existed also in Seleucia on the Tigris. The Jewish population in the East gained additional importance by the conversion of the kings of Adiabene in the first century CE.

The Economic Structure

The economic activities of the Jews in the different countries of the Diaspora were highly varied. They were in no way confined to certain occupations, as was to be the case among the Jews of Central Europe during the Middle Ages (see Part V).

Agriculture in all its forms was one of the main Jewish occupations in the Diaspora as well. Papyri discovered in Egypt give us an insight to the important role played by the Jews in the country's agriculture. In Ptolemaic Egypt we find Jews among the 'royal farmers', the military colonists, the vine-dressers, and the shepherds. They played a prominent role also in the civil service, the police and tax-collection. The same variety was characteristic of Jewish life in Egypt under the Romans. In Roman Alexandria there were leading Jewish capitalists, merchants and ship-owners who occupied an important place in the economic life of Egypt and of the Mediterranean in general. But no less marked was the Jewish presence among the artisans and the lower classes. An interesting note in Talmudic literature about the Great Synagogue of Alexandria shows the importance of the artisans within the Jewish community of the city: 'Moreover, they were not seated together, but the goldsmiths sat separately, the silversmiths sat separately, as did the blacksmiths, the metal workers, and the weavers' (Babylonian Talmud, *Succa* 51b, Tosefta Succa 4.6). Similar evidence on the variety of Jewish occupations is provided by references dealing with countries other than Egypt. It may be worth noting that in Rome itself the target of anti-Jewish satire was the poor Jews rather than the rich.

The Political and Legal Status of the Jews

Until the hellenistic kingdoms became part of the Roman Empire, the political condition of the Diaspora Jews differed according to the country in which they lived. However, we can discern some common traits in the attitudes of the various gentile governments towards the Jews. Generally, the hellenistic kings treated the Jewish religion with tolerance. The Jews enjoyed the right to associate in communities and organizations of their own, and they were permitted to maintain relations with the national and religious centre in Jerusalem, as was outwardly reflected in the annual contribution of the half shekel to the Temple (see page 267). Where the Jews were numerous, they played a part in political life as well.

The country about which we know a great deal concerning the relations between the hellenistic government and the Jews is Egypt. The greatest of the Ptolemaic kings in the third century BCE, Ptolemy II Philadelphos (285–246), was friendly in his treatment of the Jews under his rule. He freed the Jewish slaves who had been captured in Judea under his father's rule, and Jewish tradition even claimed that the translation of the Bible known as the Septuagint was undertaken on his orders. Under Ptolemy Philopator (222–204) relations between the Ptolemaic government and the Jews seem to have deteriorated somewhat, partly as a result of the situation in Palestine and partly because of the king's religious policy in Alexandria itself; but the dispute was of a passing nature. The political influence of the Egyptian Jews reached its peak in the second century BCE. Perhaps the most pro-Jewish of the Ptolemies was Ptolemy VI Philometor (180–145), whose rule also witnessed a marked increase of migration to Egypt, due to the persecution under Antiochus Epiphanes. The Jewish philosopher Aristobulus lived at the court of Ptolemy Philometor, and we find officers of Jewish descent among his prominent generals. Onias IV, the son of Onias III (the High Priest in Jerusalem), was granted permission to build a Jewish temple on Egyptian soil (the 'Temple of Onias'). The Jewish military colonists in north-eastern Egypt were subject to the rule of Onias and his descendants and were an influential military force in the Egyptian kingdom. After the death of Ptolemy Philometor, this Jewish army came to the aid of the queen dowager Cleopatra II against her rivals for the throne. In the days of Alexander Jannai, the sons of Onias IV, Hananiah and Hilkiah, gave considerable military and political assistance to the Hasmonean Kingdom.

When Rome gained control of the Mediterranean world, the majority of the Jewish nation came under the control of a single power, and the Roman state felt obliged to establish an official policy with respect to the Jews. This policy was founded on the assumption that the Jewish religion should be treated with complete tolerance. It had always been Rome's principle not to interfere with the various religions within the empire. For the most part, Roman policy was conservative and tended to preserve the status quo in the countries that became part of the empire, and the Jewish populations of the Hellenistic kingdoms were enjoying religious tolerance at the time of their incorporation into the empire. Moreover, the important part played by the Jews in the life and economy of the empire and the large proportion of Jews among the population of its eastern sections made tolerance of their religion highly advisable. The different parts of the Jewish nation were closely united, and any serious interference with the religious freedom of one of the major Jewish centres produced repercussions in others. The relations between the authorities in Rome and the royal houses of Judea – first the Hasmonean and then the Herodian – were always close. Above all, the rank and file of the Jewish people were unswervingly dedicated to their faith and were ready to sacrifice their lives in its cause. Thus the abolition of religious tolerance would have forced the Roman authorities to resort to systematic persecution, which would only too easily have resulted in a dangerous Jewish revolt.

The tolerance shown to the Jews by the Roman emperors was evident in a number of ways. The Jews were granted the right to maintain their own organizations and an autonomous administration and judiciary; and they were exempted from compulsory participation in pagan rites and from duties that would have involved violating prohibitions of the Jewish religion. The right to abstain from pagan rites even included exemption from participation in the cult of the emperor, which in those days was the principal token of loyalty to the head of the Roman state and could be refused only at the risk of being charged with high treason.

The definition of Rome's Jewish policy was the work of Julius Caesar and Augustus, who issued a series of edicts in favour of the Jews. It was Caesar who explicitly excluded Jewish organizations from the general ban against associations in Rome. More particularly, however, it was Augustus who set the pattern followed by later emperors. Agrippa, Augustus' trusted adviser, defended the rights of the

Jews against the claims of the citizens in the Greek towns of Asia Minor, and Augustus himself established the general rule that the Jews were entitled to send money to the Temple in Jerusalem and that any interference with these contributions was to be treated as sacrilege. The subsequent emperors of the Julio-Claudian dynasty followed in Augustus' footsteps, with the sole exception of Gaius Caligula, under whose brief rule (37–41 CE) the general policy suffered some serious changes. Caligula, whose madness made him believe in his own godhead, demanded that his Jewish subjects also should pay him divine honour (see page 254). His claim provided the enemies of the Jews in Alexandria with a pretext for staging a riot – the first 'pogrom' in Roman history. In the early days of Claudius' rule (41–54), there were again anti-Jewish riots in Alexandria; and among those who came to the aid of the Alexandrian Jews were Jews from Palestine. But order was restored and was not disturbed again, to any serious extent, until the Great Revolt.

The revolt had its repercussions in the large cities of the Diaspora. In Alexandria hostilities again broke out between the Greeks and the Jews, and the Roman garrison slaughtered many of the Jews. Anti-Jewish riots took place also in Damascus; in Antioch the non-Jewish citizenry attempted to deprive the Jews of their privileges but were prevented from doing so at the firm insistence of the Roman authorities.

As we have seen, the Jews enjoyed the right to maintain their own organizations in the cities and countries where they lived, and those organizations were recognized by the hellenistic and Roman authorities. The organizations were a means of fostering Jewish religion and preserving the existence of the Jewish nation in the Diaspora. From country to country the Jews designated their organizations by different names, but the differences were by no means only a matter of designation. In Alexandria, for instance, the Jews had possessed a uniform central organization since Ptolemaic times; their community was known by the name *politeuma* and was headed by elders. In the early days of Roman rule, the Alexandrian Jews were governed by an ethnarch, whose authority extended to the judiciary. Under Augustus there were apparently certain changes, and most of the powers of the ethnarch were taken over by a Council of Elders or Gerousia with scores of members. In Berenice in Cyrenaica also, the Jews were organized in a *politeuma,* which was headed by archons. In Rome the Jewish communities were centred around the different synagogues, and as far as is known there was no single organization that included all the Jews of the city. Central Jewish organizations on a national scale did not exist in the hellenistic-Roman world. To the extent that there was a central leadership of the Jews in the Roman Empire, it was based on the Jewish rulers and High Priests in Jerusalem and, after 70 CE, on the *nesi'im* in Jabneh and in Galilee.

While the Jewish centres in the hellenistic world lacked central organizations on a country-wide scale, Babylonian Jewry was marked by its strong organization led by a hereditary *Resh Galuta* or exilarch who claimed descent from the Davidic dynasty, was recognized by the Parthian kings and exercised extensive powers among the Jewish population of Babylonia.

The Jews of the Diaspora at all times maintained close bonds with the Land of Israel, and the Jews of Palestine drew encouragement from the large numbers and the devoted loyalty of their dispersed brethren.

18

Religion and Literature

The Rule of Monotheism

The outstanding characteristic of the Jewish religion during the Second Temple era was the exclusive predominance of its monotheistic belief in the same form that had developed in the preceding generations. After the extreme hellenists had failed in their deliberate attempt to create a synthesis of Judaism and the religious beliefs of the surrounding world, the rule of monotheism in Jewry was never again contested. Individuals, particularly among the upper classes in the Diaspora, might have occasionally abandoned their ancestral faith, and here and there in the Diaspora one might have found instances of religious syncretism; but these occurrences reflected not so much a desire on the part of the Jewish masses to adopt the ideas and customs of the surrounding world as the readiness of the gentile environment to absorb Jewish influences. Palestinian Jewry remained unswervingly faithful to the Jewish religion throughout the generations after the Hasmonean Revolt. Even the most extreme accusers did not include idolatry among the sins for which the generation of the destruction of the Temple was castigated. This does not mean that the development of the Jewish religion was not affected by the impact of the surrounding world on Jewish thought, customs or organizational patterns. But this influence never took the form of a conscious acceptance of foreign ideas; rather, it consisted of a largely unnoticed absorption of the general atmosphere that prevailed in the world of those days.

Jewish monotheistic concepts during the Second Temple era were markedly abstract in nature, a trend that increased as the channels closed between man and the world above. When prophecy ceased and the poetic voice of God's messengers was no longer heard, the Jew, impelled both by his own mentality and by the influence of his environment, began to rely increasingly on his intellect. As the image of the Divinity became more abstract, there was an increase in the belief in angels as the agencies that mediated between God and man. The disparity between the concept of a just Creator and the realities of the factual world contributed to the development of quasi-dualistic conceptions of the existence of God's kingdom on the one hand, and the rule of Satan on the other. These conceptions were never carried to their logical conclusions. Neither the belief in angels nor dualism was ever capable of shaking the foundations of monotheism.

The Rule of Torah and Halakhah *and the Hegemony of the Sages*

Next to monotheism the rule of the Torah, which encompassed all aspects of life, leaving nothing untouched, was one of the most outstanding characteristics of the development of Judaism in the latter part of the Second Temple era. On that point there were no differences between the major trends operating within the Jewish community. Such differences as existed related merely to the conception of what the Torah meant (the essence of dispute between the Pharisees and the Sadducees) and to its specific application in daily life. But there was no question that the Torah was always the sole foundation of Jewish life, the linchpin that held all parts of the nation together. The literature of the times is full of unqualified praise for the Torah:

> This is the book of the commandments of God and the law that endureth forever. All they that hold fast to it are appointed to life; but such as leave it shall die. Turn thee, O Jacob, and take hold of it; walk towards it, shining in the presence of its light. Give not thy glory to another, nor the things that are profitable unto thee to a foreign nation, O Israel, happy are we; for the things that are pleasing to God are made known to us (*Baruch* 4.1–5).

The rule of Torah in the Second Temple era cannot be comprehended without an understanding of the development of the *halakhah*. The *halakhah* – 'the path wherein Israel walks' – formed the main part of the oral tradition and encompassed all aspects of the Jew's personal and communal conduct. It included the order of ritual and prayer, tithes and offerings and other commandments 'dependent on the Land [*i.e.,* that can only be fulfilled in the Land of Israel]', laws of purity and impurity, of the Sabbath and festivals, of marital relations and personal status and civil and criminal law. The roots of the *halakhah* go back to far earlier times, but its main development began in the early hellenistic period and chiefly in the first century BCE. The *halakhah* grew in a number of ways. In part it was based on interpretation of the Bible, and eventually a quasi-logical system of rules was developed for deriving conclusions from the scriptural text. Other parts of the *halakhah* grew out of the legal customs and behaviour that had developed in the course of time, even if they were not backed explicitly by scriptural commandments. It was the oral tradition that, in effect, converted the Bible into the Torah – the doctrine that informed and reflected every aspect of the way of life and the aspirations of the Jewish nation.

By the end of the Second Temple era, the Torah had become part of the life of the entire people. Torah study began at an early age. Josephus (*Against Apion* 2.204) stresses the Jewish custom of teaching all children to read and instructing them on religious customs and the history of the forefathers. As a result, 'If anyone asks one of us about the Laws, he can recite them more readily than his own name' (*ibid.,* 2.178). From the time of Simeon ben Shetah onwards, we hear of public concern for education, and shortly before the destruction of the Temple the High Priest Joshua ben Gamla commanded that 'teachers of children shall be appointed in every district and in every town, and they shall be sent [to school] from the age of six or seven' (Babylonian Talmud, *Bava Batra* 21a).

The Torah was the domain of the *hakhamim* (see page 234, who developed, interpreted and promulgated it; they were the experts on law and *halakhah,* as well as being teachers and moralists. The most famous among them enjoyed enormous prestige: they were the unofficial leaders of the nation and were more influential than the official ones. The greatest of the *hakhamim* in the last generations before the destruction of the Temple was Hillel the Elder. Hillel had come from Babylonia to Palestine during Herod's reign and became the central figure in Jerusalem. He gained universal respect by his high ethical standards and was reputed to be pleasant spoken, peace-loving and accessible. Hillel was outstanding in his intellectual no less than in his moral stature. He was the leading authority in the development of *halakhah* in his days, and it was he who formulated the rules by which the oral tradition was derived from Scripture. One of his concerns was to adjust the economic laws of the Torah to the new reality of the times. Hillel had many disciples and founded the school known as the 'school of Hillel'. As leader of the Pharisees, he was succeeded by his descendants, who set their imprint on the development of the Jewish nation during the following four centuries.

Another school, which disagreed with the school of Hillel on certain controversial points of *halakhah,* was founded by the Pharisaic sage Shammai. In the consciousness of the people, Shammai has been portrayed as an excessively pedantic man, and his school was reputed to be far stricter in matters of *halakhah* than the school of Hillel.

The outstanding representatives of the school of Hillel in the final generations before the destruction were Rabban Gamaliel the Elder and his son Rabban Simon. Both lived and worked in Jerusalem and headed the Pharisaic faction in the Sanhedrin. Like Hillel, Gamaliel also instituted *halakhic* regulations on such subjects as personal status and the leap-year. Gamaliel also had many disciples and was respected by the entire nation. It was said that 'when Rabban Gamaliel the Elder died, the glory of the Law ceased' (Mishnah *Sota* 9:15). There is no doubt that the role played by Rabban Gamaliel in the life of the nation and his great prestige contributed significantly to the consolidation of the standing of the house of Hillel.

He was succeeded by his son Simon, who played an important role in the period immediately preceding the revolt and during the revolt itself. He was the supreme authority on *halakhah* for the Jews of the entire country and had the support of Rabban Johanan ben Zakkai. Rabban Simon ben Gamaliel maintained close relations with influential personalities in all parts of the country; one of his friends was Johanan of Gush Halav (John of Giscala – now Jish – in Upper Galilee). During the revolt he joined forces with the heads of the High Priest's faction, Hanan ben Hanan and Joshua ben Gamla, and was a member of the insurgents' temporary government. Next to him Rabban Johanan ben Zakkai was the most prominent personality within the school of Hillel in the last years before the destruction. He earned himself a name as a militant opponent of the Sadducean trend within the High Priest's faction.

The Synagogue

Of all the institutions developed by Judaism in the Second Temple era, the synagogue is perhaps the one that exercised the greatest influence on later generations. It has been rightly said that, in establishing the synagogue, Judaism created one of the greatest revolutions in the history of religion and society, for the synagogue was an entirely new environment for divine service, of a type unknown anywhere before, and it did not entail the ceremonial restrictions and financial sacrifices that were required for the maintenance of temples. Whether it originated in Palestine or in the Diaspora, the synagogue became the centre of religious and social life among the Jews. We know of several synagogues that existed in Palestine at the end of the Second Temple era: in Caesarea, in Dor, in Capernaum and in Tiberias; and we have records of the existence of synagogues in all the lands of the Diaspora. In Jerusalem the Jews from the various countries of the hellenistic diaspora maintained their own individual synagogues, which served as the centres of their social life; in Tiberias the synagogue was the focus of the city's public life. One of the most famous synagogues in the Diaspora was the Great Synagogue of Alexandria; and the Jews of Rome had a particularly large number of synagogues. In fact, there was no Jewish community in Palestine or in the Diaspora that did not have at least one synagogue. The synagogue was the instrument that kept Jewish tradition and the Jewish faith alive and that made them accessible to the rank and file of the Jewish people. Its functions extended to many areas: it was a house of Torah study and of prayer, but also a focus of social and cultural life. Not only was it always to remain the foremost institution of Judaism, but its pattern was adopted by the other monotheistic religions and became the prototype of the Christian church and the Islamic mosque.

Martyrdom

The faithfulness of the Jew to his religion reached its supreme expression in a willingness to sacrifice his life rather than transgress the commandments of the Torah. This readiness became an historical factor of the greatest importance – not least in that it determined the attitude of the Roman authorities towards Jewish believers (see page 280). From the days of Antiochus Epiphanes, martyrological tension was the hallmark of Judaism and of the other religions that it inspired. Though the term *kiddush ha-Shem* ('hallowing of the Name') was not yet current among the Jews of those times, the principle as such existed; and it was a characteristic that distinguished Judaism from all other religions of antiquity.

In certain circles martyrdom became connected with eschatological conceptions; the presence of martyrs was a sign that the End of Days was approaching, and the belief in the eschatological significance of the events served to justify the sacrifice. According to these beliefs, the kingdom of God draws its sustenance from the blood of the saints and their blood demands Israel's redemption:

> And in those days, the prayer of the righteous and the blood of the righteous shall have ascended from the earth before the Lord of Spirits. In those days, the

holy ones who dwell above in the heavens shall unite with one voice and supplicate, pray, praise, give thanks, and bless the name of the Lord of Spirits on behalf of the blood of the righteous which has been shed, that the prayer of the righteous shall not be in vain before the Lord of Spirits, that judgement may be done unto them, and that they may not suffer for ever. In those days, I saw the Ancient of Days when he was seated upon the throne of His glory, and the books of the living were opened before Him; and all his host in Heaven above and His counsellors stood before Him. And the hearts of the holy were filled with joy; because the number of the righteous had been offered, the prayer of the righteous had been heard and the blood of the righteous had been heard before the Lord of Spirits (*Ethiopic Book of Enoch* 47.1–4).

The Messianic Idea

It is quite impossible to understand the development of Judaism or to describe the development of political events in Judea at the end of the Second Temple era without considering the form that the messianic idea and the vision of the End of Days assumed in those times. Eschatological and messianic hopes had formed part of the heritage even of biblical prophecy. With the passing of time, the apocalypse was envisaged in many and varied forms. In Jewish eschatology at the end of the Second Temple era, national hopes mingled with a more universal vision. The End of Days was not only the time when Israel would be purified and its enemies punished but also the day when all men and all nations would be judged. Even in the physical sphere there would be a great change: this world would pass away and a new, wonderful one would arise in its place. Concurrent with the universalism there was also a development in the direction of individualism: the vision of the End of Days was not only an answer to the hope for national redemption but also to the sufferings of the individual. The fullest expression of this was a belief in the resurrection of the dead.

The one element that had perhaps the profoundest influence on beliefs concerning the End of Days was the prophecy of Daniel. In 'a time of trouble, such as never existed since there was first a nation even to that same time' (12:1), the seer prophesied the fall of the kingdoms of the world and the resurrection of the Kingdom of Israel, which would inherit their places. This conception was to remain an inseparable part of the Jewish eschatological vision, both in Israel and in the Diaspora, and it is reflected in Jewish-hellenistic literature as well as in the apocalyptic writings of Palestine.

The connexion is often stressed between the vision of the End of Days – a common expectation of the Second Temple era – and that of the royal Messiah of the house of David. Sometimes the anointed king is conceived mainly as a monarch of this world, as the national king of Israel; but at other times he is envisaged as supranational and transcendental, as in the *Ethiopic Book of Enoch*: 'For of old, the Son of Man was concealed, and the Supreme Being preserved him before his power and revealed him to the elect' (*Ethiopic Book of Enoch* 62.7). The messianic expectation also became an active factor in political life, and the entire period of the Roman governors was replete with revolts and insurrections informed by eschatological tension (as in the case of Theudas under Fadus or the Egyptian prophet under Felix). The messianic belief was a primary motive also at the time of the Great Revolt (see Chapter 19). Even the destruction could not weaken that belief. On the contrary, the most colourful descriptions of the End of Days have come down to us in the great works of the post-Temple visionaries: the Vision of IV *Ezra* and the Vision of Baruch.

Early Christianity

Among the messianic movements at the end of the Second Temple era was one that was to play a role of the greatest importance in the history of the entire human race: Christianity, whose origins are linked to the personality of Jesus of Nazareth. Like the other messianic beliefs, it developed out of the conviction that the End of Days was near; but, while the others disappeared after the death or failure of their originators, this particular movement gained in power after the crucifixion of its founder by the Roman governor Pilate.

Most of Jesus' Jewish followers in Palestine remained within the Jewish faith. Those of the first generation, such as Jesus' brother James, continued to observe the Jewish commandments, even though they differed from other Jews by believing in Jesus. But belief in Jesus and the propagation of his teachings soon spread beyond Palestine to Jews in the Greek diaspora (among them Saul, or Paul, of Tarsus in Cilicia), who in turn began preaching to Jews and gentiles in the cities of the eastern provinces of the Roman Empire (Syria, Asia Minor and Cyprus). It was the enthusiastic activity of these preachers of the new faith, in the context of the socio-political conditions and the religious atmosphere prevailing throughout the Mediterranean world in those times, that turned Christianity into a universal factor whose influence far exceeded the boundaries of the Jewish nation. In the course of this process, Christianity in its Pauline form gradually detached itself from Judaism and became a new religion, though the basic elements of the Jewish faith and the Jewish heritage remained recognizable even in Christianity's post-Pauline development. Paul himself had at one time been a pupil of Rabban Gamaliel the Elder in Jerusalem; and the foundations of Paul's doctrine, including the belief in election by God's grace, were strongly influenced by beliefs that were prevalent in Judaism and particularly among its esoteric offshoots (such as the Dead Sea sect).

From the theological viewpoint, however, Paul took the decisive step of making belief in Jesus and the atonement of mankind's sins through his sacrifice the main tenets of his ideology, attaching no value to the observance of Judaism's practical commandments. Thus he freed the pagan masses, whose hearts he won for Christianity, from the need to observe the commandments, and these new Christians, who appeared throughout the Mediterranean world as a result of the propaganda undertaken by Paul and his fellow believers, did not join the Jewish nation.

The Attraction of Judaism

Christianity would hardly have been able to spread so rapidly had the ground not been prepared by the propagation of Judaism's beliefs. In the Second Temple era, the Jewish faith expanded as it never had before and never has since. Throughout the Roman Empire and even beyond it, people adopted the Jewish faith or at least part of the Jewish way of life. Large sections of the Jewish nation made it their concern to convert the heathen to Jewish monotheism and took pride in the fact that Jewish customs were to be found everywhere:

> There is not one city, Greek or barbarian, nor a single nation where the custom of the seventh day, on which we rest from all work, and the fasts, and the lighting of candles, are not observed . . . and as God permeates the universe, so the Law has found its way into the hearts of all men. Let each observe his own country and his own household, and he will not disbelieve what I say . . . (*Against Apion* 2.282ff.).

The trend towards Judaism was to be found among different classes and nations, including the Romans. Explicit evidence of a systematic attempt to propagate the Jewish faith in the city of Rome is found as early as 139 BCE. With the increase of the Jewish population of Rome, the Jews intensified their efforts to make converts among the Romans. Although the activity of Jewish missionaries in Roman society caused Tiberius to expel them from the city in 19 CE, they soon returned, and Jewish religious propaganda was resumed and maintained even after the destruction of the Temple. Tacitus mentions it regretfully (*Histories* 5.5), and Juvenal, in his Fourteenth Satire (ll. 96ff.), describes how Roman families 'degenerated' into Judaism: the fathers permitted themselves to adopt some of its customs and the sons became Jews in every respect.

The spread of Judaism throughout the Mediterranean world was facilitated by many factors, one of which was the state of religion in the Roman Empire in general. The old Greek and Roman religions were in decline, and the situation was ripe for the introduction of new beliefs and rites imported from the East. The propagation of Judaism was further abetted by the political unity, security and close economic relations of the various areas that made up imperial Rome and which subsequently facilitated the transmission of new ideas to the different parts of the empire. Outstanding against this background was the strong attraction of Judaism as a religion that combined a belief in personal salvation with the grandeur of abstract ideas, chief among which was the belief in one God. Moreover, Judaism preached a way of life based on morality and mutual aid among fellow believers. It appealed to the emotions no less than did the mystic religions of the orient and to the intellect as much as did the philosophical systems, which addressed themselves only to a small *élite*. In addition, the Bible provided the apostles of Judaism with a literature unparalleled in any other religion.

The great cities of Syria were particularly full of Jewish converts. One of the great successes in the history of the proselytizing movement was the conversion of the royal house of Adiabene in Mesopotamia. King Izates not only adopted the Jewish faith but also sent his sons to Jerusalem so that they might gain a thorough knowledge of the Hebrew language and the Jewish religion. The members of the dynasty of Adiabene became a permanent factor in Jewish society, and some of them participated in the Great Revolt against Rome. Particularly noted for her activities in Jerusalem was Queen Helena, who established relations with the *hakhamim* of the city. The royal house of Adiabene built itself an impressive mausoleum near Jerusalem; it was famous in its time and is known to this day as the 'Graves of the Kings'.

The Hatred of Jews and the Apologists

There was, however, another side to the spread of the Jewish faith: an increasing hatred of the Jewish people and its religion among those who regarded it as a threat to the very existence of the social order that they held dear. This hostility is clearly reflected in the writings of the period, and the peak of the proselytizing movement was paralleled by an abundance of anti-Jewish sentiment in classical writings, mainly in the Greco-Egyptian literature composed in Alexandria and in the works that reflect life in the upper ranks of Roman society during the early period of the empire. Several authors accused Judaism of animosity towards the human race and claimed that it had contributed nothing to civilization. Others invented libels concerning Jewish origins and customs, together with a wide range of other accusations. The anti-Jewish trend culminated in the writings of the influential Greco-Egyptian author Apion (of the first century CE) and the famous Roman historian Tacitus (of the early second century CE).

But there were other voices in the literary world. Varro, the greatest Roman scholar at the end of the republican era, praised the Jewish method of serving God because it did not resort to statues and images. The great literary critic of the first century CE, the anonymous author of the famed treatise *On the Sublime* (pseudo-Longinus), went even further and quoted the Greek version of Genesis ('and there was light . . .') as an outstanding example of the sublime style, taking that opportunity to praise the Jewish lawgiver (Moses).

The Apocalypse

The various trends and currents within the nation found their expression in the wide spectrum of Jewish literary production in these times. Palestinian literature after the fifth century BCE marked the end of visionary prophecy and the beginning of the consolidation of the Scriptures. By the beginning of the hellenistic era, the Torah and the Prophets had already become part of the divine canon and were regarded as sacred books. In the course of time, the third section of the Bible, the Writings, also became an integral part of the canon. Biblical writing set its imprint on the entire literature of the Second Temple era, not only by way of its content but also because of its style, diction and literary forms.

There was a general awareness that the great days of prophetic inspiration belonged to the past. But one of the most serious problems that troubled the Jewish mind, as a result of the harsh times and the sufferings to which the nation was exposed, was the contrast between the glorious future envisaged for Israel and the sorrows of her actual condition – a contrast that intensified the urge to imagine an ideal world as a spiritual consolation. Thus prophetic vision was replaced by apocalyptic vision. The apocalypse seeks to reveal the mysteries of the world and the secrets of the times; the apocalyptic visionary claims to dwell in regions on high and attempts to uncover the hidden knowledge of creation and to interpret the history of man in terms of its foreordained end. He usually foresees not only universal political revolution but a cosmic upheaval that will change the entire order of the world. The ancient prophet in Israel was God's messenger who called man to repentance and to positive action. The apocalyptic visionary tended to be more deterministic; the contrast between good and bad was self-evident to him, and he fully expected the struggle to be decided by the cosmic revelation of divine justice.

Characteristic of the apocalypse is its pseudepigraphic nature: instead of acknowledging its author, the apocalyptic work ascribes itself as having been written by one of the famous personalities who lived and worked in the biblical past (*e.g.*, Enoch, Ezra, Baruch). The attempt to gain authority by pseudepigraphic attribution is not, however, confined to apocalyptic works; it occurs also in other writings of the period.

What are regarded as the classical apocalypse are the last chapters of Daniel, which were composed at the height of the persecution by Antiochus. Daniel's words were designed to be a source of encouragement at a time when the faithful Jew questioned the meaning of events and the future of the nation. The visions there present symbolic images of worldly powers that pass by one after the other until they surrender their place to the eternal kingdom of God, who shall reign over the heavens and the earth. It has been rightly noted that the Book of Daniel marked the declaration of war on idolatry on a world-wide scale and foreshadowed the major offensive of the Jewish idea, which in due time was to eradicate paganism throughout the world.

Extensive apocalyptic passages occur also in the *Ethiopic Book of Enoch,* with its wide-ranging contents and variety of themes: the Last Judgement; the story of the giants and the world of the angels; the image of the Son of Man, who is the transcendent Messiah; the world of the stars and the calendar; a symbolic survey of world history and of the contrast between Jew and gentile; calls to walk in the ways of justice and words of encouragement for the just in their uprightness; etc. The images and visions of the *Ethiopic Book of Enoch* had an enormous influence on later literature.

Another apocalypse, the *Assumption of Moses,* was written at the beginning of the first century CE and has reached us in a fragmentary version. This apocalypse culminates in a description of the kingdom of God, which will put an end to Satan. The advent of God's kingdom will be accompanied by natural upheavals, in the wake of which idolatry will disappear and an age of happiness for Israel will begin. Some of the most wonderful apocalypses (*e.g.,* IV *Ezra* and *Baruch*) were written only after the destruction of the Temple.

Wisdom Literature and the Story

Wisdom Literature, which had a long tradition in the literary past of Israel, was continued in the Second Temple era, its main representative being Ben Sira, who lived and worked in Jerusalem before the Hasmonean Revolt and whose work reflects Jerusalem society in those days. The authors of the classical wisdom book of the Bible, Proverbs, were anonymous; Ben Sira's writings, on the other hand, show us a distinct personality aware of his own importance and that of his position. Ben Sira's words of wisdom are full of poetic passages, hymns and paeans to the great leaders of the Israelite nation.

One of the most interesting genres of the literature of the Second Temple period is the novella or story. Two characteristic instances are *Tobit* and *Judith*. In style and artistic nature, these works are deeply rooted in biblical literature and show no sign of Greek literary influence. The plot of *Tobit* takes us to the Eastern diaspora and introduces the problem of the Jewish individual who places the duties of morality and religion above royal commands. The story is full of folkloristic elements, and the manner in which they are woven into the story reveals the hand of a master. The entire work provides a picture of Jewish family life in the Second Temple era.

The environment of *Judith* is purely Palestinian, and the social ambience that it reflects is that of a country town in Jewish Palestine. It is essentially an historical novella, and political events play a larger part there than in *Tobit*. Like Ruth and Esther, it has a heroine rather than a hero. Artistically, *Judith* is one of the most perfect works of ancient Jewish literature. The story is exciting and full of dramatic tension: a Jewish town, fighting for its existence against a stronger enemy, comes to life before our eyes.

Historiography

The eventful political developments of the times (such as the Hasmonean Revolt and the Great Revolt against Rome) resulted in a revival of political historiography. Some of the historians continued to follow the biblical pattern, while adapting themselves to the new spiritual climate; others imitated the example of the hellenistic historians. First mention among the former goes deservedly to the author of I Maccabees, which was written in Palestine, apparently at the end of the second century BCE, and describes the establishment of the Hasmonean state. The author, a native of the country, for the most part shares the viewpoint of the Hasmoneans. He gives proof of a thorough familiarity with all that concerns the geography of Palestine, and his presentation is clear and fluent. The entire book is written with deep sympathy for the Hasmonean dynasty, whose rise is its main theme. As an historical source for the Hasmonean Revolt, it is invaluable. The descriptive talent of the author, his fluent style, his ample documentation and the wealth of chronological data place him among the leading Jewish historians, and he is unequalled in his evocation of the spirit of a holy war that pervaded the Jewish camp during the fight against Antiochus.

Among those who adopted the ways of contemporary Greek historiography, we should mention two Palestinian historians: Joseph ben Mattathias (better known. by his Latin name, Flavius Josephus) and Justus of Tiberias. Both used the Greek language, and both belonged to the generation of the destruction of the Temple. Josephus owes his reputation as an historian to two major works: *The Jewish War* which appeared in the years 75–9 CE and describes the war of the Jews against the Romans, and *Jewish Antiquities*. Josephus seemed well qualified to become the historian of his time. Not only was he an eyewitness to the events, but he played an active role in them and was equally familiar with developments on both sides. But his advantages in obtaining material were countered by serious disadvantages in presenting that material to the reader. His objectivity and freedom of expression were prejudiced by the fact that the publication of the book was under the auspices of Titus and therefore directly connected with the imperial family; hence the book was written in praise of the Roman Empire in general and of the Flavian dynasty in particular. Furthermore, the author's political and military past in Palestine had involved him in hostile relations with many of the men and movements that had played an active part in the Great Revolt. Nevertheless, the main outlines of the war come through clearly. Josephus succeeded in writing a great work, even from the artistic viewpoint. It is pervaded by a tragic pathos commensurate with its subject and is written in a lucid, impressive style. Josephus' other historical work, *Jewish Antiquities,* relates the history of the Jewish nation from its beginnings until just before the Great Revolt. *Jewish Antiquities* is a source of primary importance on everything concerning the Hasmonean state from the days of John Hyrcanus, on Herod's reign and on the times of the Roman governors of Judea.

Of the historical work of Josephus' contemporary and rival, Justus of Tiberias, only a few fragments remain. We know that he was more deeply rooted in the Greek language and culture than was Josephus, and his historical writings also encompassed non-Jewish subjects.

The Literature of the Greek Diaspora

Side by side with the literature of Palestine, which was written mainly in Hebrew, partly in Aramaic and to a small extent in Greek (to be precise, Josephus and Justus of Tiberias, whose works were in Greek, wrote after the destruction of the Temple, and Josephus lived in Rome at the time of his writing), we also find a flourishing Jewish literature in the Greek language, written in the Diaspora countries. Greek was the main spoken and written language of the Jews in Egypt and the Roman Empire, and Jews used it for writing poetry as well as historical and philosophical works. Nevertheless, this Judeo-hellenistic literature is not merely literature written by people of Jewish origin according to Greek models but a truly Jewish literature using the Greek tongue. It focuses on Judaism and its problems and origins, rather than on the characteristic themes of Greek literature. In the main, it was designed to serve the internal needs of the Jewish community; but some of it was addressed to the outside world, with apologetic intent. In both cases it was polemical in nature, even in its more moderate aspects.

The foundation of this literature was the Greek translation of the Bible known as the Septuagint, or 'Translation of the Seventy'. It owes its name to the legendary seventy (or, more accurately, seventy-two) sages sent to Egypt by the High Priest of Jerusalem at the request of the king. The Pentateuch had already been translated by the third century BCE; in the course of time, the remaining books of the Bible also were translated into Greek. In its Greek version the Bible became the sacred book of the entire hellenistic Jewish world. In fact, few translations have had a greater influence on human civilization. The Septuagint became the instrument of Jewish religious propaganda in the Greco-Roman world. It was adopted by Christianity and became the source of many retranslations into other languages. The language of the Septuagint is basically the common Greek of the hellenistic period (the Koine), which was current in Ptolemaic Egypt; but, in their desire to translate the original as closely and faithfully as possible, the authors produced a Greek of a specific character, with a vocabulary and syntax that at times sounded foreign.

As early as the third century BCE, various Jewish authors writing in Greek had adopted the prevailing patterns of Greek literature in its many forms, filling them with Jewish content. In fact, Jewish-hellenistic literature contains most of the genres that were in common use in the literature of the period. Jewish authors, for instance, wrote Greek epics with biblical themes. The Jewish poet Philo (the Elder) wrote an epos on the foundation of Jerusalem. The few fragments that have been preserved deal with the sacrifice of Isaac, Joseph's stay in Egypt and the water sources of Jerusalem. Another Jewish epic author, Theodotus, also used biblical themes; we have fragments describing the clash between the sons of Jacob and the people of Shechem. Theodotus' work reads easily and fluently, since he employed the plain language of the Homeric epos. The only Jewish dramatist known to us from this period is Ezekiel, whose plays include a tragedy entitled *Exodus* that is based on the biblical story and shows the influence of Euripides.

The representatives of the historiographical genre who are known to us are more numerous. The first of them was Demetrius, who lived at the end of the third century BCE and wrote a book on the kings of Judah that was faithful to the contents of the Bible and composed in a simple style. Freer in his approach to the Bible as source material was Eupolemos (of the second century BCE). Unlike these writers, who describe biblical events, the greatest Jewish historian in the hellenistic diaspora, Jason of Cyrene, chose the Antiochan persecution and the Hasmonean Revolt as his themes. Jason, who had a thorough Greek education and was familiar with the life of the hellenistic world, drew on that world for his vocabulary and patterns of thought. As a native of Cyrene, he was at home with the ways of the Greek *polis*, and he even described life in Jerusalem in its terms. In form and style his five-volume history was typical of Greek historiography, but its viewpoint was dominated by a profound conviction of the superiority of Judaism. Loyalty to the Jewish faith, as Jason saw it, expresses itself in observance of the laws of the Torah. A faithful Jew never hesitates for a moment to obey the Law of Moses rather than a royal command. The purpose of the suffering with which the Jews were visited was not to destroy them but to teach them the right way, and the martyrs were convinced that their martyrdom would appease God's anger. For all his hellenistic education,

Jason showed no inclination to compromise with Hellenism in matters of religion. The Antiochan persecution was to him a war of principles, an assault by Hellenism on Judaism. Of the entire Hasmonean family, only Judah the Maccabee came alive in this work and dominated it completely. In addition to Judah, we are given portraits of Onias III, the last legitimate High Priest before the Antiochan persecution, and of the martyrs of the persecution. The common denominator among all of them was their unflinching loyalty to Judaism. Jason's work has come down to us only in the form of a summary by an unknown epitomist in Egypt. This is the book known as II Maccabees.

The distinction between historiography and the historical novel, which often pretends to be actual history, is a fine one. The latter genre is represented, for instance, by the letter of Aristeas and III Maccabees. The Aristeas letter, written at the end of the second century BCE, has as its stated subject the translation of the Bible into Greek. The story is adorned with all the devices of hellenistic style: table-talk on philosophical problems, detailed descriptions in the manner of travellers' stories, imaginary documents and so forth. In addition to its desire to glorify the Septuagint, the work reflects an enthusiastic, almost utopian feeling for Jerusalem, the Land of Israel and the Temple and a tendency to provide rationalistic explanations for Jewish religious commandments. The mood of the Aristeas letter is one of relaxed moderation, coupled with a desire not to exacerbate relations between the Jews and their neighbours.

III Maccabees was written at the end of the hellenistic era or in the early days of Roman rule in Egypt. Its subject is the persecution of the Jews under Ptolemaic rule. The anonymous author was a Jew who was faithful to his ancestral tradition and was disgusted by the very idea that the Jews should be required to surrender any part of their Jewishness in order to acquire civic rights. In his view the Jews in Egypt were living in a foreign country, and his writings hint at hopes of redemption. The book expresses the opinion of Jewish circles in the Egyptian diaspora who had adopted the Greek language and to a considerable degree also the Greek way of life, but who were not prepared to concede one iota of their principles. These circles continued to consider themselves foreigners in Egypt.

Of great influence on all later generations – Jewish, Christian and Moslem – was the emergence of philosophical systems among the Jews as a result of their contact with Greek philosophy. The first of the philosophers who attempted to explain Jewish doctrine according to the methods of Greek thought was Aristobulus (in the second century BCE). In his attempts Aristobulus resorted to an allegorical interpretation of the Torah text.

More deeply rooted in the form and style of Jewish biblical tradition is the *Wisdom of Solomon,* a pseudepigraphic work that also was composed in Egypt. The author is deeply aware that divine justice will prevail in the war against idolatry. For the author, divine wisdom is the source of all that is good in the world and the faculty through which God operates in the cosmos. The book shows clear signs of the influence of Stoic and Platonic philosophy and stresses the survival and pre-existence of the soul in a manner evocative of Platonic ideas.

Among the theoretical writings of Jewish-hellenistic literature we must also include IV Maccabees, which was written in the first century CE, perhaps in Syrian Antioch. It is a sermon on the rule of the intellect, combined with fear of God, over the emotions. The example cited by the author in support of his thesis is taken from the stories of the martyrs of the Antiochan persecution. The implication of the book is that by meticulous observance of the commandments of the Torah man can attain the same perfection as aspired to by Greek philosophy.

The greatest and most influential of the Jewish philosophers of antiquity was Philo of Alexandria (of the first century CE). Born to one of the most respected families of the Jewish community, Philo obtained an excellent Greek education in philosophy and literature. He combined a high-minded humanism with a belief in the special mission of the Jewish nation as 'priest of humanity'. Philo also wrote on general philosophical subjects, but his main works consist of an allegorical interpretation of the Torah and a series of books describing the history of the fathers of the Jewish nation and the commandments and ethics of Judaism. As a result of his doctrine of the logos, his combination of philosophy with a strongly felt religious-ethical conception and his attempt to reach a compromise between Greek thought and revealed religion, Philo earned himself a place as one of the leading authors of religious history. In fact, he is one of the great forerunners of all later theology.

19

The Great Revolt

The Causes and Nature of the Great Revolt

The powerful clash between the Jews and the Roman Empire at the end of the Second Temple era was the result of an accumulation of several factors, some specific grievances, others imponderables. In the ideological sphere there was a sharp conflict between the Jewish conception of Israel as the elect, with a glorious political and spiritual future, and the reality of the all-powerful Roman Empire, in which Judea was merely one of many subject provinces. This contrast found release in messianic hopes and the anticipation of heavenly salvation, which would bring eternal sovereignty to the Jewish nation as the heir of the Roman Empire: 'Most were convinced that it was written in the ancient priestly writings that in those times the East would gain in might and those who came forth from Judea should possess the world' (Tacitus, *Histories* 5.13). This messianic vision was the inspiration of the Jewish fighters, and until the flames rose from the Temple Mount they expected a divine intervention that would save the Temple and annihilate the enemy. This belief was promulgated to the end by prophets arising among the besieged, and to some degree it infected even the enemy armies, some of whose soldiers deserted to the Jewish side during the siege. The ideology of messianism and of the election of the Jewish people had borne a clear activist overtone among certain circles ever since Roman rule had begun. They regarded the duty to fight against Rome as a positive commandment, which should compel even the hesitant among the nation to take up arms, for the Jews had no master but God. The contrast between ideology and reality was pointed up by the very nature of the Roman Empire, with its characteristic tyranny and the paganism that pervaded even the political sphere, as in the cult of the emperor. To the Jews, Roman rule was identical with the rule of evil and of Satan. Caligula's mad attempt to impose the cult of his divinity on the Jews revived the atmosphere of the Antiochan persecution and showed what dangers the Jewish nation had to expect if Roman rule in Judea were to continue.

As has already been indicated, there were also specific aspects of Roman rule that severely offended Jewish sensitivities. Roman control of the Temple and of the Temple cult and the imposition of harsh taxes and duties, which placed a heavy burden on the population, all caused the masses to hate the foreign rulers. Most of all, the anger of the Jewish population of Palestine was aroused by the Roman administration's support of the non-Jewish, Greco-Syrian element. After its decline during the heyday of the Hasmonean Kingdom, this element had recovered with the establishment of new settlements under Pompey and Gabinius and had gained further strength under Herod and the Roman governors at the end of the Second Temple era. The garrison of the province of Judea was recruited almost entirely from the local hellenized cities, principally from Sebaste and Caesarea. The citizens of the gentile cities became something of an *élite* in Palestinian society. Relations between them and the Jews were tense. The gentiles of Jabneh and an Ashkelonite played a leading role in inspiring Caligula's measures against the Jewish religion. The residents of Dor continued to provoke the Jews even after the emperor's death, and Philadelphia was involved in border disputes with the Jews of the Peraea to the extent of engaging in armed clashes (see page 258). The disputes between gentiles and Jews in Caesarea were of historical importance, and it was not by mere chance that they were among the main factors that precipitated the Great Revolt. The tension between the hellenistic towns and the Jews assumed increasing significance during the final decades before the revolt, due to the rise of Greek and hellenized elements within the Roman administrative hierarchy under Claudius and Nero. One result was the appointment of provincials from the hellenistic orient as procurators of Judea. They naturally tended to identify with the inhabitants of the hellenized cities. It was no coincidence that Florus, the last and the worst of the procurators, was a Greek from Asia Mi. or.

It should be borne in mind that, as has already been noted, Roman rule in Judea in the last years before the revolt was generally bankrupt. Order and security, whose maintenance was the main *raison d'être* of this rule, were disturbed beyond retrieval. Anarchy reigned in Jerusalem. The villages suffered from the extortions of bandits and the roads were beset by robbers. The last governors, failing to fulfil their task, made every effort to exploit their office financially, Albinus and Florus even more so than others. In the days of the latter, as Tacitus noted, the patience of the Jews came to an end (*Histories* 5.10).

The revolt of the Jews of Palestine against Roman rule also bore the hallmarks of a social revolution. The lower classes of the large cities, mostly landless debtors and refugees from border districts, became the leaven that created the ferment at the beginning of the revolt. The social character of the revolution was particularly prominent among those extremist groups that produced such messianic leaders as Menahem the Galilean and Simon bar Giora. To them the revolt was not only a war against Rome but also a challenge to the status of the Judean upper classes, who for so long had collaborated with the Roman rulers. At first the extremists acted against the social conditions; they burned the municipal archives of Jerusalem in order to destroy the records of debts and began a campaign of terror against the main representatives of the upper classes. The latter were less than keen to revolt, and some of them made strenuous efforts at least during the first stages of the revolt to halt the movement among the masses. Many among the upper classes had vested interests in the Roman administration; but a large part, if not most, of the members of the upper strata of the Jewish community were bitterly disappointed by the administration of Florus, who had caused great injury to the wealthy Jews of Caesarea and, unlike his predecessors, had kept the priestly oligarchy of Jerusalem at arm's length. With the victory of the insurgents over the governor of Syria, the representatives of the upper classes also were carried along by the general enthusiasm. In the temporary government that was set up in Jerusalem after this victory and which was to organize the defence of the country against the Romans, a leading role was played by the former High Priest and leader of the Sadducees, Hanan ben Hanan. Other members of the High Priesthood took their place at his side, such as Joshua ben Gamla, who was related by marriage to the Boethos family. In their work for the national cause, they also had the support of Rabban Simon ben Gamaliel, the head of the house of Hillel and the leader of the Pharisees. But after the Jews had suffered heavy defeats in Galilee and the expedition that they attempted against Ashkelon failed disastrously, this group lost its power to more extremist elements drawn partly from the Zealots of Jerusalem and partly from areas outside the capital.

The Jews who took part in the revolt came from different sections of the country. Outstanding in their zeal were the Jewish refugees from the environs of the Greek cities. Thus the ranks of John of Giscala's forces in Galilee were swollen by refugees from Syria and particularly from the villages in the territory of Tyre. The leaders of the revolt themselves came from different areas. Galilee contributed Menahem, the leader of the Sicarii at the beginning of the revolt, Eleazar ben Jair, the hero of Masada, and John of Giscala. Simon bar Giora ('the son of the proselyte') was, as his name testifies, from a proselyte family, apparently from the city of Gerasa in Trans-Jordan. The man who at the beginning of the revolt made the decisive gesture of abolishing the sacrifices intended for the welfare of the emperor was Eleazar ben Hananiah, from a respected priestly family in Jerusalem. Among the commanders who were prominent at the time of the moderate leadership in the early stages of the revolt were Joseph ben Mattathias (later known as Flavius Josephus, and also from a priestly family in Jerusalem), Niger of Trans-Jordan and John the Essene.

The contribution of the Diaspora Jews to the revolt is harder to assess. We have explicit reports of the part played in the defence of Jerusalem by members of the royal house of Adiabene, and there were other Jews from the Eastern diaspora among the defenders of Jerusalem during the siege. But on the whole it seems that the Diaspora Jews, except for those of Alexandria, did not riot or, in any case, caused no diversion of Roman military forces.

If the insurgents had entertained hopes of receiving outside military assistance also from Rome's enemies, they were bitterly disappointed. True, during Nero's reign Rome was put to the test of intensive military activity in the East and protracted an indecisive war against Parthia for control of Armenia, and at one stage of the war the Parthians even defeated the Roman legions. But soon before the outbreak of the revolt the two sides settled their differences and made peace, and in the year 66 the Parthian king of Armenia went to Rome to officially receive the crown of his land from the emperor. On the other hand, just then Nero was apparently starting a military expedition beyond the Caucasus, and crack legions were moved from Europe to the East. There is no knowing to what extent the insurgents hoped to benefit from Rome's military involvements or whether they expected a renewal of tension between Rome and Parthia. In any case, the Parthian Kingdom remained on excellent terms with Rome throughout the war in Judea, and the Parthian king even sent congratulations to Vespasian after the conquest of Jerusalem. The concentration of Roman troops in the East during Nero's last days was only to the Jews' disadvantage, since it meant that there were more legions in the East than in normal years. Temporary relief came from an unforeseen quarter. From the summer of 68 to the end of 69, the Roman Empire was involved in a violent civil war in which one emperor supplanted the other, until Vespasian, the commander in the war against the Jews, took over the throne. This unexpected development gave Jerusalem a brief respite in 69, for Vespasian was waiting to see how the conflict in Italy would end before undertaking a systematic siege of the Judean capital. However, all these delays had come to an end by the spring of 70, when a mighty Roman army, under the command of the emperor's son Titus, invested the city in accordance with all the rules of siege warfare.

Jewish Palestine, closely settled by a mainly agricultural population, also had a considerable military potential. But the number of active soldiers whom the Jewish insurgents could put in the field against the regular Roman forces must not be overrated. Actually, Jerusalem itself had not much more than 23,000 armed defenders during the siege (see page 261). This force was incomparably smaller than the total manpower of the troops under Titus' command. One of the factors that prevented the effective use of the Jewish troops in the different stages of the revolt was the lack of a united leadership. The Great Revolt, unlike the Hasmonean Revolt before it and the revolt of Bar Kokhba after it, did not produce one central personality whose leadership was accepted by all the fighters. The enmity and competition between the leaders and the various factions did much to interfere with the conduct of the war on the Jewish side and even resulted in bloody clashes among the Jews.

Nevertheless, the Great Revolt was an exceptional event in the world of the Roman Empire. Judea was the only Eastern province in this era to be the scene of a long, violent insurrection. The Jewish insurgents even succeeded in gaining a victory on the battle-field over the governor of Syria and his troops, and to suppress the revolt it was necessary to use the pick of the Roman legions under the command of the emperor's own son. The valiant resistance offered by the Jews in such fortresses as Jotapata, Gamala, Masada and Jerusalem itself made a deep impression on their contemporaries. The victory over Judea was reckoned as a major military success for the Flavian dynasty, and the revolt signified an urgent need for far-reaching administrative and military changes in Judea.

The Beginning of the Revolt

The immediate cause of the Great Revolt was, as we have seen, connected with the continuously tense relations between the Jews and non-Jews in Caesarea and the procurator Florus' habitual disregard of Jewish sensitivity. When the non-Jews of Caesarea won a lawsuit concerning citizenship rights against the Jews at the imperial court in Rome, the self-assurance of the Greco-Syrian inhabitants increased. They clashed openly with the Jews, who left the city *en masse* for nearby Narbata. Rumours of the events in Caesarea produced a stormy reaction in Jerusalem, and when Florus took money from the Temple treasury fighting broke out between the Jewish crowds and Roman army units. Florus permitted his men to loot the 'Upper Market', and many of the Jews were killed (in 66). With the arrival of two more cohorts from Caesarea, the bloodshed was repeated. The Jews cut the lines of communication between the Temple Mount and the Antonia fortress, where the Roman garrison was stationed. Florus left the city. The moderates in Jerusalem, headed by Agrippa II, tried to restore calm, but the majority of the city's population was determined to tolerate Florus' oppression no longer and insisted that Agrippa and the acknowledged leaders of the people send a delegation to the emperor to lodge a complaint against the procurator. The leaders did not dare to take such action, but their reluctance only increased the influence of the militant freedom party, whose intention was to bring matters to the point of open warfare between the Jews and the Roman Empire. Following a proposal by Eleazar ben Hananiah, it was decided to discontinue the sacrifices in honour of the welfare of the Roman people and the emperor. The struggle between the moderates and the extremists ended in a victory for the latter, and the Roman garrison of Jerusalem was exterminated.

The events in Jerusalem had repercussions throughout the entire country and even beyond its borders, and bloody riots broke out in all the large Greek cities in Palestine. When it became clear that the auxiliary force stationed in Palestine could not possibly suppress the revolt, intervention by the governor of Syria became inevitable. Cestius Gallus, the legate in Syria, assembled a large force of legionaries and auxiliaries at Acco and marched against Jerusalem (in 66). The Roman force reached the outskirts of the city, but when the insurgents put up a strong resistance Gallus did not feel strong enough to take the city by force and ordered a withdrawal. The withdrawal turned into a rout for the Roman Army, which was attacked by the insurgents at Beth-horon, north-west of Jerusalem.

The political consequences of this event were enormous. Many of the Jews who had hesitated to join the insurgents gained courage. A large part of the priesthood and the Jewish upper classes also were carried along by the wave of nationalist excitement. A temporary government that united all of Jewish Palestine was set up under a single leadership. The country was divided into military districts; in Galilee, Joseph ben Mattathias was appointed commander. Beyond the confines of the Jewish section of the country, the insurgents had few successes. Their attempt to take Ashkelon by force failed despite all efforts.

The Fight against Vespasian's Legions

Nero could no longer treat the Jewish revolt with equanimity. The insurgents had endangered Roman rule in Judea, the province linking Syria with Egypt, in the heart of one of the most important parts of the empire. The defeat of the Syrian governor made it necessary to send additional legions to Judea. Their command was entrusted to Vespasian, one of the most experienced generals of the empire.

Vespasian marched into Galilee at the head of an army of 60,000 men. Against this powerful, well-trained force, the Jews could not hope to raise an army capable of holding its own on the battle-field. All they could do was hold out in their strong fortresses. The place that offered the strongest resistance to the Romans was the fortress of Jotapata in western Galilee, under the direct command of Joseph ben Mattathias (in 67). Joseph was captured during the conquest of Jotapata, but he soon managed to ingratiate himself with Vespasian and Titus and was released. After he regained his freedom, he became a follower of Titus and the historian of the entire war (see page 292).

The conquest of Jotapata and western Galilee made it easier for the Romans to engage in military operations against eastern Galilee and more distant parts of the country. One target that seemed to be of particular importance was the Jewish contingents in Jaffa, which were endangering the Roman sea-lanes along the coasts of Palestine and Phoenicia and were interfering with communications with Egypt. Jaffa was taken by a Roman column, and the Jewish ships were destroyed in a naval battle off the coast of the town. Of the east Galilean cities, Tarichaeae, to the west of the Sea of Galilee, offered particularly heavy resistance; Gamala in Gaulanitis also made a valiant stand against the Romans. With the liquidation of Jewish resistance on Mount Tabor and in Giscala in Upper Galilee, the Galilean campaign was to all intents over (in 67), and the entire Roman force was free to march against Jerusalem. Those inhabitants of Galilee who continued to participate in the campaign were refugees who had escaped to Jerusalem. Among them pride of place went to the contingents commanded by John of Giscala, one of the central figures of the entire revolt. But many other Galileans, including thousands from Tiberias, also participated in the defence of the capital.

Well aware that Jerusalem had become a gathering-point for multitudes of hardy fighters who were prepared to give their lives for their city and the Temple and that the fortifications of the city were remarkably strong, Vespasian hesitated to attack Jerusalem before having liquidated the last islands of Jewish resistance in the remainder of Palestine, though one would have thought that the situation in the city favoured the Romans and that an assault was indicated. The defeats in the field and the ambiguous behaviour of Joseph ben Mattathias had dealt a crushing blow to the official Jewish leadership. The Zealots of Jerusalem wanted to take command and oust Hanan ben Hanan, Joshua ben Gamla and the other former leaders. In the course of an armed clash that broke out between the Zealots and their opponents, the latter besieged the Zealots on the Temple Mount. The siege was lifted with the assistance of a force of thousands who had come to the Zealots' aid from Idumea, and the Zealots, seconded by John of Giscala, took control of the city. Their opponents' leaders, including the former High Priests Hanan ben Hanan and Joshua ben Gamla, were executed.

Meanwhile, the Romans had conquered virtually the entire country, including Jewish Trans-Jordan. Only the fortress of Machaerus, in the south, still put up resistance. Vespasian himself, with the main force of the Roman Army, took the toparchies of Lydda, Emmaus and Timnah. In Jericho he joined up with the column that had brought Trans-Jordan to heel. The unsettled state of the Roman Empire

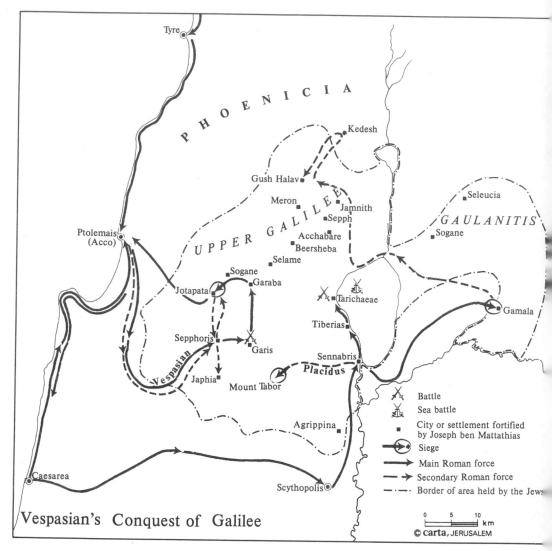

Vespasian's Conquest of Galilee

© carta, JERUSALEM

after Nero's death (9 June 68) delayed Vespasian's military operations against Jerusalem. Early in July 69, Vespasian himself was proclaimed emperor by the eastern legions, but it was only his final victory over his rival, Vitellius, in December of the same year that decided who would be the supreme ruler of the empire. Not until the spring of the year 70 was Titus, the emperor's eldest son, in a position to take charge of the campaign against Jerusalem.

The Conquest of Jerusalem and the End of the Revolt

The defenders of Jerusalem did not avail themselves of the respite in order to form a united leadership and improve their military situation. The three leaders of the insurgents – John of Giscala, Eleazar ben Simon, the priestly head of the Jerusalem

Zealots, and Simon bar Giora, the leader of the lower classes throughout Palestine, who had forced his way into Jerusalem and established himself in the Upper City – remained hopelessly embroiled in their own conflicts. Not only were they unable to agree on a joint defence plan before the siege, but they persisted in fighting one another and thus seriously undermined the military strength of the Jews and eased the Romans' task.

Titus' command consisted of the legions with which his father had conquered Galilee together with additional reinforcements. During the spring of 70, the Roman Army pitched camp near Jerusalem; the siege lasted until the end of the summer of the same year. During those five months Titus employed his military superiority to break the Jewish resistance. The attack began, as usual, by an investment of the city from the north. First the Third Wall was taken, and the Second Wall fell a few days later. The Romans could then begin to besiege the Antonia fortress, which was defended by John of Giscala, and the Upper City, where Simon bar Giora was in command. The legions began to throw up earthworks, but no sooner was the work completed than it was totally destroyed in a Jewish counter-attack. Titus decided to surround the city with a wall, which was built with great speed and cut off the remaining food supplies, causing terrible starvation in the besieged city. All the Romans' efforts were now directed against the Antonia, which was taken in the early summer and was completely razed by the Roman forces. The conquest of the Antonia opened the way for an assault on the Temple Mount, and in the beginning of Ab the Romans succeeded in overcoming the powerful resistance of its Jewish defenders. The Temple was completely burnt down on the orders of the Roman general, who intended thereby to destroy the root of the trouble and to prevent the Temple from becoming the focus of further rebellious tendencies. The burning of the Temple deprived the Jews of their last hope of victory. The remnant of its defenders fled to the Upper City, which fell to the Romans on the eighth day of Elul in the year 70.

With the complete conquest of Jerusalem, the great war between the Jews and the Romans was virtually over. A few fortresses still kept up the resistance: Machaerus on the eastern shore of the Dead Sea and Masada on the western side. Masada was defended by the last of the Sicarii, under Eleazar ben Jair, until the year 73 (or even 74). The heroic death of the defenders of Masada, who to the end remained faithful to their exalted principles and chose death by their own hands rather than capture by the enemy, was a fitting epilogue to the Great Revolt.

PART IV

The Era of the Mishnah and Talmud (70–640)

Shmuel Safrai

20

The Characteristics of the Era

The Place of the Land of Israel in the Life of the Nation

The period that we are about to consider extends from the destruction of the Temple until the Arab conquest in the early seventh century CE. At the beginning of this era, the majority of the Jewish nation lived within the domain of the Roman Empire, in the Land of Israel and in the large hellenistic diaspora, while a large minority dwelt in Babylonia and its surroundings, under the rule of the Parthian Kingdom and its successors. By the end of the period, almost the entire Jewish people and certainly all its important centres had come under Arab rule. Similarly, at the beginning of the era the centre of the nation's material and spiritual existence lay in the Land of Israel and its neighbouring countries, Syria and Egypt; towards the end of the era the centre shifted to Babylonia. The Jewish community of the Land of Israel still in some measure preserved its specific character and its sovereign position in the life of the nation, but its numbers had been sadly diminished, and it no longer retained its leading position as the centre of Jewish scholarship and creativity.

For the Jewish people it was a time of forceful and often painful political and demographic changes. In the Land of Israel as well as in the Eastern and Western diasporas, patterns of social structure and spiritual trends underwent extensive alteration. Centres and focal points of creativity that had exerted a seminal influence on the life of the nation during the Second Temple era disappeared, while new ones emerged and flourished. Modes of spiritual life, of culture and of law that were related to the Temple collapsed with its destruction. About fifty years later Jewish life in Alexandria and the other cities of Egypt foundered; Egyptian Jewry had not only been a great community that had fought for its status and rights, but was a centre of scholarly and literary activity and the homeland of Jewish-hellenistic literature (see Part III). However, after the fall of the Temple, other centres of creativity and leadership emerged in the Land of Israel – the Sanhedrin, the school of Jabneh and other places of learning. Similar centres, with a similar function and influence, developed also in the Babylonian diaspora. In all these centres economic and social conditions changed with the times, as did the nature of their activities and the scope of their influence. Their development was not uniform, but varied between the Land of Israel and the Diaspora and even between the different countries within the Diaspora.

During most of this era, however, the main centre of Jewish life remained situated in the homeland. The Jewish community there was numerically one of the largest and continued to serve as the focus for the nation's hope of returning to its ancient site and its former glory; but, over and above that, it remained the dominant element in the development of the entire Jewish history of this period. The national leadership of the Jewish people in the Land of Israel and the institutions that it established after the destruction of the Temple retained their hold on the Diaspora communities. The way of life, the spiritual and intellectual values and the social and legal patterns of the Jewish nation as a whole were formed in the Land of Israel by decisions reached in *halakhic* controversies, by specific rules and regulations, by the compilation of *halakhic* and *aggadic* literature, by the development of new terminology and phraseology, by the establishment of recognized orders of prayer and by the promulgation of the official calendar, whose dates were determined in the Land of Israel. All these matters achieved their initial validity within the Land of Israel and were subsequently adopted by the Diaspora as well. The Palestinian community remained the leaven that produced political and military fermentation and kept the hope of redemption alive.

Diaspora Jewry was not always unanimous in following the lead of the Palestinian community. But the relations between the Roman Empire and the Jews in the Land of Israel invariably swayed the relations between the empire and the other Jewish communities: if relations in the Land of Israel deteriorated and the Roman authorities imposed penalties or repressive decrees, the Diaspora was immediately affected, directly or indirectly; likewise, whenever relations between the homeland and Rome improved, so did the political standing of the Jews throughout the empire, as well as their attitude towards the government.

This period of more than 500 years was the transition from the political and social independence of Judea to the era of the Exile, in the fullest and most bitter sense of the term, when the Jews were dispersed among the nations of Europe and the Arab world as smaller or larger minorities without a territorial centre. Admittedly, the nation was not completely independent even in this period, with the exception of brief interludes of revolt. There were times when the Romans harshly persecuted the Jews in the Land of Israel. Moreover, from the religious viewpoint, the sages regarded this period as basically abnormal. The Temple, on which the system of commandments and patterns of public life depended, had been laid waste, and all attempts to rebuild it had failed. But throughout the entire era, until the Arab conquest, there were always other elements to provide a basis for national life, particularly during the end of the third and the beginning of the fourth centuries.

In the early period the Jews remained the most prominent element within the population of Palestine. If we follow the rabbinical opinion of those days, we may also include the Samaritans, who lived in the central mountain region and spread from there to the north and south, as part of the Jewish population. While there was much friction between the Jews and the Samaritans, there was more that united rather than divided them: they spoke almost the same language and had similar life styles, sharing not only the commandments and moral values that are explicitly stated in the Pentateuch but also many beliefs and practices that had developed during the Second Temple era. *Halakhah,* at least during the first generations after the destruction of the Temple, treated the Samaritans as Jews, and the Samaritans, in turn, generally participated in the military and political struggles of the Jews. For many generations after the destruction, the Jews and Samaritans together formed the majority of the population, not only in the interior parts of the Land of Israel but also in some of the border areas.

Except in times of crisis, the economic situation of the people remained normal. Agriculture was the mainstay of the economy, but many crafts flourished as well. From the middle of the second century, the Land of Israel and particularly its Jews were known for the cloths and vessels they manufactured. Until the beginning of the fourth century, most of the land was under Jewish ownership, initially in the form of independent small holdings. In the second century the Jewish farming population increased and new crops were developed. Throughout the period from the destruction of the Temple until the Arab conquest, the nation's leaders waged a constant battle to ensure that the land would remain Jewish property and that the small farmer would not lose his patrimony. For a long time they succeeded, despite the extensive expropriations by the authorities, particularly after the wars against Rome in 66–70 and 132–135, and despite the general economic and social trend in the Roman Empire and the East to encourage the formation of large estates. The rabbis would not allow a small farmer's land to be sold to a wealthier Jew, let alone to a gentile, and in various ways they made sure that the land was redeemed and returned to its original Jewish owners.

In time, however, the small holders and the Jews in general were unable to retain hold on the land. They could no longer maintain themselves by farming or preserve their village life. Consequently, they increasingly turned to commerce in the capacity of small middlemen and the economically marginal occupations and from there often to emigration. Yet, even by the end of the era, the Jews had not become completely detached from the land and from agricultural occupations. The sages attempted to encourage immigration to Israel – repeatedly stressing the importance of the commandment to settle in the Land – in order to counter the trend towards emigration that always became prevalent in times of severe economic and political crisis in the East and in the Land of Israel. These were the circumstances especially in the periods of persecution under the pagan Roman emperors and of the systematic and continuous persecution by Christian Rome.

There was always a migration movement from the Diaspora to the Land of Israel, at times restricted, at other times assuming massive dimensions. At any given time a specific Diaspora community might provide the bulk of the immigrants, but immigration never ceased; it was the nation's only means of offsetting the population decrease and of maintaining, at least in part, its demographic distribution.

Autonomous Leadership

Throughout almost the entire era, the nation enjoyed autonomous leadership. This had been revived immediately after the destruction of the Temple and again after the Bar Kokhba Revolt, and it continued to exist even during the severest persecutions, when the authorities attempted to wipe out all traces of autonomous national life. This leadership consisted primarily of the *nasi* ('patriarch') and the Sanhedrin. These two institutions encompassed all the main spheres of the community's spiritual and material life: they constituted the supreme religious authority for the Land of Israel and the Diaspora, the high court of justice and the academy that ordained the judges and Torah scholars who, in turn, promulgated regulations, interpreted the *halakhah*, decided controversial issues for individuals and communities and taught students from all parts of Israel and the Diaspora. It was the Sanhedrin that completed the codification of the Scriptures and the traditions instituted for its mode of writing, reading and translation.

The office of *nasi* existed more than 300 years after the destruction of the Temple, and, with only one interruption, it was held by descendants of Hillel, who himself claimed descent from King David. This affiliation of the ruling family to the Davidic dynasty imparted an aura of royalty to the national leadership, which thus was envisaged as a continuation of national sovereignty, providing the foundations for a renewal of independent existence. Even after the imperial authorities had abolished the Patriarchate (*c.* 429), the Sanhedrin remained in existence until the end of the era (70–640).

Though it came into existence soon after the destruction of the Temple, the power of this leadership was at first small and its sphere of influence limited, not only as far as the Diaspora and the cities of the Land of Israel were concerned but even among the sages themselves. In the course of time, however, its position became consolidated, and on behalf of the *nasi,* emissaries were sent to supervise communities in the Diaspora and to advise them of the various *halakhic* innovations introduced by the Sanhedrin. These emissaries were even authorized to appoint and dismiss community leaders.

At first the Roman authorities did not recognize the autonomous Jewish leadership. But once its authority had been fully acknowledged within the Jewish nation itself, recognition by the Roman government followed, even to the extent of enforcing the right of the *nasi* to levy taxes in the Land of Israel and in the Diaspora for the maintenance of the Patriarchate and the Sanhedrin. In fact, the Jews had begun to pay taxes to their institutions before Rome recognized them, and the practice continued even after Rome withdrew its recognition of the Patriarchate and attempted to prevent the collection of such taxes. As a result of the position occupied by the Sanhedrin and the Patriarchate in the life and consciousness of the nation, the history of these institutions formed the backbone, as it were, of the Jewish history of the period.

In general, the Diaspora accepted the hegemony of the Land of Israel, though trends towards independence emerged from time to time. Such attempts were to be found in the Babylonian diaspora; it had a long tradition of autonomous rule, exercised by its exilarch, and it possessed a singular feeling of importance, which drew its strength from a large, densely settled Jewish population with a highly developed tradition of Torah study, particularly from the end of the tannaitic era onwards (*i.e.,* from the end of the second century). But, like other centres of exile, Babylonia also acknowledged the ultimate authority of the Palestinian community. The *halakhic* missives issued by the Patriarchate were binding not only on the heads of the academies but even on the exilarch and his tribunal. The High Court (or Sanhedrin) of the Land of Israel was the highest judicial authority also for the Babylonian diaspora, notwithstanding the acknowledged authority of its own academies and courts. Until the Jewish calendar was determined in 358, Babylonia, like the other Diaspora communities, depended entirely on the rulings of the Sanhedrin and the *nasi* in the Land of Israel for determining the date of the New Moon and hence of the New Year. Only in the course of centuries, as its population and spiritual forces dwindled, did the Palestinian community gradually lose its leadership and its decisive influence over the Jewish people.

Methods and Trends in National Leadership

The rabbis developed, disseminated and instituted their own modes of social leadership. Their teachings derived largely from the concepts prevalent during the period of the Second Temple, but they also introduced many innovations that were put in force after the destruction. In the Sanhedrin, which was established after the fall of the Temple, several former elements were now absent, and the rabbis had the opportunity to revive old trends to which those elements had been opposed. For example, neither the moneyed aristocracy nor the High Priestly families were now represented. Even at the local government level, the former leading families were removed from power, which was now exercised exclusively by the rabbis themselves, who supervised the composition and operation of public institutions, including those concerned with education and charity. One of the most important aspects of their initiative in the social sphere was their concern with *halakhah* and the establishment and maintenance of a system of autonomous *batei din* or rabbinical courts. The concepts and procedures of Jewish law were given form in the first generations after the destruction of the Temple.

It was no easy task to re-establish, after the fall of the Temple and under Roman rule, the system of autonomous law courts and to induce the people to have recourse to them instead of to the legal institutions of the occupying power. But, in this field as in others, the rabbis were able not only to preserve the heritage of the past but to renew and expand it. In the political sphere the people, led by the sages, were taught not to recognize the foreign rule nor the economic system that it attempted to introduce in the country; extremists among the rabbis even instigated revolts in an attempt to regain political freedom. Several of these were large-scale rebellions and, particularly under Trajan (115–117) and Hadrian (132–135), also involved Diaspora communities; but others were on a smaller scale. In any case, political activism was never entirely absent. The more moderate element attempted, especially after the failure of several revolts, to avail themselves of favourable political constellations in order to gradually bring about complete liberation. By the middle of the third century, one discerns a measure of resignation in the attitude towards the authorities and conformity to their social and economic demands; but even by the end of the era armed attempts to regain political independence still occurred. The signs of an independent way of life in the absence of political independence had become less pronounced by the end of the era; still, they, above all else, characterize this particular period in Jewish history.

This pattern of national life was specific to the Jews in the Land of Israel; but, since the bonds between the Jewish communities in the Diaspora and the Palestinian centre remained close throughout the era, it played an important part in the development of the entire nation. The history of the different Diaspora communities, as far as it it has been documented, will be discussed separately.

The Historical Context

The new developments characteristic of the era and the manner in which they contributed to the continued existence of the Jewish nation may be summed up as follows. First, without a state and without a Temple, the people and their sense of nationhood became the focal point of the national existence, which now focused on the shaping of an organized Jewish society firmly anchored in a life governed by the Torah and its commandments. These values were the foundation and support of the nation's life and aspirations throughout its long existence as a people without a country. Secondly, this was the period in which the oral tradition was consolidated and put down in writing and in which the literature of the *halakhah* and *aggadah* came into existence.

In the days of the Temple, various trends and systems of *halakhic* thought and practice had been developed and had resulted in differences not only between the Pharisees and Sadducees but between the Pharisees and the sages themselves. The degree of religious freedom was large, and attempts to lay down and enforce a uniform view were rare. The two main Pharisaic schools, the house of Shammai and the house of Hillel, continued to exist side by side; with the exception of only a few rules, neither gained exclusive recognition, tradition acknowledging that one might live 'either according to the house of Shammai . . . or according to the house of Hillel'. After the destruction, however, there were consistent efforts to decide between the two, so that the people might have a uniform body of interpretation of the laws. Almost immediately it was laid down that the *halakhah* would follow the teachings of the house of Hillel, and the option of observing the practice of the house of Shammai was no longer open.

There was now a growing tendency to develop consistent general principles as a basis for a complete legal and *halakhic* system. The completion of this process is reflected in the creation of the classical work on the oral tradition, the Mishnah, which was compiled at the turn of the second and third centuries. The Mishnah was the main object of study, the source of *halakhic* rulings and the basis of national life and thought, and during the course of the next two or three centuries the other great compendia of the Oral Law – the Palestinian Talmud in the Land of Israel and the Babylonian Talmud in the Babylonian diaspora – built upon it. After the *halakhic* literature, the *aggadic* literature was consolidated, compiled and put into written form. While a considerable part of it was actually written after the Arab conquest, the main body of *aggadah* had already taken shape beforehand. During this era the principal prayers and benedictions also were composed and formulated, though their text was not given the same degree of finality as that of the compendia of *halakhah* and *aggadah*.

The hegemony of Palestine over the Diaspora and the manifold connexions between them also influenced these literary and religious developments. That the final versions of the *halakhah* and *aggadah* and the formulae of the benedictions were accepted and became the formative element in Jewish life everywhere was due to the spiritual centrality of the Palestinian community. Thus the religious and cultural unity of the entire nation was preserved. Even the two Talmuds, the Jerusalem (Palestinian) and the Babylonian, differ only to a small extent and are fundamentally in agreement.

21

The Jews in the Land of Israel (70–335 CE)

Recovery After the Destruction

The Great Revolt, which lasted for more than four years and involved all parts of the country, together with the various sieges, the conquest of Jerusalem and the destruction of the Temple, was a heavy blow to the Jewish people as well as to the towns and villages of the Land of Israel. Thousands were killed in the campaigns, and many towns were burnt down or razed, either in the course of the war or as acts of vengeance and intimidation. Agriculture suffered most. The areas in the hills and plains that had been planted with fruit trees lay waste. In many places Roman troops were sent out with specific orders to cut down orchards. Josephus records that in the course of the siege of Jerusalem all the trees in the environs of the city were destroyed and 'the land was as bare as virgin soil.' Pliny, the Roman naturalist who participated in the war, was particularly impressed by the destruction of the persimmon groves – the only ones in the world – for the Jews uprooted them rather than let them fall into the hands of the Romans.

However, the demographic and economic impoverishment of the population did not last; the Jewish people in the Land of Israel was not reduced to total devastation. Not only was it able to wage a great war only one generation after the destruction, but the population had to a remarkable degree recovered its numeric and economic strength by the end of the first century.

Many of those who had been captured in the war were redeemed by their brethren in Israel or in the Diaspora cities in which they had been sold as slaves. Others regained their liberty in different ways; and, while many of them settled in the places of their exile, many others returned to their homeland. Even the towns that Vespasian and Titus had conquered and, according to the records, had razed to the ground did not disappear. Jaffa was taken and totally destroyed twice: once, early in the war, by Cestius Gallus and again by Vespasian. Nevertheless, by the beginning of the second century we find it had been rebuilt and was flourishing, and an inscription has been preserved testifying to the fact that a Jew was in charge of its market. Other cities, including Jerusalem, Jodapata and En-gedi, about whose complete destruction the records are most explicit, also returned to life in the course of time. Ruined towns did not become a feature of the Palestinian landscape until after the Revolt of Bar Kokhba (135). In the hellenistic cities where the Jews were slaughtered or expelled by their neighbours (only in four of them, Antioch, Epimea, Sidon and Gerasa, did the Jews remain unharmed), we find a large Jewish population by the end of the first century. Both Jewish and non-Jewish literature show that a normal farming economy had been restored by the end of the first and the beginning of the second centuries, with the highly developed cultivation of field crops and gardens. Many orchards had been rehabilitated and new ones planted. Yet, for all its remarkable powers of recovery the nation was in serious political and economic straits. No less serious was its spiritual depression as a result of the conquest of the country, the capture of Jerusalem and the destruction of the Temple.

Writing of the year 71, Josephus says: 'At that time, the emperor sent letters to Bassus [the legate] and Labarius Maximus [the procurator], and ordered them to lease all the lands of the Jews; for he founded no cities in the country, desiring to retain all the land for himself, and settled only eight hundred veterans' (*Bellum Judaicum* VII, 6.6). As a matter of fact, there is evidence to show that both during and after the war many Jewish farmers stayed on the land, cultivated it and even owned it. Josephus' statement applied only to those lands that were actually confiscated – a considerable proportion of the lands of the Jews. In the tannaitic literature of the time, we find frequent and bitter reference to the 'oppressors' – the *conductores* who had taken over the land in many parts of the country. The expropriation took place in different forms, arousing a variety of emotions and reactions. In some cases ownership was transferred to non-Jews – as in the case of the 800 veterans who were settled in Motza, from which the former owners were expelled completely. Often the Roman authorities handed over the land to trusted and privileged persons, such as Jews and non-Jews who had sided with the Romans during the war. But in most cases where land was expropriated, the owners were not ousted but stayed on as tenants. Generally, the Roman authorities leased large tracts of land to primary tenants, *conductores*. They in turn leased it out in separate lots to farmers, who were thus forced to lease the 'field of their fathers', as the Jewish sources put it, at a high rent – usually a large share of the crop – and always risked being expelled for defaulting on the rent or on any other pretext. These 'oppressors', as they were generally referred to, were usually, but not always, non-Jews, and the Tannaitic literature of the generation after the destruction complains bitterly not only of the suffering of the farmer, who 'could more easily squeeze a penny from a rock than from the landlord', but also of the humiliation and pain at seeing the property of Jews owned by foreign oppressors. In the course of the years, the situation improved as a result of a persistent campaign to restore Jewish ownership and redeem land from the non-Jew.

The Tax Burden

Even on land that had not been expropriated, taxes had to be paid, and they continually increased after the destruction. Not in all areas under Roman possession were those who paid a land-tax required also to pay a poll-tax, but the Jews in the Land of Israel were obliged to pay both. A Roman author of the first half of the second century reported that, because of their rebellious spirit, the Jews in the Land of Israel were required to pay heavier taxes than the subjects of neighbouring terri-

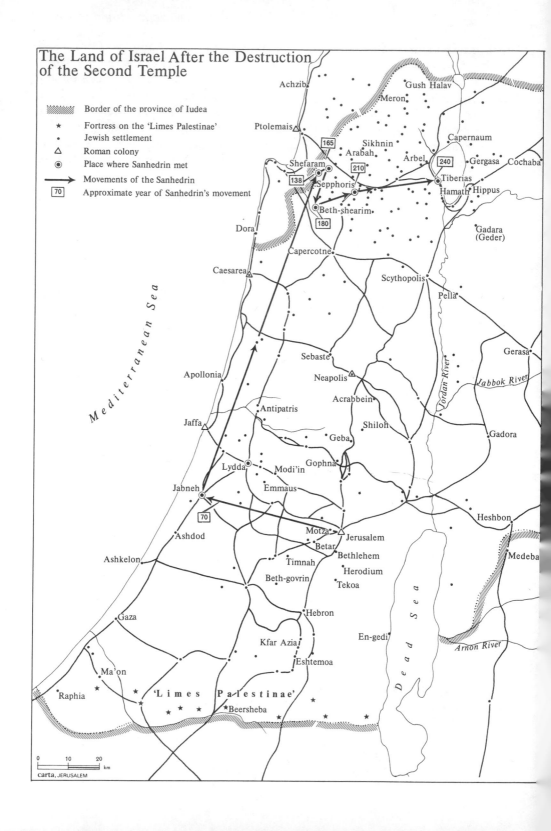

The Land of Israel After the Destruction of the Second Temple

Achzib
Gush Halav
Meron

Ptolemais
165 Sikhnin
Capernaum
Arabah
Shefaram
210 Arbel
240 Gergasa Cochaba
138
Sepphoris
Tiberias
Hamath Hippus
Beth-shearim
180
Dora
Gadara (Geder)
Capercotne

Caesarea
Scythopolis
Pella

Mediterranean Sea
Gerasa
Sebaste
Jordan River
Jabbok River
Apollonia
Neapolis
Acrabbein
Antipatris
Shiloh
Jaffa
Geba
Gadora
Gophna
Lydda Modi'in
Jabneh
Emmaus
Heshbon
70
Motza Jerusalem
Ashdod
Betar
Bethlehem
Medeba
Timnah
Herodium
Ashkelon
Beth-govrin
Tekoa
Gaza
Hebron
En-gedi
Arnon River
Kfar Azia
Ma'on
Eshtemoa
Dead Sea
Raphia
'Limes Palestinae'
Beersheba

	Border of the province of Iudea
★	Fortress on the 'Limes Palestinae'
•	Jewish settlement
△	Roman colony
⊙	Place where Sanhedrin met
→	Movements of the Sanhedrin
70	Approximate year of Sanhedrin's movement

0   10   20
km

carta, JERUSALEM

tories. After the destruction the amount of the levies demanded for the maintenance of the Roman garrisons and the civil service (*annona*) was increased. Since more troops were stationed in the country and the administration had grown, their maintenance was a heavy burden. Before the destruction the garrison in the Land of Israel had consisted only of auxiliaries, in accordance with the Roman practice of stationing legions only in border provinces; after the destruction, the Tenth Legion, which had taken part in the war, was regularly stationed in Israel and was reinforced by auxiliary troops from remote provinces. The burden fell mainly on the shoulders of the farming population. Many legal discussions in Tannaitic literature deal with issues arising from the levies to be paid on grain, cattle and every agricultural and industrial product. In addition to the taxes and duties paid in money and kind, the Tannaitic sources speak of forced labour. At the demand of various authorities – mainly the military – subjects were required to contribute their own labour and that of their animals for transport, road building and repairs and similar services. Draught animals were often impounded permanently or for a designated period.

Special mention should be made of the tax of two drachmas that every Jew in the Land of Israel and the Diaspora was required to pay to the Roman treasury as a contribution to Jupiter Capitolinus, the tutelary god of Rome, instead of the half shekel they had been accustomed to paying to the Temple treasury. This tax was based on the Roman conception that the gods of a conquered nation also became subject to Rome and that, since the gods of Rome had defeated the god of Israel, the revenue of the latter's temple was now the right of the conqueror. This belief explains why the tax was levied in the Diaspora as well as in Israel and from proselytes converted before or after the destruction of the Temple as well as from those born Jewish. Papyri discovered in Egypt show that the tax was demanded even from old women and infants. This tax was not so much a financial burden as a humiliation. For the first time in Roman history, a special tax was imposed on the Jews. Moreover, it was an indirect form of compulsory idolatry. It continued to be collected until the time of Julian the Apostate, in the middle of the fourth century, though after the first few generations following the destruction of the Temple it was no longer connected with Jupiter.

The Institutional and Spiritual Crisis

No less severe were the effects of the destruction on the institutional and spiritual life of the nation. The ravages of the war, the conquest of Jerusalem and the loss of the Temple meant that the institutions that had led the nation – the High Priesthood and the Sanhedrin – no longer functioned, and the result was paralysis and confusion. It is true that even before the destruction the sacrifices had ceased to be the main liturgical element, as the focus of religious life had to a large extent shifted to the synagogue, to Torah study, to the observance of the commandments and to charity; and the share of the High Priesthood in the national leadership and its influence on the Sanhedrin had declined. However, the synagogue and the Temple were bound together by everyday practice as well as by historical derivation: the hours of prayer were determined by those of the Temple service, and during prayer the congregation faced in the direction of the Temple; the local charitable institutions were patterned after those of the Temple; the Sanhedrin not only had its seat in the Temple but could exercise its powers only while in session in the Temple and while the Temple service continued to follow its appointed course. Thus, for example, the rabbis held that the Sanhedrin was not entitled to try capital cases unless the sacrificial services were being held as prescribed.

The destruction of the Temple not only meant the abolition of sacrifices, pilgrimages and the like, but upset many other systems of commandments. The blowing of the *shofar* and the carrying of the *lulav* were observed also outside the Temple; but only in the Temple was the *shofar* sounded when the New Year fell on the Sabbath, and only in the Temple was the *lulav* carried on all seven days of the Feast of Tabernacles, whereas in communities outside Jerusalem it was carried only on the first day. Many priestly dues and tithes were connected with the Temple or with Jerusalem: the first-born of animals, the first-fruits and peace-offerings were brought to Jerusalem, as was the second tithe, which could be eaten only within the city.

The destruction left a vacuum in the spirit as much as in the everyday life of the people. The feeling of deflation that followed the high pitch of expectancy during the revolt might well have jolted the nation's belief in its way of life and its future. Even though Judaism was not threatened with disintegration, the fall of the Temple undoubtedly produced a depression that came close to despair. On reading the Tannaitic literature of the period, one is aware of widespread dejection, pain and suffering. The same mood is characteristic of IV *Ezra* and the *Apocalypse of* [Syriac] *Baruch* (neither of which has come down to us in the original Hebrew). Both were written by Jews living in Israel some twenty-five to thirty years after the fall of the Temple; thus some of the visions recorded in them were not only conceived but actually written down under the direct impact of that event. They reflect the turmoil of the generation immediately after the destruction, as well as the first sparks of recovery. The mood of despair is evident also in the conduct of those Pharisees who abjured wine and meat or withdrew to caves to await the apocalypse with fasting and abstinence.

The transition to the new religious attitude that sought to rebuild the life of the nation, without a Temple and without its own state, on a basis of observance of the Torah and the performance of good deeds while awaiting the redemption could not have taken place under less auspicious circumstances. Spiritual recovery and the restructuring of the national entity were hampered by political and religious persecution on the part of the authorities and the heads of the non-Jewish cities in the Land of Israel and the neighbouring countries. While Rome was generally tolerant of the religions of conquered peoples, the long war with the Jews had created considerable resentment and was followed by oppressive measures that were as much religious as political in nature and which were explicitly decreed or at least condoned by the higher authorities. Until Judaism regained a legal status in the Land of Israel, the Jews of the country were officially considered *dediticii* or enemies who had surrendered themselves unconditionally.

This situation was reflected also in the attitude adopted towards the Jews living in the immediate neighbourhood of the country. An example is the history of the

Jewish community of Antioch, a large, prosperous community in one of the main centres of Roman administration in the East, the capital of a province and the seat of the governor, who was responsible also for the Land of Israel. Admittedly, Titus refused a request by the Antiochians for the expulsion of the Jews 'since their city Jerusalem has been destroyed and it is impossible to expel them. and there is nowhere else where the people are willing to admit them' (Josephus, *Bellum Judaicum* VII, 5.2). He even refused to allow the Antiochians to break the copper tablets on which the privileges of the Jews and their right to follow their own way of life were recorded. But the Roman governor assisted the inhabitants of the city who forced the Jews to commit idolatry and violate the Sabbath, 'and thus the Sabbath ceased to be observed not only in Antioch, but in all the cities of Syria.' Vespasian himself built a theatre on the site of the former synagogue in Daphne near Antioch, adding insult to injury by an inscription testifying that it had been financed 'from Jewish spoils'.

Rabban Johanan ben Zakkai

The history of the re-establishment of Jewish communal life in Palestine after the destruction is bound up with the personality of Rabban Johanan ben Zakkai. He was one of the leading sages of Jerusalem before the destruction, one of the chief Pharisees and the spokesman of the sect in its disputes and contests with the Sadducees, and he was the deputy of Rabban Simon ben Gamaliel, the head of the Sanhedrin and of the government formed in Jerusalem after the expulsion of Cestius Gallus. Letters sent from Jerusalem to the cities of Israel and the Diaspora concerning contributions and tithes bore the signature of Rabban Johanan ben Zakkai as well as that of Rabban Simon ben Gamaliel. Though a priest himself, in his teachings and precepts he chided his fellow priests for setting themselves above the common people. The pursuit of peace is an important element in his teachings. Unlike Simon, he may well have refused to take part in the revolt; it is certain that he warned the rebels against fanaticism and over-confidence and called upon them to be moderate in their behaviour towards non-Jews. A saying of his, 'Do not haste to tear down altars of gentiles, lest you be forced to rebuild them with your own hands, lest you tear down altars of bricks and be ordered to build them of stone' (*Aboth Derabbi Nathan* B, 31), apparently refers to the zeal with which the rebels, having gained control of the country, destroyed the altars of the non-Jews. Another saying attributed to him, 'If you hold a sapling in your hand and someone says to you the Messiah is there, plant the sapling first and then welcome the Messiah' (*ibid.*), also bears witness to his realistic cast of mind and his distrust of too much enthusiasm.

Rabban Johanan ben Zakkai was in Jerusalem at the time of the siege but left before the city fell. Since the Zealots kept guard to prevent all departures, his pupils resorted to subterfuge and smuggled him out in a coffin. The event made a considerable impression on the authors of the Talmudic tradition, and we have various versions of his confrontation with Vespasian and of what the emperor granted him. According to the later tradition of the Babylonian Talmud, he received 'Jabneh and its sages' and 'the succession of Rabban Gamaliel' (*Gittin* 56b). But this tradition largely reflects a later period, when 'Jabneh and its sages' was firmly established and headed by Rabban Gamaliel, the son of Simon ben Gamaliel, who laid the foundation of the dynasty of *nesi'im* who were to follow. According to earlier Palestinian traditions, it seems that Rabban Johanan was initially a prisoner and was taken against his will to Jabneh, which, along with other towns, such as Ashdod and Gophna, served as a place of detention for those who had surrendered to the Romans. What he succeeded in obtaining from the emperor also appears to have been far more modest according to the Palestinian traditions. One version relates that all he asked for was a reprieve for certain individuals; according to other versions, he asked for Jabneh in order to 'teach his pupils' or to 'perform the commandments and teach Torah'. Considering the general circumstances and the practice of Vespasian and Titus, the version appearing in the earlier sources, concerning the beginnings of Jabneh, is more likely. Rome would hardly have given permission to establish a national centre, even if only a spiritual one, in Jabneh. But, even if the official permission granted to him was very restricted, in actual fact Rabban Johanan ben Zakkai began, with or without the knowledge of the authorities, to rebuild Jewish life and to fill the void created by the destruction of the Temple. He reconvened the Sanhedrin and began to proclaim New Moons and leap-years from Jabneh.

The annual cycle of Jewish holidays is based on a lunar year, which is adjusted to the solar year by the insertion of leap-years consisting of thirteen months. Before the fall of the Temple, it had been the regular practice to establish the occurrence of the New Moon on the evidence of witnesses. Upon finding that the advent of a new moon had been properly attested, the High Court (Sanhedrin) would 'hallow' it; the information was then immediately transmitted to the Jewish communities in Palestine and even to Babylonia by means of beacons.

The resumption of this practice was, in itself, sufficient to turn Jabneh into the centre of leadership for the entire Jewish nation. Several of the rulings instituted by Rabban Johanan ben Zakkai concerned the problem of hallowing the New Moon in the House of Assembly, even though it was not meeting in the Temple, and of announcing this act to all Jewish communities. He laid down that the *shofar* should be blown in Jabneh even if the New Year fell on a Sabbath, 'in memory of the Temple'. This rule also conferred a measure of *halakhic* status on the House of Assembly in Jabneh. Another of his rulings, in the same field, stipulated that 'even if there is a President of a Court in every place, the witnesses [to the appearance of a new moon] shall testify only at the House of Assembly' (Mishnah *Rosh Hashanah* 4:4). All the practices instituted by Rabban Johanan were designed to fill the vacuum that had been created by the destruction of the Temple – some by calling for acts in memory of the Temple, others by providing ways of adjusting to the new circumstances and breaking the bond with the Temple in cases where the latter's absence interfered with the course of life.

Following are two examples of the second kind of rulings. According to the *halakhah*, the fourth year's crop of a vineyard or other plantation was to be either offered in Jerusalem and eaten there or redeemed; and in the days of the Temple it was laid down that redemption was not permissible if the vineyard was no more than a day's walk from Jerusalem. After the destruction Rabban Johanan ruled that even the fruit of a vineyard planted close to the city wall might be redeemed and eaten freely. Similarly, the *halakhah* required a proselyte to offer a sacrifice in the Temple as part of his conversion ceremony; and when the Temple was destroyed proselytes used to set aside a quarter of a *shekel* for a sacrifice to be offered when the Temple would be rebuilt. Rabban Johanan abolished this requirement of paying the quarter shekel.

To his disciples and to the people in general, who were distressed by the fall of the Temple where the sins of Israel had been atoned, he taught: 'My son, do not distress yourself, we have another atonement that is like it; and what is it? Charity: "For charity I desire, not sacrifice."'

Nevertheless, compared to what was done in Jabneh one generation later, Rabban Johanan's work and the scope of activities at Jabneh were restricted. We hear nothing about the development of relations with the Diaspora, of the supervision of communities in the Land of Israel or of concern with civil law, to mention only a few spheres in which the next generation of Jabneh scholars was to be so active. The reason was not inactivity on Rabban Johanan's part. At first he was hampered by external circumstances; for in the first years after the fall of the Temple the Roman authorities presumably kept a close watch over all that happened in Israel. In addition to withholding recognition of the Jewish national institutions and refusing them a measure of autonomous authority, the Romans restricted their activities. We know also that the Romans persecuted the descendants of the house of David, to which the dynasty of patriarchs of the Sanhedrin belonged, in order to prevent them from becoming a focus for hopes of liberation.

Conditions within the nation also were unfavourable. Only a small proportion of the sages had followed Rabban Johanan to Jabneh. Most of the leading Torah authorities who had been outside Jerusalem during the siege or had survived the fall of the city were signally absent from the first generation of Jabneh. Missing were rabbis of priestly origin who had served in the Temple and had wielded great influence in Pharisaic circles, – such as R. Zadok and R. Eleazar – and others who had greatly influenced the development of the oral doctrine – such as R. Dosa ben Harkinas, R. Judah ben Baba and the two scholars who had established schools of *halakhic* interpretation, R. Nehunya ben Hakana and Nahum of Gimzo. All of them had been active in the days of the Temple and were to be active at Jabneh after the time of Rabban Johanan. Even of his five closest disciples, only two, R. Eliezer ben Hyrcanus and R. Joshua ben Hananiah – the two who had carried him away from Jerusalem – remained with him in Jabneh. The others went their own way, including his senior and favourite disciple, R. Eliezer ben Arakh, who went to Emmaus. Apparently, most of the sages could not forgive Rabban Johanan for leaving Jerusalem during the siege and surrendering himself to the emperor's mercy. Rabban Gamaliel, who later carried on the dynasty of patriarchs, enjoyed the sages' renewed cooperation.

All this, however, does not detract from the greatness of Rabban Johanan's work in laying the foundations of the national centre that developed in the following generation. In those hard times, when the breakdown of national and religious structures was compounded by official restrictions and economic hardship, by persecution and despair, Rabban Johanan, keeping himself apart from the Zealots as much as from the priestly and financial aristocracy and to a certain extent isolated even within the world of the rabbis, laid the groundwork for new national patterns leading to spiritual and social recovery.

Rabban Gamaliel

Rabban Johanan ben Zakkai did not remain in Jabneh till the end of his life. During his last years he headed the academy at Bror Ḥayil in the south. As soon as conditions were ripe for Rabban Gamaliel to take over, Rabban Johanan was forced to leave Jabneh in order to make room for him. Rabban Gamaliel's formal installation at Jabneh could only be effected at the end of the Flavian dynasty (Domitian, Titus' brother and the last of the Flavians, was murdered in 96). The Roman authorities were fully aware of the implications of entrusting the leadership of the people to a member of the house of Hillel. No Flavian would have permitted an act so likely to raise the spirit of the nation, for they knew only too well that Rabban Gamaliel was the son of Simon ben Gamaliel, who had been one of the leaders of the revolt from the very first, and they would not have permitted him to assume any public position, let alone become the head of Jabneh. Some traditions even indicate that Rabban Gamaliel was persecuted by the Romans and was forced to remain in hiding till the advent of more propitious times.

The Flavian emperors, Vespasian, Titus and Domitian, were proud of their victory over Judea and the capture of its people. In Rome and Palestine they struck coins with the inscription *Iudaea devicta* and *Iudaea capta*. Domitian treated the Jews even more harshly than had his father, Vespasian, or his brother Titus; he strictly enforced the special taxes and the ban on conversion to Judaism in Rome. Suetonius, his younger contempory, wrote:

> In Domitian's days, the Jews' tax was collected with the utmost rigour. Those who observed Jewish customs without admitting it, and those who concealed their Jewish origin in order to evade the tax imposed on their nation, were denounced to the imperial treasury. I still remember from my early youth how the procurator, in the presence of a crowd of assistants, inspected an old man of ninety to see whether he was circumcised (*Vita Domitiani*, 12).

Another Roman historian reported that, in the year 95, Domitian ordered the execution of Flavius Clemens, a nobleman closely related to the imperial house, for Judaizing tendencies and banished his wife, Domitilla.

Under Nerva and Trajan the Romans relaxed their treatment of the Jews. Nerva even struck a coin in order to 'remove the shame of the Jewish tax'. What this 'removal' consisted of is not known, but it is evident that the Jews were no longer persecuted as harshly as before.

Jabneh Under Rabban Gamaliel

In the days of Rabban Gamaliel, the national leadership was recognized by the Roman authorities. It was not that he took office with Rome's express permission; rather, once the right moment presented itself, he became the leader of the nation, whereupon the Romans gave his leadership *de facto* or even *de jure* recognition. The Mishnah states explicitly that he went to Antioch to be invested by the governor, and there are several traditions reporting his journeys to Rome with the heads of the Sanhedrin, R. Eliezer ben Hyrcanus, R. Eleazar ben Azariah, R. Joshua and R. Akiva. The reports mention visits to the Jewish community in Rome and meetings with the heads of pagan Rome and the imperial house. Other traditions speak of imperial commissioners sent to study Jewish civil jurisprudence, which had been resumed and was now operating widely.

However, the main difference between the era of Johanan ben Zakkai and that of Rabban Gamaliel was not that the Jewish leadership under the latter was recognized by the empire but that wide Jewish circles in the Land of Israel and in the Diaspora acknowledged the authority of the Sanhedrin at Jabneh and of its head, Rabban Gamaliel, far more than they had accepted the authority of Rabban Johanan. Rabban Gamaliel was joined by all those sages who had refused to follow Rabban Johanan. Under Rabban Gamaliel the centre at Jabneh assumed most of the functions that had been exercised by the Sanhedrin during the time of the Temple.

Tradition makes no mention of journeys by Rabban Johanan ben Zakkai, but we have many reports about Rabban Gamaliel's visits to the towns of Israel. On these visits he issued rulings touching on all spheres of life and supervised the administration of the communities. It became the custom in all parts of Palestine and the Diaspora to refer matters requiring an explicit decision to the Sanhedrin and Rabban Gamaliel. Tradition places the tribunal at Jabneh on the same level as the Sanhedrin in Jerusalem: it was meritorious to present to Jabneh any question that was too difficult for the local religious authorities. The practice of sending emissaries of the *nasi* and the Sanhedrin to communities in the Diaspora, as had been customary during the time of the Temple, also was resumed. Leading sages, such as R. Joshua, R. Akiva and R. Ishmael, regularly travelled throughout the Diaspora, sometimes accompanied by the *nasi* himself. In the case of some sages, we know of only one or two such journeys: R. Joshua, for instance, is known to have visited Rome and Alexandria. Others must have spent much of their time travelling, and there are many reports about R. Akiva's journeys to distant communities.

This system of visits was also of considerable economic importance, for the emissaries brought back the moneys contributed in the Diaspora for the maintenance of the centre in Israel. But the contact with the Diaspora that was maintained by means of these visits was at least of equal importance. The emissaries provided not only an institutional connexion but also personal contact with the greatest Torah authorities of the time, acting on behalf of the *nasi*. They taught Torah wherever they went, brought the latest news from the academies in Israel, inspected the administration of the communities and their institutions and saw to the establishment of such institutions as they thought necessary, including charitable societies, schools and so forth. They had a decisive voice in the appointment of community leaders and could even depose them, if they found them inadequate.

The Development of the Halakhah

The functions of the Sanhedrin developed in three directions during this era. It became the executive organ, the source of *halakhic* interpretation and an academy for the study of Torah. The *halakhah* not only regained its force in daily life but was also developed from a theoretical and philosophical viewpoint. The teachings of the sages of Jabneh during Rabban Gamaliel's tenure show a clear tendency to summarize and consolidate the theoretical foundations of the *halakhah* and of *halakhic* law. Their concern with the practical applications of the *halakhah* – and its study in depth in search of the common principles underlying its individual cases – made a major contribution to the broadening of its influence and to the reformulation of many of its doctrines.

In the days of the Temple, *halakhic* scholars had enjoyed a considerable degree of freedom; but now the prevailing trend was towards more rigid rules. Even in the days of the Temple there had been contests of will between individual scholars and the sages as a group when the latter sought to determine the law, and on occasion they had even excommunicated individuals who refused to submit to the corporate decision. But, in general, the urge to lay down rules was not very pronounced, and the different schools of *halakhah* were allowed to go their own way. Characteristic of this tendency was the coexistence of the schools of Shammai and of Hillel, as mentioned previously, each with its own conception of *halakhah* and *aggadah*. In the Jabneh era, however, the school of Shammai was firmly ruled out of order, and it was declared that 'whoever trespasses against the teachings of the house of Hillel deserves death.' The *aggadah* attributes this ruling to a heavenly voice that was heard in Jabneh. But earlier sources show that the rabbis did not find it easy to deal with the later supporters of the school of Shammai and that the primacy of the school of Hillel was not established overnight.

This contest is reflected in the story of the excommunication of R. Eliezer ben Hyrcanus, an adherent of the school of Shammai, a conservative scholar and an individualist. He was excommunicated by Rabban Gamaliel and his followers when he refused to submit to their ruling on a point of ritual purity. The *aggadah* provides us with a vivid description of this contest between the representatives of the mainstream and an individual authority who insisted that he was in the right and was confirmed in his opinion by a revelation from heaven and by other signs. Even these, however, did not deter the rabbis. They argued that the Torah is 'not in heaven' but was given to man. The *aggadah* relates that when R. Eliezer was being excommunicated, Rabban Gamaliel was on a sea voyage and was about to be drowned in a torrent. He realized that he was being punished for the injury done to R. Eliezer, and the *aggadah* shows him standing on the ship and contending with the Almighty, maintaining that his treatment of R. Eliezer had not been for the sake of his own honour or for that of his fathers' house but 'only for Thine honour, that there shall not be divisions in Israel'. In his campaign for uniformity in *halakhah* and custom, Rabban Gamaliel dealt severely with the rulings of individual rabbis; but when, on one occasion, he treated R. Joshua ben Hananiah in a manner that the rabbis thought improper, they deprived him of the Patriarchate and replaced him by R. Eleazar ben Azariah, a priest of noble family. In the course of time, the two were reconciled, and R. Eleazar remained in office as Rabban Gamiel's deputy. Thus the presidency of the Sanhedrin reverted to the old pattern of a scholarly duumvirate.

The Role of Jabneh

Throughout the Jabneh era, from immediately after the destruction of the Temple until the Revolt of Bar Kokhba (70–132), many steps were taken that were to have a decisive influence on the coherence of the nation under the contemporary conditions. The sages were able to gain control over the different groups and trends that were competing within the nation. Sects such as the Sadducees or the Essenes were no longer heard of (see page 321). There were still a few individuals belonging to these sects, but as a social or political force contending for rule or influence in the nation they no longer existed. Decisive steps were also taken to cut off Christianity from Judaism. The various Judeo-Christian sects had generally remained within the Jewish nation, and after the fall of the Temple they even increased their missionary efforts on behalf of conversion, for the destruction of the Temple had confirmed them in their faith. Judaism, however, defended itself vigorously against inroads on the part of the Christians by refraining from all contact with them and by measures designed to strengthen belief in the eternity of the Torah and its commandments. One such measure was the insertion into the *Amidah* prayer of an additional, nineteenth benediction, *Birkat Haminim* ('benediction against the heretics'), which, in its earliest Palestinian formula, was directed primarily against the Judeo-Christians, who 'shall have no hope' in their belief that the Messiah has already appeared on earth. Of these Judeo-Christian sects, some members returned to Judaism, while others departed entirely from the Jewish nation.

In the Jabneh era regulations were laid down to ensure that the soil of the Land of Israel would remain under Jewish ownership and to protect it against conversion to common pasture for shepherds, whose numbers had increased considerably since the destruction of the Temple. The philosophy of this generation stressed the religious importance of the land and of settling on it; and under the influence of this philosophy *halakhic* rules were laid down to encourage the redemption of the land from gentile ownership.

At the academy of Jabneh, ceremonies were developed to adapt to the new conditions those festivals that could no longer be observed by pilgrimage to the Temple in Jerusalem. On Passover, even at the time of the Second Temple, the highlight was the meal of Passover eve, whose ceremonial elements and emotional connotations are clearly reflected throughout the wide range of writings that record Jewish life in those times and that have come down to us. It was and has remained an impressive component of the nation's religious and spiritual life, the occasion for recalling the departure from Egypt, which was the beginning of the nation's existence, and for giving expression to longings for future redemption. These memories and longings intermingle in a song of praise to the God of Israel, rendered in an atmosphere of intimate brotherhood. It is eminently a family ceremonial, designed to hand down those memories and emotions to future generations. While the Temple stood all these elements centred on the Passover sacrifice, and even the eating of the unleavened bread and the bitter herbs was of lesser importance when juxtaposed with the sacrifice, which formed the main part of the festive meal. With the destruction of the Temple, this entire ceremonial might well have fallen into disuse. But at Jabneh the order of the Passover eve (which in the course of time came to be popularly referred to as the *seder* or 'order') was given a new image. The scholars of Jabneh ruled that the commandment to eat unleavened bread and bitter herbs remained in force even without the sacrificial lamb; a commemoration of the sacrifice itself was instituted, and the significance of the meal was underscored by the formulation of an accompanying text, the *Haggadah*. In all essentials the order established at Jabneh is that of the *seder* as it is still celebrated by the entire Jewish people.

Under the guidance of Rabban Gamaliel, the text, order and form of Jewish community prayers (which are also obligatory for the individual) were established. Fasting on the Ninth of Ab – and apparently also on the other fast days – was known even during the Second Temple era but was practised only by small groups; after the destruction the fasts became obligatory and special prayers were formulated for such days. Moreover, it became customary to make a pilgrimage to Jerusalem on the anniversary of the fall of the Temple and to chant laments at its ruins.

One of the great works undertaken at Jabneh was a new Greek translation of the Scriptures by Aquilas of Pontus, a Roman aristocrat who converted first to Christianity and then to Judaism and became a pupil of Rabban Gamaliel, whom he accompanied on his travels. His translation was made under the supervision of the leading scholars of Jabneh, who greatly admired his work. It reflects the system of interpretation of the *tannaim* (and particularly of R. Akiva), which insists on the significance of every single letter of the Torah, including particles and conjunctions. The earlier Greek translation of the Old Testament, the Septuagint (see Part III), did not reflect the *halakhic* and *aggadic* interpretation of the Pentateuch and the Prophets that had developed since its preparation, and therefore it was difficult for Jews who used this translation to comprehend the *halakhic* lectures and *aggadic* homilies of the Torah scholars. The fact that the Septuagint had been accepted as sacred by the Christian Church and some of its phrases served the Church Fathers as the basis for their sermons may have contributed to the decision of the rabbis to provide a new translation. While the Septuagint version was not entirely rejected, the Aquilas translation was the one generally used in synagogues and in Jewish life.

Social Concepts

The outlook as well as the legislation of the Jabneh scholars reflect a pervading consciousness of the equality of all men and of the importance of all who have been created in the Divine image. Tradition summarizes the practice and ideas of the Jabneh scholars in the form of a saying attributed to them:

> I am God's creature and so is my fellow man; my work is in the city, his in the fields; I rise early to perform my labours, and he rises early to perform his; and

even as he is not vainglorious about his work, so neither am I about mine (Babylonian Talmud, *Berakhot* 17a).

This social and moral concern is encountered in all their rulings, in their concept of the equality of all before the law and in the care taken not to transgress the property rights of the individual nor to detract from his honour, whether he be prince or pauper. The teachings of Jabneh acknowledged no privileged groups or classes.

Many of the problems that had arisen in Jewish belief and practice during the course of time were studied and resolved at Jabneh. It is to Jabneh that we owe the ruling that a Jew who is compelled on penalty of death to transgress a commandment of the Torah should transgress it rather than be killed, with the exception of three prohibitions: idolatry, murder and forbidden intercourse. However, in times of official persecution designed to force Jews to abandon their faith completely, a Jew must surrender his life rather than offend even against mere custom (Jerusalem Talmud, *Sanhedrin* 3). The question of whether observing the commandments is more important than studying the Torah was answered at Jabneh in favour of study, 'for study leads to practice'. These are only a few of the many instances in which an attempt was made to reduce Judaism to its basic principles and define its contents and to use them to lay the foundations on which the nation could rebuild its life.

The Jabneh era witnessed widespread contention between the various scholars and academies, each following different trends in matters of *halakhah*, religious thought and social guidance. These disputes stimulated Jewish thinking, led to the development of varying systems of study, enriched the life of the people and in time became an element without which national life was inconceivable.

The Sages of Jabneh

Of the men who established and shaped the institutions of national and community leadership in Jabneh, none belonged to those circles that had formed the social *élite* in the days of the Temple. Those elements had completely vanished from public life. Communal and spiritual leadership was now in the hands of the Torah scholars. What distinguished the scholar was his *semikhah* ('ordination') by his peers; it was this that qualified him for his function. These sages were known by the designation 'rabbi', and from them the president of the Sanhedrin chose his executives and emissaries. The rabbis were a product of the conditions following the destruction of the Temple. Family and wealth were of no importance; this new leadership group was drawn from a wide range of social and economic backgrounds. All that mattered was learning.

In Jabneh's early days we hear mainly of two disciples of Rabban Johanan ben Zakkai: R. Joshua ben Hananiah and R. Eliezer ben Hyrcanus. R. Joshua came from a family of Levites; in his youth he had served in the Temple, and even then his outstanding personality had gained him considerable influence among the scholars, particularly those connected with the Temple. He was a poor man, earning a bare living by manufacturing needles, but his personality and leadership made themselves felt throughout the entire Jabneh era, until the early years of Hadrian's reign. R. Joshua did much to counteract the sectarian tendencies that were being encouraged by various extremist circles. The Mishnah depicts him as a confirmed individualist who insisted on going his own way and was not prepared to submit to authority or surrender the right to think and speak for himself; but in the end he accepted the views and decisions of his colleagues. For instance, he obeyed the order of the *nasi* to present himself with his staff and knapsack on the day that by his reckoning, though not by that of the *nasi,* was the Day of Atonement. We hear of him reprimanding the wealthy *nasi* for not knowing of the privations suffered by the poor Torah scholars; and an insult directed at him is given as the reason for the revolt of the rabbis against the *nasi.* R. Joshua was one of the emissaries whose travels resulted in wide-ranging contacts with the outside world (see Part III). He believed that righteous gentiles have a share in the World To Come. We find him in the role of spokesman for Judaism in disputations with Christians and other heretics. In his attitude towards the Roman authorities he was moderate, and his influence enabled him to exercise a calming effect when attempts were made to revolt against Rome.

R. Eliezer ben Hyrcanus was the son of a rich farmer and did not join the scholars until later in life. He represented the conservative trend in *halakhah* and inclined to the school of Shammai. Although *halakhic* decisions usually went against him, he had considerable influence on the shaping of *halakhic* thought and practice in his own time and in later generations. He also was one of the emissaries sent to the communities in the Land of Israel and in the Diaspora.

The most prominent figure of the Jabneh era in the first third of the second century was R. Akiva ben Joseph. He was the son of poor parents and lived as a shepherd. Only as an adult did he begin to take an interest in the study of the Torah, to which he devoted himself while making a bare living from casual labour. In his interpretation of the Scriptures, in *aggadah* and in *halakhah* he always probed for the deeper meaning, on the assumption that the Torah does not 'speak in the language of men'. In his conception every single letter was meaningful and provided a clue to the mystical significance of the specific verse. R. Akiva preached and taught in public. He had many disciples, most of whom died in the Bar Kokhba Revolt; but the survivors were the men who kept Torah and Jewish community life alive after the fall of Betar, the city near Jerusalem that was the last stronghold of the rebellion. He headed charitable institutions and travelled widely on missions to Jewish communities – to Phoenicia, Nabatean Arabia, Africa, Rome and Gaul and to Cilicia, Cappadocia, Nehardea and Media. He was a man of vision and daring in matters of social and national leadership and was one of the enthusiastic supporters of the Bar Kokhba Revolt, probably having been among those who inspired and planned it. He was executed in the course of the persecution of Jewish leaders after the revolt. R. Akiva's confidence, steadfastness and fervour during his imprisonment, torture and execution made him the exemplar of one of the most harrowing and inspiring chapters of Jewish martyrology (see Part III).

Not all of the scholars who lived and taught in Jabneh were officially ordained. Those who were not did not hold the title 'rabbi' but continued to be regarded as 'students'; and they were not appointed to office by the *nasi* but travelled from town to town as roving teachers, sometimes without a regular source of income and hence unable to raise a family. Among the latter we may single out Simon ben Azzai, a student and companion of R. Akiva and one of the great creative teachers of his time, who made his mark by his teaching of Torah in the market-place. It was the custom of the Torah scholars to teach the people not only in the academies but also in the streets and markets, 'under the fig tree and under the olive tree'.

Aside from the academy in Jabneh, *batei midrash* flourished in the towns and villages throughout the country. Such houses of study existed in Kfar Aziz in the south, where R. Ishmael taught; in Bnei Brak, which was R. Akiva's centre of learning; in Lydda, where R. Eliezer ben Hyrcanus and R. Tarfon had their schools; in Peki'in, headed by R. Joshua ben Hananiah; and in such towns in Galilee as Sepphoris, headed by R. Joseph ben Halafta, and Sikhnin, where R. Hananiah ben Tardion taught. The heads of these local houses of study regularly visited the House of Assembly at Jabneh; some even maintained their residence at Jabneh and only visited their own study-houses from time to time.

These *batei midrash* and particularly those in the villages were not permanent establishments but crystallized around the personality of an individual teacher. The adult students would meet in the evening to spend a few hours in the company of their rabbi after their day's work. Their main opportunity to devote themselves to study was on the Sabbath and on festivals, when they were joined by students who lived further away. Among the younger students, some would stay with their teachers for a number of years before marrying and – with the permission of their wives – even for years afterwards. The poorer among them would work, often for a frugal living. When the teacher died his students would join a school founded by the greatest of his pupils in the same town or elsewhere or, alternatively, the existing school of some other scholar. Particularly dedicated students were usually not satisfied to stay with one teacher but went from one scholar to another in order to acquaint themselves with different schools of teaching and practice, until they found the rabbi of their choice. Between such a disciple and his chosen rabbi there usually developed a permanent bond; for the way of life of the rabbis not only called for the acquisition of a certain body of knowledge but also involved 'serving the rabbi', that is to say, living with one's teacher as a son or servant. A disciple would follow his rabbi as he went from place to place to teach Torah or to supply the needs of a community, and the rabbi's way of life, his behaviour towards people and his manner of dealing with community affairs were learned by close observation and imitation. A rabbi and his disciples often lived communally, at least sharing a common table. Joint meals were a regular practice and offered an opportunity for learning, table-talk on a wide range of subjects and the acquisition of good manners.

Generally speaking, it was not customary in those days for a scholar to receive a salary for teaching or for occupying himself with community affairs. In fact, it was not permissible to accept remuneration for teaching Torah, on the basis of the verse 'Behold, I have taught you statutes and judgements' (Deuteronomy 4:5) and the expectation that 'What I have done without reward, ye shall also do without reward' (Babylonian Talmud, *Nedarim* 37a); likewise, it was said that 'He who takes a reward for rendering judgment, his judgement shall be invalid' (Mishnah *Bekhorot* 4:6). The typical scholar of the Jabneh era followed a trade and lived by it, spending his free time teaching and occupying himself with public affairs. It was not yet customary to exempt Torah scholars from taxes or to grant them other relief. However, not all rabbis were able to live up to these ideal standards. The sages of Jabneh even sought ways and means of compensating the scholar to some degree for having to give up his trade and livelihood – as was often the case – lest the status of rabbi become a privilege of the rich. It was declared permissible for a rabbi to accept hospitality, and some would consent to accept gifts while travelling about the country, particularly on their lengthy journeys to the Diaspora communities. Occasionally, one even hears of the people of a town in Israel or in the Diaspora undertaking to maintain a scholar so that he might settle among them. But, although the custom of providing material support for rabbis became increasingly common in the course of the tannaitic era, the ideal that one should not benefit materially from 'the honour of the Torah' was never entirely forgotten.

The 'Kitos War'

From the political and military viewpoints, the Jabneh era was by no means uneventful. Under Domitian, in the late eighties, the mood of the country was rebellious, and soldiers serving in the Land of Israel who had completed their tour of duty were not discharged. Incidents on a larger scale occurred twenty years later (c. 115–117) under Trajan's rule. Tradition refers to these disturbances as the 'Kitos War', after the Moorish general Lucius Quietus, who ruthlessly suppressed the Jewish revolt in Mesopotamia and was then sent to Judea to deal with the situation there. He was appointed procurator and remained in office until recalled to Rome and executed under Hadrian. The disturbances in Israel were actually only an offshoot of the far-ranging rebellion that swept through the Diaspora at the time.

From Talmudic traditions and epigraphic evidence we know of gatherings of Jews on the Temple Mount in Jerusalem, the spread of the rebellion to Galilee and troops being called in to deal with it, as well as the razing of a number of towns in the Land of Israel. Jewish leaders in the country were executed – including Pappus and Julianus, whose activities extended as far as the Diaspora – and decrees were issued against the Jewish religion; persecutions and deliberate provocations, such as the setting up of an idol on the Temple Mount, were encouraged. But, even in the Palestinian tradition, memories of the Kitos War have merged with those of the Bar Kokhba Revolt, which followed shortly afterwards.

The revolt of Bar Kokhba had the support of R. Akiva and other Jabneh scholars, many of whom, with their disciples, fought in the war. Since nearly all the rabbis of this generation were killed in the war itself or in the persecutions that followed it, there is no other generation of scholars that is so clearly demarcated from the next. The revolt also marked the end of the Jabneh era in the geodemographic sense, for it was followed by the devastation of Judea and the shift of the Jewish centre to Galilee.

With the accession of Hadrian to the imperial throne (117), a trend of pacification and restoration began in the East, accompanied by respect for national character and for the needs of the provinces. The Jews of Judea shared in the benefits of this trend. In the course of his efforts to rehabilitate ruined cities and devastated areas, the emperor promised the Jews that he would rebuild Jerusalem, return it to them and allow the Temple to be rebuilt. The image of Hadrian during his first stay in the orient soon after his rise to the throne, as reflected in Jewish tradition, is generally positive. Not only are there stories of promises made to the Jews, but the emperor is presented as a man who thirsted for knowledge and wished to study the Jews and their faith. The report of the emperor's activities soon spread throughout the Diaspora. Many Jews came to Jerusalem, and financial and other preparations for the rebuilding of the Temple were undertaken.

However, a few years later, the emperor changed his mind about the restoration of Jerusalem as a Jewish city and the rebuilding of the Temple. His reasons remain a matter for speculation; he may have been deterred by the emotional reaction of the Jews and a fear of the political consequences of allowing them to recover control of Jerusalem. It is also possible that his sympathy towards the Jews and Judaism had changed; from early in the second decade of the century and throughout the remainder of his reign, he displayed clear pan-Hellenic tendencies and did much for Hellenism in all the countries of the hellenistic East. Sources confirm that he detested 'foreign', *i.e.*, oriental, religions, an attitude that induced him to forbid circumcision, which he included within the category of castration, an act that was forbidden on penalty of death. The ban was not aimed specifically against the Jews, but applied in equal measure to others. Whatever the reasons, Hadrian now sought to convert Jerusalem into a pagan Roman city, without regard for its past or its place in Jewish thought and aspirations. His ambition seems to have been to construct a Greek world within the orient. Since he had lived in the East before becoming emperor (having been governor of Syria) and had been in contact with Jews, he must have been well aware of the effect his measures would have on the Jews, though he deliberately disregarded their sensitivities.

Hadrian's moves, coming as they did after the elation aroused by the prospect of rebuilding Jerusalem and the Temple, inflamed the feelings of the Jews and resulted in preparations for war against Rome. Fortifications were built in secret and, above all, arms were collected and made ready. Dio Cassius, the Roman historian whose works are our main source for the history of the revolt, reports that the Jews would intentionally damage arms that the Romans had given them to repair, so that they would be rejected on inspection and could be retained by them without arousing suspicion. As long as Hadrian stayed in or near the Land of Israel (128–132), the Jews did not revolt openly. But even then there were serious acts of terrorism, to the extent that the Roman garrison was unable to deal with the situation and an additional legion, the Sixth Ferrata, was brought in. The Sixth Legion also remained in the Land of Israel after the revolt, encamped in the Valley of Jezreel. In addition, the Tenth Legion was reinforced by recruits from nearby countries. As soon as Hadrian had left the East, the revolt broke out on a large scale, for 'the Jews in the entire world also rose and joined them, and created much trouble for the Romans, secretly or openly, and even many gentiles came to their aid' (Dio Cassius, lib. LXIX). The Samaritans, or at least some of them, also joined the rebels.

Simon, Prince of Israel

During the first stages of the revolt and the disorders that preceded it, we find – as in the Great Revolt – local heroes and various messianic and royal pretenders. As the revolt took its course, however, they were all overshadowed by the messianic figure of Simon bar Kosiba. He became the acknowledged leader of the revolt and the head of the nation, and the coins struck during the revolt are inscribed with the designation 'Simon, Prince of Israel'. Christian sources report that he was referred to as Bar Kokhba ('Son of the Star'), because of the messianic character that was attributed to him. Even R. Akiva recognized his messianic character and proclaimed, 'This is the king and Messiah!'

In caves in the Judean Desert, documents and letters from the time of the war have been discovered; these belonged to refugees from En-gedi and other places in the vicinity who had sought shelter there. In these documents we find Simon bar Kosiba, Prince of Israel, sending instructions and orders, and leases of public lands are drawn up in his name. Despite this appellation, his rule was not that of an anointed monarch; he had a priest as colleague, just as the local command of En-gedi was entrusted to a duumvirate. In fact, a number of the coins of the revolt bear, in addition to the name of Simon, Prince of Israel, also that of Eleazar the Priest – presumably Eleazar of Modi'in, one of the Jabneh scholars, whom Talmudic tradition links with Bar Kosiba and places at Betar together with him. The Sanhedrin and Patriarchate were at Betar; in fact, Rabban Simon ben Gamaliel, the *nasi* of the next generation, was educated at Betar. What the relation was between Simon bar Kosiba and the Patriarchate and whether the Sanhedrin had any actual share in the government are not known.

The Course of the Revolt

The revolt began in full force in 132. General conscription was introduced, and the Judeo-Christians who refused to bear arms were severely punished. At first the Jews fought against the Tenth and Sixth Legions and the auxiliaries. Bar Kokhba succeeded in gaining control of the whole of Judea, including Jerusalem, and of much of the rest of the Land of Israel. Wherever his control extended he introduced autonomous Jewish rule. Coins were struck with Hebrew inscriptions dated from the year marking 'the redemption of Israel', 'the freedom of Israel' or 'the freedom of Jerusalem'. Royal domains and public lands – properties that had been confiscated by the Roman authorities – were taken over by the Jewish authorities and leased by Bar Kokhba's officials in his name.

The second stage of the revolt began when Publius Marcellus, the governor of Syria, arrived with the legions of the Syrian standing army, reinforced by legions and auxiliaries stationed in Egypt and Arabia. Even against this army the Jews had the upper hand, and the Twenty-second Legion, which had come from Egypt, was annihilated and never heard of again. At this point the Jews reached the coast and the Romans launched naval battles against them.

The third and decisive stage of the revolt began when Julius Severus, the governor of Britain, arrived with his own legions and those of the Danube provinces. By then the number of legions and detachments involved in the campaign had risen to a round dozen, aside from the many auxiliary units. Galilee was lost to the Jews early in the campaign, and the whole weight of the war and its ruinous consequences were concentrated in Judea. Gradually, the rebels were pushed back to their last fortress, Betar, which lay at the edge of a range of hills south-west of Jerusalem, just below the present Arab village Bittir. Between the Great Revolt and the Bar Kokhba Revolt, the town had flourished, for after the fall of Jerusalem it had served its neighbourhood to some degree as a regional centre and a market. At the time of the revolt, the Jewish leadership moved to Betar, possibly with the intention of turning it into the headquarters of the revolt or perhaps because the rebels were then forced to leave Jerusalem. In the course of the war, it was fortified, and the Jewish sources sometimes refer to the revolt as the 'War of Betar'.

The entire rebellion lasted three and a half years and ended with the fall of Betar after a long siege in the summer of 135. According to Tannaitic tradition, Betar fell on the Ninth of Ab, the anniversary of the destruction of the First and Second Temples. With the fall of Betar and the death of Bar Kokhba, the campaign was over, though there still were skirmishes and sieges in the Judean Desert, to whose caves the fighters retreated after the fall of Betar – just as the rebels had made a last stand in strongholds such as Masada after the fall of Jerusalem during the Great Revolt (see Part III).

Of the tactics of Julius Severus and the course of the 'War of Betar' and its bitter outcome for the Jews, Dio Cassius wrote:

> He was reluctant to fight the enemy face to face after seeing their great numbers and desperate anger. Instead, his practice was to have his numerous soldiers and officers capture them singly or enclose and besiege them in their fortified places, thus depriving them of food supplies. In this way he was able, by degrees and with little risk, to frustrate, immobilize, and destroy them. Very few were saved. Fifty of the Jews' strongest fortresses were destroyed by the Romans, and nine hundred and eighty-five of their most important settlements razed. Five hundred and eighty thousand Jews were slaughtered in battles and skirmishes and countless numbers died of starvation, fire, and the sword. Nearly the entire land of Judea lay waste. . . . But of the Romans, too, many fell in this war; so many that Hadrian, in his dispatch to the Senate, refrained from using the customary introductory phrase: 'I trust you and your children are well; I and my troops are well' (lib. LXIX).

After the Revolt

The war resulted in severe demographic and territorial setbacks. The number of dead was enormous, and even greater was the number of captives who filled the slave markets in the Land of Israel and elsewhere. Particularly notorious was the Terebinth market north of Hebron, where Jewish slaves captured by Hadrian were sold in such large numbers that, according to one report, a Jewish slave could be bought for a horse's ration. Many towns and villages, particularly in Judea, were razed and never rebuilt. To a large extent the central hill land of Judea lost its Jewish population. In the tannaitic literature after the revolt, we find such recurrent phrases as 'Who sees the towns of Judea in their destruction . . .' or 'When Judea was destroyed, may it soon be rebuilt . . . .' Jerusalem was in fact built up again, but as a pagan Roman city named Aelia Capitolina, after the emperor Aelius Adrianus and the tutelary god of Rome. Jews were forbidden to live in the city and were allowed to visit it only once a year, on the Ninth of Ab, to mourn on the ruins of their holy Temple. In an effort to wipe out all memory of the bond between the Jews and the land, Hadrian changed the name of the province from Iudaea to Syria-Palestina, a name that became common in non-Jewish literature. For the Jews who remained in the country, a time of harsh religious persecution followed. Many, including leading scholars, were put to death; others were forced to flee and live in hiding, either in the country or abroad, until their return several years later.

The persecutions that followed the Bar Kokhba Revolt have found their main literary reflection in the various versions of the 'story of the Ten Martyrs', a description of the capture, torture and death of ten of the greatest scholars of the time, including R. Akiva, R. Ishmael, R. Hananiah ben Tardion, R. Tarfon, the president of the Sanhedrin shortly before the revolt, Simon ben Azzai and others. As handed down by tradition, the story has come to include earlier events that belong to the period of the destruction of the Temple or of the revolt under Trajan, such as the deaths of R. Simon the *nasi* and of R. Ishmael the High Priest; some versions also contain later elements. But the core of the tradition relates to matters that occurred after the Bar Kokhba Revolt. The story of the Ten Martyrs provided the subject-matter for numerous laments that still form part of the liturgy of various Jewish communities for the Day of Atonement, the Ninth of Ab and other fast-days.

Talmudic literature has much to relate on the systematic persecution of the Jewish religion by the Roman authorities in those days, of the executions and of the confiscations of land. A characteristic example is a saying attributed to one of the scholars of the time who taught in Babylonia and later came to live in the Land of Israel:

> Rabbi Nathan says: 'They who love and keep my commandments' – those are the Jews who live in the Land of Israel and give their lives for the sake of the commandments. Why were you killed? For having circumcised my son. Why were you burned? For having studied the Torah. Why were you crucified? For having eaten unleavened bread. Why were you flagellated? For having blessed the *lulav* (*Mekhilta* on *Jethro*).

The Romans were particularly anxious to prevent Jews from meeting in synagogues, praying or studying the Torah and maintaining communal institutions. Scholars gathering to sit in judgement or to teach, or attempting to convene the Sanhedrin were punished with the greatest severity. During this time of persecution, the Jews continued to reverence the tradition of martyrdom that had its beginnings in the Second Temple era. Hebrew literature and tradition drew much of its inspiration in this period from the national and religious devotion epitomized by such martyrdom.

The religious and social consequences of the defeat also were grave. While there are many traditions of martyrdom and of Jews living in concealment in caves and deserts so that they might observe the commandments, there are also reports of others who could not withstand the pressure and complied with the demands of the authorities. More serious was a widespread tendency to question or even deny the meaningfulness of Jewish existence and despair of the nation's redemption. Some retained a weakened form of Judaism; others abandoned the nation and found themselves a place in the gentile world of the Roman Empire, which was prospering in those days and offered ample opportunity for sharing in the economic expansion. Some even joined the authorities in their persecution of the Jews and their search for any sign of organized Jewish life. Elisha ben Abuya, one of the Jabneh scholars, who parted ways with Judaism and adopted a Roman-hellenistic way of life was the prominent example of this trend. Some traditions offer a legendary explanation of his behaviour, such as the story that he despaired of his Jewishness when he saw the tongue of Hutzpith the Interpreter, a Jabneh scholar and one of the Ten Martyrs, being dragged along by a pig. Some versions even have Elisha joining the Romans in their persecution of the Jews. Nevertheless, there were rabbis who continued to acknowledge his greatness as a scholar, as is evidenced by the many stories by his great pupil, R. Meir, who said of his own relations with him that 'he found a pomegranate, ate the flesh and threw away the rind' and who kept in touch with Elisha even after the latter had joined the pagan camp.

The Recovery

The disastrous outcome of the Bar Kokhba Revolt did much to break down the nation's consistent opposition to Roman rule. For the first time one hears voices in favour of accepting Roman authority until the time of the Redemption, though most of the rabbis – and with them the majority of the people in the Land of Israel – continued to object to foreign rule and to refuse to recognize its legitimacy. This is evidenced by the recurrent attempts at insurrection whenever conditions seemed favourable. The restrictive measures adopted by the Romans remained in full force throughout the remainder of Hadrian's reign (135–138) and were partially relaxed only with the accession of Antoninus Pius. While the new emperor did not abolish his predecessor's measures nor restore the Jews in one stroke to the position they had occupied before the revolt, there is explicit testimony in Roman law to the fact that he allowed the Jews to practise circumcision, even though the general prohibition remained in force. The abolition of the ban did not extend to the Samaritans, who for a long time continued to circumcise their children at great risk. With the relaxation of the restrictions against Jews, however, organized Jewish life again became possible.

The Centre Shifts to Galilee

The first signs of recovery appeared in Galilee, which had been less affected by the war and now became the centre of Jewish life. From now on the Sanhedrin and the Patriarchate always maintained their seat in Galilee, although they moved from place to place – for instance, to Beth-shearim and Sepphoris – until the third century, when they settled permanently in the district capital, Tiberias. Nevertheless, Judea was not entirely denuded of its academies and scholars. In Lydda there was an academy that remained active for centuries, and Talmudic literature refers frequently to 'our rabbis in the south'. The centre of leadership and of spiritual creativity was, however, in Galilee, where much of the work of collecting and completing the tannaitic and amoraic literature was performed. A leading part in the rehabilitation of Jewish community life and Torah study was played by some of R. Akiva's younger disciples, who had not yet made a name for themselves in the Jabneh era. Some of them, such as R. Judah ben Ilai of Usha and Joseph ben Halafta of Sepphoris, were sons of Galilee rabbis. Others were of undistinguished parentage, so much so that they are not even known by a patronymic.

Outstanding among these scholars, spiritually and socially, was R. Meir, who is never referred to by parentage or town and was even said to be of convert origin. He was regarded as the greatest *halakhic* authority of his time, and his influence on Mishnaic *halakhah,* which was compiled in the following generation, was considerable. His teachings include frequent praise of the Jewish nation: 'Even its sinners are called God's sons.' To him knowledge of the Torah was the greatest of virtues, outweighing all others; a learned illegitimate was to be preferred to an ignorant High Priest, even a gentile who studied Torah ranked on the same level as the High Priest. In his teachings and actions, he showed respect, understanding and love for all living creatures and, above all, for the Land of Israel and the Hebrew language. His way of life combined asceticism and pursuit of truth with an identification with the common man. Tradition relates that he was the friend of one of the great Greek sages of his day; and indeed some of his sayings indicate that he was in contact with Greek culture. We also have reports, as was noted above, of his lasting devotion to his teacher, Elisha ben Abuya, whom he did not abandon even after the latter had parted ways with the Jewish community. His wife, Bruria, a daughter of R. Hananiah ben Tardion, was also an outstanding Torah scholar, and in some cases her interpretations decided the *halakhah.*

At first the meetings of the Galilee scholars continued to bear the hallmarks of improvisation and of semi-underground conditions. The *aggadah* preserves a vivid description of a meeting of scholars in the Beth-rimon Valley; it was only years later, 'when the persecution was on the wane', that Usha was chosen as the seat of the Sanhedrin. The rabbis of the generation of Usha continued to follow the classic tannaitic tradition in every respect. Their *halakhic* innovations and legislation reflect the conditions of their time, as does the manner in which they guided Jewish community life. Most of the leading scholars of Usha lived by their own manual labour, at times tenuously.

Rabban Simon ben Gamaliel

Rabban Simon ben Gamaliel of Jabneh played no part in the first stages of the establishment of the Sanhedrin at Usha. Like many others, he had been forced to go underground and lived in hiding for several years. Later, however, we find him mentioned as head of the Sanhedrin at Usha.

The times in which Rabban Simon ben Gamaliel lived and worked were difficult in every respect. In the middle of the second century, even after the anti-Jewish laws had been relaxed, the political status of the Jews in Palestine was far from stable. The Roman authorities continued to treat them with contempt and suspicion. Worse than the political uncertainty was the economic hardship. For years there was severe poverty in the land: 'Those were the times of Rabbi Judah Ben-Ilai, when six students would cover themselves with one outer garment and concern themselves with Torah' (Babylonian Talmud, *Sanhedrin* 20a). The economic hardships of the time are reflected in various ways also in the *halakhic* rulings of this generation, several of which are reported with the qualification 'Now, since the years have become unpropitious . . . .' Even of Galilee, which had suffered less than Judea, we are told that 'Hadrian the evil-doer came and destroyed' its olive groves. One of the results of this difficult economic situation was increased emigration from Palestine.

The *nasi* and the scholars of Usha succeeded in re-establishing the House of Assembly, resuming relations with the Diaspora and regaining hegemony for Palestine. To a large degree the restoration of the Diaspora's subordination to the Land of Israel is to be credited to Rabban Simon. One aspect of the struggle that this involved is the case of the Babylonian diaspora and is highly indicative of the development of relations between the centre and the Diaspora. In the days of the persecution, when the House of Assembly had ceased to be active, the Jews of Babylonia had been forced to consecrate the New Moon and proclaim leap-years themselves. When the institutions in the homeland resumed activity, the heads of the Babylonian community claimed the right to continue to do so. Their claim was based on the allegation that one of their great scholars, Hananiah, a nephew of R. Joshua, who had left the Land of Israel or possibly had even been sent to Babylonia by the scholars of Jabneh shortly before the revolt, had been equipped with the full powers of the Sanhedrin and owed no obedience to the 'youngsters' who now headed the Assembly in Palestine. The support of the exilarch of Babylonia lent a great deal of weight to this bid for independence. The Palestinian scholars realized that such action might endanger the supremacy of the Land of Israel and lead to a complete separation between the different Jewish communities. Only by combining determination with persuasion and conciliation and by enlisting the help of Babylonian scholars was the *nasi* able to induce Hananiah to desist, and the Babylonian community acknowledged once more the authority of the Land of Israel. Rabban Simon succeeded also in securing the cooperation of the rabbis with the *nasi* and of the entire centre with the leaders of the local communities.

Tradition states that on all subjects on which Rabban Simon pronounced a ruling the *halakhah* follows him, 'for he used to pronounce in accordance with the decisions of his *beth din*' (Jerusalem Talmud, *Bava Batra* 10, 14); *i.e.,* he did not decide on his own authority alone but after consultation and discussion with the High Court. In his day the Patriarchate operated as a triumvirate that included the *nasi*, the president of the Court and a scholar of recognized standing as an *halakhic* authority. For a while R. Nathan, the son of the exilarch of Babylonia, was president of the Court. Thus Rabban Simon succeeded in obtaining the cooperation of a representative of the largest Diaspora community. His example was followed by later generations: most of the presidents of the Court in the tannaitic and amoraic eras were scholars who had come to the Land of Israel from Babylonia.

'Rabbi' and the House of Severus

The Patriarchate of Rabban Simon's eldest son, R. Judah the Prince (also referred to simply as 'Rabbi', 'our holy Rabbi' or *nasi*), was a time of economic and political prosperity for the Jewish community of Palestine. R. Judah was born while Rabban Simon was still living in hiding. The beginning of his rule as *nasi* fell within the era of the Antonines, which lasted till 192, but the majority of his term of office coincided with the Severan dynasty (193–235), and the *aggadah* records the good relations between the house of the *nasi* and the imperial family. Generally, relations between the Jews of Palestine and the Severans were good from the very beginning of the latter's rule. On the other hand, Pescennius Niger, Septimus Severus' rival, treated the Jews harshly. When the Palestinians petitioned him for tax relief, he replied that, if he could, he would tax even the air they breathed. He imposed severe penalties on the cities that supported Severus, and the urban and rural Jewish populations were made to feel his displeasure. Particularly harsh was the fate of the south and its Jewish capital, Lydda. The Tenth Legion, which was stationed in Jerusalem, sided with Niger and added to the sufferings of the Jews in this region. Thus Severus' victory came as a great relief. We have ample evidence of the nation's gratitude to the Severans. Jewish tradition depicts them favourably, and there is literary and epigraphic evidence of synagogues in Palestine and the Diaspora having been dedicated to members of the Severan dynasty – an honour that had never been shown to any Roman ruler since the fall of the Temple.

One of the reasons for the good relations between the Jews and the house of Severus was the latter's oriental origin and the inclination of some of its members towards a religious syncretism that included Judaism. Under the Severans the political position of the Palestinian Jewish community was strengthened in several ways. The right of the Patriarchate and the Sanhedrin to levy taxes for the maintenance of the centre was recognized. During the reign of R. Judah, the powers of the Jewish courts and particularly of the court of the *nasi* were reinforced and extended. They exercised civil and criminal jurisdiction and possessed means of enforcing their judgements. When necessary the court of the *nasi* even heard capital cases and imposed death sentences. The right to do so was not officially recognized by Roman law, but neither did this High Court exercise justice in secret. We have evidence to this effect in the writings of the Church Father Origen, who lived and worked in the Land of Israel in those days. In a letter written a few years after, he wrote:

> And even now, though the Romans are sovereign and Jews pay them the tax of two drachmas, the Patriarch is so powerful among the Jews, that it seems as if, subject to the Emperor's consent, there is no difference between him and the former kings of the nation, for cases are being tried without official permission, according to Jewish law, and sometimes death sentences are passed, admittedly

not completely in public, but not without the Emperor's knowledge (*Epistula ad Africanum,* para. 14).

R. Judah was a special favourite of the imperial court. He received large tracts of land from the imperial domain as gifts or in lease. Talmudic legend has much to relate concerning the close relations between R. Judah and an emperor named Antonine, the friendly conversations between them and the emperor's inclination towards Judaism. The *aggadah* even goes so far as to claim in some versions that the emperor was converted to Judaism or at least 'reverenced the Lord', which, as a technical term, means that a gentile, though neither circumcised nor converted, has adopted Jewish ways of thought and observes some of the commandments. For all their exaggeration, these stories show that there was a close relationship between one of the Severans and R. Judah. It is hard to say which emperor is being referred to, for several of the members of the dynasty were known by the name Antonine. Some think that the reference is to Caracalla (198–217), because of his sympathy for Judaism; others identify him as Alexander Severus (222–235), who was a syncretist and whom the Greek cities in the vicinity of the Land of Israel used to call the 'Synagogue Elder'.

Under the Severans the Palestinian Jews also prospered economically. The area of agricultural settlement expanded both in the north and in the south, and the Severan emperors' policy of urbanization also had a beneficial effect. Emigration was replaced by immigration from the Diaspora; the immigrants including men with experience, capital and initiative who introduced new branches of agriculture, such as the cultivation of flax, and industries connected with them, such as weaving and dyeing.

In the popular view the power and prestige of the *nasi* was the first sign of the coming Redemption. Only from R. Judah's time do we see highlighted the fact of the patriarchal family's descent from the house of David. From his day onwards the *nasi* conducted his court with all the pomp and splendour of royalty. R. Judah even succeeded in bringing the leading citizens of the towns and the rich families to his court and involving them in national affairs; under the preceding *nesi'im* there had been no contact between the heads of the larger towns and the financial aristocracy, on the one hand, and the religious leadership, on the other. Among the popular rabbis and the *Ḥasidim,* one could hear protests against R. Judah's social policy, some of the extremists even refusing to have anything to do with the *nasi*. Once, R. Judah persuaded R. Pinhas ben Jair, one of the *hasidic* scholars from the south, to be his guest at a banquet; but, when R. Pinhas arrived at court and saw R. Judah's mules in their stable, he said: 'All this the Jews must pay for,' and he never wanted to see R. Judah again.

The era of 'Rabbi', his son Rabban Gamaliel, and his grandson R. Judah *nessia* is notable for its legislation, for the summarization and conclusion of the *halakhah* and particularly for its decisions in all fields of Jewish life, in which the changes of the times are reflected. Many of R. Judah's rulings showed a tendency to relax the stringencies of the *halakhah*. He exempted parts of the north and south of the country from the tithe and the obligation to observe the sabbatical year, in which land was left fallow. He even wished to abolish the fallow year entirely, but R. Pinhas ben Jair objected and the matter was never formally discussed. The legislation of his time bears witness to his initiative, guidance and personal influence, though he also knew when to withdraw a proposal, if he saw that it would not obtain the support of his colleagues.

The Final Redaction of the Mishnah

R. Judah's activities also included the redaction and completion of the Mishnah, a summary and compendium of most of the *halakhic* material of the oral tradition. He was not the first to record the oral tradition in writing in the form of a collection of *halakhic* rulings; the *tannaim* of the Temple era and particularly of the Jabneh era and later the disciples of R. Akiva had already undertaken to do so. Entire collections or parts of collections of the teachings of these sages found their way into the Mishnah, but R. Judah's compilation was more comprehensive and wider in scope.

R. Judah collected the teachings of the early authorities, summarized the new rulings made by his own generation and the immediately preceding one and arranged them in chapters and tractates according to subject matter: *Shabbat* (Sabbath), *Pesaḥim* (Passover regulations), *Gittin* (divorce), *Kiddushin* (marriage) and so forth. The chapters of the Mishnah are now cited by their initial passages; the subjects themselves are generally arranged according to their internal logic. The tractate *Sanhedrin,* for instance, begins with the composition of the court, which consisted of a panel of three in civil cases and of twenty-three in capital cases; then it states the rules of civil procedure, followed by the rules of capital procedure. Sometimes, however, when a tractate consists of entire compendia and R. Judah wished to preserve their original form as far as possible, the tractate remains structurally incomplete.

The oral doctrine is reflected in the Mishnah in the form in which it was handed down to the final editor – as a summation of different opinions where no final decision had been reached, side by side with definite rulings handed down in earlier generations or in the House of Assembly in R. Judah's own time. As a result of the composite character of the Mishnah, there are sometimes contradictions between the formulation of a rule in a compendium reflecting the teachings of one scholar or academy and a different formulation in another compendium representing the opposite school. Sometimes *halakhic* rules are given in the form of plain statements, without mention of the source, for example: 'What blessing is recited over fruit? Over fruit of trees, one says "Who has created the fruit of the tree"' and 'A woman may be emancipated by divorce, or by the death of her husband.' Many rules, however, are attributed to their authors; and sometimes even the event that occasioned the question being raised and the name of the person who decided it or set the precedent are recorded. A large number of issues are reported as controversies. In some cases the controversy goes back to times preceding the Hasmonean Revolt or to the houses of Shammai and Hillel, even though it had already been decided whom the *halakhah* would follow; others date from the generation before R. Judah and had not yet been decided in his time. There are even controversies to which he himself was a party. The Mishnah, in short, is not so much a code edited or collected by R. Judah as a summary report in book form of what was taught and discussed in the academy and the court during his lifetime.

The circumstances of his education made R. Judah eminently qualified to act as the redactor of the Mishnah. While his father lived in hiding for fear of persecution, he grew up and studied under several of the greatest of R. Akiva's disciples. Later he also studied under his father. Thus he acquired his knowledge from several academies and was familiar with different traditions and systems. This familiarity helped him develop the eclectic and synthetic trend of his own teaching, which tended to combine elements from different traditions and systems. His modesty in teaching Torah and handing down *halakhic* rulings, his independent spirit and his high standing and long rule were all qualities that assisted him in the redaction of the Mishnah and contributed to its being accepted as a basic handbook and code of the oral tradition. While in the next generation we still occasionally find rulings being handed down that are contrary to those in the Mishnah, the other compendia that were composed before or during its time were soon overshadowed by it and forgotten. The Mishnah even came to serve as the prototype for further work in the field of Oral Law. *Halakhic* statements that had been handed down orally and for some reason had not been included in the Mishnah were collected in the same manner in the Tosefta, a series of supplements to the Mishnah that follows the order of chapters and tractates in the latter. The Tosefta is one of the collections of *beraitot*, rulings of Tannaites that have remained outside the Mishnah.

In the course of the following centuries, the Mishnah served as the foundation for the two great Talmudic works, the Jerusalem (Palestinian) Talmud and the Babylonian Talmud. The Mishnah thus became the second basis of Jewish culture, following only the Bible itself.

The Mishnah is divided into six 'orders', each dealing with a different aspect of life:

1 *Zeraim* ('Seeds') deals with agriculture: the rules of cross-breeding, of the first-fruits, which must be discarded, of the fallow year and of the portions of crops to be set aside for the Temple, the priests and the poor. This order is preceded by the section *Berakhot* ('Benedictions'), which deals with the regulations for private and public prayer.

2 *Moed* ('Festival') concerns the laws of the Sabbath and holidays.

3 *Nashim* ('Women') deals with all aspects of family life and the rules of marriage, divorce and associated matters.

4 *Nezikin* ('Torts') contains the rules of civil and criminal law and of court procedure.

5 *Kodashim* ('Sacred Matters') concerns the regulations for the Temple service, ritual slaughter and permitted and forbidden foods.

6 *Tohorot* ('Purity') deals with the laws of ritual purity.

The six orders contain a total of some sixty tractates. The editors of the Mishnah included also those rules that had ceased to be observed after the fall of the Temple – such as regulations for the Temple service, capital punishment and other matters with which the Sanhedrin was competent to deal only when in session in Jerusalem — for they regarded the conditions of their times as temporary and in force only until 'the Temple shall be rebuilt, speedily, in our times'. With the exception of a few Greek and Aramaic words and expressions, the Mishnah is written entirely in a legal Hebrew of remarkable clarity and vitality.

With the completion of the Mishnah, the history of the oral tradition reached a dividing line that was to become more clearly defined as time went on. The literature written before the redaction of the Mishnah is known as tannaitic literature, its authors being referred to as *tannaim*; works written later and included in compendia collected between two and three centuries after the completion of the Mishnah are known as amoraic literature, their authors being termed *amoraim*. Any *halakhic* ruling appearing in the Mishnah or in a *beraita* is more authoritative than one that occurs only in the *Gemara,* the later discussions that, together with the Mishnah, form the Talmud; and a ruling by an *amora* is rejected if it is found to clash with the ruling of a *tanna*. In the last tannaitic generation, the distinction between *tanna* and *amora* is not always clear. Some of R. Judah's contemporaries are not included in the Mishnah but are mentioned frequently in the extra-Mishnaic traditions, the *beraitot*. Thus, for instance, R. Hiyya and his two sons, Judah and Hezekiah, who are often mentioned in the *beraitot* and in the different amoraic works, do not appear in the Mishnah. By the following generation, however, the distinction was perfectly clear.

We possess scarcely any collections of *aggadah* that distinguish between *tannaim* and *amoraim*. The line taken by the Jewish authorities was not as sharply defined in matters of *aggadah* as it was where *halakhah* was concerned. Differing conceptions were tolerated to a far greater degree in the areas of beliefs and of ethics than in matters of practice. While certain viewpoints were held in common by all academies, the demand for uniform formulations was never as marked in these areas as it was in respect to *halakhah* and law. On the whole, this distinction has been preserved in Judaism to this very day.

22

From the Roman Anarchy Until the Abolition of the Patriarchate (235–425)

The Roman Anarchy

The fifty years (235–284) separating the end of the Severan dynasty from the reign of Diocletian were, on the whole, a period of crisis, confusion and deterioration throughout the Roman Empire. With the exception of short intervals during which the empire seemed to be at peace, the entire era was marked by an interplay of factors tending to upset the orderly course of affairs. Rome was unsuccessful in repelling the invasions of the Teutonic peoples to the west and of the Parthians to the east, to the detriment of its authority at home. During these fifty years emperors, semi-emperors and pretenders rose and fell by the dozen. Many of them were unable to establish themselves in more than one section of the empire, and even those who did often did not last out the year. The consequence was the collapse of an administration that had never been firmly established in all parts of the empire. Security was at best dubious even in the towns and villages, not to mention the highroads, and the economic conditions, particularly commerce between the different provinces, suffered accordingly.

During the third century and even later, in the first years of the autocratic monarchy, we do not hear of religious or political persecution. The persecution of the Christians in the third and early fourth centuries did not affect the Jews. Even when the emperor Decius, in the middle of the third century, ordered the entire population of the empire to report to the authorities and prove its loyalty by a sacrifice, a libation or some similar sign of participation in the cult of the emperor and had a careful record kept of these acts of loyalty, the Jews were exempted from the requirement. Similarly, there is a Talmudic tradition relating that sacrifices during the reign of Diocletian, which were compulsory for all nations, including the Samaritans, were not required of the Jews.

Taxes and Extortion

If the condition of the Jewish population of Palestine was far from prosperous, the reasons were mainly of an economic order. We hear of many complaints of economic hardship and scarcity of money in those times. The crisis was due in part to war damage and the interruption of normal commerce, but perhaps even more so to the many regular and irregular taxes and levies. As the fighting came closer, the more the authorities required the population to contribute to war levies and the greater was the arbitrariness with which these demands were enforced. The worst sufferer was the farmer, who usually paid the levies in kind. The same applied to 'crown money'. This was originally a voluntary gift, in the form of a golden crown, that the people used to present to the emperor on his accession to the throne or to a general after a victory. In the course of time, the voluntary gift became a compulsory and arbitrary tax that was imposed from time to time. Its amount was not fixed, and every emperor collected it. The more frequently emperors were crowned, the more oppressive this burden became. Another tax that accompanied the frequent insurrections and wars between the various claimants to the imperial throne was the mulct or fine. Every emperor regarded himself as the sole lawful ruler, and whoever did not assist him was held guilty of rebellion. The people could not, of course, know in advance which of the rival claimants would triumph and whom they should assist, and when the 'wrong' emperor gained or retained the throne he would fine the entire population.

The many internal and external wars of the third century occasioned frequent troop movements, and the need to billet soldiers on the march or on garrison duty also was a source of much suffering for the population. Billeting and its accompanying troubles are mentioned several times in the Talmudic literature of the period. Complaints against the evil Esau who plagues the just Jacob are mainly directed against repeated instances of extortion and robbery. Palestine was not singled out, however; the same situation is reflected also in the non-Jewish sources of the countries adjoining Palestine, namely Syria and Egypt.

The Agricultural Crisis

The farmer, as we have noted, was the main sufferer from the upheavals that followed one after the other in the East during the third century, and he suffered no less when the political situation was eventually stabilized. The legal and illegal requisitions imposed by the military were far more burdensome on landholders than on city dwellers, and so too was the new tax system introduced in the late third and early fourth centuries. As the economy of the Palestinian Jews was principally agricultural, they suffered more than did the gentiles. If an earlier age had extolled the blessings of the soil and the status of the man who tilled it, from the third century on we hear complaints of the diminishing returns of farming, of there being 'no lesser trade than working the land', and of the way in which agriculture makes man a slave to his work. The fact that farming had become less profitable was due not to natural causes but to administrative measures that, in effect, discriminated against it. The disturbed times, the steeply rising prices and the devaluation of currency made many lose interest in farming. Accordingly, we hear of fewer Jewish settlements, and once more of emigration for economic reasons being on the increase. The pressure to emigrate seems to have been stronger than any barrier the rabbis sought to raise against it; and though immigration continued, it was insufficient to offset the growing exodus from the beginning of this particular era.

Social Changes

The hardships caused by the Roman administrative system also affected the social sphere. At the beginning of the third century, changes took place that were to have a decisive effect on developments in the following centuries. In the year 212 the Antonine Constitution was introduced, giving full citizenship to all subjects of the Roman Empire, with the exception of subjugated nations. From this time the privileged status of Roman citizens, particularly in the Palestinian towns, was abolished. However, a new class distinction took its place, for the law divided all town dwellers into two classes: the 'noble' (*honestiores*) and the 'humble' (*humiliores*), the distinguishing criterion being property ownership. The rich *honestiores* were entitled and even obliged to sit as members of the town council and the communal institutions, which increasingly became instruments of the state for collecting taxes, superintending public works and so forth. The *humiliores* – the masses who owned no property – were neither required nor permitted to participate in municipal government. This class distinction became permanent even in the field of criminal law. Severe and humiliating penalties could be imposed only on the *humiliores,* while the *honestiores* were exempt from such forms of punishment. These changes also affected Jewish community life, even though the *halakhah* and the Jewish way of life (in that, according to Jewish law, all Jews are equal) deprived them of part of their sting.

By means of these innovations in urban life, the imperial administration sought to convert all the semi-autonomous cells of communal existence into a bureaucratic machinery that would be entirely at the disposal of the central authorities. The *honestiores,* who carried the burden of public office, were liable with their person and property for the different payments and services (*liturgiae*) demanded by the imperial government. In Egypt we hear of people 'divesting themselves of their property' and even fleeing abroad in order to free themselves of *liturgiae* or to avoid appointments to municipal office. Such cases occurred also in the Land of Israel after the third century, and the *halakhah* explicitly permitted flight and even emigration if one was nominated for membership in a Boule or municipal council.

Changes in Jewish Leadership

In the third century changes occurred also in the structure of Jewish public leadership. Under Rabban Gamaliel (220–230) and R. Judah (230–270) and in the first and second generations after the final redaction of the Mishnah, there was a division of power and the *nasi* no longer presided over the Sanhedrin. Until the time of R. Judah the Prince, the *nasi* had been acknowledged as the spokesman of the generation in matters of Torah and had been the head of the Sanhedrin. Even in his day (see page 339), there had been clashes between the scholars and the patriarchal court, but during his lifetime they had not caused an open break. After his death the rift widened continuously, until a situation developed whereby the *nasi* was the leader of the people and the temporal head, while the Sanhedrin was independent in questions of Torah, *halakhic* rulings and law and exercised general spiritual leadership. From the formal point of view, the *nasi* continued to be the head of the Sanhedrin, and all legislation was attributed to him; and occasionally the *amoraim* quote the teachings of a *nasi*. In the third and fourth centuries, we even see leading scholars making tours of inspection and instruction in the towns of Palestine on behalf of the *nasi*, or the *nasi* himself touring, accompanied by the leading rabbis. However, in fact power was divided, and even on the rare occasions when the *nasi* attended the House of Assembly the session was opened and closed by the rabbi or by the pair of rabbis who headed the academy.

The separation was due not to any spiritual or intellectual decline on the part of the *nesi'im* but to the increasing power of those scholars who wished to draw a line between the Patriarchate, on the one hand, and the body of rabbis and what they represented, on the other. Some of the popular, extremist rabbis complained that the *nesi'im* would appoint judges on the basis of their wealth and that they themselves were excessively rich and lived ostentatiously. More than once we learn of severe measures having been taken by the *nasi* against such rebellious rabbis.

Characteristic of the relations between the Patriarchate and the Sanhedrin were the changes in rabbinical ordination. The right to ordain and confer the title 'rabbi' was one of the most important privileges of the *nasi* and the Sanhedrin, for ordination involved not only co-optation into the Sanhedrin but also the right to sit as a single judge in cases involving fines, and in course of time it also involved the right to teach Torah in public. In the first generations after the fall of the Temple, the power to ordain was exercised by the Sanhedrin; in the time of R. Judah the Prince, it was taken over by the *nasi*. After his rule, however, it was decided that ordination required the joint approval of the Sanhedrin and the *nasi*.

The First and Second Generations of Amoraim

In the first amoraic generation, the Sanhedrin and the academy at Sepphoris were headed by R. Haninah bar Hama, a scholar from Babylonia, and the connexion between the Sanhedrin and the *nasi* continued to be close. In the second generation, however, the Sanhedrin moved to Tiberias, while the Patriarchate remained at Sepphoris. During and after the move to Tiberias, the Sanhedrin's head was R. Johanan ben Nappaha (d. 279), the most prominent figure of the early amoraic period, whose sayings are quoted frequently and whose personality has left its stamp on the entire amoraic literature. Dozens of his students attributed sayings to him, and there is scarcely any question that arose in his time on which he did not express an opinion. Unlike many of the rabbis before and after him, R. Johanan, for reasons that are not known, never visited Babylonia, although some of his disciples were accustomed to doing so. Therefore, it was they who maintained the link between the two centres and transmitted to the Diaspora the teachings of R. Johanan and the other Palestinian scholars. Another means of maintaining this contact was the many letters written to the Diaspora in the name of R. Johanan. His teachings form one of the main elements in the Jerusalem as well as in the Babylonian Talmud.

Neither the many wars between Persia and Rome in the third century, nor the state of anarchy in the eastern part of the Roman Empire disrupted the contact between Palestinian and Babylonian Jewry. The first amoraic generation maintained contacts that were more extensive, profound and frequent than those of any period before or after. Even in the middle of the third century, when the offensive of King Shapur I of Persia reached its peak and there was heavy fighting on the Roman-Persian frontier, the travels of Palestinian and Babylonian scholars to and from the Land of Israel continued without interruption.

As before, academies existed in various parts of Palestine. They were semi-autonomous and depended very little on the Sanhedrin or the academies at Sepphoris and Tiberias. Like the central academy, they served as centres for their immediate regions in such matters as the appointment of judges, religious and legal instruction and other aspects of communal life.

The centre of the southern part of the country was located at Lydda and had been founded by R. Joshua ben Levi; the centre at Caesarea was established by R. Ushaya. A smaller centre existed at Akhbarei in Upper Galilee, where R. Jannai and a group of disciples lived communally, cultivating the land together and living on its produce. These academies remained in existence for a considerable time, each maintaining its own teaching tradition and customs. On special occasions conferences of heads of academies or of scholars from several academies were convened. Particularly frequent were meetings between the rabbis from the south (Lydda) and members of the Sanhedrin in Tiberias. The two centres also cooperated in the political sphere: occasionally, the heads of the two academies would go together to see the governor in Caesarea or to Rome or they would make a joint tour of the Palestinian communities.

The International Situation

Two military events of political importance that occurred in the third century confronted the orient, including the Jews in the Land of Israel, with a choice between keeping faith with Rome or lending support to internal or external elements seeking to destroy and supplant Roman rule. First there were the long and savage wars between Rome and Persia for control of the East following the rise of the Sassanid dynasty in Persia. The first attack was mounted by Ardashir in 230–232; further attacks, some of them severe, followed in the third, fourth and fifth decades. Countries that were centres of Roman rule in the East were conquered; Antioch was taken and sacked two or three times, and many of its inhabitants were carried off into captivity. Rome's fortunes reached their nadir with the capture of the emperor Valerian by King Shapur in 260.

Neither Ardashir nor Shapur extended his campaigns to the borders of Palestine, but the great Jewish communities in Asia and Syria were highly conscious of being caught between the two rival realms, and in the Land of Israel itself the upheavals had strong repercussions. The nations of the East were divided in their attitude towards the central authorities. Among the lower classes everywhere, there was great bitterness against Roman rule because of the heavy taxes and compulsory services and because of the preferential treatment extended to the urban moneyed aristocracy. But there was opposition to Rome in ruling circles as well, due either to feelings of being discriminated against or to nationalist objections to Roman rule over the East. Some classes actually collaborated with the Persians, but there is nothing to show that the Jews – who in earlier times had set their hopes on the Persian wars and supported the invaders and later were to do so again – actually joined the Persian side in the third century. On the contrary, the Jews of Mezigath-Kaysari in Cappadocia put up a strong resistance when Shapur captured the town in 252/3, and 12,000 of them were put to the sword. This anti-Persian attitude may be explained by the fact that the rise of the Sassanids was accompanied by a Persian religious and national revival that, at least at first, led to the persecution of other religions, including the Jews of Babylonia, whose position deteriorated under Ardashir and at the beginning of Ahabor's rule. This intolerance on the part of the Persian kings made the Jews of the third century reluctant to cooperate with them, all the more so as the Persian methods of warfare were characterized by widespread destruction and looting.

While the two great empires were thus competing against each other, Tadmor (Palmyra) succeeded in gaining its independence, even attaining an influential position in the East in the years 260–272. During this short span of time, its conquests and influence also extended to Palestine and Egypt. In this desert oasis the Jews formed part of a mixed population that included Arameans, Arabs and even Persians. We have literary and epigraphic evidence, from the Second Temple era until the third century CE, of Jews from Palmyra coming to the Land of Israel and being buried there. The Jews exerted considerable social and religious influence on the ruling class, which at that time was Arab. For a while, during the rule of King Odenathus, Palmyra's influence increased under Roman protection. His wife and successor, Queen Zenobia (267–272), embarked on a campaign of successful expansion. The wide support she found in the East testifies to the strong desire for independence that prevailed in the orient in those days. Others, however, were not prepared to join Zenobia, and she did not succeed in rallying the East to her standard when the Roman emperor set out to subject Palmyra.

There are Jewish traditions that describe Odenathus, at the time when he was a successful supporter of Rome, as something of a robber baron and refer to him disapprovingly as the 'brother' (presumably, because of the oriental character of his rule) who came to the aid of 'Esau' (Rome) in his hour of weakness. R. Johanan, the spokesman of the Jews of that generation, declared: 'Hail unto him who witnesses the fall of Tadmor' (Jerusalem Talmud, Ta'anit 4). Zenobia was more favourably inclined to Judaism and the Jews. Christian traditions from the fourth century onwards have her converting and becoming 'a Jewess' – undoubtedly a legend that arose because she surrounded herself with advisers sympathetic to Judaism and gave the Jews her benevolent support. She also came to the assistance of Palestinian Jewry, and an inscription found in Egypt reports that she restored the right to offer asylum to a synagogue in Lower Egypt – a right that had first been granted by Ptolemy Euergetes (247–221 BCE) and was later withdrawn. Among certain circles the conflict between Queen Zenobia and Rome was even a source of hope that grew into messianic expectations.

The Rise of Christianity

Towards the end of the third century (284), Diocletian became emperor. For a while he succeeded in stabilizing Roman imperial rule; but, meanwhile, a new force was rising on the political horizon: the Church Militant, whose beginnings may be said to date from the recognition of the Christian religion by Constantine (313). This new factor was to have a decisive effect on the status of Palestine and of the Jews in the Roman diaspora and indirectly also on the Jews in the Persian Empire.

From this time on Palestinian Jewry had to wage a two-fronted political and religious defensive. Until then it had had to contend with the pagan world – a contest that was fought mainly in the cultural sphere, as paganism, by its very nature, admitted the existence of national religions. The Roman authorities had recognized in principle and generally also in fact the Jewish religious existence in the Land of Israel. With Christianity's rise to power and (within a relatively short time after 313) to the status of the official religion of the empire, a basic change took place in the relations between the Jews and their environment. Christianity, as a monotheistic religion, neither recognized nor tolerated other religions. One of the sages of the Mishnah foresaw the difficult times Judaism was to experience when 'the kingdom would fall to the *minim* [Christians]'. Christianity was to prove much more intolerant than Judaism, for it claimed a double inheritance from 'spiritual Israel' and from the pagan world, endowing it with both the spiritual and political right to rule.

The Church took a special interest in attempting to bring Jews into its fold; but Judaism was not proscribed in the Christian Roman Empire. Among the Church Fathers and particularly in the doctrine of Augustine (354–430), the prevailing explanation was that Judaism should be allowed to survive in order to 'bear [scriptural] witness' to the truth of Christianity. Christianity saw as its task the elimination of paganism, but it recognized the existence of Judaism in 'this world' in the belief that the general conversion of the Jews was a matter for the 'world to come'. At the end of the fourth century, there were instances of forced conversion, which were to become more frequent in the course of time, but it never became the official policy of the Christian state.

The Church, however, while not actually proscribing Judaism, consistently fostered hatred and contempt for all that was Jewish. In addition to its detestation of the Jews – a heritage from the time when the two religions had separated – the Christian world had also absorbed much of the contemptuous attitude that had prevailed among the Roman aristocracy of the pagan empire. The standard-bearers of this hatred were the Church Fathers and the monks, and its practical reflection may be found in the insulting language of imperial anti-Jewish legislation, in the decrees of rulers and administrators at all levels and in the attacks by fanatics against the Jews and their institutions. The case of the monk Barsauma of Nisibis, who roamed over Palestine with a band of followers in the years 419–422 and razed synagogues, was only one instance that had many parallels in the Diaspora.

In respect to the Land of Israel, the attitude of the Church was compounded by two additional elements. First, Christianity claimed ownership of what it regarded as its Holy Land by virtue of the Jewish past, of which it claimed to be the heir, and by virtue of the fact that Palestine contained the sites of the Crucifixion and the sepulchre of Jesus, as well as other holy sites. Second, the Christian message based itself on the premise that, with the destruction of Jerusalem and the rejection of the Jewish people by the Lord, the entire Covenant, including the promise of the Land of Israel, became vested in Christendom. The Jews were no longer the only claimants to the Land of Israel.

From the year 315 on, anti-Jewish measures were included in Constantine's legislation. One of the earliest of these edicts required Jews in the Diaspora to share in the responsibility of municipal government. This requirement not only imposed on the Jews a burden that they were reluctant to assume, but it revoked an explicit exemption that had been granted them earlier because municipal office involved idolatry – a reason that was no longer valid now. Some decrees specified that *nesi'im*, priests, presidents and elders of synagogues would continue to be exempt from municipal office. In the course of time, decrees were issued forbidding the conversion of males to Judaism. Christian or pagan slaves circumcised by their owners (as the *halakhah* requires; if the slave refuses, he must be sold to a non-Jewish owner) would be freed automatically. Another decree protected Jewish converts to Christianity against persecution by the Jews. Christian sources also report that the ban against Jewish pilgrimage to Jerusalem was imposed once again.

The Laws of Constantius

Constantine's son and successor, Constantius (337–361), was a far weaker emperor than his father had been and became increasingly dependent on his ecclesiastical counsellors, who were always concerned to prevent any Jewish influence from being exerted on Christians. As a result, his policy in Christian affairs was more explicitly anti-Jewish. His decrees extended the prohibition against Jewish proselytism to include women, forbade marriage between Christians and Jews, gave greater protection to converts to Christianity and forbade Jews to own non-Jewish slaves, whether they were Christian or not – a severe blow to the Jews in the economic circumstances of the times. In an attempt to disrupt the order of the Jewish festivals and to prevent those Christians who wished to do so from celebrating Easter on the first day of Passover, the imperial authorities prevented the rabbis from meeting to proclaim New Moons and leap-years and from sending messengers to the Diaspora communities to inform them of their decisions. These prohibitions were presumably one of the considerations that moved the *nasi* Hillel II, in the year 358, to determine once and for all a fixed calendar and send it in writing to the Diaspora communities – an act of incalculable religious and cultural importance and certainly the result of lengthy astronomical research and spiritual development. One of the consequences was that the Diaspora was no longer dependent on the monthly decisions of the Sanhedrin in the Land of Israel.

Constantius' decrees were harsh not only in content and purpose but also in language. To this legislator the Jews were nothing but a 'pernicious' or 'despicable sect' that used to meet in 'sacrilegious assemblies'. Such terminology was to become a permanent feature in the decrees of later Christian emperors.

Administrative and Social Changes

In the administrative and social sphere, the era beginning with Diocletian's rule brought far-reaching changes. The provinces were multiplied by subdivision and reallocation of territories. Palestine, one of the smallest, was eventually divided into three territories: Palaestina Prima, including Judea, Samaria, the coastal plain, Idumea and the Peraea and retaining Caesarea as its capital; Palaestina Secunda, consisting of Galilee, the Decapolis and Golan, with its capital at Beth-shean; and Palaestina Tertia, consisting of the Negev, with Petra as its capital. The civil and military powers were likewise separated. In practice this meant that each province was ruled by a civilian *praeses* and a military *dux*. The results were a multiplication of public offices and bureaucracy and a proliferating hierarchy in the official administration and apparatus. The government, its ministers and its servants assumed an aura of sanctity, which was, as it were, a reflection of the emperor's hallowed personage. The imperial subjects became slaves twice over: in theory, of the emperor; in practice, of his many and varied representatives.

The Diocletian-Constantinian system completely consolidated the crafts and bound the artisan to his trade; craftsmen were not allowed to change their trade or apprentice their sons outside it. Membership in the imperial guilds, whose sole purpose was to assure the regular collection of taxes, was made compulsory.

In this era of the empire, tenant farming became increasingly prevalent, and the small independent farmer virtually disappeared. The hardships of the new economic conditions allowed the survival of none but the great landlords, who took over the small holdings and made the former owners their tenants. The imperial laws also introduced the 'colonate', which bound the tenant farmer to the land he cultivated. Tenants who attempted to leave their land were liable to arrest and punishment, and tenant status passed from father to son. Nor were these the only respects in which tenancy turned into quasi-slavery; a tenant was not allowed to dispose of his property by sale or even as a gift without the landlord's consent. The condition of the 'imperial tenants', who cultivated imperial domains, was not very different.

In Palestine the laws of colonate were introduced comparatively late, between 383 and 388 or thereabouts, fifty years later than in most of the provinces. One reason was that the land continued to be owned by small holders and that Jewish law respected personal liberty. The central authorities took into consideration the special conditions prevailing in each province, until they believed the time was ripe for introducing the laws of Rome in the entire empire.

Changes in the Land of Israel

One cause of major demographic changes in Palestine was the reorganization of the army. Two large, separate bodies were established: the mobile *elite* troops, who accompanied the imperial court, and the border garrisons or *limitanae*. The soldiers serving in the latter were given farms and settled on the land; and these military colonies added to the security of both the borders and the towns. To some extent the prosperity of Jewish settlements in the south during this era was a result of the consequent security that prevailed on the border, but the new arrangement resulted also in a considerable increase of the non-Jewish element in the Land of Israel. Many Christian communities sprang up in towns and villages, and the large cities, which had for the most part remained loyal to Hellenism, where forced to fight to preserve their pagan identity. Constantius and his mother, Helena, who was a devout Christian and even spent her last years in Palestine, began to build great churches: one in Bethlehem in memory of Jesus' birth and two in Jerusalem in honour of his burial and ascension.

To the Jews the rise and growth of Christian power became painfully obvious through the activities of a convert named Joseph, who, according to his own testimony, had been a high-placed member of the *nasi's* court at Tiberias and was rewarded by the emperor with the title *Comes* ('Companion of Honour'). The emperor gave his support to Joseph's church-building activities in such Jewish centres as Tiberias and Sepphoris, as well as in places such as Nazareth and Capernaum, which were sacred to Christianity but where the Christians had gained no foothold. The Jews made great efforts to oppose Joseph; in Tiberias all he succeeded in doing was to build a small church, and eventually he was forced to leave the city. He spent the rest of his days in the non-Jewish city of Beth-shean.

The Revolt Against Gallus

In the year 351 the Jews of Sepphoris rose against Gallus, the Roman ruler of the East. The insurgents chose a leader, Patricius, of whom little is known, and overcame and disarmed the Roman garrison. The revolt spread to Galilee, and Lydda in the south also joined. The insurgents established their own government but did not dare to march on Jerusalem. This revolt was not an uprising against Christian rule – at all events, there were no acts of revenge against Christians or churches, and the Church Fathers, who mention the revolt, would surely have reported anything of the kind. Rather, the revolt was directed against the corrupt rule of Gallus. The insurgents had heard of the various revolts in the West and had drawn encouragement from reports of the defeat of Constantius in his campaign against Magentius, a general who had rebelled against the empire in the West. They also hoped for Persian support, for Persian attacks had become frequent at this time and in some instances were fairly successful. Gallus sent his experienced general Uriscinnus to deal with the situation, and the decisive battle must have taken place near Acco. From there the imperial army marched on the Jewish centres in Galilee, and many Jewish settlements in Galilee and on the coastal plain were laid waste. The large Jewish towns of Sepphoris, Tiberias and Lydda were rebuilt shortly after the revolt, but others were not. Beth-shearim, for example, remained little more than a hamlet. What role the Sanhedrin and the *nasi* played during the revolt is not known. Whatever their stand, they were functioning normally shortly afterwards.

Julian the Hellene

The short reign of the emperor Julian (360–363) was a time of great hope for the Jews of Palestine and the Diaspora. He adhered to the old Greek religion and sought to restore it by reducing the stature of Christianity in the empire. Moreover, he intended to re-establish the Jewish sacrificial cult, the element of Jewish religion that he prized most. Julian's attitude towards the Jews was not merely a matter of religious policy; his letters reflect personal sympathy and compassion for the Jewish people. On his way to the Persian front, in the summer of 362, he stayed in Antioch, where he proclaimed his desire to establish 'with the utmost diligence the Temple of the Supreme God' and promised to rebuild 'Holy Jerusalem, which you have for so many years longed to see rebuilt, and I shall resettle it and join you within it in rendering honour to the greatest God of all.' Of the proclamations and letters issued by the emperor in this connexion, we still have the entire text of a letter addressed to 'the community of the Jews'. His cordiality towards the Jews, his activities on their behalf and his promises for the future far exceeded anything said or done by earlier foreign potentates who wished the Jews well.

By rebuilding the Temple and restoring Jerusalem, the emperor also sought to act against Christianity, which based much of its propaganda on the destruction of the Holy City as a symbol of the forfeiture of election by the Jewish people and its transmission to the Church. Apparently, the emperor wished also to win the sympathy of the Jews in the Persian Empire before beginning his campaign in the East. In fact, Jews did actually settle in Jerusalem and began to expel the Christians from certain parts of the city. They even established a temporary synagogue in one of the colonnades near the site of the Temple. At the same time the emperor appointed one of his trusted courtiers, Aliphius of Antioch, who had previously held high office, as his special commissioner in charge of the building operations and provided him with ample allocations from the imperial treasury. In Jewish tradition the entire episode is preserved only fragmentarily and in indirect references. There are hints in the sayings of certain sages indicating that they were in favour of Julian's enterprise and thought it the beginning of the Redemption. What attitude the central Jewish authorities – the Sanhedrin and the *nasi* – adopted towards the emperor's proclamations we do not know. They would hardly have opposed the offers or actions of a gentile emperor who proposed to rebuild the Temple, but they may well have been cautious about a project that depended largely on the goodwill of a single man, a childless widower, whose court and administration included many Christians, some of whom were – openly or secretly – fanatically religious. Christian and Persian sources speak of a great revival and excitement among the Jews, of a rush to Jerusalem and of fund-raising activities from Italy to Babylonia and Persia. There is a record of thousands of Jews from Persian districts making their way to Jerusalem to take part in the building of the Temple during Julian's Persian campaign and being killed on their way by the Persians. The Persian King, Shapur II, remained suspicious of the Jews ever after.

The Christian reaction was, naturally, one of fury. Many ecclesiastical authors inveighed against the building of the Temple by a heathen emperor. More sympathetic was the attitude of the Hellenes. The pro-Jewish mood among Hellenic writers is particularly evident in the works of Libanius of Antioch, a close friend of the emperor. The building work required many preparations. In particular, it was necessary to demolish and remove the remains of the pagan temple built by Hadrian when he founded Aelia Capitolina, which had been abandoned since Constantine's days. The exaggerated reports by Christian authors of such miraculous events as a fire that destroyed all that the Jews had built, following the warnings and prophesies of Christian priests from Jerusalem, suggest that the Christians, who lived in Jerusalem in large numbers, set fire to the buildings. Meanwhile, there was no news from the emperor, and the officials in charge of the building work, including Aliphius himself, waited cautiously until contact with Julian could be established. But Julian was killed on 10 June 363, apparently by a Christian Arab soldier, and the entire episode came to an end.

However, Julian's actions left their mark on the structure of the population and the political condition of the Jews. In 363, the year of Julian's death, a Syrian source reported 'a great anger than went forth from before the Lord' and destroyed twenty-one towns of the pagans, Jews and Samaritans in the south who had taken part in 'the sin of Julian the Hypocrite'. One may assume that this 'anger' against those who participated in Julian's enterprise was helped along, if not fomented, by the Christians. The Jewish settlements in the south did not cease to exist but were reduced in number and population. In the interval between the death of Julian (363) and the rise of Theodosius I (379), which marked the beginning of Christian domination, there was no further anti-Jewish legislation. The legal status of the Patriarchate was strengthened, and there were even some edicts that improved the status of the Jews. One edict mentions that the emperor Valens (364–378) exempted officers of communities subject to 'the illustrious Patriarch [*Nasi*]' from service on municipal councils; another edict, of 368, forbade the billeting of troops in synagogues. These were good times for the Jews, possibly because the impact of Julian's personality and activities had resulted in greater tolerance towards other religions and had halted the domination of Christianity over the Roman world. Another possible reason was that Valens, belonging to the Arian sect, which by then was already in the minority, showed moderation towards the Jews and Hellenes so as not to make enemies outside the Church while he was busy fighting the Orthodox clergy.

The Worsening Attitude Towards the Jews

Under Theodosius I, his sons, Honorius and Arcadius, and Theodosius II and until the abolition of the Patriarchate (379–425), the Christian Church consolidated its position as the sole power in the empire and the empire became less tolerant towards Hellenes and 'heretics'. As for the Jews, they suffered in inverse proportion to the strength of the emperor's personality. This was not only a matter of issuing laws and edicts but also of keeping the peace and preserving justice between Jews and Christians. Characteristic of these and later times was an incident that occurred in 388. The bishop of a town on the bank of the Euphrates was among those responsible for the burning of a synagogue by a Christian crowd. The governor did not dare to punish the rioters and referred the matter to the emperor, who reprimanded him and ordered him to demand that the bishop build a new synagogue. At this stage, however, Ambrosius, the bishop of Milan and one of the leaders of the Church, intervened and forced the emperor to publicly withdraw his orders. This event occurred under Theodosius I, who was one of the strongest emperors. During his reign and that of his son Arcadius, anti-Jewish legislation was still relatively restrained, but from the time of Theodosius II the situation worsened continually. By then the inferior status of the Jews and of Judaism had been clearly established. It was reflected not so much in the edicts themselves, which were relatively mild in comparison with those of later eras, as in their formulation and in the theological preambles that preceded every edict. Even an edict designed to protect the Jews began with the comment that it is intended 'to suppress the power and insolence of the contemptible Hellenes, Jews and heretics. Therefore, all we permit is that . . . they shall no longer be persecuted and in the future their synagogues shall not be seized and burned down' (*Codex Theodosianus* XVI 8, 26 of 9 April 423).

The Abolition of the Patriarchate

Various sources from the end of the fourth century indicate that at that time the Patriarchate was still a powerful institution; the right of the *nasi* to collect contributions in all parts of the empire was recognized, and any injury to him was severely punished by the authorities. Early in the fifth century, however, the status of the last *nasi,* R. Gamaliel, deteriorated. He was accused of contravening anti-Jewish imperial edicts by building synagogues, circumcising slaves and sitting in judgement in a case between Christians. For these offences he was demoted, by an edict of the year 415, from the rank of 'honourable Prefect' and was warned against committing similar offences. Even this edict indicates the degree of power and influence he exerted on life in the Land of Israel.

However, the abolition of the Patriarchate formed part of the aims of the Church, for the very existence of this 'Sceptre of Judah', surrounded by a halo of royalty, contradicted the Christian conception of their founder as the Messiah and son of David. The leaders of the Church consistently attempted to bring the Patriarchate into disrepute with fictitious reports of its spiritual decline and moral turpitude. An edict of the Theodosian Codex issued in 429 refers to the 'Patriarchal exemption' and directs the Sanhedrins of the two Palestines to hand over to the imperial treasury the moneys that had been collected for the *nasi* with official permission. It is from this edict that we learn of the abolition of the Patriarchate – probably after the death of R. Gamaliel – and of the splitting of the Sanhedrin into two sections. The government availed itself of the opportunity offered by the death of R. Gamaliel and of his young sons and declined to confirm a new *nasi* to succeed him. With the abolition of the Patriarchate, an institution that had been maintained for three and a half centuries after the fall of the Temple, the nation lost its institutional leader, the 'remnant of the house of David'.

The Completion of the Jerusalem Talmud

In the second half of the fourth century, the Talmud known as the Jerusalem or Palestinian Talmud was compiled in the Land of Israel – mostly in Tiberias. It summarizes the entire thinking of the Palestinian scholars during the two centuries following the conclusion of the Mishnah. This era, which ran from the end of the Severan dynasty until the abolition of the Patriarchate, is known as the era of the Palestinian *amoraim* and may be divided into five or six generations, which are generally identified by the names of heads of academies or other prominent figures.

The Talmud takes the form of a commentary on the Mishnah – a commentary in the wider sense, for it often includes, over and above an explanation of the Mishnaic text, decisions on points that the Mishnah leaves open, as well as systematic or *halakhic* discussions and additions, presented as they arose in the course of academic debate or in practical life. As there is no precise record of the date of the Jerusalem Talmud's compilation or of its authors, they can only be established on the basis of the last scholars or events referred to in the body of the work. The text available to us covers only four of the six orders of the Mishnah – *Zeraim, Moed, Nashim* and *Nezikin* – and part of *Niddah*; and here and there chapters are missing. The discussions in the academies doubtlessly also included matters belonging to the missing orders, at least those that were still relevant after the fall of the Temple (such as *Hullin,* which deals with the laws of ritual slaughter and permitted foods); but how far the editing, arrangement and recording of these orders had progressed by the time they were lost is not known.

The teachings of the Palestinian *amoraim* had considerable influence also in Babylonia and are quoted in the Babylonian Talmud, although the Jerusalem Talmud never achieved as much importance outside Palestine as did the Babylonian Talmud.

23

From the Abolition of the Patriarchate to the Arab Conquest (425–640)

Difficult Times

The two centuries from the abolition of the Patriarchate until Byzantine rule in the Land of Israel was supplanted by the Arab conquerors were a difficult period for the Jews in the Land of Israel. It was a time of suffering and humiliation. The Jewish population and the number of Jewish settlements continued to dwindle, both in absolute figures and in relation to the general population of the country, and the legal status of the Jews deteriorated. The gloom was relieved only by a few weak rays of light. Compared with other eras with which we have dealt, very few records of this period have survived, although *halakhic* and liturgical writings that have come to light in recent times – following the discovery of the Cairo *Genizah* (depository for damaged manuscripts), as well as archaeological finds, such as the ruins of synagogues and inscriptions – allow us to reconstruct at least an outline of the conditions then prevailing among Palestinian Jewry.

After the abolition of the Patriarchate and the ban on the collection of funds for the Sanhedrin, we know of the existence of a Sanhedrin and an academy only in Tiberias, and their activities and influence were restricted in comparison with earlier times. For about 100 years the academy was headed by *rashei haperek* ('heads of the chapter'), who were referred to by that title also in Roman law. In the year 520, Mar Zutra, the son of the executed exilarch of that name (see page 380), settled in the Land of Israel. At first he joined the *rashei haperek*, but later we find him referred to as the head of the Sanhedrin, an office that was held by his sons and their descendants for seven generations, until the academy moved to Jerusalem after the Arab conquest.

As we have noted, anti-Jewish legislation became more frequent at the beginning of the fifth century. It was accompanied by riots staged by Christian fanatics, who attacked Jews and burned synagogues for the 'greater glory' of the Church, at a time when the rebuilding of synagogues was forbidden by law. This prohibition appears several times in the Roman edicts. The Christian population of Palestine increased in numbers. In the first half of the fifth century, during the long reign of Theodosius II, the influence of the Church expanded, affecting not only legislation but also administration. Local governors in Palestine and elsewhere in the orient were powerless against the clergy and the fanatic Christian crowds that attacked the

Jews, and even the emperor was occasionally forced by aggressive priests to refrain from protecting Jews against such injustices.

From the second half of the fifth century until the accession of Justinian (527–565), which was accompanied by a resurgence of Christian militancy, the Jews knew comparatively quiet times and their position in Palestine improved. From 438 to 527 a split in the Christian ranks brought anti-Jewish legislation to a halt. The theological dispute between the Orthodox and the Monophysites concerning the divine and the human components of Jesus' person and the division resulting from this dispute affected the domestic and foreign policy of the Byzantine Empire. The dispute was accompanied by political, civil and military clashes between the different sects within the Church, and the emperors, preoccupied with these affairs, left the Jews in peace. The monks, being engaged in rebellion and rioting against the authorities whenever the latter opposed them in religious matters, did so as well. Economically, these were prosperous times for Palestine, and the Jews shared in the prosperity, directly or indirectly. The prosperity was due not only to the emperors' enormous investments in the Holy Land but also to the great advances made in agriculture at the time. In the Negev in particular, farming spread to parts of the country that had never before been cultivated. The situation was reflected in the construction, restoration and enlargement of synagogues, remains of which have been found in the north (Beth-alpha, Hamath, Geder, etc.) and in the south (Jericho, Naaran, Ashkelon, Gaza, etc.). Though the building and decoration of synagogues were still prohibited, when the times were favourable the Jews knew how to circumvent such laws.

The Jewish Kingdom of Himyar

From Christian authors in the East we have reports of the conversion to Judaism of influential circles in the Kingdom of Himyar in Arabia and, incidentally, of the considerable influence that the centre in Tiberas exercised even then on remote Jewish communities. In Himyar, which was situated on the east coast of the Red Sea and had extended its rule over considerable portions of South Arabia, the Jews succeeded, according to these reports, in propagating the Jewish faith among the people as well as the royal family. Christian sources tell of Jewish priests (presumably, rabbis) from Tiberias who formed part of the suite of King Du Noas and served as his envoys in negotiations with Christian cities. Elsewhere we read that 'the Jews in Tiberias send priests every year and at all times to foment quarrels with the Christians.' The Christians demanded that

> the chief priests in Tiberias and in the remainder of the country be cast into prison . . . that they give sureties that they will not send letters and emissaries to the king of Himyar . . . and to tell them that unless they do so, their synagogues will be burned down, the Cross placed over them and the Christians will take control of them.

Twice the Jews of Himyar succeeded in throwing off Ethiopian domination; even in the eyes of Byzantium it was a Jewish kingdom, small but occupying a strategic position. The king of Himyar prevented Byzantine traders from passing through to India on the grounds that Jews were being persecuted in Roman lands. Byzantium was reluctant to risk a war so far away in South Arabia, but was able to persuade Ethiopia to take up its quarrel. The king of Himyar hoped for Persian aid, but there was a lull in the fighting between Rome and Persia at the time, and the Persians did not appreciate the importance of this outlet from the Red Sea being controlled by an ally of Byzantium. Du Noas fell in a battle against an invading Ethiopian army, and the Jewish kingdom came to an end.

Justinian and the Jews

Justinian began persecuting the Jews immediately after his accession (527), and anti-Jewish legislation was renewed in the very first year of his rule. The laws that had been enacted at the beginning of the fifth century were now reaffirmed, while the penalties for Jewish contraventions were increased and compensation for stolen Jewish property was reduced. In the process of selecting the old Theodosian edicts that were to be included in the new code of Justinian, some provisions that had safeguarded the rights of the Jews and the status of Judaism were omitted, and new rules discriminating against the Jews and stressing the inferior state of the Jewish religion were added. Novella 131 laid down that canon law was to rank equal with state law; another novella, from the year 537, interpreted the law so as to require the Jews to bear the full burden of municipal government without enjoying any of the honours of municipal office. Particularly burdensome was the provision that the implementation of regulations directed against the Jews and other religions was not to be vested in the provincial governors alone but was to be exercised jointly by the governors and the bishops. The law even required the bishops to have direct recourse to the emperor if they found the civil authorities negligent in implementing anti-Jewish legislation.

An important innovation, which also affected the traditional Christian approach to the Jews, was incorporated into novella 146. In one of the Jewish communities, a dispute had broken out between those who wanted to have readings from the Torah only in Hebrew and others who demanded the addition of a Greek translation. The Hebraists apparently feared that the reading of the Greek translation would replace the sermon on *halakhah* and *aggadah* that followed the Torah reading. The dispute was brought before the emperor, who took it upon himself to lay down the law on the order of synagogue services in general, with the primary intention, as the novella explicitly states, of persuading the Jews to draw closer to Christianity and to Christian hermeneutics. To that end, support was given to the party that requested the addition of a Greek translation, the latter preferably to be the Septuagint, whose use was widespread in the Christian Church, although the Aquilas and Latin translations were also permitted. The new regulations further stated: 'But what ye are wont to call *Deuterosis* [Mishnah] is entirely forbidden, and the Heads shall see to it that the law is not interfered with and is carried out properly.' This trend of interfering in the internal life of the Jewish communities and in the order of the religious service never became general in Christianity, but was, as we have seen, sometimes an influential factor.

Aggadah *and* Piyyut

In this era the spirit of the Jewish nation found expression in the *aggadah*. The *aggadah* actually dates back to far earlier times and always had gone hand in hand with the *halakhah*, both in sharing the same underlying philosophy and in the historical sense. Unlike the *halakhah*, however, the *aggadah* had never been collected in compendia. In the Mishnah and even more frequently in the two Talmuds, *aggadah* appears in the form of an accompaniment to and expansion upon the *halakhic* argument. Alongside the *halakhot* dealing with the order of prayer, for instance, we find much in the Talmud concerning the value of prayer, serving God in the heart, the customs of various scholars and the religious expectations of the Jewish people throughout the generations. *Halakhot* on alms-giving are accompanied by discourses on the importance of charity, on the ways in which it should be dispensed and on principles of social and public life. Occasionally, entire sections of *aggadah* stand on their own, with only a loose connexion established between the *aggadah* and *halakhic* sections by means of associating the *aggadah* with or attributing it to the scholar in whose name the *halakhah* is reported.

However, in the fifth, sixth and seventh centuries and even somewhat later, we find independent collections of *aggadah*. The earliest of those that have survived are *aggadic midrashim* (homiletic commentaries) on Genesis, Lamentations and Leviticus from the fifth century. In these *midrashim*, *aggadah* is the point of departure as well as the main substance. Mostly they take the form of homilies on the Pentateuch, the five scrolls and other parts of the Bible that were read in the synagogue on the Sabbath and festivals. Some of this homiletic literature interprets the text verse by verse, while some consists of entire sermons or parts of sermons based on a single verse. The prophecy of consolation in Isaiah 40, for example, which is read on the Sabbath following the Ninth of Ab, is expanded into a discourse on the nation's hope for future redemption. In more extreme instances the verse serves merely as the point of departure for a sermon that goes far afield.

The pattern of *aggadic* writing arose from the fact that the *aggadah* had, from its earliest times, been handed down mainly by means of the public sermon. The preacher used to build his discourse on the reading of the day, with which the congregation was familiar from its own study and from hearing it in the synagogue year after year. The sermon was the channel through which the thoughts of the rabbis and the wisdom of generations were communicated to the general public, including women and children. It was the main instrument of public education and of guidance on contemporary issues in political and social life. Editing and collecting the *aggadah* also satisfied the demand for professional literature for preachers and reading matter and study material for the people on the Sabbath and festivals. Among the collections of *aggadah* on the Torah are works of a type known as *Yelammedenu*, after the standard introductory formula *Yelammedenu rabbeinu* ('May our teacher instruct us'), which introduces the *halakhic* question that the preacher poses and that he answers in the course of the sermon, with the addition of *aggadic* digressions. Often the *halakhic* question is not a genuine problem requiring solution but a formal method of introducing the *aggadah*.

Unlike the *halakhah,* which has been preserved in two parallel compendia – the Jerusalem and Babylonian Talmuds – the *aggadah* and the *aggadic* books are mainly the work of Palestinian Jewry, and the scholars referred to in the *aggadah* of the amoraic period are mostly of Palestinian origin.

Another literary development in these times was the *piyyut,* liturgical poetry that was included in the prayer service, mainly on the Sabbath, festivals and other public occasions. It includes elements of *halakhah* and *aggadah,* mystical thought, prayer and even the secular songs of earlier generations. In the case of many *piyyutim* of this era, we know nothing about the authors, not even their names; but the identity of some of them has been preserved, including Jose ben Jose, R. Jannai and R. Eleazar Kalir. Their works have been incorporated into the prayer-books of the various Jewish traditions. Some *piyyutim* are recorded as having been composed for specific occasions or at the request of an individual and are preserved in collections of *piyyutim* by one or several authors. Although the amoraic era was the golden age of the Palestinian *piyyut,* the composition of *piyyutim* continued in Palestine until much later.

According to some views, the creation of the *aggadah* was a sign of intellectual decline, and the *piyyut* reflects conditions in which the teaching of Torah was banned. *Halakhah,* which was forbidden to be taught, was 'smuggled' into the prayer service, which was permitted. The *midrash* states allusively: 'At one time, when money was not scarce, people longed to hear Mishnah, *halakhah* and Talmud; nowadays money is scarce and, worse, the people sicken under their slavery, and all they want to hear are blessings and consolation' (*Shir Hashirim Rabbah* 2:14). However, such views are at best only part of the picture: political or economic conditions do not offer a sufficient explanation for the development of so rich and vital a literature. In fact, this was an era of creative *halakhic* work; and, above all, the *piyyutim* contained the strongest and severest strictures on Christianity and Rome found in the entire Jewish literature of the time.

It is more likely that the *aggadah* and *piyyut* are expressions of the accumulated spiritual wealth of the nation than of its material poverty. This era of Jewish culture in Palestine clearly shows the effect of generations of creative development. Torah education and knowledge of the Torah had penetrated deeply. There was widespread study of the Bible, of the oral tradition and of the Hebrew language, and Tiberias remained a centre for the study of the Bible and of the Hebrew language for generations after the Arab conquest. Jewish homes were full of books, and there was even a degree of return to the use of Hebrew. Many traditions that are recorded in Aramaic in the earlier literature recur in Hebrew in later homiletical collections. The return to Hebrew is reflected even in the use of Jewish names.

The Revolt Against Byzantium

In the last days of Byzantine rule over the Land of Israel the Jews made an attempt to exploit the rivalry between the powers ruling the orient – Persia, Byzantium and Rome – in order to regain their political independence. For hundreds of years they had repeatedly hoped that the redemption of the Jewish people would come with the conquest of Palestine by Persia; and now the time seemed to have arrived. At the beginning of the seventh century, the Persians set out on their conquests in the East, and in the year 614 they reached the borders of Palestine. Their approach set off a powerful messianic fermentation, which is reflected in several works written at the time whose theme is the Redemption. The Armenian historian Sebeos reported (Chapter XXIV): 'As the Persians approached Palestine, the remnants of the Jewish nation rose against the Christians, joined the Persians and made common cause with them.' The Jews assisted the invaders materially in their conquest of Galilee. From there the invading army turned to Caesarea and continued its conquests down to Apollonia, then eastwards to Lydda and from there to Jerusalem, which was captured in May 614. Jewish forces also took part in the conquest of Jerusalem. Sophronius, a contemporary monk who lived near Bethlehem, wrote in a poem: 'God-seeking strangers and citizens of the city [Jerusalem]/ . . . When they faced the Persians and their Hebrew friends/Hastened to close the city gates.'

The Persians handed Jerusalem over to Jewish settlers, who proceeded with the expulsion of the Christians and the removal of their churches. At the head of Jerusalem stood a leader whom we know only by his messianic name: Nehemiah ben Hushiel ben Ephraim ben Joseph. The sacrificial cult may even have been resumed. Jewish rule in Jerusalem lasted three years. In 617 there was a reversal of Persian policy. For reasons that are not sufficiently clear, the Persians made peace with the Christians. The Jews, on the other hand, did not, and the Persian authorities were forced to fight them: 'And they waged war against the saints and brought down many of them, and Shiroi [the king of Persia] stabbed Nehemiah ben Hushiel, and sixteen of the just were killed together with him' (*Book of Zerubabel,* page 101).

Meanwhile, the Byzantine emperor, Heraclius, had begun to build up his military strength, and in the spring of 622 he embarked on a campaign against Persia. Though the Persians remained in possession of countries that had been part of the Byzantine Empire and Persian governors resided in Antioch, Damascus, Jerusalem and Alexandria, Heraclius succeeded in reaching Ecbatana and forced the Persians to sue for peace and agree to withdraw from his conquered possessions. In 629 the emperor arrived in Palestine, preparing for the greatest hour of his life when he would enter Jerusalem and reinstate the Holy Cross. The Jews made a desperate attempt to come to terms with the new conqueror. The emperor received the Jewish leaders of Tiberias, Nazareth and the hills of Galilee, accepted their gifts, promised to pardon them and even signed a treaty with them and confirmed it on oath. One of the Jewish leaders, Benjamin of Tiberias, who was exceedingly rich, offered the emperor lodgings in his house in Tiberias, maintained the imperial court and army at his own expense and accompanied the emperor on his journey to Jerusalem. On 21 March 629, Heraclius made his triumphant entry into Jerusalem and, with a procession in the Byzantine style, proceeded to the Church of the Holy Sepulchre and returned to their place the relics of the true Cross, which the Persians had surrendered to him. The emperor, who by inclination was not anti-Jewish and had even pardoned the Jews of Edessa, who had defended the town after the Persians had abandoned it, had intended to keep his promise of clemency but was forced to break it at the insistence of the clergy.

The priests assumed responsibility for the emperor's perjury, in atonement of which they instituted a special fast, which the Egyptian Coptic Church continued to observe for centuries. The emperor ordered that the Jews be expelled from Jerusalem and its immediate surroundings. A number of Jews were accused of having killed Christians and of having destroyed churches in Jerusalem and in Galilee. Many were put to death; others fled to the desert or to Persian or Egyptian lands. In the brief interval between the return of Heraclius to Jerusalem and the Arab conquest, there were even official campaigns to convert the Jews by force, as well as persecutions on the part of Christians.

This was the final confrontation between Judaism and the Roman Empire on the political plane, for by this time the Arabs, who were to rule in Palestine for many centuries, had already appeared on the scene. The Arab conquest lasted from 630 to 640. While the Jews certainly looked forward to the fall of the 'kingdom of evil', they expected little from the victory of the Arabs. Islam was unlikely to restore Jewish rule in Palestine, for, like Byzantium, its aspiration was uncontested rule by its own religion, although the Moslem attitude towards non-Islamic sects was at that time more tolerant. At all events, we have no reliable reports of Jewish assistance to the Arabs in their conquest or of any special treatment allotted to the Jews by the new rulers. The main advantage derived by the Jews from the Arab conquest was the right to live in Jerusalem again, and even that right was restored not at the time of the conquest but only later.

After the Arab conquest, the condition of the Palestinian Jewish community was easier than it had been under Byzantine rule; but it was no longer the centre of Jewish leadership.

24

The Lands of the Diaspora

Proselytism

During the period under review, the Jewish communities outside the Land of Israel increased in size and number, one of the reasons being the proselytizing trend that began towards the end of the Second Temple era. After the fall of the Temple, this movement did not cease, and many sources indicate that it was even on the increase. It has been argued that the disappearance of the Jewish state and the destruction of the Temple made Judaism even more suited to the role of a universal religion since its national characteristics were weakened and thus it could be more easily accessible to non-Jews. Others claim that the heroism of the Jews, reflected in the war against Rome and the manner in which they retained their identity after the destruction of the Temple, aroused the admiration of many gentiles. Whether or not we accept these explanations, the existence of widespread proselytism after the fall of the Temple is uncontested. Many proselytes came from the non-Jewish population of Palestine; even more adopted Judaism in the eastern and western lands of the Diaspora, in such centres of civilization as Antioch and Alexandria and even in Rome itself. The proselytes were drawn from all social classes, from the cities and from the country. Some converted individually, leaving their homes and families; in other cases, entire families or even entire districts became Jewish. The rabbis encouraged proselytism and promoted it both directly and indirectly in the course of their travels. Only later, particularly after Christianity had come to power, was the trend reversed, not only because of the legal prohibition against proselytizing but also because the Jews preferred to live in a closed world of their own and no longer expected the fulfilment of their aspirations in the immediate future.

In addition to the long-established Diaspora communities, new ones appeared, mainly in such European lands as Spain, Germany and Pannonia.

Characteristics of the Various Diasporas

In the early part of the era, Egyptian Jewry was preponderant, by reason of both its cultural characteristics and its vitality in struggling for status and social rights. After the revolt against Trajan, of which it bore the main brunt, its population dwindled and it went into decline. The leading role was gradually taken over by Babylonian

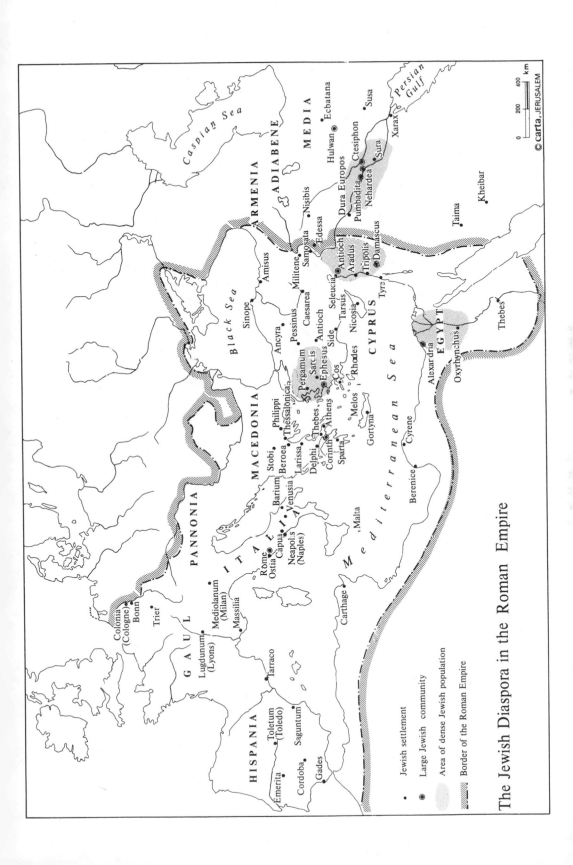

The Jewish Diaspora in the Roman Empire

- • Jewish settlement
- ◉ Large Jewish community
- Area of dense Jewish population
- Border of the Roman Empire

© **carta**, JERUSALEM

Persian Gulf

Caspian Sea

MEDIA
• Ecbatana
• Susa
• Hulwan
Ctesiphon
Xarax
• Sura
Nehardea
Pumbadita
Dura Europos
ADIABENE
• Nisibis
• Edessa
ARMENIA
• Samosata
• Militene
Antioch
Aradus
Tripolis
Damascus
Tyre
• Kheibar
• Taima
• Thebes
Alexandria
Oxyrhynchus
EGYPT

Black Sea

• Amisus
• Sinope
• Ancyra
• Pessinus
Caesarea
Antioch
Sardis
Pergamum
Ephesus
Cos
Rhodes
Side
Tarsus
Seleucia
Nicosia
CYPRUS

MACEDONIA
Philippi
Stobi
Thessalonica
Beroea
Larissa
Delphi
Thebes
Athens
Corinth
Sparta
Melos
Gortyna
• Cyrene
• Berenice

PANNONIA

ITALY
Barium
Venusia
Capua
Rome
Ostia
Neapolis (Naples)

Mediterranean Sea

Malta
• Carthage

GAUL
Colonia (Cologne)
Bonn
Trier
Mediolanum (Milan)
Massilia
Lugdunum (Lyons)

HISPANIA
Tarraco
Saguntum
Toletum (Toledo)
Cordoba
Emerita
Gades

km
0 200 400

Jewry, and by the end of the era Babylonia had become the focal point for world Jewry.

Throughout this era a distinction should be drawn between the hellenistic communities within the Roman Empire and those outside it, which were subject to Parthian or Persian rule. The differences are of both a political and a cultural order. The sources available to us seem to indicate that, after the destruction of the Temple, the Jews of communities within the Roman Empire outside Palestine were not treated as 'subjugated' populations (see page 318). However, even though they were not actually deprived of their rights, their legal status had, at least in theory, become uncertain. As we have seen, Vespasian and Titus did not accede to the demand of the non-Jewish citizens of Antioch that the Jewish citizens be deprived of their rights; but in many parts of the Diaspora the results of the Great Revolt and, even more so, of the Revolt of Bar Kokhba were clearly noticeable for a considerable length of time. On the other hand, the recognition of the Patriarchate eventually meant that the *nasi* was recognized also as the representative and leader of Diaspora Jewry, with the result that the autonomy of the communities' jurisdictions was automatically acknowledged.

The history and status of Judaism in the hellenistic diaspora, as in the Land of Israel, was on the whole determined by the Roman tradition of tolerance, as it had been shaped by Julius Caesar and Augustus and first implemented in respect to the Jews at the beginning of Roman rule in the Land of Israel. Throughout the period from the fall of the Temple until Christianity's rise to power, Jews in all parts of the empire, whatever the vicissitudes of their lot, were never deprived, theoretically or practically, of their legal status as citizens, and their main priviliges – freedom of religion and of association and the right to maintain contact with the centre in Palestine – were never revoked, though the degree to which the authorities maintained, encouraged or restricted the exercise of these rights varied. With the rise of Christianity, on the one hand, and the limitation of autonomous city government, on the other, the common features of the Diaspora communities under Roman rule became even more evident.

Culturally, this entire diaspora lay within the compass of Greek civilization. There were differences between long-established communities in the hellenistic world, such as those in Egypt, Greece and Asia Minor, and more recent ones, such as the community of Rome, where the first Jewish settlers arrived much later, just as there were differences between communities far from Palestine and those less remote, which maintained closer ties with the homeland. But, for all these differences, the Diaspora communities in the Greco-Roman world had much in common. They used Greek in writing and speech and to a large extent even within the synagogue; the Scriptures might be read in the original Hebrew followed by a Greek translation, or the Greek version alone might be regarded as sufficient. Hebrew and Aramaic were never forgotten and never disappeared completely, and they occasionally even received a boost when a new wave of exiles from the Land of Israel arrived; but most of the records that have survived from these Diaspora communities are written in Greek, whether they are literature – mostly from Egypt – or documents, synagogue inscriptions, resolutions of the heads of a community or inscriptions engraved on tombstones. Even the tombs of Roman Jews are generally inscribed in Greek. Later, however, there was an increasing tendency to use Hebrew, as the funerary inscriptions in as small a community as Venusa in southern Italy show. The organization of the communities was predominantly patterned after that of the Greek *polis,* as is reflected in the titles of office holders as much as in the manner in which they performed their office.

Compared with the hellenistic diaspora, the diaspora in the Parthian Kingdom possessed its own unique characteristics. Its status and living conditions were determined by entirely different political and economic circumstances and were embedded in a different cultural environment. That the specific nature of Babylonian Jewry was affected by its large numbers and close settlement has already been mentioned. The political conditions in the Parthian Kingdom allowed the Jews to develop an independent way of life, form of government, legal system and cultural activity to a far greater degree than was possible anywhere else outside the Land of Israel. Babylonian Jewry retained to a much larger extent the use of Hebrew in the synagogue and in daily life, and in Babylonia the Scriptures were never read exclusively in Aramaic, the Jewish vernacular of the land. The fact that Aramaic was commonly spoken also in Palestine facilitated communication between the two countries. The life of Babylonian Jewry was the direct continuation of the cultural and social life that had taken shape in the Land of Israel. It was not by mere chance that of the entire Diaspora only the Babylonian community constructed its own Talmud, parallel to the Palestinian one and based on the Mishnah, which had been compiled in the Land of Israel.

Little information has come down to us about the history of the different Diaspora communities. Often all that remains are a few fragmentary references in Jewish or non-Jewish literature or a handful of inscriptions. Of some communities we know nothing beyond the bare fact that they existed. Our information about Roman Jewry is derived mainly from Roman authors who mentioned the Jews of the city in passing. Jewish tradition also mentions the Roman Jews in connexion with incidents of Jewish history; and much has been learned as a result of the discovery of the catacombs from the first centuries after the fall of the Temple. Hundreds of funerary inscriptions tell us of the activities and status of various individuals who took part in Jewish communal life.

Ampler information is available about the Jews of Egypt and of Babylonia. As we have seen, literary activity in Egypt continued after the fall of the Temple, in the form of original Greek works as well as Greek translations of Hebrew texts written after the Great Revolt. IV *Ezra* and the *Apocalypse of* [Syria] *Baruch,* which were composed in Hebrew in the Land of Israel some thirty years after the fall of the Temple, were translated into Greek early enough to be included in the canon of the Christian Church, which has preserved the Bible tradition of Alexandrian Jewry. As a result of the role played by the Jews of Egypt and particularly of Alexandria in the Jewish revolt against Trajan, some passages about the Jews were recorded in the Jewish and Greek historical literature of the time. Documentation on the

Egyptian Jews is provided also by papyri that have been preserved; some of these illuminate minute details or major events of the revolt against Trajan, but a considerable part provides insights into the public and private life of Egypt's Jews before and after the revolt.

The only Diaspora community about which our knowledge is so ample as to enable us to describe it in every detail is that of Babylonia. At the turn of the second and third centuries, this community began to be active in the intellectual field and to play a role of importance in Jewish national life. The Babylonian Talmud, which was compiled in the course of centuries in close contact with actual life, presents us with a broad view of all aspects and problems of Babylonian Jewry; and, since this community was linked so closely with that in the Land of Israel, the Jerusalem Talmud and other works of Palestinian literature also provide us with a wealth of information about Babylonian Jewry.

Tension in Egypt

Shortly before the fall of the Temple, in the year 66, when clashes and fighting broke out between the Jews and the Greeks in the cities of Palestine and its surroundings, we hear also of disputes between the Jews and Greeks of Alexandria over civic rights – clashes that were accompanied by frequent bloodshed. Time and again the Roman governors punished many partisans of both sides, but this only added fuel to the fire.

On one occasion the Alexandrians called an assembly in order to appoint a delegation to the emperor Nero, and the Jews also appeared in large numbers at the amphitheatre. On seeing this, the Greeks cried out: 'There are enemies here who have come to spy out the city's secrets. Drive out the Jews!' The Jews fled, but three of them were captured and the Greeks prepared to burn them alive. Then the Jews attacked the amphitheatre with stones and torches, intending to burn it to the ground, and would have succeeded had they not been prevented by the governor, Julius Tiberius. First he attempted, with the assistance of a few Jewish notables, to appease the Jews; but, when they insulted him, he ordered his soldiers to kill them and loot their property. The Jews entrenched themselves in their quarter, the Delta, and resisted for a long time. Unfortunately, 5,000 soldiers happened to arrive just then from Libya and helped to overcome the Jews. The Romans put old and young to the sword and pillaged the quarter. Finally, Tiberius relented and ordered his soldiers to leave the Jews alone; but the Alexandrians who had fought together with the soldiers continued the slaughter and had to be dragged away from the corpses (Josephus, *Bellum Judaicum* II, 18.7–8).

This incident shows the difficult situation in which the Alexandrian Jews were placed. On the one hand, they had to contend with the Greek citizens for their civic standing in Alexandria, while the Roman authorities acted as referees, maintained public order and at times made an effort to conduct themselves fairly without discriminating against either side. On the other hand, the local civic struggle was occasionally compounded by the national Jewish aspect, which depended entirely on the relations between Rome and Palestinian Jewry. Every increase in Jewish national spirit in Palestine was accompanied by increased tension between Jews and Greeks in Egypt. At such times the Jews regarded the Greek residents of the cities, who were the main support of Roman rule in the East, as part of the 'kingdom of of evil', even when the Greek patriots among the Alexandrians accused the Romans of siding with the Jews.

The refugees from Palestine who arrived in Egypt after the fall of the Temple included zealots who attempted to incite the Egyptian Jews to revolt; and, while the Gerousia and the leading members of the community succeeded in preventing the Jews of Egypt from involving themselves in rebellion against Rome, it seems that at least some of the poorest Jews gave the zealots a hearing. Similar developments occurred in Cyrenaica, Egypt's neighbouring country, when John the Weaver of the Sicarii arrived there and succeeded in rousing many of the poor, while the rich and respected Jews denounced him to the governor. The insurrections gave the authorities an excuse to close the Temple of Onias, which had existed in Egypt ever since the disturbances in Palestine preceding the Hasmonean Revolt.

In the generation after the fall of the Temple, the bonds between the Jews in the Land of Israel and those of Alexandria, as well as of Egypt in general, grew closer. Among the scholars of Jabneh, there were several who came from Egypt, such as R. Johanan the Cobbler and Hanan the Egyptian; and such leading personalities as R. Joshua ben Hananiah and R. Zenon paid frequent visits to Egypt. During the sabbatical year, when the land lay fallow, the Egyptian Jews would send the portion of their crops set aside for the poor to the Land of Israel to relieve the distress of the poor there.

Such developments should not be taken as indications of despair at establishing communications with the Greek world or as a turning-away from Greek to Jewish culture. For all its links with Greek civilization, Egyptian Jewry had always kept faith with Judaism and maintained its bonds with the homeland. Individual Jews might abandon their religion and nationality for the wider horizons of the gentile world, and their allegorical interpretation of the Torah might induce them to neglect the actual observance of the commandments. However, they were exceptions and do not justify an assumption that Egyptian Jews in general sought access to the Greek world while relaxing their connexion with Judaism. Their struggle for civic rights in Alexandria was not a matter of cultural assimilation but merely an attempt to ensure their social and economic basis of existence. The founding of Jabneh was followed by an upsurge of Jewish life in Palestine and resulted in closer contacts between the Land of Israel and the Diaspora communities. The relations with the Egyptian community, the largest concentration of Diaspora Jewry, was merely one instance of this trend. The ties to their nation and homeland did not prevent Egyptian Jews from continuing their struggle for local civic rights, and we even possess a papyrus from the years 111–113, shortly before the revolt against Trajan, referring to a complaint against the Alexandrians that the Jews of the city brought before Trajan in the wake of bloody clashes arising from disputes over civic rights similar to those that had occurred before the fall of the Temple.

The Revolt Against Trajan

In 115, while the emperor Trajan was engaged in his conquests in the East, a Jewish revolt broke out in the eastern Diaspora communities behind the front. The revolt soon gathered momentum, to the extent that it became an open war that spread to Libya, Cyrenaica, Egypt, Cyprus and Mesopotamia and thus also involved the emperor's new areas of conquest (on the 'Kitos War' in Palestine, see page 330). The first signs of the war consisted of clashes between Jews and Greeks in Alexandria and Cyrene, but shortly after we hear mainly of battles with Romans and of a king whom the Jews had chosen to lead them. Evidence from many literary sources and from letters, documents and papyri that have been preserved indicates the dimensions that the war assumed in Libya and Cyrenaica and particularly in Egypt. The Romans were so sorely pressed for officers that civilian administrators were given commissions and put in command of troops recruited from among the Greeks living in the large cities and country towns. The revolt spread over all Egypt and caused considerable death and destruction. The roads were ruined and large tracts in Libya, Cyrenaica and Egypt were laid waste. Thirty years later there were still places in Egypt that remained deserted as a result of these events.

In Cyrenaica, where archaeological evidence testifies to the extent of the destruction, there are inscriptions recording that Hadrian ordered the restoration of buildings and the repair of 'the road from Cyrene to Apollonia, which was destroyed and rendered unusable in the Jewish riot'. Conditions in Libya were not very different; the Christian author Orosius wrote:

> The Jews fought many battles throughout the entire land of Libya against its inhabitants, and so sorely was the land laid waste at that time because of the extinction of the farmers, that if Hadrian had not assembled settlers from abroad and induced them to found colonies in Libya, the country would have remained empty and uninhabited.

It seems that the Egyptian villagers generally took the side of the Jews, for in those places where the peasants came to the aid of the Romans and Greeks they were greatly praised and considered to have earned special privileges. Nearly a century later, in 200, the people of Oxyrhynchus mention that 'it should also be reckoned in their favour that they are good-hearted, loyal and friendly to the Romans, as they proved in the war against the Jews by coming to the aid of the Roman armies and by celebrating the anniversary of the victory [over the Jews] every year.'

The war lasted until the end of Trajan's life (10 August 117), and even Hadrian, in his first year, had to occupy himself with putting down the revolt in Egypt. We have more or less detailed records of the war in the countries that we have mentioned, but we know nothing about the connexion between the revolt in one country and another. All we know for sure is that there was contact between the Jews of Cyrenaica and those of Egypt and that the course of events in Egypt was determined by Jewish militants who marched in from Cyrenaica. But the very fact that at one and the same time, between 115 and 117, so powerful a revolt broke out in so many distant places indicates the existence of some connexion between the uprisings; and, if there were

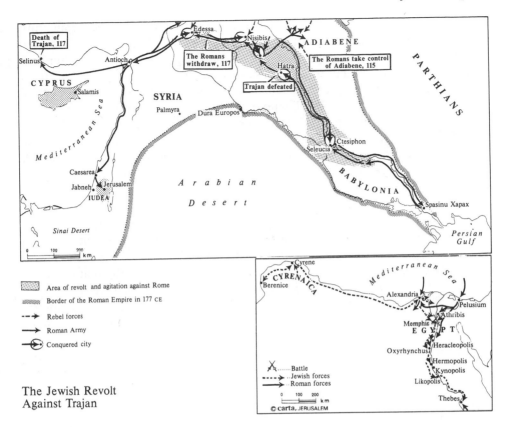

Area of revolt and agitation against Rome
Border of the Roman Empire in 177 CE
- - -▶ Rebel forces
——▶ Roman Army
——⊕— Conquered city

The Jewish Revolt
Against Trajan

no institution or organization that directed them, the Jewish people in the different Diaspora communities were at least inspired by a common aspiration. Enmity between the Jews and the Greek citizens among whom they lived was certainly not the only motive, for the revolt also affected districts in which there were no Greek cities. The aspiration that generated the unrest and the revolt was doubtless the messianic hope of establishing the kingdom of heaven once the yoke of foreign domination was thrown off, the foreigners were expelled from the homeland and its surroundings and the 'kingdom of evil' was destroyed. The participation of the non-Greek peasant masses on the side of the Jews – or at least the Jews' hope for their participation – made the prospect of victory seem reasonable. But their expectations were not fulfilled.

The collapse of the revolt had a decisive effect on the fate of the Jews in most of the countries that had participated in it. In Cyprus, where Jews had lived in all parts of the island, the entire community was exterminated, and Jews were forbidden even to set foot on its shores: 'Even if one [Jew] is forced to seek refuge there because of a storm, he is put to death' (*Dio Cassius* LXVIII, 32). The Jewish communities in Cyrenaica and Libya also suffered greatly. In Jewish historical tradition, however, only accounts of the ruin of Egyptian Jewry have been preserved. The *aggadah,*

371

in its usual vivid fashion, describes the greatness of the Egyptian Jewish community before the revolt and the extent of the slaughter during it: '"And the hands are the hands of Esau" – that is the emperor Hadrian, who slaughtered in Egypt six hundred thousand and again six hundred thousand, twice as many as had gone forth from Egypt [at the time of the Exodus] . . . so that the blood ran in the sea as far as Cyprus' (Babylonian Talmud, *Gittin* 57b). Egyptian Jewry was not annihilated completely; but, whereas it had once been a large community, long and firmly established, represented in all parts of the country and possessing a rich culture and a specific Jewish character involving a political consciousness that strove in the cultural, political and military spheres to defend its rights and position, after suffering great losses as a result of the revolt it never recovered its previous strength – as Jewish sources indicate: 'In that hour, Israel's pride was cut down, and shall not grow again until the son of David comes' (Jerusalem Talmud, *Succah* 5). The phraseology also shows the importance, for the Jewish people as a whole, that Talmudic tradition attached to Egyptian Jewry and its defeat in the revolt. In many districts the Jewish community became extinct, and there are records of Jewish property that remained unclaimed. In areas of Egypt where Jewish life had once flourished, all traces of its very existence disappeared at a single stroke. Jews continued to live in Alexandria itself, but they no longer formed an important element in the city's life. Their public institutions ceased to function, some temporarily, others forever.

The over-all effect of the revolt against Trajan on Jewish and general history can hardly be over-estimated. The rebellion of the Jews and of the other nations that had been subjugated in the course of Trajan's campaign in the East forced the emperor to abandon his last conquests and retreat; and his successor, Hadrian, gave up the remainder of Trajan's gains from this campaign and withdrew from all the conquered lands. In other words, the revolt halted Rome's expansion eastwards and re-established Parthia's position as a rival of the Roman Empire. For Jewish history these developments were particularly significant, for they meant that Babylonia and the Parthian Kingdom in general remained a refuge and fortress for Jewry and Jewish culture for centuries to come, at a time when the hand of pagan and later of Christian Rome lay heavily on the Jews and on Judaism in Palestine and in the empire in general. The Jewish revolt of 115–117 was, therefore, not only a major factor in halting Roman penetration into the East and creating a shelter for the Jewish nation, but it also helped to raise up a rival and enemy whom Rome was forced to take into consideration in so far as its treatment of the Jews was concerned.

The scholars were fully aware of this aspect of Diaspora life and, in their usual manner, they coined a phrase for it: 'It was an act of charity of the Holy-One-Blessed-Be-He when he dispersed Israel among the nations' (Babylonian Talmud, *Pesaḥim* 87b). In the same source we find them replying to a Christian that if he and his co-religionists do not annihilate Israel it is not out of the goodness of their hearts but 'because ye know not how to. Destroy them all? They are not among ye' – at least not all of them. The situation, though not operative at every moment in history, never failed to have its effect in the long run.

The Jewish community in Egypt did not recover until the end of the third century. By that time there existed, even in the country towns, Jewish institutions that concerned themselves with ransoming captive Jews from the Land of Israel. Later they provided refuge for Palestinian Jews fleeing the persecutions of the Byzantine emperors. At the time of the Arab conquest, at the beginning of the seventh century, the Jewish population of Egypt was comparatively large, though smaller than it had been in the hellenistic-Roman era. The Jewish community, which began to grow again in the era of Christian Rome, was inevitably unable to regain the degree of strength that it had achieved under the Ptolemies.

Documentary evidence from the third and fourth centuries shows an increasing use of the Hebrew language. In Ptolemaic and early Roman times, it had been customary to add a Greek suffix to Hebrew names, but at this later period names appear in their original form and spelling. However, we have too little source material on Jewish life in Egypt in this era to determine whether this phenomenon marked a return to national culture and a conscious repudiation of Greek customs and speech or was only an aspect of the general decline of Greek civilization at the time when Christianity was on the rise.

Babylonia

The Jewish community of this ancient Diaspora land had, since ancient times, consisted of 'countless myriads of which none can know the number' (Josephus, *Jewish Antiquities* 11.133). Some of Babylonia's great cities, such as Nehardea, Nisibis, Mahoza and others, were entirely, or almost entirely, populated, maintained and garrisoned by Jews. When the tannaitic tradition refers simply to the *golah* ('exile'), it means Babylonia. When speaking of the line of beacons by which the sanctification of the New Moon was announced to outlying communities, the Mishnah (*Rosh Hashanah*) describes the line that carried the report to Babylonia, ending at Pumbadita. There were places in Babylonia that possessed an ancient Jewish tradition, such as Huzal Debei Binyamin (which was presumably founded by exiles from the tribe of Benjamin) near Sura and the synagogue of Shaf Yetiv near Nehardea, of which it was said that the Divine Presence had descended upon it with the arrival of the exiles and had dwelt there ever since. The Jews of Babylonia regarded themselves as the faithful guardians of Jewish tradition and Jewish lineage, in the sense that they had not intermarried with proselytes whose conversion was suspect, with foreign slaves who had not been fully emancipated, with *mamzerim* (children of certain Jewish couples who according to *halakhah* are allowed to marry only other *mamzerim*) and the like. Where lineage was concerned the Babylonian Jews felt superior even to their brethren in the Land of Israel: 'All countries are dough [a mixture of pure and impure lineage] compared to the Land of Israel, and the Land of Israel is dough compared to Babylonia' (Babylonian Talmud, *Kiddushin* 71a).

Not all the wide area of Babylonia was closely settled by Jews, and not all Jews were considered to be of good lineage; this attribute was reserved for those who lived in the section of the land between the Tigris and Euphrates where the two rivers were connected by the main canals: on the east side of the Tigris from Naharwan and Muskeni in the north to Apamea in the south and along the Euphrates up to Ihi Dekira (Hit). The lands adjoining this district of Babylonia, such as Bei Huzae,

(Khuzistan), Mesene, Elam and Media, were regarded as 'dead', 'dying' or 'sick' as far as Jewish lineage was concerned; only Babylonia was considered 'healthy'. Among the outlying districts only a few, containing a large Jewish population – Hulwan and Naharwan in Media and Mesopotamia on the upper reaches of the Euphrates – shared the classification 'healthy' lineage.

Jewish religious and cultural life had existed in Babylonia all along, but we know little about this segment of the Jewish people before the end of the second century. The literature of the Second Temple and tannaitic eras has preserved only a few fragmentary passages about events or personalities, and almost nothing has come down to us about the literature of the Babylonian community and its influence on Jewry as a whole.

We know of several attempts by Babylonian Jewry to free itself from the hegemony of the Land of Israel, particularly at times when political conditions made it impossible for the Palestinian centre to carry on its activities. We have already mentioned Hananiah, the nephew of R. Joshua, who began to proclaim the New Moon and the leap-year in Babylonia during the critical time following the Revolt of Bar Kokhba; but even in a time of relative freedom for Babylonian Jewry, those who persuaded Hananiah and his followers to desist were Babylonian scholars. No other Diaspora community, at least from the time of the *tannaim* until the Arab conquest, was so closely linked with the Land of Israel, as was Babylonia. Many Babylonian Jews – rabbis and laymen – visited the Land of Israel in order to study Torah or came to settle there permanently; many others had their remains taken to Palestine for burial. Babylonian Jewry accepted the directives of the Sanhedrin and its leading scholars, requested their opinion on the choice of a new head of the academy when the office fell vacant and so forth. Even the exilarch generally considered himself subject to the Palestinian authorities, who constituted the highest religious and legal instance. From the end of the third century onwards, Palestinian scholars were appointed as *naḥutei* (Aramaic for those who left Israel for a time for the purpose of study), whose function was to maintain regular contact with Babylonia and to transmit to the Babylonian diaspora the teachings, decisions and rulings of the Palestinian scholars. In times of hardship in the Land of Israel, many refugees found shelter among their brethren in Babylonia. Numerous traditions are ascribed to specific scholars who are recorded as having brought them from the Land of Israel to Babylonia; such attributions appear regularly until the time of the Arab conquest. Jewish tradition, in fact, regarded it as the secret of Israel's continued existence among the nations that God had sent 'part of Jacob's descendants in exile into a place of safety, so that they might find refuge from the heavy hand of Esau'. Among those who emigrated from the Land of Israel to Babylonia were scholars whose creative work helped to raise the standards of Torah study there and contributed to the spiritual development of Babylonian Jewry.

Babylonian Jews enjoyed a large measure of autonomy in their internal affairs and continued to do so throughout this period, not only because of their consolidated position as a population group but also because of the decentralized, feudal system of government. The head of their community was an exilarch who claimed descent from the kings of Judah exiled at the time of the fall of the First Temple. It was even generally believed that the exilarchs were of a lineage superior to that of the *nesi'im* in the Land of Israel because they were of direct Davidic descent. R. Judah the Prince declared on one occasion that he would cede his place to R. Huna, the exilarch, if he should leave Babylonia and come to the Land of Israel. A late tradition claims that there were exilarchs of Babylonia even during the period of the first exile, before the fall of the Second Temple, and that the exiled king Jehoiachin was the first of them; but none of the historical sources of the Second Temple era that mention the Babylonian diaspora makes any reference to an Exilarchate. The first clear report of such an institution dates from the second century CE.

The undisturbed political condition of the Jewish community, the feudal system of government that characterized Parthia even after the rise of the Sassanids and the respect in which the Jews held the remnant of the house of David combined to make the exilarch a ruler who wielded considerable power. He ranked as a high royal official with a respected position within the Parthian hierarchy. Within the area of Jewish settlement, he enjoyed wide powers in matters of civil administration and defence and in juridical affairs, which apparently included even capital cases. As the study of Torah spread throughout Babylonia and the great academies were established, the activities of the exilarch were to some extent reduced and certain areas of public life were taken over by the academies or by scholars, at times as the result of an open or concealed contest of power. The rabbis limited the rule and authority of the exilarch, even though they did much to increase the splendour of his court. Many exilarchs had little contact with the world of Torah and even interfered with the rabbis and their teachings. Others, however, particularly in the amoraic era, befriended the rabbis or were themselves Torah scholars. In the first amoraic generation, the exilarch was Mar Ukva, who was reputed to be one of the leading scholars of his time. Huna bar Nathan, the exilarch in the days of R. Ashi, also was reckoned among the scholars of his generation. The exilarchs ruled and held court in an oriental feudal manner, with all its customary trappings and ceremonial. By comparison, the way of life of the *nesi'im* in the Land of Israel seems modest, even from the time of R. Judah the Prince, when the ancestral habits of modesty and frugality were abandoned. The teaching of Torah in the courtyards of the exilarch's palace, the annual conferences of Torah students at his residence and the manner in which rabbis stood in his presence and dined at his table all formed part of the court ceremonial. To some extent this way of life affected even that of the Babylonian academies.

In its organization the Jewish community or town in Babylonia was influenced by the Jewish towns in the Land of Israel. Charitable and educational institutions were patterned after those of Palestine. Local government was administered by seven town elders assisted by a larger council. The ultimate authority in all matters of local government was exercised by an assembly of citizens.

The decline of the Arsacids and the rise of the Sassanid dynasty (224–226) were accompanied by an upsurge of national-religious consciousness in the Persian Empire. Zoroastrianism, the traditional religion, became once again an established church; the teaching of religion and of the religious literature, the Zend-Avesta, was officially encouraged; and the priests of the Fire Cult, the magi, became a powerful clergy. The first Sassanids regarded themselves as the heirs of the great Persian kings and pursued the active policies of Cyrus and Darius. They even took steps to abolish the independence of the satraps, who ruled their provinces like kings in every respect, by attempting to secure their acknowledgement of the authority of the 'King of Kings' and to subject the administration of the entire kingdom to the control of the royal capital. These policies of the new government gave rise to religious intolerance and made inroads upon the autonomy of the Jews, who, for example, were deprived of jurisdiction over capital cases. Talmudic literature reflects in many ways the suffering inflicted upon the Jews by the new Persians. However, conditions soon changed for the better. Shapur (241–271), though in political and military matters a more determined ruler than his father, Ardashir, reverted to the traditional religious tolerance of the Persian kings and even went so far as to establish close relations with Jewish sages of his time, such as Samuel and his disciple R. Judah.

The main occupation of the Jews of Babylonia was agriculture. There were substantial landowners among them, but also many small holders and tenant farmers. The picture of both the scholars and the common people communicated to us by the Babylonian Talmud is that of an agricultural population. Jews were to be found in all branches of farming, from cultivation of the date-palm – a Babylonian staple – as well as other fruit trees, to the growing of field crops, fishing and poultry farming. There were many Jews among the artisans and among those engaged in the various forms of transport, including river navigation. Slavery played a far more important role in Babylonian than in Palestinian agriculture and crafts, among Jews no less than among non-Jews. Some Jewish towns, particularly along the Tigris, specialized in commerce. Many Jews were traders; they dealt also in those goods for which Babylonia was a transit station between the Far East and the West, particularly silk from China.

Taxation in the Parthian Kingdom and after it in the Persian Empire was comparatively heavy. A tax referred to as *taska* was levied on farmland (at the rate of one-sixth to one-third of the crop, according to the fertility of the field), and in addition there was a poll-tax or *carga*. Payment of taxes constituted a lien on the land and the person: if taxes were not paid, tenure of the land passed to the person who paid the land-tax and the tax debtor became the slave of whoever paid the poll-tax on his behalf, remaining so until he had reimbursed him for the outlay. Jews were not among the tax-exempt classes, but there are no indications of their having been discriminated against in the imposition or collection of taxes. Jewish law generally recognized the legality of the royal taxes and all that their collection implied. In this respect it was guided by the rule established by Samuel, one of the first leading Babylonian *amoraim,* that 'the laws of the kingdom are law.' Nevertheless, the rabbis regarded the tax-collector as an undesirable social element, because of the oppressive manner in which taxes were collected, though the opposition to and contempt for the publican that were so characteristic of the Land of Israel never became part of the Babylonian Jewish mentality. For all the burden of taxation, the economic situation of Babylonian Jewry was on the whole satisfactory, especially if compared to that of the Palestinian Jews.

The Babylonian Academies

A great spiritual upsurge occurred in Babylonia in the second half of the second century, almost certainly as a result of the large influx of refugees from Palestine at the time of the Bar Kokhba Revolt (132–135) and the persecutions that followed it. The Palestinians, who included some of the leading scholars, acted as leaven on the Babylonian diaspora. Many of those who went from Babylonia to the Land of Israel to study Torah returned after remaining with a teacher for a period of time. One of these students was Abba Arikha, generally known as Rav or Rabbeinu. His return to Babylonia (in 219) was a turning-point in the spiritual, *halakhic* and juridical development of the community. Rather than settling in one of the traditional centres of learning, he went to Sura, which contained a large Jewish population but little learning, and founded a great academy there. Nehardea, a cultural centre of long standing, underwent a revival in those days and also became the seat of a great academy, which was headed by Samuel, who, like Rav, also may have lived in the Land of Israel for a time. Unlike Rav, however, Samuel did not consider himself subject to the rulings of the Palestinian rabbis. Rav introduced not only the Mishnah, which had just been completed, but also the Palestinian system of study, as well as many Palestinian customs, such as the handing down of traditions and the concern with formal prayer and *aggadah*.

Jewish Babylonia was divided between Sura and Nehardea, some towns being under the influence of Sura and adopting its rulings and decisions, while others took their lead from Nehardea. Many students joined Rav's academy, and from that time the study of Torah became a common feature of Jewish life in all Babylonia. The number of regular students at Sura alone in Rav's time was 1,200. This was also the era in which the custom of *yarḥei kallah* was instituted: in the two months of the year in which work in the field came to a virtual standstill – in Adar (February/March) and Elul (August/September) – thousands of literate Jews gathered at the academies to study Torah. As in the Land of Israel the curriculum was based mainly on the Mishnah. The two academies still existed at the end of the gaonic era (the middle of the tenth century). They became the source of spiritual life and the focal points for the entire Jewish community of Babylonia, though not always to the same extent. At times Sura outshone Nehardea, while in other periods Sura was overshadowed by Nehardea or its successor, Pumbadita, where the academy was re-established after having been sacked by Palmyran regiments in 259. In the course of the centuries, additional academies were founded elsewhere and survived for longer or shorter periods, but Sura and Pumbadita remained the classical academies of Babylonian Jewry.

The founder of the academy of Pumbadita was R. Judah bar Ezekiel, who remained its head until the year 299. He was succeeded by Rabba bar Nahmani (?–320), R. Joseph bar Hiyya (?–328) and Abbaye (?–338). In the middle of the fourth century, under the presidency of Rava (338–352), the academy of Pumbadita moved to Mahoza on the Tigris; but after Rava's death the academy returned to its former seat. The Babylonian Talmud is full of sayings by Abbaye and Rava, whose argumentations are regarded as the summit of *halakhic* analysis and discussion.

Sura had a long period of prosperity under R. Huna, a disciple of Rav who headed it for forty years (257–297). Even R. Judah and the leading scholars of Pumbadita regarded themselves as R. Huna's disciples. There are many traditions in both Talmuds relating the large number of R. Huna's students and his public leadership. The Babylonian and Jerusalem Talmuds alike record his many statements on all spheres of Jewish life. After his death Sura was headed by R. Hisda until 309, but by then the main focus had shifted to Pumbadita. After R. Hisda's death Sura did not even have a president until R. Ashi came to the fore in 371; and, though the academy continued to teach Torah, its impact on Jewish life had lessened.

The Editing of the Babylonian Talmud

In the course of generations, new levels of Jewish teaching and Jewish law, based on the Mishnah, emerged and took shape in Palestine and Babylonia, in the form of discussions that almost always interpreted, expanded on or supplemented statements of the Mishnah. These were oral traditions that varied from academy to academy and from one generation to another. During the long presidency of R. Ashi at Sura (371–427), these discussions were summarized and edited in the form of the compilation known as the Babylonian Talmud, which follows the order of the tractates and chapters of the Mishnah. R. Ashi edited the material while teaching it in his academy, his editorship being attested not only by tradition but also by the Talmudic text itself.

The text of the Babylonian Talmud clearly shows the nature of this creative editing. It contains not only all that had been produced by way of interpretation and expansion of the Mishnah, but reflects centuries of thought and experience in the nation's history. While the Mishnah contains questions only of *halakhah* in an edited form, the Talmud includes large sections on other areas of national life, traditions predating the Mishnah that are not included in it and new traditions that came into existence after its conclusion. The Talmud presents the issues not in the form of conclusions and rulings but with the discussions that led to them and the investigations conducted by the rabbis in their attempt to solve theoretical or legal problems. There are sections in the Babylonian Talmud that are of interest mainly because they exhibit intellectual acuity and offer brilliant insights into legal and philosophical questions, side by side with folklore, proverbs, interpretation of dreams and the like.

We do not possess the Babylonian Talmud on the entire Mishnah, but only on the same orders dealt with in the Jerusalem Talmud, with the exception of *Zeraim* (of which the Babylonian Talmud contains only *Berakhot,* while the Jerusalem Talmud contains the entire order) and with the addition of most of *Kodashim* and all of *Tohorot* (of which parts do not appear in the Jerusalem Talmud). The Babylonian Talmud is constructed on the pattern of its Jerusalem counterpart, and the two compendia have much in common, not only because they arose on the same foundation and grew out of the same tradition but also by reason of the close connexion between the two centres of Jewish life. Palestinian *amoraim* are quoted in the Babylonian Talmud and Babylonian scholars are likewise mentioned in the Jerusalem Talmud. Nevertheless, there are many differences, first and foremost in language. The passages of the Jerusalem Talmud that are not in Hebrew are in 'western'

Aramaic with a considerable addition of Greek words; in the Babylonian Talmud they are in 'eastern' Aramaic with far fewer Persian terms. The Jerusalem Talmud is more concise and contains less detailed legal discussions than do many parts of the Babylonian Talmud. One result is that the two versions sometimes reach different conclusions; and many matters and Mishnaic passages are given different interpretations, either because of differences between Palestinian and Babylonian customs or because of varying economic and political conditions.

The subsequent histories of the two Talmuds also varied. The Jerusalem Talmud gained little currency outside the Land of Israel. At the time that the Talmud became generally known, Palestinian Jewry was on the wane and the Babylonian community was gaining power. The influence of the Babylonian *geonim* (see Part V) also weighted the scales in favour of the Talmud of their land, which they introduced and taught in all the Diaspora communities of the Middle Ages, as well as in the Land of Israel. Thus the Babylonian Talmud gained primary influence on Jewish history throughout the ages. It became the basic – and in many places almost the exclusive – asset of Jewish tradition, the foundation of all Jewish thought and aspirations and the guide for the daily life of the Jew. Other components of national culture were made known only in so far as they were embedded in the Talmud. In almost every period and community until the modern age, the Talmud was the main object of Jewish study and education; all the external conditions and events of life seemed to be but passing incidents, and the only true, permanent reality was that of the Talmud.

The final edition of the Babylonian Talmud dates from the fifth century, which was a hard time for the entire Jewish people. It was concluded and handed down to the coming generations in times of forced conversions and persecutions, in the days of R. Jose of Pumbadita and of Rabina, the last leader of Sura (499). The Talmudic tradition states that 'Rav Ashi and Rabina were the last of the Teachers' (Babylonian Talmud, *Bava Meẓia* 86a).

The Savoraim

The oral tradition refers to the teachers of the era between the *amoraim* and the *geonim* (see Part V) by the Aramaic name *savoraim* or *savorai, i.e.,* the 'explainers' or 'holders of opinion'. Accordingly, the era extending from the conclusion of the Talmud until shortly before the Arab conquest is known in the history of *halakhic* literature as the savoraite era. Jewish tradition regards the scholars who lived after the conclusion of the Talmud, that is to say, after the era of *halakhic* innovation and decision, as having been concerned mainly with explaining the *halakhah* and handing down the Jewish heritage. No books or responses similar to those of the next era (that of the *geonim*) have come down to us from the era of the *savoraim*; all we know of them and their work comes from short notes in chronicles from the gaonic era and from references in the Babylonian Talmud to some of their names, sayings and activities. In the case of some leading scholars of the post-amoraic era, sayings have been included in the Babylonian Talmud even though their authors are designated as *savoraim*. These scholars include R. Jose, R. Rahumi,

R. Aha of Bei Hattim, R. Huna the exilarch and R. Samuel, the son of R. Abahu. There are also reliable traditions from the Gaonic era to the effect that certain anonymous statements in the Babylonian Talmud are to be attributed to *savoraim*: apparently, they had a considerable share in the final formulation of many passages of the Talmud, and much of their teaching has found its way into the Talmud in one form or another – far more so than into the works of the *geonim*.

Under Yazdigar III (440–457) the fanatic priesthood of the magi gained greater influence and a wave of religious persecution swept over Persia. The Christians were persecuted more severely than the Jews, for they were suspected of sympathizing with Byzantium: but the nature of Jewish observance made the general ban on religious practices much more painful for them. In 455 an edict was issued abolishing the Sabbath. How greatly this edict affected the Jews may be gathered from the story of its repeal: 'And the rabbis proclaimed a fast, and the Holy One Blessed Be He sent a crocodile unto him in the night which swallowed him as he lay on his couch, and the decree was invalidated' (Letter of R. Sherira Gaon). Extremely severe persecutions took place during the reign of Yazdigar's son Piruz (458–485), whom Jewish tradition refers to as 'Piruz the Evil'. Synagogues and schools of Torah study were banned in Babylonia, the Jews were forced to stand trial in the Persian law courts, and Jewish children were taken away from their parents to be educated by the magi. For the first time we hear of Jewish martyrs in Babylonia. Several scholars, including Huna, the son of Mar Zutra the exilarch, were cast into prison and eventually executed (470). Many sought refuge as far away as Arabia in the south and India in the east.

The Revolt of Mar Zutra

Towards the end of the fifth century, we have reports of the founding by the exilarch of a Jewish kingdom on Babylonian territory. The report, which is found in *Seder Olam Zuta,* gives us a vivid picture of how large and widespread the Jewish population in Babylonia was and how powerful its leaders remained even in times of persecution. It also shows, incidentally, that the Exilarchate and the academies clashed over such matters as the appointment of judges: R. Huna, the exilarch, deeply offended his father-in-law, R. Haninah, the present of the academy, by refusing to confirm a judge nominated by him. However, after the exilarch had been put to death by the authorities, R. Haninah brought up R. Huna's son, Mar Zutra, and even restored to him the dignity of the Exilarchate when it was usurped by a relative.

In 495 disorders broke out all over the Persian Empire and King Kabad I (488–531) was deposed and imprisoned. Mar Zutra, availing himself of this opportunity to establish a small army of his own, founded a kingdom, apparently with Mahoza as his capital, and proceeded to levy taxes and wage wars. Throughout his seven-year reign, from 495 to 502, he had the full support of his grandfather R. Haninah. Meanwhile, Kabad regained his throne and defeated the Jewish state, and in 502 Mar Zutra and the elderly R. Haninah were crucified on the bridge of Mahoza. Shortly after the Jewish rebellion had been suppressed, Jewish institutions were ordered to be closed. The heads of the Jewish community, together with the presidents of the academies, fled to the Saba River, which joins the Tigris near Apamea, and established

The Jewish Community in Babylon in the Period of the Mishnah and Talmud

- •   Jewish community
- ★   Centre of study and leadership
- ⊛   Large *yeshiva*
- Mahoza   seat of the exilarch

© carta, JERUSALEM

an academy there, beyond the reach of the central Persian government. A son of Mar Zutra, born after the latter's death and named after his father, was brought up in secret; at the age of eighteen he went to the Land of Israel and was appointed head of the Sanhedrin (520).

Later during Kabad's reign Jewish life reverted to normal. Many Jews served as soldiers in the Persian Army. In one of the battles with the Byzantine general Belisarius, the Persian commander requested his adversary to halt the fighting during Passover, for the sake of the Jewish soldiers in his army. In the sixth century Babylonian Jewry re-established its institutions, including the office of exilarch and the custom of *yarhei kallah*.

Under Hormizd IV the magi once again became the dominant power at the royal court, and another period of hardship began for Babylonian Jewry. The central Jewish institutions were closed down, and the heads of the academy of Pumbadita moved to Piruz-Shapur near Nehardea, where the king's power had little effect (580). In the last fifty years of the Persian Empire – during the long reign of Khusroe II (590–628) and the twelve years of confusion from the time of his death until the Arab conquest (628–639) – Jewish public institutions were in operation again; the two academies had reopened and the exilarch fulfilled the duties of his office. Nevertheless, in the eyes of Babylonian Jewry, the Arab conquest offered them relief from the disturbances and irregular rule of the Persian kings. Thus the Jews came to the aid of the conquerors and welcomed their arrival.

PART V

The Middle Ages

Haim Hillel Ben-Sasson

25

Introduction

The Chronological and Conceptual Framework

From the viewpoint of Jewish history, the Middle Ages may be defined as the period stretching from the early Moslem-Arab conquests, which commenced in 632 CE, to the spiritual crisis experienced by Jewry during the second half of the seventeenth century, after the collapse of the messianic Sabbatean movement (see page 718). This period, covering more than 1,000 years, was a lengthy one even for a people as ancient as the Jews. Like every historical epoch, its relative unity consists of the dominant trends occurring within the specific society, set against the flow of events and the changing sensibility of mankind as a whole during that same period.

Throughout this epoch the Jewish people lived under the rule of Christianity and Islam, monotheistic religions that, though they had developed out of the religious concepts of Judaism itself, claimed to possess a truer comprehension of those concepts and maintained that the Jews had misunderstood them. Accordingly, their persecution and humiliation of the Jews were acts of deliberate policy – even though the two faiths had different reasons for their persecution and those reasons changed from time to time. The charges levelled by the Christians were more vehement and more intimately concerned with their own beliefs than were those of the Moslems. They condemned the Jews for having rejected their Jewish Messiah and for having crucified the incarnated son of God and accused them of spiritual blindness and religious crudity in continuing to observe the 'legalistic and materialistic' commandments of the Old Testament. The Jews, on the other hand, claimed that the worship of an incarnated son of God within a Trinity was sheer idolatry and could not be equated with the worship of the one and only God of the Torah and the Prophets. They also rejected the Christian annulment of commandments clearly prescribed in the Scriptures, whose text and meaning the Christians themselves could not deny.

The dispute with Islam was more external and less acute. Here the argument was that the Jews had refused to accept Mohammed as an emissary and prophet of God and his Koran as a sacred text; furthermore, the Jews were accused of having falsified the text of the Torah. There was no dispute as to the nature of God and no conflicting attitudes towards statues or icons. Nor did the way of life according to law differ so widely between these two religions as to give rise among Moslems to an animosity resembling that of Christian believers, whose Bible included the rebellion of the Jew Paul against the laws and practices of the Jews. Nevertheless, in many lands and in many periods the Jews suffered hostility and humiliation under Moslem rule as well, though to a lesser extreme than in the Christian realms.

What both faiths shared during the Middle Ages was their call upon Jews to join them. In those days 'equal rights' were proferred to all Jews who converted to one or the other of the two dominant religions, both of which constantly claimed that true Jewish belief demanded such conversion. Thus the fate of unabating persecution was chosen by the overwhelming majority of the Jews, who preferred to remain loyal to their faith and their people and to the heritage deriving from the early existence of the Jewish nation in its own land. Throughout the Middle Ages the Jews demanded – both from the dominant culture as well as from themselves – national and religious autonomy and cultural and social responsibility. In doing so they presented a challenge both to themselves and to the dominant society. The internal challenge gave rise to a creative spiritual force capable of offering vigilant resistance and of forging new life patterns for the community and the individual alike.

The following account begins with the Moslem conquests (chapters 26–9), which created a political area that brought the vast majority of the Jews under the rule of the Moslem caliphate. There had been no such concentration of Diaspora Jewry within a single realm since the days of Cyrus and the Persian Achaemenids. The new circumstances incidentally provided the Jews with ample opportunity for self-government, as well as advantages in their economic life. Cultural and religious activities also flourished as a result of their contact with the intellectual world of the caliphate, particularly after the hellenistic trend had become prevalent. Indeed, a modern historian has, with considerable justice, suggested that the civilization of the caliphate at this period might well be described as a hellenized Islam. West European Jewry also was greatly influenced by the way in which the Jews living under Islamic rule responded to new challenges.

The second section (chapters 30–3) begins with the First Crusade in 1096, the massacres perpetrated by the crusaders in the Rhine Valley and beyond and the readiness of Jews to incur martyrdom for the glory of God – events that had a major impact on Jewish history. The changes that followed in the twelfth century were considerable in many respects. The phenomenon of large-scale martyrdom and the mentality that it signified left their mark on the Ashkenazi Jews living in Europe north and east of the Alps and influenced the thinking of the Sephardi (Spanish) Jews. A far-reaching transformation also occurred in the economic and legal status of European Jewry, as well as in their perceptions as a result of their existence amidst the gentiles.

The third section (chapters 34–7) opens with the Black Death of 1348/9, which marked a turning-point in the history of Western Europe as a whole in the Middle Ages. The high mortality rate and the changes in the population structure, as well as its new state of mind and emotional responses, introduced a new epoch. The Jews were gravely affected by false charges brought against them accusing them of having instigated the plague; both the Ashkenazi and Sephardi cultures were seriously shaken during the period. The century and a half between the Black Death and the beginning of the sixteenth century saw the collapse of old Jewish centres as a result of expulsions and restrictions – beginning in the Iberian Peninsula – that continued until 1497. New Ashkenazi centres were established in the western Slavic countries.

The fourth section (chapters 38–41) examines the interaction of developments within Jewry and without between 1492 and 1517. From Luther's appearance until the end of the Middle Ages, a new situation emerged in Western Christianity – the permanent split created by the Protestant Reformation. During those years the Jewish communities that had established themselves within the Ottoman Empire became influential, both socially and spiritually. The establishment of these communities was the result of expulsions, chiefly from the Iberian Peninsula. Other Jewish exiles settled in and around the Netherlands; while in Poland and Lithuania there was an economic and social efflorescence of the relatively new Ashkenazi community. Culturally and religiously, the period discussed in the final chapter was marked by crises and changes indicative of the transformation of the internal and external situation of mediaeval Jewry; hence it may be regarded as the end of an epoch.

The Term 'Middle Ages' and the Problems Involved

The very term 'Middle Ages' reflects the low esteem in which the period was long held; until recently the term was used to express qualitative disapproval. The epoch fell, so it was argued, between the ancient glory of the classical period and the Renaissance, in which high hopes were vested for the progress and advancement of both civilization and society. This view, however, is no longer acceptable to historians; there is now a greater sense of historical relativity. Human achievements, differing ways of life and cultures of varying nature are assessed on their own terms and merits and on the basis of their contribution to the manifold treasures and values of humanity.

The Middle Ages witnessed important advancements in every field of human endeavor. Art and architecture produced the Romanesque and Gothic styles; religious thought and sensibility achieved overwhelming force and power. Indeed, it was one of the outstanding characteristics of the mediaeval world that social and legal disciplines had no independent authority or validity but were subordinate to religious thought. The emancipation of these fields from the authority of religion was one of the most significant contributions of the waning Middle Ages to civilization. Mediaeval philosophy was first awakened and nourished by the search for divine truth, the desire to comprehend the will of God and the meaning of His works on earth. Moreover, the Middle Ages made an important contribution to philosophy in the attempt to achieve a synthesis between the specifically religious philosophy of the period, based on the monotheistic Holy Scriptures, and the philosophies inherited from the Greek and Roman worlds, particularly those of Aristotle and his successors. The influence of their philosophy is noticeable first among Moslem thinkers and at a later period (largely through the mediation of Jewish translators and teachers) in the Christian world as well.

Politically, the mediaeval state was groping towards a greater concentration of power on the one hand and, on the other, towards the establishment of clearly defined freedoms. Consequently, the individual and the state – as understood in our times – were separated from each other by various laws and corporations. Considerable tension existed between the religious and the secular authorities as a result of the assumption by the former that the sole purpose of human institutions was to serve the will of God. As religious and often extremely ascetic institutions became involved in the affairs and passions of the world, these social tensions increased in direct relation to their all-embracing conviction that God must be served in all social matters. Most of these problems and tensions were present also in Jewish society during this period, although often with major differences in both form and content.

Specific Aspects of Mediaeval Jewish History

The Jewish Middle Ages differed in many ways from the corresponding period in European history. A major characteristic of the transition from ancient to mediaeval times, particularly in Western Europe, where change first became visible, was the decline of the city from its ancient status. In Islam too the city had lost its organizational and administrative importance for society; but in economic and religious life it played a far more prominent role than it did in the Christian West. The re-emergence of the cities and their struggle for autonomy and status in social and political life constitute a major theme in European history.

In Jewish history, however, the Middle Ages were the urban epoch *par excellence*. Erez Yisrael had ceased to be an important Jewish population centre by the very beginning of the period. As early as the eighth century, agriculture no longer provided a livelihood for most Jews in the Middle East. In the Islamic countries the cities were attracting Jews who had been compelled to abandon the villages, and the urban environment was leaving its imprint upon their way of life and thought as large numbers of Jews became town-dwellers and merchants. Those Jews who reached Western Europe, on the other hand, found a social structure in which land formed the basis of social authority as well as servitude. The Christian feudal patterns that had come to predominate in Europe prevented Jews in the Christian countries from settling on the land. As a result, the city served as their first stopping-off point and eventually became their principal place of residence and unit of autonomy.

Beyond the differences in residential and social patterns, there was a distinction between the Jewish people and its host nations in their relationship towards old and new, towards the classical and the primitive in history. The peoples who shaped the culture of the Middle Ages and dictated the conditions of existence for the Jews from positions of power – the Arabs, the Germans and the Slavs – were ethnic groups that had maintained a primitive tribal culture in the ancient world. At an earlier or later date, they had invaded the *milieu* of Greco-Roman culture or of the Christian culture that followed and had acquired its values, which were merged with the concepts belonging to their own tribal backgrounds. The Jewish people, on the other hand, was a distinct national and cultural unit of the ancient world that had entered the Middle Ages bearing all the marks of its own cultural identity, and it consciously carried with it into the new circumstances a pulsating sense of continuity with its ancient past. For Jewry, faith was the main link in the chain of continuity; while for the ruling nations around them it was a melting-pot in which they were refined, a force that succeeding in transferring the heritage of the ancient world on to them. Within Christendom tribes that were new-comers to culture in terms of their experience learned to attune their sensibilities to a belief in a humiliated and slain redeemer. Warrior tribes from the forests and the steppes had to accept values based on an ascetic ideal that demanded enthusiasm for the ascetic 'breaking-down' of the human ego. In the Islamic world the Arabs, by means of their own religious concepts and acculturation patterns, adapted the ancient culture of those they conquered to their own culture. Jewry, however, did not share in the tensions and challenges created by this fusion of cultures and civilizations.

Thus Jewish society, its faith and culture continued to live and develop in the Middle Ages in circumstances of both contact and conflict with the surrounding cultures, which were composed of a Judeo-Christian element, a waning yet still-powerful classical element and an ancient tribal element that had left its mark on their very being, even when it was latent or suppressed. The latter element was entirely absent from Jewish culture, with which the classical element had long been merged. Primitive or tribalist influences reached the national and cultural entity of mediaeval Jewry almost exclusively from the outer world.

A continuous national unity was merged with the Jews' belief in their divine election and was steadily reinforced by the urban character of Jewish life. Together, these helped to bring about a spirit of egalitarianism within Jewry, coupled with an aristocratic attitude towards the outer world. In the circumstances of Jewish social life in the cities of Europe and the Near East, Jewish law was adhered to thanks to a devoted acceptance of the firm discipline implanted in the Jewish consciousness.

During the Middle Ages, Jewish national awareness was again and again acutely confronted with the problem of divine justice in history. Under the influence of the surrounding cultures, particularly Islam initially, Jews were forced to consider the relationship between their hallowed traditions and the teachings of Plato and Aristotle. The basic tension between mysticism and rationalism in the doctrine that God's word was revealed directly to man was often brought out into the open. These challenges, as well as special frameworks for Jewish economic activity and new systems of thought, led to intense Jewish spiritual creativity and left their mark, explicitly and implicitly, on the extensive mediaeval development of the *halakhah*, in the form of legal decisions as well as in the form of legal commentaries. Essentially, mediaeval *halakhah* grew out of a combination of commentary and decision. Out of these challenges there came about new developments in philosophical thought and systems and in mystical doctrines and imagery. The oppositional stance of Jewry was expressed most clearly in its polemics with members of the other faiths. Continuity and change, as expressed in Jewry's cells of communal autonomy, bear the stamp of these dialectics of life and thought.

The Economic Life of the Jews: Basic Problems

A tangled skein of questions has developed round the nature of Jewish occupations during this period. In part they are the product of the prejudice and hatred of anti-

Semites and self-hating Jews; in part a misreading of history by idealistic reformers who projected the ideals and situations of modern times on the Middle Ages and therefore distorted the image of Jewish economic life in the Middle Ages. Many studies assume that the dominant Jewish occupation in those days was usury, whether as a matter of choice or out of habit. Some choose to speak about a Jewish 'capitalist spirit' that inspired Jewish usury; some define this 'inherent' Jewish spirit as one of enterprise and initiative; more often it is defined as rapacious and exploitatory. The truth is that variety was far more characteristic of Jewish economic life in those days than was the alleged concentration on money-lending. During the period under consideration, there were considerable changes in Jewish occupations, and the concentration of Jews in certain callings was by no means identical in different countries and at different times. Certain factors operated to cut them off from agriculture – a complicated process that can be clearly seen at work in the Middle East during the eighth century (see page 393). In Islamic countries there was a transition to the entire range of urban economic activity – handicrafts, medium- and large-scale trade and commerce, hawking and peddling at one end of the scale and high finance at the other. From tanning to medicine, no source of livelihood was missing from the spectrum of Jewish occupations.

This broad range of economic activity characterized Jewry in the Islamic lands until the end of the period and also formed the foundation of Jewish economic life in the cities of Christendom in the Iberian Peninsula. The Jews first reached Western Europe north of the Pyrenees as international traders and merchants and as financial administrators who were sometimes entrusted with the vital function of minting currency. In Christian Spain from the very beginning of the Reconquista onwards, in the cities of western Germany, which began to expand in the eleventh century, and subsequently in the Polish-Lithuanian Kingdom of the sixteenth and seventeenth centuries, the Jews were regarded as a group with proven initiative and capability in administrative affairs and matters of colonization; and each country used their skills in accordance with its own needs. Yet, of all these economic activities, the only Jewish occupation in Western and Central Europe north of the Pyrenees and in parts of Italy that has attracted the attention of observers is the granting of loans on interest, chiefly during the twelfth to fifteenth centuries. Although the Jews in these countries then constituted a minority within Jewry, finances and money-lending have come to be regarded as the economic activity most characteristic of all Jews at that period.

The main error of hostile observers, social reformers and Jewish apologists alike lies in their confusion of absolute Jewish obedience to the Torah with the actual social and economic awareness of the Jews. The development of this awareness can be seen in the deliberations engaged in by the interpreters of Jewish law from the time of Rashi (towards the end of the eleventh century at the latest). These deliberations aimed at finding a method of permitting loans on interest between Jews, as can be seen also from the efforts to establish a specific formula that would distinguish between loans prohibited by the Torah and those that could be granted. These efforts had nothing to do with the attitudes towards non-Jews, but corresponded to an urgent internal economic necessity. The formula was finally introduced in a regulation known as the *hetter iskah* ('permission by partnership') adopted in Poland and Lithuania in the middle of the seventeenth century (see pages 643–4). These exegetical and legislative efforts show that the Jews became aware at a very early point that money-lending was beneficial and fair both socially and morally, whether it was in the form of consumer loans, as generally were those advanced by Jews in their 'interest region' of Western and Central Europe, or in the form of loans for the promotion of trade, such as were made by some Jews in the Moslem East, in Christian Spain and in Poland and Lithuania.

The significant phenomenon is the interesting yet complicated chapter of the relationship between this new economic activity and the theories evolved about it. Most Jewish theorists of that period failed, out of an ingrained loyalty to *halakhah*, to acknowledge even to themselves the change in their attitude towards such monetary transactions, although the change was obvious enough from their actual behaviour as well as from their efforts to find a legal method for authorizing loans.

In a disputation with Christians held in 1500 at Ferrarra in Italy by R. Abraham Farissol of Avignon, the Jewish position on interest, as it crystallized vis-à-vis that of the Catholic Church, was clearly expressed. R. Abraham's main argument was that the structure of human society as well as the incentives for economic activity, on the one hand, and the patterns of mutual aid, on the other, had changed since the times of the ancient legislators who had discredited interest as being unnatural. The world known to him and to the clerics with whom he was debating was one of distinct nationalities, each concerned for its own interests, and of individuals, each working for himself.

> This has brought into being a new situation and new obligations, a new order of things differing intrinsically from the previous; namely [the necessity] to assist one's fellow man in return for payment due from the one in need, and not to give something for nothing to one, unless he is a pauper, when he be aided for pity's sake. . . . In other cases when a man needs something of which his comrade has plenty . . . he purchases it at a price. Hence . . . the established practice of paying for the hire of houses and workers . . . all of whom have their price. . . . For if Nature and Wisdom were to demand that aid be given to everyone who needs it so as to satisfy his wants, and that money be loaned without interest to those who need money, then Nature would also require that if anyone needs a house or a horse or work to be provided for him, they should all be supplied without payment (Abraham Farrisol, *Magen Avraham,* manuscript).

R. Abraham maintained that if the practice were different 'it would cause envy, quarrels, trouble and enmity . . . such as who should provide and who deserves to be helped. That is why the practice and rule have spread of helping and working for a fair price and an agreed wage; and on these all customs and laws are based' (*ibid.*). Thus, although theoretically he could envisage a different 'order of Nature', he could accept only a social nature in which aid is paid for in every field and charity is reserved for the absolutely poor.

For him, prices, wages and interest were socially beneficial as regulators of the relations between men in an ordered and peaceful society. He rejected the differentiation, lying at the root of the prohibition of interest, between income derived from money and income derived from anything else; and he expressly concluded from the system of payment for work or the leasing of houses that 'it follows in accordance with practice and nature that he who benefits from the money of his comrade is duty-bound to pay something back. For sometimes the lending of money can be more useful than the loaning of a horse or a house. Therefore it is natural and fitting in law to give something to the owner of the money who has loaned it to him.' He points out to his antagonist that both movable and immovable property 'come to man by virtue of money and through reckoning [*i.e.*, interest]. And just as men receive profit from their beasts or houses so it is natural and proper to benefit from interest. As the original natural order is no more . . . everything is to be done only for payment' (*ibid.*, pp. 292–3).

R. Abraham apparently could not conceive of any logical reason for the prohibition of interest, although, once having finished his argument, he set out to explain the texts in the Pentateuch that deal with loans to gentiles. In fact, during the Middle Ages the prohibition of interest was for most Jews an obligatory 'decree' for which no reason was given, and it was therefore binding only on what was explicitly forbidden. In fact, in the entire range of Jewish commentators, scarcely an argument is offered to account for the prohibition of interest (see pages 560, 644).

26

Diaspora Configuration and Jewish Occupation Patterns at the Beginning of the Middle Ages

The rapid and extensive Arab conquests transformed the structure of the Jewish Diaspora and the Jews' way of life. Almost all the Jewish people dwelt in the areas conquered between 632 and 711; more than 90% of Jewry now lived within a single empire, with a common communications network and a basically uniform set of relationships. As in the days of Cyrus and his successors, Babylonia, Erez Yisrael, Egypt and Persia were under the same authority. New areas became available for Jewish settlement, and the whole of Erez Yisrael, including Jerusalem, was reopened to the Jews. In Spain those who had been forcibly converted to Christianity were able to return to Judaism, if they so desired; and it appears that there was even an appreciable Jewish immigration to Spain from the territories of Islam.

The Shift to Cities

The new rulers, who were mostly former nomads from the arid lands of Arabia, ruined the agriculture of Babylonia by taxing according to area, instead of yield, and by neglecting the irrigation network during the early years of the conquest. The results were impoverishment and the abandonment of villages and rural areas. Furthermore, the *kharaj* (poll-tax) levied on 'infidel' peasants (see page 405) weighed heavily on Jewish villagers. By the end of the eighth century, the Jewish population and its economic structure in considerable stretches of Islamic territory had become urbanized. An ordinance of 787 issued to all Jewish settlements in a missive bearing the seal of the exilarch and the four seals of the heads of the academies stated that 'any judge who does not collect [debts from orphans] on chattels shall be dismissed.' This ordinance represented a drastic change in Jewish legal practice with respect to debt collection. Previously, the chattels of orphans had been exempt; however, by 787, the property of Jews consisted largely of movables and chattels, not land.

The transition from village to town was a result also of the economic attractions of cities in Moslem lands. The conquerors had first lived in camps, which developed into urban centres. Commerce was honoured by the Moslems; new cities were founded at central trading stations along caravan routes, and ancient cities along the trade routes gained a new lease on life. Jews settled in all these cities and sometimes developed magnificent communities, such as those of Baghdad in Iraq and Kairouan in North Africa.

In Western Europe at that time and until the eleventh century, the cities were the only places where classical culture still exerted some vestigial influence. Merchants found security within the bishop's domain and alongside or within the city walls. Jews came to Western Europe as merchants and found that urban conditions favoured their activities, providing safety and culture. Little by little the urban way of life became the Jewish form of existence in all lands. Eventually, Jews became accustomed to city life, whereas rural life became strange and unfamiliar to them. In rural feudal society there was room for only two classes: the lord, whatever his rank in the feudal hierarchy, and the peasant, who in many places was bound to the soil and to the service of his lord. Lordship, whatever its form, was a status from which Jews were barred. In the spiritual climate and the society of Christendom, it was inconceivable that a serf should be an infidel and his lord a Christian or *vice versa*.

The Jews as Colonizers

From the ninth century at the latest, the Jewish population began to grow in most countries. This growth can be seen from the spread of their communities through various lands, usually of their own free will and not under duress. In Moslem Spain there were cities that were almost exclusively Jewish, such as Lucena. It may be assumed that the Moslem conquests at first impelled Jewish concentrations along the northern shores of the Mediterranean to move further north. In Western Europe Jews were to be found in the ancient Roman cities along the waterways and the continental trade routes. The Rhine Basin served as a centre with links extending to Champagne and regions to the south. Gradually, the Jews expanded into Flanders and eastwards into what later became Germany. This expansion was encouraged by the slave trade (see page 397). In 965 'Jews and other merchants' are mentioned as having been placed by the emperor of the Holy Roman Empire (as it was then called) under the authority of the bishop of Magdeburg. In 1066, immediately after the Norman Conquest, Jews from France established a community in England, and, like the Normans, for a long time they preserved the closest possible ties with their parent community in France. As we shall soon see, the Jews played a very active role in Mediterranean and intercontinental trade, and in Western Christian countries they first appeared as a settlement of international merchants.

The Jews were not restricted to the large cities. They were to be found also in the the villages of Mesopotamia and Egypt, on the islands of the Mediterranean and Indian Ocean and at the trading stations of the caliphate. Even tiny Jewish settlements sought to maintain communal life and institutions. Thus we find a husband trying to persuade his wife: 'Come with me to my township, for my occupation and trade are there. Although my township is smaller than this one, still it has a synagogue and a bath-house and grinding mills; and it has a wall' (Responsum of the Gaon R. Zemah ben Paltoi, in B. M. Lewin, ed., *Ozar Hageonim* to Tractate *Ketubot*, para. 8, p. 372).

By the end of the eleventh century the Jews were recognized as a colonizing element in both Moslem and Christian Spain, as well as in the German Empire. The bishop of Speyer felt that his city had gained importance when he succeeded in attracting a group of Jews from Mainz to a newly added suburb (1084).

In the early Middle Ages, the Jewish faith gained additional adherents when many members of the ruling class of the Khazar Kingdom on the estuary of the Volga to the Caspian Sea, headed by their king, adopted Judaism as their religion.

Pilgrimages to the Holy Land

Links with Erez Yisrael were never severed. Jews who dwelt under Moslem rule would go there to pray and then return home. As we shall see below, the Karaites in the tenth century yearned deeply to settle in Jerusalem. Jews in more distant places also maintained ties with the homeland. A pilgrim tells his kinsman and friend of the holiness of the place and how men yearn to go there. In a letter of the eleventh century, sent from the congregation of Salonika to another community lying on the route to Erez Yisrael, we read:

> So-and-so who hails from the community of Russia and has been staying with us. . . . He met a relative who came to our Holy Jerusalem and who told him of the splendours of Erez Yisrael. His spirit has moved him to go likewise and prostrate himself at the Holy Place.

And the man knows only the Slavic 'language of Canaan'. A Jew from France who had recently lost his son relates: 'I have a great desire to go to Erez Yisrael and to Jerusalem and to end my days there.' The Slavic languages were referred to as 'the language of Canaan' on the basis of the Bible verse: 'Cursed is Canaan: A slave of slaves shall he be' (Genesis 9:25; see page 397).

Jewish Livelihoods in the Islamic Countries

A vast complex of lands and peoples had been united under Moslem rule. The Moslems viewed commerce favourably, and their fleets controlled the Mediterranean and the waterways leading to the spices and silks of the Far East. Hence the lands and seas under the rule of the caliphate became the most suitable region for the exchange of goods in the mediaeval world. Even when breaches appeared in the caliphate structure, from the tenth century on, and the safety of the travellers on the roads declined appreciably, the old contacts withstood the stress and trade continued to expand even across newly established frontiers. The diversified branches of the crafts and commerce were the main occupations of Jews in the cities. At the same time there were other Jews, in the border areas of the caliphate and in Africa, who continued to engage in agriculture for a very long time.

Jewish craftsmen were plentiful in the cities and made up a large part of the Jewish population. In fact, it appears that this economic class had existed as early as the end of the classical period. A hostile Moslem writer went so far as to claim that 'among the Jews one finds only dyers, tanners, blood-letters [*i.e.*, barbers and surgeons], butchers and waterskin repairers.' However, he was referring only to those occupations to which he wished to draw attention. More objective sources mention also Jewish blacksmiths, gold and silversmiths, harness-makers and shoemakers, some of whom were itinerant craftsmen working in Moslem villages.

Every city had Jewish shop-keepers, who dealt in everything that came to market. Jews are reported as having been among the great merchants; some sold Persian rugs to distant lands, others exported pearls from the Persian Gulf. This large-scale Jewish trade was in part intercontinental, reaching across the Mediterranean and the oceans. Jews were actively engaged in all branches of urban activity. They were also to be found in what is now termed the free professions – as physicians, astronomers, translators and the like.

'The Court Bankers'

As Jews gradually became a population group whose main economic occupations were commerce and finance, gifted individuals among them found ways and means of concentrating and organizing Jewish finance, and they began to supply funds to needy rulers. From the beginning of the tenth century, we hear of wealthy Jewish merchants who became something like 'court bankers' in Baghdad, lending large amounts to the caliph and his ministers when called upon. It appears that these vast sums were at their disposal because they served well-to-do Jewish merchants as a kind of savings bank. Jewish merchants entrusted their money to the court bankers in order to share in the profits on the large loans made by them to the rulers.

It is possible that one of the Responsa of the *geonim* preserves traces of this combination of trade and banking in the form of a model agreement between two partners:

> On such and such a day and at such and such a place we have contracted with A for the amount which B is entrusting to him, namely three thousand gold pieces, on condition that A shall add another two thousand gold pieces . . . and what may come to him more than this. *And he shall transact business with them after the fashion of the bankers, and also in other wares* . . . And A has engaged in many transactions from the beginning of the partnership until now, about ten years in all, and has earned a great deal [author's italics].

A, who is putting the money to use, declares: 'What is yours of right is your share of the profit on the five thousand gold pieces only; the rest of all my transactions have been carried out with my money and *the money of others*; and you have no share in the profits I have earned on them.' In the course of the legal discussion, the contract's use of the term '*gahbadah*' is mentioned and it is translated as 'the activity of bankers and similar matters' (Responsa, *Sha'arei Zedek,* Salonika, 1794, section 8, no. 12, fol. 96v).

This partnership between money-lending bankers and wealthy Jewish merchants – anonymous depositors in the eyes of the authorities – who served as silent partners in this field of economic activity, gave the bankers a measure of protection against their despotic clients. Arab writers explain that the caliph refrained from harming them 'in order that the merchants should be ready and willing to lend their money through the bankers when necessary'. Vizirs might be replaced arbitrarily, but as a rule the court banker remained at his post, his property untouched. Among the leading partners in this banking business during the tenth century, we find the names of Netira and his sons, Joseph ben Pinhas and Aaron ben Amram.

International Trade

A considerable part of the extensive Jewish trade followed the routes that led from the caliphate to the Far East, from where spices were brought, and to the lands of Western Europe, in the opposite direction. From the beginning of the period under consideration, the distress of Western Europe was a factor that enhanced the significance of Jewish commerce. The conquests of the Moslems and their control of the Mediterranean had cut off the long-standing commercial ties of the Germanic kingdoms in the West. Byzantine animosity to the Western Church and kingdoms, which was steadily increasing, served to complete the isolation. Jews became the international merchants of Western Europe, supplying the luxuries and spices it required and in return exporting the few commodities that were available in Europe to the wealthy territories of Islam. Some of these Jewish merchants settled in Christian lands, others remained in Islamic territory. The ties between them united these trade networks.

As early as the sixth century, the chronicles of the Frankish bishop Gregory of Tours reported the presence of Jewish communities in the kingdom of the Franks. From his account it seems that these Jews traded in luxuries, which brought them in contact with the royal court, the nobility and the upper echelons of the clergy. He regarded them as wealthy and describes a debate he held with the Jewish merchant Priscus at the royal court in the presence of the Frankish king. The Jewish merchant is shown to be in close contact with royalty, well versed in the Bible and capable of defending his faith with firmness and skill. Priscus was eventually murdered by a convert to Christianity during a period of forced conversions. This instance shows the ambiguous status of the highly cultured Jewish merchant within a primitive economic structure based largely on barter, at a time when the West was in a state of cultural decline. The Jews were foreigners, both valuable and vulnerable.

In about the year 825, Archbishop Agobard of Lyons complained of the Jewish slave trade, permitted by a special royal charter and occasionally referred to in Jewish sources as well. These slaves were almost all pagan Slavs captured by Christians and sold to Jews, who transported them to the Islamic lands. Agobard did not complain about the trade in the Slav slaves as such, for in those days no religion objected to the enslavement of members of another faith, let alone heathens. Furthermore, the the servitude of Christians to other Christians constituted the warp and woof of feudal Christian society. His objection was that the Jews refused to release and hand over to the Church those slaves who had become Christians while passing through Christian territory. He also claimed that Jews sometimes sold Christians to Moslems, a complaint that occasionally was voiced also against the Christian Venetians. The slave trade was extremely important in the economic life of Western Europe, because the supply of this welcome commodity to Moslem countries helped in some degree to balance the flow of gold from Christian Western Europe to Moslems. From our viewpoint it was important also because it brought the Jews in contact with Eastern Europe. For a long time the Slavs and their land were designated in Hebrew sources – as a result of being the slaves' land of origin – as 'Canaanites' and 'the land of Canaan'.

In the ninth century Jewish trade became more extensive and comprehensive. In the middle of the century, a Moslem writer described a Jewish merchant group known as the 'Radhanites' (a term whose etymology is not entirely clear). These merchants would depart from the southern ports of present-day France and reach the trade routes of the Islamic lands via various sea and land routes, thence proceeding to India and China, from where they brought back luxuries or items of necessity for Europe, such as spices and frankincense for the Church and silk garments for the royalty and nobility. The author speaks highly of their familiarity with languages. According to him the routes followed by their companies were fixed and well known.

Numerous gaonic Responsa, written between the ninth and eleventh centuries, bear witness to the extensive commerce engaged in by Jewish merchants in various Mediterranean ports. We learn of partnerships between Jews of distant lands (*e.g.*, between Sicilian and Egyptian Jews). Consignments of spices and fabrics were transferred from East to West. These merchants were well organized, and in the larger ports they had their own 'captain' – an official appointed by the state for its own purposes – who apparently provided warehouses, organized trading routes and methods and settled disputes. Trade apprenticeship crossed political borders and great distances: a man sent his son from the Maghreb (north-west Africa) to his brother in Egypt in order to learn the ways of commerce. In the first half of the eleventh century, R. Samuel Hanagid 'rode the sea in his youth with merchants . . . on [both] oars and wind' (*Diwan, Ben-Tehillim*, para. 8, p. 5). In his opinion the sea trade, was one of 'three things that are engaged in by all who live dangerously and are high-minded' (*ibid., Ben-Mishlei*, para. 15b, p. 246). This trade involved close ties between the merchants, most of whom were educated men. In about the eleventh century, one of them declared: 'Indeed, my father's account-book is in existence.' The *gaon* who was questioned in this connexion mentions in his Responsa that the two merchants 'used to conduct their affairs by letters which they wrote to one another. And it was their practice that . . . their letters were as binding as their words' (B. M. Lewin, ed., *Ozar Hageonim* on *Bava Kama,* p. 81). Thus we see that trade was based on agreements contained in written documents and letters, of which detailed accounts were kept.

Penetration into the Local Trade of Western Europe

In the Christian lands various economic developments occurred after the Jews had integrated into the relatively primitive feudal structure of society. At first these developments merely reflected changes in international commerce, but as time went on they assumed far greater importance in their own right. Jewish merchants began to engage in local trade, and feudal lords began to utilize their talents for the conduct of their own ramified financial and commercial affairs. We learn of the movement of Jews from the purely commercial world into the feudal world, involving complex transactions in interest, pledges and other associated dealings, from the story of one Jew

> who used to travel to many places and castles near the city where he dwelt, or
> at a distance of one or two days' journey, and it was his way of business to sell to

them and buy from . . . [the] lords of the castles. When there was no ready money to be found there they would hand him pledges of silver and gold. Sometimes he would exchange goods for the cattle they had taken from their enemies. He would buy the cattle cheaply and he would bring them home and sell them at a large profit. Such was his practice for six or seven years; but the villagers and their masters the lords took it to heart, for they said: This Jew is inciting our enemies against us for he is always available to purchase the spoils. Therefore they engage in these evil actions being assured [of a buyer for the booty]. Furthermore many of these rulers used to quarrel with the Jew . . . about the pledges held by him and over charges of usury (S. Eidelberg, ed., *The Responsa of Rabbenu Gershom Meor Hagolah,* New York, 1955, para. 36, p. 103).

This particular Jew finally disappeared without leaving a trace, but what is told of him illustrates his function within the social and economic world of the feudal barons. He exchanged wares in his possession, which doubtless he or his Jewish friends had brought from overseas for other wares, such as animals taken as spoils of war.

At about that time (*c.* 1000), we meet a Jewish family with a kind of hereditary right to conduct all branches of business of the Narbonne Hegemony (the mediaeval Hebrew term means 'episcopal diocese' or 'principality'). A father, his brothers and his son were all engaged in this administrative activity, which included managing the affairs of the *hegemon* and purchasing his requirements. Entering into transactions with the *hegemon* also was done through this family, for part of their profit derived from levying from gentiles a fee on their transactions. The feudal lord also trusted his precious metals to the Jews. The question is asked whether the Jew made a profit because 'he lent money on interest and profited by it, or exchanged [his lord's] silver and gold at a high rate and invested it, buying cheaply, or whether he exchanged his own money for silver and gold at a cheap rate and invested at a high rate'. The respondent also considered the possibility that the Jewish administrator had 'invested his money in goods, sold well and made a profit; or sold his silver and gold and placed the money in the hands of a partner to do business with, sharing half the profit'. It is also evident that the Jews held 'the salt' [industry] of the *hegemon*, but this business 'was profitable only by dint of great effort' (D. Cassel, ed., *Responsa of Ancient Geonim,* Berlin, 1848, no. 140, fol. 37v–38r). This description of the range of Jewish administrative activity shows that in Provence at that time the Jews were considered to be experts in the full range of trade and finance.

Trade and Property in Western Europe in the Eleventh Century

Money gradually began to regain importance, while the natural or barter economy steadily declined. At the same time trade began to expand, as did city life. The Jews played an important part in these developments, which suited the economic function they had fulfilled within the framework of the natural economy since the early Middle Ages. From the economic clauses of the charters issued in the cities of the Rhine Valley at the end of the eleventh century, we learn that the Jews were an important element in urban commerce. Those who wished to attract them to a city would permit them to engage in any business they desired. The few restrictions listed in the charters were in order to bar competition of Jews with the minters and money-changers, who were then a unique economic and social force. On this subject a Responsum of *geonim* tells of a Jew who had 'acquaintanceship with the Master of the Mint and was much respected by him'; while another Jew had 'refined silver which he wished to give to the Master of the Mint . . . for turning into coins, but feared that the making would be deferred'. He therefore requested that the Jewish acquaintance of the master place the silver for melting down as coinage 'in his name and on his account'. Transactions in minting metal coins were thus regular and continuous. Furthermore, the respondent considered the possibility that 'the Master of the Mint is a Jew' (*Responsa of the Geonim*, Mantua, 1567, para. 165).

The Responsa of Rashi, most of which may be attributed to the second half of the eleventh century, give a colourful and dynamic picture of Jewish occupations in Champagne and the districts of northern France and the Rhine River Valley. We learn here of transactions in land and vineyards. There is a case of a Jewess and her son who held a village and the 'tithe' from it 'as a [feudal] reward . . . like other recipients of rewards from the lords'. This means that these Jews were holding the land under certain feudal conditions. The son had sentimental ties to the estate, or at least he assumed that the claim of such ties would seem reasonable to the Jewish community and its sages, for he explained one of his actions by declaring: 'I was angry that the acknowledged heritage of my fathers should be given over irrevocably to the alien' (J. Elfenbein, ed., *Responsa of Rashi*, para. 240, p. 268). Considerable landed property, amounting to at least four vineyards and five houses, belonged to a certain Jew. In this case too an emotional attachment to the property was displayed, for he explained the terms of his will by declaring: 'I do not wish the heritage of my fathers to pass into the hands of aliens' (*ibid.,* para. 242, pp. 282–3). 'Aliens' here mean Jews who did not belong to his family.

In these eleventh-century Responsa, credit transactions also made an appearance. We learn of a Jewish commercial arrangement in which two men were active partners, while a third man and his mother were silent partners. The active partners 'undertook the toil and trouble of the partnership and engaged to do business as long as it lasted, provided that all expenditure on food and drink be chargeable to the partnership, since the activity of Reuben and Simeon was greater than that of Levi and his mother Sarah'. When the partnership was liquidated, one of the problems that arose was that it had included 'our loans to gentiles on trust', *i.e.*, without any document or pledge (*ibid.,* para 79, p. 112). From the rabbi's solution it is clear that Jewish credit to gentiles was accepted and widespread in those times; thus Rashi took into consideration the fact that it was 'indeed the local custom that he who lends money through his friend will allow the middleman a third or a quarter or a fifth. And Simeon is therefore required to share the interest according to local custom' (*ibid.,* p. 107). Indeed, in several of his Responsa we find Rashi dealing with questions concerning money earned as interest by one Jew from another and the procedure to be followed when engaging in such transactions through a gentile intermediary. Rashi's decisions often permit this escape clause from the biblical prohibition of interest from Jews.

Standards of Living

It seems that these livelihoods provided the Jews, especially those engaged in large-scale trade, with living standards that sometimes approached those of the upper strata of Christian and Moslem societies. There are reports of male and female slaves in Jewish homes in the lands of Islam. The charters granted in the Christian West permitted Jews to keep Christian wet-nurses and workers in their homes, despite Church opposition. It is impossible to draw reliable conclusions from silence; nevertheless, it is a fact that, although Western Europe suffered virtual famine for many years in the tenth and eleventh centuries, there is no hint or echo of this in the Jewish sources of the region from that period. The Jewish city dweller lived on an aristocratic level, as befitted international merchants and honoured local financiers. In the ninth century, before religious animosity had reached full force, Archbishop Agobard complained to Emperor Louis the Pious that the Jews 'vaunt themselves. . . . They likewise show us female garments which they claim were given to their women folk by the daughters of your family or by the matrons of the Court.' Whether the words 'they claim' were included only to soften the complaint in the ears of the emperor, as would appear to be the case from the context, or whether the archbishop really doubted that such gifts had actually been given, it is clear that the Jewesses of Lyons had robes as magnificent as those of the court ladies. The table laid by Rashi was far from ascetic. 'On occasion,' declared his disciple, R. Shemaiah, 'I saw brought to him on a cone-shaped vessel meat or spiced meat, or eggs fried in honey.' Rashi would recite the blessing over these sweetmeats before reciting the blessing for bread, attributing his actions to the pleasure he derived from the former: 'And he said to me . . . "This is pleasing in my eyes . . . and I find it suits me to utter blessings in praise of my Maker for those things I enjoy"' (*ibid.*, para. 86, pp. 114–15).

The height of magnificence and luxury was reached by the wealthy Jews in the lands of Islam, particularly in Moslem Spain. We know that the court bankers of Baghdad in the tenth century kept open house for numerous guests and for the poor. Similarly, the ceremonies of the Jewish leaders in Babylonia and the patronage of the leading Jews in Moslem Spain (see page 452), indicate conditions of ease and plenty. Clear testimony to this in Moslem Spain can be found in the descriptions of the life and surroundings of R. Samuel Hanagid. In his palatial home there was a 'water-fountain . . . which fell from above in the form of a dome onto a floor of marble and alabaster. And they placed lights within the dome . . . a wax candle at the head.' There was also 'a fire burning before him during winter days, with shapes of birds around it' (*Diwan, Ben-Tehillim*, paras. 113, 115, p. 89). Some scholars are of the opinion that he and his son Joseph built the Alhambra and lived there. In any case, R. Solomon ibn Gabirol, the poet and philosopher (who died sometime before 1058), has left the following description:

A palace rose above the countryside
  Built with valiant stones . . .
Its walls as thick as battlements

With balconies around . . .
The buildings decked with reliefs . . .
Laid out with alabaster floors. . . .
Windows shining from above
The countless gates and ivory doors
A pool like Solomon's, but lions stood around
Not on oxen. . . .

(H. Schirman, *Hebrew Poetry in Spain and Provence,* I, Jerusalem, 1954, no. 84, pp. 223–4)

This is a description of the palace of a wealthy Jew, presumably R. Samuel Hanagid. From the poem it is clear that the poet walked freely in the garden and the mansion he described. The magnificent fountain – one of this kind is indeed to be found in the Alhambra – is associated by the poet with the Sea of Solomon, which stood in front of the First Temple, save that is more magnificent by reason of the lions that adorn it.

27

Effects of Religious Animosity on the Jews

Islam and the Jews

The basic attitude of Christianity towards the Jews had already crystallized in the time of the Late Roman Empire, before the Middle Ages. The claim to divine election voiced by the Jews – who were a powerful rival possessing a rich past – had been associated with popular hatred and with extreme sectarian polemics as early as the fourth century. However, when the Arabs left the Arabian Peninsula and embarked upon their extensive conquests early in the seventh century, a new monotheistic religion appeared on the scene, with its own principles and attitude towards the Jews; for there is a definite distinction between the attitudes of Islam and Christianity in this respect.

The contact and struggle between Judaism and Islam lacked the intimacy and bitterness that had characterized the early relations between Jews and Christians when the latter had broken away from Judaism. Moreover, the dispute between Judaism and Christianity focused on the validity of the Law, on the question as to whether the Messiah has already come, on the incarnation and ascension of Jesus and on the nature and definition of divinity. As against these, the dispute with Islam centred on the question as to whether prophecy had ended before or with Mohammed and on the tension between two legal codes, that of Judaism and that of Islam.

Communities of Jews had long existed in Arabia and had adapted their ways of life and their communal organization to those of their neighbours – who were akin to them both ethnically and linguistically – to the extent that it is customary to refer to them as Jewish 'tribes'. The latter, together with the Christians of the region, exerted the monotheistic influences that were absorbed by Mohammed. Various indications in the Koran, as well as changes in law, custom and relationships with the Jews, show that at first he had hoped to find his main supporters among the Jewish tribes. In order to win their support, he established alliances with them and observed certain laws with regard to fasting and facing towards Jerusalem during prayers. When the overwhelming majority of the Jews refused to regard him as the final messenger of God, his frustration found expression in a cruel war of extermination. Divided politically (which may have been the reason for their defeat), as were the Arab tribes, but united by their Torah, the Jewish tribes fell with sword in hand, martyrs for their faith.

In spite of certain changes introduced by Mohammed in the course of his campaign against the Jews, the conquerors who swept out of Arabia maintained a strong faith in the unity of God, an extreme opposition to images and paintings and a readiness to view the earlier monotheistic faiths as legitimate precursors of Islam. They preserved a conception that seems to have originated with Mohammed whereby 'the Peoples of the Book', *i.e.*, Jews and Christians, were entitled to different treatment from that meted out to idolaters who had no holy scriptures. For the Moslem, therefore, the memory of battles against Jews was modified by the recognition that they shared a similar conception of the Divinity.

The Situation During and After the Moslem Conquest

Although it was mainly the fanatic enthusiasm of the Moslems that motivated and made possible their conquest of vast areas and multitudes of inhabitants, the very extent and suddenness of their success moderated their spirit and compelled the surprised victors to show consideration for the vanquished. Here again the difference between Christianity and Islam with regard to believers in other faiths was largely determined by the fact that Christianity had conquered by means of inner spiritual conversion, taking over from within the existing authorities, whereas Islam had conquered long-civilized regions by means of the sword.

The conquerors had invaded from the desert. Faced with victory, they were forced to determine anew their own self-awareness, as well as to reformulate their attitude to the vanquished, who followed various faiths and adhered to rival sects. At no time, therefore, could a situation emerge in Islam such as had appeared after a relatively short transition period in Christendom, whereby a single group, namely the Jews, constituted the only open opposition to the dominant faith. Under the Moslems the Jews were not the only heretics or non-believers. The victorious Moslems had to face problems of many kinds. Were they to dilute their Arab character by merging with the conquered who accepted Islam, or were they to preserve their own identity? Should they impose their faith on the conquered, or should they permit them to continue as they were? During the seventh and eighth centuries, life itself solved these problems, though not unequivocally. A great many of the conquered were adopted into Islam, yet subsequently had to demand – at the point of rebellion – the right of full membership in the dominant *umma* or 'community of believers'.

'The Protected People'

The need to maintain undisturbed relations with those on whom the existence of an economic structure and civilization depended gradually shaped the Moslem attitude towards those members of the 'peoples of the Book' who refused to accept Islam. The attitude toward these non-Moslems in the Islamic territories was shaped in principle in accordance with the concept of *dhimma*, meaning protection granted to them by agreement or treaty. The religious groups that were permitted to live in accordance with the terms of this protection were termed *ahl al-dhimma*, 'the protected people', while the individual infidels came to be known as *dhimmi*.

From our point of view, it is not important whether any agreement or treaty was actually signed, or whether it was a legal fiction that served as a religious instrument for crystallizing the dependent status of the infidels. In either case, from the Moslem viewpoint the latter were living under their rule in accordance with forms established by the Moslem victors at the time of conquest. The 'Terms of Omar', attributed to the great Moslem conqueror, were taken to be the archetypal relationship. Reference is made there to the 'mercy and compassion' pleaded for by the submitting infidels for themselves, for their families and for their property. Many provisions, such as the prohibitions against carrying weapons and riding horses, were based on the principle of honouring Islam and the Moslems and humiliating non-believers and their religions. The major expressions of *dhimmi* status were the poll-tax or *jizia,* which all male non-believers above the age of fifteen had to pay, and the special land-tax, known as the *kharaj.* In return, their lives and property were protected and, in accordance with the general attitude of Islam to infidels, they were assured liberty of faith and worship. They were also permitted to organize themselves as they wished, and the Jews fully availed themselves of that permission. Naturally there were changes for the better or for the worse in various places and at various times; but the principles established in the early days of Islam continued to serve as the basis for the relations between Moslem and *dhimmi* throughout the ages.

The Status of the Jews

From the Jewish viewpoint, this conglomerate of Moslem attitudes to infidels was easier to live with than the one that had been established by Christianity, particularly in the Byzantine Empire. As we have noted above, for hundreds of years the overwhelming majority of Jews lived in the Islamic territories. Although it is possible to perceive some Christian impact on the Moslem attitude towards non-believers and even towards the Christians themselves, the moderation with which the Moslems applied this influence proved to be of great importance to the majority of Jewry over a long period. Unlike the masses of Christians and pagans who joined the Moslems during the first half century or so, the overwhelming majority of the Jews under Moslem rule held firmly to their own faith.

There were variations in the attitude towards Jews. Instances will be mentioned below of Jews who, through their own talents, rose to political leadership in Moslem Spain, among them Hasdai ibn Shaprut in the tenth century, Samuel Hanagid and his son Joseph in the eleventh, and the Ibn Ezra family (which initially served Moslem rulers and later some of its members served Christian rulers). Reference has already been made to the court bankers, who played so important a role in the political economy of the caliphate and who lived like noblemen. These were favourable exceptions to the general circumstances. Moslems frequently reacted furiously to the elevation of 'degraded ones'. Sometimes the fury of the masses erupted against both the Jewish minister and his brethren, as happened in the Granada riots of 1066, when the whole congregation was killed together with Joseph Hanagid. This was a violent expression of the immanent tension and dialectic involved in the rise of a gifted member of a minority who surmounted or breached the rigid limitations fixed for the *dhimmi,* a situation fraught with both promise and danger to the man and his community.

The Sunni, the Moslem majority who had established the predominant system of law and practice in Islam, were usually more tolerant towards the Jews than were the members of the Shia, the followers of Ali. The Shiites, a minority that came to power mainly by means of revolution, showed little respect for Sunnite traditions. It was not by chance that the ruler who set out to persecute Jews (and Christians) most savagely was the Fatimid or Shiite caliph of Egypt, Al-Ḥakim B'amr Allah. In about the year 1008, he imposed savage and degrading laws, ordaining 'that the Jews shall hang from their necks the image of a calf as they did in the wilderness', and fixed the weight of the calf at 6 pounds. He also restored old prohibitions, such as those against the use of ornaments and against horse-riding. But he himself later relaxed some of these decrees, and when he disappeared in 1021 they vanished with him. From time to time both Sunnite and Shiite rulers, either of their own accord or under pressure of public opinion, would dismiss infidels from influential positions. Until the end of the eleventh century, such episodes usually proved to be passing evils. The basic attitude was in the main not changed – for better or worse – by unity in the caliphate or the latter-day break-up into separate Moslem principalities. In fact, the Jews who exerted the most influence on the affairs of Islam, such as Samuel Hanagid and his son, indeed rose to power when the Omayyad kingdom in Spain broke up into numerous principalities.

Christian Hostility

It has already been remarked that the roots of Christian religious animosity towards the Jews go back to classical times and even to the period before the Christians broke away from the Jewish people. They go down to the heart of Jewish faith and culture and were an outcome of a dispute over the identity of the Jews and their future. Christianity had emerged from the messianic ferment and the religious and social struggles of Jewry towards the end of the Second Temple period, and ultimately it moved into the non-Jewish world. This parting of ways was accompanied by the introduction of several principles and attitudes whose application as harsh reality for the Jews came centuries later, in the mediaeval world. By then Christianity was, in the eyes of Jewry, an entirely non-Jewish phenomenon, and Christian thought and imagination perceived the Jews in accordance with the views of Paul, whereby the Jews were the physical remnant of Israel but had forfeited their heritage and their election, being blinded to the light of the Church by their own wickedness. The Christian Church was the bearer of religious continuity and the 'spiritual Israel' to which divine election had been transferred.

In the fourth century, long before anything resembling the mediaeval world had emerged, the bitter polemic atmosphere among the various Christian sects added abusiveness to the Christian argument against the Jews as well. In that period sharp condemnation of the Jews, their character and their way of life was expressed in several formulations, and these eventually coloured the imagination of the pagan masses who joined the Church once it had linked itself to the imperial rulers. Christian polemics claimed and taught that the Jews were a nation whose own prophets had testified to their basic corruption, even when the Jews alone possessed the Law of God, the Torah. 'O sinful nation, people heavy with iniquity' and similar texts delivered to Israel by its prophets with chastising love were now interpreted as ancient condemnations that served to confirm present and future accusations. In this century abusive terminology towards the Jews and discriminatory laws found a place in Roman imperial legislation as well.

Pope Gregory I

The crystallization of the Church's attitude towards the Jews on the threshold of the Middle Ages can be clearly seen in the writings and letters of Pope Gregory I (590–604). He was a member of a noble senatorial family in Rome, the first monk to occupy the papal seat, a master of homiletics and miraculous tales and an administrator who carefully acted as the overseer of all Church affairs, both large and small. He has been well described by Mommsen as 'a great little man'. The decline of the old and the rise of the new was combined in all his political and literary activities, as well as in his attitude towards the Jews. It is customary to judge his attitude towards them from the administrative viewpoint, which finds expression in his letters. This approach, however, is insufficient even for an understanding of his personality. Attention must be paid also to his treatment of the Jews in his role as a theologian and a preacher. Only thus can we realize the extent to which his treatment of the Jews exemplified the heritage that he passed on to the future.

In the eyes of Gregory, the Jews were still, in principle, contenders with the Church for divine election. He interpreted the Book of Job as a condemnation of a recalcitrant Israel. In his commentary on Job, he attacked the Jews in countless parables and in vivid and detailed similes. Thus he understood the text of Job 38:14 ('It is turned as clay to a seal; and they stand as a garment') in the following manner:

> The Lord found the People of Israel – clay – when he came unto them in Egypt and they were abandoned to the ways of the Gentiles and worked with bricks. But when He brought them forth with so many miracles to the Promised Land and filled them, after they arrived there, with knowledge of His wisdom, as when He granted them such manifold secrets, mysteries in prophecy, what did He make of them if not a Seal for the preservation of His mysteries. [And yet this nation, although it possessed the words of prophecy and the mysteries they contained] after so many divine secrets, after the manifold miracles which they witnessed when our Saviour came – they loved their land more than the truth [a reference to the fear that they would lose their country to the Romans if they believed in Jesus, as stated in John 11:18] . . . they returned as it were to those bricks which they had left behind in Egypt. And that which had been the Seal of the Lord, once again became what He had abandoned. And after they had been a Seal they appeared as clay in the eyes of the Truth: and because of this impious wickedness they lost the mystery of the Logos which they had received, and preferred to enjoy only the corruption of earth.

Elsewhere, in his sermons on Ezekiel (Book One, Sermon 6), Gregory presented

Jacob as the symbol of the gentiles and Esau as the symbol of Judaism. All details in the stories of Isaac, Rebecca, Jacob and Esau were interpreted there as fore-shadowing the future election of the gentiles and the rejection of the Jews. Thus the dressing of Jacob in his brother's garments foreshadowed the fact that the gentiles would in due course be garbed in the commandments of the Holy Scriptures that were given to Esau the first-born (*i.e.*, to Judaism) to be observed spiritually, while Esau went forth to the field to hunt venison – meaning that the Jews observed the commandments only according to their letter, the material aspect that had been abolished by the coming of Jesus.

Yet this sharp theoretical and theological antagonism did not prevent Gregory in his role as an administrator from laying down precedents in accordance with Roman tradition and from practising toleration of the Jews. Admittedly he subjected the Jews to some degree of humiliation, but not to religious compulsion or to serious economic persecution. He wished to attract the Jews to Christianity and suggested economic concessions to their advantage in order to entice them, with the expectation that, even if parents had not come to Christianity for its own sake, they or their children would eventually become true Christians. This method of encouraging conversion involved offering the allurements of 'political and economic equality' (to use present-day terminology), while those who rejected the offer were pressured by humiliation and discrimination. Gregory's approach derived from his theological outlook and reflected his missionary character and his administrative technique. As we shall see below, it later served as a guide for the *moderate* attitude displayed towards Jews in the Middle Ages. Thus, in the system laid down at the end of the sixth century by one of the most hostile opponents of Judaism, the prohibition against building new synagogues and the attempt to attract Jews by material enticements were offset by laws protecting, within their humble status, those Jews who would not become Christians.

When Gregory I declared his stand at about the end of the sixth century, Christianity was the only monotheistic faith competing with Judaism; however, there was a sharp split within Christianity caused by the Germanic kingdoms that had adopted Arian Christianity. The Catholic approach itself was influenced by two co-ordinating centres: Byzantium, ruled by the emperor, and Rome, which was subject to him but had its own theories and independent attitudes.

During those very centuries of transition from one historical epoch to another, the Talmudic *halakhah* was being formulated and put on record, and the moral sermons and legendary and homiletic material of the *tannaim,* the *amoraim* and the *savoraim* took shape. At that time Christianity was repeatedly telling the Jews that their rejection of the messiah and his crucifixion had brought down upon Judaism the calamity of spiritual petrification and the curse of religious incomprehension. Yet the Jewish sages were then developing and passing on to the Jews of the Middle Ages and subsequent generations the major achievements of the Babylonian and Jerusalem Talmuds and the numerous midrashic works of the *tannaim* and the *amoraim* (see Part IV). A close examination of the works of the Church Fathers of the same period will show that the contents and the ways of thinking were largely influenced by the homiletic system and formulations of the Jewish Midrash.

Visigoth Spain

Almost on the eve of the Moslem expansion a change for the worse occurred in the status of a distinguished Jewish community in Europe, the Jews of Visigoth Spain. When the Arian kings of Spain became Catholic, they endeavoured to consolidate unity of faith among their people by forcing the Jews to convert. From the sixth century and until the Moslem conquest of Spain in 711, the Jews were subjected to every kind of legal maltreatment. This persecution, attested by the contents of the legislation of the period, was carried out despite the weakness of the state at the time and the tendency of those nobles who remained Arians to disregard its decrees. We may assume that the anti-Jewish legislation was directed at forced converts who were suspected by Church and state alike of secretly maintaining their old faith. Dire punishments, such as enslavement, execution and 'pulling out the hair' were enacted against those who continued to observe Judaism. The Jews were required to make a public profession of Christianity and of their acceptance of its ways. Methods were adopted that provided for clerical supervision of Jews when they moved from place to place. They were not permitted to educate their children, who were entrusted to Christians. In brief, in the seventh century, as later in the fourteenth and fifteenth centuries, Christian compulsion brought into being a Jewish underground of forced converts (Marranos, as they were later termed). Even after conversion the Visigoths regarded them as Jews. As was to be the case again 700 or 800 years later, there were also enthusiastic converts who reached high positions in the Church and were among the leading persecutors of their brethren. The fall of Visigoth Spain in 711 spelt redemption for the remaining Marranos. Christian chroniclers tend to place the blame for the Moslem triumph on 'Jewish treachery' and aid to the Arabs. It stands to reason that these forced converts would turn against their oppressors, but there is no evidence other than these anti-Jewish accounts.

Patterns and Attitudes in Other Christian Principalities

In other Christian countries the legal status of the Jews was more varied and less stable than it was in the lands of Islam, although the number of Jews affected was far smaller. The backwardness of the political institutions in the lands of Christendom, together with the feudal structure and conception of society, accounted to a considerable extent for this situation.

It is sometimes difficult to comprehend the process whereby the legal status of the Jews developed, because of the terminology used in those days. Much of it has been retained in European languages, but the meanings have changed. Charters and 'privileges' granted to the Jews in those years did not denote special rights or greater power for the recipient; rather, these were documents delimiting the rights of the recipient within the specific area concerned. Thus they constituted one element in the social and legal foundations of an orderly structure that was in the process of being established.

Different sectors of society had differing attitudes towards the Jews. Despite all that they shared in common, their formulations and purposes varied, leading to contradictions and compromises. Thus the aims of the Church dignitaries, who in those days were largely guided by the spirit of Gregory I in this respect, were not identical to the goals of the lower clergy or the monastic bodies, who were far more extreme. The attitudes of the rulers, who were concerned with public order and to whom the economic and social function of the Jews was important, certainly differed from those of the masses, who were animated by a simplistic Christian zealotry, as well as by local animosity towards small groups of successful and wealthy 'infidel' merchants and financiers. In due course the anti-Jewish social and religious tendencies coalesced and brought down upon the Jews the tempest of 1096. Until then, however, there was competition and tension between the varying attitudes.

The Situation in the Ninth Century

In about the year 825, in the days of Emperor Louis the Pious, the son of Charlemagne, several documents were issued specifying the rights of individual groups of Jews. Modern historians tend to attach greater importance to the views and actions of Louis the Pious than did their predecessors. It is recognized that the concepts of the empire – its unity and its Christian character – were far more significant for him and his circle than they had been for his father. Furthermore, Louis the Pious is known to have been constantly subject to the influence of the ecclesiastical leaders, who guided his actions. Much of what once appeared as his political weakness is now regarded as the outcome of increasing cultural and social maturity and leniency. Hence the terms of these documents and the complaints made by Bishop Agobard of Lyons against the spirit of the imperial policy are equally instructive.

The charters of c. 825 grant the Jews permission 'to live according to their Law'. They promised protection of body and property and permitted freedom of movement and trade, including the right to deal in slaves brought from and sold outside the empire and to hire Christians to work in their homes. Some Jews were also exempted from the laws of trial by 'ordeal of fire and water'. In general, these were documents granting rights to international merchants whose trade and presence met with the emperor's approval.

The letters of Agobard of Lyons against the Jews inform us that a special official was 'appointed over the Jewish infidels'. They also relate that when the bishop fulminated against the Jews, the imperial representatives in Lyons declared that the Jews were not held in contempt at the imperial court but were 'precious' in the emperor's eyes and were considered to be 'more worthy' than the Christians. Even if we assume that the bishop exaggerated in order to denigrate these representatives, we may still assume that they did stress the regard in which the Jewish merchants were held at court. The Jews brought two imperial documents in their favour addressed to the bishop and the viscount (vicecomes) of Lyons. According to Agobard's complaint they were given permission to build new synagogues, and market day was shifted from Saturday to Sunday for their sake. Agobard's denunciations thus complement the evidence provided in the charters to the effect that special imperial protection was granted to the Jews and that rights, such as the right to construct synagogues, were granted to communities rather than to individuals. The bishop complained bitterly about the respectable status of the Jews within the Christian community. He believed that part of this evil influence stemmed from the imperial court, where Jews were treated favourably. But the masses also praised Jewish preachers and some nobles requested their blessing. The Jews prided themselves on their ancient lineage and maintained that the laws of the Church did not require Christians to refrain from enjoying Jewish hospitality.

Agobard's complaints about the spiritual influence of the Jews and the attitude of the higher classes of society towards them were not figments of imagination. This can be seen from the conversion to Judaism of the young and learned deacon Bodo, his flight to Moslem Spain in 838–839 and his anti-Christian activity there. In brief, during the first half of the ninth century, imperial policy favoured Jewish merchants and their commercial activities, including traffic in slaves, while public opinion also was friendly, as is seen from both the charters and the denunciations.

The Norman incursions and the weakening of the central government in the second half of the ninth century no doubt helped to weaken the guarantees of safety, although the economic importance of the Jews may even have increased, as was remarked in the previous chapter. During this century there was increasing hatred and animosity towards Jews in the Byzantine Empire. During the reigns of several emperors, there had been an iconoclastic movement within the Eastern Church; it was finally defeated, but its opponents considered that it had been influenced by a Judaizing spirit. Animosity may also have increased as a result of the conversion to Judaism of the ruling class of the neighbouring Khazars and the fear that this would exert an influence on the Slavic tribes that the Byzantine Church had succeeded in converting only a short time before.

A number of compulsory conversions were imposed upon the Jews, reaching their peak in about the year 873, during the reign of Emperor Basil I. A tradition preserved by a leading Jewish family in southern Italy (then under Byzantine rule) relates:

> He thought to deaden belief in the Unity of the Creator . . . among offspring of the holy and wholesome. Eight hundred full years after the Holy City was destroyed . . . rose . . . a king named Basil . . . against the Remnant of Israel . . . to turn them away from their heritage the Torah and make them err (B. Klar, ed., *Megillat Ahimaaz*, Jerusalem, 1944, p. 20).

In this case the incitement was directed from above. The Church dignitaries who were for the retention of icons in church worship engaged in anti-Jewish polemics; three vicious sermons against the Jews were delivered by the influential patriarch Photius in the years 863–866.

The Sense of Pressure

In the West pressure on the Jews began increasing from several sides. During the tenth and eleventh centuries, Christianity became unquestionably the faith of the masses. The piety and asceticism of the reformist monks of Cluny transformed war and chivalry into Christian values and institutions, forging a sacred union of Christian men convinced that they were duty-bound to fight for Christianity and its ideals. This trend to engage in a holy war was intertwined with the knights' consciousness of being an upper class, and the higher levels of feudal society shaped the mood and trends prevailing in society. At an early stage the Jews became aware of the new meaning that chivalry had acquired. Towards the end of the tenth century, R. Simeon bar Isaac, the hymn-writer of Mainz, described the knights who

Have their fortresses on craggy peaks . . .
The hunt amid the lowering rocks . . .
Where shields are densely placed
And cuirass and helmet interlaced, . . .
Emblems limned and blazoned forth.
They battle with the flashing sword . . .
With gold and silver richly wrought . . .
The horsemen and their neighing steeds . . .
And arrows notched against the string . . .
While we pray to Almighty God,
Who maketh wars to cease.

(A. M. Haberman, ed., *Liturgical Poems of R. Simeon bar Isaac*, Berlin–Jerusalem, 1938, pp. 160–2)

The main pressure on the Jews stemmed from the penetration of Christianity into the minds and hearts of the common people, who began to regard the Jews among them as the only remaining antagonists to the generally accepted faith of the world. Christianity admitted and taught its followers that the Jews were the custodians of the Old Testament, which contained the Christian mysteries and truth. As the Jews were town-dwellers and were able to read and write (see chapter 29), their rejection of the Christian faith was regarded by the masses as a wilful denial of what the Jews, from study of their Holy Writ, must know to be true. The Hebrew *piyyutim* (hymns) of the period show how well aware the Jews were of this pressure to accept Christianity. This awareness finds expression in the call of Rabbenu Gershom, the Light of the Exile, for the rejection of Christianity: 'The mortal corrupt one [*i.e.,* Jesus] who is newly come, what guarantee can he offer to me?' Attacks and murders were carried out, as well as instances of forced conversion and martyrdom such as those that occurred in 930 at Otranto in southern Italy: 'When they were compelled by that persecution . . . Rabbi Isaiah with his own hands thrust a knife through his throat and was slaughtered like a lamb in the Temple court; and Rabbi Menahem fell . . . into the pit, and our Master Elijah was strangled' (Jacob Mann, ed., *Texts and Studies*, I, Cincinnati, 1931, p. 24). In 1007 there were persecutions in France, and there is a tradition relating that the expulsion of Jews from Mainz in 1012 led to a number of conversions in the city.

For all the pressure brought to bear upon the Jews, their value to society was still recognized. In the eyes of the central authorities, secular and ecclesiastic alike, they were usually found worthy of special rights and protection. In 1084, only twelve years before the massacres of 1096, the bishop of Speyer gave them a detailed charter that clearly indicated a desire to attract them to his city. From a Jewish document we learn that the Jews in question came from Mainz and that, in view of their experience, they sought a place where they would be assured of a wall surrounding the neighbourhood in which they would live. This was indeed promised to them by the bishop in his charter. In 1090, only six years before the massacres, Emperor Henry IV renewed the charter of Speyer and issued one to the Worms community. Despite their significant differences, both documents assured freedom of trade within the city and the right to live in accordance with Jewish religious law and practice. These rights are very clearly expressed in the 1090 documents from Speyer, whose bishop was a supporter of the emperor.

The Crusader Massacres of 1096

The First Crusade undoubtedly was the apogee of success for the papal program to lead the Christian peoples. Pope Urban II proclaimed this crusade at Clermont in 1095. Knights and feudal dignitaries of all kinds took part, together with common folk; monarchs, however, were absent. A Jewish chronicler of the twelfth century applied the words of the Book of Proverbs to the situation: 'The locusts have no king, but go forth all of them together in bands.' The campaign manifested those knightly ideals that had been sanctified by the Church and that were now diverted from Europe and fratricidal Christian wars towards a war against the infidels and the conquest of the Holy Land, 'the patrimony of the Lord'. Vengeance for the blood of Jesus was a declared purpose in crusader poetry and in the popular sermons and letters calling for the crusade, and these turned the masses of crusaders against the Jews. The twelfth-century Jewish chronicler relates that

> as they passed through the towns where there were Jews they said to one another: We are going on a distant journey to seek the House of the Weak and Perished [a Hebrew term for the Sepulchre] and to exact vengeance on the Ishmaelites; yet here are the Jews dwelling in our midst whose forefathers slew him and crucified him without reason. First let us take vengeance on them and destroy them as a people, so that the name of Israel shall no longer be remembered, or so that they should be like us and submit to the son of lewdness [Jesus] (from the chronicle of R. Solomon ben Samson, *The Massacres of 1096,* in A. M. Haberman, ed., *Massacres of Germany and France,* Jerusalem, 1946, p. 24).

The calamity began in France at Rouen, but it does not seem to have spread in that region. The Rhine Valley communities were warned but could not envisage an outbreak on a scale that would render the protection of the bishops and the emperor useless. During April and June of 1096, riots broke out in the Rhine Basin. The Jewish leaders called upon the emperor and appealed to the bishops and other lords of cities and owners of fortified places in and around the cities. They paid vast sums to these potential protectors – who in many places actually did give them fortified locations where they could defend themselves and even provided a military guard – but the cities opened their gates to the crusaders. Christian soldiers had no desire to defend infidels against their brethren who were setting forth on a holy war and, from their viewpoint, offering the Jews a choice between the true Christian faith and vengeance for their obduracy. In some places, such as Speyer and Cologne, the bishops stood firm, stopping the riots in their earliest stages and punishing rioters with death and dismemberment. But circumstances differed in other places, such as Mainz, whose archbishop, who attempted to protect the Jews, had to flee for his life from the crusaders.

The Effects of the Massacres of 1096

The Jews did their best to defend themselves with all the means at their disposal. In some places they even came out to fight at the city gates, although there was no prospect of these untrained townsmen defeating a host of trained warriors with armour. Thousands fell. The acts of *kiddush hashem* (see below), in all its grandeur, transformed the slaughter into an exalted battle in the eyes of the Jews; but the result was an increase in the number of victims. In Mainz alone more than 1,000 were slain either by the crusaders or by their own hands. Many of those who were caught refused to become Christians and were savagely tortured to death.

By the time the crusaders continued on their journey in the summer months of 1096, the majority of the Rhineland Jews had either been slaughtered or forcibly converted. On their way they continued to ravage and riot. One of the cities that suffered from their visitation, referred to as Shelo, is believed by some to be Prague in Bohemia. When the crusaders took Jerusalem in 1099, they gathered the Jews of the Holy City in a synagogue and burned them alive.

As far as their attempt to win over the Jews was concerned, the crusaders failed even in respect to the forced converts, most of whom immediately reverted to Judaism. Emperor Henry IV agreed to the return to their faith in spite of protests by the pope.

This hallowing of the Holy Name by martyrdom (*kiddush hashem*) strengthened Jewry from within, enriched it spiritually, crystallized the concepts of honour and heroism among the Jews and gave them the strength to face later trials. At the same time the Jews now realized that charters alone could not provide absolute security against mob fury. Christian religious fervour had kindled a fire in the tents of Jacob and had led to slaughter in his habitations. The blood of the Jews had, as it were, been made free for the Christian masses. In respect to legal formulations, security of life and possibilities of livelihood, the First Crusade inaugurated a new and harsh epoch for Jews in Christian lands.

Kiddush Hashem *in 1096*

All the spiritual resources and social cohesiveness of Ashkenazi Jewry were required in this hour of trial. In the tenth and eleventh centuries, the sages already sensed the increasing religious and social pressure applied by Christianity in order to achieve abandonment of the Jewish faith. The Jews had constantly responded to it with absolute rejection and contempt, but now the choice was put to them at sword point: convert or die.

Accounts of this period date from the first half of the twelfth century. Although the form of presentation and the accompanying range of ideas did not come exclusively from the martyrs of 1096, they *did* derive from their example of martyrdom, which found literary expression in the subsequent generation. The accounts of the slaughter and pillage in a vast number of communities omit almost entirely details of the physical suffering. The looting, the rapacity and the greed of the rioters are passed over almost completely. This omission was due to the intention of concentrating on the more significant aspects of what had taken place.

From the Jewish viewpoint the essence of the events of 1096 was Israel's struggle to hallow the name of God. R. Solomon ben Samson regretted the defeat in battle of the Mainz community, when 'great and small, put on armour and took weapons of war' and went forth to meet the crusader foe at the city gate. His explanation of the defeat does not stress the fact that the assailants were seasoned warriors long accustomed to armour and to the use of the sword, whereas his own people were powerful only in prayer and supplication, as R. Simeon the Great had remarked more than a century earlier when comparing the feudal paladins and the congregation of Israel (see page 412).

Belonging as he did to the days of holy wars and expeditions, R. Solomon attributed the defeat to temporary physical exhaustion deriving from piety and asceticism: 'From the multitude of troubles and the fasts they made they did not have the strength to stand against the enemy' (*ibid.*, p. 30). In these twelfth-century accounts the Jewish fighter is presented as a fearless knight. He denounces his foes and welcomes death after he has seen that his brethren 'were all slain and flung aside and trampled like the filth of the streets' and that only those who deserted their faith were saved. 'The pious Master David the Warden' mocks the crusader mob to the end. He invites the 'miscreants and . . . the townsfolk . . . to come unto me all of you'. The Christians supposed that the Jew was about to submit. The mob assembled joyously 'in thousands and myriads' around the home of the Jew; and then the pious fighter came forth and denounced the Christian faith and declared his own absolute belief in the redemption of his soul as a Jew.

> Now when they heard the words of this pious man they were greatly enraged because he reproached them and declared their shame, and they raised their banners . . . and began to shout and scream in the name of the Hanged One; and they went up against him and slew him. . . . There the righteous man fell with his household (*ibid.*, p. 36).

This provocation of the Christian mob was a declaration of war on the part of a noble man of faith, who fell on the spot to the death he invited.

An account of the Jewish women in the bishop's castle at Mainz portrays a courageous vanguard that reviled those who attacked their God and scattered money among them as a delaying action, in order to gain time to complete the mass suicide for the sake of *kiddush hashem*. The women threw stones down on the enemy and suffered the slingshots of the latter on their torn and injured faces (*ibid.*, p. 33). The wounded cried for water, but refused to accept it when called upon to accept the waters of baptism as well (*ibid.*, p. 39). In one case a youth is praised 'who hallowed the Name and did what the rest of the congregation did not do, slaying three of the uncircumcised with his knife' (*ibid.*, p. 97).

The impact of the crusader climate of opinion was so widespread that during one of the crusades the writer of a lament wrote as though crusader excitatoria (propaganda letters) were addressing the Jews:

Rise and come, they say . . .
Behold, we are journeying unto the place
A land . . . of beauty that lights up the eyes
Let us go and pillage the fortified cities and there
We shall distribute coloured cloth and embroidery to every man.
 (A. M. Haberman, ed., *Turei Yeshurun,* Yeshurun Synagogue leaflet, Jerusalem, 1966, p. 20).

Yet a fight in the open field or amid the walls of the breached castle brought the dread certainty of death, which could, after all, be escaped by conversion. Furthermore, the greatest fear of the Jews was that the children might be taken away and baptized after the adults had been slain and that they would be brought up 'in their abomination'. The cities, the walls, the fields, the armies and the rulers surrounding them were not Jewish. The ultimate choice they envisaged was a last-minute weakness leading to submission and the loss of the coming generation, or suicide in order to hallow God's name if attempts at self-defence had failed or if it were clear to begin with that there were no prospects of success.

As was only natural, many submitted in the hope of clandestinely maintaining whatever they could of their Judaism and of returning to their faith at the earliest opportunity. However, the image that became the model for future generations was that of the fighters and those who had hallowed the Name. As against conversion and crypto-Judaism, the contemporaries of Rashi called for fulfilment of the commandment of wholeheartedness with 'the Lord God of Hosts who commanded the Jew not to change the purity of his faith but to be wholehearted with Him, as is written, "Thou shalt be wholehearted with the Lord thy God"' (R. Solomon ben Samson, in Haberman, *Massacres of Germany and France,* p. 34). In this way they declared that they did not wish to live by observing the Torah secretly, but felt obligated to stand by their Law and faith openly.

Since ancient times there had been a tradition of submitting to torture and martyrdom for the sake of the faith. Ever since the time of Hannah and her seven sons during the reign of Antiochus Epiphanes, Jewry had recognized the express *halakhic* prescription that if a Jew is called upon to commit one of the three transgressions of idolatry, incest or bloodshed, he must let himself be slain rather than sin. 'In times of stress', when steps were taken to destroy Jewish unity, as distinct from measures against individuals and isolated actions, the Jew was to defy the order and allow himself to be slain even if he were ordered merely to 'change the style of shoelace' in use among Jews. The Christian society also venerated its own martyrs, who underwent torture and were prepared to perish for their sacred faith.

Yet these traditions of martyrdom did not imply mandatory mass suicide and the slaying of children. As early as the tenth century, Jews in southern Italy had recognized how insecure their position was in a world where war had become an instrument for the glorification of religion. There some turned to suicide as the way in which the Zealots of old, who were presented as the brave warriors of the Lord, had waged their war. In the *Yossipon* chronicle, compiled in that region at about 953, the Zealots offer reasons such as the glory of the Lord and the honour of the indomitable warrior in order to justify *kiddush hashem* through suicide. In the early part of the tenth century, Jews had slain themselves in southern Italy in order to escape conversion. Those who recorded these actions viewed the martyrs as an offering and sacrifice that delivered the rest of the congregation from compulsory conversion (see page 412). These records were reflections on and memories of individual actions and of past events that may actually have occurred or may have been imagined; and they exerted some influence. But the acceptance of *kiddush hashem* by means of mass suicide as an expression of wholehearted faith, as a guiding religious principle for large numbers of people, first emerged with the martyrs in the Rhine Valley in 1096.

The martyrs looked forward to seeing 'the great light' in the World to Come as merit of their sacrifice. They regarded themselves as burnt offerings, lambs selected because they were perfect and without blemish. They did not commit suicide in despair. Their vengeance lay in the expectation, passed on to the survivors, of remorse on the part of the crusaders, those fighters of another faith, when they would eventually realize their error:

> Then they will comprehend and understand and admit in their hearts that they slew us for a vanity . . . and that they have not taken a good path or a straight way . . . and they were foolish and senseless in all their deeds. They destroyed their wisdom and put their trust in their vanity (*ibid.*, p. 43).

The martyrs foresaw a day of vengeance and imminent reward in the defeat of the crusaders, a day of historic settlement that would mark the victory of Judaism.

The chroniclers gave a variety of reasons for the stand of the Jews and did not conceal the dread, the fear and the doubts that pierced them when they slew the children. Yet, by their actions the martyrs ensured the proud human stature of the humiliated Jew and his firm grip on his faith in a world where faith was a matter of pride to be defended by the sword.

Twelfth-century Jews dealt at length with this line of reasoning and with the greatness of the sacrifice. R. Solomon Yizhaki, the leading commentator on the Bible and the Talmud, generally known as Rashi, whose aged eyes saw the catastrophe and the sacrifices offered by the community at close quarters, called on the eternal and perfect Torah to appeal before God on behalf of the innocent. The shock reverberates in a magnificent hymn of this commentator, as he all but threatens the Torah should its entreaties fail. He warns that 'if there be no Israel thy praises to sing, thou art indeed silenced in every mouth and throat.' He calls on the Torah to voice its anger as befits a bereft mother: 'Approach in entreaty . . . garbed in black like a widow, demand redress for thy saintly ones . . . at the hands of . . . those who cut down thy students and ripped thy parchment sheets . . . and in their torrential rage destroyed thy habitations.' Like the crusaders, he too wishes to see victory 'in the Holy Land, explain thy lovely words for men to understand, expel . . . the arrogant in blazing wrath; while the offspring of the pious, scholars and students engage in constant studies there' (A. M. Haberman, ed., *Piyyutei Rashi,* Jerusalem, 1941, no. 6).

Thus the teacher of that generation of martyrs envisaged the expulsion of the kingdom of sword-wielders from the Holy Land and the establishment there of the kingdom of Torah, piety and study. In the name of the ideals he had inherited and on account of the human sacrifices witnessed by him, he looked in hope to the Promised Land, as did the entire world around him.

Political Response to the Massacres

When the days of terror had ended, the Jews began to ask themselves under whose protection and under what conditions they could continue to live among gentiles. It is not by chance that in the chronicles of the 1096 massacres the words of the martyrs are accompanied by lengthy addresses and conversations ascribed to bishops and rulers and by various considerations regarding the motives behind the behaviour of the townfolk. The words placed in the mouths of the Christians are actually the product of Jewish observation and the conclusions they reached, though they doubtlessly include remarks that were indeed uttered by Christians. They are given as a basis for subsequent intercession with the princes and monarchs; and they represent the views of the twelfth-century Jewish community in Germany and France about the majority society within which it lived.

According to these accounts, 'Henry the King' was enraged at the mere rumour that there were those who wished to harm the Jews. Varying and contradictory views are presented concerning the behaviour of the bishop of Mainz, who took money from the Jews but could not protect them. Thus he 'informs' R. Kalonymus the *Parness* (*i.e.,* the community leader):

> I am unable to save you; and your God has turned away from you and does not wish to leave you a vestige or remnant. And I do not have the strength at hand any longer to deliver or aid you henceforward. So now . . . either believe in our faith or bear the consequences of your forefathers' iniquity (Haberman, *Massacres of Germany and France,* p. 41).

The statement presented here indicates that the ineffectiveness of the assurances of protection given by those who granted charters and by the lords of the cities was due to helplessness, to fatalistic submission to the Will of Heaven or, in the absence of any choice, to the acceptance by the 'protector' of the crusader claim that the Jews must be punished for refusing to adopt Christianity. The following excuse is quoted in the name of the governor of the city of Mörs:

> True, at first I promised to protect and defend you as long as a single Jew was left in the world. And I have observed this undertaking. But henceforward I cannot deliver you from all these masses. . . . Be it known to you that if you do not act accordingly [*i.e.,* convert to Christianity] the city will certainly be destroyed; so it is better for me to hand you over to them than have them besiege me and destroy the fortress (*ibid.,* p. 50).

This statement gives rise to several conclusions about the relationship between the Jews and their protectors. The 'condition' of protection was sacred to the one who granted it. The reason for reneging on his guarantee is that he believed that the situation in which it was granted no longer existed, as all the Jews had been slain and 'no Jews exist any longer in the world.' (This comment, incidentally, may be taken to indicate the impression left on contemporaries by the massacres.) In addition he claimed that his city and fortress were in peril because the Jews were being protected, which was tantamount to declaring that his feudal duty to his city and its Christian inhabitants now conflicted with his obligation towards the Jews.

The Jewish narrators remembered and recorded for coming generations that there were also protectors who tried not to disappoint them. The Bishop of Trier was at first prepared to risk his life for the Jews, although as a Bavarian 'he was a stranger in the city where he had neither kin nor friend.' The Jews said to him: 'Surely you have assured us on your faith, [saying] that you would safeguard us until the king comes with his royal forces.' But he declared: 'The time I gave you was as long as any Jewish congregation remains in the whole land of Lorraine.' The bishop then went on to explain: 'It was my proper desire to keep faith with you as I promised.' Yet 'what action could he counsel when the whole world was rising against him to slay him' because he was protecting the Jews. When the Jews began to suspect that he desired a bribe, his emissary declared, 'the bishop does not desire anything of that kind' (*ibid.*, p. 54). Finally, after the heart-searching, the decision came: 'You will be destroyed . . . for . . . you cannot be saved; and your God does not wish to aid you now as he did in ancient times' (*ibid.*, p. 55). Bishop Johann of Speyer, who saved the Jews and imposed physical punishment on the rioters, is highly praised: 'For he was a righteous man among the gentiles, and the Ever-Present brought about the merit of our deliverance through him' (*ibid.*, p. 94); 'for the Lord endowed his heart to keep them alive without bribery' (*ibid.*, p. 95).

The Jews were astonished and shocked at the change among 'those who were near to us and our acquaintances' (*ibid.*, p. 29) – namely, the townsfolk, who abandoned them on the day of the slaughter. When the Jews began to reckon the sins of omission and commission on the part of the masses and their rulers, they apparently reached the conclusion that there could be no absolute faith in charters and promises, which were just so much 'parchment for covering jars'. Far more could be achieved through money and entreaty. The rulers suffered pangs of conscience, because the assurances of protection were significant enough in their eyes to warrant entering a risk – up to a point. Henceforward the Jews had to recognize the destructive force of Christian mob fury under conditions of religious and social unrest. This fact of life was known to the Jews in Western Europe from the twelfth century onwards and was basic to their relationships with the feudal and corporative world, within which and under whose protection they were to live throughout the Middle Ages.

The Conclusions of the Jews

These considerations, together with the religious fervour that had been enhanced by the example of the martyrs, led the Jews to formulate an appropriate attitude towards rulers and their decrees. It was formulated in the second half of the twelfth century, from the mouths, as it were, of the martyrs of Blois in France who were burnt to death in 1171. R. Obadiah ben Maḥir (a pseudonym it seems) reported in their name:

> For the holy ones said, there is no stranger among us. And if the rulers decree taxes and charges, it is lawful to obey the kings and make entreaty . . . to ease the burden. . . . But if their heart be turned to evil, and some worthless ones think to cause the Name of the Creator to be forgotten, to seduce those who fear Him . . . then the elect shall testify eloquently and wrathfully and declare loudly and firmly: 'On the Mount of the Lord [*i.e.*, the Mount of Sacrifice] he will appear, so let the man whom the Lord chooses be holy' [the martyr who shall suffer for the faith]. We shall disregard your lies and vanities for you are but curs. And we shall stand firm in our stronghold (S. Spiegel, ed., *Mipitgemei Haakeda*, in *M. M. Kaplan Jubilee Volume*, New York, 1953, p. 286).

Thus, on the day of trial, it is incumbent upon every Jew to sacrifice himself without submission and with a full declaration of faith. Yet it is also proper and reasonable 'to address kings and beg and entreat them' when life is normal in the Christian cities.

The Jews also drew certain military conclusions from the 1096 massacres. There was no hope of self-defence in the city, even in its fortified areas. From the Second Crusade onwards, the Jews did their best to obtain a well-fortified citadel outside the city and to remove all non-Jews. When the Jews were threatened in 1146 by riots,

> everyone left their cities and made for the fortresses, and most of the Cologne congregation gave the Bishop . . . ample money to place the fortress of Walkenburg in their hands. . . . And they sent away the governor of the fortress by means of many gifts and it was left to them alone, and no uncircumcised stranger was among them. . . . And from the time the word spread among the gentiles that Walkenburg had been handed over to the Jews who had all gathered together there [they were no longer persecuted].

This event led to the deliverance of all the other Jews who had fled to castles.

> And I the youth who write this was thirteen years old at the time in the fortress of Walkenburg . . . and the remaining Jews who were in all the lands of the king gathered together and defended their lives, and each one saved himself in the castle of his gentile friend and took his kinsfolk with him (R. Ephraim ben Jacob of Bonn, in Haberman, *Massacres of Germany and France,* p. 117).

However, under the conditions in which the Jews lived in those days, it could also be dangerous to take a castle into their own hands, as became clear when this was done in 1190 at York in England, during the riots that followed the coronation of Richard the Lion-Hearted. Shortly before Passover in that year, the Jews of York fled to an isolated castle in fear of the riots, which had spread from London. When they refused to admit the governor, in accordance with what had become established practice by then, he summoned help. On the Sabbath before Passover, the beleaguered Jews of York hallowed the Holy Name and slew themselves in the castle.

28

The Flowering of Centralized Leadership and the Rise of Local Leadership

The Exilarch (Resh Galuta)

Legend relates that Bustenai, the first exilarch under Islam, was given a wife from the family of the defeated Persian emperor. This information provides evidence that the office was retained by a member of the house of David without any interruption whatever as a result of the transition from Persian rule (see Part IV) to Moslem domination. This story must contain a kernel of historical truth, for in subsequent generations certain sections of the families of the exilarchs were considered to be of doubtful legitimacy, on the grounds that they were descended from 'the sons of the Persian woman'.

Until 825 the person recognized by the Jews as their exilarch was also the only Jewish authority acknowledged by Moslem rulers. His status was unquestioned both internally and externally. In that year disputes broke out among the Christians; they too appointed their own heads, who were recognized by the Moslem authorities. As a result of these disputes, the caliph proclaimed that any man accepted by ten infidels as their head would be accorded official recognition. In theory, this pronouncement opened the way to anarchy in leadership and to a complete collapse of the exilarch's authority. In practice, it did lead to a decline in his real power and to a measure of dependency on the two Babylonian *yeshivot* and their heads (see page 495). However, as a result of the high esteem in which Jewry held the house of David and the desire for one single authority recognized by the host society, during the entire period under consideration here, apart from relatively rare disputes, there was one sole exilarch of the Islamic diaspora.

Towards the middle of the ninth century, an Arab author wrote that from the days of Adam onwards Jews have attributed world leadership to 'the house of David, and in declaring this they claim that leadership passes from father to son'. The author provided a list of the exilarch's income. According to him, regular sums of money for each service, as well as gifts, were paid to his treasury or to those of the religious functionaries under his authority. For instance,

> when one of them weds a woman he gives him four *dirhams* in full silver; and the same amount is paid to him when they build a house. He who weds a wife may not divorce her without his approval . . . or that of his representative; and at the divorce they take four *dirhams* from the man.

According to this source, the exilarch was the guardian of children declared illegitimate by Jewish law and children of unknown parentage. When they reached maturity he was entitled to manumit them or sell them. 'And they are the ones who bear him [the exilarch], and they do not permit him to walk on foot' (Ben Zion Dinur, *Israel in the Diaspora,* I, b, Tel Aviv, 1961, 83–4).

As time passed the real influence of the exilarch may gradually have diminished, together with his share of income and his authority to grant appointments. R. Nathan the Babylonian, of the tenth century, whose letter, appended to the chronicle *Seder Olam,* gives a vivid contemporary account of Jewish institutions in this period, related that in certain regions the exilarch had the sole right of appointment: he would 'send a Judge to them by his authority and the authority of the heads of the *yeshivot'.* From those regions he received a fixed income.

Ceremonials Surrounding the Office of Exilarch

R. Nathan's account describes elaborate and carefully performed ceremonies that symbolized the uniqueness of the exilarch's office within the Jewish leadership structure. A member of the house of David became exilarch 'if the consensus of the Community favoured his appointment'. The ceremonial procession would set out from 'the home of one of the great men of the times in Babylon, such as Netira or someone similar' (meaning from the home of one of the court bankers, to whom reference has already been made); every step and every gesture was planned in detail for the ceremony that was held on the Sabbath once the [leaders] and others had reached the synagogue in Baghdad. A choir was concealed beneath a wooden tower, whose dimensions and multi-coloured cover were specified precisely. Prior to the commencement of the reading of the Torah, the exilarch entered to the festive prayer 'from the place where he was under concealment' in the middle of the tower.

> And when they see him, all the people rise to their feet until he takes his seat on the tower . . . and the head of the Sura *yeshiva* emerges behind him and takes his seat on the tower after making a deep obeisance before him, which he returns. And after that the head of the Pumbedita *yeshiva* comes forth and also bows before him and takes his seat on his left. And meanwhile all the people stand erect until the three of them are settled in their places.

The blessings pronounced for him were delivered in dramatic fashion. The cantor uttered them 'in a low voice, so that they should be heard only by those who are seated round the tower and the youths who are beneath it. And . . . the youths respond in a loud voice after him: Amen' (*Seder Olam Zuta* Chronicle, in A. Neubauer, ed., *Mediaeval Jewish Chronicles,* II, Oxford, 1895, p. 83). The exilarch served as a manifestation of the splendour of bygone days, which the Jews wished to preserve, to the extent that the Moslem government would permit a *dhimmi* people. He was 'like one of the lords of the king in his behaviour' – the reference being to the ministers of the Moslem caliph. The exilarch used to enter the royal court, speaking to the caliph 'with pleasant words until he granted his request' (*ibid.*). Thus the *resh galuta* majestically represented the Jews and performed the diplomatic function of intercession at the caliph's court. He also appointed judges, as has been mentioned, and had an authoritative say in matters of Jewish law and the organization of the *yeshivot*. His office, though maintained in the shadow of the caliphate and interwoven with the leadership of the scholars and sages of the *yeshivot*, reflected on a small scale the ancient monarchy of Judah.

The Babylonian Yeshivot *and the* Geonim

Like the exilarchate, the *yeshivot* under Islamic rule are described as a continuation of the Babylonian *yeshivot* of Sura and Pumbedita, which had functioned under the pre-Islamic rulers. It is recorded that the Moslem rulers granted them recognition almost from the moment they conquered Babylonia. However, differences in character and structure very soon became apparent. It is possible that the initial stages of these changes or a trend towards such changes had already become evident under the Persians. In any case, the specific pattern of development of the *yeshivot* under Moslem rule marks their special character as institutions for leadership and the study of Torah. These *yeshivot* were centralized to a degree unknown in the *yeshivot* of Babylonia and Erez Yisrael that had produced the two Talmuds centuries earlier. In the Talmuds we find the names of hundreds of sages whose views are cited. Only rarely is an opinion attributed to a school; and even then the school bears the name of the sage who headed it, such as 'the house of Rav', *i.e.*, the scholars belonging to the school of Rav. Only a few sages are known as heads of a school or academy. In the Middle Ages, however, we find the opposite true in almost all respects in the *yeshivot* of Babylonia and, for that matter, of Erez Yisrael. We know the names of only a handful of sages of this period, although scholars and disciples were plentiful; on the other hand, the names of the heads – the *geonim* who headed the *yeshivot* and even of those who competed and failed in an effort to obtain office – are familiar to us for most of the period and with respect to all the academies in question.

The head of a *yeshiva* was 'its mighty ruler'. He was designated the *gaon* ('pride'), which was an abbreviation of his full title, 'Head of the *yeshiva* of the Pride of Jacob'. He and he alone was its ruler within and its spokesman without. In a case of controversy over dietary laws, a message to the following effect was sent from Babylonia: Such was the opinion of the sage so-and-so, but he did not send it to you in writing because he was not the *gaon* and head of the *yeshiva*. Thus we may conclude that the *geonim* alone were authorized to communicate decisions on Jewish law and practice to other communities.

The *yeshivot* in the Islamic lands, both in Babylonia and in Erez Yisrael, occupied a central position in the leadership of the nation. They regarded themselves committed to several main tasks. Their educational function involved teaching their students as well as the entire people. They also set down final legal decisions on all issues and problems of daily life. *Yeshiva* scholars and sages interpreted and commented on the canonical literature, and the interpretations given by this collegium were binding on all. The *yeshiva* included schools of several levels, culminating in a school of higher learning. It was also an academy of qualified scholars who constituted the High Court, from which Jewish law was disseminated to all Israel.

In accordance with its character, the *yeshiva* was organized into concentric circles of full members and external participants who shared the studies and the creative achievements. As mentioned previously, there were two *yarḥei kallah,* one before Passover and one before the High Holy Days. During these two months many temporary students would gather at the *yeshiva,* as in the days of the Talmud. These periods also served as occasions for discussing and answering the questions that had reached the *yeshivot* from various communities (see page 436). The *yeshiva* also conducted classes all year round in which young men and boys were taught the Mishnah and the Talmud. Most of them were sons of the regular *yeshiva* scholars. Above them was a more advanced group of students who learnt from the senior scholars, listening to their deliberations and decisions. They were seated 'behind' the scholars, that is, behind their fixed places, without any regular positions, and they did not take part in the legal decisions.

The Guiding Principles of the Yeshiva Leadership

The structure described above, as well as the modus operandi of the *yeshivot,* shows that a serious attempt was made in these institutions to maintain a leadership of scholars and students and to base continuity and authority on hierarchical and hereditary principles. The members of the *yeshiva* were placed by a graded scale, in which each level had its own descriptive rank and title. Family pedigree also helped to determine position. These characteristics were clearly defined in express formulations.

Yeshiva status and the post of *gaon* in each of the *yeshivot* were transmitted within the strict limits of the families of scholars. A father left his fixed place in the *yeshiva* to his son or to his closest kinsman deemed worthy of inheriting the position. As we have pointed out, the office of exilarch was reserved for the house of David. In theory, the election of the *gaon* was in the hands of the entire company of permanent *yeshiva* scholars; but, in practice, most *geonim* were selected from a very restricted number of 'families of *geonim*', numbering six in Babylonia. Of these families, one traced its descent to the house of David, being a branch of the family of the exilarchs; another was a priestly family. Similarly, in Ereẓ Yisrael there were three 'families of *geonim*'. One claimed descent from the family of the patriarchate of Roman times, who were descendants of Hillel the Elder; while the other two were of priestly lineage. Of the latter, one claimed descent from Ezra the Scribe. As we shall see, in times of crisis this aristocratic circle was sometimes penetrated by outsiders. Saadiah Gaon (see page 443) was one of the few outsiders whose powerful personality brought him to the summit of leadership. But when R. Sherira Gaon, who belonged to 'the families of the *geonim*', mentioned in his 'Epistle' a *gaon* who did not belong to these families, he added a derogatory phrase, such as 'but he was not of the scholarly families, being of the merchants'.

In many cases hereditary continuity of a gaonate was assured by reserving for a suitable member of the 'ruling' *gaon*'s family the second most important office in the *yeshiva*. This was the office of *av bet din,* 'father' or 'head of the Rabbinical Court', which convened 'at the gateway' of the *yeshiva,* who was also referred to in the scholastic Aramaic of that age as the *dayyanu de-bava* or 'the Judge at the Gate'. This officer acted on behalf of the *gaon* when necessary and exerted a decisive influence in the *yeshiva*. It was only natural that he should inherit the post of *gaon*. Thus R. Hai, the son of R. Sherira Gaon, was the head of his father's court before having succeeded him as *gaon*. 'Our chosen Hai', as he was called, exerted considerable influence while his father was still alive. Hence election was in many cases merely the confirmation of a predetermined state of affairs.

The election of a *gaon* for one or another of the *yeshivot* involved the legitimate intervention of the exilarch, at least in the tenth century. Some measure of influence was exerted also by the court bankers, by virtue of their ample resources and their influence at the caliph's court – an influence that was only partly acknowledged in a formal manner. All these factors turned the election of a *gaon* into a major public occasion that often involved social and ideological struggles. Yet the principles described above were so strong that, as a rule, even the struggles were restricted to 'the families of the *geonim*'.

The Seven Rows of the Sages

The main body of the *yeshiva* – the permanent sages – was seated in seven rows in front of the *gaon* and the head of the court, ten sages in each row, and it was referred to as the 'Great Sanhedrin'. To each row was attached a specific honour and an importance of its own within the *yeshiva* and in the eyes of the people. Inclusion in one of the rows signified the importance of the individual seated there, his wisdom and his knowledge of the Torah, as well as the pedigree of those from whom he had inherited his place within the *yeshiva* hierarchy; his status was indicated by the relative proximity of the row to the *gaon*.

The most honoured sages sat in the first row. Within this row the sages were differentiated by honorific titles. R. Nathan the Babylonian reported that 'seven of them are heads of the *kallah* [see page 424] and three are *haverim* [the ancient term for scholars of saintly character]'. Each of the 'heads of the *kallah*' was 'set over ten of the Sanhedrin' and bore the title of *aluf* (equivalent in early biblical terminology more or less to 'duke' in the sense of leader). Those seated in the back rows seem to have included the *mashnin*, who taught Mishnah to the younger students.

The Torah was considered almost as a family heirloom and treasure of the sages in Babylon. When the *yeshivot* began to decline, one of the *geonim* complained that in the absence of financial support 'many sons of Talmudic scholars proceed to other crafts . . . earning wages or working.' He seems to have been certain that the breaking of the chain of scholarship in these families would shock those who heard or read his complaint and would induce them to support the *yeshiva* in order to prevent such a calamity.

The Struggles for Leadership

The immanent tension in the central Jewish institutions of Babylonia was at times liable to produce tempestuous struggles. Among the fiercest of these was the one between David ben Zakkai and R. Saadiah Gaon in the first decades of the tenth century. Almost all sections of the leadership were involved. The exilarch had endeavoured to rescue the Sura *yeshiva* from collapse. The appointment of R. Saadiah (who came from Fayyum in Egypt and was therefore known as al-Fayyumi) as the *gaon* of Sura in 928 was, as has been noted, a breach of the tradition of selecting the *gaon* from among 'the families of the *geonim*'.

In 930 a quarrel broke out between R. Saadiah Gaon and David ben Zakkai, the exilarch. On this occasion R. Saadiah Gaon was supported by 'all the wealthy men of Babylonia'. In the course of the dispute, both a counter-exilarch and a counter-*gaon* of Sura were appointed. Bitter polemics were issued in writing, and the dispute reached the courts. The exilarch emerged as victor, and in 937 R. Saadiah Gaon was compelled to reach a compromise with him.

The Methods of Leadership

Two groups of intellectual-sacral aristocracy constituted the backbone of the Babylonian Jewish leadership: the narrow circle of the family of the exilarchate and of the gaonic families and, around them, the somewhat wider circle of the families of those seated in the first seven rows of the *yeshiva*. It was in this nucleus of families of sages – to whom Torah and learning were a lifetime occupation and whose social status was determined by their rank in the *yeshiva* and in the leadership stratum – that authority was vested. This authoritative leadership was exerted through clearly defined patterns and methods that derived ultimately from a sacredness hallowed by the very quality of respect for the Torah. Both the leaders and the led were of the opinion, in their institutions and in clearly worded formulations, that there was an element of 'physical sanctity' in the *yeshiva* and that in the heads of the *yeshiva* and its sages was vested some sacral merit that rendered their blessings and curses – oral and written – particularly efficacious. It was the duty of a Jew to accord them respect and honour, both personally and as a group, because of their status and familee pedigree. This was the only period in Jewish history when the Jews regularly addressed their leadership as 'the greatness and sanctity of the honourable'. Exclusiveness was the outstanding characteristic of the class as a whole. It obligated these aristocratic families to devote meticulous care to assure continued knowledge of the Torah by their children and grandchildren and 'purity of lineage'. In their writings some compared their aristocracy to the priesthood of old. The priests too had been required to preserve knowledge and teach the people, while it was the duty of the people to maintain the priests through the tithes. And, indeed, during the greater part of the period under consideration the Jewish community granted this circle of leaders both money and honour.

The leadership fulfilled its duties to teach Torah to the people through various institutions. Torah was discussed and explained in the *kallah* months, when thousands gathered together. It was also studied more intensively by many hundreds of students, at various levels, in the schools included within the *yeshiva* structure. However, *halakhic* decisions and authoritative interpretations and comments were laid down only after receiving official approval in the deliberations of the 'Great Sanhedrin'.

The proclamation of any decision of this body was made by the *gaon* in personal terms, as decisive ruler, in the name of the hallowed association and with its authority. Only rarely do we find the *yeshiva* as a corporate body also associated with such a pronouncement.

An aristocratic and religious leadership of this kind ran the risk of petrification and degeneration. The longer its control continued and the stronger the tensions grew within its various sections, the greater these dangers became, until other forces assumed the leadership. In the tenth century we hear of an informal group that exerted great influence on the central leaders – namely, the court bankers and other wealthy men in Baghdad. When they participated in the leadership, they were described as 'the corner-stones of the congregation'. This non-aristocratic and non-academic element was able to exert influence because of its close ties with the court of the caliphate and by virtue of its intercession on behalf of its brethren. Its influence was especially great in times of contention, when its support could turn the scales in favour of one or the other of the parties.

The rule of a class of sages and their leaders, the attempt to combine sacral, hereditary and intellectual components within a single structure and the success of this attempt for centuries are a unique phenomenon in Jewish history. The rare breaches of the structure – the influence of 'the corner stones of the congregation' and the penetration of sages from abroad who rose to the very heights of leadership – and the qualitative decline and diminution of influence at the end of the epoch in no way alter the singularity and significance of the phenomenon.

Channels of Influence in the Diaspora

Each *yeshiva* had a delimited region, equivalent in extent to that of the exilarch, within which its *gaon* appointed community judges and whose inhabitants provided a regular income for the *yeshiva*. As was only natural, many of the appointed judges were local persons who had studied at the *yeshiva* or were local notables who were recommended to the central institution. In principle this system did not affect the central authority, which insisted on the right of appointment and approval, though not of proposal or selection. This attitude was clearly expressed in the tenth century by the *gaon* R. Samuel ben Hophni, when he insisted that

> the head of the generation has the duty of appointing judges over Israel. Surely you can see that Moses the enlightened prince said to Israel, 'Take yourselves wise and understanding men . . . ' and he said, 'and I shall place them at your head.' Now had they not been appointed by Moses, the choice of the nation would have been of no avail whatever. Likewise with Joshua, even though it was the Lord who chose him. Nevertheless he said to Moses, 'Take Joshua ben Nun to yourself and place your hand upon him. . . .' And this will prove that his prince-hood was only completed after the ordination by Moses. And so it was with Saul at the hand of Samuel. From this we learn that there can be no full appointment unless it is at the hands of the head of the generation and the time. True, if no such head can be found, each community should appoint that man who is best and most

fitting in its eyes (H. Taubes, ed., *Oẓar Hageonim* to Tractate *Sanhedrin*, para. 239, pp. 124–5).

From this quote we learn that at least by the tenth century the *geonim* agreed that candidates should be proposed to them and were satisfied with only the right of approval. Hence the legal principle continued to influence practice for a considerable period. Communities had, to be sure, a will and a life of their own, but they were subject to the authority and influence of the *yeshivot* and the court of the exilarch. Only in Ereẓ Yisrael did a centre arise that demanded a share in the leadership's authority; yet this assertion likewise derived from the principle of centralized authority and from the identical assumptions of a leading aristocracy. For further discussion on the influence exercised by these centres through Responsa to questions submitted, see pages 436–7.

Excommunication and Compulsion

The *yeshivot* inherited from the past and left to all Jewish communities throughout the Middle Ages an organizational and religious weapon of tremendous power: the *ḥerem* or ban, which was proclaimed in an awesome ceremony. Yet its main power derived from the spiritual attitude of the Jews throughout the Middle Ages. They held the ban to be a kind of 'net' of higher power, in accordance with the basic connotation of the Hebrew word *ḥerem*. Once it was proclaimed, the banned person was 'enmeshed' in it until such time as it was revoked. He was the object of social as well as divine punishment, for his fellow Jews would have nothing to do with him. But the main effect was that the person placed under *ḥerem* felt alienated from his innermost soul. By means of this weapon, Jewish communities were subsequently able to impose various *takkanot,* or regulations, also termed *ḥerem,* as transgressors would have the ban placed upon them. The ban could thus be imposed also on private or personal matters; for it was not the public excommunication of the individual that was the harshest part of the punishment but the fear of heavenly judgement.

Leadership Particularized

As long as central religious leadership of the Jews remained stable and the political and communications structure of the Moslem caliphate stood firm, the new social forces emerging within the Jewish community, such as 'the corner-stones of the congregation', operated within the setting of the established principles. Eventually, however, the caliphate broke up into independent kingdoms, and the ties between the periphery and the centre of the empire were broken. Then elements such as 'the corner-stones' began to function according to principles of their own and assume an independent leadership of the community. These leaders in distant countries some-times received a title from the members of the old centres in Babylonia or Ereẓ Yisrael, whose recognition and approval they still sought. This tie, however, gradually became a matter of tradition, a relic of the past that survived through sheer inertia.

The new leaders adopted modes and methods of their own. Ancient lineage and tradition were no longer important in themselves. The decisive factor was now economic and social influence, usually based on close contact between the Jewish leader and the Moslem rulers of the country.

The new leader generally rose from a position as a physician or financial adviser at the court of the Moslem ruler or of one of the leading ministers; he might have been a *katib,* a royal scribe or secretary in the Moslem West. In recognition of his service to the host society he would be appointed to conduct the affairs of the Jews within the territories of the kingdom, sometimes with the community's approval and sometimes without it. Such leaders by definition could not aim at any universal Jewish influence; their power extended only to the frontiers of the realm with whose ruler they were associated. Some of them were also scholars and sages, but that was largely a matter of coincidence and not the basis of their position.

The term usually applied to a leader of this kind was *nagid.* The rise of these regional leaders, who lacked claims to leadership based on ancestry and sacral character, was actually abetted by the success of the larger centres in Babylonia and in Ereẓ Yisrael. The knowledge of the Torah that they disseminated had steadily increased in the peripheral lands, with the result that it was no longer so necessary to consult with them. From the end of the tenth century onwards, Jewish scholarship was to be found also in communities such as Kairouan in North Africa. It was not by chance that the twelfth-century chronicler R. Abraham ibn Daud prefaced his account of the rise of the *nagid* with the story of the 'four captives', who were sent as emissaries from Babylonia, were taken captive, were liberated in due course and ultimately began to spread knowledge of the Torah in the regions where they found themselves, each of them adopting a stand independent of the centre from which he came.

The first leader to adopt this pattern was Jacob ibn Jau, who lived in Moslem Spain at the turn of the tenth and eleventh centuries. He is not in fact known to have used the term *nagid,* but what is related of his appointment and activity indicates that he was a leader of that type. Moreover, R. Abraham ibn Daud related that even before him, during the tenth century, much power in Moslem Spain had been in the hands of 'Rabbi Ḥasdai the great *nasi* . . . in whose times nobody in the world could disagree' with a sage whom he supported (Gerson D. Cohen, ed., *The Book of Tradition,* Philadelphia, 1967, p. 49). However, we have no explicit information about the actual appointment of R. Ḥasdai by the rulers to conduct the affairs of the Jews within the realm, though he did exert great influence in affairs of state and within the Jewish community. The case was different with Jacob ibn Jau. R. Abraham ibn Daud, the chronicler who wrote about him, mentioned somewhat disparagingly that he was 'one of two brothers, merchants who manufactured silk'. According to Ibn Daud's story, Ibn Jau was appointed to leadership by a king of Moslem Spain who also ruled over parts of North Africa. The king

> wrote to all the congregations of Israel to be found between Sijilmasa [in Africa] and the river Duero, which marked the bounds of his kingdom [in Spain], that he was to judge them all and was entitled to appoint whomsoever he desired over them and to collect every tax and payment which was levied upon them.

The king's instructions indicate that within this kingdom Ibn Jau had the full authority enjoyed by an exilarch or a *gaon,* and they were interpreted to mean that he was authorized to collect the taxes of the realm from the Jews. He also received public marks of honour. The congregation of Cordoba, the leading Jewish community in the kingdom, 'made an ordination for him as *nasi* [prince]'. However, this ordination, as quoted, is tinged with irony (*ibid.,* pp. 50–1).

Yet Ibn Jau seems to have been dedicated to those who were under his authority, for the hostile chronicler related that he was removed from office because he disappointed the king, who had hoped 'that he would take the money of Israel from all the congregations, both legally and illegally, and would give it to him. And because he did not do this, the king arrested him and put him in prison.' He was also faithful to the charitable tradition of wealthy Jews. R. Abraham reported the words uttered by R. Ḥanokh, the principal opponent of Ibn Jau, upon hearing of the latter's death: 'I grieve and weep for all the poor who used to be supported at his table. What will they do tomorrow?' On the other hand, his violent character can be clearly seen in the threat he made against R. Ḥanokh during his period of power to the effect that should the latter act as judge between two people, he would place him in 'a boat without oars and thrust him into the seas' (*ibid.,* pp. 51–2). Presumably this refers to the fact that R. Ḥanokh was the son of one of the 'four captives' referred to above and had himself been cast away at sea with his father. Ibn Jau was threatening to send him back whence he came.

Subsequently we hear of other leaders in various countries who bore the title *nagid.* It was first used with respect by a physician at the royal court of Kairouan and later was applied to others there. In the eleventh century the title was borne by R. Samuel ibn Nagrela and later by his son Joseph in crumbling Moslem Spain. As we shall see below, R. Samuel Hanagid (*i.e.,* the *nagid*) felt a profound sense of responsibility towards this office and believed that he was engaged in a divine mission to protect his people.

The Rise of the Southern Community

From the end of the tenth century, it is possible to observe actions and legal formulas in local communities, which began to demand rights and responsibilities of leadership never before possessed by them. At the same time they preserved a continuity with the rights and responsibilities they had enjoyed under the gaonate; however, they developed and expanded them, indulging in innovations that were sometimes revolutionary.

In his *Sefer Hashetarot* ('The Book of Deed Forms', S. J. Halberstam, ed., Berlin, 1898), the *nasi* R. Judah of Barcelona assembled specimens of ancient contracts and referred to the antiquity of several of them, which presumably dated back to the end of the tenth or to the early eleventh century. Among them we find the certificate of appointment of the head of a congregation who was chosen by the local members. This document signifies the transition from appointment of a locally chosen leader by the central authority to appointment by the local inhabitants who had arrogated to themselves the right of independent decision.

The document commences with a description of the moral and social crisis that beset the local community, to the extent that there was scarcely any difference between it and the surrounding gentiles, 'saving the name of Judaism alone'. It is quite possible that there was indeed a crisis of this kind at the place where the document was originally formulated; however, the inclusion of this tale in the formula indicates that local inhabitants felt they must provide justification for making the appointment themselves. In the words of the document, 'the elders and heads of the congregation rose and joined together with all the members of our congregation'; in other words, this was a general agreement initiated and directed by the leading members of the community. Its purpose was to choose a single head 'to give us guidance in the proper course and to instruct us in the Torah of our God . . . and in order to judge' (*ibid.*, pp. 7–8).

The document and its justification indicate that the signatories actually saw themselves in the situation referred to by the *gaon* R. Samuel ben Hophni: in their generation there was no head such as was required 'for the age and the times'; therefore, as the *gaon* had provided for such a time of decline, 'let each community choose the man who is deemed to be fit and proper.' The locality and not the centre must determine its needs in such situations and must choose its leaders accordingly.

Among the forms included in *Sefer Hasheturot*, there is a 'writ of agreement' in connexion with the allocation of taxes. 'This is drawn up by the court or the elders of the community who are familiar with all the [business] affairs of the city.' The agreement begins with the words: 'We the elders, leaders and heads of the congregation in the city of . . .' It specifies how much each individual must give as his share 'of every hundred dinars required of the congregation, whether for taxes, property rates or poll-tax . . . whether for charity or for all the requirements of the city that fall on the congregation' (*ibid.*, pp. 137–8). No special apology is offered here for taking the initiative. The local leaders seem to have been accustomed to allocating taxes, both external and intra-communal, and to have had ample experience in determining the principles and methods of allocation.

In the Responsa of R. Isaac Alfasi, which reflect circumstances during the early eleventh century in North Africa and Moslem Spain, we find a decision in principle to the effect that:

> Essentially the custom to be followed [consists] in that the majority of the congregation shall take counsel with the elders of the congregation and shall pass whatever resolution they find fit, and shall carry it out. Such is the custom even after many years have passed, and even if they themselves no longer know its origin, but the community has abided by it and has continued so to abide.

This decision is stated as an obvious matter; and its unequivocal character indicates that it reflected the practice followed in regions far from the centre, even when the gaonate was in its prime. The local heads, appointed or otherwise, always determined local custom. From this decision we learn that the components of the community's decision-making body were the same as those mentioned in the document of appointment included in the collection of R. Judah of Barcelona: the entire congregation with its elders, and not just one or the other. In contrast to the north, the idea of majority rule had already been adopted in the south (see pages 502–3). Once a regulation of this kind was adopted by the majority, a custom was established for later generations as well, even if they forgot the causes leading to its introduction.

In brief, south of the Pyrenees and west of Erez Yisrael, local communities began to emerge from the end of the eleventh century. It is possible that local leaders had begun to liberate themselves from the central authority even earlier, as a result of the tension between the Erez Yisrael and Babylonian centres. In fact, this tension had on occasion led to the establishment of two separate communities and synagogues – an 'Erez Yisrael' and a 'Babylonian' – in a single place; and strained relations between them compelled the local inhabitants to conduct their affairs independently.

The rise of a limited territorial leadership certainly contributed to the success of the local community, which developed in those countries where the territorial office of *nagid* also emerged. In addition to the interrelationship between the rise of the *nagid* and that of the local communities, the emergence of particularist units was facilitated also by the break-up of the caliphate and the crystallization of more restricted political units within Islam. The literary style used by the local inhabitants is apologetic. It appears that the social situation and the firm hand of the *nagid* caused them to submit either to the *nagid* himself or to his representative. Yet there already existed specific titles for local heads and methods of calling meetings and adopting resolutions. Whole spheres of activity, such as the allocation of tax payments, charity, the legalistic and moral regimen and provisions for study, seem to have been organized by the local residents themselves from this time forward.

The North European Leadership

In the settlements of Jewish merchants north of the Pyrenees, there was no tradition of submission to any centre at all. The exilarchs, the *geonim* and the *negidim* of the Islamic territories were far away, not only physically but also in terms of the barrier that existed between Christendom in north-western Europe and Islam. The Jews of the north were, of course, fully aware of the authority and sanctity of the ancient centres in the East, and they communicated with them from time to time. However, the connexion that did exist could not lead to submission to or real leadership by the centres because of the general geopolitical situation. Furthermore, in those regions no Jew enjoyed a status at any royal court that would enable him to be appointed or to appoint himself leader of the Jews with the support of the rulers, as happened in the cases of *negidim* in the Islamic lands. Hence this territory was virgin soil as far as leadership, traditions and institutions were concerned.

Various forms of leadership did emerge and develop here freely. From the beginning of the eleventh century, we learn of a new kind of leader, the *shtadlan* ('intercessor'), who appears in tales that may be legendary but whose details are based on actual situations. A *shtadlan* went to the pope in order to obtain protection for persecuted Jews. He announced in 'a letter with his signature that all the congregations should honour' the messenger whom he had asked the pope to send to protect the Jews. It is related also that the count of Flanders sent an invitation asking 'that the said notable should come to him bringing thirty Jews in order to settle them in his land' (Haberman, *Massacres of Germany and France,* pp. 20–1). Thus he is portrayed as an initiator of new Jewish settlement, an activity that must assuredly have involved obtaining charters, rights and the privileges of leadership.

Rabbenu Gershom, The Light of the Exile

Rabbenu Gershom ben Judah (?960–1028), who was known to the generations immediately succeeding him as 'the Light of the Exile', represented a new type of leader who came from the world of the sages and assumed authority by sheer force of personality. Rabbenu Gershom was not formally appointed, nor was he the son of an officially appointed leader. It is not known whether he held any specific communal office. In any case, unlike the *negidim,* he was not in close contact with the rulers and did not exert any influence attributable to them. Nevertheless, he exerted vast influence in his own time and upon subsequent generations through his acknowledged learning and piety, his capacity for decision-making, his talent in leadership and his readiness to utilize these qualities.

Regardless of whether the ordinances or *takkanot* attributed to Rabbenu Gershom (see pages 437–8) were actually his or were enacted in the communities during his lifetime or thereabouts, the very fact that they bear his name is the clearest possible evidence of the strength of his personal authority and his capacity to implement far-reaching measures. Nor was he unique in his period, neither in terms of his way of life nor in his personal status and activities. In those days an event took place 'at the synagogue in Mainz', where, according to a thirteenth-century source that has preserved a record of the occasion, among those present were:

> Rabbenu Gershom ben Judah the Light of the Exile, Rabbi Simeon the Great, son of Rabbi Isaac, Rabbi Judah Hacohen, author of the *Book of Laws,* and Rabbenu Judah the Great, who was the head of those who were slain, and the remainder of *the members of the Holy Yeshiva*; and they all gave instruction (Eidelberg, *op. cit., para.* 32, p. 99).

This *yeshiva* clearly differed entirely from the Babylonian model. It had no graded rows of seats, and its members are described according to their personal deeds and achievements, not in terms of office or origin.

The Local Community and the Centralist Trend

The trend towards the centralization and unification of the Jewish communities was visible also in north-western Europe. Here, however, it emerged gradually from the communities themselves. As early as the time of Rabbenu Gershom, we find that these communities adopted the practice of holding meetings of congregation members who happened to find themselves together in a port or at a market:

> The congregations that were gathered there . . . decreed by ban and oath that any person into whose possession might come any part of what had been lost in that said ship should return it to the owner of the lost property – in accordance

with the practice followed in most communities of Israel in the case of any person who loses something, whether by theft or in any other fashion. Arrangements are set in motion on his behalf and it is decreed that any person into whose hand the said lost property shall come . . . shall return it to the owners (*ibid.*, para. 67, p. 155).

Rabbenu Gershom approved of this action and explained his approval by the fact that 'Jephthah [the Judge] in his generation is like unto Samuel [the prophet] in his generation'; and he summed up by saying: 'Hence, in all that the congregations have done, their decree is valid and their actions are binding' (*ibid.*, p. 157). In his day, as we shall see, the congregation used to recognize officially the right of a Jew to preserve his commercial relations with his regular clients, eliminating competition.

A younger contemporary of Rabbenu Gershom was R. Joseph Tov Elem (referred to in French as Bonfils), who on several occasions dealt with the problems of communal taxes. On one occasion he had to deal with a question regarding the community of Troyes, which had redeemed captives not belonging to the community and subsequently demanded that other communities share in the outlay. They sent messengers to the latter and threatened that 'those who refuse will be excluded, together with all their offspring, from the community, and their bread and wine [will be prohibited]; and they imposed a fine of thirty dinars upon them.' The communities refused the messengers' demand, claiming that 'they did not have to submit to that decree since they were not members of that city, nor did they share in all its troubles.' In his Responsum, R. Joseph Tov Elem declared the autonomy of each local community, even vis-à-vis one that was greater and more important, except in cases connected with *halakhah* or when a false charge had been levelled against all Israel. 'To sum up, they cannot compel the others in any way, even if they are more numerous and greater, except in cases of suppressing transgression or if they [the representatives of the larger community] appear in connexion with a charge which may affect them all . . . since all Jews are responsible for one another' (I. A. Agus, ed., *Responsa of the Tosafists,* no. 1, New York, 1954, pp. 39–42).

Each community was therefore autonomous as far as other communities were concerned. In his opinion, numerical superiority, seniority or greater scholarship did not permit one community to impose its authority upon another. There were only two cases in which one community could intervene in the affairs of another: in order to suppress transgressions, or when cooperation was required in order to counter anti-Jewish measures (*gezerot*) adopted against several communities or liable to spread from one to another.

Towards the end of the eleventh century, Rashi specified clearly and firmly the functions of the community and its authority over its individual members. Thus when informed of a quarrel between two families in a French community, which decreed that the strife must cease, Rashi approved of this public intervention between the two families, which he termed 'a communal decree'. With the same firmness he declared that the communities were entitled to cancel 'decisions made by the ancients according to the needs of the time'. His authorization to abolish earlier decisions in the light of changing circumstances was based, in his view, on Torah law.

Indeed, there are instances of existing regulations having been adapted to the needs of the time, while others are known to have been abolished entirely. For example, Rashi was told that a certain community had 'abolished . . . every decree they had imposed upon themselves because of the threat of tribulation'. The nature of this tribulation is not made clear. Did they fear punishment from Heaven for those who had transgressed the old decrees of the congregation but could not be punished? Or did this tribulation refer to the riots accompanying the First Crusade (see pages 413–14), which would have been more difficult to face had the severe regulations been maintained? In either case, the community of Rashi's time possessed a measure of sovereignty in the regulation of its affairs, and this was recognized by the *halakhic* authorities (Elfenbein, *op. cit.,* para. 70, pp. 80–8).

Rashi raised obedience to the leaders of the community to the level of a commandment and an express *halakhic* prescription, for he decided that anyone who vows 'not to fulfill a decree of the community' *before* the community has reached its decision about it has

> sworn in vain. . . . He has dived into deep waters and brought up a potsherd; and he is not exempt from the decree of the community if they have decreed in accordance with Jewish law and the whole congregation has agreed regarding the matter. . . . For surely the oath he took was intended to bring the commandment to nought and to turn aside from the Laws of Israel. For it is written: 'Incline thine ear and hearken to the words of the wise' (*ibid.,* para. 247, 288–9).

This *halakhic* principle was derived from the words of Proverbs, an unusual source for this purpose, even in the Talmud. Its validity was based on the definition of the fundamental conditions under which a decision by local residents becomes a binding regulation that must be observed, even if it involves the breaking of an earlier vow. These conditions are that the decision be in accordance with the law and practice of the Torah and that it be unanimously adopted by all the local inhabitants.

On one occasion Rashi denounced persons who took an oath in order to escape the burden of local decisions, and he informed them that 'they swore their oath in vain, and when they uttered it they uttered falsehood; for they swore to transgress the commandment and not to observe the statutes of Hebrew law and faith, namely, of hearkening to the voice of their elders who set a fence and maintain a barrier (*ibid.,* para. 70, pp. 83–4).

Rashi's evaluation of the community, its authority and its leaders derived from his concept of unity and mutual aid, whereby all Israel are responsible for one another. When it appeared to him that any person was trying to evade this duty, he warned: 'This is not the proper way for the Holy People who follow the Holy Torah. Israel is commanded "Thou shalt restore them to thy brother" in all the physical and social fellowship of their needs; and they are warned "Thou canst not disregard," and none can say mine comes first' (*ibid.,* para. 80, p. 106).

The trend towards a centralized leadership among the communities continued in Rashi's day. The accounts of acts of martyrdom during the First Crusade, which were written in the following half century, mention that 'all the communities came to the Fairs at Cologne three times a year.' This was a gathering of community heads. 'The *Parnass* heading all . . . Master Judah ben Abraham . . . was their chief spokesman in the synagogue. . . . And when the community heads began to speak', the words of R. Judah were decisive. He is described as a model individual who suited the description of high morals given in the Psalm of David: 'O Lord, who shall dwell in thy tents. . . .' (Haberman, *Massacres of Germany and France*, p. 47). Thus in the Rhine Valley region at the end of the eleventh century there was a nucleus of leadership that held meetings, and there already existed an ideal image of the type of leader who should head them.

The Achievements of the Leadership During the Period of the Gaonate

The *yeshivot* have been considered so far from their institutional aspect, which included their methods of leadership and their promulgation of decisions, interpretation or exegesis. We have seen that several factors combined to bring these institutional and centralist aspects to an end and to reduce the power of the aristocratic intellectual leadership. As we have pointed out, one of the main factors in this decline of power was their success in spreading Jewish scholarship throughout Jewry.

The main achievements of the gaonic period lay in the spiritual field and in the shaping of the Jewish outlook and way of life. These were centuries of impressive ceremonies and gatherings, of the inculcation of Torah in the widest possible sense among large numbers of Jews and of written Responsa providing guidance and instruction for those who dwelt far away. The *geonim* transformed the Talmud into the major sourcebook of life for the overwhelming majority of the Jews. They established it with a firm hand and with considerable didactic skill. In the *yeshivot* they purposefully continued and developed the 'method of questioning', *i.e.*, the system of keen verbal discussion and debate inherited from the earlier *yeshivot* that had produced the Babylonian Talmud. The summary statements in the surviving judgements and Responsa literature of the *geonim* can therefore be viewed as a final and static stage of deliberations that were originally far more lively.

Certain gaonic Responsa and express statements indicate that the *geonim* preferred verbal instruction both in theory and in practice, with the mentor and the questioning student facing one another, to answers delivered in written form. Writing was regarded as a regrettable necessity when there was no alternative. During the tenth century the Responsa were delivered at a solemn gathering held during the spring *kallah* month. Each individual question (accompanied, as a rule, by an honorarium) was brought before the graded rows of the 'Great Sanhedrin'. A free debate ensued, in which each of the sages stated his opinion. When the deliberations and discussion were at an end, the *gaon* would instruct the *yeshiva* scribe to write the Responsum in his name, but by virtue of the authority and sanctity of the entire *yeshiva*, in accordance with his own assessment of what the sense of the *yeshiva* decision meant. Thus the decision was based on consensus. At the end of the month, after all the questions submitted had been fully discussed and clarified, they were read out to the *yeshiva* in full assembly together with the summary Responsa of the *gaon*. Following the approval, it appears, of the entire *yeshiva*, the *gaon* would sign the Responsum and send it to the original questioner. These Responsa were preserved among the communal records and became an influential social and spiritual treasury.

The *geonim* also used to send special letters to Diaspora communities in which they addressed homilies to the people and suggested improvements in their way of life. Such were the letters of R. Saadiah Gaon to the Egyptian community and of R. Hai Gaon to the *kohanim* (Jews of priestly descent) in North Africa.

Historical traditions developed in and around the *yeshivot* and were preserved in lists and notes written for various purposes. They arose also from the continuous living tradition that characterized these institutions, which had been functioning without a break for four or five centuries, if not longer. The letter of R. Sherira Gaon was a summary of one of these chains of tradition, connected with the *yeshiva* of Pumbedita. As the following chapter relates, a rationalist religious tendency began to prevail among leading circles in the *yeshivot* and possibly among all the scholars from the tenth century onwards. It clearly derived from the studies in which they were engaged. The exilarch and the *geonim,* together with 'the corner-stones of the congregation', engaged also in intercession (*shtadlanut*) on behalf of those sections of the Diaspora that lay within the Islamic territories.

The Achievements of the Northern Leadership

The *geonim* also introduced *takkanot* or ordinances. With regard to these the greatest changes came about north of the Pyrenees, in the new regions of Jewish settlement. As has been noted, it is not certain that the ordinances attributed to Rabbenu Gershom the Light of the Exile were actually his. It is even possible that their final form developed in the course of several generations and reached crystallization only after the period under consideration here. In any case, we are entitled to conclude that both socially and emotionally the commencement of the great *halakhic* transformation – namely, the shift of the Jewish family from a polygamous to a monogamous structure – took place during the tenth and eleventh centuries in north-western Europe.

The ordinances reflect two fundamental changes in family life: taking two wives was now forbidden under penalty of excommunication and, even more important, divorce of a woman against her will was abolished *de facto*. As a result, the Jewish family in Ashkenaz became monogamous. The establishment of the family continued to require the initiative of the husband, but its legal termination depended on mutual agreement between the two partners. For the rare cases in which divorce was necessary without the woman's agreement, *e.g.*, if she were mentally ill, many regulations were provided in order to safeguard her. Permission for such a divorce could be granted only with the approval of 'a hundred rabbis from three countries', which meant three territorial units, each of which was under the rule of a different sovereign, in order to prevent unified pressure on the rabbis. The husband was required to deposit financial securities for the maintenance of the woman in accordance with Jewish law.

A tendency towards monogamy had been observable since the days of the Talmud; and many moral objections had been raised against the issue of a man's divorce from his first wife. In the countries of the East as well, steps had been taken to prevent marriage to a second wife during the lifetime and continued presence of the first by the introduction of conditions into the *ketubbah* or marriage contract. These conditions required the consent of the first wife to the second marriage and imposed a monetary fine on any man purchasing a female slave or wedding a second wife without the agreement of the first. Yet it was only in the lands where the new leadership of sages and local communities had become prevalent that explicit legal provisions were made. They brought about a fundamental change in the Jewish family and distinctly marked Ashkenazi Jewish culture. There is reason to assume that the monogamous nature of the surrounding Christian families exerted an influence in this respect.

In economic life we learn from the Responsa of Rabbenu Gershom that every effort was made to eliminate competition among the Jews for a regular clientele. The safeguards assumed the form of the *ma'arufya,* whereby no Jew might enter into commercial relations with any person who was the client of another Jew. This provision was not generally adopted; but we learn that the community used to grant the right of *ma'arufya* to a sage who instructed the local congregation or to some other individual against payment of a fee.

29

Jewish Social and Cultural Life Until the End of the Eleventh Century

Arabic Influence

The Jews of the Middle Ages, as we have remarked, inherited from ancient times an entire range of viewpoints and ideals that were transmitted in an extensive literature and were preserved throughout the generations. Many of their guiding institutions were, or at least claimed to be, continuations of institutions of the ancient past. Naturally, however, the social and cultural circumstances and trends of the contemporary environment had their effect. Life in the Islamic countries, with its flow of commerce and bustling urban activity, exerted considerable influence. An equal and possibly even greater influence was the new Arabic culture, in which the Platonic, neo-Platonic and Aristotelian elements moulded much of the spectrum of thought. The Jewish literature of the period came to be dominated by Arabic, which gradually became the spoken and written language of the Jewish masses, as well as the language of study, even in matters pertaining to sacred Jewish tradition. Jewish religious philosophy, which made its appearance in the tenth century, was written mostly in Arabic. Admittedly, however, Arabic never fully displaced Hebrew and Aramaic. Furthermore, the Arabic of the Jewish scholars and merchants came to be written in Hebrew characters and acquired a style and grammar of its own, gradually becoming a Judeo-Arabic dialect.

From the eleventh century there is evidence of cultural ties within Jewry extending from Babylonia to Moslem Spain by way of the Mediterranean islands. In addition, there were communications between the *geonim* and other Jewish scholars, on the one hand, and with the surrounding Moslem and Christian cultures, on the other, throughout the period under consideration. R. Joseph ibn Aknin reported:

> In his book *Hameassef* ['The Gatherer'], Rabbenu Ḥai Gaon of blessed memory made use of the work of the Arabs . . . and he also used a stanza from a love-song to clarify a saying of our rabbis of blessed memory. . . . He also quotes the Koran and the Hadith [the extra-Koranic Moslem tradition of utterances and decisions attributed to Mohammed]. And so did Rav Saadiah Gaon of blessed memory before him, in his Arabic commentaries. . . . In this connexion, the *nagid* [Rabbi Samuel] relates . . . after quoting at length from the commentaries of the Christians, that Rabbi Maẓliaḥ ben Albassek, the *dayan* [judge] of Sicily, came from

439

Baghdad with a missive containing the biography of Rabbenu Ḥai Gaon of blessed memory and his praiseworthy practices; it related how . . . one day a Bible verse . . . was cited in discussion at the *yeshiva* and those present differed as to its interpretation. Then Rabbenu Ḥai of blessed memory instructed Rabbi Maẓliaḥ to go to the catholicos of the Christians and ask him what he knew regarding the interpretation of the said verse (A.S. Halkin, ed., *Revelations of the Mysteries and Appearance of the Lights,* Jerusalem, 1964, pp. 493, 495).

Under the impact of Arab culture and language, contemporary Arabic literary and verse forms were adopted by Jews, together with verse metres and genres. These were widely and successfully used in Hebrew and proved to be fruitful elements in the emergence of new literary styles. The Jews were also affected by the environment in their daily life, for example, in matters of fashion. At the turn of the tenth and eleventh centuries, the *geonim* noted an incontrovertible fact: 'We are scattered to all four corners of the world. And in each corner men differ in their garb, their behaviour and their adornments. Accordingly, whatsoever the people of the said place . . . do is likewise permissible to the Jews who dwell in their midst' (Lewin, *op. cit.,* on Tractate *Nazir,* p. 200).

Ideals and Principles

Within this environment of relatively free mobility, the life of the Jewish community was based on ideals and points of view shaped for and by Jewish life and culture in the Middle Ages. The Jews again brought to bear their capacity for absorbing powerful cultural and social influences – whether from Islam or Christianity – and of using them to enrich their own social and cultural life. They succeeded in this by virtue of socio-religious cohesion, a supreme Jewish value, essential for national survival since they first made contact with the mediaeval world.

In the Islamic lands the main institutions of leadership and learning in Jewry were regarded by the Jews as stemming from Divine historical will, which was the reason of and for their preservation.

Therefore the Holy and Blessed One set up two *yeshivot* for Israel, wherein the Torah is studied night and day. . . . And they confer and dispute in discussions of the Torah until they clarify matters completely and [present] the law as it truly is, bringing proofs from the Bible and the Mishnah and the Talmud, in order that Israel should not go astray in matters of Torah (*Tanḥumah,* as in Dinur, *op. cit.,* p. 81).

Based on this ideology, a sense of the sanctity of the Jewish people inspired Jews wherever they were dispersed. In the ninth century they formulated this viewpoint and placed it against the age-old belief in the sanctity of the Land of Israel: 'And should you say that the land [of dispersion] is impure – Israel is holy and does not sustain impurity. The Torah is holy and the local synagogues and houses of study are in place of the Holy of Holies and they are sustaining us now. And Israel is set apart from the gentiles' (Lewin, *op. cit.,* on Tractate *Ketubot,* p. 182).

Religious Ferment and the Doctrines of 'Anan ben David

At the end of the eighth century, 'Anan ben David set out to counter the titanic effort to base the unity of the Jewish people on the traditions of the Oral Law and on the ancient systems of the houses of study and their hallowed leadership. He adopted this simultaneously conservative and revolutionary position against the background of a victorious Islam that was undergoing change and consolidation. He appeared on the scene only a short time after the successful revolt of the Abbasids and their assumption of the Islamic leadership. With the seizure of power by this opposition, their school became dominant within the Islamic faith. At the same time the Jewish leadership stood firm, maintaining for the entire Jewish people a uniformity based on the Talmud.

'Anan was a scion of the exilarchic family. A late tradition preserved by his 'Rabbanite' opponents attributed his schism to his frustrated desire for the office of exilarch after his brother Ḥananiah was chosen instead. One of the sources explains that he was rejected because of a 'suspected blemish'. The term 'blemish' or 'disqualification' had a double meaning in the Hebrew of the Islamic world. It could mean disqualification due to doubtful lineage or due to questionable opinions, particularly among those whose views tended towards Islam. It is reasonable to suppose that in 'Anan's case the latter meaning was more applicable.

Fragments of 'Anan's *Book of Commandments* have survived. Upon reading them one finds that 'Anan was not a Karaite in the sense that he relied only on the Hebrew Scriptures, following 'the simple meaning of the Bible text' and nothing more. He specified numerous prohibitions and based customs of which he approved on expositions of the biblical text that are often presented in Talmudic style. For instance, he commanded: 'Thou shalt not wear garments made ... of animal and seed.' This is an expansion of the pentateuchal prohibition against wearing *sha'atnez,* traditionally interpreted as a mixture of wool and linen and forbidden as such in the tradition of the Oral Law. To prove his point 'Anan would engage in a radical exegesis of various biblical phrases, giving meanings even to the sounds of words in order to justify his interpretations. His *Book of Commandments* was virtually a personal Talmud developed by a solitary Talmudist, stating his individual decision to stand against the Talmudic consensus.

In essence, 'Anan's approach did not differ from that of the exilarchs or the *geonim,* either in his attitude towards the Scriptures or in his basic approach to textual interpretation and exegesis. The difference lay in his claim to absolute authority for his own personal *halakhah,* in his insistence that only the interpretations, practices and customs sanctioned by him constituted law. According to 'Anan, true believers had to withdraw from whoever did not obey him:

> Likewise father or mother, brothers or children who do not serve heaven in our fashion are persons from whom we are duty bound to separate.... Any Jew who does not observe the Torah is called a gentile.... And we must of necessity separate from them. And we are required to gather together in one place, all of us, as is written: 'Gather my pious ones to me' (E. Harkavy, ed., *Book of Commandments,* St Petersburg, 1903, p. 7).

A careful examination of 'Anan's commandments shows that many of them were ancient Jewish customs, hallowed in one region or another, which he wished to transform into universal Jewish law. For example, he required that circumcision should be performed with scissors; his doctrine put new stress on the function and sanctity of the priests (*kohanim*); the commandment of the tithe was expanded to the point that it was converted into a general tax, thus permitting the existence of a separatist community of the kind to which he aspired. In addition, distinct ascetic tendencies can be observed in his writings.

'Anan emerged as the representative of autonomous groups that existed in Jewry during the eighth century – groups with their own customs and outlook. There were certainly others before him who had fought for such regional customs and wished to maintain them. When he joined their supporters, this son of the exilarchs brought into play the weight of his personality, his deep knowledge and his systematic approach, thus establishing an opposition to the uniformity that was gradually being established under the leadership of the exilarchate and the gaonate. Even in those days there were some who justly claimed that he offered 'a Talmud of his own' to the sect that had gathered round him, which was afterwards referred to as the 'Ananites. 'Anan's 'Talmud' is exceedingly strict and homiletic in nature. He was archaistic in his approach to the hallowed concepts of the past and frequently justified his asceticism as part of the mourning for Zion. However, his surviving writings do not show any signs of messianic aspirations. He gives the impression of having been a territorialist, as it were, having tried to establish a community of his believers in a separate region, where they could sustain their uniqueness and separatism.

In the eighth and ninth centuries, both before and after 'Anan, an intense messianic fervour arose within Jewry. It was awakened by the hopes for redemption aroused by the Moslem conquests and the subsequent disillusionment. Some of these 'messiahs' fell in battle, sword in hand. The records refer to the religious and social changes to which they aspired; but, as information about them is available only in documents written by Jews who opposed them or by Moslems, it is very difficult to establish their precise religious tendencies, unlike the case with 'Anan.

The Rationalist Religious-Cultural Climate

Jewish opposition to Mohammed's claim to prophecy, on the one hand, and to Christian Trinitarianism, on the other, combined with moods that in the ninth century began to make their way from classical Greek philosophy into Moslem and Jewish thought, particularly the Platonic, neo-Platonic and Aristotelian influences. This combination accentuated the rational basis of the Jews' religious stand and was particularly recognizable when compared with the climate of the Christian religious world. In the tenth century we have internal evidence from various currents of Jewish thought indicating that this approach predominated among most of the leaders, both within the Rabbanite *yeshivot* and among their Karaite opponents. The various and, on occasion, diametrically opposed religious and social conclusions drawn by one group or another clearly show that religious creativity and thinking in those days were imbued with a rationalist tendency.

R. Saadiah Gaon (882–942)

The range and intensity of R. Saadiah's religious and social teachings and his innovations reflect in a representative way the rationalist mood that existed among the Rabbanites. The life and activities of R. Saadiah ben Joseph al-Fayyumi comprised almost all the regions, institutions and tensions of Jewry in the Islamic countries during his lifetime. He was born in Egypt, where he obtained his early education. He corresponded with the philosopher and physician R. Isaac Israeli, an Egyptian Jew who had emigrated to West Africa and whose influence is recognizable in R. Saadiah's system. He travelled to Erez Yisrael and became familiar with the *yeshivot* there. He conducted the dispute with the *gaon* Ben Meir in connexion with the Jewish calendar, objecting to the authority claimed by the Erez Yisrael *yeshivot* for their opinion and leading the supporters of the Babylonian schools. Subsequently, he was invited to head the Sura *yeshiva,* where in due course he found himself involved in extensive conflicts. He also conducted a lively, keen and unremitting debate with the contemporary Karaites.

Thus he stood at the core of the autonomous Jewish leadership and was a storm centre for conflicts. He constructed the first comprehensive system of rationalist Jewish religious thought, under the influence of Greek and Arab philosophy, in the first Jewish work of a philosophical nature since the writings of Philo of Alexandria, which had been almost completely forgotten within Jewry. The work was written in Arabic and was entitled *The Book of Beliefs and Opinions.* In this work, as in his other writings and in his actions, the spiritual and social ferment within Jewry at the time is clearly reflected. The book also outlines the philosophical and religious polemics that took place between members of the various faiths and the viewpoints that were current within the much-variegated intellectual society of Baghdad during the first half of the tenth century.

R. Saadiah's Theoretical System

The esteem in which R. Saadiah held the ancient Greek philosophers and their systems of thought can be seen even when he warns against those of their opinions that ran counter to Judaism. Even so, he referred to them as 'Aristotle and his followers ... those philosophers who were great in astronomy and the knowledge of nature in all its truth' (from his *Commentary on Genesis,* chap. 1, J. Kapaḥ, ed., Jerusalem, 1962, p. 164). He viewed the human intellect as one of the foundations of faith, a primary instrument through which the Divine Will reveals itself to mankind. Thus he explained that the Torah 'is not the source of our entire corpus of Law and teachings by itself. Apart from it we have two other sources. One of them, which has priority, is the well of intellect, while the second which follows has its starting point in tradition' (*Beliefs and Opinions,* section 3, J. Kapaḥ, ed., Jerusalem, 1970, p. 144). Hence the human intellect is the first of the three sources for acquiring knowledge of higher things, while the other two are the Written and the Oral Law. The human intellect is of particular importance; in addition to providing its own concepts, it opens a way to the proper comprehension of the other two sources and their authority. For 'every interpretation which accords with the intellect is truth; and whatever leads to that which is not in accord with the intellect is worthless' (*ibid.*, section 9, p. 268).

R. Saadiah gives a rationalistic explanation, which is both historical and psychological, of the concept of 'tradition' – the basis of Oral Law. Belief in the chain of tradition is reasonable and logical because all of human behaviour is based on either expectation or apprehension; and the source of both lies in the tradition of past experiences, in which we have as a matter of existential necessity to believe (*ibid.*, section 3, pp. 130–1).

R. Saadiah's Views on Society and History

The religious rationalism of R. Saadiah Gaon was rooted in a lively social awareness and a deep sense of history. These qualities of thought and his activities as a leader led him to pay special attention to history, to society and their structures. His thought was influenced by trends that had emerged in Judaism long before his time, as well as by the forces, the group relationships and the moral code of his environment. His discussion of these matters is marked by realism and an affirmation of the world in which we live.

Observation of the world around him had convinced him that

the purpose intended [by God in creating the world] is Man . . . for custom and construction place every worthy thing amid objects that are less worthy. . . . Our God . . . gave Man an advantage over all His creatures . . . and placed free choice as his right, and commanded him to choose the good. . . . And we find his advantage in the wisdom which was given him and which he was taught (*ibid.*, section 4, pp. 150–1).

According to R. Saadiah, man's centrality among all of Creation is not only one aspect of the religious responsibility of the intelligent creature towards his God, but it also underscores that the cultural function of man, the structure of his society and the values that underlie it derive from the Will of the Creator.

R. Saadiah listed the achievements of the practical wisdom that God granted man:

Therein [man] preserves everything that has been in the past of events; and therein he foresees most forthcoming developments; and thereby he causes the beasts to till the soil for him and fetch him its yield; and thereby he succeeds in bringing forth water from the depths of the earth to flow upon its surface, and . . . he has made himself wheels which draw it up by themselves; and thereby he succeeds in building magnificent houses and wearing fine garments and preparing pleasant delicacies and dainties; and thereby he succeeds in leading soldiers and troops for the sake of proper rule and government that mankind may live in orderly fashion; and thereby he gains knowledge of astronomy and the Zodiac and the paths of the planets, and the measure of their effects, and their distances and other matters (*ibid.*, p. 152).

Thus he suggests that man differs from the beasts mainly in his historical memory and his foresight. Man's gift of wisdom has led to economic achievements in general and to irrigation in particular (mention of which befitted a native of Egypt and resident of Iraq), the raising of an army as the basis of power and its main instrument and an awareness that orderly government is beneficial to mankind, among the other accomplishments of civilization. For R. Saadiah the arts of civilization are praiseworthy not only because they supply the essential needs of society and enable it to function, but especially because they improve life and enhance the pleasure and enjoyment of men.

The generalizations provided here regarding society, material civilization, science and the arts are clarified in detail in the tenth and final section of *Beliefs and Opinions,* which deals with 'what is good for a man to do in this world'. Here R. Saadiah discusses human urges and achievements within society. Thirteen paragraphs deal with asceticism, eating and drinking, sexual relations, spiritual love, the accumulation of money, love of children, the ordering of society, love of life for its own sake, love of power, vengeance, wisdom, work and rest. In each instance both the positive and negative aspects are presented for consideration. Reading the discussion as a whole, one finds that R. Saadiah affirms the creations of mankind in this world and man's enjoyment of life. His warnings are directed against excess and hence misuse of the advantages of life. His most severe strictures are directed against asceticism. For him human needs and passions have a constructive intellectual purpose that benefits both the individual soul and society in general, if they are pursued in reasonable measure, according to the will of the Creator. R. Saadiah's assumption is that human nature is harmed by exaggeration in any of the above-mentioned activities. The humanity of the individual can emerge only 'from the gathering together and control of the human essence', that is to say, from the shaping of the various spiritual and physical forces and resources and their consolidation in correct proportion. In his system the individual Jew is a unit of Creation. Only by imposing the authority of the intellect on human tendencies and desires can an ideal 'gathering together and control of the human essence' be achieved. Rational judgement as such is 'the basis . . . for a man to rule his attitude towards both what he loves and what he hates'.

Love and Beauty in R. Saadiah's System

Within certain circles in the society of R. Saadiah's time, Platonic love between a man and his fellow was so widely accepted that he found it necessary to express the view 'that it is the work of the Creator. . . . it has been urged that He created the souls of the creatures as spheres and divided them into two, placing each part within a different man. Therefore when either part finds its other part, it joins itself thereto.' R. Saadiah, to be sure, rejected this assumption of a natural, 'magnetic' attraction that unites two halves of a soul into a single whole, as it were, in so far as it was applied exclusively to male society. But he himself saw fit to suggest – and he was one of the first in history to do so – that such an awareness of magnetism, of two loving units completing one spiritual sphere, *i.e.,* spiritual love, applies to relations between the sexes, 'For this matter is good only with a man's wife whom he should love and who should love him for the settlement of the world.' Long before the troubadours of the European courtly tradition presented love and marriage as opposites, R. Saadiah had advised that spiritual love be made the foundation of family life. The chief purpose of marriage was, admittedly, to engender children and maintain the human race, but it should be achieved through spiritual love.

For R. Saadiah the aesthetic element in the human psyche was so important that before completing his discussion on what is best for man in this world he discussed the influence of colours and sounds on men and their moods.

R. Saadiah's Opposition to 'Contempt for the World'

The affirmation of human social creativity played an important part in R. Saadiah's system of thought; so much so that he transformed the verse in Ecclesiastes that, taken at its face value, decries the activities of man into an argument in affirmation of human endeavour. His commentary on the verse, 'I have seen all the works that are done under the sun; and, behold, all is vanity and vexation of spirit' demonstrates that he was incapable of imagining so total a negation of existence 'under the sun'. As he understands it,

> King Solomon, when saying 'vanity and vexation of spirit', is not speaking of deeds gathered together and controlled, for the Creator brought them into being. A wise man could not declare what the Creator has brought into existence as being 'vanity'. His intention was: any deed which men take by itself . . . separately, is vanity; yet when they are associated there will be no short-coming, but perfection and harmony.

R. Saadiah's acceptance of the full range of human existence was bound up with his keen awareness of the problem of right and wrong in the world, particularly when human life is ruined or destroyed. In several passages of his work, he attempted to provide a moral and rational explanation of epidemics, the destruction caused by warfare and the death of children.

R. Saadiah's Concept of Exile

R. Saadiah's consciousness of the exile was keen and bitter. He viewed it as a period of refinement and purification of Israel. In an 'Entreaty' composed by him in Arabic, he prayed:

> May it be thy will, O Lord our God, that this era may mark the end of dispersion for thy people the House of Israel, and the time for the termination of our exile and our mourning. . . . For servitude weighs upon us, and the yoke of the kingdoms has lasted very long. Day by day we diminish, growing less with the passing of time, reduced by the retreating years. . . . Thou, O Lord, hast thought to refine our ore and remove our dross, and to take away our impurities from us. Therefore thou didst exile us and didst scatter us amid the gentiles so that we sink in the roaring waters of the kingdoms; and like to the smelting of silver in the crucible, so

we have been molten in their fire (J. Davidson *et al.,* eds., *Prayerbook of Rav Saadiah Gaon,* Jerusalem, 1963, pp. 77–8).

On the assumption that in God's world there can be no endless wrong or meaningless existence, R. Saadiah saw the exile as an assurance of eventual redemption. The gentiles, to be sure, do not understand the meaning of Israel's suffering in exile; they mock those whose sufferings are borne with patience, for they do not recognize the ultimate purpose of the chastisement. The Chosen People, on the other hand, suffer, yet believe, because they know what will be the outcome of their sufferings:

> Whoever sees us in this respect . . . is astonished or thinks we are fools. For he has not been tested the way we have been and has not believed as we believe. And he [the uncomprehending stranger] is as one who has not seen the sowing of the wheat, so that when he sees someone flinging seed into the turned earth in order to grow, he regards that person as a fool, and comes to recognize that he himself is the fool only at the time of harvest (*Beliefs and Opinions,* section 8, p. 239).

When facing inwards, to the heart of the Jew, R. Saadiah explained the exile, which strikes at saint and sinner alike, in the way in which he explained other calamities of nature and history. All are intended partly as punishment for those who deserve it and partly as a trial of those who do not deserve punishment, with the aim of refining their personalities and testing their faith.

Views Characteristic of His Society

R. Saadiah's rationalist philosophy cannot be considered entirely personal. His status among the sages and his position at the head of the Jewish leadership made him highly representative of his era. Despite the numerous conflicts and disputes of his career, his rivals never objected to his philosophical opinions, although they levelled other charges against him and even suspected him of immoral deeds. Hence it may be assumed that in the tenth century the Jewish intellectual leaders within the Islamic lands were imbued with rationalistic tendencies and opinions that approved of the temporal world and favoured productive individual achievement for the benefit of the community; and R. Saadiah's *Beliefs and Opinions* may be regarded as a comprehensive expression of the views of his circle.

In fact, he was far from being the most radical rationalistic religious thinker of those times. R. Samuel ben Hophni, a *gaon* who lived after him (*c.* 997–1013), expressed extremely rationalistic views. He roundly declared that the woman of En-dor 'did not really bring [Samuel] back to life, but deceived Saul'. He admitted that Scripture certainly did attribute speech to Samuel himself, 'but it is sheer common sense that in actual fact the Scripture here merely quotes the words of the sorceress'. He was reminded that R. Saadiah had refused to interpret this passage in such a fashion because, 'He said: If this interpretation be adopted it is equally permissible to interpret every appearance of the words "And God said" and "And God spoke" in the same way.' R. Samuel responded with a statement of principle:

Whenever we find the words 'He said' or 'He spoke' and it is impossible for these to be the actual words of the person or entity to whom they are attributed, there we declare what we have declared about this story [of Saul at En-dor]. But if it is not impossible, then we should not disregard the significance of any 'He said' or "He spoke', *if it does not contradict intelligence and is not inconceivable* (Lewin, *op. cit.,* on Tractate Ḥagigah, pp. 2–5 [author's italics]).

The Karaites

The same trend towards religious rationalism produced vastly different results among those who rejected the leadership of the exilarchate and the gaonate, including those correctly termed in the tenth century as the Karaites. In the ninth century, in the interval between 'Anan and the Karaites, opposition to the established leadership found various outlets. The known leader of the opponents of the *geonim* in that century was Benjamin ben Moses al-Nahawendi (of Nahawend, in Persia). His work *Maseat Binyamin* ('The Teaching of Benjamin') is the expression of an attitude and scale of values that differed entirely in its social aspects from that of 'Anan before him and of the Karaites in the following century. He shows much concern with the status of and respect shown to local judges. Benjamin al-Nahawendi set out to protect private property on the basis of the Torah, going so far as to decide, as a matter of principle, that the sons of a deceased debtor could be sold as slaves if the family were unable to pay his debts – a decision based on the biblical story of the widow and the prophet Elisha (II Kings 4). He insisted also on ceremonial sessions in court and in the appearance of witnesses. Benjamin is said to have held philosophic views that aimed at eliminating all corporeality from the concept of the Creator. Exclusive reliance on the Scripture is far more noticeable in his opinions than in those of 'Anan.

In the tenth century we find Karaites in the full sense of the word, *i.e.*, Biblicists. We hear the views of Jews who relied exclusively on the scriptural text and their own comprehension of it. They categorically rejected the Talmud and its homiletic methods as a burden that should no longer be borne and as human invention, coming from those who deceived the people through the force of tradition and their own institutional powers. They decried the resulting elimination of direct and individual contact between the Jew and the Torah and the fact that the people were led to follow the 'evil shepherds'. The Karaites of the tenth century may well be said to have followed the principle 'Seek well in the Torah and do not depend upon my opinion,' which has been wrongly attributed to 'Anan.

The descriptions of the great tenth-century Karaite chronologist Jacob al-Kirkisani reveal the existence of a multitude of opinions and widely varying customs among those who were classified by their opponents as Karaites. The variety appears natural when it is realized that the Rabbanites applied the term Karaites to all those who opposed the rule of the *yeshivot* and the Talmud, whatever their reasons or origin may have been. The diversity between the Karaites themselves resulted from the rationalistic individualism of this trend in the tenth century.

The Karaites in Jerusalem – 'The Mourners for Zion'

In the tenth century Jerusalem became the focal point of these sectarian tendencies. Karaite thinkers of ascetic, individualistic and rationalistic orientations gathered there from all the Islamic countries, united as *Avelei Zion* ('Mourners of Zion') or *Shoshanim* ('Roses'), as their admirers called them. In the Holy City they lived in austerity, mourning the destruction of the Temple and praying for its restoration – preoccupations they held to be the core of their religious experience. From Jerusalem they disseminated their sharp polemics against the Rabbanites, the Talmud and the gaonic leadership.

This group was exceedingly creative in commentaries, polemics and historical writings. Despite all the different shadings, their work is united in its religious individualism. According to the Karaites, the individual is duty bound to rely on his own intelligence and to understand the Holy Scriptures independently. This viewpoint was clearly expressed in the proclamation written to the Rabbanites by Sahl ben Mazzliah, one of the Karaite leaders:

Know, our brethren, Children of Israel, that each one of us is responsible for his own soul. And our God will not hearken to the words of the one who justifies himself by saying, 'This is how my masters guided me'; just as He disregarded the excuses of Adam, who declared 'The woman whom thou didst give me', etc. Nor will He accept the excuse of the man who says 'my sages misled me', just as he did not accept it from Eve when she said 'The serpent misled me so that I ate.' And know ye that anyone who declares as an excuse 'I have followed the way of my fathers' will find it of no avail at all. . . . For there is no compulsion upon us to follow our fathers in all respects. But it is our bounden duty to inspect their ways and assess their deeds and judgements in the light of the words of the Torah. If we see that they follow them without change, we shall accept and obey. . . . But if their words involve any alteration of the Torah, we shall fling them away and shall enquire and investigate until we achieve the true image of the commandments of the Torah. . . .

Now ye of the House of Israel, take pity on your souls and on your children. For behold the light illumines and the sun shines. Choose yourselves the good way. And do not say: What shall we do? For even the Sons of Scripture change [*i.e.*, there are differences of opinion and practice among the Karaites]. Which of them shall we follow? The Sons of Scripture do not say that they are leaders, and they have no intention of leading the people by their own whim. But they investigate and inquire into the Torah of Moses . . . and the Books of the Prophets . . . and they also inspect the words of the predecessors. Therefore they say to their brethren the Sons of Jacob: Study and seek and search and investigate and do what becomes established for you with clear sight and remains your opinion (S. Pinsker, ed., *Likkutei Kadmoniot*, Part II, Vienna, 1880, pp. 33–4).

The proclamation constituted a call for the rejection of every earlier human authority, whether traditional or institutional, in favour of individual decision based on the application of one's intellect and conscience to the Scriptures. Neither forbears nor teachers can show the way. The proclamation used markedly individual-istic and rationalistic symbolism, proposing the method of selective investigation by the intellect.

The Theory of Cosmic and Divine Catastrophe

Even more extremist and systematic in his views was Daniel al-Qumisi of Persia, another member of the group. Al-Kirkisani reported that 'he used to accept every conclusion he arrived at through the intellect . . . and he would announce the changes that came about in his writings.' Daniel objected to the esteem in which 'Anan was held for being the first and most ancient, for in his opinion 'the later ones will find truth.' In his *Commentary on the Twelve Prophets* (J.D. Markon, ed., Jerusalem, 1957), the first complete Hebrew commentary on these prophets that has survived from the Middle Ages, Daniel maintained that since God created all things for a specific purpose, it follows that 'He gave men understanding and knowledge in order to demand an accounting of their deeds from them' (on Amos 4:13). In his opinion, the period of exile was, unlike the Temple period, an epoch in which knowl-edge of the Torah was extended and disseminated among all the people. For the

> Torah, Prophets and the other Writings . . . were not disseminated by the Lord amid all the first men of Israel, except for the priests and the Levites and the king alone. . . . But in exile He has extended the spirit of His Torah over them in order that it might serve Him as evidence concerning them, to demand judgement (on Hosea 8:12).

Daniel meant that in his time responsibility had increased, along with the increase in knowledge. Not that these were good times, but precisely because they were days of crisis, both divine and cosmic, which had destroyed the good order that had once existed in the world, he and his contemporaries had more responsibility to bear. This crisis and its dread character derived from the destruction of God's Temple.

There exists a basic document that does not carry the name of the author but closely matches the opinion of Daniel al-Qumisi and may therefore be attributed to him. It is argued there that the destruction of the Temple led to the abolition of divine justice in the apparent world order:

> For the Temple of the Lord is desolate . . . so He has made the world desolate . . . so He has made the world to be abandoned, as it were, without judge and without *Urim* and *Tummim* and without any to inquire, like the fish of the sea who have no ruler from whom the swallowed can demand justice of the swallower.

The author rejected every attempt by the Rabbanites to diminish the scale of the calamity through the use of 'a reminder of the Temple' or of a 'lesser temple', *i.e.*, the synagogue. He maintained that the synagogues of the Rabbanites during the exile constituted the worship of wood and stone, just as it had been written that this would be part of the punishment during the exile. No honour should be paid to the Holy Ark or the Torah scroll within it, nor should any curtain be spread before it.

> Nowadays the idolatrous altars of Israel . . . are the Arks to be found in all the synagogues in the Exile; and they place themselves in front of them in order to bow down before them. Likewise during the festival of Tabernacles they take a palm frond and make circuits . . . with thanksgiving and the *Hallel* prayer. . . . 'And thou shalt not bow down anymore to the work of thy hands', but they bow down today to the Torah Scroll. . . . 'And I shall break down thy *asherot*', which are the synagogues (on Micah 5:12–13).

The author opposed the hallowing of any special place of prayer in exile, for 'no place can be made holy on polluted soil.' For the true believer there is only one holy place in the world, consecrated since time immemorial for the service of the Creator: the city and site of the destroyed Temple. Consistency led the author to demand the rejection of this world, in which divine rule could no longer be observed.

Daniel insisted that public mourning for the destruction and entreaty for the redemption must continue incessantly and must be performed in Jerusalem. The aforementioned proclamation criticized both the Rabbanites and the Karaites, declaring that 'all Israel constantly pursue their profits and earnings,' and 'therefore they have forgotten Jerusalem.' The author reminded his brethren of the Christian and Moslem pilgrimages: 'Peoples other than Israel come from the four corners of the earth to Jerusalem . . . out of reverence of God . . . to pray.' He despaired of the possibility of most of the Karaites settling permanently in Jerusalem, though he hoped that they would come there for a certain period of time. He also suggested a plan for a Karaite *halukkah* system for financially supporting residence in the Holy City – such as was practised by Rabbanites there later on, from the sixteenth century – in order that the righteous and those who mourned could dwell in Jerusalem, as was fitting; for surely 'he who is the reason for wrath has to come to the gate of the Wrathful One' to pray there. Those who settled in Jerusalem would be the emissaries of the majority who remained in exile and would gain merit by maintaining them. Thus he wrote: 'And if you will not come because you are busy with your merchandise, *send five men from each city with enough to support them,* in order that we may be one association to entreat our God constantly upon the mountains of Jerusalem' (author's italics).

Daniel expressed bitterness at the material poverty of his fellow Karaites. They hear 'the shame with which they are reproached and the saying that whoever abandons the words of the Rabbanites and their festivals and ordinances will perish in poverty and distress.' Yet, from his point of view, penury 'is the sign of those who fear the Lord in Exile' (on Hosea 2:7). He saw in the practices of the Rabbanites unseemly leniency, such as the permission 'to kindle [fire] before the Sabbath [and leave it burning during the Sabbath itself] and to eat meat . . . and to drink wine and rejoice'.

The followers of ascetic, individualistic rationalism marked by an intense mourning for Zion rejected the religious rationalism of the leaders of the organized community, which also yearned for Zion but lived in exile adhering to its symbols of faith and to its clearly defined way of life. The failure of Karaism in the tenth century was due not to R. Saadiah's keen polemics but to the life-style that it offered. For the most part Jews were attracted to the unifying guidance and instruction of the centre and to the encouraging leadership of the Babylonian and Ereẓ Yisrael *yeshivot.*

Ḥasdai ibn Shaprut

In Moslem Spain, Jewish culture began to assume form from the tenth century. The ideas and ideals of Judaism were formulated in the courts of Jewish leaders and partly through the financial support they provided for poets and sages. In these places, where leadership was based not on ancient and hallowed foundations but on actual power, we hear of various tensions within Jewish society. We have already mentioned the severe punishments meted out by the heads of this society.

R. Ḥasdai ibn Shaprut, whose activities and political influence lasted from about 940 to 975, reached a high position under the Omayyad caliphate during its period of unity and eminence. He was a famous physician, a translator from Greek and a successful diplomat. The Babylonian *yeshivot* granted him the title *resh kallah,* and he, a wealthy man, supported the establishment of *yeshivot* in Spain and invited scholars from other countries to head them and teach in them. Yet he also displayed the despotism characteristic of ministers in Islamic courts. When he became angry at the Hebrew grammarian and poet Menaḥem ibn Seruq, not only did he withdraw his patronage, but also, as Ibn Seruq complained in his poem-letter to him, 'they beat me before your eyes divesting me of my robe on the holy day of rest and plucking my hair on the holy Sabbath. . . . And on the festival day . . . you ordered my home to be destroyed . . . not by gentiles but by their own [Jewish] hands.' When the poet complained he received this harsh reply: 'If you did wrong . . . I have already meted out punishment to you; and if you have done no wrong I have already led you to eternal life.' This tyrannical behaviour on the part of his patron led the poet to protest in proud defence of his honour and in the name of human equality:

> Hearken now to my words, mighty *nagid* and lord! You are made of the same stuff as I, and He who made me is your Maker. . . . And though justice be delayed now, I await the day of judgement, the day when I rise up forever, that day when we stand together . . . the day when there can be no pretext and the mighty cannot resort to force.

The pride of the individual remains unshaken. Though he may be broken and full of complaint, he declares that he is not simply waiting for the Day of Judgement but argues:

> Son of man, hear me . . . You should know the law!
> The wise one has before him
> The path of morals and the way of faith
> Which he who hears correctly
> Admits and accepts
> For himself and itself.
> That is the glory of the strong
> And their praise.

Now when you said 'if you did wrong
And if you have done no wrong',
Is it proper to judge on an 'if'?

Here the appeal is not only to justice and right but also to the element common to the powerless poet and the all-powerful *nagid,* namely their common culture, as well as the glory and praiseworthy characteristics of the patron. The pride of the cultured individual leads Menaḥem to declare:

Must I cry out to you?
And before you must I shed tears?
. . . Or my spirit submit to you?

Indeed for the violence done:

I weep
And for the false judgement
Tears fall from my eyes.
   (Schirman, *op. cit.,* pp. 11–19)

The Cultural Climate in the Tenth and Eleventh Centuries

Behaviour of this kind was not restricted to relations between literary patrons and impoverished scholars and sages. A Responsum of R. Isaac Alfasi, dating from the eleventh century, deals with a man who sold silk to another for 950 gold pieces. In due course the vendor quarrelled with the purchaser, who denounced the other 'before Judah, who was a notable at that time; and . . . the notable gave orders and they imprisoned him . . . and beat him and inflicted all kinds of torment on him'. The Jewish notable demanded 500 gold pieces as the price for setting his fellow Jew free after having tortured him in his own prison. But it came about that 'after some time there was persecution in that country,' and the violent notable was killed, together with the other Jews who had been been concerned, with the exception of the one who had been imprisoned (Ms. Adler, no. 1765, *Responsa of R. Isaac Alfasi,* Schechter Jewish Theological Seminary, New York, fol. 26).

   Amid the social tension the ideals and yearnings for the redemption were preserved. Between the years 956 and 961, when R. Ḥasdai was at the height of his career, he sent a letter (apparently drafted by Menaḥem ibn Seruq) to the king of the Khazars in which he expressed his delight at their military victories. He also requested information about the kingdom and expressed a yearning for redemption and hope for deliverance. The verse introducing the letter stated:

Those sad for [the delay] of the time will declare to God:
The time we yearned for has come,
The Tabernacle of David and City of God
Will spew out the gentiles
And the Remnant shall see with its own eyes
The heights of the Citadel

And the son of Jesse will reign for ever!
   (Schirman, *op. cit.*, pp. 7–8)

Even those who doubt that this letter was actually sent by R. Ḥasdai ibn Shaprut agree that it was composed in his time and imitates the style of Menaḥem (whose name is included in acrostic form). In any case, it expresses the mood that prevailed in the latter part of the tenth century.

Patronage of Torah and wisdom was not restricted to notables in the royal service, although they undoubtedly originated and perpetuated the practice. R. Isaac Alfasi tells of a scholar 'who used to dwell in the east of France . . . far from Spain for many years, and left his wife and children where they were and willed to journey in the land of Spain through the communities, and came to a certain city where he preached in public'. His sermon was successful, for 'five of the leaders of the community . . . besought him to fetch his wife and children to that city and dwell among them.' They had to entreat him earnestly before he responded favourably. 'And they made a binding agreement with him that these five would give him twenty-four gold pieces . . . every year for three years.' They also specified his duties, and the definition indicates the contents of the Jewish culture sought by 'the leaders of the community'. They wished him to instruct them in '*halakhah,* Mishnah, Scripture, and the interpretation of the weekly portions in the Pentateuch and whatever else they might wish'. Eventually they all agreed and commenced with Tractate *Berakhot,* which they studied for four days each week; 'and on the fifth they read Scripture, and on the sixth the interpretation of the weekly portion.' But one of them claimed, 'I cannot comprehend the depth of the *halakhah* and I do not desire to.' He refused to pay his share of the wage unless they studied more Mishnah and less Talmud (*Responsa of R. Isaac Alfasi, op. cit.,* para. 223).

R. Samuel Hanagid

The personality that epitomized the spiritually and materially wealthy upper class among the Jews of Moslem Spain was R. Samuel ibn Nagrela, designated by the title *nagid,* who was born in 933 and is known to have still been alive in 1056. His actions and point of view are representative of the aristocratic circles of Jewish society at that time. His political achievements, the opportunities afforded him for action among and for his own people and the nature of his activities were largely a result of the decline of the Omayyads in Spain during the eleventh century and the emergence of petty warring kingdoms and principalities.

In many respects the courts of these political bodies resembled those of the Italian principalities during the Renaissance. Rulers, lords and even the principalities lacked deep roots, security, stability and continuity. Survival depended upon talent, effort and the capacity to seize a fleeting opportunity. The protagonists had to rely almost entirely on personality, tenacity and charisma. In Moslem Spain, as in Italy, political uprootedness occurred amidst an old and rooted cultural tradition. This convergence made cultural creativity and innovating personalities an important political asset, building up glory for the usurper and bolstering his precarious base.

This configuration channelled emotion and thought towards rational and critical deliberation on the individual and society alike – their motivations, strengths and weaknesses, the way to gain influence over them and the way to manipulate them.

As we have noted, R. Samuel Hanagid's life style reflected the opportunities inherent in these qualities, forces and tensions among leading Jews within the small Berber kingdom of Granada in the eleventh century. He is reported to have been an overseas trader and to have led a life of luxury, as previously described (see pages 401–2). Even before he reached the summit of his career, he had held various administrative and political posts.

R. Samuel Hanagid was also a brilliant poet. Both Arab history and Jewish legend bear witness to his outstanding Arabic style and his beautiful calligraphy. 'He was at home in Greek philosophy,' declared an Arab historian, and 'in the various branches of mathematics. His knowledge of astronomy exceeded that of the astronomers. He also knew all there was to know about geometry and logic.' His contemporaries recognized him as a great Talmudic scholar; his works include a number of commentaries on the Talmud and Responsa to *halakhic* questions. He maintained contact with R. Ḥai Gaon in Baghdad and with the sages of North Africa. In one of his poems, written after he was delivered from his enemies, he vowed to write a work on *halakhah* in which he would define matters agreed by law:

> In pure speech and choicest word,
> And rescue truth from the grave
> And bury everything absurd.
> (*Diwan, Ben-Tehillim, op. cit.*, para. 107, p. 82)

Here, in effect, was a description of Maimonides' *halakhic* compendium, known as the *Mishneh Torah* or *Yad Haḥazaka*, presented several generations before Maimonides was even born – a work that would summarize and make easily available all that was straightforward and generally accepted in Jewish tradition, while 'burying' whatever was complicated and twisted in presentation.

The *nagid* was also a military commander who many times led the Moslem armies of his king into battle. Several of his poems record impressions of the fighter gained at the scene of battle, as well as accounts of the actual fighting:

> Swiftly we engraved on their flesh
> Fine words with pens of iron
> With our arrows and spears
> Filling their bodies like quivers.
> Warriors reeled, not from wine
> But drunken with their own heart's blood.
> And they who had borne the banners aloft
> Were borne themselves to the grave.
> (*Ibid.*, para. 103, p. 76)

His poetry reflects the light and movement on the battlefield:

Horses speed back and forth like adders from their lair.
The spears flash like lightning through the air.
The arrows are drops of rain, and the swords gleam brightly.
   (*Ibid.,* para. 10, p. 9)

R. Samuel expressed the thoughts of a man living in constant tension, awaiting victory or defeat:

I lodged a heavy force in a fort
Destroyed by warriors of old.
Beneath its owners did sleep.
And I said in my heart: Where are
The peoples who dwelt here of yore?
Where are the builders, destroyers and lords,
The paupers, princes and slaves?
They now rest in their graves
In the depths of the earth.
If they arose and came forth
They would pillage our very lives.
True, my soul, like then
On the morrow I may join
These hosts lying here.
   (*Ibid., Ben-Kohelet,* para. 132, p. 275)

R. Samuel's Social and Cultural Views

R. Samuel's great scholarship and dedication to the Talmud did not prevent him from voicing scathing criticism of scholars whose external appearance or behaviour were not to his liking. He mocked those who 'imagine that by fringes and beard and tall turbans a man is qualified to head a *yeshiva*'. The noise of their study at a distance reminded him of 'the bellow of bullocks'. Similarly, their behaviour within the synagogue, when the students nodded their heads and debated the words of the Talmud, 'while the master prolongs explanations', annoyed him. His attitude towards external form and the manner of study of the sages and their disciples is etched in heavy sarcasm at the close of his poem on the head of the *yeshiva* who:

Blesses God for creating him man and not woman, to whom I did say,
Is your soul from the males? Why, God bears witness you are a female.
   (*Ibid., Ben-Tehillim,* para. 73, pp. 50–1)

This was neither culture nor proper behaviour, and so this could not be a sage nor the Jewish culture desired by R. Samuel. For him the most praiseworthy culture was his own, for which he praised a scholar whom God:

Made wise in his Scripture and faith
Which are set high above wisdoms all

And schooled in the wisdom of Greeks
And in Arab learning as well.
  (*Ibid.,* para. 91, p. 63)

Experience and a basically rationalistic approach had taught R. Samuel that:

Good sense fashioned in you will last,
With good sense you learn and acquire
As light above an oil-lamp
Remains, and the blaze of a fire.
  (*Ibid., Ben-Mishlei,* para. 1072, p. 248)

R. Samuel fulfilled the obligation to aid the poor, particularly scholarly sages and poets. Indeed, he was the Maecenas of his age. For example, he supported the poet and philosopher R. Solomon ibn Gabirol, even though their relations were strained.

R. Samuel's view of the politics and the character of the petty kingdoms of his time can be seen from his philosophy of three stages of statehood:

When the state begins it is harsh, for
  all rebels are instantly slain.
If any revolt when it is firm, he suffers,
  but not death's bane.
When 'tis calm and at least like to Tyre, then
  it remains so a while ere it fall
Like a fig from a tree which at first
  is hard and tart to the taste.
And so it remains for some days, though
  its hardness with moisture is laced.
And when it grows full and handsome and ripe
  from the tree it will certainly fall.
  (*Ibid., Ben-Mishlei,* para. 739, p. 207).

His own experience and the struggles of his *milieu* had taught him the need for risk and daring in the struggle for existence. Thus he advised:

Take risks when you aim for power,
And defeat the foe with the sword.
  (*Ibid.,* para, 988, p. 239)

At the same time he recognized the need for tact and diplomacy. Although he was the minister of an autocrat, he advised that it is to the advantage of the ruler to maintain proper relations with the people and that the best ruler is he

Who forgives his people's misdeeds
And toils for the good of the poor.
  (*Ibid.,* para. 44, p. 124)

R. Samuel regarded his own political function as a divine mission to safeguard his people in the lands whose rulers he served. Foes of the rulers and of himself were enemies also of the Jews. He correctly assessed all the perils involved in loyally serving the tyrant while simultaneously attending to the welfare of his brethren and to his own status and honour among them. He warned of the consequences of inciting society against him:

> Their letters are sent through the towns
> To spread of me report.
> Yet they aim to destroy by their lies
> Not me only but the loved of the Lord,
> The orphan, and woman with child.
> (*Ibid., Ben-Tehillim,* para. 10, p. 8)

At the same time he was sure that he was also generally esteemed among Jews for his personality and standards. He assured himself that, when he died, in every city people would say 'Come and mourn for this man, unique in his days for Torah and counsel' (*ibid.,* para. 24, p. 19). He wrote these words while still young. The fate of his son Joseph, who was slain in a Moslem attack in 1066, which was followed on the very same day by the slaughter of the community of Granada, may be seen as confirmation of Samuel's assessment of the degree to which the community depended on him and on his status. Yet it may also be regarded as an indication of the jeopardy in which a member of a minority placed his brethren when he was prepared to serve a tyrant.

The Budding Ashkenazi Culture

In the tenth and eleventh centuries, the emerging communities of Western Europe north of the Pyrenees formulated a set of social ideals that was based on ancient Jewish national tradition but also reflected their particular structure, society and relationships with the Christian environment. Quite early on norms to guide this fledgling Jewish culture were established. These ideals and norms are expressed in one of the hymns of R. Simeon the Great, according to whom the sages of Torah are

> Rulers o'er its treasures who advance by its light,
> Doing its work, indeed, the very dusty spade work,
> Not enjoying its honour or crown,
> Nor using it as tool or diadem
> But wishing to study, preserve and teach,
> They keep sleep away from their eyes,
> And teach wisdom according to the Torah.
> (Haberman, *Liturgical Poems,* p. 186)

A deep knowledge of the Torah, guidance by personal example and preoccupation with instruction should be the qualities of those in positions of authority. Stress was put on the importance of serving the people out of a sense of duty and not for the sake of material benefit or public recognition – an expectation that would have been inconceivable at that time in the world of Babylonian Jewry. It is true that sages recognized as teachers of the community were sometimes given preferential treatment in certain kinds of transactions, so that they would be able to devote themselves to the study and teaching of Torah. Thus Rabbenu Gershom decided 'that the community has to make provision for this scholar whose craft is the labour of heaven . . . in order that he should not be disturbed in his study' (Eidelberg, *op. cit.*, para. 68, pp. 160–1). Yet there was a qualitative difference between the granting of special commercial concessions of this kind and the officially set remuneration of the Babylonian scholars. It was the duty of these sages to lead 'the remnants of the holy people', who had not themselves been privileged to 'draw on the spring of the Torah or enjoy her kinship', to quote R. Simeon.

He also described an ideal behaviour for the common people. They had to perform 'their transactions in good faith . . . and be concerned for every commandment . . . being called sons of the Living God . . . coming to the House of prayer . . . and accustomed to show kindness' (Haberman, *Liturgical Poems*, p. 187). These two sets of duties and standards – for the sages and for the common people – became the guiding lights of Ashkenazi Jewry throughout the Middle Ages.

Study of the Torah in Early Ashkenaz

The ideal of devotion to study was in large measure already being realized in these early days. The extent can be judged from a case, brought to Rabbenu Gershom for decision, concerning a dispute between two Jews over the ruin of manuscripts. One had left 'some books with the other as security on a loan, but when he came to redeem them he found they were worn and . . . claimed: they were new books but you studied them and lent them to others and they became yellowed from smoke.' The other replied: 'The condition on which I loaned you money on them was *to study and teach from them, and to lend them to others*' (Eidelberg, *op. cit.*, para. 66, p. 153).

These details incidentally provide information on the type of illumination used during study. The manuscripts became yellowed because they were studied with the aid of smoky lights or torches. It also appears that the money-lender considered it a merit on his part to have lent the manuscripts for others to study as well; and he claimed that he took them as a pledge for this express purpose. In the Christian society of that region and period, such a dispute might have developed, if at all, only between one scholarly monastery and another or possibly between a cathedral school and a monastery school; it is most unlikely that it would occur between ordinary laymen.

The extent of book knowledge derived from parental concern for the education of their children. We are told of a teacher who made the following complaint to his employer before Rabbenu Gershom: 'You came again and again to me and took me to your home to teach your three sons. You gave me three pounds a year for them, and if fellow pupils from outside were added to your sons, would raise it to ten pounds' (*ibid.*, para. 71, p. 164). Thus the class that appeared reasonable to the father was one containing up to ten pupils. He was prepared to house it in his home, in order to ensure the education of his own sons. Furthermore, the teacher's tale shows that the father provided one of his sons with additional education, for the teacher said to the father: 'You sent me to be with your son and to instruct him, and to introduce him to the gates of the sages morning and evening' (*ibid.*, p. 165). It seems that the father sent his son to another city, together with the teacher, in order to 'introduce him the gates of the sages' in that place; and he undertook to pay the teacher the expenses involved. An effort of this kind and the existence of 'gates of the sages' open to those who wished to study were unimaginable then in lay Christian society, even among the aristocracy.

The Scriptures were a central subject of study among Ashkenazi Jews in these early days. The teacher stated: 'You told me to stay in your house and teach your son the whole of Scripture as I saw fit.' He was of the opinion that he had done so 'until the pupil had completed the Scriptures' (*ibid.*, p. 166). The style and terminology of the scholars of that period also indicate biblical influences.

R. Solomon Yizḥaki (Rashi; 1040–1105)

The creative strength of the group that laid the foundations of Ashkenazi Jewish culture is clearly and forcefully displayed in the works of R. Solomon, better known as Rashi. Not only did he make a major contribution to Jewish cohesiveness within the Christian realms, which were steadily growing more hostile in the period during which he wrote, but he also exerted an influence throughout Jewry, and not only within the area of Ashkenaz, that has lasted until our own times. This impact was achieved almost entirely through his commentaries on the Bible and the Talmud, which combine the traditions and pedagogic methods of preceding generations in a lucid, succinct and illuminating presentation. His comments incorporate the essential teachings of Ashkenaz until his own times. He himself bore witness to the influence of his teachers: 'Indeed, I grow from a great tree, Rabbi Jacob ben Rabbi Yakar; and although I never actually heard this from him, at all events *my heart and outlook and understanding come from him*' (Elfenbein, *op. cit.*, para. 59, p. 57). His interpretations have come down to us in the form of *incipits* from the text followed by his commentary.

In his commentary on the Scriptures, he has so perfectly combined his own comprehension with the spirit of the Bible and that of the Midrashim – the homiletic and interpretative literature that preceded, accompanied and followed the two Talmuds – that it is often difficult to differentiate between his own words and the text he is quoting. The commentary is imbued with a moral spirit and includes words of consolation taken from the *aggadah* (the non-legal sections of the Talmuds); it pulsates with a desire to explain the scriptural text in the most direct fashion possible. Rashi's spiritual vigour enabled him to combine these two aspirations within a single commentary, although he sometimes found it necessary to state the homiletic significance of a passage alongside its simple meaning. When he himself was uncertain he was careful to refrain from offering a definite opinion. For example, he declared at the commencement of his commentary on the prophet Zechariah:

The prophecies of Zechariah are very obscure indeed. They contain visions resembling dreams that require interpretation; and we are unable to determine the true interpretation until the Righteous Teacher comes. Yet to the best of my ability I shall set out to interpret the texts one by one on the basis of the closest scrutiny.

In his succinct and clearly expressed comments on the Talmud, Rashi succeeded in combining concepts of and keys to the most complicated and casuistic topics. His commentaries summed up the past and opened the door to the future, enabling his successors to follow his beaten path towards comprehension of the Bible and the Talmud. The creative achievement of exegesis and legal construction, which we shall discuss in connexion with the Tosafists of France and Germany in the twelfth and thirteenth centuries, is to be seen as a combination and broadening of methods and trends for which Rashi opened the way.

30

The Status and Economic Structure of Jewish Communities, 1096–1348

European Jewry's Awareness of Its Expansion

The massacres of 1096 considerably changed the political status of the Jews and affected their religious and social thinking, even though their geographical distribution changed very little. After Emperor Henry IV permitted the forced converts of 1096 to return to Judaism, communities were restored in most places. In the following centuries the Jews of Germany began to spread towards the east and the south-east, establishing communities in the cities of those regions. Thus Rothenburg, on the Tauber River, became a centre of study and communal leadership during the thirteenth century. It appears that the hundreds of congregations in Bavaria and Franconia, which were destroyed by massacres, particularly during the dreadful half century from 1298 to 1348, were the result of this expansion in the twelfth and thirteenth centuries. Even if we assume some exaggeration in the reported numbers of communities destroyed and of the Jewish residents, the figures still testify to the spread of Jewish centres. Jews began to make their way into the regions of the western Slavs, and into Poland in particular, from the thirteenth century. In the year 1264 a Polish prince granted a charter to Jews residing in his lands.

The Jews of Germany were well aware of this movement into new regions. R. Eleazar ben Judah (1165–1238), one of the leaders of the Ḥasidei Ashkenaz, discussed climatic differences and regional characteristics as factors affecting the relations between nations:

> The Holy and Blest One has decreed that there should be summer and winter. Now what is the use of a *severe* winter? . . . Sometimes it is an advantage, like the snow which blankets the seeds. And furthermore God created warm places. Now if there are wars and disputes those who dwell in warm lands cannot . . . be in a cold place; and they can flee, one nation from the other . . . and nation is separated from nation by rivers or mountains or seas or *forests,* in order that they should not come to battle one against the other. That is the meaning of the verse in Psalms, 'The Lord has founded the earth with wisdom, establishing the world by His wisdom' (R. Eleazar ben Judah, *Hokhmat Hanefesh* ['The Wisdom of the Soul'], Safed, 1915, fol. 22v).

This *ḥasid* was clearly well aware of a move towards colder lands and towards the forests. He was interested in the offensive and defensive relations between nations, the advantage of barriers between them and the possibilities of finding refuge in times of war by emigration. In the twelfth century the Ḥasidei Ashkenaz prepared regulations for Jews who

> when they came to set up houses in the forests suffered from a pestilence because the spot was set apart for demons; for as long as human beings were not customary there, they used to die. They asked a sage what they should do. He told them: choose the plot for yourselves.

A ceremony was to be conducted by 'ten men with a Torah scroll over all the ground' of the area selected. The verses to be recited as they went to each part of the plot, until the whole area had been covered with the Torah Scroll, are recorded. 'And finally let them say: On the authority of the Omnipresent and on the authority of the Torah and Israel who observe it, no harmful spirit male or female shall be permitted to come to this place now or forever' (J. Wistinetzky, ed., *Sefer Ḥasidim,* Frankfurt a.M., 1924, para. 371, p. 113).

This tale clearly indicates Jewish participation in the clearing of forests and settlement in what was originally woodland. The ceremony with the Torah scroll and the recitation of certain verses were meant to banish the evil spirits from what had been their domain.

The *ḥasidim* found it necessary to advise 'people who wander through the land seeking a place to dwell – let them closely observe the established burghers of that town, and carefully observe the gentiles', their moral standards and their way of life. For, 'if Jews dwell in that town, their sons and daughters will behave like them [the gentiles]; for in most towns, as the gentiles behave, so do the Jews' (*ibid.,* para. 1301, p. 321).

In England changes in settlement occurred as a result of trends and measures peculiar to that country, which was the most centralized and authoritarian of the West European kingdoms of this period. We know of the spread of Jewish communities there in the twelfth century, by the end of which they numbered in the dozens, with many located in the main towns. Jewish expansion continued in the early thirteenth century. However, the savage fiscal exploitation by the rulers, the animosity of the population and the authorities and changes introduced in financial methods (see pages 474–5) were followed by a total expulsion of Jews from England in 1290. It is estimated that about 16,000 Jews left, most of them proceeding to France and Germany. No Jews were again to be found in England until the second half of the seventeenth century.

In France the situation of the Jews deteriorated from economic success and wide expansion at the beginning of the period to sustained persecution culminating in expulsion at the end. Available sources indicate that several towns in France contained two Jewish streets, one of wealthy Jews, the other of the less wealthy. Contemporary Christian sources sometimes complain of the ostentation of Jewish homes and life-styles. The conditions governing economic and social developments and the circumstances of life in general in southern France were very favourable, especially until about 1230 (see chapter 33 on the style of life enjoyed by R. Judah

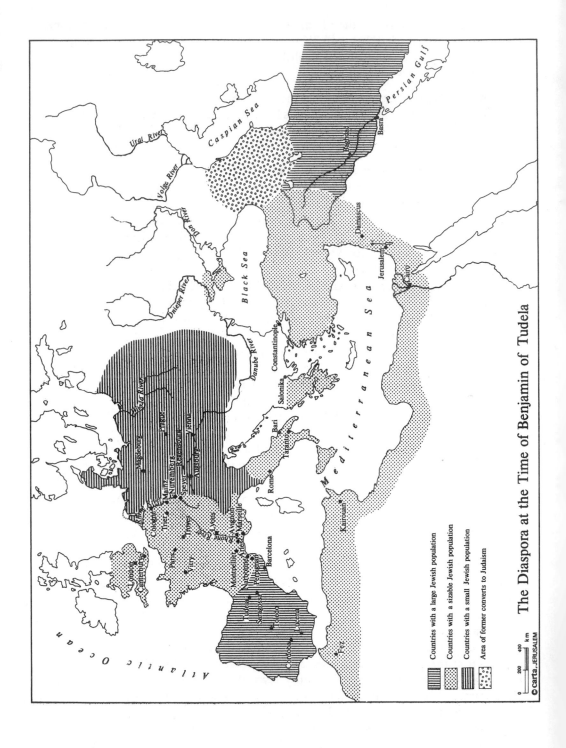

The Diaspora at the Time of Benjamin of Tudela

Countries with a large Jewish population

Countries with a sizable Jewish population

Countries with a small Jewish population

Area of former converts to Judaism

km

0   200   400

© Carta, JERUSALEM

Atlantic Ocean

London
Canterbury

Cologne
Trier
Mainz
Nuremberg
Speyer
Regensburg
Augsburg
Vienna
Magdeburg
Prague

Paris
Troyes
Vitry
Sens
Vienne
Avignon
Marseille
Montpellier
Narbonne
Perpignan

Tudela
Saragossa
Barcelona
Toledo
Lucena
Córdoba

Fez
Kairouan

Rome
Bari
Taranto
Salonika
Constantinople

Jerusalem
Cairo
Damascus
Baghdad
Basra

Mediterranean Sea

Black Sea

Caspian Sea

Persian Gulf

Ural River
Volga River
Don River
Dnieper River
Danube River
Vistula River
Elbe River
Rhône River
Rhine River

ibn Tibbon). In cities like Narbonne there were wealthy veteran families that preserved their own traditions and high judicial status. In the second half of the twelfth
century, Benjamin of Tudela (in his *Itinerarium,* M.N. Adler, ed., London, 1907)
could still list eight important communities when he travelled through southern
France. According to his account, these communities clearly enjoyed economic
well-being and social stability.

From the thirteenth century a number of French kings began to expel the Jews
or to restrict their freedom of movement. They sought to achieve the latter objective
by agreement with local rulers, who were to return to their original masters any
Jews who fled. These developments reached their peak in the major expulsion of
1306. In 1315 Jews were called back, as they had been after earlier expulsions, but
only a few returned. The dreadful persecutions of the early fourteenth century,
which culminated in the massacres of 1348, brought the period of great creativity
of mediaeval French Jewry to an end.

In Italy, Benjamin of Tudela passed through thirteen Jewish communities (*ibid.*),
the most important of which was Rome. Presumably, there were many more communities in Italy. Between 1290 and 1293 the Jewish communities in the Kingdom
of Naples were almost entirely destroyed and with them the ancient Jewish centre
in southern Italy, which had been the cradle of Ashkenazi culture. A preaching
campaign by Dominican monks, expulsions and acts of slaughter caused many
Jews to surrender their faith. In 1294 tax remissions were granted to 1,300 heads of
Jewish families that had converted. This was one of the largest group conversions
recorded in Jewish history (see pages 408–9 on the Jews in Visigoth Spain and pages
568–70 on Spanish Jewry in the fifteenth century). It indicates that the number of
Jews in southern Italy alone must have amounted to at least 10,000.

The persecutions in southern Italy corresponded with others of a similar nature
that were carried out at about the same time in France and England. The rulers of
Naples during that period were of the French house of Anjou. When they issued
their first expulsion order in southern Italy in 1288, they issued a similar order in the
area under their rule in France. Thus, between 1288 and 1294, the ancient Jewish
community of southern Italy, along with its *yeshivot* and traditions, was reduced to
dust; the Jews of England were expelled *en bloc;* and imminent expulsion threatened
French Jewry. These developments constituted a co-ordinated effort to eliminate
Jews from most kingdoms of Western Europe, particularly those that were undergoing centralization and unification. Papal Rome remained a relatively quiet retreat
for Jews, having maintained the old traditions with respect to the treatment of
Jews. This state of affairs had an effect on several principalities and kingdoms near
the papal state.

In the Byzantine area, on the islands south of Europe and on the continent itself,
Benjamin of Tudela found over twenty communities (*c.* 1165). He reported of
Constantinople: 'There are no Jews among them in the city, for they transferred
them beyond an arm of the sea . . . where there are about two thousand Rabbanite
Jews. And there are about five hundred Karaites to one side, with a division between
them' (*ibid.*, p. 16). There were also several more communities that Benjamin did
not visit. In 1204 the Byzantine Empire was conquered in the course of the Fourth

Crusade. Hence Benjamin's description portrays the situation of the Jews under the rule of Byzantium prior to its dismemberment.

Under the rule of the crusaders and particularly in Erez Yisrael, Benjamin found only a few Jewish communities, with small populations. On the other hand, he saw and, even more so, heard about vast Jewish communities in Iraq and beyond. He was told of their congregations and holy places. From his account it seems that Egypt also had a substantial Jewish community. In general, it appears from his descriptions – which in this respect have found greater confirmation than the account of the traveller R. Pethahiah of Regensburg – that the Islamic territories contained more Jewish settlements and a larger number of Jews than were to be found elsewhere.

Journeys to the Holy Land

The movement of Jews towards the Holy Land increased in the thirteenth century, particularly from the Western lands. As early as 1141, R. Judah Halevi (see pages 531–2) had left Spain for Erez Yisrael. This move was an expression of his conviction concerning the sanctity and centrality of the land for the Jewish people – a doctrine that was to influence many subsequent generations. In 1211, 300 rabbis proceeded to Erez Yisrael from England and France, and additional groups followed. In 1267, R. Moses ben Nahman (Nahmanides [see page 532]) went to the Holy Land. Jews used to take an oath together and establish partnerships with the aim of settling and making a living together there. This was not a mass movement; however, considering the distances and difficulties involved, it represented a considerable and sustained group effort, whose spiritual impact was felt well beyond its own dimensions.

Spain

Moslem Spain and the Christian monarchies of the Iberian Peninsula are barely treated in Benjamin's account because Spain was his starting point as well as his point of return; hence he devoted little attention to it. However, there is ample information about the decisive changes in Jewish places of residence during this period. Two political and religious movements caused the centre of gravity of Jewish life and population in this region to shift from Moslem territories to Christian kingdoms. The process began with a movement of Jews from the Moslem principalities in the south to the Christian lands of the north. This movement was due to the Reconquista, the regaining of the Iberian Peninsula by the Christians from the Moslems, which was conducted on a considerable scale during the twelfth century. In response the Moslem Almohades ('Proclaimers of the Unity of Allah') invaded Spain from North Africa to defend the purity of Islam and Moslem dominion. They meted out harsh treatment to the Jews of Africa and subsequently to those of the Iberian lands, where the Moslem invasion, together with the Reconquista, resulted in serious transformation and damage due to war.

Various circumstances, which will be discussed below, had led to the full participation of Spanish Jews in the economic and cultural activities of the kingdoms in which

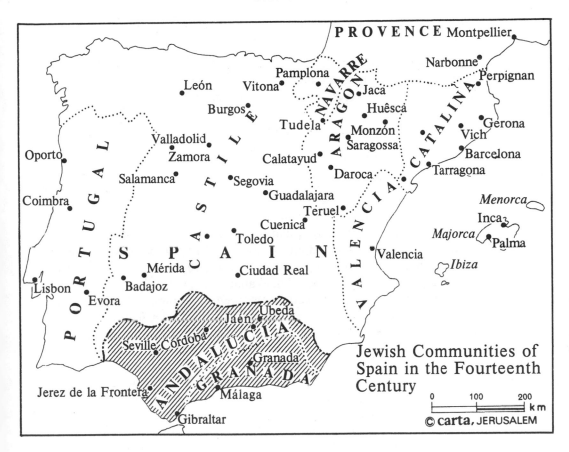

Jewish Communities of Spain in the Fourteenth Century

© carta, JERUSALEM

they lived (see page 468). Their participation in the Reconquista at the close of the eleventh century and during the twelfth century stemmed from the decline of Moslem power and the collapse of the Moslem kingdoms. From the middle of the twelfth century, as has been noted, an additional factor came into play – the religious ardour of the Almohades, who drove the Jews northwards. According to the account of R. Abraham ibn Daud, a contemporary chronicler, the Jews fled from the Almohades *en masse* and under difficult conditions. Some Jews turned to the Christians 'and sold themselves to help them flee from the lands of Ishmael, while others fled naked and barefoot'. It was under these conditions that the figure of the courtier Judah ibn Ezra the *nasi* emerged. A member of a family that had for many generations held high office in the Moslem kingdoms, he now transferred his allegiance to the Christian king of Castile, who put him in command of a frontier fortress. Judah turned his fortress into

a city of refuge for the exiles . . . and in his home and at his table the children of the exile found rest. He fed the starving and gave the thirsty to drink and clothed the naked and provided beasts for all who stumbled [*i.e.,* he gave the weak horses to ride in order to proceed northwards] until they reached the city of Toledo,

467

because of the awe and honour in which Edom [the Christians] held him (Cohen, *op. cit.*, p. 71).

Few of the Jews of the Moslem lands fled southwards, but those who did included the aristocratic family of Maimonides. The mainstream turned to the north. But sooner or later, with the success of the Reconquista, Christian rule also reached those who did not flee.

Jewish Participation in the Reconquista Colonization

The Jews were granted shops, gardens and fields in and around the cities conquered by the Christians from the Moslems. The Christian kings regarded the Jewish notables, familiar as they were with Moslem culture, as an important political and cultural factor; therefore the Jewish population was an exceedingly desirable element in the resettlement of the conquered cities, which had largely been abandoned by their Moslem inhabitants. The kings correctly assumed that the Jewish masses would be faithful to them, and they willingly allocated extensive quarters for their use. These quarters were usually in locations that were favourable for commerce and easy to defend. Indeed, some quarters were well fortified; the Jewish quarter of Tudela, for example, was virtually a separate, fortified city. In 1170, in a document enumerating the rights granted to the Jews of Tudela, the king promised that he would see to the repair of the walls of their quarter; but they in return were required to defend it against his enemies. They were also authorized to defend themselves there against their own enemies. If their assailants were slain in the course of such defence, the Jews would be exempt from all punishment. This charter indicates that at that time the king regarded the Jewish quarter as his own stronghold within the city. Until the end of the thirteenth century, the Tudela community used to lease the fortified market of the city, with its goldsmith and shoemaker shops. In another city, the Jews received from the king, after his conquest in 1266, a total of ninety-nine houses for themselves. The orders of chivalry and the monastic orders of Spain pursued the same policy of securing Jewish participation in the resettlement that accompanied the Reconquista.

Jewish Commerce in the Indian Ocean

In the Moslem Orient the Jews remained an integral part of the economic life of the city. Documents found in the Fostat *Genizah* reveal that large-scale Jewish trade in the Indian Ocean continued in the twelfth century, as is implied in the Responsa of Maimonides, which date from that period. These merchants used to come to the ports of Egypt, South Arabia and India, while Yemen served as their central transit station. Some of them established a metal-utensils 'industry' there. So far scholars have found recorded in these documents seventy-four commodities that Jewish merchants brought from the east in their ships and 103 commodities that they took back with them from the west. This fact clearly explains the ties between Egypt and Yemen, which have been revealed in Maimonides' 'Epistle to Yemen' (see page 535).

Jewish Economic Activity in Christian Spain

Lists of taxes paid by the Jewish communities in Christian Spain show that Jews engaged in the entire range of urban occupations there too. In the Christian kingdoms Jewish physicians, translators and those experienced in administration, particularly the handling of monetary affairs, played an important role. Thus members of aristocratic and educated Jewish families that had fled from Moslem Spain came to occupy leading positions in the royal courts as administrators of royal finances, physicians, advisers, and as translators of Greco-Arab philosophy and philosophic literature into the languages of the Western world.

The Livelihoods of Jews in the Byzantine Empire

In the Byzantine Empire Jews earned a living in a variety of ways. At Crissa, Benjamin of Tudela found 'only about two hundred Jews, sowing and harvesting in their plots and on their soil', *i.e.,* a Jewish village. At Thebes he found 'about two thousand Jews, who are the best at making garments of silk and purple in the land of the Greeks' (*Itinerarium, op. cit.,* p. 12). Elsewhere he found Jews 'engaged in making silk'. Echoes of the social tension among those engaged in different economic activities can be heard in Benjamin's account of the Constantinople community,

> among whom there are craftsmen in silk and many merchants and many wealthy men. . . . They dwell in a burdensome exile. And most of the enmity comes about because of the tanners who make leather and fling their filthy water into the streets at the entrance to their homes, polluting the street of the Jews. And therefore the Greeks hate the Jews, *whether good or bad,* and make their yoke heavy upon them and beat them in the streets (*ibid.,* pp. 16–17).

This information certainly did not reach him from the tanners; it was how wealthy Jews explained to themselves and to others the animosity of the Greeks towards the Jews. It resulted from the filthy habits of those who followed such a despicable craft, and because of them all Jews, good and bad, suffered. In this context 'good' meant the silk-maker or physician, and 'bad' meant the miserable tanner, blamed as the cause of this animosity.

Jews engaged in the same range of crafts in the crusader countries. Benjamin mentioned dyers and silk-makers. The emperor Frederick II brought Jews to Sicily in order to introduce plants and crafts that the country had not known before. These Jews came from the Balkans, as well as from the island of Jerba off the coast of North Africa.

The Transition to Money-Lending in Ashkenaz

After the First Crusade a decisive economic change occurred in the lives of the Jews dwelling in the north-western and central European countries. The range of their livelihoods gradually narrowed, until on the whole they were dependent on one branch alone. This phenomenon, itself a result of social and political conditions that were affecting the Jews unfavourably, had grave consequences in the social sphere and in the realm of their security. The declining safety of the Jews once society at large had become accustomed to seeing their blood shed with impunity, the worsening attitude of Christian society as a result of the steady increase in incitement and animosity from the twelfth century onwards, the rise of cities and general developments with respect to money and credit all combined with the ecclesiastic prohibition of interest to transform Jewish life and to produce its singular and damaging economic and social character.

Little ready money was available for the economic needs of Western and Central Europe. A large quantity of precious metals had been withdrawn from circulation and immobilized in the form of regalia for the courts and the nobility and of church and monastic utensils. From the time of the Crusades onwards, the Italian cities had been developing their commercial relations with Moslem countries and the lands beyond that supplied spices – a trade that grew steadily. This process not only extruded the Jewish merchants from their intermediary function in the international trade of the Mediterranean area, but, owing to its scale and the prospects of vast profits, it also attracted most of the ready money available in Christian society. In these commercial transactions one could also invest money in partnerships or in purchases made in advance, which made it possible formally to evade the prohibition of interest. The clearing of forests and the development of the textile industry in northern Europe, together with the wool trade of the Cistercian monks, depleted the limited local cash reserves. What remained in the hands of Christian capitalists was loaned out, subject to the payment of various forms of legal or illegal interest, in order to finance the large-scale political and military activities of the expanding and developing kingdoms. In effect, channels of investment had been found for the available capital in Christian hands that were more remunerative than loans to the needy, as well as being religiously and legally acceptable.

The Jews in north-western Europe and Italy were increasingly excluded from the expanding commercial activity. They no longer enjoyed the security conditions required for long journeys. Jews and rulers alike sought legal and political formulae that would secure a modicum of safety for Jews (see pages 478 ff.). Meanwhile, the merchants and the Christian cities in which they lived and traded were organizing themselves on the basis of social ties reinforced by Christian oaths of mutual loyalty – the municipal *conjuratio*. The mediaeval city and its guild of merchants or craftsmen were Christian associations; indeed, the merchants' guild was sometimes called *ecclesia mercatorum*. The nature of these social cells and of their objectives would have made admission of an infidel a subversion of their very foundations. In those days cities and guilds used to demand a monopoly on economic activity, each according to its own area of specialization. This Christian character and monopolistic trend of the flourishing city life, together with the physical insecurity of the Jews, served to eliminate them from commerce and the crafts.

The Jews still had ready money available from their former engagement in extensive international trade. Now they could no longer invest in commerce; but one field of credit had not been provided for, namely, consumer loans. A monastery that required money for construction costs that had risen above original expectations; a knight or a priest who had become involved in protracted litigation; a family, one of whose members had become ill; a captured knight, for whom ransom was needed; a priest or monk who needed cash to cover expenditure that he did not wish to report to his superiors or that the latter were not prepared to cover; a small craftsman or shopkeeper who needed money for business purchases; a peasant with a bad harvest – these were some of the parties who began to turn increasingly to the Jews. A cross-section of those who had recourse to the Jews in the twelfth century can be found in the list of debtors and their debts recorded by Aaron of Lincoln in England (see page 473).

At this time the Church began intensifying its campaign against usury and usurers. Its stand particularly affected those who advanced loans to consumers. The Jews considered themselves to be outside the ecclesiastical sphere of competence and did not accept the Church's moral authority; according to the Torah, they held interest loans to be prohibited only to their Jewish brethren. In due course, however, their moral and social sense led them to regard interest as benefiting all who required it.

The combination of these circumstances caused the granting of loans on interest gradually to become the main Jewish occupation in the cities of England, France, Germany and northern Italy, as well as in Bohemia and Poland, when Jews first settled there. This state of affairs commenced as early as the twelfth century in England and France, but not before the thirteenth century in Germany.

The Character of Jewish Interest Loans

This source of livelihood was profitable. Like any rare commodity, money was expensive, and therefore the interest rate was high. An interest of 33% or more was customary, and sometimes the rate was considerably higher. Furthermore, the very nature of a consumer loan made it difficult for the borrower to repay both the principal and the interest. Thus the interest usually accumulated and was added to the principal, with the debtor required to pay compound interest. On rare occasions loans were granted on a bond or verbal promise alone – on credit – but, as a rule, a pledge was required. If the borrower were in serious need, the lender could assess the value of the pledge according to his own judgement. As a rule it was specified that after a certain period of time – usually one year, one month and one day – the lender would be entitled to sell the pledge. Sometimes the borrower would see his pledge sold before his eyes after he had paid part of the interest and then ceased paying, and he had no recourse. Their money-lending transactions gave the Jews additional sources of livelihood: trade in second-hand objects, which were in great demand among those who were not well to do, and the use and repair of pledged objects.

The Jew stood apart from Christian society. He did not always know the person bringing the pledge; nor was he especially interested in knowing him, particularly if the latter agreed to let him have the pledge at the lowest possible valuation. Hence a Christian thief or murderer might find a convenient 'hiding place' for his spoils by giving them as a pledge for a loan. The law in Christian countries provided that if a stolen object were found in any man's possession, the claim that he had purchased it or given a loan on it would not obviate his duty to return the article to its legal owner without compensation. He was obliged to seek out the thief and collect from him. Under this law Jews would not have been able to lend money on pledges, as there could be no security in the pledge itself. Therefore, they requested and received, in the charters granted to them, express authorization from kings and other authorities to the effect that pledged objects found in the hands of a Jew, even if stolen, would remain in his possession, provided he swore that he had given the loan in good faith and had received the article without knowing that it had been stolen. His good faith in the transaction would protect him against the duty of returning the object, unless the original owner paid him the amount of the loan.

Jew-haters declared that this right gave Jews the privilege of partnership with thieves. Even an outstanding jurist such as Pope Innocent III could write at the beginning of the thirteenth century that 'the doors of the Jews are open to thieves until the hour of midnight.' Furthermore, with the value of coinage in those days dependent upon the quantity of precious metal it contained, Jews were frequently charged with 'clipping coins', *i.e.,* scraping the outer edges of coins and removing a thin layer of silver or gold, which the innocent Christian borrower would not notice. As we shall see these incidental phenomena of money-lending reinforced the negative image of the Jew and added to the characteristics of a cruel oppressor who exploited the weakness, innocence and kind-heartedness of his Christian neighbours.

The vital importance of consumer credit, of which Jews were the chief suppliers in and around the mediaeval Christian city, became apparent particularly when they were persecuted or expelled. Many European cities pillaged and expelled Jews for exploiting the citizens with their interest charges and then themselves invited the Jews back after a few years because the townfolk could not manage without the loans. The fact is that when a few Christian money-lenders remained in such cities without Jewish competition, they treated the borrowers far more harshly.

Jewish money-lending was important for the Christian kingdoms. It was easy to impose high taxes on the money that accumulated in Jewish hands, and sometimes the kings simply confiscated part or all of the Jews' property. Occasionally the rulers would share Jewish capital with their non-Jewish subjects by proclaiming a remission of the debts owed to Jews. Pope Innocent III wrote in one of his letters that 'certain princes . . . who are ashamed to take usury themselves, admit Jews to their cities and villages, where the latter become their agents for collecting the usury.' One may almost refer to Jewish money-lenders as 'officials' of the Christian rulers, for whom they engaged in money-lending, while in return the rulers abused them for doing so. Eventually, it became proverbial that the Jewish money-lenders were like sponges: they were 'immersed' as it were in Christian money, and when they had absorbed enough the rulers would squeeze out the money into their own coffers.

The English Monarchy and Jewish Money-Lending

In those days, England was the best-administered territory in Western Europe, and both public opinion and the views of the nobility played a considerable role there during the thirteenth century. The economic function of the Jews and the perils it entailed can be seen with particular clarity in this country.

From the destructive riots of 1190, the king of England learnt that when Jews were slain their *starrs,* or documents recording loans, were either pillaged or burnt. As the king regarded himself as the legal heir of 'his Jews', it followed that he had lost his own money, *i.e., the* debts owed to the murdered Jews. There were some who claimed that the Jews, who could read and write, sometimes falsified the *starrs* to their own advantage. In order to eliminate such possibilities, the kings of England established *archae-*'coffers' in central cities of the realm and placed them under the special guardianship of two trustworthy Christians and two trustworthy Jews. Thereafter every record of a debt to a Jew was written in two exact copies, known as chirographs. The Jews were required by oath to hand over to these *archae* one copy of each document, which was placed in the sealed coffer. The guardians alone were authorized to remove the copy, on the express instruction of the lender or by order of the king or his representative. Thus the king of England was able to supervise, for purposes of both taxation and confiscation, all loans granted by the Jews; at the same time the Christian borrower was safeguarded against forgery, and in the event of riots and massacres the royal treasury would not suffer loss. The officers of the exchequer could collect the debts of the murdered Jews on the basis of the chirographs in the coffers. Incidentally, this procedure offered a degree of indirect protection to the Jews, as the borrowers knew that murder would not enable them to escape payment of their debts. In the thirteenth century there were twenty-seven such *archae* in England. They were situated in all the important Jewish centres, primarily in London but also in York, Oxford, Lincoln, Leicester and Winchester.

The trend towards supervision of Jewish financial transactions and documents developed also in France, where centralized government was gradually emerging in the first half of the thirteenth century. As early as 1206 King Philip Augustus, with the approval of leading princes, 'owners of the Jews', appointed special officials to record documents of indebtedness and place a seal on them. Special fines were threatened against those who gave incorrect information about the amounts or the conditions of the loans. The same royal order fixed the rate of interest that Jews might charge in France, and they were prohibited from accepting as pledges blood-stained or wet objects and church vessels and property (which were prohibited also by Jewish *takkanot*). Later royal ordinances, issued from 1223 onwards, indicated a desire to abolish Jewish usury as far as possible.

The Jews engaged in extensive monetary transactions in these realms, and their methods were highly developed. They frequently established widespread partnerships in order to collect the capital for financing loans. Wealthy Jews also used to employ agents in distant places, usually kinsmen. The size of the loans granted by the wealthier lenders can be judged from the transactions of Aaron of Lincoln. In the second half of the twelfth century, he granted loans in twenty-five English counties, in seventeen of which he had his own agents. Nine monasteries received loans for building purposes, and money was lent also to build two cathedrals. When he died in 1185, 430 persons throughout England owed him a sum total of £15,000, which was equal to three-quarters of the annual revenue of the English exchequer. The Jews had extensive financial connexions in France too. In the thirteenth century their enemies claimed that large parts of Paris 'belonged' to Jewish money-lenders.

Church Opposition to Jewish Money-Lending

From about 1230 onwards, on the initiative of ecclesiastic circles, efforts were directed at terminating all Jewish transactions involving the payment of interest. Raymond de Peñaforte, the Spanish Dominican scholastic and legal authority, declared that Jews should be prohibited from taking interest and that it was their duty to return what they had already taken. This attitude became popular among Christian scholars and influenced rulers and legislators. Indeed, from 1230 onwards French laws concerning the Jews reflect a desire to abolish Jewish usury.

In 1239 a decree of Prince Archambaud de Bourbon expressed the religious and economic outlook:

> By the will and with the consent . . . of the King of France, for the salvation of my soul and the souls of my predecessors, I hereby resolve and require that all Jews who wish to dwell in my land henceforward shall make their livings from permissible activities and commercial transactions, refraining completely from the extortion of usury.

The prince's concern for his own salvation and that of his departed ancestors finds expression also in other laws of the period. In 1253, Louis IX of France sent orders from his crusader camp in the Holy Land to expel from his country all Jews, save those engaged in manual labour. There were no positive results from these orders, which only produced financial extortion, social oppression and bodily injury.

In 1261 the prince of Brabant, wishing to secure his soul's salvation, gave instructions in his will to expel from his land all Jews and all Christian money-lenders (known as *cahorsini*), except those who would give up usury and turn to commerce. His widow, who inherited the principality, asked the opinion of the leading Christian scholars of the day regarding this matter. Thomas Aquinas, in his reply of March 1274, based himself on the assumption that the Jews were destined to eternal servitude on account of their transgressions, whence derived the authority to exact taxes from their property:

> It is true, as the laws declare, that in consequence of their sin [of rejecting and crucifying Jesus] Jews were destined to perpetual servitude, so that sovereigns of states may treat Jewish goods as their own property; save for the sole proviso that they do not deprive them of all that is necessary to sustain life.

However, those who benefited from Jewish property were profiting from usury. Therefore, 'they would do better to compel the Jews to work for their living, as is done in parts of Italy [presumably, he was referring to the situation in southern Italy and Sicily (see pages 567–8)], rather than to allow them to live in idleness and grow rich from usury' (A.P. D'Entréves, *Aquinas, Selected Political Writings*, Oxford, 1952, pp. 85f.).

About a year after the deliverance of this theologically based decision, King Edward I of England took steps to put it into practice. In 1275 he published a 'Law regarding Jewry' (*Statutum de Judeismo*), which categorically prohibited the practice of usury on the part of Jews. Henceforth no debts bearing interest were to be collected.

On the other hand, the law expressly permitted the Jews to be merchants and craftsmen. Furthermore, for a period of fifteen years from the promulgation of the law they were allowed to lease lands for a period not exceeding ten years for purposes of cultivation. All these arrangements were made, as suggested by theologians, for the salvation of the ruler and for the benefit of Christianity; there was no intention of bettering the Jews or their lot. Even after the enactment of this law Jews were permitted to reside only in those cities that had possessed, before 1275, *archae* for preserving records of debts that incurred interest. At the same time the requirement of wearing the 'badge of infamy' (see page 485) was made stricter.

For the Jews of England the result of the new measures was a worsening of their situation in all respects. The rulers appear to have recognized this, for before the decision to expel the Jews in 1290, a proposal was made to permit them to practice usury again, subject to various restrictions, the most important of which was the stipulation that interest might not accumulate more than three years. Expulsion brought the matter to a close, without the proposal ever having reached the lawbooks.

The aim of prohibiting Jews from engaging in usury continued to occupy the thoughts of legislators. King Alfonso xi of Castile apparently was influenced by the English example of 1275, and in 1348 he decreed that Jews and Moslems in his kingdom were forbidden to loan money on interest. He also prohibited them from collecting their debts. On the other hand, he permitted each Jew and Moslem to purchase land for himself for appreciable sums. To be sure, he distinguished between the southern part of his realm and the north, where they were permitted to purchase less. Neither Jews nor Christians desired this law, and in 1351 the Cortes or Parliament of Castile demanded its abolition.

As long as the political, economic and social organization of Christian society was based exclusively on Christian cohesiveness, there was no hope of abolishing Jewish usury without completely undermining the existence of the Jews. The intention behind the laws was the same everywhere, but their effects varied from country to country and from decade to decade, in accordance with the circumstances of the Jews. In England the laws were enacted at a time when the situation of the Jews was steadily growing worse; while in France, despite the difficulties of their position, the Jews had not yet reached such a desperate state. Altogether different was the situation decades later in Castile, where usury was not the main livelihood of the Jews.

Other Jewish Occupations

Although money-lending was a livelihood for most of the Jews within the boundaries of Ashkenaz, there were still some who earned their living in other ways, even in England. In France, and particularly in the German or Holy Roman Empire, we hear, as late as the thirteenth to fifteenth centuries, of Jews who traded in wool and transported it via the Rhine River. Jewish merchants purchased various goods in the Rhine district and sold them in Hungary. During the twelfth and thirteenth centuries, we hear of merchants – 'travellers to Russia' – who, with their caravans and freight, reached the heart of the Slavic east. However, only a minority was involved in such activities.

In the south-eastern part of the Holy Roman Empire, as early as the beginning of the fourteenth century, Jews were engaged as middlemen in the trade between villages and towns. They peddled urban products in the villages and brought village produce to the urban markets. Indeed, they increasingly invested their capital in transactions of this kind, as will be related in greater detail below.

31

Changes in the Legal Status and the Security of the Jews

The Situation After 1096

During the period under consideration, established trends continued to exert influence, sometimes in different combinations and with the addition of new social and economic elements or constellations. The majority of the Jews in Western Europe north of the Pyrenees were, as we have seen, compelled to engage in money-lending. This function made them considerably important in the eyes of rulers, who required ready money; but, at the same time, it often brought down upon them the fury of the population, which saw that it could molest and even murder Jews with impunity. The cities in which Jews dwelt claimed and received an enhanced political and legal status. Under the influence of the religious and social ferment endemic to the cities in the twelfth to fourteenth centuries, the townsfolk emerged as an actively hostile element to the Jews.

In the course of the struggle between Church and empire in Western Europe, which began with Pope Gregory VII, the Church exhibited revolutionary tendencies accompanied by a style of popular preaching that spoke directly to the masses – on occasion against the rulers. This struggle and the methods employed, which were initiated by the leadership of the Church and aimed to enhance its status, were implemented mainly by monks and the lower strata of the clergy. The ecclesiastic authorities held firm to the principle that the Jews must be allowed to exist, but in humiliation; even a pope such as Innocent III was liable to introduce a vulgar anti-Jewish vein in his letters against the Jews. The Fourth Lateran Council, which he headed, suggested that the Christian masses should be activated against Jewish money-lending without regard to the civil authorities.

The emperor remained the 'protector of the Jews' after 1096 as well. Henry IV expressed his opinion of the riots and forced conversion to Christianity with utmost clarity when – in fundamental opposition to the Christian doctrine of the time – he permitted forced Jewish converts of 1096 to disregard their baptism and return to Judaism, for which he was rebuked by the pope. Yet the rulers also were influenced by the teachings of the Church, particularly after a decline in the economic utility of the Jews, as we have seen with respect to Jewish money-lending. Towards the beginning of the fourteenth century, a new danger was added as rebellious peasant bands began to include the Jews as one of their targets.

'Jewish Servitude'

After the handful of charters and the earlier protective measures had proved almost useless – as had been demonstrated in 1096 – the rulers began to seek new methods for protecting the Jews. In 1103 an attempt was made to include them in the 'Peace of the Land of Mainz'. This provision for 'territorial peace' originated in Christian concepts of 'the Truce of God' in the Christian lands, which were being torn apart by knightly and feudal wars. It aimed at protecting those members of Christian society who did not bear arms and did not engage in fighting. The attempt to include the Jews did not survive long in the empire, for the very concept of 'territorial peace', being Christian by definition, seems to have militated against the inclusion of the Jews.

Charters were again granted to the Jews. From this period onwards they reflect ecclesiastic pressure aimed at humiliating the Jews as much as possible and excluding them from activities such as money-lending, which, from the Church's viewpoint, ran counter to their proper position among Christians. Particularly strong was the objection to the participation of Jews in any profession that would secure them a respected status among the Christians or authority over them. Henceforth incitement of the mob was increasingly employed as a method of applying pressure. It should be borne in mind that the highest 'secular' rulers largely belonged, by education, way of thinking and religious and social complexion, to the cultural *milieu* of the masses. In those days the new money-lending function of the Jews played an increasing part in the charters granted them.

The charters and the conditions under which they were formulated reflect the gradual emergence of a new concept, one that was found also in papal letters and in the attempts to incite the masses – namely, the concept of Jewish servitude. This concept combines a theoretical basis for humiliating the Jews, while increasing their subjection to the will of the authorities. At the same time it assured the Jews greater governmental protection, deriving from both the interests of the rulers in protecting these 'serfs' who contributed so much to the treasury, as well as from concern for their own status and prestige within their countries.

The first formulation of this attitude occurred in Christian Spain, where as early as 1176 the laws of the city of Teruel expressly specified that 'the Jews are the serfs of the king and the absolute property of the royal treasury.' The conditions of the Reconquista period were favourable to the Jews and thus restricted possible negative repercussions from this servitude. Though even in the kingdoms of the Iberian Peninsula various practical conclusions were drawn from this concept, they were less extreme and harsh than they were to become when the Reconquista drew to an end.

In France Jewish serfdom was handled in an interesting fashion; it was one of the aspects of the country's political divisions in the early thirteenth century and its gradual unification. Documents from French lands show the rulers of the various principalities and duchies each referring to 'my Jew' and requiring that the latter be returned should he flee elsewhere. Between 1198 and 1231 the king and princes 'owning Jews' promised one another on eighteen separate occasions to return their respective Jews. William of Brittany, a legal expert and publicist who lived from 1217 to 1294, declared that the ruler is entitled to take from the Jews whatever they have, 'if he so desires . . . as being the belongings of slaves'. A royal order of 1230 that was countersigned by 'Jew-owning' princes and dukes stated: 'Nobody whosoever may keep the Jew of another Lord; and wheresoever a man shall find his Jew, he shall be entitled to seize him by right, as being his slave and property.'

In Germany, too, it was resolved in the second half of the twelfth century that 'the Jews belong specifically to the Imperial Chamber.' Emperor Frederick I made use of this concept of ownership by the Imperial Chamber when he specified the principles of his government and its duties vis-à-vis all the subjects. In the Preamble to the Confirmation of Rights of the Jews of Regensburg, dating from 1182, he declared:

> It is the duty of our Imperial Majesty, as well as a requirement of justice and a demand of reason, that we rightly preserve his due to each one of our loyal subjects, not only the adherents of the Christian faith but also those who differ from our faith and live in accordance with the rites of their ancestral traditions. We must make provision for them to maintain their customs and secure peace for their persons and property. For this reason we announce that [we are] deeply concerned for the welfare of all Jews who dwell in our Empire, who are known to belong to the Imperial Chamber by virtue of a special prerogative of our dignity.

Emperor Frederick II related to the concept of 'the serfdom of the Jews' mainly out of his struggle with the pope for the leadership of Christendom. He first coined the description of the Jews as 'the serfs of our Chamber' in Sicily, and from 1236 he extended its use throughout the Holy Roman Empire north of the Alps. He also countered ecclesiastic claims to authority over the Jews by stating in the same year that 'according to the accepted law, the Jews are directly subject to us, both in the Empire and also in our Kingdom.' In 1237 he stated in the Charter to the City of Vienna that it was also on account of the 'unbearable sin' of the Jews that he, as the heir of the Roman emperors, was their lord, 'since Imperial authority imposed everlasting servitude on these Jews from ancient times as punishment for the sin' of crucifying Jesus. Practical conclusions benefiting the rulers were reached by Henry III of England in his *Mandatum Regis* of 1253: 'That no Jew remain in England unless he do the King service; and that from the hour of birth of every Jew, whether male or female, serve Us in some way.'

Since the days of the Church Fathers, the Church had claimed that the true image befitting Israel, which had refused to recognize Jesus and had slain him, was that of Cain, who had murdered his brother. The dispersion of the Jews had brought upon them both fear and lasting serfdom. The comparison of the Jew to Cain was consistently disseminated by preachers. It also formed the ideological groundwork for the rulers in their own definition of Jewish serfdom. However, it was on the basis of this comparison that the Church claimed for itself the right to exercise over-all control of the Jews throughout Christendom. At the same time it was willing to delegate the task of direct supervision of this serfdom to the Christian rulers in their respective territories. Accordingly, Innocent III declared in 1205: 'God is not displeased but rather finds it acceptable that the Jewish Dispersion shall live and serve under Catholic kings and Christian princes.' From its exalted position of spiritual overlordship, the Church considered itself privileged to guide and instruct all believers in their attitude towards the Jews. Occasionally, this guidance was used to protect them. Thus, for example, in 1199 the same pope published a *Constitutio pro Judaeis* ('Constitution for the Jews'). Employing phraseology borrowed from letters by earlier popes dealing with the same subject, the edict, or constitution, of Innocent III provided that the Jews should not be harmed bodily and that the status quo of the Jews should be retained and not be changed either to their advantage or to their disadvantage. This protection was given to them 'in accordance with the clemency that Christian piety imposes . . . following in the footsteps of our predecessors'. In accordance with this piety he commanded in particular that force not be used in order to compel Jews to accept Christianity 'for surely none can be believed to possess the true faith of a Christian who is known to have come to Christian baptism not willingly but by force.'

The pope expressly forbade that Jews be slain or wounded or that their property be damaged and their festivals profaned: 'No man shall disturb them by means of stick or stone. . . . In opposition to the wickedness and avarice of evil men, we decree that no man shall presume to desecrate or reduce the cemeteries of the Jews or, with the object of extorting money, to exhume bodies buried there.' The pope imposed a ban of excommunication on all who contravened the provisions of the constitution. As we shall see, however, there were passages in the letters of Pope Innocent and in the decisions of the council headed by him that were capable of negating the protection afforded by the edict. In any case, the constitution undoubtedly reflected the traditional attitude of and the principles officially adopted by the heads of the Church with regard to the Jews. Thus Jewish serfdom as advocated by the Church included both grave disabilities for the Jews and a measure of protection, which, though carefully defined, was applicable only to certain aspects of life.

In summation it may be said that the ideological basis for Jewish serfdom lay in the general principles that had been adopted by Christianity with respect to Judaism, which were formulated with increasing severity and asperity as the Church achieved increasing control over the thoughts and attitudes of Western Christendom. During the thirteenth century the hostile attitude led to practical demands by the Church and to counter-demands by the monarchs, which derived from the principle of protecting all subjects, regardless of faith, as well as from considerations of material advantages for the rulers and their countries. The combination of factors, together with the tensions between them, led to the crystallization of the 'serfs of the Chamber' formula regarding the Jews. By ensuring the social, legal and personal humiliation of the Jews, the formula offered legal and material advantages to the rulers; but it also advanced the interests of the Jews by providing them with a clearly defined formulation on which they could rely for protection of life, limb and property. Some believe that it was not by chance that this concept was adopted in the 1230s and specifically by Emperor Frederick II, at a time of strong imperial resistance to the growing influence of the Church.

It is reasonable to assume that the views and aspirations of the Jews regarding their security and legal status affected the formulations concerning them, as well as the provisions of the charters issued by the civil authorities and the Church. The Jews had no choice but to acquiesce in whatever fate or status was accorded them. However, since the continuation of their relatively peaceful existence was at stake, they set out to obtain in various ways those provisions held to be desirable; and certain of the charters' formulations may be viewed as an outcome of their representations. (Some of their viewpoints have already been quoted on pages 418–20.) The rulers would graciously accede when they had a personal interest in the economic functions and activities performed by the Jews, which gave the latter a certain bargaining power and a means of exerting some influence. Jews who were in close contact with the royal courts served as *shtadlanim* or intercessors for their people – the diplomats of a social group whose only power lay in its economic function. The Jews also benefited from the immanent aim of government to maintain law and order in its territories, although the rulers often were incapable of achieving this under the conditions prevailing in the Middle Ages and in view of the legal and moral attitudes towards the Jews that had become rooted in the minds of kings, churchmen and Christians in general in the course of the preceding generations. Intercession was relatively productive at times in realms that favoured the Jews; but it also had some influence in times of trouble even within the *milieu* of mediaeval north-western Europe in this period.

The Jews were well aware that the authorities did not fully exploit their serfdom. They were deprived of freedom of movement only in exceptional cases, which were regarded as arbitrary acts of tyranny. Rarely were they deprived of the right to family inheritance. Their serfdom consisted of two main elements: the imposition of special taxes, together with economic exploitation, frequently to the point of pillage; and the protection afforded them by the authorities. From the viewpoint of the general populace, their legal state of serfdom accorded with and substantiated the ecclesiastic and popular view of the degradation and wickedness of the Jews; the Jews, however, grew to appreciate the actual diminution of their state of servitude.

The Libels

During this period a new phenomenon emerged in the relations between Christianity and Judaism – the levelling of false charges. The latter came to overshadow all other aspects of and introduced a new horror into the lives of the Jews. By its very nature this phenomenon constituted a vicious circle: each false charge added to the terrifying image of the Jew, and the worsening of that image lent greater credence to constantly renewed accusations. The charges grew out of the popular religiosity and superstitions of the Christians and were sustained and disseminated by monks and priests. Times of social ferment in the towns and countryside and periods of general cruelty within society as a whole favoured the belief in Jewish cruelty and in the need to act cruelly towards Jews.

There were two main libels, whose effects were to increase the number of Jewish victims and to give free rein to the debased instincts of the populace. These were the *blood libel* and the *libel of desecrating the host*. The blood libel was the older of the two, having been levelled in a slightly different form against the Christians of the second century. In 1144 the Jews of Norwich in England were accused of having murdered a Christian child. From that time on charges of this kind were levelled against Jews all over Europe. The explanation and logic of those who believed the accusation were that, once the Jews had crucified Jesus, they thirsted for pure and innocent blood. Since the formerly incarnate God was now in heaven, the Jews aspired to the blood of the most innocent of the believers, *i.e.*, the children, the tender Christians. As a result of this reasoning, the season of the most blood libels or charges of ritual murder was that of the Passover festival, which was close in time to the Passion of Jesus.

Various elaborations were added in the course of time. In Norwich it was claimed that the Jews had tortured their victim and crucified him. In 1255 the Jews of Lincoln were accused of having crucified a Christian boy and, after having taken him down from the cross, of having removed his intestines, apparently for purposes of witchcraft. In 1286 in Munich it was charged that the Jews, in the words of a Jewish lament, 'slay diverse Christian children, injuring them in all their limbs . . . cruelly drinking their blood'. Jewish acts of sadism and drinking the blood of the corpses were added here to the general horror.

Many Christians believed these libels to be the literal truth. Public proclamations, even from the highest quarters, were of no avail in destroying the belief. In 1235 the Jews of Fulda were charged with ritual murder. Emperor Frederick II resolved to investigate the matter thoroughly. First he called on the heads of the clergy. After failing to receive an unequivocal answer from them as to the truth of the charges, he decided to hold a special convention of Jewish converts to Christianity in order to ask them whether there was any basis for the accusation. Letters sent to various countries inviting respectable converts to the gathering still survive. On this occasion it was declared with the utmost clarity that Jews did not harm Christian children and did not need blood for their rituals. In 1236 the emperor published a special statement announcing the results of his investigation. Pope Innocent IV, the emperor's enemy, also denounced the blood libels as unfounded. But it appears that the overwhelming majority of Christians in the West did not believe the findings of the investigation or the declarations of the emperor and the pope, and the libels continued.

The dangerous potential of the charges hovered over the Jewish community, particularly in the area in which Ashkenazi Jews lived. It found expression at festival times, or joyous or mournful occasions, at times of social disturbances among the Christians and when there was exceptional tension between them and the Jews. Throughout the centuries dealt with here and in those that followed, many Jews were cruelly slain as a result of the libels. Entire communities were wiped out or were compelled to move elsewhere. Even when the Jews were spared destruction and torture, the social and psychological damage remained and left its mark. The result was that within the West European cultural *milieu* of the Middle Ages the Jew came to be viewed as a menacing demon.

This image can be found in *The Canterbury Tales,* written by the great English poet Geoffrey Chaucer, who was born in 1340, fifty years after the expulsion of the Jews from England. Chaucer completed the work in about 1387, almost a century after the Jews had been expelled. The 'Prioress' Tale' tells of an innocent Christian child, the son of a widow, who was walking through the Street of the Jews singing songs in praise of Mary, mother of Jesus. The Jews seized and murdered him. The crime was miraculously revealed, and the whole community of Jews was put to death. The story indicates that the absence of Jews did not affect the outlook of the poet or of the average English pilgrims whom he described. The cultural heritage had survived; what is repeated here is the blood libel of Lincoln, which occurred well over a century earlier.

The desecration of the host libel was levelled against the Jews only after the Fourth Lateran Council had decided in 1215 that according to Christian dogma the bread and wine of the sacrament are literally transubstantiated into the body and blood of Jesus. Christians began to believe in the miraculous power of the host, in its potency as a charm or for magical purposes. The inner logic of the Christian attitude towards the Jews manifested itself. The Jews had always been known to be wicked. They had once slain the incarnated God who came to redeem them, the very Christ now working in the mystery of transubstantiation and the host. What else could one expect but that these wicked people would sin by defiling the host? The first recorded charge of this kind dates from 1243, from a place near Berlin. The charge usually ran as follows: a Jew was supposed to have bribed or persuaded a Christian man or woman to provide him with a piece of the host. This was then taken to the home of the Jew or to the synagogue. There it (*i.e.,* Jesus) was tortured, either by an individual or by the community. It was stabbed and trampled upon. The Jews would run a risk in order to fulfil their desire 'to torture Jesus again'. When a Jew was suspected of such action, he would be subjected to grievous torment. Whether or not he 'confessed', he was usually burnt and his family and community punished. Entire areas of Jewish communities were devastated as a result of this libel. If a map marking the appearance of the libel is examined, most of the places where the charge originated and was levelled are found to lie within the German Empire.

The charge of desecrating the host shows even more clearly than the ritual-murder charge how the Christians viewed the Jews in the Middle Ages. The Jews were held to be fully aware of the fact that the sacramental act of the Christian priest brought about the mystery and miracle of the transubstantiation of Jesus in the bread. Yet, although they knew of this highest mystery of Christianity, not only did they not admit it, but they also did everything possible to strike at God and to profane Christian sanctities.

Jewish Stereotypes in Christian Art

Christian society in this period tended to be influenced emotionally and conceptually by stereotyped images of individuals, peoples and religions. Centuries earlier the Christian Church had begun to rely on painting and sculpture in order to inculcate the principles of its faith; 'the walls of the churches became the popular Scriptures. Subsequently, when the Gothic style developed, the stained-glass windows and the statuary and reliefs on cathedral portals and on the walls began to reflect and preach a world view and morality for Christians. While the Church succeeded in spreading its views by these means, which were highly effective for the illiterate, it suffered a religious and cultural loss by giving material form to abstract ideas and thus reducing the capacity to draw fine distinctions. Spiritual concepts were presented in wood, stone, glass and paint. Everything was done to enable Christians to grasp what was being expressed. One specific colour was always used to display sanctity, another to signify impurity. One side of the church was restricted to figures from the Old Testament, another side to those from the New Testament.

Church painting and sculpture are addressed to the senses and aim to create an impression of realism. Scenes of the Jews torturing Jesus and of the Wise Men giving Judas Iscariot money for his betrayal were painted and carved, frequently showing garments and lineaments that identified the Jews in these scenes with those then living among the Christians. In the course of time, when the diabolic nature of the Jews had pervaded the Christian imagination, stonemasons and painters began giving the demons and wicked angels whom they carved and painted the appearance of contemporary Jews. Later these artistic propaganda methods were supplemented by morality plays. The stage managers were instructed and the actors were encouraged to present the play in such a manner that the wicked Jews of the past would resemble their contemporary Jewish neighbours. The portrayal of the synagogue found a permanent place among the stereotyped images of Christian sculpture and painting. It was portrayed as a woman with blindfolded eyes, the veil sometimes taking the form of a snake or scorpion to indicate wilful blindness. She bore marks of shame and waywardness on her face and in her disarrayed hair and clothes. In her hands she usually had a 'broken reed as a support' and fragments of the tablets of the Law. She was faced by the Christian ecclesia, whose face was lovely with youth and victory and who held the symbols of Christian salvation. In Western Europe this comparison of the synagogue and the ecclesia was found in cathedrals in areas containing a local Jewish community, which is indicative of its propagandist nature. Most of the morality plays produced by the Christian community included a scene showing a debate between the synagogue and the ecclesia, which served the contemporary Christian author as an occasion for castigating the Jews for their sins of the past and their wilful errors of faith in the present.

The visual presentation of Church preachings and the dramatic stereotypes that were generally employed fed the hatred for the Jews and further blackened their image among the Christian population, to such an extent that the Jew almost certainly appeared worse in the view of the public than in the thinking of the Church leaders. The lofty art of the Christian Middle Ages, both the Romanesque and the Gothic, carried within it a venomous animosity towards and misrepresentation of those who believed in the Old Testament.

The Church and the Jews in the Thirteenth Century

During this century the ecclesiastic hierarchy became increasingly aggressive towards the Jews. As has been remarked, the Church's general trend towards domination led it to try to secure control over the Jews of the West. Its words and deeds alike show that it had adopted for itself popular anti-Jewish attitudes. In those days the heads of the Church faced large-scale internal ferment, which found expression in the new mendicant orders of the Franciscans and Dominicans. The Church was fighting the empire. It had engaged in a war of extermination against the Albigensian heresy in the south of France. The general bellicosity and extremism of the Church were also exhibited in its attitude towards the Jews. Pope Innocent III, who both initiated and marked the apogee of Church activity in this century, did not refrain from employing rumours that reached him when writing about the Jews. A rumour about a student who was found slain near the home of a Jew led him to the general statement that Jews secretly kill Christians. We have already quoted him on the connexion between Jews and thieves. He did not hesitate to describe the Jews 'as the popular saying had it, like a mouse in a pocket, like a snake round the loins and like fire in the bosom.' On the other hand, he formulated the 'Constitution for the Jews' referred to above.

Innocent did not forget the Jews at the Fourth Lateran Council, convened by him in 1215, which adopted several resolutions about and against them. The Council ordained that the Jews must wear a mark on a clearly visible part of their garments to distinguish them from Christians. The reason given was mainly to prevent them from mingling with the Christians, which might lead to sexual relations with them. Yet the regulation included an ironic hint that this enactment merely fulfilled the requirements of Moses, who ordered the Jews to wear a mark upon their garments (the fringe, or *zizit*) that would distinguish them from the gentiles.

This regulation marked the appearance in Christian lands of the 'badge of infamy', which Jews were required to wear. Other ordinances instructed the people, under clerical guidance, to combat Jewish usury by various measures laid down in the regulations, to force the Jews to obey the injunctions of the Church with regard to usury and to refrain from conducting business with Jews who did not abide by Church instructions. By these measures Innocent intended to strike simultaneously at the Jews and at the emperor and monarchs who protected them and who profited from the taxes levied on usury. This anti-Jewish measure was in perfect accord with his general purpose to incite the masses against the monarchs and all who did not obey him.

The combined effect of the spiritual tensions in Christianity, the ever-sharper polemics against the Jews and the efforts of the Church to impose its discipline on all Christendom gave rise, on the occasion of denunciations by Nicolas Donin, an apostate from France, to a succession of stormy disputations concerning the Talmud that began in 1240. The first disputation, held in Paris, actually constituted a trial, at which the Jewish sages were permitted only to defend themselves. The purpose of the event was to condemn the Talmud and to seek its eradication. In the same year the pope ordered the Church authorities and the rulers to seize all copies of the Talmud on a certain Sabbath and to hand them over to the Dominicans for examination. The order is known to have been carried out in Paris, the seat of the disputation. Some years later manuscripts of the Talmud were burnt in several other places. In 1240 the Jews were also accused of rejoicing at the approach of the Tartar hordes, as though they marked the coming of the Messiah. In 1241 there were savage riots against the Jews of Frankfurt, who fell in courageous self-defence.

In 1247 the Jews succeeded in obtaining from Pope Innocent IV a declaration stating that the Talmud was an absolute necessity for the Jews, if Judaism were to continue to exist as a separate religion, and that the burnings of the Talmud were to cease. When the heads of the Church spoke up in defence of the Jews, as they did on a number of occasions in the thirteenth century, condemning physical violence on the part of the mob or the rulers, they did so in the spirit of the 'Constitution for the Jews' devised by Innocent III, and they stressed that the Jews were to be protected 'only on account of the humane feelings' of Christianity and not because they had any intrinsic right to protection.

The religious and social tensions were especially obvious in north-western Europe and in the programme of the Church authorities throughout the thirteenth century. The measures adopted against the Talmud helped to reinforce the evil image of the Jews, for the Talmud was declared to be a source not only of heresy but also of blasphemous expressions against Divinity, as well as a fount of nonsense, of contradictions and of immoral social doctrines.

Fifty Years of Horror in Ashkenaz (1298–1348)

During the twelfth and particularly the thirteenth century, seeds of hate were sown by means of mass incitement through the stereotypes that Church art introduced, the various libels and the denunciation of the Talmud. The seeds bore their bitter fruit between 1298 and 1348 in the region of the Ashkenazi communities. False charge followed false charge, massacre followed riot. A charge of desecration of the host in Roettigen in 1298 set the wave of persecution, under the leadership of the Jew-hater Rindfleisch, on its destructive path across the whole of Bavaria and its neighbouring regions. Bands of peasants afterwards assailed the Jews in this region. Social unrest in Christian society thus found an outlet. As early as 1298 R. Asher ben Jehiel (known by the acronym Rosh) feared that the flames of destruction would not leave a single Jew on German soil.

The animosity and persecution reached their peak during the Black Death, in the massacres of 1348–9. This plague descended upon Europe, familiar as it was with epidemics of all kinds, on an absolutely unparallelled scale and with shattering results. In many places more than half of the population perished within a brief period. Rational explanations of the catastrophe were unknown. People were overwhelmed and stupefied by a disaster with which they could not cope. Nowadays it is known with absolute certainty that the plague was spread by rats that had carried it by ship from Asia to Europe. In those days scapegoats were sought. At first suspicion rested on other groups, but finally it settled on the Jews. The general fear was supplemented by the age-old animosity. The Jews were accused of poisoning the wells in order to destroy the whole of Christendom. In Switzerland, Jews were tortured until they produced the demanded confession. News of the guilt of the Jews was broadcast so rapidly that in some places Jews were exterminated even before the plague arrived.

Hatred reached dimensions hitherto unknown. From Christian Spain to Poland,

Jews were slaughtered and burnt; but the worst massacres occurred in the German Empire. Intelligent Christians were prompt to see the injustice involved. In 1348, Pope Clement VI spoke out against 'the infamy that certain Christians have been incited by the Devil to find the cause of the plague, whereby God has smitten the Christian people for their transgression, in acts of poisoning on the part of the Jews'. The pope denied the truth of the charge.

> in the light of the fact that this plague has struck different parts of the world, both amid the Jews themselves and also among other nations where Jews do not dwell at all; and it is raging in accordance with the hidden will of God; and it is absolutely unthinkable that the aforesaid Jews have performed so terrible a deed (Dinur, *op. cit.*, II, 2, pp. 628–9).

The papal statement did not have the slightest effect. The condemnation and slaying of the Jews formed part of a general psychosis; they were the product of fear and the offspring of the many false charges that had been levelled against the diabolic Jews, whose evil image had been deeply etched into the imagination of the masses by various means long before 1348. Some cities then swore not to admit Jews into their walls – 'forever'. In actual practice 'forever' did not last more than a few years. But this fact in no way reduced the overwhelming animosity demonstrated by the decision. The scale of the slaughter can be seen by the fact that among those Jews who returned to the cities were groups whose vast majority were widows and young orphans.

Christian Spain

For most of this period, the situation of the Jews in the kingdoms of Christian Spain was far better than that of the Jews in any other Christian region. Those effects of the Reconquista that had benefited the Jews (see page 468) now combined with the established practice of Jewish participation in economic and cultural life, which was acceptable to many Christians in those times. As a result, Jewish life there differed considerably from its counterpart in Ashkenaz.

In the Kingdom of Aragon, Jews were welcome and even sought after. In 1247 a proclamation was issued by the king assuring his protection for all Jews coming by land or by sea to settle in certain districts of his country. The congregation of Perpignan considered itself 'a desirable vineyard . . . planted by the right hand' of this king. The kings also granted extensive privileges to many communities. Jews were of political importance in the kingdoms, and scholars and members of the liberal professions still played a significant role in Christian society and at the royal courts. State documents were sometimes signed with a Hebrew name and even in Hebrew script.

From 1257, Judah ben Lavi de la Cabaleria occupied a high post in the city of Saragossa. In 1260 he was appointed to an office equal to that of minister of finance for the entire kingdom; and he was not the only Jew to occupy a prominent position in state affairs. From the end of the thirteenth century, however, the influence of Jews began to decline in Aragon, and they no longer occupied such high offices. Even while Jews enjoyed a high standing, religious animosity found expression in decisions of the Cortes, such as that of 1241 against the Jews and their practice of usury. In 1250 there was a ritual-murder charge in Saragossa, although such occurrences were rare in Spain.

In Castile the Jews held a firm position among the higher officials throughout this period. The physicians of the Ibn Waqar family were very close to King Sancho IV and were among those who served as witnesses to his will. Naturally, the positions of these courtiers as well were subject to sharp personal fluctuations. One of the indications of both the relatively firm legal and social status of the Jews and the social tension within the Jewish community was the authorization granted by the government, at the request of the community, to execute informers. This authority was used on a number of occasions, with the approval of the rabbis.

R. Moses ben Naḥman (Ramban or Naḥmanides) and the Barcelona Disputation (1263)

The difference between the position of the Jews in Christian Spain and that of French and German Jewry can be seen by comparing R. Moses ben Naḥman in the Great Disputation at Barcelona in 1263 with R. Jehiel and his companions at Paris in 1240. In France the Jews were defendants against an accusation; but Naḥmanides relates of the disputation in Aragon that when King James I asked him to debate with the convert Pablo Christiani, he answered: 'I shall perform the command of my lord the king if you will grant me permission to speak as I wish.' When the Dominican Raymond de Peñaforte wished to make the condition 'as long as you do not say insults', Naḥmanides replied: 'I am not prepared to be subject to your restriction, but I shall say all I desire in the matter under debate, just as you say all you desire. I intend to speak in a decent manner, but it will be of my own free will.' According to Naḥmanides, 'they gave me permission to speak as I said.' In Paris the Talmud was dismissed as false and evil, while in the Barcelona debate Naḥmanides devoted much time to proving that not all the *aggadic* statements or homiletic remarks of the sages are binding on Jews. For in Spain an attempt was made to use the Talmud and Midrashim to prove the truth of Christianity. It seems that the close contacts between Jews and Christians led to this attempt. As we shall see (pages 558–9), the contents of this major debate show how free Naḥmanides felt himself to be; and indeed he proved an aggressive disputant on this occasion.

The year 1348 brought astonishing developments for the Jews of Christian Spain. Widespread rioting broke out in Aragon, and in some cases the courts actually tortured Jews. The next chapter records the reactions of the communities to this situation. By the close of this period, at about 1348, there was a growth of Christian fanaticism in the two major Christian kingdoms of Spain and a decline in the influence of the Reconquista period that had previously worked to the advantage of the Jews.

Islamic Lands

Throughout this period the earlier conditions continued to prevail in the Islamic countries. But the collapse that followed the Mongol invasion, together with the general decline of and the conflicts between the Moslem kingdoms, had their effect. Maimonides' comments in the twelfth century about the Moslems indicate that within the uppermost circles of Jewish society, particularly those that were closest to the Moslems, the degradations imposed by the rulers were very keenly felt. The persecution by the Almohades in Spain and North Africa and the religious persecutions in Yemen were also to prove significant.

32

Leadership by Local Institutions and Scholars

'The Writ of the King Stands'

In the Diaspora Jewish leadership functioned with the approval of the secular authorities and by reliance upon them. At the same time Jewish leadership always strove to retain internal autonomy for Jewish law and, within its sphere, juridical power over individuals. Dependence as well as jealous autonomy demanded a clearly defined attitude towards the law of the realm and the civil courts and judges of the host country. To arrive at this definition required that Jews take a stand and formulate their own conceptions on kingship and rule. Jewish thought on these subjects reflected contemporary opinions regarding political and social institutions in the host society. In theory, the views of Jewish sages on this matter revolved mainly around the Talmudic saying that 'the law of the realm is law' – its general sense, its limitations and its implications for the law of the host society. There were numerous opinions on this point, which together constitute a considerable body of political theory on kings and kingship. Here let us focus upon one case that exemplifies the political theory of the Jews in the Middle Ages, both as an aspect of the basis for autonomous Jewish leadership and as a facet of the political thought prevalent in Western Europe at the time.

In the mediaeval kingdoms the concepts of centralization and the exclusiveness of one single legal system within principality boundaries were very insecurely based. The concept of the state in modern thought has little relevance to those political entities. Between the sovereign and the individual living in his territory stood various corporative relationships, such as those of the guilds of craftsmen or merchants for their members, the city or the community for their citizens and the university for its professors and students. Specific legal statutes were defined by charter or by custom for the member of every corporation, or for members of other similar entities. These intended to mark the antiquity, true or imagined, of the institutions and of the political and legal concepts and systems by which they lived. In the Middle Ages the antiquity of a system of law and order was regarded as a mark of its intrinsic superiority and as justification for its applicability.

Ancient law was considered *ipso facto* good law, and, as such, was fully acceptable. Custom played an important role as an accepted fount of proper order and authority in social and political life. If a custom could be proved to be *mos majorum,* of the ancients, its value increased accordingly. There were set limits for the ruler, his actions and authority, drawn on the lines of customs and practices of earlier days. The struggle of kingship against these time-honoured limitations, the attempts at innovation and the disputes with various corporations marked the gradual transition of the political and legal systems from mediaeval modes to those of the early modern period.

There were two aspects to the issue of 'the law of the realm' as it concerned Jewry. One involved the competence and authority of Jewish *halakhah* when it clashed with the law of the land; the other involved clarification of the nature of kingship and its legal authority. A comprehensive and original consideration of these problems was formulated by rabbis in Provence towards the end of the period under consideration here. On the basis of Talmudic opinions, one of them declared:

> From this it can be seen that in respect of matters prohibited under the heading of robbery – if the king of the land wills to decree the very opposite, then the legal prohibition of robbery and violence is removed, and we are entitled to act as we desire, the barrier being removed (A. Sofer, ed., *Responsa of the Sages of Provence*, Jerusalem, 1967, para. 174, p. 419).

A prohibition of this kind ceased to be binding on the community if the sovereign had abolished it. The granting in principle of such a prerogative to the ruler, modern as it is in a certain respect, was restricted in two ways. There was a sphere of action that lay within the competence of the ruler and another sphere that did not. The laws of the land were valid for Jews only in respect of 'what the king is required to do . . . in matters between him and the people, but it may be that in matters between one individual and another not one of our laws is to be abrogated in favour of the law of the realm.' Thus a clear distinction was made between the public sphere, pertaining to the king on the basis of his sovereignty over his subjects, and the sphere of private law, which 'may be' a sphere not included in the royal prerogative. It thus remains the affair of the Jewish community and an area within which the community is required to act in accordance with its own law. The community's law is binding on its members and is not the affair of the king.

The second restriction derived from the merits of ancient, 'good' law, as against the legislator's wish to introduce innovations, 'for the saying that the law of the realm prevails does not apply to matters which do not come from its good laws' (*ibid.*, p. 420). The law of the realm is valid only in respect to its own affairs, within the orbit of its existing system of laws. With regard to the king's protection of merchants and trade – a category that included Jews, on account of their involvement in business affairs – this Provencal rabbi is prepared to recognize legal innovations for the better ordering of commerce and to give them preference over Jewish law. For

> business affairs in which there is innovation afresh every day can justly be said to depend on the conditions under which they are negotiated, and in such instances novelty plays its part. Thus it may possibly be said that what the king has set as the law of the realm will be accepted by all people in the country as an absolutely determining condition in all their affairs and negotiations. It is a condition relating

to monetary matters, where a condition accepted is binding, even if it is opposed to what is written in the Torah (*ibid., p.* 421).

Trade and commerce are dynamic, changing activities, and their methods are based on agreement. Without some generally accepted innovatory power, it would be impossible to introduce order into this world of change and of free will. The sage was therefore of the opinion, admittedly with hesitance, that Jewish merchants are entitled to follow the law of the realm rather than the Torah. The *halakhic* concept of an 'economic stipulation', which is valid for those who have agreed to use it in their transactions, also made it possible to view the laws of the realm as a similar condition accepted by those engaged in monetary affairs.

In the stable and systematic legal area of testimony, this rabbi demanded a kind of immunity for the laws of Israel by virtue of the Torah and by the right of antiquity as an element in law. On this basis the law of the realm would not be binding on Jews with respect to the laws of evidence. For the gentiles' law of evidence is not only a very ancient one but is specific to their nature, and Israel at the time of receiving the Torah was explicitly removed from subordination to this law in favour of the law of God. Thus the rabbi stated:

And we the offspring of Abraham have been set apart from them and been hallowed . . . and since this is part of their ancient laws and behaviour, far be it from us to act on them and call this the law of the realm. But [the legal system and law of evidence of the Christians] is the law of the sons of Noah [only] (*ibid.*).

The criteria applied by this scholar show that he was familiar with the legal theory of the contemporary gentile society. By means of distinctions, some of which were based upon the *halakhah* and others which employed legal, social and economic concepts of the period, he utilized both the concepts of Judaism and those of the merchant community, as well as economic and legal innovations and the concept of antiquity. He appears to have divided the latter into two: the antiquity of the just laws that are binding on the king, which nullifies his innovations; and the primal antiquity of 'the law of the sons of Noah'. The latter does not apply to Israel because, by the acceptance of the Torah, we 'have been set apart from them and have been hallowed' thereby. As a result, he was in a position to be flexible towards the law of the realm, accepting the requirements of the legal and social realities around him and, at the same time, preserving whatever he considered sacred in the laws of Israel.

The second sage who participated in this discussion was of the opinion that the Talmudic *amora* Samuel accepted the authority of the civil law through lack of choice under the economic and social conditions of life in exile.

This concept [that the law of the realm is binding] took root only out of inevitable necessity because we are subjected to them. We have no alternative in matters pertaining to the state, such as monetary litigation, but to behave according to the rules set by the ruler of the realm, who determines its norms, of necessity, whoever he may be. This holds true as long as they do not contradict any of the commandments of the Torah proper, even though they may run counter to certain sayings of the scribes, and as long as they concern only financial matters. And they [the scribes or sages] proclaimed [the very 'dicta of the Scribes' that is abrogated by agreement, out of the need to obey the law of the realm] and they also confirmed [that 'the law of the realm is binding'] (*ibid.*, p. 427).

This scholar regarded the area of activity 'pertaining to the state' as being by its very nature determined by 'the ruler of the realm, who establishes its norms . . . whoever he may be'. This piquant definition of the legislator applies equally to those who established the 'good' ancient law and to every ruler who introduces new legislation. Since living in exile 'we are subjected to them', there is no escape from this necessity. But Jewry may submit to this political and economic situation only insofar as 'the 'dicta of the Scribes' permit it. Together with this full submission in an area that by its very nature belongs entirely to the sovereign legislator of the realm, there was a firm insistence not to give way even by one iota with respect to the Torah itself. 'You should know that we do not accept their witnesses, judges, or assessors on the basis that the law of the realm is law.'

In the midst of this tension, the following distinction was made. What the first scholar regarded as a removal from one legal sphere to another is presented by the second as an outright rejection of a situation against which, politically speaking, nothing would avail. The first scholar removed the matter of legal evidence from the sphere of competence of the law of the land, while the second scholar used this removal as proof of the fact that Jewish submission to the ruler of the state is limited by the words of the Torah. The second scholar considered that the authority of sovereign law derives from the area under the ruler's sway, as everybody who comes within it, even if not a permanent settler, is required to obey his laws (unless the king has expressly exempted the foreigner). Therefore, 'if the king has established a law, it is valid throughout his land even for those who are not from there, and certainly it is the law of the realm' (*ibid.*, p. 428).

The discussion among the Provençal scholars is a segment of the range of opinion that developed in the Jewish communities of Western Christian countries in the Middle Ages regarding the nature of secular sovereignty and law. In Provence, the contact between the Jews and the surrounding culture was closer than it was in the areas to the north and to the east, but the attempt to define those areas governed by *halakhah* and those under the jurisdiction of the secular authorities established a dialectic tension even here. The tension assumes many forms and touches upon several distinctions. We find differentiations made between the antiquity and the 'goodness' of the several laws; there is a distinction between the authority of the monarch and that of the corporation. Above all, for Jews, there is that claim for their exemption from the law of the realm on the basis of the specificity differentiating their entity from the gentile one. Within Torah law itself there is the gradation between the 'words of the Torah' proper and the enactments of the scribes. The practical aim of all the debaters was to maintain the independent law of Israel as far as was possible under gentile rule and at the same time to enable Jews to live peacefully under the authority of their legitimate rulers.

The New Yeshiva

The process of change in the *yeshivot,* which began in the tenth and eleventh centuries, and the struggle over the character of the scholar (see the criticism of R. Samuel Hanagid on the character of the sages in his times on page 456) reached their peak with the fundamental transformation that came about in the nature of the *yeshiva* virtually throughout the entire Diaspora. The type of *yeshiva* that existed in Babylonia and Erez Yisrael, based on an aristocratic hierarchy of intellectual families whose profession was the study of Torah and whose leadership derived from the sanctity of their study, was no longer to be found and apparently had never taken root anywhere in Europe. From the twelfth century onwards, the *yeshivot* of Spain and Germany no longer exhibited the exclusivism and claims characteristic of the *yeshivot* in Babylonia and Erez Yisrael. It is true that every country had its aristocratic scholarly families; but their status never approached that enjoyed by such families in Babylonia and Erez Yisrael. Towards the end of the twelfth century, a keen struggle was waged between the rising and the declining leaderships.

The Theory of the Yeshiva *Leadership*

In this conflict R. Samuel ben Eli represented the views of the older leadership. His opinion is expressed in direct debate with the representatives of the new leadership and in his glorification of those who represented the older institutions. In a letter – a kind of pastoral epistle – sent by the *gaon* to 'Our dear, select and choice brethren of the holy congregations throughout the Land of Syria, the princes of each Congregation and their learned sages and the other Congregations, great and humble' (S. Assaf, ed., 'Letters of R. Samuel ben Eli and His Contemporaries', *Tarbiz,* 1, [1930], 63), he declared:

It is known unto them, may they be blessed, that the place of the *yeshiva* is the Throne of the Torah which is like the Throne of Moses our Master, may he rest in peace in each and every era. And indeed the word '*yeshiva*' [which means 'seat'] is derived from the verse 'and Moses took his seat to judge the people,' and that is the place which is appointed for the study of the Torah and its Talmud and for passing on the *halakhah* from age to age from the time of Moses our Master. . . . For by its means are preserved the laws of Israel and their faith is strengthened in order that they may not err or veer from the truth. . . . Indeed the *yeshiva* is the seat of Moses our Master, and therein is the faith of Israel kept intact. And whoever opposes the *yeshiva* opposes the Lord of the Torah whose throne the *yeshiva* is; and he also is opposed to Moses our Master, may he rest in peace, whose seat it is (*ibid.,* pp. 64–5).

The etymology to which the institution's name is attributed is indicative of the continuous and absolute sacredness claimed for it by the head of the institution. The *yeshiva*'s self-image as the guardian of orthodoxy and the view that opposition to the *yeshiva* constituted opposition to God, the Torah and Moses reflect the sense of inner strength still possessed by the Babylonian *yeshivot* in the twelfth century.

Furthermore, in this same letter, the *gaon* proceeded, in the great name of the *yeshiva,* to question the authority of the exilarch. He told his readers,

> You know how the Lord was wroth with Israel when they sought themselves a king in the days of Samuel . . . and as for the king, indeed they chose him because they needed someone who would go forth before them into battle and war. Now in the days of the exile they have neither king, nor war, nor any of those things which make a king necessary; and they have no need save of one who shall guide them, instruct them, teach them the commandments of their faith, judge their cases and decide the *halakhah* (*ibid., pp.* 65–6).

Here is a clear presentation of the claim that in the Diaspora the *yeshiva* and its head are the only authority by which the Jewish people is to be guided.

This latter-day *gaon* insisted on the observance of ceremony. In a letter that he sent in advance of his son-in-law, who was travelling as his emissary, he instructed the communities as to how they were to receive this religious dignitary:

> When they hear of his impending arrival let them go forth to meet him . . . and let him enter with honour surrounded by many people. And when he comes to the synagogue, let them call out before him while he sits majestically in a seat of splendour with fine drapes as befits the fathers of the Courts, and with a pillow behind him. And he has a signet ring with him wherewith to seal (*ibid.,* p. 62).

The *gaon* warned the members of the communities that 'he will impose the ban on all who are impudent to him . . . for his word is our word . . . and his honour our honour. And he who is blessed by him is blessed by us. And whosoever he excommunicates is excommunicated [as though] from the gate of the *yeshiva*' (*ibid.*). The sanctified authority and the ceremonial meticulousness, the power to ban or bless and the formality of the signet-ring bearing the seal of the Head of the *Yeshiva* were all basic components of the *yeshiva* leadership.

The Sages' Demand for Authority

The demand for authority by the new spiritual leaders can be fully discerned in the words of Rabbenu Moses ben Maimon (1135–1204), known as Rambam or Maimonides. When exiled from Spain to Egypt, he discovered that the new system that had developed in Europe differed distinctly from the old, which still remained dominant in the East. In express opposition to the reverence in which the *yeshivot* were held and with contempt for their very methods and aspiration, Maimonides called for a leadership by more spiritual figures. He rejected the past while offering new patterns for the future. Several passages in his commentaries (on the Mishnah) insist on an absolute prohibition of payment of any kind for studying and teaching Torah. He censured the *yeshivot* because their members were earning a livelihood from 'quotas' exacted from the people. In a letter to a pupil of his he implies that the aristocratic and institutional traits of the gaonate must corrupt the character of the office holders, and he employed homiletic exegesis to discredit the demand of *yeshiva* scholars for financial support. As many *tannaim* and *amoraim* of the Talmudic era were craftsmen and lived in poverty, it is impossible to suppose that, had they requested financial support from their contemporaries, they would not have received it. Thus it follows, claimed Maimonides, that they never demanded such support, because they regarded it as a transgression.

Maimonides also rejected the assumption of the *yeshivot* that the Talmudic education they provided was the one and only method for achieving true scholarship in Israel. He stressed that the Talmudic sages themselves spoke slightingly of 'the modes of argument of Abbaye and Rava'. In marked contrast to opposition to the *yeshivot,* Maimonides respected the office of the exilarchate both in theory and in practice, publicly according it full honour.

It is by no means certain that Maimonides himself occupied the office of *nagid* in Egypt. Many scholars believe that he did, and the office was undoubtedly held by his descendants. In any case, he was the acknowledged leader of his people. His signature is the first to appear on a writ of ordinances for the Jews of Egypt; and his 'Epistle to Yemen' shows that the Yemenite Jews, who maintained close commercial ties with Egyptian Jewry (see page 468), regarded him as the leader and comforter to whom they turned in times of distress. Questions were addressed to him from various places in the Diaspora, as though he were a *gaon;* and towards the end of his life queries came from as far away as southern France, so widely were his writings disseminated. Some honorifics applied to him date, to be sure, from the days and social climate of the *geonim*; yet the main terms of praise are personal, lauding his talents, activities and renown.

Social Tension in the Sephardi Communities

There were a number of institutions in Spain that aimed at centralized leadership and a number of social forces that aspired to it. The monarchy in Castile recognized the office of the 'rabbi' (*el rab*) or, as he was sometimes called, 'the court rabbi' (*rab de la corte*). As a rule, he came from one of the leading Jewish families. When in addition to holding his official position, he was an outstanding Torah scholar and of high character, the Jewish community also recognized him as 'the head of the Spanish exile', as in the case of R. Don Todros Halevi Abulafia. In Aragon the Alconstantini family used to supply a *nasi* and judge for the whole kingdom. However, owing to internal disputes the king abrogated this family prerogative in 1232, under the influence of Naḥmanides. Several communities united in a *collecta* for purposes of taxation. The attempts to set up a central leadership for the entire kingdom will be discussed below.

Despite the tendency towards centralization, the development of Jewish life in the Christian kingdoms of Spain gradually led Jewish affairs to be maintained and conducted largely by the local communities themselves, subject to the guidance of the leading sages of the town. The wide differences in the social and economic levels of the Jewish town dwellers in Spain and the emergence of a class of Jewish courtiers led to tension and to numerous transformations in the structure as well as in the objectives and policies of the communities. The struggle had many facets, all of which derived from the central conflict between the aspirations of the aristocratic families, which usually belonged to the courtier circles, and the efforts of the middle class and the poor to achieve leadership and to establish the policies they desired, which usually were those advocated by the spiritual circles that tended toward mysticism.

The Taxation Conflict

An issue that, in view of the social situation, was bound to become a focal point in this conflict was the principle whereby taxes should be assessed. The Jewish community, as a corporative body, received from the royal authorities the duty and right of levying from the Jews the taxes owed to the realm, as well as any additional taxes to meet communal requirements. The authorities imposed taxes on whatever basis they found convenient – usually on a *per capita* basis or on the basis of a general valuation of property, but sometimes the imposition of taxes was purely arbitrary. The Jewish leaders would always attempt to persuade the authorities to reduce the total amount. Once the amount had been fixed, the government was not concerned with the methods used in assessing individuals or in distributing the tax. On occasion, if called upon, the authorities would help the community to collect the tax, but the methods of imposition and collection were left to the community itself.

In Spain a major source of tension was created when those in royal or ministerial favour attempted to gain personal or family charters in order to evade their share of the tax burden. Jewish leaders fought firmly and bitterly against this practice on the part of individuals with ample financial resources.

A second dispute arose over the principles of assessment, with the differences of opinion corresponding to the economic and social stratification of the Jews. The lower levels as a rule supported the method of declaration, whereby a man gave an oath regarding his taxable property. These declarations were, to be sure, checked, and instances of punishment for false reporting have been recorded; but the checking itself was not a problem as the poorer elements were sure they could obtain a fair assessment by this means because of the awe in which oath-taking was held. On the other hand, they were not sure of the objectivity of the communal leaders, who in most places and at most times belonged to the wealthy and powerful elements, in spite of the struggle to obtain representation for other classes. The upper circles favoured the method of assessment of the property of each man by a valuation committee to determine how much he should pay. Another point of conflict within the communities concerned the composition of such a committee. Members of the lower classes demanded that representatives of the middle and lower classes be included among the assessors.

A third dispute revolved around the question whether to impose taxes on the basis of wealth or on a *per capita* basis. This debate was particularly widespread when a tax was imposed for security purposes or to avert an impending evil.

The fiscal and social conflicts were complicated by the new spiritual outlook that reached these communities from the commencement of the thirteenth century (see chapter 33 on the conflict over the works of Maimonides). As was to be expected, the constitutional struggles within the communal institutions were intertwined with the fiscal conflicts.

Communal Institutions in Spain

In Castile the local communities were led by 'elders' (*mukdamin*) and rabbinical judges. In this country, as has been pointed out, there was a central institution consisting of the office of *el rab*. Intercommunal meetings were held during the fourteenth century in Castile and they gradually became the focus of leadership. In Aragon many and varied titles were employed, the most common being 'trustees' (*ne'emanim*) and *mukdamin,* whose use clearly shows the influence of the Christian patterns. In this kingdom there was relatively little centralized authority.

The Jewish electoral systems in the various communities and kingdoms depended in each period on the degree of influence of the different social strata. In some places the approval of the entire Jewish population was necessary before the community could take action. On the other hand, there were places where it was expressly provided that only members of the few aristocratic families were authorized to sign ordinances (*takkanot*). Between these two extremes were numerous variations. In important communities, such as Barcelona and Saragossa, social struggles are clearly indicated by the frequent changes in the complexion and structure of the institutions and by the submission of their disputes to the royal authorities for decisions regarding the election of the representative bodies.

In this period the Jewish sages, basing themselves on the Talmudic principle of emergency legislation, permitted themselves to pass judgement and to impose fines and punishments for which there was no authority in the Mishnah and Talmud. Already in the twelfth century, Maimonides had testified that in Moslem Spain it had been the practice to hand over informers to the secular authorities for execution. This practice continued in Christian Spain during the thirteenth and fourteenth centuries. The rabbis used to pass death sentences on informers. Women who engaged in sexual transgressions were sentenced to punishment by amputation. The communities, on their appeal to the government, received permission to sentence informers to death. Even the Ashkenazi rabbi Asher ben Jehiel imposed capital punishment in Spain in the fourteenth century.

The close ties with Christian society and the ample economic resources available to certain Jews created the need for various sumptuary regulations prohibiting excessive display in clothing and jewellery. Care was taken to establish institutions that would supervise social and moral behavior and assure adherence to the dictates of the *halakhah* and the concepts of Jewish morality. Naturally, the interpretation and application of these concepts depended on the views of the leading circles. In the thirteenth century a 'moral reform' movement with an anti-rationalist tinge emerged in the Spanish communities. Its leaders, who included Rabbenu Jonah of Gerona, preached penitence and particularly stressed the need for constant supervision of the individual by the community. They demanded that the body elected for the purpose of moral supervision over the behaviour of the individual (*berurei averot*) be broadened and strengthened.

The personal authority of recognized scholars was decisive in certain matters. For the most part they belonged to the old aristocratic families, even if they themselves were not courtiers. In fact, the struggle against the rule of these families was led by the scions of these families. One of the heads of the anti-rationalist circle, whose complaint to the king led to the abolition of the leadership of the Alconstantini family in Aragon, was Naḥmanides. He himself belonged to an aristocratic family and was linked by education and activity to court circles. The same applies to the other main leaders of the 'moral reform' movement. Particularly noticeable was the family of R. Asher ben Jehiel, which had come from Germany. He and his sons after him helped to reshape the communal leadership, the *halakhah* and the theoretical and moral outlook of Spanish Jewry, largely by the impact of personality and knowledge of the Torah.

The Council of Aragon Communities of 1354

The political theory of the Jewish communal leaders in Aragon at the end of the period under consideration here was clearly expressed in the resolutions of the Council of Aragon of 1354. The fact that the resolutions were never actually implemented reflects the state of tension and disunity within local Jewish society, but it does not diminish their importance as a plan agreed upon by the responsible leaders at a time of acute external danger, as well as internal tension that had been mounting during the past few generations. The resolutions of the Council bear the imprint of the methods used by Jewish *shtadlanim* and reveal their familiarity with the political situation and the ideology of the Christian royal court and of the papal court at Avignon.

Six years after the riots of 1348, the Jewish leaders of Aragon declared at the Council: 'We have seen the helplessness of the communities . . . in obtaining their specific needs . . . if one does not help the other.' Nevertheless, the resolutions indicate that those who attended the meeting feared that those who had stayed away would appeal to the government authorities and oppose the establishment of a central leadership, for sharp measures were proposed against anyone who might attempt such action.

The Council chose 'selectmen' (*nivrarim*) for the purposes of interceding 'in all matters affecting the communities in the Kingdom . . . two for the communities of Catalonia and two for the communities of Aragon and one for the communities of Valencia and one for the communities in the Island of Majorca if they should approve'. These representatives had to prepare the budget and distribute the burden among the communities. The financial report was to be presented by the 'selectmen . . . each to his own kingdom; by which we mean, those who are in Catalonia to Catalonia', etc. It was hoped that once their plan had been realized and 'when all the communities become one body and we all have one purse', the leaders of the Jews would be in a position to obtain better protection for them from the host society, while at the same time establishing good order within the Jewish community.

The persecutions that the Jews had undergone six years earlier were attributed to the incessant Christian effort to compel Jews to abandon their faith: 'With their lies and incontinence they have brought false charges, in order that [Jewry] should indeed abandon the well of living water.' Those who had withstood authorized torture were considered to have shown 'the strength . . . to stand in the hall of trial';

while those who had broken down and converted were accused of being 'weak-hearted and soft by nature'.

The leaders maintained that internal communal order could be achieved only when permission was obtained from the king 'to eradicate thorns from the vineyard . . . and to remove . . . denunciators and informers'. This passage obviously referred to the execution of informers. The communities were prepared to pay for this permission. Those assembled also wished for 'a charter from our Lord the King' that would permit the collection of money from the communities to meet the needs of the central organization and another charter against those who might try to overthrow the central leadership. It seems that these internal arrangements were recorded here because they were concerned with protection against the outer world. There was, however, a further set of resolutions that regulated the internal life of the community, for the communities were required 'to behave according to all those practices and regulations to which the delegates of the communities had agreed and which they had written down in a book signed by them, or according to all that the selectmen would agree'. Unfortunately, this 'signed book' has not survived.

The Jewish leaders in Aragon had two diplomatic addresses to which they turned: the royal court of their country and the papal court in Avignon, which were closely connected. In having recourse to the king, they were relying on the continuity of royal protection, 'for since olden times he and his fathers, his ancestors and forbears, have been gracious monarchs in whose shadow we have lived amid the gentiles'. They made the king their emissary, as it were, to the pope; while at the same time they would send delegations of their own directly to the papal court. The leaders were well aware that the general mood there was favourable to the Jews (see the statement of Pope Clement VI on page 487). They complained of the fanatical Christian mob, which, as experience had only recently taught, 'when there be plague, when there be famine will shout . . . saying, all this is by reason of the sin of Jacob, let us exterminate them.' The Jews requested that the pope reprove the Christian people, who should learn, when 'one of the judgements' of the Lord comes down on mankind, to be more firm in their observance of the Christian faith, 'in which it is a principle to guard us like the apple of their eye, for we dwell here, relying on their fidelity'. The resolutions show that the *shtadlanim* were well aware of Christian institutions and legal concepts. The Council appealed to the pope to 'inscribe a law and judgement in his edicts which are called Decretals' that would make it impossible to blame the Jewish community as a whole in the event of one of its members harming a Christian. It asked also that the oppressive and harmful acts that Christians customarily engaged in against Jews during their festivals should cease.

The most daring and fundamental request to the pope was 'that he should explain that the general inquisition into heresy should not be applied to the Jews', except in the case of a Jew who rejected 'what is held equally by all faiths'.

But in respect of the difference between the religions – even if a Jew supports a Christian who is a heretic in his own faith – the stigma of heresy should not spread to the Jew. *For it is impossible to classify as heresy on the part of the Jew what he holds to be justified according to his own faith* [author's italics].

In effect, the leaders were asking that Jewish opposition to the principles of Christianity or to Christian religious rites not be defined as heresy, since for the Jew this opposition constituted orthodoxy. Even if he supported a Christian heretic, he himself should not be tried and punished as a heretic. The king could punish a Jew who abetted Christian heresy, but the matter should not be the concern of the ecclesiastical Inquisition.

This request constituted a demand for Jewish religious autonomy in the fullest sense of the word, with a clear declaration of basic opposition to Christianity. The demand also reveals the fear that the trials of the Inquisition caused in those days. The Jewish definition of what fell within the sphere of competence of the Inquisition and what did not largely corresponded to the definitions of the inquisitors themselves. The Council resolved to take action to ensure that those who provoked attacks against Jews would be punished, 'since violent gentiles cannot be chastised by words alone, and vengeance is therefore important'. It also requested that laws be passed for the protection of Jews by the Cortes and that Jews be released from various financial and administrative exactions and injustices (I. F. Baer, *Die Juden im christlichen Spanien,* I, Berlin, 1929, para. 253, pp. 350–8).

The Council programme, which was never implemented, was based on the leaders' awareness of the precarious status of the Jews and was intended to strengthen their position through the application of some Christian concepts drawn from the institutions of the monarchy and the contemporary Church, while at the same time protecting Jewish autonomy in religion and internal affairs.

The Leadership in Ashkenaz

The political theories of Ashkenazi Jewry after the massacres of the First Crusade in 1096 have already been described (see pages 418–20). They served as a guide for Jewish relations with the Church and the secular authorities during this entire period. From the twelfth to the fourteenth centuries the communities of Ashkenaz underwent extensive institutional and conceptual development. The local community gained a more definite character, both externally and internally. Various provisions and ordinances were instituted to create within the walls of the city its own legal authority and to foster the idea of an exclusive right on the part of the community members to live in their place of residence. Both these matters constituted innovations. As we shall see, there were conflicting tendencies regarding the right of settlement – one municipal, the other Jewish. These developments were in response to the autonomy granted to the Jewish community by the Christian rulers.

It is possible that the formulae in the charters that permitted the Jews 'to live according to their law' derived from a Christian reworking of the formulae used by the hellenistic rulers, who granted autonomy to the Jews in their cities, allowing them 'to live in accordance with the laws of their forefathers'. Christians were capable of recognizing the unique character of Jewish law in these communities, but, in accordance with their own view that the Christians were 'the true Israel', they refused to acknowledge Jewish law as the ancient 'laws of the forefathers' of Israel. Accordingly, just as Jewish autonomy in the hellenistic world was one among the many autonomous *polytheumai* of the system, so in the mediaeval city, whether it was under the rule of a bishop or, later, an independent conjuration of the citizens, Jewish autonomy fell within the framework of the corporations, which were permitted to stand between the individual and the sovereign in the Middle Ages.

Unanimity or Majority Rule

Between the twelfth and thirteenth centuries two contradictory opinions emerged regarding the method of adopting a decision that would be binding on all members of the community. We have seen (page 431) that R. Isaac Alfasi in the eleventh century spoke of a majority decision as the obvious method. At the end of the eleventh century, however, Rashi specified that regulations must be adopted unanimously in order to be considered fair and binding (see page 435). His grandson R. Jacob ben Meir Tam still insisted on such unanimity in the twelfth century. Compulsion could be used against an individual only if he himself had originally participated in the unanimous decision and later rejected what he had formerly agreed to as a member of the community. On the other hand, various regulations of the twelfth century, which were attributed to the much earlier Rabbenu Gershom, stipulated the alternative basis for validating a regulation.

One of these provided that, 'if members of a community are establishing an ordinance to help the poor or for any other purpose, and the majority of those worthy to decide have agreed to it, the others may not abolish the ordinance' (L. Finkelstein, *Jewish Self-Government in the Middle Ages,* New York, 1924, p. 121). Thus the majority was entitled to impose its view on a minority that opposed it. Furthermore, the wording of the passage indicated that both the majority and the minority included only the 'worthy' members of the community. It seems reasonable to assume that in the twelfth century the 'worthy' man was one who possessed a sound knowledge of the Torah, an established economic position and a reputation as an honourable man, all of which were reflected in his participation in the burden of taxes and the giving of charity.

The differentiation between the 'worthy' (*meliores*) and the 'unworthy' was to be found also in the Christian cities that were taking shape in that period. In Church institutions men were speaking of the authority of 'the better [*sanior*] part or the greater [*major*] part'. In other words, in both the Jewish and non-Jewish society in those days, an attempt was being made to give a qualitative meaning to the acceptance of the opinion of a numerical majority as overriding. Both in town and community, this tendency merged together with the aims of the patrician class or upper social stratum. Thus it should be remembered that the majority mentioned by Alfasi in the eleventh century and the majority referred to in the twelfth-century regulations of Ashkenaz was a majority of the 'worthy' people, *i.e.,* the narrow social group that conducted the community's affairs. Similarly, the biblical injunction 'after many to wrest' (Exodus 23:2) was applied only in court decisions based on the majority opinion of the expert scholar-judges, who passed judgement sitting as a rabbinical court.

It was in the Jewish community-city of the Middle Ages that Jewish legal and political thought for the first time adopted the principle of basing decisions on a numerical majority of those domiciled within the walls of the city and bearing responsibility for the maintenance of Jewish life in that place. In the thirteenth century the Ashkenazi scholar R. Eliezer ben Joel Halevi, known as Rabiah, decided in favour of majority decision, either of the members of the community or of the leaders. In theory, these two principles – unanimous agreement and majority rule – continued to clash with one another in the mediaeval Jewish community. In actual practice, however, majority rule seems to have been the method adopted.

The Institutions of the Ashkenazi Community

The thirteenth century witnessed the emergence of well-defined institutions in the local Ashkenazi communities. In a document from the community of Cologne, dating from 1301, 'the leaders and the Warden [*parnass*] and all the community of the Jews' speak together. Responsa of the same period also refer to 'the Guardian' (*epitropos*) of the community.

R. Meir ben Barukh (1220–93), known as Maharam, who lived in Rothenburg, provided much information on the life, institutions and practices of the Jewish community. A case was brought before him involving a dispute in a community whose members 'are unable to agree on the choice of leaders by unanimous agreement'. R. Meir decided that if it were impossible to reach unanimous agreement 'let them follow the majority.' In the course of presenting this *halakhic* decision, he described the structure and functions of communal institutions. A community has 'to choose its leaders . . . to choose cantors . . . to provide a charitable fund . . . to appoint the *gabbayim* ['officials'] to build a synagogue . . . to purchase a house for weddings, to purchase a house for craftsmen and to provide for all the needs of the congregation' (M. Bloch, ed., *Responsa of Maharam,* Berlin, 1891, para. 865, p. 320). From this decision we learn that communal office-holders were chosen by election but that R. Meir still regarded majority decision only as a last resort.

In the communities of Ashkenaz during the thirteenth century the force of the *herem* or excommunication (see page 428) was supplemented by punishment meted out by the gentile authorities. The large Jewish communities on the Rhine ruled at their synod that if a man resisted the ban for forty days and did not take steps to have it lifted, his property would be handed over to the rulers. In general, those times left to later generations patterns for the local community that crystallized in the trials of actual situations, as well as through theoretical *halakhic* deliberations. These patterns increased the hold of the community over the individual. The central leadership was marked by both the activity of Talmudic scholars and rabbis, who were sometimes appointed by the authorities, and by a lay leadership, which in the Rhine region and in France met at assemblies during fairs and markets and obtained written approval for its decisions.

Distribution of the Tax Burden

The conflict that we saw in Spain over 'declaration' versus 'decision' as the method of assessing taxes existed also in Ashkenaz, but to a lesser extent. In Ashkenaz we

hear of the ideal modified by reality in respect of taxes. R. Simḥah of Speyer, a sage and
ḥasid of the thirteenth century, related:

> I have heard that my uncle Rabbenu Kalonymus of saintly and blessed memory
> was in close touch with the royal palace and gained access to the court. When
> the king demanded a tax from the Jews, he would help them reach a fair com-
> promise, and after that would request the king to deduct a third or a quarter as
> his own share. For he used to tell the king: I serve you with loans and many
> other matters. I wish you to release me from the tax; yet it is my duty to pay
> together with them. Although the king would agree to deduct his share from the
> tax, he would afterwards pay it together with the Congregation (Solomon Luria on
> Tractate *Bava Kama,* Jerusalem, 1887, para. 460, p. 74).

Here was a *shtadlan* who negotiated with the king and exploited his personal services
to the king in order to aid the entire community. First he dealt with the practical
aspect of reaching a 'fair compromise', which meant a considerable reduction of the
total tax demanded; then he attended to the moral aspect of voluntarily contributing
his share.

In order to facilitate tax-collection in the thirteenth century, a 'tax-ban' was
proclaimed. In the regulations of the Speyer, Worms and Mainz Assembly (*Va'ad
'Shum'*), held in 1220, it was decided that 'he who takes an oath before the congregation that he has only so much money and is afterwards found to have more . . . will
be inadmissible as a witness and his oath will not be accepted.' In the Friedburg
community, during the same century, economic measures were adopted against those
making false statements. It is related of a member of this community that when 'they
found he had transgressed the regulation and possessed more then he had declared,
the congregation took the additional sum away from him'. Furthermore, it appears
that the confiscated amount was shared among the other members of the community, for 'one of the rich men said: I give you my share, which is more than
sixteen marks' (Bloch, *op. cit.,* para. 127, p. 205). It is not known whether all communities adopted stringent measures, but it is clear that as a rule they endeavoured
to ensure a fair distribution of the tax burden among all members. *Takkanot* attributed to Rabbenu Gershom provide that an appeal against the tax imposed
could be lodged before the court only after the amount assessed by the community
had been paid.

The Competence of the Local Rabbinical Courts

The increasing urbanization of the Jewish communities and the difficulty of communication between them led to the introduction of the ban or *herem* of the rabbinical
court. The Talmud had assumed the existence of a central supreme court exercising
authority over all members of the nation, wherever they might dwell. In mediaeval
Ashkenaz, however, there was no such body, nor do we know of the existence there
of such an institution in earlier times. Great scholars and sages exercised some of the
functions of a high court on various occasions, but no court or *yeshiva* ever achieved
permanent status as the supreme authority of the region. Contemporary trends in

the Christian cities led each community to set up a court of its own, whose judges lived in the community. In any case, the insecurity that followed the First Crusade constituted a serious obstacle to the establishment of a supreme court, as it was dangerous for Jews to travel between cities.

From this combination of factors, each community came to regard itself as an independent region with respect to judicial authority; and whoever came to the community fell within its judicial competence. Regulations provide that 'if a man passes through a community where there is an ordinance of competence for the local court and he is summoned to court in accordance with the ordinance . . . he is subject to the ban [*herem*] until he comes and pleads in court' (Finkelstein, *op. cit.,* pp. 118–19). R. Samson of Sens, a French scholar of the twelfth century, declared that it made no difference whether the person 'passing through there' was the plaintiff or the defendant, 'and he cannot say, let us go to the higher court' (Alexander Süslein Cohen, *Sefer Ha'agudah,* Cracow, 1571, 51 B).

A transformation had occurred in the legal and organizational concepts of Jewry. The centrality of the Jewish courts in Ashkenaz was entirely nullified by ordinances and decisions of this kind, and the autonomy of the local community was institutionalized in the field of law as well. One centralizing factor still remained, but it depended entirely on the personal prestige of an outstanding scholar to whom communities would turn with particularly difficult problems. This recourse sometimes bore the character of an appeal against the local court. However, as such authority stemmed from reputation rather than from any official appointment, it was unstable and could hardly serve as the foundation for a central authority.

The Right of Settlement

The urbanization of the communities also found expression in the ordinance on 'Right of Settlement' in the community. In addition to enforcing its own laws, the mediaeval European city constantly endeavoured to impose its sovereignty over the entire area within its walls. It insisted that no one was entitled to settle there without the permission of the municipal authorities. As a rule, the city prevented strangers from settling unless they made a special payment or brought some special benefit to the city. The regulations varied from place to place, and the demands of a city with a predominantly merchant leadership differed from those of a city managed by craftsmen; but the basic principle was identical in all cases, and it was reflected in the provisions introduced by the Jewish communities within the cities.

We find a classic example of the existing attitude in the Responsum sent from the heads of the Rome community in answer to a question submitted from Paris in the first half of the twelfth century (on the status of Rome as a centre of Jewish leadership, see page 507). The Paris community reported a claim based on 'the Decree of Settlement which had been instituted lest a man set himself up in a city apart from the townsfolk who were there at the time and the children then born to them, males and not females' (the right of domicile was automatically inherited only by sons, and not by daughters or sons-in-law). The community in question had 'decreed that no person shall remain permanently in the city or within a radius of fifteen leagues around it without their permission, save they and their offspring'. The leaders of the Rome community declare in their reply that as far as they are concerned the closing-off of the city in such a fashion 'is something which we do not practice'; but they added: 'You bear witness to four kingdoms – France, Lorraine, Burgundy and Normandy – which follow this regulation.' The individual who had lodged the complaint argued: 'As for me, I am a member of the city and you are a member of another city. And I desire that you should not earn any more in the city, but leave the city . . . my inheritance and heritage' (S. D. Luzzatto, ed., *Bet Haozar,* section I, Lvov, 1847, fol. 57r–58v). Thus, at that time, the Jewish cities in the north tended to close their doors, while the Jews of the south did not recognize such a practice.

In the course of time, the attitude towards this matter was divided in the north too. Yet the tendency towards exclusivism continued, out of the desire to accept only those who were already resident in the community or whom the members found desirable in light of the advantages they brought to the area and its residents. This attitude was opposed by the rabbinical ruling (which, it would appear, lay behind the latent astonishment of the Rome leaders) that the gates of a community should be closed only to Jews who are morally and socially harmful and should be open to all other Jews. The conflict involved both social and moral issues, confronting the local unit, concerned exclusively with the welfare of its townsfolk, with the broader concept of 'all Israel' (*klal Yisrael*), which regards every Jew as a fitting member of every Jewish community, wherever it might be. The latter viewpoint required local inhabitants to provide some special reason in order to disqualify a fellow Jew from joining them.

Tension increased during periods of persecution. On the one hand, the inhabitants of a place unaffected by the riots or massacres wished to maintain their separate group; on the other hand, their sense of brotherhood impelled them to absorb their suffering fellow Jews. The Hasidei Ashkenaz transformed the 'Right of Settlement' into a moral and religious concept; they wished to close off their 'good' community in order to preserve the pedigree and high morality of its members and to assure that it would not be unfavourably affected by strangers.

Interruption of Prayers as a Method of Social Protest

The ordinances of the twelfth and thirteenth centuries show that in the small communities of Ashkenaz there existed a practice whereby a Jew who felt that he had been wronged was permitted to make an 'authorized scandal'. He was entitled to interrupt the prayers of the community or prevent the reading of the Torah until he received a promise that the wrong done to him would be righted or that the community would consider his complaint. Various ordinances speak of this practice as an accepted custom that the leaders were attempting to curtail. By its very nature, a custom of this kind could take root only in small communities, where each person knew all the other members and their problems. This may explain why the custom was never established in the larger communities of Spain, while it was accepted throughout the area of Ashkenazi Jewish culture, including Poland and Lithuania, as well as in some Moslem countries, and extended into the modern era. There is a basis for the practice in the Talmud, but its admission in one Jewish area and its rejection in another indicates that local social conditions determined its acceptance.

Economic Regulations

Reference has already been made to the *ma'arufya,* the right to a specific client, which played a considerable role in Jewish social and economic life from the eleventh century onwards. In Ashkenazi Jewry it was not accepted everywhere nor at all times, yet it was always potentially available. The social and spiritual tendencies that brought this regulation into being also produced those regulations of the twelfth and thirteenth centuries that forbade one Jew to compete against another in renting an apartment from a non-Jewish householder. This prohibition became increasingly important for the Jewish communities when, willingly or unwillingly, they became restricted to the residential area of the *Judengasse* or *Platea Judaeorum,* which eventually became overcrowded due to population growth. To prevent evasion of the regulations, it was provided that for a specified period of time after a Jewish tenant had left a dwelling, no other Jew was permitted to rent it.

Such regulations reflected the attitude that one Jew should not try to deprive another of his livelihood and that money should not be transferred through competitive means from Jewish to non-Jewish hands. The general economic ethos in Western Europe in the Middle Ages also was opposed to competition, and attempts were made to restrict it as far as possible for reasons of general social morality.

The Councils and the Trend Towards Centralized Leadership

Reference has been made to a central leadership based on a meeting of community heads and sages representing the unified local communities. After the Jewish centre in the Rhine Valley had experienced the destructive effect of the First Crusade, a search began for different methods of leadership and for new foci of activity. These varied as issues rose and fell in importance, the initiative coming sometimes from one centre and sometimes from another.

At the beginning of the twelfth century, as we have seen, the Jews of northern France appealed to Rome to decide an issue concerning residence in the community. It appears that in those days Rome was a centre of authority and of guidance for the Jews of northern France, as it was for western Christendom. In the letter referred to, those who had initiated the ordinance restricting settlement in the community described themselves as 'the least of the flock which is in Paris ... and we turn submissively towards our rabbis who are in Rome for their agreement. . . . If they agree to our decree, then our decree is valid.' Apparently, they sent a copy of their regulations to Rome and received a reply and confirmation of its validity, for the men of Paris continued: 'We have decreed according to the approval of a certain epistle which was brought from the south. This decree will be enacted by the Torah

Scroll, by the 613 Commandments, if our rabbis in Rome approve, and what they establish will be established.' In the second half of the twelfth century, the decision also gained the approval of Rabbenu Tam, who supported it as 'a fair decree and an ancient decree' (Finkelstein, *op. cit.*, pp. 168–9). Here we see a process whereby the regulation of a community was referred to the centre for approval, after which the community gave the regulation sanctity by taking an oath on the Torah scroll before putting it into effect.

At this time the Jews of northern France were concerned with maintaining the unity and stability of the family. The main provision of ordinances sent to the Roman centre for approval was the decree 'that no son of Israel may leave his wife for more than eighteen months without her knowledge and without faithful witnesses [who can attest that she has agreed], save in accordance with the *bet din* [court] of the nearest city'. Even on this eighteen-month period, various restrictions and conditions were imposed. 'Seven worthies of the city' were entitled, according to their judgement, to permit the husband to be absent 'for the needs of the wife, to collect his debts, and for the purposes of study, writing and business', which were regarded as sufficiently urgent reasons to justify absence for a limited period. The regulations also contained additional sections to protect women (*ibid.*). The fact that Rabbenu Tam approved this regulation several generations later shows that it had spread from Paris throughout northern France, which in turn indicates that identical problems had arisen throughout the region. The authority of Rome and the subsidiary authority of Paris were decisive.

In the second half of the twelfth century, the ties between the Jews of north-western Europe and those of Rome were severed, and the centre of leadership moved to France itself. In this period *takkanot* were enacted by councils of sages and community leaders, headed by Rabbenu Tam. This central leadership used methods of its own to gain authority and to obtain approval for its actions. The leaders knew that not all of those authorized to participate in the council were present. It is also clear from the ordinances that not all districts listed as approving had representatives present who actually approved. However, the regulations were declared valid on the assumption that 'of those mentioned here some have already agreed; though there are others whose views we have not heard. But the matter is urgent, so we depend upon our knowledge of them. The greater [in scholarship and leadership] deign to hearken to the lesser' (*ibid.*, p. 153).

Another manuscript of the same ordinances describes the method used for obtaining the approval of those not present at the session at which the ordinances were enacted: 'This writ . . . which they decreed . . . they sent through the whole Exile which is in the Kingdom of France and Lorraine [the Rhine Valley] and Ashkenaz [chiefly central Germany], and to many in Sepharad [probably many communities in Provence] . . . the great and generous ones have signed this missive' (*ibid.*, p. 159). It follows that the focus of leadership in the second half of the twelfth century was in France and that this centre wished to establish its authority from Germany on one side to Provence on the other. The general approval of the communities dispersed over this extensive area was obtained in two stages. First the initiators and those who came at their invitation met at an assembly where the ordinance was adopted.

Afterwards the text of the ordinance was circulated among the communities in order to obtain their approval. Those authorized to sign constituted 'the great and generous ones'. Perhaps this expression should be interpreted to mean the Talmudic sages and the wealthy. It may be assumed that this particular method was employed because, while the communities of northern France had recovered from the shock of 1096, the roads were not yet safe and it was dangerous for Jews to travel considerable distances.

The assemblies were occupied with the problem of public order and, it appeared, with the tensions resulting from the conflicts within the leadership. Those who promulgated the ordinances strongly condemned the moral decline that had spread within Jewry. Under the leadership of Rabbenu Tam they declared war against

> the licentious ones among our people, some of whom have elevated themselves to put vision in their mouths when there is destruction in their hearts, while others accustom [people] to transgression, denouncing in secret as well as openly through gentiles, princes, and simple men – and both alike are intent on acts of transgression (*ibid.*, p. 152).

The authors of the regulations are clearly set against two kinds of transgressors: those who denounce men about private matters 'in secret and openly', and those who approach the non-Jewish rulers for the sake of 'words of vision', meaning some public and religious purpose. It is reasonable to assume, in the spirit of those times, that 'the licentious ones among our people' sought to gain power over the communities by enlisting the aid of the non-Jewish authorities. The regulations indicate a social struggle within the communities between two groups. The leadership condemned both those who turned to the gentiles in order to harm individuals as well as those who appealed to them for public or religious purposes. Both groups were equally sinful in the eyes of the assembly, as can be seen from the fact that the authors of the regulations called 'on all those who have acquaintance with the [authorities of the] kingdom to compel with the aid of gentiles any one who [presumes] to transgress a single one of these our ordinances' (*ibid.*, p. 155). Probably some of those with 'vision in their mouths' had appealed to the rulers to appoint them as heads of the communities, for the assembly stated, *inter alia,* that

> we have banned, excommunicated and decreed that no man may be permitted to assume power over his fellow Jews through the king, prince, or judge in order to punish, fine or compel them either in secular or religious matters, for there are some who pretend to be pious, yet lack even modesty (*ibid.,* p. 154).

They appear to have been opposing persons who had demanded leadership for themselves on the grounds of some special piety they claimed to possess, which Rabbenu Tam and his companions denied.

These conflicts typified the tension involved in the pursuit of Jewish self-government, which, on the one hand, meant the rule of Jewish law within the Jewish community but, on the other hand, was dependent upon those in contact with the gentile authorities in order for it to operate. Most of the clauses of these ordinances dealt with the problem of Jews who informed on their fellow Jews in private matters.

In the second half of the twelfth century the focus of initiative in ordinances of autonomy shifted around; sometimes we find it further south, among 'our great rabbis who dwell in Narbonne'. Jews dwelling in the north of France turned to some of the elders of the south and upon hearing from them stated 'we who dwell in Troyes and Rheims accepted it for ourselves and sent our messengers to those within a day's journey' (*ibid.,* p. 164). In the second half of the twelfth century, therefore, Rabbenu Tam was not always the initiator and focus of leadership. Sometimes action was taken by an assembly of scholars and community heads in his city, and sometimes the rabbis of Narbonne in the south took the initiative. The Jews of a certain region united to pass this initiative on to their own district within the ambit of a distance of 'a day's journey'. The ordinances circulated at the time were concerned with what was then an urgent issue in the Christian cities as well. At that time the mortality rate in childbirth was very high. These regulations, like many municipal regulations, dealt with the inheritance of the dowry and jewellery of a woman who died soon after marriage (*ibid.,* pp. 163–5).

The Councils of 'Shum' (Speyer, Worms and Mainz)

In the thirteenth century the situation in the Rhine Valley improved, and a central Jewish authority began to reconstitute itself. Three sets of ordinances have survived that were enacted from 1220 onwards by the scholars and the community leaders of the region at councils that are known to have been convened by the so-called Shum communities (the Hebrew initials of Speyer, Worms and Mainz), though the signatories included scholars and leaders from other communities as well. At the last of the three councils, the participants recorded that 'when the leaders of the people gathered together we decreed . . . by the precious [Torah]; and all the people joined in the covenant' (*ibid.,* p. 225). It is clear, then, that both the territorial range and the method of obtaining approval for regulations were more restricted in the thirteenth century than they had been during the previous century. In addition, the three leading communities were expressly designated as the centres of authority and justice for the other communities. All three councils specified that 'an informer's oath shall be unacceptable and he shall be excommunicated by all the communities until he restores [what he gained unjustly from] his fellow-Jew and has likewise done penance in Mainz and in Worms and in Speyer' (*ibid.,* p. 226).

These thirteenth-century ordinances were 'roof regulations' whose purpose was to guide communities concerning the authority of the *halakhah* and to define their competence and the limits of their authority. They included provisions regarding taxation and instruction as to the degree of celebration permitted young men at weddings (*ibid.,* pp. 226–7). Various standing orders were issued to the communities; for example, that 'informers must be cursed every Sabbath' (*ibid.,* p. 227). The measures that heads of communities might take with respect to individuals were restricted: 'The *parnass* [community head] may not impose a ban in secret, nor withdraw a ban without the knowledge of the congregation, nor may the rabbi by virtue of his office; but the ban shall be imposed or withdrawn in the presence of the congregation' (*ibid.,* p. 228). On the other hand, two of the councils ordered individuals 'to bring the tithe in accordance with what the congregation shall prescribe' (*ibid.*, p. 230). Also included among the regulations was the congregation's guidance for the individual; for example, the requirement that he refrain from shaving his beard, that he avoid food cooked by gentiles and that he not let his hair grow long; and arrangements were suggested whereby loans on interest could be made to Jews (*ibid.*, p. 225). The last assembly decided that 'whoever transgresses any of these ordinances shall be under the ban of all the communities. And if he remain disobedient for a full month, his money shall be handed over to the king' (*ibid.*, p. 231).

The Elite Groups

During the Middle Ages the leadership of Jewish society was almost always in the hands of clearly defined and cohesive groups. In some regions their internal structure and their economic foundations were fully evident, as were the social and spiritual ideals that guided them. The opposition to their way of living and the suggestion of new methods of leadership and spiritual activity as a rule also emerged from and were guided by those same ruling circles. Throughout the Diaspora the leadership circles were known for their aristocratic family consciousness, although the rigidity of the ancient Near East ('Babylonian') Jewish aristocracy had vanished (see pages 494–6). In all areas there were specific families that led and guided the people for centuries; some of them even 'specialized' in particular areas of public and spiritual activity. Thus we hear of the close ties between the Alconstantini family and the kings of Aragon; and we hear of the Ibn Ezra family, which was prominent in court life (see page 467), as well as spiritual and intellectual life (see chapter 33). The Tibbonid family was preeminent in cultural activity, especially as translators (see page 519). Rabbenu Jonah Gerondi and Naḥmanides, who were in conflict with the court Jews, both belonged to aristocratic families. In France the house of Rashi – his grandsons and their offspring – exerted considerable influence for hundreds of years, and the Ḥasidei Ashkenaz were headed by a distinguished family.

From the end of the twelfth century, the great majority of the Jews in the Iberian Peninsula lived in the Christian kingdoms. There, as in the Moslem territories, the leaders of the Jewish communities were the wealthy merchants, from whose ranks came the financiers who were in close contact with the rulers and held posts in the royal service. This group also included the physicians, particularly those who treated the royal and noble families, as well as the translators from Arabic into Latin. Despite the differences between the members of the various professions in standards of living and in education and culture, they shared common ideals and a common style of life. During the period under consideration here, the leaders of the Jewish communities of Provence (*i.e.*, southern France) very much resembled their counterparts in Spain.

Below this circle, with respect to material resources, were the scholars and sages – the biblical and Talmudic authorities – as well as the poets, the slightly less-successful physicians and so forth. Many of these were supported by patrons belonging to the ruling class and paid court, as it were, to the Jewish courtiers. The relations between the two groups were close and at the same time tense. Those who were under patronage did not enjoy 'crawling on all fours' before their patrons. R. Abraham ibn Ezra, himself a member of an aristocratic family, whose private circumstances made him a candidate for patronage, complained:

> Before dawn I call at the potentate's house,
> And am told he is out with his horse,
> At evening I'm back and this time I hear
> His lordship is sleeping, of course.
> It seems he is riding or sleeping all day
> And I must be patient perforce.
>   (Schirman, *op. cit.*, II, p. 575)

The situation in which such a man might find himself is illustrated by the following lines of Ibn Ezra:

> I have a coat resembling a sieve
> For winnowing barley or corn.
> I'm weary of stitching together its holes
> And patching the spots that are torn.
> If a fly were to land on its coarse ragged cloth
> It would soon fly off elsewhere in scorn.
>   (*Ibid.*, p. 576)

Yet, culturally, poor men of this element formed an integral part of the leading circle and often stood at its centre, particularly in matters of faith and philosophy. Their spiritual pride was not in the least affected by their poverty or dependence on the wealthy. Thus Ibn Ezra ended the poem on his coat with the following entreaty:

> Exchange it, O God, for the robe of renown
> (Better stitched) with pride to be worn.
>   (*Ibid.*)

In the spiritual and social ferment that is discussed in the next chapter, the Jewish courtiers and their spiritual and intellectual followers usually acted as a united group, imbued with and influenced by the surrounding gentile culture. Their opponents, including those from their own ranks, claimed that their way of life was marked by a desire for material comfort and by a virtual disregard of daily Jewish practice.

Towards the end of this period, a new and rival ruling group emerged wherever this circle held sway. Middle-scale merchants and poor scholars formed the economic and social backbone of the new group. Its leaders were drawn from the younger members of the established group who had withdrawn from their circle. What distinguished the opposition was its ideological unity more than its origin or economic activity. Its members were more mystically oriented and inclined towards moral severity (see chapter 33). Their comments on communal affairs were keen and abrasive. The struggle between the two circles provided the social setting of Jewish cultural life in Spain and Provence from the thirteenth century onwards.

After usury had become the basis of Jewish economic life in Western Europe north of the Pyrenees (see page 469), the effective cultural leadership of Ashkenazi Jewry passed to the sages and scholars, who usually combined a wide knowledge of the Torah with material prosperity. The heads of the communities were frequently also great sages of the Torah. The Ḥasidei Ashkenaz constituted an opposition to this leadership, from which they had emerged. They differed not in their style of life but in their demand for absolute consistency and uprightness in the way of life that the entire leadership declared it desired. The leaders, those in official positions as well as those in opposition, exerted influence more by their scholarship and personal example than by their economic or political impact.

In brief, the leading circles throughout the entire range of Jewish culture were still small, closely knit groups. At this period Jewish life in Europe displayed a new trend towards open and formal leadership. The leaders in Ashkenaz were closer to the rest of the community in occupation and standard of living than were those in Spain, where the gap was wider.

The Magnanimous Leadership of the Sages and Scholars

In spite of the generally accepted picture of humility and self-effacement on the part of the individual Jewish sages of this period, the views of many of them reveal a strong need to have their 'magnanimity' expressed socially and accorded recognition by the public. When Rabbenu Tam, in the twelfth century, gained the impression that a scholar in Provence had not treated his opinion with due respect and had issued a ruling that contradicted his own, he warned him:

> I bid you not to split up our kingdom into splinters, for we drink from the spring of Rabbi Solomon [*i.e.,* Rashi, his grandfather]. Through matters that are of no account do not cause turmoil in his area. Do you regard us as mere binders of sheaves or rushes by some lakeside, insensitive about the honour of our grand-sire? Brethren, do not do evil. . . . And I request all the disciples of our Master Rabbi Solomon not to treat the Eastern Gate [of the Temple] lightly; and if they do not hearken, their souls will bear their punishment (*Sefer Hayashar,* Berlin, 1858, no. 45, 83, 85).

Thus Rabbenu Tam demanded absolute authority throughout France by virtue of the tradition and status of his grandfather, as well as for the sake of unity of custom and faith. On this point he always took a firm stand. He prohibited others from correcting the Talmudic text, yet he introduced his own corrections. He objected to those who disagreed with his grandfather, though he did so himself. He held that the leader of the age, *i.e.,* he himself, was entitled to alter and innovate, while others were duty bound to obey him because of his knowledge of the Torah and his inherited dynastic authority. His *halakhic* decisions and interpretations were often innovatory, tending to facilitate commercial relations with non-Jews; and he permitted himself to introduce decisions of far-reaching significance concerning other problems of social and economic life. Yet he was strict with regard to some matters. In his commentaries and *halakhic* decisions and at the assemblies that he headed (see pages 508–9) he thought and acted as the head of Jewry in France and, to some extent, even beyond it – from Provence in the south to German Ashkenaz in the east.

In about 1269 the twenty-year-old scholar Menaḥem Hameiri wrote *Hibbur Hateshuvah* ('Tractate on Repentance'), a systematic study of the moral behaviour of man. The fifth chapter contains an instructive discussion on humility. To the author 'this matter of humility does not at all involve lowliness of spirit.' He specified four types of pride, three of which are permissible and even desirable for certain persons and under certain conditions; only the fourth kind is absolutely forbidden. The first permissible type is the pride of 'high office', for

> in its nature it does not include ill-intended pride, but when a person feels that he has lofty qualities and political leadership has been entrusted to him, as is well known that the well-being of the community calls for a leader and the absence of leadership would damage it, he will turn the accident of his elevation to a desirable end.

It is right for a man to show self-esteem if he senses in his soul that he has more suitable qualities than others and if his function as a leader requires that he do so, for 'to tell the truth it is proper for every ruler to show the people that he is superior'. A king who acts with complete humility is a sinner because he inspires others to disobey him. Therefore, 'it is fitting that a king should crown himself with this quality for the purpose of leadership and the continued functioning of statehood. And if he does not act in accordance with this principle he will be acting falsely to his soul and will turn his honour into shame.' In principle, haughtiness is fitting only for kings; but R. Menaḥem Hameiri was of the opinion that the Jewish leaders of his time – and he later became a leader in his own community – also should be haughty, because leadership of the people required this trait:

> Since this quality is admissible in all respects to kings and rulers, part of it should devolve upon every leader to whom some authority is entrusted, depending always on the authority in his hands. . . . And from this aspect a portion of it is permissible to the leaders of the community.

The second permissible kind of pride is that of 'loftiness of spirit', meaning that the sage refrained 'from being in constant friendship and company with the mass of people. Let him behave . . . as though holding himself precious. Let him not bend his back to serve the worthless, nor give his face to be trampled upon by the multitude and the ignorant.' A scholar who does not behave in this manner deserves to be considered a commoner. Also permissible is pride in the good esteem in which one is held, 'so that a man should not be so abject as to be careless of himself and engage in worthless deeds and develop despicable qualities'.

The only kind of pride that must be absolutely rejected by all is the self-pride of the sage or public official who disregards fairness and objectivity and does not honour truth. Hameiri totally condemned this kind of pride:

> It is proper for every man to keep away from such a person . . . if the latter supposes . . . that he is by nature more lofty and elevated than his fellow men and more intelligent than they, and if he hates and despises everybody who denies his

superiority or views, not because the truth has been revealed to him ... but because he imagines he is above all those whose opinions differ from him in respect of wisdom or rank. His purpose is to destroy all other opinions even if they be true ... and when the truth be against him, he will disagree with the truth too and will combat it (A. Schreiber, ed., *Ḥibbur Hateshuvah,* New York, 1950, chap. 5, pp. 118–41).

Status Symbols Within the Leading Class

In Ashkenaz social standing was given recognition in ceremonies connected with the fulfilment of commandments, and people insisted on the right to perform these commandments as a form of public honour. One such person turned to the Ḥasidei Ashkenaz of Regensburg – hardly the right address (see page 548) – to demand judgement against twelve persons who had donated more than he had to charity and as a result took for themselves the honour of winding up the Torah scroll in the synagogue after the public reading. The plaintiff declared that 'the transgressors, growing powerful, sought honour and glory for themselves in winding up the Torah scroll, and connived to increase their prestige and took counsel and agreed together.' He assured the *ḥasidim,* 'thanks to God, it is within my capacity to make them change their mind,' while he vilified these donors to charity, 'for there are some among them who do not know even a single verse of the Torah, and I don't intend to say even worse against them', and explained the reasons for his complaint as follows:

> I am not acting for the sake of my own honour. ... But I have become zealous for the insult to the Torah; moreover I am concerned for what will develop from this. For if five or six begin to roll up the Scroll, in a year's time others will say we wish to do the rolling, until murder will be done among them. Therefore pay attention to this matter ... and know, that if you declare your opinion I can do the rolling in spite of them (Wistinetzky, *op. cit.,* para. 1592, p. 390).

The Ḥasidei Ashkenaz quite astonished the questioner, R. Ephraim ben Meir, with their answer (see page 551). He would have been better satisfied had he been appealing to Maimonides in the twelfth-century Orient. Maimonides was asked about one who claimed a permanent right to precedence in being called to the Torah reading:

> This right was known with him and his forefathers; the rest of the community demanded to be called up to the Torah reading instead of him. ... They claimed: there can be no rights over the Torah; and no one should be kept from it. [Maimonides answered] If the man who wishes to ascend in place of him is greater than he in wisdom and fear of God, let him ascend, and then what the Congregation said will be correct: that the goings-up to the Torah are not acquired by inheritance only. But if he is his equal and like him, then the heir to this 'right' is more deserving for the sake of peace. But if the one who wishes to go up is less than the former, there is no way to allow this under any conditions (J. Blau, ed., *Responsa of Maimonides,* Jerusalem, 1960, para. 243, pp. 444–5).

R. Kalonymus ben Kalonymus, a sage of Provence and a translator into Latin, visited Italy and was familiar with the various circles of Jewish society there. He left us some pen portraits of the early fourteenth century that mock various kinds of social ostentation. Yet, behind the mockery it is possible to identify, as in a distorting mirror, the views and opinions of those who demanded honour and respect. In his satire entitled *Even Boḥan* ('The Touchstone'), he voiced the claims of the wealthy *shtadlan*:

There is none other than me. I decide yes or no. With my own strength I made this city in which the people now dwell. I preserved it so that it should not be abandoned when most people thought of running away . . . in time of danger and the hour of distress. . . . I weigh money into the Emperor's coffers like precious jewels. And money will answer everything. . . . Can one who has no money defer an evil decree? And can he who does not have the wherewithall close the breach? (A. M. Haberman, ed., *Even Boḥan,* Tel Aviv, 1956, p. 36).

The *shtadlan* demanded to be honoured by the community by virtue of his intercessions and his financial outlay for its commonweal.

33

Social Life and Cultural Achievement

Main Sources of Tension

The crusaders' battle for the faith cast its shadow on the thought and consciousness of the period under consideration here. The honour of a faith such as Judaism, which did not possess military force to support it, was difficult to maintain in this atmosphere of holy war. It was not by chance that R. Judah Halevi gave his work of religious disputation, *The Kuzari,* the subtitle 'A Book in Defence of the Despised and Humiliated Faith'. In a world in which national consciousness was just beginning to emerge and was still intertwined with religious awareness, the problems of the election of the Jews and the question of acceptance unto Jewry by means of conversion were concomitant aspects of the problem of the honour and faith of the Jewish people. Below are recorded various instances of different and even contradictory solutions to the issue of the nation's character and the nature of its election.

The rationalist comprehension of man, world, Torah and God, which had increasingly predominated in the gaonic period, now became the subject of an increasingly bitter conflict in which many factors were involved. Meanwhile, trends towards a mystical view of God and the universe, which had constantly been present in Judaism, found a new and perfected theoretical and literary expression in opposition to rationalism. Rationalism, too, steadily became more sharply defined. R. Abraham ibn Daud, one of the leading thinkers of the twelfth century, expressed the situation of the rationalist:

> In these times of ours there will sometimes be found one who studies philosophy a little, but who does not have the strength to hold both lights in his hands – the light of faith in his right hand and the light of philosophy in his left – for when he kindles the light of philosophy the light of faith goes out (S. Weil, ed., *Sefer Haemunah Haramah* ['The Book of Exalted Faith'], Frankfurt a.M., 1852, p. 2).

This inner conflict was also stressed by Maimonides, the greatest rationalistic philosopher of Judaism. In the introduction to his philosophical *magnum opus Moreh Nevukhim* ('Guide to the Perplexed'), which was written in Arabic, he declared that the work was intended for readers who have 'studied the wisdom of the philosophers and are familiar with their works, and whom the intelligence of such humans has drawn to dwell in its habitation, and who are distressed at the simplistic explanations of the Torah'. But his contemporary R. Judah Halevi warned:

> Look well indeed my friend and comprehend
> And turn aside from traps and snares.
> Be not misled by Greek philosophy
> That offer only flowers and never fruit,
> Declaring that the earth is not firm set,
> Nor are the tents of Heaven spread on High,
> Nor did Creation's work ever begin,
> Nor will the moon's renewals ever end.
> Hark how confused are all their wisest words
> Built on a base of void and blind as well
> For you'll return with empty, shaken heart
> And mouth that's full of empty argument
> Then why should I seek paths that are at best
> Circuitous and forsake the main highway?
>   (Schirman, *op. cit.*, II, pp. 493–4)

Halevi was still secure in the social and spiritual atmosphere of the upper-class intellectuals in Spain. Doubts such as those that had awakened within him and the intellectual conflicts that R. Abraham ibn Daud and Maimonides endeavoured to solve by a synthesis of philosophy and faith helped to bring about anger and a feeling of bitterness within the emerging mystic circles. Questions regarding the anthropomorphic descriptions of God in the Scriptures and the attitude to be adopted towards the messianic era and bodily resurrection were not simply theoretical matters but the foci of spiritual and social maelstroms.

Until the beginning of the twelfth century, Jewish creativity had developed largely against the background of Moslem culture (see pages 442–58), being either influenced by it or in conflict with it. During the period discussed here, however, the influence of the Christian environment was beginning to make itself felt, and the effects of Jewish resistance to it became increasingly recognizable. The struggle between rationalism and mysticism in this period reflected the opposing influences of Islam and of Christianity. The Jewish exile presented itself to the Jew as a central issue to be faced in his own personal life, in the arguments of his Christian antagonists and in the constant and degrading pressure imposed by the Moslems, even though the latter did not always indulge in the massacres and grave social injustice of Christendom. The debate with Christianity and with Islam produced a literature of disputation valuable for its explicit statements and even more for its contribution to Jewish self-understanding.

The Cultural Climate and Level of Education in South-western Europe

The cultural and spiritual climate within the upper circles of Moslem Spain combined devotion to the study of Torah with attention to aesthetic sensibilities. This combination is evident in the following story:

I was told by one of the elders of Granada, may their souls rest in Paradise, that they once sat enjoying themselves at a banquet in one of the lofty corners of the chamber in which some of the most magnificent and important men of those times were gathered, with Rabbi Judah Halevi, may he rest in Paradise, among them; and they engaged in honourable and pleasant conversation. While they were admiring the wisdom of the Creator, as seen in all His Creation, there appeared a beautiful woman dressed in all her finery; and they marvelled at her beauty and praised the Lord, may He be exalted, for the perfection of His works. While they were still admiring her lovely face and figure, she began to talk to her companion, and they heard her saying harsh things in a harsh voice. When Rabbi Judah Halevi heard this voice he said: 'The mouth that held us is the mouth that frees us' [a pun on the Talmudic phrase 'The mouth that forbade is the mouth that permits']. And all who heard him admired his wisdom in applying the words of our rabbis of blessed memory to this poetic matter (R. Joseph ibn Aknin, *Hitgalut Hasodot* ['Revelation of the Secrets'], A.S. Halkin, ed., Jerusalem, 1964, pp. 177, 179).

This aristocratic *milieu* of scholars and notables was shaken by the invasions of the Almohades. Yet even those who fled northwards took something of this atmosphere with them and re-established it in their new abode.

The physician R. Judah ibn Tibbon, who was born in Granada in Moslem Spain in the year 1120 and moved in the middle of the century to Lunel in Provence – where he died in 1190 – left his son R. Samuel (who translated the works of Maimonides from Arabic into Hebrew) an ethical will that is highly instructive from the social and cultural viewpoints. He advised his son, *inter alia,* as follows: 'My son, as far as you can, honour yourself and your household and your children with good garments, for it does not befit a man that his garb should be unworthy of his calling. And give less to your belly and more to your back' (J. Abrahams, ed., *Hebrew Ethical Wills,* I, Philadelphia, 1948, p. 66). Aesthetic form was important to him for a more fundamental reason:

My son, when you write something go back and read it again. . . . And do not let haste prevent you from returning to correct even a brief letter. Be careful not to err in language, grammatical structures, and conjugations or in the masculine and feminine forms . . . for a man bears blame for his errors and he is remembered all his life because of them. And the sages said: Who displays his nakedness so that it is seen by all? Of course the one who writes and makes mistakes in doing so (*ibid.,* p. 68).

Calligraphy was important to the father who offered his son this advice:

And make your script and writing beautiful. See that the work of your pen is well done and that the ink with which you write shows up well. And let your letter be the best of which you are capable. . . . For an epistle is beautiful in its script, while the beauty of penmanship lies in the pen, epistle and ink, and beautiful lettering indicates the quality of the writer. . . . For as I told you, writing is one of the significant forms. The more careful a man is to improve it, the more handsome it is. . . . And may your God give you understanding and make you right in all your ways (*ibid.*, pp. 69–79).

A note of piety can be heard in this caution regarding beautiful script and writing materials. It seems as though the whole of life is included in this concept of 'forms, and the more careful a man is with it the finer it will appear' before both God and man alike.

R. Judah related that he spent a large sum of money to have his son taught calligraphy. He was proud of his efforts to educate his son:

> I sought as far as the ends of the earth and brought you a teacher of secular wisdoms. And I did not spare outlay or fear the danger of the roads. Indeed, I would have been in almost the very worst of situations together with you on that journey if the Lord had not been with us (*ibid.*, p. 57).

Instruction in sciences was a matter in which divine providence had aided him and for which he was prepared to run risks. The son was educated in his father's profession, medicine; and his father sought to inculcate in him the ethics of the profession:

> My son, receive all men graciously and when you visit the sick, let your tongue be a healing for them. If you receive payment from the wealthy, then heal the poor without charge and the Lord will pay your recompense and give you your wage. . . . And you will be honoured by great and small, by Jews and gentile. And you will gain a good name both near and far (*ibid.*, p. 67).

Observance of professional ethics is required vis-à-vis every man, Jew and non-Jew alike.

Personal status was important for the father, and he advised his son to treat it so. In his ethical will he several times expressed pride at the respect shown to him and the honour in which he was held. Humility was not one of his favourite virtues, and he did not teach his son to favour it: 'You see the great sages who seek and endeavour to enjoy my company and presence from the ends of the earth, and who are eager to see me and my books' (*ibid.*, p. 58). 'At your wedding you were more honoured than all your companions, and you were honoured by the community who imposed neither tax nor burden upon you. You were respected by the lords, knights, bishops, priests and monks on my account' (*ibid.*, pp. 66–7). This indulgence in self-esteem was accompanied by the requirement to act with delicacy and courtesy towards one's wife and brothers and towards society in general.

The Cultural Climate in the Orient

The level of education was considerably high even among the less wealthy groups and in Moslem countries besides Spain. From a question addressed to Maimonides, we learn of the situation of a girl who was married off at the age of nine. The description makes it clear that the couple was poor and that the wife led a harsh life with her husband:

As long as she has been with him he has not lit a lamp for her, neither on weekdays nor on the Sabbath nor on a festival. And she only sees lamplight if she enters the home of his mother or his brother, for she dwells with them in one courtyard (Blau, ed., *op. cit.,* para. 34, p. 50).

Yet the woman was educated. 'She has a brother who teaches little children Bible, and she knows Bible too. She asked her brother to allow her to teach the children Bible with him in order to gain something with which to maintain herself and her children.' She engaged in this profession for six years together with her brother. 'After that it came about that her brother went on a journey. She took his place and took the children and taught them Bible and continued thus for four years,' becoming the chief teacher in this educational institution. She explained:

My livelihood is not like others so that if I abandon it today, I shall regain it to-morrow. If I leave the pupils even for a single day, I shall seek but not find them, because their fathers will take them to other Torah schools. And as for my oldest son . . . men bring him their sons only because of me, because he is still a lad. . . . And if I should cease teaching the little ones . . . my sons and I will remain and be lost (*ibid.,* p. 52).

We hear much about the education of girls in Islamic countries. Blind men had an advantage in this respect, because people were readier to send their daughters to study with them. In a touching letter from Egypt that seems to date from the first half of the twelfth century, a woman wrote on her deathbed:

I tell you, my sister – may the Lord receive me as your ransom – that I have fallen into a grievous disease and there is little possibility of recovering from it, and indeed I see dreams that announce my end. . . . My lady, if the Lord on High should decree my death, my greatest wish is that you should take care of my little daughter and make an effort for her to study. Indeed, I know that I am imposing a heavy burden on you. For we do not have the wherewithal for her upkeep, let alone the cost of tuition. But we have an example from our mother and teacher, the servant of the Lord (S. D. Goitein, *Methods of Education,* Jerusalem, 1962, p. 66).

Here is an instance of a Jewish family that was certainly not well-to-do in which the women of two generations were educated and saw to the education of their daughters.

The works of the great Jewish poets of this epoch, the philosophy and the type of leadership bear witness to a high level of culture and education. It seems that this cultural creativity was shared by Jews of every class in Moslem Spain and the lands of the East, though there is, in the nature of things, little information available about this.

The Cultural Milieu and Level of Education in North-western Europe

In the Ashkenazi communities of north-western Europe there were relatively few differences among the social strata. The general educational level was high. One of Abelard's students, a twelfth-century monk, reported in one of his commentaries:

> The Jews, out of their zeal for God and their love of the Law, put as many sons as they have to letters, that each may understand God's Law. . . . A Jew, however poor, if he had ten sons, would put them all to letters, not for gain, as the Christians do, but for the understanding of God's Law; and not only his sons but his daughters (B. Smalley, *The Study of the Bible in the Middle Ages,* Oxford, 1952, p. 78).

In the communities of Ashkenaz, the child was introduced to the study of Torah by means of a solemn and symbolic ceremony. The Ashkenazi Jews, who were so highly praised by the monk for their pursuit of learning, had a practice in the twelfth century whereby

> as soon after the circumcision as they desire [a quorum of] ten assemble and take a Pentateuch; and the babe in the cradle is finely arrayed as on the day of circumcision. They place the book upon him and say: 'May this one fulfil what is written in this'; and they say, 'And He shall give thee' and all the verses of the Blessings . . . and they place an inkwell and a scribe's reed in his hand in order that he may be privileged to be a swift scribe in the Lord's Torah (S. Hurvitz, ed., *Maḥzor Vitry,* Nuremberg, 1923, para. 507, p. 628).

Thus while still an infant the Jew was brought in contact with the hallowed objects of study, which are seen as sacred and potent symbols of learning, as though the child would thereby absorb the love of Torah and desire to study it.

When the parents brought the child to begin learning, the whole family celebrated the occasion with symbolic ceremonies, which were marked by a mingling of didactic methods with expressions of belief in the sanctity of the Torah:

> They write the letters of the Hebrew alphabet on a board for him; and they wash him and dress him in clean garments, and they knead him three loaves of fine wheat in honey. . . . And they boil him three eggs and bring him apples and other kinds of fruit, and seek a worthy sage to conduct him to the school house. He covers him with his prayer-shawl and brings him to the synagogue, where they feed him with the loaves of honey and the eggs and fruit; and they read him the letters. After that they cover the board with honey and tell him to lick it. Then they lead him back to his mother (*ibid.,* para. 508, p. 628).

Of this ceremony the people of that period used to say, 'It is as though they have brought him to Mount Sinai.'

Information has also reached us about the educational methods employed in those days: 'And then they begin to teach him; first they entice him but finally use a strap on his back . . . and they accustom him to sway his body as he learns.' These methods and ceremonies continued to be in use from the twelfth century in France and from the thirteenth century in all of Ashkenaz. The same ceremony was recorded by the illuminators of Jewish manuscripts early in the fourteenth century.

In due course we shall discuss the stringent ascetic tendencies among the Ḥasidei Ashkenaz. Mention has already been made of *kiddush hashem,* or the hallowing of the Holy Name by death, and the dread and glory that it involved. At the same time,

Jewish family life, including that of the ascetics and leaders, was in general a combination of fear of heaven and joy of life. Even children's games were of great value in the eyes of an ascetic family head. R. Eleazar ben Judah, one of the leading Ḥasidei Ashkenaz, lamented his wife, 'the pious Mistress Dolce', who was slain by the crusaders in 1196, together with their two young daughters. In phrases borrowed from the final section of the Book of Proverbs, yet with details undoubtedly taken from actual life, he described this worthy woman:

> Crown of her husband, daughter of nobles . . . her husband's heart trusted in her, she fed him and clothed him in honour to sit with the Elders of the land and garner Torah and good deeds . . . all the time she was with him, she made him books from her toil. . . . She sought for white wool to spin fringes. . . . She spun thread for phylacteries, scrolls and books. She was as swift as a deer to cook for the children and to do the will of the students. . . . She sewed together about forty Torah Scrolls . . . adorned brides and brought them [to the wedding] with honours. The sweet one [Dolce] would wash the dead and sew their shrouds. Her hands stitched clothes for the students and repaired torn books. She opened her hand to the poor and gave food to her sons and daughters and husband. She made wicks [for the candles of the] synagogue . . . and recited Psalms. She sang hymns and prayers . . . reciting the account of the making of frankincense, and the Ten Commandments. In all the cities she instructed women and sang sweetly, coming early to the synagogue and staying late. Throughout the Day of Atonement she stood singing and taking care of the candles. . . . She opened her mouth with wisdom and knew what is forbidden and what is permitted. . . . On the Sabbath Day she would sit enquiring, absorbing her husband's words. . . . Wise in speech was she . . . buying milk for those who studied and hiring teachers by means of her toil. . . . She ran to visit the sick . . . fed her sons and urged them to study . . . rejoicing to perform her husband's will, and never at any time angering him (Haberman, *Massacres of Germany and France*, pp. 165–6).

This lament is not only a memorial to an exceptional woman who was loved by her husband but also a description of the domestic atmosphere among the sages in those days. The woman participated in the life of Torah and prayer not only through her services to the students and the head of the *yeshiva*, but also by praying, listening to sermons, educating the children and performing those good deeds that fell within the sphere of the woman, such as leading brides under the canopy and preparing the dead for burial. The details are surrounded by a gentle air of deep personal esteem.

Of his elder daughter, who was thirteen when murdered, the father wrote that she had 'learnt all the prayers and melodies from her mother. She was pious and wise, a beautiful virgin. She prepared my bed and pulled off my boots every night. Bellette was nimble about the house and spoke only truth, serving her Maker and spinning and sewing and embroidering' (*ibid.*, p. 166). The bereaved father also remembered the deeds of his younger daughter: 'Each day she recited *Shema Yisrael* and the following prayer. She was six years old and could spin, sew and embroider, and entertain me by singing' (*ibid.*, pp. 166–7).

The family and home life of the Jew in the lands of Ashkenaz thus combined devotion to the Torah and gentleness (see pages 552–3 for details on the ḥasidic doctrine on the role of love in married life) and mutual honour and respect in familial relations. The Tosafists of France addressed the women of their households as 'Lady'. It may be assumed that the educational level in all groups of the community was more uniform here than in Spain and the Islamic countries.

The Attitude Towards Books

Books were honoured and esteemed throughout the Diaspora during this entire period, and there was much evidence of this esteem as early as the tenth and eleventh centuries. In the twelfth century R. Judah ibn Tibbon reminded his son: 'I honoured you by giving you many books, and you never needed to borrow a book from any man. . . . And in most of the books you have two or three differing texts, and what was more I made books for you in all sciences' (Abrahams, op. cit., p. 57). The father and the son found honour in increasing the number of their books, and R. Judah advised his son to adopt towards them an attitude of profound respect and loving care:

My son, make books your companions and make your bookcases and shelves your groves and pleasure gardens. Graze in their beds and cull their flowers . . . and if your soul grows weary and exhausted, move from garden to garden and from flower bed to flower bed. . . . For then your will shall be restored and your spirit will become beautiful (ibid., p. 63).

Books offered R. Judah aesthetic pleasure and spiritual renewal. He instructed his son on how to treat the books in his library: 'And place them all in good order so that you should not grow weary in seeking a book when you need it . . . ' He also suggested that a separate catalogue be prepared for each bookcase (ibid., p. 81).

Emanuel of Rome, who was born in the second half of the thirteenth century and died some time before 1336, described in the eighth book of his Maḥbarot ('Fascicles') how manuscripts were regarded by a contemporary group of 'wise, moral, and understanding men'. In accordance with his usual practice, he related events imaginatively and mischievously. A man brought

fine books that were load enough for a brace of mules . . . from Toledo where he spent seven years, and he brought back books more precious than gold. Some of them were in Hebrew and some of them were in Arabic. As soon as I heard of this, I yearned to know the names of those books, and he showed me a parchment on which the names of the books appeared in order, and there were about a hundred and eighty.

According to his account, these books were 'closed away in certain barrels with seal upon seal upon them'. After the owner of the books had departed for Rome, Emanuel and his companions broke the barrels open and selected 'the choicest and most precious of the books, and copied ten of them out'. When the man returned and complained, Emanuel responded with an eloquent letter in which he wrote that 'our dry souls yearned and longed for the voice of new knowledge, and our thoughts declared: . . . all things pleasant are there, the choicest of knowledge and perfect poesy, go down and break some out for us from there so that we may live and not perish' (D. Yarden, ed., *Maḥbarot Emanuel,* Jerusalem, 1957, pp. 161–6). He advised the book-dealer to accept the situation without protest, because 'it is better for you to be silent and speak pleasantly and say that you lent us the books out of generosity.' From Emanuel's account we learn that books were transported from Spain to Italy. Whether the incident occurred as related or was partly a product of Emanuel's imagination, it certainly expresses the attitude of the Italian Jews towards Hebrew books.

The Ḥasidei Ashkenaz demanded that books be treated as sacred objects. From their writings we learn that considerable attention was given to this matter. They required 'the purchaser of books not to say that any book was not worth its price', for to do so was to cast aspersion upon it. 'But let him say, this is how much I am prepared to pay; if you like, you can give it to me' (Wistinetzky, *op. cit.,* para. 665, p. 176). In those days there were men in Ashkenaz who built up large libraries. The *hasidim* sought to assemble collections that were as complete as possible, hoping they would be preserved by their families after their deaths; and 'the righteous ones used to sigh for fear that their heirs would sell their books.' However, one *hasid* explained the breaking-up of libraries after the death of the collectors from the viewpoint of another *hasidic* attitude, whereby a man's books were considered to be merely loaned to him and he was forbidden to keep them exclusively for his own use. To those who complained at the dispersal of a collection the sage answered:

> Do not sigh. I shall tell you the sin on account of which the books are not in the hands of the heirs. The reason is that the deceased did not lend his books to others. For he said, I am old and if they blur the letters they will be erased and I shall be unable to see them. But a man should not think thus, for it is better for a man that people should study his books and the letters should become illegible than that the book should be in a hidden place where nobody studies them (*ibid.,* para. 673, p. 178).

The Tosafists and Their Work

It is clear that this cultural *milieu* of Jewish society formed the foundation for Jewish spiritual achievement. However, the relationship between the cultural base and the structures built upon it is not always evident, particularly when information is available only in fragmentary form. Thus, for example, one cannot state with certainty what of the cultural heritage of the Jewish aristocracy of Spain contributed to the works of Maimonides, which were written largely in Egypt, or to what extent the culture of the Jewish lower classes in Egypt, previously referred to, influenced this philosopher to devote so large a part of his work to guiding and instructing the Jewish masses. Below we shall mention works by *élite* groups such as the Ḥasidei Ashkenaz, whose intention was to serve as a guide and example for the entire people, and we shall observe the formulation of mystical lore, which aimed at revealing a small part of the Kabbalah to the community at large.

One creative current dedicated all its energies to the traditions revealed in *halakhic* and *midrashic* literature. It specialized in Talmudic exegesis and analysis, in legal discussions and the practical application of law and in commentary on the Torah and the Prophets. This group, known as the Tosafists, originated among French Jewry and spread throughout Ashkenaz, exerting a powerful influence on the Jewish culture of Spain as well. The school gained its name from its main achievement, the *Tosafot* – additions. Formally speaking, these consisted of additional notes and analytic comments on and elucidations of earlier Talmudic commentaries, particularly that of Rashi. A study of the work shows that behind this modest name lies a considerable degree of spiritual independence and a structural approach comprising many creative participants and cases. The authors called their works *Tosafot* on account of their acceptance of the principle that earlier generations were superior to their own. As the Talmud had already been commented on by Rashi, they were entitled only to formulate supplementary comments and had to concentrate on the words of the *Kuntres,* as Rashi's commentary was called in those days. In fact, however, the *Tosafot* form the 'Talmud of France', a development of *halakhic* discourse in accordance with the methods and objectives of the Talmud. With sharp, penetrating minds, the Tosafists analysed the topics, problems and concepts of the Talmud for the benefit of students, who were in every area of Jewish life, and particularly in the sphere of Ashkenazi Jewry, a substantial portion of the adult male population. Their method added new dimensions to the theory and practice of *halakhic* method. Some of their methods of study resembled those of the Christian scholastics, who were just beginning to develop at the universities that were established in the major cities of Western Europe.

The works of the Tosafists include much more than the texts available in print, as some of their writings have been preserved only in manuscript form. They used the technique of question and answer – one sage raising the problem, while others provided the solution – in accordance with Talmudic tradition. The debate may be contained within a single passage, with a quotation from the Talmud as the *incipit.* Rashi's commentary is organized in the same way, for this was the normal method of exegesis in the Middle Ages, based on explanations and comments on earlier authorities. However, as in the case of the Talmud, if a student links together the separate sayings of a leading Tosafist, he will find that they form a coherent system of thought bearing the hallmark of the individual.

The spiritual world of the Tosafists was marked by their legal acumen coupled with a deep love of *halakhah* and of the moral attitudes inherited from their ancestors. Deliberations that seem academic and abstruse at first sight in fact often provided the spiritual basis for communal life. Hence their innovations were by no means purely academic. Some of the questions presented to the Jewish legal authorities in those times – *e.g.,* problems regarding trade with Christians and its relevancy or irrelevancy to the ancient laws governing contact between Jews and idolaters, loans given on interest, Sabbath observance in a climate where houses had to be constantly heated, etc. – were solved in accordance with the *halakhah* by the keen insight of the Tosafists, while long-established formulations were transformed so as to conduct Jewish life in the circumstances of a changing society. It is sometimes evident that even radical departures were made, although innocently, in the belief that the innovation expressed the actual opinions of the great predecessors. On rare occasions, an innovation that was believed to be beneficial was introduced with the clear knowledge that it altered the character of long-standing *halakhic* usage.

In due course the discussions of the Tosafists reached the other areas of Jewish culture, remaining until the present day a subject of study in the *yeshivot*. Their works represent a major contribution to the entire corpus of Jewish thought on the part of Ashkenazi culture and particularly that of France in the twelfth and thirteenth centuries.

The collective nature of the discussions, the method of joint study and the means of presentation, which placed the fragmentary phrases of several scholars together in brief passages, did not obliterate the remarkable personalities of the scholars involved. Particularly prominent were two brothers, R. Jacob, known as R. Jacob Tam or Rabbenu Tam, and R. Samuel, known as Rashbam, the sons of R. Meir, Rashi's son-in-law. They lived close together and are prominent among the Tosafists. The former allowed himself to innovate and criticize earlier authorities but, as noted previously, prevented others from doing so, on the grounds that they lacked his authority. It is not a matter of coincidence that many important ordinances of the twelfth century bear the name of Rabbenu Tam. Nor should we regard as an empty legend the contemporary story that relates that Christian knights dragged him out and attempted to inflict the 'wounds of Jesus' upon his flesh, in order to take vengeance upon the acknowledged leader of the Jews for the alleged transgression against the messiah. Unquestionably, he acted and led as the 'Bishop of the Jews', possessing exceptional stature.

The spiritual independence of R. Samuel was possibly even greater than that of his brother, Rabbenu Tam. In his commentary on the Torah, he rejected all the *midrashic* or homiletic literature, including the work of his grandfather. He sought the simplest and clearest meaning of the text in the fullest sense, sometimes even disregarding those interpretations set out in *halakhic* tradition. Rashbam wrote his own commentaries on various tractates of the Talmud, appearing as 'a second Rashi' rather than as an analytical Tosafist. Although he participated in communal activities and the enactment of ordinances, he seems to have been primarily of an academic bent.

As one regards both the common and the divergent views of the Tosafists engaged in the exoteric aspects of the Torah and Jewish tradition, it becomes clear that the teachings and opinions of mediaeval Jewish scholars will be best presented within the context of the problems then facing Jewry and the 'programmes' proposed by individuals or groups as solutions to social and spiritual problems.

The Significance of the Exile

The generations that experienced – either personally or vicariously – the crusades, the persecutions of the Almohades, the 'normal' humiliation at the hands of the Moslems and the slaughter by the Christians inevitably sought some meaning for the suffering of the Jewish people and a reason for the weakness of the nation chosen by God. When R. Abraham ibn Ezra considered the situation of his people in the twelfth-century Diaspora, he could see only the weakness of the persecuted, a weakness that derived not from nature but from habituation to social degradation. In his opinion, servitude itself could destroy a man's capacity for self-redemption:

And why should not they [the generation of the Exodus] fight for their lives and their children? The reason is that the Egyptians were masters of Israel, and the generation that left Egypt had learnt from their youth to bear the yoke of Egypt, so that its spirit was crushed. And how could it now do battle against its master? Besides, Israel was indolent and unskilled in war. Indeed you can see that Amalek came with few men, yet had it not been for the prayer of Moses he would have overcome Israel. But the Lord himself, who does great deeds and plans mighty acts, saw to it that all the males who departed from Egypt perished because they did not have the strength to wage war against the Canaanites – until there arose a new generation, the generation of the wilderness, *who had not seen exile and had an exalted spirit* (from his commentary on Exodus 14:13 [author's italics]).

Ibn Ezra, it will be recalled, left his native Spain and wandered through Italy, France and England. To a man in London he expressed the view that several passages in the final portion of the Book of Genesis were written in order 'to strengthen men's hearts regarding Erez Yisrael and make it more precious in their eyes, so that they should be there in their lives and their deaths. For most of the commandments can only be performed in Erez Yisrael' (see his commentary to the last portion of Genesis, M. Friedlander, ed., London, 1877, p. 65).

The doctrine of R. Judah Halevi regarding the Exile, the Redemption and Erez Yisrael is far more comprehensive and complex. He viewed the world around him with the echoes of martyrdom ringing in his ears. On the occasion of a wedding, he praised those who hallowed the Holy Name, addressing them as

You who went . . . for the unity of His Name to shed your blood; and you dedicated your souls to the fire for His sake, and can be compared to your Father Abraham. . . . Now this is your way since bygone times and forever, and it is the way of your children ever afterwards.

The heroism of the martyrs gave him the strength to overcome the feeling of humiliation that so oppressed his friend and contemporary Ibn Ezra. But he was well aware of the fact that in the eyes of the gentiles Israel was indeed held in contempt because it was degraded in exile. In his work *The Kuzari* he wrote: 'The Kuzari said in his heart: I shall enquire after Edom and Ishmael [Christendom and Islam], for one of these two religions is undoubtedly desirable. But as for the Jews it is enough to see them in their degradation and small numbers, and that they are despised by all' (section I, para. 4). Indeed, Jewish social life is notable not for its material achievements but for the sacred spiritual pursuits that elevated Jewry from the depths into which it had sunk. R. Judah Halevi was convinced that the exile had injured the Jewish sense of life. He has the king of the Khazars say that He who gave the Torah 'set the Sabbath and festivals for the greatest of reasons, to leave you your quality and grandeur. But for them, not one of you would wear a clean garment, nor would you have any assembly to commemorate your Torah because of your spiritual degradation in the long-continued Exile' (section III, para. 10). The ordinary Jew suffered from 'the general distress' of the entire nation:

> The confusion of the person who takes to heart the length of the Exile and the dispersion of the nation and what has happened on account of the poverty and paucity of numbers ... comes to ask 'can these bones live?' and this because we have been destroyed as a nation and our memory is forgotten (*ibid.*, para. 11).

Jewish creativity had also suffered as a result of the Exile: 'Hebrew ... has met the same fate as its speakers. It has been impoverished in their poverty and diminished by their small numbers, in spite of its natural superiority over all other languages' (section II, para. 67–8).

R. Judah Halevi's consciousness of the exile was intensified by the situation of Spanish Jewry in his time, part of which was settling 'in the regions of Edom', while part dwelt as of old in 'the borders of Arabia' – as he poetically described the distribution of the Jews between Christian and Islamic principalities. He lived through the changes that followed the crusade then being fought in Spain (namely, the Reconquista) and he knew of the war of the crusaders in Erez Yisrael. He recognized the religious sincerity of both the Christians and the Moslems. Prompted by the two armies that did battle with one another, with worthy intentions on both sides, Halevi's king of the Khazars is made to set out to seek the path to the truth. In a dream he was informed that 'your intention gains the approval of the Creator, but your deeds are not desirable.' When the philosophers argued before him the absolute superiority of good intention, the king disproved their arguments by reference to the crusades, pointing out that:

> undoubtedly there can be a deed which is desirable in itself, yet not so according to logic. Otherwise why should Edom and Ishmael, who have divided the inhabited world, be waging war against each other? Each of them has dedicated his soul to God, each fasts, prays, and lives ascetically, yet sets out with the purpose of slaying the other, believing that this slaughter is a great and virtuous deed and brings him close to the Creator.... And each of them believes that he is on the way to Paradise. And to believe them both is impossible for the intellect (section I, para. 2).

The piety of both sides was not cited merely for the sake of debate; R. Judah Halevi was highly sensitive to manifestations of faith and piety by members of other religions. He would awake to morning prayers at

> The sound of a people crying,
> Praying with perfect heart,
> Arise, why do you slumber?
> Strangers pray, while you sleep apart.
> (J. Zemora, ed., *Complete Poems,* Tel Aviv, 1946, Book V, 17, p. 215)

Thus he was aware of the sincere religious devotion among the crusaders as well as among the Moslems in the mosque nearby.

In Spain, Jews were hurt in the course of the Reconquista wars, of which Halevi wrote: 'Seir and Kedar [*i.e.,* Christendom and Islam] . . . may fight their wars but we are the ones who fall.' This statement opened his lament:

> On the city, that held three-score
> Merchant-princes, the might of Israel . . .
> The day the city was breached . . .
> Slaughtered by the vengeance of the sons of Seir
> Lifeless lie heaps of dead
> After the sword of vengeance
>   has passed
> Then captivity, hunger and thirst
>   approached the Children of Israel
>   (*Ibid.,* Book X, 1, pp. 593–6)

He shared in the sufferings of his brethren but also bemoaned the absence of Jewish military might:

> Amid the hosts of Seir and Kedar
> Israel's host appears no more . . .

In order to overcome this feeling of weakness and desperation, R. Judah developed his own theory on the selection of Israel. It involved the physical election of Erez Yisrael, which is located in a region that 'has equable and temperate climates'. Of all the lands within this choice region, 'the most central and desirable is the Land of Canaan, the country of prophecy.' The Jew has to aspire to this land not only because of its sanctity and not only because of his degradation in exile, but also because the very situation of exile involves an ambiguity in its very essence. Halevi placed a disparaging remark about the Jews in the mouth of the king of the Khazars, who said, 'You are degraded in this world and will also be degraded in the world to come.' But the Jewish sage replied, 'You condemn us for our poverty and misfortune, yet these have been the pride and greatness of other peoples', a reference to the holy figures of Christianity and Islam (*The Kuzari,* section I, para. 113).

However, Halevi did not accept easy answers or rest content with half-truths. Humility is a fitting religious value for all faiths, but only on the condition that it is a voluntary manifestation of abnegation and the abasement of the spirit. Thus, the Jews' argument 'would be true if your abnegation came of its own free will; but it is imposed upon you, and *if you could, you would slay*' (*ibid.,* para. 114). This argument, which incidentally reveals the same desire for physical resistance and self-defence as was expressed by Ibn Ezra and Maimonides, gave R. Judah an opportunity to penetrate deeply into the psychology of the ordinary Jew suffering in exile:

> The majority among us do not accept poverty and submission to God for the sake of His Torah . . . but the minority among us do hold this opinion; yet there is a recompense for the majority because they bear the burden of exile in an intermediacy between sheer compulsion and full free will.

The term 'intermediacy' is most significant. It is indicative of the fact that from the spiritual viewpoint the ordinary Jew is in an ambivalent situation, compulsion and free choice being intermingled in his acceptance of the exile and its implications. R. Judah proves the existence of an element of choice by the fact that the Jews are surrounded by religions that rest content with a mere declaration by an individual of his acceptance of the religion. If the Jew in exile 'were to wish to join with his oppressor, he need only say a word without any effort at all' (*ibid.*, para. 115). It follows that there is an element of choice.

Elsewhere in his book Halevi was even more precise, arguing that the choice in exile is free choice,

> for important persons amongst us could eliminate the contempt and slavery from their souls by a single word which they could utter without difficulty; and then they could become free men, higher in status than those who have held them in servitude; and the only reason they do not do this is to preserve their Torah (*ibid.*, section IV, para. 23).

Halevi was expressing the feelings of the aristocratic circles, who regarded themselves as equal in all respects to the Christian and Islamic nobilities but rejected the advantages of membership in those groups for the sake of their belief in God.

Accordingly, Judah Halevi preferred to dwell in the desolate Erez Yisrael:

> Better a day in the land of God
> Than a thousand on foreign soil,
> The ruins on the Holy Mount
> Than coronation hall.
> For by these I shall be redeemed
> And by those held in thrall.
> (Schirman, *op. cit.*, II, p. 491)

The cruel enslavement that he rejected was the courtly life of the upper class:

> Who can think himself content
> Subject to an idol king?
> Like a swallow longing for the sky
> But tethered by a string.
> Templed by the alien gods
> Under the dominion of Philistine, Arab or Hittite,
> Culled to do their will and betray God's
> To forsake the Creator and serve creatures.
> (*Ibid.*, p. 498)

Halevi appears to have been arguing against those who rejected migration to Erez Yisrael. In his poems and *The Kuzari,* he presented the arguments of those who claimed that the Holy Land was in ruins, that the Christians were ruling over it and that Jews should not abandon the graves of their fathers in Spain and journey afar. He himself recognized the difficulty of renouncing his social success, his circle of friends and his disciples. Nevertheless, his negation of life in exile finally prevailed;

to the Kuzari's argument against journeying to the Holy Land, the sage responded:

> The Land of Canaan is uniquely dedicated to the God of Israel; and only there can the commandments be fully observed, since many of them are connected with Erez Yisrael. Heart and soul can be clear and pure only in the place which they know is dedicated to God (section V, para. 23).

Halevi himself practised what he preached. His pilgrimage in the year 1141 was a public and communal event, apparently intended as an open demonstration. The arrival of the esteemed poet was a festive occasion for the Jews of Egypt, who welcomed him with ceremonies and banquets.

When R. Moses ben Naḥman (Ramban or Naḥmanides 1195–c. 1270) arrived in Erez Yisrael in 1267, he sang the praises of Jerusalem in a poetic epistle that informed those in Spanish exile of the splendours and the everlasting sanctity of the Land, of its degradation in the absence of its sons and its natural longing for their return. Jerusalem is the place

> wherein the world was set firm and whence the foundations and boundaries of the earth first branched out . . . whence prophecy goes forth and is spread abroad to the souls of the offspring [Israel]. . . . From there Israel gets uplifting and sustenance . . . and where the Temple Mount is great and holy, hallowed for the Sanctuary. . . . Indeed, these are the least praises of the city. . . . And this day I have seen her holiness and also a harsh vision. Within the city I found one oppressed and suffering Jew. He is a dyer and has his fill of contempt, and at his home gather both great and small, not enough to complete a quorum for prayer. Yet there are not enough for a community, neither wealthy and propertied, nor even the poor and the needy. . . . I compare thee to a woman whose son has died at her breast and the milk gives her pain, so she suckles small puppies. . . . Thy very foes feel sorrow for thee and remember thee afar and glorify the Holy City saying, 'She is given to us as an inheritance.' And when they come to you and find all that delights the eye, they flee as though from the enemy when there is none to pursue. Yea abandoned is the whole of the spacious and fertile land, for they are not worthy of thee, nor art thou a footplace for them (from the end of his commentary on the Pentateuch).

Here too the eternal bond between the Jew and the Holy City and the state of ruin of the city were contrasted to the abject condition of the Jews living there at the time and the attitude of the crusaders towards it. However, Naḥmanides added a point stressed also in his commentary on the Torah, namely, that aliens cannot settle in the land because it does not wish to give them of its bounty. Rather, it is awaiting its sons; hence the desolation of the land is in itself a promise to Israel. At the sight of the holy ruins, Naḥmanides, in the manner of R. Judah Halevi, reminded his God and the Holy City of the martyrs who had died in God's name. He recalled

> the blood of . . . the saints and the innocents who gave their souls to death for Thy name's sake, and placed their heads beneath the sword, offering Thee their human sacrifices which they turned into sweet fragrance . . . for they were glad

and rejoiced. One said: 'I am the Lord's, belonging to the Rock of Israel my Creator; I shall sacrifice myself, my flesh and my blood. And I give my firstborn for my sin, the fruit of my belly for the transgression of my soul.' Their spirits rejoiced . . . from father to sons, it was a heritage from Sinai to offer their souls as free-will peace-offerings for acceptance before the Lord (*ibid.*).

This thirteenth-century leader was praising the practice of slaying one's own children rather than allowing them to fall into the hands of Christians. Facing the Temple Mount and remembering the martyrs of the Diaspora, he complained bitterly to God of the situation of the Jews in the exile: 'Those who cleave to the Living God You have set amid the gentiles, despised and abased. And the many peoples battle against them, flaying their very skins from off them . . . despoiling and looting. You have smitten them with an enemy's blows' (*ibid.*). Such was Naḥmanides' view of the situation in the Diaspora when he left his native land for the land of his fathers. While he had still been living in Spain, however, his assessment had been more favourable in terms of the physical and spiritual existence of those Jews who remained there: 'We are left few in number amid every people. . . . But taken together we are numerous, God be praised' (from his commentary on Deuteronomy 4:27). At that time he saw little economic difficulty in the Diaspora. In his opinion the curses found in Deuteronomy were intended only as 'a reference for those generations at the time of the Destruction of the Second Temple, when steps were being taken to destroy them entirely' (on Deuteronomy 28:42). The curse of the Spanish exile seemed to him to consist mainly of the Jewish dread of persecution: 'Our fears in the Exile come from the nations who constantly persecute us.' As far as the material conditions of life were concerned, 'since we have been in Exile in the lands of our enemy, our efforts have not been wasted, for in these countries we live like the gentiles who dwell there, or even better than they' (*ibid.*).

The longing of the Jews of Spain for Ereẓ Yisrael and their questions concerning the exile and the Messiah grew more urgent as their position steadily declined. The Kabbalists of the thirteenth century had already begun to view the exile in terms of a divine cosmic catastrophe, the flaws and defects in the position of Israel reflecting the flawed and defective state of the universe as a whole. The Redemption of Israel meant the redemption of the universe. The struggle between Israel and 'Edom' was a struggle between good and evil, pure and impure. Every Jew who pursued good helped to liberate the sparks of the primal 'Great Light' held captive in the 'husks'. According to kabbalistic belief, at the very commencement of cosmic history the vessels into which the divine light had entered in such abundance proved incapable of containing it and shattered, sparks of that light remaining within the sherds. The good deeds of Israel would, in due course, release those sparks and bring about the 'correction' of the cosmic catastrophe, and at the restoration of cosmic order the state of Jewish exile would be rectified. Rationalist circles continued to conceive of the Exile and the Redemption within the old frame of reference, *i.e.,* the restoration of the Kingdom of Israel and the vision that the Jewish people, when redeemed, would serve as an example and focus for the spiritual and intellectual salvation of the world.

The outstanding teacher of this rationalist school was Maimonides. Strongly opposed to the apocalyptic descriptions of the 'birth-pangs of the Messiah' and of a world that would be entirely different in the eschatological future, he declared:

> Let no man suppose that in the days of the Messiah the natural order of the world will be in any way changed, or that there will be any innovation in the created universe; but the world will continue after its fashion, and as for Isaiah's verse, 'And the wolf shall lie down with the lamb, the leopard and goat together,' it is a parable and an enigma. It means that Israel will dwell secure amid the wicked idolaters who are likened to a wolf or leopard . . . and all will return to the true faith. . . . Indeed, all such passages regarding the Messiah are parables. And in the days of Messiah the King all men will know what the purpose of the parable was, and what matter was indicated therein. The sages said: 'There is no difference between this world and the days of the Messiah except in respect of servitude to alien kings' (*Yad Haḥazaka,* Laws of Royalty, XII, para. 1–2).

Not only did Maimonides reject outright the mystical descriptions of the days of the Messiah, which in his opinion were fantastic and exaggerated, and defer to the future the comprehension of the biblical texts that describe those times in miraculous terms, but he also repeatedly stressed the human and regal character of the Messiah. On this matter as well, the style and spirit of his words were those of legal decisions as well as of a polemic tract:

> Do not permit yourself to suppose that the King Messiah needs to perform signs and wonders or to bring innovations into the world, or resurrect the dead, or anything of that kind. It is not so. . . . If a king of the house of David arises who is learned in the Torah and fulfils the commandments like David his forefather in accordance with the Torah and the Oral Law, and if he commands all Israel to observe the Torah and he repairs its breaches, and wages the Wars of the Lord, then indeed he qualifies as the Messiah. If he has done these things successfully and built the Temple in its rightful place and gathers together the dispersed of Israel, then indeed he is assuredly the Messiah. And he will bring the Restoration of the World, to serve the Lord together (*ibid.,* XI, para. 3–4).

In describing the era of the Messiah, Maimonides rejected the desire for vengeance and world domination, stressing instead hopes for a world of material ease and spiritual, religious and intellectual richness. It was on this positive note that he ended his great *halakhic* work.

Maimonides' naturalistic and intellectualized conception of the Redemption was a product of both his basically rationalistic approach as well as of his concept of the type of leaders God sends to mankind. He developed his doctrine of prophecy and the Messiah under the influence of Greco-Arab philosophy. Here greatness of intellect and learning are essential prerequisites for prophecy. Yet, while intellectual as well as moral accomplishments are necessary conditions, they are not in themselves sufficient qualifications for prophecy. Unlike his predecessors among the Arab philosophers, Maimonides left to the Divinity the right of 'veto': the man who has reached these heights of human achievement is potentially capable of prophecy, but whether or not he does prophesy depends on the Divine Will. In his view it is also possible for a man to be a 'prophet unto himself . . . able to prophesy for himself in his heart, expanding . . . and extending his knowledge and thought until he knows what he never knew previously of those great matters'. Miracles are not the hallmark of prophecy. The Messiah must inevitably be a prophet, a man who has reached the pinnacle of wisdom. When a question was sent to Maimonides from Yemen regarding a man who had appeared there claiming to be the Messiah, he answered that since this man had not formerly been a sage he could not possibly qualify as a prophet and, *a fortiori*, should not be believed to be the Messiah. He advised his questioners to treat the claimant as a madman.

Maimonides regarded the exile as a mighty spiritual and social contest. The camp of truth, *i.e.*, the host of Israel, had constantly been surrounded by foes wishing to destroy the truth that Israel defended. In earlier days the kings of various nations had employed only the method of coercion; in later times they attempted to win by seduction. The innovation introduced by Christianity and afterwards by Islam lay in the combination of coercion and seduction, which accounted for the fact that the Jewish war was so difficult to wage in his era. He was convinced that Israel would emerge victorious, because Israel's victory would signify the victory of truth. Maimonides seems to have actually believed that the Messiah would come in his own days.

To sum up, in the Jewish world of the twelfth to fourteenth centuries, there was considerable concern over questions regarding the exile, the Redemption and the sanctity of Erez Yisrael. The intensity of emotion did not extend over wide circles; but those groups that occupied themselves with these matters exerted great influence among the people – whether of a mystical or rationalistic character.

The Idea of Election

The Jews recognized the fervency of the Christian and Moslem believers who confronted them (see the comments of the Ḥasidei Ashkenaz concerning the moral influence of the Christian burghers on the Jews, on page 463, and those of Judah Halevi regarding the effect that the religious feeling among members of other faiths had on the Jews, on page 529). Jewry was constantly wrestling with the claims of Christianity and Islam, each of which purported to be the sole true religion faithful to the will of the God of Israel. Under these circumstances it was only natural that the question of the election of Israel should become an immediate and crucial one. The problem appears to have become particularly acute during the twelfth century.

The rationalist rabbi Abraham ibn Daud based the belief in Israel's election on the fact that the faith was given to Israel by Divine Will in a complete form, without any need for Israel to undertake the efforts required of gentile philosophers in order to reach it:

> And while they groped towards monotheism for thousands of years, it was given to us by Divine Revelation for confirmation through the Prophets. So when we recite 'Blessed art Thou O Lord who chose us from all the nations,' there is no reason for any rational being to wonder at this. For this most worthy faith which

comes so hard to other nations was given to us at the first without any toil. And if it has reached others too, it has come to them from us (Weil, *op. cit.*, p. 63).

In effect, he justified Israel's claim to election on the grounds that it was the first nation to accept a pure, monotheistic faith.

For R. Judah Halevi, who was keenly sensitive to the issue of exile and the national degradation of the Jews, such a solution was insufficient. His concept of the election of Israel was based on a singular combination of a mystical, anti-rationalistic approach to the relationship between man and God and a naturalistic conception of the election of individuals and a nation by God. According to his view, outstanding individuals who have much in common with the group to which they belong but who possess some superior quality or qualities may be elected from among their group. It is on this principle of election that the hierarchy of God's creations and creatures is based. Under the influence of the Greco-Arab scientific disciplines of his time and as a physician who throughout his life had dealt with healthy and unhealthy bodies, he conceived of a scale of being, which begins with the mineral kingdom. The vegetable kingdom is superior by reason of the capacity to grow. The animal kingdom is on an even higher plane by virtue of the ability of animals to move and associate. Among the animals, man ranks highest because of his faculties of speech and understanding; and Israel, the peak or crown of Creation, stands elected above the rest of the human race by virtue of the gift of prophecy, which is restricted to Israel alone. For polemic purposes Halevi gave the latter point a central place in his work *The Kuzari*, which describes the king of the Khazars' conversion to Judaism and his acceptance of the true faith of Israel even though he consciously cannot achieve that highest quality, which is peculiar to Israel.

According to Halevi, the process of election was operative in the human race even before the people of Israel came into existence. In every age, since the time of Adam, God would elect special persons who were outstanding in their generation, 'all others being like a husk'. In the days of Shem, the son of Noah, election was given a geographical base in 'the land of prophecy', becoming the patrimony of the children of Shem and, in due course, the heritage of Israel. In the age of the patriarch Jacob, the quality of election was extended; 'the sons of Jacob are elected, all of them are worthy of divine concern . . . and here began the application of divine concern with a complete congregation after it had been found only among individuals'. The people of Israel were given this privilege not because of their personal qualities and lineage alone, but because they were eventually to be entrusted with the land of Canaan, 'that place which is designated for Divine concern'. From that time Israel became eternally elect. A bad Jew bears within himself the latent or slumbering qualities of election and singularity, which pass from him to his good son or grandson. Even under the conditions of exile, 'the quality of prophecy' remained vested in Israel. For this quality to pass from potentiality into acuality, the Jews have to return to the land of prophecy – Erez Yisrael – and act in accordance with the prophetic teachings, *i.e.*, the Torah of Israel (*The Kuzari*, section I, para. 95).

Even when Jews are not in their own land and prophecy is withheld from them, there is a significance to their election. Israel in exile was, to be sure, 'a body without head or heart . . . and not a body but scattered bones. . . . Nevertheless . . . these bones . . . still have in them some qualities of life, and have been vessels for head and heart and spirit and soul and intelligence' (*ibid.*, II, para. 29–30). Halevi demonstrated the superiority of this people by reference to its vitality. Even the memory of many other nations had been forgotten, but Jewry continued to exist. 'We are not to be compared to the dead. We are like a sick patient of whom all the physicians have despaired but who yet hopes for a cure by some miracle or change in the established order' (*ibid.*, para. 34). The sufferings of Israel in the exile resulted from its centrality for mankind and its unique and eternal election. In Halevi's opinion there was no contradiction between the assumption that Israel was exiled from its land on account of its sins and the assumption that the passages in Isaiah (53ff.) that tell of the servant of the Lord who suffers for the transgressions of others refer to Israel. He explained the compatibility, after his fashion, in medical terms: 'Israel among the nations is as the heart among the members of the body – it is more sensitive to sickness than all of them and is healthier than all of them' (*ibid.*, para. 36); thus the deficiencies of the other 'members' of mankind injure Israel.

As though to controvert this opinion, Maimonides expressed the view that the Jewish nation had been chosen because of the free will of its fathers and sons and their acceptance of the true faith. Israel is, in effect, a 'nation of proselytes'. Maimonides was asked by Obadiah, 'the righteous proselyte', a convert from Normandy, whether in his prayers he should include himself as one of the elect by referring to 'our father Abraham'. Maimonides replied:

> Obadiah, wise and understanding righteous proselyte, may the Lord repay your deeds and may your reward be complete from the Lord God of Israel under whose wings you have come to take shelter. . . . You should recite the prayers in their normal form and not change a word. Just as every Jew prays and recites blessings so you are fit to bless and pray. . . . The essential point is that our father Abraham was the one who taught all the people and gave them wisdom and informed them of the true faith and unity of God and rejected idolatry and confounded its ways and brought many under the wings of the *Shekhina* and taught them and instructed them and ordered his children and household after him to keep the way of the Lord. . . . Therefore whosoever converts to Judaism until the end of all generations, and whosoever unifies the Name of the Holy and Blest One as it is written in the Torah, he becomes a member of the family and one of the disciples of our father Abraham, may he rest in peace. And he has brought them to the right path just as he brought back his own generation with his words and teachings. In this way, he has brought back all those who shall convert in the future through the testament he ordered of his sons and household after him. It follows that our father Abraham, may he rest in peace, is the father of his fit and worthy offspring who follow his ways, and the father of his disciples and of every person who converts to Judaism. . . . Since you have come under the wings of the *Shekhina* and joined Him [God] there is no distinction here between us and you, and all the miracles that have been performed were, so to say, performed for us and you. . . . There is no distinction whatsoever between you and ourselves in any respect.

Most certainly you have to recite 'Who has chosen us' and 'Who has given us' and 'Who has given us a heritage' and 'Who has set us apart', since the Creator, may He be exalted, has already chosen you and set you apart from the nations and has given you the Torah. The Torah being for us and for all proselytes . . . and know that most of our forefathers who left Egypt were idolaters there, mingling with the gentiles and learning from their deeds, until the Lord sent Moses our teacher, may he rest in peace, master of all the Prophets, and set us apart from the nations and placed us under the wings of the *Shekhina,* together with all the proselytes, and gave us all one law. And do not let your pedigree be light in your eyes. While we trace ourselves back to Abraham, Isaac, and Jacob, you trace yourself back to the One who spoke and the world came about. . . . Indeed it should be clear to you that you have to say 'Which the Lord swore to our Fathers that he would give us' and that Abraham is a father to you and to us and to all the righteous who follow in his ways. . . . Such are the words of Moses son of Rabbi Maimon of blessed memory (Blau, *op. cit.,* para. 293, pp. 548–50).

Maimonides indicated two stages in the 'conversion' of Israel, the first commencing when Abraham recognized the true God and taught the monotheistic concept to all who were prepared to accept it, without distinction as to race, and the second occurring when Moses found the offspring of the patriarchs engaged in idolatry and brought them back to the true faith at Sinai. Those who have received the Torah by conscious choice are particularly honourable. The differences between the views of Maimonides and of R. Judah Halevi on the character of election came to exert an influence throughout the Middle Ages and even later.

Rationalists and Mystics

The religious rationalists of the twelfth century were, as has been noted, aware of the inner tension between the faith of the heart and the philosophical concepts of the intellectual approach. The major attempts to achieve a synthesis of the two – the *Sefer Haemunah Haramah* of R. Abraham ibn Daud and the *Moreh Nevukhim* of Maimonides, both written in Arabic – aimed to eliminate the contradictions and to strengthen faith. They also endeavoured to ensure that this faith would not contradict human reason.

The immanent tension of the rationalists was compounded by the need to defend their systems against the steadily growing circles that opposed rationalism and a synthesis with Greek philosophy. The dynamics of the Aristotelian system, on the one hand, and the glow of mystical awareness, on the other, joined together to create agitation in the world of Western Christendom. In the cities, which were awakening to increased activity during the twelfth and thirteenth centuries, and in the universities that were gradually emerging in cities such as Paris, there was, from the twelfth century onwards, a growing struggle between the Aristotelian approach, transmitted from the Islamic world (frequently via Jewish scholars, translators and rationalist philosophers), and the traditional Christian views. In the thirteenth century, some scholars at the University of Paris even rejected the belief in heaven and hell, in the traditional sense. They tended to base Christian thought on what could be apprehended by the intelligence and confirmed by theological consideration. This trend among the university scholars is sometimes described as 'Latin Averroism', after Averros or Ibn Rushd, the Moslem philosopher whose opinions strongly influenced this current of thought. The beginnings of the rationalist approach in Christianity were already visible in the twelfth-century teachings of Peter Abelard, which were opposed by a powerful mystical trend for which Bernard of Clairvaux had broadened the way with his attacks against Abelard. The struggle became more acute during the thirteenth century, when the study of certain Aristotelian works was prohibited and certain viewpoints were declared anathema. The conflict also had social and regional aspects, as the supporters of Christian rationalism centred in the cities and universities, while the citadels of mysticism lay within the walls of the monasteries and among circles subject to the influence of popular monastic preachers.

The rationalists of the twelfth and thirteenth centuries believed, along with R. Abraham ibn Daud, that

> what the philosophers call the active intelligence . . . had been known far earlier by the prophets as the Holy Spirit. Thus Scripture says: 'Indeed it is a spirit in Man, and the breath of the Almighty which makes them understand it.' . . . The 'spirit in Man' is the human intellect, while 'the breath of the Almighty' is the Holy Spirit (Weil, *op. cit.,* p. 58).

The identification of biblical terms with philosophical concepts and the attribution to the human intellect of so central a position found expression in many areas of creativity. In some cases this was because the opposing trend presented its own claims. In his commentaries, R. Abraham ibn Ezra declared his guiding principle to be 'that rational deliberation is basic, because the Torah is not given to one who lacks reason. And the angel that mediates between man and his God is his intelligence' (introduction to his commentary on the Torah). These religious philosophers were continuing in greater depth and detail the tradition begun in the tenth century of explaining away every instance of anthropomorphism in biblical texts, that is, any expressions that might lead one to suppose that God has a physical or corporeal form. They also sought to deny the concept of 'partnership' by reinterpreting biblical expressions that might lead to the conclusion that God had partners in the work of Creation or in the direction of the universe. These two efforts, which also had a polemic anti-Christian purpose, led the rationalist philosophers to interpret verses containing ambivalent expressions as parables and enigmas. The mystics were not alone in their opposition to this homiletic tendency, for the *halakhists* regarded extreme exegesis of this kind as a rejection of the plain sense of the biblical text and as an allegorization that deprived the Torah of its real significance and thus was liable to negate the requirement to observe commandments.

The influence of the systematic Greco-Arab philosophy on some Jewish philosophers was so great that they considered Talmudic dialectics and the casuistic method of questions and explanations to be unnecessarily wearisome, leading only to confusion. Written in beautiful Hebrew, Maimonides' great work, *Yad Haḥazaka,* was intended to guide the people in the path of the *halakhah* by preserving the essence of the Talmud while discarding the husk of unsystematic discussion,

> so that the Oral Law as a whole shall be set out for all without queries or answers, not with one saying this and the other that, but clear-cut decisions . . . according to the law . . . so that all the laws may be manifest. . . . So that a man should not require any other work whatever for any of the laws of Israel, but this work shall be a compendium of the entire Oral Law. . . . Accordingly I have called this work *Mishneh Torah* ['Deuteronomy'] because a man should study first the Written Torah and afterwards study this . . . and does not need to read any other book apart from them (from the Introduction).

He hoped his presentation of a systematic codification and guide that eliminated the unnecessary and the complicated would aid future generations of Jews. Scholars from his own time until the present day who have studied this work have confirmed that he has indeed summed up – sometimes in a single word or sentence – every point of the Oral Law and its earlier interpretations.

For Maimonides the *halakhah* encompassed an attitude towards the world, the foundations of knowledge (the first of the fourteen parts is entitled 'The Book of Knowledge') and a theory of state and society (displayed in various sections, particularly in the laws of the Sanhedrin and the laws of monarchy in the final book). His codification and its declared purpose angered many sages, and even his supporters and commentators could not agree to his elimination of Talmudic debate; in fact, they reintroduced Talmudic casuistry in their interpretation of his work. Thus his desire was not fulfilled but his intention testifies to his rationalistic mode of thought.

The school of Maimonides issued a ban on mystical literature. Inquiring about an early work entitled *Shiur Komah* ('Dimensions of the Height or Body'), a questioner cited R. Ḥai Gaon, who wrote that its 'subject matter is one of the secrets of the sages of blessed memory, dealing with fundamental natural or divine matters'. To this Maimonides responded,

> Never have I thought that this is one of the works of the sages . . . indeed, far be it from having been theirs. . . . In brief, erase this book and cut out all memory of its contents – to do so is to fulfil the commandment 'And ye shall not mention the name of other gods'. . . . For he who has height or body is undoubtedly another god (Blau, *op. cit.*, para. 117, pp. 200–1).

In the *Mishneh Torah* he declared categorically that any comprehension of the Deity involving even the slightest measure of corporeality must be regarded as absolute heresy.

Meanwhile, the mystical current began to emerge with increasing force, presenting its alternative view of the universe and of Divinity. Like all mystics, the Jewish ones aspired to come close to God rather than to understand Him. They yearned for the Living God, and their visions and revelations arose from this aspiration for contact with God. For them the Torah was a revelation filled with mystery, a guide on the path to truth. This path is opened by means of language. One of the leading mystics, Joseph Gikatilla, followed Naḥmanides, who wrote that the believer must concede that the Torah is not 'conventional in its language', 'for if you were to say that the language of the Torah is like other languages, we would be denying the divinity of the Torah, the whole of which [including its linguistic garb] was given by the Divine Power', and 'the Torah would be acquired without soul' (from his 'Essay on the Inner Meaning of the Torah', in H. D. Chavel, ed., *Selected Works of Naḥmanides,* II, Jerusalem, 1963, pp. 467ff.). According to the mystics, there is a symbolic significance even in the musical rhythm of the vowels, the letters, the punctuation and the cantillation marks of the biblical text. The *Zohar* ('Radiance'), the basic work of kabbalistic literature, explains:

> 'And the wise shall be radiant', like the vowels that are melodious and whose melody attracts the written letters and vowel-signs to follow them and proceed in motion behind them like soldiers behind their king. . . . 'As the radiance', the melody of the cantillation signs; 'the firmament', the spreading of the melody. . . . 'And they that justify the many', these are the punctuation marks . . . on account of which the statement is made 'This shall be radiant', letters and vowel points which give light together (*Zohar* on Genesis).

To the music of this mystical harmony played on the instruments of the Hebrew language, the mystics set out to reveal the secrets concealed within the Torah.

Nature, for them, had a layer of mystery that constituted its true significance. Maimonides had endeavoured to explain miracles in natural terms and present his own philosophical concept of man and the cosmos as *halakhah* in order to increase man's love for the Creator, through the recognition of God's wisdom revealing itself in the natural order. For a mystic such as Naḥmanides, however, the Creator cannot be identified through the regular movements of Creation because, for the mystic, there is no fixed or established natural system:

> For a man has no share in the Torah of Moses our teacher until we come to believe that all actions and occurrences are miracles. There is nothing of the natural way of the world in them, whether they happen to society or to the individual. . . . Everything comes about by decree from High (from his commentary on Exodus).

The real meaning of any commandment, therefore, lies within its mystery.

The literature of the Jewish mystics of the Middle Ages appeared first in Provence and afterwards in Christian Spain. Ancient foundations were used to construct a new edifice. Part of the literature was intentionally presented in the form of collective works. The most widely accepted work in this literature is the *Zohar,* which seems to have been written and compiled mainly in thirteenth-century Spain and is commonly believed to have been given its final form by R. Moses de Leon. It is written in a unique Aramaic and claims to consist of the words of many Mishnaic *tannaim* and Talmudic *amoraim,* particularly R. Simeon bar Yoḥai, to whom the work is traditionally attributed, and his disciples. In a slightly different style, such attributions to ancients were to be found before the *Zohar* in *Sefer Habahir* ('Book of Brightness') and after the *Zohar* in the works *Sefer Hakanah* ('Book of the Reed') and *Haplia* ('The Wonder'), contemporary writings that were attributed to individuals from the past.

The purpose of Naḥmanides' commentaries, the *Zohar* and the works of the mystics of Spain and Provence in the twelfth and thirteenth centuries was to give a written and comprehensible form, for those whose frame of reference was conventional language, to the mystics' aim and achievements in their heavenly visions and their penetrations into the secret strata of the Torah. The literature was produced by an extremely small group of mystics who reported visions and occult interpretations by word of mouth. The spirit of the times and the need for polemics against the rationalists led the mystics to express themselves in part in a fashion that could be comprehended by the general public.

Certain ideological links existed between the rationalists and the mystics, but all bridges were burnt between their main representatives. The conflict became more acute because it inevitably involved the question of the kind of general education permissible for a Jew. These spiritual struggles were frequently complicated by social tension; thus, among the Jews of the Iberian Peninsula and its vicinity, not only were varying viewpoints and interpretations at loggerheads, but the social factions within the communities were likewise in competition.

The Maimonides Controversy

The opposition that arose against the writings and philosophy of Maimonides at the end of his lifetime continued and grew stronger during the early decades of the thirteenth century. The first serious conflict flared up around 1232, when the opponents of the rationalists first publicly contested his opinions. This dispute spread through Provence and the whole of Spain, and the sages of northern France also intervened in sharp opposition to him. However, the supporters of Maimonides gained the upper hand in a series of bans and counter-bans.

Naḥmanides adopted a conciliatory stand in this dispute. He wrote to the sages of northern France expressing his esteem for their basic intentions: 'Our Rabbis of France, we are your disciples and from your waters do we drink.' His letter indicates that the sages of northern France 'had all agreed to ban and excommunicate every man who raised his hand to study the *Moreh Nevukhim* and "The Book of Knowledge" [the section of philosophy that introduces the legal compendium, *Yad Haḥazaka*] . . . until they are put away forever'. Naḥmanides explained to them that they were unacquainted with the cultural climate and the social circumstances of the intellectual circles of Spain and Provence: 'You are set in the bosom of faith, planted in the courtyards of tradition, fresh and luxuriant.' The words of Maimonides in the works that they had barred were not intended for them: 'Did he give himself toil on account of you, *geonim* of the Talmud? He was as one compelled to construct a book by which to escape from the philosophers of Greece, to withdraw from Aristotle and Galen. Have you heard their words, have you been led astray by their proofs?' Naḥmanides sang the praises of Maimonides, emphasizing above all his distress at the fact that the leading circles, from which he himself originated, had become steeped in courtly traditions and deeply influenced by the alien culture. Naḥmanides therefore felt compelled, both spiritually and socially, to advise these revered sages to moderate their objections.

Provence was, at the time, the battlefield on which the Catholic Church was waging its war against the Albigensian heresy. The Dominicans were energetically investigating the heresy and burning its books. According to the account of the rationalists – a version accepted by R. Abraham, the son of Maimonides, among others – the latter's opponents drew the attention of the Christian inquisitors to the heresy in the writings of Maimonides. According to another version the Dominicans, on their own initative, took advantage of the internal Jewish dispute. In any case, the works of Maimonides were burnt by them in 1232. This act shocked even his opponents, and there is a reliable tradition that relates that Rabbenu Jonah Gerondi repented of his share in the dispute. The inquisitorial fires extinguished the flame of communal strife. When the Talmud was burnt only a few years later, there were some who regarded this as a punishment meted out to the house of Israel for the burning of Maimonides' works.

As a result of the singular value attached by Jews to study and the constant tension between Jewish and Greek philosophy, displayed even by those who endeavoured to build a bridge between the two, the main point of argument, even in the first controversy, turned on the question of general culture: which books should be studied and which prohibited? While the controversy died down, the factors that had produced it continued to exist, steadily becoming more pronounced. The rationalists did not surrender their aims and aspirations and the mystical trend continually grew stronger.

By the beginning of the fourteenth century, some scholars in Provence claimed that certain preachers of the rationalist school were explaining Talmudic legends and even biblical accounts in an extremely allegorical spirit. They claimed, for example, that one preacher had declared that 'Abraham and Sarah represent Matter and Form.' The social tension between the middle and lower classes, which gathered round the *halakhic* scholars and the mystics, steadily increased at the sight of the opulent and, according to the moralists, dissolute way of life of the upper classes, most of whose members were inclined towards Maimonides and rationalism.

This time it was not easy to persuade the heads of Spanish Jewry to demonstrate opposition to the dominant mood of the Provence communities. The exchange of correspondence published in the collection *Minḥat Knaot* ('Offering of Zeal') reveals that R. Solomon ben Abraham Adret (Rashba) hesitated a long time before taking action. After clashes in which the influence of R. Asher ben Jehiel (who had come to Spain from Germany) was brought to bear on the side of those opposed to Maimonides, two bans were pronounced in Barcelona in 1305. Those who issued the bans displayed a spirit of compromise similar to that of Naḥmanides in the earlier controversy. In one ban they required

> that no member of our Congregation shall study the books of the Greeks which were written regarding the science of Nature or of the Divinity, no matter whether these were written in their own language or had been translated into some other language, from this day and for fifty years, until the said member of our Congregation be five and twenty years old. . . . But from this decree of ours we exclude the science of Medicine although it also stems from the science of Nature.

The works of Maimonides and other Jewish rationalists were not explicitly included in the ban, and the prohibition against studying Greek philosophy was only imposed upon those under age twenty-five. The second ban was issued against those who went to extremes in allegorizing the Scriptures.

> For one of them said when preaching publicly in the synagogue as though in surprise: 'What reason did Moses have to prohibit pork? If it is because of its poor quality, the sages have not found its quality so bad.' And one of them said: 'The purpose of the commandment of the phylacteries is not to place them actually on the head and the arm, which serves no useful purpose, but only that a man should understand and remember the Lord.'

Books by such commentators were ordered to be burnt and banned to the public.

In contrast to the relative restraint shown by the anti-Maimonides group, his rationalist followers took a totally uncompromising position. R. Menaḥem ben Solomon Hameiri (1249–1306), who wrote a comprehensive and systematic commentary on the Talmud entitled *Bet Habeḥirah* ('The Temple'), issued a counter-ban to the one signed by the Rashba. He reminded Maimonides' opponents of their failure in the initial controversy, warning them that by their ban they would only widen the breach and would not achieve their objective. Furthermore, he declared as a matter of principle that times could not be set during which a man should learn Talmud and Jewish philosophy or should study other philosophies: 'You, your honoured self, know that there are various chambers and inclinations within a man, one tending this way and one that.' From the psychological viewpoint he suggested that there are some who tend towards study of the Talmud while others incline towards philosophy, according to their innate talents and spiritual readiness for a specific study. Secondly,' Hameiri continued, 'this age [*i.e.,* twenty-five] is the one at which man has millstones round his neck [*i.e.,* a wife and children to support]; and whatever has not yet been inscribed within him by that age will be written upon sand.' For this reason he rejected any age restriction. He also defended the value of secular wisdom. Believing that man tends to study what interests him, Hameiri warned the authors of the ban: 'I also see . . . an obstacle, that in yet another seven years . . . or whatever number it may be, each person will seek what suits him according to his temperament,' and, in any case, the coming generation would ignore a prohibition against secular studies.

An epistle in content and length, a veritable tractate defending the viewpoint of the rationalists, was included in the Responsa of the Rashba as 'An Apologia', though it is far from apologetic in tone and argument. According to this treatise, the greatest contribution of Greek philosophy to Judaism was its re-establishment of pure monotheism in Israel,

> for one of the most widely known phenomena was the popularity of a corporeal view of God in earlier ages almost throughout the entire Diaspora. . . . However, in all ages there were *geonim* and scholars in Spain and Babylon and the cities of Andalusia who, through their familiarity with Arabic, were able to savour the philosophies of Greece in so far as they had been translated into that language. Hence they began to clarify many views in their doctrines, above all the unity of

God, and to eliminate that tendency towards corporeality, particularly by means of theoretical proofs borrowed from those philosophical works.

This protagonist of rationalism assured the authors of the ban, headed by the Rashba,

> that the hearts of the people cannot be turned away from philosophy and the books devoted to it as long as they have a soul in their bodies. . . . Even if Joshua the son of Nun had commanded it with his own mouth, they would never be prepared to obey. For they intend to fight for the honour of the Great Rabbi [Maimonides] and his books, and will dedicate their money, their offspring, and their spirits for his holy doctrines as long as the breath of life is in their nostrils. And thus they will command their children after them throughout their generations.

By the time the second controversy had subsided, it seemed to the leaders of Spanish Jewry that the religious approach they were offering the people was prevailing; but, in fact, in both Provence and Spain influences were penetrating from Ashkenaz that militated against the school and its teachings. The doctrines of the *halakhists* and of the Ḥasidei Ashkenaz were being disseminated in Spain by R. Asher ben Jehiel and through the sermons being preached there by the French rabbi Moses of Coucy. Mystical doctrine had sufficient appeal to compete with the influence of philosophy. The struggle continued in subsequent generations, with the balance increasingly tilting in favour of the anti-rationalists.

The Doctrines of the Ḥasidei Ashkenaz

In Ashkenaz a small group of scholars and élitists had developed an entire system in which positive and critical aspects were uniquely combined with a social and mystical outlook. During the second half of the twelfth century and the entire thirteenth century, a group emerged within Ashkenazi Jewry that was small in number but qualitatively of considerable significance. These were the *hasidim* or 'pious ones', who were motivated by a strong fear of sin and endeavoured to live in a simple and strict fashion. Their basic doctrine was of a dual nature – stern and demanding towards themselves, but lenient and gentle towards Jewry as a whole. Occasionally, they voiced severe criticism of those who led the people astray, but not of the people themselves. The aim of the *hasidim* was to educate Jewry towards a completely moral life. They fought for goodness and uprightness in human relationships and demanded the maximum from themselves in order to provide an example that would inspire and elevate the rest of the people.

The *hasidim* formed a closed and select circle that willingly and enthusiastically established exacting standards for itself. 'Righteous men may set up boundaries and impose fines on the pious and godfearing. . . . Even though the majority of the community are unable to comply with those limitations, they themselves accept them of their own free will' (Wistinetzky, *op. cit.,* para. 786, p. 197). From the outset they were headed by the members of an aristocratic family: R. Samuel Heḥasid, his son, R. Judah Heḥasid, and their kinsman, R. Eleazar ben Judah of Worms, the author of the *Roke'aḥ* ('Balsam'). Their teachings were formulated collectively, their main work being the *Sefer Ḥasidim*. Though the work is attributed to R. Judah Heḥasid, its structure and the content show that it is a product of generations of work. It consists of a collection of tales interwoven with moral teachings. Most of their words, particularly those included in this volume, were aimed at influencing the heart, the imagination and the intelligence of the reader.

The Ḥasidei Ashkenaz had their own esoteric and mystical doctrines. Like most mystically oriented groups, they were greatly preoccupied with the manifestation of Deity in the universe. They devoted much attention also to the power contained in the names of God and in the letters of the Hebrew alphabet, as well as to combinations of letters that could influence higher universes and spheres of being (see page 541 for corresponding views expressed in the *Zohar*). Of particular interest, from the historical viewpoint, are the conclusions they reached, on the basis of their cosmic theories, as to the proper structure of man's spiritual world and as to the pattern of human life. Their attitude combined extreme contempt for the material world with extreme realism vis-à-vis nature and human society.

The Ḥasidei Ashkenaz believed that the temporal world surrounding humanity is replete with demons and evil spirits. The dead, too, walk the earth and exert an influence upon it. While the body is alive, it is menaced from within by active elements of corruption; meanwhile, the forces of darkness lie in wait for the soul. Impurity and death ceaselessly pester the living soul, attempting to seduce it. R. Eleazar, the author of the *Roke'aḥ,* conceived of man's homage to the devil in the following terms:

A man who gives himself to a demon goes leaping backwards with his hands behind him. And he delivers himself from the domain of the Creator to that of the demon. And the demon treats him well, but finally causes him to fall. And they [the demons] are in the forest where little nuts grow (R. Eleazar ben Judah, *Ḥokhmat Hanefesh*, fol. 14r).

According to the *hasidim*, the Jewish community consists not only of those living in the Jewish street but also of the dead in the graveyard. The latter did not wish to be abandoned by the living, and at night their souls came to pray in the synagogue. The living and the dead together constituted the one body-mystic of Jewry in each locality.

These beliefs bear the impress of fears and superstitions that were emanating from the German Christian environment. The influence of Christian monasticism can be seen in the *hasidim*'s high regard for asceticism, which they valued first and foremost as a form of penance for a man's transgressions. In their view a man should break his spirit and torment his flesh in proportion to all the forbidden pleasures he has enjoyed – whether carnally or through his mind and emotions – until the 'weight' of the penitence weighs on him so that it removes his sins. Moreover, self-mortification could have its own value and reward. Yet, as Jews, the *hasidim* were limited in their pursuit of asceticism, because family life was the foundation of Jewish morality and celibacy constituted a failure to observe the Torah's ruling. The tension within this movement that resulted from having to cope with the influence of Christianity in this respect is much in evidence in hasidic thought and imagination.

Prayer, probably more than anything else, revealed the double standard of maximalistic self-demand, on the one hand, and leniency towards other Jews, on the other. The *ḥasid* is required to utter his prayers with intellectual and emotional intensity and to apply the melody most suited to the subject matter of the prayer:

> Draw out every word, so as to concentrate in your heart on whatsoever is uttered by your lips . . . with rhythm and the sound of the melody and in a loud voice. . . . And when you pray, add whatever is relevant to the specific blessing. . . . And if you cannot add, seek ye out melodies. Pray in the chant which you find sweet and pleasant . . . for words of entreaty and request let it be a melody that makes the heart weep . . . for words of praise, one that makes the heart rejoice, in order that your mouth may be full . . . of love and joy for the One who sees your heart and blesses it with bounteous affection and jubilation (Wistinetzky, *op. cit.*, para. 11, pp. 7–9).

Individual prayer included counting the letters, which were regarded as keys to the kingdom of Heaven. According to the *ḥasid*,

> Benefit accrues to me before the Holy and Blest One when I draw out my words. In the same psalm I count on my fingers how many letters *aleph* there are and how many letters *bet;* and after that when I return home I consider its meaning, why there should be precisely that number in that specific psalm or prayer (*ibid.*, para. 1575, p. 386).

Commentaries were actually produced in which the authors counted and numbered each letter, linking one to another 'by hooks and loops' of reasoning. The *ḥasidim* opposed any change of wording and the removal or addition of a single word, as these might alter the hallowed numerical structure of the letters. For them their prayer was an experience that cemented a formal and mystical enumeration, combining intention, melody and the construction of secret systems from the letters of the holy tongue, together with a freer attitude during prayer, which enriched it with new formulations and appropriate melodies.

With regard to the prayer of the simple folk, the attitude of the *ḥasidim* differed:

> If somebody comes to you who does not understand Hebrew, but is God-fearing, or a woman, tell them that they should acquire the prayers in a language they understand. For prayer consists only of comprehension by the heart, and if the heart does not understand what comes from the mouth what value has it? Therefore it is better to pray in the language that one understands (*ibid.*, para. 11, p. 9).

Love of the Creator was one of their main principles, filling their entire universe. The *ḥasid* was required

> to serve and love the Lord . . . since the soul is full of love and that love is united with joy, and that joy drags his heart away from the pleasures of the body and the delights of this world, and thus that joy is more powerful and gains control of the heart. . . . And all the affection and delight of the heart by one who loves the Lord with all his heart and all of whose thoughts are directed to perfoming the Creator's

will, to benefit the community and to hallow the Name. . . . And that love prevents a man from disregarding Torah for the sake of trifles such as amusing his children or enjoying the sight of women, or conversing, or strolling at random; and it causes him to sing sweet songs in order to fill his heart with joy at the love of the Lord (*ibid.*, para. 815, p. 206).

The true *ḥasid* was not concerned with the pleasures of this world because he achieved personal satisfaction and pleasure by performing his duty to the utmost, putting his love and joy into his performance.

Ḥasidic thought sometimes combined holy simplicity with radical criticism, without any contradiction between the two. This holy simplicity, which penetrated to the foundations of faith, led the *ḥasidim* to reflections on the justice of the Torah Law. Alongside the latter and sometimes even in opposition to it, they upheld a 'heavenly law'. Only in the latter, they claimed, could one find the full measure of spirituality and justice required of man. Torah Law constituted a minimal norm. The *ḥasid,* however, required himself to act in accordance with the maximum – namely, the principles of heavenly law. According to Torah Law, for example, a robber must restore to the victim the full value of the stolen goods. This judgement was not sufficient in ḥasidic doctrine:

> The robber has to think of the distress he has caused [to the robbed one] and all dependent upon him and the deprivations which he has caused them; and he should pay them back both according to the full damage he has caused, secondary results included, as well as according to the character and status of those robbed. . . . And he should add from his own money in return for the pleasures he derived from the stolen property, and should take on penitence in measure to counterbalance these pleasures. . . . The depth of this repentance . . . can be imparted only to the one who feels true remorse and wishes to be clear before the Holy and Blest One (*ibid.,* para. 22, p. 26).

According to Torah Law, there is a limit to responsibility; one who is under thirteen years of age or who is mentally unbalanced is not legally responsible for his actions. The *ḥasidim* concluded otherwise: 'Whatever sins you remember . . . you have to pay for,' irrespective of age, or of the mental condition under which the deed was committed (*ibid.,* para. 216, p. 77).

This attitude finds an even more radical expression in civil cases:

> When two come for judgement before the sage, if the said two are quarrelsome and contentious, the sage shall conduct the case according to Torah Law, even though it may seem to warrant an opposite decision according to the laws of Heaven. But if those two are good and God-fearing and accept the counsel of the sage, let him apply the laws of Heaven, even though they may be contrary to the laws of the Torah (*ibid.,* para. 1381, p. 337).

As the *ḥasidim* considered the matter of punishments stipulated in the Torah, they came to the conclusion that 'not from the measure of prescribed punishment [in the Torah] can one ascertain what is [the gravity] of commandments, [neither] their true punishment or reward' (*ibid.*, para. 157, p. 67). It is evident that the essential scale of importance of the commandments cannot be gauged from looking at the Torah punishments, as

> what the Torah punished by death in some cases and not in others was based on human conventions of what is shameful, and not according to what is spiritually and emotionally involved in the act itself. Thus the daughter of a priest who engaged in whoredom was sentenced to death by burning, but the daughter of a common Israelite by strangling; yet the passionate intent [*yezer*] involved is identical (*ibid.*, para. 43, p. 42).

'Therefore the commandments cannot be compared according to their punishments' (*ibid.*, para. 1046, p. 262). When they considered the *halakhah*, the *hasidim* stressed the inner, 'true' aspect of matters rather than their external appearance. The laws given in the Torah were expressed in terms of human conventions and could not illuminate essential values.

This attention to the inner aspect of things found expression in a penetrating criticism of the social order. They asked why there was no equality in the distribution of wealth in the world. The concentration of much property in the hands of a few was viewed as an act of injustice, as it were, on the part of Providence, which 'gives to one what could support a hundred'. If the rich man 'does not give to the poor . . . the poor will come and cry to the Lord: "You have given to this one what could maintain a thousand."' However, the *hasidim* found an explanation and a solution for the concentration of wealth in the concept of trusteeship, according to which the rich man receives his wealth, in part, as a trust from God for the poor:

> I have allowed you wealth in order that you should give as much of your wealth as [the wealth] permits to the poor. Since you have not given it I shall take it back from you as though you robbed them and as though you denied my pledge. For I entrusted this wealth to you in order that you should distribute it to the poor (*ibid.*, para. 1345, p. 331).

They also sought other explanations for financial inequality:

> If you see a wealthy wicked man with whom the children of great sages colligate, know that . . . it is not because of his merits that they make matches with him but because of the merits of his forefathers and mothers, or because the sages had formerly held him in contempt (*ibid.*, para. 237, p. 80).

The merits of the fathers and compensation for suffering may therefore also account for an evil man's wealth.

R. Eleazar ben Judah probed even further into the question of inequality. He saw that

> in this life there may be one who is not God-fearing, but who has a sharper mind than a God-fearing person. For the way of this world is in honouring one above his fellow. Just as a wealthy man has what he desires even though he does not fulfil the will of God as his riches would permit, because it has been determined

that he should enjoy in this world the honour accruing from his wealth, so that the descendants of the nobles would colligate with him, the same in Torah-learning: an undeserving one is honoured through it, for this was willed in Heaven. As riches were given to the undeserving, to bring him to hell, so an undeserving scholar who causes people to sin, judges falsely, despises the good, envies and hates them and 'rules with a heavy hand' – for the righteous man falls down before the wicked – is successful, for his words are listened to in this world, and he has disciples who abet him and is victorious over his worthier opponents. However, in the world to come, the world of the spirit, the righteous are given increased wisdom according to their fear of Heaven. To the degree they penetrate deeply into God-fearing, in that measure, in that world to come, the righteous one will be granted greater wisdom to prevail in debate, in analysing questions, as well as in harmonizing answers. And it is according to his pronouncement that the judgement of this world will finally be settled (R. Eleazar ben Judah, *op. cit.,* fol. 10r).

Thus intellectual gifts and natural capacity, including mastery of the Torah, are like possessions and property and do not always serve to a man's advantage. Sometimes, like material belongings, they are given in order to lead a man astray and bring him low. In the next world, however, intellectual gifts and scholarship will be granted to one according to the degree that he has immersed himself in the fear of Heaven, and the justice lacking in this world will be present there. Learning is a supreme value and intellectual gifts are important, for in the next world these will be the reward of the righteous. In this world, however, there is an unequal distribution of all possessions, spiritual and material alike.

These were not merely academic musings. According to a theory of R. Eleazar, 'it is decreed that each generation shall have its own thorn in its side.' The righteous and the 'thorn' engage in a constant struggle to influence the community. When the righteous one fails, it is because 'the townsfolk do not deserve to obey the good, therefore their hearts are made to incline to evil in order that they may be led astray.' R. Eleazar lived in a community that valued books and religious poetry. Apparently, he considered some of the writers of such books and hymns 'thorns', for he continued in the same vein: 'And furthermore evil people compose books for generations to come; and they write hymns to be uttered for generations, while the good ones do not achieve the same . . . so that the coming generations will also be unworthy and will also be led astray.' Even among the builders of public institutions and the *shtadlanim,* he found 'thorns':

> And likewise an evil man is permitted to profit in the world and establish a synagogue or graveyard or something else great, so that coming generations do not benefit from the deeds of the good. But for good persons, God does not desire that their deeds should be performed on behalf of those who are not worthy (*ibid.,* fol. 23r).

This theory of the eternal struggle between the 'thorns' and the righteous for leadership is radical and bitter, for it expresses criticism not only of evil contenders for leadership, but also the view that their popular success is due to the innate unworthiness of the given community or 'generation'. It also expresses eloquently the view that good deeds are not in themselves evidence for the good intentions of the doer, be his creativity expressed in good works of leadership, scholarship or liturgy.

The *hasidim* offered realistic and detailed criticism of the established order of society. When R. Ephraim, already referred to, lodged an appeal against the men who had offered more money for charity than he would offer and thus deprived him of his long-established right to roll up the Torah scroll, he received a response from the *hasidim* of Regensburg that must certainly have astonished him: 'Although their intention is not for the sake of Heaven but to be honoured . . . since a benefit accrues to the poor, he should not refuse it to them . . . for if he does refuse it . . . he is robbing the poor.' Regarding his desire to fulfil the commandment, they explained that if he gave charity even without performing the act of rolling up the scroll, he would receive the reward for the latter act, as if he had indeed performed it:

> Now as for the one who rolled and wrapped the Torah Scroll hitherto and whose intention is for the sake of Heaven: if he gives to the poor that money which he was accustomed to donate to the synagogue when binding up the Torah Scroll, he is as meritorious as though he had actually bound it up . . . since he would willingly perform the task now but refrains for the sake of the poor.

Furthermore, he should not fear future disputes for, if he sets a personal example of renunciation, he will prevent additional disputes of this nature (Wistinetzky, *op. cit.,* para. 1593, pp. 390–1).

The *hasidim* objected to the injustice of formal equality in taxation of the rich and poor alike, expressing their opposition by reference to biblical times: 'If there is a poor Israelite and a wealthy priest, how is it possible that the poor man is required to pay his tithe to the wealthy?' After offering 'simple' exegetical criticism of the law of the Torah on tithes, they turned to the situation in their own communities, questioning the justice of an equal, formalized distribution of the tax burden within the congregations of Ashkenaz, which demanded 'to give so much from each pound'. Such a system was improper because 'sometimes the poor man who pays is poorer than the one who receives.' In their opinion the collection of contributions to the Temple and the imposition of taxes in their own times was determined 'according to human conventions', as people were liable to evade fair payments if individual assessments were made. The *hasidim* knew of no way to solve the problem within the framework of the existing communal leadership. Instead, they suggested that 'the good should return to the poor in secret all that the latter give, without the evil people knowing about it' (*ibid.,* para. 914, p. 226), which in effect meant that they would have liked a progressive tax. What they were actually suggesting was the imposition of an additional charge on themselves, but they did not know how to introduce the practice into communal life.

The view that certain kinds of pride are justifiable in the case of the leader and the scholar was totally rejected by the *hasidim.* They had no apprehensions concerning extreme humility; on the contrary, the more extreme it was the better it was in their eyes. The recommended form of behaviour for the *hasid* was to always be among those who do not return an insult:

They shame him and insult him while he remains as though he were deaf and dumb. . . . not shaming any man. . . . And the true strength of the ḥasidic spirit is that although they mock him, he does not surrender his Hasidism nor his intention of acting for the sake of Heaven (*ibid.*, para. 975, p. 241).

They firmly believed that 'there is no quality so good in the world for preserving those who employ it and aiding them to gain all that is good, and keeping all evil away from them, as the power of humility for the sake of Heaven' (*ibid.*, para. 14, p. 9). The essence of humility was, of course, its inner aspect, not its external form. The truly humble man even has to behave with those marks of external pride which the proud impose upon him in their hearts. With penetrating honesty, the *ḥasidim* found an excellent expression for dialectical tension that arises when humility becomes an accepted value of the entire society. In such a situation it may happen

that others make an honour of humility . . . as for instance if they are greater than he is but do not wish to walk ahead of him, as though they are saying, 'We are humble.' But he feels ashamed because he has to walk ahead of them . . . since they may say how impudent is this fellow who walks in front of those who are greater than he is. . . . This is great humility, for he consents to be shamed in order to honour them (*ibid.*, para. 815, p. 206).

Sexual life and drives, together with family life and matrimonial relationships, was a topic that occupied an important place in ḥasidic doctrine. The *ḥasidim* openly and frankly described the power of sexuality, its temptations and dangers. Love between man and woman was considered a positive and necessary part of normal family life (see the opinion of R. Saadiah Gaon on this subject, on pages 445–6). They related:

A certain man fasted for a long time in order that God would give him a woman he loved; but his fasting and prayers were of no avail. He said to a sage: 'Consider, I have fasted and wept to no purpose.' The sage explained to him why his prayers were not answered and consoled him: 'Assuredly the Lord had matched for you one who does not find favour in your eyes,' but 'because of your fasts and prayers you may come to love this one [*i.e.*, the woman he had married without loving] and you will be happy together' (*ibid.*, para. 1137, pp. 287–8).

The *ḥasidim* spoke with understanding of the love that throbs in a man's soul. One of them

used to pray: 'Lord of the Universe, it is revealed and known before Your seat of glory that *my soul* loves a certain woman, not because I desire her sinfully for I do not yet know her. *Now if it is your purpose that I should love her, may Thy will be blessed, and I shall suffer as seems good in your eyes . . .*' And out of his love for her, he said: 'Lord of the Universe, how can I possibly take any other woman? For I may cause her evil and may come to hate her on account of my love for the other one' (*ibid.*, para. 1136, p. 287 [author's italics]).

The *ḥasidim* explained that 'sometimes Heaven causes a man to love a woman and a woman to love a man even though he does not take her.' There may be various reasons for this heavenly decree of unrequited love. 'Sometimes a man loves because his offspring and hers are destined to wed,' in which case the love may be fulfilled in the next generation.

The concepts of love found in the poetry of the troubadours were thus transplanted by the *hasidim* into a domestic, family framework. The world of chivalry considered marriage and love incompatible; the Hasidei Ashkenaz, on the other hand, accepted from this world the notion of spiritual suffering in love – though it is hard to determine through which channels this influence reached them – but interwove it with Jewish family life.

Good family stock also was particularly valued as a contributing factor in successful marriages. The ban on settlement within communities (see pages 505–6) was even justified as a means of perpetuating the families of good lineage that had settled together in certain places in order to avoid marriages with those of less suitable stock. Also highly valued was a knowledge of Torah on the part of the bridegroom. On the other hand, towards men who married women only for their money there was an ironical attitude. Such a man in a hasidic tale was made to utter the resignatory 'blessing for death' on his marriage, while he blessed God for 'a good tiding' upon hearing the sum that this undesired wife would bring in dowry (*ibid.*, para. 1127, p. 285).

In spite of their bitterness towards the non-Jewish population, the *hasidim* sought some sign of a slightly humane attitude on the part of their neighbours to justify teaching the need for honesty in the relations between Jews and gentiles. They advised that, 'if Jews and gentiles have made a condition among themselves to support one another and the gentiles helped the Jews with all their hearts, let the Jews do the same to the gentiles' (*ibid.*, para. 1849, p. 445).

Martyrdom, the hallowing of God's Name, held a central position in their thought, and praises were sung of the martyrs. The *hasidim* spoke of their longing for martyrdom, recording the disappointment of a man who wished to hallow the Name but was never privileged to do so and reckoning how much smaller his portion would be than that of his comrades who did hallow the Name, for he died peacefully in bed while the others were 'the leaders of the slain'.

The hasidic outlook was perhaps best exemplified by the injunction to serve God 'with all the depths of your thoughts' and was illustrated by the story of Rabbenu Jacob ben Yakar, who used to clean the space in front of the Holy Ark with his beard; and when the congregation would turn with requests to the king or to the authorities, he would remove his boots before praying, saying, 'I am a poor man; let them go [to the king] with their money while I go [before God] with mercy and entreaty' (*ibid.*, para. 991, p. 245). Hence the profundity of hasidic thoughts find expression only in actions that combine absolute humility with a manifestation of a truly personal relationship in serving the Creator and sharing in the troubles and distress of all Israel.

Disputations with the Christian World

The Hasidei Ashkenaz offer the best possible evidence that the very barrier between the Jewish and Christian worlds was also their meeting-place and that this meeting-place was the area of tension. We have mentioned that the *ḥasidim* cautioned against the influence of the Christian environment on Jewish morals. In describing the culture of Spanish Jewry, attention was drawn to the close ties between the Jews, particularly the upper stratum, and the surrounding culture. Similarly, 'the magnanimity of spirit' of sages such as Rabbenu Tam and R. Menaḥem Hameiri and the ḥasidic doctrine of humility had their parallels within the surrounding Christian world.

Emanuel of Rome opened his *Book of Lament* with a description of his reaction to a Christian cathedral:

> We entered the great temple of the Christians; and round the temple were the graves of the mighty kings, the princes, and the lords. On each of them were written fine phrases and sweet laments, carved of the rock of intelligence, taken from the pearls of wise utterance and interwoven with the diamonds of good words. . . . They subdue the hearts of those that hear them and they cause the eyes to weep while all pride will surrender and submit and knee will bend and kneel (Yarden, *op. cit.,* p. 383).

Although the Christian edifices undoubtedly made a favourable impression on Emanuel, as a rule the external splendour and sacral claims of the churches left the Jews with a sense of spiritual despondence. Both the Jews and the Christians had learnt from the Scriptures about the glories of the destroyed Temple in Jerusalem; and that served as a starting-point for debate and deliberation as to the status of the splendid church.

In *Megillat Ahimaaz* ('The Chronicle of Ahimaaz') completed in 1054 in southern Italy, it is related that the Hagia Sophia Cathedral in Constantinople was the subject of a debate of this kind. This motif was repeated in Germany as well. In the north, in Western Christendom, the Jewish reaction was far more extreme than it had been in Byzantine Italy. Perhaps the early Romanesque and Gothic cathedrals were more difficult to tolerate, as in and around them the Jews could see not only external pomp but also widespread adoration of the hallowed place itself. *Sefer Niẓaḥon Yashan* ('Book of the Old Debate') tells of

> Rabbi Kalonymus of Speyer, for whom the wicked King Henry [III, 1030–56, one of the builders of the great cathedrals in Speyer, Worms and Mainz] sent after he had finished building the ugly abyss [*i.e.,* the cathedral] in Speyer. The king said to him: What more can there have been in the building of the Temple than this, that they should have written so many books about it?

The Jew first requested assurance that he would not be punished for his answer and then replied that, despite all his wealth, the king could not possibly hire as many building workers as Solomon had employed and that the Temple had been larger than the cathedral. But the sting of the answer came at its close, when R. Kalonymus referred to the sanctity of the building:

> After Solomon built the Temple and completed it . . . it is written: 'And the priests could not stand to serve because of the cloud, for the glory of the Lord filled the House of the Lord.' But if an ass were to be loaded with vomit and dung

and were to be led through this abyss, it would not be harmed at all (*Niẓaḥon Yashan* in J. Wagenseil, ed., *Tela Ignea Satanae,* I, Nuremberg, 1681, pp. 41–2).

Jews recognized that they were often influenced, willingly or unwillingly, by their Christian surroundings, The Ḥasidei Ashkenaz referred to both positive and negative moral influences of the Christian townsfolk dwelling side by side with the Jews. When they wished to illustrate the high degree of dedication to the service of the Creator required of a Jew, they pointed to the fealty of knights about to wage war for their lords as a fitting comparison, itself taken from Christian literature.

Yet none of these influences diminished the fervour of the polemic activity. Theories were developed concerning the relative value of the monotheistic religions that did not accord in all respects with the pure Jewish faith (see the remarks of Maimonides on page 559) and the higher status of the Christians and Moslems compared with ancient idolaters (see the opinion of R. Menaḥem Hameiri on page 560). In the religious and moral field, Christian influence frequently became visible when some ancient Jewish institution or concept was revived or re-emphasized as a result of current modes among the Christians. In some cases it must be assumed that similarities between the social and religious aspects of Jewish and Christian daily life gave rise spontaneously to parallel developments, and that there was no appreciable direct influence.

Religious debate arose as a result of the efforts of the dominant religion, whether Christian or Moslem, to eliminate the religious error of its subordinate neighbour. However, the Jews were not always the respondents; occasionally, they initiated the debate. This was particularly true in Islamic countries, where Jews and Christians were religious minorities. The opinion conveyed by Maimonides to his son was, in fact, an ideal for all Jewry with regard to their attitude towards their neighbours: 'My father and teacher of blessed memory', recalled R. Abraham,

> interpreted the injunction to Israel to be 'a kingdom of priests' as meaning that in the same way as the priest of each community is the leader and the outstanding example for the members of that community to follow, finding the right path through him, so, God says, by observing my teaching, be you the leaders of the world. Your relationship to other nations is as the relationship of the priest to his community. Let the world follow in your footsteps and imitate your deeds and proceed in your paths (E. J. Weisenberg, ed., *R. Abraham's Commentary on Exodus* [19], Letchworth, 1959, p. 302).

Aware of their duty to serve as a model society, the Jews would sometimes risk their lives by taking the initiative in contesting the dominant religions.

During the period under consideration here, the disputations took two different forms, one of which was the 'private' debate between a Jew and his Christian neighbour. The sight of a cathedral, the reading of a passage from the Scriptures or the Gospels or some occurrence might give rise to such a debate. *Sefer Niẓaḥon Yashan* contains fragments of debates of this kind recorded by a Jew in Hebrew. Sometimes it is clear that the arguments were intended as guides and patterns for later debaters; and it is reasonable to assume that they sometimes record only what the Jew would have liked to say to Christians had he been free to fully express his view, for it is unlikely that some of the recorded arguments were actually voiced to Christians with impunity (as in the case of R. Kalonymus' comments on the Speyer cathedral). The reader is occasionally left with the impression that the Jewish writer is discussing the pressures placed on him by the realities of the surrounding Christian environment and that he is actually speaking to himself. In some of their details, these notes reflect the anti-clerical moods and opinions then current in Christian society. The contents of *Sefer Nizahon Yashan* date from the twelfth and possibly the thirteenth century. The actual wording and spirit of the Hebrew and their sharp bitterness are indicative of the lively contact and mutual acquaintanceship that existed at that time between Jews and Christians living within the area that now constitutes Germany and France.

The style and spirit of the debates, which vacillated between abuse and apparent friendship, have been presented in a Hebrew paraphrase of the words of the Christians, and reveal their Christological and allegorical interpretations of the biblical text, as against the Jewish *halakhic* approach:

> Many are the verses which they apply to the Crucified one, telling us: You fools! We know that the Law was given to you and not to us. So why do you not respond to its true character? And why do you not take to heart the nature of this law, which commanded you to obey strange commandments ... you are indeed brute beasts not to understand what this sign and hint really means (Wagenseil, *op. cit.*, p. 19).

The Jews were well aware of the Pauline formulation current among Christians that attributed blindness to the Jews. Christianity gave an allegorical explanation to the verse relating that Moses veiled his face, 'arguing that it represents the curtain that has been hanged on our faces, *i.e.*, that we do not understand the commandment of the Lord God, which they claim is to believe in Jesus' (*ibid.*, p. 40).

In these private conversations, Jews attacked the Christian interpretation of the Scriptures, their form of worship and the doctrines of their faith. The theological and exegetical argumentation was supplemented by social criticism, particularly on the celibacy of the clergy and the monks. Jews had always believed that celibacy ran counter to the will of the Creator, expressed by the creation of two sexes, and was a needless provocation of sexual desire and its passions. In the Islamic lands, Maimonides' son attacked the monastic system on the grounds that it established two ways of life, one for the elect and the other for the majority of the people. It was for this reason that R. Abraham gave the following interpretation of the Lord's commandment that Israel should be a holy people:

> In every other community there are pious men separated from the rest of the people, even among the idolaters. Such are the priests among the people of India and among the Christians, while the rest of the community remains in its promiscuity ... as is generally known. ... Therefore God said: 'Behold yourselves, you shall, *all of you,* be holy,' meaning that part of you shall not be pious and separated [from the ways of the world] while the other part of you are adulterers

and criminals. For all Israel are bound by all the commandments (Wiesenberg, *op. cit.*, p. 302).

In northern Europe, as well, celibacy was one of the most sensitive issues in Christian society. Jews used to insist that while the monks and nuns fulfilled their vows they were sinning at heart, for 'the monks and nuns . . . are consumed with lechery, burning within, longing for sexual intercourse but unable to engage in any. And that is conflagration' (Wagenseil, *op. cit.*, pp. 43–4). The Jews based themselves here on the saying of Paul that it is better to take a wife than to burn (with lust). At the same time they voiced doubt, which was widespread in Christian society as well, as to whether the monks actually abided by their vows of celibacy, charging that, 'if they do not increase and multiply openly and legally, they have their fill of adultery in secret' (*ibid.*, p. 43).

Jewish debaters referred to yet another criticism of Church practice, widespread in Christian society – employing the words of the prophet Isaiah, which were particularly suited to the target of their criticism – namely, the acquisition of landed property by the churches and the monasteries:

'Woe unto them that join house to house . . .' these are the priests and monks who have seized all the land, and join house to house, and lay field to field until they have left others no place whatever. 'And yea are placed alone in the midst of the earth' – that is the situation in their cloisters (*ibid.*, p. 82).

To the argument often flung at the Jews that they failed to attract others to their faith, they retorted:

As for their question whether there are proselytes among us? They shame themselves and their faith by asking this, for when a wicked Jew apostatizes . . . he liberates himself from all commandments . . . and adopts the life of the passing fashion. His evil deeds are therefore no cause for surprise. But those proselytes who have adopted Judaism have undertaken the duty of circumcision and all the other positive commandments. And furthermore, for fear of the violence of the Christians the proselyte is compelled to flee from place to place and deprive himself of all worldly good and to flee for his soul abroad lest the uncircumcised smite him and slay him . . . and the woman who converts also cuts herself off from all worldly pleasures. Yet despite this they come to shelter under the wings of the *Shekhina*. They clearly do this only because they understand that there is nothing tangible in their faith. . . . Therefore the Christians should be ashamed when they refer to the lack of proselytes (*ibid.*, pp. 242–3).

This estimate of the converts is almost identical with the comments written by Maimonides to R. Obadiah, the Norman proselyte (see pages 537–8).

In the course of debates, Christians used to ask, 'Why are most of the gentiles white and handsome while most of the Jews are black and ugly?' The Jewish debater was prepared to accept the aesthetic standard of his *milieu*, which held that blonde is beautiful. He explained the difference in complexion by the fact that Christian women had sexual intercourse during menstruation, thus passing on some of the redness of the blood to their children's complexion; furthermore, when the gentiles engage in sexual intercourse 'they are surrounded by beautiful paintings and give birth to their likeness' (*ibid.,* pp. 251–2).

The Jews were also accused by their gentile neighbours of murdering Christian children and drinking their blood. To this blood libel they responded

> that there is no people for whom murder is so strongly prohibited as it is for us, and we are warned even against the murder of gentiles. . . . Likewise we have more prohibitions against blood than any people, for even meat that has been ritually slaughtered is in addition salted by us and drained off, and we take great pains to remove all blood.

After having explained the absolute baselessness of the accusation, the Jewish debater stated the true purpose for which the charge was levelled: 'But you make these false charges against us in order to have an excuse for slaying us because we fear the Almighty' (*ibid.,* pp. 257–8).

R. Jehiel of Paris, persecuted and accused, referred to the situation of the Jews under Islamic rule when he had to defend the Talmud publicly in 1240. He who touches the Talmud, he stated,

> touches the apple of our eye. And if you bring fury down upon us – why, we have been flung to the ends of the earth. This Torah of ours is to be found in Babylon and Media and Greece and Ishmael, and among the seventy peoples beyond the Rivers of Ethiopia, there you will find it. Our bodies are indeed in your hands, but not our souls (his *Disputation,* R. Margalioth, ed., Lvov, undated, p. 13).

When Nahmanides debated in 1263, he spoke to the gentiles without restraint, but he faced a severe internal problem. His Christian disputant in Spain had set out to give a Christological interpretation to several Midrashic legends, and Nahmanides was compelled to adopt definitions that approached the views of his rationalist Jewish opponents (see page 544). He drew a distinction between the Talmud, which he described as 'an explanation of all the commandments of the Torah', and the *aggadot,* which, he claimed here, are found in

> a book . . . called Midrash, meaning Sermons; just as though the Bishop were to stand and deliver a sermon and one of his listeners saw fit to write it down. And as for this book, if anybody believes it – all well and good; while if anyone does not believe it, no harm is done ('The Disputation of Nahmanides' in Chavel, *op. cit.,* p. 308).

In presenting his case Nahmanides declared before the king, in whose presence the disputation was held, that human existence since the time of Jesus had not constituted 'the days of the Messiah'. Indeed, the mentality and values of Christian chivalry contradicted those of 'the latter days':

> For the rule of Rome did not arise through Jesus. . . . Before they believed in him, Rome ruled over most of the world; indeed, after they accepted the Christian faith they lost many principalities. And now the worshippers of Mohammed have

more dominion than you. And likewise the prophet says . . . 'Nation shall not lift sword against nation, neither shall they learn war any more.' Yet from the days of Jesus until now the whole world has been filled with violence and pillage. The Christians, moreover, shed more blood than other nations; and how hard it would be for you, your Majesty . . . and for these knights of yours if they were not to learn war any more (*ibid.,* p. 311).

Gradually, as a result of generations of disputation, the debate came to focus on several focal points of biblical interpretation, such as the significance of the passages in Isaiah on 'the servant of the Lord'; the meaning of the verse in Genesis, 'and the older shall serve the younger'; the question as to whether Jacob, when crossing his hands to bless the sons of Joseph, was making the first sign of the cross as a token for later generations; and the real significance of many terms describing God that appear in plural form. These issues formed the subject of disputations with Christians not only in Christian kingdoms but also in the Islamic lands. We hear of them from R. Abraham, the son of Maimonides, who tells: 'I silenced them [the Christians] in all disputations . . . as we taught them [a Jewish understanding of] "until Shiloh come" [Genesis 49:10].' He adds: 'They insist on this passage, as, except for it, they did not find in the Torah any mystifying passage like the several they have found in Prophets and Psalms, which they explain falsely' (*R. Abraham's Commentary on Exodus, op. cit.,* p. 202). In several other places of this commentary, we find traces of polemics against Christianity.

Within Jewry there were rationalistically oriented circles that related to the significance of the success of Christianity and of Islam. In the twelfth century Maimonides had dealt with this subject in his major *halakhic* work, *Yad Hahazaka,* in the section entitled 'Laws of Kings and Their Wars' (at the end of Chapter 11; this passage is found only in manuscripts and in printed editions that were not subject to Christian censorship, such as the one printed at Constantinople in 1509). Maimonides explained that

> all these matters . . . are only to ease the path of the Messiah and to put the whole world right and serve the Lord together. . . . In what way? The world is already full of the words of the Messiah and the words of the Torah· and the commandments. These matters have spread to distant islands and many peoples . . . and they discuss these matters and the commandments of the Torah. Some say these commandments were true but have been abrogated for these times and were not given for future generations; and others say, there are hidden matters here and they are not as simple as they seem, but the Messiah has already come and revealed their mysteries. Now when King Messiah truly comes and prospers and is exalted and rises high, they will all repent at once, knowing that their beliefs were false.

Why, however, did the Lord choose to prepare the world for the complete truth by means of a period of rule by half-truths and false beliefs? Maimonides continued:

> This has led to the destruction of Israel by the sword, and the dispersion and degradation of their remnant, the replacement of the Torah, and the misleading of the greater part of the world to serve a god other than the Lord. But the thoughts

of the Creator of the Universe are not for flesh and blood to comprehend, for our ways are not his, nor are our thoughts his thoughts.

According to Maimonides' theory, Christianity and Islam were established in order to prepare the gentiles to accept the authority of the Torah and its binding commandments.

In the thirteenth century one of Maimonides' great admirers and protagonists, R. Menaḥem Hameiri of Peripignan (see page 544), developed a doctrine of religious toleration. In many places in his *Bet Habeḥirah* ('The Temple'), a major commentary on the Talmud, he draws a sharp distinction between 'the ancient gentiles, worshippers of isols', whom, according to the *halakhah,* Jews must avoid, and 'the nations who are marked out by ways of faith', *i.e.,* the nations that follow Christianity and Islam and do not fall into the category of idolaters. 'There is no brotherhood between idolaters who are not subject to the dictates of faith and the nations which are marked out and defined by their faith' (*e.g., Bet Habeḥirah* on *Bava Meẓia* in H. Schlesinger, ed., Jerusalem, 1959, p. 5). Based on this distinction, Hameiri reached the practical conclusion that wherever the term 'thy brother' is used in the Torah it includes anyone believing in God (*ibid.,* p. 100). The commandment to help unload 'the ass of thine enemy' applies 'most certainly to a personal enemy within Israel, and those like them' (*i.e.,* Christians and Moslems).

Hameiri's approach had a direct bearing on the daily activities and the livelihood of the Jews: 'It is always prohibited to deceive people in buying and selling, even if it is not actual deception, and the prohibition holds true for dealings with both Jew and gentile, above all in matters of coinage, in which most people are not expert' (*ibid.,* p. 193). He viewed his own source of livelihood, money-lending, as a beneficial service for those in urgent need of money.

> In any case morality and precept apply even to lending money to a gentile against interest. Since he has come to you, do not send him away empty-handed; however, you are certainly not required to make a loan without charge. And there are some who explain that this was the intention of the sages when they explained [in the Midrashic work *Sifri*] that 'Thou shalt take interest of the stranger' is actually a positive commandment and not just a permitted act (*ibid.,* p. 267).

Other rabbis, even if they had not reached the same level of toleration, none the less upheld the ideal that the Jews both as a society and as individuals should serve as an example for the other nations of the world; and they insisted that Jews were therefore required to conduct their social and commercial relations with the neighbouring gentiles in model fashion. In the thirteenth century R. Moses of Coucy in France, who travelled and preached in Spain as well, related:

> I preached to the exiles of Israel that those who lie to the gentiles and steal from them profane God's holy Name; for they cause the gentiles to say 'Israel has no Law'; and it is said: 'Let not the remainder of Israel do wrong or speak falsely or give utterance to deceitful words' (*Semag,* Venice, 1547, Prohibitions, II, fol. 7v).

34

The Collapse of Old Settlements and the Establishment of New Ones, 1348–1517

The Communal and Economic Position in the German Empire

The Black Death marked the end of an epoch and a turning-point for the Jewish communities of central Europe, as old anti-Jewish tendencies again began to emerge at an increasing rate. Hatred and fear of the Jews were universal during the period of the plague, which began in 1348 (see pages 486–7). At first sight it might appear that this hatred was promptly compensated for, as various districts began to allow Jews to return to their cities, even while they were being slaughtered elsewhere. From 1349 we hear of the admission of Jews at an increasingly rapid pace into cities from which they had been expelled 'forever' or into cities that had sworn not to admit them for at least another 200 years. However, readmission was motivated by and based on social assumptions and carried out in legal terms that, taken together, indicate a definite worsening in the settlement situation and the economic, social and legal status of the Jews, particularly in north-western and central Europe.

An analysis of the reasons that induced the bishops and the cities to readmit the Jews indicates that the latter were urgently required for various purposes, chiefly economic ones. In the first stage, the Jews had been massacred or driven away; their residential districts had been burnt down, either by the Jews themselves or by the Christian masses, or had remained standing while their real estate and the debts owed to them were left behind. Various groups began to compete for possession of the spoils, the remaining buildings and the plots of land. The townsmen who had murdered and pillaged promptly came to an agreement with the rulers whereby they were forgiven the massacres and the property of the Jews was handed over to them. As a rule the emperor and princes agreed to this arrangement in return for high fees. Thus the cities undertook large financial burdens in order to enjoy the spoils of their deeds against the Jews. However, the emperor, the princes and the bishops soon felt the lack of the very considerable taxes that the Jews had been paying them annually. The townsfolk quickly discovered that there was no substitute for the Jewish loans on interest, which were required for consumer purposes, both major and minor. They turned to Christian money-lenders, but the latter raised their interest rates in the absence of Jewish competitors.

Thus the cities found themselves burdened with debts due to the departure of

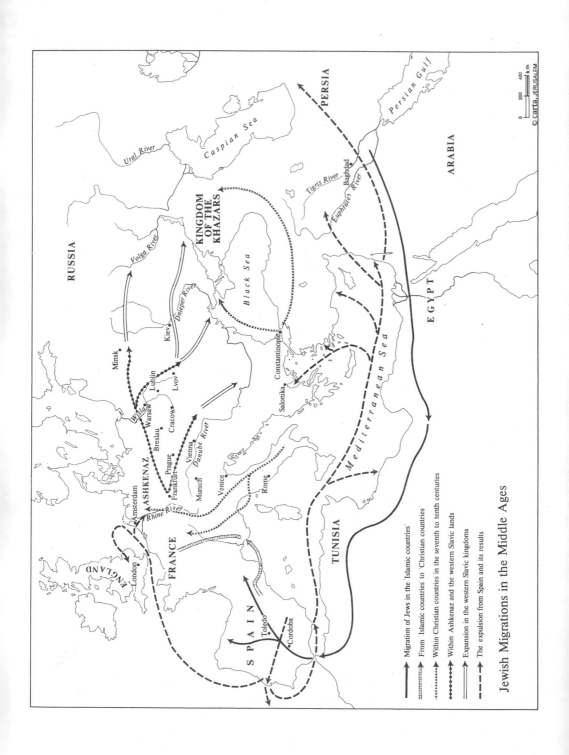

Jewish Migrations in the Middle Ages

RUSSIA

Caspian Sea

Ural River

Volga River

KINGDOM OF THE KHAZARS

Black Sea

Dnieper River

Kiev

Minsk

Lublin

Warsaw

Lvov

Wisła

Breslau

Cracow

Prague

Vienna

Danube River

Frankfurt

Munich

Venice

Rome

ASHKENAZ

Amsterdam

Rhine River

Constantinople

Salonika

Tigris River

Baghdad

Euphrates River

PERSIA

ARABIA

Persian Gulf

EGYPT

Mediterranean Sea

TUNISIA

FRANCE

ENGLAND

London

SPAIN

Toledo

Cordoba

→ Migration of Jews in the 'Islamic countries'

⟶ From 'Islamic countries' to 'Christian countries'

⟶ Within Christian countries in the seventh to tenth centuries

⟶ Within Ashkenaz and the western Slavic lands

⟹ Expansion in the western Slavic kingdoms

--→ The expulsion from Spain and its results

0   200   400
km

© Carta, JERUSALEM

an economic and social element whose presence was valued only after it had vanished, whereupon they sought the return of the Jews. The cities, sometimes together with a more central authority – such as a bishop or a prince – granted the Jews protection in return for a considerable sum of money, payable upon admission, and the payment thereafter of a heavy annual tax. However, Jews were no longer admitted permanently but only for a fixed period of time – three, five or ten years. This arrangement left the experienced rulers of the cities with the option of cancelling the Jewish right of domicile and withdrawing their protection whenever they saw that the masses were again rising against these aliens.

Several of the charters of admission even contained a special clause stipulating the 'right' of the protector to cancel his protection, subject to, for example, a fortnight's advance notification. The time restriction of the settlement right was intended primarily as a means of extorting more money from the Jews with every renewal of the right of domicile. When Jews were expelled from any given place, those who expelled them frequently attempted to prevent all further contact with them. Thus there was 'the case . . . of Master Eberlin, who confirmed an oath to his wife . . . to visit the graves in Landshut. After the expulsion, the graves were closed off and no Jew was permitted to visit them – not even by bribery – but they continued to go in secret, furtively, and in danger of their lives' (*Responsa of R. Israel Bruna*, Salonika, 1798, no. 245, fol. 99v). This repeated rupture of local ties and the consequent precarious atmosphere became typical of Jewish existence in the cities of the German Empire, as was the increased financial burden placed on the Jews in the form of new payments or higher rates of taxation.

In theory the emperor retained his sovereignty over the Jews, who were still called 'serfs of the exchequer' (*servi camerae*). However, various German cities endeavoured to change this state of affairs by the introduction of formal measures. In Mainz and Speyer, the sites of two ancient and large Jewish centres, the Jews officially became the 'property' of the cities. The Speyer town council recorded that it re-admitted the Jews in the year 1352:

> We have been privileged to receive this kindness which has been done to our city of Speyer by the Holy Roman Empire, whereby the Jews and the community who will now be dwelling with us in Speyer, henceforth and forever, shall belong to us and to our city and shall be ours in respect of body and property.

Most of the German cities did not obtain a legal formulation of this kind, but in practice their domination of the Jews steadily increased, a process of which the Jews themselves were aware.

In the fifteenth century R. Jacob Weil decreed that a Jew's right of residence in any given place was based on the fact 'that the burghers had given him permission to settle there'. Accordingly, a certain woman was not entitled to settle there, as 'the burghers had not given her the necessary permission'. A Jew had 'the aforesaid right and privilege because he pays a tax to the burghers' (*Responsa of R. Jacob Weil*, Jerusalem, 1959, no. 118, p. 78). The members of the community, who opposed the admission of this Jew, had already bound themselves with close ties and on pain of excommunication that none of the congregation shall endeavour to settle a stranger among them. And if some kinsman should come to one of them and request him to intercede on his behalf with the burghers, he shall give notice of this to the community so that they may resist with all their force (*ibid.,* no. 107, p. 72).

These new rulers of the Jews were far more hostile and less generous than the formal central authorities had been. This was particularly noticeable in those cities where the local authorities had to share their income from the Jews and their power over them with the neighbouring archbishop or prince. In general, the latter was less exacting towards the Jews and tried to protect them more than did the towns-folk or the local magistrate.

The readmitted Jews were resettled in streets different from those they had formerly lived in, an act that worsened their situation in two respects. As a rule, the new site was less centrally located and less convenient than the place where they had lived before 1348; and the closing-off of the Jews within their own special street was carried out with far more strictness than it had been before the Black Death.

These trends – the efforts of the city to control those who dwelt within its walls, its assumption of control over the Jews from the central authority, the restriction and enclosure of the Jewish places of residence and the financial extortion – had all existed before 1348; but the new circumstances accentuated these tendencies and led to their forceful implementation on a far more extensive scale.

The Restoration of the Jewish Communities

The Jews who were invited to return to the cities under these harsh conditions and at so high a price were at first usually refugees from the 1348 massacres who had fled to the villages and the estates of the nobles. A new community would generally be composed of widows and their children, as adult males were very few in number. There were some districts, such as northern Germany, where Jewish communities were barely, if at all, restored. Even where they were re-established, expulsions, whether of brief or prolonged duration, became a recurrent phenomenon of communal life. In the fifteenth century, R. Moses Mintz ended a detailed Responsum on a *halakhic* matter with the statement that he was writing at a time of 'expulsion and seizure ... for the time given us by the Bishop [of Bamberg] has come to an end, and he refused to allow a time extension, not even for a day nor an hour' (*Responsa of R. Moses Mintz,* Salonika, 1806, no. 49, fol. 50v).

These communities, intermittently restored and destroyed, whether by expulsion or by riots, repeatedly faced complicated problems of population policies and of domicile, which had to be solved in accordance with constantly changing local conditions. We referred above to a community that had sought to discourage new settlers. But in the year 1456/7, R. Moses Mintz recorded that 'in this city the responsible householders are few in number and the burden [of taxation and upkeep

27 Part of a business letter from the eighth century written in Persian in Hebrew characters, found during excavations in east Turkistan, testifies to details about Jewish commerce during that period.

28 An eleventh-century wooden door, with sixteen carved panels, from the Ezra Synagogue in Fostat, Egypt, in which (according to tradition) the Rambam worshipped.

29 Caricature of a Norwich Jew on the ramparts of the local castle (1233), from the Public Record Office.

30 This entry of the Forest Roll of Essex, England, includes the earliest dated sketch of a mediaeval Jew (1277). The badge on the cloak is a representation of the two Tablets of the Law, and all Jews were obliged to wear it at the time.

31 A Christian depiction of the Jewish slave trade. A bishop is redeeming manacled Christian slaves from Jewish merchants in a bronze relief from the door of the church in Gniezno, Poland (twelfth century).

Opposite 32 A capital from the monastery of San Martin in Fuentidueña, Spain, from the second half of the twelfth century. The Jew, the Son of Darkness, is depicted as an owl, while the Christians, Birds of Light, peck at his skull. Such anti-Jewish symbolism was common during the period.

33 A 'Synagogue' sculpture from the Trier Church (*c.*1250). Note the veil over the eyes, the displaced crown, the broken staff and the upside down Tablet of Law.

Opposite 34 Hannah and her seven sons before their tormentors *above*, among the symbols of *kiddush hashem*, from a Hebrew prayer book (fourteenth or fifteenth century) in the Hamburg Library.

ריאשרן נתה נחה וער וער ואשר חשה בתורה

ומיזב להרוג שטה איבד וזיהיר בעבירות טהריד ב

ומהב כבבש אלוה מיזהיר זמם אפתה השביעי קה

קטנב זהב אעשרד אליי נב זיבגהיר לי לבמישה ה

קונב זירז העלב הטוב לבהר

וזק הרגבי לפיה מאהר זנה

זיהזי להשתלות לא אהר

הב ורידר מושל רשע הול

חזק מזחהן בלי פטע הסן

הלד ולכמלב שיעשע הזה

הורונב משפטי בניה המפשה

נפשה על ניזנה הלפה והשב

ריהה לקוניה המבטי אבגיר

לעבוד הסיריב אילו והריגש

זבורי הנוז פרוני בלתה וכור טפס עוד בירון

מרה טיפטופי אשר לא יבדה טיפיש ידנ הור

ישרא טיבב זוכר שפיר יהורי טיביה וקירוז כביר בר

שריה ובכוה יהקבר בשליי זורי יזה לוה אנו

מזשהב הזי לאשו לאשו קהיש מזנו

כזשהקב להרבי טורהב סהרב נב

יהיר וניש א שיכו

יהב לבולב מהקואות ביב

incepit et ob quam causam et ad
quem finem tendant. et quia sine
mine potui super hijs informari
uolo regiftrare qd probare nō
valerem. Cde modo facti qd ui
di et audiui intendo poftea face
re mentionem.

De captione et destructione iu
deorum.

Anno .dni .ccc.xlix. capti fu
erunt iudei et in carceribus
et pulchombus vniuerfaliter
pofiti in omnibus locis vbicuq̃
morabantur. Ratio autem cap
tionis fuit. Quoniam vehemens
fuspicio erat super eos qd ipfi po
pulum criftianum malioqs per
venenum teftruere intebantur

et qd venenum in puteis. in fon
tibus in aquis fecrete proijciebant
prout poterant. et hoc fecerunt
in pluribus locis ficut fama et
rumor cois laborabat. Erant
autem inter eos quidam de fecta
eox aftrologi fubtiles et periti qui
fecundum curfum ftellarum pre
noftabant eis mortalitatem

Opposite 35 The burning of Jews (1349) in an illumination from a chronicle written on the Black Death between 1349 and 1352.

Above 36 An illuminated Bible manuscript page written in Burgos, Spain (1260). Note the lavishness of the ornamentation.

Left 37 The wall carvings and stained-glass windows of the fourteenth-century synagogue in Toledo, which became the Il Transito Church after the expulsion of the Jews from Spain.

Above 38 View of the exterior of the Altneuschul in Prague, built during the last third of the thirteenth century, the oldest extant synagogue in Europe. Next to it is the meeting place of the Jewish community, used towards the close of the Middle Ages.

39 The receiving of the Torah at Mount Sinai in the view of *Ḥasidei* Ashkenaz, in an illumination from a manuscript of the Pentateuch executed in Regensburg at the beginning of the fourteenth century.

40 Jews sucking and embracing 'the Jewish swine', the hateful caricature of the Jew, in a wood relief on a chair rest in Cologne Cathedral (fourteenth century).

Opposite 41 The Four Sages in conversation in Bnei Brak, actually a portrait of mediaeval Jewish sages, in an illumination of the Erna Michael Haggadah, Israel Museum.

Above 42 The expulsion of the Jews from Frankfurt (1614), following the riots against the Jews there, shown in an etching from a historical chronicle written in 1642.

43 The veneration of Shabbetai Ẓevi by the Jews of Smyrna from a late seventeenth-century travel book.

of the community] is heavy upon us, so we are seeking householders to share the burden with us.' It may be assumed that after 1348, many communities faced the problem of attracting additional members.

The residential requirements of the Jews were fully exploited by the burghers. It was reported in the aforesaid city and year that 'the townsfolk here owned houses in the vicinity of the synagogue, which they rent to the Jews. When one of the houses becomes empty, then any Jew who needs a house must rent that house from them' (*ibid.*, no. 39, fol. 34r).

The uncertainty resulting from exploitation and extortion became even more widespread as a result of various libels. Any internal Christian religious ferment also could endanger the position and residence of the Jews. For example, the Hussite Revolt in Bohemia and Moravia, from the beginning of the 1420s, operated against the interests of the Jews by leading to increased suspicion and religious zealotry, particularly among the German population and the Catholic circles of central Europe. The successful rabble-rousing of the Italian monk Johannes da Capestrano, who preached against the Hussites in central Europe at the beginning of the second half of the fifteenth century, helped to harm the Jews and undermined the position of important Jewish communities, such as Breslau in Silesia. Under such circumstances one is surprised not at the occasional slackening of Jewish vitality but at the capacity of the Jews for social and spiritual regeneration.

Jewish communities tended to move away from old centres and ancient cities towards new sites. Some Jews settled in the villages and on the estates of noblemen in the vicinity of the old cities. Others headed for the southern and eastern regions of the empire, proceeding to Austria, Bohemia, Moravia, Silesia and beyond, to Poland. The move to the east formed part of the larger eastern settlement movement by western colonists. It gradually transformed the regions of the western Slavs, particularly Poland, into an area of Jewish settlement, a centre that steadily increased in numbers and occupational variation, as we shall see below. In the course of this shift eastwards, the Jews were brought into the areas surrounding large cities or into smaller towns and were no longer concentrated at the focal points of imperial trade and politics. On the other hand, the fact that the Jews formed part of the larger settlement movement in the western Slavic areas meant that they, together with the Christian German burghers who arrived in the same wave of settlement, were newcomers to the cities, particularly those of Poland. As strangers, they had to prove themselves by displaying their usefulness to the ruling agricultural nobility. New economic, social and spiritual opportunities, as well as problems, had to be faced by these Jewish settlers in the new types of settlements and circumstances in which they found themselves.

Jewish Sources of Livelihood in the German Empire

Money-lending remained the main Jewish occupation and had indeed played a large role in the Jews' return to the cities. At the same time the Jews began to turn to several new sources of livelihood, under the pressure of their difficult conditions and the increasing instability of Jewish money-lending in the fifteenth century. They were able to enter new branches of activity due to the change in the economic character of the Christian cities, whose inhabitants were growing less grain and vegetables for their own consumption and were becoming customers for the agricultural produce of villages and estates both near and far. Those who grew crops and raised livestock were interested in having their produce handled by experienced persons for profitable sale in the urban markets. Both the townsfolk and villagers were interested in ensuring a regular trade of agricultural products. The transfer of food from distant places to the cities benefited the large estates that produced for the urban market, while also requiring the services of middlemen operating between the city, the village and the estates.

These developments enabled Jews to engage in the trade of crops as well as in peddling in the towns and villages. Their new economic activities were facilitated by their settlement in villages near the cities and in the estates of the nobles who accepted them when they were expelled from the cities, as well as by their penetration into new regions in the south and the east. Under the new conditions it was also difficult to restrict membership in the crafts to guild members. The consumer became a more significant factor within the walls of the city. As a result, Jews began to engage in handicrafts, although they entered through the 'back door' of the economic structure and the urban society. In the fifteenth century R. Israel Isserlein described 'women who wash veils for Christian women . . . that work which is done by women to the veils before laundering, when they hem the edges'. There were also 'women who spin thread in order to sew garments with them, and make their living at this craft' (*Terumat Hadeshen*, Warsaw, 1882, no. 152, p. 46). The activity of women in economic life included their participation in village trade. These women, however, were not the only ones engaged in the crafts. In 1514 the city council of Leitmeritz testified that 'among the Jews in our city there are poor people and also a few who make their living from handicrafts only' (G. Bondy and J. Dvorsky, eds., *Urkunden u. Regesten . . .* , I, no. 347, Prague, 1906, p. 222).

Several Responsa inform us of the purchase and sale of wine by Jews, and R. Israel Isserlein mentioned a city where the Jews 'were accustomed to sell wines to non-Jews slightly more cheaply than if they were selling them to Jews' (Isserlein, *op. cit.,* no. 204, p. 61). Various Jewish and non-Jewish documents describe both directly and indirectly the cultivation of vineyards by Jews for the production and sale of wine. Jews also appear to have been innkeepers, while engaging in trade on the side.

The livelihood of the Jews within the German Empire still depended on money-lending, but it was steadily growing more variegated as Jews began to engage in handicrafts, peddling and brokerage within the villages and between the villages and the cities. By virtue of the gradual penetration into trade, and under the pressure of the living conditions within the empire, the Jews who moved eastwards into Poland tended to engage increasingly in commerce and handicrafts. As we shall see (pages 580–3), these trends produced a new economic and social development among the Jews of Poland, as well as considerable tension between them and the burghers of German origin.

The Jews of Italy and their Occupational Pursuits

In the fourteenth and fifteenth centuries a new kind of Jewish settlement arose in Italy, spreading from Rome to the cities in the centre and the north of the country. Jewish immigrants from Germany and France joined these established communities – particularly those in the north – on condition of a concession that would enable a Jew to open a loan-bank for the townsfolk. Banks of this kind are referred to in Jewish sources as 'shops'. The city fathers would lay down detailed conditions governing the business which were agreed to by both sides – the Jewish lender and the gentile borrower – and were known as the *condotta, i.e.,* 'behaviour'. The *condotta* was fixed for a specific period. The Jew would either make a large, single payment or would undertake to pay a heavy annual tax in return for the privilege of being the municipal lender. He himself was required to invest a certain amount of capital in the bank. Thus, for example, a capital of 3,000 ducats was fixed at the opening of the bank in the city of Fano in 1439 and 5,000 ducats at Urbino in 1464. The conditions for accepting pledges and the rate of interest also were prescribed. As a rule, the interest rate varied between 15% and 25% and was far lower than the rate charged by Christian money-lenders. These financial transactions led to other commercial activities and to the development of various crafts, such as those of the goldsmith and the silversmith, tailoring and the repair of clothing. Sometimes a wealthy Jew would obtain a *condotta* in several cities. Generally, these communities were fairly small in size.

Not all the Jews in Italy were engaged in finances or handicrafts. R. Joseph Colon, for example, had to deal with a question that reveals the demanding and exhausting occupations in which Jews engaged, some of which brought them and their families into close contact with Christian society. The problem concerned a *kohen* (a Jew of priestly descent) who 'dwells in the city of Pavia'. In the year 1469/70, his wife left him and threatened to convert to Christianity. According to the husband's account, she did so because he was 'an innkeeper in Pavia', and she had demanded that he leave this source of livelihood, declaring, 'I do not wish you to be an innkeeper anymore' (*Responsa of R. Joseph Colon,* New York, 1958, no. 159, p. 166). In Rome life was more settled and varied, both socially and professionally. But in other Italian cities as well, we have evidence of Jewish participation in a variety of urban callings, including medicine and the crafts.

The Jews of Italy eventually came to attribute hatred of Jews to their successful and expanding money-lending. This explanation was also forced on them by the Franciscans, who waged a campaign against them and their loans on interest, and was reinforced by the penetration into Jewish thought of the negative Christian attitude towards usury.

A clear picture of the economic and social conditions in southern Italy can be found in a letter written by R. Obadiah Bertinoro, a commentator on the Mishnah who later settled in Erez Yisrael. According to his description, which applied to the situation in the years 1487–8:

Palermo [in Sicily] . . . has about eight hundred and fifty Jewish householders all gathered in one street, very well situated. And they . . . are poor craftsmen of different kinds, copper and iron smiths and porters and men engaged in all kinds of heavy work. They are despised by the gentiles, being all ragged and filthy. And they must wear a red cloth as broad as a gold piece on their hearts as a sign. The royal working-duties are very burdensome for them, since they are required to work for the king whenever there is need for them, such as in dragging the fishing boats ashore, building up embankments, or things of that kind (A. Yaari, ed., *Letters from Erez Yisrael,* I, Tel Aviv, 1943, p. 104).

In Messina he found a similar, albeit slightly better, situation: 'There are about four hundred [Jewish] householders dwelling separately in their own street. They are wealthier than those who dwell in Palermo and are all craftsmen, though some of them are also merchants' (*ibid.,* p. 108).

Coming from northern Italy, this scholar reacted with shock and disgust to the conditions in the south, from which we may deduce that a large gap existed between the conditions in the north and in the south of the country. It may be that the Jews of the south had preserved the handicraft traditions and the variety of Jewish activities that were widespread in those parts of the Mediterranean basin ruled by the Moslems.

The Economic and Social Crisis in Christian Spain

The events of 1348 cast a heavy shadow over the lives of Spanish Jews and made a deep impression upon them (see pages 499–501). In fact, their position was still relatively stable, and the deterioration in the status of the Jewish court circles, particularly in Aragon, had not as yet left its mark on the general situation. In Castile the Jews suffered during the struggle between Enrique de Trastámare and King Don Pedro. The French and English mercenaries of both sides, who had become accustomed to looting and pillage during the Hundred Years' War in France and were savagely anti-Jewish, caused much harm to the Jewish communities in the cities that were besieged or occupied by them in the years 1366–9. Some of the communities were compelled to pay considerable sums to both sides. Thousands of Jews died in the course of the sieges and the battles, and massacres of Jews took place in several places. Even after Don Pedro had fallen in 1369 and Enrique II had become ruler of Castile, the distress of the Jews persisted. The effect of the persecutions, the extortion of money and the sale of Jews into slavery continued for a long time. Henceforth their situation deteriorated even more sharply, both in Castile and in Aragon. The year 1378 witnessed the beginning of a long series of religious incitements, centred in Seville, stemming from opposition to Jewish success in economic and state financial functions.

A combination of circumstances in 1390 created a notable decline in the situation of the Jews. The king died and was succeeded by a minor. The Archbishop of Seville also died in that year, and the conduct of this central ecclesiastical region was entrusted to an extremely anti-Jewish archdeacon who, since 1378, had consistently preached fiery sermons against the Jews. These developments provided the political background for the anti-Jewish riots that flared up in Seville in 1391. The Christian principalities of Spain had faced economic hardship since the end of the fourteenth century, and this caused much social tension in the cities, particularly in years of famine and high prices. The emotional setting was determined by the increasing social tension that marked Christian Spain at the end of the fourteenth century, particularly in the cities of Castile. The latter's autonomy was steadily being restricted in favour of the central authorities, who were themselves engaged in internecine dynastic quarrels. This was compounded by the bitter struggle with the Castilian nobility, which was not prepared to allow the king to impose his authority upon it and had begun to evince anarchic tendencies. The nobility's sense of pride and of class distinction became violently extreme. The patrician group, as crystallized in town society, adopted the ideals of chivalry, a development that produced an ever-widening gap between them and the common citizens, who reacted with their own anarchic assertions of their honour.

Under these circumstances the events of 1390–1 led to an outburst of urban Christian pride, which assumed violent forms against the Jews as soon as royal power had weakened, and ended in the riots and crisis of 1391. The wave of attacks on Jewish communities commenced in Seville and spread through the entire country. Some Jews suffered martyrdom, others were killed during the attacks and many were converted to Christianity (on the social and spiritual effects of these events see pages 583–4). Many communities that survived the conversions and riots collapsed from the burden of the blood-money they had paid to the mobs and the rulers in order to escape massacre and forced conversion. Jewish society was impoverished not only economically but spiritually as well, for an appreciable proportion of its leaders abandoned the open practice of Judaism and became Christians, withdrawing their wealth and their spiritual assets from Jewry.

From that year until the expulsion, about a century later, the Jews of Christian Spain lived under the relentless pressure of recurring and terrifying crises. The rabble-rousing and rancour were nourished not only by the old hatred of the Jews occupying official posts and of their economic position but also by a fresh envy of the New Christians, *i.e.,* the Marranos or forced converts, who enjoyed equal rights in all respects with the rest of the Christian population and steadily infiltrated into the new sources of livelihood and social positions, thus enraging the 'old' Christians. The anti-Jewish legislation of the authorities and the incitement of the Church also affected the Jews socially and economically. Moreover, the persecuted Jews were now split even further by mutual suspicion, as well as by the inevitable tension between the Jews and the forced converts (see pages 620–1).

The Jewish occupational structure in the Spanish kingdoms had not basically altered, but the Jews' scope of activity and prospects of success steadily grew smaller. Royal decrees affected old and honoured occupations and changed the way of life of those engaged in them. The situation was summarized in 1415 by R. Solomon ibn Laḥmish Alami in his *Iggeret Mussar* ('Letter of Reproof'):

Evil has befallen us . . . throughout the length and breadth of the provinces of Castile and in the Kingdom of Catalonia in the year 1391 . . . and for twenty-two years thereafter those who were left in Castile were a parable and a by-word, their situation becoming ever worse. . . . They were required to change their garments, and various trades and leasings and crafts were denied to them. . . . Those who had lived comfortably in their homes were expelled from palaces of ease and delight . . . and all Jews dwelt in shacks both in summer and winter, in shame and misery . . . for they had not learnt crafts wherewith to make a living. And further because of their ruin and distress . . . they were not included among the craftsmen . . . and so it happened in the Kingdom of Aragon to the remaining communities when a new king rose against them to enact new discriminations (A. M. Haberman, ed., *Iggeret Musar,* Jerusalem, 1946, pp. 39–40).

Other documents indicate that this moralistic description may have been somewhat exaggerated, but there was certainly a sharp change for the worse.

The existence of the converted New Christians and the problems they created for the Church and the rulers (see pages 586–7) caused Christian leadership to regard the Jewish communities as the source of the converts' obstinacy in persisting in Jewish ways. In 1412 a legal attempt was made to restrict the places of Jewish domicile in order to isolate and confine the Jews. An appreciable Jewish emigration from Spain began – including both unconverted Jews and Marranos – to North Africa and other Moslem countries. Emigration to Ereẓ Yisrael increased during the fifteenth century, and copies of requests for support by the Spanish communities for those who departed for the Holy Land have survived.

The Expulsion from Spain

After the establishment of the Inquisition and the creation of the United Spanish Kingdom, upon the marriage of the Catholic monarchs Ferdinand and Isabella, the kingdom defeated the remaining Moslems in the southern part of the Iberian Peninsula and conquered Granada. The Catholic rulers then ordered a general expulsion of those Spanish Jews who had not converted. The latter were allowed three months in which to depart, the period ending in the summer of 1492 (the seventh day of Av, according to the Jewish calendar). Legend has recorded the date as the Ninth of Av, the day of mourning for the fall of Jerusalem and the destruction of the Temple. Many Jews converted, including members of the upper classes; but tens of thousands left Spain and went into exile. Over 100,000 Jews proceeded to Portugal, where they met with a bitter fate, and only part of this number fled from there to Moslem countries. About 50,000 Jews left Spain at once for the Moslem countries and Italy; they suffered considerably both on the way and when they reached their new refuge.

In spite of the many crises that had arisen between the years 1391 and 1492, the Jews expelled from Spain left the country with the feeling of being uprooted from their fatherland and of being forced to abandon a good and enviable way of life. Even the terrifying forced conversion in Portugal – which admitted the masses of expelled Jews and then, after separating the children from their parents, compelled them, with inhuman cruelty, to accept Christianity – did not cause the Jews to forget how good their lives had been in the kingdoms of Spain. In the opinion of some prominent Jews among the exiles, the situation of Spanish Jewry had been far more favourable and tranquil than that of any other community until the expulsion.

After the bitter disappointment in Portugal, this Sephardi diaspora spread throughout Italy and the lands of Islam, while some, particularly the converted Jews, proceeded to the Netherlands, where they eventually created a social and cultural *milieu* of their own. In due course the Spanish exiles rose to very considerable social and spiritual achievements and established communities of a unique character in areas as far apart as Amsterdam, on the North Sea, and Safed, perched amid the hills of Galilee (see pages 633–9).

Jewish Settlement in Eastern Europe and the Barrier of Muscovite Russia

Throughout this period an increasing number of Jews settled and established communities in the western Slavic countries of Bohemia, Moravia and Poland. Various evidence shows that in these countries, and in Poland in particular, the Jews found relatively better conditions for their economic and social life. The major effects of this development on Jewish economic history can be observed in the sixteenth and seventeenth centuries (see pages 641–4), but their foundations were laid during the period under consideration here. However, the eastern boundary of this Jewish migration was fixed at the end of the fifteenth century. During the last quarter of that century, a widespread religious movement, generally called 'the Judaizing Heresy', arose in Russia and made a deep impression. Whether or not the Jewish share in this movement was considerable, the Russian authorities considered, apparently with some justice, that it was due to the influence of Jews. When the movement was subsequently suppressed, the Russian rulers decreed that no more Jews were to be admitted into Russia. From that time until the partition of Poland at the end of the eighteenth century, not only were professed Jews barred from Russia, but Russian military forces adopted the practice of exterminating Jews in the territories that they conquered.

Pilgrimages to and Settlement in Ereẓ Yisrael

The persecution in Spain led to a marked revival of emigration to Ereẓ Yisrael. The emigrants and pilgrims included Marranos who wished openly to atone for their conversion by living in the Holy Land. Italian Jewry maintained close ties with Ereẓ Yisrael and followed developments there with constant concern. From the Responsa of R. Joseph Colon, we learn that contributions were regularly sent to Jerusalem and that special officers were appointed for this task in Italy. When a synagogue was destroyed in Jerusalem and its members 'were compelled to borrow much money at interest from the gentile . . . two notables sent to all the ends of the Exile to request help in paying off the said debt' (*Responsa of R. Joseph Colon, op. cit.,* no. 5, p. 15).

Towards the end of the century, even closer ties were established by a number of outstanding people who left Italy for Erez Yisrael and described the situation they encountered there. The banker and merchant R. Meshullam of Volterra described the various congregations and communities he came across in 1481. In Gaza there were about fifty Jewish 'craftsmen, some of them notable and worthy men. And they had a handsome little synagogue and vineyards and fields and houses.' Among the Jews of Gaza, he found two whom he described as Sephardim even before the expulsion from Spain. In Hebron he discovered only 'about twenty Jewish householders'. In Jerusalem there were about 250 families. His chief interest was devoted to the Holy Places, the landscape and the buildings. From R. Meshullam's account it is clear that among the Jerusalem notables were several who were designated by the term 'Ashkenazi', *i.e.,* who hailed from northern Europe. He used the term *'sheikh'* to refer to the Jewish judges.

R. Obadiah of Bertinoro, who arrived in the Holy Land in 1488, was far more interested in the social situation. His letter from Jerusalem provides an extensive account of the Karaites and the Samaritans living there and in Egypt. He records finding 'about seventy Rabbanite householders at present in Gaza . . . where there is now an Ashkenazi rabbi called Rabbi Solomon of Prague'. In Hebron he found 'about twenty householders, all of them Rabbinite, about half of whom come from the Marranos who had recently arrived to shelter under the wings of the *Shekhina*'.

The poverty and squalor of the Jerusalem community shocked him:

> There are now only seventy households left, all poverty stricken and with no livelihood . . . and he who has or can find himself food for a year is called wealthy in this place at the present time. Many elderly and lonely widows, Ashkenazi and Sephardi and of many other tongues, are to be found there, seven women to each man (Yaari, *op. cit.,* p. 127).

He wrote disparagingly of the heads of the community and their methods of leadership; and about the destroyed synagogue referred to above, he related,

> the courtyard in which the synagogue stands is very large indeed and within it are many houses, all of them a *hekdesh* [alms-house] of the Ashkenazim in which Ashkenazi widows are wont to dwell. And there are many courtyards in Jerusalem in the Street of the Jews, all of them a *hekdesh*. But the elders sold them all and not one is left except the *hekdesh* of the Ashkenazim, which they could not sell because it is assigned to the Ashkenazim and their portion, and none of the other poor have any share in it (*ibid.,* pp. 129–30).

R. Obadiah also described his own living conditions and his impressions of the city and its climate:

> I have taken a house here in Jerusalem near the synagogue. And my bedroom on the upper floor is in the wall surrounding the synagogue. The courtyard which contains my house has five tenants, all of them women, and no male save one who is blind; and his wife serves me when I need it. But I must give thanks to the Lord who has blessed me until now so that I have not fallen ill like all the others who came with me. For most of the people who come from a far country to

Jerusalem take to their beds because of the difference in climate and its change-ability from moment to moment from hot to cold and from cold to hot. All the winds of the world come and blow in Jerusalem. And they say that before any wind proceeds to the place whither it wishes to go, it comes to bow down before the Lord in Jerusalem. And blessed is He who knows the truth (*ibid.*, p. 137).

These descriptions of Ereẓ Yisrael at the time of its resettlement by immigrants from Spain and of Jerusalem in its decline should be borne in mind when the development of the Jewish community there in the sixteenth century is considered (see pages 633–9).

The Economic Basis of the Communities in the Oriental Countries

Jewish documents, external sources and descriptions left by travellers present a picture of communities containing large Jewish populations engaged in every branch of urban economic activity. This picture pertained to North Africa, of which we are informed in some detail by the Spanish Jews who fled there and as far as the Island of Rhodes, which was still in Christian hands in the fifteenth century. Differences did exist between one place or region and another. However, apart from the very poor situation of the Jews in Rhodes and Byzantium, the Jewish communities in these lands included wealthy social circles that were in close contact with the authorities and directed the affairs of large communities, whose members included shopkeepers, pedlars and every kind of craftsman.

35

Popular Pressure Against the Status of the Jews

The Emotional and Social Climate

From the second half of the fourteenth century until the beginning of the sixteenth, most of European Jewry suffered from two developments in contemporary Christian society. Although they were basically opposed to one another in origin, these developments had a combined effect on the status of the Jews, since they activated elements and trends within Christian society that came to determine the position of the Jews.

Christian unity had begun to break down in central Europe. The tension between the clergy and the other classes steadily increased, creating an atmosphere dominated by mutual suspicion; fear came to dominate in popular religious feeling. Nationalism now emerged as a force involved in religious differences. The Hussite Revolt, for example, expressed both religious opposition to the dogma and leadership of the Church hierarchy, as well as Slavic resistance to the Germans' claims to superiority. In the cities, a struggle was being waged between the aristocratic patrician families and the craftsmen guilds. While the central authority of the Holy Roman Empire was crumbling, the princes, dukes and counts, as well as the municipal authorities, had begun to assume the trappings of dominion and sovereignty. Among the masses piety was both increasing and becoming more confused. Society was endeavouring to purify its structure and ideals and to restore unity within the universal Catholic Church, or the universal empire that should rule over Christendom. Whether these visions of the ideal church and empire of the past were founded in reality or a product of the imagination is irrelevant; whether the proposals for betterment were realistic or utopian is unimportant in this context. Every aspiration to return to a former purity is, by definition, a revolt against the existing situation. Society was embroiled in spiritual and social turmoil, caught between the trend towards division and aspirations towards unity and harmony, between a sense of degeneration and a yearning for the grandeur and glory of the past.

Many of the anti-Jewish libels and accusations, as well as the deliberations concerning the Jews, were influenced by the tensions gripping north-western and central Europe. At the same time the trend towards Christian unity was advancing in Spain, and the spirit of the Church Militant was prevailing on an increasing scale. During this period the kingdoms of Spain exhibited strength, in spite of internal warfare and the weaknesses referred to previously (see pages 568–9). The marriage of 'their Catholic Majesties' Ferdinand of Aragon and Isabella of Castile set the seal on the process of Christian unity; and the conquest of Granada in 1492 by the united forces of Castile and Aragon converted the whole of Spain into a Christian country. In that same year Columbus set out on his royal mission to discover the western passage to India and thereby open a new route for trade and for further Christian conquests. This confident religious zeal aspired to purity of faith, which was viewed as an ideal that could and should be achieved immediately by means that were then at the disposal of Christian society. The tradition of the Reconquista, which had generally treated the Jews as partners in the cultural and social life of the Christian kingdoms, not to mention their economic life, now appeared to be a dangerous anachronism. Thus the Jews of the Iberian Peninsula were the victims of Christianity's renewed confidence, of its trend towards unity and of the constantly mounting spiritual force based on zealous faith.

The Situation in the Holy Roman Empire

After 1348–9 the emperors began delegating control over the Jews to the local rulers and, even more so, to the cities that had readmitted them (see page 563). However, they never completely renounced their right to extort benefits from the Jews or to exercise legal sovereignty over them, as was demonstrated by King Wenceslaus. In June 1385, after several unsuccessful attempts on his part to restore his income from the Jews, Wenceslaus reached an agreement with the League of Swabian Cities whose main point was that in return for 40,000 guilders to be paid by the cities, the king would cancel a quarter of all the debts owed by the Christians, no matter who they might be, to the Jews. The cities were authorized to collect the other three-quarters as they desired. Generally they appropriated the latter sums for themselves. Although the Christian borrowers were not released from their debts, their money would not be paid out to Jewish creditors, as debts to the Jews were cancelled. Most of the Jewish capital in circulation was thus taken over by the townsmen among whom the Jews lived. Only a few Jews managed to reach an agreement with the cities to return a part of their money. In many cities, among them Nuremberg, the Jews were imprisoned and their property was confiscated. According to various estimates, Nuremberg, after paying 15,000 guilders to the emperor, profited from debts owing to the Jews by a total of 60,000 guilders, a sum greater than the total annual income of the city.

Before long, however, people were once more in need of loans from the Jews, who, in spite of their tremendous losses, still retained some capital in their hands. In 1390 the emperor again announced a remission of debts owed to the Jews, but this time, it appears, only in part of the empire. On this occasion the remission of debts was proclaimed according to the cities and areas in which the borrowers lived. As a result of this change, the Jews found more protectors in 1390, since there were cities whose 'own Jews' lost their debts while the burghers obtained no advantage.

In spite of the temptations of this outright robbery, the damage to the credit system and to the receipts from taxation was apparently so considerable that the practice was abandoned. At the beginning of the fifteenth century, the Jews were even expressly promised that no further remissions of debts would be proclaimed. It is characteristic of this era that these promises were undertaken only for a specified period. Even this elementary right was given a temporary character – a quality that marked everything granted to the Jews.

Throughout the late fourteenth and early fifteenth centuries, anti-Jewish riots and libels against the Jews continued to occur throughout the empire. They were not of a general character, but would occur first in one district and then in another. For the Jews they always meant loss of money and serious disturbances, quite apart from the heavy loss of life as a result either of riots or of death sentences handed down by Christian courts.

The Attitude of the German Cities: The Case of Regensburg

With the growing trend towards capitalism among the leading citizens and the increasing sense of bitterness among the lower classes, the hatred of the German townsfolk towards the Jews became even more pronounced. In Nuremberg the aims of the patricians were realized. While objecting on legal grounds to the interest charged by Jews and sending legalistic queries to ascertain whether the latter were entitled to charge interest at all, the rich men of Nuremberg themselves openly practised usury, although chiefly on large loans. From 1473 the town council engaged in continuous and open efforts to expel the Jews. In 1498 it achieved its purpose when the emperor approved the expulsion. Although the initiative had come from the city fathers, the expulsion was approved by the lower classes as well. The Nuremberg city council served as an example to many other German cities that expelled the Jews, motivated by a combination of embryonic capitalism and popular religious animosity.

The situation in Regensburg was far more complicated and historically instructive. In this city, which was in a state of social and economic decline, the town council acted against the Jews largely out of a sense of bitterness over its own decline and in response to the pressure applied by the lower classes. Between 1475 and 1519 Regensburg's affairs highlighted the legal complexity of 'ownership of the Jews', as in the mutually exclusive yet interconnected matter between a city and a local prince (of Bavaria in this case) and the imperial authority. The Jews requested imperial protection, but the city opposed the application with a variety of arguments. In 1476 it replied to the emperor's demands by declaring that the city 'regards the Jews of Regensburg as *its* Jews, because they are surrounded by a wall and gates in its free city.' But it also acknowledged the emperor's sovereignty over them (R. Straus, ed., *Urkunden und Aktenstücke zur Geschichte der Juden in Regensburg,* Munich, 1960, no. 216, pp. 67–8). At the same time a lawyer put forward a more fundamental claim on behalf of the city, namely, that the Jews were the slaves of *all* by reason of their transgressions, and no charter of rights could release them (*'Item quod Judaei propter demerita sua post passionem Domini venditi sunt non Caesari sed omnibus indistincte, ut generales servi omnes haberentur, non quod propterea aliquod privilegium sortiretur'* [*ibid.,* no. 323, p. 105]). In 1507, the city formulated in detail its claims to authority over the Jews (*ibid.,* no. 760, pp. 264–5). When necessary the city took advantage of the suzerainty of the Bavarian princes. In 1476 the latter claimed that they had a long-standing lien of ownership over the Jews, for a period of 147 years, which had been confirmed by all the kings (*ibid.,* no. 284, p. 90). The worsening attitude towards the Jews was also expressed in libels, particularly of ritual murder, which arose under the influence of the Trent Libel (see page 580).

In 1500, about nineteen years before the expulsion, an agreement was proposed between the Jewish community and city of Regensburg. Its provisions show that the Jews sought protection chiefly against blood libels and other accusations and against tax extortion and an agreement safeguarding their loans on interest and their general way of life. The city, however, demanded that the Jews pay special high taxes, abstain from engaging in handicrafts (such as tailoring), depend on the townsfolk for basic foodstuffs and refrain from trading in pledges and removing those in their possession beyond the walls of the city. The proposed agreement was rejected by all parties.

In the course of this prolonged struggle, which lasted for decades, the Jewish community displayed great talent for self-defence, having recourse to various Christian legal authorities to defend their position. The last lawyer to represent the Jews was the famous jurist Zasius. Towards the end of the struggle, when hope for agreement was fading and matters had reached the point of public debate, the Jews forcefully argued their case against the city and its claims, sometimes employing irony and even exhibiting aggressiveness. In July 1518, one year before the expulsion, the Jews asserted, *inter alia,* that Regensburg was indeed declining. They knew the reason, but it had not yet been proved that the transactions of the Jews had caused the decline. The Jews could not be held responsible for crime in the city, as there were many criminals in other cities where no Jews lived. While it was true that Jews were engaging in various crafts, they did so only within the limits permitted to them and they earned small profits, bearing a heavy burden imposed specifically upon them. In their reply the Jews presented a detailed justification of their practice of various occupations, together with the complaint that the unfavourable attitude of the authorities 'is the thanks the Jews receive because against their own considered wishes and judgement they make loans without interest or at only a nominal interest to the craftsmen of Regensburg at the urgent request of the latter'. The memorandum ended with the following words:

> If it is desirable and necessary to keep Jews, then it is also necessary to keep
> them in a humane fashion . . . and to fulfil the promises made to them. That the
> Jews should be kept in Regensburg . . . and treated in a humane fashion . . . is
> proved . . . by our liberties. . . . We declare that we are Jews and not better than
> Jews are (*ibid.,* no. 988, pp. 355–61).

In another memorandum the Jews stated that they were not required to justify the practice of usury as it had been permitted to them by both the emperor and the Church since time immemorial. Furthermore, they called upon the city to apologize because it maintained a house of ill repute, which was prohibited by common agreement. 'If Jewish usury is so full of poison and evil,' the Jews asked, 'why is it accepted so willingly by Christians, priests and laymen alike, including the Masters of Regensburg themselves?' (*ibid.*, no. 993, p. 367).

The pleas, the legal aid, the desire of the emperor and the princes for profit and the irony of the Jews were of no avail. In 1519 the Jews of Regensburg were expelled from their community, which, according to one of their memoranda, had existed over 1,500 years. The synagogue was pillaged and later transformed into a church. Thus for the Jews of Regensburg the impoverishment and decline of the city led to the same consequences as economic success and expansion had brought upon the Jews of Nuremberg.

The Religious and Social Onslaught by the Franciscans

During the fifteenth century the Franciscan monks were very active in fomenting hatred of the Jews, particularly in Italy but also beyond its borders. For a long time the Franciscan order had been torn by a bitter struggle between those who advocated strict adherence to a life of poverty and asceticism and those who were more lenient – a struggle accompanied by sharp theological differences. The Franciscans worked in the cities, where the poor were their most ardent admirers. Unlike the Dominicans, who were concerned primarily with theology based on theoretical concepts alone, the Franciscans cultivated a simple and popular piety. In Italy this piety was often accompanied by a pedantic legalism. The members of both wings of the Franciscan order were itinerant preachers who exerted considerable influence over the masses in wide areas and were particularly concerned with the problem of economic exploitation of the poor.

Questions of commerce, fair profit and interest occupied a prominent place in the thought and sermons of these preachers. These issues were discussed against the background of urban society in Italy, where trade flourished and money was pursued with an insatiable appetite. Theoretically, their deliberations were based on moderate formulations regarding trade and capital profit, but popular feeling rejected the more moderate tendencies. Bernardino da Siena, one of the greatest preachers, whose anti-Jewish animus was intertwined with complex social concerns, devoted twenty-three sermons in Latin and several in Italian to economic matters. He was sharply opposed to open usury. At the same time he did not regard a man compelled to loan money at the demand of the state – in accordance with the practice in Venice, Florence and Genoa – and forced to receive interest on his loan as a usurer, as he was under compulsion. Thus he supported a series of financial measures that were then customary in the Italian city-states. But he bitterly condemned other attempts to evade the prohibition of usury. His sermons display a familiarity with the commercial and financial methods of his time.

On these matters Bernardino vacillated between the old and the new. Only in respect of the Jewish money-lender did he demand a full and consistent application of the prohibition of usury. In his attitude towards the Jew, the economic factor was supplemented by a religious animosity that produced vehement rancour. Thus he said of the Jews, 'In respect of abstract and general love, we are permitted to love them. However there can be no concrete love towards them.' Thus the concept of love, which Christianity claimed as a central doctrine, was restricted when it came to Jews; and the Jews' practice of money-lending at interest was one of the reasons offered by the preacher for his personal animosity towards each individual Jew.

The Monti di Pieta Loan Funds

Jewish success in the field of credit in northern and central Italy served, therefore, as a focus for Franciscan activity. As a measure against the Jewish 'shops', from the middle of the fifteenth century the Franciscans advocated the establishment of loan funds, with Christian money, in order to provide loans on pledges to needy Christians, thus redeeming them from the claws of the Jewish usurers. In other words, Jewish usury was to be countered with its own methods – an additional indication of the ambivalent attitude of these friars towards interest. From 1462 onwards many 'piety funds' were established in places where Jews practised money-lending. In some cases this led to the expulsion of the Jewish money-lenders; in other instances the Jewish 'shop' functioned alongside the Christian fund. In due course these Franciscan institutions created a difficult problem for their founders, who discovered that without the imposition of some rate of interest and without persons with expertise in loan transactions the money of these funds was dissipating. However, canon law prohibited interest in any form, and most certainly as a permanent practice. Only at the beginning of the sixteenth century did the pope decide, after prolonged debate, to allow the funds to charge a low rate of interest.

John of Capistrano (1386–1456), 'The Scourge of the Jews'

The Franciscan tradition of cruel animosity towards the Jews, in the manner displayed by Bernardino da Siena, was now supplemented by an appeal to combine the social objectives of the Franciscans with political-inquisitorial activity. The leader both of this social activity and of the intensified hatred of the Jews was a disciple and admirer of Bernardino, John of Capistrano (both were in due course canonized by the Catholic Church). From 1417 onwards Capistrano conducted a preaching campaign against the Jews which was paralleled by influential propaganda activity in the ruling courts – including that of the pope, since he was a legal scholar with inquisitorial powers. The combination of talent and authority in Capistrano, a man familiar with the law and a leader in the attempt to eradicate heresy, provided him with ample resources and abundant opportunities to assail the Jews. Various libels and expulsions were a direct result of his influence. He even obtained the cancellation of charters issued in favour of the Jews. In the kingdom of Naples, the impact of his anti-Jewish influence was felt long after his time, while the miserable situation of the Jews in Palermo and the whole of Sicily (see page 568) was largely a consequence of his activity.

Eventually, Capistrano extended his anti-Jewish efforts beyond the borders of

Italy. In a campaign conducted in the cities of Austria and Germany and as far as Poland to destroy the Hussite heresy and restore the true Christian faith, Capistrano incited his audiences against the Jews, and in his sermons in Germany he claimed to have been told that the Jews spread a 'dreadful' idea among Christians: 'The Jews declare that every man can be saved by his own faith, which is impossible.' In 1453 Capistrano was actively involved in a ritual-murder libel in Breslau, as a result of which several Jews were burnt at the stake and the community was expelled from the city.

Bernardino da Feltre and the Trent Blood Libel (1475)

An admirer and disciple of Capistrano, Bernardino da Feltre, represented a third generation of Jew-baiting Franciscan preachers. Towards the end of the fifteenth century, he preached against the Jews in many places in Italy. In 1475 he preached in Trent, on the German frontier. His sermons produced a strained atmosphere, falling on fertile ground that had already been saturated with anti-Jewish feeling due to German influence. A rumour spread in Trent about the disappearance of a two-year-old infant named Simon, whereupon the usual charge was levelled against the Jews. The entire community was arrested and subjected to torture, which led to conflicting confessions. Those sentenced were promptly executed, while the remaining Jews were expelled. The impact of the libel was felt far and wide, as we have learnt from the case of Regensburg. The pope at first refused to authorize the adoration of this 'victim of the Jews', but in due course he withdrew his opposition. In 1582 the infant Simon was officially proclaimed a saint of the Catholic Church. (In 1965 the Church withdrew its canonization and acknowledged that a judicial error had been committed against the Jews of Trent in this trial.)

The Status of Jews in Poland-Lithuania

Jewish migration to the Kingdom of Poland and the Grand Duchy of Lithuania continued throughout the period under consideration here. When Capistrano presented a threat even to the Jews of Poland, sages from Germany wrote:

> Never has it been so necessary to unite as now. . . . You have heard how that priest has even stricken those who dwell under the King of Poland . . . who have so long since been regarded as a remnant and a refuge for the Jews in exile; and no one would have believed that this foe and oppressor would reach the gates of Poland (I. Halperin, ed., *Polish Jewry*, II, Jerusalem, 1954, p. 234).

Thus by the middle of the fifteenth century, it had long been believed by Jews in Germany that Poland was the safest place for Jews. This impression persisted even after people knew of the anti-Jewish riots that erupted there during the Black Death and in 1407.

The economic and social success of Polish and Lithuanian Jewry, which began to develop during this period, was based on both political and economic foundations. The social traditions of the city and trade guilds of the burghers, who were of German origin, had not yet fully struck root in the new soil, while urban life in Lithuania was even less developed. Political changes in Poland and the vicinity made the international transit trade particularly important for all sectors of Poland's urban economic life. The Jews increasingly participated in trade relations that had already been established with Hungary and Bohemia-Moravia, on the one hand, and with the Italian commercial colonies and trade 'factories' along the Black Sea coast, on the other. Internal commercial needs, then already patterned mainly on the economic interests of the Polish nobility, also favoured the Jews, who penetrated deeply into the various branches of Polish urban trade, their prospects improving after the conquest of Constantinople by the Turks in 1453. The overland route through Poland, which linked the Ottoman Empire with central and western Europe, became vitally important for international trade. The Jews took pride of place among the great merchants who travelled from Constantinople to Lvov and further west and among those who proceeded from Lvov to Constantinople and the lands to the east. The Jews played an increasingly important role in the textile trade with the merchants of Western Europe, in the sale of produce from the Moslem East and in the large-scale purchase of grain and cattle in the Polish markets and their export westwards, both overland and by river and sea routes. The fabrics and luxuries offered by the Jewish merchants made them welcome among the Polish nobility.

As the Jews in the Polish cities found their way into all branches of commerce, their success led to increasing tension between them and the townsfolk, particularly in the capital city. In 1485, under the pressure of the townsfolk, the leaders of the Jewish community in Cracow signed a document stating that:

> with the agreement of the members of the congregation, we have undertaken . . . not to engage in any commerce . . . nor may we take any goods . . . from merchants to be sold by us to other gentiles, with the exception of pledges previously given to us which are already overdue. These we may sell in our houses whenever an opportunity arises. But we shall not be permitted to bear or move those pledges or sell them in the streets or markets within the city, except on two specified days in the week. . . . However, poor Jewesses may sell every day the kerchiefs and jewellery which are their own handiwork (*ibid.,* pp. 235–6).

From this statement we learn that an attempt was made to force the Jews out of their positions within the field of commerce and back into their own corner of money-lending, allowing them to sell abandoned pledges, and that the occupations of poor Jewesses included handicrafts. The Jews' renunciation of commercial activity received official confirmation. In 1492 the city translated the declaration into German in order to publicize the information among all the merchants and craftsmen. This municipal announcement tends to support other evidence indicating that the Jews did not cease to engage in trade even after the renunciation had been imposed upon them.

In 1494 riots broke out against the Jews of Cracow. When the town council complained to the royal authorities, the Jewish leaders were arrested. After a short but sharp legal exchange at the royal court, the antagonism of the ecclesiastic authorities prevailed, and the king ordered that the Jews be expelled from Cracow. In 1495, the Jews left the capital and settled in the neighbouring suburb of Kazimierz.

If the townspeople believed that expulsion would rid them of Jewish competition, they were soon disillusioned. From their new base, the Jews continued their efforts to penetrate into trade and commerce and proved very successful. Cracow was not the only Polish city in which the townsmen of German origin struggled against the Jews for control of trade. The widespread nature of the struggle shows that the Jews were turning to commerce in all the main cities of Poland. Nor was Cracow the only place in Poland and Lithuania from which the Jews were expelled.

In the Grand Duchy of Lithuania, the legal formulations regulating the status of the Jews were laid down in the second half of the fourteenth century in accordance with the charters of Poland, with which the grand duchy was then in the process of cementing a union. Thus in 1388 the Grand Duke Vitautas (Witold) specified for the Jews of the duchy rights 'like those possessed by the Jews of Lvov'. One year later he decreed that 'the other rights and liberties which were given by us in a charter to the Jews of Brest-Litovsk [Brześć] in 1388 also apply to . . . the Jews of Grodno.' In fact, however, the economic, social and political status of the Jews in the cities of Lithuania was then very different from that of the Jews in Lvov or any other Polish city. Apart from the 'other [formal] rights and liberties', the charter granted to the Jews of Grodno in 1389 testifies to the fact that they were full burghers in their cities from all practical aspects, enjoying all economic and settlement rights. The area of domicile allocated to them was situated next to the town citadel – in the municipal market and by the river flowing through it – an excellent and central location. In respect of transactions, the grand duke permitted the Jews

> to keep in their homes all kinds of provender, and likewise to sell any kind of liquor . . . to conduct and engage in trade and buying and selling . . . equally with the townsfolk; to engage in various crafts . . . to use plough-land and pasture which they now possess or which they shall acquire in the future.

Their wide range of occupations and their equal status with the townsfolk in the spheres of commerce, crafts and agriculture were granted to the Jews of Lithuania not only because of the grand duchy's need for settlers who would develop its cities and trade, but also, in all probability, by virtue of the traditions of Jewish economic and social life within the former Duchy of Kiev and Byzantium – from which part of the Jewish community of Lithuania had apparently come in earlier days. It may be because of this derivation that we find Jewish merchants from Brest-Litovsk among the leading dealers in pigments in Poland and Lithuania and that early in the sixteenth century they included people who were regarded as experts in a particular kind of pigment – occupations that may have represented a continuation of the tradition of Jewish crafts and commerce in the Byzantine Empire and in the Mediterranean basin. The community of Brest-Litovsk benefited from the strengthened ties between Poland and Lithuania. Some of its wealthy Jews combined tax-farming with large-scale trade in the cities of western Poland.

Towards the end of the fifteenth century, it seemed that the great flood of expulsions would uproot Lithuanian Jewry as well. In 1495 a general expulsion of

Jews from the grand duchy was decreed; but here, as in the cities of Poland, they were evicted only for a short time. In 1503 Jews were permitted to return to Lithuania after undertaking to pay for the annual upkeep of 1,000 horsemen, a duty that was afterwards waived. In granting them permission to return to Lithuania, Alexander, the king of Poland and the archduke of Lithuania, stated: 'We have permitted them to dwell in all places in our estates and cities where they were formerly to be found . . . to give . . . them their House of Prayer and graveyard, and likewise the farms and fields . . . as before.' No restrictions of time or other conditions accompanied the permission to return, which restored the *status quo ante*, whereby Jews were allowed to own land and movables. The expelled Jews returned and demanded the money that had been owed to them, for the archduke further stated that the Jews 'had pleaded before us that many dukes and nobles, boyars and burghers in the district of Grodno owed them money or goods and were refusing to pay them; therefore . . . you shall order whatever is owing to them to be paid' (*ibid.*, p. 236). The attempt to expel the Jews from Lithuania had failed. Henceforth their settlement began to prove successful, both economically and socially.

Developments in the Kingdoms of Christian Spain (1391–1492)

During the century between the riots of 1391 and the total expulsion from Spain in 1492, the fate of the Jews, with respect to both their legal status and their security, was determined by the Christian desire for maximal political and religious unity. The success in compelling large numbers of Jews to come to the baptismal font encouraged repeated attempts – employing a mixture of spiritual influence and social and economic pressure – to induce more Jews to convert. Certain friars, such as Vicente Ferrer, specialized in this area. The disputation at Tortosa (see page 587) was conducted chiefly in order to effect the conversion of large numbers of Jews, and it was prolonged in order to achieve this purpose.

At the same time, the influx of these New Christians (also called Conversos or Marranos, a term of abuse meaning 'swine') into Spanish society led to extreme tension, both religious and social, within the established Christian social structure. Ecclesiastic qualms of conscience about acquiring believers by force, together with the behaviour of many of the converts, led to suspicions that the converts' adoption of Christianity was only a cover behind which they led as full a Jewish life as possible. Christian circles suddenly realized that the converts now enjoyed equal rights and had begun to penetrate into all the occupations and social positions that had formerly been closed to them as Jews. Both society and the Church had brought upon themselves the problem of forced converts, and many were of the opinion that a potentially destructive Jewish underground now existed in their midst. The outcome of these apprehensions was the Spanish Inquisition. Those Jews who had remained true to their faith found themselves being driven into Christianity under the combined pressure of preachers, laws and riots, while at the same time they were suspected of being a source of Jewish influence and inspiration among those who had already converted. Hatred of the Marranos and of the Jews were mingled in a strange and intense fashion.

Furthermore, hatred of Jews was fomented in Spain by incitement on the part of certain fanatic converts who wished to destroy Jewry in order to give their brethren the spiritual benefits they themselves had received. Much of the anti-Jewish incitement was conducted by such converts, some of whom, as we shall see, even called for massacres. They were also the initiators of much anti-Jewish legislation.

The problems of Spanish Jewry during this period were unique, as they were tied, to a large degree, to the problems that lay at the heart of Christian society. The Jewish community sought to restore its ruins and protect itself against depredations of the host society, while the Christian world maintained that the existence of openly practised Judaism endangered its own achievements amidst Jews and made it incapable of totally assimilating the converts. The other side of this entanglement was that many Christian problems, particularly that of the Marranos, were regarded by Jews as their own internal problems. Thus the period of gradual separation between Jews and Christians in Spain was, simultaneously, the period in which they were most closely involved with one another.

Anti-Jewish Legislation

As a result of anti-Jewish incitement and the pressure of the increasingly acute problems in the triangular relationship between Christians, Marranos and Jews, the kings of Aragon and Castile introduced a number of laws whose declared religious purpose was to isolate and degrade the Jewish communities. As early as 1380, King John of Castile had prohibited Jews from reciting in their *Amidah* prayer the passage condemning heretics:

> Because it has been explained to us that the Jews . . . speak evil in it regarding the Christians and the priests and the faithful dead, we . . . prohibit . . . any individual from saying it henceforward, and they shall not keep them written in their books . . . and if anyone shall recite this prayer . . . or respond [*i.e.,* say 'Amen'], he shall receive one hundred strokes in public; and if it shall be found written in the prayer-book or any other book, he shall be fined three thousand gold pieces. And if he does not have money for the fine, he shall receive one hundred strokes in order that they may know henceforth that we shall treat harshly whoever abuses the Christian faith.

In the same regulations, the king deprived the Jews of the right to judge their own criminals and forbade them to circumcise their Moslem slaves (Baer, *op. cit.,* II, para. 227, pp. 221–2). Even the clause dealing with criminal law was influenced by theological reasoning, for granting the right of jurisdiction in criminal cases to Jews 'is a great iniquity . . . for as was said by the prophets, they lost all power and all freedom with the coming of our Lord Jesus of Nazareth' (*ibid.*).

In 1412, King John II passed several laws that commenced with a statement concerning the royal duty 'to seek the best method . . . so that Christian believers . . . shall not be brought into any errors as a result of close contact with the infidels.'

The laws, enacted in order 'to remove the Christians . . . from every . . . heresy', required that Jews and Moslems in the cities of Spain reside in separate quarters surrounded by walls. Certain professions, including medicine and the sale of food-stuffs to Christians, were barred to them. Jews were forbidden to engage in tax-farming or tax-collection. The prohibition against judging their own criminals was repeated; and the laws once again stressed that it was forbidden to interfere with anyone who wished to adopt Christianity. Detailed instructions were provided about the kind of clothing that infidels were forbidden or obligated to wear. The use of honorific titles for Jews was prohibited. Jews were required to grow beards and to refrain from shaving. Many crafts were closed to them, and many restrictions were imposed on social contact between Jews and Christians. Although the laws of 1412 always mentioned Moslems and Jews together, the Jews were the real target of this legislation. The trend to degrade, restrict and isolate the Jews continued until the issuance of the Order of Expulsion, which marked its apogee.

Anti-Jewish Incitement

The spiritual father of the fanatical incitement against the Jews was Abner of Burgos, a Jewish kabbalist and scholar who converted to Christianity in about 1321, upon experiencing a deep religious and spiritual crisis, and became known as Alfonso of Valladolid. His anti-rationalist stance and his despair of the Jewish question found expression in his polemics – some written in Hebrew, others in Spanish – which contain a complete doctrine of denunciation of the Jews and of their laws and morals. Jewish Oral Law, he maintained, constituted a code of robbery, usury and deception. Redemption would come to the Jews when they accepted the belief in the messiah who has already come. Various sayings by the Talmudic sages regarding the signs of the Redemption were interpreted by this apostaté to mean that the Jews must be deprived of the easy livelihoods of usury and medicine, that they must be deprived of their autonomy and that they must be terrorized and subjected to harsh laws. Only then would they merit redemption. As Professor Baer summarizes,

> In such malice-filled homilies did the apostate portray his personal vision of the Latter Days. . . . The plan that the enemies of Israel were to carry out in its entirety in the year 1391 is outlined here for the first time. The aging fanatical apostate who wrote these diatribes launched his holy war himself, not only in words but also in deed (Y. Baer, *A History of the Jews in Christian Spain,* I, Philadelphia, 1961, p. 354).

The leading and most zealous apostate after 1391 was the former R. Don Solomon Halevi, who, after his conversion, became Bishop Pablo de Santa Maria of Burgos. After converting, together with his young children – one of whom inherited the episcopal see of Burgos from his father – Pablo studied theology and became one of the leading disputants against the Jews and opponents of Judaism. He too debated from the standpoint of a mystic vis-à-vis sceptical rationalists. One of the Jews who debated with him, Joshua Lorki, also converted in due course, becoming

Geronimo de Santa Fé. He was the main disputant with the Jews in the debate held at Tortosa in 1413–14. This group of fanatic apostates helped to initiate the persecution of the Jews and were most active in encouraging conversions.

Hatred of the Marranos and the Riots Against Them

Towards the middle of the fifteenth century, the 'old' Christians began to recognize the problem they had created for themselves by forcibly imposing Christianity on masses of Jews. The main campaigns were those of 1391, the results of the successful preaching of Vicente Ferrer, and the wave of conversions during and immediately after the disputation at Tortosa. Families were torn apart. The wife of Pablo, the bishop of Burgos, remained a faithful Jewess. Sometimes tense and delicate relationships developed within the divided families. Ties stretching back over many generations did not simply snap at a moment's notice upon conversion.

Nor did the Christian's attitude towards his neighbour change as soon as the latter converted. At the outset the Christians may have supposed that in the course of time the converts would be swallowed up within the larger Christian community. But, as decades passed, it became clear that a large proportion of the converts had no desire to be assimilated, while the Christian community showed no desire to absorb considerable parts of the convert masses. Thus arose the problem of the Marranos and their image within the larger Christian community. Suspicion on religious grounds and economic or social competition, the old contempt for the obstinate Jew and the new contempt for those who had abandoned the faith of their fathers and, under the threat of physical violence, had readily joined the group possessing greater rights were all elements that combined to make the convert a figure as much despised as was the Jew – and possibly even more so.

Various tractates dating from the middle of the fifteenth century onwards, which Professor Baer has summarized in his work on the history of the Jews in Christian Spain, contain harsh statements concerning the behaviour and character of the Marranos. A racial note began to appear in the absence of any open religious distinction between the 'old' Christians, who were 'good and faithful' and the New Christians or Marranos, who were 'wicked and treacherous'. The only remaining distinction within the Christian Church and society was that of origin. Under these circumstances the concept of 'purity of blood' (*Limpiezza di sangre*), *i.e.*, a lineage that included no New Christians, gradually began to develop. The Church itself never officially recognized these racist ideas, not even in Spain. Several of the converts who had risen to high positions in the Christian Church and society engaged in sharp debate against this point of view, which contradicted the principles of Christianity. They also pointed to the converts who were faithful and devoted to their new religion. But among the Christian masses, including some of the writers and thinkers of the Church, as well as members of the higher social circles, these racist views struck deep roots.

Practical consequences ensued. In 1449 violent clashes, commencing in Toledo, broke out between 'old' Christians and Marranos. The camps divided along racial lines, but there was a strong economic and social undercurrent. The movement began among the lower classes and later gained the support of the nobles. The homes of leading converts were burnt down, and some of the converts themselves were arrested and burnt at the stake. They were accused of secretly observing Judaism and of engaging in treachery, deceit and monetary extortion. All new converts were prohibited from occupying any office of power whatsoever and from serving as witnesses within the city or its environs. Satires against them were distributed. This movement, however, did not eliminate Marrano influence in the highest circles of the royal court, in the universities and in the higher echelons of the Church. The struggle and tension between these two sections of the Christian community were to continue for many generations, even after the Jews had been expelled.

The Disputation at Tortosa (1413–14)

This disputation, a prolonged and particularly exhausting affair for the Jews, was largely an extension of the missionary activities of Vicente Ferrer. It was he who had converted Joshua Lorki. The schismatic Pope Benedict XIII, who then resided in Aragon, was known to be interested in the conversion of Jews by means of debate (his library included the writings of Abner of Burgos). Preparations for the disputation began as early as 1412. Representatives of the Jewish communities were ordered to come to Tortosa at the beginning of 1413. It was an imposing and solemn occasion. The Jewish representatives were numerous and talented, but the decisive element in the debate was the social threat to the Jews and the economic pressure upon them. It should be remembered that the disputation was initiated at a time when Jews were being isolated in special quarters.

Speaking on behalf of the Christians, the former Joshua Lorki presented two main topics for discussion: the Messiah and the Talmud. Many of the arguments against the Jews were taken from the work *Pugio Fidei* ('Dagger of Faith') by Raymond Martini, who had set out to prove from Midrashim and sayings of the Talmudic sages that the Messiah had already come. Sometimes the Christian disputants responded to the answer offered by the Jews with fury and threats. One session followed another. In April and May 1414, participants began to consider 'the problems of the errors, heresy, blasphemy and abuse of the Christian religion' in the Talmud. On this issue as well, the Jews stood firm in their own defence. But when they saw that the pressure upon them was continuing and that the very prolongation of the disputation was harming the Jewish communities and their faith, they declared that they did not wish to defend those sayings of the sages that sounded like heresy – clearly a tactical measure adopted to free themselves from the futile and destructive struggle at Tortosa.

In 1415, as a result of this disputation, various decrees were introduced in Aragon that resembled those enacted in Castile in 1412. Many Jewish leaders converted, including honoured elders. Thus the debate rendered the problem of conversion even more acute, both quantitatively and qualitatively – though it also had fruitful effects on the outlook of the Jews (see pages 617–19).

The Inquisition

The Inquisition was a legally constituted court, according to its own definitions and philosophy. In order to understand the nature and motivation of its activity, its power and the dread that it produced, it is necessary to regard the Inquisition from its own point of view and to consider the justification given for its establishment and activity. The starting-point of the Inquisition's world view was love. In conducting his investigation, the inquisitor was acting out of love for the soul of the believer in an attempt to prevent him from sinning and leading others astray – though the individual may not have realized that he was causing himself injury. The inquisitor was filled with love of the accused arraigned before him. When he found himself compelled to exclude a person from the Church, he was, in his own eyes, simply pruning off diseased and wilted branches from the vineyard of the Lord of Hosts. If he were compelled to ask the secular authorities to execute the sentenced person, he was, in essence, performing an act of surgery, amputating a diseased member that spread its poison through other parts of the body. Such was the logic of the Inquisition. It permitted the inquisitor to hear detailed evidence in the absence of the accused, for he was as much the representative of the accused as he was his judge.

The institution and principles of the Inquisition were already long established when they were given a new and more intensive form towards the end of the fifteenth century. The zealots of the Christian Church in Spain maintained that in their struggle against the crypto-Judaism of the Marranos, the episcopal and papal inquisitions acted too slowly and showed too much leniency. Instead, the zealots desired a sovereign Spanish institution that would deal with the plague in the context of the grave local conditions. In 1482 the pope was still trying to maintain control over the Inquisition and to gain acceptance for his own attitude towards the New Christians, which was generally more moderate than that of the Inquisition and the local rulers. In the years 1482–3, the inquisitorial measures and royal decrees against the Jews grew increasingly severe.

The year 1483 proved decisive, for the Jews were then expelled from every part of Andalusia and in the autumn of that year the Dominican Tomás de Torquemada was appointed inquisitor-general of both Aragon and Castile. It was he who set the patterns of behaviour for the Spanish Inquisition. Wherever a new inquisitorial court was established, a 'term of grace' lasting thirty or forty days was proclaimed, during which the inquisitors received confessions and voluntary evidence. A study of the documents of the Inquisition shows that as a result of this procedure, a Marrano who had secretly remained faithful to Judaism or who did not behave as a devout Christian was caught unawares in the net that had been spread around him. As a rule, the suspect would confess during the term of grace to trifling transgressions. At the same time his neighbours and acquaintances would report their suspicions concerning his behaviour. For instance, they might claim that they had not seen smoke rising regularly from his chimney on Saturdays; or that the members of his household purchased large quantities of vegetables before the time of the Passover festival; or that he, along with other New Christians, purchased meat from a Marrano butcher. The sons and daughters of converts married among themselves, and they maintained contact with professing Jews. When a convert was arrested after the term of grace, his inquisitors would suggest that he should provide a list of defence witnesses. These often turned out to be witnesses against him, for he would call on his Christian neighbours to testify to his public behaviour as a Christian. While the witnesses might do so, they would also voice their suspicions that he remained a Jew in secret.

The Inquisition, like other courts of the period, employed torture in order to compel the accused to tell the truth. We possess a document from the end of this period showing how some of the Marranos who had secretly remained faithful to Judaism turned their torture into a form of martyrdom. According to this document, spiritual and psychological techniques were used in order to overcome the effect of the pain and to shift from a denial to an affirmation of Judaism, first inwardly and finally openly. A member of that generation offered advice to the Marrano who was about to be 'put to the question' and to undergo the tortures of the Inquisition:

> When they take him forth to suffer pain and torture . . . with harsh anguish . . . at that time let him concentrate, and in his imagination place the Great and Awesome Name between his eyes . . . with this he may rest assured at heart that he will stand the test . . . and although this is far from logical, yet it has already been proved by experience.

The Marrano was advised to concentrate his thoughts, in the course of the torture itself, upon the four Hebrew letters composing the Divine Name, which he was to picture in his imagination. Doing so would make it easier for him to bear the torment.

The sage who had heard of this method of resistance had also been informed that the moment of spiritual crisis came when the victim was told that the torments would be terminated if he wholeheartedly accepted Christianity. A fitting response to this temptation was laid down in the course of the fifteenth century:

> The moment of his resolution to Hallow the Name by martyrdom is when they wish to torture and question him . . . and they tell him that if he exchanges his honour they will let him alone. . . . Indeed, I have found that what one of the pious wrote should be his answer: 'What are you asking of me? Indeed I am a Jew. A Jew I live and a Jew I die. Jew, Jew, Jew!'

Such a reaction on the part of the Marrano caught between the pain of torture and the lure of conversion constituted a protest that closed off all routes of escape. This path was held in high esteem in the eyes of professed Jews. The writer quoted here considered that

> possibly . . . the soul of the martyr who makes his soul one with God and constantly increases his love, giving his grave to the wicked and his body to be consumed by fire, has been described by the wise king in his wisdom: 'Who is this that comes up from the wilderness, cleaving to her beloved' [Song of Songs 8:5]. For every divine utterance is tried and tested; and the soul cleaves and

falls limb by limb and piece by piece (*Megillat Amraphel,* pub. G. Scholem, Jerusalem, 1930/1, pp. 153–5).

Not all converts, not even the majority, chose this way. Many of them, particularly the wealthy, succeeded in escaping from the claws of the Inquisition without being compelled to confess. A large number made a confession and did Christian penance. Yet the activities of the Inquisition against the crypto-Jews continued for generations, even after the expulsion.

Two years before the expulsion, a blood libel was brought against the New Christians – the case of 'the Holy Child of La Guardia'. In the confused trial, several Marranos were accused of having crucified a Christian boy. According to the charges, they had endeavoured to obtain the Christian Host for the purpose of performing witchcraft with it and with the heart of the crucified boy in order to cause all the Christians to perish of rabies. All the accused were burnt in 1491. From the historical point of view, the important aspect here was the Inquisition's exploitation of a charge that had no factual foundation. Whether the inquisitors intended it or not, this charge helped to prepare the ground for the expulsion of the professed Jews and to increase the animosity towards the Marranos. The preaching and debating that commenced with Vicente Ferrer and the Tortosa Disputation continued in various forms and degrees of intensity until the expulsion.

The Inquisition was not aimed solely at the New Christians. At every trial suspicions were voiced against the community of professed Jews, and efforts were made to obtain from the authorities new decrees against them. The mass animosity, which prepared Christians to believe any evil of the Jews and the New Christians alike, had assumed a distinctly racist tone. There were still Jews who held honoured posts at the royal court and Jewish leaders who maintained close contact with the court of Queen Isabella, such as the aged chief rabbi Don Abraham Senior. As was mentioned earlier, he converted at the time of the expulsion. Spanish folk traditions have preserved a legend concerning attempts by the leading Jews to pay vast sums in order to secure the cancellation of the decree of expulsion. These sources relate that the fiery fanaticism of Tomás de Torquemada rendered all such efforts futile.

The Position of the Jews on the Eve of the Christian Reformation

At the beginning of the sixteenth century, the Jews of central Europe were subject only to partial, and in large measure temporary, expulsion, whereas the Jews of Western Europe, from Spain to England, had been expelled from almost every country. Within the Holy Roman Empire, the relatively small Jewish communities of Alsace were beginning to occupy a central position in Jewish life, for the older and larger communities of other areas had lost their status and suffered constantly from mass persecution or had been expelled altogether. Thus, for example, at the beginning of the sixteenth century, a rabbi from Alsace, Johanan Luria, related: 'A certain priest came and said to me: Jew, what is this yellow-coloured badge which you wear on your clothes and what does it signify?' The Jew gave a proud and firm reply. The Christian then asked why the Jews did not wear their *ẓiẓit* [ritual fringes] openly. The sage explained that the reason was the insults and attacks directed against them daily by the Christians:

> Ever since we have settled among you, you have regarded us as contemptible . . . every day there are those among you who will snatch away the *ẓiẓit* so that they are damaged and so our gain in wearing them openly becomes a loss. We have therefore to wear them secretly so that they should at least be visible in our homes (H. H. Ben-Sasson in *Zion,* 27 [1962], 168–9).

The Polemics Regarding the Talmud Between Johannes Pfefferkorn and Johannes Reuchlin

In Germany several Jewish apostates engaged in persecuting their former co-religionists. With the printing press facilitating the spread of varied and opposing opinions, these apostates began to assail the Jews by printing books against them (see page 585). In addition to writing against the Jews, one of them, Johannes Pfefferkorn, decided to renew the idea of destroying the Talmud because of its anti-Christian passages. In the climate of nascent humanism in Germany, however, the decision was no longer in his hands or in those of his patrons, the Dominicans of Cologne. In 1509 he obtained an order from Emperor Maximilian for the confiscation of Jewish writings. However, the emperor also commanded to seek the advice of the universities of Mainz, Cologne, Erfurt and Heidelberg and also to consult the Dominican inquisitor of Cologne, the convert Victor of Carben, and the Christian philologist and jurist Johannes Reuchlin. The latter opposed the burning of the Talmud, his reason being that the Talmud, as well as the books of the Kabbalah, contain much material that is of service to Christianity and confirm its claims to truth. In any case, he believed they should be preserved because they contain important information. In presenting his argument, the philologist and humanist declared that Hebrew was 'a miraculous thing', that none of the translations (of the Bible, etc.) matched up to the original and that Hebrew literature should be studied in its original tongue. He believed that the Kabbalah contained Christian mysteries (this was likewise the opinion of the famous Italian humanist Pico della Mirandola). Reuchlin also cited legal considerations, beginning with Roman law, and even recalled that in ancient times Judaism and Christianity had been considered 'two sects' by Roman imperial law. In accordance with that law, he noted, Jews had held citizenship in the Roman Empire (*concives imperii*). Likewise, they were entitled to defence, in accordance with their charters of rights and imperial law.

From this point on, the focus of polemic activity shifted beyond the subject of the Jews to the contest between the German humanists and their scholastic opponents, whose citadel of strength lay within the Dominican order. Appeals and counter-appeals to the emperor and the universities, as well as treatises for and against the stand of Reuchlin, issued from the printing presses from 1509 onwards.

The Talmud was not burnt, and the Jews have remembered Reuchlin for this ever since. It was at this time that the humanists published the *Epistolae Obscurorum Virorum* ('Letters of Obscurantist Men'), mocking the Dominicans and parodying their confused Latin style. Both the popular religious hatred and the humanistic reasoning evidenced in this controversy were to re-emerge in various forms after 1517, in the strife that marked the period of the Reformation and Counter-Reformation.

36

Jewish Autonomy from the Black Death to the Reformation

Community Leadership Within Ashkenaz

After the Black Death and the massacres that accompanied it, the communities within the region known as Ashkenaz had to deal with the problem of restoring the basic order of Jewish society. Because of the frequent expulsions and changes in the Jews' places of residence (see pages 561–5), the reconstruction of Jewish community life was a recurrent problem. It is evident that the Jews turned to tried and tested forms, and for the most part community life was re-established according to recognized precedents. In several areas, however, old concepts no longer suited the new circumstances. The concept of prohibition of settlement, for example, changed considerably in communities that required new settlers because of the instability of their tenure of domicile, in some places, as well as of their very security and status. As we shall see, the power of the rabbis expressed itself in a new mode under the changed conditions. Select information about the community structure at the end of this period comes from Regensburg. In about 1498 the community was headed by a group of ten members, while its regulations were passed at a meeting of the thirty-one 'boni viri of the community and of [the rest of] those who dwell in the street of the Jews'. This leadership set out to restore order in the ancient and persecuted community, their chief objective being to settle quarrels and prevent appeals to the gentile authorities. Here it is twice stated that decisions were passed 'by a vote of the majority' (Straus, op. cit., no. 676, pp. 228–30).

Smaller communities were headed by fewer members. The community of Schweidnitz received permission in 1370 to choose four leaders every year. If the community could afford to do so, it was entitled to select a 'bishop' (i.e., a dayyan or judge in matters of Jewish law) every year or two. When the community was not in a position to do so, the four elected leaders would serve as judges according to Jewish law, sending difficult questions to a competent scholar. In this charter the principle of majority decision was expressly specified, for it provided that the opinion of the majority was to be decisive in the conduct of communal affairs, and no individual could reject the majority decision (Bondy and Dvorsky, op. cit., no. 145, pp. 74–5). 'We . . . the heads of the holy community of Cracow . . . with the approval of all members of the congregation', who signed the deed of renunciation of trade in 1485 (see page 581), were also four in number.

'The worthy and wise persons, our Masters the magistrates and council of the City of Worms' were not satisfied with the undertaking given by the leaders of the congregation in monetary matters. Apparently, they demanded the signature of all earners 'who are Jews of Worms . . . who are assessed for [taxation] who dwell .here . . . old and young'. Their document was signed by thirty-five Jews (*Book of Documents of Worms,* II, no. 217). In negotiations about rights with city authorities, which must certainly have been frequent, the spokesman for the Jews was 'Rabbi Meir of Jeschenau, who is the intercessor here and is established [as intercessor] by the burghers' (*Responsa of R. Moses Mintz, op. cit.,* no. 39, fol. 34r). Thus the leadership and representation of the Jewish community, in both internal and external matters, would vary according to its structure and numbers, the demands of the magistrate or burghers and the provisions in the charters.

The subject of taxation appeared repeatedly on the agenda of these communities. They had their own detailed forms for taking an oath. 'When a person in Austria is required to swear, he goes to the cantor and the beadle and gives them the fee as prescribed there for a man from whom they will hear the oath.' The Austrian Jews copied the practice in Venice, requiring that the oath be made in the presence of ten Jews. It was in this fashion that a man would take an oath when he 'came to reduce the value . . . that the assessors had assigned him'. It is clear that assessment by means of 'decision' was the primary method of fixing taxes and that it could be countered by an oath confirming the financial statement listing all one's possessions, which the apellant was required to submit to two of those before whom he swore (Joseph ben Moses, *Leket Yosher, Yoreh De'ah,* J. Freimann, ed., Berlin, 1904, pp. 36–7).

As was only natural, the struggle over payment of taxes reflected the economic and social tension of the time. Thus it is related that when 'a community had together agreed to select five persons to assess every man and woman and to set the tax according to that assessment', there rose 'two wealthy brothers, influential in the community, and demanded that two of the five chosen . . . should be of their group' (Isserlein, *op. cit.,* no. 344, p. 138). The capacity of a few wealthy persons to oppose communal authority is clearly indicated in the reasons given by R. Israel Isserlein for submitting to their demands:

> When the wealthy and arrogant chose the assessors . . . they are more ready to accept the latter's decisions. Order is maintained and they will not demand more appeals in their arrogance. . . . But there is no reason to be overly cautious with members of the middle class in such matters, since in any case they will accept the decisions and will not cause trouble (*ibid.,* p. 139).

R. Israel consoled himself with the fact that, even if the demand of the wealthy were accepted, only two of the assessors would come from their group and that middle-class members would be in the majority (*ibid.*). To us this evidence is important because it shows the preponderance of wealth over majority decision in some cases and that it was sometimes necessary to take this fact into consideration so that order would be maintained. It was evident to the rabbi that causing such a disturbance was beyond the power of the middle class, despite its numerical preponderance.

The Theory of Communal Leadership in Ashkenaz

R. Israel Isserlein again stated that the essence of the community and the source of its authority over its members stems primarily from the concept of its constituting a partnership empowered to carry out their common duties. He took the view that 'the members of the city and the men of the community who join in paying the taxes have every legal aspect of partnership' (*ibid.,* no. 343, p. 138). The fact that the burden of taxation was shared by all members was both a sign of communal cooperation and the actual legal expression of partnership, which was the basis of authority in the matter of tax-collection and in other financial affairs and of the community's right to impose its decisions upon individual members who disagreed with it. Likewise, 'in every matter where the many have a claim against the individual – even if these are not connected with taxes and royal levies – the majority is always to be regarded as having the contested subject in its possession' and is to be given preference over the individual (*ibid.,* no. 341, p. 132). The officers of the community gained authority over the individuals primarily as heads of this 'partnership'.

In Alsace communal-leadership theory was formulated harshly, in a way that R. Israel would presumably have opposed. In matters of communal leadership 'the understanding is as follows . . . the heads, the elders and the officers . . . indeed stand for all Israel,' and ordinary folk have no share in leadership. This point of view held that it is impossible to conduct communal affairs by continually turning to the general public for its opinion, 'for agreement does not emerge well from the commonalty'. Even in calling on the community to repent, it was necessary for 'everything to be done by the leaders'. The protagonist of this viewpoint argued that a distinction must be drawn between the individual's share in the Torah and the public mastery of the Torah when Torah is enacted in public, 'for all Israel has a share in the Torah but [the Lord] has set only the elders over them [the Torah laws] and not the vulgars. For how can pearls be cast before those who trample upon them?' The common members of the communities should show their leaders the respect due to royalty, for, 'although we have no king or princes . . . the leaders and heads of the age take the place of the king'. The royal stature of the leadership was a prerequisite condition for the proper functioning of the nation, 'for nothing can be agreed or succeed without the heads and leaders'. What the latter decide is valid even if the public objects for

> [when] a leader engages . . . in a matter affecting the commonalty, then the latter . . . are not to say: 'He wishes for this but we do not approve of it . . . ' for the patriarch of the age is the age . . . and it is proper . . . that the leader of the age be like its patriarchal head. . . . He represents the generation even when he works to their disadvantage. This is easy to understand.

Having once understood that the will of the leader prevails in all communal matters, whether or not the community agrees, 'we learn from this that all the regulations and agreements made by the *boni viri* of the city are binding on the masses even against their will.' That is how the world has behaved since early times. Thus 'Eve herself was not explicitly commanded not to eat from the tree; but since Adam was the head and accepted the command, everyone was required to accept it' (Ben-Sasson, *op. cit.*, 175, 176, 184, 185).

Such views led not only to greater exercise of authority on the part of community leaders but also to abuse of their position. In some communities there were also tendencies towards overbearing rule. R. Jacob Weil was asked about a 'warden who was appointed over the community. After twenty years there were complaints against him – should he give a financial report to each and every one' of the members of the community? In his Responsum the rabbi drew a distinction between two methods known to him by which a warden could gain power in the community. One way was that the man 'is appointed by the community which chooses him to be warden according to their opinion'. In this case he is not obligated to present an account. On the other hand, 'when he is not appointed by the opinion of the community but by the rulers, or by force and violence, as when everyone fears him and nobody is entitled to speak or protest against him, then it is obviously necessary for him to provide an account.' However, the account should not be presented to each individual, 'since, as is known, certain matters on which it is necessary to expend communal money . . . should be revealed only to the modest [*i.e.,* the circumspect].' Thus sharp theoretical condemnation is softened by the recommendation of secrecy and by entrusting certain actions of the leadership and the control of its budget to selected individuals only. At the same time, the rabbi uttered a bitter complaint about 'this great scandal in most communities; that the wardens oppress and tyrannize the people forcibly, not for the sake of heaven but for their own benefit, discarding their own yoke and placing it on the necks of the unfortunate' (*Responsa of Rabbi Jacob Weil, op. cit.,* no. 173, p. 120).

From details on institutional matters and clauses in the ordinances, it becomes clear that, in theory as well as in practice, there was a close resemblance between the Jewish community leadership of the later Middle Ages and the Christian city magistrate as far as power and control were concerned. In the cities, however, the clash between different elements was far more acute, and there were violent conflicts between the power-hungry patricians and the craftsmen and 'the ordinary little people', who also demanded power. In the Jewish communities the patrician theory, whereby authority was to be exercised by the well-to-do scholars, and the opposition of the moralists and the public to rule by a privileged few arose within a setting that contained no genuine class distinctions. Differences in the level of wealth, as well as of education, were to be found among those engaged in identical occupations and following the same life style. So with the *yeshiva*: just as it provided a unifying factor for those who studied within its walls, so it served to set them apart from others. An external sign of the differentiation and unification alike can be seen in the honorific titles that these educational institutions then began to grant.

Scholars as Established 'Leaders' in the Communities of Ashkenaz

It appears that after the catastrophe of 1348–9 – after the waves of massacre and hatred joined the effects of the Black Death to cause disintegration of settlement, economy and security for Jews – and during the difficult period that followed in the next few generations in the cities of Germany, it was increasingly felt that of all its possessions, nothing was left to Jewry except the Torah and that it was therefore necessary to elevate those relatively few who studied and possessed knowledge of the Torah. The authority of the scholars and sages became a factor providing continuity and stability to the otherwise ravaged Jewish social structure. Their status within the leadership and in the public eye began to rise and was indicated in various social nuances and institutional practices. Correspondingly, the self-respect of the scholars steadily increased. One of the outstanding figures of the fifteenth century stated that 'Talmudic scholars have become objects of sanctity on account of the knowledge of the Torah within them' (*Responsa of Mahari Segal,* Hanau, 1610, no. 1, p. 3).

The institutionalization of the revered status of scholars can be recognized from the use of established stereotyped forms. The communal rabbis were honoured with the title 'leader', a designation that actually described their role. One scholar wrote to his friend: 'I wish to inform you that I have requested the Gaon and Exilarch [this honorific title had again come into use] our master the rabbi, Rabbi Isserlein . . . to write to you that you should have the full standing of Leader, Judge, and Decider' (*Leket Yosher, op. cit., Yoreh De'ah* p. 37). As a rule, a 'leader' was elected during the intermediary days of Passover. If he resided in another city, he was invited by letter. 'The congregation of Vienna sent' a letter to R. Israel Isserlein announcing that they had elected him and asking that he come 'to settle his home and dwelling' in their city. R. Israel wrote his acceptance during the same intermediary days of Passover, and 'his answer was written without any change of script [though change was held fitting when anything not absolutely necessary was written during that semi-festival period] . . . because providing a scholar to be a leader of a city was a necessity for the community' (*ibid., Orah Hayyim,* p. 105).

A communal rabbi tended to view himself as the sole 'Master of the Place' (the technical Aramaic term was *mara deatra*), and he would not suffer another scholar to reside or 'lead' in his city. As late as the fifteenth century, this tendency had to contend with the earlier traditions. R. Israel Isserlein protested against those who wished to exercise exclusive authority in their own cities, stating that 'the crown and dominion of the Torah . . . lie abandoned for any who wishes to have its merit.' He believed that those who opposed the entry of another scholar in the city did so for reasons of 'livelihood . . . because of the money that comes to the pocket of the leaders from divorces and *halizah* and hearing the oaths of women and the payment for the blessings of betrothal and espousal' (*Pesakim u-Khetavim* ['Decisions and Writings'], Warsaw, 1882, no. 128, p. 25). Yet reports of a struggle during the first generations following the Black Death clearly indicate that this tendency towards monopoly was on the rise.

It was sustained and supported by the institution of *semikhah* or 'ordination' of scholars and sages, which was well defined and established in Ashkenaz at this period. It may be assumed that there had always been methods whereby individuals and communities could distinguish the sage entitled, in the opinion of his scholarly equals, to instruct and give guidance in accordance with the *halakhah*. During this period, recognition took on the form of written confirmation and the application of specific titles, such as *morenu* ('our teacher'); a demand for special respect; and the right to be a 'leader' and to head a *yeshiva*. *Semikhah* was defined by the Sephardi rabbi Isaac ben Sheshet (Ribash) as 'the custom of France and Ashkenaz, where the rabbis ordain their pupils with the degree of rabbi when they see that they have attained knowledge to give instruction, and they give them permission to set up a *yeshiva* in any place and to judge and teach' (*Responsa of R. Isaac ben Sheshet*, Riva da Trent, 1558, no. 271, fol. 192v). As time went on an aura of hallowed authority attached itself to the act of ordination. R. Moses Mintz maintained that 'every rabbi and expert has been ordained a rabbi by a preceding rabbi all the way back to Moses our Master . . . a rod and strap had been given in his hand . . . and no householder . . . may in any way question the words of the rabbi' (Ben-Sasson, *op. cit.*, 179). Thus a virtual *halakhah* on 'the chain of ordination' arose and had considerable influence, even if it had no historical basis. It led the ordained person to demand respect and to feel superiority towards 'a boor and householder', who did not possess this *semikhah*. The head of the *yeshiva* was the elect among the circle of those ordained, whose members had a strong sense of their right to hold power and exercise authority over the people. In Alsace R. Johanan Luria preached at the turn of the fifteenth and sixteenth centuries to a newly appointed *yeshiva* head:

> There still remain sages with as great a knowledge of the Torah as you or more, so whence came this greatness to you of being appointed head of the *yeshiva*? The text in Psalms says 'Thou lovest righteousness and hatest wickedness' . . . the greatness of Moses our Master . . . and the Levites was that they had the firmness of heart to castigate the wicked . . . therefore thou hast been annointed with the oil of gladness above thy comrades by being appointed head of the *yeshiva*. For the head of the *yeshiva* is called a king, to make it known that the merit of the age lies in those who are firm of heart for the sake of heaven, and not those who are pleasant to people whatever they may do (*ibid.*, 186).

The sage is elected from the 'tribe of Levites', that is, those already ordained, on account of his firmness and readiness to lead the generation with a strong hand.

In due course doubts were expressed regarding 'the Ashkenazi ordination'. It was appealed against as early as the fourteenth century, when an attempt was made to use it for purposes of buttressing the authority of the central leadership in France. It was particularly objected to by scholars and sages among the exiles from Spain, who met it in Italy and other countries within the bounds of Ashkenaz, when the local ordained rabbis claimed superiority. In Ashkenaz itself, ordination continued to be used until modern times, and it was an institution basic to the study of Torah, social organization and rabbinical authority.

The 'leader' functioned in every field of life in his city. Not only did he conduct a *yeshiva*, he also dealt with all weddings and divorces (so much so that in France in the fourteenth century, some were nicknamed 'the Wedding Rabbis', either because they were accused of engaging primarily in this lucrative activity or because they engaged in match-making on behalf of their *yeshiva* students). Many of the arrangements and regulations of the local community were undertaken with his approval, under his supervision, or on his initiative. Among these were acts which constitute a clear mark of autonomy in the mediaeval city, such as the selling of liquor. 'On one occasion the *boni viri* of the community came from Neustadt to the Gaon [Rabbi Israel Isserlein] to obtain correct measures for wine and oil, and he provided them; for the measures had been forgotten. For the Jews had a large measure unlike the gentiles, because they did not have to pay excise.' After consultation with these community leaders, the rabbi sent his beadle to a Christian craftsman and ordered wooden vessels 'and the craftsman prepared them accordingly. And after they had scorched a mark at the top of the measures, he gave them to the beadle and whoever wished to sell wine would go to the beadle, who gave him the measure. When he did not need the measure he would return it . . . to the beadle. It seems the measures for oil and milk were of iron or tin' (*Leket Yosher, op. cit., Orah Hayyim*, p. 139). Here is an illustration of a whole area of communal control over measures. It is clear that the rabbi was the one who decided all details in this area from beginning to end. Furthermore, his beadle carried out and supervised regulations of this kind.

Sometimes the rabbi would be responsible for revitalizing the community and restoring its social activities. At the end of this period, R. Moses Mintz relates that

> before I came hither to the community of Bamberg, this place was like a broken and breached wall . . . and there was no man who thought of improving local affairs and regulating them. And the congregation were like sheep that had no shepherd, and . . . there was no money in the charity fund, neither at the synagogue nor at the cemetery [thus we know of two centres for charity, which were neglected in the absence of a community rabbi] . . . and at all times the poor came . . . and said: 'Clothe us or feed us,' and wailed bitterly and none paid them attention. . . . In addition, when it was a matter of doing the last rites for the dead, there was no provision there . . . and this caused the dead to be left lying.

This anarchic state of affairs – the description of which indicates the elementary duties of a Jewish community in Ashkenaz with respect to public administration and charity – existed in Bamberg in the summer of 1469. In praise of himself, R. Moses Mintz says, 'I made many ordinances' and imposed authority 'to be observed by men, women and children, young and old together'. Among these he records the ordinance that laid the foundation for a permanent charity fund. This regulation required that 'every man and woman shall give to the fund a quarter of the tithe . . . by his faith and soul . . . on whatever he earns [*i.e.*, 2.5% of his income] . . . by interest or by wares . . . and the warden or charity warden shall collect it every month from every man . . . and shall go with the closed box from house to house' (*Responsa of R. Moses Mintz, op. cit.*, no. 60, fol. 57r).

Attempts to Introduce a Centralized Leadership in Ashkenaz

The authority vested in the community rabbis produced a natural tendency towards centralization of leadership. The scholar, to be sure, was satisfied with his position as the leader in the city that had chosen him; but the tradition of Responsa and the resulting *halakhic* interaction gave rise to a desire to exert a more far-reaching influence, depending on the scholarship of the individual and the degree of recognition he enjoyed in the immediate vicinity and beyond. The recurring troubles and the pressures of various rulers, whose fields of interest formally or informally overlapped the limits of Jewish local autonomy, strengthened the tendency among Jewish communities towards unified self-defence and joint intercession. In the aftermath of riots, blood libels and expulsions, very often within relatively short periods of time, the communities were in need of guidance from some definite centre. Together, these factors outweighed the contrary tendency to separatism, which resulted from increasing submission to the Christian cities and the destruction of the old communities that had been recognized as centres for generations.

A certain practice seems to have been more widespread in the fifteenth century than the surviving sources would suggest, namely that the communities used to regard the 'small Jewish groups round about us' as satellites. An indication of this relationship was that the people of the small outlying communities 'are connected with our cemeteries'. As a rule, the ordinances governing the communities were binding only on those who dwelt within its walls, and, therefore, other communities in the vicinity were not included: 'Our regulations do not apply to them. And if they transgress against our regulations, we do not impose fines upon them because they are not included within the rule of our regulations.' But in certain circumstances '[the larger communities] used to wish to include the small communities around them within the regulations involving matters which are of public importance'. It may be assumed that an aspiration of this kind would come about at a time of external danger or internal crisis, whether spiritual or social. For this purpose, a set pattern was established: they 'then fixed a certain day; and the communities and settlements which were to be included within the regulations met together, sending two or three from each city and preparing the ordinances and sending letters through all the vicinity to be read by proclamation before the public, cautioning them.' This proclamation served as a warning of punishment in the event of transgression (*ibid.*, no. 63, fol. 59v). Thus we see that there did exist the practice of small communities, through committees of representatives, being incorporated under the leadership of a large community. The representatives were summoned by prior agreement and, in large measure, they followed the practice of the committees and councils of the late twelfth century (see pages 563–4).

The sages were an important factor in these committees and councils as well. R. Israel Isserlein relates: 'I saw a written ordinance enacted for the purpose of collecting a heavy tax . . . the congregation of Neustadt and all the communities and their residents [possibly 'the smaller communities'] of the lands of Styria. And that writ was drawn up by two *dayyanim* and other scholars and it was in the year 1415/16' (Isserlein, *Terumat Hadeshen,* para. 342, p. 136). R. Jacob Weil relates that 'when we were gathered in Nuremberg many ordinances were formulated. And this was one of them: if one party to a suit wishes to plead in German, then the other must also plead in German' (*Responsa of R. Jacob Weil, op. cit.,* no. 101, p. 69). Another Responsum indicates that the communities met in Nuremberg in order to negotiate with the authorities the amount of the tax imposed yearly on the Jews of the empire. On occasion the rulers discouraged any central Jewish representation in such matters. 'And if the king's counsellors required, they were compelled to meet them, each community on its own' (*ibid.*, no. 147, p. 95).

The conflict between the authority of the sages in their own localities and the trend towards central leadership was revealed by the dispute regarding the Bingen synod in 1455. Prior to the meeting of the synod, the following negotiations took place between those who initiated it and the rabbis who were invited. R. Veibisch, one of the chief antagonists of the resolutions adopted on this occasion, 'wrote . . . that he first wished to know clearly and not in hints, in detail and not in general terms, what they wished to ordain and what remedy they wished to initiate . . . that he did not intend to come unless he first saw the character and quality of the ordinances.' R. Seligman of Bingen, the guiding spirit of the synod, 'wrote to him that he himself did not yet know what would be discussed and what would be enacted'. Another initiator explained to Rabbi Veibisch 'that it was not his desire that the ordinances should be enacted by their actual synod meeting; and likewise it was not his intention to sign in a hurry, even if there should be agreement on the matter, but only with deliberation and in consultation'. However, when the synod did meet, it in fact acted on and resolved various 'ordinances and decrees'. Furthermore, one 'umbrella' ordinance of this synod specified 'that if any doubt should arise regarding the sense of the wording of the ordinances in the other lands . . . Our Master Rabbi Bing Seligman should be their interpreter'. The communities in general and their sages in particular strongly opposed this supreme authority of interpretation. We learn from the opponents in what measure this synod was an assembly of communal rabbis and their representatives, for the aforesaid R. Veibisch complains that 'he sent . . . his son thither [to Bingen] for the day of the Synod . . . only to show his respect for Rabbi Seligman, to accede to his request and not in order to sign. And the fact that he [the son] signed on behalf of his father . . . was on account of his awe and the imposing threats which Rabbi Seligman employed' (Isserlein, *Pesakim u-Khetavim*, no. 252, p. 55). The opposition to this synod was widespread, vitiating its influence and objectives.

The Rabbis of the Lands

Rabbis who were recognized and accepted as *halakhic* authorities, and particularly those who were communal heads, sometimes tended to expand their areas of influence. R. Johanan ben Mattathias of France complained to the sages of Catalonia that R. Meir Halevi of Vienna, whom he described as 'rabbi of Ashkenaz', had granted authority to R. Isaiah ben Abba Mori 'over the whole kingdom of France in its entirety [and] that if anyone rises to set up a *yeshiva* without his authority, then his divorces and *halizot* shall be disqualified and all their [those who will obey decisions of rabbis unauthorized by R. Isaiah] cooking vessels shall be *trefa* [ritually taboo]; and that Rabbi Isaiah's dominion shall be over the whole land of France' (*Responsa of R. Isaac ben Sheshet, op. cit.*, no. 270, fol. 192r). Thus R. Meir of Vienna had appointed a Chief Rabbi for the whole of France. What is of interest is the fact that R. Johanan demanded this authority for himself because his father

R. Mattathias had led the Jewry of France before him. And although he complained of the Ashkenazi intervention, he himself called the Catalonians into the dispute.

There were also occasions when scholars were appointed by the rulers as rabbis over all the Jews within the principality, or part of it. In this way the rulers aimed at establishing a central authority among the Jews that would assist in the collection of taxes from them. The sages, in turn, would accept this appointment in order to extend their control over the communities by virtue of the power stemming from the secular appointment. In 1407 a certain R. Israel received an appointment of this kind; in 1426, three rabbis were appointed on behalf of the emperor, one of them being Jacob Moellin, called the Maharil. In 1435, R. Anselm was appointed as rabbi on behalf of the realm for all the western regions of the empire; and although he was involved in a dispute with R. Israel Bruna, we do not find that this matter is raised against him in the course of their disagreements. In the year 1490 there appears 'Meir the Jew, the Jewish rabbi [*Mistr*] for the Kingdom of Bohemia and the Margraviate of Moravia' as chief of those providing security for payment of the annual taxes by the Jews of Moravia (Bondy and Dvorsky, *op. cit.*, no. 285, p. 167). In Poland, in 1503, King Alexander appointed R. Jacob Polak as 'rabbi of the Jews'. The king granted him 'full authority to settle according to Jewish law . . . disputes between any Jews, to eliminate any quarrel, to rectify what is corrupt, to improve morals, and to exercise . . . other functions involved in the office of rabbi'. This 'leader' of the Jews of Poland was formally granted the powers to which the sages and scholars of Ashkenaz were accustomed. The king ordered the Jews of Poland to accept R. Jacob over them 'as rabbi according to your law . . . to submit to his authority in all matters touching on his office' (Halperin, *op. cit.*, p. 236). This act clearly spelled anew the conception of territorial and state rabbis appointed by the rulers of the realm, after the fashion of the Middle Ages.

Leadership and Synods of Italian Jewry

In Italy as well, certain changes could be observed in the leadership of the communities as a result of the settlements that were being created around the *condotti* (see page 578) and the incitement of the Franciscans (see page 567). In all communities except Rome, which was more stable, the decisive element in the rise of the leadership became the personal power of the wealthy individual who held the 'shop'. There was also a recognizable tension between the old families and the new arrivals from France and Germany, who aspired to leadership and status in the community, and this was true of Rome as well. The 'newcomers' were called *Transmontani* ('those from over the mountains') and only in 1524 did the established Jews come to terms with them in Rome, and they were accepted into the leading circles.

Anti-Jewish measures and dangers of all kinds led to the establishment of a central leadership by synods in Italy, too. From 1399 onwards, there are records of actions taken by assemblies of community heads and sages. Preparations for unified intercession with the pope, on the one hand, and guidance of the communities, on the other, ensured that the various synods were held at frequent intervals (in Bologna in 1416 and at Forli in 1418). It seems that various regional synods, such as the synod of the communities of Marches in 1420, were held in order to implement the decisions of the Forli meetings. In the middle of the fifteenth century, there were further gatherings for defensive purposes, to counter, for example, the attacks of John of Capistrano (see page 579). In the early part of the sixteenth century a large number of such synods met as a result of numerous internal and external problems related to the expulsions from Spain and southern Italy and the subsequent arrival of large numbers of refugees. During the fifteenth and early sixteenth centuries, there was virtually a continuous series of synods to solve special problems that arose; some of these synods based themselves on the decisions of their predecessors.

The Rabbinate Structure in Spain

The status of the rabbis in the Spanish communities never, even at the most critical times, reached the degree of institutionalized authority that was achieved by the communal rabbis thanks to the formal 'ordination' in Ashkenaz and in Italy. R. Isaac ben Sheshet (Ribash) defined what was required by a rabbi in a small community: he should have 'more than enough [knowledge] to be able to judge, instruct, teach pupils, preach, and express himself effectively, both in writing and verbally'. He provided this definition when casually asked by 'that honourable congregation which rabbi or *dayyan* I would choose for them of those in the country and which they could induce to come to them' (*Responsa of R. Isaac ben Sheshet, op. cit.,* no. 287, fol. 204r). These scholars, *dayyanim,* preachers and teachers were sometimes faced by considerable opposition from the more powerful householders. Their outstanding representatives in the fifteenth century, such as R. Nissim and R. Isaac ben Sheshet, had to face sharp antagonism. R. Isaac ben Sheshet explained to a scholar guidelines for estimating the nature and importance of a community, with all its advantages and disadvantages, in reply to a rabbi who was about to decide whether to stay in a community near Valencia or leave it for Teruel: 'I cannot comprehend your intention; how you could think of leaving that worthy community where there are many intelligent and understanding men, double and four-fold what there are in Teruel, while the congregation as a whole is larger than there. And even if there are some whose intention is to grieve you, still you have many who strive for you and are zealous on your behalf' (*ibid.,* no. 445, fol. 352r).

The insistence on being a recognized communal rabbi was to be found in Spain as well, although there it adopted a more moderate form than in Ashkenaz. R. Isaac ben Sheshet rebuked Rabbi Ḥasdai Solomon of Valencia for 'your quarrels with the learned Rabbi Amram ... for it is befitting on your part to honour him ... because you have come *into his bounds;* and even if your presence there is not proper in his eyes it would not make him hate you, were it not that he has been great in that kingdom for forty years; and he sat alone on the seat of instruction. And he did not desire that a second rabbi should enter his house and he fears that you may decide differently from him in respect of the laws ... and that which he dreaded has come upon him.' R. Amram was a leader who issued legal decisions, and not the head of a *yeshiva,* for R. Isaac goes on to explain: 'Indeed, I am not surprised if he sometimes says things that are not sufficiently detailed and precise ... since he does not study the

Talmud constantly with intelligent students but only reads the judicial literature and compilations morning and evening' (*ibid.*). The external marks of respect were important in the relations between the old adjudicator, the communal leader, and the young teacher who had invaded his territory. R. Isaac's advice to R. Ḥasdai is that 'it would be good to honour him publicly and treat him with respect; and behind the door and the doorpost, when you are by yourselves, make him understand his error and he will undoubtedly recognize your value' (*ibid.*).

There is a bitterly satirical description, written by Solomon Bonafed, of a rabbi of Saragossa in the first half of the fifteenth century, through which we can learn what was regarded as praiseworthy in public appearance and leadership in Saragossa of that period. The rabbi in question, Joseph ibn Jeshua, was a Sicilian who had been accepted as leader and teacher in this large community and was honoured elsewhere as well. According to his satirist, he had a poor physical appearance, but he used to proceed 'amid the congregation and community in a prayer-shawl fringed with eight long threads and five knots . . . and when he goes to the house of prayer with a company of his friends his head knocks against his shanks, mourning and bowed of head in a fine linen shroud . . . head low . . . humble heel' (H. Schirman, ed., *Koveẓ al Yad* ['Miscellany'], New Series, IV, Jerusalem, 1946, p. 17). Not only were his garments, behaviour and actions those of obvious piety and humility, but also the man 'would hallow himself amid the mass . . . and I have heard say that he would not eat from a vessel that a Jew [who was not observant enough in his view] had used . . . and on the Great Sabbath [before Passover] . . . he would preach for six hours regarding the laws of *ḥaroset* and parsley . . . to display his casuistry . . . and try the people with enigmas . . . wondrously inventing eighty different ways of making food unfit to eat . . . and spending the whole day in fetching and carrying . . . matters, the usage of which is forbidden' (*ibid.*, pp. 18–19). This strict rabbi and casuistic preacher also used to teach Aristotle, engaged in astronomy 'and was proud to Heaven in medicine' (*ibid.*, p. 21). Bonafed was forced to confess that 'the people who walk in darkness honoured him with their silver and gold . . . and placed him as head over them' (*ibid.*, p. 31). No matter how much animosity distorted this characterization, it still implies that the ideal rabbi and leader was a man who inspired, by his personal example, his ability in argument, his teachings, his sermons and his many pupils and disciples.

The Communities of Spain

The tension between the social elements of the Jewish communities regarding leadership, which has been described above, continued to cause divisions during this epoch and, in some measure, grew even more acute. In the large community of Barcelona, until 1386 the leadership was in the hands of a small group composed of several aristocratic families, which constituted the council of 'The Thirty'. In the 1370s and 1380s they were described as 'Thirty men supervising all the affairs of the congregation concerned with taxes and compulsory payments, and the choice of a community magistrate. . . . The election of the aforementioned Thirty takes place once every three years.' The electors were appointed according to 'a seal [*i.e.*, charter] from our King which empowers the three trustees and the Court to make the choice of the thirty men' (*Responsa of R. Isaac ben Sheshet, op. cit.,* no. 228, fol. 153v). This leadership structure was of a circle within a circle, one electing the other, while both together conducted all the affairs of the Jewish community in Barcelona. The council of 'The Thirty' would control most of the institutions, 'the trustees and their trustees and the law-court and those who check the accounts and the charity wardens'. The numerous institutions and the variety of functions and terms describing them did not prevent full control by the oligarchy. The election of the executive offices was carried out as 'The Thirty decide and establish a mode of behaviour . . . for the whole Thirty . . . to be placed in ballot. Three of them, those who come first by lot, make a selection of the others' for the various communal offices listed above (*ibid.,* no. 214, fol. 144r).

Sometimes there were divisions within this restricted group, and the lower classes eventually brought pressure to bear. In 1386, when there was a move towards democracy in the city, it was decided that henceforward the three trustees and council of 'The Thirty' should be elected from all three classes – upper, middle and lower – and full equality was all but granted to the third class. A small Council of Eighteen was specified; it would consist of five representatives of each class and the three communal trustees. The oligarchic control of offices was also undermined by the provision that the trustees should be elected for one year only and should be eligible for re-election only after an interval of three years. But the superior position of the aristocratic circles within the society and the struggle between them and the lower classes did not cease, and it was accompanied by acrimonious and bitter social criticism (see page 616).

In smaller communities the poor achieved even fewer rights than in the larger ones, and oligarchic rule continued to prevail. Social grievance also grew to considerable proportions in places where no specific institutional expression was given to the struggle between the classes. The tension is also reflected by the constant activity within the communities of 'the elected [to supervise on] transgressions' (*brurei averot*), whose task was to supervise the individual's way of life and who had the power to bring people to judgement and to impose punishment for breaches of *halakhah* or morality.

The income of the community came from excise taxes on wine and meat, which were usually farmed out. When, for example, the town of Huesca received a royal order ' . . . that every man, no matter what his faith, who is not a permanent resident of the city should leave the city and its walls within three days, and this was done', the reason that the communities preferred this indirect taxation became clear. The tax-farmer then came and demanded the return of his lease money 'because most of the charges on meat and wine are paid by persons who are not permanent residents in the city' and, following their expulsion, he had lost the income on which he had counted when he paid the community in advance (*ibid.,* no. 426, fol. 344v – 345r). In other words, this indirect excise on food consumption produced a considerable income from those consumers who were not permanent members of the community and hence eased the burden of the residents. In order to consolidate this income, the communities sometimes decreed 'that no man wherever he be shall under any conditions whatsoever be permitted to bring wine here from elsewhere . . . except . . . the wine which has been legally paid for when made . . . to the excise-farmer . . . and they undertook that all the wine so brought shall be prohibited for use like wine that is used for idolatrous purpose' (*ibid.*, no. 262, fol. 180r).

On occasion the community 'elected twelve men to make and ordain regulations for declarations of one's property'. The activities of those appointed to receive such declarations included fixing the date by which the statements must be made. Disputes regarding these matters were frequent, and among the questions sent to R. Isaac ben Sheshet was whether they might alter provisions made by themselves, including deferment of the date for making the declarations (*ibid.*, no. 457–61, fol. 359r–361v). When a man came to R. Isaac ben Sheshet to ask a question regarding tax affairs, the rabbi first refused to answer him because 'I fear lest there is some dispute among you regarding the declarations and you belong to one group. And it would not be fitting to answer you until I am questioned by both groups together, particularly as you have not brought any letter from the community magistrate' (*ibid.*, no. 473, fol. 371v). The communities sometimes exercised an influence over very extensive areas and did not hesitate to put aside even ancient *halakhic* principles.

A Responsum sent to Granada indicates the situation in Moslem Spain at that time and relates the activities of certain associations formed for specific purposes, but acting in cooperation with the leadership. This Responsum records that

> a community perceived there was difficulty in digging graves and needed to hire diggers . . . and in order that there should always be people ready to perform this duty they made ordinances providing for the setting up of a certain association . . . and agreed that when a man died who was well-to-do, thirty pieces of silver should be taken from his property, and if he was fairly well off, then between ten and twenty, while if anybody was without means he would be buried free of charge. And these sums of money, together with others which it was the practice to collect at every burial and during every month, should be set aside for all the burial requirements of the needy – the bier and the shrouds. But if there is any member of the association who is needy and shall be required by lot to dig, let him be paid like a day labourer . . . on the day that he is so engaged, for the upkeep of his household. And among the paragraphs of the regulations there is also provision that money shall be withdrawn from this fund for the redemption of captives and for such charities as are necessary according to the judgement of the Elder [a central authority who also conducted affairs in the community of North Africa at that period]. And the wardens and *boni viri* of the city and all the community agreed to this and acted accordingly for some time (*Responsa of R. Simeon ben Ẓemaḥ Duran,* part III, Amsterdam, 1738, fol. 5r).

Theory of Leadership in Spain

The principles of leadership in Spain were developed by leaders and rabbis of the aristocratic families who guided the communities and whose legal education and political trend of thought were largely influenced by the views current in the Christian environment. The social criticism, which emanated largely from the opposition mystical circles (see pages 542–5 and 614–17), also bears the mark of this influence.

During the most difficult period for Spanish Jewry, R. Isaac ben Sheshet set out to contradict

> what may be claimed . . . that as the charter [of Barcelona] was vouchsafed by the King to the community, therefore a Jew is not to be judged in accordance with our Torah but only according to the laws of the gentiles, for on this assumption it was granted by the King. . . . And the community too [acted on this assumption] as they accepted . . . that [it was] on the cognizance of the king's intention . . . and the plenipotence granted in the charter is to do in agreement with the judges of his [the king's] people, only that they [the Jews] should be judged by their sages (*Responsa of R. Isaac ben Sheshet, op. cit.,* no. 228, fol. 155r).

In reply to this hypothetical claim he wrote:

> There is no doubt that even without the seal of His Royal Majesty . . . this community would have had the right to enact ordinances in accordance with the Torah, and to ban and excommunicate and fine the transgressor independently . . . but since the awe of the King . . . was upon them lest the rulers might claim, 'you have taken authority to yourselves without royal permission', and in order to threaten the transgressor so that he should fear the wrath of the king, for that reason they obtained the will of His Royal Majesty . . . on that charter (*ibid.*).

From this we learn that, as a matter of principle, the communal regulations derive from Jewish law and the decisions of the Jewish judges are based on that primal Jewish authority. The charters were seemingly requested from the king only in order that the communities should not be falsely charged with presumption and excessive independence and to supplement Jewish enforcement of the regulations with the punitive power of the state. However, R. Isaac adds, although the appeal to the secular authority is not legally necessary for enacting the ordinances, once it has been obtained it is binding on the community, and thereafter it should not depart from the limits specified by the king.

> Obviously the intention of the community refers only to what is specified in that document and what is valid under the laws of the gentiles, in accordance with their experienced scholars, who do not warp judgement, and the ordinances enacted should not be extended beyond the power they have from the king . . . in accordance with the gentile authorities (*ibid.*).

Thus the law of the state, according to the interpretation of the royal judges (once their approval has been asked), constitutes a limit on the legislative activities of the community. 'And even if their ordinance be worded more comprehensively than the limit granted by the king's terms, this wording is not to be followed, but rather the spirit of the authority granted by the royal seal . . . but not more than that. For if they do more than is empowered according to the royal learned judges, they will be punished by them.' However, practical political considerations aside, Jewish law sufficed as the authoritative source of the autonomy of the communities and their right to conduct their affairs according to their own concepts and courts.

In the fifteenth century, there are indications that Jewish legal autonomy continued to be exercised in criminal cases as well, although they were subject to the influence of the legal concepts and methods of Christian jurists. In order to preserve this autonomy, the Jewish courts sometimes even issued death sentences where these were called for. The heads of the community (*mukadamin*) of Teruel asked R. Isaac ben Sheshet what he thought should be the proper punishment for an informer, who, under Jewish law, was liable to the death sentence. At the beginning of his Responsum the rabbi declared: ' . . . let the fire of their zeal go forth, and if it finds thorns . . . let it destroy them in the vineyard of the Lord of Hosts'. He also justifies the acceptance of a confession on the part of the accused as a basis for finding him guilty, though this is not in accordance with Talmudic law. His reason was that

> the court does not now have authority to judge criminal cases save by royal authorization. It is necessary therefore to justify the sentence likewise for the royal judges who are not of our faith, in order that they should not suspect us of judging without justice or trial. For nowadays . . . criminal cases are judged only in accordance with urgent necessity, since our capital sentencing has ceased within our own jurisdiction. . . . Accordingly, it has been the practice to accept the confession of the transgressor even in criminal cases, in order that the matter may be clarified from his words as well as by circumstantial evidence, if there is no proper testimony (*ibid.,* no. 234, fol. 162r–v).

All these trends find clear expression, in a world where both the main trend of Christian political thought as well as ideas and needs of Jewish society aimed at central leadership, in the actions of the Grand Synod of the fifteenth century convened in Valladolid.

The Valladolid Synod of 1432: Its Actions and Aims

Between 22 April and 2 May 1442, a synod of the communities of Castile met in Valladolid. The tendency towards centralized leadership had always been stronger in Castile than in Aragon. This came as a result of the powerfully centralist aspirations of the kingdom itself, which found their strong expression in those very cities where there were Jewish communities, and by virtue of the office of *rab de la corte* (see page 496), the 'court rabbi' – at this time, Don Abraham Benveniste. The ordinances agreed upon by this synod are instructive not only with respect to the trends that the participants wished to ensure for the future, but, as Isaac Baer states: 'A good deal could doubtless be learned from them regarding not only the conditions prevailing at the time of their adoption, but also the organization of the Castilian communities in the days of their last glory – especially in the fourteenth century. For the reformers were bent solely on restoring the communities to their former high estate and rebuilding the structure that had been destroyed in 1391' (Baer, *A History of the Jews in Christian Spain,* p. 261).

The expressed motivation of the synod shows that here, too, there was the compound desire for independent Jewish leadership coupled with the aspiration to gain approval of the non-Jewish authorities and influence the views of the Christian community. The deliberations evince a marked consideration for the opinions of the non-Jewish rulers, as they repeatedly refer to them and endeavour to explain to them the objectives of the synod. In general, diplomatic considerations shaped many of the arguments and formulations. The ordinances commence with the enumeration of precedents for action being taken by communities with the approval of the authorities. For 'in times gone by the ancient kings would grant authority to the heads of the communities . . . that they shall legislate . . . fitting ways wherein all the members of the communities should walk . . . and thus the Torah was firmly based and every community was well established.'

These ordinances, written for the most part in Spanish, relate that Don Abraham invited the communities 'to send trustworthy people from amongst them to safeguard the ways of justice and to take counsel together. And the communities . . . did as he ordered. And some of them sent missives to the noble rabbi . . . to confirm and accept for themselves whatever . . . he would arrange. And some sent faithful representatives on their behalf.' This synod, like the Synod of Aragon 100 years earlier (see pages 499–501), was not attended by all those invited. In Castile, however, letters of agreement and acceptance were sent in which 'the noble rabbi' is presented as the vital and decisive spirit in the assembly and its activities. Those present are described as 'a number of scholars who came from several communities . . . and good representative men . . . with several authorizations . . . which they brought . . . each individual from the members of his community and . . . several good men who had access to the court of our lord, the King.' The participants, therefore, were there either by virtue of their knowledge of the Torah, because they represented a specific community, or because they were courtiers who could act for the benefit of the Jewish community at large. They defined the purpose of their regulations as being 'matters . . . related to Divine Worship . . . and the honour of the holy Torah and the service of the King . . . and the prosperity of the communities . . . and to their benefit'. The meeting took place 'in the Great Synagogue . . . which is in the Jewish square'. According to the official formulation, the ordinances were approved 'by the agreement of all, without any dissenter', so that the demand for taking a unanimous decision was fulfilled.

For the most part, the ordinances had the character of 'comprehensive instructions', aimed at indicating how each community should proceed for the commonweal in its specific locality. Hence, the first concern of the ordinances was with the study of Torah – as 'the Torah is what maintains the world' – a traditional Jewish reason for concerning oneself first and foremost with learning, and also because, at the time in question, 'those who study Torah have grown lax in most places and sustained themselves with great difficulty. And for this reason the pupils are growing steadily fewer. . . . In order to restore the crown as of old' instructions were issued. Thus the restoration of the status of the Torah and of those who studied it was the declared purpose and constant ideal.

The synod required each community 'to ordain and collect among themselves a contribution for the study of the Torah'. This 'voluntary contribution' was in fact to be an indirect consumption tax on the amount and weight of slaughtered animals and on the amount of wine consumed. The synod gave detailed specifications of the payment to be demanded as this communal surcharge. 'And we ordain this [levy for] the study of the Torah on meat and wine to be imposed on the price of the meat and wine in order that the purchasers shall pay the tax.' They also required a regular payment towards the study of Torah to be made on the occasion of every wedding and circumcision, 'as soon as it is certain tnat the newborn is lifeworthy'. Also 'let the heirs of any dead person male or female aged ten years and upwards give the garment that he wore next to his shirt or else ten gold pieces for the study of the Torah, and whatever the heirs wish to give in addition. And whosoever adds to these amounts, may he be blessed.' The synod ordered the communities to take care that this tax for 'the study of Torah' should be farmed out like the other com-munal levies. It provided for a period of thirty days for the implementation of these measures in places where they were not yet in force. The synod imposed the duty on the communities in order to maintain 'scholars [and] Torah teachers to be appointed over the community' to teach adults, as well as to provide good teachers for children of school age in proportion to the size of the population; and to ensure that those engaged in these duties earn a decent wage. The duty of maintaining a *yeshiva* and providing instruction there is also specified. (The number of pupils in an elemen-tary class is restricted to twenty-five if the teacher has no assistant and to forty if he does have one.) The synod required the communities to maintain a permanent prayer quorum of ten and imposed severe punishments on any person engaging in quarrels in the synagogue.

With respect to the choice of judges and other appointed functionaries, the synod was influenced by a sense of decline and crisis, 'by reason of our sins . . . there has been a decline in the number of God-fearing scholars who know the Torah, have full faith and are fit and worthy to act as judges according to the Torah.' This problem 'caused our predecessors . . . to depart in their ordinances from the specifications of the Talmud in selecting judges'. The members of the synod themselves would also not be meticulous about these specifications, since a lack of judges and appointed officials was liable to produce a situation whereby 'one man would swallow the other alive . . . and where there is no true judging there is no peace and there is no harmony'. The function of these judges is 'to judge claims, appeals and complaints and to punish transgressions'. The synod outlines a brief period of ten days during which communities without such judges should meet to elect them. In communities where they were already appointed, there must also be a meeting within ten days of the expiration of their term of office to select new judges. 'And the same applies to all other appointed functionaries, such as treasurers . . . and other officials.' The synod gave detailed instructions also on the functions of the judges, the hearing of evidence, the seat of the courts and the restrictions on judicial power.

The synod dedicated a special section of its regulations to 'the matter of informers'. The reason given in writing was certainly for the eyes of the authorities only, as the synod stressed the right of judgement that the king granted the Jews 'by his grace . . . in order that our judgements, both civil and criminal, shall be conducted in ac-cordance with the laws of Israel'. It carefully bases its stand on this delicate matter upon four arguments, two of which were that 'the Jews safeguard their Torah thereby; . . . [and] that the judges [in the secular courts], although very wise and just men, are not familiar with our laws.' Following this section was a series of measures to be taken and punishments to be imposed against various forms of appeal to non-Jewish courts and of denunciation, or informing, 'whether direct or by saying things that are liable to harm a Jew in a place where there are people who are not of our faith'. Among the sharp measures the synod proposed was that if an informer is known to persist in this evil practice, 'his forehead shall be branded with a white-hot iron seal on which is engraved: Informer'. The punishment of 100 lashes and expulsion was suggested, while if anybody were proved to be an informer three times, 'let steps be taken to execute him'.

After proposing measures against other infringements on Jewish autonomy through appeal to non-Jews or by application to them, as opposed to Jewish communal authority, the ordinances expressly opposed the acceptance of appointments in Jewish communities on the basis of 'writs from his royal Majesty . . . or our lady the Queen . . . and equally from other lords and ladies'. At the end of this section, the synod specifies 'that no Jew may maintain in his service . . . in his home on a regular basis any Christian woman, either on a wage or without payment'. This regulation is in accordance with an ancient ecclesiastical requirement; it was enacted by the Jewish synod to avoid the numerous mishaps that might result from such service opposed by the Church.

The fourth section of the Valladolid ordinances is dedicated to the problem of taxes, especially evasion of payment and assuring that the community's burden would be equally distributed among its individual members. The justice and injustice of tax arrangements is taken into account, and there is also the element of tax evasion, which was seen as a defiant assertion against Jewish autonomy. The fifth section is dedicated to sumptuary laws aimed at the excessiveness in clothing and jewellery displayed by the women of that time (Baer, *Die Juden im christlichen Spanien*, II, no. 287, pp. 280–97).

37

Spiritual and Social Creativity

*The Philosophy of Leading Circles in Spain from
1391 Until the Expulsion*

Contrary to current belief, Jewish rationalism did not become muted in Spain
during this period, nor did its ideals lose their hold. For a considerable part of this
century, with the exception of the *halakhic* approach, the rationalist approach was
the only one to maintain its momentum of creativity. Nor was its expression one of
weakness or defeatism; rather it spoke with religious and philosophical resoluteness,
and the standard of its formulations remained equal to that of earlier generations.
They may even have improved on earlier formulations in their clear determination
to strengthen the faith of the beleaguered Jews and to restore their hopes during that
difficult period. For the greater part of the fifteenth century, the rationalists were the
group that guided Spanish Jewry in all questions related to society and the conduct
of its life.

R. Abraham Bivach (Bibago) used rationalism in these times as the hallmark of
Jewish uniqueness, so as to explain the misery of Israel and its lack of worldly
success.

> The Jewish nation alone is attracted towards pure intellect. . . . This being so . . .
> the Jewish nation stands among the nations like the intellect among the elements of
> the soul, and as this intellectual element . . . cannot establish its superiority over
> them . . . likewise the Jewish people is in poverty and degradation, among the
> other nations. For the path leading upwards is disliked by the multitude. Moreover,
> the intellect is in exile among the elements of the soul . . . for it comes unto us
> [human beings] from the universe of intellect 'as a stranger and sojourner in the
> land'. . . . The Jewish nation has been exiled . . . at present in Edom (Abraham
> Bivach, *Derekh Emunah* ['The Path of Faith'], Constantinople, 1522, fol. 22r).

This is actually a paraphrase of R. Judah Halevi's description of 'Israel amid the
nations is as the heart among the members of the body' (see page 537). The image
was deliberately transferred from 'heart' to 'intellect' so that Israel among the nations
would be viewed as an intellectually aristocratic nation within the 'multitude' of
gentile believers. Indeed, R. Abraham Bivach stressed that the election of Israel is
the election of the son

who is to be innocent and upright, dwelling in the tents of wisdom and understanding and behaving according to the higher and worthy ways, always reading and studying books of knowledge, and perfecting his intellect. . . . He will undoubtedly love . . . his more exalted portion, which is the human intellect . . . and that is why there is a blessing recited on being called to the reading of the Torah: 'Who has chosen us from all peoples and exalted us above all languages and has hallowed us with His commandments'; for this is the essential love and true providence . . . in accordance with the most perfect and lofty portion, which is the intellect, when He ordained commandments and beliefs for His people whereby their intellect emerges from potentiality to actuality (*ibid.*).

He considers, therefore, that not only is the election of Israel intended to set it apart in terms of higher values and a scholarly way of life, but that the giving of the Torah and the commandments was for the purpose of developing the intellect 'from potentiality to actuality' – an educational method, as it were, intended to nuture 'reason'. R. Abraham was opposed to those who 'say that there are sages among our people who stepped beyond the pale [of Jewish life] and are wicked and sinful. To this we answer . . . that we also see others who do not know or comprehend rational philosophy at all, but who are called scholars and sages because they have delved deep into the wisdom of the Holy Talmud according to the letter, even though they do not understand its deeper wisdom, the chosen utterances which are true divine wisdom, and, lo and behold, among them are exceedingly wicked sinners' (*ibid.*, fol. 45r). Not only does he justify failings of Jewish philosophers by pointing out similar flaws among the 'sages of the holy Talmud', but parenthetically he criticizes the Talmudists for not perceiving the spirit of the Talmud but only the 'letter of the law'. R. Abraham claimed this was because they did not comprehend the true 'inner' sense of the Talmud. (In this connexion, see the opinion of an earlier kabbalist who shares this line of criticism, page 615.)

In addition to *Derekh Emunah,* other rationalist works – such as *Sukkat Shalom* ('Tabernacle of Peace') by R. Abraham Shalom and *Sefer Ha'ikkarim* ('Book of Dogmas') by R. Joseph Albo – called both for piety as well as for the rational understanding of the dogmas of faith; they preached the orthodox way of life based on the philosophic reasoning behind the *halakhah*. This attitude to the Law was, in their view, a shield against Christianity and heresy. This literature evolved in part from the central role played by the rationalists in the defence of Judaism during the continuous disputation with Christianity in Spain at that time.

The criticism of the rationalists voiced by members of the generation of the expulsion must be regarded as primarily an expression of bitterness towards the Jewish leadership, which had not stood the ultimate test. Those who led the defence carried the burden of responsibility for the defeat.

Only five years before the expulsion, in 1487, the leaders of Spanish Jewry strongly maintained that religious rationalism and the Jewish culture it sponsored – as well as the life style of the upper classes – were outstanding Jewish values to which they could point with pride. In a letter to the Jews of Rome and Lombardy, they placed in the same category with Torah scholarship the virtues of general rationalist enlightenment and the efforts of Jews within court circles ' . . . to find favour in the eyes [of the rulers]. . . . Wise and respected men combine their knowledge of Bible, Mishnah and Gemara with the alien culture for the glory of heaven.' As for actual *halakhic* decisions 'we rely mainly on Maimonides of blessed memory . . . the wisdom and Torah which he learnt, taught, and wrote, provided that our great rabbi Rabbenu Asher does not disagree with him' (Baer, *Die Juden im christlichen Spanien,* II, no. 360, p. 385). This was the position that the leaders of Spanish Jewry took both internally and vis-à-vis other Jews, but it was eventually overcome in the assault of hostile forces from both within and without.

Kabbalists as Spokesmen for the Opposition During the Fourteenth and Fifteenth Centuries

What has come down to us from the writings of Spanish Jewry and evidence of its inner life as related in the available sources indicate that after the great efflorescence of mystical literature during the thirteenth century (see pages 540–2) there was a pause both with respect to written works and in the formation of kabbalistic schools almost until the expulsion itself. The centre for the study of these doctrines was, at that time, the *yeshiva* of R. Isaac Canpanton; however, only his *halakhic* works have survived.

After the expulsion, kabbalistic activity revived and its influence increased. It seems to have been revived initially by students of the Canpanton circle, but the only systematic expression that has been preserved from the period between the beginning of the fourteenth century and the expulsion is an anonymous work by an author writing in the second half of the fourteenth century who called himself Kanah ibn Gedor. His system, as found in his works *Sefer Hakanah* and *Sefer Haplia,* offers a unique programme for Jewish religious life. On the one hand he systematically sets out to refute established principles of the Talmud, using Talmudic methods of argument in doing so; on the other hand, he gives vent to bitter social criticism. Theological ferment and the desire for innovation can be sensed, for example, in the way he argues whether or not the commandments are binding during the period of the exile. For the God of Israel

> has sold them and exiled them and they have gone among other nations. Now there can certainly be no mouth or tongue to declare that they are bound by the commandments of their Lord . . . and this being the case they are no longer bound to His service . . . as God is true and there is no injustice in Him, He should not judge them at all. . . . Incest is permissible, as are forbidden foods. And the whole of the Torah is now a matter of willing acceptance, and we [Jews] are not bound by it nor subject to any obligation or punishment (*Sefer Hakanah,* Poryck, 1786, fol. 15v).

The urgency of the discussion and the frame in which it was presented are revealed from the words of the interlocutor in this debate, who insists that the Torah is binding in exile as well. For otherwise the sages of the Talmud have explained the Torah to us in vain; in vain have they made their decrees . . . and if we had been exempt they would not have troubled to prepare the sixty-one tractates of the Talmud as they would have been in vain. And they would have converted in order to acquire honour and power for themselves. And they would have married gentile women. For Rabina and Rav Ashi [the redactors of the Babylonian Talmud] dwelt outside the Land of Israel (*ibid.*, fol. 16r).

The material and social reasons for conversion, which had been imputed to those abandoning Judaism during the critical days of Spanish Jewry, are here presented as the logical conclusion to be drawn from the abrogation of the Torah and commandments in the exile. On the other hand, the unique Jewish experience and the creation of the Talmud (as explained above) served Ibn Gedor as evidence for the continued validity of the commandments in his days. However, the Talmud, in its literal sense, is, in his eyes, far from being perfect. The study of Talmud without an understanding of its inner secrets is dangerous and harmful: one 'who has studied Torah and Talmud without studying them properly, without any knowledge of their deeper roots, as so many do nowadays, is like one with a tumour in the intestines which the doctors cannot heal because it has produced metastasis' (*ibid.*, fol. 23r). This is likewise true for the *aggadic* passages: 'All the sayings are mysteries; their discussions, which seem simple, are like the lid placed on a pot so that the majority should not know what is within. For who would believe that Sarah scratches Abraham's head and their faces are red while they sleep . . . but all these are hidden secrets' (*ibid.*). Both the *aggadic* subjects chosen by him to mock their simple meaning, as well as his argumentation against accepting them literally, are almost identical to the choice and arguments of the philosophers. The difference is that the latter sought reasons for the commandments and made use of allegory, while this author follows the paths of the mystics and reveals the hidden meanings of the Torah. The literal meaning is sharply rejected by philosophers and mystics alike.

When the author of *Sefer Hakanah* set out to lay bare 'the inner meaning of the laws of damages', he listed a series of laws that are logically unacceptable (*ibid.*, fol. 123ff.). His choice of examples and the critical spirit and style with which he attacks them in order to point out their inner contradictions are very close to Christian criticisms of the *halakhah*. Yet even before Ibn Gedor attempts to explain the inner meaning of the *halakhot,* the pressure that Christian opinion must have exerted on him is forcefully expressed: 'These and similar *halakhot* are heard by the Christians among whom we are placed; and they make light of us and say that Israel has a law that is full of nonsense. And even the ignorant ones among us mock our Torah, to say nothing of those who disbelieve the words of the sages' (*ibid.*, fol. 124v).

The author of *Sefer Hakanah* expresses a radical demand for the equality of women in fulfilment of the commandments and in divine worship: 'He who hears the words [of the sages of Israel] will cry unto God and ask the Holy and Blest One: why did You create poor woman who has neither reward nor punishment because she is exempt from certain commandments?' (*ibid.*, fol. 22r). The questioner is pleased by his perception in being shocked by the words of the ancient sages: 'Blessed be the

Lord who has given us intelligence that cannot tolerate their [the sages'] words' (*ibid.*). The Talmudic authorities taught that women are exempt from performing certain commandments, and the author uses the identical passages to prove that women are obligated to perform them. The scholars of old expounded the term 'your sons' as sometimes meaning children (which includes females) and sometimes only males. 'And I see that they construct everything as they desire. And in that case I, too, shall construct as I desire' (*ibid.*, fol. 22v). His exposition reflects his sense of respect towards women:

> Worst of all, it is not enough that she has been debased to the very ground since she has been exempted from the commandments of the King, but has been compared to a slave by the statement, 'whatever commandment is required of a woman is required of a slave as well.' Now for Heaven's sake, tell me, my master, how a slave can be compared with a woman? For the woman is free and of the seed of Israel, while the slave is a Canaanite of the seed of an unfit gentile (*ibid.*).

The author of this work has no way of proving the truth of the literal text of the Talmud as against 'the contrary Talmud' that he presented in his argument. The interlocutor explains the fact that women are exempt from commandments that must be performed at a specific time by using the kabbalistic argument that these commandments point to '*Binah* [Wisdom, one of the ten kabbalistic *Sefirot*] . . . which is above the earthly circumference'. Yet even this mystical distinction cannot exempt women from the study of Torah. This exemption is 'a decree of the King', not subject to reason, and is based on the words 'your sons'. 'And were it not expressly stated "your sons", I would claim that the woman is duty-bound to study because of her excellence' (*ibid.*, fol. 22–3).

The writer also goes to considerable length in objecting to the eating of meat: 'My son, abstain from ritual slaughter . . . alas, you ignorant . . . why do you not understand . . . that there is more intelligence . . . in beasts than in you' (*ibid.*, fol. 120r). For all the basically kabbalistic reasons for his opposition to the eating of meat, it would seem that his objection derives also from his campaign against luxuries: 'Woe to those who rejoice in the display of colourful garments.'

These attacks on material pleasures form an integral part of the bitter social criticism to be found in Ibn Gedor's books. This criticism is expressed partially in the form of satirical stories about contemporary leaders of the community.

> The proud, who are physicians, so carefully insist on eating delicacies. Woe unto you, ignorant multitude who go down to perdition. And when you see scholars and sages you flee from them, and where you see the proud, who eat fat meat and drink spiced wine, you enslave yourselves and engage in feeding with them . . . and they imagine that they have acquired benefit for their souls. Alas for you, ye righteous ones in that wicked age (*ibid.*, fol. 10r).

With the approach of the expulsion and the collapse of the community's social structure and its leadership, complaints against the rationalists increased, on the grounds that their explications of religion had awakened doubts and shaken the Jews' confidence in their faith. But until the actual expulsion, these arguments came only from the opposition. The eclectic character of the contents of the *Sefer Hakanah* and *Sefer Haplia* only make this particular author's opposition more representative of the general attack.

Judeo-Christian Disputation in Spain

At the Tortosa Disputation the Jews were under strong social pressure; and this pressure, coupled with fresh memories of 1391, encouraged the Jews to view the disputation as a potential source of serious physical harm to their communities. Under these difficult circumstances, the Jewish representatives behaved with considerable acumen and courage. R. Zerahiah Halevi Ferrer was particularly outstanding. The Christians preferred to begin with biblical and *aggadic* passages proving that, with Jesus, the Messiah had already come, but R. Zerahiah demanded a consideration of the 'conditions' for authenticating the Messiah. In the course of the prolonged debate on the subject of the Messiah, the Jewish representatives insisted again and again that the essential differences between Judaism and Christianity did not lie in the question of the actualization of the Messiah. Judaism prescribes a set of definite characteristics for its awaited saviour. He is to be a royal man and not an incarnated God; with regard to atonement for 'original sin', there is no connection between the coming of the Messiah and the atonement of mankind for the 'original sin'. The simple meaning of Bible verses should be the spirit of their letter and not any allegorical interpretation; the Messiah will come as king to restored earthly Jerusalem, denying messianic import to the image of 'celestial Jerusalem'. The prolongation of Jewish exile is a Divine mystery – all reasons given for its duration until that time were simply moral consolation, stemming from human vision and arbitrary decisions of interpreters of such mysteries. The Jews concluded their argument with a methodological and moral consideration of the attitude to interpretation: a fragment may not be taken out of context and certainly is not to be interpreted against the pervading spirit and immanent principles of its context. Hence no one may take isolated Talmudic sayings and interpret them in any authoritative sense without believing in the Talmud as a whole and submitting to its authority.

In the course of the disputation, R. Astruc Halevi argued the incompatibility of the two sets of messianic patterns – the Jewish versus the Christian. The Messiah of whom the Christians speak is not the Messiah whom the Jews are awaiting; for the Messiah of the Christians is an incarnated God and came to save human souls, while the Jew does not envisage any such Messiah. He awaits a human being of high moral quality whose 'work of Redemption will be to lead the Jews physically from servitude to freedom, to bring the nation to permanent victory, to rebuild the Temple and to maintain it in its exaltation.'

Rabbi Zerahiah Halevi summed up for the Jews by claiming that Christians and Jews agree that the principles of their faiths cannot be proven but are a matter of belief alone. Moreover, the writings sacred to each religion must be interpreted according to its own principles and not according to the principles of any other faith. Therefore, if, for example, the Talmudic legends contain something apparently opposed to the principles of the Jewish faith, it cannot be interpreted in an isolated manner, in order to contradict the principles of Judaism, but must be made subject to those principles.

The sermons and writings of Jewish scholars in Spain during the second half of the fifteenth century, and even during the early expulsions, continue to respect the Christian culture and to recognize the dangers to Judaism inherent in such respect. This respect for the achievements of Spanish Christian civilization was not restricted to the rationalists alone. Outstanding anti-rationalists were also imbued with an awareness that this civilization was of a high calibre.

The debating method employed by the moderate rationalists can be deduced from the account of R. Abraham Bivach. He relates 'what happened to me with one remarkably wise man in my youth at the table of the King Don Juan in the Kingdom of Aragon. He asked me: Are you a Jew and philosopher? I answered him: "I am a Jew who believes in the Divine Torah and I am not a philosopher, though I have pursued the wisdom of philosophy to the best of my ability"' (Bivach, *op. cit.,* fol. 96v). In the course of the discussion R. Abraham defined his point of view, which is 'as is to be found among the disciples of Maimonides'. In contrast to the Christian belief in a God who delivers mankind from original sin through his death, R. Abraham presented the Jewish belief in a future human Messiah. This question was, as was noted above, the central theme of the Tortosa Disputation and the focus of Christian missionary preaching.

The questions of Exile and Redemption grew steadily more acute with the mounting ferocity of the persecutions and with the increasing apostasy of Jews to Christianity. The Jew needed no public debate, private conversation, or preaching monk to raise these questions for him; the bitter realities of life in Spain placed the problems of Exile and Redemption before him with a clarity that could not be surpassed.

R. Abraham formulated the faith in the coming of the Messiah in clearly Maimonidean terms, stressing that the only difference between the current situation and the days of the Messiah would be the end of servitude to alien kingdoms. Bivach stressed as part of this conception that the Messiah would be succeeded by his offspring, 'for the Teacher [Maimonides] did not believe that people would live eternally after the coming of the Messiah' (*ibid.*), who will be only 'a brave, wise, and pious king', the founder of the dynasty of the Kingdoms of Israel (*ibid., fol. 96r*). The envisaged achievements of the Messiah, as formulated by R. Abraham, reflected the immediate problems of Spanish Jewry during this time. He is assured to be 'the Redeemer who will gather together the dispersed and far-flung of Israel . . . so that not a single one will be left unredeemed but will depart as a free man from Exile to the land wherein he shall serve his God. . . . All Jews will be redeemed, not a horse-shoe will remain behind. And all of them will go to the Land of Israel' (*ibid.*). The Redemption takes on an explicit trait of liberation from the pressure to convert.

Polemical literature, composed with an anti-Christian and propagandist intention, was written during the period between 1391 and the Tortosa Disputation by Profiat Duran, also known as the Efod. The best known of these is his satirical letter to an apostate, which is known by its recurring refrain, 'Be not like thy fathers', and his more comprehensive work *Kelimat Hagoyim* ('The Shame of the Gentiles'). In his ironic manner, he argues that apostasy arises from sheer weariness of the rational religious quest of Judaism and the search for refuge in the mysticism of Christianity. The apostate is made to assume 'that thy forefathers left a heritage of falsehood, constantly following vanity, that they lost their reason in their manifold investigations. . . . I comprehend from another part of your letter,' the Jewish polemist writes ironically, 'that the Holy Spirit hovers over your face in your dreams, and when you awake, it converses with you. . . . Human reason did not attract you to sojourn in his abode [a figure of speech used by Maimonides at the beginning of his work *Moreh Nevukhim*] which is a habitation of darkness. . . . You thought it to be an alien and cruel serpent's venom, an eternal enemy to faith . . . and whoever said that reason and belief are two lights is a scroundrel. Reason plays no part among us . . . it does not know where light dwells. . . . It is faith that mounts aloft' (A. Poznanski, ed., *Iggeret al Tehi Keavotekha,* Jerusalem, 1970, pp. 32, 34).

By rejecting rationalism the convert reaches a belief unpalatable to good Jews. The whole intellectual system of the rationalist upper classes in Spain is presented here as the hallmark of Judaism, and, in contrast, the acceptance of Christianity involves the rejection of such rationalism. In the opinion of the Efod, the Jewish comprehension of Scripture is marked by a philosophical approach, and therefore he calls on the apostate: 'Be not like thy fathers who dug deep into the tale of the Creation to expound the hidden secrets and wisdoms therein, drawing conclusions that were in agreement with philosophy . . . and so they developed their theories. But you are not so, you do not enter into any reasoning about it. Take the matter simply; but add the spiritual punishment of Man for his disobedience' (*ibid.,* p. 72).

The Efod states that he wrote *Kelimat Hagoyim* under the influence of R. Ḥasdai Crescas, who himself wrote a polemical work against Christianity. The Efod was asked to 'answer thereby in accordance with the mode of argumentation of the opponent, for that is the true and decisive response in matters of this kind' (*Kelimat Hagoyim,* 'Dedicatory Letter to R. Ḥasdai Crescas' in A. Poznanski, ed., *Haẓofeh be-Ereẓ Hagar,* III, Budapest, 1913, p. 102). The Efod regarded Jesus and the Apostles as only 'in error', but those who followed them as 'misleaders' (*ibid.,* p. 104). He had heard 'from men familiar with the wisdom of Kabbalah that Jesus of Nazareth and his disciples were kabbalists, but their knowledge of the Kabbalah was confused. . . . And when I went through the tales of the erring ones I found support for this explanation,' for in the early Christian writings there are terms similar to those of kabbalistic doctrine. But 'the intention of the kabbalists in this is that of the philosophers' (*ibid.,* pp. 143–4). Jesus and his disciples seemed to him to resemble forced converts who were ignorant of Judaism. 'Undoubtedly Jesus and his disciples and apostles were not learned . . . and for this reason the Jews called those who believed in Jesus Marranos [*i.e.,* 'changers', from the Hebrew verb to change, used also to denote apostasy], because they used to change the meaning of the verses and present inadmissible explanations of the Torah' (*ibid.,* IV, 1915, p. 47). They were simple people who knew Bible texts only through listening to sermons, and because of their ignorance they used to confuse what they heard' (*ibid.*). Relics of this confusion are still to be found, in his opinion, in the quotations from the Bible that are included in Christian prayers.

The Problem of the Marranos

The conversion of many Jews from 1391 onwards raised a number of problems for both the Christian Church and Christian society (see page 586), as well as for the faithful Jews in Spain. Few chose martyrdom; many resolved 'to leave that kingdom . . . and cross the seas. This was done by many who wandered afar to the ends of the world, some to the ends of the East and some to the ends of the West, to deliver their souls from hell and serve the Lord.' This was how R. Isaac described the emigration from Spain (*Responsa of R. Isaac ben Sheshet, op. cit.,* no. 88, fol. 43r). The emigrants were not always openly declared Jews, and the fact that many Marranos also endeavoured to flee increased Jewish dissatisfaction with those who did not leave. 'Surely it is plain to see that the Marranos could have escaped and fled for their lives, as so many of them did' (*Responsa of R. Simeon ben Ẓemaḥ Duran, op. cit.,* I, no. 63, fol. 31r–v). However, the same sage continues:

> But it is hard to say thus for many reasons; therefore I shall come to their defence. For it may be unfair to say they could have saved themselves . . . as there may have been compelling reasons to detain them. Perhaps they could not find the money to pay ships' captains who demand high prices; or because they feared that the matter might be revealed for their sins and bring physical punishment upon them; or that they made every effort to flee, but the time was not ripe and they failed; or some other matter prevented them (*ibid.*).

This was part of the spiritual effort made by the community of professed Jews to understand the motivation of their apostatized brethren, so as to differentiate correctly between the various nuances and refrain from lumping them all together. Some had indeed converted out of enthusiastic conviction, and their subsequent persecution of and missionary preaching to their fellow Jews helped to increase the bitterness towards all who became Christian. Many others, however, converted only under compulsion; while still others had mixed feelings and motivations. If it were difficult for the 'old' Christians to judge the faithfulness of the New Christians to the Church, it was even more difficult for the Jews to assess the measure of their faithfulness or animosity towards Judaism. The Jews were well aware that some of the converts relied on the biblical examples of Na'aman (who bowed down in the House of Rimmon) and Queen Esther (who did not reveal her origin) in order to justify their ostensible submission, while remaining faithful to the God of Israel in their hearts.

Some Jews resented this ideology of crypto-Jews. It would seem that it was with this self-justification of Marranos in mind that R. Abraham Bivach came out and stressed that the long duration of the exile cannot be attributed to false belief. Such wrong beliefs also existed during the First and Second Temple eras; men who err in their hearts are, then as now, punished individually in hell, after death, and not collectively by exile in this life. Exile is prolonged out of evil deeds of idolatry. 'For they do in idolatry genuflect and prostrate and burn incense and the like. Hence, when the Holy Writ threatens exile as punishment for idolatry, it is not for the wrong belief – this is punished in hell – but indeed for the practical matters joined to and deriving from this wrong faith . . . for exile is the punishment of prostration. Thus it is verified that actual sinful deeds . . . compelled the expulsion of Israel from their land' (Bivach, *op. cit.,* fol. 22v).

The value of inner faith was not rejected by all Jewish sages. In the Responsum quoted above, R. Simeon ben Zemah Duran extends his considerations beyond the factors that are directly liable to deter the convert from fleeing and compel him to remain within Christianity:

> And I say further even if we know that there is not . . . any fear of flight, as when the wicked king . . . has sent word throughout his kingdom that they may leave, even in that case we should not condemn the one who does not depart but stays there . . . for they may fear that the permission given them is only to test them and see whether they have converted by force or of their own will; and if they flee they will be slain. . . . All this we may say regarding these Marranos, since this is reasonable . . . for their beginning proved that they were compelled. Give them the benefit of the doubt until you see them transgressing against the Torah in a place where there is no danger . . . (*Responsa of R. Simeon ben Zemah Duran, op. cit.,* no. 63, fol. 31r–v).

The attitude of most Jews towards the Marranos was based on these principles, though occasionally some felt otherwise. Yet some – like Bivach – claimed that actions were what counted, the intention was not decisive and the deeds of the converts were evil. Others – like Simeon Duran – attached major importance to the intention, even if it were not expressed in action. Naturally, these attitudes changed in the course of time with the increasing gravity of the Jewish situation in Spain. After the expulsion this problem was to become one of the central issues for Sephardi Jewry.

The Spiritual and Social Atmosphere in Ashkenaz

The Jewish communities that consolidated themselves in Ashkenaz after the Black Death restructured a settled form of life and a set of ideals within a relatively brief period, and certain circles were very strict in implementing them.

In the fifteenth century, the 'first *hasidim* of Neustadt', in Austria, were held in high esteem. Their general attitudes and manner of life can be judged from the tale of R. Shalom of Austria:

> In his days there was a certain householder . . . who behaved with great piety at home. He had a special room . . . in which he ate meat dishes and likewise a special room for dairy foods. And he would insist that the gentile who used to fetch him water should wear a white robe, and in a number of other such matters he would make a hedge and a fence in order to keep at a distance anything that was prohibited. In his home he also brought up two orphan brothers. . . . And he was one of the first *hasidim* of Neustadt (*Sefer Maharil,* Sabbioneta, 1556, fol. 119v).

The strict observance of the law was widespread in the circles of such pietists. We learn that 'the wife of the rabbi in a certain city wore fringes at all times,' even though this commandment is to be kept by men only. This great rabbi explained that he did not raise any objection for fear 'that she would not obey me' (*ibid.,* 'Laws of Fringes and Phylacteries', fol. 110r). This also reflects the tendency towards the equality of women in religious life that was popular among the kabbalists in Spain (see page 616).

When the communities were more firmly established, R. Jacob Moellin, who was active among the older communities of the Rhine district, formulated a scale of values for public service for the members of the various classes. The underlying principle was to '"turn away from evil and do good" so that a man should not say . . . I shall not do evil nor shall I do good. That is why the Bible prescribed "And do good", and there is no finer good than charity, which is the basic commandment on account of which the world exists.' This commandment can be carried out in various ways and with regard to the individual's capacity:

> If the man is a scholar, let him show kindness by teaching Torah to people without charge. And let him be pleasant in his relations . . . at all times, ready either to judge or to instruct without delay. If a man is wealthy and his words are listened to by the authorities, let him be prepared to recommend the needs of people before the rulers. But if a man is poor and needs his money, let him in any case try to do whatever good he can on his own. And if he is in need and must make a living from others by his toil, let him take no more than his worth, and ask less from a Jew than from a gentile, and ask less from the community than from individuals. And indeed . . . the essence of charity is troubling oneself for the community (*ibid.,* 'Laws of Passover', fol. 3r).

Diplomatic activity on behalf of Jewry was seen as the proper service of the upper class, while teaching and judging should be performed by scholars. The person engaged in manual tasks appears last in this classification, as one 'in need and who must make a living from others by his toil'. In the eyes of the rabbi, his situation is worse than that of 'the poor man', who is described as one with little wealth, all of which is invested in the necessity of making a living. The assumption is that a 'needy' craftsman works for both Jews and non-Jews, and individuals and community alike are liable to require his services.

In the explanation (R. Jacob Moellin heard from R. Meir Halevi of Vienna) of the Talmudic remark that R. Judah Hanasi used to honour the wealthy, there is evidence of the social tension of the time. The explanation contended that 'as Rabbi Judah himself was exceedingly rich, he accustomed himself to honour the wealthy in order that people might learn that they too should honour him for his wealth and not for his knowledge of the Torah. For he did not wish to make use of the Crown of the Torah' (*ibid.,* fol. 116r). 'When [R. Israel Isserlein] saw a certain householder who had enough to live on but chased after money day and night, was always thinking of riches and his dealings were not in good faith, the Gaon said "Do you want to grow rich by sheer force; that is amazing. [His exact, colloquial words are quoted: *Wil Du mit Gewalt reich werden; das ist ein Wunder.*] There are even sages who are not worthy of wealth, which is a gift from heaven"' (*Leket Yosher, op. cit., Oraḥ Ḥayyim,* p. 32).

A more extreme reaction is to be found in an anonymous sermon, which, as its contents indicate, originated in the circles of poor scholars. According to this sermon, the wealthy are found to be unfit 'to receive the Torah' because of the pride that is an integral part of riches.

That is why it was made the practice to read the Book of Ruth at the Feast of Shavuot which marks the time when the Torah was brought down to Israel: to teach that the Torah was only given by being 'brought down' and by poverty. And the tribe of poverty was given in the portion of the Torah, for if the wealthy are engaged therein they become proud. But as those who study the Torah are poor and modest and humble, they behave in a humble fashion although they are scholars (Ben-Sasson, *op. cit.,* 175).

In domestic life there was also more enjoyment than is usually assumed. R. Jacob Moellin 'permitted twigs of trees cut off during summer to be placed in water on the Sabbath, to give pleasure on the Sabbath' (*Sefer Maharil, op. cit.,* fol. 38v). R. Israel Isserlein relates that 'I heard at the *yeshiva* [*i.e.,* in his youth] from one of the great scholars that in bygone days at Krems . . . the rabbi of the city who was one of the great men of those times, together with all the worthies of the congregation . . . went walking along the bank of the River Danube after eating the Sabbath feast' (Isserlein, *Terumat Hadeshen,* no. 1, p. 9). Nor was such a walk the only relaxation. In the days of R. Israel Isserlein 'most people, including even the strictest, were accustomed to gather on the Sabbath day after leaving the synagogue and to exchange news concerning the affairs of kings and lords and the course of the wars.' The rabbi certainly permitted this 'if people take pleasure in it . . . as indeed do many', but he was apprehensive since he had seen on many occasions that some of those conversing 'do not take pleasure in such talk and rumours but do this to please their companions who have joined them' (*ibid.,* no. 61, p. 25).

It seems that the Jews wore the same clothes as gentiles, at least when they were travelling, for it is told that 'Jews lodged in a certain inn belonging to non-Jews. And there were many non-Jews there. And when they sat down . . . to eat . . . they did not know that there were Jews with them in the inn' (*ibid.,* no. 239, p. 84). Jews also went out 'to see the pleasures of the uncircumcised when they bet and raced their horses, whoever came first winning gold'. The rabbi permitted this because this was not for pleasure, but 'to learn the craft, how to purchase horses that can run fast in order to escape from the enemy; and so I have seen from people known by their pious works' (*Responsa of R. Israel Bruna,* no. 71, fol. 32r).

From R. Jacob Moellin's tale of a certain incident in his own city of Mainz, we learn that there was a lively social life in the *yeshiva*: it seems that 'an important young scholar . . . had lads, students and friends at his home who ate there for payment . . . and he used to teach them the straight sense' of the Talmud and something of the discussions. This 'student hostel' was kept in order by a widow servant. At night 'four of the students met together to hear difficult problems discussed by their master', the householder. One of them 'was engaged to a worthy maiden of good family, and his father was very rich, owning ample' property. The lad was about sixteen years old, and in spite of his engagement, he jokingly 'wedded' the servant widow (*Responsa of R. Jacob Moellin,* no. 101, fol. 37r–v).

The Varied Cultural Elements

Despite the general view to the contrary, the scholars and leading personalities of Ashkenaz Jewry in those days were well acquainted with secular works and regarded with favour elements of culture and attitudes that are usually thought to be characteristic only of Spanish Jewry. The eminent debater and Bible commentator R. Yom Tov Lipmann Meulhausen, who wrote his *Sefer Hanizahon* ('Book of Disputation') *c.* 1420, attacks the restriction of study to the Torah and Talmud alone.

> And if the slave should say, 'I love my Lord' in Heaven 'and my wife, the hind of love, and I study Torah, Talmud and later authorities, and I love the Lord and His Unity, and His faith is engraved in my heart and I am able to comprehend one thing from another, so I do not need to study others or the wisdom of the ancients,' let him take to heart . . . that this will not be enough for the great scholar (*Sefer Hanizahon,* Genesis, T. Hackspann, ed., Aldorf-Nuremberg, 1644, no. 2, pp. 5–6).

And as though he had come to an agreement with the school from which R. Abraham Bivach came in Spain, the Ashkenazi sage declares elsewhere:

> Many of the degrees of wisdom can be found among the sages of Greece . . . and from this do not make the error that those degrees are forbidden, namely natural science and astronomy and philosophy, for these are branches of our faith and lead to the love of His Blessed Name and the fear of Him . . . and this is not Greek wisdom but the wisdom of all who are wise (*ibid.,* Judges, no. 136, p. 91).

The Yeshivot *in Ashkenaz*

The *yeshiva* students in Ashkenaz differed widely in their social origin as well as in their material resources. The youngsters were sometimes critical and complained about their teachers and the heads of the *yeshiva,* but despite this, the *yeshiva* – even more than the Christian university where the social phenomena were much the same – was the anvil on which the scholarly world was shaped and, in turn, formed the culture of Ashkenazi Jewry. The *yeshivot* remained what the universities had originally been – a circle of students gathered round a single teacher, who usually specialized in a single subject that was a combination of piety and religious law.

Various sources depict a group of students united round their master, living with him in a certain intimacy and sharing even in his home and family life. The youngsters would accompany their master when he emerged into the 'Jewish street' on festive occasions. When R. Israel Isserlein 'was in good health he went with all the lads to the community synagogue' for the reading of the Book of Esther at Purim. In general, however, 'he was loath to leave his own synagogue [where he taught his students] but would pray there. Even when he left the city, he would tell the students to continue praying there' (*Leket Yosher, op. cit., Orah Hayyim,* pp. 31–2). The students used to eat at the table of this rabbi, 'and on Sabbath Eve he washed his hands first and his wife followed him and after her all the students' (*ibid.*, p. 33). 'And thereafter [following the Sabbath hymns sung at the table] he gave each of the students a slice of pie' (*ibid.*, p. 36). Next to the synagogue and the rabbi's home was the students' house, and the rabbi required a married student to come and eat there with his friends but only after reciting *Kiddush* (the Sabbath benediction) at home in order that his wife should also hear the blessing (*ibid.*, p. 51). The *Havdalah* ceremony at the end of the Sabbath was performed by the rabbi for both his family and his students.

> And he gave the spice-box to his wife and afterwards took it in his hand and all his sons and daughters-in-law and grandchildren came and smelt the spice-box in his hand. And after that he gave it to the students. And I remember that he would wait until they had all smelt it. And if it was difficult for him to stand, he would sit down until they had all finished (*ibid.*, p. 57).

Thus, at the same time that the student studied Torah with his teacher, he likewise learnt good behaviour and meticulous performance of the commandments, the way in which a sage and scholar should live and the correct behaviour for the respected head of a family.

Rich and poor alike came to the *yeshiva*. We learn that 'a certain Jew owed the student charity fund three pounds', which he had vowed for the students' upkeep. He himself was not well-to-do for 'he did not have the money to pay' this vow (*ibid.*, *Yoreh De'ah*, p. 15). Sometimes wealthy members who had been given the honour of participating in the *yeshiva* feast at the rabbi's table would pay for the board of poor students. Such a man participated at the *yeshiva* of R. Abraham Klausner 'in his feast with the young men . . . and he paid the regular sum of one gold piece to help the students' (*ibid.*, *Orah Hayyim*, p. 97). At the same time, there were 'those wealthy and pampered youngsters who provided their own tables. When they were seated in their places, they would turn the table whichever way they wished, with many books upon it'. To be sure, R. Israel Isserlein, the head of the *yeshiva*, did not approve of this arrangement; he preferred toiling for the Torah even in looking for the books. He 'said . . . they have not done well. On the contrary, when somebody needs a book and can obtain it only with great difficulty, it helps him to remember what he wished to learn' (*ibid.*, *Yoreh De'ah*, p. 39). In any case this indicates both the variety of students to be found in the *yeshivot*, as well as the conflict between 'technical aids' as opposed to personal toil in didactics.

The students tended to wander from place to place and from rabbi to rabbi quite frequently. This practice of wandering in study was widespread also among the Christian university students of the time. A large number of students was therefore a cause of pride for the *yeshiva* head, or 'holder of the *yeshiva*' as he was often termed in those days. If he were well-to-do, he attracted students not only by his knowledge of the Torah but also by the support he could promise them. 'Rabbi Abraham of Katzenellenbogen' proudly declared to his teacher R. Israel: 'I expended on the students . . . twice as much as I earned from all sources in my rabbinical office. And if I did not pay any youngster what I vowed to give him for his upkeep, he may demand it before . . . my master, and whatever the Gaon required of me . . . I would pay. . . . I have already requested my honoured master . . . to send me students of long standing, and I shall undertake to give them whatever he imposes upon me, and so I shall do this very day' (*ibid.*, p. 26). It is told of another sage 'that he became impoverished and could not maintain students as he was accustomed . . . in spending money for days and years in the upkeep of his *yeshiva*' (*ibid.*, p. 38). This readiness on the part of the teachers to support their students clearly indicates the great social significance attached not only to the commandment of supporting those who study the Torah, but also the honour and pride that a group of students, preferably of 'long standing', gave their master. Naturally there were *yeshiva* heads and sages who themselves made a living from instructing the students and included board and lodging in the charge for instruction. But the esteem in which these were held was also according to the number of their students.

Quarrels would sometimes break out among the youngsters. In the *yeshiva* of R. Meir Halevi, for example, 'one honoured student of the *yeshiva* in his anger flung a plate at the head of the attendant who served the lads.' The rabbi wished to place a ban on him, 'and the whole company toiled very hard indeed before the wrath of the master died down' (*Sefer Maharil, op. cit.*, fol. 116v). At the *yeshiva* of R. Jacob Halevi, the attendant's son insulted a student, and the head of the *yeshiva* placed a ban on him. His sin was forgiven only after he had begged for pardon in public, 'when the rabbi was approaching the *yeshiva* with more than fifty students. The attendant stood there with his son and they begged forgiveness . . . from the rabbi and from that student and from all the students in the *yeshiva*' (*ibid.*).

The same R. Abraham mentioned above, in connexion with his payments to the students in his *yeshiva*, was also troubled by their tendency towards dissipation. One of them 'always furtively drank from a barrel of my wine . . . late at night after midnight he opened my foodstore and stole bread and meat and other foodstuff from it.' According to the evidence of this *yeshiva* head, this was but an extreme case of wanton behavior in the *yeshiva*.

> I am not opposed to all the students studying with me in any respect, but sometimes I find it hard to bear their frequent drinking bouts and interference in various matters in order to annoy the householders. . . . For by such actions the glory of the Lord and of the *yeshiva* will be diminished on every side. . . . Within one brief period, twenty students fought together. And Shalom Bruner . . . hit Sussman his brother-in-law . . . and all those who were beaten cry for justice but there is no redress, there is neither justice nor judge. In all faith, I refrain from judging them on account of the informers among the students (*Leket Yosher, op. cit., Yoreh De'ah*, p. 26).

One may assume that many contemporary university teachers would have agreed with him. However, in the main, the energy and high spirits of the *yeshiva* students were dedicated chiefly to the lively debates that developed in the course of their study.

During the fifteenth century, the *yeshivot* of both Ashkenaz and Spain developed the new *pilpul*, the pursuit of fine legal distinctions in the Talmud. Those who fostered it wished to develop intellectual methods of analysis among the *yeshiva* students by encouraging them to discover apparent contradictions between various hallowed sources and to reconcile them in order to reach the *halakhic* decision required at a given time. This development actually expressed a desire to liberate Jewish legal thought from old concepts and patterns. Various *yeshivot* in Ashkenaz developed their own specific techniques of analysis (*ḥillukim*), which were then known by the name of the communities where those *yeshivot* functioned. During these debates the behaviour of the 'pilpulists' and of the youngsters in the audience was very often noisy and unaesthetic. The teachers too often did not express themselves with restraint. Sometimes the way of teaching, exegesis and legal decisions of one authority was rejected with ridicule as incompetent analysis; but more often than not the *pilpul* method of his opponent was put forward as the basis for another understanding and decision. The *pilpul* served as proof of ability and as a basis for social prestige. The rules of these methods were set out in systematic works.

Pilpul was widespread both in the schools of Spain as well as in those of Ashkenaz. In Spain we find evidence for *pilpul* in systematic works on method, while in Ashkenaz we find descriptions of actual debates in descriptions of *yeshiva* life there. The fact that there was opposition to this method, yet an almost universal acceptance of its formulas, indicates that Jewish life was inevitably sustained by the decisions reached through *pilpul* no less than by the appetite for acute intellectual discussion that it fostered. It is possible that at least a portion of the bitter opposition of some 'pilpulists' themselves to *pilpul* can be attributed to the fact that they sensed the permissive and disruptive force of this exaggerated acuteness.

38

Jewish Settlement and Economic Activity in the Sixteenth and Seventeenth Centuries

The Background

Towards the close of the Middle Ages, a number of factors encouraged Jews to settle in various regions and establish centres there. These factors were not uniform in their influence and had different effects, some bringing harm and extrusion, on the one hand, and benefit and alleviation, on the other. Yet jointly they formed the background to Jewish settlement. The population of Europe had been increasing from the twelfth century onwards and did not require Jews to settle its cities. In the area North of the Pyrenees the economic function of the Jews had become increasingly narrow and specialized, conflicting with the aims of the Christian community. The Black Death had slowed down this process through the reduction in population, although it rendered it more acute in other respects, by adding to the existing horrifying traits and behaviour attributed to the Jew the terrifying image of the Jew as a poisoner of wells. In any case, the gap in the population was rapidly filled during the second half of the fourteenth century and the 100 years that followed, while the economic and social crisis, the mood of suspicion and the violence, which grew during this period, combined to worsen the Jewish position.

Demographically and economically, the major and minor expulsions of the late fifteenth and early sixteenth centuries were merely the violent expression and final incentive for the shifting of Jewish settlement to new places in Eastern Europe and the Mediterranean region. Socially, however, as a result of the Christian attitude towards the Jews, this period marked the peak of the cruelty and xenophobia that struck Europe as a result of the terror engendered by the Black Death and that continued for centuries afterwards.

Before 1348 the general socio-religious climate in Europe had been one of vitality and creativity; after the cataclysmic experience of the Black Death, the structure seemed to remain intact, yet the living spirit was gone and the force of humaneness was spent. The effects of these developments were not focused on the Jews alone. Some historians regard this 'breaking of the chrysalis' as one of the main factors in the split within Western Christianity at the time of the sixteenth-century Reformation. Yet, the Jews' isolation, their baleful image and their political and physical weakness turned them into an incomparably convenient scapegoat for contentious social forces.

Meanwhile, new demographic and social conditions were crystallizing in Poland and Lithuania in Eastern Europe, as well as in the Ottoman Empire. In the latter, urban life was not yet part of the national and political structure, as was true of Poland and Lithuania; moreover, the cities had neither the tradition nor the ability to stand independently against the will of the ruler in the Ottoman Empire. For the Jews who came to these cities, it was therefore easy to obtain the positions and economic functions they desired – as long as it was convenient for the rulers. Further- more, from the second half of the fifteenth century onwards, these kingdoms were on the rise, each in its own area and after its own fashion.

It should be borne in mind that the expulsions from Europe had their source in the economic and social crises of the fourteenth and fifteenth centuries. Yet at the time that the Jews were expelled from Spain, and subsequently from Portugal, even more far-reaching changes were coming about in Europe, changes portending economic expansion and social success. The year of the expulsion was also the year in which Columbus discovered the New World. This discovery, together with the opening of the route around Africa to India, brought about the 'price revolution' in Western Europe, which consisted mainly in an increasing demand for agricultural produce from Eastern Europe to meet the requirements of the commercial and manufacturing centres that were established in the West. This led to rising prices for agricultural produce and the development of trade between the various countries of Europe, alongside the growth of colonial trade. As a result of the new territorial discoveries, Europe's international trade began to shift from the Mediterranean Sea to the Atlantic Ocean. At first glance it would appear that the Jews had been almost entirely eliminated from the Atlantic region just when it became the focus of economic and settlement activity. The peoples of the south, such as the Portuguese and Spaniards, who were the first to benefit from the discoveries, as well as those living further north – the English, the inhabitants of the Low Countries and the French – who began to participate increasingly in this new trade and in the sea voyages shared one quality: scarcely any professing Jews were to be found in their countries. Yet the rise of the various forms of Protestantism and the movement of the New Christians to the Netherlands, and from there to north-west Germany and England, were in due course destined to change this state of affairs and to lead to the reappearance of Jews along the Atlantic coast.

A map of Jewish population centres during this period reveals that in the sixteenth and seventeenth centuries Jews were concentrated in the two large kingdoms that were to be increasingly successful for the greater part of the epoch. The Kingdom of Poland-Lithuania was Christian, while the Ottoman Empire was Moslem; but within these two territories, masses of Jews benefited considerably from the indirect results of the discoveries in the New World and the development potential of these extensive political and economic empires. In 1515 the Ottoman Empire gained con- trol of Erez Yisrael; in 1517 Egypt was conquered. Thus regions populated by Jews, and the land to which Jews had always aspired, were incorporated into the larger framework of an empire that, until its defeat at the siege of Vienna in 1683, con- tinued in the main to expand successfully in Europe as well.

The Kingdom of Poland and the Grand Duchy of Lithuania was also undergoing a period of economic and social expansion. After defeating the Germans in the West, Poland achieved full unification with the Grand Duchy at the Union of Brześć (Brest-Litovsk) in 1569. From then until 1648, the Polish nobility was engaged in establishing peace and exploiting the spacious and fertile lands to the south-east of the kingdom, which included the greater part of present-day Ukraine. The victories in the West gave Poland an outlet to the Baltic Sea by means of the network of rivers and connecting canals. This provided a route to the West for the timber and agricultural produce of the areas that were being developed in the East. As we have noted, this produce was in considerable demand in Western Europe. The markets and roads of Poland also served the overland transit trade between the Ottoman Empire and Central and Western Europe. In the Polish-Lithuanian Kingdom the Jews served as a kind of 'counter-burgher class', a group that was highly desirable to the dominant Polish nobility on account of its commercial and administrative capacities. In the Ottoman Empire, the Jewish exiles from the Iberian Peninsula engaged in vigorous economic and cultural activity, turning the Jewish community, which even previously had engaged in manifold activities in Islamic cities, into an even more influential and variegated society.

In due course, the communities of the New Christians in the Netherlands, particularly in the Protestant section that had revolted against Spain, began to participate increasingly in the economic and settlement activity that derived from the geographical discoveries. They also established ties with Germany, Poland-Lithuania and the Ottoman Empire, thanks to their Jewish brethren in those countries. From the Netherlands, groups of one-time Marranos, or their descendants, settled in north-west Germany and England, and these new western settlements were also economically and socially successful. In both regions these re-integrated Jews played an important part within the newly expanding capitalism of the period. The Jews of Italy also found their place within these commercial and social ties, which spread from the centre in the Netherlands to Poland and Lithuania by way of Germany, and from there to the Ottoman Empire. From the latter, by another route – partly by land and partly by sea – ties were re-established by way of Italy with the successful Jewish centres in the Netherlands, north-west Germany and England. In the seventeenth century, the Jewish settlers on the American continent and in the West Indies came from north-west Europe. The exiles from Spain and Portugal maintained commercial, political and social contacts with those countries.

To sum up, in this dynamic situation the Jews succeeded in penetrating into fresh branches of livelihood, especially in Poland-Lithuania and north-west Europe. Out of the destruction of the period of expulsion at the end of the fifteenth century, from the days of crisis in Germany, the Jews succeeded in emerging to engage in a vast economic and demographic thrust, as part of the general colonizing and economic dynamism of the sixteenth and seventeenth centuries.

The Early Settlements of the Spanish Exiles

The exiles' goal was to find refuges where they could live an open Jewish life. They first headed for Portugal, which was closest and was also attractive because of its cognate language and culture. In 1497, however, they found themselves confronted by a new decree demanding compulsory conversion to Christianity. Whoever could do so, fled to another country. The flight from Portugal continued even more steadily than that from Spain during the whole of the sixteenth and seventeenth centuries.

As early as 1492, some of the exiles had made their way to the shores of North Africa. A precedent had already been established during the flight from Spain following the riots of 1391 (see page 572). In some of the ports of North Africa they found Portuguese rulers and a familiar linguistic and cultural *milieu*. In these places there was some degree of cooperation between the Portuguese authorities and the openly professing Jews or Marranos even after the compulsory conversion in Portugal itself. These Portuguese outposts along the African coast needed the merchants and skilled craftsmen among the Jews, so that little attention was paid to the laws of the Inquisition. Among the leading groups of Jews in these Portuguese enclaves there were several families, such as that of Benzamero, who became 'court factors' to the rulers. Naturally this led to a certain tension between the local Moslem Berbers and the Jews who helped the Portuguese. This tension at times was even reflected in the relations between the exiles and the old, established Jewish population, which tended towards the Moslem environment. The attitude of the exiles towards the veteran members of the Jewish communities to which they came was usually one of superiority – as though they looked down on them from a higher culture, a better organized social order, a loftier faith and richer customs, which in their opinion they had brought with them from the Iberian Peninsula (see pages 570–1).

The exiles also reached the North African regions that were in Moslem hands. There the welcome they received varied from one ruler to another, but everywhere their sufferings during the period of absorption were considerable. The ruler of Fez was remembered, however, with particular warmth. He was 'one of the God-fearing ones among the nations of the world, who admitted the Jews expelled from Spain and treated Israel well until his death [in 1505]. For God established him over the Kingdom of Fez to enable us to live' (R. Abraham Terutiel, continuation of *Sefer Hakabbalah* in A. Neubauer, *op. cit.,* I, Oxford, 1887, p. 1). About 20,000 souls were absorbed in Fez, where the exiles rapidly began to succeed in their affairs and purchased property. One of them relates that as early as the year 1498 'the Lord blessed us abundantly so that we built houses with upper stories adorned with paintings and carvings. And the Lord blessed us with *yeshivot* . . . and beautiful synagogues . . . with Torah Scrolls clad in silk and satin . . . and with silver crowns' (R. Ḥayyim Gagin, *Eẓ Ḥayyim,* in J. M. Toledano, *Ner Hama'arav,* Jerusalem, 1911, p. 55). These splendid private homes and public buildings reflect the economic achievement of Jews within only six or seven years after their expulsion from Spain.

The Establishment of the Sephardi Diaspora in the Ottoman Empire

A considerable stream of exiles from Spain overflowed into the Ottoman Empire. Once the latter had annexed Ereẓ Yisrael, it became a lodestone for Marranos who wished to repent and return to their former faith. The chronicler R. Elijah Capsali, a contemporary of the expulsion and a member of the older Jewish population in the Ottoman Empire, relates that during the period after 1492 'there came to [the Ottoman Empire] thousands and myriads of the expelled Jews so that the country . . . was filled with them' (M. Lattes, ed., *Seder Elijah,* Padua, 1896, p. 13).

The road from the Iberian Peninsula to the Balkans and Asia Minor, and frequently from there to Syria and Ereẓ Yisrael, was long, arduous and perilous. The exiles often established their own transit stations, such as the ports and cities of Italy. The physical distress and sudden impoverishment were hard to bear. One of the exiles who found a haven in the Ottoman Empire related that he arrived after 'all their money had been consumed by the cost of their wanderings . . . amid a people who did not understand their language.' According to this witness, family relationships also broke down on the way. For 'the men arrived without wives and wives without husbands.' This undermined religious family law 'since each one being alone did his best to find a helpmate . . . without being particular . . . whether the relationship was permissible.'

The sultan at the time of the expulsion, Bayezid, welcomed the refugees fleeing from the fanatical Christians. As recorded by a Jewish contemporary 'the Sultan sent men ahead and spread the word through his kingdom in writing as well, declaring that none of his officers in any of his cities dare to drive the Jews out or expel them, but all of them were to welcome the Jews cordially' (*ibid.,* p. 12). It can be assumed that this imperial protection and the order granting right of domicile were issued through the influence of the leaders of the long-established Jewish community in the Ottoman Empire. This community and its leaders also went to considerable effort to provide material aid for their exiled brethren. 'Then the communities of [the Ottoman Empire] wrought greatly . . . giving money like stones for the redemption of captives . . . in those days the noble . . . Moses Capsali did much in Constantinople . . . making the rounds of the Congregations and compelling each man to give the amount that was proper for him' (*ibid.*). The aid was given through a genuine concern for their fellow Jews, but it produced a feeling of superiority on the part of the local Jews, who saw themselves helping the down-trodden exiles and graciously granting these unfortunates both status and recognition. When the Spanish exiles had established themselves – and they did so relatively quickly in the Ottoman Empire as well – the cultural and social pride of these Jews from Spain and Portugal quickly reacted against the local Jews.

Yet not all the exiles required aid. In the Ottoman Empire as well, there were some who immediately entered court circles. Such was the physician Joseph Hamon, who arrived in Turkey from Granada 'and for about twenty-five years served [as a physician from 1493] in this royal household during the days of the king, Sultan Bayezid, and also as a trusted friend to his son . . . Sultan Selim . . . and who entered the breach to deliver Jews from overwhelming perils' as is witnessed by the funeral address delivered after his death in 1517 (H. H. Ben-Sasson in *Zion,* 26 [1961], 27). The dates show that he became royal physician and a courtier immediately after his arrival in the Ottoman Empire. His son Moses is known to have followed him in this exalted office.

Success was not restricted exclusively to medical and court circles. It seems that in the Ottoman Empire it was felt that the absorption of the exiles from the West provided social, cultural and even military advantages. Among the exiles there seem to have been skilled iron-casters and makers of gunpowder, who assisted the empire professionally. R. Elijah Capsali reported that the Lord had blessed 'the Turks because of the Jews . . . for thanks to the Jews the Turks conquered great and mighty monarchs. . . . The Jews taught the Turks how to use all kinds of destructive weapons, batteries and field cannon. And through them the Turks grew mightier than all the peoples of the world.' He had also heard that the son of Sultan Bayezid, 'Sultan Selim, loved the Jews very much indeed, for he saw that through them he could smite nations . . . for they made him a great many batteries and weapons' (from his *Chronicle,* in *I. Baer Jubilee Volume,* Jerusalem, 1960, p. 224).

It is a fact of military history that the introduction of fire-arms into the equipment of the Turkish Army came at about the time of the admission of the Spanish exiles into the Empire. The Turkish victories over the Mamelukes and Persians at the beginning of the sixteenth century are usually attributed to their use of fire-arms. From Capsali's statement it would therefore appear that the Spanish Jews who came to the Ottoman Empire included experts in such fire-arms, and they helped considerably in the task of equipping the Turkish forces.

The exiles gradually dispersed throughout the main cities of the Empire. Many synagogues were to be found in Constantinople during the sixteenth century. In this city they settled in quarters where Jews had not formerly resided. Salonika also became one of their main centres, and similarly Adrianople and Smyrna (Izmir). The exiles also established themselves in smaller cities. Expulsions from southern Italy helped to diversify the Jewish community and increase the various congregations in the Empire. In the Greek city of Arta, which was not particularly large, 'four communities settled which came from the expulsions in the kingdoms of Spain, Portugal, Sicily, Calabria and Apulia'. These congregations settled down alongside 'the congregation of residents who had dwelt there since earlier times, established in their fine houses and courtyards' (*Responsa of Benjamin Ze'ev,* no. 303).

Settlement in Erez Yisrael

Jews had left Spain for Erez Yisrael throughout the century between 1391 and the expulsion (see page 572). In the course of the sixteenth century the Jewish community of Erez Yisrael was enlarged not only by those who had left Spain to preserve their Judaism, but also by New Christians from Portugal and Spain who were drawn there in order to return to Judaism and to do penance for their defection at the holy places. This group increased, particularly after Erez Yisrael became part of the Ottoman Empire in 1516. The constant flow was not only a factor in the settlement of the area, but also a force that helped shape the consciousness of communities deriving from descendants of Spanish exiles in the Orient. The kabbalist R. Hayyim Vital noted in his *Sefer Hahezyonot* ('Book of Visions'), written at the end of the sixteenth or beginning of the seventeenth century, various facts indicating the effect of this phenomenon on the thinking of the Sephardim in Syria and Erez Yisrael

(*Sefer Haḥezyonot,* A. Eshkoli, ed., Jerusalem, 1954, pp. 244–9, and see below, pages 693–4).

Those Jews who arrived with the early stream of settlers, including craftsmen and traders, continued to engage in their previous occupations. A member of the generation of the expulsion 'who dwells in the holy city of Jerusalem, Samuel ben Joseph Pijo', relates that he and his family and friends had suffered greatly before reaching their haven, but that they also suffered dreadful losses after settling there. He sadly declares 'of all the family of my father's house none are left save I . . . they have all been buried in the Valley of Jehoshaphat in Jerusalem . . . and also of the entire family of Rabbi Moses Navarro of blessed memory neither scion nor memory is left. For only his wife remains, behaving as one demented.' However the letter bearing these sad tidings is chiefly concerned with the statement that it is possible to live a normal economic life in the cities of the Holy Land. The writer calls on people to join them: 'Whoever wishes to come, let him come, for here they can spend their entire lives supporting themselves by their handicrafts. And these are the crafts which are suitable – goldsmith and silversmith, tailor and sewer, carpenter, harness-maker, weaver and blacksmith; while as for buying and selling – everyone whom the Lord has graced with a little money. And also to tell the truth, everybody who knows how to study will find a sufficiency here, for . . . I who have no craft except my studies obtain my needs through studying the Torah' (Yaari, *op. cit.,* no. 28, pp. 180–1).

After the political changes of 1516–17, the Jewish community of Ereẓ Yisrael benefited from the country's inclusion within the Ottoman Empire and its links with the commercial centres, with the Jewish community in Egypt to the south-west and, even more so, with that of Syria to the north. In this new situation the community of Safed, which had had no significance earlier, became a major national and cultural centre (see page 661). The exiles chose it for settlement because of several circumstances. It was the Jewish centre closest to Syria and the route by which Jews arrived from other provinces in the north-western part of the Ottoman Empire on their way to the land of their fathers. Safed was not sacred to any other faith. Neither Islam nor Christianity had any claims there. From the Jewish point of view, Safed lay close to the numerous graves of *tannaim* buried in Galilee. Particularly attractive was the Tomb of R. Simeon bar Yoḥai, 'the author of the holy *Zohar*', which was at Meron nearby. All these factors gave Safed an aura of Jewish sanctity. Its successful economic relations with Syria to the north and the local rural hinterland enabled this community to establish a broad economic and social base.

The tension between Safed and Jerusalem was not merely the outcome of a differing cultural and religious atmosphere (see below on the dispute regarding the restoration of the ancient *semikhah*). The economic and social characters of the two communities were quite different. During the 1520s the traveller Moses Bassola found in Jerusalem 'a congregation of all kinds', *i.e.,* communities of different origins and traditions, 'in all about three hundred householders', or heads of families. But within this abnormal community there were also about 'five hundred widows who had a special status. They . . . make an ample living because they do not have to pay any tax or burden, and the community is supported by them; for when they die all their property is taken by the community unless they have heirs. And most of the public needs are met by this.' But the male family heads depended largely on charity, which they obtained from various sources. At the time the Jerusalem community had 'more than two hundred souls recipients of charity . . . And much charity comes to them from Egypt and Turkey and other places'. Within Jerusalem itself the Ashkenazim were more dependent on alms than the Sephardim (A. Yaari, ed., *Travellers' Tales from Erez Yisrael,* Tel Aviv, 1946, p. 149). In 1650 a Jew from Prague noted that in Jerusalem 'some Sephardi Jews had dwellings and shops . . . and among them are many craftsmen . . . but we Ashkenazim do not know the languages in which to speak with the gentiles; and therefore we do not engage in commerce' (*ibid.,* p. 283).

This was not the situation in Safed, where living conditions were, on the whole, normal and well established. Yet, even there, alms played an important function, particularly for the scholars who dedicated themselves to the study of Torah. The city grew rapidly both in population and sources of livelihood. In 1522 more than 300 householders are spoken of in Safed – a population equalling that of Jewish Jerusalem. By the middle of the sixteenth century travellers already report the presence of 8–10,000 Jews in Safed, most of them Sephardim. By the early seventeenth century there were some 20,000 Jews in the city, and according to certain authorities the number even reached 30,000.

Even at the first stages of this growth, Moses Bassola was impressed by the economic opportunities it offered. He particularly stressed the trade in grain, textiles and haberdashery between Safed, Damascus and Beirut. He was also impressed by the Jewish hawkers and pedlars in the surrounding villages and the opportunities for craftsmen. He thought that 'in general this countryside is far more commercial than Italy' for Jews (*ibid.,* pp. 138–9). The scholars of Safed also had their ties with the agricultural environment, which we learn from the story of a Rabbi Moses against whom the complaint was lodged that he was not always engaged in the study of Torah. For he goes out 'to the villages to bring in the honey of his bees . . . and his new wine and his oil and his grain' (R. Gottheil and W. Worrell, *Fragments from the Cairo Geniza,* New York, 1927, p. 257).

In Safed a Jewish textile industry developed. The use of credit increased, and there are complaints of interest being taken by Jews from Jews in spite of the ancient prohibition. The leading sages, both *halakhists* and mystics, also participated in the economic activity. R. Jacob Berab (see page 664) was a wealthy dealer in spices, whose transactions involved great sums of money; even the sainted R. Isaac Luria (see pages 696–9) dealt in pepper and other wares. In the stories of wonders and miracles that occurred in Safed we find an echo of the tensions between employers and their Jewish workers in the large textile workshops.

The rate of economic development made an impression on all observers. In 1535 an Italian Jew was impressed enough to note 'that as in Italy improvements are being made and new plantations planted and the community is growing every day, so it is in this city. Anyone who saw Safed ten years ago and sees her now must marvel. For Jews are coming plentifully all the time and the garment-making industry is increasing every day' (Yaari, *Letters from Erez Yisrael,* p. 184).

During the sixteenth century an attempt was actually made to establish another

Jewish centre in Galilee, at the site of ancient Tiberias. This attempt is connected with the work of Doña Gracia (Hannah) and Don Joseph Nasi (see page 658). Documents in the Turkish archives indicate that the initiative derived more from Doña Gracia than from her son-in-law Don Joseph, although at the time Jewish public opinion attributed it to him. As early as 1561, a traveller found a Jewish community in Tiberias, which regarded Doña Gracia as its patroness. In June 1560 an order was sent to the Governor-General of Damascus and the Director of Waqf (lands dedicated for religious purposes) stating that

> an application has been submitted: there is a district known by the name of Tiberias ... in which are to be found subterranean structures of the infidels [apparently the Crusaders], and houses within the fortress. ... Near the houses there lies a large lake and several hot springs nearby. Water of special qualities flows there, and there is a deserted bath-house. There are date-palms beyond number and places suitable for the manufacture of silk and the planting of sugar cane. Every year a thousand, two thousand, or three thousand Moslems, Jews and Christians come ... to bathe. If such a number of people gather when it [the bath-house] is in ruins, what income can be received when it is restored? [The applicants] have declared: We undertake to pay a sum.

The person submitting this application, as becomes clear from an additional document, dated 1566, was Doña Gracia, for the document states: 'A Jewess named Gracia has undertaken [to pay] a fixed annual sum of one thousand gold pieces [as rent for Tiberias], together with several villages around it.' The order requires a wall to be built and water to be brought to Tiberias as soon as possible. It refers to 'the physician David, who is in charge of these matters on behalf of the aforementioned Gracia Nasi' (U. Heyd in *Sefunot*, 10, [1966], documents 1–2, 202–5).

When these permits were obtained from the Turkish authorities, Don Joseph Nasi called on the Jewish communities in other countries. The community of Cori in Italy recorded the impression that Don Joseph's appeal made on their small congregation. They relate 'that he is asking for Jewish craftsmen in order to resettle and restore the land'. They had heard that 'he had arranged for ships and subsistence in several places such as Venice and Ancona' in order to bring the Jews over to Tiberias. They also understood that he had chosen Tiberias specifically 'since it was from the Lord, as the region of Tiberias had been granted to him, which our blessed God has chosen to make a sign and wonder in respect of our Redemption and the deliverance of our souls, as Maimonides declares' (D. Kaufman in *Jewish Quarterly Review*, 2 [1890], 307–8). Thus an attempt was made to establish a settlement in the place that was traditionally declared to be the place from which the Redemption of Israel would come, in addition to the purpose of developing a normal economic life.

The Chronicler Joseph Hacohen recorded that in Tiberias Don Joseph Nasi appointed 'his attendant Joseph ben Adret to build up the city walls'. There was Moslem opposition to this but it was over-ruled by the authorities. The construction of the wall was completed in 1565; then 'Don Joseph gave orders to plant a vast number of mulberry trees to feed the silkworms, and he also commanded wool to be brought from Spain to make garments [in Tiberias] like the garments which are made in Venice' (*Emek Habakhah* chronicle, M. Letteris, ed., Cracow, 1895, pp. 145–7). This activity was therefore half settlement and half messianic yearning, and it was entirely directed by the large and wealthy family of Jewish courtiers from the Iberian Peninsula who continued to maintain their positions of trust in the Ottoman Empire. Jewish craftsmen, plantations for growing silkworms and Merino wool from Spain were intended to serve as the economic foundation. Calls were sent out to the entire Mediterranean region, as is shown by the letter of the Cori community.

When Don Joseph Nasi, Duke of Naxos, died in 1579, the Tiberias venture was continued by Don Solomon Abenaes, Duke of Mytilene, another Turkish Jewish courtier who also originated from Spain. He entrusted matters to his son, who was, however, more enthusiastic than his father desired. By 1598 the Tiberias community was already in a state of crisis. In Galilee, in Safed and in the Tiberias experiment a firm economic foundation was laid for remarkable spiritual and social activity.

The Sephardim in North-west Europe

The Netherlands, while still under Spanish rule, became, thanks to their geographical location, a centre of commercial activity in the area of the Atlantic Ocean. Many of the New Christians found it convenient to move from the Iberian Peninsula to this northern region, which was somewhat distant from the reach of the Spanish and Portuguese Inquisitions, and where there was little likelihood that they or their past would be known. Many wealthy and noble Marranos came to Antwerp and Amsterdam and achieved economic success. The wealthy ones took an active and notable part in the commerce of Antwerp, Amsterdam and Bruges, and the physicians and craftsmen engaged in their respective professions.

With the approach of the Protestant Reformation, the situation changed in many respects. In the region where the Reformation succeeded, Jews were permitted to live openly in their faith. The Calvinists, to be sure, struggled with this problem, but as a rule they tended to permit them to live as Jews. In modern Belgium, to the south, Catholicism finally remained dominant, and the Jewish community of Antwerp shrank steadily. But there was a community of professed Jews in Amsterdam from 1602 – or, according to some, from as early as 1591. From 1608 it had its own rabbi and was actively engaged in every field of commerce. Their commercial activity prospered remarkably, not only because of their ties with Jews in Central and Eastern Europe, on the one hand, and Italy, North Africa and the Ottoman Empire, on the other, but because of the close ties they enjoyed with Portugal and the kings of the very country that had expelled them. Their diamond trade, for example, was based entirely on the purchase of raw materials from Portuguese sailors.

There were very wealthy men among the Dutch community, and Jews were shareholders in the Dutch East India Company. By the end of the seventeenth century, they indeed held almost one-quarter of its shares. In 1688 a Jewish merchant gave Prince William of Orange a loan of two million Dutch gold pieces without interest, which enabled him and his wife Mary to proceed to England and become its joint rulers. Amsterdam had Hebrew printing presses and was a centre of the Jewish book trade.

In 1601 the Marranos of Spain and Portugal, which were then united, obtained permission to leave their countries and sell their property, which increased the exodus from Portugal. Colonies of 'Portuguese' merchants left Amsterdam, Portugal and Spain for north-west Germany, settling in Hamburg, Altona, Glueckstadt and neighbouring cities, in Denmark and in other countries of the north-west. They came to settle as Christians, but lived as Jews. They preserved their ties with Portugal and prided themselves on their family ties with the Christian nobility of that country, while, on the other hand, they secretly established themselves as Jewish communities. This we learn from information provided by the spies of the Inquisition and the complaints of the authorities. Sometimes the agents of the Portuguese court were in fact the heads of the secret Jewish communities. In due course these gradually emerged into the open, and their membership grew.

In 1646 there were approximately 100 families in Hamburg, who were active in the trade between Germany and the Iberian Peninsula. A large part of Germany's trade in so-called colonial goods was in their hands. They were in constant touch with their brethren in Amsterdam and established contacts with the Ashkenazi Jews who came and settled alongside their congregations. Both the Portuguese and the Marranos who fled from there benefited considerably from this ambivalent connexion. The Marranos were excellent agents and intermediaries and were successful in the Levant and spice trade, particularly between the Iberian Peninsula and these distant regions. They also linked the trade of Portugal with the North European countries. This also accounts for the otherwise strange fact that the overseas Marranos in their far-flung dispersion aided in restoring Portuguese independence from Spain in 1640.

The resettlement of the Jews in England actually began in Amsterdam. Here various messianic hopes and tidings along with the religious aspirations of the more extreme Protestant and Puritan sects in England helped to bring about this resettlement. The activities of R. Menasseh Ben Israel (see pages 653–4) were of considerable importance in this connexion. In England itself there was considerable public opposition, but the propaganda for the return of the Jews had its effect. Economic considerations carried considerable weight in this propaganda. Attention was drawn by the pro-Jewish propagandists to the success of Amsterdam and of the Netherlands in general after the reception of the Marranos and Jews there – a feat that Cromwell's England greatly envied. These facts served to demonstrate that the return of the Jews would promote English trade and commerce. Menasseh Ben Israel informed his English readers:

Hence it may be seen that God hath not left us; for if one persecutes us another receives us civilly and courteously; and if this Prince treats us ill, another treats us well; if one banisheth us out of his country another invites us with a thousand privileges; as divers Princes of Italy have done, the most eminent King of Denmark and the mighty Duke of Savoy in Nissa. And doe we not see that those Republiques doe flourish and much increase in trade who admit the Israelites? (*The Hope of Israel,* London, 1652, sec. 33. in L. Wolf, ed., *Menasseh Ben Israel's Mission to Oliver Cromwell,* London, 1901, pp. 50–1).

In this way the expulsion turned full circle, and the success of the refugees was transformed into a reason for renewing their residence. Here also was the root of the claim in modern times that the Jews brought special benefits to an urban capitalist economy.

The Jews of Italy

In those regions of Italy where Jews were left, they felt the full weight of the Catholic Counter-Reformation movement. The fragmentation of the country into numerous principalities produced the effect that there was neither unity nor consistency in the policy towards the Jews. In spite of this, a certain pattern can be discerned in the history of the Jewish communities. It initially found expression in the confinement of the Jews to special quarters outside of which they were not permitted to live. This policy began in Venice, where in the year 1516 the Jews were closed off in the area known as the 'Ghetto' (*i.e.,* 'the Foundry'). As the number of Jews in the city increased steadily during the sixteenth century, additional quarters were allocated to them and were given the same name. In due course the word 'ghetto' became a general European term for the enclosed quarters where Jews were compelled to live. In addition, during the sixteenth and early seventeenth centuries there were a number of expulsions from Italy.

The ghetto in Rome had very poor housing and sanitary conditions. Nevertheless, the community continued to exist and grow. In 1655 there were close to 5,000 Jews in Venice, which was the largest Jewish community in the country. The community of Mantua in Lombardy was of considerable importance. Exceptionally favoured were Pisa, and in particular Livorno, where in the course of time an important Jewish centre developed with neither a ghetto nor specific economic restrictions.

Marranos developed a lively overseas commercial trade in Ancona until 1556, when they suffered severe persecutions initiated by the pope. However, the reaction of the Jews (see pages 667–9) indicates the importance of Jewish maritime commerce for the ports of Italy and the Jewish awareness of their value in this field. Commercial transactions, interest-loans, trade in old clothes, the growing overseas traffic, medicine and crafts constituted the Jewish livelihoods in Italy during this period.

The Jews of Poland-Lithuania

During the sixteenth and the first half of the seventeenth centuries (until 1648) the number of Jews in this kingdom increased steadily. Here for the first time Ashkenazi Jewry achieved a substantial growth in population, and new communities arose in steady progress. Although at that time certain Polish cities were granted the privilege *de non tolerandis Judaeis* ('not to suffer the presence of Jews'), the Jews nevertheless continued to reside in or next to most of the important old cities of the country and established themselves in many new centres – some in the 'private cities' founded by the great Polish nobles, and others in the villages and estates that they leased from the nobility. The Jews travelled a great deal on the roads, fulfilling a central function at the major fairs of the realm, such as Lublin and Jaroslaw. Jewish merchants were active abroad in the fairs of Germany to the west and in the trade centres of the Ottoman Empire to the south-east.

In both old and new cities the Jews maintained normal economic, urban activity. In 1521 the proconsul and consuls of the City of Lvov (Lemberg) wrote to their fellow city counsellors in Poznan (Posen) complaining 'that the infidel Jews have robbed us and our merchant citizens of almost all our sources of livelihood . . . they alone engage in commerce, go out to the small towns and villages, and do not permit anything to reach Christian hands'. This the city-fathers regarded as a breach of the conditions on which the Jews had been allowed to settle and to the detriment of Christian urban life. By their appeal they wished to obtain the united action of Christian townfolk against the Jews. However, they were unsuccessful against the Jews. They continued to engage even more effectively in commerce and, as we shall see below, penetrated into new and emerging economic areas. In 1618 an anti-Jewish burgher, Sebastian Miczyński, wrote a diatribe against the Jews describing their trade:

> In Lvov, in Lublin, in Poznan and particularly in Cracow, not to mention Vilna, Mohilev, Slutzk, Brest-Litovsk, Lutsk and elsewhere, the Jews have in almost every brick house five, ten, fifteen or sixteen shops. These shops are full of merchandise and all kinds of wares . . . they go to other countries from which they import sundry goods to Poland . . . when goods of any kind reach Poland the Jews quickly purchase everything. . . . In addition they export goods . . . to Hungary, to Moravia . . . and to other places. . . . They trade in spices and all kinds of grain, in honey and sugar, in milk products and other foodstuffs. There is scarcely any kind of goods, from the most expensive to the cheapest, in which the Jews do not trade. . . . They do not rest satisfied with sitting in shops and doing business. Some of them actually go round the market, the houses and the courtyards peddling their wares. . . . They entice . . . the buyers . . . and attract them to the Jewish shops promising them good bargains (*Zwiercidlo Korony Polskiey,* Cracow, 1618).

He complained therefore not only about competition in the shops and the large-scale import and export business, but also of the initiative taken in peddling and attracting customers to the Jewish shops. He continues by listing the transactions of large Jewish merchants whom he names, such as a certain 'Jew . . . Bocian' who 'apart from other transactions and apart from his shipping goods to Danzig, has . . . seven shops in Cracow and agencies almost everywhere in Poland. His transactions are on the scale of three or four hundred thousand gold pieces, for there are no wares in which he does not deal. There is a Jew . . . Moses who imports various goods from Frankfurt, Leipzig, and the Netherlands from which the merchants of Cracow formerly used to purchase goods, but now they purchase them from this rascal' (*ibid.*). Miczyński complained of Jewish initiative at the fairs and of their trade with the cities of Germany and the Netherlands. He complained that the wealthy Jewish merchant 'sits like a devil . . . on a chair in his shop and he has dozens of Jewish huntsmen dressed in rags who by artificial means attract and entice noblemen and others to purchase from him' (*ibid.*). The scale of his transactions is considerable, while those of the Christian merchant shrink steadily. In brief, even if we discount this description as an exaggeration resulting from animosity, there still remains reliable evidence of Jewish success in large-scale commerce, of the Jews' central position in the import and export trade, so that in Poland-Lithuania the Jewish merchants and craftsmen constituted something like a Jewish 'Third Estate' corresponding to the Christian urban Third Estate, yet more successful.

This success derived largely from the Jewish ties with the Polish nobility, whose power in the state was steadily increasing. Despite the religious fanaticism of this Catholic nobility, which also increased during the period under consideration here, and in spite of the incitement of the clergy, the nobility found the Jewish urban class useful and therefore was willing to support it. This support may largely be attributed to the fact that as the Jews penetrated into new livelihoods, with which we shall deal below, they became the advisers and economic stewards of the nobles. Jew-haters complained that almost every Polish noble had 'his' Jew, who advised and guided him in his business affairs.

The New Sources of Livelihood – the Arenda

From the 1569 Union of Brest-Litovsk onwards – after in firmly united Poland-Lithuania the rule over the Ukrainian steppes became the concern of Poland – the Polish nobility began to pacify and secure the roads and the wide expanses of the present-day Ukrainian steppes. Parallel to the pacification and, to a large degree, as a result, they began to cultivate these expanses, to develop the crops, the rivers and the fish-ponds; farther north, in Lithuania and White Russia, the nobility also developed the forest products of pitch and timber, for which there was a great demand in Western Europe. These economic aspirations on the part of the Polish-Lithuanian nobility also led to increasing exploitation of the peasants on their estates. However, all this activity required financing. A nobleman with economic initiative would first turn to a Jew in order to receive a loan from him for the development of his estates. As the pacification of the south-east regions of the country was successful, and as the economic measures showed favourable results in the crop-yield and the produce of the forests, there came about an increasing exploitation and oppression of the peasantry, together with a greater demand for systematic and commercially rational administration of the estates. As a rule the Polish noble was not interested in devoting himself to such matters. His power and status came from being the head of the military arm and from his political authority. Hence, from the first settlement in the steppes of the Ukraine, noblemen tended to leave their estates 'in pledge' to the Jewish lender. In the course of time this pledge came to include the management of estate affairs by the Jewish lender, who received part of the income pending repayment of the loan.

Settlement in the Ukraine increased at a rapid pace. Jews participated in it, and their numbers grew accordingly. From twenty-four settlements with about 4,000 inhabitants in that region before 1569, the number of Jews shortly before 1648 had grown to 115 communities and 51,325 residents, according to an official count. Indeed, there is reason to assume that there were even more Jewish settlements and Jews within the territory. During this period the Jews and Poles moved from 'pledges' to the Arenda system. In essence this system allowed a person to lease a group of estates at a fixed rate and for a specified number of years (usually three), or a single estate or section of an estate, in order to manage it and receive the income. In 1595, for example, Abraham son of Samuel leased from Duke Gregory Koszyrski and his wife a complete 'key' (a group of estates, in the language of the sources) according to the following conditions: The lessors gave

> the worthy Master Abraham son of Samuel and his wife . . . and to their offspring our estates as specified below, namely the town . . . and therewith [certain estates and villages] . . . and the following monetary payments that come from them, from their mills, lodging places and inns [for the sale of all] liquors, and mead; likewise the regular duty on the city together with the Boyars and all the persons whether required or not required to provide labour therein, who dwell in those towns and villages, their plough-fields, their labours and their waggons, the tax on grain, on beehives . . . on fish ponds, mills and the payments for them, whether these are already in existence or shall be built in the future, together with the lakes, places for beaver hunting, with the fields, the meadows, the forests, the woods, the threshing floors . . . and in general with all the various sources of livelihood, for five full and consecutive years . . . for the specified sum of money . . . five thousand Polish *złoty* [gold pieces] which sum has been paid into our hands in full for five years.

Thus the Jew received the complex of small towns, villages and estates to be administered solely by him. By this document he was likewise authorized 'to hold and receive all receipts whatsoever from the said estates, and to use them, to judge and sentence . . . all our subjects, to punish by money fines or by sentence of death those who are guilty or who disobey in accordance with their evil deeds.' A Jew who leased such a 'key' usually settled other Jews, poorer members of his family or acquaintances, on the various estates and sometimes in the various economic facilities of the estates, such as inns, flour-mills or fish ponds. Thus this large leasehold system brought about the settlement of single Jewish families in the villages as innkeepers or stewards of estates or of special activities within them. As was only natural, the Jew who lived in a village not only sold liquor and commodities to the peasants but also purchased their agricultural produce. In brief, the Arenda brought the Jews into agricultural life – not in actually tilling the soil but in management and commercial transactions over the produce. Village Jews enjoyed a considerable measure of material benefit, although their presence there gave rise to various social and religious problems (see page 683).

The administration of these estates led to a state of tension between the Jewish managers and the village serf population. As we shall see below (page 682), the Jews had some consideration for the feelings and status of these serfs, in spite of which the latter viewed them as the exploiting arm of the Polish nobles and behaved towards them with animosity. Feelings ran particularly high in the Ukraine, where security in the fields and on the highways, as well as the other manifestations of the nobles' rule were for them innovations. The enmity was enhanced because the serfs in these regions were generally of the Eastern Orthodox faith, while the nobles were Roman Catholics. These tensions, which derived from the character of the Arenda, found horrifying expression in the massacres that took place in 1648–9 (see pages 656–7).

The Arenda also involved tax-farming. In 1580, it is true, the Council of the Land of Poland, the central institution of Jewish autonomy there, issued a warning against large-scale customs and tax-farming and the leasing of royal mines, because of the enmity that these might create on the part of the Polish nobility. Yet as late as 1623 the Council of the Grand Duchy of Lithuania (the other central institution of Jewish autonomy) still held that the Jews benefited from holding leases of customs and taxes. In Poland, too, Jews remained customs officials and also partners of Polish nobles or of Armenians, who were the official tax and customs farmers. Tax-farming was supplemented by the trade in goods passing through the customs stations and the upkeep of lodging-places for the merchants who were delayed there. This economic variety continued after the catastrophe of 1648 as well, although the problems involved became more difficult and complicated, and the leasehold conditions grew steadily more burdensome for the Jewish lessee. The arrangement of 'hold on the Arenda', whereby a Jew was forbidden to compete with another who had already leased an estate for three years, in order to prevent cut-throat competition, became more complicated and difficult to implement after 1648, with the considerable diminution in the number of estates available for lease.

Jewish control of the export of agricultural produce from Poland and Lithuania helped Jews within the German Empire to become a key element in the supply of foodstuffs and agricultural produce to the armies of the rulers, princes and dukes of Germany. This indirectly helped to bring about the rise of the *Hofjude* ('court-Jew') in the German Empire during the seventeenth century.

The rapid development of Jewish business in Poland and Lithuania brought about considerable tension in the area of credit. Both Jewish moralists and Jew-haters complained of this – each from their own point of view. All contended that Jewish merchants stretched their credit transactions to the point of bankruptcy. The ordinances of the Councils of the Lands of Poland and Lithuania deal at some length with the 'runaways', *i.e.,* those who went bankrupt and fled from their places of residence. In the discussions of the moralists and in the ordinances, there is a clear awareness of the danger that the Jewish merchant may lose his good name, which they held to be important for the maintenance of the Jewish economic structure as a whole. It appears that the Jews had considerable credit with the merchants from the Netherlands and Germany who came to Polish ports such as Danzig. We also find that Polish Jews developed a special type of credit document, known as the *mamran,* which was the equivalent of a letter of credit and could easily be passed from place to place and from hand to hand. It was not by mere chance that in the year 1607 Polish and Lithuanian Jewry introduced the *heter iskah,* a regulation whereby one Jew was allowed to participate in the transactions of another by advancing money in return for a specified percentage on the capital invested. This was introduced, as is explained in the preamble to the relevant regulation, because 'it has become a widespread practice . . . in these lands to make loans and engage in transactions and advance money on various kinds of wares.' In this situation one of the leading Jewish thinkers of the time, the Chief Rabbi Judah Loew (known as the Maharal) of Prague, who also lived in Poland for many years, came to the conclusion that 'certainly the truth is that interest benefits both [the borrower and the lender]; saving that the [scriptural] prohibition of interest was not intended to harm business transactions but was a divine decree promulgated in the Scriptures. . . . If he has nothing better, then it is preferable that he shall engage in money-lending rather than do nothing' (*Ḥiddushei Aggadot,* 'Homiletical Novellae', on *Bava Meẓia;* and see pages 389–92).

Jewish Occupations Within the German Empire

The Jews of Bohemia and Moravia engaged in livelihoods more or less like those of their brethren in Poland and Lithuania. In the German parts of the empire, however, the situation was different. The expulsions, as we have noted, had earlier destroyed the old communities. Though the Jews suffered greatly during the Reformation, they nevertheless gained opportunities to penetrate into new occupations. Ties with Poland and Lithuania, on the one hand, and with the Netherlands and the Sephardi communities of north-west Germany, on the other, gradually brought Jews back into the major branches of trade and commerce during the seventeenth century. Towards the end of that period, Glueckel of Hameln records in her autobiography that her father, who lived in Hamburg, 'traded in jewellery and, like a Jew, in anything else which could be profitable'. But she relates of her husband after their marriage: 'We did a little business . . . and we had dealings with the small farmers and lent money on pledges. But my husband of blessed memory would not be content with this and from the hour of our marriage planned to settle in Hamburg,' that is, near the business centre of the Portuguese Jews. When he succeeded, he began to trade in gold jewellery, and this was his practice: 'He ran about all day from house to house buying up gold, which he sold either to the smelters or to the merchants, and he used to earn well.' In due course he also began to deal in diamonds on the scale of thousands of gold thalers. His business brought him connexions even with Moscow.

The children of this couple married the children of court-Jews. The latter position could be achieved in various ways. One might begin as a supplier of jewellery to a ruler and go on to provide agricultural produce to the army, after which there might be participation in diplomatic missions. In the trade in precious stones, much depended upon the personal relations between the *Hofjude* (court-Jew) and the local ruler.

The commercial practices of the Middle Ages gradually began to break down in the course of these economic and social developments. R. Jair Ḥayyim Bacharach was called upon to deal with the problem of a group of vendors of clothes and textiles who used to study together every day with a certain scholar and who had jointly agreed 'that whatever disputes came about between the members of the group in respect of unfair competition and trespassing on trade rights of others' should be brought for decision to their teacher who conducted the Talmud lesson. However, competition was increasing between them and their warden said to them: 'Why waste the time and cost involved in legal decisions as well as time in quarrelling, seeing that in addition much goes undiscovered, as one does not know the unfair competition of the other; for instance, talking to one's established clients and the disparagement of each other's goods. . . . This breach cannot be repaired, as the transgression has already become deeply rooted. Therefore let us agree together that we permit infringement among ourselves in whatever way it comes about.' In this we see the emergence of modern-style competition and the crumbling of mediaeval trade ethics. The Jewish merchants themselves recognized this, even though the rabbi was not prepared under any condition to agree that guild morality should be terminated.

39

Changes in the Legal and Social Status of the Jews

Significance of the Christian Reformation in Jewish History

The importance of the Reformation in Jewish history was to increase steadily. The Reformation did not achieve its declared purpose of bringing all Christians together in a reformed faith of purity, which its leaders believed had existed in the early Church. The Catholic Church likewise did not achieve its aspiration of eradicating the new heresy. This meant the disappearance of that ideological and practical unity of Western Christendom that suffocated Jewish existence within its confines. From that time on in Western and Central Europe there was no longer any spiritual power that claimed control over all of Western Christianity – and whose claim could be regarded as unchallengeable. After the spiritual and social hegemony of the Catholic Church had been displaced in the revolutionary tempest, it was impossible for any one of the other churches to exert a spiritual and social authority resembling that of the mediaeval church. Hence, the Jews had ceased to be the only open non-conformists in the cities and kingdoms of Europe. Henceforth they dwelt side by side with Christians with differing views, which were mutually regarded as heretical. Doubtless all the Christian Churches throughout this period theoretically agreed that the disbelief of the Jews was worse than any of their respective heresies, equalled only by that of the Moslems; however, by then this question had become a matter of degree. In addition, there were a number of small groups, such as the extreme Puritan sects of England, the various Anabaptist sects and the antitrinitarians of Poland and Transylvania, as well as outstanding spiritual individuals like Sebastian Franck in Germany, who remained outside the major church frameworks. This sectarian divisiveness and the expression of individualist opinions would in due course undermine all tendencies to compulsion or religious intolerance.

An additional and no less important advantage for the Jews derived from the fact that all the Protestant sects turned to the Scriptures as the ultimate authority. The humanist tendency to return to source documents (see page 591) took on a religious aspect here. For the Christian the Bible consists of the Old and New Testaments alike. However, the aspiration to build a better Christian society and an improved state led several Christian sects and leading Protestant thinkers back to the systems and aims of the Law as expressed in the Old Testament in the behaviour of the judges, prophets and kings of Israel. The Hebrew Scriptures and the Hebrew language became religious, social and political assets of prime significance in Protestant society and culture.

Here too the new interest in the scriptural text produced ambivalent attitudes to the Jews. There were some who tended to treat them more severely and to punish them on the basis of certain biblical verses; but others, as a result of their studies of the Bible and of Hebrew, tended to respect the Jews, to take an interest in their way of life and to appreciate their past and its continuity. In the Netherlands and England these tendencies were to lead in due course to a very favourable outcome for the Jews. Another change that favoured them was the fact that the Protestants were not tied by mediaeval precedents of the popes and the church, the priests and the monks. Even the Protestant missionary efforts, as we shall see below, led them to be less hostile towards the Jews than had their Catholic predecessors. Admittedly, this led to disappointment: when the Jews refused to be impressed by the new 'purified' Christianity of the Reformation and were not tempted to convert by the friendlier attitude, Reformation leaders rose to vent their denunciation. The popular character of certain Reformation leaders and trends worked to the disadvantage of the Jews, for it gave free and powerful expression to the anti-Jewish hatred of the common people.

It was not fortuitous that the Peasants' Revolt of 1525 in Germany and its leaders were imbued with a murderous and active hatred of Jews. The great influence of the cities and burghers on the Reformational sects militated against the Jews for the greater part of the period and in most areas of Europe. The civic anti-Jewish traditions, particularly among the craftsmen, found authorized and lively expression in the world of religion. The trend towards innovation and the weakening of former ties worked both for and against the Jews. The tradition of protection of Jews against drastic injury by the pope and the various ecclesiastical heads in their respective countries and by emperors and princes lost its value in the eyes of extremist innovators.

In contradiction to the Reformation's declared objectives, its critical approach, its humanist appeal to sources and to individual judgement and its disruption of old values and systems helped to liberate and consolidate secularist trends that were essentially anti-religious. Although the Christian Reformation was diametrically opposed to the secularization of life, it, together with the Catholic Counter-Reformation, indirectly had the effect of giving rise to secularist trends. Naturally this also worked to the advantage of a comprehensive tolerance that was prepared to include the Jews as well.

The abolition of priestly celibacy and the elimination of monasticism – trends that were shared equally by all Protestant schools of thought – did much to eliminate indirectly a tangible distinction between Jews and Christians in everyday life. Since the overwhelming majority of the Protestants also disliked the icons and many of the rituals of the earlier Church, Jewish and Christian life and worship became less alien to each other. At the same time the tendency of the Protestant churches, particularly those of the Lutheran denomination, to entrust authority and supervision of church and spiritual life to the civil authorities, restricted religious and cultural authority everywhere and for all concerned. The effect on the Jews was twofold: these groups gave in to the ruler and his opinions simply because he was the ruler, but in the course of time this proved dangerous to all minorities; yet sometimes a ruler used his authority to defend the Jews, and this increase in secular authority always tended to weaken Church-motivated anti-Jewish legislation.

Martin Luther and the Jews

The Augustinian friar who broke the power of the Church in Germany remained in his innermost self and in his faith a man of the Middle Ages. The man whose actions led to transformations in most European countries was a German in all respects. His spiritual and propagandist style, his reactions to men and to events, are well defined by Ignaz von Döllinger: 'Never did there appear a German like that Augustinian monk who lived in Wittenberg, who had so deep and intuitive an understanding of his people and was so fully comprehended by them in return, being absorbed within them, as it were. In his hands the essence and spirit of the Germans were like clay in the hands of the potter.' These three elements – his concervative revolutionism, his revolutionary mediaevalism and his instinctive Germanism – determined his attitude towards the Jews as well.

While still a monk Luther was interested in the Jews. In the lectures he delivered on the Book of Psalms in the years 1513–16, he discussed them at length, in clear mediaeval terminology. Although he tended to support Reuchlin in 1513 (see page 591), his attitude towards the Jews as such was ambiguous. In general, during the period before his Reformational activities, he did not believe that the Jews would change their faith. It seems, however, that once he began to preach a new style of Christianity, he began to hope that it would attract the Jews as well. In 1520 he spoke out against those who persecuted the Jews and brought libellous charges against them: a Christian must feel and suffer the pain of their stiff-neckedness and they must always be prayed for; cruelty makes Christianity repugnant to them; the theological claim that the Jews were the serfs of the emperor was nonsense; those who persecute the Jews are like those foolish children who scratch out the eyes of Jews in pictures as though that will help Jesus. In 1523, this essentially missionary approach of hoping for the conversion of the Jews while sympathizing with their sufferings, reached its peak in a pamphlet Luther published under the title *Jesus Christ Was A Jew By Birth*. This work was intended to answer those who charged Luther with Judaizing tendencies while at the same time to preach Christianity to the Jews, but it also contains further arguments against their maltreatment.

> For our fools – the popes, the bishops, the sophists and the monks – these coarse donkey-heads, have hitherto treated the Jews in such a way that any man who is a good Christian could well turn into a Jew. And if I were a Jew and saw such stupid rascals as these leading the Christian faith and giving instruction in it, I would sooner be turned into a swine than a Christian. For they have treated the Jews as though they were curs with nothing in common with humanity. They continue

to abuse them and take away their money even after they have baptized them as Christians. They have not taught them Christian doctrine, nor the Christian way of life but simply placed them under papistry and monachism. When they [the converts] see that the arguments of the Jews are well-based in Holy Writ while those of the Christians are only idle chatter without any Holy Writ, is it possible that they should have the heart to be good Christians? I myself have heard from God-fearing Jewish converts that if they had not been privileged to hear the tidings of the Evangelism in these days they would have remained Jews in the mask of Christians all their lives long . . . I hope that if the Jews are treated in a friendly fashion and are instructed from Holy Writ, many of them will become worthy Christians (*Das Jesus Christus eyn geborner Jüd War,* Wittenberg, 1523, pp. 1–2).

The critical review of the past, the offer of better treatment in the present, the courteous tone in which the missionary preaching is presented, all display the hope that the Jews would respond to the call of the Reformer. But the hope was not fulfilled. Henceforth the development of Luther's attitude towards the Jews paralleled his progress from religious leader and preacher open to debate and tolerance to a tyrannous and domineering Church head who could not suffer opposition. It was not towards the Jews alone that he changed his attitude from attempts at convincing in amity to cruelty and contumely. It was in this way that, even before his change of attitude towards the Jews, he began to write of the peasants and of rival Protestant groups.

Luther's change of attitude from the late 1530s onwards began to resemble that of Mohammed towards the Jews about 900 years earlier (see page 403). Both these religious innovators had hoped that the superiority of their faiths and their adherence to the Jewish Bible would win the Jews over to their beliefs. When they were disappointed, the popular social trends of their respective environments led them both to anti-Jewish cruelty. And both of them gave full expression to this animosity. Not only did the Jews not turn to Luther's faith, but they even declared their hope that the change in Christianity would bring all Christians, including Luther, over to Judaism. It may be assumed that Luther was not lying when he wrote in 1543 in a diatribe 'About the Jews and their Lies' (*Von den Jüden und ihren Lügen*) that

three learned Jews came to me in the hope that in me they would find a new Jew because we here in Wittenberg have begun to read Hebrew. They had even imagined that because we Christians have begun to read their books, this would swiftly change us. When I debated with them, they behaved after their fashion and offered me their interpretations; and since I compelled them to return to the text of Holy Writ, they evaded the written word and said that they must believe their rabbis just as we believe in the Pope and the Doctors, and so on. And indeed I had pity on them and wrote them a Letter of Recommendation for the journey, so that they should be allowed to travel freely therein for the sake of Jesus. But it became known to me that they described Jesus as 'the hanged one'. . . . Therefore I do not wish to come into further contact with any Jews (in W. Linden, ed., *Luther's Kampfschriften gegen das Judentum,* Berlin, 1936, p. 144).

About five years earlier, Luther had actually heard of Jewish influence among Christians in Bohemia and had written against them. The Reformer returned to his original opinion about the stubborn Jews and the hopelessness of bringing them to better ways. As a ruler and propagandist, however, in 1543 he offered a complete plan for dealing with them.

What should we Christians do with that rejected and accursed people the Jews, whom we cannot suffer, because they are among us and we know so many of their lies, abusings, and curses. . . . Nor do they allow us to convert them. If we wish to deliver some from the fire and the ashes, we must employ a sharp kindness together with prayer and the fear of God. . . . I shall offer my faithful suggestion: first, that we burn their synagogues with fire; and what cannot be burnt shall be buried with earth, so that no man shall ever more be able to see any stone or remnant of it . . . secondly it is necessary to uproot and destroy their houses in the same way, since there we find they do the same as in their synagogues, and house them under some roof or other or in a cowshed like gypsies, in order that they may know that they are not lords in our land as they claim, but in exile and captivity . . . thirdly it is necessary that all their prayer books and their books of the Talmud shall be taken from them . . . fourthly, that their Rabbis shall be forbidden on pain of bodily punishment and death to teach henceforward . . . fifth, that the Jews shall be absolutely forbidden to move on the roads . . . sixth, that they shall be forbidden their usurious transactions and all their ready money and precious belongings of silver and gold shall be taken from them and placed under deposit . . . seventh, that the young and healthy Jews and Jewesses shall be given mallets, hoes, and spindles and shall be required to earn their bread by the sweat of their brow. . . . There is room for apprehension, to be sure, that they are liable to harm us . . . if they should serve us or work for us. . . . Let us therefore use the simple wisdom of other peoples like those of France, Spain and Bohemia . . . and expel them from the land forever (*ibid.*, pp. 201–5).

This detailed plan and its style, like that of the book in which it is suggested, actually shocked several people who were close to Luther and his views. This plan almost places Luther in a class with the likes of Hitler. But the vitality of the movement he called into being and the circumstances under which it operated had the effect that for the greater part of the period following him, and in most sections of the Lutheran world until the twentieth century, more attention was paid to the Luther of 1523 than to the Luther of 1543.

During the very time that Luther adopted his savagely anti-Jewish stance, his circle included those who maintained their friendly approach to the Jews more consistently and systematically than he did. In about the year 1540 the Reformer Andreas Osiander issued an anonymous work that attacked the blood libels and their charges of ritual murder. In this pamphlet he disproves, item by item, the so-called 'proofs' of Jewish guilt and responsibility for slaying Christian children. He also accuses the monks and priests of libelling and persecuting the Jews and points to the economic motivation for such persecution. He relates that 'the Jews themselves as a result of their ample experience have coined the saying that it is not good for a rich Jew and a poor nobleman to be neighbours' (*Schrift über die Blut-beschuldigung,* hsg. v. M. Stern, Kiel, 1893, p. 44). In spite of the vicious preachings of Luther, in spite of the mass hatred of Jews, in spite of the religious wars that laid Germany waste until 1648, there were relatively few anti-Jewish riots during that period. Luther's incitement was largely cancelled out by the spiritual and social direction imposed on his followers in their conflict with the Catholic Counter-Reformation.

The Persecution of the Jews and Their Status at the Beginning of the Reformation

The hatred of the German masses and the animosity of the Reformation towards the Jews after the mid-1520s gave rise to much social persecution. The emperor of Germany was then Charles V, who was also the leader of the Catholics and King of Spain. Although Jews were still not admitted to Spain, within the bounds of the German Empire the Jewish leaders regarded the emperor as their benefactor and protector against the Protestants. In those days the great *shtadlan* and leader of German Jewry was Joseph (Joselman) of Rosheim in Alsace (see page 687). In his diary (published by J. Kracauer in *Revue des Etudes Juives,* 16 [1888], 85–95), he reveals the nature of the struggle for Jewish rights and the atmosphere that had changed even among rioters and persecutors, and which was beginning to incline towards discussion and persuasion. In general Joseph of Rosheim relied on the imperial authorities for protection against the populace. In spite of this, he relates that during the 1525 Revolt of the Peasants in Alsace

> they intended to swallow us alive, and attacks had already begun in some lands ... by the mercy of God I came to them in a house of the clergy called Altdorf, and there I spoke to their hearts with the Book [the Bible] clearly, and to the leaders of their forces who cried out against the raising of hands against the Jews. Many missives were also written to every city and land, and although they finally went back on their words and to their barkings, in any case this proclamation brought easement and deliverance to the Jews until the time came for their defeat (*ibid.,* p. 89).

Thus the intercessor for the Jews was able to convince the leaders of the rebels within their own camp and with the aid of the Bible. Later, to be sure, they changed their minds and wished to riot, but nothing came of it. This possibility of debating and convincing by 'the Book' was one indication of the cultural climate during the Reformation.

By 1537 Luther's hatred of the Jews was undeniable and well known. Joseph of Rosheim accuses Luther of being responsible for the order issued by the Duke of Saxony expelling Jews from his land; yet even here there is room for both legalist and biblicist argumentation. Joseph obtained 'outstanding documents from the other wise men of the nations [*i.e.,* Reformation leaders] and the place of Strosspurk [*i.e.,* the town councillors of Strasbourg]' (*ibid.,* p. 92). With the aid of these letters of recommendation, he debated with the Protestant scholars, and though he did not succeed in having the expulsion from Saxony rescinded, he did succeed in having the expulsion from Brandenburg withdrawn. And all this was due to 'the Disputations where I stood before many wise men, the wisest of the nations, to convince them that things were not as Luther . . . and his followers claimed from the words of our holy Torah' (*ibid.*). Thus Joseph of Rosheim used proofs from the Scriptures before a Protestant public and achieved a degree of success. With the emperor his main argument was the continuity of the imperial privileges, and at heart he identified himself with the humanist concept of the equality of the human race. Those were the foundations of his general arguments before the emperor and his counsellors, together with the legal claim based on the ancient charters. In the Articles he proposed to the Reichstag of Augsburg in 1530, he included the basic assumption of equality of Jews and Christians before the law 'as is likewise indicated by Natural Law; for there is no difference between human beings on earth' (L. Feilchenfeld, ed., *Rabbi Josef von Rosheim,* Strasbourg, 1898, Beilage III, p. 156). In the same context he argued that 'after all we are also human beings who were created by Almighty God to live upon earth and to dwell and work among you and with you' (*ibid.,* p. 157). In 1548 he wrote in a supplication to the heads of the city of Colmar, ' . . . to be sure we do not share the same faith, but in spite of this we are human beings whom God Almighty created to dwell besides other human beings on earth. . . . Likewise the accepted written Laws, both canon and civil, show clearly that we poor Jews, equally with other peoples upon earth, must be shown mercy and given tolerant treatment. Just like the Roman Emperors, so our most gracious lord likewise has the will and grace to treat us gently at all times' (*ibid.,* Beilage XXIV, p. 198).

The Situation of the Jews in Germany at the Time of the Reformation

Jews dwelt in many German cities and principalities during the sixteenth and seventeenth centuries in spite of Luther's destructive proposals; and respected and wealthy Jewish communities were even added in the north-west of the kingdom. The Jews also penetrated into large-scale commerce, into army supply, trade in jewellery and precious stones, until some of them became court-Jews. Throughout this period popular animosity towards Jews continued to seethe and ferment. An instance of the threat to the Jews by the masses and the assistance provided by the central government can be found in the experiences of the Jewish community in the large city of Frankfurt on Main.

Throughout the sixteenth century the masses continued to show their hatred of the Jews while the patricians protected them with the emperor's aid. Early in the seventeenth century relations between the patricians and the masses became very tense, and this was reflected in the treatment of the Jews. In 1612 the craft guilds demanded that the number of Jews in the city should be restricted and the rate of interest lowered. The Town Council rejected this demand and was supported by the emperor. In 1613 a commission proposed in secret a plan for the Jews that combined economic, social and religious elements: according to this plan the criterion for admitting a Jew to the city would be his wealth. Every Jew with less than 15,000 gold pieces was to be expelled from the city, and a forced loan was to be imposed on the remainder. No more Jews were to be admitted to the city. The rate of interest was to be reduced to 5% or 6%. The Jews left in the city would be required to hear a Christian sermon once a week.

Steps were actually taken to implement this plan, and sixty Jews were expelled. The emperor intervened and ordered that they should be readmitted, and the Town Council agreed. The masses led by Wintz (Vincent) Fettmilch then burst into the Jewish quarter on 22 August 1614. The Jews closed the gates of their quarter and defended themselves. One gate was broken down, and for thirteen hours the masses robbed and looted the homes of the Jews. A total of 1,380 Jews gathered in the cemetery to await help and prepare for any eventuality. Fettmilch permitted them to leave the city, and armed burghers accompanied them in order to protect them on their way out. Meanwhile the pillage of the houses continued. The robbers, according to the words of a contemporary Hebrew lament, took

> beds, gold and silver and ready money, also household belongings and clothes and jewels made by craftsmen together with much good wine . . . and the precious Holy Books . . . the wicked villains kindled fire wherewith they burnt the revered books, and baked dry meat on them . . . books of parchment both new and old, that were worth several thousand . . . they sold to a certain craftsman so that he should bind other books with them. They also carried away excellent wares. Likewise they took bonds and certificates of debts and placed them all on the waggon.

The description of the pillage indicates the property and cultural conditions in the Frankfurt Judengasse at that time. The emperor intervened, cancelled the expulsion, suppressed the revolt and ordered the execution of Fettmilch and his companions. The Jews were conducted back to the city under military protection and with orchestral accompaniment.

The Attitude Towards the Jews in England at the Time of Their Readmission

It has already been pointed out (see page 638) that one of the reasons for readmitting the Jews into England was that the experience in the Netherlands had proved that Jews bring considerable economic benefit to their places of residence. This, however, was not the only consideration. A range of ideas and emotions combined to produce favourable public opinion. Among the radical sects of Cromwell's time there were some that regarded the Civil War and the distress of England as a punishment for the expulsion of the Jews, and these proposed that the cause be removed in order to alleviate the consequences. R. Menasseh Ben Israel of Amsterdam and some of his Christian sympathizers in England expressed the belief that the remains of the Ten Tribes were to be found in the New World. According to this eschatology, the coming of the Messiah was delayed by the fact that Jews were not to be found at the 'end of the earth', as the Norman name of England, Angleterre, was interpreted by them.

In addition there was an increasing trend towards toleration on the part of some radical circles. In 1644 Roger Williams had published a work specifically denouncing religious persecution and in favour of tolerance, in which he expressly demanded that the Jews be permitted to display their capacity for good citizenship by granting them equal rights, even though they rejected Christianity. In even more extreme groups, particularly the extreme Puritan sect known as the 'Fifth Monarchy Men', it was suggested that the Jews should even be helped to redeem the Land of Israel. These smaller sects gave expression to the far more moderate mood to be found in many other circles. Yet there were conservative groups in the City of London that voiced opposition. R. Menasseh Ben Israel published pamphlets to influence the English to allow the Jews to return and found supporters among men close to Cromwell; but in 1655–6 they met with mass resistance expressed in violent demonstrations.

The decision was nevertheless taken in 1656 to permit the Jews to return to England. The resistance prevented public promulgation of the decision, but this proved to be advantageous for the Jews. Cromwell wished to readmit them subject to various degrading restrictions, but, as the official resolution never became law, Jews who were already in England continued to live there even after the Restoration of the monarchy without being restricted by specific legislation. In practice they were granted economic equality, but had no political rights until the middle of the nineteenth century. Meanwhile the populace gradually became accustomed to them, respected them because of the new interest in the Old Testament and the Hebrew language and, in general, preserved a friendly attitude towards them.

The Status of the Jews in Poland-Lithuania

In Poland-Lithuania the Jews continued to be considered 'serfs of the Royal Chamber' throughout the period under consideration. The Catholic Church displayed the same animosity towards them here as in other countries, and its influence increased steadily from the end of the sixteenth century. In spite of this the Jews in this principality gained a unique legal and social status, which caused several favourable conditions for Jewish life and activity precisely at the time when the Catholic Counter-Reformation was achieving its maximum success in this area of Europe. Naturally, the economic activity already described played a major part in consolidating this status. However, it was interwoven with a number of religious and social factors that favoured the Jews until 1648.

During the sixteenth century Poland-Lithuania served as a haven for radical Protestants. Even antitrinitarians found shelter there and disseminated their views with an appreciable amount of public expression and missionary success. Important sections of the Polish nobility were highly cultured, and many wealthy and leading families traditionally maintained contact with Italy and Switzerland. Their ties with Bohemia also helped to introduce heretical opinions. Thus the country was in a state of cultural flowering and religious ferment. During the first half of the seventeenth century, these factors continued to be significant. Jews and Christians alike recognized this unique character of Poland.

In brief, the special circumstances existing in Poland-Lithuania, the strength of the Protestants there until the beginning of the seventeenth century and the social conditions that initially worked for religious tolerance towards them indirectly fostered a better attitude towards the Jews. On the other hand, both the Protestants and their moderate Catholic opponents would cite the position of the Jews as a reason for improving the position of the Protestant heretics on an *a fortiori* basis, *i.e.,* if life is made so easy for the Jews, it should be made even more so for those who share the basic beliefs of Christianity.

The political and social support for the Jews, even when the attitude towards the Protestants became more severe, emanated from the Polish nobility, the *Szlachta,* which was all powerful in the kingdom (see page 641), and particularly from the magnates who formed the highest rank of the nobility. In spite of their hatred for Jews, they found the Jewish 'Third Estate' convenient for their economic and social requirements. Even when long-established cities obtained the right not to tolerate Jews, they nevertheless came to dwell in such exempt cities within the town-estates and houses of magnates who were legally exempt from the authority of the munici-pality. These enclaves within municipal boundaries were known in Polish legal terminology as *Juridica.* Even in cities where Jews were permitted to live, there were many who settled within the estates of such nobles. The cities fought against this, sometimes successfully, but their opposition only led to closer ties between the Jews and the magnates.

Jews also settled on the estates of nobles and gentry lying outside the cities, thus escaping both the urban congestion as well as the restrictions that the municipal authorities imposed on their commerce. Little by little Jews began to settle in 'private cities' (in size these were often only townlets) founded by the nobility, where they received special privileges. The owners of these cities would give Jewish settlers houses, gardens and building materials for synagogues, while the Jews participated in the defence of the city. In Rzeszów, which belonged to the Lubomirski magnate-family, it was required of the Jewish settlers 'that every householder shall have as many guns as the number of men, and that he shall keep cartridges and three pounds of gunpowder for each gun'. The community was also required to maintain a store-house for gunpowder, cannon balls for light cannon and four such cannon 'for their synagogue and a Jew who shall look after these guns and shoot with them'. This was also why fortified synagogues were built in the eastern provinces, on the roof of which there were embrasures and places for fire-arms. Jewish participation in defence and the training for this purpose was widespread in the eastern part of the realm. These new 'private' townlets and cities were overwhelmingly Jewish from the start. They, too, did much to establish close ties between Jews and nobility. In theory the king still exercised authority over the Jews, who were legally his prop-erty. In practice they were increasingly subject to the protection and good will of the magnates. This situation, combined with the economic progress, proved very favourable for the Jewish community until 1648.

From time to time, to be sure, there were various troubles. In the years 1539–40 there spread a 'Conversion Charge', when an informer charged that Jews were secretly converting Christians to Judaism and sending them to the Ottoman Empire to live there as Jews in safety. In the religious ferment then characterizing Poland, such conversions were not entirely out of the question. After persecution, restrictions and searches resulting from this charge, the trouble abated, as the harm inflicted on the Jews seriously interfered with economic life, and Jewish complaints therefore found an attentive ear. From time to time there were also charges on a smaller scale. The Jews in the large cities suffered from the pupils in church schools, particularly the Jesuits. The gathering of rioting pupils was a frequent and menacing aspect of Jewish life. The communities actually collected *Schüler Gelt* for the schoolmasters and their pupils so that the latter should not run riot. In the south-east of the kingdom, where Jewish settlement was fanning out, they sometimes suffered from the revolts of peasants and Cossacks against the rule of the Polish nobility. The Councils (see page 683) passed special resolutions to provide funds for 'vengeance'; that is, for putting the machinery of Polish law into operation against those who murdered Jews on the roads. Yet in spite of the dangers, the position of the Jews in Poland continued to improve from the legal and security standpoint, as well as socially and economically, until 1648.

The Massacres of 1648–9

At the close of this period of relative success, expansion and an increase in the range of occupations, the Jewish community suddenly suffered the dreadful shock of the murderous riots that accompanied the Cossack Revolt under the leadership of Bogdan Khmelnitski (known to the Jews as 'The Wicked Khmel'). The success of this revolt, the alliance struck between Khmelnitski and the Tartars and the character of the clash of the Cossack forces – which regarded themselves as an army of nobles in their own right – with the army of the Polish nobility all combined to worsen the situation. The Cossacks rioted against the Jews with a terrible cruelty. All those

> who could not flee . . . were slain and were martyred with unnaturally cruel and bitter deaths. Some of them had their skins flayed off them and their flesh was flung to the dogs. The hands and feet of others were cut off and they were flung unto the roadway where carts ran over them and they were trodden underfoot by horses. And some of them had many non-fatal wounds inflicted on them, and were flung out into the open so that they should not die swiftly but should suffer and bleed until they died. And many were buried alive. Children were slaughtered in their mothers' bosoms and many children were torn apart like fish. They ripped up the bellies of pregnant women, took out the unborn children, and flung them in their faces. They tore open the bellies of some of them and placed a living cat within the belly and left them alive thus, first cutting off their hands so that they should not be able to take the living cat out of the belly . . . and there was never an unnatural death in the world that they did not inflict upon them (N. Hanover, *Yeven Meẓulah,* Tel Aviv, 1966, pp. 31–2).

The cruelty of the Cossack rioters established terrifying patterns, and as a result many Jews preferred to flee to captivity under the Crimean Tartars. This was also a harsh fate, but final deliverance by Jewish redemption of captives at the slave markets of Turkey was a foreseen possibility. In many cases the Jews of the Ukraine, who were accustomed to self-defence, took a very active part in the defence of their cities. In the fortress of Tulchin about 2,000 Jews bravely defended themselves, until they were betrayed by their Polish allies.

The Massacres of 1648 and 1649 brought ruin to the Jews in the greater part of the Ukraine. The destruction meted out by the Cossack Revolt was afterwards compounded by the Muscovite invasions of Poland, which also brought harm to the Jews. The vast number of refugees brought about fresh problems for the communities that had not been affected. After 1648 and 1649 there began a large-scale Jewish migration from the East to Germany and the Western countries.

These massacres and their effects placed the leadership and the social relationships governing Polish and Lithuanian Jewry (see pages 680–1) under a severe strain. The impulse towards economic and social expansion was checked, although many Jews still succeeded in prospering through the Arenda. And Jews continued to make up the urban population of Poland, alongside the Christians, until the Nazi Holocaust (see Part VI). But the degradation and the restrictions of development increased steadily.

The masses of captives who were redeemed in the slave markets of Constantinople strengthened the awareness of Jewish unity among both the Jews of the Ottoman Empire and those of Poland-Lithuania – the two major centres of Jewish life in those days. These closer ties were accompanied by a common feeling of the instability and temporary character of any success in the Diaspora and the steadily increasing menace of dispersion as such (see pages 703–7 on the messianic movement of Shabbetai Zevi).

Jews in Italy During the Catholic Counter-Reformation

In Italy the Counter-Reformation operated powerfully and effectively against the Jews and joined forces with the urban animosity that already existed. When Cardinal Caraffa became Pope Paul IV in 1555, a period of persecution and degradation began. In that year the pope issued a stern Papal Bull imposing severe hardships on the Jews. He began to persecute the Marranos who lived in Ancona, having them tortured and afterwards causing a number of them to be burnt at the stake (see page 667). Economic restrictions and insults were also common both in the papal territories and in other cities and principalities. Jews were increasingly penned into ghettos. This policy was continued, with certain changes and ameliorations, by the popes who came after him.

The fragmentation of Italy into city-states and duchies, and the competition between the rulers, served here, as in Germany, to prevent these activities from reaching any final resolution. The degradation of Jews within Italy was severe and served to embitter their spirits accordingly. Nevertheless they gradually became accustomed to their situation, and the attacks upon the Talmud and the censorship imposed upon it and other Jewish books were ameliorated as a result of Jewish activities and caution.

The Status of the Jews in the Ottoman Empire

In the Ottoman Empire, the exiles from Spain were, as we have seen, favourably received. All indications show that in spite of the Islamic tradition of humiliating Jews and in spite of actions taken against individuals and communities (which were frequent under the despotic and capricious Ottoman rule, particularly during the revolts of the Janissaries), the Jews of the Ottoman Empire generally enjoyed favourable conditions and opportunities for economic activity. The upper class was sometimes on friendly terms with the rulers and wielded considerable influence. In the courts of the sultan and his viziers there were Jewish financiers, physicians and advisers with high incomes. There were also Jewesses who exercised influence through the women of the sultan's harem.

We have already cited the high position attained by Joseph Hamon the physician, whose son Moses was also influential. As a result, he obtained a letter from the sultan in 1552 addressed to the Doge of Venice, in which Sultan Suleiman demanded that the widows and daughters of two Jews who were kinsfolk of Moses Hamon should be permitted to leave the Christian lands and come to Istanbul. This referred to Doña Gracia Nasi and her daughter Reyna. These two wealthy women succeeded in reaching the Ottoman Empire in 1553, where they were joined by a kinsman who had returned to Judaism and adopted the name Joseph Nasi. In the year 1566 Don Joseph was granted the title of Duke of Naxos by Sultan Selim II, in whose court he wielded vast power. Emissaries of Christian rulers to the sultan would first turn to him in order to succeed in their missions (see page 636 on the family's activities in establishing Tiberias).

40

Autonomy: Institutions and Trends

The Synagogue Community of the Spanish and Portuguese Exiles

The exiles from Spain and Portugal carried along a sense of unity and pride in their Sephardi past and even in the localities from which they came. When they first resettled in the lands of their dispersion, they adopted, as we have noted, a haughty attitude towards the long-established Jewish inhabitants whom they found there. At first, while they were exiles in need of help, the local residents were still able to stand up for themselves; but that situation did not last very long. The liturgical customs of Spanish Jewry were valued by those who had left the country and were carried on by their descendants. Within a generation or two the newcomers from Spain had established a firm economic and social base. From it they asserted their claims for cultural domination and social superiority over the resident Jewish communities. Samuel of Medina, a rabbi who belonged to the exiles' circle, wrote:

> The essence of prayer is that it shall be in a beautiful language and familiar to all – wise and discerning men as well as to fools. Therefore, as is generally known, all the prayers of the Sephardi rite are only those that were ordained by the sages. And even the *piyyutim* [later hymns in verse], which we recite in addition to the prayers proper, were composed by Rabbi Judah Halevi, of blessed memory, and by Rabbi Solomon ibn Gabirol, of blessed memory, or by Rabbi Abraham ibn Ezra, of blessed memory – all in perfect Hebrew that can be understood by all. . . . Because of this, as written above, it seems to me that whoever abandons other prayer rites and adopts that of Sepharad should not only not be reproached but should be praised. For who knows, perhaps if their ancients [of the other rites] had seen the Sephardi prayer rite they would have done likewise [*i.e.*, accepted it] for the reason I have mentioned (*Responsa of R. Samuel of Medina* on *Orah Ḥayyim*, Lvov, 1862, no. 34, fol. 8v).

This opinion was given when 'in the kingdom of Turkey . . . the customs of prayer have become confused; and almost all have turned to the prayerbook of the Sephardim. For they are the majority in this kingdom, and their prayers are pure and sweet. And all or most have abandoned their rites and follow that of Sepharad as it is now practised in the city . . . Salonika' (*ibid.*). Thus we see the reflection of the newly established Sephardi influence. One or two generations after the Spanish exiles had settled there, they began to remodel the local Jewish culture in the image of their traditions.

The division that came in the early stages of this intrusion was replaced by a new life-style and structure based on the hegemony of Sephardi Jewry. The strain showed even more clearly in the area of community leadership. The various congregations that were founded after the exiles' arrival tried in some places to work together as one community, with majority-decisions binding on the minority. This compromise did not take root everywhere. Tension grew when the long-established Jewish inhabitants began asking for how many generations an exile should still be considered as one of the 'expelled', whether Spanish or Portuguese. In one place an attempt was made to solve this problem:

> The congregations of one city reached an agreement whereby anybody who came to the city and whose parents or he himself had been born in Italy – even though his grandfather came from Portugal, Castile, Aragon or some other kingdom – would join the Italian congregation. But if his father had been born in one of the aforesaid kingdoms, even though he himself was born in the land of Italy, he would go only to the congregation that spoke the language of those of his kingdom (*Responsa of R. Moses of Trani*, Lvov, 1861, no. 307, fol. 56v).

Thus, while the first and second generations still bore the stamp of the expulsion, the third generation had to be absorbed. However, 'the members of the Aragon congregation protested, maintaining that if someone knew he was Aragonese or of some other language, it was not proper or fitting that he should go over to the Italians merely because he and his father had been born in Italy.' As far as the Aragonese were concerned, their Iberian character was permanent.

The rabbi from Safed who responded to this query accepted their view, because 'Aragon is an independent community with a court of its own,' *i.e.,* the communal independence of a synagogue-congregation was well-nigh absolute. An additional reason of his was that a transfer from one congregation to another meant loss of charity money for the poor of the abandoned congregation. A third consideration was that any mutuality in this agreement existed only on paper and was purely formal. Yet, while there were men from Aragon who had children and grandchildren in Italy, this did not mean that others would cross over from an Italian to an Aragonese congregation: 'It is a known fact that no Italian can be imagined who went to Aragon, and there he and his father were born. For there are no Jews in Aragon for the past seventy years, and we are assured that no Jew will ever set his tent up there again. For the Blessed God is gathering the dispersed of Israel in the near future in the Land of Israel' (*ibid.*).

This insistence on the eternity of Sephardi synagogue autonomy did not necessarily mean the rejection of the majority decision of a city's congregations; it was a refusal to bow to the gradual extinction of the continuity of the Sephardic identity. While this autonomous structure led to much divisiveness within Jewish city life, as well as to considerable tension between the various congregations, it nevertheless prevented a complete estrangement between groups that had to live as close neighbours within the city confines. In times of large-scale mobility and growing mutual acquaintance of the Jewish life-styles and philosophical outlooks that had evolved by the end of the fifteenth century, the synagogue-congregation made possible a secure form of autonomy – first for the various Sephardi congregations, but soon also for their host congregations – in rites, culture-patterns and social responses; yet it prevented any one of them from imposing its own communal and ritual way of life on another. Autonomous solutions of this kind were to recur during the nineteenth and twentieth centuries at times of religious divisions and large-scale migrations within Jewry (see Part VI).

The Holy Community of Safed

The combination of the cultural and religious strength of the Spanish exiles, the normal economic groundwork and the new form of voluntary lifelong association with the synagogue and the 'language', as well as the vitality of new and emerging cultural and social trends, became the pillar on which the unique community of Safed was based in the sixteenth and early seventeenth centuries.

We shall deal below with the rich creativity of Safed in most fields of Jewish thought and life. To begin with, however, we shall consider the methods of leadership in which Safed also offered patterns of its own. These were based on an intense feeling of community in serving the Creator by ardent worship in associations and synagogues. It seems likely that Safed or some community that was influenced by it must have brought to R. Moses of Trani the question

> regarding the agreement reached by certain men to become one association, united wholeheartedly, to pray together at a special place and at fixed times, and they will not be entitled to separate or cease praying together at any time, not by reasons of animosity. . . . They shall only pursue peace and each one shall help his neighbour. . . . And at any rejoicing of any one of them or the reverse they shall honour him and make him glad; and if anybody sets out to injure any one of them improperly they shall rise to aid him; and in case of any false charge (heaven forbid) against any one of them, the whole group shall stand together with him, so that they shall all be one society to aid one another (*ibid.,* no. 151, fol. 10v).

The desire of these men to join together, to experience common rejoicing, mutual encouragement and aid and common prayer were focal points of the unity. These Safed associations shaped customs and established patterns of behaviour that in due course were to be adopted in the majority of Jewish communities, while others remained peculiar to those specific groups. In Safed 'there is an association which goes at the close of every Sabbath to sing and dance and gladden bridegroom and bride' (S. Schechter, *Studies in Judaism,* Philadelphia, 1928, p. 298). Within this holy community of Safed there were established special practices for welcoming the Sabbath; outstanding members of the community 'go out every Sabbath Eve into the field or to the courtyard of the synagogue and all of them welcome the Sabbath dressed in their Sabbath garments' (*ibid.,* p. 295). According to one description 'several groups went out on Sabbath Eve while it was still day, dressed in white garments, to welcome the Sabbath'. They recited the psalm 'Ascribe to the Lord, ye sons of might', the hymn *Lekhah Dodi* ('Come my love'), 'A psalm and song for the Sabbath day' and *Boi Kallah* ('Come O Bride'). From Safed there spread the custom of special study on the night of Shavuot, 'for on this night after the meal each congregation gathers in its own synagogue and they do not sleep all night long but read the Torah, the Prophets and the Scriptures, the Mishnah, the *Zohar* and Sermons . . . until the light of morning. And then all the people immerse themselves in the morning before prayers' (*ibid.*).

These group practices were influenced by outstanding individuals. A personality of this kind introduced the practice of the *Tikkun Ḥaẓot,* or midnight penitential prayers:

> there was one here in Safed . . . named our honoured Master Rabbi Abraham Halevi. . . . Every midnight he would rise and make the round of all the streets and raise his voice and cry in a bitter voice: 'Rise in honour of the Blessed Name, for the *Shekhina* is in Exile, and our Holy Temple has been consumed by fire, and Israel is in great distress.' He would proclaim many things of this kind; and he would summon each of the scholars and sages by name and would not move away from the window until he saw that he had already risen from the bed. And by the hour of one after midnight the whole city would resound with the voices of those studying the Mishnah and the *Zohar* and the Midrashim of our rabbis of blessed memory, and of psalms and prophets and hymns and entreaties (Yaari, *Letters from Erez Yisrael,* p. 205).

In Safed 'there are men of piety and good deeds who at each watch of the night preach sternly of humility and repentance and the gravity of sin. And men turn in repentance to their Lord. There are pious people who go round all the houses to inspect the *mezuzot* in case some are unfit for use, and they give *mezuzot* to the poor . . . from the charity fund' (Schechter, *op. cit.,* p. 300). In the same Safed 'most of the townsfolk leave an earlock one finger wide from above the ear, and some leave a width of two fingers'. And another tradition about this Safed practice explains: 'The reason for this commandment is that only thereby can a man be recognized as a Jew, whether alive or dead' (*ibid.*). Among other customs originating in Safed and observed till the present day was that of the monthly 'Minor Day of Atonement': 'For they hold a watch on the Eve of the New Moon, gathering in synagogues and houses of study and spending most of the day in prayer and tears, clad in sack-cloth and ashes' (*ibid.*).

Responsa, descriptions and tales of Safed also contain evidence of social tension. There were disputes about the distribution of charity among the various synagogues and among those from various countries. The *Sefer Haḥezyonot* ('Book of Visions') of R. Ḥayyim Vital, the great disciple of R. Isaac Luria (see pages 693–4) is an incomparable source, reflecting the social and personal tension to be found among even the kabbalists. Yet he too conveys that singular atmosphere of unity through association that characterized Safed's communal life. Thus he mentions that in that year [1570] some of the devoted and pious scholars and sages of the city of Safed all agreed to meet together in the synagogue each Sabbath Eve, where each one of them would relate his deeds both good and bad before them all, stating what he had done during that week. For in this way a man would become ashamed of himself and would cease to sin (*Sefer Haḥezyonot, op. cit.,* p. 52).

R. Ḥayyim himself made use of this group organization in order to disseminate his own doctrines and those of his master, R. Luria. Ten sages signed a covenant that

we have undertaken to be together in association, to serve the Lord, may He be blessed, and to engage in His Torah by day and night in all that we will be taught by our teacher the sage and divine rabbi, our honoured master Rabbi Ḥayyim Vital . . . and we shall study the True Wisdom with him and shall be faithful in spirit and keep secret everything that he shall say to us. And we shall not distress him or entreat him too much regarding matters which he does not wish to reveal to us, nor shall we reveal to any other person any secret of all that we shall hear from him in this way of truth, nor of all that he has taught us in the past . . . and this undertaking is by a grave oath . . . and the duration of this undertaking is from today and for ten consecutive years (*ibid.,* p. 254).

This closed group of students that engaged in the study of the mysteries were following the pattern of the Safed societies and its charismatic leaders and itself became one of the cornerstones in the leadership established in Safed.

Naturally Safed had a more general leadership. It had its problems of transgressors, discipline and punishment. And the rabbi relates: 'I was summoned to the council of the sages, counsellors, and leaders of Safed with regard to Jacob Zarkon who had shown signs of heresy as well as homosexuality. And they gave permission to the leaders of the congregation . . . that he should be punished with the help of the gentiles and he was imprisoned by them and they flogged him.' When the man requested to be released from the gentiles 'the appointed officers told him: We wish you to leave the city and cease to pollute the land with your evil deeds' (*Responsa of R. Moses of Trani, op. cit.,* no. 22, fol. 5r). Thus the Safed community used the most extreme measures, to which only an exacting community would have recourse, and employed them as a punishment against heretical and sexual deviation. The application to the gentile authorities to punish that Jew, the imprisonment and beating, and the subsequent insistence on expulsion from the city for the purpose of 'burning out the evil' from among the good inhabitants all show that the sages and leaders of Safed imposed discipline in the tradition of the communities of Spain in their golden age. It might even be correct to say. on the basis of this incident, that the punishment imposed and the expressions used towards the person punished was not devoid of an inquisitorial flavour.

However, the singularity and greatness of Safed lay in its voluntarism and individual forms of social life, rather than the community leadership of the 'counsellors and leaders . . . of the congregations', who functioned here as they did in other Jewish centres with synagogue communities.

The Attempt to Restore Ordination

The fiery religiosity of Safed and the awareness of the creative and charismatic power of its leading figures gave rise to an attempt to re-establish an ancient institution of leadership as the accepted fount of authoritative *halakʰʲc* decisions – namely, the *semikhah* (see Part IV). Undoubtedly, those who wished to renew it were imbued with messianic hopes. They wished to restore sacral leadership as of old and the full authority of the *halakhah*. Theoretically, they relied on the authority of Maimonides, who held that in certain circumstances it was possible to renew the institution of *semikhah,* provided it met with the approval of all the sages and scholars of the generation.

The initiator of this plan was the great, confident and wealthy scholar R. Jacob Berab (see page 635), and he himself was the first to be so ordained. Most of the scholars of Safed supported him, and he ordained four sages who, in the course of time, ordained seven others. One of those ordained by him was R. Joseph Caro, who in due course would successfully introduce his codification of Jewish Law as the authoritative *halakhic* guide.

R. Jacob's action was taken in 1538, forty-six years after the expulsion from Spain. The restoration was the result of many factors. At the time messianic fervour ran high in Safed, partly due to the personality and preachings of Solomon Molkho (see page 701). The penitent Marranos sought an authoritative institution competent to decide on and impose proper modes of penitence. There was an ardent desire to make the Land of Israel the centre from which the *halakhah* would go forth and spread to all parts of the Diaspora and to attract people 'to come from the ends of the earth' to this centre. And there was the hope that by the restoration of this hallowed institution they would succeed 'in restoring the crown as of old', thereby awakening the mercies of Heaven to restore all the glory of the nation, bring about its Redemption and re-establish its kingdom, as in bygone days. All these were background elements leading to the steps taken by R. Jacob Berab and his companions.

One of the opponents of this measure summed them up as follows:

> As the main reason leading our brethren who dwell in Galilee [*i.e.,* in Safed] to take this step is that they moan and groan at the helplessness of those who bear the banner of the Torah; and particularly in this our Land which is desolate by reason of our sins, from which Torah once went forth to all Israel; but now 'Israel is grown poor' and the violent and evil-tongued have grown powerful and none inquire and none ask; therefore they [*i.e.,* the inhabitants of Safed] have said, Come let us return to the Lord and raise the banner of the Torah. And they will come unto us from the ends of the earth to honour the God of the Land. For they will say, there are mighty judges in Israel 'and Israel prevails'. And we shall do our best to restore the crown as of old. Perhaps the Lord will show grace to our remnant and will show mercy unto us again as of old ('Responsum of R. Moses de Castro', *Sefunot,* 10 [1966], 147).

Although the initiative was taken by Safed, it is evident from the above that the scholars of Jerusalem recognized its importance and significance. The scholars of Safed sent a letter to Jerusalem, and, their opponent remarks, when the Jerusalemites heard 'these tidings, our hearts rejoiced and our honour was glad and our spirits revived and we uttered praise and thanksgivings unto the Lord, may He be blest, who has kept us alive and sustained us and brought us to discuss and deal with such a matter . . . since this matter is of vast significance and touches on us ourselves and on others' (*ibid.*).

However, institutional and conceptual conservatism won out against the trend in Safed towards restoration and innovation. The Jerusalem scholars, headed by R. Levi ben Ḥabib, vehemently opposed the attempt, and the conservative opponents won after a keen dispute. R. Jacob Berab and his ordained disciples, with R. Joseph Caro among them, seem to have held their ground for some time longer, continuing to ordain and to use the term 'ordained'; but the practice ceased even during the lifetime of R. Jacob Berab's disciples.

The restorational and messianic intentions underlying the renewal of the *semikhah* doubtless merged with the continuing messianic ferment from which it originated. As the idea of *semikhah* did not find general acceptance, it also does not seem to have attracted many people to the Land of Israel. Those who initiated the practice never regretted having done so – on the contrary, they regarded themselves as having been privileged to participate. The *maggid* of R. Joseph Caro (the spiritual guide, or 'the soul of the Mishnah', as he believed, which instructed him) told him in a dream-vision one night, five years after he had been ordained by R. Jacob Berab: 'I shall elevate thee to become a prince and leader of all the Exile of Israel in the kingdom of Arabistan. And since thou didst dedicate thy soul to the restoration of the crown of *semikhah* as of old, thou shalt merit to be the ordained of all the sages of the Land of Israel and elsewhere; and I shall restore the *semikhah* as of old at thy hand' (*Maggid Mesharim,* Vilna, 1875, p. 57).

Five years after the objections voiced by the scholars of Jerusalem, R. Joseph Caro thus saw the source of his leadership in the fact that he had been ordained. In his efforts to 'restore the crown of *semikhah* as of old' (a phraseology which in itself is evidence of the restorative intention and the sense of achievement involved), he experienced a feeling of dedication and hoped that he would be privileged to complete the task. In any case the Safed court demanded a special and central position for itself. Sixteen years after the attempt to revive the ancient practice, R. Joseph declared: 'At the present time, the court of this city [Safed] is the one authorized for the people and has greater wisdom and numbers than any place of which we have heard; and from the four corners of the earth they do send their questions and accept the terms of the Responsa. This being so, it has the legal authority of the Great Court, particularly as the communities have acknowledged its authority (*Responsa of R. Joseph Caro,* no. 17). This mode of expression is less resolute than ought to have been accorded the authority of hallowed ordination by those who had obtained it; nevertheless, it displays a stand and tone of voice that constitute an echo of that great claim made by R. Jacob Berab, and this more moderate claim for the central authority of Safed spread through the communities and produced a profound effect.

The Codifications

R. Jacob Berab turned R. Isaac Alfasi's compendium of the Talmud into a primary source and made a scholar's familiarity with it a prerequisite for ordination. By doing so R. Jacob, in his desire to restore an institution that would ordain scholars worthy of a seat in the Sanhedrin, followed the attempts that had been made from time to time – since at least the end of the tenth century – to summarize the Talmudic discussions in simple, clear and authoritative *halakhic* decisions. We have already discussed the attempt made by Maimonides to turn his *Mishneh Torah* into the sole authority for *halakhic* decision, as well as the energetic resistance to his attempt (see page 540). At the beginning of the fourteenth century a further attempt was made to issue a code of authoritative *halakhah*. R. Jacob ben Asher did not claim that his work could replace the Talmud, but wished it only to stand *alongside*. He therefore did not include in it all the laws of Jewish life, as Maimonides had done, but omitted those, such as the laws of kings, which were a matter for the future. This work is known as *Sefer Haturim* ('Book of the Rows', referring to the rows of precious stones on the breastplate of the High Priest), and it consists of four sections: (1) *Oraḥ Ḥayyim* ('The Way of Life'), containing the laws of daily life governing the Jewish individual from the time he rises in the morning to serve the Creator until he goes to sleep, after reciting his night prayers, with the detailed order of prayer, the laws governing the reading of the Torah and those practices that constitute the duties of the individual, including Sabbath and festival laws; (2) *Yoreh De'ah* ('Instruction in Knowledge'), containing all the laws of prohibitions, including monetary prohibitions such as usury; (3) *Even Ha'ezer* ('The Rock of Aid'), containing the laws of matrimony and family life; (4) *Ḥoshen Mishpat* ('Breastplate of Judgement'), containing laws of economic matters. Thus R. Jacob not only excluded those laws that were in abeyance during the exile but also every systematic presentation of a religious outlook or philosophy. It is possible that he did this in order to avoid controversy. Among the detailed laws, there are various moral sayings and reasonings based on his specific outlook. This work enjoyed considerable success and became the foundation for all subsequent *halakhic* codifications and compilations.

R. Joseph Caro (1488–1575) acted with the deep sense of leadership and responsibility that he had acquired from his teacher R. Jacob Berab. He also had a singular mystical power. It was his belief that when he dreamed at night he was visited by 'the Soul of the Mishnah', which was his *maggid* or spiritual guide, transmitting instructions to him as from on high. Caro was an outstanding authority on *halakhah*. In him we find, therefore, a mystic who was active and productive, a keen and widely versed *halakhic* and Talmudic thinker, and a religious leader who held that he bore the authority of those ancient and ordained scholars who had originally been seated in the Sanhedrin. While still living in Adrianople in the Balkan Peninsula, he had already headed a *yeshiva* and had begun to write a commentary of his own to the *Sefer Haturim,* which was called *Bet Joseph* ('The House of Joseph'). In 1525 he settled in Safed where he was privileged thirteen years later to obtain ordination from R. Jacob Berab. This entitled him in his eyes to struggle together with his master for the establishment of the institution of *semikhah*. In 1542 he completed his own *Bet Joseph* at his *yeshiva* in Safed. In 1555 he prepared a summary of this commentary as an independent work of *halakhic* authority – the *Shulḥan Arukh* ('The Prepared Table'). It was arranged in the style of the *Sefer Haturim*, in brief paragraphs, each stating a specific *halakhah* and its practical application. As a rule R. Joseph followed the *halakhic* principles and customs of the sages of Spain and the practices of Sephardi Jewry.

In Poland at about this time, R. Moses Isserles, the rabbi of Cracow (known as 'Rama', *c.*1520–*c.*1572), was preparing a commentary of his own on the *Sefer Haturim*, which he called *Darkei Moshe* ('The Ways of Moses'). This was a formulation of the *halakhah* and customs of Ashkenazi Jewry. When R. Joseph Caro's work was published and reached Poland, R. Moses Isserles prepared a summary of all the differences between his *halakhic* decisions and those of R. Joseph, using the same form of paragraphs to comment on or disagree with those in the *Shulḥan Arukh*. In this way he spread his Ashkenazi *Mappah*, or tablecloth, on the Sephardi 'set table'. These two have merged in the printed editions of the *Shulḥan Arukh* as it was recognized thereafter throughout Ashkenaz. Among the Sephardim, however, *halakhic* decisions follow only R. Joseph Caro.

These two were not the only authorities who tried to prepare *halakhic* compendia. They both also had their critics, both on matters of principle and with respect to the details of their decisions. Like R. Isaac Alfasi and Maimonides, they also acquired commentaries and supra-commentaries on the detailed aspects of their conclusions. Nevertheless, the works of R. Joseph Caro and R. Moses Isserles became the practical guides to Jewish individual and communal life from the end of the sixteenth century onwards. Only at the beginning of the nineteenth century, with the advent of the Reform movement (see Part VI), were other practical and philosophical approaches established towards the *halakhah* and the Jewish way of life.

Technical factors also promoted the success of these works: the invention of the printing press enabled these books to be widely disseminated immediately after their publication; previous works had been available only in manuscript form. The closer ties and increased communication within the Diaspora also helped promote their popularity, and in the case of R. Joseph Caro this was supplemented by the authority and sanctity of Safed, as well as his own personal charisma.

The Ancona Affair

In 1556 Pope Paul IV continued to persecute the Jews and put on trial a group of Marranos who lived in Ancona, a port of the Papal States. They had been granted right of residence because of the commercial advantages they brought to the territory. Persuaded by Doña Gracia and Don Joseph Nasi, the sultan intervened on behalf of the Marranos, but to no avail. Some of them fled from the city and found refuge in Pesaro, a rival port. The pope stood firm. Twenty-four male Marranos and one female who remained steadfast to their Judaism went nobly to the stake. Twenty-seven who confessed and submitted were sent to hard labour in Malta, but succeeded in escaping on the way.

The incident shocked the whole of Jewry. It seems that there must have been many attempts at intervention within Italy itself, but there are few records of these. In the same year, resolutions were recorded by 'The Small Council' of Venice 'to engage in a certain matter for the public benefit which . . . it is not fitting to enter in the book'. They sent messengers to Verona 'to select two of them who should not be halted by rain, snow, cold, or heat . . . our Father and King . . . annul all harsh decrees against us'. In Verona the community agreed to send 'two men to be with them there in Venice . . . since it was their intention to engage in a certain enterprise for the general welfare; and this is a hidden secret which can be revealed only to the discreet and cannot be written in the book' (I. Sonne, ed., *From Paul* IV *to Pius* V, Jerusalem, 1964, p. 149). In Italy it was therefore possible to try to obtain help, yet they were afraid to call the incident by its name even in Hebrew and even in internal Jewish documents.

Doña Gracia decided to engage in open commercial war from the Ottoman Empire against the Papal States by proclaiming a commercial boycott of the port of Ancona. The intention was not only to punish Ancona but also to reward Pesaro, which had agreed to receive the refugee Marranos. This was a first and daring attempt to use the commercial strength of the Jews in the maritime trade of the Mediterranean as a lever to benefit those who helped them, while dealing a blow to those who harmed them. The initiative came from the 'Great Lady' and her group, but she required the support of the scholars. The rabbis of Italy naturally could not express their opinion openly; but we have the views of scholars living elsewhere. A dispute arose between those who supported Doña Gracia's boycott and those who opposed it.

Discussions of the matter evoked contrary viewpoints, but they all aimed at shaping a Jewish policy on the issue. The protagonists of the boycott argued in the name of the Marranos who had fled from Ancona to Pesaro that the boycott offered 'two achievements: one, avenging the blood of our murdered brethren . . . and second that those who had gathered together in Pesaro . . . should live in security'. For the Duke of Urbino who ruled there would see 'how many . . . good advantages would accrue in establishing traffic and commerce in his country' by shifting Jewish trade from Ancona. They state that the Duke actually admitted them because he was told that the Jews would boycott Ancona; if they do not do so now 'he will grow enraged and will make a condign end of the Jews dwelling under him' (*ibid.*, p. 156). However, there were still Jews living in Ancona who were opposed to the boycott because they felt that the pope must not be enraged. There were many Jews among his subjects, and he would strike at them if he perceived any contemptuous act towards him on the part of the Jews who dwelt in Turkey. They explained that the Duke of Urbino would be satisfied with the commercial advantages he gained from those Marranos who had settled of sheer necessity in his port. He would not punish them if they did not boycott Ancona, for 'he is a wise and understanding man and knows that it is beyond the capacity of these poor Jews to compel all Israel' (*ibid.*).

R. Joshua Soncino, who heard the arguments of both sides, decided against the boycott for the following reasons: it was not clear where the danger was greater – whether to the professing Jews in Ancona who continued to dwell there, in the event that the boycott were imposed, or to the Marranos who had settled in Pesaro if it should not be imposed. Furthermore, he did not see that this was a case for fulfilling the commandment of 'avenging the . . . blood of our brethren'; for the victims here were Marranos who had followed Christian practice in public. They committed a grave error when they had gone over to open Judaism under Christian rule. The rabbi wished to establish a Jewish policy towards Marranos in this respect: 'If I could find somebody to support me, I would declare that a ban must be imposed on every person forcibly converted in Portugal who takes up residence under some ruler or duke in the Christian lands. For although they are spoken to smoothly and are flattered at the time . . . when their time comes, action will be taken against them.' His conclusion was therefore that agreement to this boycott was 'a matter for personal decision. He who wishes to support it can do so, while he who does not may refrain' (*ibid.*, p. 157).

A very different stand was taken by the Sephardi rabbi Joseph ibn Lev. He formulated the boycott as 'an abiding and binding agreement whereby no Jew resident in Turkey may trade in Ancona'. He described those calling for the boycott not as the refugees in Pesaro – as R. Joshua defined them – but as 'a few persons who are zealous on account of the burning of those saintly persons' (*ibid.*, p. 155), thus stressing the idealism of the boycott promoters. He records the reasons for vengeance, the favourable attitude of the Duke of Urbino, and the consideration that if Ancona is not boycotted, the refugees in Pesaro would be unfavourably affected; he then added the following religious and nationalistic reason: 'Most certainly the Name of Heaven has been profaned by the Pope who lords over that place.' He thus suggests that the burning of the martyrs was regarded by those who called for a boycott as a profanation of the Name of Heaven and the honour of the God of Israel. He further complains that the pope is 'evil . . . and deeds which have never been done before have been done by him, such as burning the Talmud in contempt'. The pope's generally hostile attitude towards Judaism was thus sufficient reason for a general commercial campaign against him. Moreover, if the Duke of Urbino saw that the promise of boycotting Ancona was not kept, he might hand over the refugees 'to the Pope, who is demanding them from him in order to sentence them to death'. The opinion of R. Joseph ibn Lev is that the majority of the communities were entitled to compel the minority to participate in the boycott (*ibid.*).

The attempt failed because of internal Jewish differences, the same phenomenon that had led to the failure of reviving the *semikhah*. These two attempts, one at reviving a hallowed ancient institution and the second at employing commercial strength as a political force, came from circles of former Spanish Marranos. Both of them, the restoration of ordination and the attempt at the commercial boycott, together with the new interest in codification, reflected a desire to unite the congregations of Jewry throughout the Diaspora in a common way of life based upon *halakhah* and upon joint action through economic strength.

The Beginnings and Sources of the Councils of the Lands

The tendencies towards unity expressed in the aforementioned attempts of the Sephardi diaspora achieved considerable success in the establishment of a number of central institutions for conducting Jewish affairs in certain large countries. Reference has been made above to repeated attempts to create a central Jewish leadership through meetings of scholars and community heads. We have noted the existence of councils and synods of this kind, their activities and ordinances, in Germany, in Aragon and Castile in Spain, and in Italy. A 'council' (*vaad*), according to the termi-nology of the Middle Ages, means a gathering or assembly intended for some specific purpose. Thus these central institutions were by definition not permanent institutions. Even if they met quite frequently and established a sense of continuity, they still retained a temporary nature stemming from the time of their initial development.

The greatest continuity and range was achieved by councils such as those established in the Western Slavic countries, in Poland and Lithuania, as well as in Bohemia and Moravia. Their success in these regions was due to several factors. As we have seen (on page 655), the Jewish community in Poland-Lithuania was involved in a process of expansion during the sixteenth and the first half of the seventeenth centuries. Jews were leaving the 'royal' cities for the new 'private' towns of the nobility and created many new communities, some of which flourished and prospered even more than the established ones. The leaseholds in the villages produced a network of small Jewish settlements, sometimes consisting of no more than two or three families. The old communities claimed authority over the new. A successful community tended to claim similar authority over those that were unsuccessful. And all communities claimed authority over 'the surrounding areas', *i.e.,* over those groups of families who were dispersed around the established communities.

From the beginning of the sixteenth century the Polish authorities wished to shape a central Jewish leadership, to whom they turned to collect taxes from the Jews who were now dispersed throughout the realm. The attempt was first made in the appointment by royal authority of central or chief rabbis. In the year 1503, R. Jacob Polak was appointed the Rabbi of Jewry in Poland. King Alexander proclaimed that 'by reason of his dedication to and deep knowledge of the Law of Moses and all its practices' he had granted 'this letter of appointment . . . to elevate him and appoint him as Rabbi of the Jews'. The king awarded him 'absolute authority to sit in fair judgement for the settlement of disputes between all Jews, to right what is wrong, to improve morals and fulfill . . . other functions connected with the office of Rabbi in accordance with the said Torah'. The Polish king likewise commanded all the Jews of his kingdom, whether resident on his own estates or those of his magnates, 'by all the severity of the law to recognize the said Jew . . . as Rabbi in accordance with your Torah, to take care and submit to his discipline in all matters touching on his office' (Halperin, *op. cit.,* p. 236).

The Jewish population in Poland continued to grow, while the centralizing power of the royal court diminished. In the middle of the sixteenth century, the royal authorities of Poland tended to show a considerable measure of tolerance towards differing faiths and opinions and were inclining towards granting self-government to regions and various groups of residents. The matter of the Chief Rabbinate passed from the decision of the state to the Jews themselves. In the year 1551, King Sigismund Augustus granted permission to the Jews of 'Great Poland' to choose 'the Chief Rabbi and religious Judge at any time required, whenever . . . the office of Rabbi or Judge shall become vacant' (*ibid.*, p. 238).

The trend towards centralization in Jewish leadership continued, while Jewish autonomy expanded. Even the authority granted to the Chief Rabbi, to be elected by the Jews themselves, began to be couched in more respectful terms. The king now gave him 'the absolute authority to judge, investigate, and inquire, to give judgement without appeal in respect of all the Jews . . . who are within the region of his jurisdiction; to impose punishments and bans in accordance with the Torah of Moses and its customs, and to engage in all other matters touching on religion'. This extensive authority was granted to him at the request of the Jews themselves, for the king goes on to remark:

> We expressly repeat and confirm what was declared by those self-same Jews be-fore us – and in case any of the said Jews shall dare to behave negligently towards the punishments and bans imposed upon him by the Rabbi or the Judge or the other heads of the Jews, and shall not take care to submit himself to their judgments within a month, he shall be handed over to us to be punished by death, and all his property shall be confiscated for the benefit of our Treasury (*ibid.*, pp. 238–9).

The king likewise ordered his lords and nobles to aid the rabbi and not the Jews who might try to challenge his authority. It appears that R. Moses Isserles also held a rabbinical post with similar powers confirmed by the state. And it may be assumed that he was also chosen by the Jews, in accordance with his opinion with respect to rabbis appointed by the state, as stated in his *Responsa* (no. 123).

In Bohemia and Moravia in 1577 the community heads and rabbis of Prague signed an ordinance concerning the election of their chief rabbi. The signatories in-clude the Maharal of Prague and his brother R. Sinai, and it is based on the authority of previous sages. The main points of this agreement are 'that no man shall assume high office save with the approval of the majority of the community, as is the custom in all quarters where Jews dwell'. Furthermore, 'that no man shall assume any office in this congregation, neither of head nor of rabbi nor of judge nor of any office whatso-ever, saving for the duration of one year; and at the end of each year all the offices shall be renewed in accordance with the ordinances'. These ordinances were brought be-fore the emperor, who was reminded 'that Moses, who was the first of all the prophets and their foremost, and all of whose words were the utterance of God and His com-mandments, told the community when he wished to appoint heads and commanders over them, "bring wise and understanding and known men . . . and I shall set them at your head"' (Bondy and Dvorsky, *op. cit.*, no. 772, pp. 558–9). Additional documents show that during those years there was an internal and external struggle in Prague for the independence of the community in selecting their leaders, particularly concerning the part to be played by the rabbis in this election.

In Poland-Lithuania, Bohemia and Moravia, the state therefore took an interest in Jewish leadership. In these realms the Jews also insisted on complete independence in the choice of their representatives, in accordance with the best traditions of Jewish autonomy.

The Leadership of the Councils of the Lands

From the second half of the sixteenth century onwards, there are increasing signs that Jewish leadership was passing to elected heads and great scholars, who were regarded as leaders and representatives of the 'lands' or 'states', as extensive areas of Poland and Lithuania came to be termed. In the year 1567, there is express mention of two heads who dealt with all tax affairs 'in the name of all Jewish communities in . . . the Duchy of Lithuania.' From about 1569 we have ordinances enacted by 'select men from all the lands of Lithuania', who defined their actions as being performed in the name of 'all the communities of the states of Lithuania whose authority has been invested in us' (I. Halperin, *East European Jewry*, Jerusalem, 1968, p. 49). The same ordinances that mention the 'select men . . . of Lithuania' provide for meetings to be held once every three years and 'nine heads of states and three rabbis were elected' as a first step (*ibid.*). This number of representatives may indicate that Lithuania had already instituted three 'communities [that are] heads of courts'. In any case the Council of the Land of Lithuania was constituted on this pattern of three ruling communities from 1623, when there was an agreement signed by the three communities constituting the Council – Brest-Litovsk, Grodno and Pinsk – marking out the 'boundaries and surroundings' of those regions under the jurisdiction of each. After some generations these three were joined by two more partners – Vilna and Slutsk. In any case, only a handful of communities controlled and determined the affairs of the Council of Lithuania.

In Poland the structure was different. There the communities joined together as 'districts' even before the Council of the Lands of Poland was organized. Thus, for example, the district of 'Great Poland' began to take shape as early as 1519 and was in due course headed by the community of Poznan (Posen). Other regions seem to have come into being only in the second half of the sixteenth century. In any case, by the end of the 1570s we hear of 'the Rabbis of the Three States' of Poland and 'the Judges of the Three Lands'.

The Local Community

Both in Poland and Lithuania, the Councils were established on the groundwork of the local community organization, particularly of those in the large cities. In 1595 the community of Cracow approved a series of ordinances that reflect the institutions and life of that large community. They were written in Yiddish, with a considerable admixture of Hebrew words and sentences (M. Balaban, ed., 'Die Krakauer Juden-gemeinde-Ordnung von 1595 und ihre Nachträge', *Jahrbuch der Jüdisch-Literarischen Gesellschaft*, Frankfurt a.M, 10 [1913] 296–360; 11 [1916], 88–114). Cracow was the chief community in the region of 'Little Poland' and one of the leading communities in the Council of the Lands. In the year when the ordinances were enacted, this community had 'four heads, five [*boni viri*], fourteen *kahal*, three lower judges . . . three secondary judges . . . three tertiary judges . . . three keepers of accounts . . . five wardens [*gabbayim*] . . . five notables in charge of the orphans . . . and wardens of the state tax on alcoholic beverages' (*ibid.*, 10, p. 316). The ordi-

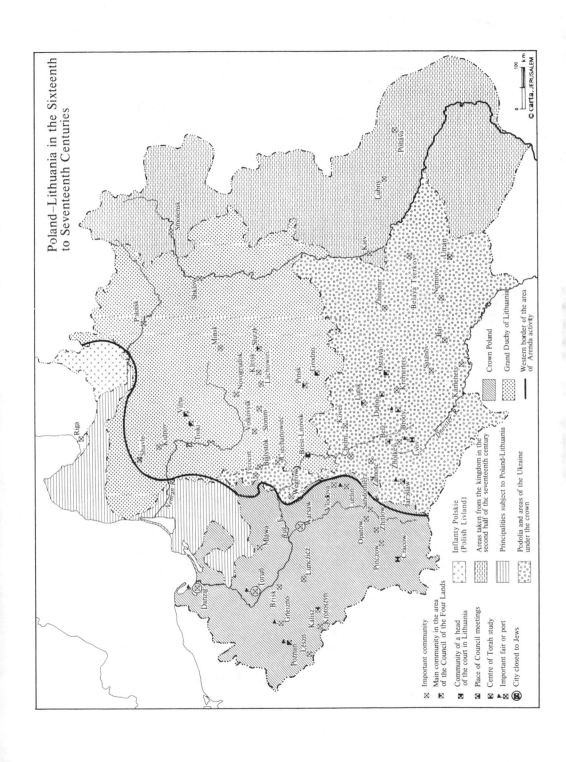

Poland–Lithuania in the Sixteenth
to Seventeenth Centuries

Riga

Shavle
Smolensk
Polotsk
Shklov
Minsk
Kaunas
Vilna
Novogrudok
Troki
Kleisk · Sluzk
Lachowiec
Tykocin
Volkovisk
Slonim
Grodno
Pinsk
Bialystok
Brest-Litovsk
Ciechanowiec
Lubny
Kiev
Zhitomir
Belaya Tserkov
Uman
Nemirov
Bar
Suano
Ostrava
Kremenets
Kamenets
Łuck
Dubno
Brody
Kovel
Chelm
Belz
Lvov
Zholkev
Jarosław
Zamość
Lublin
Sandomierz
Opatów
Żółtów
Uchanów
Warsaw
Węgrów
Cracow
Pińczów
Lunczice
Brisk
Łowicz
Mława
Gnezmo
Poznan
Leszn
Kalisz
Krotoszyn
Toruń
Danzig
Lubny
Połtava

Crown Poland

Grand Duchy of Lithuania

Western border of the area
of Arenda activity

100   km

© carta, JERUSALEM

Inflanty Polskie
(Polish Livland)

Areas taken from the kingdom in the
second half of the seventeenth century

Principalities subject to Poland-Lithuania

Podolia and areas of the Ukraine
under the crown

⊠ Important community

⊠ Main community in the area
   of the Council of the Four Lands

⊠ Community of a head
   of the court in Lithuania

⊠ Place of Council meetings

⊠ ▲ Centre of Torah study

⊠ ▲ Important fair or port

⊗ City closed to Jews

nances clearly specify the range of activities and precise authority of each group of community officials, for example, 'the wardens are required to visit, each of them during the month that he carries out his function, all the houses under their supervision for purposes of charity, and the bath-house and the butcher shops at least once during their month of office; and they are required to supervise the way matters are arranged, and likewise [to oversee] the bath-attendants and the butchers' (*ibid.*, p. 341). The authority of the three grades of judges (*dayyanim*) is specified according to the amount of money involved in cases of dispute. The 'lower' judges were authorized to deal with any dispute whatsoever 'from the value of a farthing up to and including ten gold pieces' (*ibid.*, p. 331). The 'secondary' judges were authorized to deal with disputes concerning amounts 'from ten . . . to one hundred gold pieces' (*ibid.*, p. 332). 'The tertiary High Judges' were authorized to deal with any dispute involving more than one hundred gold pieces (*ibid.*, pp. 332–3). There were many heads of *yeshivot* whose status depended on the academy they ran (often using private resources) and their student body. Over all the judges and scholars teaching in the city was the Head or 'Father' of the Court, who was the Chief Rabbi of the city. He was its spiritual leader and the head of the town's principal *yeshiva*, which was always maintained by public funds. In a leading city like Cracow or Poznan, the Head of the Court was also the Chief Rabbi of the region. In due course the Cracow community also maintained a town preacher whose function was to preach to the people in the synagogue and who held a respected position in the community.

Those elected in Cracow included minor officials such as 'beadles and the cantor for the old [main] synagogue . . . bath-house attendants, ritual slaughterers, the chief beadle of the congregation and beadles and teachers for the [minor] synagogues' (*ibid.*, p. 323). The community also appointed a '*shtadlan* [intercessor] to accompany whoever needed him' (*ibid.*); that is, the *shatdlan* did not represent the Jewish community vis-à-vis the state, the ministers, or the city, as he had previously; this was now the function of the heads of the community. The *shtadlan* was appointed for minor daily affairs 'in order to ease the burden of negotiations by the leaders, who are unable to intercede on behalf of each and every person. The needs of our people are numerous, they are impatient. So let him [the *shtadlan*] accompany each individual who so requires, to the judge, or the clerk or the official or the customs officials or the town councillors, or to any place that may be necessary' (*ibid.* p. 328). Thus this community provided its members with a kind of advocate who interceded with the lower level of gentile authorities.

The Cracow community also provided assessment committees that fixed the amount of taxes that each member had to pay to the state and for the upkeep of the community. The methods used by these committees were carefully regulated, as were their methods of checking declarations of property. All functionaries of the community were headed by the monthly warden, and during his month of office, he was indeed the ruler of the community. He supervised all office-bearers and, together with the Head of the Court, gave guidance, took part in legal cases and represented the community in general.

The Cracow ordinances of 1595 show that the Jewish communities in Poland considered themselves entitled and even required to oversee the whole range of

Jewish life, to offer guidance, to supervise behaviour and even to inflict punishment when a Jew deviated from the straight path. Regulations covered commerce and commercial practice, the rate of interest on loans to gentiles, which was not less than 12%; who should receive charity, who should give it and when it should not be given; when Jews should refrain from entering the streets of the gentiles, how they were to react when insulted; how to behave in order to obtain their merchandise cheaply; what should be done in order to prevent rubbish and manure from being flung in the streets from over the wall. 'Neighbours are required to inform the officials who are required to demand the fine' from the person who transgressed the regulations governing cleanliness (*ibid.,* pp. 359–60).

Other communities had similar regulations. In 1629 in Poznan, 'the residents in the Trees Street complained bitterly because they pay most of the money for [the removal of] refuse but the refuse was not being removed from their street at all'. The *kesherim* ('selectmen') of Poznan, an advisory institution to the community, composed of 'elder statesmen' who had formerly served as community leaders, advised, in response to this outcry, that 'the community is required to appoint special officers in the Trees Street who will supervise the removal of the refuse and the cleaning of the street as is done in the Synagogue Street. And the refuse money they collect from the Trees Street shall be used specifically for the removal of refuse from this street' (D. Avron, ed., *Pinkas Hakesherim,* Jerusalem, 1966, para. 108, p. 21). A year afterwards the same community of Poznan passed an even more comprehensive regulation: 'In each street there shall be special officials, two appointed in each street; they shall be in charge of the affairs of their street. The two shall collect within their street for the needs and expenditures of that street in order that the camp of Israel may be holy' (*ibid.,* para. 141, p. 28). Three years later the *kesherim* established that 'the community ... are required to appoint officers in each separate Jewish street, as has been customary long since; and the refuse and removal fee shall be collected by them as is the practice' (*ibid.,* para. 216, p. 43). Thus the cleaning of streets was an old and long-established requirement and the constant concern of the Poznan community heads.

Such arrangements show that the heads of the communities used to keep careful check on those matters with which their ordinances dealt. Various instructions detailed by the communities show considerable awareness of the character of the problems with which they tried to grapple. In Cracow, for example, they determined the methods of teaching to be adopted and the principles in accordance with which the teachers were to be paid. What emerges clearly is the differentiation according to the subjects taught: a sliding scale was used, specifying payment by the hour but also establishing the number of hours to be taught in accordance with the difficulty of the subject. The attempt to restrict the teacher's rights regarding his hours of teaching is itself instructive. It is a characteristic expression of the community's authority over the individual, so that he should do nothing to his own advantage which might harm the group as a whole. In this case, the teacher was not to earn more than was compatible with satisfactory instruction (Balaban, *op. cit.,* 10, pp. 99–100).

The budgets of the communities in Poland were aimed primarily at protecting the Jews against harm from the gentile environment. More than 70% was expended on monetary contributions and gifts for potentates and dignitaries, for intercession and mediation actions and litigation against persons who had injured Jews. Of the remaining 30%, about half was spent on administration and salaries and about half on charity. In Poznan during the first half of the seventeenth century, salaried staff included physicians, the *shtadlan*, cantors, beadles, attendants, midwives, Jewish and gentile watchmen and the scribe. In this city the highest salaries were paid to the Head of the Court and the community preacher. Charity items included a considerable sum for poor brides – both for dowries and for the weddings.

The community leaders were formally elected for one year, with the exception of certain functionaries whose posts required expert knowledge and special status, such as the Head of the Court. The latter was usually elected for three years and was usually re-appointed for three more years. Elections generally took place during the intermediate days of Passover. There was a small group of electors: it has been calculated that, in general, the proportion of persons with voting rights in each community did not exceed 11–12% and sometimes fell as low as 4–5%. The voters usually elected arbitrators from their own number, between five and nine as a rule. These met and elected the communal offiers. In the elected institutions in practice the functions were conducted in monthly succession. Hence the term for the leading *parnass* is 'the *parnass* of the month'; this monthly rotation was usually also in effect for the wardens. The individual therefore usually carried out his duties during 'his' month, after which he became a member of the institutional council like the rest, until his term to take an active lead came round once again.

Many communities also had various guilds and associations that people joined on a voluntary basis. In the year 1640, for example, the barbers of Cracow, who were also barber-surgeons in those days, united in a craft guild. Its main purpose was to prevent journeymen from engaging in the profession until they had worked long enough to be recognized as established craftsmen. They therefore provided that no member 'is entitled to keep with him more than one lad to teach him the craft; and that he [the lad] shall join him for three consecutive years. And during two full years the said lad is not entitled to let blood for any man whatever in the world. And likewise in the third year he may let blood only if his master is standing by him, so as to learn his craft in the best way, so that he should not faint or be negligent in his work.' Yet together with such regulations of a strictly professional character, the barber-surgeons also provide that a chest should be made 'in order to collect charity among themselves according to the generosity of each one, week by week'. They also bound themselves to a fair price level and fixed regulations to prevent internal competition. This group also had a social character, as they 'undertook . . . to live in brotherhood and friendship with one another, and to rejoice affectionately at the three festivals, to be fully glad and joyous with a glad and cheerful heart' (F. Wetstein, *Kadmoniot mi-Pinkasim Yeshanim,* Cracow, 1892, no. 9, pp. 28–9). Together with such guilds we also hear of associations to fulfil the last rites for the dead (*Ḥevra Kaddisha*), for visiting the sick, for reciting Psalms together, and so on. It is possible that the social tendencies emanating from Safed influenced the establishment of such associations during the second half of the period.

Methods and Practices of the Councils of the Lands

The large communities were well organized within their cities, although smaller ones no doubt were less fully developed than places like Cracow and Poznan. It was on this firm basis of the closely knit local community that the complicated structure of the central territorial leadership of Polish and Lithuanian Jewry was based in the late sixteenth and early seventeenth centuries. During the latter half of this period a similar organization appears to have developed in Bohemia and Moravia, although its regulations are known only from 1651 onwards. In Poland and Lithuania the large community usually controlled its environs. These, as we have remarked, consisted of neighbouring townlets and villages in which there was no organized Jewish community or where the organization was still new and weak. In the course of time, these communities and their environs organized into a bloc of the entire region, known as a *galil* or district. In a broader context, this was called a 'state' (*medinah*) or 'land' (*erez*). The representatives of the communities in a district used to meet regularly at the District Councils. The rabbi of the chief community in the district was regarded as the Head of the Court of the entire district and was known as 'The Head of the Principality Court'. The District Councils and their institutions enacted ordinances and laid down instructions. Sometimes a chief community would call representatives of subordinate communities to pass ordinances *ad hoc*. Thus, for example, in the year 1602 'the heads of the people met together, the heads and leaders of the holy congregation of Vladimir [in Volhynia] . . . with the arbitrators of each community, these being all the smaller communities of the territories belonging to the holy congregation of Vladimir, who were selected from the communities to sit with our Head of the Court to take steps to prevent the profanation of Sabbath and festivals' (H. H. Ben-Sasson in *Zion*, 21 [1956], 195).

In Poland, the heads of the States and their rabbis customarily met at the fairs of Lublin and Jaroslaw. It may be assumed that at first there was a gathering of 'the Judges of the Lands', which was a court of major scholars from the main communities of the various Lands whose authority was acknowledged. It was called upon to decide during these fairs various matters affecting Polish Jewry as a whole, disputes between the Lands themselves, or between communities, and appeals made by individuals against decisions made by other rabbis or courts. The deliberations of this court inevitably assumed a certain public and political character. The heads of the various States gradually joined the judges, they began to work together and thus developed the 'Council of the Lands' of Poland, at least in the form known to us from 1580 onwards. It is also referred to as 'The Council of the Four Lands', although its structure was sometimes based on a division into more than four Lands. This Council consisted of two 'Houses': (1) the heads of the principalities, selectmen and representatives of the territories, forming a kind of Parliament of Polish Jewry; and (2) 'the Masters of Justice of the Four Lands', the institution that grew out of 'the Judges of the Lands' and that became a sort of Supreme Court of Polish Jewry, consisting of a collegium of elected judges.

We learn of the relations between these two bodies – *i.e.*, the 'Parliament' and 'Supreme Court' – from the preamble to the ordinances regarding the *hetter iskah* (the legal formula permitting Jews to take interest-bearing loans from one another) and the regulations for Sabbath prohibitions issued in 1607. These regulations were adopted 'when the leaders and heads of the people from three Lands were met together and devoted their attention to the situation of the country'. It describes in detail how they deliberated on what was amiss in the life of the Jews. They therefore took the initiative in passing ordinances. In order to draw them up, however, they 'chose rabbis from the large congregations', and the latter were the ones who actually formulated them. At the same time 'the heads of the principalities undertook . . . that each within his own territory would impose the observation of whatever would be ordained' (H.H. Ben-Sasson, *Hagut Vehanhagah,* Jerusalem, 1959, pp. 259–60). The task and authority of enforcement and execution of ordinances drafted by the rabbis was entrusted to the leaders – one has to assume that actual power rested with them – just as governance of the society and the accompanying initiative was in their hands. This division of activities was not always strictly observed, but as a rule there was satisfactory cooperation between the parliamentary and judicial sections of the councils.

In Lithuania the leadership structure differed in several respects. 'The Council of the Principality of Lithuania' or 'The Council of the Principality' was not structured on Lands. Three, four and finally five major communities were the main constituents of the Council, which consisted of the community heads and rabbis and was divided into the two chief sections described above. Though 'spokesmen' were permitted to appear on behalf of the other communities, they could not take part in the deliberations, as they were not on the council. Although there are several indications that the Council of Lithuania may have preceded the Council of the Lands of Poland, we have information on its activities only from the year 1623 onwards. The two Councils of Poland and Lithuania continued their activities even after the period dealt with here and were abolished by the Polish authorities in 1764 (see Part VI).

The ordinances of Moravia in 1651 mention, and occasionally quote, earlier ordinances, but their 1651 compilation is the first to survive intact as the work and resolve of councils conducting Jewish affairs in this region. We learn that 'six persons were selected . . . to serve as heads of the State; namely, in each territory there will be two . . . heads of the State, so that in all there will be six heads of the State . . . and they shall have coercive authority to ban and punish sinners and rebels, and shall conduct their leadership strictly'. Another six persons were chosen to collect taxes – again, two in each territory. The selection was carried out in an interesting fashion. Each of the communities constituting the Council sent emissaries to the 'Council of Reappointment' where 'it was resolved to gather together . . . to reappoint heads of State and selectmen'. The representation of each community was fixed according to its share in the tax. The Council of Reappointment met at first as if it were a convention of separate territorial 'councils', 'emissaries from the Upper Territories together and emissaries of the Central Territory together and emissaries of the Third Territory together. And each territory separately was required to select from among them five intelligent, understanding and informed men.' These fifteen persons formed a kind of enlarged committee that dealt with the affairs of the principality both separately and together with the heads of the principality. In order to elect the heads of the principality all the emissaries and all the office-bearers who had been elected at the previous council came together and then again separated according to the three territories. They placed slips in a ballot box and withdrew them one by one until nine arbitrators had been chosen. These nine arbitrators chose the six heads of the principality, two from each territory; and the six tax-assessors were selected on the same principle. Only in the last resort did the referees decide according to the majority, and they did their best to achieve unanimity (I. Halperin, ed., *Ordinances of Moravia,* Jerusalem, 1951, para. 24–45, pp. 11–16). The Councils of Poland and Lithuania usually endeavoured to meet at regular intervals – the Councils of Poland twice a year and the Council of Lithuania every two years – but they were not always able to do so. The regional councils also endeavoured to meet at regular intervals. The Councils, particularly in Poland, had a complete hierarchy of functions and titles. They would appoint 'a *parnass* of the house of Israel of the Four Lands', who headed the Council in both internal and external affairs. One of the principality heads was always selected for this office, and not one of the rabbis. Next to him in rank was the 'trustee of the House of Israel of the Four Lands', who was the treasurer and chief secretary of the Council. This office carried a salary, and rabbis were also appointed to it. The trustee was under the authority of the '*parnass* of the house of Israel'. Another honourable and important post was that of the '*shtadlan* of the house of Israel', who received a large salary and was required to be present at all times at the royal court or at the meeting-places of the State Sejms in order to present the Jewish view on matters coming before the authorities. The Council also had a 'writer' or secretary and in the course of time there was need for several. The function of the tax-assessors was important. The Council of the State of Lithuania had generally parallel functions and offices, but for a considerable time it was headed by the rabbi of Brest-Litovsk.

The proportion of persons among all the householders in the communities with the right to vote for the Council varied according to the size of the community and the number of smaller communities under its authority. None of the residents of these small communities, who constituted one-quarter and possibly one-third of the Jews of Poland, had any voting rights. At the very most the right of election to the Councils belonged to some 5% of all householders and at times it fell as low as 1%. In Lithuania their participation was even more restricted.

The representatives of the chief communities at the Council of the Lands were elected by different systems and at different times, which varied from one community to another. In some communities they were elected by seven arbitrators during the intermediate days of Passover. In some they were elected by all the higher echelons of the communal apparatus, 'by the magistrate at full table'. And in some they were elected by a body of thirty or thirty-two persons, consisting of the heads of the community together with 'outstanding individuals', chiefly wardens and judges. Representatives of the districts were usually elected by 'district arbitrators', or by the communities. Elections in the constituent Lithuanian communities were first conducted by a body of eleven to sixteen persons: heads, notables, and the leading persons of that community. In due course, elections were in the hands of a group of 'twenty-seven persons', whose composition corresponded to that of the thirty-two in Poland.

In the formal view of the Polish authorities the Councils were the tax-farmers for the entire Jewish population of the country. They conducted negotiations concerning the rate of taxes, and their collection was entrusted to them. However, many sources indicate that the state authorities were well aware that the Councils served as institutions of Jewish autonomy in the full sense of self-government. They tacitly acquiesced in this fact but were not prepared to give any official confirmation of their autonomous status. As the bodies responsible for state taxation, the Councils allocated the tax to be paid by all the Jews of the kingdom of Poland and all those of the Grand Duchy of Lithuania among the various communities and districts. Assessment as well as collection were based on lists and evaluations prepared by the communities. Sometimes the Councils intervened in the communities to ensure justice and fairness in the distribution of the tax. In 1627, for example, the Council of Lithuania decided to send 'emissaries' to the communities 'to establish . . . in each district a fair and true amount . . . the rich will pay more and the poor less'. However, this aspiration towards a true distribution of the tax burden was accompanied by the need for effective collection. For the Council required the said emissaries 'to choose from the society two or three of the wealthy members from whom all the monies to be collected shall be demanded . . . and to entrust those . . . rich men with a rod of power . . . to collect every requisite amount' (S. Dubnow, ed., *Pinkas Hamedinah*, Berlin, 1925, para. 125, p. 30).

As the situation of the Jews grew worse in Poland and Lithuania, particularly after the Massacres of 1648 and 1649, it became steadily more difficult to collect the taxes. The Council employed all kinds of methods to make collection more efficient, but the methods proved unsuccessful. The difficulty in balancing the Council budget was that its expenditure was based neither on the taxes that had to be paid to the government nor on allocations for internal Jewish needs. It is reasonable to assume that the major portion of its expenditure went for defence, diplomatic intercession, money contributions and other requirements calling for prompt actions, and that these sums were kept secret from the authorities, with no recorded details even in Hebrew. Requirements of this kind always came suddenly, so that it was difficult to foresee or balance the budget for such expenditures. It was not through lack of economic acumen but through the unique legal and social position of the Jews and its deterioration in the course of time that the Councils were always deeply in debt. A study of their registers shows that they endeavoured to keep their accounts balanced by various credit devices, which became more daring and hazardous from year to year. Hence the tension and difficulties in collecting taxes grew steadily worse as the debts of the Councils and the communities increased.

This is particularly striking in the case of the Lithuanian Council, of which we possess a complete register of ordinances. In addition, it refused to permit smaller communities to participate in the central leadership, and, as a result, the latter wished to break the yoke of the central Council. The individual communities gradually established their own form of income based on indirect taxes placed on consumer articles. This was called the *korobka,* or, 'shopping basket'. At first this tax was levied chiefly on slaughtered animals, on every head of cattle or poultry consumed. Later certain communities began to levy this tax on income as well. This innovation made the traditional sources of income of the central authority even less practical than before.

The Councils also directed the communities between their official sessions. Here as well the system of operation is particularly clear for Lithuania, where the communities that made up the Council agreed on methods of consultation by correspondence when action was necessary between sessions. They arranged which community should write first and to which community the document should finally be returned. As a rule, both the right of initiative and of final confirmation was granted to the community of Brest-Litovsk. When a new community, such as Vilna, attained the right of participating in the Council, the order of correspondence was rearranged:

> When the heads of the holy community of Brześć [Brest-Litovsk] send letters to communities they should act according to the ancient ordinance for transmission in this order: first to the community of Grodno, which will express its views and send it on to the community of Pinsk, and the heads of the holy community of Pinsk will send their opinion and the opinion of the holy community of Grodno to the holy community of Brześć. With regard to transmission to the community of Vilna their practice shall be . . . that in respect of money they shall likewise send to the holy community of Vilna; and they shall send all the opinions to the holy community of Brześć (*ibid.,* para. 699, p. 168).

The new member, Vilna, was therefore at first permitted only partial participation in this system of correspondence, restricted to budgetary and financial matters alone.

In theory the Councils regarded themselves as responsible for conducting the affairs of the Jewish communities and instructing them with respect to all matters that might arise. As a rule, to be sure, they were careful not to intervene in the relations between a community and its individual members, but there were exceptions even in this, particularly in Lithuania. There was a far greater tendency for the Councils to intervene in relations between communities and districts. The letter and spirit of the Council ordinances show that these bodies saw themselves as general mentors to the local communities and as their instructors in practical matters. They framed 'standing regulations' to provide a framework for communal behavior. The Councils felt they were called upon to regulate matters arising from innovations in economic activity, in Jewish society and in life-style; and, as we have noted, they generally did this with the approval of leading scholars in session at the Court of the Council. However, many hints in the provisions of these Councils indicate that their demands often exceeded the response from the communities. The Council's claim to central authority was never fully implemented, nor were most of its aspirations.

As far as social relations and general attitudes are concerned, the ordinances of the Councils, especially in Lithuania, reflect a marked oligarchic tendency. Their ordinances regarding public discipline, which were intended for those who might try to rebel, are sharp in their wording and threaten severe punishment. This style reflects not only the aims of the rulers but also points to the existence of an opposition to the ruling circle, which seems to have been comparatively strong within the communities and grew steadily more forceful towards the end of the period under consideration.

When the innovations in the economic life of Poland became an integral part of the Jewish economic situation (see page 641), the Councils established a number of pertinent ordinances: for example, 'the right of prior claim on the Arenda' and the right to renew a leasehold (see page 643). This was in order to prevent competition between Jews when leasing estates or economic facilities within an estate (*e.g.,* a mill or an inn) from a Polish noble. As far as the nobleman was concerned, the objects he offered for lease were placed on a free market of competitors. In practice, however, the market was closed, as his offer was always responded to by one Jew only, the former lease-holder. As has already been remarked, the effectiveness of this ordinance diminished considerably after the Massacres of 1648–9.

The Councils were also aware of *halakhic* problems connected with credit, on which the expanding Jewish economy was increasingly dependent. Charging interest from other Jews became an acceptable practice to *halakhists* and moralists (see the opinion of the Maharal of Prague, page 644). In order to make the new economic situation comply with Torah law, the Council of 1607 required the scholars who had met there, headed by R. Joshua Falk – whose name was attached to these regulations for generations – to prepare a detailed system of rules that would set down the correct method of borrowing and lending at interest in accordance with the *halakhah*; this became the well-known *hetter iskah* method. They were also concerned with the economic and moral problems deriving from the fact that Jews, as representatives of the lord and owner of an estate, in fact became masters of peasants who, in turn, had to work on the Sabbath. A gathering of the community of Vladimir and its environs in 1602 considered this problem and proclaimed that the said 'hard labour . . . as is generally known . . . is prohibited, but a Jew shall release the village gentiles from work they have to do on Sabbaths and festivals. . . . Let the Jew see to it that the norm [*i.e.,* the number of days that the peasants were legally required to dedicate to the estate] . . . shall be performed on weekdays and not on Sabbaths. And if the villagers are obligated to work every day of the week . . . then . . . he shall waive his claim and permit them to rest on the Sabbath and festivals entirely.' The duty of entirely renouncing one-seventh of the working days of the serfs, at a time when the general tendency of the Polish nobility was to burden their serfs as much as possible, is explained by the heads of these communities on the grounds that it offers a sense of liberty, a participation in the fate of the serfs and an expression of the success and economic plenty of the Jews in those places and at those times. In the opinion of the regulators, the serfs were to be exempted from work on the Jewish days of rest if there were no alternative because

> while living in exile and in the Egyptian captivity our forefathers . . . themselves chose this Sabbath day for rest before they were commanded concerning it. They were aided by Heaven to establish it as a day of rest for all ages. And therefore in a place where gentiles are in the service of Jews, it is incumbent upon us to fulfil the commandment of the Torah and of the sages. Far be it for us to rebel against

the source of all blessing [the Lord] by means of the good with which He has blessed us. And let the name of Heaven be hallowed and not profaned, heaven forbid (Ben-Sasson in *Zion*, 21 [1956], 205).

They did not always make their decisions with such firmness and social generosity, but the various ordinances of the Councils, the District Councils and individual communities show that all these problems concerned them deeply. They dealt not only with serf-labour on the Sabbath day on estates leased out to Jews, but were also concerned with problems of pigs and other ritually inedible beasts, which the Jew received as part of the inventory of livestock, with the opening of inns on the Sabbath and with similar problems.

It seems that the Councils also did their best to reduce the number of bankruptcies and to punish those who were responsible for them, as well as to prevent unfair competition between Jews in acquiring non-Jewish clients. The Councils passed many ordinances regarding the study of Torah, the upkeep of *yeshivot* and their students and concerning supervision of sermons and preachers. They attempted also to pass sumptuary regulations dealing with festive clothing and public feasts. The express reason for this was to avoid arousing gentile envy of the Jews. It is possible that an additional reason was to prevent waste and licentiousness. There are some who suspect that the regulators wished to ensure that the poor should not adorn themselves or appear in public in a fashion that did not befit their social station.

The achievements of the Councils were appreciable with respect to the protection and defence of Jews. The Polish nobility actually suspected that they had succeeded in persuading members of the Polish Sejm (or parliament) to make use of their veto power in order to interrupt deliberations when there was a danger that decisions might be passed to the detriment of the Jews. This suspicion, expressed mainly by Jew-haters, was doubtlessly exaggerated, but may have had some basis in fact. From the ordinances of the Council of Lithuania it is clear that the latter was always on the watch to exact 'vengeance'. This meant that the Council covered part of the expenses required to induce the Polish courts to punish any person guilty of murdering a Jew. The amount of their participation was determined by the economic position of the victim's family and of the community in which he lived.

To sum up, between the second half of the sixteenth century and the second half of the eighteenth century (see Part VI), there functioned in Poland-Lithuania, Bohemia and Moravia a system of autonomous Jewish institutions based on a trend towards territorial concentration of leadership. Their aspirations in this respect exceeded their achievements, yet their accomplishments were still considerable. From their ordinances and activities we can perceive a vigilant social initiative, which recognized all dangers and reacted to old and new alike by methods whose elasticity and realism were outstanding. Their range of activities, their organization and structure, and their budgetary framework should be assessed not only in terms of what they tried to be, but also from the fact that their responses were to challenges offered by chance occasions and their activities were mostly in response to what was being wrought by others.

Social Tension and Council Leadership

In the ordinances, as well as in the sermons and moralist literature of Poland and Lithuania, we find a constant fear of divisive quarrels. Such factiousness is described as a permanent element in community life. It appeared, on the one hand, as deriving from individual aspirations for power, and, on the other hand, as attempts on the part of the lower classes to demand justice for themselves. The language of the heads of the Lithuanian Council towards the latter is exceedingly sharp.

> They are idlers, therefore they sit around with the worthless . . . and they talk scandal and laugh and joke at the deeds of the Seven Worthies of the city. . . . It is the duty of the leaders in each and every congregation to break the fangs of these evil-doers with severe punishments that should bring them to the very gates of death, to set them apart . . . with every force at their disposal (Dubnow, *op. cit.*, para. 59, p. 12).

The bitterness was doubtlessly nourished by the control exercised by the large communities over the small surrounding communities – a control that was far more absolute in Lithuania. But it was also sustained by the class interests of the upper echelons. From the ordinances we learn of a certain paternalism on the part of the wealthy circles towards the poorer groups. An interesting expression of this was found in certain ordinances that deal with charity for 'bringing brides under the bridal canopy', and, at the same time, with questions of female domestic servants and wet-nurses in Jewish homes. Among the Jewish public, many of whom were growing wealthy, there was an increasing demand for Jewish domestic help. Jewesses were desired both on account of their reliability in respect to the ritual food laws of *kashrut* and also because the moral and social danger of introducing young Christian women into their homes as servants was clearly recognized. There was an ancient and hallowed tradition that the community was required to support the daughters of the poor, to give them dowries and clothing, in order that they might be able to wed when they reached marriageable age. The communal leaders of Cracow combined these two objectives in the year 1595. They provided that 'if the daughter of a poor man or woman shall reach the age of ten years and they refuse to permit her to enter service [as a domestic servant], then if he or she has been receiving an allowance [from the charity fund] they will not receive it any more. And when the said daughter marries he will not receive anything as a contribution to her wedding, even if he no longer receives an allowance' (Balaban, *op. cit.*, 10, p. 345). Forty-three years later, the Council of the State of Lithuania ordained that it was the duty of poor girls from the environs of the large communities 'to enter into service for three years'. 'Poor virgins from the vicinity . . . are not to be given anything until they have in hand . . . some visible proof from the leaders of the community that they have served in the homes of householders dwelling within the community for a period of three years from the time that they were twelve years old, since this age is fitting for domestic service.' They also required that whatever money such a girl has earned during the three years 'shall be given to the Treasurer of the city and not to her father; and if she wishes to make herself a Sabbath dress from her wages, let her not do so without the knowledge and approval of the Treasurer' (Dubnow, *op. cit.,* para. 128, p. 32).

Here the class attitude towards the people from the environs can clearly be seen. The details of the ordinance point out the paternalistic assumption that neither the poor girl nor her father know what is good for them. The worthies seem to have assumed that they were doing a favour to a girl from a poor home and a small community when they required her to serve in the home of a decent householder in a large community, where she would learn the manners of good families as well as the value of money.

Yet there were also bounds to class considerations of this kind. We find a very interesting example of a conflict between a desire to exploit the poverty of a young couple for the convenience of a wealthy young family and the deeply rooted Jewish morality involved in fulfilling the commandments of regular familial cohabitation and the setting-up of a family. The Council of Lithuania in the year 1637 expressed itself against 'a man . . . who wishes to give his child to the home of the wet-nurse or to keep her and her husband in his home, when the wet-nurse is required to take oath or give her hand not to engage in sexual intercourse with her husband' (*ibid.,* para. 326, p. 69). The aim of such an arrangement was to ensure that there would be a continual supply of milk from the Jewish wet-nurse for the rich child without any interruption caused by pregnancy. The Council specifies, 'we hereby annul the said promise, and she or her husband is entitled to annul the agreement.' The Council would annul an agreement of this kind 'even when the agreement shall have been made with the approval of her husband'. It also expressly prohibits 'any man from hiring a Jewish serving woman or wet-nurse who needs to be with her husband'. In spite of this the Council was prepared to agree to an arrangement of this kind, which prevents sexual relations between a married couple for a long period, if 'there are urgent medical reasons for it according to an experienced physician'. If it is to the advantage of the child that has come into the world, 'everything is permissible, and the giving of the hand in agreement is valid' (*ibid.*).

The ordinances of the Councils and the communities also indicate another kind of social tension between the permanent residents and the various beggars. In particular they were apprehensive regarding vagabonds and vagrants. The ordinances of Lithuania give express warnings to such persons, particularly stressing the preachers among them. They were forbidden to speak from the synagogue dais without the specific permission of the community representatives, and they were charged with moral transgressions. The poor used to complain about such hard-heartedness. An expression of this tension can be found in the record of the *kesherim* of Poznan, who constituted one of the leading institutions of the community. They noted in their register,

the outcry of the masses at the large number of collections for the various funds . . . and for this reason many of them who cannot give are shamed. . . . And above all the women [protest against] those women who gather at the entrance to the women's section of the synagogue and let none of them depart unless she puts money [into a box or plate held by the poor women]. They sometimes also jeer at the women after this fashion: 'You have money for food, but not for putting here?' The congregation is therefore required to make an end of the charity-plates at the entrance at once (Avron, *op. cit.*, para. 446, p. 88).

Yet the whole gamut of deeds and regulations of the communities and the Councils make it clear that conflicts of this kind, in spite of the bitter feelings they aroused on occasion, were only incidental to the life and morality of the communities. The magistrates regarded themselves bound, in accordance with the Torah, to be concerned for all their Jews. Thus it was laid down in 1651 in Moravia:

> The leaders selected by the Jews of the country . . . shall take no active step whatever to extricate themselves from the trouble and burden of their leadership . . . and shall act in their high office for the sake of Heaven, and shall follow the path of the good, and then they shall prosper wherever they turn. And they shall themselves follow in detail the intercessions both for this country and for any other with our lord his Imperial Majesty, the Emperor and the ministers of the crown. And let them not be detained by rain or snow, nor rely upon others, and let them be industrious for the sake of Heaven, and may the good deeds of their fathers come to their aid (Halperin, *Ordinances of Moravia,* para. 50, p. 18).

Identical ideals are formulated in other Councils and by the communities.

In the leadership there was a tension of a different kind: between the rabbis, for whom the study of Torah was both an ideal and a life occupation, and the wealthy, respected householders, who directed communal affairs because the voters in communities and Councils had elected them to that position. The scholars complained when these lay leaders dared to allocate to themselves the authority to impose punishments for ordinances they had ordained, without the authorization of the scholars. They complained even more when the community heads simply exercised legal powers, as happened in many instances. During the 1620s R. Joel Sirkes of Poland wrote two letters to 'the nobles of the Land . . . namely the heads and leaders of the Land who are meeting in Council at the Lublin Fair', by which he meant the heads of the Council of the Lands of Poland. In the second letter he offers a complete set of detailed regulations to prevent the heads of the Lands from using the sanction of a *herem* (excommunication) without the authorization of scholars. 'Who has permitted you to proclaim excommunication against the entire community without the approval of the sages? And although you have been elected and deputized from all the communities in the realm, it is nonetheless conceivable that there is scarcely any validity in any of the penalties of the *herem* which you are imposing.' He advises them not to make any further use of excommunication as a punishment, but to make use of a system of 'secular' punishments. 'I do not say that ordinances should not be ordained . . . for certainly all that you have ordained until now and will continue to ordain is an urgent necessity. But you must specify in the ordinances . . . that anyone who transgresses against them will be fined such and such an amount of money, or will suffer some physical punishment, or will be expelled from the kingdom or handed over to the civil authorities as you see fit for the good of the generation' (Joel Sirkes, *Additional Bayit Ḥadash Responsa,* Korzec, 1785, no. 43, fol. 22v–23r).

The Maharal of Prague very sharply assailed the practice of community heads infringing upon the authority of the rabbis as judges. He finds a hint confirming his attitude in the Torah, writing 'it is possible that the Torah alluded to this in the commandment: "Thou shalt not plant an *ashera* for thyself which the Lord thy God doth hate" for the letters comprising the word *ashera,* a grove or tree planted for purposes of idolatry, are identical with the letters of the word *harosh* (the head). "Which the Lord thy God doth hate" refers then to the *ashera* or the head that is hated by the Lord thy God.' He relates having heard 'that the Head and his peers and those like him say "You are not our head of Court whom we are required to obey." And it is very hard to suffer their yoke.' He is of the opinion that because of such unqualified lay-courts 'people no longer have recourse to judgement according to the Torah', and he advises 'that he who fears God should be sensitive about this and not come for judgement before them [the lay judges]'. And it is not injustice alone that he fears. He describes how a leader of this kind, 'when he thinks that somebody is not behaving respectfully towards him and does not wish to be subject to him, he humiliates and distresses and persecutes him; and in his worthlessness he insults worthies and scholars, being of the opinion that these worthies and scholars do not wish to be subject to him.' His animosity reaches the point where he relates that 'my spirit cooled and the fire blazing in my heart was extinguished ... when I saw that they have neither offspring nor grandchild ... celebrated among the scholars or holding a place among the students' (*Gur Aryeh,* a commentary on Exodus).

It is possible that the situation was particularly grave in Moravia. Several of the scholars of Poland and Lithuania legitimized and confirmed the existence of these lay-courts. Yet this tension did not prevent fruitful and productive cooperation for the good of Jewry even in the ruling circle.

Jewish Leadership Within the German Empire

In the early part of the sixteenth century, the great *shtadlan* R. Joseph of Rosheim (1478–1554) was the leading Jewish figure within the Holy Roman Empire. We have already spoken of his success in employing new methods of intercession with the Protestant rebels and his conservative and confident approach towards the Imperial Catholic rulers (see pages 651–2). During the ferment that followed the emergence of Luther, R. Joseph journeyed from place to place every year to obtain the renewal of charters, to ensure the annulment of anti-Jewish decrees and to answer complaints and charges against the Jews. He employed various means towards this end. To Protestants 'I spoke to their hearts from the Bible.' Before the Imperial rulers and lawyers in the case of a blood libel in Moravia 'I had to produce all the ancient ratifications [charters and Papal Bulls] from the Popes and the Emperors to the city of Günzburg. There I copied them together with an apology in a manuscript and sent it to the King and his attendants so that they learnt the justice of our cause' (Kracauer, *op. cit.,* p. 90), *i.e.,* he presented a legal and historical argument based on the position adopted by leaders of the Church and state in previous generations.

In 1530 R. Joseph submitted 'paragraphs and ordinances' as 'the Emissary of all the Jews' to the Reichstag, which met in Augsburg. He relates that these ordinances were enacted at a general Council 'where the elected heads of many places and quarters' came together and resolved 'in the name of all of Jewry to pass fitting ordinances suited to the said Jewry, as they ordained and resolved'. These included an obligatory reduction in the rate of interest; an undertaking not to add interest to the principal (*i.e.*, not to charge compound interest); caution and fairness with regard to the pledges taken by the Jews; an undertaking not to grant loans to young unmarried sons of the burghers or to their daughters, attendants or servants, and not to purchase anything from them without the approval of the father or mother of the household. (This system was renewed for the Jews in the time of Napoleon, see Part VI.) They recommended moderation in collecting debts from orphans and widows and an undertaking to perform justice for Christians who brought complaints against Jews to the heads of the Jews and their judges. R. Joseph regarded it as a personal achievement that by proposing these ordinances to the emperor and the Reichstag he had prevented the issue of anti-Jewish decrees, which the authorities had been about to issue.

The stance of R. Joseph as the leader of Jewry was exceedingly cautious. When Solomon Molcho came to Regensburg in 1532 on behalf of David Reubeni to propose that the emperor 'should summon all the Jews to go to war against the Turk' (a formulation of the proposals of David Reubeni and Solomon Molcho which does not appear in this form in their own records), R. Joseph called these proposals 'strange ideas'. He relates: 'Hearing what was in his mind I wrote a letter to him and warned him not to rouse the Emperor lest the Great Fire consume him. And I removed from the city . . . in order that the Emperor should not say I was helping him in his ideas and activities'. He feared the harm to Jewry as a whole that might result from this daring attempt. Yet when Molkho died, he wrote of him that 'He died sanctifying the Name and faith of Israel, and he turned many away from sin. His soul rests in the Garden of Eden' (*ibid.*, p. 91). Although he recognized the potential danger from the emperor and warned against it, he reached the conclusion at the end of his life that the aim of the Lutherans was 'to riot against us and uproot that nation of Israel so that it should not be a people any more, by sundry kinds of harsh decrees and by destruction'. He also became increasingly aware that the Jews ought to pray for the peace of the Catholic emperor and the success of his forces against the Lutherans. When the Protestants were defeated by the emperor's army in 1547, he regarded this as a sign that 'the Lord had seen the suffering of His people, so he sent His angel, merciful rulers, to give strength and power to our Lord, the Emperor Karlein' (H. Fraenkel-Goldschmidt, ed., *Joseph of Rosheim, Sefer Hamikna,* Jerusalem, 1970, p. 74).

R. Joseph's leadership of the German Jews was strong and firm, and he directed Jewish economic activity so that it would be suited to the purposes of the central Christian authorities. With respect to the authorities, he used various methods to achieve success in the areas with which he concerned himself. But after Luther's rancorous writings of 1543 (see pages 649–51), he leaned towards a cautious submission to the protective rule of the Catholic emperor, for he felt that the hopes of the Jews depended on him.

The Council of 1603

After the death of R. Joseph of Rosheim the activities of the Jewish leadership in Germany declined. Early in the seventeenth century an attempt was made to conduct the affairs of Jewry within the German Empire after the style of the central Councils, which were just beginning to prove successful in the Slavic countries to the east. A Council of delegates and sages from most of the German communities met together in 1603 in Frankfurt on Main, a city with a history of continuous Jewish settlement from its beginnings. Those who met described themselves as 'heads of the people, communities and quarters . . . by the decree [this being a *halakhic* decision calling for the meeting of the Council and approving of its resolutions] of our Rabbis the sages of Ashkenaz' (M. Horovitz, ed., *Die Frankfurter Rabbiner versamnlung vom Jahre 1603*, Frankfurt a. M., 1897, p. 20). This session of the Council was referred to as 'when the Heads of the People gather together, the Tribes of Israel who are in all the Districts of Ashkenaz' (*ibid.*, p. 27). Those who dare to oppose its ordinances 'will revolt against the emissaries of the dispersed ones of Israel' (*ibid.*, p. 28). The purpose of the Council was defined in a way that indicates the beginnings of a permanent institution intended to prevent incipient anarchy. For those assembled came 'to meet and study the needs of the commonweal and to . . . legislate in accordance with the needs of the times, in order that the holy people may not be as a flock that has no shepherd' (*ibid.*, p. 20). The problems that faced Jewish autonomy are evident from the stern regulations against those who take their cases to gentile courts. Severe penalties are prescribed for those who dared to do this. The Council set out to re-establish proper communal methods of tax assessment and prescribed the duty of electing assessors in 'each community and quarter'. In order to ensure a regular income for Jewish defence needs, 'the rabbis of Ashkenaz have agreed to collect once a month from every man according to his material worth, one *pfennig* in the hundred from the month of Tishri 5365 [1605] and thereafter.' All the communities were required to transfer this tax to several main communities, and evasion on any excuse whatsoever was to be severely punished. The tax was levied 'in order that the total sum shall be accumulated from all the places . . . to select men who are personable and fit to appear in royal courts, to come and go at a propitious hour on behalf of the congregation of the Lord according to the need of the time with the help of their Deliverer who has not forsaken them'. The Council also prescribes exactly how the money is to be guarded: 'Let all the silver coins collected be placed at once in one closed chest intended specially for this purpose. And each of those set to manage these matters shall have a key to the said chest, and one shall not take out anything without the knowledge and approval of his colleague. . . . Let them act in good faith' (*ibid.*, pp. 21–2).

Like the Council of 1530, that of 1603 issued several ordinances with the aim of eradicating business practices that were morally unsatisfactory or that angered the host society. The Council denounced 'the wicked Jews' who deceived their gentile customers, 'making use of new coins some of which are completely worthless . . . they put them out deceitfully to blind the eyes of those who receive them in place of other coins that resemble them.' In addition to such trickery in money-changing, the

Council denounced 'those who demand payment of debts with dishonest documents and words'. The Council expressed its dissatisfaction that, as a result of such deeds, the gentiles comment, 'Where is the God of this people?' (*ibid.*, p. 24) rather than saying, 'the remnant of Israel will not deceive.' The Council warned against those who purchased stolen goods from gentiles and threatened to excommunicate 'anybody who has dealings with a notorious thief, purchasing from him or lending him money on any object'; it also pointed out the 'great trouble' caused to all Jewry in their times by these wicked deeds by a handful of Jews (*ibid.*, pp. 24–5).

As in Poland-Lithuania, in Germany, too, at that time attention was drawn to the danger to all Jewry from those who exploit credit, go bankrupt and give other Jews a bad name by 'the sound of a great commotion, the outcry of the gentiles at wicked men to be found among us . . . who come with false devices to purchase on credit or take loans from the gentiles which they do not intend to repay. And by this they cause much enmity . . . between the gentiles and ourselves. In addition this causes great profanation of the Name of the Lord.' The Council threatened excommunication and the cutting of all economic ties with anyone who could be suspected of deliberately declaring bankruptcy (*ibid.*, p. 25).

The Council of 1603 set out to regulate the methods of attestation for the rabbinate. It renewed an old ordinance 'that throughout Ashkenaz no rabbi shall be ordained as *Morenu* ['our Master'] save by the approval of three scholars, each heading a *yeshiva* in Ashkenaz . . . in order that the name of our Holy Torah may not be profaned' (*ibid.*, p. 24). The Council also endeavoured to determine the competence of the various rabbinical courts, establishing 'that no scholar, rabbi, head of a Court, or Court shall tresspass on his colleague's jurisdiction regarding anything . . . that is already subject to the authority' of another institution (*ibid.*, p. 27). The Council required supervision of ritual slaughterers. It called on Jews to refrain from using milk or wine purchased from gentiles, as their preparation was not under proper supervision. As in the ordinances of Poland-Lithuania, the Council ordered 'the removal of an obstacle from the way of our people, when women go alone to the homes of the uncircumcised and by unfrequented paths' (*ibid.*, p. 26). It also cautioned against imitating gentile clothing and demanded restraint with respect to luxuries.

This Council represented a serious and systematic attempt to unify the Jews of the empire into a country-wide entity; to establish a special tax fund for the needs of diplomatic intercession; to supervise economic transactions and ensure economic morality under the control of the Jews themselves, and to regulate the affairs of the rabbinate and the *yeshivot*. But the Council did not last. The reason may have been that it was denounced at the time as a kind of plot against the rulers, for the participants were actually brought to trial on a charge of high treason against the state.

41

The Social Ideals of Jewry at the End of the Middle Ages

Dilemmas Posed by the Expulsion from Spain

Many of the Sephardi exiles were troubled for generations after their expulsion by the thought that the Jews had been expelled from the Iberian Peninsula without attempting any armed resistance. Some told themselves that the dispersion of the Jews in small groups within the gentile cities made them helpless victims of the latter and prevented them from offering any real resistance. R. Joseph ibn Yaḥya contends that when Haman proposed that the Jews should be expelled from ancient Persia, he argued 'there is no reason to fear that on the day of their destruction they will create a disturbance in the kingdom or resist those who rise against them. For not a sound will be heard when they are destroyed, since they are scattered, a few here and a few there.' Nor would their expulsion have any harmful effect on daily life, Haman explained to the king: 'Do not suppose that you will make any part of your kingdom bare [by expelling the Jews] . . . for . . . their dispersion keeps them completely isolated, for there are only a few of them here and there, thus their commonalty is incapable of uniting' (*Commentary on Esther*, Bologna, 1538, fol. 37r).

These reflections were formulated by R. Simḥah (Simone) Luzzatto in an apologetic statement whose central motif is submission to the expulsion.

> The Jews . . . never desire to try new ways of raising the status of their people in general. For they believe that every recognizable change that relates to them . . . derives from a Higher Cause and not human effort. The Decree of Expulsion from Castile and other neighbouring kingdoms . . . involved nearly half a million people . . . including men of high intelligence and counsellors of state . . . yet among this great number there was not even a single man who dared to offer any firm and energetic council that they save themselves from that bitter Expulsion. But they were dispersed and scattered throughout the whole world, which is a decisive proof that the Jews tend . . . towards submission and obedience to their rulers (*Essay on the Jews of Venice*, Jerusalem, 1950, pp. 122–3).

Two other sages of the period, the Sephardi exile R. Solomon ibn Verga in the sixteenth century and the Italian R. Judah Aryeh of Modena in the seventeenth century, summed up the reasons for the distress of the Jews as a combination of religious resignation, rationalist irony and the pessimism of beaten men who live on by sheer miracle and have come to rely on miracles for their salvation. But they are saved only when they prove deserving, and their downfall is thus understood as natural. Solomon ibn Verga wrote that:

> The Jews, when they first found favour in the eyes of God, had Him fighting their wars, as is known to all . . . and therefore they did not learn the stratagems of war because they had no need of them. And so we find it said of them in the Book of Judges 'No shield was to be found nor javelin.' But when they sinned God turned his face from them, and they remained vulnerable in all respects. They did not know the weapons or methods of war, and the Divine Will was no longer with them . . . and so they fell like sheep without a shepherd (Solomon ibn Verga, *Shevet Yehudah,* E. Shohat, ed., Jerusalem, 1947, p. 44).

Although this was ostensibly said regarding the defeat of the Jews in biblical days, the words clearly bear the impress of his feelings about the contemporary situation of the Jews. The Italian rabbi expounded the biblical text, 'Israel has transgressed and they also sinned against my covenant' in the following way: 'Thereby they returned to the natural order, and it is natural that they should be defeated by these nations, for they are the least of nations and weak' (Judah Aryeh of Modena, *Mi-Dvar Yehudah,* Venice, 1602, fol. 38r). Just as this pessimism derives from the world of faith so it ultimately undermines faith.

The exiles were also tried and tested by their messianic hope, which seemed very far from fulfilment. The response to this challenge was not only an awakening of messianic fervour. Even R. Isaac Abrabanel, the leader of the Spanish exiles who repeatedly gave expression to ardent messianic hope, recorded what must have been his innermost feeling in writing that

> in the days of the Redemption . . . I shall relate how I used to say in those days [*i.e.,* in the times of despair that followed the Expulsion] . . . all the Prophets who prophesied about my Redemption and salvation are all false . . . Moses may he rest in peace was false in his utterances, Isaiah lied in his consolations, Jeremiah and Ezekiel lied in their prophesies, and likewise all the other prophets. . . . Let the people remember . . . all the despairing things they used to say at the time of the Exile (*Zevaḥ Pessaḥ,* Constantinople, 1505, fol. 35r).

The problem of the attitude towards the Marranos also became more acute and complicated. Those who had abandoned their fathers' graves, their homes, their property and their ties with the land and culture of Spain, which they loved and cherished, in order to remain loyal to Judaism were naturally stern in their attitude to those who, at the price of pretending to accept Christianity, had continued to possess all that the exiles had surrendered. Harsh and bitter words were directed against the Marranos on the very eve of the expulsion. At that time, even their sufferings under the Inquisition seemed to be a well-deserved punishment. About two years before the expulsion, R. Joel ibn Shuaib proclaimed

> these words with regard to those who have abandoned the Torah and left the community . . . that the blessed Lord may reject them . . . and destroy them

utterly. . . . May he reject them with both hands as smoke is blown away . . . for they thought that they would be separated from the fire by separating themselves from the Congregation; so the Lord separated them for evil from all the tribes of Israel as the smoke is separated from the fire and rejected. . . . Let them fall by that from which they hoped to escape and be consumed by the fire, utterly lost in this world and the next . . . because they were of the seed of Israel and wickedly separated themselves from them (Commentary on Psalms, Salonika, 1569, fol. 155r).

The Marranos, in this view, are a section of the people that had sought the obliteration of their Jewishness and got more than they bargained for – total oblivion. In his commentary, R. Joel addressed the converts directly, as it were, explaining to them what they could expect after adopting Christianity: 'Although you have forgotten your God, you will not rest; for the enemy desires to destroy you under any circumstances. . . . There is no refuge or salvation, neither on earth nor in heaven' (*ibid.*, fol. 103v–104r).

Not long after the expulsion, arguments in favour of the Marranos began to be heard, particularly after Portugal forcibly imposed Christianity on those who fled there. The Jews who escaped shared in the anguish of the Marranos there. A scholar who arrived in Salonika in 1500 declared: 'I and all the people of this generation are obligated to be distressed and concerned and grieve all our lives for our fathers and brethren who have suffered the great destruction of Spain, because they wish to come and serve the Lord but are not permitted to depart, so that they serve other Gods under compulsion' (Josef Gerson, *Ben Porat Josef,* ms. British Museum, Or. 10, 726, fol. 166r). The same man clearly formulated the point of view of the Marranos, that forced conversion is the dreadful climax of the condition of exile and was decreed on Israel together with exile itself: 'Everything was destined and declared from the beginning by Moses in our holy Torah . . . see, if we engage in idolatrous worship, Moses said "And there you will serve other gods of wood and stone" . . . and so it is, literally, as we have seen with our eyes . . . for it is real idolatry . . . and in that case the Lord may He be blessed has fulfilled what He decreed against us for our transgressions, and therefore there is no cause for astonishment' (*ibid.*). This theory gives a predestined reason for the compulsory religious conversion and an historical-religious significance to the Jewish religious underground.

In the course of time various theoretical and practical problems influenced the attitude towards the Marranos. In spite of this, they and their way of life formed exceedingly active factors in the conduct of Jewish communal affairs, and in Jewish religious action and thought. Within the Jewish community at large there actually developed a certain sentimentality towards the Marranos and their ties with Judaism. Most of these were legend or fantasy, but even if they had little to do with the actual life of the Marranos, they are of interest in showing what Jews thought of them. Early in the seventeenth century the great kabbalist R. Ḥayyim Vital reports in his *Sefer Haḥezyonot* what he was told by a physician 'who was an attendant of the King of Spain. Once when he gave him water for washing before a feast, a priest came and told the king of dreams he had dreamt, in which angels came and told the priest, "Go and tell the king that he is indeed likewise a new Christian, and the grandson of . . . a Jewess; so why does he hate and slay the Jews who are Marranos just as he is."' According to this tale the king kept the priest in his palace as a prisoner. 'And all this on account of the nobles who are jealous of the Jews. And indeed they whispered together all the time, the king and the priest, in secret regarding our Torah.' Furthermore the Marrano priest outlines a policy for the Marrano King of Spain, the main point of which is the splitting of the Catholic camp and an alliance with the Protestants. Moreover, the priest tells his king: 'Indeed, before he died your father commanded you to avoid making war on the King of France, for as long as he is well there will be peace for all the Christian [i.e., Catholic] nations. But now make an end of this policy in order that the destruction of the Christian realm shall begin.' And indeed, the king obeyed him and caused the King of France to be slain 'by a stratagem, through a trusted man'. (Can this refer to the murder of the French King Henry IV?) The priest also 'advised him out of the mouth of the angels how he should make peace with the nation of Flanders', the angels explained to the Spanish king that the struggle 'for these past eighty years' with the Protestants of the Low Countries 'causes much harm and damage to the King of Spain', and it would be impossible to achieve peace with the Dutch unless he first made peace with the ruler of England, 'and after that through him the peace will come'. R. Ḥayyim Vital adds many more stories on this topic. Men came from Spain, presumably Marranos, and told of further prophesies, of signs and tokens in the Heavens. One of the additional prophecies specifies that after the death of the Grand Inquisitor and the King of Spain 'there will arise many wars in the world and the faith of the abject Jewish nation will arise, and will be exalted forever.' R. Ḥayyim testified that with his own eyes he had seen 'the written version that came from Spain itself' (Sefer Haḥezyonot, op. cit., pp. 244–9).

This series of tales contains many elements that refer to the political struggles of Western Europe during the Wars of Religion of the Counter-Reformation period. In Safed and Damascus, where R. Ḥayyim lived, these stories aroused great interest, because the picture of Marranos enjoying power and strength and working for their faith in secret found a responsive chord. Many Jewish chronicles in that period tend to attribute the rise of Protestantism in various parts of Europe, such as the south of France, to the presence of the offspring of Marranos in those places. The children of those upon whom Catholic Christianity had been forcibly imposed had now, it was argued, arisen and broken its unity and were avenging themselves on the Catholic rulers by means of the Wars of Religion.

As we have noted (see page 659), the departure from Spain led to considerable social and cultural tension between the exiles and the Jewish communities that admitted them. The culture of Spanish Jewry displayed considerable strength and in many places came to dominate the local Jewish culture. But in those regions and Jewish cultures where this did not happen, a certain tension existed. The exiles held in low esteem the Jewish surroundings to which they came. This was particularly true in Italy, where they confronted the culture of Ashkenazi Jewry. R. Isaac Abrabanel mocked the Hebrew style and speech 'in the Land of Ashkenaz . . . in the mouths of their rabbis . . . although they are . . . numerous, their speech is . . . a mockery and travesty that has neither rhyme nor reason'. The Ashkenazi *semikhah* of rabbis was also ridiculed by the Sephardi scholars. The Ashkenazi scholars retorted with criticisms and complaints about the offspring of Marranos whose Jewish culture was tainted by the Christian culture of their surroundings, yet who dared to criticize the style of life and literary creativity of the Ashkenazim, who had never adopted the culture of their environment. In Safed and other places influenced by Sephardi culture, this tension disappeared. In this respect the great Ashkenazi sage R. Isaiah Horowitz from Poland was typical when he described in his work *Shenei Luhot Habrit* ('The Two Tablets of the Covenant') how the practices of the Sephardim, which he had observed in Jerusalem, Safed and Hebron, could serve his Ashkenazi brethren as a model. He disseminated their philosophical and moral viewpoints with considerable force and praised the leading Sephardi scholars and sages

Divinity, Existence and Exile in the Doctrine of Safed

The creative power of exiled Spanish Jewry, the spiritual force that was released by the shock of expulsion, and the psychological strength of Marranos and their offspring in reaction to the dread of forced baptism all found expression in the way of life and doctrines of the sages of Safed at the height of its vigour. We have already referred above to the character of leadership in this community and its voluntarist trends. On the social foundation that the settlers in Safed had established in the sixteenth century and on the basis of the thoughts and spiritual experience of those generations, the structure of Jewish mystical thought began to rise again. The Kabbalah – as the Jewish mystic doctrine began to be called henceforward – began to show signs of creativity shortly before the expulsion from Spain, after a prolonged interval since the mid-fourteenth century. Following the expulsion, this doctrine began to spread far and wide. Furthermore, those engaged in it no longer found it necessary to restrict it to narrow circles. True, we have cited above a small group of students who undertook to keep their master's teachings secret (see page 663). Their master recorded that his own teacher, R. Isaac Luria, had said to one of his disciples before his death:

> Tell the scholars in my name that from today and henceforth they should not engage at all in this wisdom which I have taught them. For they have not understood it properly and may, God forbid, come to heresy and spiritual destruction. Indeed R. Hayyim alone should engage in it by himself, whispering it in secret. [The disciple] said to him: And is there no hope for us then? But he said to him: If you so deserve, I shall come and teach you (*ibid.*, p. 230).

But R. Hayyim did teach others, and other disciples of Luria spread the secret doctrine far and wide. For these cirles were convinced that preparation for the coming of the Messiah required a study of the *Zohar* and the other kabbalistic works. 'And from the year 1540, it is a most choice commandment that old and young should engage therein in public. . . . For in virtue thereof Messiah the King will be coming, and not in virtue of anything else' (Introduction by R. Abraham Azulai to his commentary on the *Zohar*).

The doctrines of Safed were based on a number of outstanding personalities whose qualities had impressed themselves on the consciousness and imagination of the people no less than on a broad system of mystical and theoretical views. Of these figures the central and primary one is that of R. Isaac Luria, 'the holy Ari', who died in 1572 at the age of thirty-eight. His doctrines, disseminated by his remarkable disciples, left a very deep impress on the Jewish world. His image is surrounded by a luminous sanctity. Wonders were related about his birth and circumcision. When his father wept on this occasion, 'Elijah of blessed memory came towards him and said: Do not weep, servant of the Lord. Go to the altar and make your sacrifice which is wholly for the Lord, and be seated. . . . And I shall sit in your lap and in my hands I shall hold this child' (M. Benayahu, ed., *Sefer Toledot Ha-Ari,* Ben-Zvi Institute, Jerusalem, 1967, p. 152). His education and the roots of his greatness were linked with the vestiges of Sephardi learning possessed by the Marranos – who sometimes did not know what treasure they possessed. According to legend, while the young R. Isaac was at a synagogue in Egypt he saw a man holding a book full of 'great mysteries'. When he asked the man what was in the book, the other answered: 'What can I say . . . for I am of the Marranos. And because I saw that each member of the congregation holds his prayerbook in his hand, for very shame I took hold of this book . . . but I do not know what is written therein' (*ibid.,* p. 153).

In these folk-tales, R. Isaac ascends to the Upper Assembly of Heaven. They also contain sections that reveal aspects of life in Sephardi Safed along with the fine and delicate spirit of their hero. It is related there 'how the wise men of Safed appointed ten men to check transgressions [see page 663]. . . . Now one day . . . one of these officials rose early . . . and opened his window to see whether the dawn had risen, in order to proceed to the synagogue and be one of the first there, as was his practice. Now he saw a certain woman' going forth from her courtyard dressed in her finery. The official rose and followed her and saw her enter the courtyard of a man who was suspected of adultery. And the official said, 'Indeed it is now evident that this woman' is a wanton harlot. And he proceeded to the synagogue, where as soon as prayer was over he told the beadle to bring together 'the ten who were appointed to prevent transgressions'. The beadle did so, and the official rose to recount what he had seen that morning. Yet before he opened his mouth the Ari spoke first and said to him: 'Close your mouth, do not speak . . . for the woman whom you saw . . . is . . . clear of all sin.' She had gone in the early dawn so that people should not see her, but only because in that courtyard was a man who had come from the West and had brought her a letter with a pledge from her husband. 'Then that scholar prostrated himself at the feet of the Ari of blessed memory and said to him: I obey you, forgive me. And the Ari said: Why prostrate yourself to me? Go and prostrate yourself before that woman and beg forgiveness of her for having suspected someone fit and worthy' (*ibid.,* 159–60). Here the suspiciousness of the official and the inquisitorial watch and ward are contrasted with the simple intuitiveness of the mystic. Some of the tales relate how he went to welcome the Sabbath clad in white garb; how as he listened to the twittering of birds he heard the voices of saints who had come to teach the truth. Such tales leave the impression of his position as a true prophet.

There is the story of a man who confessed his sins and was found to deserve death by fire. The man 'promptly purchased wood for the pyre. And the rabbi said, our sentences are not like those of the peoples of the world' (*i.e.,* unlike the Inquisition, which burns human beings at the pyre), but requires pouring molten lead down the throat. To which the man answered: 'Act according to your knowledge, Master. And he sent at once to fetch lead,' which they placed on the fire. Then he told the man to recite the death-bed confession, and so he did. When he had ended, 'the rabbi told him, lie prostrate on your back; and he did so. Straighten out your legs, said he . . . Open your mouth; and he opened it. Close your eyes tightly. And he did so. Now the rabbi had sweet water ready, and he poured it down his throat . . . and said to him: The Lord has likewise removed your sin, you will not perish. And he raised him at once and prepared a list of penitential practices for him . . . and sent for his wife and children; and the man was a full and perfect penitent' (*ibid., p.* 239). Popular belief linked the Ari with messianic hopes. Yet, most of all, the people saw the Ari himself as a gentle and holy man.

The mystic doctrines emanating from Safed, and particularly from the school of the Ari, gave cosmic and human significance to the Exile and the Redemption. Theirs was a doctrine with ancient foundations; but the particular formulation and emphasis gave them a new mystical significance. Their starting-point was the question: 'If the Godhead is in all, and all is filled with it, how can there be any place in the universe which is not God?' The answer they found involves 'the mystery of *zimzum*' (withdrawal, shrinking). When God, the *En-Sof,* or Boundless and Infinite, determined to create the Universe, He, as it were, withdrew, or reduced, Himself in order to leave space for His universe – a dark void. Hence the Creation is not an expansion of the Godhead, but its recoil or concentration within itself.

Gershom Scholem has pointed out with some justice that though the kabbalists never stated it expressly, 'this first action of *zimzum* creates the impression of a primal Exile. God did not so much reveal Himself, as exile Himself into the recesses of His Being' (*Sabbetai Zvi,* Tel Aviv, 1957, p. 25). In this universe there are various *Sefirot* (spheres of emanated light) radiating plentitude of Divine influence. These *Sefirot* are vessels containing the overwhelming Divine irradiation. However, only the first three *Sefirot* could adequately contain the primal Divine Light. When the radiation reached the six lower *Sefirot,* their capacity failed them and the Light shattered them. Sparks of the primal Divine Light were trapped in the fragments of these vessels, some of which mounted aloft, while others descended and sank. Those that sank are the *Klippot,* or husks, which were transformed into the forces of impurity and evil. Their strength derives from the sparks of Divine Light that are still trapped within them. This is Exile – the light entrapped within the broken vessels and subjected to evil. The *Shekhina,* the Divine Presence, is itself in Exile, and therefore the universe is flawed. But when the sparks that are trapped in the broken vessels will be redeemed, the Exile of the Light will be at an end, and the human and cosmic Redemption will come about. That will be the hour of the Jewish national redemption. The Torah and the commandments are the means given by God to those who serve Him on earth – namely, the Jewish people – whereby they can repair the cosmos. By performing the commandments and avoiding transgression, they can perfect not only the souls of the Jews but of the whole world, by delivering and redeeming the Divine Light. The purpose of the Exile is to work constantly towards the Redemption of the Light from the place of its captivity, to deprive evil of its power. That, according to the Kabbalah, is the mission of each and every Jewish soul.

The efforts of the individual are liable to constant repetition through the generations, for the Lurianic kabbalists believed in the transmigration of souls. The condition of Jewry, the continuity of the individual Jewish souls in their various incarnations, the sufferings undergone by Israel in Exile, all have functions of their own to perform in the 'Mystery of Perfection'. The days of the Messiah mark the culmination of this process. R. Isaac Luria gave Jewry a new myth for comprehending its existence, both in achievement and in tribulation. The Jewish predicament involves the whole significance of human history, and both are aspects of the mystery of Creation. The failures of the individual and of the community can never be final or absolute, but only one stage in a succession of incarnations, a ceaseless process that will inevitably 'perfect the universe as the Kingdom of the Almighty'. Thus those who followed this doctrine regarded themselves as duty-bound to disseminate it; for through it, they revealed to the ordinary Jew not only the purpose of his distress and suffering but also the lofty significance of every detail of the commandments. It is no accident, therefore, that the doctrines of the Ari were spread not only in systematic and philosophical kabbalistic works but also in the extensive literature of homiletical preachings.

In one of the first of these works, completed in Safed in 1575, the author explains in the terminology of kabbalist doctrine 'that these garments [i.e., of the universe as it exists, which is an analogy taken from the *Zohar*] contain representations of all things existent; and they constitute the roots [within the existent universe] from all the lower worlds. And when the roots are lit up by the commandments that Jews perform below, there are mercy and goodness in the world; but when Israel does not act in perfection below, then all the garments absorb severity and darkness.' He explains that, according to his teacher, this is the reason why the *Hekhalot* books (which are among the earliest kabbalistic works) call God the 'Wretched Monarch', '. . . for there is nothing more wretched and shameful than that man should use to sin against Him that very life which God breathed into his body in order that he should use it in God's service. It may be compared to a king who gave his servant money to buy bread to eat; but the servant went and spent the money on a stick with which to beat his master. Can there be a worse servant than that?' This attitude makes it possible 'to comprehend the punishment for transgressing against any prohibition in the Torah. For the prohibitions are fences and hedges to hold "Samael", the personification of evil, in check and not let him free; but he who transgresses unties those bonds. Therefore he causes evil to himself, for he will be consumed by suffering in this world, or the next world if he should not suffer in this.' In this order of things, where Satan is visualized as a cur that is tied up but may bite, the *Shekhina* is the Mother of the Exiles and awaits her 'sustenance' from the commandments that her sons perform.

And you should know that all the miracles that have been performed for us, and whatever is done each day and whatever shall be done, is all through the *Shekhina* who is linked with us, and she is the merciful Mother. . . . It is fitting that everyone should hasten to be joined to her love in order to awaken the Higher Love which links the *Shekhina*. All this awakening depends upon the deeds of the righteous, even at the time when the Temple was still standing . . . how much more so now, by reason of our manifold transgressions in this great and bitter Exile where the *Shekhina* is not nourished by the sacrifices but receives merely a little sustenance from the deeds of the righteous. Men are obligated to support her against her falling, she being 'the fallen booth of David', which collapses further each and every day, and all this by reason of our transgressions, as is said in Scripture: 'and because of your transgressions your mother was sent away.' For by iniquity she falls, and by good deeds she is raised and supported. . . . This being so, since the *Shekhina* requests the children of Israel to support her, that support assuredly depends upon us, namely on the *Yihudim* [spiritual unifications through formulas deriving from biblical verses] in our prayers and Torah study, which are an aid and support for her. . . . And this is the desire of the *Shekhina*: that we should always remember her in *Yihudim,* whether by prayer or by fulfilling commandments, such as acts of loving-kindness and other good deeds, or by engaging in the study of Torah.

This doctrine is imbued with the tenderness of extending aid to the mother *Shekhina,* who suffers with her children in exile. This doctrine raises love both as a human emotion and mystic power at one and the same time.

For love is the glory of the soul, as she glorifies in the glory of joy that she has in her God and is joined with the radiance of the fear of the Lord when she achieves the splendour of her majesty. The light of her yearning for her Maker mingles with the love of her passion, a yearning desire to be crowned with the diadem of beauteous, clear and pure thoughts. And she shall moan in her great and exultant gladness for her friend, that most high friend, and shall be joined with the ties of affection. And she shall inquire and investigate the steps that lead to illumine with the light of life. . . . In that hour she will be hallowed with the sanctity of the Holy of Holies, and then in her fullness of love find favour before the King who is King of Kings. And at that time she shall grow fully existent and beautiful and resplendent with the glorious vigour and power and forceful majesty of love. And then the Most High will single her out and make her radiance shine, bringing her into the Chambers of Radiance and binding her in the circle of life.

Erotic overtones, fine aesthetic feeling and glowing faith combine here to produce a mosaic of love, joy, beauty and sanctity. These moralists also preached the practical conclusions to be drawn from the mystical doctrine of the *Klippot*.

Our sins cause the Holy and Blest One to garb Himself and His *Shekhina* in ten husks. . . . And that husk which our sins have caused the Holy and Blest One to put on will be required of us. . . . How, then, can the Jew rejoice when he knows how many barriers upon barriers his sins cause God and His *Shekhina* to garb themselves in; and that is the reason for the length of our Exile. . . . And because of this our rabbis of blessed memory said 'that Israel can be redeemed only through Repentance' in order that the *Klippot* may be broken.

This ethical system thus derives at every stage from the concepts of kabbalist theory. The tension of Exile versus Redemption, the horror of the *Shekhina* being in Exile and the Light trapped within the *Klippot* are used to guide and instruct each and every Jew in his deeds at every moment, since these are the deeds that repair and perfect the universe and bring it to the ultimate restoration, or alternatively defile man and universe, causing the Jew to be cruel towards his mother, the *Shekhina*, and preventing his soul from rejoicing in the union between the higher love and beauty.

There was ample tension in the world of the Safed kabbalists. *Sefer Haḥezyonot* of R. Ḥayyim Vital, the leading disciple of the Ari, shows that there were various drives and forces struggling within him. Here he recorded his own dreams and those that others dreamt about him. Almost all of them point to the greatness of R. Ḥayyim in this world and in the World to Come. But his hatred of rivals, his aspirations and desires also find expression in these dreams. There was one in which he saw how 'the body of Moses was brought to the synagogue, and it was almost ten *ells* long. And they prepared a long bench there with books upon it. And upon them they placed the body of Moses. And I saw that his body was clad in his garments. And when they set him down on the bench it changed from what it had been and became transformed into a Torah Scroll . . . stretched out lengthways, like a long letter spread along the length of the bench' (*Sefer Haḥezyonot, op. cit.*, p. 78). In this dream there is a clear identification with R. Ḥayyim himself.

Messianic hopes that get caught up in a period of spiritual tension are also expressed in violent and sensuous terms. In the year 1562 'I dreamt that I was standing on the summit of the tall mountain that lies west of Safed . . . and I heard a voice announcing: "The Messiah comes!" And behold the Messiah stood before me and blew the ram's horn. And thousands of myriads of Jews gathered around him. Then he said to us: "Come with me, and you will see the vengeance for the destruction of the Temple." So we followed, and he fought there and smote all the Christians who were there.' (We are not sure whether he used the term 'Christians' because, as one of the offspring of the Spanish exiles, he regarded them as the main foes of Jewry – even though he was well aware of the fact that the Moslems ruled over the Temple Mount in his times – or whether he used this term because he was careful, even when he wrote his diary, not to record the name of the Moslems, who were the rulers of Ereẓ Yisrael.) He continues, the Messiah '. . . entered the Temple and also slew those who were there . . . and we purified and rebuilt the Temple on its foundations and the daily sacrifice was offered by the High Priest. And he resembled my neighbour R. Israel Halevi. So I asked the Messiah: How can a Levite be a priest? And he answered me: "You were in error when you thought him to be a Levite, for indeed he is a priestly *kohen*." After that he took a Torah Scroll from the Temple building and read therein. And I awoke' (*ibid.,* p. 41).

In these visions and dreams, the personalities and spiritual ideals underlying the concepts of the mystic doctrines find their expression. In this visionary world, the near becomes far and the distant draws near. The seer perceived the Lord of all the prophets lying before his eyes, becoming a book, changing into a man. The High Priest appears to him in the likeness of his neighbour in Safed. The concept of the mansion of the Temple appears to him in his dream as the Holy Ark that contains the Torah Scrolls of the synagogue in which he prays. These spiritual and emotional forces are in themselves an expression of the power of the kabbalist circle that disseminated the doctrines of the Ari. Within a relatively short time, the Lurianic Kabbalah and its disseminators were to become the foundation for a powerful messianic movement.

The Messianic Leadership

From the beginning of the sixteenth century, various individuals claimed their leadership over all Jewry by virtue of their redemptive mission. One of these seems to have been the Ashkenazi rabbi Asher Lemlein, who called the congregations of northern Italy to repentance at the beginning of the century. More interesting was the man who called himself David Reubeni, prince of the royal house of the tribe of Reuben. He combined the ancient belief that the last Ten Tribes dwelt with overwhelming military and political power beyond the Mountains of Darkness, prepared to come to the aid of their Jewish brethren, with the Christian aspiration to establish a 'Second Front' to conquer the Moslems. He appeared among the communities of Italy in the 1520s and reached Portugal and its Marrano communities before vanishing in the 1530s. In Portugal he led the New Christian Diogo Pires to circumcise himself and become the Jewish kabbalist and visionary Solomon Molcho. Together they came before the emperor in Germany, where Solomon Molcho died a martyr's death by burning, while David Reubeni vanished – as befitted his mysterious character. He left a diary behind him, which shows that even more important than the real man – about whose origins historians are still in dispute – was the image he wished to present. In his manner of living and in his tales he presented the likeness of a Jewish paladin, ascetic and God-fearing, diplomat and preacher, who both attracted and repelled communities through the imaginary personality he projected.

Shabbetai Zevi and his prophet Nathan of Gaza are the most outstanding figures in this period of messianic ferment. The style they adopted was crucial to their success. The prophet Nathan of Gaza sent instructions calling for harsh penitence, which were accepted literally and obeyed by people in distant lands, from Amsterdam to Yemen, from the eastern frontier of Poland to the outlying villages of the Atlas mountains in North Africa; and in most places they were accepted willingly and enthusiastically. The few opponents had to lower their voices. They had to remain silent in the synagogues when benedictions were uttered for Messiah the King.

These benedictions were based, interestingly, on the formulas established and used by the Jews for their gentile rulers, coupled with formulations of messianic adoration.

> And this is the form of the blessing: May He who giveth victory to kings and dominion to princes and whose Kingdom holds sway over all the Universes . . . who maketh a Covenant with David his servant to establish his royal throne forever, may He bless and guard and preserve and aid and elevate and increase and raise ever higher our Lord and King the Holy Rabbi righteous and saved, namely Shabbetai Zevi, anointed by the God of Jacob, may his glory be exalted and his kingdom set on high . . . may his horn be raised in honour and the diadem of his God be on his head . . . may his name live forever, may his name be bright before the sun and may people bless themselves thereby. May all the peoples recognize him. May our eyes behold and our hearts rejoice at the rebuilding of our Temple and our glory, the Holy Place of the Lord that thy hands have established, and so may it be His will and let us say, Amen (J. Sasportas, *Zizat Novel Zvi*, J. Tishby, ed., Jerusalem, 1954, p. 62).

The keenest and fiercest of his opponents admits that he and those like him

> all stood in awe and fear, and each one went his way – the believers because of the awe of their kingdom and the honour of the king whom they accepted. As for us, we feared and dreaded the claim to dominion without power, and for the sake of peace, lest there should be some scandal in the synagogue. . . . And I also saw that I was [isolated], only a grain of sand in the country. And all the Torah scholars and their students took their stand against me. . . . So I had to rise and stand when they rose. And when they responsed Amen to each benediction and praise, I would respond Amen after them to each curse I uttered. . . . So each one said Amen according to his intention and opinion (*ibid.*, p. 132).

The feeling of pride and the sense of liberation from the yoke of strangers that Shabbetai Zevi had imbued were so strong that after Shabbetai Zevi converted to Islam, this same opponent, R. Jacob Sasportas, expressed his feeling that Israel had once more lost its honour and that the hope which they had in their hearts had come to nothing:

> Now that joy and gladness has been taken away from the whole house of Israel . . . on this it is fitting to weep, on this it is fitting to mourn. For our joy has been transformed to sorrow, and in secret our soul doth weep because of the overwhelming pride of the nations and because of the pride of Israel that has been taken away. For the flock of the Lord thought that they would have one king over them and one shepherd for all. But now our hopes have been dashed at their very birth and the many slaves from among the nations are bursting forth . . . and the least of them . . . spits and laughs in our face because we set our hopes on falsehood . . . and there has been more than enough shame and anger since the honour of the Torah has been profaned and flung to earth (*ibid.*, p. 212).

In earlier generations, to be sure, there had been messiahs who had claimed that they would redeem Israel (see page 442), but their claim had never been so widely accepted, and the people had not obeyed their orders nor honoured their self-elevation to such a great degree. For only a few years – but years that were emotionally and intellectually intense – Israel had had its Messiah the King, a prophet of God; it had experienced a feeling of independence. To a certain extent this had meant a revival – albeit brief – of the ancient forms of biblical leadership. At the same time it served, after a fashion, as a preparation for later trends and developments, for following a single charismatic personality and his claim to lead and save.

Even if one rejects the assumption of a link between the Sabbatean ideology and that of the Ḥasidism founded by R. Israel Ba'al Shem Tov (see Part VI), it is clear that the very possibility of achnowledging absolute reverence for a *zaddik,* and for his sons after him, had its roots in the seventeenth century. It is even possible that the response of the Jewish people to a figure like that of Theodor Herzl in the nineteenth and twentieth centuries had its roots in the people's reaction to the success of Shabbetai Ẓevi.

The Messianic Movement of Shabbetai Ẓevi, 1665–6

Attention has been drawn above to the trends of leadership shown in this movement. Its founders were young. The central figure himself, the son of Mordecai of Smyrna, was born in Asia Minor in 1626 and died in 1676 at the age of fifty. When he claimed the title of Messiah and attracted the masses of Jewry, he was therefore less than forty years old. The prophet of the movement and its guiding spirit and ideologist, Nathan of Gaza, seems to have been born in the year 1644 and died in 1680 at the age of thirty-six. He was therefore about twenty-one years old when he set out to announce the coming of his Messiah and to lead Jewry towards repentance. The messiah was a Sephardi, the prophet an Ashkenazi. The messiah had an attractive, captivating personality, and his emotions and imagination seemed to have been greater than his intellect. Gershom Scholem, the authority on the Sabbatean movement, has drawn the conclusion that although it was influenced by the forces of Lurianic Kabbalah, 'it is impossible to claim that he himself represented the power of the Kaballah and its new and renascent thought in his own time. And though he served as a transmitter of that cause, it was not consciously that he did so. . . . The general atmosphere within Jewry was more decisive in shaping the movement than the peculiar spiritual state of the youthful kabbalist Sabbetai Zvi' (Scholem, *op. cit.,* p. 95).

The young scholar from Smyrna had a kabbalistic method of his own more or less following that of the *Zohar.* Yet that was not the most important factor. His character was soft, tending to changeability. His admirers speak of periods when he had 'the great illumination', which could be seen on his face and in his readiness to perform great and revolutionary deeds. They also speak of periods when 'the visage was averted', meaning times of depression, of humility and regret for the revolutionary deeds he had performed before.

Nathan of Gaza always displayed a firm and consistent stand. He was consumed by the fire of the vision he had seen and which had not been fulfilled, but he refused to show remorse because of the light that had been brought to the house of Israel.

Nathan was consistent in his asceticism. He reveals himself in his writings and in the impressions gained by those who were in touch with him as a man of great intellectual power. The force that brought him to be a prophet was the same as the force that had given rise to R. Joseph Caro's *Maggid*, identical in principle with the psychological complex that attributed to the 'dream master' of R. Hayyim Vital and his circles the many colourful visions they saw. But Nathan translated these dreams for himself and the masses of Jewry as tidings of Redemption – a redemption which he identified with actual persons and events. From the ecstasy of the solitary ascetic he became a prophet for the multitude. In due course he related how he was privileged to proclaim 'to the congregation of Israel, our Redemption and the salvation of our souls'. He was granted this privilege at the time when he was

> closed in purity and sanctity in a special room. After I had prayed, whispering and weeping greatly, while I was engaged in entreaties, behold a spirit passed before me so that the hair of my flesh stood on end. . . . I saw the *Merkava* [the heavenly chariot of Ezekiel, one of the two main themes of early Jewish mysticism] and I saw divine sights all that day and all that night and then I uttered a true prophecy like one of the prophets – 'Thus saith the Lord' – and in my heart was clearly engraved about whom my prophecy had been, and likewise that he must be alive and live forever . . . and I have never seen so great a vision as this until now. And the matter remained hidden within my heart until the Redeemer [*i.e.,* Shabbetai Zevi] proclaimed himself in Gaza and claimed the name of Messiah. And then I was permitted by the Angel of the Covenant to proclaim what I had seen and the truth of what was known to me (*ibid.,* pp. 166–7).

He did not abandon this vision even after his messiah changed his faith, but went wandering from community to community, preaching the power of faith, calling for repentance and purity of spirit in the name of the converted messiah. His formidable personality and public failure are together revealed in the letter that he was compelled to sign at Venice in the year 1668, two years after the collapse of the movement. All that a firm and strict rabbinical court could extract from him was: 'Although I have declared that I saw the *Merkava* as Ezekiel the prophet saw it and the prophecy declared that Shabbetai Zevi is the Messiah, the Rabbis and Geonim of Venice have ruled that I am in error and there was nothing real in that vision. I have therefore admitted their words and say that what I prophesied regarding Shabbetai Zevi has no substance' (Sasportas, *op. cit.,* p. 267).

The report of Nathan's prophecy came some seventeen years after the Jewish Ashkenazi captives of the Ukrainian communities, who had fallen into the hands of the Tartars during the Massacres of 1648–9, had reached the Jewish communities of the Ottoman Empire (see page 657). In the communities that had redeemed them, the leading circles were Sephardim, who were still under the impress of the exile from Spain and the resultant crisis at the end of the fifteenth century. The Lurianic doctrine of the Restoration of the Universe as an act of simultaneous universal and Jewish redemption had been spreading steadily in various forms among both the higher and the lower levels of the community. The commercial ties throughout the Jewish Diaspora were growing steadily closer, and communication had improved. Accordingly, the doctrines and leaders of the movement could appeal to various spiritual forces and tendencies at the same time. The demands of the prophet Nathan for perfection and penance awakened the ascetic zeal of both individuals and masses and made him into a unifying element in the movement. It is related that outstandingly wealthy men as well as scholars in Amsterdam asked him to inform them of the proper ascetic practices suited to the 'roots' of their souls and did their best to fulfil those practices no matter how harsh they were. Books were written for the masses, some of them in the contemporary Yiddish, giving instructions how to carry out acts of penitence; and the books sold swiftly. A Polish priest relates that the Jews 'at that time fasted several days a week on account of their messiah, and some of them all week long. They gave no food to their little children. They immersed under the ice in winter, and there they uttered a prayer that had only recently been composed. During the winter many Jews perished because of their immersions in the dreadful cold. They went to their synagogues every day, and there they conducted prayers' (Scholem, *op. cit.,* pp. 495–6).

At the 'court' of Shabbetai Zevi, on the other hand, in the years 1665–6, even during his imprisonment in Gallipoli, there was ample external pomp. At times of 'the Great Illumination' he would promise vengeance against the gentiles and stress that in particular he would avenge himself on the murderers of Poland and Lithuania. When the spirit rested upon him, he would distribute lands, principalities and kingdoms among his followers. In this court there was an emotionally charged atmosphere that was almost erotic. The lists of sins and transgressions with which Shabbetai Zevi was charged either as instigating or performing includes numerous commands to transform fast-days for the destruction of the Temple into festivals of feasting in honour of the messiah and the Redemption. These deeds express his sense of strength, his belief in his mission and in himself. His foes accused him of 'permitting the murder' of his rivals, this likewise being an expression of his sense of messianic majesty. Until the time of his conversion, he was also accused of 'pronouncing the Divine Name as it is written', an act belonging to the Messiah and the days of Redemption; 'of eating the forbidden fat and giving it to others to eat and profaning the Sabbath'. The two latter accusations, if true, would prove a clearly antinomian tendency, a sense of liberation from the shackles of traditional Jewish Law. The various stories about the marriages of Shabbetai Zevi and of licentiousness, including sexual orgies, at his court, in so far as they are correct, express a kind of religious archaism, which sensed the ritual aspect of such deeds, just as they expressed a revolt against Jewish law (see Part VI regarding the sexual practices of the sects that continued the Sabbatean tradition, such as the Frankists).

Penitents and seekers of liberty – rich and poor, scholars and the ignorant – thus united round this movement with its wealth of ancient and hallowed symbols and with its ample supply of charismatic figures, each of whom appealed to a different type of person. This movement came at a time when Ashkenazim and Sephardim alike were experiencing the kind of suffering that was termed the 'birthpangs' of the Messiah's coming. It called on Jewry not only in the name of 'The Anointed of the God of Jacob' but also in the name of the true prophet. Several documents of the movement recorded the year 1666 as 'the first year for the renewal of prophecy and majesty'.

This was a comprehensive national movement by virtue of the more developed means of communication and the shared consciousness, a mass movement carried along by the extremely individualist trend of a handful of young leaders. With respect to its symbolic and mystical foundations, it was both ancient and mediaeval, even in its revolutionary and antinomian tendencies. On the other hand, its emotional character and its social and psychological qualities were completely inspired by tendencies that would grow even stronger in later times, including its call for ascetism and conservatism.

The crisis of the movement came about through pressure on the weakest of its leaders, Shabbetai Zevi himself. On being threatened with great physical punishment and even death, in 1666 he adopted the faith of Islam. The Jews who saw him entering the sultan's palace thought that he was about to remove the crown from the ruler's head. Their disappointment was bitter when they learnt that the messiah had adopted his faith, Islam. Their own crown had fallen from their heads. It seems that after his conversion he fell into a state of deep personal depression, from which he eventually recovered. It may be assumed that his faithful prophet Nathan encouraged him in this. Nathan, in fact, retained the respect and honour of extensive Jewish circles even after the conversion. The vacillating moods, the various letters and the strange actions performed by Shabbetai Zevi after his conversion and until his death are more matters for his personal biography than for the history of the movement. A small group of those who believed in him also converted. They and their offspring developed in due course into the Doenmeh sect in Islam, which survived for many generations (see Part VI).

The greater part of Jewry was shaken to the core. The blow was even greater than the crucifixion of Jesus had been to his followers. As Gershom Scholem has pointed out, it is difficult to compare the death of Jesus with the conversion of Shabbetai Zevi. Jesus had paid the highest price that could be demanded from a man, but Shabbetai had not. 'The paradox of a traitorous Messiah is far greater than that of an executed Messiah' (*ibid.*, p. 683–4).

The various communities did their best to ensure that he would be forgotten. They erased what had been written about him in communal registers and books. This shock undoubtedly led to a search for new paths differing from those of the messianic movements and eventually to implementing the hope of resettling Erez Yisrael and redeeming the Jewish nation in modern times (see Part VI).

Gradually a complete symbolical system was developed in order to justify Shabbetai Zevi's conversion to Islam and to maintain belief in him as the messiah. It seems that the first direct reaction can be found in the words of the prophet Nathan in a letter concerning the fast of the Ninth of Av, which he wrote soon after the conversion:

> Whoever believes in the great, holy, and awesome Sabbath [a glorifying pun on 'Shabbetai'] is beauteous [Zevi] for all Sabbaths. And although he has put on the pure Turban, that is not a profanation of his sanctity. He is holy and all the deeds of the Sabbath are holy. It is necessary to believe likewise that the *Shekhina* has ascended to her original seat and does not dwell in Exile . . . nor is it mentioned

in the words of our sages of blessed memory that the Lord had sworn that the *Shekhina* would not depart from the Exile save together with the people of Israel. Hence . . . she no longer requires our aid; and we must yet be redeemed while she must ascend, since an enhancement of the principle of Sabbath has entered the universe, therefore it is regarded as though we have been redeemed even though we are still in Exile and Messiah the King is oppressed among the *Klippot*, to cleanse all that we have sinned, to perfect all that we have blemished. Since we have merited this, that the *Shekhina* is no longer in Exile . . . now a great and mighty illumination has been added to her . . . this being so, it is not fitting to complain or to awaken any envy or weeping or mourning, since she dwells in joy. To be sure, the fast [of the Ninth of Av] deserves to be observed in order to share in the grief of Israel, until the matter shall be fully and entirely revealed and we shall have the power to make it a complete festival (A. Amarillo in *Sefunot,* 5 [1961], 253–4).

Here the Lurianic concept of *tikkun* or restoration has been deliberately split into two parts. The *Shekhina* has been redeemed, while Israel still awaits its restoration. In more secular terms, the sense of inner freedom possessed by the believer in Shabbetai Zevi now found expression in the belief that the cosmic Divine Redemption had been achieved, although it was not visible in this world. This separation of the political and physical liberation of Jewry from the salvation of the *Shekhina* from Exile and of the cosmos from the effects of the *Shekhina's* Exile would in due course separate the desire to work for the redemption of the people from a concern with the *Shekhina* and her condition (see Part VI).

After Shabbetai Zevi's conversion, when matters became more complicated and his believers were searching for answers, they adopted a Marrano image that the messiah is like a worm that bores into a tree or an apple in order to consume it from within. Accordingly he entered Islam in order to destroy it from within. They experienced, in fact, a sense of nihilism. All that was left of their idealism was faith in a messiah who was concealing himself. Those who continued to believe secretly in Shabbetai Zevi were consumed by doubts; there are some who believe that from them sprang the tendencies towards heresy and dissolution among Jews in modern times (see Part VI).

The Sabbatean movement brought the Jewish Middle Ages to a climactic crisis. It was an attempt at creative rebirth in keeping with the tendencies of the mediaeval world, yet it spelled the virtual destruction of the Jewish world of the Middle Ages by an extreme demand for individualism. It combined the fervour of a comprehensive mass movement with the alien fires of despair and doubt.

Ashkenazi Concepts of Jewry and Its Destiny

During the sixteenth and the first half of the seventeenth centuries the Jews in Ashkenaz – Germany, Italy, Bohemia and Moravia, and Poland-Lithuania – formulated systematic concepts regarding the destiny of Jewry. These thinkers, even those who were basically mystics, adopted a rationalist approach. Here, too, individualism found expression, but it was less fervent and insistent than that of the Sephardi kabbalists and messianists. Here too the bitter pain of expulsion, persecution and insult cut deeply; however in this part of the world it involved confronting a new situation created by the Reformation.

The *shtadlan* R. Joseph of Rosheim recorded for his own use and for the benefit of later generations a summary reworking of what had won his approval in a book written by R. Abraham Bivach, the Spanish rationalist (see pages 612–14). An anonymous Jewish religious disputant of the same period advised his brethren how to conduct religious disputations with Christians of the biblicist Reformation camp. The Jewish approach has to be rationalistic, not a blind reliance on the Bible:

> Do not begin a disputation with them by quoting passages from the Bible, *but only by way of nature, the heart, and reason.* One has to believe, and there must be a unity which directs the entire Universe. . . . And this is what you should do to purify and refine them and talk to them – suppose there were no Bible in existence, what could we do? . . . For their faith is based on our Prophets and Holy Scriptures, and if we have no Prophets, they have no proofs to present. . . . But we have a principle and foundation even without any Book of Scripture, and that is in nature: that we believe in God's unity and greatness from His very activity; and because whatever is done every day could not be done save by His Will (H. H. Ben-Sasson in *Harvard Theological Review,* 59 [1966], 389).

From the evidence of several sources, we may conclude that in Ashkenaz the study of the Spanish Jewish philosophers was widespread, particularly among the Jews of Alsace during the early part of the sixteenth century.

In Italy R. Obadiah Sforno, the great physician, philosopher, Talmudist and Bible commentator, developed a system of his own, which combined rationalism with a touch of mysticism. In accordance with the best traditions of this trend he explained the Nazarite practices described in the Torah as intended to exclude the asceticism practised in the Middle Ages: '*He shall refrain from wine and mead* – he shall not mortify himself with fasting which reduces the ability to serve Heaven as was said by those of blessed memory: And let him not torture his body by flagellation after the fashion of the hypocrites. But let him keep away from wine in order to diminish passion and master his evil inclination, and he will not weaken himself at all.' One of his major principles is that the entire human race is beloved of the Lord and should be brought to serve Him. In his commentary on the Song of Moses in Deuteronomy he goes so far as to explain that the choice of Israel from among the nations was the result of a failure of the divinity in history and was not a primary intention on God's part.

> When Moses said 'Remember the days of old' he wished to explain this in relating the past and the future, stating first how the intention of God had been to achieve this purpose for the whole human race 'in the days of old and the years of bygone generations'; and how when He did not succeed in this, the Lord wrought greatly by raising Israel to high degree. Israel's transgression with the golden calf and the sin of their stiff-neckedness is that God intended to hallow

Israel and His own Name in His universe through them, so that they should serve as luminaries to the human race, to explicate and to instruct, as He said, 'For mine is the whole land and ye shall be for me a kingdom of priests.' But they wantonly destroyed all this through the calf.

And in the final section of Moses' blessings he explained the words '"*Likewise He loves nations*", although you hold the nations in affection according to your words, "And ye shall be unique to me amid all the peoples", this being a declaration that all mankind is unique for you, as the sages of blessed memory said in the Ethics of the Fathers: "Beloved is Man who is created in the Divine Image."' To sum up, Sforno's teachings express a clearly humanist doctrine, deriving from Jewish sources and developed into a comprehensive humane approach.

A philosophical approach aiming to encourage and guide the people was developed by R. Judah Loew ben Bezalel (1525–1609), known as the Maharal, or the High Rabbi, of Prague. He based the religious and social essence of Exile on concepts that are surprisingly close to the organismic nationalist theories of nineteenth-century Europe. In his opinion,

> Exile is a change and departure from the natural order, whereby the Lord situated every nation in the place that best suited it. . . . The place they deserved according to the order of existence was to be independent in Ereẓ Yisrael . . . just as every natural entity is not split into two. . . . And since the Jewish nation is one undivided nation, though it is more dispersed than all the other nations . . . the dispersion is unnatural. . . . Furthermore, according to the order of being, it is not fitting that one nation should be subjugated by another . . . for the blessed Lord created each nation for itself . . . according to the natural order it is not fitting for Israel to be under the rule of others (*Neẓaḥ Israel,* Prague, 1591, fol. 2r).

The concepts of the integrity of the natural unit, of national concentration in a particular land and of the demand for independence and political liberty combine, in the Maharal's opinion, to produce the unequivocal certainty that the central phenomenon of Exile itself will lead to its self-destruction: as this phenomenon destroys the natural order of national life, it cannot continue forever. For should it so continue, the concept of national order would no longer prevail; and a principle is not to be changed by a deviation. There are laws governing the existence of independent nations, and they are the guarantee that ultimately the existence of Israel must likewise be in accordance with those laws. For 'whatever departs from its natural position has no stability in a position that is not natural for it. . . . If it were to stay there . . . the unnatural would become natural, which is impossible . . . and therefore the Exile is in itself an indication of the Redemption' (*ibid.*). As long as Exile lasts there is a justification – though unnatural – for it. This he formulates in a manner basically in accordance with the kabbalistic concepts of the flawed cosmos; yet his formulation includes the conception of national elements that are intrinsically opposed to one another. For the Maharal there is a natural division between Edom and Israel, 'as between water and fire, which although they have neither knowledge nor will are nevertheless opposed by nature; and so are Jacob and Esau'. Esau, or

Edom, are taken here to represent the Western Christian world, following the Talmudic use of the term for Rome. As they are opposed to each other, each of them wishes to dominate the entire universe – and Heaven. Esau and Jacob 'each desires that the entire existence which is this world shall be his . . . as well as the world to come, and would disqualify his rival.' The present success of Esau is because his flawed and defective character is suited to the flawed and defective condition of this world. Therefore 'he has through quarrelling obtained his share, namely this world with its disgrace and shame . . . and to which he is near; but Jacob is far from it, being withdrawn from the dirt.' Israel's future victory is therefore assured by the very process of the improvement of the world. When this world will be worthy of Israel, Israel will rule over it.

Poland and Lithuania also had their rationalist-mystical trend, which found expression in *Torat Haolah* ('The Doctrine of the Offering'), the semi-philosophical work of the great sixteenth-century *halakhist* R. Moses Isserles (see page 667). In this work he symbolizes the hierarchical value of the commandments through the structure of the Temple and its various sections. Yet he is of the opinion that for nine-tenths of the commandments the reasons revealed to man are the material and social advantage they ensure. 'For in truth the commandments enjoined in the Torah are mostly based on physical requirements and the behaviour of human beings to one another. And although they are also of spiritual benefit, still their principal benefit is also explained in terms of human needs, or those of the body.' This scholar also quoted Aristotle in support of a *halakhic* decision and was fiercely assailed for doing so by one of his contemporaries. In his view there is also considerable value in the economic wealth granted to a man, which should be regarded as a gift of God. And he tends to account for the existence of the righteous poor by assuming that the Lord knows that by their inborn character these just men would not be able to pass the test of wealth, and he therefore leaves them in poverty. These views were shared by some of his contemporaries. The general mood from the second half of the sixteenth century, to be sure, tended increasingly to abandon rationalism. A clear example of this can be seen in R. Moses Isserles' outstanding disciple, R. Abraham Horowitz, who wrote in his youth a markedly rationalistic commentary on Maimonides' 'Eight Chapters' (part of Maimonides' commentary on the Mishnah). In his old age, however, he discarded it for another, in which he wrote that with respect to sundry matters his present commentary, which is not rationalist, 'is the root, while the earlier one is uprooting'.

In the third quarter of the sixteenth century, it was still possible for R. Eliezer Ashkenazi, who reached Poland from Egypt by way of Cyprus, Venice and Prague, to become a very influential rabbi and Head of the Court in leading Polish communities. With him he brought to Poland a forcefully keen intelligence tending towards free criticism and religious rationalism, though not without a measure of mysticism. He told those who listened to him that with regard to the principles of faith it was their duty to decide as their reason directed.

> For in all that affects human faith . . . each one of us . . . is bound until the end of all generations to investigate the secrets within the words of the Torah and to

conduct his faith in the straightest and most correct way . . . and to accept the truth from whatever source, once we know of it. And let not the opinion of others, though they preceded us, hinder us from inquiry. . . . We are guilty if we slacken in investigating the secrets of our Torah, and declare that as 'lions' have already mastered them, we should accept their words as they stand. . . . But it is fitting for us to inquire and inspect with the eye of our reason and to write down our opinions for the benefit of those who come after us, whether they will agree with us or reject our opinions, for reasons that are proper for them though they have not been revealed to us (*Ma'asei Adonai,* Venice, 1583, fol. 169r).

Social Criticism

The flourishing social life, the economic success of certain groups and the resultant tension between those who had succeeded and those who had not combined to produce intense spiritual activity and social thought, accompanied by keen and penetrating criticism. Not everybody was prepared to accept R. Moses Isserles' line of reasoning, according to which the good but poor man is denied wealth in order to escape its temptations. There were scholars who observed the cupidity and ostentation of those who had grown rich, and they gave different explanations amounting to a sharp comdemnation of wealth and an outright denial that it was a positive gift of God. R. Ephraim Solomon of Luntshits, the leading preacher and moralist of Poland in those days, hated the wealthy in that country and strongly condemned their way of life. In his various collections of sermons he returns again and again to this main theme, which may be summed up in his own words: 'To retort to those misguided ones among our people who enjoy all the good and passing successes.' It should be borne in mind that his books are the record of hundreds of sermons, which he preached on countless occasions, including those he pronounced before the Council of the Lands of Poland. In his opinion 'the wealthy . . . are generally the powerful. They use brute force to establish their dominion over the scattered sheep of Israel, the oppressed people among them.' The poor of Israel, he argues, find themselves in grievous exile under this powerful and wealthy group, with their lust for domination and their callous attitude to others. In his opinion a man aspires to wealth because he wishes to be honoured; but wealth leads on to pride. 'For the proud in spirit normally wish for riches, whereby they can display . . . the splendour of their greatness. But all wealth leads to arrogance.' R. Ephraim repeats again and again that he is expressing 'the doubts that arise in the hearts of all men who give careful thought to God's ways. When they see some good man suffering . . . their reason is powerless to explain that anguish. . . . And whoever gives thought to this must clearly declare that there is room to complain at such a perverted state of affairs.' Even the earlier explanation of the Hasidei Ashkenaz (see page 549) that God gives wealth to those who possess it as a 'deposit' or 'pledge', whereby the wealthy man supports the poor, no longer satisfied those who agreed with R. Ephraim Solomon. 'In any case the poor man . . . has reason to complain of the nature of judgement: why should such a sentence be given by the Holy and Blest One that his fellow-man be given a double share of wealth in this world, and then, because he supports me, he will be delivered from the punishments of hell (*Gehinom*) as well, while I have nothing. Let me have the wealth and I shall be delivered from hell by giving him.'

R. Ephraim insisted on a two-fold confrontation. He compared the success of the wealthy Jews to that of the gentiles, and the abasement of the poor Jew to that of Israel in exile. By these comparisons he could argue: 'You wealthy Jews with your Jewish faith must admit that the success of the gentiles is no proof that God approves of them and not of Israel. And you, God-fearing Christian believers, have to agree that the success of the wicked wretches among you is no proof that God has chosen them.' The two groups to whom R. Ephraim is opposed – the wealthy Jews and the gentiles of the world, face an inner duty to admit

> that all who receive this [material] success . . . are not assured of salvation and mercy as they have thought . . . it is like a son . . . whose father never trained him. . . . Once he saw his father holding mouldy bread and rotten meat and he asked his father to give them to him . . . what did his father do? He flung the bad food to the dogs. . . . Such are worldly benefits in the hands of the Lord. . . . The Holy and Blest One flings them to the dogs, giving temporal success to the wicked. . . . And this assumption is a decisive answer to the lawless wealthy among our own people and the gentiles.

Here R. Isserles' pyramid of social values has been stood on its head. Riches are evil by definition and are generally given to those who are evil.

Another subject that was central to R. Ephraim's thinking was hypocrisy. His descriptions show that he was conscious of its presence in the Jewish society of his time. In a number of his sermons, and particularly in his book *Oraḥ la-Ḥayyim* ('A Way for Life'), he surveys the good deeds and institutions of his contemporaries and finds that though outwardly they appear to be good, they are spoilt by the unworthy purposes of those who lead them. From this confrontation of wholesome exterior with bad intentions, he concludes that in his generation 'all commandments begin and end in counterfeit'. The very importance attributed to good deeds, to the study of Torah and to prayer in an age steeped in the pursuit of wealth and material success causes people to perform good deeds in order to gain material and social reward, which Jewish society presents to those whom it regards as righteous and as scholars in the Torah. Therefore 'in this topsy-turvy generation all deeds have been spoiled . . . since the hypocrites . . . have become numerous and show so many qualities of piety openly, when all their purpose is to achieve respect and honour . . . or sometimes their desire is money and they hope to achieve it by asceticism.' He prefers to assess deeds by their inner intention and the doers by their true purposes. There is a fear that the so-called piety of a materialist community distorts the true piety of the soul by reimbursing it with worldly rewards.

The Jews During the Counter-Reformation

In the early part of the seventeenth century, Venice, then the largest Jewish community of Italy and the home of the first ghetto, had a rabbi who felt it necessary, for the purpose of influencing the surrounding Catholic society, to offer the non-Jewish world a picture of the Jewish community, its characteristics and aspirations, which in his opinion would persuade the non-Jews to treat the Jews well or at least to cease to harm them. Yet no comprehensive nor systematic presentation was possible without an extensive response to the prevalent social and political concepts of Italian Catholicism.

The work in question, written by the rabbi and *halakhist* R. Simḥah Luzzatto, is the 'Essay on the Jews of Venice', which was written in Italian in 1638. The declared purpose of the writer was 'to draw attention to the benefit which the members of the Jewish nation who dwell in Venice . . . bring to this city'. In addition to the economic advantages, however, he relies on the antiquity of his people. He uses terms and concepts taken from the humanists and the Church alike:

> Just as the remains of an ancient statue is of value for the lover of antiquities because it was made by Phidias or Lysippus, so it is fitting that the remains of the ancient Hebrew people should not be scorned, even though its appearance has been marred by the mishaps that have befallen it during its long exile; for it is generally known that aforetime, in the days of its glorious past, this nation received from the Great Master craftsman both its political constitution and the way of life (Luzzatto, *op. cit.,* p. 79).

He explains to the rulers of Venice that it is to their advantage that the Jews, rather than others, should accumulate the profits from commerce, 'for the Jews have no homeland of their own, to which they might wish to transfer the wealth they have gained in the city and they do not have permission to purchase real estate in any place; which is not the case with other merchants' (*ibid.,* p. 87). He finds it fitting to inform the Catholic rulers of the city:

> This people has a very weak and debilitated spirit and in its present condition is not fitted for any political dominion. The Jews engage in their own private affairs and are very little, if at all, concerned with their public matters. Their economical habits verge on miserliness. They esteem the past and pay very little attention to the course of contemporary affairs. Many of them have simple manners and only a few dedicate themselves to the sciences and the knowledge of languages. In observing their faith (as others argue) they go too far in certain respects and tend towards an exaggerated meticulousness. As against these defects you will find that they have qualities worthy of esteem: firmness and boundless constancy in their faith and in the preservation of their religion; unity in the dogmas of their faith . . . extraordinary courage, if not to the point of imperilling themselves, then at least in suffering distress; a singular familiarity with the Holy Scriptures and their meaning; charity and loving kindness towards men, and hospitality towards every one of their nation even if they are strangers and aliens. The Jew of Persia shares in the distress of the Italian Jew. . . . They are careful to preserve the purity of their race, protecting it from every admixture. Many of them are exceedingly shrewd and can negotiate the most difficult of transactions. They behave humbly and respectfully towards any man who is not of their own faith. Their sins and

crimes almost always derive from the lowly and disgusting rather than from cruelty and viciousness (*ibid.,* p. 106).

Many of these arguments – economic usefulness, diligence, faithfulness – were also used by Menasseh Ben Israel in the Netherlands and in England. There, however, he spoke to a Christian *milieu* where sections of the population were prepared to treat the Jews honourably in respect for their past, their culture and their character. In a Catholic environment, the Jewish apologist was compelled to stress his readiness to be humiliated; he had to agree that he was petty and low if his arguments were to be accepted by the masters of Venice.

Disputation and Tolerance During the Wars of Religion

Social thinking among Ashkenazi Jewry of the sixteenth and seventeenth centuries was greatly influenced by the developments that followed the Reformation and the conflicts within the Reformation leadership. The reactions during the early days of the Reformation have already been described above, with the Jewish stress being placed on 'nature, heart and reason', as against biblicist arguments of the Protestants. As time passed the Protestants split among themselves; yet the continued existence of Protestantism shattered the unity of the Christian world, which had borne down so heavily on the Jews of the early Middle Ages. In Poland-Lithuania, and also Bohemia and Moravia, there were many minor Protestant sects, some of them exceedingly critical of official Christianity. At a gathering of Protestants in Poland in 1567, it was said that 'an evil influence' was being exerted on the Lublin community by certain persons who came from Lithuania and preached against the divinity of Jesus and in favour of accepting certain precepts of the Jewish Torah. The leader of this 'Judaizing' trend was the Christian scholar and preacher Szymon Budny. His translation of the Bible differed in many details from the accepted Christian version. He specifically followed the Hebrew, basing himself on his knowledge of Jewish commentaries. On the other hand the Jewish disputant R. Isaac Troki used many of the arguments of Budny and his friends in arguing against other Christians. These Polish Judaizers were the extreme wing of a far larger group, known as the 'Polish Arians' who rejected the divinity of Jesus. Bohemia and Moravia also had individuals and sects of an extreme Reformational character, who, like the extremist sects in Poland, demanded an extension of tolerance.

The Jewish disputation with Christianity in Poland is comprehensible only against this background. R. Isaac Troki, the major disputant, was actually a Karaite, yet in his work *Ḥizzuk Emunah* ('The Strengthening of Faith') there is no sign of any separate Karaite position in the debate with the Christians, and he argues as a spokesman of all Jewry. There is a recognizable affinity to the views of the extreme Christian sects referred to above. Not only does he expressly quote the translations and treatises of their leaders, but he utilized the situation of Christianity in Poland and Lithuania in order to reply to the Christians, particularly the Catholics.

This atmosphere of moderate discussion in a world with many sects and viewpoints inevitably introduced a different attitude towards religious compulsion as such, even among people with a basically intolerant outlook. We have dealt above with the gulf that the Maharal of Prague saw as existing between Israel and Edom. In spite of this, when the Maharal set out to protest against the censorship of books imposed by the Catholic Church (which particularly affected Jewish books), he included in his argumentation several principles concerning questions of toleration and religious compulsion. From the viewpoint of Jewish culture, it is important to note that these ideas were promulgated by this Jewish scholar more than half a century before the famous protest made by the English poet John Milton in his *Aeropagitica* against the imposition of any limitations on writing and printing. In the 'Seventh Well' of his *Be'er Hagolah* ('Well of Exile,' Prague, 1598), Rabbi Loew lists four forces – or, in his terminology, 'sects' – that lead to the 'negation of religion'. Of these, the third is that force which he saw as splitting the unity of the peoples around him. 'It is religious fanaticism, when religion produces division within a nation, creating animosity and hatred within that nation. . . . For each separate nation has its own specific religion. And through religion it is that nation' (*ibid.,* fol. 44r). Accordingly, he pleads that each nation should be permitted to preserve its own faith, by which he meant that the Jewish nation should be allowed to remain united in its ancient faith. The fourth injurious factor derives from religious compulsion, and from his experience he saw it as an expression of political tyranny entering the field of religious free-will.

> For insofar as every religion in the world accepts the sovereignty of the King of Kings – that in itself stands against the concept of human monarchy. For if a king of flesh and blood decrees something against religion, his decree is to be disregarded and only the King of Kings is to be obeyed; and this is a rejection of the decree of his royal authority. Now there may be a man who violently wishes for royal power, desiring people to be utterly subjected to his authority, to obey him, and disregard the commandments of that king who is King of Kings. This is 'a wilfully wicked kingdom', for it is with malice that he wishes to rule over the people and display excessive governmental rule; . . . for he requires people to accept his decree even if it contradicts the decree of the Blessed Lord; and there can be no greater malice than that, as has been the practice of many kings. They impose decrees against the Jewish religion to demonstrate their rule over them. . . . And they undoubtedly did this because the observing of the religion which is decreed by the King on High draws men away from the authority of a human king. . . . And they so greatly desired to show great power as to demand that their decrees must be obeyed and those of the Eternal King be disregarded (*ibid.,* fol. 44v–45r).

The argument itself is intended to apply to Jewry, but its content and line of reasoning are taken from the general situation around him. He who imposes his own decrees on religion is an absolutist tyrant aiming at nullifying the autonomy of faith under its only sovereign, God. The oppressive ruler refuses to come to terms with the world of believers. His compulsion is entirely political, while the person suffering for his faith is defending the freedom of his religious conscience, which is subservient to God alone and with which Man has no authority to interfere. Here is a Jew employing the range of argument of the small extremist Christian sects that had revolted against the compromise reached during the sixteenth century by Protestant and Catholic rulers, whereby *cuius regio eius religio,* 'He who holds the region determines the religion.'

These general principles serve as an introduction to his argument against the censorship of printing. The rabbi explains to the powerful ruler 'that for the good of inquiry and knowledge it is not fitting to suppress whatever is opposed to his opinion'; in particular, it is necessary to permit the expression of ideas that are not intended to annoy 'but to state what the writer believes. Even if they contradict the beliefs and faith of the ruler, the writer should not be told: "Do not speak and keep your mouth shut." For that way there will be no clarification of faith' (*ibid.,* fol. 45v).

He explains that in such instances it is better to invite the opponent to express whatever he has in mind. There are several reasons for this. In case of suppression, the opponent can argue that 'if he were allowed to speak he could say more'. He then appealed to the chivalry of the ruler. 'Every knight who wishes to contend with any other to show his bravery desires his opponent to be as strong as possible. And then if the contender defeats him, he appears the better knight. But what bravery is there if the challenger is not permitted to stand up and fight?' (*ibid.,* fol. 46r). He reiterated that silencing those who are opposed to a particular religion is not a mark of strength, but rather a sign of weakness. Christians, he pointed out, permit the publication of the works of pagan philosophers who wrote against religion; he insisted that the entire concept of censorship is new. Moreover, he hints that compulsion leads only to an underground protest or hypocrisy. 'And the moralists have said: Beware of the secret enemy . . . who is unlike the one who states his beliefs, and who can be answered and dealt with by words. . . . There is no certain knowledge when people do not believe in religion and are far from it because they do not have one heart and thought in that religion' (*ibid.*).

The whole range of the Maharal's thought shows that he called for greater tolerance in the outer world than he would agree to practise within Jewry. Yet the details of his argument and their basis in practical and theoretical affairs, as well as their close resemblance to the arguments of the Christian sects, serve to show that the thinking of Jews in the Slavic lands was deeply imbued with the idea of toleration.

Theories of Education

In Ashkenazi Jewry of this period, and particularly among the scholars who spent most of their lives in Slavic countries, we find criticism of old and many suggestions for new methods of education. In due course the Maharal of Prague was regarded as the leader of this school, as his contemporaries and followers acknowledged, and he returned to the subject in a number of his works. Several of his contemporaries and his successors of the following generation declared that in this respect they followed in his footsteps. He objected primarily to the lack of a system for advancing pupils from the easy to the more difficult subjects. He placed great value on the subject of the Mishnah, the basic text of the Babylonian and Jerusalem Talmuds, in which he felt there was sanctity, a simple style and a pattern of living.

The dedication of time to the study of the Mishnah would direct the mind of the student to simplicity, and when he proceeded later to the study of the Talmud, his fine argumentation (*pilpul*) would aim at the truth. 'And I had already begun to instruct people to have their sons taught Mishnah first . . . but it did not last.' Since his own views ran parallel to those of his brother, R. Ḥayyim, he explained to those who wished to sharpen their minds through *pilpul* that 'it would be more fitting for them to engage in a craft which requires skill, such as carpentry, in order to master the subtleties of the Torah . . . for the keenness that comes from learning a craft is of the same kind as keenness for Torah; for both wish to arrive at the truth by keenness of mind.'

Some of his successors went even further. The remarks of the Polish scholar R. Jacob Horowitz, the brother of R. Isaiah and the son of R. Abraham (see page 710) are instructive in this respect. In his glosses to his father's ethical will, *Yesh Noḥalin* ('Some Inherit'), he censured the Jews of his time for not being sufficiently familiar with the Scriptures.

> Even though, because of our many sins, vision and revelation are no longer found in our midst, there being no prophet or seer with us, nevertheless their words still endure, though they themselves have passed away. And we are duty-bound to hearken unto their words, which are the words of the Living God. It is immaterial whether we hear the words of the prophets themselves from their own lips; or whether their words are alive and with us, reliable and delightful for ever and unto eternity. Therefore we must hearken to their words and cleave to them and toil and believe in their words which are uttered in truth. . . . And if one does not study them and know them and grow familiar with them, how can one hearken to their voices and obey? And even those for whom Talmud study is their life occupation – it is impossible that any study whatsoever should completely defer the study of Scripture, namely of the Bible from beginning to end; but he should be well versed in it (*Yesh Noḥalin,* Amsterdam, 1701, fol. 25v).

R. Jacob agrees with the Maharal about the importance of the Mishnah, but he maintains that the Scriptures have priority. He proposed a change in the curriculum not for the didactic reason of proceeding from the easy to the difficult, but for reasons of basic religious principle – a summons to return to the Scriptures because of their prophetic vitality.

This criticism of education thus involved the cultural content and the value assigned to the various historical strata. It indicates the problems faced by the highest level of Jewish scholars in those regions. The group did not consist only of professional rabbis. Men who had studied at the *yeshivot* and afterwards engaged in practical pursuits played a considerable part in it. David Gans, the great chronicler of Ashkenazi Jewry, was a pupil of R. Moses Isserles in Cracow and afterwards studied under the Maharal in Prague. His chronicle, *Ẓemaḥ David* ('The Plant of David'), published in 1592, was intended, as he explains 'for householders like myself'. The structure of the work shows that these laymen attributed to general history a value of its own. This chronicle is divided into two separate parts, Jewish history and the history of gentile nations and emperors. The two parts show how far the author is rooted in his country. He is proud of magnificent Prague and is particularly fond of Bohemia and Bohemian history. He uses many quotations, including page references, from Christian chroniclers, and explains that he found it necessary to relate so much about the rulers of the gentile nations because 'you will find certain morals in the history of the emperors; and they . . . are more easily accepted by simple folk when we tell them: "This is what Emperor So-and-so said".' R. Menaḥem Mendel of Berestechko, a hamlet of Volhynia in eastern Poland, demonstrates a comprehensive familiarity with all the branches of learning on which various works in Hebrew were then available.

The changes in cultural and educational values were therefore marked by a certain continuity of past patterns of Ashkenazi culture (see page 708). They derived chiefly from the forces operating in that society during the sixteenth and seventeenth centuries. Many of these proposals and criticisms foreshadowed programmes to be adopted in later eras (see Part VI).

Ashkenazi Thought at the Close of the Middle Ages

The range of creative activity in each of the scholars and circles quoted above displays different segments of thought. In spite of this, certain of these sections combine into one influential and formative entity that was equally subject to influences from within Ashkenazi life in the period under consideration – and far more than is usually supposed.

In the Ashkenazi *milieu* of Italy and Poland-Lithuania, from R. Joseph of Rosheim to the Maharal of Prague, there is a current of thought whose rationalistic content and educational trend is clearly recognizable even in circles which use mystical concepts and kabbalistic terminology. All these thinkers reflect in their writings the economic and social forces operating within the community. Jewish society was largely influenced by its spiritual and material successes, variegation and achievements. The main influence from the gentile surroundings is the atmosphere of humanism of the later Reformation, the culture which had advocated a return to Scriptural sources. The challenges deriving from Jewish society and the influences of this environment sometimes conflicted with one another. Nevertheless the challenges produced a synthesis rather than a clash. The influence of Safed also gradually made itself felt (as can be clearly seen in the case of the Horowitz family), until the rise of the Sabbatean movement.

The Path to the Modern

In Italy, on the one hand, and in the Netherlands, on the other, there were Jewish thinkers who were induced by the changes and crises in Jewish history to challenge the very foundation of Judaism, as they had been shaped during the Middle Ages. In his book *Shaagat Aryeh ve-Kol Sakhal* ('The Lion's Roar and the Voice of the Fool'), the Venetian scholar Judah Aryeh of Modena ironically, and in a form which allowed him to escape responsibility, noted basic arguments against the *halakhah* and the duty of obeying it. His own style of living, with its varied occupations and numerous contacts with the gentile world, suggests much of the same sceptical and ironical mood. He was not alone in such behaviour and views, although his extremism and his caution were exceptional.

In Italy this attitude was the fruit of the influence of the later Renaissance, with its affirmation of life and abandonment of barriers. In the Netherlands, however, parallel ideas arose largely because of the vacillation between Christianity and Judaism experienced by the Marranos. There were converts, particularly among the later generations after the expulsion from Spain, who had imagined the Judaism for which they secretly longed while under Christian domination as something very different from what they found when they actually returned to it. In their minds Judaism was identical with freedom of thought and criticism, with a breaking of the ecclesiastical yoke. They had become accustomed to offering criticism, either secretly or openly, of the Catholic Church as well as of its legends and laws, its clergy and ways of life. When Marranos of this kind reached the Spanish and Portuguese communities in the Netherlands, particularly Amsterdam, they found a Jewish society that had learnt by bitter experience what contact with non-Jewish culture in Spain had done to their forefathers; it was now conducting its own affairs in a Calvinist environment and had accordingly introduced a system of stern supervision of the individual, his way of life and opinions. It was difficult for the Marranos not to criticize both the Jewish *aggadah* and *halakhah,* and they found it hard to accept the control of individual life-styles by the rabbis and heads of the community after they had so strongly objected to such control by the ecclesiastical authorities in the Iberian Peninsula.

This type of Marrano is represented by Uriel da Costa, who fled from Christianity but could not find his place within the Jewish community. He was born in Portugal to a noble family of Jewish origin. He studied Canon law at a Jesuit university and took clerical vows. At the same time he began to feel that he could find no spiritual salvation in Christianity. As a result he decided to leave Portugal and persuaded his mother and family to flee to Amsterdam together with him. There they accepted Judaism. In Amsterdam, however, he revolted against the principles and commandments of the Oral Law and published treatises to defend his views, becoming a focus for polemics. Treatises were also published against him, and finally the congregation excommunicated him. He lived in isolation for several years, banned by his brethren.

In his isolation his views became even more radical, and he rejected the foundations of the Torah and the *halakhah;* but his desire for the company of Jews led him to declare that he had repented. He was compelled to agree to be flogged in the synagogue and to engage in public penance of a degrading kind. His rebellious temperament was deeply wounded by this submission to social discipline, for which he saw no spiritual justification. Soon after his public penitence, he committed suicide.

Far more deeply rooted in Judaism and a far sterner fighter than da Costa, was Baruch Spinoza (1632–77). He is the first Jew who is known to have rejected the Jewish faith and withdrawn from the society of his Jewish brethren without adopting another religion. Spinoza studied Torah with the rabbis and scholars of Amsterdam, and the impress of his studies, particularly of Maimonides, can be seen in his writings. He also refers to the messianic movement of Shabbetai Zevi, which had a powerful effect on Amsterdam Jewry. When Spinoza began to express his views in public, he clashed with the rabbis and leaders of the Amsterdam community, who excommunicated him in 1656. However, he did not remain completely isolated, but found himself a circle of Christian friends who held him in high esteem. The only effect of the ban was to remove him from the society of Jews. He earned a living by polishing lenses, while becoming one of the outstanding figures of world philosophy. He introduced his own system of divinity and morality, investigating the relationship between God and Creation and developing a pantheistic point of view. His thinking influenced and continues to influence many leading philosophers throughout the world. However, the desire for objectivity, which characterized his investigations of abstract questions, deserted him when he came to consider the relation between state and religion. His discussions of this relationship reflect the complex of tensions and animosities within the Jewish community of Amsterdam, on the one hand, and the ideas prevalent in Western Europe during the second half of the seventeenth century, on the other. In this respect the only work that Spinoza published (and published anonymously) in his lifetime is of particular importance. The others all appeared after his death. This work, which was printed in 1670, bears the Latin title *Tractatus Theologico-Politicus*. The purpose of the treatise was 'to explain that in a free state every man should be entitled to think what he wishes, and also to declare what he thinks'. In its historical and religious outlook, the entire work is dedicated to a critique of the Bible, and the work sets out to settle accounts with the Jewish people and their traditions. The opinions and expressions of the ancient Roman historian and Jew-baiter Tacitus and the reproaches of the early Church Fathers combined in Spinoza's consciousness when he wrote about his people's past. His own desire for liberty of conscience and his rejection of the Torah was tinged with his animosity towards the *halakhah* and *halakhists* and found expression in his characterization of the Torah and the Jewish people. One aspect of this approach is his tendency to view many Jewish laws and historical events as national and political matters affecting only the Jewish nation.

In Spinoza's opinion the Torah has no spiritual value save for those aspects that it shares with Natural Law and that are therefore binding on all mortals. 'The sacred ceremonies, as found in the Old Testament at least, were laid down for the Hebrews alone and were so adopted to their kingdom that for the greater part they could be performed by the entire society but not by individuals. . . . Therefore they have no relationship at all with happiness . . . but they are concerned . . . with the temporal peace of the body and of the kingdom.' Nor is the Torah obligatory for the Jews since the destruction of the Temple. 'After the abolition of their kingdom the Jews are bound by the Law of Moses no more than they were before the initiation of their society and state.' The obduracy of the Jewish leaders and their hatred of other nations had led them to act in defiance of this truth. The Pharisees continued to observe the laws of the Torah even after the destruction, 'more with the intention of opposing Christianity than of finding favour in the eyes of God'. The sages and scholars of Jewry also held fast to the Torah because of their desire to rule. It would seem that the leaders of the Amsterdam Jewish community served Spinoza as a measuring-rod by which he judged all the leaders of his people throughout the ages.

According to him, the Jews hate all other peoples. This hatred has become second nature to them because they foster it every day in their liturgy. Their manner of worshipping God not only differs from that of other peoples but is also contrary to them. He views the entire period of the Second Temple as one long civil war. Even good qualities that he may find in his brethren derive from their evil nature. The unity of Jewry and their present affection for one another derive from their hatred for all other peoples, and as a result all other peoples hate them. The destruction of their kingdom was because the Lord also hated them and gave them 'statutes that were not good and laws by which none could live'. He quotes the prophet Ezekiel in order to express this Christian opinion of the Torah and what it inevitably brought on the Jews who followed it. He is also of the opinion that 'when the Lord agreed that the Levites rather than the first-born should serve him after the sin of the Golden Calf, the Lord at that time wished not for their well-being but to punish them.'

Even the Maranno foundation of the Jewish community within which he had lived, and that was the direct intellectual source from which he had drawn his ideas, was attributed by him not to the spiritual strength of the persecuted Jews but to a change in the attitude of the Christian rulers towards them. He points to a difference which, in his opinion, is to be found between the behaviour of the converts in Spain and in Portugal. In Spain, where the Jews (*i.e.,* the New Christians) were permitted to occupy every position in the state, they assimilated, whereas in Portugal, where they were excluded from government posts, they did not assimilate. From which it follows that is is not worthwhile for the Christians to persecute the converted Jews nor to discriminate against them. Persecution restores them to their Jewish error. Good treatment may help to bring about their disappearance. Perhaps Spinoza even wished to hint that it was not worthwhile for the Christians to persecute the observant Jews, since persecution would strengthen them in their hatred; whereas a friendly attitude would lessen this hatred and bring them closer to the other peoples. He seems to imply that the martyrs who were tortured for their faith in Portugal, of whose bravery and self-sacrifice his brethren in the Amsterdam community were so proud, were simply a product of an unwise policy on the part of a single Christian kingdom and victims of their own desire for pomp and power. Spinoza makes no attempt to conceal his rancour towards the mediaeval life of the Jews and the religious and social phenomena of their ancient past from which mediaeval Jewry had drawn its strength.

He did not, however, entirely reject Jewish nationality and statehood. He considered the possibility that the Jews might return to their land and their kingdom even though he did not know how such a thing could actually come about. The embitterment of this philosopher was the first sign of the future revolts against the laws of the Torah, the nation's past and the communal structure. Like many of these rebels, Spinoza was more successful among Christians than among his Jewish contemporaries. In his own times he remained an isolated thinker cut off from the Jewish camp.

It is clear, therefore, that many tendencies and currents in modern Jewish history were emerging at the close of the Middle Ages, not only through the rise of indivi-

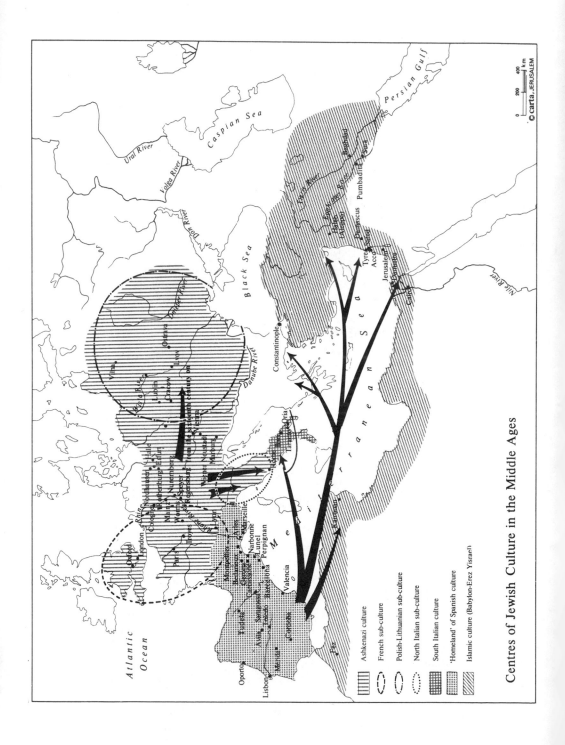

Centres of Jewish Culture in the Middle Ages

Ashkenazi culture

French sub-culture

Polish-Lithuanian sub-culture

North Italian sub-culture

South Italian culture

'Homeland' of Spanish culture

Islamic culture (Babylon-Erez Yisrael)

Atlantic Ocean

Caspian Sea

Ural River

Volga River

Don River

Black Sea

Danube River

Dnieper River

Mediterranean Sea

Persian Gulf

Tigris River

Euphrates River

Nile River

Constantinople

Vilna

Ostrog

Lublin

Lvov

Prague

Cracow

Vienna

Regensburg

Nuremberg

Rothenburg

Fürth

Speyer

Worms

Mainz

Frankfurt

Trier

Cologne

Koblenz

Neustadt

Mainz

Marburg

London

Oxford

Paris

Troyes

Lyons

Arles

Marseille

Montpellier

Béziers

Lunel

Narbonne

Perpignan

Barcelona

Valencia

Cordova

Lucena

Seville

Granada

Malaga

Toledo

Saragossa

Avila

Tudela

Oporto

Lisbon

Fez

Oria

Bari

Otranto

Taranto

Damascus

Aleppo (Halab)

Tyre

Acco

Safed

Jerusalem

Baghdad

Sura

Pumbadita

Damietta

Cairo

Carta, JERUSALEM

0   200   400
km

dualism, the crises immanent within the kabbalists of Safed and the messianic movement of Shabbetai Zevi, nor through the stand adopted towards the gentile environment during the Reformation and the periods of material and social success among Ashkenazi Jewry, but also because of the criticisms expressed by various thinkers in Italy and the Netherlands.

The Jewish Middle Ages went out, as it were, with the intensification of its specific modes of faith and hope to the pitch, a point where they clashed head on with reality and foundered on its rocks. Yet, the fires of the late seventeenth century consumed the excesses more than the norms. Continuity survived even that crisis in Jewish life. Much of the wreckage served both as a transition to the modern and as a means of preserving the old. The change in reality and in ideas was the challenge, but it also shaped the response. Thus, the first steps of the modern Jew were steeped in the mediaeval; and in this interaction of mutation and conservation, much of the mediaeval continued well into the modern period.

PART VI

The Modern Period

Shmuel Ettinger

42

Introduction

The Main Trends of Modern Jewish History

The condition of the Jews in modern times bears little resemblance to the situation during the Middle Ages. The social, cultural and economic conditions of the Middle Ages allowed the Jews a special status, both in their own view and in the eyes of the Christian and Moslem peoples among whom they lived; they enjoyed the status of a religious community and a closed social corporation. In modern times, however, circumstances changed. These included the emergence of centralized states that demanded absolute control over their subjects without the interposition of mediaeval-type corporations; the crystallization, within these states, of modern cultures and languages that suppressed local dialects and particularist aspirations; multi-branched economic networks that brought in their wake revolutionary changes in living habits and in the social order. The principles of legal equality, of the right of the individual to equal opportunity and of representative government that allowed the participation of the general public in important political and social decisions and mass networks of public and state education were also major influences towards radical social change. In fact, any one of these factors could have brought an end to the separate existence of the Jews.

The Jews were few in number at the dawn of the new age (less than one million in the mid-seventeenth century). Their considerable talent for adapting themselves to new developments, to the way of life and to the language of their environment; the desire of many of them to escape from the suffering entailed in being affiliated to Judaism and even in bearing the name 'Jew'; the great eagerness with which the economic entrepreneurs and intellectuals among them greeted new ideas; and the great hopes they pinned on the subsequent changes encouraged their integration and assimilation. And those unable to assimilate seemed doomed to become the fossilized remnant of a historical group with a rich and glorious past – a new version of the Samaritans or Karaites.

The historical development in fact proved to be very different. The number of Jews did not decrease; it multiplied at an extremely rapid pace, until it totalled nearly 17 million before the Second World War. They settled in large, important centres in Europe and the United States, where they created communities of outstanding intellectual, social and economic quality. In addition, their descendants have exerted considerable influence over the cultural and social life of the modern world by playing an active part in the political and ideological struggles of the times. Anyone perusing the thousands of publications – books, pamphlets and articles – dealing with Jews, Judaism or the 'Jewish question' that have been printed in European languages would find it difficult to claim that the Jews forfeited their focal position in European life during the modern period. In the course of time, they began to establish public organizations and political parties, and socialist trends appeared at the same time that a militant and resolute Zionist movement began to aspire to and organize its efforts towards the renewal of Jewish statehood. The Holocaust in the early 1940s, and the rise of the State of Israel at the end of the same decade are indisputable testimony to the fact that, for many of the gentiles who surround them as well as in the view of the majority of the Jews themselves, their communal and national uniqueness has never ceased to be significant.

It is not surprising that many people, both Jews and gentiles, friends and enemies, have continued in modern times to occupy themselves with the riddle of the endurance, survival and renaissance of the Jews. They ask why larger groups and equally strong cultures and civilizations – the Persians in Moslem culture and the Greeks in Roman-Byzantine culture – have vanished or have been absorbed while the Jews have remained Jews. Whatever their biological origin may be (there is no doubt that people of different stock joined the Jews through the ages), in their own consciousness and in that of their surrounding environment they remain 'sons of Abraham, Isaac and Jacob'. This endurance has aroused wonder and admiration, as well as jealousy and hatred. When one of Friedrich II's courtiers was asked by his monarch how he knew that there was divine providence in the world, he cited as overwhelming proof the survival of the Jews. On the other hand, for many scholars the persistent survival of the Jews constituted an ideological obstacle to their otherwise comprehensive historiosophical theories, and they dismissed this phenomenon as lacking in historical significance ('a living fossil' as Toynbee puts it). This view is apparently based on the assumption that if facts do not fit in with a theory then ignore the facts! Rigid dogmatists such as Stalin and his heirs – who established their own definition of the concept of nationhood – arrived, through their scholastic casuistry, at the negation of the very existence of the most ancient historical nation at the very time that it was demonstrating its extraordinary force for self-renewal.

The explanations of those scholars who have recognized the significance of Jewish existence can be divided into several categories. There are those who, sometimes out of a clearly Christian prejudice, offer modern extensions of the theological explanations propounded by the Church and by Christian dogma. This well-known belief holds that the Jews continue to exist as living proof of the verity of the Gospels and of Christianity. In other words, until the coming of Jesus, the Jews enjoyed a meaningful historical existence as the framework through which the appearance of Jesus was awaited; now, having rejected him, they live a life of slavery and degradation and exist only in order to prove that Christianity was no human invention. According to this view, Jewish existence since Jesus lacks historical significance because the Jews were left behind by history.

When this theological explanation began to lose its hold over the intellectuals of the seventeenth and eighteenth centuries, a new approach emerged, which endeavoured to explain Jewish survival not on religious-dogmatic grounds but from the economic aspect. According to this theory, the Jews were the transmitters of commerce and barter in a feudal society based on a natural and closed rural economy. This economic and social fact lent them their uniqueness and their cohesive force. Hence, the young Marx could claim in 1843 that Jews continue to exist not in spite of history but because of it, in that they symbolized capitalism and proceeded to renew it each day. The German economist and sociologist Sombart went so far as to argue that Judaism, in its very essence, was a religion of merchants and that there was a close resemblance between its laws and the 'spirit of capitalism' (without considering that the basic principles and rules of their religion had been formulated in a period when the Jews were farmers, living on their own land). Not one of these experts was prompted to ask why, in that case, the Jews had not disappeared from the world with the emergence of cities and the rise of the capitalist class in Europe; after all, the social world surrounding the Jews then began to resemble what, according to their argument, constituted the basis of Jewish uniqueness. In fact, the Jews became a significant factor in the economic life of Europe and continued as a group with a specific character *after* capitalism had established itself and had become dominant in most European countries. No less unfounded is the claim that the Jews continue to exist because of the hatred of the gentiles, who were unwilling to accept them into their midst (as if the absorption of the Jews had not been the declared aim of the Christian and Moslem nations for hundreds of years).

The common denominator of all these theories was the assumption that the Jews existed in order to fulfil a certain need in the society around them. On the other hand, they treated the Jews as the mere object of historical events, an inert body maintained only by the influence and developments of an alien world around it. However, it is evident that, even according to these views, Jewish existence is of importance and perhaps of universal significance in the life of other nations, which in a way echos the ancient theological theories.

It is impossible to deny that the Jews themselves – even those who recognize the existence of a Jewish nation in modern times – have been affected by the attitude of modern European theorists. In response, some of the founding-fathers of the Zionist movement were impelled to emphasize the biological element in Jewish survival. Aḥad Ha-Am, the Hebrew essayist and philosopher (1856–1927), claimed that the Jewish people did not exist for any specific purpose, but, like any other living body, as a result of its 'survival instinct'. The actions of Aḥad Ha-Am and other thinkers like him undoubtedly refuted their theories. If an objective and unconscious 'survival instinct' had been the source of Jewish endurance, there would have been no need for a nationalist movement and the revival of the Hebrew language and culture, nor for polemics against the enemies of the nationalist idea; the 'instinct' would have operated in any case. It would therefore appear that only by examining the social and psychological factors that affected the Jews as a group will we be able to understand the processes at play within the Jewish nation, particularly in modern times.

Internal Jewish life underwent profound changes in the transition from the Middle Ages to modern times. Formerly the Jews had wandered from West to East, from the more developed countries to the more backward ones, until by the seventeenth century the great majority of them were concentrated in the Polish Kingdom and in the Ottoman Empire. They then reversed direction: in the eighteenth and nineteenth centuries Jews began to move from the East towards the West, to the main economic and cultural centres of Europe and the United States. From the last quarter of the nineteenth century onwards, millions of Jews were caught up in this migration. It was this movement to new centres, more than any other factor, that brought about a change in the way of life and in the occupational structure of the Jews, created new social strata and destroyed the old social patterns of organization. Against the background of the political and legal changes that had been taking place from the time of the French Revolution in the countries of Western and Central Europe, this great wave of migration led to the disintegration of the Jewish community, *i.e.,* the corporative community organization that, from the end of the Middle Ages, had been displaying increasing symptoms of inflexibility and fossilization and that exercised powerful control over the life of the individual Jew. European political and social thought from the eighteenth century on was unwilling to accept the continued existence of mediaeval corporations and particularly those bodies, such as the Jewish community, that were 'suspect' and whose nature was incomprehensible to the European mind. The Jews now faced an alien and, for the most part, hostile environment, either as isolated individuals or as members of voluntary associations, while they approached it as supplicants willing to pay a high price for acceptance.

Despite the rapid dissolution of historical Jewish frameworks, this period witnessed an intensification of the anti-Semitic propaganda that claimed that all Jews everywhere maintained strong clandestine ties in order to gain control over Christian nations. This propaganda was furthered to no small extent by the remarkable success of many Jews in swiftly assimilating into the culture of various European countries, in learning their language and in winning for themselves prominent positions in economic and cultural life, in social movements and even in politics. All the spiritual qualities and traits that had evolved throughout the lengthy history of Jewish suffering and vicissitude were now to bear fruit in their capacity for adaptation to new conditions: their intellectualism and respect for learning, their rapid grasp of facts and their analytical ability. The Jews, who had been town-dwellers for hundreds of years, had developed these qualities more than even the population of the more advanced European countries. Mutual aid and solidarity – even without the rigid community framework – were much more developed among the Jews than among their neighbours. Sober reality aroused among many of them a permanent discontent with the existing situation and a stubborn resolve to 'remake the world into the Kingdom of God' by creating social and human harmony. Paradoxically, however, we find among the Jews examples of both extremes: the greatest smugglers and criminals existed side by side with the greatest scientists and artists; successful bankers and capitalists who had overcome social prejudices found themselves together with extreme revolutionaries; conservatives anxious to preserve the status quo at all costs and fearful of any daring or initiative lived side by side with fighters for emancipation and heroic warriors against tradition. Only against this background can one comprehend the strange phenomenon in many European countries at the end of the nineteenth century of voices being raised in defence of the hapless European against the all-powerful Jew. This renewed hostility towards the Jews, which advanced almost simultaneously with their legal emancipation, placed many Jews in a most difficult predicament; their increasing desire to be accepted by the society around them roused apprehension within that society, and their hand outstretched in friendship often encountered curt rejection.

As a result, Jewry stood at the crossroads. There were those Jews who thought the only way to persuade other nations that they were true Germans, Frenchmen or Poles was to renounce their origins, their historic traditions, their national culture and religion. For them assimilation and conversion were the sole cure for that hereditary disease – their Jewish origin. Others tried to differentiate between the national elements of their Jewish affiliation and its religious or spiritual aspects. They claimed that in the light of legal emancipation they belonged not only to the body politic of their country of residence but also to its national framework, while from the religious and moral point of view they remained Jews. And lest their Jewish loyalties be regarded as a stubborn unreasonable adherence to a meaningless past, they stressed the universal message of Judaism for mankind as a whole, its pure monotheism and consistent moral principles. They believed that these offered a solution to the problems of European society, embroiled as it was in contradictions and struggles, an answer that Christianity had failed to provide after nearly 2,000 years of rule. Another, more radical school of thought maintained that neither adjustment to European society nor altercation with it would help solve the problems of the Jews; what was needed was a fundamental reform of the existing order. Among these people there were some who advocated social radicalism and believed that in the new society that would rise in Europe after the purifying revolution, racial or community affiliations would no longer be of any importance and each individual would be judged on his own intrinsic value. There were yet others who chose the path of nationalistic radicalism out of the belief that a change in the existing situation could only be brought about through the systematic and organized exodus of the Jews from European society to a country of their own, where they would become 'a nation like all other nations'.

This myriad of opinions also demonstrates how full of contradictions Jewish national development has been in modern times. On the one hand we find the centripetal force driving individual Jews and various groups within the people to identify themselves with the Jewish past and with all Jews throughout the Diaspora, and on the other hand we see the centrifugal tendency pulling them apart and bringing them closer to their alien surroundings. In fact all Jews, with the exception of the inhabitants of the State of Israel, live on two planes; they are part of the societies and states among which they live and with which they share political loyalty, cultural and social creativity and economic activity, but at the same time they share in the lengthy historical, religious and cultural heritage of spiritual kinship to the Jewish community as a whole. There were periods, particularly in the second half of the nineteenth century and at the beginning of the twentieth century, when the centrifugal tendencies predominated. But the spread of modern anti-Semitism and the Nazi Holocaust led to a radical change: if deliberate flight from Judaism was no protection against the Jewish fate, then what point was there in abandoning a rich and ancient historical tradition?

These contradictory trends are not the product of modern times, but are characteristic of Jewish history as a whole. The Jews have never stagnated throughout their lengthy history because, despite the claims of various historiosophical theories, they are not merely a historical remnant nor a relic of the past but rather a living social organism, consciously struggling for existence and the right to develop. They have not stagnated because at no period in their history have they barricaded themselves against the social and cultural development of other nations, nor cut themselves off from the influence of other civilizations, but rather they have confronted them, both resisting their influence and absorbing their riches. A close scrutiny of the various strata of the Hebrew language or of the legal concepts and social patterns created by the Jews over the generations will bear out this assumption. Yet, one cannot overemphasize the tremendous force of historical continuity and of enduring conscious historical existence. This fact has transformed the Jews into an outstanding and unique historical phenomenon, which cannot be contained within the conventional patterns of the various rationalistic theories. Dostoevski, who could scarcely be suspected of great sympathy for the Jews, and who accused them of constituting a 'state within a state', put it as follows:

> It is not sufficient to attribute the *status in statu* only to persecution and to the instinct for survival; even the tenacity of the survival instinct could not have sufficed for four thousand years. It would have wearied of preserving itself for such a lengthy period of time. The strongest civilizations in the world never attained even to half of those four thousand years, and lost their political force and tribal image. The primary cause here is not the instinct for survival alone, but a driving and motivating idea, something universal and profound, and it is possible that mankind is not yet capable of passing final judgement upon it.

As a nation that had already achieved eminence in creativity and organization at a time when the European peoples were taking only their first steps in history and whose spiritual heritage formed the cornerstones of their culture, it was not surprising that the world outlook and self-awareness of the Jews should differ fundamentally from those of the peoples around them.

43

Migration and Economic Activity in the Seventeenth and Eighteenth Centuries

The Change in Direction of Migration

The processes that marked the transition in Europe from the Middle Ages to modern times and that laid the foundation for future changes did not, at the time, actually alter the status of the Jews or improve their conditions. The invention of the printing press, the great geographical discoveries, the shifting of the main commercial routes from the Mediterranean Sea to the Atlantic Ocean and the increase in the importance of northern Europe, as well as the political consolidation of European states, the Reformation and the religious wars resulted in religious, political and social ferment; and the truth of the old maxim that times of ferment are times of trouble for the Jewish people was demonstrated once again.

The expulsion of the Jews from the countries of Western Europe that commenced at the end of the thirteenth century had almost been completed by the beginning of the sixteenth century. In the seventeenth century there were only two main areas inhabited by considerable numbers of Jews: the Polish-Lithuanian Kingdom and the Ottoman Empire. Apart from these, there were Jews in relatively few towns of Germany and Italy. The total number of Jews in the world in the mid-seventeenth century was less than one million, and they were divided more or less equally between Sephardim (Jews originating in the Iberian Peninsula and members of the oriental communities) and Ashkenazim (Jews of Central and Eastern Europe). A change in Jewish dispersion began to be discernible at the end of the sixteenth century and became even more evident in the seventeenth century. At that time both the descendants of the Marranos (forcibly converted Jews persecuted by the Inquisition) and refugees from the Thirty Years' War and the 1648–9 Cossack rebellion led by Khmelnitski came to settle in the commercial centres that were developing in the West. They were very few in number, but, nevertheless, they represented the beginning of a great change of direction in Jewish migration. In place of wandering eastwards to economically backward and sparsely populated countries where their main economic and social function was urban settlement, estate management, innkeeping and petty trade, they began to move westwards to the centres of rising capitalism. This trend not only marked the beginning of a decisive change in the geographical dispersion of the Jews but in their economic activity in modern times; it was the preparation for their rise to importance in the economic, social and intellectual life of Europe during the nineteenth and twentieth centuries.

The Centres of Sephardi Jewry

The first Jewish settlers in the West were groups of refugees from the Iberian Peninsula who reached the northern countries and, at first under the guise of 'New Christians', set up communities in Antwerp, Amsterdam, Hamburg and London. Another branch of the same migration movement established new Jewish centres in France, in Bordeaux and its surroundings. Some Jews settled in Paris (until the eighteenth century under the guise of Christians), in Livorno in Tuscany, Venice and several other Italian cities, where Jewish communities existed during the Middle Ages.

These Sephardi Jews, who were mostly educated people of social standing, had fled Spain and Portugal and returned to Judaism. They did not find it difficult to establish contacts in their new places of residence; they merged into the social and cultural life, expanded their spheres of activities far beyond matters of commerce and finance, and even exerted considerable influence in political affairs. At the same time they remained deeply involved in Iberian affairs: they played an active part in the struggle of Portugal, which declared its renewed independence from Spain in 1640, in the wars of the Dutch and even in the forays of the North African pirates against Spanish shipping.

The close ties between the New Christians in the Iberian Peninsula and the Sephardi Jewish centres in northern Europe, Bordeaux, Italy, Constantinople and Salonika, the towns of the Levant and North Africa, created an important economic and social network based on family ties, tradition and language. In several respects it may be compared to the German Hanseatic League in the Middle Ages. One of the fundamental reasons for the increase in the economic importance of Sephardi Jews was the monopoly that the Spanish and Portuguese governments held over trade with their numerous overseas colonies. Spices and precious metals that arrived from these colonies were earmarked mainly for the developing markets of northern Europe, but because of the War of Liberation of the Netherlands against Spain, the lengthy state of hostility between Holland and Spain, as well as the war between Spain and England, the direct marketing routes were blocked. Trading was entrusted, for fixed periods, to trade companies, mostly run by New Christians, which carried out commercial deals for these governments. Thus the Christian kingdom that had expelled them found itself relying on the aid of its own exiles in order to benefit its economy, and also helping them to consolidate their position in their new places of residence in Europe.

Jews in Mediterranean and Colonial Trade

The settlement of Sephardi Jews in several of the key Mediterranean ports increased their commercial influence in this region. They expanded Dutch trade in the seventeenth century, and through their activities, Livorno gradually became a key port for trade with the North African coast. This encroached on the interests of French traders, and the merchants of Marseilles and nearby ports were constantly voicing complaints against Jewish competition. Many Jews served in North African ports as revenue officers and wholesale traders. They wielded considerable power and their ties with Jewish centres in Europe were of great economic and even political importance.

In the Levant ports on the eastern shore of the Mediterranean the Jews were also influential. They were active as middlemen in trade with Europe, and most of the representatives of the Dutch and English commercial firms in the Levant were Jews. At first the Jews of England were not permitted to participate in the activities of the British Levant Company, which claimed that because of the extensive influence of Jewish merchants in the East, its trade was in danger of being taken over by the Jews. In 1753 the prohibition was lifted, but those Jews who joined the company were not permitted to employ Jewish agents in the East. In practice, English merchants could not possibly operate in the East without the mediation of Jews. In a letter of an eighteenth-century merchant connected with the Levant trade, the writer made the following observation:

> The merchant can no more shake off his Jew than his skin. . . . The merchant cannot be without a Jew nor change that he hath. . . . It is not a little convenience that is had by these appropriated Jews; for they serve in the quality of Universal brokers, as well as for small or great things.

The Jews also achieved considerable importance in the activities of the Dutch East India and West India companies.

The Jewish role in trade and pioneer settlement was no less weighty on the American continent. A number of Marranos made their way to the Spanish colonies in central and southern America and Inquisition trials against them were common in the sixteenth and even seventeenth centuries. During the Dutch attempts at settlement of Brazil, in the fourth to sixth decades of the seventeenth century, a Jewish community grew up at Recife whose members carried out economic and even military tasks on behalf of the Dutch authorities. When the Dutch retreated before the Portuguese in 1654, this group of Jews moved to the Dutch colony of New Amsterdam (which became, ten years later, the British colony of New York) and were the first Jewish settlers in North America. Jewish communities also grew up in the British and French colonies on the Carribean Islands. In British-held Jamaica, the governor claimed in 1671 that His Majesty can have no more profitable subjects than the Jews and the Hollanders '. . . for they have great stocks and correspondents cannot find any but Jews that will adventure their goods or persons to get a trade'.

The Jews of Bordeaux, who enjoyed the support of the French authorities, took an active part in French colonial affairs. The Gradis family of Bordeaux, for example, excelled in economic activity and in particular in maritime trade from the end of the seventeenth century. It established two important commercial centres in the islands of Santo Domingo and Martinique. But the family's foreign trade activities were most extensive in Canada. They helped to consolidate French rule in this colony, and, during the wars between France and England in the mid-eighteenth century, they equipped privateers and thus helped maintain contact with the besieged colony.

Certain of the Jewish settlers in the British colonies in North America also took part in colonial trade activity. The outstanding among them in the second half of the eighteenth century, and particularly after 1770, was Aaron Lopez, a resident of

Newport, Rhode Island, who had 'above twenty sail of vessels' engaged in sugar trade with the West Indies and trading in rum, slaves and other such colonial commodities of the time.

Nevertheless, the number of goods in which Jews could trade was limited. The main one was sugar, which was being increasingly supplied to Europe from the plantations of Brazil and the West Indies. The Gradis family was one of the main sugar importers to France through the port of Bordeaux. The proliferation of sugar refineries in various European countries during the eighteenth century drove Jews out of this branch of commerce, and the experiments in extracting sugar from beets, conducted in the second half of the century, reduced its importance in colonial trade. A similar situation was created in the coffee, cocoa and tobacco trades, where the government monopoly and the domination of the merchant guilds led rapidly to the withdrawal of Jews from trade in these products.

The situation was different with regard to diamonds and precious stones. At the beginning of the eighteenth century Jews were purchasing some 80% of all the diamonds imported by the Dutch East India Company, as against 8% of all other commodities. The great majority of the diamond merchants in London at the end of the eighteenth century were Jews, and though the import of diamonds was, in actual fact, the monopoly of the East India Company, Jewish merchants also purchased the quantities smuggled in by numerous seamen. The discovery of diamond mines in Brazil seriously affected the monopoly of the East India Company. It went so far as to boycott the Brazilian diamonds, but Jews played a considerable role in introducing Brazilian diamonds to European markets. As a result of their standing in the diamond trade, they also became more prominent in diamond polishing. The Jews of Livorno also traded in corals, and their district became famous for its coral-jewellery industry.

The change in colonial methods and the gradual transfer of the adminstration of the colonies to governmental agencies finally put an end to the activities of the Jews in these fields. This is also one of the reasons for the waning of the economic influence of the distinguished Sephardi families in Europe after the French Revolution.

'Court-Jews' in the German States

The Thirty Years' War impelled the numerous German states to begin introducing centralized and absolutist administration, though they were somewhat later in this than other countries of Western Europe. One of the main obstacles to this change was the lack of an officialdom independent of the Estates and capable of serving the needs of the central government without favouritism. Yet another hindrance was the vigorous opposition of the patriciate of the big commercial cities to centralization and to new economic methods based on mercantilist theories. German rulers therefore chose to recruit the aid of the Jews to help implement their policy, particularly as purveyors to the army and the court, thus obviating the need to rely on the approval of the Estates. These Jewish agents of the rulers were known as *Hofjuden* ('court-Jews').

There were some court-Jews whose only task was to supply luxury goods to the courts of the rulers, and above all precious stones and jewellery. But coin-minting was a more important economic function. Since most of the coins in the seventeenth and eighteenth centuries were cast in silver, the expansion of economic activity and the widening of circulation led to a shortage of this metal, and one of the more important tasks of the Jewish minters was to supply the metal itself. Consequently, the reduction in the amount of silver contained in coins, which was, for example, a deliberate act of policy on the part of the Prussian King Friedrich II during his numerous wars, was widely regarded as the result of 'Jewish cheating'.

But the central task of most of the court-Jews was that of purveyors to the army. The strengthening of military forces was one of the tested methods by which smaller rulers tried to consolidate their political standing, but even the German emperor had recourse to court-Jews for supplying the army. Samuel Oppenheimer fulfilled this function at the end of the seventeenth century, in the troubled times when the Turks were besieging Vienna and during the numerous wars against the French. The court-Jews who had connections with supply sources of potash (for the manufacture of gunpowder), grain, fodder and horses, particularly in Poland, were capable of outfitting the armies on terms with which other suppliers could not compete.

The financing of the court and the army was of even greater importance. Samson Wertheimer, and his son Wolf after him, exerted considerable influence over the financial policies of the empire. They advised on taxes and levies, raised funds and provided subsidies and fulfilled those tasks that, in the modern centralized state, are carried out by ministries of finance. This activity strengthened the ties between the court-Jews and the rulers, and thus the political influence of the former grew. Diego Teixeira, a Marrano who returned to Judaism and settled in Hamburg, was the banker and representative of Christina, former queen of Sweden, in the mid-seventeenth century. Duarte Nunes da Costa was extremely active at the same time on behalf of independent Portugal. Behrend Lehmann, the court-Jew of the Duke of Saxony, helped him to be elected to the throne of Poland at the end of the same century. Because of these contacts, the court-Jews, both Ashkenazim and Sephardim, could exert diplomatic pressure in order to defend their brethren, as when Maria Theresa expelled the Jews of Prague in 1744–5 but eventually agreed to allow their return.

A court-Jew who became an initiator both of policy and its execution was Josef Suess Oppenheimer, known as 'the Jew Suess'. During the short reign of Karl Alexander, the Duke of Wuerttemberg (1733–9), Suess was the main planner and implementor of the radical reforms in state affairs. With the aim of increasing state income in order to maintain a strong army despite the opposition of the Estates (thus becoming an active factor in German politics), Suess brought about the dismissal of the state council and the establishment of a ministerial council responsible only to the Duke. The ministers were selected on his advice and were mainly foreigners. Suess proposed the establishment of a court treasury independent of the Estates, the sale of titles and an accounting department headed by a Comptroller General. He introduced police methods for handling the people, particularly in matters of tax collection, and concentrated on the development of industry and, above all, the manufacture of gunpowder. These methods earned him the hatred of large sections of the population. After the sudden death of the Duke, Suess was arrested, tried, and sentenced to death. He rejected a proposal that he convert to Christianity, and though he was not an observant Jew, died with the prayer *Shema Yisrael* on his lips.

The court-Jews were mainly active in Germany, but in the eighteenth century several Jews appeared in similar capacities in France, England and Russia. This group of court-Jews, which was numerically small but influential in political life and in Jewish society, served, as the Jewish courtiers in mediaeval Spain, as a kind of bridge for the cultural and social integration of the Jews into their surroundings, a process that, at the end of the eighteenth century and in the nineteenth century, encompassed a wide section of Jewry.

New Economic Activity in Central and Western Europe

The fact that the Jews remained outside the framework of the trade guilds and corporations (a situation they were forced to accept, despite its disadvantages, because of the Christian character of these mediaeval corporations) now made it easier for them to engage in the distribution of new goods such as cotton, silk and china manufactured in workshops and factories. The Jews played an active part in the trade fairs in southern and northern France. The large fairs in eastern Germany – at Leipzig, Breslau and Danzig – served as a meeting point for Jewish traders from Germany and Poland, and, thus, in the eighteenth century, barter trade between Poland and Germany became increasingly concentrated in the hands of Jewish merchants. Jewish capitalists in Germany often financed major deals, while the importance of Jews as money-lenders decreased considerably. They also began to play a prominent role in insurance (particularly marine insurance) and the stock exchange, and the second half of the eighteenth century witnessed the development of Jewish family banks, the importance of which became evident in the nineteenth century.

Even at the beginning of the modern era, however, the monopoly held by the guilds and trade corporations served as a hindrance to the entry of Jews into new branches of production. The new mercantilist tendencies of the various governments and the military supply needs that should, in theory, have encouraged the economic activities of the Jews, actually handicapped them to a large extent (here, too, mainly in the manufacturing sphere) because of the intervention of government officials and the strict supervision they imposed on all forms of production. Jews therefore did not attain importance in industry, with the exception of diamond polishing. In several Italian cities they took part in the development of the silk industry, which later also developed in Prussia. Jews also owned factories for the manufacture of textiles, hide processing, silver and gold plate, cigars and so forth.

Arenda, City Trade and Fairs in Eastern Europe

In the Polish-Lithuanian Kingdom the main economic task of the Jews was still the sale of agricultural produce and the supplying of goods to villages and estates. Thus there was a striking difference in the eighteenth century between the economic activities of Jews in the West, where they were connected with cities and states, and in Eastern Europe, where they were connected with villages. From this point of view, the activities of the Jews in the Ottoman Empire resembled those of Western Jews.

Arenda (the leasing for economic exploitation of feudal estates, or some branches of them, for several years, generally from an absentee landowner) was still of primary importance as a livelihood for the Jews of Eastern Europe. These were not the Arendas of complete estates as in the sixteenth and seventeenth centuries, but were concentrated on smaller branches – mills, fishponds, and, above all, the sale of alcoholic beverages. This last was the monopoly of estate owners. As it was practically the sole luxury item of the primitive rural economy, it served as a major source of income for the estate owner. The lessor, in the great majority of cases, was also the innkeeper and, to a large extent, the village trader, buying from the farmers their surplus produce and supplying their few outside needs such as salt, iron and tools.

The Jew's relationship with the owner of the estate was generally as agent or 'factor', supplying the owner or manager with the necessary commodities and luxury items and purchasing the estate's produce. The number of Jewish 'factors' in Poland in the eighteenth century was extremely large, and they were employed not only by estate owners but also by other people of standing and even institutions, like, for example, the theatre in Warsaw. Since the Polish economy in the eighteenth century was based on the estates, it is not surprising that a considerable part of Polish foreign trade was concentrated in the hands of Jews. A further result of this tie between the Jews and the rural economy was the dispersal of the Jewish population: in the mid-eighteenth century some 30% of all Polish Jews lived in villages and estates.

But in Eastern Europe as well as in Central Europe, the Jews were mainly town-dwellers. Not only were they of equal importance, both numerically and with regard to their economic task, to all the rest of the urban class (the majority of whom, in Poland, were not of Polish origin), but in many towns in eastern Poland they were almost the sole element engaged in urban economic activities. In these towns, which were under the private ownership of magnates and aristocrats, the squire derived only a small income from the fees of the inhabitants. And since the prices of agricultural produce were generally very high in West European markets, the squire would in some towns require his subjects to perform agricultural work instead, leaving the urban occupations to the local Jews. Very few towns enjoyed the economic support and political protection of their squires and were encouraged to engage in trade and crafts. And even then it was sometimes convenient for the squire to support Jewish trade, since the Jews had better foreign contacts, paid well and made no political demands whatever. Thus the trade operations of the Jews in Brody, for example, flourished with the help of the squires, and this town consequently became an important trade centre in eighteenth-century Poland, as well as the largest Jewish community in the country. Under these favourable conditions many towns in eastern Poland were transformed into predominantly Jewish towns. The homes of the Jewish residents were clustered around the town square, in which their shops and workshops were located, while the Christian residents resided in suburbs, where they lived semi-agricultural lives. This was the source of the growth of Jewish towns and townlets – of the Jewish *shtetl* as a type of social settlement – that left their mark on the organization of Jewish society in Eastern Europe until the Nazi Holocaust.

It is not surprising that Jews controlled urban trade in Poland and, in the eighteenth century, even a considerable proportion of the crafts. In the 'royal towns', which were administered by officials of the king and in most of which the Christian citizens had their own internal, autonomous organization, the Jews played an important role, despite the bitter war that the other residents waged against them. Jews who settled in suburbs or *juridikas* (buildings or quarters outside the jurisdiction of the town) competed with the urban guilds and corporations and developed new and unconventional trade methods. These activities were regarded by the citizens as immoral, one reason they became the avowed enemies of the Jews. The extent to which Jews controlled urban trade is attested by the claim of a foreign visitor to Poland at the beginning of the eighteenth century that as he had arrived on the Jewish New Year he was unable to obtain any of the goods he wanted.

One of the factors that encouraged the activity of East European Jews in trade and crafts and helped them overcome the pressure of the guilds and trade corporations were the fairs or annual market days, at which the monopolistic rights in force throughout the year were temporarily waived. Most of the agricultural transactions were concluded at fairs, and, as a result, several of the towns in the East, such as Dubno or Berdichev, achieved economic eminence in the eighteenth century. At the fairs contracts were signed, credit arrangements were made, and retail and whole-sale trade flourished. The social significance of the fairs was also considerable. There, it will be recalled, the Polish representatives of the Council of the Four Lands met, marriages were arranged and social gatherings held.

In short, there was a clear differentiation in the seventeenth and eighteenth centuries between the economic activities of the Jews in the East and in the West. In the East they continued to engage in activities connected with the estate and the village (the main importance of the town and townlet lay in their role as buyers and sellers for the villages), while in the West they were turning to international and colonial trade and to activity connected with the centralist aims of the rulers – mainly financial counselling, the recruitment of funds and financial administration. The former were perpetuating traditional forms of economic activity as evolved in Eastern Europe from the sixteenth century onwards, while the latter were taking part in the rising capitalistic developments, which were to alter the economic and social organization of European society. But in both regions the activities of the Jews furthered the political and economic aims of the rulers and thus brought down upon their heads the wrath of the urban elements, who were beginning to demand additional rights and, in the West, even participation in government. The strengthening of the town element also increased the importance of the Jews in the eyes of the rulers and intensified competition, hostility and charges of Jewish exploitation and immorality. But despite the differences between the economic activities of the two geographical divisions of Jewry, there was contact and cooperation between them: the Jews of Europe needed the help of the Jews of the Islamic countries for Mediterranean trade, while the latter utilized the trade contacts of the European Jews for their purposes. The Jews of Poland made use of the credit of German Jews, while the latter, in their turn, needed supplies provided by their Polish brethren. The basis for future differences in development had already been created, but cooperation still existed.

44

The Attitude of European Society in the Seventeenth and Eighteenth Centuries

The Twofold Effect of the Reformation

The religious Reformation of the sixteenth century destroyed the unity of the ecumenical Christian church, which had existed, at least in theory, throughout the Middle Ages, and led to the proliferation of churches and religious sects. The splinter groups failed to accept the principle of religious tolerance; on the contrary, they attacked each other violently, fighting the 'heresy' and 'satanic schemes' of their rivals. The Counter-Reformation and the religious wars that took place in Europe during the second half of the sixteenth century and the first half of the seventeenth century produced dual results: increased religious fanaticism and a deepening schism on the one hand, but at the same time an awareness that problems of faith could not be solved by force. Thus a political basis was created for compromise between the opposing religious trends and for the possibility of maintaining Catholic and Protestant states side by side. But the compromise of 'faith is determined by the ruler' not only failed to alleviate the tension but actually aggravated the situation of religious minorities within the states. In the second half of the seventeenth and the beginning of the eighteenth centuries, there was no obvious difference between members of the Protestant and Catholic churches as far as their attitude towards the Jews was concerned.

The Spread of Religious Tolerance and the Growing Respect for the Jews

Religious tolerance did not emanate from the churches but from several marginal religious schools of thought and from the theories of great thinkers, who began to question the connection between religious truth and political rule. Such views were expressed several times in the turbulent years of civil war and Puritan revolution in England. One of their most vehement spokesmen was the preacher Roger Williams, founder of the colony of Rhode Island in North America. In an essay published in London in 1644 he claimed that 'true civility and Christianity may both flourish in a state or kingdom, notwithstanding the permission of divers and contrary consciences either of Jew or Gentile.' Hence his conclusion that 'it is the will and command of God that, since the coming of His Son, Lord Jesus, freedom of religion, a permission of the most Paganish, Jewish, Turkish or anti-Christian conscience and worship, be granted to all men, in all nations and all countries.'

The basic principle of this concept also found expression in the famous essay by John Locke, 'Letter Concerning Toleration' (1689), in which he wrote, *inter alia*: 'There is absolutely no such thing under the Gospel as a Christian commonwealth.' There was in early Christian times no connection between state and church. The church was 'a voluntary society of men, joining themselves together of their own accord in order to the publick worshipping of God.' And hence the conclusion: 'Neither pagan, nor Mahometan nor Jew ought to be excluded from the civil rights in the commonwealth because of his religion.' Thus the basic theory of religious tolerance was formulated at the end of the seventeenth century, although this in no way meant that tolerance was practised within the framework of states. At the most, enlightened circles in Europe in the eighteenth century accepted the call for tolerance as expressed in the speech of the Jew in *The Spirit of the Laws* by Montesquieu:

> If Heaven has had so great a love for you as to make you see the truth you have received a singular favour; but is it for children who have received their father's inheritance to hate those who have not? If you were wise, you would not put us to death for no other reason than because we are unwilling to deceive you. We believe that the God whom both you and we serve will not punish us for having suffered death in a religion which he formerly gave us only because we believe that he still continues to give it.

More influential in the seventeenth century than the explicit statement in essays of this type that the Jews deserved to be tolerated, was the rising importance of Hebrew and Jewish literature in the spiritual life of Europe. There was an increase in the number of learned Christian Hebraists at European universities, and special chairs of Hebrew and of Jewish studies were established. The Bible became more important as an authority for political thought, and the society and state of ancient Israel were held up as an example of an enlightened political society. The Mishnah and the teachings of the Jewish sages were often consulted as authorities in legal or theological questions by such great scholars as Lightfoot and Selden, and mediaeval Jewish philosophy and thought were hailed as important achievements in the realm of rationalist theology and studied by many contemporary thinkers.

It is true that the study of Judaism was often undertaken merely as an aid to polemics and that the most important Hebraists engaged in anti-Jewish religious debate and argued in favour of the conversion of the Jews; nevertheless, because of this preoccupation and study, the prestige of Judaism and of the Jews grew in enlightened circles. Even those who dreamed of the conversion of the Jews, such as the German theologian Johann Christoph Wagenseil, defended them against attack and libel. An anti-Semitic book such as *Das entdeckte Judentum* (Jewry Exposed) by the orientalist Johann Eisenmenger, which was published in 1700 and was a source of quotations for anti-Semites in generations to come, was not widely distributed in its day, and the author himself was arrested by the authorities.

Mercantilist Theory and Jewish Apologetics

The spread of the new political and economic thought also contributed to the changing European attitude towards Jews. 'The welfare of the state' became an accepted principle in wide circles: people were to be judged not by religious affiliation but by their usefulness to the state. As the expansion of the population and commercial activity aimed at increasing the prosperity of the state were among the basic tenets of the accepted mercantilist theory at the end of the seventeenth and beginning of the eighteenth centuries, the economists who advocated this method should, in theory, have supported the integration of the Jews into the society. But, in fact, several of the more important proponents of mercantilist theory in Britain and Germany, such as Sir William Petty or Johann Joachim Becher, were among the enemies of the Jews, holding that they brought more harm than advantage. Still, few economists of the period paid attention to the activities of the Jews.

The main proponents of the rights of the Jews for utilitarian reasons were the Jewish apologists. In 1638 Rabbi Simone Luzzato published an essay in Italian entitled 'Essay on the Jews of Venice' in which he enumerated all the advantages his and other states could derive from the presence of the Jews: 'Wherever the Jews live, trade and dealings flourish'. They developed new branches of the economy, did not purchase real estate and did not seek power. These are also the central arguments of Menasseh Ben Israel in his 'Humble Addresses' to Cromwell to permit the return of the Jews to England. The dispersal of the Jews had not made them 'a despicable people, but as a plant worthy to be planted in the whole world . . . being trees of most savory fruit and profit'.

The reverberations from the writings of the Jewish apologists can be assessed from the remarks of Sir Josiah Child, head of the British East India Company, who, in a treatise published in 1693, proposed that Jews settling in England should be naturalized. Holland had acted after this fashion and thus attained considerable economic success. The impact is even more evident in a pamphlet by the deistic philosopher John Toland, who suggested *Reasons for Naturalizing the Jews in Great Britain and Ireland* (1714). He listed all the advantages that the Jews might bring to the country and explicitly based himself on Luzzato. A similar thread runs through the writings of Montesquieu on the subject, when he emphasizes the importance of the Jews to European trade in the Middle Ages: Christian theologians had prohibited loans at interest and trade and thus helped transfer it to the Jews. Kings were in the habit of expelling Jews and expropriating their property, and the Jews therefore invented the letter of exchange, in order to transfer their money from country to country. In this way the property of the rich merchants became unseizable. Commerce, by this method, became capable of eluding violence and of maintaining its ground anywhere. Henceforth it became necessary for princes to govern with more prudence. They were placed in a situation in which it was to their interest to be humane and virtuous. Without explicitly saying so, Montesquieu aroused in readers of his influential book the impression that the Jews were fulfilling an extremely positive role in the economic development of European countries.

The European Enlightenment and the Jews

The spread of the ideals of the Enlightenment in the countries of Western and Central Europe throughout the eighteenth century brought about a profound change in the attitude of the educated class of Europeans towards the Jews. But this new approach was not lacking in ambivalence. Though ready to recognize the equal value of each individual as a 'human being', whatever his origin or religious affiliation, it was totally unwilling to accept the existence of historical groups that sought, for whatever reason, to preserve their separate identity within the state. Furthermore, the demand of certain Jews to be accepted into European society while belonging to the 'separatist' Jewish group was regarded as hypocritical.

As a young man the well-known German writer Gotthold Ephraim Lessing wrote a play entitled *The Jews* (1749) with the sole purpose of proving that even among the Jews there were decent and honest people worthy of esteem. In *Nathan the Wise* (1779) he depicted the Jew as a proponent of natural religion, opposed to positive religions both in theory and in practice. To the accusation levelled against the Jews that they had introduced the religious split between human beings and were the first to regard themselves as the 'chosen people', Nathan replies: 'I did not choose my people nor you your people . . . I am a man first and a Jew second and you are a man first and a Christian second.'

The philosopher Herder, on the other hand, after defining the Jews as 'a parasitic plant, clinging to almost all the European nations and sucking their marrow to a lesser or greater extent' envisaged the day 'when it will no longer be asked in Europe who is a Jew and who a Christian, since the Jew will also live according to European laws and will contribute his share to the good of the state'. The most succinct formulation of this approach was that of Clermont-Tonnerre, voiced during a debate in the French National Assembly in December 1789:

> We must not permit the Jews to constitute a separate political body or class in the state. It is necessary that each of them individually be a citizen. But, it will be claimed, they do not want this. Very well, if they do not want it, let them tell us so, and then it will be necessary to expel them. We cannot allow there to be in the state a group of non-citizens, a nation within a nation. But, in fact, it is clear that this is not their wish at all.

The Negative Attitude of Deists and Philosophical Rationalists

The opposition to recognizing the Jews as a group with the right to exist within the framework of European society did not emanate for the most part from fears of political disloyalty, of 'the state within the state' or 'nation within a nation'. It grew mainly out of the struggle of enlightened elements against the rule of the Church. The English deists, supporters of natural religion and opponents of all revealed religions, were the first to claim at the beginning of the eighteenth century, out of their desire to undermine the principles of the Christian churches, that the Jewish Bible was a fabrication, that their forefathers and heroes were immoral scoundrels and their prophets were narrow-minded fanatics who engaged in religious persecution. The Jews, they believed, had always been a barbaric, cruel and corrupt nation. Many of the violently anti-Jewish arguments of the Church Fathers were raised once again in the extensive deistic literature, with the rather transparent aim of attacking Christianity by undermining the foundations of its progenitor, Judaism.

Voltaire imported this method into France. In the entry on 'Jews' in his *Philosophical Dictionary* (1756), he wrote:

> Large nations cannot take their laws and beliefs from a small, unknown and enslaved nation. . . . Anyone who claims that the Egyptians, the Persians and the Greeks took their knowledge from the Jews is like someone who claims that the Romans learned their crafts from the inhabitants of lower Brittany. . . . Their residence in Babylon and Alexandria, which allowed individuals to acquire wisdom and knowledge, only trained the people as a whole in the art of usury. . . . In short, they are a totally ignorant nation who, for many years, have combined contemptible miserliness and the most revolting superstition with a violent hatred of all those nations which have tolerated them. Nevertheless they should not be burned on the stake.

One member of Voltaire's circle, the materialist philosopher Holbach, defined the Jews in terms that have served anti-Semites throughout history:

> The revolting policy of the Jewish legislator (Moses) has erected a stone wall between his people and all other nations. Since they are submissive only to their priests, the Jews have become the enemies of the human race. . . . The Jews have always displayed contempt for the clearest dictates of morality and the law of nations. . . . They were ordered to be cruel, inhuman, intolerant, thieves, traitors, and betrayers of trust. All these are regarded as deeds pleasing to God. In short, the Jews have become a nation of robbers. . . . They have become notorious for deception and unfairness in trade, and it may be assumed that if they were stronger, they would, in many cases, revive the tragedies which occurred so frequently in their country. . . . If there are also honest and just people among them (which cannot be doubted) this means that they [*i.e.,* the few honest Jews] have rejected the principles of that law clearly aimed at creating trouble-makers and evildoers.

The German philosopher Fichte combined these two arguments regarding the moral corruption of the Jews and the fact that they constituted 'a state within a state' into a vicious indictment against them. In a book published in 1793 he vehemently opposed the granting of rights to the Jews, as they were 'a hostile and powerful state, in constant war with other states and in several of them severely oppressing the citizens'. He did not believe in their ability to become loyal citizens of countries of their residence. 'Give them civil rights? I see no other way of doing this except to cut off all their heads one night and substitute other heads without a single Jewish thought in them. How shall we defend ourselves against them? I see no alternative but to conquer their promised land for them and to dispatch them all there.' If they were granted civil rights they would 'trample on the other citizens'.

745

It is not surprising that the proponents of these theories believed in the eighteenth century that every effort should be made to free the Jews and the whole world from the disaster known as Judaism. As Kant noted in *The War of Faculties* (1798): 'The euthanasia of Judaism can only be achieved by means of a pure, moral religion, and the abandonment of all the old legal regulations' (*i.e.,* of Judaism).

The 'Improvement' of the Jews as a Method of Integration

A substantial section of the educated class in the eighteenth century nevertheless believed that it was possible to find ways of improving the Jews so that they could be absorbed and integrated into European society – even without altering their religion and beliefs. The Jews, it was argued, had many flaws and were infinitely inferior to the Christians. Yet it was the duty of Europeans to help reform them, as the laws of mediaeval Christian rulers and the persecutions by the church were what led to the Jews' isolation and their preoccupation with trade and money-lending, which were the causes of their moral corruption. The plans put forward included far-reaching changes in the economic occupations of the Jews, their way of life and their communal organization. In his book on the *Civil Reform of the Jews* (1781) C. W. Dohm proposed that they be granted equal rights and complete freedom in choice of occupation – although, above all, they should be encouraged to engage in crafts. He also proposed freedom of worship and the opening of synagogues, the abolition of special Jewish quarters (ghettos), admittance into schools and permission to engage in science and the arts. At the same time he advocated the prohibition of commercial book-keeping in Hebrew in order to increase mutual trust and prevent deception. He also favoured supervision to ensure that Jewish schools should not be infiltrated 'by anti-social attitudes towards those who think differently . . . [and that] some of the pure and holy truths of the religion and moral theory of rationalism [be nurtured], in particular the respect of all citizens for the state and acknowledgement of their obligations towards it'. Dohm also warned that Jews should not be encouraged to train for state service and suggested that if a Jew were equal in qualifications to a Christian, the latter should be preferred. His point of departure was, naturally, the belief that Jews had a tendency to be dishonest and were afflicted with greed and that their religious tradition was imbued with hatred of Christians and of the state. A new educational method was required, therefore, under efficient government supervision 'to prepare the coming generations, at least, for a more moderate attitude towards those with different views'.

Dohm's book greatly influenced enlightened writers in other countries in their discussion of the Jewish question and their proposals for the reform of the Jews. These proposals differed in detail. The French cleric Abbé Henri Gregoire, who was awarded a prize by the Society of Sciences and Arts in Metz for his 'Essay on the Physical, Moral and Political Renaissance of the Jews' (1789), proposed the dissolution of Jewish communities and their transformation into private associations, occupied only with questions of religious worship and not with political or social matters. All Jewish gatherings would be chaired by a government representative and all deliberations would be conducted in the language of the country. Abbé

Gregoire was the sworn enemy of all local dialects, but especially of the 'German-Hebrew-Rabbinical jargon which the Jews of Germany employ and which only they understand, the main aim of which is to increase their ignorance or camouflage their lust'. In short, Gregoire wanted to restrict to the minimum all those factors differentiating Jews from their surroundings. In 1785 a Polish author had proposed that the Jews be forbidden to use their language in any document whatsoever, so that it would die out naturally. They should also be prohibited from wearing special clothing, from selling alcohol, and, above all, in order to reform them completely, they should be conscripted for military service.

Discussions About the Jews at the Time of the French Revolution

In the French National Assembly and the Batavian (Dutch) National Assembly the old as well as the new attitudes of various social groups towards the Jews became, for the first time, a weighty political factor in determining their legal status. Generally speaking no one was willing to advocate openly the idea of depriving Jews of their 'human rights', *i.e.,* freedom of movement and the right to choose their place of residence and occupation. The controversy revolved around the problem of political and civil rights. In the course of the discussion in the French National Assembly (December 1789), the clergy and the conservatives claimed that 'the word *juif* is not the name of a [religious] sect but of a nation which has laws of its own, according to which it has always acted and wishes to continue to act. If you define the Jews as citizens, it is as if you had said that Englishmen and Danes could be French citizens, without papers and naturalization and without ceasing to be Englishmen and Danes.' On the other hand, according to the radical delegates, as represented by Robespierre, 'The evil qualities of the Jews emanate from the degree of humiliation to which you have subjected them' and 'any citizen who fulfils the conditions of eligibility you have laid down, has the right to public office.'

Abbé Gregoire initiated vigorous action and published 'A Motion in Favour of the Jews', but the opponents were many. There was an increase in the number of attacks on the Jews in the right-wing press, and various works were published vilifying them. On the other hand, the left-wing press encouraged those who demanded equal rights for the Jews, even to the point of reproaching the National Assembly for its hesitation. The Jacobin clubs and several of the district communes in Paris passed resolutions in favour of the Jews, and the City Council of Paris even sent a deputation to the National Assembly for this purpose.

Similarly, in the Batavian National Assembly in 1796 there were those who claimed that 'the Jews were banished from the Land of Canaan and their hope is to return to the land of their fathers. Therefore they are as strangers in all other lands and unworthy of being dwellers in a republic, for they stand and yearn with all their hearts for the coming of the Messiah, who will be a mighty king'. As against these, the supporters of the granting of rights to the Jews replied that 'the Jews are human beings as we are and their deeds bear testimony that they have participated as have all inhabitants of Batavia in electing representatives of the people' (*i.e.,* the National Assembly).

'And this they were asked: Are the Jews now to be thought as a people or a nation on their own. . . . On this too they were questioned: To whom is the name of people to be given: to a group of people of one state or to people of one faith? It was found that those who were Jews by faith, were not called a nation unto themselves since they have no state of their own.'

It seems, therefore, that there were many fluctuations in the attitude of Europeans towards the Jews during the seventeenth and eighteenth centuries. For the advocates of religious tolerance and for those who called for separation of church and state, Jews constituted an example of existing discrimination. The former, regarding religion as a matter for the individual conscience and not for the public, paid no attention to the faith of the Jews or to the extent of their willingness or capacity to integrate in European society. In contrast, those influenced by the secular state theory and the arguments of the mercantilists advocated tolerance towards the Jews, and even the granting of civil rights to them, out of admiration for their commercial abilities, economic initiative and political loyalty. A state interested in enlarging its population and economic prosperity would find it to its advantage to accept Jews. The writings of Jewish apologists proved effective in influencing several political writers in Europe.

Another reason for the changing European attitude towards the Jews was the increased interest in their political, legal and philosophical traditions, which began to play an important part in European spiritual life from the seventeenth century onwards. But the revolt against revealed religions, the antagonism to the Bible and the criticism of church tradition and organization, which became more intense in the eighteenth century, changed this attitude from esteem to hostility. The English and French deists and the radical materialists diverted their war on the Church and narrowed in on Judaism as the progenitor of Christianity. Attacks on Judaism were employed as a useful tactic: it was easier to undermine the foundations of Judaism and to debase it than to come out openly against the established religion. In the course of their campaign, they reverted to the arguments of Jew-haters of previous generations and did not differentiate between the ancient Israelites and the Jews of their day. It is possible that they were displaying the ignorance of historical development, which indeed characterized eighteenth-century thought, but it is also possible that in their eyes the ardent loyalty of the Jews to their ancient tradition, which was thought to be dark and corrupt, was in itself regarded as suspect. Thus the European Enlightenment absorbed into its philosophy of respect for all men, including those born Jewish, and of respect for freedom of conscience and opinion, certain reservations as regards Judaism. They saw it as the false creation of priests and rabbis and, in regard to the Jews themselves, as a group claiming the right to a separatist existence. Even those intellectuals who were opposed to attacks on Judaism and to religious polemics believed that the reforms they were proposing for the Jews – in their appearance, way of life and occupations – would lead the Jews themselves to abandon their old superstitions. And to the extent that these remained, they would be the personal affair of the individual. The right of the Jews to exist as a group was still accepted only by millenarians, who hoped for universal mystical salvation and who claimed that the return of Israel in body, whether to Christianity, to their own country or even to both together, was the precondition for the universal salvation promised in Christianity. In any case, in the political polemics regarding the status of the Jews at the time of the French Revolution, when the principle of separation of church and state was generally accepted, their opponents claimed that the Jews were a separate nation and not only a religious entity and, therefore, unable to claim any political rights. Their supporters, on the other hand, agreed to accept them into society as individuals who would be expected, to a greater or lesser extent, to disavow their heritage.

45

Legal Status in the Absolutist States and During the French Revolution

The Pressure of Centralization versus Particularism

The organization of European society in the Middle Ages was basically corporative, *i.e.,* each social group or corporation had its own clearly defined political and social status and all the groups existed side by side, although their rights sometimes conflicted. The solution to these clashes was generally reached through the custom of the land or by force. In the Islamic countries the situation was similar, particularly after Turkish rule was consolidated. Under these conditions the Jews were considered to be one of these corporations, playing a marginal role in society and suffering discrimination. There was no fundamental contradiction between their separate existence as a group with their established right 'to live according to their laws' and the general political order (see Part V).

The strengthening of centralist and absolutist trends in the countries of Europe from the sixteenth to eighteenth centuries brought about a far-reaching change in this situation. The absolutist rulers were anxious to break down all the corporative barriers that cut them off from their subjects and to introduce uniform legal and administrative procedures. Jurists in the seventeenth and eighteenth centuries, particularly in the German states, began to argue against the existence of corporations in general and the autonomous Jewish community in particular. Under the new circumstances the very existence of the Jews as a separate corporation constituted an anomaly contradicting the main trend of political development. These changes were particularly noticeable in the German states. There problems of public law and state administration had become urgent because of the growing clashes between the antiquated framework of the Holy Roman Empire and the aspirations of the individual states and constituent political bodies, as well as between the rigid conservatism of the Estates and the urban patriciate and the growing force of the rulers who were striving to achieve absolute power. This development was to leave its mark on the legal status of the Jews in Western and Central Europe until the period of Emancipation and to serve as a powerful factor in moulding Jewish self-awareness and organizational patterns in modern times.

All the new processes were extremely important because they pointed out the direction that historical development was taking. In a practical sense they did not influence the majority of Jews until the nineteenth century because, as noted above, the great majority of Jews were concentrated in the Kingdom of Poland-Lithuania and in the Ottoman Empire, in both of which the new political processes had not yet manifested themselves.

The Status of the Jew in a Disintegrating Poland and a Weakened Turkey

In theory there was almost no change in the legal status of Polish Jews from the fifteenth century until the partitions of the country in the second half of the eighteenth century. In actual fact, however, there were far-reaching changes during this period. One of the developments that characterized the political system of Poland was the declining influence of the monarchy and the increasing power of the nobility, which, for all intents and purposes, ruled the country and consequently reduced it to a state of anarchy (a famous saying of the period was that 'Poland was based on anarchy'). In practice, therefore, the status of the Jews of Poland was determined more by the attitude of the various groups of nobles and burghers than by the privileges that each king reaffirmed.

Under these circumstances, the undermining of the central government and the slackening of the social responsibility of the nobility had a detrimental effect upon the Jews in the eighteenth century. The Jews were generally protected by the landowners and, in particular, by the more eminent nobles or magnates, for whom the payments exacted from the Jews served as an important source of income. The patronage of a nobleman, and particularly of a great magnate, safeguarded the existence and livelihood of the Jews and protected them against the pressures of the other classes (the clergy, the urban middle class and the peasants), who were, in the main, hostile towards them. But at the same time, the Jew was completely at the mercy of the squire and totally dependent on his will or whim. The tormenting of Jews by these landowners – who flung them into pits or seized their children for conversion – were common occurrences in the eighteenth century. And if they acted in this manner towards their 'own' Jews, their behaviour towards Jews under the protection of their noble rivals was naturally even more brutal.

Those Jews who did not live on the estates or in privately owned towns, but rather in the large royal towns, were involved in bitter conflict with the burghers, and particularly with the craft guilds, since Jewish craftsmen in various branches tended to interfere with the monopolistic status of the former. Relations deteriorated further when Jewish craftsmen in the privately owned towns began to offer manufactured goods for sale at the fairs or market-days held in the larger towns. The transition that was taking place at that time among artisans, from work for a private client to the preparation of a stock of goods for sale at markets, was to the advantage of the Jews, who were excluded from the framework of the craft guilds. But, at the same time, it led the conservative Christian craftsmen to regard them as undermining principles sanctified by tradition. The townsmen, on the other hand, could not ignore the new and more efficient economic techniques, and in the smaller towns they sometimes feared that the departure of the Jews would ruin their economy. They therefore came to various arrangements with them, and there were even cases of cooperation between Christian and Jewish inhabitants; occasionally Jewish crafts-men were even granted access to the urban guilds.

The clergy was the driving force behind the persecution of the Jews in Poland. They demanded rights of jurisdiction over the Jews, which they had never previously held, and sometimes succeeded in forcing the Jews to attend church sermons. At every possible opportunity the clergy would incite an urban mob or students to anti-Jewish riots; the tried and tested means of incitement were blood libels.

In the second half of the seventeenth century and during most of the eighteenth century, there were numerous cases of anti-Jewish libels culminating in torture and brutal executions. These libels became more frequent in the 1740s and 1750s in eastern Poland, and nearly every year had its blood libel, with the aim of arousing the religious fanaticism of the mob. This situation obliged the Council of the Four Lands to dispatch a special emissary to Rome to ask 'His Excellency the Pope and the other Christian sages who sit in religious judgement to order the rulers of the land, its priests, and judges not to hearken to words of falsehood and calumny such as the sense and the mind reject, all the witnesses thereof being speakers of falsehood who have been bribed by haters of Israel.' One of the cardinals, Ganganelli, wrote a refutation of the blood libels, which was approved in 1760 by Pope Clement XIII. The intervention of the Pope halted the wave of blood libels, but did not put an end to the anti-Jewish activities of the clergy.

Although the peasants were the most oppressed class in Poland, those living in the eastern region of the country succeeded, even under the conditions of anarchy prevailing in the eighteenth century, in finding political expression in the Haidamak movement. The Haidamaks were gangs of Cossacks and peasants who robbed merchants on the broad highway and sometimes even attacked towns and townlets. They regarded themselves as the heirs of the Khmelnitski movement (see Part V). From the 1720s onwards there was scarcely a year in which such gangs did not appear, and in 1734 and 1750 the Haidamaks even succeeded in capturing several small towns in eastern Poland and in murdering and robbing both Jews and Poles. The worst outbreak was that of 1768, when the clashes between rival groups (named 'confedera-tions') among the Polish nobility reached its height. Several gangs under the leader-ship of Zhelezniak invaded eastern Poland and one of them attacked the important fortress of Uman, where many nobles and Jews from the vicinity had sought shelter. Gonta, the Cossack leader who was in charge of the fortress, joined the marauding units together with his men, and the combined force perpetrated widescale slaughter in the town. The number of victims, according to certain sources, reached 20,000, including thousands of Jews. Jews and Poles were also murdered in other towns during the same year.

Despite the lack of political stability in the Polish state (or perhaps because of it), the Jews were regarded as one of the recognized classes of Polish society; their alienness was therefore not so conspicuous, as all the other classes, with the exception of the nobility, also lacked political rights. Among the nobility, particularly in its upper echelons, there were certainly many who regarded the Jews with somewhat less contempt than they accorded the serfs. It is likewise possible that their attitude towards the Russian Orthodox church, the 'slave religion' (followed by the majority of the peasants in eastern Poland) was more negative than their attitude towards Judaism, particularly after 1764 when this 'slave religion' dared to raise its head and demand equal rights (with the political connivance of Russia and the concurrence of the new monarch who obeyed its behests). In any case, it is a fact that all the severe restrictions operating in the German states – the curtailing of residence rights, their denial to the second generation, strict supervision of occupations – were almost non-existent in Poland; and even in those places where certain prohibitions existed, the laxity of the political regime made it easier for the Jews to evade them. The arbitrary whims of the magnates and the dangers embodied in the political anarchy were in some respects less harmful to the Jews than the rigid administrative measures legislated by the absolutist regimes. The partition of Poland therefore constituted a great shock to the Jews, since they were now exposed to all the pressures that had already been introduced in centralized states.

The situation was similar in the Ottoman Empire. In the second half of the seventeenth century there was a change for the worse in the status of the Jews. They continued to hold important positions in economic life, but the weakening of the rule of the sultans meant that the latter could not guarantee efficient protection. Like all other subjects, or perhaps more so, the Jews were at the mercy of the arbitrary will of ministers and local officials. In the eighteenth century the situation worsened. The rapid deterioration of the great empire constituted a gloomy chapter in the history of the Jews in the East. In many places their property and even their persons were attacked with impunity. The Janissaries (an unruly unit of the Turkish Army), who took over the Turkish capital and began appointing and deposing sultans, set fire to the Jewish quarter of Constantinople several times in order to rob the residents under the pretense of extinguishing the flames. Gangs of robbers roamed the provincial towns and highways unchallenged. Also religious fanaticism increased, and various restrictions were imposed on the Jews with regard to clothing, places of residence and so on.

In the Moslem 'West' – the countries of North Africa that formed part of the Ottoman Empire – there was also a change for the worse. There were still Jews in these countries who enjoyed the favour of the regime and held important positions in trade and financial affairs, but sometimes even these became the victims of extortion. The situation of the Jews was particularly grim in interregnal periods, namely during the wars between the various claimants to the throne; the Jews were then at the mercy of the mob. The most inferior Moslem regarded himself as licensed to attack Jews who did not enjoy the protection of Moslem courts.

The Equivocal Attitude of Absolutism

In Poland and Turkey, as we have noted, the Jews found part of the political framework and their sufferings emanated, in the main, from the weakness of the regime and from conditions of anarchy, while in the absolutist states there was increasing tension between the corporative structure of Jewish society and the aims and aspirations of the regime. These governments were no longer interested in encouraging and nurturing internal Jewish autonomy, as they had in earlier periods, but now sought to reduce it. In several areas in the eighteenth century restrictions were imposed on internal Jewish jurisdiction, such as the prohibition of excommunication. In Germany, and even in Poland, government officials claimed in their memoranda that the community framework no longer served the interests of the Jews as a whole but was an instrument for domination and exploitation by the rich and powerful, and the entrusting of Jewish affairs to general officials would be to the benefit of the Jews. On the other hand, the absolutist state was not yet ready to dispense with the Jews as a separate group within the state: it needed the special taxes levied on them and the income derived directly from discrimination against them (including restrictions on residence, movement and marriage), as well as their economic connexions and the services they were capable of supplying. The rulers also wanted to use the special status of the Jews as an instrument against the urban patriciate that was demanding participation in government: the absolutist regime sometimes utilized the Jewish corporation as a means of baiting other corporations.

Hence, there was an implicit contradiction in the attitude of the absolutist rulers towards the Jews. There was yet an additional contradiction in the religious and moral sphere. On the one hand, the absolutist states of the seventeenth and eighteenth centuries preserved the traditional attitude, formulated in Christian Europe, whereby the Jews were regarded as harmful aliens who should be treated with suspicion, restrained in all areas and prevented from establishing contact with Christians. On the other hand, there was a prevalent view – based on experience and on the more modern political and economic theories – that the status of citizens should not be made dependent on religious affiliation, as well as the fact that there were distinct advantages to be derived from people active in trade and crafts. Thus we find that certain rulers established contact with Jews not only for their own advantage but also for social reasons, and yet immediately repented and repudiated their actions when threatened by the clergy with hell-fire. The Jews were therefore dependent on the arbitrariness of the rulers, and their stability was thus undermined.

There was another characteristic of centralized regimes that was to the advantage of the Jews and at the same time had an adverse effect on their lives. On the one hand, increased centralizing trends and improved administrative methods added to the security and convenience of the general population, including the Jews; but, on the other hand, the officials were thus afforded the opportunity of imposing stricter and more efficient supervision over the implementation of various anti-Jewish restrictions.

Supervision of Jews in the German States

An outstanding example of the status that the absolutist state was willing to allocate to the Jews in economic and social life is to be found in the statutes for Prussian Jews enacted by Friedrich II in 1750. He permitted the transfer of the residence rights by Jewish fathers to only one of their sons; the Jews were forbidden to engage in occupations of the burghers; they were precluded from melting gold and silver or selling cattle, except for their own needs; they were forbidden to trade in wool, to brew brandy or other liquor, or to trade in any but kosher wines; they were prohibited from trading in hides and processing tobacco. On the other hand, they were permitted to handle precious stones and metals, luxury cloths, horses, furs, wax and honey, goods imported from Poland, tea, coffee, chocolate, snuff, etc. In brief, they were allowed to exploit foreign-trade contacts that other merchants did not possess and to trade in new goods that could not be supplied by the usual methods. The criterion for tolerance was the degree of advantage that the state treasury was likely to derive – the richer the Jew the more useful he was. Not all Jews were equally 'tolerated', and it is not surprising that the payment that was extracted from the Jew for the right to live in the state was known as *Toleranz*.

In the Catholic Habsburg Empire the traces of the religious anti-Jewish tradition were more evident, as was the influence of the clergy and of the urban classes over the authorities. Clear evidence of this fact is provided by the two expulsions of the Jews from Austria at the end of the seventeenth century and during the eighteenth century, a measure that all other European countries had long since renounced. The Jews of Vienna were expelled in 1670, and on this occasion the hatred of Emperor Leopold I for the 'enemies of Christ' was the decisive factor. In contrast, the expulsion of the Jews of Prague in 1744–5 by Queen Maria Theresa was based on rumours of the disloyalty of the Jews of this town during the French and Prussian conquest. In actual fact these accusations were proved false but a scapegoat was needed on whom to pin some of the blame for Austria's military *débâcles*. The Prague municipality even intervened on behalf of the victims, noting that their expulsion would seriously affect the town's economy. The decision was reversed in 1748 only after the intervention of the diplomatic representatives of England, Holland and other countries, under the influence of court-Jews and Jewish bankers. But aside from the expulsion orders, the states ruled by the Habsburgs (Vienna and Lower Austria, Hungary, Bohemia and Moravia) maintained a severely restrictive policy towards their Jews as to numbers, places of residence and freedom of movement.

The partitions of Poland in 1772, 1793 and 1795 brought hundreds of thousands of additional Jews under the rule of Austria, Prussia and Russia. This disrupted all previously existing conditions. For the Jews, who were already accustomed to their old framework, this change-over constituted a worsening of conditions, while among the new rulers the consequences of the partitions intensified the ambivalence and anomaly of their attitude towards the Jews. Russia, which in theory had prohibited the residence of a single Jew for hundreds of years, now found itself with the largest Jewish population in the world. At first it tried to preserve the situation that had prevailed in the Polish state before the partitions. As a precautionary measure, Prussia prohibited the Jews of the annexed districts (the Grand Duchy of Posen) from moving to other parts of the state. The Queen of Austria tried several times to reduce the Jewish population of Galicia by expelling the 'beggars'.

'Integration of the Jews' by the Enlightened Absolutists

A further change was brought about by the emergence in several countries of rulers of a new type, known as the 'enlightened despots'. The political concept of 'enlightened absolutism' valued the welfare of the state above all and regarded the absolutist ruler as the first servant of the state. But it also maintained that the public good and the interest of the subjects were one and the same. The 'enlightened' rulers therefore strove to bring the Jews closer to the state and to integrate them within it. On the advice of several politicians and philosophers, they believed that this could be done by the reformation of the Jews through education, their redirection to new and useful occupations and the granting to them of 'human rights', *i.e.,* the abolition of the grave discriminations against them in matters of personal status. It is a fact that in the 1780s the 'poll tax' was annulled in most countries and various concessions were granted as regards residence, movement and the choice of occupations. The Jewish communities naturally feared innovations, which they thought could only take the form of new restrictions on their autonomy, and exerted the full force of their influence in order to maintain the old order.

According to the *Toleranzpatent* granted by Joseph II to the Jews of Vienna in early 1782:

> Since the beginning of our reign we have made it one of our most important aims that all our subjects, whatever their nationality or religion, since they are accepted and tolerated in our states, should share in the public welfare which we are endeavouring,to nurture, enjoy liberty in accordance with the law, and encounter no hindrance in obtaining their livelihood and increasing their general industry by all honourable means.

On the other hand this document explicitly stated that the king was strongly opp(;ed to increasing the number of Jews. He would continue to 'tolerate' the Jew only in accordance with his 'degree of usefulness', namely the extent of his prosperity. At the same time he believed that it was possible to derive advantage from the Jews and to integrate them into the framework of the state. The main purposes of the 'letters of tolerance' granted to the Jews in various parts of his state included nullification of movement and residence restrictions; concessions as regards occupations (the right to learn crafts, establish factories and engage in the liberal professions); the right to employ Jewish and gentile domestic servants 'according to the needs of their occupation'; the right to send their children to general schools and to establish their own schools; the abolition of several religious restrictions, such as the compulsory wearing of a beard and the prohibition against going outdoors during Christian festivals. But to counterbalance these concessions there were also 'reformatory' tendencies that could only be interpreted by the Jews as harsh restrictions: the prohibition of Arendas; compulsory attendance at public schools and the determination of a minimum marriage age of twenty-five for those who had not completed schooling; compulsory military service; prohibition of the use of Hebrew and Yiddish in various documents; restriction of internal Jewish autonomy by the cancellation of the legal and economic power of the communities; and intensified police control to ensure implementation of these regulations.

The new enactments were regarded as so revolutionary that they encountered the opposition not only of the Jews but also of many state officials. After the death of Joseph II in 1790 the latter implemented very few of them. Joseph's heirs reverted to the previous policy and even revived some of the old restrictions, but they did not abandon his general aim, which was to integrate the Jews into the life of the country.

The changes in the status of Jews in Russia were wrought at first through the general administrative amendments introduced by Catherine II. In 1778 Russia was divided into provinces and their inhabitants were classified into various categories: the rich Jews were registered as merchants and included in the guilds, while the remainder were classified as 'burghers'. Their inclusion within guilds and craft corporations along with the general population created the problem of their participation in the representative institutions of these corporations. Thus Russia became the first country in Europe in which the Jews were allowed to elect and be elected to guild councils and municipalities, even though this development aggravated the tension that already existed between the urban element and the Jews. On the other hand, in 1782 the authorities decided that merchants and burghers must reside in towns and not villages. Thus they laid the foundation for the demand, which later became more emphatic, that the Jews be banished from the villages – one of the central trends in Russian policy towards the Jews throughout the nineteenth century. The attempts of Jewish merchants to trade in central Russia engendered friction with the local merchants as well. One of the consequences was a law in 1791 prohibiting the Jews from permanently leaving the newly acquired provinces, and this created the notorious Pale of Settlement.

After the accession of Alexander I to the throne, a special committee was appointed in 1802 to study the question of Jewish status. Two views were expressed at the committee: one claimed that it was necessary to change the way of life of the Jews and 'reform' them before assimilating them; the second argued that the conferring of rights should come first. The outcome of the discussions was the 1804 statute, which was influenced by similar legislation in the German states. The fundamental assumption of this statute was that the Jews, as they were presently situated, constituted a harmful factor, and that their habits and life-style could only be changed through altering their condition. The statute of 1804 opens with the preamble:

> Because of the complaints which frequently reached us and the Ruling Senate regarding injustice and various disturbances affecting the agriculture and industry of the inhabitants of those districts in which Jews reside, we have found it necessary – in the ukase to the Ruling Senate issued on 9 November 1802 – to establish a special committee to examine relevant matters and to find means of ameliorating the condition of the Jews.

The decree was therefore aimed at protecting the inhabitants against the injurious activities of the Jews by improving the situation of the latter. It ordered the Jews to leave the villages within three to four years (to prevent them from exploiting the peasants) and prohibited them from engaging in leasing, innkeeping and the sale of alcohol. Anyone violating this decree was to be fined and a third violation would be punished by banishment to Siberia. The statute also defined the area in which Jews were permitted to reside and added to the provinces annexed from Poland several areas in southern Ukraine and on the shore of the Black Sea, which were sparsely populated and which the Russian Government wished to settle. Thus it established 'a border within a border', an area of Jewish settlement that was closed on the east lest the Jews infiltrate the 'main' Russian areas. The Jewish Pale of Settlement endured until 1917.

The measures for 'reforming' the Jews included the opening of public schools to Jewish children and permission for Jews to establish their own schools; the stipulation that within a limited time all documents be written in one of the languages of the country (and not Yiddish or Hebrew) and that only those acquainted with one of these languages be eligible for election to municipalities and rabbinical posts; the encouragement of Jewish farmers by allocating areas of land in southern Russia for Jewish settlement without this entailing serfdom. Loans were promised for the establishment of factories, and craft guilds were forbidden to exclude Jewish artisans.

Of all the numerous clauses of the 1804 statute the only ones of practical value were those relating to expulsion from the villages and aid in agricultural settlement. The expulsion commenced in 1807 and at the same time the establishment of agricultural colonies began in the Kherson district. But only a very small percentage of the exiles were absorbed into the colonies. Many government officials opposed the expulsions and claimed that the towns inside the Pale of Settlement were already crammed full of Jews with no regular sources of livelihood. The authorities then suspended the expulsions as well as the agricultural settlement, and a special commission was appointed to examine the question of Jewish residence in the villages. The commission reported that 'as long as White Russian and Polish landowners continue to maintain administrative methods based on the sale of liquors, and as long as they continue to encourage drunkenness, this plague cannot disappear and will even increase from year to year. Its results will remain the same, whether the innkeeper is a Jew or a Christian.' The commission came to the conclusion that the Jews were not causing harm to the villages, but were rather useful for purveying commodities, maintaining links with the town and transmitting post.

The Tsar did not approve the commission's report, but the political situation and the wars with Napoleon, which broke out shortly afterwards, postponed implementation of the 1804 statute. The Russian authorities renewed their anti-Jewish edicts in the second (more reactionary) half of the reign of Alexander I.

The Constitutional Legislature and the Jews: Their Status in Holland and England

The two European countries that did not withhold 'human rights' from the Jews – that is, did not restrict their movement, residence and occupations – were Holland and England, states with a constitutional legislature. In both these countries there was an established religion, and members of other faiths, the Jews among them, were merely tolerated. This was of importance only with regard to political rights. The positive aspects of the attitude of the constitutional legislature towards the Jews, as compared with that of absolutist regimes, are particularly striking if we recall that the Jewish communities of Holland and England were relatively new, and it might have been claimed, with some justification, that Jews were indeed aliens.

As early as 1657 Holland officially recognized the Jews as subjects of the republic, although they still remained outside most of the guilds and did not hold public offices, as these entailed a Christian oath. In England the process of naturalization was much more protracted. At the end of the seventeenth century the Jews were exempted from paying the alien duty, but those Jews who had not been born in the country were still not recognized as citizens. As aliens they were precluded from purchasing real estate and shipping vessels, which greatly hindered their commercial activities. Their economic operations also encountered the opposition of the merchant guilds.

It has already been noted that various voices were raised in England calling for the naturalization of Jews coming from abroad. The first stage in this process was the 1740 act that permitted 'foreign Protestants and others' (including Jews) to be naturalized in any of His Majesty's colonies in America after seven years of residence. Furthermore, the Jews were permitted to omit from the oath administered to applicants for naturalization the words 'upon the true faith of a Christian'. In 1753, both houses of Parliament passed a similar act for the Jews of Britain, but, as a result of the public clamour that this aroused, the government proposed in the same year that the law be repealed. Jews were able to become freely naturalized only after the annulment in 1826 of the Christian oaths and ceremonies surrounding the naturalization procedure.

Despite the failure of the naturalization act, the process of integrating the British Jews continued. Several taxes formerly levied on Jews were abolished, and Jews were now granted the opportunity of joining merchant companies, the stock exchange and the liberal professions. During the second half of the eighteenth century the English courts accepted the authority of rabbis and the validity of Jewish matrimonial laws in wills and deeds, and the existence of the Jewish community was legally recognized. (At first the courts invalidated wills that bequeathed money to synagogues, but in due course they began to approve them.) However, until the 1830s, the Jews were not permitted to join municipal corporations, nor were they allowed to hold public or political office, although they enjoyed the franchise.

Legal Equality in the United States and Revolutionary France

The aim of the 'enlightened' absolutist rulers was to absorb the Jews into the state; yet, as a result of their countries' historical heritage and the clash of interests between the indigenous social classes, the measures they employed were hesitant and self-contradictory, and in the final analysis the results were scarcely evident. On the other hand, the revolutionary social processes that emerged at that time, and which decisively changed the face of these countries, in fact created the basis for rapid integration.

Those legislators who accepted the principle of emancipation, namely the legal equality of the Jews, did not go into the details, roots and development of their legal status, but based themselves on a general political premise that was an offshoot of the principles of religious tolerance and of the separation of church and state recognized by the American and French revolutions. In the United States these principles were accepted without specific mention of the Jews. The United States differed basically from its European counterparts in that it did not share the historical heritage

759

of the Middle Ages, and, in the first stage of its existence, its political leadership was entrusted to men imbued with the ideals of the Enlightenment. Furthermore, the Jewish community in the American colonies was a tiny minority. According to the Act for Establishing Religious Freedom passed in Virginia in 1786:

> No man shall be compelled to frequent or support any religious worship, place, or ministry whatsoever, nor shall he be enforced, restrained, molested, or burthened in his body or goods, nor shall otherwise suffer on account of his religious opinions or belief; but that all men shall be free to profess and by argument to maintain their opinion in matters of religion, and that the same shall in no wise diminish, enlarge, or affect their capacities.

And the sixth article of the Constitution stated that 'No religious test shall ever be required as a qualification to any office or public trust under the United States.' This approach sufficed to safeguard the legal equality of the Jews, although in several states there was a lengthy struggle for the practical implementation of these principles.

The only European country at that time in which the emancipatory approach was crystallized and became the accepted basis of the political order was revolutionary France. At the end of August 1789, the National Assembly, in the *Declaration of the Rights of Man,* assured that 'No man should be molested for his beliefs, including religious beliefs, provided that their manifestation does not disturb the public order established by law.' Yet the National Assembly did not pursue this concept to its logical conclusion as regards the legal status of the Jews. The abstract principles on which this clause was founded, which reflected the spirit and aims of the revolution, were counterbalanced by the interests, traditions and concepts of wide sectors of the population, particularly in Alsace-Lorraine. In Alsace there was a deeply rooted tradition of hatred towards the Jews, 'who are moneylenders and blood-suckers', and anti-Jewish feelings on the part of the clergy. When the National Assembly returned to the question of Jewish emancipation in December 1789, during the discussion of the necessary conditions for 'active citizenship' (*i.e.,* full political rights), strong opposition to Jewish equality was expressed, and, in the end, no resolution was passed. The Sephardi Jews of Bordeaux, who enjoyed extensive social contacts and honourable economic status, were granted in January 1790 the rights of 'active citizens', but for the Jews of Alsace-Lorraine the process was more protracted. Only at the end of September 1791 did the Assembly pass the general law enfranchising all Jews.

The revolutionary army carried the French Revolution's gospel of liberty and equality to the countries it occupied. (One should nevertheless differentiate between those countries in which the occupation authorities enforced a change in the attitude towards the Jews, and those in which the revolutionary ideals were absorbed by society and the indigenous population began to introduce changes on its own initiative.) When the French expelled the pope from Rome in 1798, the special laws relating to the Jews were revoked; the same occurred in the Cisalpine Republic, south of the Alps. But in the same year several Italian territories were restored to Austria under the Treaty of Campoformido, and once again the Jews were stripped of their rights. In the end the captured Italian territories were annexed to the French Empire, under the name of the Kingdom of Italy, and French legislation was enforced there, but after the Napoleonic era the former situation was restored. In the Helvetian Republic (Switzerland), established by the French, the legislative assemblies rejected the proposal that they grant equal rights to the Jews. On the other hand, the Batavian (Dutch) National Assembly accorded equality to all Jews 'who wish to utilize it', because of the guarded attitude of most Dutch Jews towards emancipation (which entailed loss of internal autonomy). In 1808 the Kingdom of Westphalia (established by Napoleon in Germany after the Tilsit peace treaty) granted equal rights to Jews, but after Napoleon's downfall this state disintegrated and the laws passed under French influence were repealed. One of the states that arrived at the principle of emancipation out of internal considerations was Prussia. After the military defeats of 1806–7 there was public unrest, and the ground was prepared for a number of liberally inclined political amendments, including the granting of civil rights to the Jews. The edict establishing these rights, published in March 1812, declared Jews to be 'countrymen and citizens' of the state. All civil obligations, including military service, were imposed on them. Their matrimonial laws were placed under the jurisdiction of government courts, although the legislature recognized the validity of marriages solemnized according to Jewish law. The principle of equality was legally maintained in all spheres, with the exception of government service.

Departure from the Emancipatory Principle: Napoleon and the Jews

As we have noted, the emancipatory approach was based, from the first, on general political principles. The first clash between the implementation of these principles and hostile forces on the political scene occurred shortly after the establishment of the French Empire by Napoleon. The emperor regarded the Jews as a nation rather than a religion, but, nevertheless, he did not contemplate expelling the Jews, as he was more interested in their 'reformation' and consequent integration into the framework of the state. The problem emerged in all its severity when the inhabitants of Alsace-Lorraine once again raised the question of debts owed to the Jews. The problem reached the Council of State, where it was proposed to introduce special laws for the Jews, a measure contradictory to the principle of legal equality. The majority of the Council rejected the suggestion, but Napoleon himself weighted the balance in its favour. As a result of these discussions, it was decided to institute remission of all debts to the Jews for a period of one year and to convene an assembly of Jewish notables to discuss the attitude of Jews towards the state.

The convening of the Assembly of Jewish Notables took place in July 1806, and twelve questions were submitted to it. They related to Jewish matrimonial laws (the attitude of Judaism towards polygamy, the validity of divorces granted by governmental courts and mixed marriages), the attitude of Jews towards France and the French people, the authority of Jewish autonomous institutions and problems of usury and of Jewish occupations. A committee appointed from among the Assembly formulated the replies and endeavoured to conciliate the authorities. On the basis of these replies, there convened, in February 1807, the 'Great Sanhedrin' consisting of rabbis and leading lay personalities, whose function was to give religious sanction to the replies of the Assembly of Jewish Notables, and the Sanhedrin passed nine resolutions in this spirit. Its task, according to Napoleon, was to represent the 'organization of the Mosaic religion' in the state.

In March 1808, two edicts were promulgated in order to regulate the position of the Jews in the country. The first introduced a hierarchical organization of communities in France: all individual and communal Jewish affairs were concentrated in the hands of a central consistory in Paris, which was supposed to help the authorities control the affairs of each individual Jew. The second edict (subsequently known by the Jews as the *Décret Infâme*) imposed control over Jewish loans, required Jews to obtain special permits in order to engage in trade, forbade Jews from other areas to settle in north-east France and prohibited the provision of replacements for military service (this latter was allowed to other conscripts). The grave deviation from the principle of emancipation involved in the 'Infamous Decree' did not lie merely in the restrictions it imposed on the Jews but in the very act of legislating special laws for the Jews. Furthermore, in the arrangements that Napoleon made for the 'Mosaic religion' within the framework of the French state, it was clear that the state enjoyed preference over religion. According to the organizational code of the consistories, the rabbis were enjoined to see to it that the Israelites (as the Jews were called by those who wanted to avoid insulting them) '. . . should regard military service as a sacred task, and they should inform them that during the period in which they dedicate themselves to service the Torah exempted them from observing religious injunctions which cannot be reconciled with it.' The wide powers granted to the communities contradicted, to a certain extent, the principle of equality. But the Jewish organization should not exploit these powers to achieve its own aims; it existed only for the needs of the state authorities.

All Napoleon's activities, like those of other absolutist rulers, were aimed at inducing the Jews to integrate in the state, or, according to the final paragraph of the 'Infamous Decree':

> The instructions in this order will be implemented over a period of ten years in the hope that at the end of this period, under the influence of the various measures undertaken with regard to the Jews, there will no longer be any difference between them and other citizens of our Empire. But if, despite all this, our hope should be frustrated, implementation will be extended for whatever length of time seems appropriate.

Napoleon's new policy towards the Jews was treated with some ambiguity outside the borders of France. In the Duchy of Warsaw (created out of central Poland in accordance with the Tilsit peace treaty), the granting of equal rights to the Jews was postponed in 1808, on the basis of the 'Infamous Decree', for ten years. Yet, at the same time, emancipation was being granted to the Jews of Westphalia.

After the defeat of Napoleon, there was an especially strong reaction in several of the Italian states, where the Jews were deprived of all their rights and returned to the ghettos; in the 'Free Cities' of Germany – in Frankfurt the Jews were returned to the ghetto; and in Lübeck, where a total expulsion took place. The Germanic

Federation, which discussed the Jewish question at the Congress of Vienna in 1815, did not decide on a return to the conditions prevailing before Napoleon's conquests, but preferred to discuss 'how to achieve the civil amelioration of those professing the Jewish religion in Germany, insofar as possible by general agreement (of all the states), and particularly how to give them and safeguard for them, within the states of the Federation, the possibility of enjoying civil rights in return for accepting all the obligations of citizens'. But 'for the time being we have secured for members of this religion those selfsame rights granted to them by the various states of the Federation'. During the discussions there were those who proposed leaving to the Jews those rights granted them 'within' the various states, *i.e.,* those rights granted not by the states themselves but by the French under Napoleon. But most of the states were unwilling to maintain laws that had been forced upon them, and the Congress therefore decided on the phrase 'by the states', thus invalidating Jewish emancipation throughout Germany, with the exception of Prussia.

The economic, social and political changes in Europe during the seventeenth and eighteenth centuries were slow to influence the legal status of the Jews. Throughout this period those subscribing to mediaeval concepts fought fiercely and ultimately were successful in dominating the Jewish question. Whether directly or indirectly, several of the changes that did occur, particularly in the centralized states, actually aggravated the consequences of this point of view. Only at the end of the eighteenth century did the emancipatory approach, advocating the full equality of the Jews and basically rejecting the mediaeval attitude, prevail in various countries.

The development in approach to the Jewish question was influenced by the particular character and aims of the regime involved. Absolutist rulers mainly acted according to the old, hostile approach; they were also influenced by the desire to abolish corporations in the state and by the theories of mercantilism, which advocated deriving the greatest possible economic benefit from enlarging the population and controlling its activities. The 'enlightened' absolute monarchs supplemented – or, at times, replaced – these aims by the desire to 'integrate' and 'reform' the Jews. The constitutional governments did not restrict individual liberty or economic activity, but wrestled with the question of political rights. In the Polish-Lithuanian Kingdom and the Ottoman Empire we find a totally different development: the disintegration of the central government was what affected the situation of the Jews. The partition of Poland altered the status of the Jews within its borders and even forced the benefitting kingdoms to display a new attitude towards them. The transition to complete legal equality occurred at the end of the eighteenth and the beginning of the nineteenth centuries, when the American and French revolutions introduced new political principles as the basis for defining the status of Jews.

46

The Internal Struggle in East European Jewry

The Intensification of Social Conflicts

In the mid-seventeenth century, the foundations of the great Jewish centre in Poland-Lithuania were shaken by the Cossack revolts, the Khmelnitski massacres (1648–9) and twenty years of warfare between the Poles and the Russians and Swedes, accompanied by various forms of persecution. The relative tranquillity enjoyed by the Jews of Poland ('the Jewish paradise' according to a verse satire of the time) vanished without a trace. A period of harassment and blood libels, which lasted till the end of Poland's existence as an independent state in 1795, was initiated. Nonetheless, the Jewish community continued to grow, as did internal competition for sources of livelihood. The social tensions that had existed within Jewish communities in earlier periods were now aggravated and transformed into real social hostility – a confrontation between the ruling class of the wealthy and the scholars and the wider strata of the lower classes and the poor.

The Waning Influence of Autonomous Jewish Institutions in Poland

The inevitable result of all these developments was to damage the position of the community organization. The weakness of the Polish central government and the political anarchy in the country restricted the ability of the higher Jewish institutions – the provincial councils and the Council of the Four Lands (see Part V) – to impose their authority over the total Jewish population and over the individual Jewish communities. They were obliged to distribute large sums of money for various kinds of bribery, to prevent blood libels, to buy protection or the cooperation of officers or officials, and it was therefore necessary to place a heavier burden on the local community. Despite these measures the individual community was often left on its own and was forced to raise additional funds for self-protection. On the other hand, there was growing interference by the Polish authorities, and particularly the Minister of Finance and his emissaries, in Jewish affairs and increasingly strict supervision of all gatherings and tax-collection. The Jewish leaders were forced to conceal a large part of their activities and their income, and this encouraged corruption among the leaders as well as aggravating the suspicions of outside elements.

The heavy burden of debts on the communities and councils served as the background for the quarrels and grievances between the various Jewish organizations.

For all these reasons, the government began to lose interest in the Jewish institutions, both as a steady source of considerable income and as an instrument for conducting Jewish affairs. When criticism of government mismanagement and the authority of the corporations increased in the mid-eighteenth century, the Polish Sejm decided, in June 1764, to abolish all the councils and to impose on the Jews a poll-tax of two *zloty*, to be collected by the authorities themselves from each and every community. This signalled the end of the official recognition of the central and provincial institutions of Jewish self-rule, which had endured for nearly 200 years. But the revocation of the juridical status of the Jewish councils did not lead to direct contact between the individual Jew and the governmental agencies, nor did the regime itself aspire to such far-reaching reform of Jewish life. It only hoped for higher income (this hope was realized in the first few years of the new programme), and because of the debts of Jewish institutions it was convenient for the government to continue to preserve a form of recognized Jewish representation. It is not surprising that the central and provincial councils continued to impose their authority even after their formal abolition, though to a lesser extent than before.

The Internal Struggle in the Polish-Lithuanian Communities

Consequently, from the end of the seventeenth century onwards, there was an increasing number of rebels who sought the protection of the nobles against the Jewish leadership. Towards the middle of the eighteenth century there were numerous decrees excommunicating 'any man of Israel who approaches a landed squire in order to obtain exemption from tax'. There were severe disputes between the communities, especially between large communities and those of the small towns around them, for each endeavoured to shift the great part of the tax burden on the other.

There was an increase in the instance of recourse to non-Jewish courts, not only in individual disputes, but in controversies between communities. In 1721 all the Lithuanian communities appealed to the Treasury tribunal against the five main communities, which dominated the Lithuanian council, claiming that the latter had collected illegal taxes from them and that the tax burden was unequally distributed.

Social tension was also evident within each community. The prominent families competed among themselves for leadership, influence, appointments and honour. The coveted titles of *haver* (comrade) or *morenu* (our teacher), which were granted for distinction in learning, were often bestowed on the undeserving. At times, people lacking the necessary learning or experience were appointed to the rabbinate through the aid of powerful relatives or supporters, or because they offered payments or loans to the needy community. The embarrassing situation often arose whereby a distinguished rabbi exerted little influence over his community, as he was dependent on the powerful members, while less worthy rabbis ruled the community with an iron hand. This was not an entirely new phenomenon, but the difference lay in the proliferation of instances of corruption and in the growing tension between the various sections of the Jewish population. Furthermore, this development led to a reduction in the community's capacity for action, particularly with regard to economic ethics; it proved helpless, for example, in protecting the rights of an individual with *hazakah* (established claim to possession) or in preventing economic competition. The sense of unity and of mutual responsibility was weakened. In the second half of the eighteenth century, unprecedented criticism was levelled against the community organization in general. An extreme example of this mood was the complaint submitted by some of the townspeople of Shavle in Lithuania to the official in charge of estates:

> We, the Jewish residents of Shavle, declare, with tears in our eyes, that we have need neither of a rabbi nor of leaders since they . . . engage in extortion and plotting and are destroying us utterly, and since they are connected among themselves by family ties, they rob us of our last coins only in order to enrich themselves . . .

The decline in the authority of the community generally brought with it a change in methods of tax collection. The direct taxes or *sekhumot*, which became increasingly difficult to collect, grew less important, while the importance of the *koropki*, or indirect taxes, increased. These were imposed on various commodities or on trade deals. The indirect taxes had existed from the second half of the seventeenth century, but only in the mid-eighteenth century did they become an important element in the budget of the communities. There were some places in which direct taxation was completely abolished; in Cracow the following regulation was passed in 1771: 'Since there are several people who have been registered in the list of tax-payers who are unable to fulfil their obligation and to pay out either a large or small sum in one payment, or from whom it is difficult to collect, or who do not give at all, it has been decided to introduce a *koropka* . . .' The communities that were unable to collect direct taxes adopted the indirect taxation method by imposing it on various commodities and, above all, on meat. Since supervision of the dietary laws (*kashrut*) was entrusted to the community, this provided a new method of maintaining the community income level and the individual's dependence on it for kosher food.

Public Criticism of the Social Order and the Leadership

The ruling stratum had in the seventeenth century already begun to fear the crystallization of an opposition force in the communities. More and more decrees were issued against 'gossip-mongers' or those 'who gossip and jest about the deeds of the town notables', *i.e.*, against those criticizing the leadership. These edicts warned against 'plotting with one another against the status and deeds of the town worthies' and were aimed at preventing an organized opposition, but the very proliferation of decrees attests to their ineffectiveness.

The most cohesive opposition framework was that of the artisan societies, which convened separate *minyanim* (private synagogues or prayer-houses) and sometimes also elected their own *maggid* (preacher) or rabbi. Thus they attempted to liberate themselves from the patronage of the community. Under the conditions of social tension in the eighteenth century, even those societies originally established for the purpose of engaging in charitable work took on the character of opposition cells. The *kahal* (*i.e.*, leadership) tried to obstruct these societies by exercising its right to appoint their *gabbai* (treasurer), but even this form of supervision did not produce the desired results. In some places the community leaders employed more vigorous measures: in Dubno in Volhynia all the societies were abolished, and in Ostrog, in the same province, the enrolment of new members was prohibited for six years. Simultaneously, the leadership endeavoured to prevent the opposition from exerting influence over community affairs. The already limited franchise was restricted even further. In actual fact, an infinitesimal percentage of members of the community participated in the election of the *borerim* (arbitrators) who appointed the new *kahal*. In some places there were explicit regulations prohibiting the participation of artisan representatives in the arbitration committee.

It is therefore surprising to note the extensive circulation of *musar* ('ethical instruction') literature in eighteenth-century Poland; it contained a strong element of social criticism, it chastised the rich and powerful, pointed out their failings and demanded their correction. Not only were many copies printed and distributed, but they evidently received the *haskamah* (official authorization) of important rabbis and scholars, who were distinguished public leaders, since no printer would have dared to produce a book without such approval. Social criticism appears to have become an integral part of the inner life of the Jews in Eastern Europe. This helps us understand the paradox that one of the *parnasim* (leaders) of the Council of the Four Lands in the 1720s bestowed on R. Berakhia-Beirekh ben Eliakim Getz the 'force and power to be a preacher in all the four lands of Poland under its authority, to lay down regulations and to improve public morals in each community. He may preach without the approval of a rabbi or leader and without protest and hindrance, and woe to whosoever opens his mouth against him on any matter, great or small. He should be honoured and respected in every way as is fitting for a sage and scholar such as he (may his like flourish in Israel) and helped to complete his work, which he bears with him in written form, since he has composed several works with his holy mind, and has beheld the *haskamot* of many great sages and rabbis from the lands of Germany and Poland and Moravia . . .' Rabbi Berakhia was one of the sharpest critics of those rabbis and leaders who betrayed trust and severely castigated them in his book *Zera Beirekh Shelishi* on the Talmudic Tractate *Berakhot*. (The above quotation appears in its *haskamah*.)

Mystical Ferment: Jacob Frank and His Sect

Jewish society in Poland, which was willing to accept even extreme social criticism, rallied to counter-attack when attempts were made to undermine its faith and religious views. Mystical ferment – particularly on the part of the Sabbatean remnants – which had never died out in Eastern Europe and which flared up against the background of the social tension and leadership crisis, therefore encountered the vehement opposition of all sections of the Jewish public.

In the 1750s Jacob Frank emerged as the new and energetic leader of the Sabbatean remnant in Poland. Frank was born in Podolia, wandered extensively and became attracted to Sabbateanism in Salonika. In 1755 he returned to his native province, rallied a number of the faithful around him, taught them several Sabbatean concepts and organized festivities that deteriorated into sexual orgies. The deeds of this group soon came to light and an excommunication edict was published against them. The Bishop of Kamenets, seizing on this as an opportunity for attacking the Jews, demanded a religious disputation between the Jews and the Frankists. The latter were defined as 'Jews opposed to the Talmud', believing in the incarnation of God and in the Trinity and denying the redemption of Israel in Jerusalem. The disputation was held in June 1757, and the Frankists were naturally declared to be the winners. Consequently, copies of the Talmud were publicly burned by the hangman. However, shortly afterwards, the bishop who had defended the Frankists suddenly died, and the Jews were able to resume their persecution of the sect. Frank himself had already fled to Turkey, where he succeeded in obtaining a safe-conduct from the King of Poland. He and his supporters now approached the Archbishop of Lvov and requested a new disputation with the Jews. This debate was held in the summer of 1759, and this time the Frankists claimed that the Jews used Christian blood for ritual purposes. Frank expressed his readiness to convert to Christianity but wanted permission to maintain a separate sect. His demands were rejected by the church authorities, but it was already too late to cancel his and his supporters' baptism. After Frank had converted, together with several hundred of his followers, he was incarcerated in the Czestochowa fortress for thirteen years, lest he exert evil influence over them. But the sect continued to exist secretly and even developed its own beliefs. Frank combined the kabbalistic Sabbatean tradition with traces of political thought: Poland was the chosen land, and in order to achieve his goal it was necessary to employ military force; he claimed that he wanted to establish a great Jewish army and to exploit the political differences between various states.

After the Russian armies entered Poland during the first partition (1772), Frank was released and settled at Offenbach in Germany. After his death the sect was headed by his daughter. It died out at the beginning of the nineteenth century.

The Ba'al Shem Tov and the Beginnings of Ḥasidism

A no less bitter but more protracted controversy arose around the new mystical sect that emerged among Polish Jewry and which was connected with the personality of R. Israel ben Eliezer Ba'al Shem Tov ('Master of the Good Name'). The Ba'al Shem Tov (1700–60) was born in Podolia and was apparently of humble origin. In his youth he was a synagogue sexton and an assistant teacher. After several years of solitude and meditation, even before his *hitgalut* (the revelation of his true mission), he became a *ba'al shem,* or miracle-worker, curing with amulets and charms, and he continued to engage in this practice even after he became the leader of a sect. The main tenets of his beliefs are clearly known to us although he left no written works apart from a few letters and a series of sayings noted down by his disciples. But there can be no doubt that his main power lay not in his teachings, but in the force of his personality.

The Ba'al Shem Tov established contact with the ascetic kabbalists of his day, and apparently also with the Sabbateans. In that period there were many, even among the young, who delved into the Kabbalah. As a result there was a prolific emergence of esoteric mystical theories. Extreme asceticism also was widespread. Solomon Maimon, the Lithuanian youth who was to become a Kantian philosopher, relates that there were young scholars who hastened their own deaths through extreme ascetic practices. The Ba'al Shem Tov introduced a change of direction by guiding the individual kabbalist from self-castigation and seclusion to leadership of the community, thus moulding a new type of Jewish leader, the ḥasidic *zaddik*, or righteous one.

This new concept of the *zaddik* altered the image of Jewish leadership. According to ḥasidic belief, 'the *zaddik* is the foundation of the world': the whole world was created only for him, and he controlled all riches – spiritual and material – and could even change a decision of God Himself. His task was to lead the community; otherwise his mission forfeited its entire meaning. Whatever degree of spiritual elevation he himself achieved, he could never change the worldly order and hasten salvation as long as he acted alone, since 'the generation is not worthy'. What is more, if detached from the people, his spiritual advancement could have the opposite effect – namely, the masses might be chastised for not having emulated him. The world could not live up to the criteria according to which the *zaddik* conducted his life, and therefore the very fact of his strict devoutness might lead the world to be judged with severity rather than with mercy.

Particular importance was therefore attached to *devekut* (attachment to or communion with God) as understood by Ḥasidism. The *zaddik* adhered to God, on the one hand, and the people, on the other, and was thus a *memuza*, or intermediary, mediating between the people and God. He bore responsibility for the entire community and therefore had to 'descend' from his exalted spiritual level in order to raise the people up with him. In descending, he adopted what appeared to be a simple and common form, mingling with the people in the market-place, conversing with them, but remaining throughout in a state of *devekut* to the other world, his sole aim to raise the people to a higher level. The basic assumption of Ḥasidism was that 'there is no place empty of Him': divinity exists in all spheres, and therefore the central objective of the *zaddik*'s leadership was to release the divine sparks hidden in all the shells (*Kelipot*) of the material world.

Out of opposition to and rejection of asceticism there emerged the emphasis on the joys of divine worship. As the Ba'al Shem Tov himself said: 'That physician is best who administers medicine within a drink as sweet as honey.' Joy was a fundamental tenet in ḥasidic teachings. The asceticism and sorrow of a devout few only evoked the Divine attribute of stern justice (which the world could not endure), for the world was thereafter condemned for failing to resemble them. It is quite possible that this stress on joy and the special ḥasidic way of life arising from it helped to attract the masses, and particularly the young, to Ḥasidism.

At a relatively early stage the Ba'al Shem Tov began to believe that his teachings could serve as a guide to the people and bring Redemption nearer. In the great mystical vision he experienced on the New Year in 1747, in which he saw the ascension of his soul to Heaven and which he describes in his famous letter to his brother-in-law in the Holy Land, the Messiah promised that he would come 'when your [the Ba'al Shem Tov's] learning is known and revealed in the world and your springs flow out', *i.e.*, when the ḥasidic beliefs became widespread. Yet, he was not certain which path to take in order to achieve this goal. When the Ba'al Shem Tov died in 1760 his name was well known and he had adherents in many places, but they did not yet constitute a 'movement'.

The Crystallization of the Ḥasidic Movement: The Maggid of Mezhirech and His Disciples

The Ba'al Shem Tov's disciples were mostly drawn to him after a period of extensive soul-searching and self-examination. Although several of them were *maggidim* (preachers), it would be difficult to pinpoint a social characteristic shared by all of them. They included scholars as well as the unlearned, notables as well as simple people. Two of them stood out above the rest and left their mark on the development of the movement. R. Jacob Joseph of Polonnoye was the Ba'al Shem Tov's faithful disciple who continued his traditions; his *Toledot Jacob Joseph* (1780) was the first ḥasidic book published. But he was not chosen to head the movement after the death of the founder. The task evolved on a man who had joined the Ba'al Shem Tov only a short time before: R. Dov Baer (?–1772), the *Maggid* of Mezhirech and Rovno (the great *Maggid* in ḥasidic tradition). The *Maggid* transferred the movement's centre from remote Podolia to Volhynia, began to gather numerous young disciples around him and even sent out emissaries to spread ḥasidic teachings in distant regions – Galicia, White Russia, Lithuania and central Poland.

Even in towns where their supporters were few, the *Maggid's* pupils maintained separate places of worship. Prayer played an important role in ḥasidic lore; it was regarded as the main link with the upper spheres and, therefore, more important than religious study. This was a daring departure from the customary attitude of Jewish society in Poland and Lithuania in earlier generations and even in the eighteenth century, where the study of Talmud was held as the highest ideal. Ḥasidism also initiated among its followers prayers according to the Sephardi prayerbook adopted by R. Isaac Luria in Safed (*Nusaḥ Ari*), which differed from the established Ashkenazi version used by Polish Jews. Hence also the importance of *kavvanah* (inner devotion), the fervour during worship, including cries and strange movements.

Certain kabbalistic beliefs led the *Ḥasidim* to insist on carrying out the ritual slaughter of animals with specially polished knives instead of the normal sharpened knives. It was related even of the Ba'al Shem Tov that he strictly observed his own methods of slaughter and examined the knives. This led the *Ḥasidim* to choose their slaughterers from among members of their own community. Communal meals also played a central role in the ritual of the movement. The Sabbath or festive meals held by the *rebbe,* at which he would preach (generally on verses from the Portion of the Week) became important ceremonies in the life of the community. The *se'udah shelishit* (the meal eaten towards the close of the Sabbath) later became the most important occasion for the recitation of the rabbi's teachings, the telling of stories about the *zaddikim* (merely the relating was regarded as a sacred act) and the chanting of special ḥasidic melodies.

When the *zaddikim* began to limit their trips to far-flung communities, it became customary for the believers to travel to the *rebbe* on holidays and Sabbaths; the

The Spread of Hasidism in the Early 1770s

Expansion of Hasidism
.... Area in which Hasidism established itself
—·—·— Political border

© carta, JERUSALEM

0   50   100
km

rebbe's court and its customs took on an importance of their own in the life of the
sect. Special ceremonies were evolved and every movement or word of the *rebbe* was
of significance to his disciples. All these factors helped turn the hasidic groups into
a cohesive community.

There is reason to assume that there was a division of opinion in the hasidic movement between those who advocated centralization, meaning one single leader for
the movement, 'one spokesman for the generation', and those who held that each
of the *zaddikim* should be a leader in his own right. This may have been one of the
bones of contention between R. Jacob Joseph and the *Maggid* of Mezhirech. In any
case, the *Maggid* introduced a clearly decentralized trend, according to which every
hasidic community had its own leader and leadership was handed down from the
rebbe to his disciple. The dynastic principle, according to which the son inherited
from his father, prevailed only at a later stage of the movement's development and
under completely different conditions.

The *Maggid's* disciples, who played an important part in the hasidic movement,
included R. Levi Isaac of Berdichev, who followed in the footsteps of the Ba'al Shem

771

Tov as the 'pleader of Israel's cause'. In Galicia Ḥasidism was disseminated by the *maggid* R. Jehiel Michael of Zloczow and by R. Elimelech of Lyzhansk, who emphasized the *ẓaddik's* responsibility for his flock. The latter's disciple, R. Isaac Jacob 'the seer of Lublin', and R. Israel of Kozienice introduced Ḥasidism into central Poland.

In White Russia and Lithuania the new beliefs were spread during the *Maggid's* lifetime by R. Aaron 'the Great One' of Karlin, and at the time the *Ḥasidim* in general were known as Karlinites. At about the same time another disciple, R. Menaḥem Mendel, led his ḥasidic communities in Vitebsk and Minsk, and later headed a large group of *Ḥasidim* who made their way to the Holy Land in 1777. The most important figure in that region was R. Shneour Zalman of Lyady (Lozna). He was a great Talmudic scholar and eventually evolved his own school of ḥasidic thought known as *Ḥabad* (the Hebrew acronym for 'wisdom, understanding and knowledge'), expounded in his book *Likutei Amarim,* or *Hatanya.* The *Ḥabad* system placed greater emphasis on intellectual and theoretical teachings than on the emotions. It endeavoured to restrict the *ẓaddik's* role as intermediary between the faithful and God to spiritual matters alone. There can be no doubt that R. Shneour Zalman's activities took place in a region in which traditional ideas were strongly entrenched and influenced his views, and they also contain something of the 'rationalist' approach of the Lithuanian Jews, of whom he was one.

The Struggle Against Ḥasidism: The Gaon of Vilna

There is no record of the struggle against Ḥasidism and its adherents until the death of the *Maggid* from Mezhirech. But evidence has been preserved of the cooperation between community leaders and ḥasidic leaders in the 1760s. After the outbreak of persecution of the *Ḥasidim* by the Jewish leadership in Poland in the early 1770s, the heads of the Dubno community made an agreement with R. Jacob Joseph and his followers for joint action on the 'ransom of captives', that is, the freeing of a Jewish lessee (*arendar*) seized by one of the nobles. There were similar cases of cooperation elsewhere, particularly with regard to the safeguarding of *ḥazakah* (preventing competition between Jews in economic matters).

The campaign against Ḥasidism began in Vilna, which was known as the 'Jerusalem of Lithuania', the most important centre of religious study in Poland in those days. Even here there existed a small community of *Ḥasidim,* headed by a noted scholar and the town *maggid.* When the existence of this group was discovered in 1772, the *Ḥasidim* were excommunicated and their leaders punished or even banished from the town. The Vilna community addressed a letter to all other communities, calling on them to ferret out and excommunicate the *Ḥasidim.* The community of Brody, the largest in Poland, also decided on excommunication and was followed by other communities. The Brody excommunication prohibited the existence of separate *minyanim* of *Ḥasidim,* prayer according to the *Nusaḥ Ari,* ritual slaughter with specially polished knives and so forth. This decree had little effect on the situation of *Ḥasidim* in the south of Poland, in Podolia, Volhynia and the Ukraine, but it made their life more difficult in Lithuania and White Russia. Some of them concealed their activities or left their homes. The controversy was renewed when the *Hasidim* began to publish their own books on their own printing presses, without the approval of the community rabbis. The book *Toledot Jacob Joseph,* in particular, infuriated the opponents of Hasidism, and in 1781 Vilna once again announced the excommunication of 'the sect' in the name of 'the great and renowned ones of our community . . . together with the rabbi, the great sage of our community, and together with the great devout and famed *gaon,* Rabbi Elijah'. The document banned contact with the *Hasidim* and the renting of apartments to them, and the faithful were ordered to drive them out. All the Lithuanian communities joined in the excommunication. In consultations held between the communities of various districts in the following years, the excommunications were reiterated and made even more severe. The opponents of the *Hasidim* sent out emissaries to various places, including Germany and Bohemia, where rabbis were also persuaded to apply excommunication.

Despite the external and internal crises that afflicted Jewish society and its leadership in the eighteenth century, it was still strong enough to withstand this rising wave of religious fervour. The creative and conservative forces of this society rallied around the Gaon, Rabbi Elijah of Vilna, who was one of the greatest Jewish scholars of all times. He did not hold a rabbinical post in Vilna – he was supported by the community in order to enable him to devote all his time to study – but he was recognized as a leader, and his guidance was requested by Jews in many countries.

R. Elijah of Vilna wrote commentaries on the Mishnah and the Talmud, and his biblical exegesis was distinguished by its conciseness and simplicity. He even wrote studies in mathematics, astronomy and grammar as an aid to Bible study. But he was also a mystic who lived in a state of spiritual tension. He wrote books on Kabbalah and, according to his most devoted disciple, R. Hayyim of Volozhin, 'Elijah the prophet was revealed to him'.

The Gaon of Vilna opposed the hasidic claim that God could be worshipped in the temporal world through both the good and the evil impulses that exist in men. He believed that this approach blurred the limits between the secular and the sacred, the forbidden and the permitted – an attitude alien to his strictly ascetic approach. He was convinced that emphasis on inner devotion and deviation from clearly designated law would lead the *Hasidim* to transgress against the Torah. Their argument that study of the sacred texts other than for their own sake was valueless and could only lead to excessive arrogance appeared to him to undermine the basis of religious learning. He believed that study even for purposes other than pure devotion would develop into study for its own sake; otherwise, study would be totally neglected. The concept of the *zaddik* as an intermediary between God and the people appeared to him to be simple idol-worship, particularly since he regarded many of the great leaders of Hasidism, including the Ba'al Shem Tov, as ignoramuses. Thus, several of the basic assumptions of Hasidism and all of its lore proved repugnant to him. He refused to regard this movement as merely transgressing, as did the community leaders. The Gaon declared that 'all those who follow this path never return – it is heresy'. He was dissatisfied with the lenient punishment meted out by the leaders of the Vilna community on the hasidic *minyan* there, and he 'sent for the community leaders and was angered against them. Why had they imposed so slight a punishment?

773

If I were able, I would do unto them as Elijah the prophet did to the prophets of Baal.'

The Lithuanian communities and rabbis obeyed him. All the attempts of the ḥasidic leaders R. Menahem Mendel of Vitebsk and R. Shneour Zalman of Lyady to meet with him for clarification and discussion were unsuccessful. Towards the end of the Gaon's life, the *Ḥasidim* apparently began to spread rumours that he had repented of his opposition to their beliefs. This roused him to publish a letter in the summer of 1796, in which he announced: 'I shall stand on my guard as in the past, and it is the duty of anyone who is known by the name of Israel ... to repel them and persecute them with all kinds of persecution.'

The Gaon died during the Feast of Tabernacles in 1797. The opponents of the *Ḥasidim* claimed that 'the sect' in Vilna held 'a feast and festivities' after his death, and this aroused their fury. Leaders of the Vilna community announced in all the town's synagogues on the last day of the festival that 'whosoever follows in their footsteps and acts as they do ... will no longer be regarded as a son of Israel and will be like a stranger in everything ... that man shall be driven out of this holy community ...'

Since they regarded the *Ḥasidim* as outside the pale and not constituting part of the Jewish people, it was permitted to denounce them to the authorities. And, in fact, a complaint was submitted that the *Ḥasidim* and their leader, R. Shneour Zalman, were disloyal to the authorities, despised the gentiles and had been smuggling money to Turkey (in fact, these were funds for the Jews in Palestine). R. Shneour Zalman was arrested and brought to St Petersburg, but he was soon released and the authorities were ordered not to harass the Karlinites. But because of renewed denunciation, this time on the part of R. Avigdor Ben Ḥayyim, rabbi of Pinsk, the ḥasidic leader was re-arrested and called upon to answer a series of questions. Certain *Ḥasidim* also carried tales to the authorities, claiming that part of the money collected as tax by the Vilna community was being utilized for persecution of the *Ḥasidim*. Only after the authorities became convinced that there was no political aspect to the dispute did they release R. Shneour Zalman for the second time.

Apart from excommunications and tale-bearing – and possibly because of the failure of these methods – various anti-ḥasidic polemical writings began to be published in the late eighteenth century. The polemicists, R. Israel Leibel, *Maggid* of Novogrudok in Lithuania, R. David of Makov and others, scorned the *Ḥasidim*, their way of life and their belief in their *rebbes*. But the struggle was not an easy one, because, in the meantime, the *Ḥasidim* were becoming stronger and had begun to harass their opponents and to obstruct the distribution of their books.

Ḥasidism and the Autonomous Institutions of East European Jewry

Ḥasidism did not advocate social change and did not deliberately introduce it. But as it developed into a significant social factor in the life of East European Jews, it left its mark on the structure of Jewish society and its leadership. Nor did this movement affect the accepted patterns of Jewish society. Even in those places where it was dominant, the traditional community endured. The movement did not alter the balance of social forces within the community, and certainly did not improve the status of the lower classes as compared with the upper echelons. But the consolidation of the ḥasidic movement transferred to the new framework some of the religious and social interests that had formerly been concentrated solely within the community.

In the communities within the sphere of influence of Ḥasidism, the importance of the rabbi waned, and he was no longer the supreme spiritual authority, becoming more a teacher and an expert on religious law and living in the shadow of the *ẓaddik*, who enjoyed supreme authority. The preachers (*maggidim*), who had filled an important role in the spread of Ḥasidism, also almost completely disappeared from ḥasidic society. Both were replaced by the ḥasidic *rebbe,* who taught his disciples religious matters and ḥasidic lore, advised them on the truly pious way of life and guided them in their business and family affairs. The community framework, which had once encompassed every aspect of Jewish life, now lost a considerable part of its content, and thus the dependence of the individual on the community was weakened.

The *rebbe* intervened in appointments to community posts, particularly that of the ritual slaughterer. The ḥasidic *ẓaddik* was not connected with any particular community, but operated from outside. This was an innovation as compared with earlier periods; then each community had jealously preserved its independence and would not permit outside elements to interfere in its affairs. Even the councils could not force their decisions on the individual community, but were compelled to compromise or to demand religious arbitration. The *rebbe* influenced the communities and individuals by force of his status or his contacts with divine powers – that is, through his curse or blessing. His independence of community organization enabled him to rise above the interests of the local community and to act, in a fashion, like the councils of the past – to endeavour to protect general Jewish interests such as *hazakah,* ransom of captives, funds for the Holy Land or the organization of opposition to violent elements and to oppressive decrees issued by the authorities.

These changes meant that the previous ruling stratum forfeited much of its importance and influence in those regions where Ḥasidism held sway. The prosperous and the scholarly were also obliged to accept the authority of the *rebbe,* and although in due course a ruling class emerged in ḥasidic communities as well, it was not nearly as powerful as its predecessor. The masses, who had acquired a certain degree of influence during the struggle between Ḥasidism and its opponents, demanded a say in public matters, and their influence indeed increased. The view of the Jewish community as 'one body' and the demand for contact between the masses and the *ẓaddik,* which were the cornerstones of Ḥasidism, boosted the confidence of the individual Jew and considerably restrained the inter-community struggle that raged among Polish Jewry throughout the eighteenth century.

This struggle also left its mark on the communities of Lithuania, the stronghold of opposition to the *Hasidim.* The Gaon of Vilna's war on Ḥasidism did not end in victory, but it consolidated and bolstered Lithuanian Jewry. It also served as a pretext for crystallizing new sources of creativity and education, *i.e.,* the great *yeshivot* (academies of talmudic study).

It may be deduced from the above that the growth of Ḥasidism not only failed to undermine the already shaken foundations of Jewish autonomy in Eastern Europe but in several respects actually strengthened and reinforced them. The ḥasidic communities and the Lithuanian *yeshivot* constituted a barrier against the infiltration of the *Haskalah* (Enlightenment movement) into this region, maintained the unity of the majority of the Jewish community on traditional foundations and produced a gap between the Jewish communities of the East and the West throughout the nineteenth century.

47

The Jewish Community in Western and Central Europe

The New Communities

Unlike the Jewish communities of Eastern Europe, the Near East and North Africa – most of which had existed consecutively for hundreds of years – the communities of Western and Central Europe were, in the main, founded in the seventeenth and eighteenth centuries. Only a very few of them, such as Frankfurt on Main, Prague, or Worms, had existed continuously from an earlier period.

A few of the new communities were created by the descendants of refugees from Spain or Marranos who continued to flee the Iberian Peninsula in these centuries as well. The majority, however, were formed by Jews from Eastern Europe and the villages and small towns in Germany, who began to move to the important urban centres. Hence, there was great dependence of the majority of the new communities of Germany on the authorities, who, as was mentioned earlier, made their residence conditional on heavy financial payments – unlike the situation in Eastern Europe, where the community itself generally determined the conditions for 'settlement rights' (*i.e.,* the conditions on which one could join the community).

Sephardi Communities in the Seventeenth and Eighteenth Centuries

Those communities composed of descendants of refugees from Spain won official recognition in several European countries in the seventeenth century. Even in those towns that already had Jewish communities, the Sephardim established their own communities and wrote up their community ledgers in Spanish or Portuguese (only in the eighteenth century did some of them begin to use the language of the country). The new form of community organization preserved some of the features of the pre-Expulsion period, and it is not surprising that the basic regulations of the Sephardi communities (the *askamot*) were very uniform.

The Sephardi community was headed by an executive body (*ma'amad*) generally appointed for one year, which appointed its own successor. Anyone appointed to the *ma'amad* or as *gabbai* (treasurer) was obliged to accept the office, and refusal entailed heavy fines. Generally speaking, anyone who disobeyed the community leaders could expect a fine or even excommunication (the most notorious cases being the excommunication of both Uriel da Costa and Baruch Spinoza by the Amsterdam community. The *ma'amad* determined the various taxes to be levied from members of the community, decided when they were permitted to have recourse to gentile courts and maintained the communal institutions.

As it was based on common Sephardi origin (the descendants of the Spanish Jews viewed themselves as a *nacion* [nation]), the Sephardi community rejected other candidates for membership and sometimes even inflicted punishment on members of the *nacion* who married Jewish women from outside the group. Leadership of the community was generally in the hands of a small number of distinguished families, who in time developed into a closed oligarchic group. But despite its organizational rigidity, the Sephardi community was not particularly stable with regard to Jewish tradition. Many members, particularly in the seventeenth century, were descended from the Marranos who had returned to Judaism, and sometimes, as in Bordeaux and its surroundings, they continued to appear in the Christian world as New Christians. These Jews were educated from childhood in the spirit of the Catholic religion, and even after their return to Judaism their knowledge of Jewish tradition was limited. There were those among them who found their regained Judaism so remote from what they had envisaged in their old homeland that they were bitterly disillusioned, and although they did not retire from Jewish life or leave the community, they became indifferent towards Jewish affairs. Others taught their children Spanish customs and culture rather than Jewish traditions. It is not surprising, therefore, that the Sabbatean revival met with greater response in the Sephardi communities. The idea of a messiah who changed and annulled laws, and so resembled the Christian concept, was more easily assimilated in Sephardi than in Ashkenazi communities. This mood can also help explain the success of one of the Sabbatean preachers, Nehemiah Hayyun, in the Sephardi community of London during the early eighteenth century. On the other hand, those with deep roots in the two cultures made various attempts at philosophical and even religious synthesis in those years. This served as the basis for the spiritual ferment in these communities during the seventeenth century, which, in content, anticipated rationalist theories and the ideals of the Enlightenment and even left its stamp on the development of European thought in that period.

Court-Jews as Jewish Leaders in the German States

The great majority of the communities of Germany were, as we have noted, new or restored. Many were created when one of the rulers took a court-Jew into his service and the latter brought his assistants, agents and servants with him. These constituted the nucleus of the community, which was augmented by other Jews who joined with the ruler's permission. In other places, particularly in southern Germany, the Jews would unite in a body known as a *Landjudenschaft,* led by the 'Council of the Land', which represented them and directed their affairs. In many places the court-Jew served as a *shtadlan* (go-between or official representative of the community), and this title was sometimes preserved in one family for several generations.

The new communities preserved the traditional organizational framework of the Ashkenazi communities, but the strict supervision by the authorities over the burghers and the severe restriction of freedom of movement and sources of livelihood left their stamp on the community organization as well. There was internal jurisdiction, but here too the state officials sometimes intervened. The considerable dependence of the community on the court-Jews also had a generally negative effect. A court-Jew could sometimes exploit his intimacy with the authorities in order to further Jewish interests, or to neutralize official intervention in the internal affairs of the community, but more often than not the hostility of various sections of the gentile population towards the court-Jew, the servant of the absolutist ruler, was extended to all the Jews. The court-Jew's loss of favour was also likely to be reflected in the fate of the community as a whole.

For all that, the organizational pattern of Jewish communities in the German states was not wholly new. The changes and struggles connected with the consolidation of centralist and absolutist methods in these countries were not the only impetus; the new organization was the result of the adjustment of the old autonomous Jewish institutions, formed in the Middle Ages, to new circumstances. There was actually an internal contradiction in their development: under the influence of their surroundings and with the support of the authorities, they developed representative autonomous bodies – 'councils of the land' and regional congresses – but the consequence of their organizational success was that legal experts and government officials began to protest against the very existence of autonomous Jewish institutions. These, they claimed, constituted a 'state within a state' and their main aim was to perpetrate the rule of the rich and powerful at the expense of the Jewish masses.

In fact, even in these communities, an upper class consisting of the rich and learned took over control. They sometimes failed to hold elections of councils and representatives at the proper times, and even made long-term appointments. On the other hand, this stratum, which undoubtedly wanted to perpetuate its dominant rule, undertook the burden of maintaining all the community institutions – the religious court, the *talmud Torah* (religious school), the *hekdesh* (hospital) and the assembly hall – and was ardently dedicated to the task of maintaining the Jewish way of life. The *talmid hakham,* or scholar, was still the accepted ideal of the Jews of Central and Eastern Europe in the seventeenth and most of the eighteenth centuries. Court-Jews and other prosperous members of the community married their daughters to scholars, and several of the greatest rabbis of that period were the offspring of such unions. One of these, R. David Oppenheim, was appointed at an early age Chief Rabbi of Moravia and, in 1702, Chief Rabbi of Prague. He was renowned mainly for his great library of books and manuscripts, some of them extremely rare. Oppenheim even thought of turning his collection into a public library, but feared expropriation and the intervention of the clergy, who often censored sections of Hebrew books and manuscripts. His sons lost possession of the collection, and in the early nineteenth century it was acquired by the Bodleian Library in Oxford.

Spiritual Ferment

The main spiritual conflicts at the end of the seventeenth and the first half of the eighteenth centuries arose in response to the activity of the Sabbatean remnants. The communities of Central and Eastern Europe several times launched attacks on the Sabbateans and even excommunicated them. The conflict became particularly bitter in the 1750s, when one of the greatest religious scholars of the generation, R. Jonathan Eybeschuetz, was accused of being a Sabbatean. He headed a *yeshiva* in Prague, then became a rabbi in Metz and eventually served as rabbi of the three communities of Altona, Hamburg and Wandsbek. R. Jacob Emden (the son of Rabbi Zevi Ashkenazi, who was known for his fierce campaign against Sabbateanism at the beginning of the eighteenth century) claimed that Shabbetai Zevi's name was inscribed on amulets that Eybeschuetz had distributed to his community. R. Jonathan, who had studied Kabbalah and was apparently connected in his youth with Sabbatean groups, denied the accusations, but Emden attacked him violently in a series of books and pamphlets. In these works he exposed the activities of the Sabbateans in Germany and Poland. The controversy eventually reached the Polish 'Council of the Four Lands', which rallied to Eybeschuetz's defence. This struggle, which caused a split among the community leaders in Central and Eastern Europe, also had a detrimental effect on their status vis-à-vis the Jewish public and weakened the autonomous organization as a whole.

The Cultural and Social Ties with the Non-Jewish Surroundings

The process of drawing closer to the non-Jewish world exerted an immeasurable influence on Jewish life; slow and protracted, it eventually wrought profound changes in the spiritual world and the internal organization of the Jews in both Central and Western Europe. There were various factors that made this process more rapid in Western and Central Europe than in Eastern Europe or the Near East. The fact that the Jews were few in number and were dispersed in small communities weakened the sense of affiliation to a strong and cohesive Jewish society and drew them closer to their surroundings. Because of the excessive financial demands of the Central European rulers, only the rich were able to obtain 'letters of protection', while the poor were expelled from these countries from time to time. The relatively high standard of living among Western Jews, the need to maintain contact mainly with the higher classes of the gentile population and frequently even with the ruling circles, fostered a certain resemblance in patterns of living and thought, as had occurred in mediaeval Spain. On the other hand, the spread of secular influences in the non-Jewish world and the waning of church influence also had their effect. An atmosphere was created in which Jewish attempts to assimilate were often greeted with understanding and even welcomed. Nor should we disregard the influence of the Sephardi Jews, a considerable number of whom were born Christians, who had lived for lengthy periods in gentile surroundings and were brought up according to the latters' concepts and ideas, so that emulation seemed natural to them. Their status was such that the Ashkenazim in Sephardi centres tended to follow in their footsteps.

The first manifestations of *rapprochement* between the Jews and their surroundings were in outward appearance (the shaving of beards, wearing of wigs, etc.), clothing and private and public behaviour. Similarity in appearance generally led to social proximity – participation in social gatherings, card-games and various family cele-brations. But even in the West, the social assimilation was limited to a relatively narrow circle. The most obvious influence was cultural, and, above all, learning the lan-guage of the country. To a certain extent this had existed in previous centuries, in order to facilitate commercial contacts and dealings with the authorities. But the change in conditions in this part of Europe at the end of the seventeenth century and during the eighteenth century brought about a shift in values. The ability to read a newspaper, for example, not only served a practical purpose but also increased the prestige of the educated Jew in the eyes of his community. In the 1730s and 1740s knowledge of the vernacular was an inseparable part of the education of the young Jew of good family in Central Europe, and there were also many families that taught their daughters French. The behaviour of the rich and the notables was gradually copied by all sections of Jewish society, and knowledge of the language spoken in the country of residence gradually became common in the Jewish community.

There was also a change in the attitude towards Christianity and gentile society. The theory was voiced that Christianity should be regarded not as idol-worship but as a religion suited to the gentiles. Among the Sephardim there were even those who questioned the concept of the 'chosen people' and queried whether the Jews were still expected to await the coming of the Messiah and Redemption in the Holy Land. In this spiritual and cultural atmosphere there was growing opposition to the Oral Law, and religious observances were no longer strictly followed. In short, during the eighteenth century there were certain circles among the Jews of Western and Central Europe who moved from an outward assimilation to their surroundings to social contacts and, thence, to taking root in the culture and language of the non-Jewish world. There were some who began to doubt some of the basic concepts of the Jewish religion. This socio-cultural process, which generally affected the upper echelons of Jewish society, necessarily left its mark on internal Jewish organization.

In the Sephardi communities this assimilation was reflected in the large number of mixed marriages between Jews and non-Jews, the offspring of which were invariably brought up as Christians. Notables who for lack of interest refused to share in the burden of holding communal office broke off contact with the communities and sometimes even baptized their children. But even in the German communities, those sections in Jewish society that had come into close contact with the non-Jewish world began to display special sensitivity to the discrimination and humiliation implicit in the Jewish condition. A considerable number of these chose conversion or the modernization of Jewish society as ways of furthering their own integration into the society around them. Consequently, not only was the community organization weakened from within, but it was also deprived of the social stratum from which Jewish community leaders had formerly emerged. This class now began to concen-trate its attention and hopes on activities and developments occurring outside Jewish society. The ideological justification for this change was provided by the ideals of the Enlightenment, which spread rapidly in the eighteenth century. And although only a very limited group of German Jews really deserved to be denoted *maskilim* (*i.e.*, the Enlightened), their prominence rapidly won them extensive and steadily increasing influence over German Jewry.

The Beginnings of the Jewish Enlightenment
(Haskalah): *Moses Mendelssohn*

The Jewish Enlightenment movement (*Haskalah*) was an offshoot of the European Enlightenment and resembled it in that it elevated the individual, the 'human being', and aspired to liberate him from historically evolved social and religious frameworks. In giving to man his pride of place, the Enlightenment claimed that the human mind was the criterion for all natural and social phenomena. The proponents of the Enlightenment found themselves, therefore, at variance with traditional values and institutions, tending to regard the past history of mankind as a compilation of errors resulting from ignorance, from over-reliance on authority and from exploitation of the ignorant masses by leaders greedy for power and riches.

The singularity of the Jewish *Haskalah* lay in its emergence against the background of the social and cultural integration of the Jews to their surroundings. Not only did the Jews absorb the cultural values of European nations, but some of them even began to write creatively in European languages. This was not new in Jewish history; Jews had written in foreign languages before, and many outstanding works of Jewish and general content had been written in the past in Greek, Arabic, Spanish and Italian. However, the basic tenets of Judaism had constituted the focal point of these works, even when they were imbued with a spirit of extreme rationalism; their purpose then had been to prove that the truth of Divine revelation could be demonstrated by reason and that Jewish tradition could be justified in this fashion. Among eighteenth-century *Haskalah* circles, the touchstone for understanding and evaluation was drawn from the spiritual riches of the surrounding culture, and, therefore, even among those *maskilim* who in theory remained true to Judaism, the movement became an expression of universal spiritual aims. A considerable number of them arrived, relatively soon, at clearly deistic concepts, advocating what was known in the eighteenth century as 'natural religion' and opposing all revealed religions.

The spiritual father of the *maskilim* was the prominent philosopher Moses Mendelssohn (1729–86). He was the son of a scribe, a writer of holy scrolls, from the town of Dessau, and from his youth displayed outstanding abilities as a student of mediaeval Hebrew philosophy. On moving to Berlin, he devoted himself to the study of German literature and acquired knowledge of Latin and European languages. He met the famous German writer Gotthold Ephraim Lessing in the mid-1750s and was drawn into German Enlightenment circles under his influence. Lessing even began publishing Mendelssohn's philosophical writings that had been written in German.

Mendelssohn's philosophical theories serve, in the history of Jewish thought, as a link between mediaeval rationalist philosophy and eighteenth-century ideas. The starting-point of his theories was the truth of Divine Revelation as manifested in the 'Giving of the Law' on Mount Sinai. His purpose, however, was not to derive universal religious truth from them, as these could be arrived at through reason, but rather to determine a way of life and organization for the Jews as a group that would be capable of serving as an example to all men. The injunctions imparted to the Jewish people by revelation formed the 'divine constitution'. The laws and injunctions of

Judaism were closer to natural religion than the dogmas of any other religion. Generally speaking, Mendelssohn accepted Spinoza's definition that the Jewish religion was the political constitution of the Hebrews, but, unlike Spinoza, he did not regard this as a limiting factor or a defect but sought to emphasize the universal significance of this corporate constitution. The commandments of the Jewish religion could not, because of their unique character and lack of sensual expression, become pagan symbols, even though their significance was mainly symbolic. This had ensured, on the one hand, that through the centuries the Jews would not stray far from natural religion, and, on the other hand, that they would not have to create a dogmatic network of doctrines binding all members of the religion, as had happened in Christianity. It was precisely because Jewish religious obligations had taken the form of practical commandments that the sphere of beliefs and opinions remained, according to Mendelssohn, open to discussion and clarification. At the same time, no change in beliefs and opinions, and not even formal conversion to another faith, could exempt the descendants of those who had stood at the foot of Mount Sinai from the obligation of strictly observing these laws. Thus Mendelssohn endeavoured to connect faithful observance of religious injunctions (the symbols uniting all pure believers in one specific framework) with tolerance and the widest possible freedom of opinion.

The Activities of Mendelssohn and His Circle

At first Mendelssohn refrained from active intervention in the life of the Jewish community, but in the 1770s he changed his mind. In 1778 he began to publish his German translation of the Pentateuch with a Hebrew commentary (*Biur*) based on rationalist principles. This project, which in theory was aimed at bringing Mendelssohn's children to a closer understanding of the Bible, became, for many young Jews, a short cut to the German language and culture as well as to a rationalistic interpretation of the Scriptures. It is not surprising that the *Biur* encountered the vigorous opposition of conservative elements in Judaism.

But even more far-reaching in consequence was Mendelssohn's adherence to the principle, accepted in European Enlightened circles, of the separation of state and religion. In his book *Jerusalem* he emphasized that only the state could exert coercion, while religion (the church) should be based on persuasion. Hence powers of coercion and control should not be entrusted to church frameworks. The practical implication of this theory was the undermining of the authority of the internal autonomous organization of Jewry. Mendelssohn was opposed to the community's right to impose excommunication on its members and to its legal jurisdiction.

Despite these opinions, Mendelssohn did not encounter fierce opposition on the part of the Jewish leaders or rabbis in Germany. This was partly because he was an observant man, partly because of his standing in German society, and partly because of his defence of the Jews against various hostile elements. The same was not true of the activities of his disciples and close associates. Hartwig (Naphtali Herz) Wessely (Weisel), David Friedlaender and Naphtali Herz Homberg were eager to reform and adapt Jewish society, particularly in the field of education.

When Joseph II's *Toleranzpatent* was issued in early 1782, Wessely published an essay in Hebrew entitled 'Words of Peace and Truth', which was a draft proposal for the reform of Jewish education. His main demand was to increase secular education at the expense of Jewish studies and to direct the majority of Jewish boys, after the first stages of study, to learning crafts and practical occupations. In theory, this was merely a proposal for making certain changes in education, but in practice it was a profound, even decisive, turning-point for the Jewish outlook. Wessely's work aroused fierce reaction among traditionalists. The establishment of Hevrat Doreshei Leshon Ever (The Society of Friends of the Hebrew Language) and the issuing of a Hebrew journal by the name of *Hame'assef* ('The Gatherer') in 1783 to preach these new ideas – albeit moderately and sometimes disguised – intensified the split in Jewish society.

After Mendelssohn's death in 1786, and particularly from the 1790s onwards, the public controversy between *Haskalah* circles and their opponents became sharper. In their Hebrew publications the *maskilim* continued to maintain a moderate tone, but their German writings were anti-traditional and even deistic. Negation of the Talmud and the *mitzvot* (religious injunctions) was almost universal; the declared ideal was 'pure Mosaism' or 'natural religion'. This circle accepted and concurred with the theory advanced by anti-Semites throughout history that loyalty to Talmudic tradition and the observance of *mitzvot* separated the Jews from their neighbours and prevented them from fulfilling their obligations as citizens of the state. The 'advancement' of the Jews, not merely civil and moral but also religious (*i.e.,* the need to adapt the Jewish religion to the needs of the state, and in the view of several of them, even to convert as a group) became a popular slogan. On the other hand, the great majority of the *maskilim* did not cut themselves off from Mendelssohn's spiritual heritage; they continued to regard 'pure' Judaism as preferable to Christianity and sometimes envisaged its future importance by interpreting Jewish messianic aspirations in universal terms as an epoch of reason, liberty and fraternity.

The Haskalah *in Jewish Society*

The *maskilim* began to publish critiques of Jewish society and to advance proposals for reform. As a result of the violent opposition of the rabbinical authorities to even the mildest of reforms, the *maskilim* ceased to believe in the possibility of influencing the Jews from within. They too, like their non-Jewish counterparts, came to the conclusion that the Jewish masses would not help change the face of Jewish society. On the other hand, they had confidence in the beneficial influence of 'enlightened absolutism' and called for its intervention in Jewish affairs. This served as the basis for their propaganda methods – both internal and external. Within the Jewish community they published philosophical works in the rationalist spirit, endeavouring to disseminate a knowledge of history and science and criticizing both the 'stubborn' traditionalists and the 'unconcerned'. As regards the non-Jewish world, they were constantly approaching the authorities with proposals and plans for altering the Jewish way of life. The Jewish masses, particularly in those parts of Poland annexed to Prussia and Austria, regarded any official intervention in Jewish autonomy as 'an evil decree'; thus the activities of the *maskilim* antagonized the Jewish community as

Centres of the Enlightenment and Stages of Its Expansion

Expansion of the Enlightenment

- ▦ through 1750
- ▓ through 1800
- ▤ through 1850

Centres of the Enlightenment

- ✪ up to 1750
- ★ up to 1800
- • up to 1850

a whole. But their estrangement only strengthened the adherence of the *maskilim* to the state authority and their dependence on it; the latter remained, in fact, their main support.

Memoranda and proposals by Jewish *maskilim,* all of whom were in some way connected with the Berlin group, fulfilled an important role in all the discussions held by the Russian, Prussian and Austrian authorities. It was they who proposed introducing changes into the organization of Jewish society and the Jewish way of life in order to adapt it to the demands of 'reason' – namely, to those of the society in which they lived. Their proposals related, above all, to several vital spheres in which they believed that reform could prepare the Jews for the necessary changes: education, livelihood and religious commandments.

Education

Many of the plans thought up by the *maskilim* concerned educational problems. The main purpose of Wessely's 'Words of Peace and Truth' and the subsequent publications was to make 'humanistic learning' (*i.e.*, secular studies) as important as 'Divine Law' (*i.e.*, the Scriptures, the Talmud and religious-legislative and ethical literature), and even to grant priority to the former. If the greatest of scholars lacked worldly knowledge and was unacquainted with 'manners, learning and nature', then his education was flawed. The educated man should acquire general knowledge and the achievements of general culture.

As we have noted, this implied a basic change of values in the life of the Jewish individual. *Talmud Torah*, the study of Torah not for the purpose of achieving any particular aim but for its own sake, was the accepted ideal in Jewish society. The entire spectrum of life, of livelihood and of family affairs was, at least in theory, subordinate to this high ideal. The *maskilim* did not dare to attack the principle of study openly, but they placed new emphasis on the introduction of secular studies and the changing of teaching methods. They maintained that it was important to study the Hebrew language and its grammar prior to studying the Bible. Not all young boys should continue their studies and specialize in Mishnah and Talmud, they claimed, but only the more talented, who were planning to become rabbis; the others should learn crafts. The implication of this was that study of the Talmud should be left to the few and that *Talmud Torah* would cease to be the general ideal.

The *maskilim* stressed particularly the importance of 'pure' language and the need to study grammar. There was in this something of the humanistic heritage of the Enlightenment as a whole. In the early stages this approach provided the impetus for the renaissance of biblical Hebrew, and even laid the foundations of secular Hebrew literature. But this trend very soon clashed with the second aim of the *maskilim*: inculcation of the language of the country. Since there were more rationalist writings in European languages than in Hebrew, the young *maskilim* soon began to abandon their Hebrew studies. Hebrew soon became the means of expression only for that intermediate generation, with its traditional education, that had found its own way to the general Enlightenment. In the second generation of *maskilim* in Germany, knowledge of Hebrew was already on the wane. This transitional period was protracted when the *Haskalah* spread to Galicia and Russia, but the basic trend remained unchanged.

The *maskilim* were the initiators and main organizers of the new Jewish schools established in Germany and Austria either with government support or by official demand. The first such school, Ḥinukh Nearim (The Free School) was founded by Berlin *maskilim* in 1778. They tried to apply their educational theories in this Berlin school and in the Frankfurt Philanthropin (1804).

When the Austrian authorities in Galicia tried to disseminate the *Haskalah* by coercion at the end of the 1780s, Herz Homberg, one of Mendelssohn's disciples and an ardent *maskil,* was appointed chief inspector of these schools. He composed special textbooks for studying the basic tenets of the Jewish religion and called for government censorship of Jewish books. He also threatened with official punishment those rabbis who refused to cooperate with him. But the entire Jewish public, with the exception of the small group of *maskilim,* opposed this compulsory 'Enlightenment', just as they would oppose a similar plan by the Russian authorities in the 1840s. For them these schools were hotbeds of heresy. In actual fact, and in contradiction to the aims of many *maskilim,* these schools did not strengthen the attachment of their pupils to the values of Judaism but served everywhere as instruments for the integration and cultural assimilation of the Jews as individuals into the society around them.

New Sources of Livelihood

One of the main problems that preoccupied the *maskilim* was the great discrepancy between Jewish sources of livelihood and those of the gentiles amongst whom they lived. They regarded this difference as an obstacle to integration. This concern on the part of *maskilim* occurred simultaneously with the upsurge of physiocratic economic theories highlighting the importance of creative occupations, particularly those connected with agriculture, and belittling trade and barter. The *maskilim* believed that commerce had corrupted the moral qualities of the Jews and that its abandonment would further their moral reform.

Both Jewish and non-Jewish proponents of the Enlightenment devised numerous methods for changing Jewish occupations and for introducing 'productivity'. They did not regard the Jews as responsible for their situation, but rather, in the words of the Paris Sanhedrin, 'the children of Israel . . . were forced almost to abandon crafts and agricultural work which they had loved in ancient times, and this only because of the suffering and vicissitudes which overtook them with no balm or haven for their souls . . .' They hoped that within a short time the Jews' livelihoods would begin to resemble those of the rest of society.

Their hopes were not realized. Despite the concessions that the 'enlightened' rulers granted the Jews in the learning of crafts and the establishment of factories, considerable influence was still wielded by groups of merchants and artisans who feared the Jews and opposed their entry into new occupations. Agricultural settlement involved considerable problems, since the opposition of local peasants was no less violent than that of the Jewish communities. The latter were not anxious to abandon traditional sources of livelihood and did not regard the conversion of their children into peasants and artisans as a desirable aim. The Jewish masses viewed the *maskilim* proposals that leasing and innkeeping be prohibited as catastrophic. As a result, not only did the Jewish public fail to support the demands of the *maskilim,* but these proposals actually delayed the acceptance of other *Haskalah* objectives. The main barrier, however, was the *Haskalah* attitude to the traditional observance of the religious commandments.

Religious Reforms

Mendelssohn had demanded that Jewish burial customs be amended and that the dead be buried only after three days (considerable space was devoted to this problem in *Hame'assef*). But when the radical attitude to religious affairs began to take hold, the *maskilim* no longer discussed such questions on their own merits (since they were convinced that there was no point in observing any religious injunctions whatever), but rather as a means of adapting the Jewish way of life to the demands of the non-Jewish surroundings. And since they knew how sensitive the Jewish community was to any attack on tradition, they tried, in this sphere as well, to find shelter behind the policies of the authorities. When the Assembly of Jewish Notables and the Sanhedrin were convened in France and the authorities demanded that they define the attitude of the Jewish religion towards the state, the *maskilim* began to speak out in support of reform of the Jewish religion. The Sanhedrin, out of a desire to conciliate the authorities, but also under the pressure of the *maskilim,* passed several resolutions according to which, whenever there was a conflict between the demands of the state and of religion, the former should prevail; in any case Jewish law would not apply during military service. The Sanhedrin also decided that 'the law of God includes both religious and political injunctions . . . and the latter have not been valid since Israel with all its tribes ceased to be a nation dwelling apart,' that is, since it ceased to exist as an independent state. Although the resolutions did not state which were the political injunctions, these remarks served to remove religion from the sphere of human relations and from the connections between the individual Jew and his community.

The first attempts to introduce changes into religious ritual were also made with the aid of the authorities. After Jerome, king of Westphalia and brother of Napoleon, established a central consistory for the Jews of his state in the capital, Kassel, in 1807, the leader of this body, Israel Jacobson, a friend of Friedlaender, began to introduce changes in the book of prayer and in the ritual. The main changes were the omission of certain prayers, the preaching of a sermon in German, changes in marriage customs, religious confirmation for boys and girls and so forth. Jacobson wanted to make Jewish ritual observances resemble Protestant ceremonies as closely as possible in outward appearance. When civil rights were granted in Prussia in 1812, Friedlaender also proposed certain changes in synagogue worship in Berlin. He demanded the replacement of the 'dead Hebrew language' by German and the removal of references to Zion and Jerusalem from the prayerbook, since the Jews, as free Prussian citizens, had only one homeland for whose peace and welfare they should pray.

The aim of all these reforms was to remove as much as possible the barriers dividing the Jews from the non-Jews, but also to bring the *maskilim,* and especially the young among them who were no longer interested in synagogue prayer, closer to Judaism. The aim was to prevent conversion, which the *maskilim* regarded as an act of treachery and hypocrisy, since the mysteries of Christianity and its dogmatic principles were even more alien to their spirit than the practical injunctions of Judaism.

When the ideals of the Enlightenment began to spread, prominent Jews took up arms against them. The chief among them was the rabbi of Pressburg (now Bratislava), R. Moses Sofer (Hatam Sofer). The main objective of these opponents was to strengthen internal Jewish organization, 'to restore former glories' and to suppress those who were trying to undermine tradition. However, in this period when conversion was rife, religious stringency could no longer bring back those attracted to the *Haskalah;* rather, it drove them to make a complete break with Judaism. In fact, the 'faithful guardians of Israel' during that period and even later employed defensive methods in order to preserve their immediate environment from the influx of *Haskalah* ideals and *a priori* renounced those who had already gone over to the *Haskalah* camp.

Even though the *Haskalah* movement was maintained for some time (in fact till the second half of the nineteenth century) by only a small circle within the Jewish people, and even though the hopes that they had pinned on the help of the authorities were dashed, this movement played a role of primary importance in modern Jewish history. The *maskilim* clearly realized that the problem facing increasing numbers of Jews was how to preserve their Jewish identity within the framework of a society that was abolishing corporative frameworks and establishing universal principles for the granting of rights and imposing of obligations. The *maskilim* were the first to seek solutions to this problem, and although they did not achieve their aim, they induced Jewish society to seek out new ways for itself.

48

Demographic Changes and Economic Activity in the Nineteenth Century

Natural Increase

The nineteenth century was a period of rapid increase in population in all European countries, but the numerical growth of the European Jewish communities far exceeded the average. The number of Jews in the world at the beginning of the century was estimated at two and a quarter million, of whom some two million lived in Europe. At the beginning of the 1880s there were nearly seven million Jews in Europe out of a total of seven and a half million in the entire world. The Jewish rate of increase was twice as fast as that of the non-Jewish population, and several scholars have spoken of the 'demographic miracle' of the Jewish people in the nineteenth century.

The main reasons for the rapid increase of population in Europe during that period were the amelioration of sanitary conditions and improved medical treatment for the sick. The situation in the towns, which in previous centuries had been hotbeds of disease and epidemic, improved as a result of the revolutionary changes in water supply, in sewage and in garbage disposal. But the specific character of Jewish society, with its religious and cultural traditions, also left its mark. The main cause of Jewish natural increase was not fertility – proportionally there was no significant difference from non-Jews in number of births, and, in fact, towards the end of the nineteenth century, the relative fertility in the Jewish population was lower – rather, there was a drop in infant and adult mortality among Jews as a result of devoted care of the sick.

The average life-span of Jews was considerably higher in the nineteenth century than that of non-Jews. For example, a survey carried out in Frankfurt in 1855 showed that the average life-span of Jews was forty-eight years and nine months and of non-Jews thirty-six years and eleven months. In Pest, Hungary, in 1871, the number of children up to the age of fourteen constituted 33% of the Jewish population, while only 10% of the non-Jewish population. There can be no doubt that the greater stability of the family, the smaller number of illegitimate children, the infrequency of venereal diseases, the higher status of the woman within the family, the care lavished on babies and small children, abstinence from alcohol, the readiness of the individual and the community to undergo considerable economic sacrifice in order to help others and the lengthy tradition of charitable deeds combined, among the Jews, to serve as the basis for their demographic development. All these elements encouraged a high rate of natural increase in a period when several factors were exerting a damaging influence on the demographic balance. On the one hand, the difficult political and social conditions in several countries impelled some 200,000 Jews to convert to Christianity during the nineteenth century, and on the other hand, the amelioration of the status of the Jews in other countries led to an increase in mixed marriages, the offspring of which were, for the most part, lost to the Jewish people.

It is worth noting that only as a result of the new developments in nineteenth-century Europe did the social framework of the Jews, as well as their traditions, have such a beneficial effect from the demographical point of view. The fact is that the rate of Jewish natural increase in preceding centuries was incomparably less than in the nineteenth century. Additional proof of the influence of the European social and cultural progress on Jewish demography is the much lower rate of increase in the Jewish communities of Asia and Africa, which had not yet been affected by the social and cultural processes of nineteenth-century Europe. These Jews numbered less than half a million at the beginning of the century and only 750,000 at the beginning of the 1880s. Thus the percentage of Sephardim and members of the oriental communities within the Jewish people decreased from more than 20% at the beginning of the century to 10% in the eighties.

Migration and Urbanization

The high rate of natural increase in Europe created the problem of surplus population and impelled many people to emigrate. This affected particularly the Jews, as they were restricted as to residence and occupations and suffered from the hostility of both peoples and governments. In the nineteenth century the Jews began to migrate overseas, particularly to the United States. This migration, which in the eighteenth century had consisted of individuals, now became a mass movement, especially among the Jews of Central Europe. Added motivation for migrating to the United States was provided by the failure of the 1848 revolutions, on which many Jews had pinned hopes for equality and integration. The Jewish press of the time was emblazoned with the slogan *Auf nach Amerika!* ('On to America'). This emigration swept along with it certain socially active elements and radicals, who later laid the foundations of the Jewish community in the United States. At the end of the 1860s, immigrants from Eastern Europe began to arrive as well.

However, until the 1880s, the main flow of Jewish migration was not across the Atlantic but from Eastern to Western Europe and from the densely populated areas of Lithuania and White Russia in the Pale of Settlement to the Ukraine east of the Dnieper and to the 'New Russia' on the shores of the Black Sea. There were German Jews who migrated to France or England, and Polish and Galician Jews who migrated to Germany (although there were even some who migrated to southern Russia), but the mass movement, encompassing hundreds of thousands, was internal: from the Grand Duchy of Posen (whose Jewish population thus shrank in the nineteenth century) to other parts of Germany; from Galicia to other parts of the Austro-Hungarian Empire; and from the northern Pale of Settlement to Poland and further south. Thus, large sections of European Jewry shifted from relatively remote areas to the great centres, and from culturally and technologically backward regions to more developed ones.

Despite these wanderings, which led to the creation of numerous Jewish communities in the new countries, the great majority of the Jewish people was still concentrated, at the beginning of the 1880s, in a small number of countries: Russia (four million),

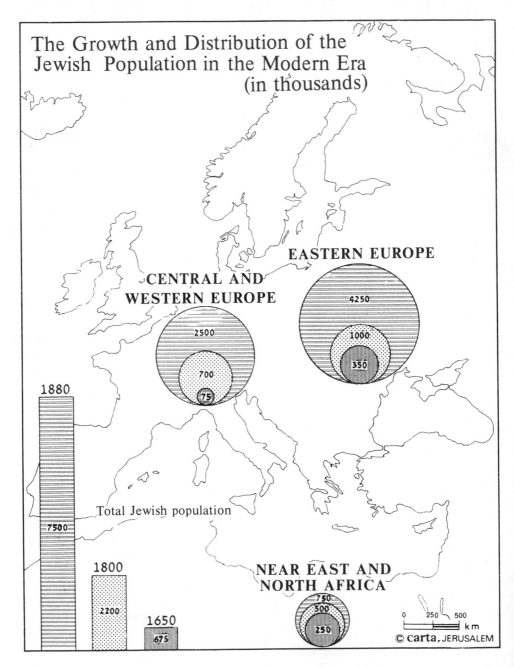

The Growth and Distribution of the Jewish Population in the Modern Era (in thousands)

EASTERN EUROPE

CENTRAL AND WESTERN EUROPE

2500

700

75

4250

1000

350

1880

Total Jewish population

7500

1800

2200

1650

675

NEAR EAST AND NORTH AFRICA

750

500

250

0   250   500
k m

© carta, JERUSALEM

Austria-Hungary (one and a half million), Germany (550,000), the Ottoman Empire (300,000), and the United States (250,000).

Almost all the emigrants were concentrated in large towns, and the great majority found their way to the cities. Those Russian Jews who were expelled or forced out of the villages also settled in towns. Thus the Jews fit into the general process of urbanization that Europe was experiencing in the nineteenth century. But in this too the Jews – who had been town-dwellers for generations – did not resemble the rest of the population. The great majority of the new urban class were ex-villagers, and, in the first stages of their wanderings, they continued to maintain contact with the village. Accordingly, the adjustment of the Jews to the new conditions was more rapid, and the emergence of large Jewish centres in the towns was a relatively short-term matter. This aroused the wonder of the Jews themselves and the amazement of others. At the beginning of the nineteenth century there were no more than three or four Jewish communities in the world consisting of over 10,000, while in the period under discussion the number increased rapidly. At the beginning of the 1880s some 125,000 Jews were living in Warsaw, while cities like Vienna, Odessa, Budapest, New York and Berlin had Jewish populations of over 50,000 each.

The Changes in Occupation and Social Position

These basic processes – natural increase, migration and urbanization – left their mark on Jewish economic activity and considerably altered the character of Jewish society. As long as the Jews lived in relatively backward areas, remote from centres of economic and political life, their main sources of livelihood were based on contacts with the feudal estate, the purchase of the agricultural produce from the landowners and peasants, as well as the supply of industrial goods to them, and contacts with the authorities. The capitalistic development that accompanied the Industrial Revolution had almost no effect on their lives. But to the extent that the Jewish masses moved to the large commercial and industrial centres and were concentrated in those cities that were economically important, their economic activity became tied up with the new processes. Meanwhile, in the former places of residence, increasing numbers of Jews lost their previous sources of livelihood and were forced to look for new ones or to emigrate. Some of the richer Jews rapidly adjusted to the new conditions and began to play an active part in the new capitalistic developments, while the great majority were forced to pursue the arduous and wearisome path of searching for and adapting to new occupations entailing physical labour. They became artisans and labourers in workshops and factories, unskilled workers (waggoners, porters, janitors, etc.) or lived by their wits by engaging in brokerage and incidental services. It is not surprising that as a result there was an increase in the number of those in need of charity, and even of beggars and criminals. On the other hand, there were the first manifestations of the emergence of a Jewish working class – in the textile, food and tobacco industries. All these factors produced far-reaching changes in the image of Jewish society. In earlier periods there had also been sharp differences between the economic development and occupational structure of the Jews in Central and Western Europe and those in Eastern Europe; then, too, there had been a contrast between the way of life of the rich and the poor, but the common suffering, the harsh discriminations and the sense of a common destiny had maintained the internal cohesion of Jewish society. The nineteenth-century processes, which led to class polarization, threatened to undermine the basis of Jewish solidarity.

Not only did a yawning economic and social gap open up between the very rich – bankers, industrialists, holders of government monopolies and railway builders – and the poverty-stricken masses struggling for survival, but there was also a deep cultural and religious breach. The great majority of the common people remained faithful to Jewish tradition (at least until the beginning of the great migration in the eighties), to their spoken tongue (Yiddish) and to ideas and beliefs consistent with a traditional Jewish education. The majority of Jewish capitalists, on the other hand, began to cut themselves off from Jewish tradition and culture and to assimilate into the culture around them. This development intensified the contrasts and worsened relationships within Jewish society. Each stratum sought its own method of fulfilling its particular aspirations, and social polarizations developed into extreme ideological differences.

The Abandonment of Rural Occupations

Among the economic changes we have mentioned, the most vital was the reduction in the number of Jews who earned their living from estates and villages. At the beginning of the nineteenth century a very large number of Jews in Russia and Galicia were still estate lessees or 'factors' (agents) of landowners. Several forces combined to invalidate the importance of this source of livelihood: the Polish revolts against Russia in 1830 and 1863, which led the Polish nobility to flee the country, leaving their lands to expropriation or abandonment; the government restrictions in Russia and Austria aimed against Jewish lessees and innkeepers, and their expulsion from the villages in Russia; the freeing of the serfs in Austria and Russia and the emergence of a prosperous stratum among the peasants themselves, who began to engage in money-lending and commerce and drove the Jews out of the villages. In Germany the rise of a similar class in the villages led to a decrease in the number of rural Jews engaged in money-lending and trading in farm animals and agricultural produce.

This process, which commenced in the first half of the nineteenth century, was accelerated during the second half. An attempt was made by several rich Russian Jews to remain within the sphere of these occupations despite the difficulties involved, and they tried to re-establish themselves in the liquor trade. In the forties the authorities declared alcohol to be a state monopoly, which was to be leased out to the highest bidder, and the purchasers then sold it through their Jewish agents, who owned inns and taverns. But this arrangement endured only until the 1860s. After that, the number of Jewish innkeepers rapidly decreased, until, in the 1890s, this occupation had totally disappeared from the range of Jewish occupations in Russia. The legal status of the Jews of Galicia was more favourable, and they were not dispossessed at such a rapid pace from this economic branch. The number of Jews who made their living from the village was larger in Galicia, but there was a relative decrease there as well. Less Jews now engaged in peddling, making their way from village to village from Sunday to

Friday; nevertheless, there were still Jews both in Russia and Galicia (and to a lesser extent in several areas of Germany) who bought agricultural produce from the villages and supplied them with goods from the towns.

In that same period there were also Russian Jews who made a living from agriculture, including those Jewish farmers whom the authorities had begun to settle in agricultural colonies in the south. These farmers were always few in number and not all of them actually engaged in agriculture. Nevertheless, thousands of farms were established during the nineteenth century, not only in the southern colonies but also in villages in White Russia and Bessarabia, and auxiliary farms were developed near large towns all over the Pale of Settlement.

Commerce and Crafts

There were several crafts in which Jews had established a foothold in the course of generations, and in the countries of the Moslem East Jewish artisans played an important economic role. In Europe, however, the craft guilds maintained their monopolistic status and rejected Jewish attempts to gain entry. In Eastern Europe Jewish artisanship developed through bitter struggles with the urban element, and even though the Russian authorities at the end of the eighteenth century were supposed to aid in integrating the Jews into the general urban frameworks by altering their legal status, the main reason for the proliferation of Jewish craftsmen in the nineteenth century was their expulsion from other sources of livelihood and their high rate of natural increase.

Most Jewish artisans could not raise sufficient funds to purchase quality tools, nor was there anyone from whom they could learn their craft – with the exception of some few occupations that Jews had pursued for generations (for example, tailors, hatters and jewellers). Many of them therefore only carried out the simplest tasks and competed with non-Jewish artisans only in price. In addition, the large number of Jewish artisans (in Russia at the end of the nineteenth century they totalled, together with apprentices and workmen, some half-million) led to bitter internal competition. They were therefore among the first to emigrate to new lands.

To a certain extent, the well-established tradition of organization restrained internal competition. Craft associations, which had achieved considerable importance in East European Jewish life in the eighteenth century, succeeded in part in maintaining their status and traditions through the nineteenth century, despite the tremendous increase in the number of artisans. The houses of study and synagogues belonging to the various trades (tailors, furriers, etc.) continued to exist, and many new ones were opened. Within these associations the tradition of mutual aid and of the furthering of common interests endured.

Natural increase was the main reason that, despite the changes in the occupational structure of the Jews, there was no decrease in the relative number engaged in trade. However, the branches and forms of commerce did change: as the merchant guilds grew weaker there was an increase in the number of Jewish shopkeepers, wholesalers, exporters and importers in the towns. Despite their gradual detachment from occupations connected with the estate and the village, the majority of East European Jewish merchants still traded in foodstuffs and agricultural produce. Even during the second half of the century they controlled most of the trade at the agricultural fairs in the Ukraine and Galicia. They also played an important role in the large commercial firms (including shipping companies) organized in Eastern Europe for the export of grain and agricultural produce to Western Europe.

In West and Central European countries in the 1880s, more than 50% of Jewish bread-winners were traders, while in Eastern Europe they constituted only a little over one-third. Internal and foreign trade in the Pale of Settlement were mostly concentrated in Jewish hands. A similar situation prevailed throughout the nineteenth century in the Ottoman Empire and the countries of North Africa, but there the Jews mainly engaged in retail trade, while wholesale trade was in the hands of Christians (Greeks and Italians).

Jewish trade in the nineteenth century was characterized by attempts to improve commercial methods through advertising and, above all, by concentrating on two extremes – luxury goods and popular commodities. At times the Jews played an important role in distributing new types of goods from new sources. On the other hand, their importance waned in the area of maritime and colonial trade, in which they had been prominent in the seventeenth and eighteenth centuries.

Thus we see that, despite all the changes, the great majority of the Jews in the nineteenth century engaged in trade and crafts. However, this period also marked the entry of rich Jews into new branches of trade and economy, and the emergence both of a Jewish working class in the workshops and factories and of a Jewish intelligentsia in cultural activities and liberal professions, primarily in the framework of non-Jewish society. And all these sources of activity and livelihood, which were in their infancy until the 1880s, were subsequently to become major factors in Jewish life.

Banking

The wealthy Jews were naturally active mainly in the financial field, but their methods of economic activity in the nineteenth century differed from those of the court-Jews and the lessees of mints and other government monopolies during the previous century. Banks attained great economic importance at the beginning of the nineteenth century, and several Jewish bankers became extremely influential, successfully competing with non-Jewish banking houses in the floating of government loans, in the granting of loans to governments and other such activities.

The great majority of Jewish bankers, who established branches all over Europe and wielded considerable influence in all the important capitals, were descendants of German court-Jews and financiers. Jewish banking families from Frankfurt, Mainz, Hamburg, Vienna and Berlin advised kings and governments on financial matters, helped establish national banks (in Austria, Belgium, Russia, Poland and Germany), construct railways and develop towns. But in the second half of the nineteenth century most of the private banking families in Vienna, Paris and Berlin, with the exception of the Rothschilds, broke away from Judaism, and were assimilated into the European nobility.

The most important of the Jewish banking-houses was the House of Rothschild.

Its main sphere of influence after the Napoleonic Wars was in securities and, above all, in underwriting various government loans. For a lengthy period there was almost no important government loan in Europe in which the Rothschilds did not lend a hand. Other Jewish financiers were active also on stock exchanges.

The financial success of many Jews came to them, as before, largely through their contacts with the authorities. One of the prominent German bankers in the second half of the nineteenth century was Gerson von Bleichroeder, Bismarck's financial adviser. He helped Bismarck raise funds for the Prussian war against Austria (1866) and, at Bismarck's request, immediately after the war with France and the latter's defeat, he conducted the negotiations over the five-million-franc reparation demanded of the defeated country. During the Second French Empire the Jewish banker Achille Fould served as Napoleon III's Minister of Finance. In the same period government support was extended to the Péreire brothers for the establishment of a new kind of bank, the Crédit Mobilier. This bank employed new methods of raising funds – namely, the selling of shares to the general public – and thus accumulated large sums in circulation. It rapidly went bankrupt but, nevertheless, inaugurated a new era in investment methods. When Disraeli thought up the scheme of purchasing Suez Canal shares for the British Government, it was the House of Rothschild that implemented it.

In the second half of the nineteenth century, the share company replaced the private bank, and, in most European countries, banking-houses were transformed into limited companies that financed the new industries. This development lessened the importance of personal ties and naturally weakened the influence of the private banking families. In the process the economic power of the thin stratum of Jewish bankers was likewise reduced. But the new banking institutions, stock exchanges and insurance companies served as the arena for the economic activities also of rich Jews at the end of the nineteenth and beginning of the twentieth centuries.

Railways

One of the main spheres of financial activity that occupied Jewish bankers was railway construction. In all the countries of Europe, with the exception of England, Jewish bankers played an extraordinary role in building the foundations of this new network of transportation. In this area, too, it transpired that the contacts between the Jewish financiers and the authorities were of great importance, as railways were usually constructed on the basis of government concessions and control.

The main railway networks in France, Belgium, Austria and Italy were financed by the House of Rothschild. The Chemin de Fer du Nord in France is an example of one of their more important projects. The Chemin de Fer du Midi was built by the Péreire brothers, who also constructed the first railway lines in Spain and Tunis. German Jewish bankers and contractors played an important part in the construction of Prussian and Rumanian railway networks.

Most of the Russian railway network was built between 1850 and 1870 by Jewish contractors, the most important of whom was Samuel Poliakov. This activity created considerable employment for the Jews of the Pale of Settlement and elsewhere, as Jews served as agents, assistants and suppliers to the main contractors. They also played an important part in the operation of trains, on both the technical and the commercial side. But the Russian Government soon began to purchase the railway lines from the private owners and thereafter to take them over, and one of the first steps of the Russian railway authorities after the purchase was the eviction of Jews from this branch.

Baron de Hirsch, who later distinguished himself in projects for Jewish settlement and aid, was the main builder of railways in the Balkans and the Ottoman Empire. Even in the United States, Jewish banks played a part in the construction of railway lines, especially after they succeeded in obtaining from Germany capital investments (mainly Jewish) for this purpose.

Industry

In those countries – such as England, France and the United States – in which industries had been established or consolidated before Jews attained recognizable economic status, the Jews did not exert much influence on this sphere of economic activity. In France, for example, Jewish capital was active in urban development – including the modernization of Paris – rather than in industry. The situation was different in those countries that began to develop their industries after Jewish capitalists had already achieved economic influence. These included the countries of Central and Eastern Europe, and Jews there played an active part in consolidating various industries. They were prominent in the industrial development of southern Germany and the Rhine region in the 1830s and 1840s; in the second half of the nineteenth century, Jews in Germany were to be found in the machine, copper and oil industries. Jewish industrialists in Russia were of more significant importance in the food (particularly sugar), textile and tobacco industries, but they were also active in coal-mining (in connexion with railways), the production and marketing of crude oil and precious metals; in addition, Jews were prominent in river-shipping and urban development. But despite the important standing of Jewish capitalists in various industries, they tended not to employ Jewish workers (even in textiles), and therefore Jewish workers in these countries were employed mainly in small industries (see page 868).

Liberal Professions

One of the characteristic signs of the change in the social structure of the Jews was the large number engaged in the liberal professions. This phenomenon was generally the outcome of legal emancipation, which enabled them to serve as lawyers or university teachers. Before emancipation there were some Jewish publishers, journalists, writers, musicians and actors, and it was only in the second half of the nineteenth century that their number in the liberal professions multiplied, giving this group new importance within the Jewish community.

Government service was closed to Jews despite their legal emancipation, and only in a few countries (such as Holland and France) did considerable numbers serve in government posts. In Russia a small number of Jews was allowed into the bureaucracy during the sixties, but, from the second half of the seventies, discrimination again prevented this development to continue.

Jews came closest to the culture and language of their surroundings in Central Europe. The widest stratum of Jewish intelligentsia existed there, and Jews exerted considerable influence over cultural life and public opinion through the press. In France, too, Jews played a prominent part in developing popular journalism. The important press agencies of Europe (Reuter's in England, Wolff in Germany) were founded by Jews. In journalism, the arts and the theatre, the role of Jews in these countries greatly exceeded their proportion to the total population. In the English-speaking countries, Jewish entry into these fields was slower and occurred in stages.

In Russia, until the 1860s, only a few Jews were acquainted with the Russian language. And even though in the sixties and seventies there was an increase in the number of Jews attending and graduating from secondary schools and higher institutions, they still constituted an infinitesimal proportion of the Jewish population. It is not surprising, therefore, that the percentage of Russian Jews in the liberal professions in that period was almost nil. Even in the Germanic countries, 'professionals' did not account for more than 3–4% of Jewish bread-winners.

The transformation in the structure of Jewish society, which brought in its wake changes in the life-style, culture and organizational patterns of the Jews, was, on the one hand, the result of the exceedingly high rate of natural increase among European Jews in the nineteenth century and, on the other hand, the consequence of the legal restrictions, capitalist development and emigration that induced Jews to seek out new sources of livelihood. On the surface this seemed to be a development parallel to that which Europe was undergoing: population expansion, urbanization, the dwindling of rural occupations and the rise in urban occupations as a result of the emergence of a capitalist economy. However, because of the unique social traditions of the Jews and their special status in Europe, these processes were far more marked in Jewish historical development and later produced revolutionary results, in both the structure of Jewish society and the attitude of other nations.

49

The Struggle for Emancipation in Western and Central Europe

The Principle of Equal Rights in the West

The political situation in Europe after the Congress of Vienna (1815) was injurious to the legal status of the Jews; but here too there was a difference between Central and Western Europe. In the Central European countries, powerful social forces arose in opposition to the principle of emancipation, thus slowing down the integration of the Jews, while in the countries of Western Europe, the emancipation ideal continued to gain ground. In Holland and in Belgium (which was separated from Holland in 1830), Jewish equality was maintained throughout this period. In France, the Restoration monarchs declared Catholicism to be the state religion, but the Jews did not suffer discrimination as a result – beyond the restrictions already included in the 1808 'Infamous Decree' of Napoleon (see page 762). The desire of the Restoration government to observe the principle of Jewish equality in full was demonstrated when the decree expired in 1818, and agitation began throughout Alsace for its renewal. Some of the press exploited the opportunity for attacks on the Jews, and it was claimed that the lifting of restrictions would lead to tension in the region; but these threats did not affect the government's stand and the decree was not extended. The Alsace region remained a hotbed of anti-Semitism, and every new social upheaval (such as the 1830 and 1848 revolutions) led to renewed outbursts of hatred, and, in some places, even to pogroms. Nonetheless, from the legal point of view, French Jews did enjoy equal rights.

After the Revolution of July 1830, the French Government proposed that the Jewish religion in France be placed on terms of equality with the Christian churches. (The latter's clergy received salaries from the government.) The two legislative bodies approved the proposal, and, from the beginning of 1831, rabbis began to receive state salaries. In 1846, as a result of the protracted efforts of a Jewish lawyer, Adolph Crémieux, the special Jewish oath in law courts, one of the last relics of discrimination, was abolished. From then on there were no specific laws for the Jews, and no legislation singled out the Jews as a separate group. The 1848 revolutionary constitution contained a general prohibition of preference based on title, class or religion in public appointments.

The establishment of the emancipation principle in Western Europe in this period

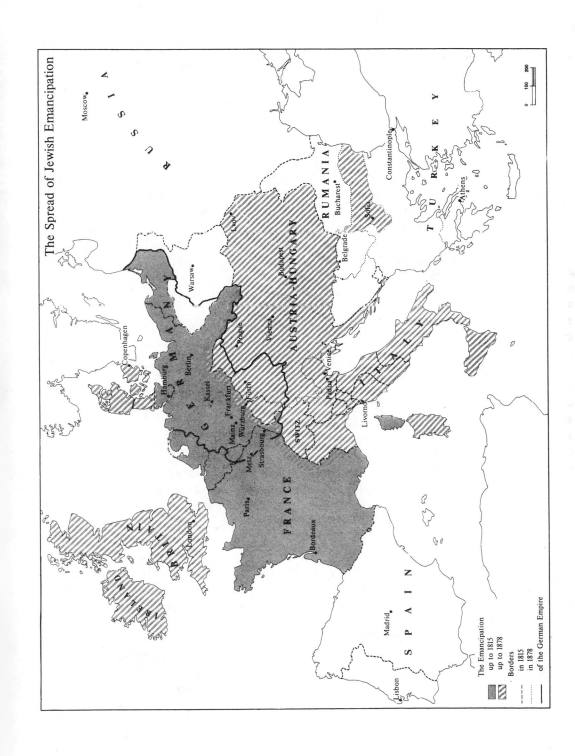

The Spread of Jewish Emancipation

RUSSIA

Moscow

GERMANY

Copenhagen

Hamburg
Berlin

Warsaw

Lvov

AUSTRIA-HUNGARY

Budapest

Vienna

Prague

Kassel
Mainz Frankfurt
Würzburg Fürth

Metz
Strasbourg

SWITZ.

RUMANIA

Bucharest

Belgrade

Sofia

Constantinople

T U R K E Y

Athens

BRITAIN

IRELAND

London

Paris

FRANCE

Bordeaux

Padua Venice

I T A L Y

Livorno

SPAIN

Madrid

Lisbon

0   100   200

The Emancipation
up to 1815
up to 1878

Borders
in 1815
in 1878
of the German Empire

robbed it of the revolutionary aura it had in previous periods; thus, Jewish emancipation was separated from political radicalism. From here on even monarchies and conservative regimes felt they could grant the Jews equal rights without undermining the foundation of their rule. This example weakened the arguments of those opposed to Jewish rights in other European countries and therefore furthered Jewish emancipation as a political principle.

The Struggle for Equal Rights in England

There were no special laws in England defining the status of the Jews. In theory, every Jew born in England was a full citizen. There was, however, a practical obstacle to the enjoyment of political rights: the oaths that had to be taken by all candidates for public, government or corporative office. Every candidate was expected to swear by 'the true faith of a Christian'. This same oath was required in order to receive a university degree, to purchase certain types of real estate, and sometimes even in order to be placed on the electors' registry. In 1828–9 the British Parliament passed several laws abolishing restrictions on Catholics and other minority Christian sects (dissenters), but the oath was not altered, and thus the Jews remained the sole restricted minority group.

While the Catholic Emancipation Bill was under discussion, a petition was submitted to Parliament requesting the abolition of anti-Jewish restrictions. In 1830, the Whig M.P. Robert Grant pleaded unsuccessfully for such a law. When the Reform Parliament was convened in 1833, Grant introduced the bill again, and this time it was supported by prominent members, such as the noted politician and historian Macaulay. The bill passed all its readings but was blocked by the House of Lords; the reigning monarch, William IV, supported the opponents of the Jews. The bill was re-submitted several times in years following but was doomed to failure.

In the same period (1830s–1840s), the Jews did succeed in obtaining other rights through a series of regulations and partial bills. It is worth noting that the City merchants, who had been the sworn enemies of the Jews during the outcry against the 'Jew Bill' in 1753, later took the initiative in lifting several legal restrictions. In 1831 it was decided that anyone who wished to be admitted to the freedom of the City of London, which enabled a man to engage in retail trade, could take the oath in a fashion that would not affect his religious faith. The Jews were later granted entry into municipal office and to the Bar and were enabled to serve on juries. After the founding of University College, London in 1837, Jews were permitted to study there for degrees. This was still forbidden in the universities of Oxford and Cambridge because of the religious test required there, demanding an oath of loyalty to the principles of the Anglican Church. (These restrictions were finally abolished in 1871.) In the same year (1837), Moses Montefiore, a businessman noted for his charitable enterprises, was elected as sheriff and knighted by Queen Victoria.

Parliament's support for abolishing discrimination against Jews proved, beyond a doubt, that English public opinion was generally ready to accept the gradual emancipation of the Jews. By the 1840s the last of the disabilities had actually disappeared, with the exception of the restriction on the right to sit in Parliament.

The removal of this restriction became the specific aim of a certain group of Jews, consisting primarily of the more wealthy City merchants.

In 1847 Baron Lionel de Rothschild was elected to Parliament by the City of London. There was no law prohibiting Jewish membership, but no Jewish member would have been able to take his seat because of the nature of the oath administered to new members. The Prime Minister seized on this opportunity to propose that discrimination in this field be abolished, and the House of Commons concurred by a large majority. Once again, however, the passage of the bill encountered strong opposition in the House of Lords. Prominent supporters of the bill included Benjamin Disraeli, Robert Peel and William Gladstone, who had formerly opposed the idea but now transferred sides. Rothschild renounced his seat but was re-elected, and once again the House of Lords vetoed the bill passed by the Lower House. A year later, Sir David Salomons was elected to Parliament and tried to gain entry by taking the oath and omitting the controversial phrase. He was forcibly removed from the chamber, and a heavy fine was imposed on him. It was only in 1858, after thirteen bills had been rejected, that both Houses passed a bill allowing each House to determine its own form of oath. Thus the House of Commons was able to change the oath for the benefit of Jewish members, and the latter were able to take their seats.

In practice, this completed the legal emancipation of the Jews in England, but as there was no formal separation between state and church, this equality did not take the form of a general definitive declaration. Even under the bill eventually passed, certain honours remained closed to Jews (as they did to Catholics), but this did not affect the actual legal rights of the Jews.

Discussion of the 'Jewish Question' in Central Europe Before the Revolutions of 1848

In contrast to Western Europe, where emancipation advanced with relative ease, the process encountered many difficulties and obstacles in Central Europe. The 'Holy Alliance' of the monarchs of Russia, Prussia and Austria left its mark not only on the form of government in the various Central European countries but also on the mood of the public. The German struggle against Napoleonic rule was depicted as the achievement of the 'German spirit' in its struggle against the 'French spirit'. Among many educated Germans and German youth, all the rationalist and universalist concepts of the eighteenth-century Enlightenment were regarded as the fruit of the 'alien spirit'. On the other hand, these circles began to absorb romantic ideals, which led them to search for historical roots for their social corporations and government institutions and to the idealization of the Middle Ages. The 'Christian state', based on the traditions of the past and endeavouring to preserve its concepts and institutions, was therefore regarded in these circles within the German states as the supreme goal.

This mood administered a heavy blow to the Jewish *maskilim*, who could not find a place for themselves in this conceptual framework and regarded it as a betrayal of the noblest aims of human thought and culture. In an earlier period Enlightened circles had served as a meeting-place for Jews and non-Jews, as a force drawing the

Jews closer to the society around them; now these very circles produced the most vehement enemies of the Jews, and ideals suffused with anti-Jewish hatred. The integration of numerous Jews into the social and cultural life of Germany was not to the liking of many elements in that country. It was against this ideological and social background that the controversy over the 'Jewish question' flared up anew.

Immediately after the Congress of Vienna, pamphlets and books began to appear that, for various reasons, refuted the Jewish demand for citizenship in the German states and pointed to the danger facing Germany and the Germans from the assimilation of the Jews. These and similar claims were actually a continuation of attacks in polemical literature from the beginning of the century. Others came to the defence of the Jews and claimed that they were beneficial to the state, that their loyalty was unquestioned and that they did not yearn for another homeland. One of the outstanding characteristics of this renewed Jew-hatred was that people with varied and contrasting approaches – romantics and rationalists – prophesied in the same strain. The most prominent opponents of the Jews were Friedrich Ruehs, professor of history at Berlin University, and the Kantian philosopher from Heidelberg, Jakob Fries. The former claimed that those Jews who were loyal to their political religion constituted a 'state within a state' and were therefore incapable of being loyal citizens of a German state. This implied that only by rejecting their Judaism would Jews qualify for German citizenship, and that only the destruction of Judaism as a religion could reform the Jews. Judaism was a relic of an ancient barbaric period, 'a proliferating sickness of peoples, whose force increases through the power of money'; Judaism was a danger to the nations of Europe from the political, economic, and even moral point of view – Jews were the leaders of gangs of robbers and dealers in stolen property. Fries concluded: 'If the Jews do not leave Judaism, they will be obliged to remain irrevocably in their miserable condition. It would be an immeasurably important deed to liberate our people from this plague.' This was the style employed by noted public personalities.

The *Mirror of the Jews,* written by Hartwig von Hundt-Radowsky, was a totally unbridled pamphlet aimed at inciting the masses: 'No people in the world has so excelled in evil and the lust for revenge, in cowardice, arrogance and superstition, in usury, cheating and theft, as the Jews. All Jews – whether rich or poor, educated or ignorant – are members of a united gang of criminals.' His proposals, submitted in a spirit of mockery, were to sell the Jews to plantations or mines, to castrate them or kill them ('I myself do not regard the killing of a Jew as a sin or crime, but as a mere police offence'), or to banish them to 'the Promised Land in which milk and honey flow and in which big grapes grow. With the help of several thousand cannon it would be easy to push the fleas past Turkey . . . '

The *Mirror of the Jews* was only one of dozens of pamphlets that appeared from 1815 on, and this general anti-Jewish incitement undoubtedly stirred up the riots that broke out during the summer of 1819 in several regions of Germany. The appearance of the *Mirror of the Jews* was part of increased incitement after the outburst of the riots and explicitly referred to them. The new movement was known as *Hep! Hep*!, after the battle cry of the rioters. It was started by a mob in the town of Würzburg (Bavaria), which broke into the homes and shops of Jews, looted them and destroyed the property. Only military intervention put an end to the riots, but the urban mob demanded that the Jews be expelled from the town. From there the riots spread to other Bavarian towns and even to other parts of Germany (Frankfurt and Hamburg). In Heidelberg (Baden) several professors and students came to the defence of the Jews after the police refused to do so.

The July Revolution of 1830 strengthened liberal trends in Germany. From these circles emerged supporters for extending Jewish rights; they spoke up during the debates in the *landtags* (provincial parliaments) of several states in southern Germany, such as Bavaria, Württemberg and Baden (although most of the Baden liberals and their leader von Rotteck opposed equal rights). The opponents of the Jews reacted with renewed fury to this trend, emphasizing the nationalist nature of the Jewish religion that had led to the separation of the Jews from the rest of society. This was, for example, the view of H. E. G. Paulus, the liberal theologian from Heidelberg. Hence, there arose the argument that even if it were wrong to demand Jewish conversion to Christianity as a condition for equal rights, it was at least permissible to expect the Jews to amend their religion and adapt it to the demands of society. This attitude was accepted also in various liberal circles outside Germany and led them to make equal rights for Jews conditional on their religious reform. The renowned leader of the Hungarian liberation movement, L. Kossuth, claimed that Jews should not be granted equal rights as long as they observed their dietary laws and other customs that set them apart from their surroundings. These arguments were countered mainly by Jewish *maskilim,* and above all by Gabriel Riesser, who for some time fought for complete Jewish emancipation.

The enemies of the Jews also included proponents of discrimination based on absolutist political thought. Thus, for example, a pamphlet, *On the Attitude of the Jews Towards the Christian States,* published in 1833, proposed that the rights of the Jews should be extended gradually, as they became educated and more useful (*i.e.,* prosperous), while the Jewish masses should continue to exist as 'tolerated' elements, lacking all rights. This proposal was published in the Prussian state, in which equal rights had theoretically been granted to the Jews in 1812.

In the 1840s there was widespread preoccupation with Jewish emancipation. Conservative elements attacked the threat that the Jews posed to the 'German essence' and claimed that the problem was not one of 'Jewish emancipation' but rather of 'the emancipation of Christians from Jewry'. An extreme advocate of this attitude was the converted Jew Friedrich Julius Stahl, who, in his book *The Attitude of the Christian State Towards Deism and Judaism* (1847), denied the political rights of all those who did not accept the Christian faith, since it was the duty of the state to fulfil its Christian aims. But the radical school of thought that lay to the left of liberalism also produced violent opponents to the Jews and to Judaism. The 'young Hegelians' Bruno Bauer, Ludwig Feuerbach and Friedrich Daumer, who voiced radical criticism of Christianity, also tried to direct their shafts against its progenitor, Judaism, as the source of all the evils in the religion of Christ. They contrasted the destructive and unnatural 'Asiatic' influences, which Judaism had bequeathed to Christianity, with the beneficial Greek influences. These thinkers claimed that Judaism contained a certain egoistical and gastronomical element (as every mention of God in the Bible is connected with eating) and that human sacrifice was one of the important constituents of ancient Hebrew worship, thus influencing Christian religious symbolism. There were even those at the time who found a connexion between this explanation and the blood libels.

From this adverse criticism of Judaism it was a small step to denigration of the Jews themselves. In his book *On the Jewish Question* (1843), one of the leaders of this circle, Bruno Bauer, denied the rights of the Jews to emancipation on the grounds that they had always been opposed to progress and had insisted on remaining a separate people even though their nationality was chimerical. Until they were released from both their religion and their imaginary nationality there was no point in granting emancipation. In any case, even in their existing situation, they controlled the stock exchanges and wielded influence at court, and therefore even a change in their legal status would not make any difference in the nature of the Jews.

Bauer's pamphlet aroused extensive reaction, mainly on the part of several Jews who tried to refute them. One of those who accepted Bauer's argument – though not his conclusions – was the young Karl Marx. In an article entitled 'On the Jewish Question', in reply to Bauer and published in the same year, Marx claimed that the separation of state and religion could bestow legal emancipation on the Jews without their having to renounce their Judaism; but this only proved that legal emancipation was much less valuable than general human emancipation. Marx thus attempted to release the problem from its 'theological husk', and to examine the social essence of Judaism. He fully accepted Bauer's claim that the Jews exerted control through their money, but this was not all. The Jew had changed the social order. 'Through the Jew and beyond him money achieved world power, and the practical spirit of Judaism became the practical spirit of the Christian peoples.' Jewish existence should therefore not be regarded as a mere anachronism but as one of the manifestations of the practical streak in human nature – egoism. 'Judaism has been preserved not despite history but thanks to history. Civil society constantly gives birth to the Jew.' The history of bourgeois civil society was the history of the Judaization of the European nations. 'Money is Israel's jealous God, and they can have no other God . . . the God of the Jews has become secular, the God of the world. The credit note is the practical God of the Jews'; 'What is contained in the Jewish religion in its abstract form – contempt for theory, for art, for history, for man as an end in himself – this is the practical, deliberate viewpoint of the financier. . . . The imaginary nationalism of the Jew is that of the merchant, of the financier in general . . . ' Hence, as a step towards liberating society, Judaism should be eliminated: 'The social emancipation of the Jew is the emancipation of society from Judaism.' Here we find not only the view that commerce and money are the essence of Judaism, but also a vehement contempt for the spiritual creation of Judaism and the call for its elimination as a prerequisite for the liberation of all mankind, including the Jews. It was a carbon copy of the demands of conservative Jew-haters in an earlier age.

We should, of course, take into account that these anti-Jewish remarks had their source in the general aims of the radical circles, which aspired to abolish religion in general. But the way in which Bauer and Marx described Judaism certainly did little to further Jewish integration into the larger society; on the contrary, it intensified

806

society's opposition to and revulsion for the Jews and supplied Jew-haters with a whole variety of new arguments. However, simultaneous to the harshening of the attitude towards the Jews and Judaism on both right and left, there was increased support for the Jews in certain liberal circles.

The Legal Status of the Jews in Central European Countries Before the Revolutions of 1848

As we have noted, the political reaction that followed in the wake of the Congress of Vienna was felt most strongly in the German states. In most of these states, conditions for the Jews reverted to what had prevailed before the French conquests. In Frankfurt the Jews were concentrated in the ghetto again, and several 'Free Cities', including Bremen and Lübeck, went so far as to expel them. In Bavaria the old restrictive laws remained in force. In Prussia – whose area was almost doubled after the Congress – it was decided that the 1812 Emancipation Law would be applied only to those areas that had formed part of the state at the time of legislation, while in the areas annexed subsequently, the Jews would be dealt with according to the laws of the previous rulers (which were generally severely repressive). The legal situation therefore varied from place to place: in old Prussia the Jews were regarded as citizens of the state, while in the newer provinces they were 'tolerated' or 'protected'. In the Rhine area, which had formerly been under direct French rule, the Prussian authorities extended the 'Infamous Decree' for an unlimited period. And as if this were not enough, the Prussian regime rendered the 1812 law meaningless during the 1820s by barring the Jews from government and municipal service and from academic posts. This discrimination particularly affected the educated Jewish class and those closest to Christian society and its culture. Hence, there was a twofold reaction: on the one hand, a higher rate of conversion resulted, while, on the other hand, a militant spirit of opposition was aroused.

In Austria the situation reverted in theory to the conditions defined in Joseph II's *Toleranzpatent,* but in actual fact previous restrictions were restored in several spheres. The regime strictly observed all regulations restricting the number of Jews and burdened them with taxes ('tolerance' fee, meat tax, candle tax, etc.). It also kept a strict eye on Jewish occupations on the pretext that 'the customs, way of life and occupations of the Jews should be rendered harmless'. The authorities claimed that they were thus contributing to the abolition of Jewish separation and isolation, but, in fact, they themselves were fostering these qualities – although they did increase their intervention in Jewish internal affairs. The inflexible official policy was particularly evident in the capital, Vienna, in which only 200 families enjoyed the right of settlement, while thousands were forced to live under the guise of temporary or illegal servants, dependent on the mercy of the corrupt police. In the Papal State and the Kingdom of Sardinia, the Jews were even confined again to the ghettos, and economic disabilities and restrictions of movement were partly restored. There were even cases of the seizing of Jewish children for forcible conversion.

In the 1830s the Jews of most German states endeavoured to renew their demands for equal rights. But although voices were raised in several state assemblies in support of these claims, the weakness or hesitation of liberal circles was detrimental to the cause. There was almost no state (with the exception of Kurhessen) in which the Jews achieved their aim. In Hungary, the Diet decided in 1840 to grant the Jews rights equal to those of all other non-aristocratic inhabitants, but the Upper House would not approve this resolution and proposed as a substitute the cancellation of the 'toleration fees' and of restrictions on places of residence, occupations and the purchase of real estate. The central authorities in Vienna reduced the proposed concessions even further.

In the forties the principle of Jewish emancipation won wider public support and was taken up by certain sections of the German bureaucracy. In 1843 the Landtag of the Rhine province passed a resolution in support of Jewish equality and approached the Prussian monarch on this matter. Similar resolutions were passed by other *landtags*. Eventually the united Prussian Landtag approved a new comprehensive law defining the status of the Jews. This was actually a reaffirmation of the 1812 law, with the omission of several clauses. The Law on the Status of the Jews (1847) granted rights equal to those of Christian subjects 'to the extent that there is no instruction to the contrary in this law'. The Jews were permitted to serve in government and municipal posts 'apart from those connected with judicial, police or executive authority'. Jews were permitted to serve as teachers in several types of schools and as professors of medicine, science and linguistics in universities, but were barred from teaching religious subjects and the humanities. The restrictions on their movement and on occupations were also lifted.

In short, there was an 'eve of reform' mood in most of the states of Central Europe, and several concessions were actually granted. Most of the governments made promises to the Jews and carried out reforms on their behalf most unwillingly, more as a concession to a swelling tide of public opinion in their countries. But before the authorities in those countries could take their first hesitant steps, the 1848 revolutions broke out, and the problem of Jewish emancipation took on a new form.

The Effect of the Revolutions of 1848 on European Jewry

The revolutions of 1848 had a strong effect on the process of emancipation of the Jews of Central Europe. The Jews played a prominent part from the very first days of the revolutions in Berlin and Vienna. They were among the first victims in battle and were buried in mass graves together with other revolutionaries. In Vienna there were Jews among the leaders of the National Guard and the Students Legion, of which the outstanding were Adolf Fischhof and Joseph Goldmark. When the Kaiser left Vienna, Fischhof was appointed head of the General Security Committee that ruled the city.

In the all-German parliament convened in Frankfurt in May 1848, there were several Jewish representatives, including the veteran of the battle for Jewish rights, Gabriel Riesser, who was elected deputy-speaker. Generally speaking, the revolutionary parliaments of Germany and Italy did not regard Jewish rights as self-evident. There were protracted discussions on the subject, and at times vigorous opposition was expressed on the grounds that Jews 'do not belong to the body of the nation'. Riesser succeeded in guaranteeing that the future constitution would contain a clause granting legal equality to all men whatever their religion.

In the Austrian Diet the Jewish delegates conducted a campaign for the annulment of the special Jewish taxes and for complete civil equality, but the assembly was dispersed before completing its discussions. In the Hungarian Diet even the liberal Kossuth regarded equal rights for the Jews as 'premature'. It was only at the end of July 1849, a few days before the final failure of the Hungarian revolution, that the Diet passed a resolution granting equal rights.

Generally, the masses, particularly in the Catholic countries, were vehemently opposed to the emancipation of the Jews. They wanted freedom *from* rather than *for* the Jews. The masses regarded the Jews as a force no less hostile than the hated governments, and at times even more so. Consequently, the 1848 revolutions were accompanied by anti-Jewish riots in many places. Hatred of Jews was particularly strong in those countries where the Jews were believed to identify with the oppressor nation; in Bohemia and Moravia, for example, the Jews were thought to support the Germans because they spoke German and were steeped in German culture. And, in fact, at the end of April riots broke out against the Jews of Prague.

At the same time there were similar outbursts in various Hungarian towns, and in Pressburg (Bratislava) the inhabitants demanded the expulsion of the Jews from the town. Eventually, the Jews were forced out of the Hungarian National Guard under the pressure of hostile public opinion. A wave of riots also swept various German states, particularly in the south. In Alsace, in which each revolutionary awakening was accompanied by anti-Jewish riots, there were attacks in 1848 as well, and the rioting masses were suppressed only by military force. In Rome there was violence towards the Jews after the gates of the ghetto were opened and Jews were allowed to settle all over the town.

The revolutionary forces were suppressed everywhere, but the panic-stricken governments hastened to grant their peoples constitutions 'of their own free will'. These constitutions were intended to placate the liberal circles that had supported the revolutionaries and that had firmly advocated the principle of the equality of all inhabitants. Some of the constitutions therefore included clauses which, for all practical purposes, guaranteed equal rights to the Jews. The constitution that Franz Josef of Austria granted his people on 4 March 1849 stated that 'civil and political rights are not dependent on religion'. The inclusion of the equality clause in the constitutions granted by monarchs helped gain recognition for the emancipation principle even in right-wing circles and thus completed a process that had commenced in France. When monarchal rule was reconsolidated after the revolutionary upheavals and the 'reformed' Prussian constitution was published in early 1851, one of its clauses recognized the Christian faith as the official state religion. But as the authorities did not dare erase Clause 12 of the 1848 constitution, which recognized the equal status of *all* religions, the two contradictory clauses existed side by side within the same document.

In conclusion, the revolutionary period produced a general recognition of the principle of emancipation in Central Europe, but this same period also brought to light the difficulties entailed in implementing this principle. As long as the question was discussed in uninational countries such as France or Holland, it was clear that the precondition was the ending of Jewish 'separatism' – namely, renunciation of their national identity and their internal autonomy and an attachment to the ruling nationality as equals. The advocates of equality emphasized therefore that Judaism was an exclusively religious trend and not a separate nation. But in multi-national countries this did not suffice. The demand that Jews renounce their communal identity led to complications, since it was in no way clear into which of the national groups in the country the Jews were expected to assimilate.

Riesser and Goldmark, who never tired of proclaiming that the Jews were only a religious group, aspired to their integration into the German nation and culture, and the demand for Jewish emancipation therefore seemed to them consistent with the desire for the political unification of Germany. In a united Germany the Jews would take their place as equals. There were also non-Jews who emphasized the importance of the Jews as part of the indigenous German element, but the events of the 1848–9 revolutions refuted this simplistic approach. The revolutions produced widespread nationalism in many peoples; in Austria, for example, the Jews faced, for the first time, the difficult choice between identification with the Germans or with the Hungarians, the Poles or the Czechs – nations whose political and cultural aspirations were in complete contrast to those of the Germans. At a time when most of the Jews of Hungary identified with the aspirations of the Hungarian nationalist movement, the political and cultural proclivities of Jews in parts of Poland and other Slavic countries were directed towards the stronger German element; this inevitably roused Slavic hatred of the Jews to a new pitch. The Jewish support of the Hungarians also aroused the fury of the southern Slavs, who were ready to cooperate with the Austrian authorities against Hungarian nationalism. In those regions of Poland included in the German states, the Jews were divided, some supporting the Poles and others the Germans. There was even a certain internal tension as a result.

One can thus understand why many Jews, including Fischhof, were among those who hoped for cooperation between the various nationalities within one national framework. It was as a result of this dilemma that the first signs of the renewed concept of internal autonomy and the defence of minority rights appeared. Within the framework of the multi-national state it was very difficult to delineate clear territorial borders. What was envisaged, therefore, was autonomy not for a particular territory populated with members of a certain nation, but for a national unit, and for historical partnership based on cultural unity and common destiny. This political situation and the development of these ideas led certain people to regard the Jews not as a mere religious group but also as national partners. These ideals, which were to prove of considerable influence in the future history of Europe, were the outcome of the complex problems that were the result of the 1848 revolutions.

Despite certain advances that the Jews made in 1848, the final outcome was the dashing of the great hopes they had pinned on the revolutions. This was a bitter blow for Jewish liberals, not to speak of the radicals among them, and the emigration of many of them to the United States was the natural consequence of their disillusionment.

The Victory of Legal Equality in Central Europe

The 1850s were years of political reaction. Only a few governments actually dared to revoke the rights of the Jews and to revert to the pre-1848 situation (as did Pope Pius IX, who returned Rome's Jews to the ghetto), but in most of the countries of Central Europe administrative discrimination was introduced. In Prussia the Jews were excluded from serving in government posts. In Austria restrictions were placed on the purchase of real estate and Jews were prohibited from entering the liberal professions. In several German states there were restrictions on movement and occupation. But none of these regulations, which generally took the form of temporary decrees, endured. The problem of Jewish equality in these countries was connected with political and economic problems of the first order, and, as a result, the Jews attained complete legal equality in this part of Europe within a few years.

When Bismarck came to power, the Prussian Government began to implement the unification of Germany by force. The German liberals had always aspired to this, and the common dream created the basis for cooperation between the Junker leader and the liberals. To this end Bismarck was willing to offer certain concessions to the liberals on such matters as the Jewish question. After the victory over Austria in 1866 and the establishment of the North German Confederation, a liberal majority was crystallized in the united Reichstag. In November 1867 this body passed a resolution banning religious discrimination, and in July 1869 a law was passed in united Germany establishing that 'all restrictions of civil and political rights still in existence and emanating from religious differences are hereby cancelled . . .' This law enabled the Jews to enter government service, including the judicial network and teaching posts in all government schools. In the other countries of the German Empire, the law was only applied after the completion of unification.

In Austria the liberal trend became discernible at the beginning of the 1860s. Several of the restrictions directed against the Jews were abolished, but complete equality was attained only with the introduction of the new constitution in 1867. The annulment of the agreement with the Vatican in 1868 removed matrimonial law and education from church control and greatly facilitated the institutionalization of legal equality without regard to religious differences. A similar law was passed in Hungary, but the Hungarian Government demanded, as a condition, certain reforms in the Jewish religion. Despite the legal equalization, the actual implementation of the laws encountered opposition in various parts of Austria-Hungary because of the strained relations between the nationalities.

In Italy, apart from the Sardinian Kingdom, in which equality had prevailed since 1848, the legal situation of the Jews grew worse; and in the Papal State there were even more restrictions than before. This policy aroused the indignation of European public opinion, which was particularly incensed by an incident that occurred in Bologna, still under papal rule. In 1858 the police kidnapped a six-year-old child from the Mortara family on the pretext that the maidservant had secretly baptized him during an illness. The child was snatched away from his parents and handed over to a monastery. Despite many appeals by Jews and the pressure of European public opinion, the child was never restored to his family.

Jewish rights in Italy became closely connected with the country's unification around the Sardinian Kingdom. As the state grew, annexing additional Italian regions, Jewish equality was extended. When the pope's secular rule was abolished in 1870, and Rome was declared to be the capital of a united Italy, the Jews of the city were also granted legal equality.

One of the states that persisted in its opposition to equal rights was Switzerland, which even prohibited the residence of Jews within its borders. They were allowed to reside only in the Canton of Aargau, but without civil or political rights. In 1856 the Council of Swiss Confederation granted the Jews of Aargau freedom of movement throughout the country, but the local population opposed this move, and anti-Jewish sentiment swept over Switzerland. At the end of 1862, a referendum was held on the question of rights for the Jews, and the great majority of the participants voted against the proposal. This led to the abrogation of the law passed by the Council. The restrictions imposed on Jews entering the country from outside Switzerland led to disputes with other states. In the 1850s and 1860s the United States, England, Holland and particularly France demanded – in vain – that Switzerland abolish various prohibitions against Jewish citizens of their countries visiting Switzerland for business purposes. Only under the 1874 Federal Constitution were the discriminations removed, and the principle of equality was then accepted in Switzerland. This completed the legal emancipation of the Jews throughout Central Europe.

50

The Struggle for Emancipation in Eastern Europe

Attempts at Forced Integration

During the period that the Jews were conducting a campaign for full legal equality in the countries of Western and Central Europe, Russia was beginning to reconsider its former aim of integrating, by moderate means, the Jews into the life of the country. The reaction unleashed in Europe after the Congress of Vienna and the new mood of religious mysticism of Alexander I were both reflected in the attitude of the regime towards the Jews.

Napoleon's campaign against Russia put an end to the two main methods whereby the Russian Government had attempted to change the way of life of the Jews and the organization of their society – expulsion from the villages and the founding of agricultural settlements in the south. But the basic aim of preventing 'acts of injustice and interference in the agriculture and industry of inhabitants of those districts in which Jews reside' (as expressed in the preamble to the 1804 statute) – namely, the so-called protection of the peasants against Jewish exploitation – remained the declared policy of the Russian Government both during the second half of Alexander I's reign and throughout the reign of Nicholas I.

Despite the loyalty of the Jewish population towards Russia during the French occupation, official distrust was intensified rather than weakened. Expulsions from the villages were renewed and the Pale of Settlement was reduced; Jews were banned from living in the fortified towns along the western border and in those port towns that served as naval bases. In 1825 a statute was published expelling the Jews from a strip approximately 36 miles wide along the western border, with the exception of those towns and villages containing Jewish communities.

Tsar Alexander was convinced that conversion of the Jews to Christianity was the best method of integrating them into society. His intention was to encourage the transition to Christianity by granting concessions to converts, such as the right of settlement anywhere in the country, the granting of agricultural land and even permission to engage in the manufacture of alcohol – the traditional Jewish occupation against which previous edicts had been directed. Since even conversion was not likely to bring the Jews closer to Russian society, with its closed corporations and classes, the Tsar had the idea, in 1817, of founding under his personal patronage a 'Society of Israelite Christians'. But this proved unsuccessful; there were few converts, and the Society was dissolved in 1833. On the other hand, among peasants and merchants in several provinces of central Russia that were closed to Jews, there appeared during these years groups of Judaizers who observed the Sabbath and various Jewish customs and rejected the basic tenets of Christianity.

The Cantonist Decrees

Nicholas I, who ascended the throne in December 1825, employed more severe measures in order to 'reform' the Jews and force them to convert or assimilate. In 1827 an ukase was published abolishing the financial payment formerly exacted from the Jews as a substitute for military service and extending conscription to them as an inescapable obligation. Some concessions were granted to Jewish merchants, artisans and farmers. At that time there was a standing army in Russia, and the period of service was twenty-five years. On the pretext that the Jews were unaccustomed to military service, the minimum age for conscription of Jewish recruits was lowered to twelve (and children of eight or nine were also sometimes seized), and they were 'prepared' for service at cantonist institutions – namely, special schools run by brutal drill-sergeants, generally of peasant stock. The government hoped that the uprooting of these young boys from their surroundings, their transfer to central Russia and their military education would lead them to forget Judaism and to convert. Since the authorities were convinced of the inferiority of the Jews and the ability of the military framework to inculcate a basic education among the simple masses, they hoped that military service would create among the Jews a nucleus of people who would be Christian in religion and Russian in education. These would serve as a bridge-head for the Jewish masses and lead them along the path of assimilation.

Terror reigned in these cantonist units. The children, who found it impossibly difficult to adapt themselves to the brutal barrack life and to the lengthy marches into the interior of Russia (a number died of disease and the vicissitudes of the journey), were also starved, beaten and persecuted in order to force them to convert. Nicholas himself displayed great interest in the progress of this attempt at conversion and called for even harsher methods. Pressure was particularly strong in the early 1840s. The Holy Synod (the supreme church institution in Russia) published new instructions to priests serving in cantonist units in order to speed up 'preparation' for conversion. Whole units were forcibly baptized. These 'achievements' involved terrible sacrifice; many cantonists chose to die for the sake of their religion. One of them related in his memoirs that only two members of his unit persevered in their Judaism till 1845. All those who had refused to convert had committed suicide: three by cutting their throats, two by hanging, others by drowning. There were numerous cases of mass suicide by drowning for *kiddush hashem* (the sanctification of the Name) during the ceremonies that the priests held while baptizing the boys in the river. There were also many who could not endure the persecution and pretended to accept Christianity while secretly observing Judaism. If discovered, they were sent to remote monasteries for 'reform'.

Yet none of these methods furthered the regime's policies. Those Jews who converted did not become leaders of the Jewish community, but were rather cut off from it and totally assimilated into their new surroundings. The main effect of the canonist decrees was to intensify hatred among the Jewish masses for the cruel regime and to exacerbate social differences within the community. The community as a whole bore responsibility for providing recruits; therefore, its powers were extended to this end. According to the conscription regulations 'the community is entitled, as it sees fit, to choose any Jew for army service, for arrears of debt, for vagrancy and other disturbances of the public order which cannot be endured in the community'. This led to horrifying corruption. The community leaders would hand over all those who dared disobey them, or who displayed oppositional tendencies. A new character appeared in Jewish lore: the *khapper* ('kidnapper'), who seized little children in the street or in the homes of widows and the poor in order to fulfil the community quota of recruits or to rescue the sons of the rich and powerful from service. Many families lived in constant dread of the kidnapping of their children.

The 1835 Statute and the 1840 Committee for the Jews

The general policy towards the Jews was reformulated in the days of Nicholas I in the 1835 statute. This was actually a repetition of the 1804 statute without the clause specifically referring to expulsion from the villages. However, in the definition of the borders of the Pale of Settlement, several districts were specified in which Jews were permitted to reside only in towns and cities, but not in villages. Jews were excluded from the city of Kiev as well as the 36-mile strip along the border. They were also ordered to register under a regular family name, and marriage was prohibited under the age of eighteen. The employment of Christian domestic servants was prohibited. This statute also reiterated the concessions granted to Jewish artisans and farmers (as regards military service as well). As a result, thousands of families submitted requests to become candidates for agricultural settlement, particularly after the authorities drew up a programme for Jewish settlement in Siberia. But shortly after its publication the plan was abandoned, and even those Jews who had already left for Siberia were arrested and sent back, under police escort, to the Pale of Settlement. Several thousand more Jews were settled in the southern region.

At the end of 1840, a special government committee was set up in Russia to determine measures 'for the basic reform of the Jews of Russia'. This committee found that 'the Jewish disregard for the civil order is based on their religious distortions; believing in the baseless traditions of the Talmud as if they were divine injunctions, they regard their sojourn outside of Palestine as imprisonment ... daily awaiting the arrival of the Messiah ... ' The committee therefore proposed 'to influence the moral education of the young generation of Jews through Jewish schools in a spirit opposed to the present Talmudic teaching; to abolish the *kahal* [Jewish communities] and to subordinate the Jews to the general administration ... to prohibit the wearing of special Jewish garments ... to classify the Jews by oc-

The Pale of Settlement in 1835

St Petersburg.
Volga River
Riga
Moscow
Dvinsk
Polotsk   Vitebsk
Vilna
Grodno   Minsk   Mohilev
Lomza   Bialystok   Bobruisk
Plock
Wegrow   Slutsk   Gomel
Warsaw
Kalisz   Lodz   Brest-Litovsk
Piotrkow   Radom   Pinsk
Chernigov   Lublin   Vladimir
Kielce   Zamosc   Lutsk
Dubno   Zhitomir   Kiev
Ostrava   Poltava
Berdichev   Kremenchug
Kamenets   Dnieper River
Uman   Yekaterinslav
Bug River   Elisabetgrad
Kishinev   Nikolaev   Melitopol
Odessa   Kherson
Simferopol
Danube River   Svestopol   Yalta

Provinces in which settlement in villages
was forbidden

Area of 50 versts along the western border,
where new settlement of Jews was forbidden

★ City forbidden to Jewish settlement

⊛ City forbidden to new Jewish settlement

0   100   200
k m

© carta, JERUSALEM

cupation into the useful, *i.e.,* merchants, artisans, farmers, and those without
permanent occupations . . . restrictions should be imposed on the latter, including
the obligation to provide three times as many recruits for the army'. These proposals
contained, in a nutshell, the 'Jewish policy' that Nicholas continued to pursue until
his death in 1855.

Education by State Coercion

The authorities then began to intervene in Jewish education (calling this activity 'moral education'). At the beginning of Nicholas I's reign in July 1826, supervision was imposed on the printing of Hebrew books according to general censorship regulations. The *maskilim* wanted to direct the brunt of government control against hasidic literature and proposed to the authorities that they impose censorship on Hebrew books in general, both those printed in Russia and those imported into the country. To a great extent it was a result of their influence that an edict was issued in 1836 introducing general censorship on Hebrew books and prohibiting the maintenance of Hebrew printing presses, with the exception of two, in Kiev and Vilna, where there were special censors for the purpose.

At the same time the Russian Minister of Education approached several of the *maskilim* in Germany to advise him what measures were required in order to raise the standard of education among the Jews. He reached the conclusion that the main obstacle to their education was the 'greed of the rabbis and the false, prejudiced belief that the Talmud was vital to the Jews'. He therefore decided that it was necessary to establish special schools for Jewish boys, like those that already existed in Odessa, Kishinev and Riga, in which 'instruction was far removed from the spirit of the Talmudists'. Various *maskilim* suggested to him that he introduce these changes by coercive methods.

According to the recommendations of the Committee for the Jews – an institution established by the authorities to deal with Jewish affairs – it was decided in 1841 to open such schools. The Minister of Education approached Dr Max Lilienthal, the director of the Jewish school in Riga and a young German-born *maskil,* and asked him to head this educational project. On the Minister's suggestion, Lilienthal set out on a tour of the communities in the Pale of Settlement so as to recruit their support. He encountered distrust everywhere, even though he explained that the authorities had the good of the Jews at heart and promised that if he found any signs of activity directed against the Jewish religion he would resign. According to the description of Benjamin Mandelstam, a *maskil* and writer of the time, the members of the Minsk community

> reproached Lilienthal severely, saying: 'Troubler of Israel, why have you come to us to damage what is sacred and destroy our youth? Do you wish to convert us as you have converted our brethren in Vilna?' And the best of them advised him: 'Cease from this work, for it is an evil decree of the king to give a new Law to our sons. There are among us many worthless and foolish people whom we can buy up to take the place of our sons in these schools, just as we do for the army; but as to hearkening to the voice of those who would drive us away from our people and to take our children and offer them up to the Molech of the *Haskalah,* the abomination of the Children of Israel – that we will not do.'

Lilienthal met with greater success in the south, but generally speaking – with the exception of a small group of *maskilim* – the Jewish community regarded these schools as constituting an evil decree. Eventually Lilienthal (and some of the *maski-*

lim) realized that the fears of the Jewish community had been well founded; the authorities did not have Jewish interests at heart, but intended rather to manipulate the beliefs and concepts of the Jews and even to induce them to convert. A secret memorandum, written by the Minister of Education and approved by the Tsar, stated that the aim of the schools was to 'purify the religious concepts of the Jews'. Lilienthal fled from Russia in 1845.

Government schools as well as two rabbinical seminaries in Vilna and Zhitomir (in addition to that existing in Warsaw since 1826) were established nonetheless. The directors were Christians and only the Hebrew subjects were taught by Jews. The establishment of the schools brought in its wake severe persecution of the *heder,* or elementary religious school, and of the *melamdim* who taught there. The Jews protected themselves by every means at their disposal – above all, by bribing officials. Most of the lists of pupils that the local authorities submitted to the Ministry of Education were fabricated. In actual fact there were few – mainly sons of the poor – who were sent to the 'Molech of the *Haskalah*'; these were later to become the first Jews who were closely acquainted with the Russian language and culture.

Taxes on Traditional Clothing

The Committee for the Jews regarded the traditional Jewish garments as extremely harmful, 'creating a sharp differentiating line between the main population and the Jews' and, therefore, they wished to ban these garments altogether. Several of the Vilna *maskilim* urged the government to prohibit these garments completely, but this suggestion was not accepted. The authorities were content to impose taxes on all those found wearing the clothes in question. The tax imposed in 1844 was neither permanent nor uniform, and an 1848 edict referred specifically to the tax on the skull-cap. A general prohibition against the wearing of Jewish garments was published in 1850, but was difficult to implement. More specific regulations were published in 1853 and included the *kapota* (long robe), and headgear like the *streimel* (fur hat) and skull-cap. Men were forbidden to grow sidelocks and women to shave their heads, (as they used to beneath their headcovering). The local officials exploited these regulations in order to exact payment from the Jews, but after the death of Nicholas I in 1865 the regulations were rescinded.

The Abolition of the Kahal

A measure on which the authorities pinned great hopes was the abolition of the *kahal,* that is, the government recognition of the autonomous Jewish organization. An order to this effect was published at the end of 1844, and supervision of Jews and collection of taxes from them (including the *koropki*) was now entrusted to the municipalities and to the police. The authorities did not intend thereby to grant the Jews a status equal to that of other inhabitants, nor did they cancel their special obligation to recruit cantonists, nor cease to appoint tax collectors from among the Jews. These tax collectors, together with the synagogue treasurers, became the new leaders of the Jewish community in Russia. The leadership had always been in the hands of a small social stratum, but this intervention narrowed it even further. The important role of the *khappers* and *ba'alei taksa* ('tax collectors') in the new leadership discredited it almost completely in the eyes of most Jews.

The 'Classification' Plan

The harshest measure employed in the 'reform' programme or government decrees was the proposal to classify the Jews into groups in order to differentiate between the minority of 'useful' Jews who should be tolerated and the majority of 'exploiters and parasites' against whom strict measures should be employed. According to this plan the Jews were divided into five categories: merchants, farmers, artisans, permanent townspeople (*i.e.,* property-owners and religious ministrants), and town-dwellers 'whose residence was not permanent'. The last category, which included waggoners, goldsmiths, apprentices, etc., was the 'useless' one. The plan also provided for the tripling of the conscription quota from the 'useless' elements, their expulsion from the villages and restriction of their movement even within the Pale of Settlement. The Tsar agreed to the plan and ordered that the recruitment quota be increased fivefold, but certain important officials opposed it.

Moses Montefiore, who visited Russia in 1846, tried to persuade the authorities to postpone its implementation, but his pleas went unheeded – even though local officials and the Council of State had also recommended delay. The Tsar was adamant, and the plan was published at the beginning of 1851. All Jews were obliged to equip themselves with documents attesting to their categorical affiliation. There was a frantic rush among the Jews to obtain documents declaring them property-owners, and such papers were obtained in return for heavy bribes. Only the Crimean War and the death of Nicholas prevented the implementation of this programme.

In short, in the first half of the nineteenth century, the Russian regime made considerable efforts to integrate the large Jewish community into the legal, economic and social frameworks of the state, even though its economic standing and influence on urban life in western Russia had lent it considerable importance. These efforts were made on the assumption that it was possible to compel the Jews to convert and to eradicate their unique national and cultural traits by force or through various harsh measures, a policy abandoned by all other European states. But all official efforts met with failure. The heavier the decrees imposed, the firmer and more stubborn was the determination of the Jews to withstand them. There is no one area where it is possible to state that the authorities advanced in any way towards their goal. Only with the liberal trend that emerged with Alexander II's ascension to the throne was there a shift in the attitude of some Jews. This opened up the possibility of Jewish integration in several spheres of Russian life.

Integration of the Jews in the Period of the 'Great Reforms'

The Russian *débâcle* in the Crimean War forced the Russian authorities to introduce far-reaching changes in the political order. The 'great reforms', which encompassed most spheres of Russian life, directed attention also to the status of the Jews. The

Committee for the Jews, which had existed since 1840, came to realize that all the measures employed during the reign of Nicholas I had failed to achieve their aim. The chairman of this committee drew the attention of the new Tsar, Alexander II, to the fact that certain restrictions were hindering the assimilation of the Jews into the general population. In response, the Tsar ordered in 1856 a re-examination 'of all existing regulations regarding the Jews, in order to adapt them to the general purpose of integrating this people into the basic, rooted population, insofar as the moral condition of the Jews permits this'. Immediately upon his ascension to the throne, Alexander had approved the recommendation of the Committee to ease the conscription arrangements of the Jews. In the summer of 1856, the cantonists were abolished, and the Jews were made equal with the rest of the inhabitants as regards conscription.

In the examination of the laws relating to the Jews, the first and main problem that arose was the residence restrictions, *i.e.*, the Pale of Settlement. Many Russian bureaucrats supported the abolition of the Pale and the granting to the Jews the right to settle all over Russia. The Minister of the Interior also supported this idea, but the Committee rejected the proposal, and the Tsar supported its decision. The Committee's argument was that the cancellation of residence restrictions and equalization of rights could only be granted simultaneously with the spread of secular education among the Jews, a change in their way of life and their direction to 'useful' occupations. Thus, the government's method of dealing with the Jewish question was upheld in the reign of Alexander II as well: the acceleration of the pace of change in Jewish life through the encouragement of 'useful' Jews, *i.e.*, a continuation of the policy of the absolutist rulers of the eighteenth century.

With this aim in mind, the authorities began to implement the reforms: Nicholas I's secret order of 1844, banning all Jews from serving in government posts, was repealed in 1856 for university graduates and in 1862 for physicians and pharmacists without degrees. In 1859 Jewish merchants of the 'first guild' (meaning those paying the highest taxes) were granted the right to reside outside the Pale of Settlement. In 1861 these rights were extended to Jewish residents possessing university degrees, in 1865 to Jewish artisans, and in 1867 to soldiers who had served in Nicholas' army, as well as their descendants. In Russian Poland the Jews were permitted in 1862 to purchase real estate and to settle in all towns and cities.

All these concessions were actually directed at a very small section of the Jewish population, and they failed to solve the problem of the Jewish masses crammed into the Pale of Settlement with no opportunity of earning a livelihood. This phenomenon aroused the concern of prosperous Jews, and in 1862 they appealed to the authorities to ease the restrictions still burdening the great majority of the Jewish population. In this request the notables expressed the hope that the authorities would gradually lift restrictions from all Jews, rather than single out small groups among the Jews.

The Intensification of Anti-Semitic Trends

The main reason that the authorities hesitated to extend rights to the Jews lay in the profound distrust that the Tsar himself felt towards them. In due course this approach was strengthened by the change in attitude of certain public circles and of the bureau-cracy. This was primarily as a result of the 1863 Polish revolt and the attempt upon the life of the Tsar in 1866, which brought to an end the liberal tendencies in Russian public life. On the other hand, the Slavophiles and Ukrainian nationalists began by the early sixties to represent Jewry as the main opponent of Christianity and as an obstacle for the Slavic striving for liberation from German domination and, hence, as a most dangerous antagonist.

The Polish revolt substantiated the stand of those who believed that only the em-ployment of a firm policy against the minority nations within the Russian Empire could rebuild the strength of the state, while concessions could only encourage anti-Russian rebellion. Before the revolt, important officials had recommended the dissemination of Russian culture among the Jews and the expansion of their spheres of livelihood, and they had proposed that the process of Russification of the western regions be based on these principles. But from the mid-sixties onwards there was a change in attitude. The press in the western regions also began to express reservations regarding the granting of rights to Jews, and the anti-Semitic propaganda of the Slavophile circles wielded considerable influence.

A book written by the Jewish apostate Jacob Brafman also increased distrust of the Jews. His *Book of the Kahal* was a translation of the minutes of the Minsk Jewish community during the last years of the eighteenth and first years of the nine-teenth centuries. Brafman wrote an introductory volume containing poisonous propaganda against the Jews who, he claimed, constituted 'a state within a state', their main aim being to subjugate and exploit the general population. His book won a favourable audience among official circles.

This change in the attitude of government circles made itself felt in the Urban Statute published in 1870. In contradiction to the proposal that restrictions be abolished, the new statute reaffirmed that not more than one-third of the members of a municipality could be Jews (even in those towns with a Jewish majority) and banned Jews from holding the post of mayor.

The new aims of the ruling circles in the seventies were particularly evident in measures theoretically directed against 'Jewish separatism'. The Minister of Educa-tion discovered that the establishment of special schools for Jews was setting Jewish youth apart from their non-Jewish surroundings, and therefore he ordered, at the beginning of 1873, the closing of these schools (established in 1844); the rabbinical seminaries were turned into institutions for the training of teachers. The rapid increase in the number of Jews in the general institutions of learning aroused the resentment of considerable sections of Russian public opinion, and anti-Jewish articles began to appear very frequently in the press. The widely circulated paper *Novoye Vremya* ('New Times'), which was then changing from a liberal to a re-actionary line, published an article in 1880 entitled 'The Jews Are Upon You', in which it described the danger emanating from the increasingly prominent role being played by the Jews in Russian culture and in Russian public life.

Anti-Jewish developments had begun to occur during the sixties, but now they were intensified. In 1871 a pogrom broke out against the Jews of Odessa; it was instigated mainly by Greek merchants, out of commercial rivalry. During the war between Russia and Turkey (1877–8), many articles were written attacking the Jewish purveyors for supposedly robbing the government and causing harm to the army. Certain authors, writing in a popular style, filled their books with savage anti-Jewish provocations. In 1878 a blood libel was levelled against several Jews in Kutais in Caucasia, and even though they were exonerated, many papers discussed whether Jews really used Christian blood.

Throughout the seventies there was a turn for the worse in public opinion, which became even more hostile towards the Jews than the government bureaucrats. The underlying reason was the spread of Slavophile ideas to the general public, particularly during the Balkan war. This ideology emphasized the uniqueness of Russia as opposed to the West, and Jews were accused of disseminating corrupting influences and exploiting the 'basic population'. It was at the time of this intensified incitement (1880) that two members of the Committee for the Jews submitted a memorandum in which they noted that it was incorrect to regard the Jews as a non-productive population, as the local bureaucracy held a positive view of their economic activity; therefore, the correct procedure in solving the Jewish question was through their gradual advancement towards complete equality of rights. Otherwise, the authors warned, revolutionary ideas would prevail among the Jews. Although most members of the Committee tended to favour the extension of Jewish rights, there were influential circles that hindered this move. The murder of Alexander II marked the end of even a semblance of liberal leanings; it opened up an era of open warfare on the Jews.

The Jewish Situation in Rumania

In many respects the situation of Rumanian Jews resembled that of the Jews of Russia. In the principalities on the Danube in the first third of the nineteenth century, the Jews suffered various discriminations (particularly with regard to occupations and the purchase of real estate) and were obliged to pay special taxes. In the 1840s the Rumanians stepped up their struggle with the Turkish regime and were anxious to win the few Jewish intellectuals to their cause. During the 1848 revolutionary ferment, the demand for equal rights for the Jews was raised. The political parties, which were then organized around the problem of the unification of the Danube principalities into one kingdom, outdid each other in their promises to the Jews.

After the idea of unification prevailed, the Jews played an important part in the economic development of the state. Duke Cuza, who headed the state, declared that he was opposed to religious discrimination and promised gradual emancipation. His opponents among the landowners endeavoured to depict his entire liberal attitude as 'Jewish policy', injurious to the state. Thus, anti-Jewish incitement became one of the important factors in the evolvement of the Rumanian state. When Karl Hohenzollern was proclaimed ruler in Cuza's place (1866), he proposed the granting of civil rights to the entire population, whatever their religion, but this suggestion met with violent demonstrations against the Jews and deteriorated into open pogroms.

While the Rumanian legislative assembly was discussing the question of Jewish emancipation, demonstrations were held in the streets of Bucharest. The mob burst in and dispersed the assembly; later the Choral synagogue was destroyed and a number of Jews were attacked. The assembly subsequently passed a law determining that only Christians could become citizens, and the government declared that it had never intended to grant the Jews civil rights. From then on the Rumanian regime was characterized by its cruel persecution of the Jews.

In 1867 the government of Bratianu began to expel Jews from the villages; poor Jews were driven out of the country as vagabonds. When a cholera epidemic broke out in the same year, various elements accused the Jews of spreading the disease and used this charge as a pretext for persecuting them. The situation became so harsh that the foreign consuls intervened and demanded an explanation from the Rumanian Government. In July of the same year several Jews were expelled from Galati (Galatz) across the river to Turkey. When the Turkish border-guards refused to grant them entry, they were sent back to the Rumanian shore where they faced the bayonets of Rumanian troops, and, as a result, several drowned in the river. The consuls of all the powers (including Russia) protested to Bucharest against this act of barbarism, and the British Foreign Secretary denounced the Rumanian Government in the House of Commons. Bratianu's government was obliged to resign.

This event led to an outburst of fury against the Jews. Many members of the legislative assembly proposed that a law be passed prohibiting the Jews from residing in villages and restricting their residence in towns. The government wished to avoid any discussion of the matter since it feared the intervention of foreign powers. The visit to Rumania of two prominent Jewish personalities, Adolphe Crémieux and Moses Montefiore, in 1866–7 brought new promises from the authorities to stop the persecution – but they were never kept. Intervention from abroad aroused popular anger even further. The country was swept by a new wave of pogroms, and a particularly savage one occurred in Galati in October 1868. The government came to the defence of the Jews – on the ground that they were aliens and that appropriate measures could therefore not be employed against them for fear of foreign intervention. Renewed restrictions and pogroms in 1872–3 aroused protests in many states in Europe, and the United States Secretary of State appealed to all the signatories of the Convention of Paris (1858) to intervene on behalf of the Jews. The first step in this direction was taken by the Turkish Sultan, who was nominally supreme ruler of Rumania. He warned the Rumanian Government that if it proved incapable of maintaining order, the Ottoman forces would undertake the task. This time the interventions proved effective, and the pogroms ceased until 1877. But administrative persecution did not cease, and economic restrictions against the Jews were intensified.

The Berlin Congress: Emancipation of the Jews as a Recognized International Principle

The suffering of Rumanian Jewry aroused Jewish communities and organizations to turn to the Berlin Congress of 1878, where representatives of the Great Powers were meeting to discuss the outcome of the Russo-Turkish war, in order to persuade the Rumanian Government to bestow equal rights on the Jews. Rumanian government-circles also hinted that international pressure was the only way of influencing the masses in this direction. There were even some Jews who hoped they would succeed on the same occasion in arranging for an extension of the rights held by Russian Jews. Bismarck promised to raise the problem of Jewish rights at the Berlin Congress, and in several countries the issue was indeed discussed in parliament. Several Jewish organizations sent delegations and submitted memoranda to the participants in this Congress.

During the Congress' deliberations, the French representative proposed that recognition of the independence of the new Balkan states (Bulgaria, Serbia and Rumania) be made dependent on a specific declaration on their part that they would grant equal rights to *all* citizens. The Bulgarian and Serbian representatives agreed, and the Turkish delegate announced that the principle was in accordance with the general legislation of his country. Nor did the Rumanian delegates declare their explicit opposition. Only the Russian representative declared that the Jews of Berlin, Paris and London could not be compared with those living in Bessarabia, Rumania and Russia.

Bulgaria and Serbia approved the Berlin treaties and introduced the requested amendments into their constitutions. The Rumanian Government ignored the resolution and, as a result, Great Power recognition of its independence was delayed. But despite the fact that the Berlin Congress did not succeed in changing the legal status of Rumanian and Russian Jewry, it proved to be of great significance in the struggle for Jewish emancipation. The question of Jewish rights emerged from the framework of internal national considerations and was transformed into a recognized international principle. Moreover, the Great Powers not only accepted it, but also actively demanded its implementation. There were certain countries that violated this principle, but these were vigorously condemned by European public opinion.

51

Integration into the Non-Jewish World in the Nineteenth Century

The Problem of Jewish Status in the Alien World

The integration of the Jews to the European way of life was one of the decisive processes in nineteenth-century Jewish history. In this period each and every Jew living in one of the European countries was confronted with the problem of his attitude both towards his own people and society and towards the people among whom he dwelt. There were many and varied methods of solving this problem – ranging from unquestioning loyalty to Jewish tradition by means of firm opposition to any possible influence emanating from the non-Jewish world to complete assimilation within the environment and complete detachment from historical ties. Most Jews chose neither of the extremes, but preferred a series of varied attempts at simultaneous loyalty to both frameworks and a desire to be integrated into both.

As we have already noted, this integration was not merely a question of external imitation – as had sometimes occurred in the eighteenth century – but constituted an acceptance of the criteria of Christian society and culture in the sphere of beliefs and values. The tradition of hatred for and contempt of the Jews fostered by the non-Jewish world also had its effect: a considerable number of Jews were eager to demonstrate their complete detachment from their origins and their utter loyalty to European culture by denying their past and religion. But their blatant willingness did not facilitate their assimilation. The host culture regarded acceptance of the Jews as an act of generosity and assumed that the Jew, with his flawed heritage, having only recently recognized the spiritual world and values of European society, should humble himself and be content with a marginal status. They failed to realize that the very attraction of the non-Jewish world for these Jews was based on their desire to escape the status of a marginal group that suffered discrimination and to achieve equal status in a society constructed on rationalist foundations, in which the individual was important in his own right and judged on his own merits.

European society, for the most part, was ready to allot the Jew one of the lower rungs on the social ladder. Even the more liberal elements anticipated that, at most, the Jews would come to resemble their surroundings, *i.e.,* most of them would be peasants, workers and perhaps some merchants, while a small number might, in time, become government officials and members of the liberal professions. But the great majority of the Jewish public did not seek to identify with the alien environment by abandoning their traditional sources of livelihood. Even the minority of the young and educated that did so aspire were only attempting to become part of the social *élite;* they regarded themselves worthy of status by virtue of their talents and education. Therefore, the controversy over integration became, to a large extent, a question of different ways to achieve the goal.

The nature of this controversy changed during the nineteenth century. At the beginning of the century, when only a few individual Jews sought entry to European society, there was greater readiness to accept them. But as soon as the ambitious *maskilim* formed a social group with its particular cultural achievements and strong communal awareness, opposition towards them began to increase.

Conversion

The first stage in the attempt of the *maskilim* to become fully integrated into their non-Jewish surroundings was through the extreme step of conversion. This was an accepted method of sundering ties with Jewish society and joining the Christian majority. In the Middle Ages and at the beginning of modern times only a few took this path (except in periods of forced conversion). In the second half of the eighteenth century there was an increase in the number of converts in Sephardi communities in Europe; and in the last years of that century and the first years of the nineteenth century, there was an increased rate of conversion in Germany as well. Among Russian Jews this process commenced in the forties and fifties, most of the converts being cantonists who were forcibly converted, but there was also a considerable number of graduates of government rabbinical seminaries and institutions of higher learning who hoped to advance their careers in this way.

There can be no doubt that the great majority of Jewish converts in the nineteenth century acted because of the legal and social conditions in which the Jews lived in the various European countries. Some converted in order to obtain government and academic positions or in order to marry a Christian; others took this step in order to enter into political life. As the Jews obtained legal equality, the number of converts dropped. But it is important to note that even in those countries that officially introduced legal equality for Jews, there was still concealed discrimination and there were still those who hoped to escape it by becoming Christians. They regarded conversion – as Heine put it – as a ticket of admission to European society. To them Judaism was 'a historical error', an insignificant relic of an ancient period. They could not believe in the continued existence of Jewish society and despaired of reforming it; as they could not adjust to it, they strove to escape it. As for the ancient heritage of Judaism, which had left its mark on every one of them, they regarded it as a shameful hereditary disease ('Judaism is not a religion, it is a catastrophe'), and sought the remedy in conversion. Several of the converts tried to neutralize the gravity of the step they had taken by endeavouring to dismiss the religious significance of Christianity, regarding it, in the words of the great German historian Theodor Mommsen, as 'the only word expressing the character of today's international civilization in which numerous millions all over the many-nationed globe feel themselves united'.

However, under the conditions prevailing at that time in European society, the 'remedy' of conversion sometimes proved harsher than the 'disease' itself. From the moral point of view, conversion was difficult to justify, particularly for those who held rationalist views: all the complaints they were nursing against Judaism and its customs could also be voiced against Christianity and its mysteries. And even those who, on the basis of Hegel's teachings, regarded Christianity as a higher stage in the development of the universal spirit were forced to admit that, according to the new radical criteria, both symbolized values that were no longer valid. It was difficult, therefore, to justify conversion according to the accepted criteria of the *maskilim*. As Gabriel Riesser said:

> No, it is no fanatical principle which leads us to reject contemptuously the idea of conversion, but the simple eternal truth that we cannot permit our lips to utter that in which our soul does not believe. As a result, the problem of religious conversion is, first of all, the struggle between truth and falsehood, between sincerity and hypocrisy, between honesty and vulgarity.

The social problem proved even greater than the moral obstacle. The converts knew that they were abandoning a Jewish society undergoing difficult strains and that their brethren regarded them as deserters and traitors. Hence, there was a sense of shame that characterized many of them ('May all converts suffer a mood like mine,' Heine once said). Nor did they feel better in Christian society. Their demands for equality, and even for honourable positions, was regarded by most Christians as 'typical Jewish insolence'. In some cases the conversion only accentuated the Judaism of the convert rather than concealing it. He uprooted himself from one society and was not permitted to put down roots in the other. It is not surprising that most of the converts reacted with particular sensitivity to the contempt they encountered. This explains why many of them were attracted to ideological and social radicalism – to what at times amounted to savage criticism of the existing social order – and yearned for the ideal society in which man was not judged by such 'incidental' characteristics as his origin. But even in this attitude there are some traits of an ancient Jewish tradition not to be reconciled with the present and to pin hopes on a messianic future.

Those converts who chose Christianity out of complete identification with its principles became the greatest enemies and persecutors of Judaism, just like their mediaeval counterparts. They became fanatic believers in the 'Christian state' and 'Christian society' and claimed that there was no room for Jews within the framework of Europe. The converts who did not attribute religious significance to conversion, after sensing their own detachment from both Christian and Jewish societies, sometimes cast nostalgic eyes on their past. They would not return to Judaism, but they began to take pride in their origin (*e.g.,* Disraeli) or in Jewish creativity (*e.g.,* Heine). There were some converts, like the well-known orientalist Daniel Chwolson in Russia or the theologian Selig (Paulus) Cassel in Germany, who came to the defence of the Jews in times of need. It is not surprising that this aroused anger in anti-Semitic circles, and it was argued that the converts were a most dangerous element, as they were the agents of 'world Jewry' within Christian society.

Cultural Assimilation

From the mid-nineteenth century onwards, conversion ceased to be the main method of integration into European society for the Jews and was chosen only by the few. Cultural assimilation and a spiritual and ideological identification with the state replaced it. This change was the result of a lengthy process in which knowledge of the indigenous language and culture was acquired – a process that had commenced in Western Europe in the eighteenth or even in the seventeenth century. Nevertheless, throughout the eighteenth century most communities still wrote their ledgers in Hebrew or in a Hebrew mixed with Yiddish. Jewish cultural works were almost all written in Hebrew, whether in rabbinical style or in the new style of the *Haskalah*, while the spoken language in the Ashkenazi communities was Yiddish.

For the individual Jew entrance into the world of European culture meant the abandonment of Hebrew and Yiddish. The replacement of Hebrew by other languages and of Yiddish by the 'pure' language of the country became the central slogans of both Jewish and non-Jewish advocates of the Enlightenment. This trend was furthered by the special schools established for Jewish children and the increase in the number of Jews attending public schools. The change in the language of their culture also transformed the spiritual world of the Jews and altered their creative activity. The sermons of rabbis and sages and the popular Yiddish literature aimed at the masses began to yield their place to works written in the spirit of European literature of the time. The small amount of Hebrew that remained among the Jews of Western and Central Europe was confined wholly to the sphere of religion. To the extent that any other Jewish culture reached them, it emanated from Eastern Europe, where the Jewish communities perserved their traditional creativity.

The first sphere in which the Jews became active in European languages was the press, as this area was not under the supervision of the government or of traditional institutions that hindered Jewish activity. The Jews played a particularly important part in the liberal and radical press, as this fitted in with the aims of Jewish political activity. They also possessed several traits that particularly suited them to journalism: a rapid grasp of facts, agility, extensive contacts. From the middle of the nineteenth century, several important newspapers in Germany and France belonged to or were run by Jews. Some of these Jewish journalists helped to develop journalistic techniques and to increase newspaper circulation. The publishing experience possessed by some Jews proved helpful here. Their success in the world of journalism provided the pretext for claims about 'Jewish control of the press' and statements about their 'alienness to the spirit of the nation'. As an example of the lack of roots of the Jewish journalist in the country of his residence, critics would cite one of the more important journalists of the era, Henri de Blowitz, who is claimed to have introduced the technique of the newspaper interview. He was a Bohemian Jew, brought up on German culture, who served as the London *Times* correspondent in Paris, and the secret of his success was his cosmopolitanism.

As the Jews took root in the culture of their surroundings, they also became more important in the field of literature. Ludwig Boerne (1786–1837) and Heinrich Heine (1797–1856) exerted considerable influence on the cultural life of Germany. They were regarded as the spiritual leaders of the Young Germany movement, although most of the members of this group were non-Jewish.

The extensive musical tradition of the Jews made it easy for them to play a prominent part in the development of European music; Disraeli once said that 'the most inspiring singers, most graceful dancers and most delicate musicians are the sons and daughters of Israel'. In the nineteenth century the Jews produced several important composers (such as Mendelssohn-Bartholdy, Meyerbeer, Halevy, Offenbach). They were also active in the dissemination of musical education: thus, for example, when Bach had been forgotten for more than a hundred years, Mendelssohn revived his work; the Rubinstein brothers organized musical education in Russia; Joseph Joachim and Leopold Auer created schools for violinists. From the middle of the nineteenth century many of the great musical performers were of Jewish origin. In the second half of the nineteenth century, all four of the violinists who won the title of 'soloist to his Imperial Majesty' in Russia were of Jewish origin. In the theatre and opera Jews also played a prominent part (for example, the actresses Rachel and Sarah Bernhardt).

Another sphere of artistic expression – which was actually alien to Jewish tradition – was painting and sculpture. But by the second half of the nineteenth century there were distinguished Jewish artists, such as the painters Jozef Israels (1824–1911) in Holland, Camille Pissaro (1830–1903) in France, Max Liebermann (1847–1935) and Lesser Ury (1861–1931) in Germany and the sculptor Marc Antokolsky (1843–1902) in Russia.

Other Jews played no less important roles in science: there was a well-established Jewish tradition of medical practice and of medical research. Jews advanced rapidly in the more theoretical sciences (such as philosophy and mathematics), which did not necessitate direct contact with scientific institutions. The corporative nature of many of the universities, a heritage of the Middle Ages, prevented the Jews from gaining entry to academic positions (particularly in the humanities) even when they theoretically enjoyed equal rights. Despite these obstacles, however, the number of Jews at universities increased in all faculties. (The number of conversions for the sake of academic careers was also relatively high.)

In short, Jews now began to play a prominent part even in those spheres from which they had formerly been remote, both from the point of view of practice and of tradition. In the West and Central European countries, cultural concepts and values created in Jewish society were rapidly replaced by the cultural treasures of Christian European society. This was a revolutionary phenomenon in that it differed from parallel developments throughout most of Jewish history. Formerly, when Jewish society came into contact with alien cultures, it would either contend with them or endeavour to create a synthesis between the opinions and concepts evolved by Jewish society and those absorbed from outside. In the nineteenth century, however, many of the *maskilim* and even spokesmen of Jewish society chose to renounce their historical heritage of their own free will, sometimes out of contempt and in order to root themselves in the culture of their environment. Only at the end of the century were the first attempts made to create a renewed synthesis between Jewish and European creativity.

National and Political Identification

Cultural assimilation and the adoption of the concepts and values of Christian European society led many Jews to re-evaluate the significance of their affiliation to Judaism and to increase their identification with the states and nations among whom they lived. What was new in this approach was not the loyalty of the Jews towards their gentile countries and rulers – this had existed in earlier periods – but the contradiction that many of them suddenly felt between this loyalty and their affiliation to Judaism.

This sense of contradiction was created during the era that centralizing trends were being intensified in Europe. Educated Jews, who yearned for equal rights in the countries of Europe, took these theories very seriously, since they implied that *individuals* formed the state, not members of a group or corporation (though this was not yet feasible since, in most of Europe, class and corporative representation was still strongly entrenched). Under the conditions prevailing in the first half of the nineteenth century, the educated Jew was pushed back into his own social framework even in those countries in which he had, in theory, been granted civil rights. This came as a shock to those accustomed to regard themselves as equals of those educated Christians who shared their views. These *maskilim* had often declared that their Judaism was of absolutely no political or national significance. At the beginning of the nineteenth century, they increasingly claimed that no separate political or national loyalty could be attributed to Judaism, that the people among whom they lived were their brethren and that the state was the only homeland to which they were loyal 'till death'. As an expression of the sincerity of their beliefs, they proposed that all mention of the Messiah and of the Return to Zion be removed from the prayer-book.

In the Jewish liberal and radical circles that came into being somewhat later, the prevalent view was that there was an identity between Jewish aims and the general political goals for which corresponding non-Jewish circles were fighting. In Germany these circles associated the hope of Jewish acceptance into the surrounding society with the unification of the country and the triumph of liberal ideals. Gabriel Riesser (1806–63), for example, attacked those who accused the Jews of maintaining allegiance to another homeland.

> Where is that second homeland which calls us to its defence? To claim that our forefathers came here thousands or hundreds of years ago is an inhuman and tasteless charge. We did not come; we were born here and we have no claim to any other homeland. If we are not Germans then we have no homeland.

During the Revolution of 1848, Riesser was in favour of the political unification of Germany. He then declared 'Give me Jewish equality in one hand and the realization of the beautiful dream of Germany's political unification in the other . . . and I will unhesitatingly choose the latter, for I am convinced that unification also encompasses equality.'

Just as in Jewish liberal circles in Germany the aspirations of the Jews were identified with the political hopes of that country, so French Jewish radicals and socialists linked the liberation and advancement of the Jews with the triumph of the great principles of the French Revolution or the spread of Saint-Simonist ideals.

The struggle for Jewish integration into the non-Jewish environment was, as we have noted, to a large extent a struggle for a place in European society. It is understandable, therefore, that for the Jews the chances of achieving an honourable position in rigidly fixed social frameworks, of being accepted as equals in those conserative and clerical circles that advocated the 'Christian state', were almost non-existent. As a result, an increasing number of Jews began to pin their hopes of success for advancement on the triumph of forces of reform and revolution. This belief was so strong that, in time, the difference between Jewish interests and radical aspirations became blurred. Consequently, the Jews began to play an increasingly important role in political life. In some Jewish circles the struggle for specific Jewish rights and status was regarded as a sign of narrow-mindedness; the more radical the group, the stronger was their conviction on this point. They were convinced that the question of the furthering of Jewish interests could only be settled as part of a comprehensive campaign, so that any special emphasis on Jewish affairs was inevitably futile. If society as a whole were reformed, all its defects would be corrected – including discrimination against Jews. This belief was particularly strong in a later period among the Jewish socialists.

The outcome of this development was the indifference that many politically active Jews began to display towards Jewish affairs. In keeping with this attitude, neither Achille Fould (1800–67), the French conservative, nor Eduard Lasker (1829–84) and Ludwig Bamberger (1823–99), liberal leaders of the German Reichstag, nor Ferdinand Lassalle (1825–64) and Johann Jacoby (1805–77), the German socialists, were particularly active on behalf of Jewish interests, and they only supported them to the extent that Jewish problems formed part of more general political questions. As the legal situation of the Jews improved, this indifference among politicians of Jewish origin towards their own people increased. A belief that the specific problems of the Jews would form part of a general solution was the characteristic sign of the national and political assimilation of the Jews in their countries of residence.

Social Assimilation and Its Problems. The Idea of the 'Jewish Mission'

There were actually very few obstacles to the cultural assimilation of the Jews into European society, thanks to the ideals of the Enlightenment and to government policy. Because only a relatively small number of Jews attached themselves to European culture at the end of the eighteenth and beginning of the nineteenth centuries, there was no social group that opposed this process of cultural integration. The situation changed to a large extent when there was a considerable increase in the number of Jews achieving national and political identification with the non-Jewish world and, hence, attaining to political activity and influence. The desire for cultural integration began to grip wider circles of the Jewish community; in fact, it encompassed all the Jewish groups in Central and Western Europe. This led to extensive contact between the Jewish and Christian middle classes in those countries and, in turn, highlighted the competitiveness, suspicions and reservations of the surrounding non-Jewish world. The educated European townsman, who had become accustomed to regarding the Jews as inferior and alien to the social and political framework, was incapable of accepting them as equals and shrank from the fervour of the Jewish desire to assimilate to the non-Jewish world.

The Jews began to sense the force of their rejection by European society, but refused to renounce their ideals of equality and the dream of a rational and reformed society. They could not return to activity within the precarious framework of the Jewish community and they therefore began to seek out a new justification for their desire of equality and of integration. One of the most characteristic expressions was the ideal of the universal 'Jewish mission' – namely the special message that the Jews and Judaism bore to the nations of the world.

At the end of the eighteenth and the beginning of the nineteenth centuries, individuals began to offer a universal interpretation of Jewish messianic faith, claiming that the messianic era would be an epoch of peace, liberty and fraternity among men, whatever their origin or religion. In the first quarter of the nineteenth century, several of the *maskilim* began to accentuate the importance of the Jews as a culture-bearing nation in the past (like the Greeks or the Romans), the debt Europe owed them in this respect, and the significance of the scientific, rational 'Jewish idea' – the outstanding proponent of which was Spinoza's philosophy. This was both a justification and an explication of separate Jewish existence throughout the centuries (since some of those Enlightened European circles that had been influenced by English deists and French materialists never tired of stating that Jewish allegiance to a separate group existence was pointless obstinacy). This great historical and spiritual heritage also substantiated the demand for integration into the upper, rather than the lower, echelons of European society.

The next stage in the development of the Jewish self-awareness within these circles was the claim that only pure Jewish monotheism and the moral principles that had evolved in Jewish society from its beginnings could save Europe from its spiritual morass and from the maze of social contradictions and struggles. This entailed emphasizing the importance of the Jews and Judaism to European society, and the significance of the Jewish contribution to its development and welfare in both past and present. But this argument also constituted a veiled – or, sometimes, an explicit – criticism of the dogmatic foundations of Christianity and its mysteries, especially its failure to solve the vital problems of man and society after 2,000 years. It is worth noting that even among Jewish converts to Christianity there were many who supported this view.

The idea of a 'mission' was widely accepted in Jewish circles in Western and Central Europe. But this method of expressing loyalty to European culture and the advancement of society elicited a spirited reaction from both clerical and radical circles, which regarded it as a manifestation of 'Jewish arrogance' and of the Jews' desire to maintain their own separate existence. To no small extent it also strengthened suspicions of the existence of secret 'Jewish aims' and prepared the ground for the intensification of anti-Semitic trends. The process of Jewish integration into European life was, therefore, a complex dialectic of acceptance and rejection, of desire to assimilate and consolidation of Jewish self-awareness at the same time.

52

Ideological Changes in Jewish Society in the Nineteenth Century

As a result of the political changes that occurred in Western and Central Europe, the integration of the Jews into their environment and the cultural orientation of these trends, most Jews accepted the ideals of the *Haskalah* and began to concentrate their efforts on the social, religious and cultural spheres, on adapting their organizational patterns and way of life to that of the world around them. Consequently, the great majority of the Jews of these countries favoured reform in all these spheres, and there were few who opposed them. In Eastern Europe, on the other hand, most Jews remained loyal to the old frameworks and their traditional way of life, and the *maskilim* were a small, persecuted minority. The first signs of disillusionment with the *Haskalah* appeared before it had had time to spread, laying the foundation for radical and even revolutionary ideology in the national and social sphere during the seventies and eighties.

During this century there was no real agitation for reform among the Jews in Islamic countries, nor were there problems of integration – with the exception of certain fluctuations under the influence of the imperial powers and their culture. In this respect, they differed from European Jewry.

The Religious Reform Movement in the West

The first attempts to introduce reform into religious ritual were made by Israel Jacobson – mainly within the framework of the consistory in the Kingdom of Westphalia during the first decade of the nineteenth century – and by several rich Berlin Jews at the beginning of the second decade; neither endured. The Westphalia consistory disappeared when the state was dissolved after the defeat of Napoleon, and the conservative Prussian monarch Friedrich-Wilhelm III closed the private houses of worship in Berlin.

The first reform temple was founded in Hamburg in 1818. The service was conducted according to the ritual of the Berlin reformers, the number of prayers recited in German was increased and all prayers referring to the coming of the Messiah or the Return to Zion were omitted. The Hamburg community leaders were opposed to these innovations and prohibited worship in the temple and from the new *siddur*, or prayerbook. This opposition sparked off an extensive literary controversy, mainly in Hebrew. A very few rabbis (including Aaron Chorin, rabbi of Arad in Hungary, who had dreamed of reforming religious worship for years) supported the reformers, while dozens of others, headed by the great scholars of the generation, R. Akiva Eger of Posen, R. Mordecai Banet of Nikolsburg (and Brünn) and R. Moses Sofer of Pressburg (Bratislava) were totally against the reforms. The main opposition was not directed against the reforms themselves, since several of them, such as prayer in the language of the country, could even be justified according to religious sources. The fury was directed against the fact that young people with no standing in the religious world had taken it upon themselves to offer instruction in religious law and to change Jewish law and custom. How could these young *maskilim* dare to raise their hand against the sacred traditions!

The Hamburg temple continued to exist, but very few similar institutions were established until the second half of the 1830s, when a new generation of university-educated rabbis arose in Germany, and many community members, particularly the leaders, displayed a readiness to appoint them to rabbinical posts. From then onwards the number of German rabbis ready to contemplate some degree of religious reform grew from year to year. The most important of these was Abraham Geiger (1810–74), who may be denoted the spiritual father of the reform movement. Geiger was opposed to arbitrary amendments introduced by the young rabbis of his generation on their own initiative. His aim was to find general principles for differentiation between fundamental and marginal principles in Judaism. He therefore called for a scientific approach to the general question of Jewish tradition. In his view, the essence of Judaism was the religious-universal element. All the remainder was the fruit of historical conditions, particularly those that had influenced the Jews during their exile. Those injunctions and customs that were not an essential part of Mosaic Law, but the product of later periods and, therefore, unsuited to modern society, should be abolished.

A new controversy on questions of reform was sparked off when the orthodox rabbi of the Breslau community refused to cooperate with Geiger, who was elected his deputy in 1838, and particularly when the rabbi of Hamburg, Isaac Bernays, revived the prohibition against employing the prayerbook used in the reform temple. This time many reform rabbis supported Geiger and the temple prayerbook. Outstanding among the extreme reformists was Samuel Holdheim (1806–60), who at that time published a book entitled *On the Autonomy of the Rabbis*. He wrote that as it was clear to him that the state should deal with problems of a political and social character, the authorities had the power to decide which problems were under their jurisdiction and which could be entrusted to the Jewish community. He believed that the government should deal with matrimonial, Sabbath and festival laws and all problems arising between man and man. Only questions of religious worship should be left to the authority of rabbis and Jewish religious institutions because synagogue worship was the most important part of Jewish religious life. Holdheim's proposals thus undermined the traditional structure of the Jewish community, rejecting most of its established functions.

Since the proponents of reform could not arrive at agreement among themselves – neither as regards those details in need of reform nor in determining the principle on which reform should be based – it was proposed that rabbinical gatherings be convened, and their decisions would serve as the authoritative source for the introduction of changes in Jewish ritual.

Conferences of Reform Rabbis

The first conference of German reform rabbis was convened on the initiative of Ludwig Philippson, editor of the *Allgemeine Zeitung des Judentumus,* an extremely influential weekly founded in 1837. At the first meeting (Brunswick, 1844) Philippson proposed the approval of the resolutions of the French Sanhedrin (see pages 761–2), which was regarded by the reformers as a religious authority; the gathering also permitted intermarriage with Christians.

At the second rabbinical conference (Frankfurt, 1845), differences of opinion in the reform camp came to light. The extremists wanted to reduce the religious value of the Hebrew language and were opposed by the rabbi of Dresden, R. Zacharias Frankel, who regarded such a step as an abandonment of Jewish historical traditions. When he saw that the resolution on Hebrew was going to be accepted by a majority, Frankel left the meeting. In due course, he rallied round him several supporters who advocated 'historical positive Judaism', as the conservative approach of Frankel and his supporters was called. The activities of this group were mainly concentrated in the Breslau rabbinical seminary, which Frankel founded (1853) and headed for many years, and the scholarly periodical *Monatsschrift für Geschichte und Wissenschaft des Judentums.* Frankel's departure lessened the prestige of the conference and made it more difficult for it to declare itself a supreme religious authority. Nor did the third conference (Breslau, 1846) succeed in attaining this central objective: the creation of a religious authority capable of giving public sanction to religious reform. Nevertheless the reform theories continued to spread, and in many parts of Germany separate reform communities arose, which broke away from the old, orthodox communities. From Germany the movement spread to Hungary (where it was headed by Leopold Loew) and moved to the United States and certain West European countries. But the political events of 1848 delayed its further consolidation by some twenty years, particularly since some of the reform rabbis were active in the revolutions and were therefore suspect later in the eyes of the authorities. Quite a number of rabbis emigrated to the United States during these years.

The reawakening of the reform movement commenced at the end of the sixties. A convention of reform rabbis, held at Kassel, decided that the time was ripe for a 'synod' of rabbis, scholars and community leaders in order to establish a supreme institution for the reform movement. These two synods (Leipzig, 1869; Augsburg, 1871) displayed no inclination to introduce further far-reaching changes in religious legislation, with the exception of the abolition of *halizah* (the ceremony of release from levirate marriage obligations, Deuteronomy 25:7) and a certain easing of Sabbath laws. On the other hand the synods issued emphatic statements to the effect that Judaism in no way contradicted the basic tenets of modern society, that it aspired to understanding between religions, and other such conciliatory announcements aimed at the non-Jewish world. They proposed the establishment of general schools unaffiliated with any religious framework and demanded the right of religious instruction for each child – including Jewish children – according to his religion.

At that time most German Jewish communities were beginning to favour reform. In the same period the reformers in Hungary, who constituted a minority of the Jewish population, tried to force their opinions on the rest of the Jewish population with the aid of the government; but this plan failed because of the vehement opposition of orthodox elements. In the United States reform trends were augmented by rabbinical reformers who arrived from Germany; in 1869 the first conference of reform rabbis was held in the United States.

The basic principles of reform were formulated and consolidated in this period. Israel's mission was not to remove itself from other nations and re-establish a separate kingdom, but rather to unite with all other earthly creatures on the basis of common faith in one God. Therefore, as it is written in the Talmud (*Pessahim* 87b), 'God did mercy the children of Israel in scattering them among the nations.' He had sent them out among the nations to disseminate belief in one God and thus to serve as a 'nation of priests' for the entire world. The world had need of Israel's existence, and the pure belief of that nation, the universal religious and moral belief, which other nations have not yet attained. Needless to say, they continued to adhere to the belief of the first reformers that any custom, law or prayer that hindered Israel's mission should be changed or abolished.

Modern Jewish Scholarship

The reactionary period that followed the Congress of Vienna and the appearance of anti-Jewish literature, which emanated from Enlightened German circles, brought about a change of values among the *maskilim*. The dream of a rapid *rapprochement* between Jews and Christians on the basis of the spread of Enlightenment theories proved an idle hope. Young *maskilim* began to question why large sections of Christian society displayed hostility towards them, despite the fact that they had acquired extensive knowledge of European culture and had adopted its manners and behaviour.

These *maskilim* tended to think that this continued hostility resulted from European society's ignorance of Judaism, its history and its contribution to European culture. Thus these circles set themselves a dual aim: to adapt Jewish concepts and behaviour to those of European society and to 'show the beauty of Shem in the tents of Japhet'; or, in other words, to present the treasures of Jewish creativity to the non-Jewish world. The way to achieve these aims was to reveal the sources of Jewish religious customs and literary works. It was mainly for this purpose that the Verein für Kultur und Wissenschaft der Juden (Association for Jewish Culture and Science), which laid the foundation for modern research in Jewish studies, was founded in 1819.

The association was headed by several young men, including Dr Leopold (Yom Tov Lipman) Zunz (1794–1886), who became known as the 'father of modern Jewish scholarship'. Heine was also a member for a time. But the association rapidly realized that its meetings were not influencing the attitude of Christian society towards the Jews, and in 1824 it was dissolved. Most of its members converted so as to be able to enter the academic world; the first among them was Eduard Gans (1797–1839), chairman of the association and later Professor of Legal Philosophy at Berlin University.

Zunz continued to engage in scientific study, at first with the aim of furthering Jewish integration into the non-Jewish world. In 1832 he wrote *Sermons of the Jews* in order to prove that the prohibitions that the Prussian authorities had imposed on sermons in German were groundless, because during long periods Jews had preached in various vernaculars; in 1837 he wrote *On Jewish Names* in order to demonstrate that Jews had always been called by foreign names. But despite the tendentiousness of Zunz's studies, their scholarly importance remains unquestioned to this day.

Abraham Geiger gave Jewish studies a new impetus. According to his method, all reform should be based on objective criteria drawn from scientific research. This belief that all Jewish concepts, injunctions and customs, with the exception of several general rational truths, were the fruit of historical development, led Geiger to heavy criticism of Jewish worship and law and to the demand that they be exchanged for religious legislation suited to the spirit of the times. This approach, distinct from its central aim, provided strong impetus for critical study of Jewish history and literature.

Leopold Zunz, Zacharias Frankel, Abraham Geiger and Moritz Steinschneider (1816–1907) introduced modern research methods into various spheres of Jewish studies, while Marcus Jost (1793–1860) and Heinrich (Hirsch) Graetz (1817–91) did the same for modern Jewish historiography. Graetz's work *A History of the Jews from Ancient Times to the Present Day* in thirteen volumes (which took him from 1853 to 1876 to complete) was both valuable and influential in Jewish education and, in parts, is significant to this day. All of the above wrote their works in German.

Nachman Krochmal, known by his Hebrew acronym, Ranak (1785–1840) and Solomon Judah Rapoport (Shir, 1790–1867), both from Galicia, were the founders of modern Jewish learning in Hebrew. The former, in his book *Moreh Nevukhei Hazeman* ('A Guide to the Perplexed of the Time'), which was published by Zunz in 1851, evolved a historiosophical method for understanding Jewish history; while the latter, in a series of studies, established his own approach to several chapters of Jewish spiritual life.

The dream of these and other scholars in the field of Jewish studies was to set up special research institutions. Geiger was the first to create a 'scientific theology' for the Jews while striving to establish a department of Jewish theology to be attached to a university, like the existent departments of Christian theology. No such department was created, but rabbinical seminaries were established by several trends of Judaism, which were to serve not merely for the training of rabbis, but also as research institutions. Towards the end of the nineteenth century it was also proposed that an Academy of Jewish Studies be set up. Besides the academic impetus, there were practical aspirations associated with these institutions. Just as Christian faculties of theology were asked to rule on religious problems, so it was now hoped by some of the reformers that the department or academy they hoped to found would serve as a supreme religious authority, with its judgements based on scientific research and commanding wide acceptance.

Reservations Regarding Reform and Rationalism in the West

Even among those influenced by the Enlightenment there were some who expressed reservations about the idea of integration into non-Jewish society and wondered if it were worth the price exacted. Samuel David Luzzatto (Shadal, 1800–65), who greatly admired Jewish tradition and was also influenced by the romantic moods prevailing in European society at the beginning of the nineteenth century, criticized not only the extreme rationalism of the *maskilim* of his day, but also the great mediaeval thinkers, such as Maimonides and Ibn Ezra. In his view, Judaism, which was based on emotion, could not be reconciled with the rationalist elements of Greek culture. He therefore expressed doubts as to the possibility of Jewish integration into the surrounding society and the chance of attaining emancipation at the cost of renouncing Jewish tradition. On the other hand, Luzzatto was willing to agree to slight changes in religious custom; he maintained close contact with the German Jewish scholars, wrote for their publications and, despite all his differences of opinion with them, was closer to the *maskilim* in Central and Eastern Europe than to the traditionalists. His approach reflected the spiritual tradition of the Jewish community of Italy, from which originated in the sixteenth and seventeenth centuries some of the ideas that later became basic tenets of the *Haskalah*.

Another opponent of religious reform was R. Samson Raphael Hirsch (1808–88) the founder and leader of the new orthodoxy in Germany (the Frankfurt style 'neo-Orthodoxy', as it was later called). Despite their differences and the fierce struggle between them, there were certain elements common to both Hirsch and the reformists, as both emerged from the world of the *Haskalah*. Hirsch, like the reformers of his day, believed that the religious ideals of Judaism and of universal ethics were identical. He too favoured emancipation and cultural integration into Christian Europe. The difference with him lay in his view of the Torah and his definition of the mission of the Jew. According to Hirsch, Torah implied observance of all religious injunctions, however small, and the regulations and decisions of Talmudic sages should be treated as if they were part of the law given to Moses on Sinai. The Torah was the essence of Judaism, and it was the task of Judaism to maintain it in its traditional form. He who observed it was the ideal man carrying out the will of Providence.

Although Hirsch recognized the election of Israel, the basis of his belief was not Israel as a nation, but the individual Jew. He offered a solution to Jewish existence under the conditions of emancipation. By observing God's will, by fulfilling his special mission, the Jew would take pride of place in human society. Hirsch attributed spiritual essence not only to the 'Jewish nation' of his day, but he believed that in ancient times Jewish existence had also had only one meaning – its religious mission. Judaism, like the Torah, was not a historical phenomenon but an eternal metaphysical one – hence the clash between his view and the historical approach of the reformists. This belief led Hirsch to call on the faithful to separate themselves from the 'evil flock', and to regard only his supporters, the neo-orthodox, as *Klal Yisrael*, the people of Israel, within Germany, while all other groups were to be classified as dissenters. In actual fact his supporters were a small minority, and they themselves had dissented from the main body of German Jewry.

The Haskalah *in Eastern Europe (Galicia and Russia)*

The *Haskalah* in Galicia was mainly the outcome of the attempt made by Joseph II to influence the way of life of the Jews by official means; for example, by establishing government schools for Jewish boys that helped disseminate a knowledge of German. But active circles of Jewish *maskilim* appeared in this area only at the beginning of the nineteenth century. Even in Russia, where there was no state intervention at the time to stimulate the desire for integration and enlightenment, *maskilim* emerged at the end of the eighteenth century.

The father of the Russian *Haskalah* was R. Isaac Baer Levinsohn ('Rival', 1788–1860), whose book *Te'udah be-Yisrael* ('A Mission in Israel', 1828) advocated changes in Jewish education and contained a compilation of sayings by Talmudic scholars and sages in praise of agricultural work, physical labour and the study of the vernacular. The Russian *maskilim* founded several schools in the 1820s and 1830s (in Warsaw, Uman, Odessa, Kishinev and Riga), in which the language of instruction was German; they also initiated projects for Jewish agricultural settlement.

With regard to their central aims – the dissemination of secular culture among the Jews and the economic and moral reform of the people – there was no difference between the *maskilim* of the East and their Western counterparts. But as a result of contrasting conditions, the way in which the movement spread and the status of the *maskilim* in Jewish society were totally different in the two regions. In Eastern Europe there was no influential social stratum in the Jewish community that aspired to closer contact with the non-Jewish world and culture, as there was in the West. The East European Jewish community was shocked at the slightest deviation from tradition and from accepted patterns of behaviour and thought. Those attracted to the *Haskalah* were few in number and were afraid to undertake any public campaign. In the early stages their one desire was to escape and join the *Haskalah* centre in Berlin. Only those economically and socially independent of the community were in a position to demonstrate openly their attraction to the *Haskalah;* in other words, it was a movement based on the wealthy and their associates. Adherence to the *Haskalah* in Eastern Europe entailed a large degree of detachment from the Jewish community. The latter viewed the spread of the *Haskalah* as a means of abandoning Jewish frameworks, while the *maskilim* saw themselves as persecuted by fanatics – hence, the bitter nature of the struggle over this movement in Eastern Europe.

The difference in the cultural level and in the nature of the Jewish environment in Western and Eastern Europe was also responsible for the weakness of *Haskalah* forces and religious reforms in Eastern Europe, as well as for the vagueness of their aims. The Jew of Eastern Europe did not feel inferior to his environment, as did the Western Jew. The level of education of the peasants and even the townsmen, among whom the Jews of Eastern Europe lived, was low and was not likely to attract the Jew to try and integrate into it. (There were exceptions: the town of Lvov in Galicia had a predominantly German culture, while Warsaw was steeped in Polish culture.) The *Haskalah* influences that infiltrated East European Jewry came from the cultural centres of the West, and above all from Berlin. This heightened the sense of continuity and unity of the *Haskalah* movement throughout Europe, which was generally influenced by the secular German Enlightenment; in fact, the cultural language of most East European *maskilim,* until the 1860s, was German.

Consequently, in its early days, the East European *Haskalah* generally resembled the Berlin *Haskalah*. The *maskilim* wrote in Hebrew, and as the assimilation process of the Jews in the East was very slow, the revived Hebrew culture was not easily supplemented by the language and culture of the environment. Thus the foundations were laid for the growth of a new secular Hebrew literature. Joseph Perl and Isaac Erter in Galicia, Isaac Baer Levinsohn, Abraham Lebensohn (Adam Hacohen), Mordecai Aaron Guenzburg, Abraham Mapu, Judah Leib Gordon (Yalag) and Moses Leib Lilienblum (Malal) in Russia, founded the new Hebrew literature and journalism. This literature was directed not merely at a limited circle of people who were identified with the basic principles of the *Haskalah,* but also at a wider public of Hebrew-readers, including *yeshiva* students.

In their desire to influence the masses, East European *maskilim* also wrote in Yiddish, the folk language to which the Western *maskilim* were fiercely opposed (though several plays were written in Yiddish by the German *maskilim* at the end of the eighteenth century). Israel Axenfeld and Solomon Ettinger, Isaac Joel Linetzky and Shalom Jacob Abramowitsch (Mendele Mokher Seforim) were the fathers of Yiddish literature, the central objective of which was to disseminate *Haskalah* ideals and to expose the defects of Jewish society.

Another distinguishing feature of the *Haskalah* in Eastern Europe was the fact that it did not absorb ideas connected with religious reform. Since the process of assimilation was very gradual, there were no widespread demands for reform for the sake of emulating Christian society. Those individuals who assimilated into the culture of their surroundings generally converted or totally removed themselves from Jewish problems. And even those who doubted the value of tradition did not dare to voice their views openly. Only in the new settlement in the eastern Ukraine and in 'New Russia' (mainly in Odessa) was there evident, at a relatively early period, some relaxation in the observance of religious customs. It is not surprising that the sole voices raised in favour of religious reform – such as those of Joachim Tarnopol in his book *An Attempt at the Contemporary and Cautious Reform of Judaism,* written in Russian, or of Lilienblum in his article *'Orḥot Hatalmud'* ('Ways of the Talmud'), both of which appeared in 1868 – failed to spark off a reform movement. At the end of the 1860s and in the 1870s several Hebrew writers, among them J. L. Gordon, expressed open and savage criticism of blind adherence to tradition.

The fact that the *maskilim* were few in number and their social force was limited hampered them in their battle against the community leaders, particularly the ḥasidic *ẓaddikim*. In order to hold their own in this uneven contest, they were inclined to rely on the authorities and to cooperate with them. They attacked internal Jewish autonomy not only on ideological grounds, but mainly in order to weaken the force of the opposing camp, which ruled the communities.

The fact that the *maskilim* were on the side of the authorities in Russia at a time when children were being conscripted for military service by official decree, aroused doubts in the Jewish mind regarding the loyalty of the *maskilim* to their people. The curtailing of traditional Jewish livelihoods (and above all innkeeping and leasing), which the Jewish community regarded as a harsh decree, was considered by the *maskilim* to be a step towards reconstruction of economic life – even though this did not hinder certain rich Russian Jews, who were also prominent *maskilim,* from operating as lessees of the government brandy monopoly. The tax imposed on the community for maintaining government schools for Jewish children was regarded as an intolerable burden. But it was the rabbinical seminaries set up by the government in Warsaw, Vilna and Zhitomir to train a new generation of teachers – and in which many *maskilim* taught – which constituted overwhelming proof for most Jews of the eventual consequences of *Haskalah* beliefs. Many of the graduates of these seminaries had never intended to serve as rabbis, and quite a few later converted. Bitter criticism was voiced by the *maskilim* themselves against the character of those graduating from these seminaries.

Traditionalists in the East: *Ḥasidism, the Lithuanian* Yeshivot *and the* Musar *Movement*

After the bitter struggle that raged in the East European community at the end of the eighteenth century and in the first years of the nineteenth century between Ḥasidism and its opponents, the two camps began to make peace. The opponents of Ḥasidism (the *mitnagdim*) realized that they did not have the power to uproot this 'sect' and to drive it out of the Jewish community. The death of the Gaon of Vilna deprived East European Jewry of the central personality who had lent the struggle its moral and official sanction and had united all the opponents of Ḥasidism. Furthermore, both camps were shocked at the strengthening of destructive forces, endangering the existence of traditionalist Judaism: the absolutist regimes with their 'reform' decrees from without, and the *maskilim* from within. The conciliation also resulted from the fear that if the authorities recognized the separate existence of the ḥasidic communities, as it had recognized the ḥasidic prayer-house, Jewish internal autonomy would be weakened, and the income of the communities would be affected.

The abatement of the struggle with Ḥasidism weakened cohesion within the ḥasidic movement. There was increased class differentiation within the ḥasidic communities, and a certain social tension was created. The number of *zaddikim* increased, and competition between them became intensified. The dynastic principle prevailed, with the son automatically inheriting his father's function as *zaddik*. The 'courts' began to bicker with one another, and squabbles between the disciples of various *rebbes* became a common phenomenon. But there were also dynasties that became firmly entrenched and had many disciples, since they branched out. For example, the descendants of R. Israel Ruzhin (who was himself the great-grandson of the *Maggid* of Mezhirech) established a large and cohesive network of 'courts', as did the *zaddikim* descended from R. Nahum of Chernobyl, one of the more important disciples of the *Maggid*. In Poland, the court of the Gur *rebbe* was extremely influential.

The *mitnagdim* also found ways of uniting, particularly through the new *yeshivot* (academies for religious study) set up in Lithuania in the nineteenth century. In the past the *yeshiva* had been the school of an important rabbi, and the more renowned he became, the greater the number of young men who flocked to him to study. But this institution was dependent on the personality of the rabbi and had not yet achieved great importance in community life. R. Ḥayyim of Volozhin (1749–1821), the disciple of the Gaon of Vilna, laid the foundation for the new type of *yeshiva*, which was supported not by the community of that town alone, but by many and distant communities. The *yeshiva* enjoyed autonomous status, and within a relatively short period it became a kind of supreme authority for the Jewish community of Lithuania not merely on legislative problems but also with regard to daily life.

Other *yeshivot* sprang up on the Volozhin model, mainly in small towns such as Mir, Telz, Slobodka or Eishishok, and they developed their own systems and way of life, as well as their particular image of the scholar and of the ideals of *yeshiva* study. The *yeshiva boḥer* (student) was evaluated by his diligence and his intellectual grasp in his studies. These *yeshivot* were not schools for rabbis, but a society of students of the Torah, whose graduates were supported financially to serve as an example for all Jews. From these institutions there emerged a new leading stratum for Lithuanian Jewry – the *ba'alei batim* (propertied class), with spiritual proclivities implanted in them in the *yeshivot* – that was capable of standing up to Ḥasidism. Not only did all the great sages of the age such as R. Joseph Feimer (Joseph Slutzker), R. Joseph Baer Soloveichik, R. Naphtali Zevi Judah Berlin (Hanaziv), R. Isaac Elhanan Spektor and others emerge from the *yeshivot*, but under the influence of education in these schools, study of the Torah began to encompass wider sections of the people, and the criteria prevailing in the *yeshivot* also began to be accepted by other sections of the population.

In time, a feeling of crisis gripped the leading social group in Lithuanian Jewry. A keenly critical faculty made itself felt, producing criticism of the values and customs of Jewish life; the emotional forces that Ḥasidism symbolized appealed to the young; embryonic *Haskalah* tendencies broke through here and there, though still in almost clandestine fashion, and were generally opposed. The *musar* (ethics) movement that arose in Lithuania was aimed at bolstering a weakening edifice and fulfilling the needs of the younger generation. Its leader, R. Israel Salanter (1810–83), emphasized the importance of studying ethical matters and fostering the atmosphere and feeling that should envelop all deeds and base them on fervour. While Ḥasidism was rooted in the joy and ardent devotion of the masses, the exponents of *Musar* concentrated on the cohesive quality of sorrow and on the importance of study. The movement was aimed at the general public, and women were also included. For this purpose R. Israel founded the *musar shtibel* ('prayer-house of the *musar* movement') where the believers prayed and studied such literature as Moses Luzzatto's *Mesillat Yesharim* ('The Path of the Upright') and Baḥya ibn Paquda's *Ḥovot Halevavot* ('Duties of the Hearts'). The exponents of *musar* tended to engage in self-examination and to express contempt for 'the vanities of this world'.

The movement did not meet with success among the middle class but was absorbed by several of the Lithuanian *yeshivot*, in which it developed its own specific educational methods and even succeeded in creating its own atmosphere. The *musar* literature was taught in the *yeshivot* with a mournful but fervent intonation. The *mashgi'aḥ* (supervisor) was transformed from an executive official to a moral leader of the *yeshiva* students, taking the place of honour next to the head of the *yeshiva*. The 'talks' of the *mashgi'aḥ* consisted of lessons in religious and ethical behaviour. Prayer was also chanted with the same intonation and fervour. In time members of the movement expressed the view that the study of ethics was more important than Talmud and, as a result, were attacked by several important rabbis.

The Struggle Between the Maskilim and the Traditionalists

As we have noted above, there was a harsh and protacted struggle in Eastern Europe between the great majority of the Jewish public, who were loyal to tradition, and the *maskilim*. It was the *maskilim* who sparked off the controversy, since they regarded the condition of the people as shameful and offensive and sought to rescue it from its degradation. They were confident that they would eventually prevail and that the governments and societies of their countries of residence constituted powerful allies. On the other hand, the weakening of Jewish autonomy discouraged the traditionalists. For generations their authority had been based not only on the authority of Jewish law and the sanctity of its framework but also on the support of the regime for Jewish leadership. This support was now removed to a large extent from them and transferred to the *maskilim* – the 'upstarts'. The traditionalists were depicted by the *maskilim* as stubborn rebels unwilling to cooperate with the authorities in their plans, and the supporters of tradition were generally forced to take up a defensive stand.

The struggle was generally conducted on two planes, the public and political on the one hand, and the ideological and literary on the other. The new Hebrew literature that developed in Galicia was mainly polemical, and anti-ḥasidic satire was very popular among the *maskilim*. Joseph Perl and Isaac Erter each wrote a work that contained savage criticism both of the hypocritical *ẓaddikim* and of the ignorant and exploited masses. Perl helped the Galician authorities to persecute the *ẓaddikim* and to confiscate the ḥasidic literature smuggled in from Russia. The Galician *maskilim* conducted a constant struggle against the 'obscurantists' and against the defects in internal Jewish organization. Isaac Erter and Joshua Heschel Schorr founded the newspaper *Heḥaluẓ* ('The Pioneer'), which was aimed at fighting prejudice and stagnant tradition, daring to criticize even the foundations of Talmudic law. There were various objectives within this circle as well, and there were some *maskilim* in Galicia who were against recruiting the aid of the authorities for the purpose of forcing *Haskalah* on the Jewish masses.

The situation in Russia was similar. R. Isaac Baer Levinsohn wrote a Yiddish satire entitled *Hefker Velt* ('A Lawless World'), which criticized the Jewish community. Many poems by J. L. Gordon and novels by Perez Smolenskin were written in the same spirit. In Yiddish literature the element of social criticism played a particularly important part. But the struggle went beyond mere literary polemics. As we have noted, the authorities consulted some of the *maskilim* and recruited their aid in attempts to change the organization of Jewish life. As early as 1816 David Friedlaender of Germany wrote a special memorandum 'On the Reform of Polish Jewry', in which he proposed the reorganization of Jewish education, the abolition of the community and a campaign against Ḥasidism. When the Russian Government began to execute the above-mentioned plan to open special schools for Jewish children, it consulted Jewish *maskilim* in Germany and placed a German-Jewish *maskil*, Dr Max Lilienthal, at the head of the project. The *Haskalah* circles in Russia hoped that the time had come for them to take their rightful place in Jewish life. The general opposition of the Jewish public to the government's plans aroused the anger of the *maskilim,* and they submitted new coercive schemes to the government.

It was only in the 1870s, when radical trends appeared among the *maskilim* and the number of young Jews engaged in revolutionary activity increased, that conservative Jewish circles in Russia decided that the time had come to make approaches to the authorities. Some of them claimed that only those loyal to Jewish tradition could be regarded as loyal to the government and that the *maskilim* were dangerous. But these attempts did not alter the basic attitude of the government towards conservative Jewish circles, and the rift between the various camps in Russian Jewry intensified.

The Beginnings of National and Social Radicalism in the East

At the end of the 1860s and in the 1870s, many of the *maskilim* in the East began to display a certain amount of disillusionment with the ideals of *Haskalah*. Many of the active members of the movement who had taken as their slogan 'Be a man in the street and a Jew in your own home' discovered that the idea was not feasible. The young people who had been brought up in the spirit of the *Haskalah,* on which the old generation of *maskilim* pinned their hopes for the moral and cultural renaissance of the people, chose the path of assimilation, detaching themselves from the sufferings of the people and from its age-old traditions. The *maskilim* now asked themselves in despair whether all their efforts had been in vain and began to comprehend that slogans alone could not solve the problems of the people they wished to lead. In 1862 Moses Hess, one of the more important German socialists, drew up a plan for the political and national renaissance of the Jews in their ancient homeland. His book on this subject bore the title *Rome and Jerusalem.* He regarded France as the loyal ally of the Jewish people in this project. But in the same years a number of orthodox rabbis, such as Zevi Hirsch Kalischer, Judah Alkalai and Joseph Natonek, proposed similar plans, and David Gordon propagated them in his periodical *Hamaggid*.

There were also those, like Perez Smolenskin (1842–85), who began to criticize the very ideological foundations of the *Haskalah*. Smolenskin attacked Mendelssohn, the Berlin *Haskalah* and all those who regarded the Jews as merely a religious sect, denying their national element. He himself regarded the Jews as a nation – its distinguishing features concentrated in the spiritual sphere – whose foundations were the Hebrew language and messianic hopes. Those denying the national spirit of

Judaism were denying and betraying their own people. In 1868 Smolenskin founded the journal *Hashaḥar* ('The Dawn'), in which he conducted a campaign on two fronts: against the conservative obscurantists and against those *maskilim* who rejected the traditions of their forefathers.

In these same years a new group appeared among the Russian *maskilim* (influenced by the radical Russian writers such as Chernishevsky and Pisarev) that began attacking *Haskalah* literature for its detachment from the true problems of life. Instead of preoccupying itself with casuistic hair-splitting over words and literary forms, they claimed literature should instruct readers in materialistic thought and social utilitarianism. It should explain that knowledge of the sciences was important, while all Jewish studies were worthless. Proponents of this view included Abraham Uri Kovner in the sixties, and Moses Leib Lilienblum and Judah Leib Levin (Yahalal) in the seventies. The two latter were attracted to the socialist ideas that began to spread among Jewish youth during those years.

Jewish socialist circles first emerged in Russia among students of the rabbinical seminary in Vilna in the 1870s. Aaron Samuel Liebermann (1845–80), who was later known as the 'father of Jewish socialism', was connected with these groups. When he was forced to flee from Russia (1875), Liebermann founded, together with several other Jewish emigrants, the Hebrew Socialists Society in London (1876) in order to 'disseminate knowledge of socialism among the Jews wherever they may reside . . . ' He published a pamphlet addressed to 'The Young Men of Israel', which was directed against those *maskilim* who cooperated with the government. In 1877 Liebermann founded in Vienna the first Jewish socialist paper in Hebrew, *Ha'emet* ('The Truth'). This paper was filled with criticism of *Haskalah* literature for its detachment from life. The paper closed down in the same year, after only three issues had appeared. Liebermann's work was carried on by Morris Vinchevsky (Ben Netz), who published a Hebrew socialist journal, *Asefat Ḥakhamim* ('Assembly of the Wise'), in 1878.

Those who were attracted to national or social radicalism in the seventies were few in number, but they were the forerunners of the great revival that was to encompass the entire Jewish community of Eastern Europe in the 1880s.

53

The New Patterns of Jewish Organization in the West in the Nineteenth Century

Under the influence of the assimilatory tendency, the outlook and the activities of the reform movement, Jews in the West gradually began to believe that there was no longer a single Jewish nation. They reasoned that Jews in various countries were linked solely by origin and religion and that the importance of these ties was waning. The accepted claim in these circles was that in order to adapt himself to the modern state and society the Jew ought to become a Frenchman or a Pole 'of the Mosaic persuasion'. Furthermore, they believed that the social processes in Europe at large would inevitably lead to an undermining of the national element in Judaism, as nationality was based primarily on culture and affiliation, and, in their opinion, for the Jewish individual, these two elements were associated with his environment and his country of residence. But at that same time, as we have noted, there began to appear in Jewish society the first signs of the strengthening of communal awareness and of the crystallizing of solidarity between Jewish groups in different countries. The clearest expression of this consolidation was the awakening of European Jewry at the time of the Damascus blood libel. From 1840 onwards the old and the new were intermingled, remoulding the cells and patterns of leadership: in Jewish society in this period, self-proclaimed assimilationists sometimes served as the leaders and servants of the newly reunited Jewish community.

The Influence of the Damascus Libel

In 1840 a Capuchin monk in Damascus vanished without a trace. His fellow monks spread a rumour that he had been murdered by Jews as part of their religious ritual. The French Consul in Damascus tried to exploit the affair in order to consolidate French influence in the Levant, particularly in the light of the conquests of the Egyptian ruler Mohammed Ali, and did everything possible to ensure that the investigation would rely heavily on the monks' charges; in other words, he helped foster the charge. Several Jews were arrested by the authorities and cruelly tortured. One of them 'confessed' and pointed to seven community notables as planners of the murder. On the basis of this 'confession' many members of the community were arrested, and, after torture, several confessed, one died of his injuries, and another converted. The French Government expressed its support for its representatives in the East. When Crémieux submitted a question on this affair to French Premier Thiers (the historian), the latter evaded the issue. On the other hand, several statesmen in England and Austria came to the defence of the Jews and tried to exert pressure on Mohammed Ali to release the prisoners; but the French Consul-General in Alexandria persuaded him not to succumb to the pressure of the Great Powers. When it transpired that the authorities had no intention of investigating the true reasons for the Damascus murder or of conducting an open trial for the arrested Jews, a Jewish delegation composed of Montefiore, Crémieux and the well-known orientalist Solomon Munk left for Egypt to appeal to the authorities there. European public opinion also protested on behalf of the victims, and under this pressure Mohammed Ali was obliged to release the prisoners.

The Jewish reaction to the Damascus affair is justifiably regarded as a turning-point in the history of Western Jewry in the nineteenth century. On the one hand, many Jews became aware of the deep-rooted hostility of the Catholic Church towards them, to the point where it was willing to employ measures such as blood libels. Furthermore, even a government that had proclaimed Jewish equality, and even implemented it to a large extent, proved willing to support a blood libel merely because it believed that this might further its political aims overseas. On the other hand, the weight and force of Jewish solidarity were revealed: Crémieux, who was steeped in French culture and had begun to make a name for himself in political life – and whose identification with France was not open to question – regarded it as his obligation to come out against the policy of his government. He even took part in a Jewish delegation that acted on behalf of general Jewish interests, even though it included Jews from countries with which French relations at the time were not particularly cordial.

From the time of the Damascus Affair it became clear that there existed such a thing as European Jewish opinion, which was ready to raise its voice against an attack on Jews anywhere. Despite their cultural and national integration, the bonds of unity and mutual responsibility among Jewish communities had not weakened; the ties between them had merely taken on new form. Yet, other trends, opposed to the concept of Jews as a single community, also began to spread and grow stronger at this time among European Jews. This is attested to by the letter of the young Abraham Geiger to his friend Derenburg in reaction to the departure of the Jewish delegation for Egypt. His attitude towards the delegation was negative. He regarded it as a relic of an emotional approach that was not suited to new conditions.

> For me it is more important that Jews be able to work in Prussia as pharmacists or lawyers than that the entire Jewish population of Asia and Africa be saved, although as a human being I sympathize with them.

It is possible that much of the concern of the Jews of Central and Western Europe for their brethren in the East emanated from their realization that as long as the 'Jewish question' existed, even in some remote location, they could not be sure of their own total integration into their surroundings. This induced many of them to become active for the dissemination of education among their brethren in the East, to fight for their rights, for the changing of their means of livelihood and even for their emigration. There were some among them who connected this philanthropic activity with the hope that if the image of Eastern Jews were altered, hostility and opposition towards the Jews of Europe would disappear. But whatever the motives of the renewed expressions of solidarity – whether positive, through a sense of identification with the sufferings and hopes of Jews everywhere, or negative, through a desire to eradicate the stereotype image of the Jew in order to avoid reminding the non-Jewish world of the origin and identity of the candidate for assimilation – the result was the weakening of the trend towards detachment from Jewish affairs and the strengthening of cohesive and unifying factors, as well as the substitution of new forms of Jewish contact for the old ones. This last development made itself felt in the changing forms of Jewish organization in the nineteenth century.

The Press as a Unifying Factor

The Jewish press played a role of paramount importance in the strengthening of ties between Jewish communities in the various countries from the 1830s onwards. It conveyed information on the Jewish situation and directed the attention of the Jewish public to general Jewish problems. This press appeared in the West in the languages of the various countries – German, French, English and Dutch – and everywhere served as evidence of the cultural integration of the Jews and their allegiance to the countries of their residence. The most influential papers were *Allgemeine Zeitung des Judentums* in Germany and *The Jewish Chronicle* in London. In contrast, the press in Eastern Europe was mostly Hebrew and was attached to a declared objective (as attested to by the sub-heading of *Hameliz*) of being 'the mediator between the people of Jeshurun [*i.e.*, Israel] and the government, between faith and the *Haskalah*'. In other words, it had taken as its aim to influence the Jewish public in the spirit of moderate *Haskalah* and to cooperate with the authorities. The most important papers in Hebrew were *Hamaggid,* founded in 1856 in Lyck, Prussia, *Hameliz* of Odessa and *Hacarmel* of Vilna, both established in 1860, and *Hazefirah,* founded in 1862 in Warsaw.

The Damascus Affair aroused the Jewish press to an extensive discussion of general Jewish problems, and this issue continued to remain alive even after the incident. The French-language weekly *Archives Israélites,* which began to appear in Paris in 1840, preached the establishment of a society for the dissemination of *Haskalah*. In 1853 it proposed for the first time that a Jewish congress of representatives from all countries be convened in France in order to discuss general Jewish problems.

International Jewish Organizations

The strongest impetus for international Jewish organization was provided by the Mortara affair in 1858, the kidnapping of a six-year-old Jewish child from the home of his parents in Bologna by the Papal guard (see page 811). In reaction to this terrible affair it was claimed that against the tyranny of the Pope 'Jewish civilization should also found its own parliament here [in Paris] to discuss its reactions.'

In May 1860 a group of Jews convened in Paris and appealed to world Jewry to organize a worldwide alliance with the aim of defending Jewish honour, encouraging physical labour, opposing ignorance and prejudice, striving towards Jewish emancipation and its consolidation through the moral and spiritual improvement of the Jews. To the query why there was a need for a separate Jewish alliance, the organizers replied that each great religion, with the exception of Judaism, had government or state representation: 'Judaism is a word and a banner which, from the moral point of view, unites millions of human beings scattered all over the world.'

The association that was established was called the Alliance Israélite Universelle, and its slogan was the Talmudic expression 'All Israel is responsible one for the other.' Several hundred Jews from France and other countries, as well as some non-Jews, responded to the call of the founders. The Alliance immediately re-opened the Mortara case and began to act against discrimination of Jews in Switzerland and Rumania. It also endeavoured to arouse the Great Powers to intervene in Rumania when riots again broke out at the end of the sixties (see page 823). In addition, the Alliance Israélite soon began to establish schools, particularly in various parts of the Ottoman Empire. It began to publish information on the state of the Jews in various countries and to grant aid to immigrants and to agricultural settlements. Within the framework of this activity, Charles Netter founded the Alliance Israélite agricultural school, Mikveh Yisrael, in Palestine in 1870.

But the Jews soon displayed a tendency to transfer Jewish activity from general international frameworks to centres of Jewish organization within each country. This was mainly motivated by the anti-Semitic slander campaign that nicknamed the Alliance Israélite 'the world Jewish government', 'the world *kahal*', etc. The war between Prussia and France in 1870, which intensified the difference between the powers and discouraged the tendency of public opinion to support European unity, also hindered cooperation between the Jews of hostile countries. The Alliance Israélite's international character was naturally also affected. In 1871 the Anglo-Jewish Association, known in Hebrew as Agudat Aḥim (Association of Brothers), began to operate in England, and in 1873 the Viennese Israelitische Allianz zu Wien was organized. These associations operated in the spirit of the original Alliance and in close cooperation with it.

An outstanding example of the all-Jewish cooperation of national organizational frameworks in the spirit of the Alliance Israélite was the activity of the Jewish delegation during the Berlin Congress; it was organized on the initiative of the Alliance Israélite, submitted a memorandum to the representatives of the participating states and played an important part in obtaining the inclusion of a clause in the peace treaty with the new Balkan states ensuring equal rights to Jews. When the Rumanian Government violated the treaty, the Jewish organizations resorted once more to extensive diplomatic activity to persuade the Great Powers to exert pressure on the Rumanian Government to implement the clause and grant equal rights to its Jews.

The Changes in Community Organization

The old corporative forms of community organization began to disintegrate in Western and Central Europe in the eighteenth century. The *maskilim* claimed that they should be replaced by free and voluntary association for the purpose of communal worship. This view, which was accepted in several circles, did not really affect the form of community organization in most countries of Europe. Of greater importance was the centralized-hierarchical consistory system that Napoleon introduced in France and that was totally opposed to these voluntaristic trends. This example influenced countries such as Holland, Belgium and several southern German states, and deterred still other governments from introducing far-reaching changes in Jewish community organization.

Nevertheless, the process of Jews integrating into the gentile environment led to the weakening of the community's influence over them and their lives. The gravest consequence, from the point of view of internal Jewish organization, was the fact that active and 'enlightened' elements in Jewish society no longer displayed any interest in community life but devoted their energies and aspirations to attaining status and honours outside the Jewish environment. Thus, in the first half of the nineteenth century, the community began to lose its importance, without losing its powers.

The activities of the religious reformers aroused renewed interest in community life. They even succeeded in bringing some of the more indifferent *maskilim* close to Jewish events and developments. The disillusionment of the latter with the aloofness of the non-Jewish world and its unwillingness to absorb them also had an effect. The reform and liberal communities now became the most active in this sphere, while orthodox elements, which were on the defensive, began to seek a separate organizational form, suited to their needs. Thus the conservative trends utilized modern, libertarian principles for the establishment of separate organizational cells, while the forces of innovation, which were sometimes secular by nature, made a perceptible contribution to the reconstitution of unity and cohesion.

A characteristic example of this development was the organization of the Hungarian community. On the initiative of the reformists (and with the support of the Minister of Religion), a general Jewish congress was convened in 1868 in order to entrust the community leadership to the reform wing. The orthodox element thereupon established an association of Shomrei Dat (Guardians of Religion), and it was they who now spoke in the name of freedom of conscience and the right of the individual to belong to whichever community he preferred. The regime accepted this principle, and the Hungarian communities were split almost everywhere into orthodox and neological. The divided communities were united only by their trend into national associations, which, in many ways, constituted a cohesive force in Jewish life.

A similar situation was created in Germany. When the *Kulturkampf* broke out there between Bismarck's government and the Catholics, the orthodox leader Samson Raphael Hirsch joined forces with the liberal Jewish statesman Eduard Lasker and they succeeded, in 1876, in bringing about legislation permitting Jews to leave the community without abandoning the Jewish religion. This sanction of division led to the creation of separate orthodox communities in Germany.

In those countries that had followed the French example there was also change. In Holland, the Supreme Church Council, which had operated on a centralized basis, was abolished in 1848, and in 1870 an inter-community co-ordinating committee, representing all the communities in their dealings with the authorities, was established. A similar situation was arrived at – though through different means – in those countries, like the United States and Britain, where affiliation to the community framework was free and voluntary from the outset. In England, representatives of the community had met regularly from the eighteenth century onwards, and in time a permanent representative body, the Board of Deputies, was established. When Moses Montefiore was elected president of the Board (1835) it began also to represent Jews throughout the Empire and to act on behalf of Jews all over the world. But in Britain as well, the communities organized themselves by religious affiliation. At the end of the 1860s the great majority of the synagogues in London joined the orthodox United Synagogue organization, under the jurisdiction of the Chief Rabbi, while the reform and Sephardi synagogues remained outside this framework.

In the United States there was no community organization in the traditional sense of the word, and the synagogues were headed not by rabbis but by cantors, few of whom were learned men. It is not, therefore, surprising that the first Jewish organization there was created not in the religious but in the social sphere. In 1843 the B'nai B'rith order was founded in New York on the Freemason model; its objective was to foster moral conduct and fraternity among Jews. In fact, it was an organization based on mutual aid and solidarity – a particularly important institution in a country of immigration; it developed rapidly, and in the 1880s it began to open lodges outside the United States. Under the impact of the Mortara affair, a community organization was established in 1859 in the United States, which resembled the British Board of Deputies. This organization was known as the Board of Delegates of American Israelites and was active, together with other Jewish organizations, in various countries on behalf of the Jews of Russia, the Orient, the Balkans and Switzerland. When community organizations in the United States began to be established according to religious trend, the Board of Delegates was absorbed into the reform movement.

Developments within the Jewish communities of Western and Central Europe brought about an increasing breach between the Jewish belief that their main loyalty belonged to the countries and nations among whom they lived and the political and social realities that impelled them to act as part of a larger Jewish entity in order to defend Jewish interests. It transpired, in due course, that the nuclei of activists contained the force that was to counter-balance assimilatory tendencies. But the innate contradiction between belief and reality did not emerge in all its severity until the 1880s. New forces, which began to operate in European and in Jewish society at the end of the seventies and the beginning of the eighties, highlighted this contrast, brought it to the attention of wider Jewish circles and thus ushered in a new era in modern Jewish history.

54

The Failure of Emancipation, the Struggle for Survival and National Rebirth (1881–1948)

New Trends in Jewish History

There has been no more dramatic period in Jewish history than the years between 1881 and 1948 – a relatively short span of time when measured against the annals of a nation. During those years the Jewish people underwent enormous changes and agonizing tribulations, yet, at the same time, manifested an extraordinary vitality. The threat to the very survival of the people had never been as great as it was in the 1930s and 1940s; but in no earlier period, not even during the Hasmonean Rebellion, had so many Jews been ready to engage in a social and political struggle to ensure that they – and they alone – would remain the arbiters of their own fate and that of their brethren. This heightened awareness, coupled with the improved methods of communication and transport (which ensured the swift spread of information and a knowledge of the intensity of the struggle), produced a supreme example of Jewish unity in thought and deed. In contrast to the lengthy tradition developed during the Middle Ages to divert the resentment of alien rule and the sufferings of the Diaspora into the inner world of the spirit and abstain from political activism (a tradition only interrupted by infrequent messianic movements), mighty forces now awoke in the people. These forces, operating at a social and political level, transformed a scattered, divided and mortally wounded people from a passive entity into an active and independent political and social force.

At the beginning of this period the majority of the Jewish people still lived within the traditional frameworks and maintained their historical way of life. Relatively few had drawn close to the European environment, had become acquainted with its culture and values or had sought to be accepted within them. Even these few, who served as an example and ideal for many others and were eventually to be imitated by them, were still, in the main, proud of their origin and of the contribution the Jewish people had made to human culture. At the same time they were unanimous in their view of the future: the Jews were destined to be assimilated into European culture and to be included unreservedly within the national frameworks of the gentile world – except perhaps in matters of religion and morality, where the Jews had a unique mission to fulfil as a separate group. Almost all of them realized, however, that the road to integration would not be smooth and that many obstacles lay in the path. The benighted clergy, traditional enemies of the Jews, continued to incite

853

their people against them; there was still an ignorant, prejudiced mob ready to attack the Jews at the word of any rabble-rouser. Certain governments continued to discriminate against the Jews at the urging of hostile groups, or in order to distract the attention of the mob to a convenient and acceptable target; there were still hesitant liberals, who advocated half-measures and secretly feared Jewish competition – or, as they termed it, 'Jewish domination' – and who laid down rigorous conditions for the acceptance of Jews in the nation. There were, in fact, certain conditions that Jewish supporters of assimilation could have accepted and justified, such as the abolition of all religious injunctions, which created 'Jewish separatism'; but they could not accept the demand for identification with the national and religious myths of European nations in place of the ideal of a universal rationalist society, the dream of those eighteenth-century philosophers who had been the spiritual mentors of the Jewish *maskilim*. Many gentile radicals still insisted on regarding all Jews as capitalist exploiters and Judaism itself as the lowest grade of human culture, a relic of barbaric worship and materialistic 'egoism'. They claimed that as long as the individual of Jewish origin failed to reject his shameful heritage he was not worthy of being regarded as a member of progressive society. Despite these reservations and obstacles, it appeared to these few Jews that human society was progressing towards salvation and liberation; and all the *maskilim,* identifying completely with the great ideal of a free and enlightened society, were firm in their belief that no force could resist the triumphant march of progress.

The situation was totally different at the end of this sixty-year period. The developments that eventually led to the Holocaust not only changed the physical, geographical and social status of the Jewish people, but also revolutionized their Jewish consciousness, creating a profound psychological metamorphosis that led large sections of the people to self-reckoning and to consequent ideological change. The belief in progress, in the benevolence of nations, in Christian and humanistic tradition was shattered. All nations had failed to save helpless millions from extermination, nor did they – neither during the years of catastrophe nor later – make the denunciation of mass-murder and genocide a central theme in their education. Rather, they frequently turned a blind eye to the terrible suffering of the Jews or hushed it up. The few heartwarming examples of assistance and sacrifice only served to emphasize the general disregard, the blank wall of rejection and hostility that the Jews encountered almost everywhere that the Nazi conquerors and their allies trod. The gates of all countries were locked and barred when the great wave of Jewish refugees began to flow across Europe in the 1930s, and they remained closed in the terrible days of liquidation of the ghettos, of extermination camps and of ramshackle rescue ships foundering in the depths of the sea.

The Soviet Union, which had created a powerful partisan movement behind the frontlines, was 'unable' to come to the aid of the ghetto fighters nor even to restrain the rampant anti-Semitism in partisan units – which, in turn, not only failed to rescue those Jews who faced extermination, but even attacked Jewish units or 'family camps' in the forests. Great Britain, which incessantly bombed enemy soil, was 'unable' to bomb the death camps and the railway tracks leading to them. America, for all its mighty influence in many parts of the globe, was 'unable' to exert itself in order to open the gates of Palestine to the persecuted Jews or to find them a place of refuge.

The reason for all these omissions was the fear that open support for the suffering Jews would arouse latent, or even overt, anti-Semitism in the particular countries or harm their interests in the Arab world or elsewhere. This development demonstrated the truth of the claim that had been voiced for some time by Jewish nationalist, and even socialist, circles – namely, that as soon as problems arose, the first thing liberals or radicals would be ready to sacrifice were the special interests of the Jews. Therefore there was a need for an independent Jewish policy to safeguard Jewish interests. This explains why the Jewish community of Palestine (the Yishuv), which at the time of Hitler's coming to power in Germany consisted of some 200,000 people and whose political situation was precarious, absorbed more victims of persecution than the United States of America.

What were the factors that strengthened and intensified the change in the situation and beliefs of the Jews during this period? There can be no doubt that the willingness of the non-Jewish world to absorb Jews was considerably limited from the beginning. Individual *maskilim* or those wealthy Jews who had advocated a total rejection of the historical heritage of their people naturally succeeded in completely assimilating into the corresponding strata of Christian society; but for the Jewish community as a whole this was not a solution. The great majority of Jews diligently strove to preserve their national character, their way of life, religion and customs, and this struggle naturally hindered their acceptance into the alien environment, which was for the most part unwilling to absorb those Jews who continued to maintain their distinctive traits. Particularly intense – and steadily growing – was the opposition of the European middle classes. These townsmen had been the enemies and competitors of the Jews for generations. As the Jews drew closer to the culture and customs of the Christian environment, as they began to resemble other town-dwellers in their way of life and sources of livelihood, the areas of contact and friction increased and the old tension was naturally aggravated. The friction was intensified by the natural increase of the Jews: from 7.5 million at the beginning of the 1880s to 11 million at the beginning of the twentieth century, and more than 16.5 million at the outbreak of the Second World War. The same effect was achieved by the great westward movement of the Jews and their concentration in large population centres. Hundreds of thousands – even millions – emigrated, mainly from Eastern Europe overseas or to the west of the continent, where they clustered in the large cities, the important centres of economic and cultural life. Thus their singular qualities, the result of a different historical development, were particularly highlighted.

The peculiar Jewish ability to adapt to alien surroundings operated in two opposing directions. With astounding rapidity the Jews acquired the languages of their countries of residence, penetrated into the gentile culture, adopted its national aspirations and even its values. This helped them to attain cultural and social significance and led to extensive economic, cultural and even political activity, as European society was then based on principles of equal rights and equality of opportunity. But most European countries – although they resigned themselves to Jewish integration, whether on principle or in order to utilize the Jews' abilities in various spheres – reacted with anger and hostility towards those Jews who achieved distinction and to the Jewish demand for a status commensurate with their abilities. Such reservation and suspicion led many non-Jews to discern special communal Jewish characteristics even in those areas in which the Jews themselves had ceased sensing any difference between themselves and their surroundings. As a result of this tendency normal competition between merchants, bankers or journalists (most of whom were, of course, non-Jewish) was depicted with 'scientific' generalization as a struggle for survival and a battle for power between 'the Jews' and 'the basic population'. The personal problems encountered by non-Jews in their professions were explained as created by 'Jewish domination'. Once again the European public became sensitive to the image of the alien and hostile Jew, an image that successfully served as the basis for various ideologies aimed at resisting 'the Jewish threat'.

An additional factor in the deterioration of the non-Jewish attitude towards the Jews was the extensive and vigorous activities of the Jews themselves on behalf of their own integration and rights. Jewish associations were established for the dissemination of education to help students acquire the indigenous culture; Jewish organizations appeared to combat anti-Semitism and discrimination, and they fought for the attainment of full integration into the political, social and cultural life of the majority group. There can be no doubt that these societies and organizations came close to achieving their declared aim. But the very fact of their separate framework and their activities on behalf of a specifically Jewish aim – even if this aim was to eradicate all that set them apart – aroused non-Jewish suspicions as to their true objective, as well as strengthening their awareness of Jewish common interests and the contacts Jews maintained among themselves. Thus we find that the deliberate efforts of the Jews on behalf of their integration and the eradication of their specific group characteristic actually strengthened this singularity and fostered a sense of Jewish solidarity. In short, the strong desire of the Jews to assimilate, their energetic activity in this direction and their partial success were among the main factors that aroused Europe to reject them and set them apart.

Among the Jews themselves very few were clearly aware, at the beginning of this period, of the acute changes that had occurred in the attitude of the society around them and of the dangers this entailed. The majority still hoped for equality before the law, which they regarded as the main source of their security and status. For hundreds of years they had evolved the concept, accepted by enlightened Europeans, that their special status was the result of discriminatory laws and regulations, which had set them apart from the rest of the population. It was therefore customary throughout the nineteenth century to regard the 'Jewish question', *i.e.,* the discussion of the place of the Jews in the state and in society, as a basically legal problem and as a matter of juridical definitions and administrative regulations, and it was not realized that this 'question' was gradually moving from the formal, legal realm to the social and psychological sphere. In any case, it was difficult for the great majority to conceive that this same problem might become gravest within the framework of those very countries that had declared the equality of all citizens before the law.

The few who first sensed this began to offer various solutions to the Jewish question in a nationalistic spirit: there were those who proposed autonomous status for the Jews, mainly in multi-national countries; there were those who searched for a 'country of their own' for the Jews, in which they could establish their own state and develop their own particular culture; others dreamed of the renaissance of the Jews in the land of their fathers, which would constitute a haven, a spiritual centre for the Diaspora, or an independent Jewish state with its people 'a nation like all other nations'. The anomalies and difficulties of Jewish existence within the countries of Europe gradually led to the consolidation of a clear national consciousness in large sections of the Jewish people. Its main objective was twofold, and at times even self-contradictory: on the one hand it was reflected in the revolt against the historical traditions of the people, abhorrence of its restrictive and debasing 'Diaspora' forms and in the desire to replace it by a new national culture, suited to modern conditions; on the other hand it found expression in the desire to elevate this historical tradition, to revive it in various spheres and to bestow upon it new significance.

The process of intensification of anti-Jewish feeling and the desire of considerable sections of European society to reject the Jews was more rapid than the process of consolidating independent national consciousness, particularly against the background of the great upheavals that European society experienced in the twentieth century. One of the main reasons that so large a number of young Jews and of Jewish intellectuals took an active part in socialist and communist revolutionary movements lay in their hope that a basic change in the form of European society and a reform of its fundamental defects would pave the way to the removal of obstacles dividing Jews from non-Jews. In other words, they advocated the solution of the Jewish problem through their integration into the free and enlightened society that would be created through the longed-for revolution, rather than through the difficult method of removing obstacles in an old and conservative society, and rather than proposing national renaissance, which appeared utopian and fanciful.

Those who aspired to an ideal society and were ready to offer up any sacrifice in order to obtain it, those who believed that this would redeem mankind of all its flaws, including the curse of the 'Jewish question', were due to be bitterly disappointed. It was not only in Germany, the bulwark of European socialism, that a considerable portion of the working class – the force that was supposed to carry out the changes – in fact supported Hitler and his anti-Semitic schemes; in the Soviet Union, which advocated socialism as a political and social way of life, official anti-Semitism appeared towards the end of Stalin's life, and, as a result, the remnants of Jewish culture in that country were eradicated. Jewish writers, artists and public figures were exterminated, and barbaric plans were drawn up for the expulsion of all Russian Jews to Siberia.

However, not only the Jews were stunned by the Holocaust and the revival of anti-Semitism. The unbearable sufferings of the Jewish people during the Second World War and the masses of Jewish displaced persons who wandered over Europe moved world public opinion. The indifference towards the fate of the Jews and their abandonment during the war and in the years when the Nazis were coming to power, served to many as a lesson and as proof that the Jewish question called for a radical solution. Many nations concurred with the proposal that an independent Jewish state be established in Palestine and gave it their support. After the establishment of the State of Israel, Jews from most of the countries that had been under Nazi rule, with the exception of the Soviet Union, emigrated to the new state. Europe, in which the great majority of the Jewish people had lived before the Holocaust, ceased to be the greatest Jewish centre, although there are still considerable numbers of Jews in the Soviet Union, France and England. The importance of the State of Israel as a Jewish centre and a focus of Jewish activity far exceeded the relative size of its population within the total world Jewish population.

Simultaneously with the political and territorial transformations there also occurred a far-reaching change in the function of the Jews in their non-Jewish surroundings. In the period of the rise and flowering of capitalism, European society had needed the financial experience of the Jews, their initiative and economic inventiveness. In modern society, based on industrial development and high technological standards, there was a growing need for new scientific forces and intellectual abilities. Thus academic institutions were opened to Jews, and all at once (or so it seemed), the Jews attained importance in science and technology, literature and art. Despite the tremendous difference in political structure, social order and cultural traditions between the United States and the Soviet Union, the Jews were enabled in both countries to achieve in very large numbers status and influence in scientific and cultural pursuits. But here too there was no guarantee that this was the way to peaceful integration. It was no longer impossible that this hope even concealed a future threat.

In its day, Nazism deposed the Jews from all their positions in the academic world, in scientific institutions, hospitals and theatres. In the preceding centuries there had also been states and rulers who courted the Jews and exploited them for their own needs – opened up before them possibilities of extensive activity in periods of expansion and then rejected them, and even persecuted and expelled them, at times of regression and crisis, after they had completed what had been expected of them. One of the basic aims of the prophets and founders of the independent Jewish state was to create new political and social conditions through which the Jewish people could develop their national culture without interruption and, at the same time, make their own particular contribution to world culture without ever being forced to hear the slogan 'The Jew has done his work, the Jew may go' disguised under the pretext that this same Jew was a 'Bolshevik' or 'homeless cosmopolitan', a plotter for 'international domination' or a dangerous visionary.

The establishment of the State of Israel, and the ways in which the Jewish people have fashioned their spiritual and social image within it, is an example of a rare realization of a utopian vision in human history. It is possible that its existence is not only a vital need for the Jews but also a bold historical experience that offers hope for all mankind, in that it is proof that noble aspirations can be realized in relations between human beings and not only with regard to natural forces. Furthermore, there can be no doubt that the establishment of the State of Israel ushered in a new era in the history of the Jewish people.

55

Demographic Changes and Economic Activity at the End of the Nineteenth and Beginning of the Twentieth Centuries

Natural Increase and Its Effect

From the beginning of the 1880s and up to the outbreak of the First World War – a period of some thirty-five years – the natural increase of the Jews was higher than in any other period and reached nearly 2% annually. This was comparable to the most fertile of European nations and well above the European average. At the beginning of this period there were 7.5 million Jews in the world and at its end more than thirteen million. In other words, the Jewish people almost doubled their number in less than half a century.

In this period the East European custom of marrying off young boys at a tender age no longer existed; a very small percentage of men married under the age of twenty. Nor were the Jews distinguished by a particularly high rate of fertility (in the number of live births); the high rate of increase was largely the result of the low death-rate, particularly among babies in the first year of life. Thus, for example, in European Russia (not including Poland) the population movement (per 1,000 souls) was as follows in 1904:

	Births	Deaths	Increase
Jews	30.2	14.2	16.0
Russian Orthodox	51.7	31.8	19.9
Catholics	35.8	21.9	13.9
Moslems	44.0	30.6	13.4
Protestants	25.9	15.3	10.6

The death-rate for children under the age of one year was 40% among the general population and less than 25% among the Jews. Only at the end of the period was there a gradual decrease in the number of births among the Jews, on the one hand, and a decrease in the death-rate of the general population on the other, and both together reduced the Jewish rate of increase and the proportion of Jews in the general population.

The difference in demographic development between the Jews of the East and the West is particularly noticeable in this period. Jewish increase in Prussia in the last years of the nineteenth century was 0.8%, while in European Russia it totalled 1.7%, and in Galicia some 2%. At the end of the period the natural increase of East European Jews was three to four times higher than that of the veteran Jewish residents of Central and Western Europe. This was manifested in the age composition of Jewish communities in Western Europe, as there was an increase in the percentage of the middle-aged and old. In immigrant centres in the West the situation was different: in London, at the beginning of the twentieth century, there was an annual 3% growth among Jewish immigrants, and in several cities in the United States the rate was even higher.

Mixed marriages also accentuated the difference between East and West European Jews. In the years 1908–12, the percentage of mixed marriages among French Jews was 6.54%, among the Jews of Germany 5.16% and among Dutch Jews 4%, as against 0.8% among Rumanian Jews, 0.62% among Russian Jews and 0.45% among Turkish Jews. This situation also affected natural increase: mixed marriages are generally characterized by a low fertility rate and only a very small percentage of the descendants of these marriages identify themselves with the Jewish people.

This relative decline of the Jewish population of the West could not affect the demographic development of the Jewish people as a whole, since the great majority of the people lived in the East European communities and the immigrant concentrations in the United States. At the end of the period under consideration, namely at the outbreak of the First World War, there were some 5.5 million Jews in the Russian Empire, more than 2.5 million in the Austro-Hungarian Empire, 2.5 million in the United States and some 300,000 in Rumania. All in all, in these four centres – three of them in Eastern Europe and the fourth composed of immigrants from the other three – there were some 11 million Jews. On the other hand, there were some 600,000 Jews in Germany, 250,000 in England, 100,000 each in Holland and France, and some 45,000 in Italy – altogether slightly more than one million Jews in Western Europe. The natural increase of the Jews of the Near East and North Africa, who then totalled some 800,000, was still limited because of the high death-rate, but was also higher than that of Western Europe.

Migration as a Decisive Factor in Jewish Life

One of the fundamental changes in Jewish life in the period under review was the enormous movement, mainly from Eastern to Western Europe and overseas, and above all to the United States of America. This migration was the consequence of demographic, economic and political developments. The high rate of natural increase created population surpluses that could not be absorbed in the traditional Jewish occupations. Capitalist development, which commenced at a rapid pace in Russia after the liberation of the serfs in 1861, and also reached Galicia and Austria at about the same time, opened up new sources of livelihood for a small number of Jews, but caused deprivation to greater numbers, as it had eradicated many of the traditional occupations. This development was exacerbated by the expulsion of the Jews from the villages and their eviction from occupations connected with the rural economy. Many Jews became artisans and there was fierce competition among them, while others became day-labourers and, in fact, remained without livelihood. These two groups, the artisans and the hired labourers, provided the main candidates for emigration. Under the backward conditions of Galicia, the increase in sources of livelihood could not catch up with the growth of the Jewish population, particularly when the Poles began to organize rural cooperatives and other economic institutions in order to exclude the Jews from economic life. In Rumania the government and population conducted an economic war on the Jews, the declared aim of which was to drive them out of the country, while in Russia, oppression and harsh decrees were the official method of 'solving the Jewish problem'.

Persecution was no less effective a factor than the economic causes. The great wave of Jewish migration commenced with the flight from pogroms. In 1881 thousands of Jews fled the towns of the Pale of Settlement in Russia and concentrated in the Austrian border town of Brody, in overcrowded conditions and deprivation. With the aid of Jewish communities and organizations, some of these refugees were sent to the United States, while the majority were returned to their homes. Jewish organizations to a large extent later lost control over migration, and it became based on individual initiative, as family members who had established themselves in the New World brought over their relatives. A factor of considerable importance in encouraging emigration, even after the first panic of the pogroms had died down, was the disillusionment of the Jews of Russia and Rumania with the hope of obtaining legal equality, or at least ameliorating their condition. This emigration movement was largely a 'flight to emancipation'.

The effect of political discrimination on migration is attested to by the increase in the number of emigrants after each new wave of pogroms. Migration from Russia increased greatly after the expulsion from Moscow in 1891 (in 1891 some 111,000 Jews entered the United States, and in 1892, 137,000, as against 50–60,000 in previous years). In the worst pogrom year, from mid-1905 to mid-1906, more than 200,000 Jews emigrated from Russia (154,000 to the United States, 13,500 to Argentina, 7,000 to Canada, 3,500 to Palestine, and the remainder to South America and several West and Central European countries). Between 1881 and 1914 some 350,000 Jews left Galicia.

Members of other nationalities, particularly from Southern and Eastern Europe, also emigrated in large numbers in this period to the United States and other overseas countries, but Jewish migration was different, both in dimension and in nature. From 1881 to 1914, more than 2.5 million Jews migrated from Eastern Europe, *i.e.,* some 80,000 each year. Of these, some two million reached the United States, some 300,000 went to other overseas countries (including Palestine), while approximately 350,000 chose Western Europe. In the first fifteen years of the twentieth century, until the outbreak of the First World War, an average of 17.3 per 1,000 Jews emigrated from Russia each year, 19.6 from Rumania, and 9.6 from Galicia; this percentage is several times higher than the average for the non-Jewish population.

The characteristic feature of Jewish migration was the migration of whole families. The percentage of children among Jewish immigrants to the United States was

The Diaspora in the Modern Period

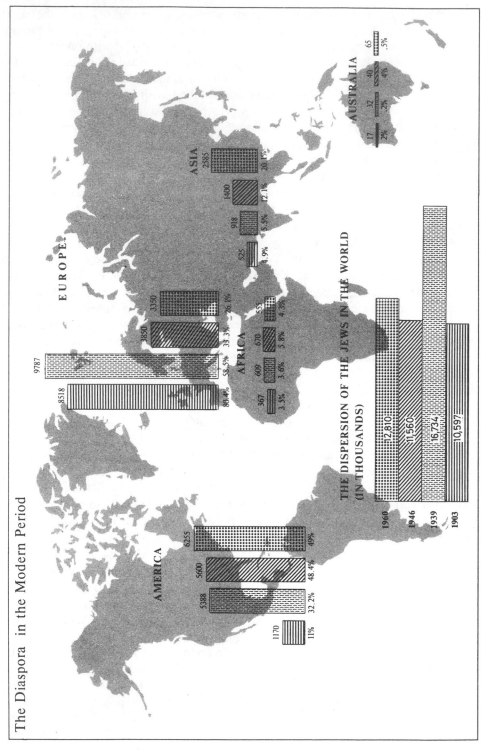

EUROPE

9787 — 58.5%
8518 — 80.4%
3850 — 33.3%
3350 — 26.1%

AMERICA

6255 — 49%
5600 — 48.4%
5388 — 32.2%
1170 — 11%

ASIA

2585 — 20.1%
1400 — 12.1%
918 — 5.5%
525 — 4.9%

AFRICA

55 — 4.3%
670 — 5.8%
609 — 3.6%
367 — 3.5%

AUSTRALIA

65 — .5%
40 — .4%
32 — .2%
17 — .2%

THE DISPERSION OF THE JEWS IN THE WORLD
(IN THOUSANDS)

1960 — 12,810
1946 — 11,560
1939 — 16,734
1903 — 10,597

862

double the average, a fact which demonstrated that the uprooting was permanent. And in fact, in the last few years before the First World War, only 5.75% of Jewish immigrants returned to their countries of origin, while among other immigrants about one-third went back. Nearly half of the Jewish immigrants had no defined occupation, *i.e.,* no permanent source of livelihood, as against some 25% of the other immigrants, but of the other half, about two-thirds were skilled artisans (mainly tailors) as against only one-fifth of the general immigrant population.

A further distinguishing feature of Jewish migration was that from the outset it displayed clearly ideological tendencies. A considerable number of the younger immigrants, members of the intelligentsia, were motivated not only by the desire to find a new refuge or a place in which there were greater chances of success; their departure constituted a protest against the discrimination and injustices they had suffered in their old homes and reflected their ardent desire for a place in which they could live independent and free lives. From the beginning, controversy existed between the 'Palestinians' (Hovevei Zion, Lovers of Zion), who believed that independent existence of the people was only possible in their ancient homeland, and the 'Americans' (above all the Am Olam group), who hoped to establish a Jewish state as one of the states of the union to serve as the background for an autonomous territorial, national experience, or who claimed that the 'Land of Freedom' was the most suited to the free development of the Jews, even without an autonomous frame-work. It was not the ideological argument but the conditions of absorption that determined the direction of migration for the great majority of those forced to flee from their countries of residence.

The New Centres

Despite the huge dimensions of Jewish migration (in the first fifteen years of the twentieth century, Jews accounted for 10% of immigrants to the United States), it did not produce great changes in the situation of East European Jews from the demographic or economic point of view, for migration absorbed only the natural increase. But in historical perspective it constituted a turning-point in the development of the Jewish Diaspora, as new centres began to emerge outside Europe. At the outbreak of the First World War there were some 2.5 million Jews in the United States, some 100,000 in Argentina, approximately 85,000 in Palestine, some 75,000 in Canada, some 50,000 in South Africa and approximately 20,000 in Australia.

The Jewish community in the United States became an important factor in Jewish life in this period. The attempts to found agricultural communities there failed and the hopes of a separate national unit also vanished, but new forms of Jewish life were nevertheless consolidated. The great majority of the immigrants settled in the port-cities on the East Coast and in several industrial towns. Their natural tendency was to settle near their relatives or *landsmen,* and therefore as immigration increased, so did the overcrowding in the Jewish areas of residence. Urban concentrations, later referred to as ghettos, were created, which were reminiscent of the way of life in the Jewish centres of Eastern Europe. This was caused not only by the familial nature of Jewish migration but also by the concentration of religious institutions and mutual-aid organizations, which served many of the newcomers in these areas; there was also the feeling that they were residing 'among their people' and not in an alien environment, whose language and customs were strange.

The continuous migration and the concentration in large towns affected the occupational structure and social relations in the new centres. The great majority of the immigrants, uprooted from their old homes and their sources of livelihood, arrived in their new homes penniless. Jewish immigrants came last among all migrants in the amount of money per capita they brought with them to the United States, and therefore they underwent an arduous process of adaptation to new conditions. Some of them became pedlars, offering their goods for sale from door to door, and sometimes wandering far from their own homes, while most of them were forced to turn to exhausting physical labour. This transition constituted a crisis, not only because many of them were unaccustomed to physical labour, but also from the psychological point of view, since in many cases this involved non-observance of the Sabbath. Many of the immigrants were absorbed into the clothing industry, partly because a number of them had been engaged in this occupation in the 'old country' and partly because even those who lacked experience could easily learn the simple tasks of wholesale tailoring. They engaged in piecework, under conditions of harsh exploitation, in small, dark, airless 'sweatshops'. As the immigrants flowed in, the situation of the 'greenhorns' became increasingly difficult. It was these arduous working conditions which impelled the Jewish workers to establish the first trade unions. Organization of labour and gradual acclimatization raised the standard of living among the immigrants, and they soon attained a higher income level than they had enjoyed in their old homes. This helped them to bring across their relatives, or to send them financial aid, so that to a large extent this immigration was self-absorbing. Aid from relatives in the United States became a factor of no small importance in the lives of quite a number of East European communities, and in time this habit of supporting relatives and persecuted Jews became one of the important foundations of American Jewish society.

The Effect of Concentration in Towns

The high rate of emigration overseas greatly reinforced the process of urbanization. Of the eleven cities with populations of more than 100,000 Jews at the outbreak of the First World War (which together accounted for one-quarter of the total world Jewish population), immigrant centres took first place. In New York there were 1,350,000 Jews, in Chicago 350,000, in Philadelphia 175,000 and in London more than 150,000. The large centres in the 'old world' were Warsaw, with 350,000 Jews, Budapest, with more than 200,000, Odessa, Vienna and Lodz, with more than 150,000 each.

This concentration in towns and in cities had a considerable influence on the Jewish way of life and on relations with the non-Jewish environment. The Jews were prominent in the large world centres and their economic, cultural and social activities were clearly apparent. The Jewish vote became an important political factor in the United States, and their influence increased. But this concentration also strengthened anti-Semitic trends. Despite Jewish concentration within new ghettos, a large non-Jewish public came in close contact with them, and their distinctive qualities became more obvious. At the same time the Jewish immigrants began to acquire the culture of their environment; a large percentage of second-generation immigrants turned to higher education, the number of those engaged in the liberal professions grew, and cultural assimilation increased. The concentration in large cities therefore affected Jewish life in two directions: on the one hand it weakened the influence of tradition, increased cultural assimilation and rapidly integrated the Jews into the life around them; on the other hand conditions and relationships were created that strengthened the Jewish sense of solidarity and of common destiny. The Jewish impact on economic and cultural life strengthened the desire to belong to the Jewish community. The existence of an intellectual Jewish society deflated the desire, which had gripped Jewish *maskilim* in earlier times, to flee from Judaism. The large concentrations even created conditions for the temporary flourishing of Jewish creativity and the Jewish press, mainly in Yiddish.

Changes in Economic Activity

In Eastern Europe during the period under review, the falling away from rural occupations continued among Jews, as did the transition to a typically urban economy. The development of capitalistic relations in the village, the eviction of the Jews from the Russian villages, the high rate of emigration and agricultural cooperation reduced the role of the Jew as a mediator between town and village. Only in Galicia did the great overcrowding of Jews in towns and townlets lead to settlement in the villages in the eastern section of the region. At the beginning of the century, 14.3% of Galician Jews were still engaged in agriculture, and the situation was similar in Carpathian Russia.

A trend that slightly hindered the transition to typical urban economy was the ideology of productivity fostered among the *maskilim* and in the nationalist movement, which called for the direction of the Jews to agricultural settlement. In Russia at the end of the nineteenth century, some 3.6% of the Jewish population lived off the soil as farmers and agricultural labourers. In Russia and Poland in 1900, Jews owned more than five and a half million acres of land. The national renaissance movement in Palestine, which also advocated the return to the soil, succeeded by the time of the First World War in setting up some forty settlements, with a population close to 10,000. In Argentina, the Jewish Colonization Association (founded by Baron de Hirsch in 1891) began to settle Jews on the land, and by 1914 the number of Jewish agricultural settlers in the country had reached 12,000. But all these endeavours exerted little influence on the social and occupational structure of the Jews in general before the First World War.

At the end of the nineteenth and beginning of the twentieth centuries, there was a decrease in the economic importance of Jewish financiers in most countries. There were still large Jewish banking-houses (Kuhn, Loeb and Co., J. & W. Seligmann, Speyer and Co., in the United States; the House of Rothschild, the Schuster and Cassel families in England; the French Rothschilds; the Warburg family in Germany), but the extensive development of state banks, joint-stock banks, discount and other limited companies greatly reduced the economic significance of the private Jewish 'family' banks. A number of important Jewish banking families (such as Mendelssohn, Bleichroeder, Koenigswarter, and Bischoffsheim) converted to Christianity and became divorced from the Jews and their problems. Obviously this too weakened the status of the Jews in the world of finance. Nevertheless, when the Russian Government, at the beginning of the twentieth century, wanted to obtain new loans in the international financial markets, the head of the Council of Ministers sent out special letters to the House of Rothschild in London and Paris and hinted that the Russian regime intended to ameliorate the condition of its Jews. But the ability of Jewish bankers to influence Russian policy towards the Jews through financial pressure was very limited during that period.

Jews also played only a small part in industrial development in the West at this time. In the United States, Kuhn, Loeb & Co. took part in the construction of railway networks and played a role in the development of electricity and telegraph services; the Guggenheim family played a prominent role in the mining industry. In England the Mond family founded chemical industries and actively participated in the establishment of one of the greatest industrial concerns of the time – Imperial Chemical Industries. Generally speaking, however, Jews did not play a large part in the industrial development of these countries at that time. Of greater importance were the Jewish firms engaged in German industry. Such important enterprises as Ludwig Loewe in the arms industry, Emil Rathenau's A.E.G. (General Electric Company), the Hirsch Copper and Brass Company and a whole series of other Jewish businesses were important to the German economy. Jews were also prominent in book and newspaper publishing. In Germany the Mosse family published many newspapers, among them the prestigious *Berliner Tageblatt,* and the Ullstein Verlag (publishing house) was one of the biggest in the country; in the United States the *New York Times* was owned by a Jewish family.

Jews continued, however, to play a central role in the economy of the more backward countries, such as the Austro-Hungarian Empire and Russia. Until the First World War the Jews were prominent there in banking and insurance, despite the demand of the Russian authorities to restrict the number of Jews among the directors of share companies. In Austria as well as in Hungary, the Jews were active in heavy industry, in coal-mining, oil and chemical industries. In Russia Jews played a prominent role in the food industry: in 1909 more than 100 of the 300 sugar factories in the country were under Jewish ownership. By the early nineties the factories of the Brodsky family were producing about one-quarter of all the sugar manufactured in Russia, and it was they who set up and managed the syndicate for sugar export. Exports of other agricultural produce and of timber were also for the most part in Jewish hands, as were many of the flour-mills and tobacco concerns. In the textile centres of the Pale of Settlement, in Lodz and Bialystok, Jews were active both as employers and as labourers. With the outbreak of the First World War they became more important in the metal industry as well, primarily because of their extensive ties with firms outside Russia.

Changes in the Occupational Structure

The demographic and economic processes mentioned above left their mark on the occupational structure of the Jewish people as a whole and on their intra-social relations. As a result, the disparity between the economic situation of the various Jewish communities became more acute during this period. While the standard of living of the Jews in the West, and particularly in Germany, rose rapidly, the increased overcrowding and competition in the East led to further impoverishment of the masses.

In the countries of the West (apart from immigrant centres), Jewish pedlars almost completely vanished, and there were fewer artisans, while the number of those engaged in trade and in the liberal professions increased. At the beginning of the twentieth century, more than half the Jewish bread-winners in Germany were engaged in trade (though their proportion in German trade as a whole dropped from 5.7% in 1895 to 4.2% in 1907 and 3% after the war). In Italy about one-fifth of the Jewish bread-winners were engaged in the liberal professions or in government and municipal bureaucracy. In Austria, of the total Jewish labour force in 1900, 11.4% were engaged in agriculture, 27.8% in industry, 43.7% in trade and transportation, and 16.2% in liberal professions and government service. In Vienna there was a particularly large percentage active in literature, the press, the arts, theatre, etc. In Hungary at the beginning of the twentieth century Jews constituted some half of the physicians and chemists, one-third of the lawyers, some 40% of the writers, 20% of the actors, musicians and sculptors.

In Russia at the end of the nineteenth century, the percentage of Jews in the liberal professions was very small. Some 31% of the Jewish bread-winners were engaged in trade and 36.3% in industry and manufacturing. There were 500,000 Jewish artisans and apprentices. At the end of this period there were some 150,000 manual labourers, of whom approximately 70,000 were factory workers. The main concentration of those engaged in industry and manufacturing was in Lithuania and White Russia (40% of the Jewish bread-winners there). The plight of artisans in Eastern Europe was alleviated somewhat when the Jewish Colonization Association (ICA) and other philanthropic organizations began to extend credit to them for purchase of raw materials and preparation of stock. In the decade before the First World War, Jewish citizens in Russia set up hundreds of mutual-loan and cooperative societies that assisted in the purchase of raw materials, helped finance seasonal work or prepare goods for fairs, extended financial support at times of illness, and so on. These associations also helped the small trader.

The new centres of immigration stood halfway between the countries of the West and the East as regards occupational structure. On the one hand, the process of 'proletariazation' was, as we have noted, rapid and harsh, and the percentage of Jews who supported themselves and their families by manual labour was particularly high. In New York in the 1890s three-quarters of the Jewish bread-winners were engaged in manual labour, as hired workers or artisans. In London, and even in Amsterdam, a Jewish proletariat also emerged in this period. But as a result of the extensive economic opportunities in the important economic centres, this proletariat was unstable, and its composition was in constant flux. As the Jewish immigrants adapted to the conditions of the new countries, greater numbers began to abandon manual labour, only to be replaced by new immigrants fresh off the boat. The veteran immigrants then turned once again to middle-man services, and above all to trade. The second generation played a much smaller role in manual labour than had their parents.

Nevertheless, the crystallization of a Jewish working class in Europe and in the New World exerted considerable influence on the development of social forces among the Jewish people in the period under review. This was a drastic departure from the period in which the entire nation had seemed to constitute one class, *i.e.,* a middle class of merchants and financiers of various kinds. As a result of the new processes, the Jewish people now began to approximate to the condition of a 'normal people', revealing a social structure similar to that of other nations, more than in any other period of their exile among the Christian nations of Europe. The Jewish working class, which from the first was characterized by a tendency to organization and social activity, served as a counter-balance to the social hesitation of the Jewish bourgeois circles and was a most important element in the independent national and social activity initiated by radical Jewish youth.

But the consolidation of a Jewish working class was hampered by several obstacles, originating in the economic and social conditions of East European Jewry and in the historical traditions of the Jewish people. It was extremely difficult for the Jewish worker to compete with the non-Jewish labourer in Eastern Europe; the latter had only recently left his village and, in most cases, had left his family behind to work the soil, so that he himself was able to manage on a small wage. The extensive organization of Jewish workers was, in a certain sense, to their disadvantage, as employers preferred the non-Jewish workers to Jews with their long tradition of working-man societies and social consciousness. There were also problems resulting from Sabbath observance.

For all these reasons non-Jewish employers did not employ Jewish workers, and even Jewish employers only took them on in smaller enterprises, where there was a need for skilled labour and resourcefulness. As mechanization spread, the work of the individual worker became simpler and more mechanical, and Jewish employers also began to prefer non-Jewish labour. This was so common that when the textile factories in Bialystok began to shift over to mechanical looms, the Polish workers demanded that the Jewish weavers be dismissed, since they were supposedly only allowed to work on hand-looms. Clashes between Polish and Jewish workers in the textile centres of Lodz and Bialystok became a common occurrence.

The Jewish tendency to economic independence also undermined the stability of the working class. Workers wanted to save money or to obtain dowries in order to rise from the status of wage-earner to that of independent artisan – although this sometimes entailed a drop in standard of living. Jewish women (who constituted the majority of workers in the tobacco and knitting industries) regarded their work as a temporary evil until they married. Despite the numerical increase in the Jewish proletariat, there was constant change in its composition in Eastern Europe. A son who continued in his father's occupation as a worker was a rarity, while dynasties of artisans were common.

Numerical growth, geographical dispersion, concentration of considerable sections of the people in large towns, changes in occupational structure and social relations transformed the image of the people during this period and created conditions for extensive activity in political, social and cultural spheres. But no less impetus was provided by the change in the attitude of European society towards its Jews.

56

Modern Anti-Semitism and the Appearance of Anti-Semitic Parties

Integration of the Jews into the Non-Jewish World and the Reaction

The process of legal emancipation in Central Europe was concluded in the 1860s and 1870s: the concept of equal rights of all citizens, irrespective of origin and religion, was recognized as a binding principle in European political thought. The Jews of Europe were convinced that the 'Jewish question' had thus been solved. To their great surprise they discovered that the non-Jewish world was still holding aloof from them; discrimination continued to reign in various spheres, and for the European the Jew continued to be a Jew – although from the legal point of view he was now a Frenchman, German or Englishman. It thus transpired that the accepted Jewish view (deeply rooted in the political traditions of European Jewry) that their special status constituted a basically legal problem was erroneous, or at least inexact; it was only a part of a more intricate problem.

This development was in part the result of the anti-Semitic social and cultural traditions of the nations of Europe, which had survived the political and legal changes, and, in part, a reaction to the integration of the Jews to their surroundings, its rapidity and perceptible success. In the eighteenth and nineteenth centuries, when Europe was debating the question of Jewish emancipation, its proponents had claimed that the way of life of the Jews, their seclusion, special occupations, places of residence, were all the fruit of discrimination and persecution practised by the rulers, the church and the towns over hundreds of years. When these were removed, when the Jew was accepted as an equal in his surroundings, his communal or individual uniqueness would disappear and the 'Jewish question' would vanish. But the way in which the Jews assimilated into the non-Jewish world during and after the struggle for emancipation did not justify these assumptions. The process of integration in various spheres of life helped bring the Jews closer to their environment, but did not erase the communal and psychological characteristics of most Jews – sometimes even accentuating them. As large numbers of Jews moved to the important cultural centres and became absorbed into influential professions and spheres of life, their presence became more visible, and when they proved successful they became the object of greater envy and hatred than in previous periods.

The Unique Traits of Modern Anti-Semitism

As we have noted, no less important in the evolvement of modern anti-Semitism was the centuries-old European tradition of hatred of the Jew and his image, as embedded in the European consciousness. Hatred of Jews is an ancient phenomenon, originating in the basic difference between the monotheistic minority and the mighty pagan empires and in the struggle that Judaism conducted in the early days of Christianity against the latter's tendency to attract masses of idol-worshippers through adjusting to their customs (see Part IV). The New Testament displayed anti-Jewish overtones, and these were intensified in the writings of the Church Fathers. Hatred of the Jewish people left an indelible mark on European Christian culture and on the minds of Europeans. Every religious and social upheaval in Europe during the Middle Ages and at the dawn of modern times was accompanied by anti-Jewish outbursts, manifested in persecution and in pogroms. Nevertheless, modern anti-Semitism has displayed certain features that distinguish it ideologically and organizationally from traditional anti-Jewish feeling -- from which it has, albeit, drawn inspiration.

Early anti-Jewishness was primarily directed against the 'evil doing and infidelity of the Jews' – namely, their specific religious customs, way of life and occupations. They were 'murderers of Christ', who needed Christian blood for their strange rituals. But to the extent that they repented of their 'evil ways' or 'saw the light' (*i.e.,* converted to Christianity) their infidelity vanished. The same was true in the social sphere. The Jew was a parasite, a greedy money-lender, a leech sucking the blood of the Christian people, plotting against the regime; but if he became a loyal Christian and left his past behind him, he was at once reformed.

Modern anti-Semites hold a different view. They claim that the destructive 'Jewish spirit' has infiltrated European nations through those Jews who have most closely approached their surroundings in beliefs and way of life. These anti-Semites speak of the alien and oriental 'Jewish essence' as opposed to the 'Aryan Christian spirit' of the peoples of Europe. Neither can change their nature and therefore they are condemned to eternal hostility or opposition.

The explanation of this conflict is based on the qualities of the 'Jewish race', a concept borrowed from the anthropological and linguistic terminology to which social significance was attributed in the second half of the nineteenth century. Hence, also, the word for the new anti-Jewish feeling: 'anti-Semitism', *i.e.,* opposition to the qualities of the Semites – even though it was clear even to its proponents that this was directed against the Jews alone. The rapid absorption of the new term in the press and in daily language demonstrates the extent to which public opinion in Europe, and particularly in Germany, was ready for this ideology. The racist argument was given particular weight in the propaganda of anti-Semites after they had determined – supposedly on the basis of scientific study, a type of argument highly esteemed by modern man – that racial characteristics were stable and could not be altered or eradicated.

Modern anti-Semitism has also displayed organizational innovations. In the past, anti-Jewish outbursts were only by-products of political and social developments. As the Jews had existed outside the framework of Christian society, even the anti-Jewish outbursts were not the result of a specific plan to fight the Jews, nor did anyone claim that the status of the Jews in the state or in society could affect the general fate of the nation. It is possible that the inferior and oppressed status of the Jews in those times prevented the masses from accepting such arguments. Modern anti-Semitism is characterized by the proliferation of organizations or political parties that are specifically anti-Semitic – namely, with the central aim of combating the Jews and their influence; associations that are ready to construct their entire policy around the question of the attitude towards the Jews and to regard the solution of the 'Jewish question' as a way of solving all the problems of society.

The Ideological Roots of Modern Anti-Semitism

The growth of the new movement aroused the amazement of liberal and radical circles, which generally supported Jewish rights and regarded hatred of the Jews as 'a relic of the barbaric Middle Ages'. There can be no doubt that the second half of the nineteenth century was an epoch of advancement in rational scientific thought and in the spread of education among wide sections of the European population. Why, therefore, did the vestiges of prejudice flare up just at this time? The reason lies in the resubstantiation that some of the important ideological streams of the eighteenth and nineteenth centuries lent to anti-Jewish tradition.

It has already been noted (see pages 744–6 and 805–7) that the attacks against Judaism and the Jews by English and French deists in the eighteenth century and by the 'young Hegelians' in the middle of the nineteenth century led the anti-traditionalist circles, the proponents of rationalist thought, to take up an extremely negative attitude towards those Jews who had not totally detached themselves from their historical or religious traditions. European socialists, almost all of whom had drawn inspiration from this spiritual tradition, continued this negative attitude or else found a connexion between the social function of the Jews in the economic sphere and the nature of the Jewish religion and its injunctions. They therefore emphasized the role of the Jews in the development of European capitalism, and those who regarded this as a negative social development – such as Fourier, or Proudhon – displayed open hostility towards the Jews. One of Fourier's disciples, Alphonse Toussenel, published a book in 1845 entitled *The Jews, Monarchs of the Age.*

The anti-capitalistic struggle of many socialists therefore displayed a clearly anti-Jewish tendency, whether consciously or not, and this was reflected in the plans and actions of various socialist parties. It was accepted that 'anti-Semitism is the socialism of fools', but it was followed by an explanation that it is a stage in the maturing of the worker and the common man towards socialism, the stage in which he sees only a part of the social picture and not the entire framework of social relations. It was only the appearance of radical, mass anti-Semitic parties, which propagandized among the workers and competed with the socialists, that led the Social-Democratic parties to dissociate themselves from anti-Semitism. From the 1880s onwards it became apparent that those parties and socialist groups that regarded capitalism as an essential, transitional stage were more opposed to anti-Semitism than those that totally negated capitalism. But the identification of the Jew with capitalism remained in force and served as an important element in the absorption of anti-Semitic propaganda by the population of Europe.

The romantic ideals that emerged in political thought, historical concepts and literary works at the turn of the nineteenth century helped to consolidate national consciousness and led to the worship of the 'national spirit' and the creation of national myths. The idealization of the Middle Ages and the strengthening of the religious traditions that emanated from these ideologies led many of the advocates of such theories to oppose Jewish emancipation. Now that the ideals of emancipation had triumphed, they served as a convenient instrument for expressing public resentment of the very fact of Jewish equality or the ways in which it was implemented.

One of the ways in which national self-awareness was forged in certain countries was by directing hostility against those elements regarded as different or alien, and hatred of the Jew became a typical reflection of national loyalty. The strengthening of historical consciousness, under the influence of romantic ideals, lent this opposition a basic ideological significance (the 'spirit of Christianity' as against the 'Jewish spirit', the 'Aryan' race versus the 'Semitic' race, etc.). This trend won support in the opposite camp of those who advocated scientific positivism, the influence of which increased in the second half of the nineteenth century.

The tremendous achievements in the exact sciences and their utilization in the sphere of philosophical ideas, morals and society led to the idea of 'social Darwinism', which depicted human history as the incessant struggle of individuals and groups for survival and, through this struggle, natural selection leading to the survival of the fittest. The term 'race' was borrowed from the natural sciences and was taken to represent a human group with certain common biological and cultural characteristics, shaping the development of society and culture. Racial differences were cited to explain differences in political orders, in cultural achievement and in moral and social values. Under the influence of scientific determinism, the claim that racial characteristics were fixed and immutable began to be voiced. For most advocates of these theories the outstanding example of the struggle between races was the clash between the Semites and the Aryans. This created the so-called scientific basis for the anti-Semitic claim that hatred of the Jews was natural.

In actual fact, national romanticism, socialist aspirations, scientific positivism and even social Darwinism in themselves had nothing to do with the 'Jewish question'. They were among the main ideological currents in European thought in the nineteenth century and were anchored in the general processes of European development. Nevertheless, because of their historical influence, they became factors of great importance in preparing nineteenth-century Europeans for the absorption of certain elements in anti-Semitic ideology.

The Social Roots of Anti-Semitism

Just as ideological changes prepared the way for the intellectual and emotional assimilation of anti-Semitic arguments, so did social developments in Europe in the second half of the nineteenth century create the background for the activity of anti-Semitic organizations. This was a period of democratization of methods of government and the consolidation of representative government and of the general franchise in most Central and West European countries. As a result, wider sections of the population began to exert influence over their governments. Political parties emerged, competing among themselves for votes, and therefore obliged to take note of the traditions, values and beliefs of the people. This added weight to the anti-Jewish tradition, which had deep roots in wide sections of European society. The spread of popular education, which encompassed the great majority of the people in most European countries in the nineteenth century, and the resulting mass circulation of the popular press also helped augment anti-Semitism; the impact of propaganda and of shallow slogans was now wider.

This was also the period when the 'free society' was being consolidated, based on economic competition, opposition to government intervention in the activities of the individual and the abolition of the monopolistic status of certain historical frameworks, *e.g.,* the guilds and the craft associations. This situation was advantageous for the Jews, who had been excluded from the old frameworks; they were more open to economic innovations that entailed a certain amount of risk and had long been accustomed to sidestep the coercive control of absolutist governments. The peasant masses, on the other hand, who were uprooted from their natural surroundings and therefore flocked to the towns, and the townsmen, who were deprived of the protection of the old frameworks, which had restrained competition and determined 'fair prices', felt lost and helpless; the ground seemed to be slipping away from under their feet. The reform movements established in the seventies and eighties were an expression of the yearning of the middle and lower classes for government patronage and for protective measures. There were growing demands for reversal of the 'liberal-Manchester' (free trade) approach and a return to governmental intervention in economic affairs. It was claimed that economic liberalism only profited the big capitalists, the 'gilded International' – the Jews.

Use of the stereotype 'Jew' or the 'typical Jew' as the personification of negative individual and group characteristics was also connected with the social and political changes occurring in Europe at the time. The intensification of differences between states and of inter-party strife led to the increased utilization of stereotypes that appealed to the imagination and the emotions rather than to understanding and reason. The power of the Jewish stereotype resulted from the fact that it combined the remnants of the mediaeval image of the 'evil Jew', the images created under the impact of new ideological currents, and the fear aroused in the European towndweller by the integration of the Jews into society and their steady advancement. Opponents or competitors declared Rothschild to be the symbol of Jewish domination of the stock exchange and the world of finance, while Disraeli allegedly symbolized Jewish domination of politics; Marx and Lassale symbolized Jewish revolutionary plots, Boerne and Heine controlled radical literature and journalism, Sarah Bernhardt dominated the theatre, and so on. Although most of these people were remote from Jewish problems, and even hostile towards Jews, they were the examples of Jewish domination. Moreover this led to an accentuation of the theory that Jews were hostile towards all Europeans and ambitious to dominate the world.

These elements needed only a social impetus in order to be transformed into an active political force in the form of anti-Semitic parties. The impetus was provided as a consequence of the *Kulturkampf,* conducted in Germany around the question of the 'dual loyalties' of Catholics, during which spiritual and cultural uniformity was declared to be the supreme ideal of the German nation, and as a result of the grave economic crisis that occurred in that country in 1873.

Organization of the Anti-Semitic Movement in Germany and Austria-Hungary

As a result of the crisis, several anti-Semitic writers appeared who blamed the Jews for Germany's problems. This accusation was first levelled by the Catholic journal *Germania,* which declared that the Jews were to blame for the sufferings of the German people. This point was elaborated by Otto Glagau, an anti-Jewish journalist. Another journalist, Wilhelm Marr, published several inflammatory pamphlets depicting the problems of the state as a life-and-death struggle between Judaism and Germanism, with the former gaining the upper hand. It was he who is said to have coined the term 'anti-Semitism'.

In 1878 the preacher at the Imperial Court in Berlin, Adolf Stoecker, founded the Christian Social Workers' Party, the main objective of which was to combat the influence of Social Democracy among the workers. The party achieved only limited success, and in order to increase its popularity Stoecker began to intersperse his speeches with anti-Semitic comments. The success of this tactic led him to put forward a complete anti-Semitic programme in September 1879 in a comprehensive anti-Jewish speech ('What We Demand of Modern Jewry'). From then onwards the party concentrated its efforts on anti-Jewish incitement.

Germany now became the centre of anti-Semitic activity. At the end of 1879 and in 1880 many anti-Jewish pamphlets and articles were published. The historian Professor Heinrich Treitschke attacked the refusal of the Jews to assimilate into German culture and society, their desire to create a 'mongrel' German-Jewish culture and the incessant flow of Jewish immigrants from Poland. It was he who coined the phrase – adopted by all later anti-Semites – 'the Jews are our misfortune.' Because of Treitschke's respected status, his remarks aroused widespread controversy. At the same time several publications were devoted to the racial aspect of the Jewish question. The most extreme was that of the former socialist Eugen Duehring. He not only attacked the various characteristics of the Jewish race, but also attempted to offer a 'scientific' explanation for the blood libels: they supposedly originated in the human sacrifices offered up by the ancient Hebrews and endured because of the desire of Jewish leaders to bind each individual to the Jewish community by making him an accomplice to a crime.

In August 1880 a petition began to circulate, calling for the closing of Germany to Jewish immigration, the dismissal of Jews from posts involving administrative authority and the separate registration of Jews in all statistical surveys. The petition was submitted in April 1881 with some quarter of a million signatures. But there was no ideological uniformity in the 'Berlin Movement', as this anti-Semitic trend was called. It was a confused combination of conservative romantics and racial-radicals (such as Henrici), the former shying away from the declarations of the latter that Jews should be physically assaulted. The elections to the Reichstag in that year constituted a disappointment for the anti-Semites, as not a single candidate of their list was elected.

The emergence of the anti-Semitic movement in Germany influenced other countries, particularly in Eastern Europe; if such a movement could arise in enlightened Germany, then it was even more likely to emerge in backward states. One of the leaders of the Russian Slavophiles, Aksakov, wrote in June 1881:

> The anti-Semitic movement, this anti-Semitic alliance created recently in Germany, in the country which leads European culture, is not the outcome of religious intolerance, crude ignorance, reaction, etc., as our naive 'liberals' think. It is a characteristic feature of the times, attesting to the awakening of public awareness, which may have come too late. In any case, the Western European Christian world will be faced in the future, in one form or another, with a life-and-death struggle with Jewry, which is striving to replace the universal Christian ideal by another, Semitic ideal, also universal, but negative and anti-Christian.

The first 'international' congress of anti-Semites was held in Dresden at the end of 1882. The congress published a 'manifesto to the governments and peoples of the Christian countries which are in danger because of Jewry'. This document called for the establishment of committees to combat the Jews in every town; all of these should unite in one 'international Christian alliance', so as to counterbalance the Alliance Israélite Universelle. At the second congress, in 1883, an attempt was made to declare Duehring's theories to be the movement's binding ideology ('the racial theory of the greatest thinker in the world is the rock on which Jewry will be dashed to pieces'). But the proposal failed because of the opposition of those anti-Semites who refused to base their movement entirely on racism.

In Hungary the parliamentary deputy Istóczy began to deliver anti-Jewish speeches in 1875 and to demand the expulsion of the Jews from the country. On the day the Berlin congress opened in 1878 he proposed that the Powers be advised to establish a Jewish state in Palestine and to send all Jews there. In Austria, at the same time, Schoenerer, an advocate of the inclusion of Austria in the German Empire, proposed that an onslaught be launched on 'Semitic control of money and words' (*i.e.,* finance and the press). The Hungarian anti-Semitic movement won more extensive support because of the Tiszaeszlar blood libel. In September 1882 anti-Jewish riots broke out in Pressburg (Bratislava), which were suppressed by the army. The anti-Semitic faction in the Hungarian Diet then consisted of seventeen members. But, all in all, the anti-Semites did not win extensive political influence in these countries during the 1880s.

Yet, the anti-Semitic movement did not encounter widespread public opposition in its early days, save in Jewish circles. After the first manifestations of organized anti-Semitic activity, prominent representatives of liberal circles in Germany, including scientists and politicians, published a manifesto on November 1880 denouncing anti-Semitism and calling it a 'national disgrace'. But even among these protesters there were many who claimed that the Jews held themselves aloof, maintained separate organizations, had not assimilated into the Christian world and, therefore, aroused the opposition of the masses.

The Rise and Decline of the Anti-Semitic Parties

After Bismarck began to rely on the Conservative Party to run the country, there was an increased tendency to bar Jews formally from public and government office. Jewish officers were not promoted, the Ministry of Justice prevented the appointment of Jews to judicial positions, and the Ministry of Education did likewise with government teaching positions. The hostile attitude towards the Jews prevailing in academic circles precluded them from obtaining university posts.

The alliance between the Conservatives and the National Liberals strengthened this tendency, which became particularly marked after Wilhelm II ascended the throne and the influence of the officer corps increased. The Conservative Party included in its new programme of December 1892 a clause calling for war on 'the destructive Jewish influence over our national life'. The Conservatives began to compete with the anti-Semites for influence over the masses. In the 1893 elections to the Reichstag, the anti-Semites gained a quarter of a million votes and sixteen deputies. But as the government, and even the Kaiser himself, spoke out against the unrestrained anti-Semitic propaganda – which supposedly operated to the advantage of the Social Democrats – their parliamentary decline soon commenced (in 1898, thirteen deputies; in 1903, only nine). It should be emphasized that the reservations were directed at the propaganda methods rather than the actual ideology.

When the anti-Semitic onslaught was renewed, an Alliance for Repelling Anti-Semitism was founded (1890), headed by several politicians and scientists, mainly members of the Progressive Party. This alliance published a large amount of material aimed at refuting anti-Semitic arguments. The Social Democrats also began to oppose anti-Semitism. But anti-Semitic ideas continued to spread in the press, in pamphlets and in 'scientific' articles. Particularly widespread circulation was achieved by a book written by H. S. Chamberlain, an Englishman totally assimilated into German culture, entitled *Foundations of the Nineteenth Century* (1898), which depicted history as a struggle between the Aryan and Semitic races. The former were allegedly creative and constructive, the latter harmful and destructive. Hundreds of thousands of copies of this book, which lacked any scientific foundation, were distributed and greatly influenced the German intelligentsia. The Kaiser himself read it aloud to his children and proposed that it be included in the programme of studies in officer cadet schools. Thus anti-Semitism gradually became an essential part of the ruling ideology.

In this same period anti-Semitism also increased in Austria, and particularly in Vienna. In 1890 thirteen anti-Semitic deputies were elected to the Diet, but the movement received its greatest impetus when Karl Lueger, a former Democrat, joined and began to preach a 'Christian Socialist' ideology, claiming to be protecting the rights of the 'little man'. In 1895 the anti-Semites and anti-liberals won a majority in the Vienna municipality, and Lueger was elected mayor. Emperor Franz

Josef refused to confirm the appointment, but was obliged to do so after Lueger was re-elected for the third time in 1897. The mayor exploited his position in order to discriminate against the Jews in various spheres. In 1907 there were 131 anti-Semitic deputies in the Austrian Reichsrat; this faction fought to introduce the *numerus clausus* (a fixed numerical proportion) for Jewish pupils, together with a series of other discriminatory proposals.

As a comprehensive political force, the *specifically* anti-Semitic parties began to decline both in Germany and in Austria-Hungary, but their ideas spread far and wide – to non-party circles, to the economy, among youth, even to sports.

Anti-Semitism in France and the Dreyfus Affair

In France the first signs of anti-Semitism appeared at the beginning of the 1880s, when the struggle between the republican-radical camp and the monarchal-clerical elements became more acute. The immediate reason for anti-Semitic propaganda was the collapse of the Catholic Union General Bank, in which many small Catholic investors lost their savings. The director of the bank blamed 'Jewish capital' for the bankruptcy, and several issues of anti-Jewish papers appeared. But anti-Semitic ideas became more influential after the publication, in 1886, of Edouard Drumont's book, *Jewish France*. This work purported to depict the historical clash between Aryans and Semites, describing the destructive influence of the Jews over French history and their decisive influence over political life after 1870. It called for a social revolution to be based on the division of Jewish property. Hundreds of thousands of copies of the book were sold, and anti-Semitic activity followed. Anti-Semitic student associations and other such bodies were organized. Particularly active were the lower echelons of the clergy, who were sensitive to social problems and who organized a 'Christian-Democratic' movement. Many socialists also took part in this propaganda campaign.

The anti-Semites became active in parliament as well. In 1891 one of them proposed that the Jews be expelled from France, and thirty-two deputies supported him; but the proposal was never placed on the agenda. From the beginning of 1892 an anti-Semitic daily paper, *Libre Parole,* appeared under the editorship of Drumont. He exploited the collapse of the Panama Company to increase his influence. As several Jewish financiers were involved in the affair, Drumont regarded it as proof that the Jews were corrupting France. But after some time interest in this affair waned, as did anti-Semitic preoccupation with it.

There was a renewed outbreak of anti-Jewish sentiment at the end of 1894, when a Jewish officer, Alfred Dreyfus, who had served on the French General Staff, was arrested on a charge of espionage. Anti-Semites began to claim that this provided additional proof of 'Jewish treachery'. Their propaganda, abandoning its social nature, was transformed into patriotic incitement and attacks on the ideals of the French Revolution. The Minister of War hesitated at first, but later decided to bring Dreyfus to trial before a court martial. By means of forgery and political pressure, Dreyfus was found guilty and sentenced to exile on Devil's Island for the rest of his life. The socialist leader Jaurès, who later came to Dreyfus' defence, claimed at the time in the National Assembly that the light sentence resulted from the influence of the Jewish bourgeoisie. But a staff officer named Picquart revealed that the central document on which Dreyfus' conviction had been based had actually been written by another officer and that a certain Colonel Henri, assigned to counter-intelligence, had forged documents, apparently with the knowledge of his superiors, in order to pin the blame on Dreyfus. After this revelation Picquart was dismissed from his post and sent to Algeria. A Jewish journalist, Bernard Lazare, published a pamphlet entitled *A Judicial Error – the Truth About the Dreyfus Affair* (1896).

Rumours began to circulate some time later about various happenings in the General Staff, and a public outcry was raised which lasted three years (1897–9). The anti-Semites claimed that there was a Jewish conspiracy in France, the aim of which was to humiliate France and its army. Most of the political parties were opposed to a retrial, but the public was divided into two main camps – the Dreyfusards and the anti-Dreyfusards. This split reflected the struggle between social forces, as consolidated since the establishment of the Third Republic, but the 'Jewish, question' now became of central importance. On 13 January 1898 Clemenceau's paper, *L'Aurore*, published an article by the renowned writer Emile Zola, entitled 'J'Accuse'. In this article Zola accused the General Staff of a miscarriage of justice and of shielding the true spy. In reaction there were anti-Semitic riots in French and Algerian towns. At the new elections, most of the Dreyfusard candidates were defeated, but the new War Minister, Cavaignac, who was the sworn enemy of the Dreyfusards, ordered a re-examination of all documents in the Dreyfus file, and thus the forgeries were discovered. Henri, the officer who had carried out the forgeries, committed suicide in prison. Nevertheless, the army chiefs continued to oppose a retrial, and the public controversy became even more violent. Eventually a new trial was held in August 1899; Dreyfus' guilt was reaffirmed by a majority, but it was recommended that his sentence be reduced, and the President pardoned him. (He was totally exonerated only in 1906.)

The consequences of the Dreyfus Affair were of vital importance to the political future of the French Republic. It led to a decline in the influence of military and ecclesiastical circles and to the strengthening of radical elements. Shortly after the termination of the affair, a law was passed separating religion and state in France. But the Dreyfus Affair was also valuable as regards the attitude of French society towards the Jews, as it dealt a heavy blow to the organized anti-Semitic movement in France. But the anti-Dreyfusard camp became even more firmly entrenched in its anti-Semitic beliefs and was an important element in the crystallization of the ideology of the right-wing group Action Française, which emerged shortly afterwards. The radical and anti-clerical camp, on the other hand, began to comprehend the public and political threat embodied in anti-Semitic propaganda.

The anti-Semites remained influential only in Algeria. They drew inspiration from the anti-Jewish feelings among the Arabs, who were opposed to the civil rights granted to the Jews by the French, and among the French settlers, who in 1882 had already founded anti-Semitic associations and issued anti-Semitic journals. The outbursts reached their height during the Dreyfus Affair, when Algiers elected an anti-Semitic mayor. Drumont and other leaders of anti-Semitism stood as candidates for the National Assembly in Algerian districts. During the 1897 pogroms in Algerian towns, military force was employed in order to suppress the rioters. At the 1898 elections, four anti-Semites were elected in the six Algerian electoral districts. They did not succeed in winning re-election in 1902, but hostility towards the Jews continued to grow. As the Jews came closer to French culture, Arab hatred of the 'traitors' who were consolidating French rule grew stronger, while the settlers regarded them as competitors and rivals.

The difference between the public reaction to anti-Semitism in Germany and Austria-Hungary and that in France was to have a decisive effect on the future political regimes in those countries during the twentieth century and on the future of the Jews within them in the period between the world wars, and particularly during the Nazi Holocaust.

57

Anti-Semitism as Official Government Policy in Eastern Europe

'Southern Tempests'

We have noted that in the 1870s anti-Jewish sentiment increased in Russia both in ruling circles and among the masses. The growing economic activity of Jewish capitalists and the growing number of Jews in secondary schools and higher institutions served as a pretext for the claim that Russia was in danger of Jewish domination and that it was necessary to protect the 'basic population' of the Empire, *i.e.,* the Christians of Russia, against Jewish scheming. But during the lifetime of Alexander II, when politicians and bureaucrats of liberal propensities exerted a certain amount of influence, there was no basic change in official policy towards the Jews. The change occurred after the murder of Alexander by revolutionaries in 1881. His successor, Alexander III, who was totally under the sway of his tutor, the reactionary Pobedonostsev, declared that he would follow the policy of consolidating autocracy and would therefore oppose any concessions to liberal trends. Liberal ministers were accordingly dismissed from the government.

In the brief period between the murder of the Tsar (1 March 1881, according to the Julian calendar then in force) and the announcement of the aims of the new reign (29 April 1881), violent anti-Jewish riots broke out in south-west Russia, in the Ukrainian provinces, which were referred to by Jewish writers as 'southern tempests'. They commenced in the middle of April in Elizavetgrad, spread rapidly to several other towns and villages, and a few days later reached Kiev, the capital of the region. At the beginning of May, a pogrom occurred in Odessa, which lasted for three days. All in all, the pogroms of spring and summer 1881 affected more than 100 Jewish communities. Generally speaking they consisted of looting: gangs composed of local townsmen and peasants would plunder Jewish homes and shops. But there were also cases of rape and murder. Those Jews who had placed their trust in the protection of the authorities were helpless and, in most cases, offered no resistance. Only in Odessa, which had learnt the lesson of the 1871 pogrom, were there manifestations of self-defence, led by students. The authorities displayed total incompetence as well as an unwillingness to defend the Jews and, in several cases, as in Kiev, army units stood idly by while the rioters wrought havoc all around them.

The very fact that the pogroms spread so rapidly seems to indicate that there was some guiding hand involved. It is possible that this was the work of a clandestine group of courtiers (the Holy Brotherhood, as they were called), who had set them-selves the task of combating revolutionary terror and who hoped, thereby, to sway the authorities. This theory is substantiated by the fact that among the heads of the rioting gangs were people who had arrived in the Ukraine from central Russia. But we should not underestimate the influence of local conditions. In the southern Ukraine there was particularly intense competition and tension between the strong urban Christian element and the prosperous peasants in the villages (who after emancipation began to engage in trade and money-lending) and the Jews, whose economic activity had expanded considerably in the sixties and seventies. In an area that was characterized by age-old anti-Jewish sentiment and in which folk songs and legends glorified pogroms, such activity now served as the pretense for anti-Jewish agitation. Some of the educated class in the Ukraine, who sought to encourage Ukrainian nationalism through the revival of old traditions, fanned this mood among the masses. The conditions were ripe for outbursts against the Jews, and it is possible that only fear of the authorities had held them off so long. When the new Tsar ascended the throne and rumour had it that the reins had been slackened, that the Tsar permitted attacks on Jews in revenge for the murder of his father by Jewish revolutionaries, the pogroms commenced. The hesitant and evasive objections of the regime strengthened the belief that it had given its blessing to the rioters.

The central authorities, who at first feared that the anti-Jewish outbursts were the fruit of revolutionary propaganda, were reassured when a special emissary, sent to examine the situation on the spot, refuted this view. Apparently on the initiative of the new Minister of the Interior, Ignatyev (who was a Slavophile), this emissary everywhere helped spread the rumour that the pogroms were an eruption of 'the anger of the people' against 'Jewish exploitation'. This proved particularly convenient for the new ruling clique and for Ignatyev himself, who wished to discredit the liberal reforms of the previous reign and to encourage the autocratic tendencies of the new Tsar. In a memorandum he submitted to the Tsar, Ignatyev claimed that ' . . . the main cause of this movement [*i.e.,* the pogroms] lies in the economic situa-tion. During the previous twenty years, the Jews have taken over trade and industry, purchased areas of land by sale or lease, and by means of their unity have succeeded in exploiting the main body of the population, particularly the poor, hence arousing them to a protest, which has found distressing expression in acts of violence.'

The ruling clique therefore decided to make anti-Jewish feeling the basis of its policy of *rapprochement* between the authorities and the people. For this purpose an edict was published in August 1881 establishing special commissions in each district of the Pale of Settlement, with the participation of representatives of the various classes, in order to examine the harm caused by Jewish economic activity to the 'main inhabitants'. As these commissions were composed of representatives of those classes hostile to and competing with the Jews, and the instructions given them were worded in an inimical tone, it is not surprising that the great majority of these bodies reached the conclusion that restrictions should be imposed on the economic activities of the Jews so as to prevent them from causing harm to the general population. Nevertheless, there were some commissions that recommended that the

Jews be granted the right to settle anywhere in Russia, in order to alleviate the overcrowding in the Pale of Settlement.

Since the attitude towards the Jews had become a clearly political instrument, certain elements now began to exploit it in order to achieve various political objectives. At the end of 1881, pogroms broke out in Warsaw, possibly aimed at winning the Poles over to the Russian regime, or to demonstrate to the world that not only the Russians objected to the Jews. Unlike the Russian authorities, however, Polish public figures strongly condemned the pogroms.

A particularly severe outburst, initiated by the local bureaucracy, raged in the spring of 1882 in the town of Balta on the Russian-Rumanian border, and the rioters killed and wounded many Jews. The authorities were apparently startled at this manifestation of 'local initiative', and, at the end of May 1882, they dismissed Ignatyev from his post and appointed in his place Dmitri Tolstoy, a reactionary of the old school who frowned upon the use of mobs to implement policy. In fact, after his appointment, the pogroms ceased for the most part, although there were sporadic outbursts in 1882 and during the next few years. The last pogrom of the eighties occurred in 1884 outside the 'Pale' at Nizhny Novgorod, where several Jews lost their lives.

The 'Temporary Rules' and the Formulation of Anti-Semitic Policy

Ignatyev's last act before his dismissal was to formulate anti-Jewish decrees on the basis of the recommendations of the district commissions. They were issued in the form of 'Temporary Rules', published on 3 May 1882, prohibiting town Jews from settling in villages (even in the 'Pale'), from purchasing real estate outside the towns, from leasing estates and agricultural land and from opening their businesses or shops on Sundays and Christian holidays. It was clear that the regime had chosen a cruel and extreme method of implementing an anti-Semitic policy, which it described as 'protection of the basic population against Jewish exploitation'. These regulations severely affected the livelihood of the Jews, who had always eked out a precarious living in the overcrowded conditions of the towns of the 'Pale', where the conditions were aggravated by the high rate of natural increase. But even more harsh than the economic effect of the new regulations was the attitude of the local authorities towards the Jews. The local bureaucracy regarded these new decrees as an open hint of the central authorities' intentions and, together with the police – who were in any case corrupt – they now began to harass the Jews and to exploit them through blackmail and demands for bribes, out of the firm conviction that the Jews were 'fair game'.

The way in which the 'protection of the basic population' was interpreted in practice is demonstrated by the closing-down in 1884 of the Jewish craft school in Zhitomir, the first of its kind in Russia, which had been opened in 1862. The pretext for closing the school was that it afforded the Jews unfair advantage, since the 'main population' did not have such schools. In fact, the regime was making it clear that it was not obliged to concern itself with the Jews. Ignatyev declared at the beginning of 1882 that 'the western border is open to the Jews', *i.e.,* the authorities wanted as many Jews as possible to leave Russia. The true architect of Russian government policy at that time, the Procurator of the Holy Synod (Head of the Ministry in charge of church affairs) Pobedonostsev, is credited with the remark that one-third of Russian Jews would emigrate, one-third die out and the remainder convert to Christianity.

Despite these tendencies, the authorities often declared – at least outwardly – that it was necessary to find a way of solving the 'Jewish question' through normal legislation. A Supreme Commission for the Revision of Current Laws in the Empire Concerning the Jews was established at the beginning of 1883; it was known as the Pahlen Commission, after its chairman, Count Pahlen. This commission spent five years collecting extensive data on the Jews, their status and economic activity. Eventually the majority of its members reached the conclusion that the rights of the Jews should gradually be extended, in order to equalize them to the rest of the population. The Tsar, however, did not accept these recommendations and concurred with the minority view, which called for the continuation of restrictions.

Although several senior officials endeavoured, even in the eighties, to discuss the Jewish question objectively, Russian public opinion generally became increasingly anti-Semitic. Some of the anti-Jewish trends were inspired by the German anti-Semitic movements, others were aroused by the tendency to emphasize Russian uniqueness and the basic difference between the social and political development of Russia and that of the West. The Slavophiles were the first to take up this stand, but revolutionary Narodnik circles and supporters of the anarchist Bakunin were also attracted to these views and took them a step further. The Jews were 'aliens' and 'parasites' who exploited the Russian people out of their own sense of solidarity; they also schemed with their brethren in the West, endeavouring to introduce into Russia the 'corrupt spirit of the West' and the destructive influence of capitalism. In such an atmosphere it is not surprising that the pogroms were interpreted as a reflection of the will and anger of the people.

With few exceptions, the Russian press neither condemned the pogroms nor dissociated itself from them. The greatest writers of the time, such as Turgenyev and Tolstoy, kept their silence. Only the well-known radical writer, Saltykov-Shchedrin, who had joined Nekrasov and others of the same camp in savagely denouncing the Jews in the seventies, now repented, and in the summer of 1882 published a passionate article defending the persecuted Jews.

The executive committee of the revolutionary party Narodnaya Volya issued a leaflet in Ukrainian in August 1881 in which it called on the peasants to rise up against their Jewish oppressors and against the 'Tsar of the *pans* [*i.e.,* nobility] and the *Zhids*'. The organ of the same movement published an enthusiastic article on the anti-Jewish mood prevailing in the villages. Not all party members agreed with these articles, but the great majority regarded anti-Jewish outbursts as presaging the peasant uprising.

In this atmosphere additional restrictions against the Jews were accepted as a natural step. Some time before the publication of the 'Temporary Rules' of May 1882, the War Ministry published an order restricting the number of Jewish army doctors to 5% of the total 'since they do not perform their tasks with complete loyalty and because of their undesirable influence over the sanitary service in the army'. This accusation constituted a bitter affront to Jewish physicians, who had taken part in the Russo-Turkish War and had even been mentioned in dispatches for their devotion to duty. A campaign then commenced for the dismissal of Jews from other government services, and no new Jewish candidates were accepted. From 1889 onwards, a Jew who wished to engage in private legal practice needed the special permission of the Minister of Justice, and even the most distinguished of Jewish lawyers were forced to work for many years with the status of 'assistant advocates'.

Jewish youths were particularly affected by the restrictions imposed on entry into secondary schools and institutions of higher learning. The change in the attitude towards the Jews was particularly evident here, as the dissemination of Russian culture and education among Jews had been a primary measure employed by the authorities from the 1840s onwards to bring the Jews closer to the state and the society around them. The incentives previously introduced to attract young Jews to non-Jewish institutions were abolished in the seventies, and in 1875 the Ministry of Education expressed the view that it was impossible to absorb all the Jews in educational institutions without depriving the Christian population. But the idea of a *numerus clausus* for Jewish students was first raised in 1881 or 1882. From 1882 to 1884 several higher institutions of military medicine, mining and transportation decided that only 5% of their students should be Jewish. In July 1887 the Minister of Education published a circular restricting the number of Jewish pupils in secondary schools and higher institutions to 10% of the total number of students within the 'Pale', 5% in towns outside the 'Pale' and 3% in St Petersburg and Moscow. Several institutions were completely closed to Jews. The *numerus clausus* had become official policy.

Particularly burdensome to the Jews was the 1886 regulation that imposed heavy fines on the families of young Jews who failed to report for military service. There were many young men among the immigrants to the United States, and, as the great majority of them left Russia illegally, their names were not removed from the lists of those liable for military service; their families were therefore obliged to pay fines when the time came for their sons to be conscripted. The Jews also suffered from the complex regulations regarding 'residence rights' outside the Pale of Settlement. The police harassed those Jews who lived outside the 'Pale', extracted various payments from them and organized special night-raids. Attempts were also made to give several small towns the status of villages in order thereby to expel the Jews. The worst catastrophe in the series of expulsions was in Moscow in 1891: in order to 'purify the sacred historic capital' it was decided to expel Jewish artisans who were residing there legally, on the basis of regulations dating back to Alexander II. This decision affected some 20,000 Jews, some of whom were banished like criminals, in chains and with police escort. This event further undermined the confidence of the Jews in a regime capable of transgressing its own laws.

Mob Rule in the Reign of Nicholas II

Nicholas II, who came to the throne in 1894, made no basic changes in the policy towards the Jews during the early days of his reign, although several more oppressive restrictions were added. But the renewal of public opposition to the Tsar's autocratic rule, and disappointment at the fact that the new ruler had not introduced liberal reforms, changed the public mood, particularly among the intelligentsia. In the last years of the nineteenth century and first years of the twentieth, liberal and revolutionary parties were organized in Russia, and their influence began to be felt in political life, leading to changes in the political situation as a whole. This became evident in the shift in attitude of a considerable section of Russian society towards the Jews. Opposition circles came to realize that anti-Semitism had been the deliberate policy of the regime, aimed at consolidating its rule and influence over backward sections of Russian society. They therefore decided that it was their duty to oppose this policy. People such as the philosopher V. Soloveyev, the writers Korolenko and Gorki and many others spoke out against the persecution of the Jews. The protests of liberal and radical circles against official anti-Semitism led the authorities to claim that the Russian revolutionary movement was a Jewish plot, being carried out with the aid of Russia's enemies. Thus the government of Nicholas II chose to fan anti-Semitic sentiment among the masses as a means of creating a political weapon.

The Tsar, who was imbued with a hatred of the Jews, also supported this policy. The government began to finance the publication of anti-Jewish newspapers, and attempts were made to organize pogroms and blood libels. As the revolutionary terror increased, the wave of anti-Semitic propaganda was intensified. Particularly outstanding in its virulence was a local paper published in Kishinev, the capital of Bessarabia. In the same town a clandestine anti-Semitic organization was established, supported by local government officials. The incitement and organization bore fruit, and in April 1903 a terrible pogrom broke out in Kishinev. It differed from the pogroms of the eighties in that this time the rioters concentrated on murder, rape and torture. According to an official report, more than fifty people were killed and over 500 injured, while hundreds of homes and shops were plundered and destroyed.

This savage conduct shocked enlightened public opinion in Russia, as well as throughout the world. The Russian Liberation Movement, *i.e.,* the opposition parties, blamed the government for the pogrom and rallied for an active struggle against the persecution of the Jews. But the greatest transformation occurred in the mood of the Jews themselves: it was brought home to them cruelly and unequivocally that they could not rely on the authorities, even for simple physical protection. The consequences swiftly appeared: when pogroms broke out in the summer of 1903 in Homel in White Russia, groups of young Jews successfully defended themselves. But the authorities did not remain idle: this time they intervened, arresting the Jewish defenders so that the rioters were able to continue their acts of murder and wanton destruction under police protection. At the trial subsequently held, the main defendants were the young members of the Jewish self-defence organization.

When the war with Japan broke out in 1904 and the Russian Army suffered a series of crushing defeats, the anti-Semitic press accused the Jews of sympathy for the

Japanese and of disseminating revolutionary propaganda to undermine the Russian position. In order to combat the increasing revolutionary ferment, the regime set up 'patriotic' organizations loyal to 'the Tsar and the fatherland', and their spearhead was composed of armed gangs of rowdies known as the Black Hundreds, whose objective was the annihilation of revolutionaries and Jews. These hooligans commenced their activities in 1905 with street attacks on Jews and with pogroms, in which army and Cossack units participated. None of these activities succeeded in suppressing the revolutionary spirit. The Tsar was obliged to agree to concessions and to announce the establishment of an advisory assembly, the Duma. In drawing up the statutes for the elections to the Duma, an attempt was made to deprive the Jews of the franchise, on the grounds that they were not full citizens. But the authorities retreated from this policy under pressure of public opinion. The Tsar's greatest concession, which undermined the principle of autocracy, was granted when he was forced, on 17 October 1905, to issue a manifesto guaranteeing the basic freedoms of his citizens. In reaction, the Union of the Russian People and the Black Hundreds organized mass 'patriotic processions' with portraits of the Tsar borne aloft. These processions soon deteriorated into mass riots directed against the Jews. As investigation later uncovered, the leaflets inciting to riot were clandestinely printed on a press at police headquarters and were financed by a special secret fund administered by the Tsar himself. The riots swept over dozens of towns, leaving hundreds of corpses in their wake. In Odessa the pogroms raged for four days and more than 300 Jews lost their lives. Jewish self-defence organizations hit back hard at the attackers. Individual members of the Russian intelligentsia also joined these units and some were even killed. In several places Russian workers came to the defence of the Jews against the rioters. But this activity was suppressed with the aid of army and Cossack units. Police and army personnel took part in the pogroms at Bialystok and Siedlce in 1906 and were later even awarded honorable mention or medals. The Duma appointed a commission of enquiry to clarify the causes of the Bialystok pogrom, and this body eventually pinned full blame on the authorities. The right-wing press responded by claiming that many of the Duma deputies were Jews or Poles elected with the aid of Jewish money. The Russian Orthodox Church took an active part in this anti-Semitic propaganda.

The revolution ended in 1907, with the consolidation of the dictatorial rule of Stolypin. All agitation was suppressed by the regime, and for fear of mass outbursts the riot movement was also largely restrained. Stolypin was anxious to check the anti-Jewish policy in order to restore confidence in Russia within the international monetary markets. The Council of Ministers even decided on several legal concessions to the Jews, but the Tsar refused to approve them.

The Intensification of Anti-Semitic Incitement. The Beilis Blood Libel

The pogrom movement was checked to some extent, but various propagandists continued their campaign against the Jews in the Duma, in the press and at public meetings. At a conference of associations of nobles in 1911, the participants demanded that Russia be rid of the Jews. At the same conference, 'experts' claimed that the Jews needed Christian blood for the observance of their religion. And, in fact, shortly afterwards, a Jew named Mendel Beilis was accused in Kiev of the murder of a Christian boy for ritual purposes. The libel was concocted by the Union of the Russian People, and although the police knew the identity of the true murderers, they cooperated with the Minister of Justice and his office and for two years prepared 'testimonies' of various underworld figures and 'experts' so as to provide legal substantiation for the accusation. Beilis was put on trial only at the end of 1913. The Minister of Justice reported personally to the Tsar throughout the trial. Public opinion in Russia and abroad regarded this trial as a struggle between the regime and opposition forces, and the 'Jewish question' became one of the central problems of Russian life. The best lawyers in the country came to Beilis' defence and clearly exposed the ignorance of the prosecution's 'expert' witnesses, while the liberal and revolutionary press revealed how the Minister of Justice had staged the trial. A protest movement arose in several European countries and in the United States. Despite the tendentious composition of the jury (mainly near-illiterate peasants), Beilis was acquitted for lack of evidence, although there was no clear-cut decision with regard to the blood libel itself. The public accepted this verdict as a defeat for the regime and a triumph for liberal and radical public opinion, which had for the most part supported the Jews throughout the trial. The Beilis trial was one of the high points of the public struggle over the 'Jewish question' in Russia.

Public opinion in Russian Poland, in contrast to that in Russia, was hostile towards the Jews. During the Beilis trial it affirmed its belief in the truth of the blood libel. The main nationalist party (National Democrats, or Endeks, as they were called after the initials of the party's name) began to organize an economic boycott against the Jews, placing guards outside Jewish shops as a means of enforcement. Polish nationalists (even from the liberal camp) were particularly opposed to the demands of Jewish parties for national rights and national autonomy. At the elections to the Fourth Duma in 1912, Warsaw Jews voted not for the nationalist candidate but for a Polish socialist, and Polish public opinion generally regarded this as an act of provocation and treachery.

Jews as Scapegoats During the First World War

The situation of Russian Jews deteriorated after the outbreak of the First World War. The military action on the Eastern, *i.e.*, Russian, front was conducted in the area of the Pale of Settlement, with its dense Jewish population. The Russian military authorities suspected that this population sympathized with the Central Powers and was hostile towards Russia. Consequently, as soon as the invasion of Austrian territories commenced, they began expelling Jews from Galicia and Bukovina on the instructions of the General Staff, and Jewish hostages were taken in order to ensure the allegiance of the community as a whole. The military authorities claimed that the Jews were transmitting information to the enemy. Polish anti-Semites, including some who were in contact with the Austrian Army, conveyed to the Russian commanders accusations that the Jews were engaging in espionage on behalf of the Austrians. After the Russian defeats and retreat in 1915 these same Poles accused the Jews of spying for the Russians. All these accusations culminated in death sentences by court martial. In many places in the battle areas the Cossacks conducted pogroms against the Jewish population. Thus, in addition to the usual vicissitudes of war, the Jews also endured the deliberate anti-Semitic policy of the Russian military authorities. As a means of emphasizing the disloyalty of the Jews, on 5 July 1915 all publications printed in Hebrew lettering were prohibited. This, too, was an act of cruelty against a population of millions, of which the great majority knew no other language.

When the military situation of the Russians became desperate as a result of the German attack, the Supreme Headquarters ordered the expulsion of masses of Jews from areas close to the front. Hundreds of thousands of Jews, including women, children and old men, were ordered to leave their homes on twenty-four or forty-eight-hours' notice. The pressure of Jewish refugees was so great that in 1915 the authorities 'temporarily' permitted the entrance of Jews into Russia proper, outside the Pale of Settlement, with the exception of the capital cities. At a time when the Russian Army lacked ammunition and vital supplies because of transportation difficulties, dozens of trains were deployed to convey expelled Jews. The official explanation was the disloyalty of the Jews, and it brought a savage anti-Jewish incitement based on their supposed profiteering, their desire to undermine the stability of the currency, etc. It transpired that the authorities were planning to make the attack on 'Jewish treachery' an important component of their policy, but the revolution that broke out at the beginning of March 1917 brought about the downfall of the Tsar and a basic change in policy.

Government Anti-Semitism in Rumania

The attitude of the Rumanian Government and of the great majority of the Rumanian people towards Jews after the Berlin Congress was a repetition on a smaller scale of developments in Russia. Nor can it be doubted that the Rumanian rulers derived encouragement from events in Russia in determining their anti-Semitic policy. When the Berlin Treaty of 1878 obliged Rumania to bestow equal rights on all citizens, irrespective of nationality and religion, the Rumanian Government tried to persuade the Powers that there was no need to grant civil rights to 'hundreds of thousands of aliens' *en bloc,* but that this should be done step by step. A special commission was set up, and it managed, in the last two decades of the nineteenth century, to grant rights to only a few hundred Jews. Despite the denial of their rights, all civil obligations, including that of military service, were imposed on the Jews.

Various economic restrictions were also imposed on them, with the declared aim of favouring the (Rumanian) 'native son' over the (Jewish) 'foreigner'. The Jews were forbidden to engage in the sale of tobacco and liquor. The prohibition of peddling caused considerable hardship to the Jewish masses. A 'foreigner' who wished to engage in trade required a special permit from the authorities. He was not permitted to serve as a bank manager, and if he set up a factory he was obliged to guarantee that for several years at least two-thirds of his employees would be Rumanians.

In share companies the majority of the shares had to be held by Rumanians. Jew
were excluded from employment in any public service and were not allowed
practise as lawyers. Only in cases where no Rumanian was interested in opening
pharmacy in a certain region were Jews granted a license to do so.

The Rumanian authorities interfered in particular with Jewish education. T
Jews were obliged to pay school fees, while Rumanians were exempt from paymer
Jewish students were accepted in secondary schools and higher institutions or
after all the Rumanian candidates had gained entry (in actual fact there was
numerus clausus of some 5–7.5%). When the Jews tried to develop their own netwc
of schools, the Ministry of Education placed numerous obstacles in their pa
(All these legal restrictions were imposed on the Jews during the eighties.)

The Rumanian Government also financed public anti-Semitic activity.
'international congress' of anti-Semites was convened in Bucharest in 1886 with 1
moral and financial backing of the government (only a few delegates actually ca
from abroad). In 1895 an Anti-Semitic Federation was founded in the count
and one of its first registered members was the Minister of Education. The statu
of this association declared that it would employ every possible means to ma
life intolerable for Rumanian Jews. This body organized riots in several towns dur
the last few years of the nineteenth century. In 1907 the villages were afflicted b
series of agrarian riots, and the first victims were Jews. This movement progres
from the robbing of Jewish lessors to the holding of pogroms in towns and town
with the open support of representatives of the authorities. But when the ri
spread, and the peasants began to attack landowners as well, the panic-stricl
regime hastened to suppress them.

As a result of the Balkan wars, a new area, with its own Jewish population,
annexed to Rumania in 1912. The Rumanian Government at first guaranteed
maintain the civil equality that these Jews had previously enjoyed, but retreated
the face of anti-Semitic public opinion and, above all, the pressure of the stude
Attacks on Jews actually increased during the First World War.

58

The Growth of the Jewish National Movement and the Burgeoning of Independent Political Activity

The Nature of Jewish National Resurgence

The emergence of the Jewish national movement was undoubtedly a decisive turning-point in modern Jewish history. The trend towards integration into the general society and the achievements of Emancipation led the Jews to an increasing identification with the peoples and nations among whom they lived. However, even in those countries in which there were numerous obstacles to integration and emancipation, and even in orthodox circles, where no doubt had ever been cast on the uniqueness and election of the Jewish people, no need was felt for independent political activity or for political objectives relating to the Jewish people alone. In the second half of the nineteenth century certain nationalist philosophers appeared and within a short time had drawn up an extremely radical programme: (1) all Jews, everywhere, constituted one nation whose unity was based not only on common memories, religion and cultural vestiges, but also on hopes for a shared future to be built upon a national and political programme; (2) national-political activity should be carried out independently by the Jewish people through the consolidation of special Jewish frameworks and the uniting of all national forces for the achievement of these objectives. The Jews should seek out allies, but they alone were capable of bringing about the victory of their ideal, and they alone could ensure their own redemption and future.

What factors led to the rise of national ideals in the 1860s and 1870s and to the crystallization of a national movement in the 1880s? Some originated in the processes affecting only Jewish society, and some in the developments characteristic of general European society at the time. In this period the unification of Italy and Germany were completed, and the national movements of the Slavic peoples, and especially of the Balkans, attained recognition and even political success. The consolidation of national ideologies and movements in the political life of Europe focussed greater attention on the unique cultural and ethnic traits of national units and led to an accentuation of those qualities distinguishing human beings from one another, rather than those uniting them. One of the main reflections of this development was the revival of anti-Jewish traditions and an upsurge of anti-Semitism, which made it even more difficult for the Jew to identify with his surroundings. But the *maskilim* were influenced to no less an extent by the positive example of those nationalist movements that had achieved their objectives. Why, they asked, should the Jews be regarded as inferior to the Serbs, the Bulgarians or the Rumanians, who had all achieved political independence?

Internal Jewish developments revolved around disillusionment with the universalist ideals of the Enlightenment. These had not brought about the establishment of a new society based on rationalistic concepts, nor did lasting peace reign among nations. Among the Jews these ideals had only induced a considerable number of young Jewish intellectuals to abandon the heritage of their forefathers and the treasures of Jewish culture and to attach themselves to alien cultures. East European Jewish intellectuals, who now realized that the ideals for which they had been ready to abandon Hebrew language and culture were not being implemented, began to wonder what purpose there was in their beliefs. Even those who, under the impact of the advancement of European society, had transferred their open or hidden messianic yearnings to the sphere of the political and social ideals of the society in which they lived now refocussed their aspirations on Jewish society; and it transpired that messianic belief was still a powerful force for a considerable number of Jews – both *maskilim* and traditionalists.

The nationalists did not deny the fundamental principles of the former *maskilim*, nor did they renounce their ambition to bring the Jews closer to the Enlightenment and to arouse in them a desire to change their occupations, their way of life and moral image. But they did despair of the possibility of achieving this within the framework of European countries, where each Jew was trying hard to be a German, a Frenchman or a Russian 'of the Mosaic persuasion'. They hoped, instead, to realize their aims within a self-contained Jewish framework – either a sovereign Jewish state with a Jewish majority, or an autonomous Jewish unit within a larger framework – without harassment by anti-Semites or government discrimination. They offered this plan to all Jews, or at least to those Jews who were suffering from legal and social discrimination or from obstacles in achieving emancipation and therefore desired to be 'a nation like any other'.

From the outset, therefore, the Jewish national movement was afflicted by dialectical tension: its internal justification lay in historical resurgence and in reliance on the achievements of a glorious past, while its plan for the future was based on the integration of the Jewish people into the world around them and on collective abandonment of all that had, for centuries, differentiated Jews from other nations. It is possible that this tension, this fusion of historical tradition and modern aims was what lent the Jewish national movement its force and stability. An additional and very significant factor was that the national movement made Jewishness a source of individual pride: from the end of the eighteenth century the Jewishness of a scientist, artist or statesman had been regarded by European society as a disability, a sign of alienness. The very mention of the fact that some prominent person was a Jew constituted an insult, while for a Jew to identify himself as such was regarded as an act of courage and sacrifice. The national movement enabled the Jew to be active in all spheres of life, with his Jewishness being regarded as a natural factor. Thus the national movement made the Jew equal to people of other nationalities from the social point of view and with regard to his self-image.

The Idea of Return to Zion

The newly emergent nationalist movement for the most part associated its yearnings with Palestine, the historic homeland of the Jews, but there were also those who considered the possibility of national renaissance elsewhere, even within a self-contained framework in an existing centre of Jewish residence. In the past the most loyal advocates of the return of the Jews to their historic homeland had been members of various Christian sects, who mentioned such projects in their writings in the seventeenth and eighteenth centuries. In the nineteenth century a political factor was added: several politicians in England and on the European continent began to think that a Jewish state should be set up in Palestine as part of the political settlement that they expected would follow the death of the 'sick man of Europe', *i.e.,* after the disintegration of the Ottoman Empire. Thus, they believed, Palestine would serve as a barrier between Turkey and Egypt, and the Jews – who did not have affiliations in the area – would be best suited for this task.

One of the Jews who at the beginning of the nineteenth century became attracted to the idea of a Jewish state was Mordecai Manuel Noah in the United States. He proposed establishing such a state under the name of 'Ararat' in the vicinity of New York, but in the 1840s even he returned to the original consideration of Palestine. The idea of a return to Zion as the first step towards the redemption of the Jewish people was advocated by R. Zevi Hirsch Kalischer and R. Judah Alkalai; and in the 1850s R. David Gordon began to disseminate this idea in *Hamaggid*. In the sixties Dr Chaim Lurie established in Frankfurt-on-Oder a society for the settlement of Palestine.

The German socialist thinker Moses Hess formulated a programme based on political and historical considerations in his book *Rome and Jerusalem* (1862). He pinned his hope of a Jewish political revival in Palestine on the political support of France, which had formerly extended aid to the unification of Italy. Hess believed that the Jewish people were endowed with national characteristics that would enable the Jewish state to serve as a social and spiritual example to other peoples. The historian Heinrich Graetz was convinced by Hess's arguments and became his ardent supporter. But all these projects met with little response among the Jewish public in the West.

In his journal *Hashahar* ('The Dawn'), the Hebrew writer Perez Smolenskin was then publicizing his views on the spiritual foundations of Jewish nationalism. (*Hashahar*, which appeared in Vienna, and *Hamaggid*, published in Lyck, East Prussia, were in fact both directed at the *maskilim* in Russia.) But it was only at the end of the seventies that Eliezer Ben-Yehuda (Perlman) published an article in *Hashahar*, in which he wrote that nationalism could not be fostered without a spiritual centre to serve as the basis and focal point of the renaissance of the national spirit, and that such a centre could be established only in Palestine. In the summer of 1880 an association for the settlement of Palestine was set up in Bucharest, Rumania. Enthusiasm grew after the publication of Laurence Oliphant's plan for the settlement of Palestine by the Jews, but it gained momentum only after the outbreak of the pogroms in Russia in the spring of 1881.

The Emergence of the Ḥibbat Zion (Love of Zion) Movement

The 'southern tempests' had had a powerful effect on Russian Jewry. The fact that there was no section of Russian society ready to come to the defence of the Jews, who had had to face the rioters and the hostile authorities alone, came as a severe shock to Russian Jews, and particularly to the young and to the assimilated intelligentsia who had grown close to Russian society and culture and now felt that their proferred hand had been rejected. The *maskilim* began to return to their people; they appeared at the synagogues and took part in public fasts. Some of them began to feel that the time had come to act on behalf of their own people, and they joined the youth and student associations that had advocated nationalism even before the pogroms, such as the Jewish student association of St Petersburg. The latter held a reception for 'our national scribe', Perez Smolenskin, during his visit to Russia at the beginning of 1881.

Many nationalistic groups arose in 1881, some of them on a radical national and political basis, as was natural against the background of the radicalism that characterized Russian youth as a whole during the same period: 'There can be no salvation for Israel if it does not found a government of its own in the Land of Israel' (from the statutes of the Aḥvat Zion, Brotherhood of Zion Society in St Petersburg); 'It is necessary to seek out for all the wanderers a special, isolated place where comrades can gather together until, in the course of time, all matters of state, law and administration will be in the hands of the Hebrews alone, and everything will be determined by the word of their mouth. . . . Only then will the conduct of the state be in the hands of the Children of Israel, if they constitute at least a majority of all the residents of that country in number' (from the statutes of Kibbuẓ Niddeḥei Israel, Society for Gathering the Dispersed of Israel in Minsk); 'The objective of the society is the economic, national and spiritual renaissance of the Hebrew people in Syria and Palestine' (from the statutes of the Bilu [an acronym for 'House of Jacob, come and let us go', Isaiah 2:5] society). In Rumania there were more than thirty associations for settlement in Palestine at the end of 1881, and at the beginning of January 1882 a conference of representatives of all these bodies was held in Foscani and elected a central committee to reside at Galati.

Only a few of these associations resembled Bilu in regard to their objective of mass immigration of their members to Palestine. The majority sent representatives 'to search the country' and several even to purchase land for future settlement. During the great flight of Russian Jewry at the time of the pogroms, which encompassed many thousands of Jews, only a few hundred immigrated to Palestine, and many of these did not succeed in settling there. The Alliance Israélite warned against panic-stricken flight to Palestine, and the Turkish authorities hastened to prohibit the entrance of Jews into Palestine for settlement purposes.

The great achievement of the national resurgence at the beginning of the eighties was the crystallization of a national ideology. It was formulated by a group of writers, such as M. L. Lilienblum, J. L. Gordon, J. L. Levin and L. Levanda, who